Tuttle

Learner's
Chinese-
English
Dictionary

Tuttle

Learner's Chinese-English Dictionary

SECOND EDITION

LI Dong 李冬

TUTTLE Publishing

Tokyo | Rutland, Vermont | Singapore

The Tuttle Story: "Books to Span the East and West"

Many people are surprised to learn that the world's leading publisher of books on Asia had humble beginnings in the tiny American state of Vermont. The company's founder, Charles E. Tuttle, belonged to a New England family steeped in publishing.

Immediately after WWII, Tuttle served in Tokyo under General Douglas MacArthur and was tasked with reviving the Japanese publishing industry. He later founded the Charles E. Tuttle Publishing Company, which thrives today as one of the world's leading independent publishers.

Though a westerner, Tuttle was hugely instrumental in bringing a knowledge of Japan and Asia to a world hungry for information about the East. By the time of his death in 1993, Tuttle had published over 6,000 books on Asian culture, history and art—a legacy honored by the Japanese emperor with the "Order of the Sacred Treasure," the highest tribute Japan can bestow upon a non-Japanese.

With a backlist of 1,500 titles, Tuttle Publishing is more active today than at any time in its past—still inspired by Charles Tuttle's core mission to publish fine books to span the East and West and provide a greater understanding of each.

Published by Tuttle Publishing, an imprint of Periplus Editions (HK) Ltd.

www.tuttlepublishing.com

Library of Congress Control Number: 2004115974
ISBN 978-0-8048-4527-4

North America, Latin America and Europe
Tuttle Publishing
364 Innovation Drive,
North Clarendon,
VT 05759-9436 USA.
Tel: 1(802) 773-8930
Fax: 1(802) 773-6993
info@tuttlepublishing.com
www.tuttlepublishing.com

Asia Pacific
Berkeley Books Pte. Ltd.
61 Tai Seng Avenue #02-12,
Singapore 534167
Tel: (65) 6280-1330
Fax: (65) 6280-6290
inquiries@periplus.com.sg
www.periplus.com

18 17 16 15   6 5 4 3 2 1   1505CM
Printed in China

TUTTLE PUBLISHING® is a registered trademark of Tuttle Publishing, a division of Periplus Editions (HK) Ltd.

Contents

A Guide for Learners of Chinese

This dictionary is for learners of Chinese as a foreign or second language. It is designed to be a teaching/learning aid to the growing communities of teaching and learning the language. More specifically, this dictionary aims to help those learners who wish to sit for the **New Chinese Proficiency Test** (**New HSK** 新汉语水平考试), the Chinese government-sponsored, international standardized test, as it gives detailed treatment of all the 5,000 words in the prescribed Word Lists from Level 1 to Level 6. A further 1,000 very useful words are covered in the dictionary to allow for flexibility of the vocabulary requirement of the HSK.

In the following pages I offer the essentials of the Chinese language and, along the way, advice on how to make the best use of this dictionary.

1   PRONUNCIATION

1.1   The Pinyin Romanization System

The pronunciation of Chinese words is transcribed in this dictionary using the internationally recognized Chinese romanization scheme called *pinyin*. Every Chinese word in this dictionary is accompanied by its *pinyin* spelling so users will know how it is pronounced.

Pronouncing Chinese syllables normally involves three elements: vowels, consonants and tones. Modern standard Chinese, known as *Putonghua*, uses about 419 syllables without tones and 1,332 syllables with tones.

1.2   Vowels

1.2.1   Single Vowels

There are seven basic single vowels:

a	similar to *a* in *ah*
e	similar to *a* in *ago*
ê	similar to *e* in *ebb* (this sound never occurs alone and is transcribed as **e**, as in **ei, ie, ue**)
i	similar to *ee* in *cheese* (spelled **y** when not preceded by a consonant)
o	similar to *oe* in *toe*
u	similar to *oo* in *boot* (spelled **w** when not preceded by a consonant)
ü	similar to German *ü* in *über* or French *u* in *tu*; or you can also get *ü* by saying *i* and rounding your lips at the same time (spelled **u** after **j, q, x**; spelled **yu** when not preceded by a consonant)

1.2.2   Vowel Combinations

These single vowels enter into combinations with each other or the consonants of **n** or **ng** to form what are technically known as *diphthongs*. These combinations are pronounced as a single sound, with a little more emphasis on the first part of the sound.

You can learn these combinations in four groups:

Group 1:	diphthongs starting with **a/e/ê**	
	ai	similar to *y* in *my*
	ao	similar to *ow* in *how*

an	
ang	
en	
eng	
ei	similar to *ay* in *may*

Group 2: diphthongs starting with **i**

ia	
ie	similar to *ye* in *yes*
iao	
iou	similar to *you* (spelled **iu** when preceded by a consonant)
ian	
ien	similar to *in* (spelled **in** when preceded by a consonant)
ieng	similar to *En* in *English* (spelled **ing** when preceded by a consonant)
iang	similar to *young*
iong	

Group 3: diphthongs starting with **u/o**

ua	
uo	
uai	similar to *why* in British English
uei	similar to *way* (spelled **ui** when preceded by a consonant)
uan	
uen	(spelled **un** when preceded by a consonant)
ueng	
uang	
ong	

Group 4: diphthongs starting with **ü**

üe	used only after **j**, **q**, **x**; spelled **ue**
üen	used only after **j**, **q**, **x**; spelled **un**
üan	used only after **j**, **q**, **x**; spelled **uan**

1.3 Consonants

Consonants may be grouped in the following ways.

Group 1:   These consonants are almost the same in Chinese and English.

CHINESE	ENGLISH	
m	*m*	
n	*n*	
f	*f*	
l	*l*	
s	*s*	
r	*r*	
b		pronounced as hard *p* (as in *speak*)
p		*p* (as in *peak*)
g		pronounced as hard *k* (as in *ski*)
k		*k* (as in *key*)
d		pronounced as hard *t* (as in *star*)
t		*t* (as in *tar*)

Group 2:   Some modification is needed to get these Chinese sounds from English.

CHINESE   ENGLISH

j	as *j* in *jeep* (but unvoiced, not round-lipped)
q	as *ch* in *cheese* (but not round-lipped)
x	as *sh* in *sheep* (but not round-lipped)
c	as *ts* as in *cats* (make it long)
z	as *ds* as in *beds* (but unvoiced, and make it long)

Group 3:   No English counterparts

Chinese **zh**, **ch**, and **sh** have no English counterparts. You can learn to say **zh**, **ch** and **sh** starting from **z**, **c** and **s**. For example, say **s** (which is almost the same as the English *s* in *sesame*) and then roll up your tongue to touch the roof of your mouth. You get **sh**.

1.4   Tones

Chinese is a tonal language, i.e. a sound pronounced in different tones is understood as different words. So the tone is an indispensable component of the pronunciation of a word.

1.4.1   Basic Tones

There are four basic tones. The following five-level pitch graph shows the values of the four tones:

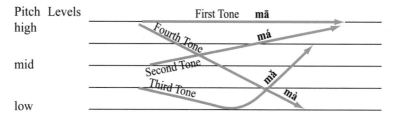

The **First Tone** is a high, level tone and is represented as ˉ, e.g. 妈 **mā** (meaning *mother, mom*).

The **Second Tone** is a high, rising tone and is represented by the tone mark ′, e.g. 麻 **má** (*hemp* or *sesame*).

The **Third Tone** is a falling and rising tone. As you can see from the pitch graph it falls from below the middle of the voice range to nearly the bottom and then rises to a point near the top. It is represented by the tone mark ˇ, e.g. 马 **mǎ** (*horse*).

The **Fourth Tone** is a falling tone. It falls from high to low and is represented by the tone mark ˋ, e.g. 骂 **mà** (*curse*).

In Chinese speech, as in English speech, some sounds are unstressed, i.e. pronounced short and soft. They do not have any of the four tones. Such sounds are said to have **Neutral Tone**. Sounds with the neutral tone are not marked. For example in 爸爸 **bàba** (*daddy*) the first syllable is pronounced in the fourth tone and the second syllable in the neutral tone, i.e. unstressed.

1.4.2   Tone Changes

Tones may undergo changes in actual speech ("tone sandhi"). The third tone, when followed by a first, second, fourth or neutral tone sound, loses its final rise and stops at the low pitch. Followed by another third tone sound, it becomes the second tone. This is a general rule and the notation of third tone sounds remains unchanged.

For example, in 所以 **suǒyǐ** (*therefore, so*), notation remains the third tone for both syllables, but the word is actually pronounced like **suóyǐ**.

Two important words 不 **bù** (*no*) and 一 **yī** (*one*) also undergo tone changes. You will find the details of their tone changes under these entries.

1.5 Syllables

1.5.1 Chinese Syllables: Distinct Units

Normally a consonant and a vowel merge to form a syllable in Chinese. Every syllable is a distinct unit in speech. Learners should say each syllable clearly and give full value to most syllables in speech. The general impression of Chinese speech, described in musical terms, is staccato rather than legato (which could be used to describe English).

1.5.2 Syllable Division Mark

As Chinese syllables are distinct units and should not be liaised with preceding or following syllables, a syllable division mark (') is sometimes used to avoid confusion, e.g. **shí'èr**, **píng'ān**, **tiān'é**.

2 WRITTEN CHINESE

2.1 "Chinese characters," a unique writing system

Chinese is not written in letters, like **a**, **b**, **c**, nor does it use an alphabet. Chinese is written in logograms, known as 汉字 (**Hànzì**) and generally referred to as "Chinese characters."

Each Chinese character is pronounced as a syllable and, with few exceptions, has distinctive meaning or meanings. Though there are tens of thousands of Chinese characters, only a couple of thousands are in frequent use – the first 1,000 Chinese characters cover about 90% of daily communication.

2.2 The composition of Chinese characters: Meaningful components

Chinese characters may be composed of parts, some of which convey certain meanings. The presence of such components gives you some clue to the meaning of characters. The ability to **recognize** these components is both useful and interesting. See List 1 Meaningful Character Components on page xvi.

2.3 The writing of Chinese characters

STROKES

Each Chinese character is written by a number of strokes, with the sole exception of 一 (which means "one"). The table below shows the basic strokes.

Stroke	Writing the stroke	Examples
Héng	left to right 一	千 主 女
Shù	top to bottom ∣	千 山 北
Piě	top (right) to bottom (left) ノ	千 人 么

Stroke	Writing the stroke	Examples
Nà	top (left) to bottom (right)  ╲	人 木 又
Diǎn	top to bottom ╲	主 心 习
Tí	Bottom (left) to top (right) ╱	习 打 北
Strokes with hook	left to right, top to bottom  �→╰ ┐╯ ┘╰	买 打 以 心
Strokes with turn(s)	 ╰ ┐ ╮ ╯	山 马 女 么 又
Strokes with turn(s) and hook	 ╰ ╗ ╰ ╮ 乙	北 习 认 马

STROKE ORDER

For the character to look correct, its strokes should be written in the correct order. Knowing the order will also help you remember characters. The general rules of stroke order are as follows.

Rule	Example	Stroke order
Top before bottom	三	一 二 三
Left before right	什	 丿 亻 仁 什
Horizontal before vertical/downward	天	 一 二 于 天
"Enter the room, then close the door"	日	 丨 冂 月 日
Vertical stroke before sides/bottom	小	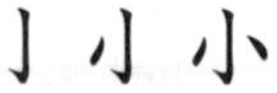 亅 小 小

2.4 Simplified and Traditional Characters

The Chinese government simplified hundreds of Chinese characters in mid-1950s by reducing the numbers of their strokes. Such simplified characters are called 简体字 **jiǎntǐzì**. This dictionary uses *jiantizi*. Traditional versions (also known as complicated characters) are still used in Taiwan and Hong Kong, and they are shown where applicable, e.g.:

xué 学 Trad 學

3 VOCABULARY

3.1 Words in this Dictionary

This dictionary gives detailed description of the 5,000 words prescribed for Level 1 to Level 6 of **the New Chinese Proficiency Test (New HSK 新汉语水平考试 Xīn Hànyǔ Shuǐpíng Kǎoshì**), the Chinese government-sponsored, international standardized test. Over 1,000 more words are covered, to further develop learners' vocabulary power.

3.2 The importance of Chinese characters

Most Chinese words are made up of two or more characters; the component characters usually determine the meaning of words. It is widely accepted by teachers and students of Chinese that in order to understand the meaning of a word, one should first of all learn the meanings of its component characters. This dictionary treats Chinese characters as individual items and gives them clear definitions, with the exception of a very few which are not used alone in Modern Chinese.

3.3 Word-formation methods

Chinese words are very transparent, i.e. the way a word is formed tells a lot about its meaning. Therefore it is very helpful to know the ways words are formed, as it facilitates understanding of words and makes learning more interesting.

This dictionary analyzes word-formation methods of headwords, whenever it is practical to do so. We recognize five methods of word-formation.

Compounding (shortened to "comp"): the components of a word are complementary to each other in meaning and are of the same status. For example:

    cáifù 财富 [comp: 财 property, fortune + 富 riches] **N** wealth, fortune

Modification ("modif"): one component modifies the other. For example:

    báitiān 白天 [modif: 白 white + 天 day] **N** daytime

Verb+object ("v+obj"): the word has a verb-and-object relationship. For example:

    chànggē 唱歌 [v+obj: 唱 sing + 歌 song] **v** sing songs, sing

Verb+complementation ("v+compl"): the word has a verb-and-complement relationship, that is, the first component is a verb and the second one modifies it. For example:

    kànjiàn 看见 [v+compl: 看 look + 见 see] **v** see, get sight of

Suffixation ("suffix"): the word contains a suffix. For example:

    bēizi 杯子 [suffix: 杯 cup + 子 nominal suffix] **N** cup, mug, glass (只 zhī)

3.4 Definitions

In most cases English equivalents or near equivalents are given as definitions. For example:

    bāngmáng 帮忙 **v** help, help out

For grammatical words that have no English equivalents, concise explanations are given in brackets. For example:

    de 的 **PARTICLE** (attached to a word or phrase to indicate that it is an attribute. 的 **de** is normally followed by a noun.)

After the definition of a noun, the specific measure word used with the noun is shown, if it is one of headwords in the dictionary. For example:

diànnǎo 电脑 [modif: 电 electricity + 脑 brain] N computer (台 tái)

When no measure word is shown for a noun, you can use the default measure word 个 gè.

The dictionary also show antonyms after the definition of common adjectives and some nouns. For example:

gāo 高 ADJ tall, high (ANTONYMS 矮 ǎi, 低 dī)

3.5 Example Sentences

Words become really meaningful only when used in sentences. **A major feature of this dictionary is the thousands of example sentences that amply illustrate the meaning and usage of words.** Great attention was paid to the composition of the sentences to make sure they are

(1) idiomatic,
(2) communicatively useful, and
(3) within the controlled vocabulary of this dictionary.

These sentences are accompanied by their *pinyin* and English translations. In some cases a second translation is provided in brackets to aid comprehension and idiomatic expression.

All this makes this dictionary an essential aid to teaching and learning Chinese.

4 GRAMMAR: Main Features

4.1 Topic+Comment Structure

The basic principle in making Chinese sentences is to follow the "topic+comment" structure. "Topic" means the subject matter you want to talk about, and "comment" is the information you give about the subject matter. To make a Chinese sentence, you simply first mention the subject matter you want to talk about, and then say what you have to say about it. For example, you can say 这件事 zhè jiàn shì (*this matter/affair*) first as the "topic" and then add "comment":

这件事 我不清楚。 **Zhè jiàn shì wǒ bù qīngchǔ.** *I'm not clear about this matter.*

这件事 我很了解。 **Zhè jiàn shì wǒ hěn liǎojiě.** *I know this matter well.*

这件事 谁都不知道。 **Zhè jiàn shì shuí dōu bù zhīdào.** *Nobody knows this matter.*

这件事 我不感兴趣。 **Zhè jiàn shì wǒ bù gǎn xìngqu.** *I'm not interested in this matter.*

这件事 最近社交网站都在谈。 **Zhè jiàn shì zuìjìn shèjiāo dōu zài tán.** *Social media are all talking about this matter these days.*

4.2 Ellipsis of Sentence Elements

Chinese speakers may leave out words that are supposed to be understood, and therefore need not be spoken. Subjects and conjunctions are often omitted. For example, you may translate the English sentence *If you like it, you may buy it, but if you don't like it, you don't have to.* into the Chinese sentence 喜欢就买，不喜欢就别买。 **Xǐhuan jiù mǎi, bù xǐhuan jiù bié mǎi.** Compare the two sentences, and you will find that some English words, such as *if, you, it,* and *but* are not translated.

4. 3 Word Classes: Flexibility, No Inflection

Chinese words do not have inflections, i.e. they do not change to indicate grammatical categories. For example, the verb 做 **zuò** (*to do*) is invariably 做 **zuò**; there is no past form or any other inflected form of this verb. Neither do Chinese words normally have formal markers of word class. Consequently, it is rather easy for a word to be used in more than one word class. This relative flexibility in word classes, however, does not mean that Chinese does not have word classes (see Section 4.5).

4. 4 Measure Words and Particles

Measure words (量词 **liàngcí**) and particles (助词 **zhùcí**) are two word classes found in Chinese but not in English and most other languages.

Measure words are usually required when a noun is modified by a numeral. For example, 两书 **liǎng shū** is unacceptable; you must use the measure word 本 **běn** between the numeral and the noun: 两本书 **liǎng běn shū** (*two books*). Furthermore, Chinese nouns require specific measure words to go with them. For example, the noun 书 **shū** (*book*) must be used with the measure word 本 **běn**. See List 2 Measure Words.

In Chinese grammar, particles are words attached to other words or at the end of a sentence to indicate grammatical concepts or to express emotions. For example, the particles 了 **le**, 着 **zhe**, 过 **guo** are attached to verbs to indicate, respectively, whether the actions denoted are completed, in progress or past experiences.

4.5 Word Classes

Following are brief explanations of the basic terms in Chinese grammar used in this dictionary. (A word of warning: it is a rather complicated matter to define grammatical terms accurately. Here we will be content with some very general but useful ideas.)

ADJECTIVE	a describing word, a word that describes people, things or actions, typically used before a noun.
ADVERB	a word that modifies a verb, an adjective or another adverb.
CONJUNCTION	a word used to link two words, phrases or sentences, indicating certain relationships between them.
IDIOM	a set phrase, the meaning of which cannot be readily derived from its components.
INTERJECTION	a word that expresses strong emotions.
MEASURE WORD	a word that connects a numeral to a noun. Measure words are a special feature of Chinese; a list of measure words is included in the front matter.
MODAL VERB	a word used before a verb to indicate necessity, possibility, willingness, etc.
NOUN	a naming word, a word that names people, animals, plants, things, ideas, etc.
NUMERAL	a word that represents a number, typically used with a noun.
ONOMATOPOEIA	a word that imitates the sounds of a thing or an action.
PARTICLE	a word used with another word, phrase, or sentence to indicate certain grammatical meanings or to express strong emotions.
PREPOSITION	a word used before a noun or pronoun to indicate time, place, direction, manner, reason of an action, etc.
PRONOUN	a word that is used in the place of a noun, a verb, an adjective, etc.
VERB	an action word, a word that indicates what somebody does or feels.

5   CULTURAL AND USAGE NOTES

As a dictionary for learners rather than a mere wordlist, this dictionary goes out of its way to give essential information on cultural context, pronunciation, grammar and usage of words. For example:

lǐwù 礼物 [modif: 礼 gift + 物 thing] N gift, present (件 jiàn)

…

> NOTE: Chinese modesty requires that you belittle your present, describing it as 一件小礼物 yí jiàn xiǎo lǐwù *a small/insignificant gift*. Upon receiving a present, it is bad manners to open it immediately. The recipient is first supposed to say 不用不用 búyòng búyòng *You didn't have to* and then express thanks for the gift, describing it as 这么好的礼物 Zhème hǎo de lǐwù *such a nice gift*, e.g.
> ■ 谢谢你送给我这么好的礼物。 Xièxie nǐ sònggei wǒ zhème hǎo de lǐwù. *Thank you for giving me such a nice gift.*

There are hundreds of such notes in the dictionary.

6   HOW TO LOOK UP A WORD IN THE DICTIONARY

6.1   By *Pinyin* Romanization

This dictionary arranges headwords alphabetically according to *pinyin*. So if you know how a word is pronounced, you can find it easily, just the way you will look up an English word in an English dictionary.

6.2   By Radical

Very often, however, you do not know the pronunciation of a word when you come across it in reading. In that case you can find it either by its radical or the number of its strokes.

Radicals (部首 bùshǒu) are certain component parts of characters that have been used in Chinese dictionary-making for nearly 2,000 years. Characters sharing a radical are grouped together under the heading of that radical. To find a character in a dictionary, follow these steps:

(i)   In the **List of Radicals**, look up the character's radical according to the number of strokes in the radical. This gives a Radical Index number.

(ii)   Turn to the number in the **Radical Index**

(iii)   Locate the character according to the number of remaining strokes needed to write the character (i.e. number of total strokes minus radical strokes = remaining strokes). You will find the pinyin by the character.

For example, to find 活:

(i)   The radical group of 活 is 氵, which has three strokes. In the **List of Radicals**, look up 氵 in the section marked "3 strokes":
        3 strokes
        氵 33

(ii)   Turn to number 33 in the **Radical Index**.

(iii)   As there are nine strokes in 活, and the radical has three strokes, six strokes remain to complete the character 活 (9 − 3 = 6). Look in the section "6 strokes" and locate 活:
        6 strokes
        活 **huó**

(iv)   Turn to **huó** in the dictionary:
        huó 活 …

6.3   By Number of Strokes

Unfortunately, looking for a character by its radical is not an entirely satisfactory method as learners may not always know which part of the character is the radical. Therefore, this dictionary includes a **Stroke Index** to aid the learner further. Simply look for the character according to the number of its strokes, and then locate the character by its first stroke.

For example, to find 活:

(i)   There are nine strokes in 活. Go to the section of nine strokes.

9 strokes

(ii)   As the first stroke of 活 is " 、 ", locate 活 under " 、 ".

、

…

活 **huó**

(iii)   Turn to **huó** in the dictionary.

huó 活...

6.4   By English Meaning

To find out the Chinese equivalent or near-equivalent of an English word, use the English-Chinese Word Finder, which is practically a handy English-Chinese dictionary. Chinese equivalents or near-equivalents of over 6,000 English words are listed alphabetically in the Finder.

For example, to find out what *airport* is in Chinese, turn to "A" in the Finder and locate *airport* in the list of words beginning with "A":

airport **fēijī chǎng** 飞机场 *55*, **jīchǎng** 机场 *86*

The entry for 飞机场 **fēijī chǎng** is found on page 55 and the entry for 机场 **jīchǎng**, on page 86.

It is my firm belief that learners of Chinese will find this dictionary a valuable learning aid.

List 1
Meaningful Character Components

Most of Chinese characters are made up of two or more component parts. "Significant graphs" (义 符 **yìfú**) are components that suggest the meaning of characters. Hence, learning the meaning of these component parts will deepen your understanding of characters you know, and help you guess the meaning of unfamiliar characters. The following is a list of such meaningful character components.

冫 = freezing, ice (e.g. 冰 **bīng**, 冷 **lěng**, 寒 **hán**)

讠, 言 = word (e.g. 语 **yǔ**, 词 **cí**)

八 = dividing (e.g. 分 **fēn**, 半 **bàn**)

刂, 刀 = knife (e.g. 利 **lì**, 剩 **shèng**)

力 = muscle, strength (e.g. 男 **nán**, 办 **bàn**)

阝 (on the left) = mound, steps (e.g. 院 **yuàn**, 附 **fù**)

阝 (on the right) = city, region (e.g. 部 **bù**, 邮 **yóu**)

氵, 水 = water (e.g. 河 **hé**, 海 **hǎi**)

忄, 心 = the heart, emotions (e.g. 情 **qíng**, 怕 **pà**)

宀 = roof, house (e.g. 家 **jiā**, 室 **shì**)

广 = roof, hut (e.g. 庭 **tíng**, 店 **diàn**)

门 = door, gate (e.g. 闻 **wén**, 间 **jiān**)

土 = earth (e.g. 场 **chǎng**, 城 **chéng**)

女 = woman (e.g. 妇 **fù**, 妈 **mā**)

饣, 食 = food (e.g. 饭 **fàn**, 饱 **bǎo**)

口 = the mouth, speech, eating (e.g. 问 **wèn**, 吃 **chī**)

囗 = boundary (e.g. 围 **wéi**, 园 **yuán**)

孑, 子 = child (e.g. 孩 **hái**, 学 **xué**)

艹 = plant, vegetation (e.g. 草 **cǎo**, 菜 **cài**)

纟 = silk, texture (e.g. 组 **zǔ**, 纸 **zhǐ**)

辶 = walking (e.g. 道 **dào**, 过 **guò**)

彳 = path, walking (e.g. 行 **xíng**, 往 **wǎng**)

巾 = cloth (e.g. 布 **bù**, 带 **dài**)

马 = horse (e.g. 骑 **qí**)

扌, 手, 攵 = the hand, action (e.g. 拿 **ná**, 擦 **cā**)

灬, 火 = fire, heat (e.g. 烧 **shāo**, 热 **rè**)

礻, 示 = spirit (e.g. 神 **shén**, 祖 **zǔ**)

户 = door, window (e.g. 房 **fáng**)

父 = father (e.g. 爸 **bà**)

日 = the sun (e.g. 晴 **qíng**, 暖 **nuǎn**)

月 = the moon (e.g. 阴 **yīn**, 明 **míng**)

月, 肉 = flesh, human organ (e.g. 脸 **liǎn**, 脚 **jiǎo**)

贝 = shell, treasure (e.g. 贵 **guì**)

止 = toe (e.g. 步 **bù**)

木 = tree, timber (e.g. 树 **shù**, 板 **bǎn**)

王, 玉 = jade (e.g. 理 **lǐ**, 球 **qiú**)

见 = seeing (e.g. 视 **shì**, 现 **xiàn**)

气 = vapor (e.g. 汽 **qì**)

车 = vehicle (e.g. 辆 **liàng**)

疒 = disease, ailment (e.g. 病 **bìng**, 疼 **téng**)

立 = standing (e.g. 站 **zhàn**, 位 **wèi**)

穴 = cave, hole (e.g. 空 **kōng**, 窗 **chuāng**)

衤, 衣 = clothing (e.g. 裤 **kù**, 袜 **wà**)

钅, 金 = metal (e.g. 银 **yín**, 钱 **qián**)

石 = stone, rock (e.g. 碗 **wǎn**, 磁 **cí**)

目 = the eye (e.g. 眼 **yǎn**, 睡 **shuì**)

田 = farm, field (e.g. 界 **jiè**, 里 **lǐ**)

禾 = seedling, crop (e.g. 种 **zhǒng**, 秋 **qiū**)

鸟 = bird (e.g. 鸡 **jī**)

米 = rice (e.g. 糖 **táng**, 精 **jīng**)

竹, 竹 = bamboo (e.g. 筷 **kuài**, 笔 **bǐ**)

舌 = the tongue (e.g. 话 **huà**, 活 **huó**)

舟 = boat (e.g. 船 **chuán**)

酉 = fermentation (e.g. 酒 **jiǔ**)

走 = walking (e.g. 起 **qǐ**)

⻊, 足 = the foot (e.g. 跳 **tiào**, 踢 **tī**)

List 2
Measure Words

Measure words are a special feature of Chinese. A particular measure word, or set of measure words, occurs with each noun whenever one is speaking of numbers. The measure word may function like a collective noun (like a pride [of lions] or a school [of fish]) or may be related to the shape of the object. Noun phrases using measure words often have the structure "number + measure word + noun," e.g.

- 一把刀 **yì bǎ dāo** *a knife*
- 两道难题 **liǎng dào nántí** *two difficult questions*

Some measure words occur with verbs, and may be related to the frequency or duration of the action. For verbs, the expression may have the structure "verb + number + measure word," e.g.

- 看了三遍 **kànle sān biàn** *read three times*
- 去过两次 **qùguo liǎng cì** *have been ... twice*

bǎ 把 for objects with handles; a handful

bān 班 class (in school)

bèi 倍 fold, time

běn 本 for books

bǐ 笔 for a sum of money

biàn 遍 times, indicating the frequency of an action done in its complete duration from the beginning to the end

cè 册 volume (books)

céng 层 story, floor

chǎng 场 for movies, sport events

chǐ 尺 a traditional Chinese unit of length (equal to 1/3 meter)

cì 次 time, expressing frequency of an act

cùn 寸 a traditional Chinese unit of length (equal to 1/30 meter)

dào 道 for questions in a school exercise, examination, etc.; for things in the shape of a line

dī 滴 drop (of liquid)

diǎn 点 o'clock

dù 度 degree (of temperature, longitude, latitude, etc.)

duàn 段 section of something long

dùn 顿 for meals

duǒ 朵 for flowers

fēn 分 Chinese currency (1 分 **fēn** = 0.1 角

jiǎo = 0.01 元 **yuán**), cent

fèn 份 for a set of things or newspapers, documents, etc.

fēng 封 for letters

fú 幅 for pictures, posters, maps, etc.

gè 个 the most commonly used measure word for nouns that do not take special measure words, or in default of any other measure word

gēn 根 for long, thin things

gōngchǐ 公尺 meter (formal)

gōngjīn 公斤 kilogram

gōnglǐ 公里 kilometer

háng 行 used with nouns that are formed in lines; line, row, queue

hù 户 used with nouns denoting households and families

huí 回 number of times

jiā 家 for families or businesses

jiān 间 for rooms

jiàn 件 for things, affairs, clothes or furniture

jiǎo 角 Chinese currency (0.1 **yuan** or 10 **fen**), ten cents, a dime

jié 节 a period of time

jīn 斤 *jin*, unit of weight equivalent to half a kilogram

jù 句 for sentences

Measure Words

kē 棵 for trees
kè 克 gram
kè 刻 quarter of an hour
kǒu 口 for members of a family
kuài 块 for things that can be broken into lumps or chunks; for money; *yuan*, dollar
lǐ 里 a Chinese unit of length, equivalent to 0.5 kilometers
lì 粒 for rice, pearls
liǎng 两 a traditional Chinese unit of weight, equivalent to 50 grams; ounce
liàng 辆 for vehicles
liè 列 for trains
máo 毛 a Chinese money unit, colloquialism for 角 **jiǎo** (= 0.1 元 **yuán** or 10 分 **fēn**)
mén 门 for school subjects, languages, etc.
mǐ 米 meter (colloquial)
miàn 面 for flat objects
miǎo 秒 second (of time)
míng 名 for people, especially for those with a specific position or occupation
mǔ 亩 a traditional Chinese unit of area, especially in farming (equal to ⅕ hectare or 667 square meters)
pái 排 for things arranged in a row
pī 批 for a batch of goods, and for things/people arriving at the same time
pǐ 匹 for horses
piān 篇 for a piece of writing
piàn 片 for a thin and flat piece, slice
píng 瓶 a bottle of
qún 群 a crowd/group of

shēn 身 for clothes
shǒu 首 for songs and poems
shuāng 双 a pair of (shoes, chopsticks, etc.)
suì 岁 year (of age)
suǒ 所 for houses, or institutions housed in a building
tái 台 for machines, big instruments, etc.
tàng 趟 for trips
tào 套 a set of
tiáo 条 for things with a long, narrow shape
tóu 头 for cattle or sheep
wèi 位 a polite measure word for people
xià 下 used with certain verbs to indicate the number of times the action is done
xiàng 项 item, component
xiē 些 some, a few, a little
yè 页 for pages (of a book)
yīngchǐ 英尺 foot (as a measurement of length)
yīngcùn 英寸 inch
yuán 元 the basic unit of Chinese currency (1 元 **yuán** = 10 角 **jiǎo** / 毛 **máo** = 100 分 **fēn**), dollar
zhāng 张 for paper, beds, tables, desks
zhèn 阵 for an action or event that lasts for some time
zhī 支 for stick-like things
zhī 只 for animals, utensils, or objects
zhǒng 种 kind, sort
zuò 座 for large and solid objects, such as a large building

List of Radicals

1 stroke

Radical	No.
、	1
一	2
乙乚	3
丨	4
丿	5

2 strokes

Radical	No.
亠	6
冫	7
冫氵讠	8
二	9
十	10
厂	11
匚	12
匕	13
卜	14
刂	15
冖	16
冂	17
勹	18
刀	19
力	20
八	21
亻	22
人	23
儿	24
几	25
又	26
凵	27
厶	28
廴	29
卩	30
阝(on left)	31
阝(on right)	32

3 strokes

Radical	No.
氵	33
忄	34
小宀	35
宀	36
忄广	37
辶	38
门	39
辶	40
工	41
干	42
土	43
士	44
上	45
艹	46
卝	47
大	48
寸	49
扌	50
口	51
囗	52
巾	53
山	54
彳	55
彡	56
夕	57
夂	58
犭	59
彐	60
尸	61
已	62
己	63
巳	64
弓	65
女	66
子	67
纟	68
马	69
	70

4 strokes

Radical	No.
灬	71
文	72
方	73
心	74
户	75
斗	76
王, 玉	77
木	78
犬	79
歹	80
瓦	81
车	82
比	83
日	84
曰	85
贝	86
见	87
父	88
攵	89
牛	90
手	91
毛	92
气	93
片	94
斤	95
爪	96
月	97
欠	98
风	99
殳	100
火	101
礻	102
戈	103
水	104
止	105

5 strokes

Radical	No.
石	106
业	107
目	108
田	109
皿	110
四	111
钅	112
矢	113
禾	114
白	115
用	116
母	117
鸟	118
疒	119
立	120
穴	121
礻	122
示	123
去	124
疋	125
皮	126

6 strokes

Radical	No.
老	127
耳	128
西	129
页	130
虫	131
缶	132
舌	133
竹	134
自	135
舟	136
衣	137
亦	138
羊	139
米	140
耒	141
艮	142
羽	143
糸	144

7 strokes

Radical	No.
走	145
里	146
足	147
身	148
豸	149
角	150
言	151
辛	152
束	153
非	154
酉	155
豆	156

8 strokes

Radical	No.
佳	157
青	158
鱼	159
雨	160
齿	161

9 strokes

Radical	No.
革	162
是	163
食	164
音	165

10 strokes

Radical	No.
鬼	166

11 strokes

Radical	No.
麻	167

12 strokes

Radical	No.
黑	168

Radical Index

All characters are listed here under their radical plus the number of additional strokes needed to write them.

1 、

1–5 strokes

义 yì
之 zhī
为 wéi/wèi
半 bàn
永 yǒng
主 zhǔ
州 zhōu

6–11 strokes

举 jǔ
登 dēng

2 一

1–3 strokes

一 yī/yí/yì
七 qī
丁 dīng
亏 kuī
三 sān
万 wàn
下 xià
与 yǔ
于 yú
丈 zhàng
才 cái
互 hù
井 jǐng
开 kāi
天 tiān
五 wǔ
无 wú
牙 yá
尤 yóu
长 zhǎng
专 zhuān
不 bù/bú
丰 fēng

4–6 strokes

击 jī
龙 lóng
平 píng
世 shì
丙 bǐng
丛 cóng

东 dōng
而 ér
夹 jiā
亚 yà
再 zài
至 zhì
更 gēng/gèng
来 lái
丽 lì
两 liǎng
求 qiú
严 yán

7–12 strokes

事 shì
肃 sù
表 biǎo
面 miàn
甚 shèn
衰 sāng/sàng
昼 zhòu
哥 gē

3 乙

1–7 strokes

乙 yǐ
乞 qǐ
飞 fēi
丑 chǒu
民 mín
买 mǎi
承 chéng

4 丨

3–6 strokes

中 zhōng
旧 jiù
且 qiě
申 shēn
史 shǐ
师 shī
串 chuàn

7–12 strokes

畅 chàng
临 lín
虐 nüè

鉴 jiàn

5 丿

1–5 strokes

了 liǎo/le
九 jiǔ
及 jí
久 jiǔ
丸 wán
习 xí
乡 xiāng
也 yě
川 chuān
书 shū
乌 wū
乏 fá
长 cháng
瓜 guā
乎 hū
丘 qiū
生 shēng
失 shī
乐 lè/yuè
年 nián
农 nóng
向 xiàng
血 xuě/xiě

6–13 strokes

囱 cōng
乖 guāi
乳 rǔ
垂 chuí
鼠 shǔ
舞 wǔ

6 亠

1–7 strokes

亡 wáng
六 liù
市 shì
交 jiāo
亦 yì
产 chǎn
充 chōng
亩 mǔ

京 jīng
享 xiǎng
夜 yè
哀 āi
亮 liàng
亭 tíng

8–15 strokes

帝 dì
离 lí
衷 zhōng
高 gāo
商 shāng
率 lù/shuài
就 jiù
豪 háo
赢 yíng

7 冫

决 jué
冰 bīng
冲 chōng
次 cì
况 kuàng
况 kuàng
冷 lěng
冻 dòng
净 jìng
悄 shāo
凉 liáng
凄 qī
准 zhǔn
减 jiǎn
凌 líng
凑 còu
凝 níng

8 讠

2–6 strokes

计 jì
讥 jī
认 rèn
诛 zhū
订 dìng
记 jì
让 ràng
讨 tǎo

训 xùn
讯 xùn
议 yì
讲 jiǎng
论 lùn
设 shè
许 xǔ
讽 fěng
访 fǎng
识 shí
诉 sù
译 yì
诈 zhà
诊 zhěn
证 zhèng
词 cí
话 huà
评 píng
试 shì
诗 shī
详 xiáng
询 xún
诚 chéng
诞 dàn
该 gāi
诧 chà

7–12 strokes

说 shuō
诵 sòng
诬 wū
误 wù
诱 yòu
语 yǔ
课 kè
谅 liàng
请 qǐng
谁 shéi/shuí
谈 tán
调 tiáo
谊 yì
读 dú
诽 fěi
调 diào
谎 huǎng
谜 mí
谋 móu

谓 wèi
谍 dié
谦 qiān
谢 xiè
谣 yáo
谨 jǐn
谬 miù
谴 qiǎn
谱 pǔ

9 二

二 èr
些 xiē

10 十

十 shí
升 shēng
午 wǔ
千 qiān
支 zhī
毕 bì
华 huá
协 xié
克 kè
卑 bēi
兢 jīng
卖 mài
直 zhí
卓 zhuó
南 nán
罩 zhào
真 zhēn

11 厂

厂 chǎng

2–10 strokes

历 lì
厅 tīng
厉 lì
后 hòu
压 yā
厌 yàn
辰 chén
厕 cè
厘 lí

厚	hòu
盾	dùn
原	yuán
厨	chú

12 匚

巨	jù
匹	pǐ
区	qū
臣	chén
医	yī
卧	wò
匪	fěi

13 匕

北	běi

14 卜

上	shàng
卡	kǎ
占	zhàn

15 刂

3–5 strokes

刊	kān
划	huá/huà
列	liè
刑	xíng
则	zé
刚	gāng
创	chuàng
利	lì
判	pàn
删	shān
别	bié
到	dào

6–10 strokes

刮	guā
剂	jì
刻	kè
刷	shuā
制	zhì
刺	cì
剑	jiàn
削	xiāo/xuē
剧	jù
剖	pōu
剥	bō
副	fù
割	gē
剩	shèng

16 宀

写	xiě
军	jūn
罕	hǎn
冠	guàn
冤	yuān

17 冂

内	nèi
同	tóng
册	cè
肉	ròu
网	wǎng
周	zhōu

18 勹

勺	sháo
勾	gōu
勿	wù
句	jù
匆	cōng

19 刀

刀	dāo

2-6 strokes

切	qiē/qiè
矛	máo
召	zhào
色	sè
争	zhēng
免	miǎn
危	wēi
兔	tù

7-13 strokes

剪	jiǎn
象	xiàng
劈	pī
豫	yù

20 力

2-5 strokes

力	lì
劝	quàn
加	jiā
务	wù
劣	liè
动	dòng
劲	jìn
励	lì
男	nán
努	nǔ

助	zhù

6-11 strokes

势	shì
勉	miǎn
勇	yǒng
勘	kān
舅	jiù
勤	qín

21 八

八	bā

2-5 strokes

公	gōng
分	fēn
分	fēn
兰	lán
共	gòng
关	guān
兴	xīng/xìng
并	bìng
谷	gǔ
兑	duì
兵	bīng
弟	dì

6-13 strokes

具	jù
其	qí
典	diǎn
单	dān
首	shǒu
兼	jiān
前	qián
兽	shòu
奠	diàn
曾	céng

22 亻

1–5 strokes

亿	yì
化	huà
仅	jǐn
仁	rén
仍	réng
什	shén
仇	chóu
代	dài
们	men
他	tā
仙	xiān
仪	yí
仗	zhàng

仔	zǐ
付	fù
何	hé
伙	huǒ
价	jià
件	jiàn
任	rèn
伤	shāng
似	shì/sì
伟	wěi
伪	wěi
休	xiū
优	yōu
传	chuán/zhuàn
份	fèn
仿	fǎng
伏	fú
伴	bàn
保	bǎo
倍	bèi
估	gū
你	nǐ
伸	shēn
体	tǐ
位	wèi
佣	yōng
住	zhù
作	zuò
伯	bó
伺	cì
但	dàn
低	dī
佛	fó

6–9 strokes

供	gōng
佳	jiā
侥	jiǎo
例	lì
侣	lǚ
佩	pèi
侨	qiáo
使	shǐ
侠	xiá
依	yī
侦	zhēn
侄	zhí
侧	cè
俭	jiǎn
倒	dǎo/dào
俊	jùn

俩	liǎ
便	pián
侵	qīn
俗	sú
信	xìn
修	xiū
便	biàn
促	cù
俄	é
俘	fú
侮	wǔ
候	hòu
健	jiàn
借	jiè
俱	jù
倦	juàn
倔	jué
倾	qīng
倘	tǎng
债	zhài
值	zhí
俯	fǔ
倡	chàng
假	jiǎ/jià
偶	ǒu
偏	piān
停	tíng
偷	tōu
做	zuò
偿	cháng

10–14 strokes

傲	ào
傍	bàng
傅	fù
储	chǔ
博	bó
傻	shǎ
像	xiàng
催	cuī
僻	pì
僵	jiāng
儒	rú

23 人

人	rén
入	rù

1–10 strokes

个	gè
介	jiè
今	jīn
以	yǐ

从	cóng
仓	cāng
令	lìng
会	huì/kuài
伞	sǎn
众	zhòng
金	jīn
命	mìng
舍	shè/shě
禽	qín

24 儿

儿	ér
元	yuán
兄	xiōng
光	guāng
先	xiān
宪	xiàn

25 几

几	jī/jǐ
凡	fán
秃	tū
虎	hǔ
凭	píng

26 又

又	yòu
双	shuāng
友	yǒu
叉	chā
反	fǎn
圣	shèng
发	fā
对	duì
变	biàn
艰	jiān
受	shòu
叔	shū
叛	pàn
叙	xù
难	nán
释	shì
叠	dié
聚	jù
敲	qiāo

27 凵

凹	āo
凶	xiōng
出	chū

Radical Index

画	huà	随	suí	治	zhì	渴	kě	恼	nǎo	宏	hóng

画	huà

28 厶

么	me
云	yún
允	yǔn
台	tái
县	xiàn
参	cān
能	néng

29 廴

延	yán
建	jiàn

30 卩

卫	wèi
危	wēi
即	jí
却	què
卷	juǎn
卸	xiè
印	yìn

31 阝 (on left)

2–6 strokes

队	duì
阶	jiē
阳	yáng
阴	yīn
阵	zhèn
防	fáng
阿	ā
陈	chén
附	fù
际	jì
陆	lù
阻	zǔ
降	jiàng
陌	mò
限	xiàn
降	xiáng

7–11 strokes

险	xiǎn
院	yuàn
陡	dǒu
除	chú
陪	péi
陶	táo
陷	xiàn
隆	lóng

随	suí
隐	yǐn
隘	ài
隔	gé
隧	suì
障	zhàng

32 阝 (on right)

那	nà
那	nèi
邻	lín
邮	yóu
部	bù
都	dōu
都	dū
鄙	bǐ

33 氵

2–5 strokes

汉	Hàn
汇	huì
汁	zhī
池	chí
汗	hàn
江	jiāng
汤	tāng
污	wū
沟	gōu
没	méi
沐	mù
汽	qì
沙	shā
沉	chén
沧	cāng
泛	fàn
河	hé
沮	jǔ
泪	lèi
怜	lián
泥	ní
怕	pà
泡	pào
泊	pō
泼	pō
浅	qiǎn
泄	xiè
泻	xiè
沿	yán
泳	yǒng
油	yóu
沼	zhǎo

治	zhì
注	zhù
沸	fèi
法	fǎ

6–8 strokes

洪	hóng
浑	hún
活	huó
济	jì
浇	jiāo
洁	jié
津	jīn
浏	liú
浓	nóng
派	pài
洽	qià
洒	sǎ
洗	xǐ
洋	yáng
洲	zhōu
洞	dòng
测	cè
海	hǎi
浸	jìn
酒	jiǔ
浪	làng
流	liú
涉	shè
涂	tú
消	xiāo
涌	yǒng
浴	yù
涨	zhǎng
浮	fú
淡	dàn
混	hùn
渐	jiàn
淋	lín
清	qīng
深	shēn
渗	shèn
涮	shuàn
淘	táo
添	tiān
淹	yān
液	yè
渔	yú

9–10 strokes

湖	hú
滑	huá
溅	jiàn

渴	kě
渺	miǎo
湿	shī
湾	wān
温	wēn
游	yóu
渣	zhā
滞	zhì
滋	zī
渡	dù
港	gǎng
滚	gǔn
溜	liū
滤	lǜ
满	mǎn
漠	mò
溶	róng
滔	tāo
溪	xī
源	yuán
滨	bīn

11–17 strokes

漏	lòu
漫	màn
漂	piāo/piào
潇	xiāo
演	yǎn
波	bō
滴	dī
澳	ào
潜	qián
潮	cháo
澄	chéng
激	jī
澡	zǎo
瀑	pù
灌	guàn

34 忄

1–8 strokes

忆	yì
忙	máng
怀	huái
快	kuài
忧	yōu
怪	guài
性	xìng
怖	bù
恨	hèn
恒	héng
恢	huī

恼	nǎo
恰	qià
悔	huǐ
悄	qiāo
惯	guàn
惊	jīng
惧	jù
情	qíng
惋	wǎn
惜	xī
悼	dào
惦	diàn
惨	cǎn
惭	cán

9–13 strokes

慌	huāng
愧	kuì
愉	yú
愤	fèn
慎	shèn
慢	màn
懂	dǒng
憾	hàn
懒	lǎn

35 小

小	xiǎo

1–5 strokes

少	shǎo/shào
尖	jiān
杀	shā
尘	chén
当	dāng/dàng
肖	xiào
余	yú
尚	shàng
尝	cháng
恭	gōng
党	dǎng
常	cháng
辉	huī
慕	mù

36 宀

2–5 strokes

宁	níng/nìng
它	tā
安	ān
守	shǒu
宇	yǔ
宅	zhái

宏	hóng
牢	láo
完	wán
宝	bǎo
官	guān
审	shěn
实	shí
灾	zāi
定	dìng

6–13 strokes

宫	gōng
客	kè
室	shì
宣	xuān
宗	zōng
害	hài
家	jiā
宽	kuān
宴	yàn
宾	bīn
宰	zǎi
寂	jì
寄	jì
宿	sù
寒	hán
寓	yù
富	fù
塞	sāi
赛	sài
察	chá

37 爿

壮	zhuàng
状	zhuàng
将	jiāng

38 广

广	guǎng
庆	qìng
库	kù
序	xù
庄	zhuāng
床	chuáng
庙	miào
庞	páng
应	yìng/yīng
底	dǐ
店	diàn
府	fǔ
废	fèi
庭	tíng

度 dù	适 shì	寺 sì	**45 上**	薄 báo/bó	托 tuō
席 xí	送 sòng	在 zài	上 shàng	蔑 miè	扬 yáng
座 zuò	逃 táo	地 de/dì	**46 艹**	薪 xīn	执 zhí
康 kāng	退 tuì	场 chǎng	*1–7 strokes*	藐 miǎo	扮 bàn
庸 yōng	选 xuǎn	坝 bà	艺 yì	藏 cáng	把 bǎ
廉 lián	追 zhuī	坏 huài	节 jié		报 bào
腐 fǔ	逛 guàng	坚 jiān	花 huā	**47 廾**	护 hù
	逝 shì	均 jūn	劳 láo	弄 nòng	技 jì
39 门	速 sù	坑 kēng	苏 sū	弃 qì	抗 kàng
门 mén	透 tòu	块 kuài	芽 yá	奔 bēn	拟 nǐ
2–10 strokes	途 tú	坛 tán	荐 jiàn	弊 bì	扭 niǔ
闪 shǎn	造 zào	址 zhǐ	茎 jīng		抛 pāo
闭 bì	逐 zhú	坠 zhuì	苦 kǔ	**48 大**	批 pī
问 wèn	递 dì	坐 zuò	茂 mào	大 dà	抢 qiǎng
间 jiān/jiàn	逗 dòu	坟 fén	苗 miáo	太 tài	扰 rǎo
闷 mēn	逢 féng	垄 lǒng	若 ruò	夫 fū	投 tóu
闲 xián	通 tōng	坡 pō	英 yīng	头 tóu	抑 yì
闹 nào	逮 dài	坦 tǎn	苍 cāng	夸 kuā	找 zhǎo
闻 wén	逻 luó	型 xíng	范 fàn	奇 qí	折 zhē/zhé
阅 yuè	逼 bī	幸 xìng	荒 huāng	奉 fèng	抓 zhuā
阐 chǎn	道 dào	垫 diàn	荤 hūn	奋 fèn	扯 chě
阔 kuò	*10–13 strokes*	城 chéng	茫 máng	奖 jiǎng	扶 fú
	遗 yí	埋 mái/mán	荣 róng	类 lèi	抄 chāo
40 辶	遇 yù	*8–17 strokes*	药 yào	牵 qiān	抖 dǒu
2–5 strokes	遍 biàn	基 jī	荧 yíng	奏 zòu	抚 fǔ
辽 liáo	遏 è	培 péi	荡 dàng	套 tào	拌 bàn
边 biān	遥 yáo	堂 táng	获 huò	奢 shē	抱 bào
达 dá	遭 zāo	堆 duī	莫 mò	爽 shuǎng	拔 bá
过 guò	遮 zhē	堕 duò	茶 chá	奥 ào	拐 guǎi
迈 mài	遵 zūn	堵 dǔ	草 cǎo		拣 jiǎn
迄 qì	避 bì	堡 bǎo	*8–15 strokes*	**49 寸**	拘 jū
迁 qiān	邀 yāo	塔 tǎ	菌 jūn	寸 cùn	拒 jù
巡 xún		堤 dī	萌 méng	寻 xún	拉 lā
迅 xùn	**41 工**	塑 sù	苹 píng	夺 duó	拦 lán
还 hái/huán	工 gōng	塌 tā	营 yíng	寿 shòu	抹 mǒ
近 jìn	功 gōng	填 tián	著 zhù	耐 nài	拧 níng
进 jìn	巧 qiǎo	境 jìng	菜 cài	封 fēng	拍 pāi
连 lián	左 zuǒ	墙 qiáng	黄 huáng	辱 rǔ	披 pī
违 wéi	巩 gǒng	增 zēng	萝 luó	尊 zūn	揉 róu
迎 yíng	式 shì	壁 bì	落 luò		抬 tái
远 yuàn	攻 gōng	壤 rǎng	葱 cōng	**50 扌**	拖 tuō
运 yùn	项 xiàng		蓝 lán	*1–5 strokes*	押 yā
这 zhè/zhèi		**44 士**	蒙 mēng	扎 zhā	拥 yōng
返 fǎn	**42 干**	士 shì	蒸 zhēng	扒 bā	择 zé
迟 chí	干 gān/gàn	壳 ké/qiào	蔼 ǎi	扑 pū	招 zhāo
迫 pò	旱 hàn	声 shēng	蔽 bì	扔 rēng	抵 dǐ
述 shù		壶 hú	蔓 màn	打 dǎ	抽 chōu
6–9 strokes	**43 土**	辜 gū	蕉 jiāo	扛 káng	担 dān
迹 jì	土 tǔ	喜 xǐ	蔬 shū	扣 kòu	拆 chāi
迷 mí	*1–7 strokes*	鼓 gǔ	蕴 yùn	扩 kuò	拨 bō
逆 nì	圾 jī	嘉 jiā		扫 sǎo	

Radical Index

Radical Index

胎	tāi					碗	wǎn	畔	pàn	铸	zhù

Radical Index

皂 zào
的 de
皇 huáng
皆 jiē
魄 pò

116 用
用 yòng
甩 shuǎi
甭 béng

117 母
母 mǔ
每 měi
毒 dú

118 鸟
鸟 niǎo
鸡 jī
鸦 yā
鸭 yā
鸽 gē
鹅 é

119 疒
2-5 strokes
疗 liáo
灯 dēng
疤 bā
疯 fēng
疾 jí
疲 pí
疼 téng
症 zhèng
病 bìng
6–12 strokes
痕 hén
痒 yǎng
痛 tòng
痹 bì
瘦 shòu
瘤 liú
瘫 tān
瘸 qué
瘾 yǐn
癌 ái

120 立
立 lì
4-9 strokes
亲 qīn

竖 shù
竞 jìng
站 zhàn
童 tóng
竭 jié
端 duān

121 穴
究 jiū
穷 qióng
空 kōng/kòng
帘 lián
窃 qiè
突 tū
穿 chuān
窍 qiào
窄 zhǎi
窝 wō
窗 chuāng
窜 cuàn

122 衤
初 chū
补 bǔ
衬 chèn
衫 shān
被 bèi
袍 páo
袜 wà
袖 xiù
袱 fú
裤 kù
裙 qún

123 示
示 shì
票 piào
禁 jìn

124 去
去 qù
丢 diū

125 疋
楚 chǔ
疑 yí

126 皮
皮 pí
皱 zhòu

127 老
考 kǎo
老 lǎo

128 耳
耳 ěr
取 qǔ
耸 sǒng
耻 chǐ
耽 dān
聊 liáo
聋 lóng
职 zhí
联 lián
聘 pìn
聪 cōng

129 西
西 xī
覆 fù

130 页
页 yè
2-5 strokes
顶 dǐng
须 xū
顾 gù
颂 sòng
预 yù
顿 dùn
颁 bān
颈 jǐng
领 lǐng
7-13 strokes
频 pín
颗 kē
顺 shùn
颜 yán
额 é
颠 diān
颤 chàn

131 虫
3-6 strokes
虫 chóng
虹 hóng
蚂 mǎ
虽 suī
蚊 wén
蛇 shé
蛋 dàn

蛮 mán
蛙 wā
7-15 strokes
蜂 fēng
蜡 là
蜜 mì
蝇 yíng
蝴 hú
蝶 dié
融 róng
蠢 chǔn

132 缶
缺 quē
罐 guàn

133 舌
舌 shé
乱 luàn
敌 dí
甜 tián
舒 shū
辞 cí
舔 tiǎn

134 竹
竹 zhú
4-6 strokes
笑 xiào
笔 bǐ
笨 bèn
笼 lóng
符 fú
第 dì
筹 chóu
筋 jīn
筛 shāi
筑 zhù
等 děng
答 dá
答 dā
策 cè
7-14 strokes
简 jiǎn
筷 kuài
签 qiān
管 guǎn
算 suàn
箭 jiàn
篇 piān
箱 xiāng

篮 lán
籍 jí

135 自
自 zì
臭 chòu
鼻 bí

136 舟
舟 zhōu
舰 jiàn
航 háng
舱 cāng
船 chuán
艇 tǐng
艘 sōu

137 衣
衣 yī
衰 shuāi
袭 xí
袋 dài
装 zhuāng
裹 guǒ

138 亦
赤 chì

139 羊
羊 yáng
美 měi
养 yǎng
差 chā/chà/chāi
羞 xiū
着 zháo/zhe/zhuó
群 qún
羡 xiàn

140 米
米 mǐ
料 liào
粉 fěn
粒 lì
粗 cū
粘 zhān
粮 liáng
糊 hú
糖 táng
糕 gāo

糟 zāo
精 jīng

141 耒
耕 gēng
耗 hào

142 艮
良 liáng
既 jì

143 羽
羽 yǔ
翅 chì
翘 qiào
耀 yào
翻 fān

144 糸
系 jì/xì
紧 jǐn
素 sù
索 suǒ
累 lèi
紫 zǐ
繁 fán

145 走
走 zǒu
赴 fù
起 qǐ
赶 gǎn
越 yuè
趁 chèn
超 chāo
趣 qù
趟 tàng

146 里
里 lǐ
重 chóng/zhòng
野 yě

147 足
足 zú
趴 pā
距 jù
跃 yuè
践 jiàn
跑 pǎo

跌	diē	**150 角**		**154 非**		雄	xióng	霞	xiá
跟	gēn	角	jiǎo/jué	非	fēi	雅	yǎ	霸	bà
跪	guì	解	jiě	罪	zuì	雌	cí	露	lù
跨	kuà	触	chù	靠	kào	雕	diāo		
路	lù							**165 音**	
跳	tiào	**151 言**		**155 酉**		**158 青**		音	yīn
踊	yǒng	言	yán	配	pèi	青	qīng	章	zhāng
蹲	dūn	警	jǐng	酝	yùn	静	jìng		
踢	tī			酬	chóu			**166 鬼**	
踪	zōng	**152 辛**		酱	jiàng	**159 鱼**		鬼	guǐ
踩	cǎi	辛	xīn	酷	kù	鱼	yú	魅	mèi
蹬	dēng	辟	pì	酿	niàng	鲜	xiān	魔	mó
蹦	bèng	辣	là	酸	suān				
		辨	biàn	醉	zuì	**160 雨**		**167 麻**	
148 身		辩	biàn	醋	cù	雨	yǔ	麻	má
身	shēn	辫	biàn	醒	xǐng	雹	báo		
躬	gōng	瓣	bàn			雷	léi	**168 黑**	
射	shè			**156 豆**		零	líng	黑	hēi
躲	duǒ	**153 束**		豆	dòu	雾	wù	墨	mò
躺	tǎng	束	shù			需	xū	默	mò
		赖	lài	**157 隹**		霉	méi		
149 豸				焦	jiāo	震	zhèn		
貌	mào					霜	shuāng		

161 齿	
齿	chǐ
龄	líng

162 革	
革	gé
鞋	xié
鞠	jū
鞭	biān

163 是	
是	shì
匙	shi
题	tí

164 食	
食	shí
餐	cān

Stroke Index

This index lists all characters in this dictionary according to the number of strokes used to write them. Characters with the same number of strokes are grouped together according to the first stroke used. These groups are listed in the following order:

1. 一 (including ⺂ ⺄)
2. 丨 (including 丿 丨)
3. 丿 (including 丿 一 丨)
4. 丶 (including 丶 ㇏)
5. ㇕ (including 乛 乙 ...)
6. ⺄ (including ...)

Within each group, characters are arranged alphabetically according to *pinyin*.

1 stroke
（一）

一	yī/yí/yì
乙	yǐ

2 strokes

厂	chǎng
丁	dīng
二	èr
七	qī
十	shí

（丿）

八	bā
儿	ér
几	jī
几	jǐ
九	jiǔ
人	rén
入	rù

（㇕）

刀	dāo
己	jǐ
了	le/liǎo
力	lì
又	yòu

3 Strokes

才	cái
寸	cùn
大	dà
干	gān/gàn
工	gōng
亏	kuī
零	líng
三	sān
士	shì
土	tǔ
万	wàn
下	xià
于	yú
丈	zhàng

（丨）

巾	jīn
口	kǒu
上	shàng
小	xiǎo

（丿）

川	chuān
凡	fán
个	gè
及	jí
久	jiǔ
么	me
乞	qǐ
千	qiān
勺	sháo
丸	wán
夕	xī
义	yì
亿	yì
广	guǎng
门	mén
亡	wáng
源	yuán
之	zhī

（㇕）

叉	chā
飞	fēi
马	mǎ
尸	shī
卫	wèi
习	xí
也	yě
已	yǐ
子	zǐ/zi

（㇕）

女	nǚ
山	shān
乡	xiāng

4 Strokes
（一）

不	bú/bù
车	chē
歹	dǎi
丰	fēng
夫	fū
互	hù
井	jǐng
巨	jù
开	kāi
历	lì
木	mù
匹	pǐ
墙	qiáng
切	qiē/qiè
区	qū
犬	quǎn
太	tài
天	tiān
厅	tīng
瓦	wǎ
王	wáng
无	wú
五	wǔ
牙	yá
艺	yì
尤	yóu
友	yǒu
元	yuán
云	yún
扎	zhā
支	zhī
专	zhuān

（丨）

贝	bèi
长	cháng
见	jiàn
内	nèi
日	rì
少	shǎo/shào
水	shuǐ
同	tóng
长	zhǎng
止	zhǐ
中	zhōng

（丿）

币	bì
仓	cāng
仇	chóu
从	cóng
乏	fá
反	fǎn
分	fēn/fèn
风	fēng
父	fù
公	gōng
勾	gōu
化	huà
介	jiè
今	jīn
斤	jīn
仅	jǐn
猫	māo
牛	niú
片	piàn
气	qì
欠	qiàn
仁	rén
仍	réng
什	shén
升	shēng
手	shǒu
乌	wū
午	wǔ
勿	wù
月	yuè

（丶）

订	dìng
斗	dòu
方	fāng
户	hù
火	huǒ
讥	jī
计	jì
六	liù
认	rèn
为	wéi
为	wèi
文	wén
心	xīn
忆	yì

（㇕）

办	bàn
尺	chǐ
丑	chǒu
队	duì
孔	kǒng
劝	quàn
书	shū
双	shuāng
引	yǐn

（㇕）

比	bǐ
幻	huàn
凶	xiōng
以	yǐ
与	yǔ
允	yǔn

5 Strokes
（一）

扒	bā
本	bēn
丙	bǐng
布	bù
打	dǎ
东	dōng
功	gōng
古	gǔ
击	jī
节	jié
可	kě
厉	lì
龙	lóng
灭	miè
末	mò
平	píng
扑	pū
巧	qiǎo
去	qù
扔	rēng
石	shí
示	shì
世	shì
术	shù
未	wèi
右	yòu
玉	yù
正	zhèng
左	zuǒ

（丨）

凹	āo
北	běi
旦	dàn
电	diàn
叼	diāo
叮	dīng
归	guī
号	hào
甲	jiǎ
叫	jiào
旧	jiù
卡	kǎ
另	lìng
目	mù
且	qiě
申	shēn
史	shǐ
帅	shuài
四	sì
叹	tàn
田	tián
兄	xiōng
叶	yè
业	yè
由	yóu
占	zhàn
只	zhī/zhǐ

（丿）

白	bái
包	bāo
册	cè
斥	chì
丛	cóng
处	chǔ/chù
匆	cōng
代	dài
冬	dōng
犯	fàn
付	fù
瓜	guā
乎	hū
饥	jī
句	jù

7–8 Strokes Index

兔 tù
妥 tuǒ
往 wǎng
委 wěi
物 wù
侠 xiá
欣 xīn
依 yī
鱼 yú
岳 yuè
胀 zhàng
侦 zhēn
征 zhēng
知 zhī
侄 zhí
制 zhì
质 zhì
肿 zhǒng
周 zhōu

丶

宝 báo
变 biàn
波 bō
怖 bù
诧 chà
炒 chǎo
衬 chèn
诚 chéng
单 dān
诞 dàn
底 dǐ
店 diàn
定 dìng
法 fǎ
房 fáng
放 fàng
废 fèi
沸 fèi
府 fǔ
该 gāi
怪 guài
官 guān
河 hé
话 huà
剂 jì
肩 jiān
京 jīng
净 jìng
沮 jǔ
卷 juǎn
刻 kè
空 kōng/kòng
泪 lèi
怜 lián
帘 lián
炉 lú
盲 máng
庙 miào
闹 nào

泥 ní
怕 pà
庞 páng
泡 pào
泼 pō
泊 pō
浅 qiǎn
衫 shān
审 shěn
诗 shī
实 shí
视 shì
试 shì
详 xiáng
享 xiǎng
泄 xiè
泻 xiè
性 xìng
学 xué
询 xún
沿 yán
炎 yán
夜 yè
泳 yǒng
油 yóu
育 yù
沼 zhǎo
治 zhì
注 zhù
宗 zōng

𠃌

承 chéng
孤 gū
驾 jià
艰 jiān
建 jiàn
降 jiàng
届 jiè
居 jū
录 lù
弥 mí
陌 mò
迫 pò
屈 qū
述 shù
肃 sù
弦 xián
限 xiàn
驻 zhù

𠃊

参 cān
姑 gū
贯 guàn
姐 jiě
经 jīng
练 liàn
妹 mèi

绍 shào
绅 shēn
始 shǐ
细 xì
线 xiàn
姓 xìng
织 zhī
终 zhōng
组 zǔ

9 Strokes

一

按 àn
帮 bāng
甭 béng
标 biāo
玻 bō
残 cán
草 cǎo
茶 chá
查 chá
城 chéng
持 chí
春 chūn
带 dài
挡 dǎng
荡 dàng
垫 diàn
栋 dòng
毒 dú
封 fēng
赴 fù
革 gé
故 gù
挂 guà
厚 hòu
胡 hú
荒 huāng
挥 huī
荤 hūn
挤 jǐ
荐 jiàn
砍 kǎn
枯 kū
挎 kuà
括 kuò
栏 lán
厘 lí
茫 máng
面 miàn
某 mǒu
耐 nài
南 nán
挠 náo
挪 nuó
拼 pīn
牵 qiān
轻 qīng
荣 róng

甚 shèn
拾 shí
柿 shì
树 shù
耍 shuǎ
挑 tiāo/tiǎo
挺 tǐng
挖 wā
歪 wāi
威 wēi
咸 xián
相 xiāng/xiàng
巷 xiàng
项 xiàng
鸦 yā
研 yán
药 yào
要 yào
荧 yíng
珍 zhēn
挣 zhēng/zhèng
政 zhèng
指 zhǐ
拽 zhuāi
砖 zhuān
柱 zhù
奏 zòu

丨

背 bēi/bèi
尝 cháng
点 diǎn
哆 duō
罚 fá
骨 gǔ
贵 guì
哈 hā
虹 hóng
哄 hǒng
将 jiāng
奖 jiǎng
界 jiè
咳 ké
临 lín
蚂 mǎ
骂 mà
冒 mào
哪 nǎ
虐 nüè
趴 pā
盼 pàn
品 pǐn
省 shěng
是 shì
竖 shù
思 sī
虽 suī
贴 tiē

哇 wā
畏 wèi
胃 wèi
峡 xiá
显 xiǎn
响 xiǎng
削 xiāo/xuē
星 xīng
哑 yǎ
咽 yàn
咬 yǎo
映 yìng
咱 zán
眨 zhǎ
战 zhàn
昨 zuó

丿

拜 bài
胞 bāo
保 bǎo
便 biàn
饼 bǐng
钞 chāo
重 chóng
促 cù
贷 dài
待 dài
胆 dǎn
独 dú
段 duàn
盾 dùn
俄 é
俘 fú
复 fù
钙 gài
钢 gāng
钩 gōu
鬼 guǐ
很 hěn
狠 hěn
皇 huáng
急 jí
俭 jiǎn
剑 jiàn
饺 jiǎo
狡 jiǎo
俊 jùn
看 kàn
俩 liǎ
律 lù
贸 mào
勉 miǎn
秒 miǎo
胖 pàng
盆 pén
便 pián
侵 qīn

钦 qīn
氢 qīng
秋 qiū
泉 quán
缺 quē
饶 ráo
牲 shēng
胜 shèng
狮 shī
食 shí
适 shì
顺 shùn
俗 sú
胎 tāi
侮 wǔ
狭 xiá
香 xiāng
卸 xiè
信 xìn
修 xiū
须 xū
叙 xù
钥 yào
盈 yíng
狱 yù
怨 yuàn
钟 zhǒng
种 zhǒng/zhòng
重 chóng/zhòng
追 zhuī

丶

哀 āi
疤 bā
扁 biǎn
测 cè
差 chā/chà/chāi
穿 chuān
帝 dì
洞 dòng
度 dù
疯 fēng
宫 gōng
冠 guàn
恨 hèn
恒 héng
洪 hóng
恢 huī
活 huó
浑 hún
济 jì
浇 jiāo
洁 jié
津 jīn
举 jǔ
觉 jué
客 kè

12–15 Strokes Index

A

ā 阿 PREF (used to address certain relatives or friends to convey sentiment of intimacy) 阿爸 ābà daddy / 阿婆 āpó (maternal) granny

Ālābówén 阿拉伯文 N the Arabic language (especially the writing)

Ālābóyǔ 阿拉伯语 N the Arabic language

āyí 阿姨 N mother's sister ■ 我妈妈有一个姐姐, 一个妹妹, 所以我有两个阿姨。 **Wǒ māma yǒu yí ge jiějie, yí ge mèimei, suǒyǐ wǒ yǒu liǎng ge āyí.** *My mother has an elder sister and a younger sister, so I have two aunts.*

NOTE: (1) 阿姨 **āyí** is a form of address used by a child for a woman about his/her mother's age. It is also common to put a family name before 阿姨 **āyí**, e.g. 张阿姨 **Zhāng āyí**. (2) 阿姨 **āyí** is also used by adults and children for domestic helpers and female nursery staff.

ā 啊 I INTERJ (used to express strong emotions such as surprise, admiration, regret, etc.) oh, ah ■ 啊, 海风多么凉爽！ **Ā, hǎifēng duōme liángshuǎng!** *How refreshing the sea breeze is!* II PARTICLE (attached to a sentence to express strong emotions such as surprise, admiration, regret, etc.) ■ 海风真凉爽啊！ **Hǎifēng zhēn liángshuǎng a!** *How refreshing the sea breeze is!* ■ 北京的冬天真冷啊！ **Běijīng de dōngtiān zhēn lěng a!** *How cold the winter in Beijing is!*

āi 哀 V & N grieve; grief, sorrow (See **bēiāi** 悲哀.)

āi 哎 INTERJ (used to attract attention or express surprise) ■ 哎, 你还在玩电子游戏? **Āi, nǐ hái zài wán diànzǐ yóuxì?** *Oh, you're still playing computer games?*

āiyā 哎呀 INTERJ (used to express surprise or annoyance) ■ 哎呀, 我说了半天, 你怎么还不明白? **Āiyā, wǒ shuō le bàntiān, nǐ zěnme hái bù míngbai?** *Goodness, I've been explaining for ages; how come you still don't see the point?*

āiyō 哎哟 INTERJ (used to express pain or pity)

āi 唉 INTERJ 1 (as a sigh) alas ■ 唉, 孩子又病了。 **Āi, háizi yòu bìng le.** *Alas, the child is sick again.* 2 (as a response) yes, right ■ 唉, 我来了！ **Āi, wǒ lái le!** *Yes, I'm coming!*

ái 挨 V undergo (some painful or unpleasant experience) ■ 那个小偷挨了一顿打。 **Nàge xiǎotōu ái le yí dùn dǎ.** *That thief was beaten up.*

ái 癌 N cancer 肺癌 fèi'ái lung cancer / 胃癌 wèi'ái stomach cancer

áizhèng 癌症 N cancer 得了癌症 déle áizhèng have contracted cancer

ǎi 蔼 TRAD 藹 ADJ friendly, amiable (See **hé'ǎi** 和蔼.)

ǎi 矮 ADJ (of a person or plant) of short stature; short (ANTONYM 高 **gāo**) ■ 他虽然长得矮, 但是篮球打得挺好。 **Tā suīrán zhǎng de ǎi, dànshì lánqiú dǎ de tǐng hǎo.** *Although he's short, he's a good basketball player.* ■ 妹妹比我矮一点儿。 **Mèimei bǐ wǒ ǎi yìdiǎnr.** *My younger sister is a bit shorter than me.*

ài 隘 TRAD 隘 ADJ narrow (See **xiá'ài** 狭隘.)

ài 爱 TRAD 愛 V 1 love ■ 我爱爸爸妈妈, 爸爸妈妈 也爱我。 **Wǒ ài bàba māma, bàba māma yě ài wǒ.** *I love my mom and dad, and they love me too.* 2 like, be fond of ■ 她爱表现自己。 **Tā ài biǎoxiàn zìjǐ.** *She likes to show off.*

ài bú shì shǒu 爱不释手 IDIOM love (something) so much as to be unable to let it go, fondle admiringly

àidài 爱戴 V love and esteem

àihào 爱好 [comp: 爱 love + 好 like, be fond of] V & N like, be interested in, have as a hobby; hobby, interest ■ 我爱好旅行, 爱好了解世界各地人民 的风俗习惯。 **Wǒ àihào lǚxíng, àihào liáojiě shìjiè gèdì rénmín de fēngsú xíguàn.** *I like traveling; I like getting to know the social customs and practices of peoples all around the world.* ■ "你有什么爱好？" "我的爱好比较广泛, 不过我最大的爱好是玩电子游戏。" **"Nǐ yǒu shénme àihào?" "Wǒde àihào bǐjiào guǎngfàn, búguò wǒ zuìdà de àihào shì wán diànzǐ yóuxì."** *"What's your hobby?" "I have many hobbies, but my favorite one is playing computer games."*

àihù 爱护 [comp: 爱 love + 护 protect] V care for and protect, cherish ■ 父母都爱护自己的孩 子。 **Fùmǔ dōu àihù zìjǐ de háizi.** *All parents care for and protect their children.* ■ 我们应该爱护我 们之间的友谊。 **Wǒmen yīnggāi àihù wǒmen zhī jiān de yǒuyì.** *We should cherish our friendship.*

àiqíng 爱情 [comp: 爱 love + 情 feeling, affection] N romantic love ■ 年轻人都希望获得爱 情。 **Niánqīngrén dōu xīwàng huòdé àiqíng.** *Young people all yearn for love.* ■ 婚姻一定要建立在爱 情的基础上。 **Hūnyīn yídìng yào jiànlì zài àiqíng de jīchǔ shang.** *Marriage must be based on love.*

àirén 爱人 [modif: 爱 love + 人 person] N husband or wife ■ 我和爱人结婚十年了。 **Wǒ hé àirén jiéhūn shí nián le.** *My husband (or wife) and I have been married for ten years.*

NOTE: 爱人 **àirén** as *husband* or *wife* is only used in Mainland China as a colloquialism. On formal occasions 丈夫 **zhàngfu** (husband) and 妻子 **qīzi** (wife) are used instead. Now there is a decreasing tendency to use 爱人 **àirén** in China. In its place 先生 **xiānsheng** and 太太 **tàitai** are used to refer to *husband* and *wife*, a long established practice in Taiwan, Hong Kong and overseas Chinese communities. For example: ■ 你先生近来忙吗? **Nǐ xiānsheng jìnlái máng ma?**

Is your husband busy these days? ■ 我太太要我下班回家的路上买些菜。**Wǒ tàitai yào wǒ xiàbān huíjiā de lù shang mǎi xiē cài.** *My wife wants me to buy some vegetables on my way home after work.*

àixī 爱惜 v cherish, value highly
爱惜自己的名誉 **àixī zìjǐ de míngyù** treasure one's reputation

àixīn 爱心 [modif: 爱 love + 心 the heart] **N** love, compassion

àimèi 暧昧 ADJ ambiguous, dubious

ài 碍 TRAD 礙 **v** hinder (See **fáng'ài** 妨碍.)

ān 安 ADJ peaceful, safe

ānjìng 安静 [comp: 安 peace + 静 quiet] **ADJ** quiet, peaceful, serene ■ 这里很少有车开过，环境很安静。**Zhèlǐ hěn shǎo yǒu chē kāiguò, huánjìng hěn ānjìng.** *There is very little traffic here. The environment is very peaceful.* ■ 请大家安静！**Qǐng dàjiā ānjìng!** *Please be quiet, everyone!* ■ 这位老人只想过安静的生活。**Zhè wèi lǎorén zhǐ xiǎng guò ānjìng de shēnghuó.** *This old man only wants to live a quiet life.*

ān jū lè yè 安居乐业 IDIOM live and work in peace and contentment

ānníng 安宁 [comp: 安 peace + 宁 peaceful] **ADJ** calm, composed

ānpái 安排 [comp: 安 to settle, to arrange + 排 to arrange, to put in order] **v** arrange, make arrangements; plan ■ 大学生一般都很忙，因此必须安排好时间。**Dàxuéshēng yìbān dōu hěn máng, yīncǐ bìxū ānpái hǎo shíjiān.** *University students are generally busy people, so they must plan their time well.* ■ 董事长下个月去中国旅行，请你安排一下。**Dǒngshìzhǎng xià ge yuè qù Zhōngguó lǚxíng, qǐng nǐ ānpái yíxià.** *The chairman of the board is going to China for a trip next month. Please make the arrangements.*

ānquán 安全 [comp: 安 peace + 全 complete, all-around] **I N** security, safety ■ 开车安全第一。**Kāichē ānquán dì yī.** *When you are driving, safety is the most important thing.* **II ADJ** safe, secure ■ 在这里夜里一个人在街上走，安全吗？**Zài zhèlǐ yèlǐ yí ge rén zài jiē shang zǒu, ānquán ma?** *Is it safe to walk alone in the streets here at night?*

ānwèi 安慰 [comp: 安 make peace + 慰 comfort] **v** comfort, console ■ 他们失去了心爱的女儿，心情悲痛，朋友们都来安慰他们。**Tāmen shīqùle xīn'ài de nǚ'ér, xīnqíng bēitòng, péngyoumen dōu lái ānwèi tāmen.** *They are in deep sorrow as they have lost their beloved daughter. Their friends have all come to comfort them.*

ānxiáng 安详 [comp: 安 peace + 详 calm] **ADJ** (of facial expression) serene, composed

ānxīn 安心 [v+obj: 安 make peace + 心 the heart] **ADJ** relaxed and content ■ 她不安心在小学教书，她想当电影演员。**Tā bù ānxīn zài xiǎoxué**

jiāoshū, tā xiǎng dāng diànyǐng yǎnyuán. *She is not content to be a primary school teacher; she wants to be a movie star.*

ānzhì 安置 [modif: 安 safely + 置 to place] **v** find an appropriate place (for people)

ānzhuāng 安装 [modif: 安 safely + 装 to install] **v** install, fix
安装空调设备 **ānzhuāng kōngtiáo shèbèi** install an air-conditioner

àn 岸 N bank or shore (of a river, lake, or sea) ■ 河的两岸是一个个小村子。**Hé de liǎng àn shì yí gège xiǎo cūnzi.** *The river is flanked by small villages.*
海岸 hǎi àn coast / 上岸 shàng àn go ashore

àn 按 PREP according to, in accordance with ■ 按计划，这座工厂将在明年四月建成。**Àn jìhuà, zhè zuò gōngchǎng jiāng zài míngnián Sìyuè jiànchéng.** *According to the plan, the factory will be built by April next year.* ■ 我一定按你说的做。**Wǒ yídìng àn nǐ shuō de zuò.** *I will definitely do as you say.*

ànmó 按摩 v & N massage

ànmóyuàn 按摩院 N massage parlor

ànshí 按时 [v+obj: 按 according to + 时 time] **ADV** according to a fixed time, on time ■ 学生要按时完成作业。**Xuésheng yào ànshí wánchéng zuòyè.** *Students must finish their assignments on time.* ■ 你得按时吃药，病才会好。**Nǐ děi ànshí chī yào, bìng cái huì hǎo.** *You've got to take the medicine on time, or you won't get well.*

ànzhào 按照 PREP according to, in accordance with (same as 按 **àn**)

àn 案 N case, plan

ànjiàn 案件 N case, legal case
民事案件 **mínshì ànjiàn** civil case / 刑事案件 **xíngshì ànjiàn** criminal case / 调查案件 **diàochá ànjiàn** investigate a (police) case

ànlì 案例 N legal case, precedent case
案例分析 **ànlì fēnxī** case analysis, case study

àn 暗 ADJ dark, dim ■ 房间里太暗了，你要看书得开灯。**Fángjiān li tài àn le, nǐ yào kàn shū děi kāi dēng.** *The room is dim. You've got to turn on the light if you want to read.*

ànshì 暗示 [modif: 暗 dark + 示 indicate] **v** drop a hint, hint

áng 昂 v hold (the head) high
昂起头 **ángqǐ tóu** hold the head high

ángguì 昂贵 [comp: 昂 holding high + 贵 expensive] **ADJ** very expensive, costly ■ 物价昂贵。**Wùjià ángguì.** *The prices are exorbitant.*

āo 凹 ADJ concave, sunken, dented

āotū bùpíng 凹凸不平 ADJ rugged, full of bumps and holes

áo 熬 v stew, boil

áoyè 熬夜 N work late into night, burn midnight oil

ào 奥 ADJ deep, profound

àomì 奥秘 [comp: 奥 deep + 秘 secret] N deep secret, profound mystery
探索奥秘 tànsuǒ àomì explore a mystery

ào 傲 ADJ arrogant (See **jiāo'ào** 骄傲.)

ào 澳 N deep waters

Àodàlìyà 澳大利亚 N Australia

B

bā 八 NUM eight ■ 八八六十四 **Bā bā liùshísì.** *Eight times eight is sixty-four.*

bābudé 巴不得 V wish for eagerly, be extremely anxious (to do something)

bājie 巴结 V cosy up, fawn on

bā 扒 V 1 strip off, take off (clothes, etc.) **2** hold on to, cling to

bā 疤 N scar

bá 拔 V pull out, pull up

bá miáo zhù zhǎng 拔苗助长 IDIOM pull up a young plant to help it grow (→ spoil things with excessive enthusiasm)

bǎ 把¹ MEASURE WORD **1** (for objects with handles)
一把刀 yì bǎ dāo a knife
2 a handful of
一把米 yì bǎ mǐ a handful of rice

bǎ 把² PREP (used before a noun or pronoun to indicate it is the object of the sentence) ■ 请你把这封信交给李先生。 **Qǐng nǐ bǎ zhè fēng xìn jiāogěi Lǐ xiānsheng.** *Please deliver this letter to Mr Li.* ■ 我可以把车停在这里吗? **Wǒ kěyǐ bǎ chē tíng zài zhèlǐ ma?** *May I park my car here?*

bǎguān 把关 V check on, ensure

bǎshǒu 把手 N handle, handrail

bǎwò 把握 I N being certain and assured, confidence ■ 你有成功的把握吗? **Nǐ yǒu chénggōng de bǎwò ma?** *Are you sure of success?* II V seize (an opportunity) ■ 我们一定要把握这个时机。 **Wǒmen yídìng yào bǎwò zhège shíjī** *We must seize this opportunity*

bǎxì 把戏 N **1** acrobatics, juggery **2** trick, swindle

bà 爸 N dad, daddy, papa

bàba 爸爸 N daddy, papa ■ 我爸爸工作很努力。 **Wǒ bàba gōngzuò hěn nǔlì.** *My father works hard.* ■ 爸爸, 这个星期五晚上我想用一下你的车, 行不行? **Bàba, zhège Xīngqīwǔ wǎnshang wǒ xiǎng yòng yíxià nǐ de chē, xíng bu xíng?** *Daddy, I'd like to use your car this Friday evening. Is it all right?*

bà 罢 TRAD 罷 V stop

bàgōng 罢工 [v+obj: 罢 stop + 工 work] V stage a strike, down tools

bà 霸 V & N dominate, rule by might; tyrant, tyranny, hegemony
恶霸 èbà local tyrant

bàdào 霸道 [modif: 霸 tyrant + 道 way] ADJ & N overbearing, high-handed; tyranny, hegemony

bà 坝 TRAD 壩 N dam (See **dībà** 堤坝.)

ba 吧 PARTICLE **1** (used to make a suggestion)
■ 我们一块儿去吃中饭吧。 **Wǒmen yíkuàir qù chī zhōngfàn ba.** *Let's go and have lunch together.* ■ 今天太冷了, 别去游泳吧! **Jīntiān tài lěng le, bié qù yóuyǒng ba!** *It's too cold today. Don't go swimming, OK?* **2** (used to indicate supposition) ■ 你是新加坡来的张先生吧? **Nǐ shì Xīnjiāpō lái de Zhāng xiānsheng ba?** *Aren't you Mr Zhang from Singapore?* ■ 你对这个地方很熟悉吧? **Nǐ duì zhège dìfang hěn shúxi ba?** *You're familiar with this place, aren't you?*

bāi 掰 V break off with hands

bái 白 I ADJ white ■ 下雪以后, 路上一片白。 **Xiàxuě yǐhòu, lù shang yí piàn bái.** *The road was all white after the snow.* ■ 她穿白衣服特别好看。 **Tā chuān bái yīfu tèbié hǎokàn.** *She looks especially beautiful in white.*

NOTE: In Chinese tradition, white symbolizes death and is the color for funerals.

II ADV in vain, without any result ■ 他根本不思改进, 你说了也白说。 **Tā gēnběn bù sī gǎijìn, nǐ shuōle yě bái shuō.** *He does not want to improve his work at all. You said all that in vain.* ■ 我忘了在电脑里保存文件, 一个晚上的工作白做了。 **Wǒ wàngle zài diànnǎo lǐ bǎocún wénjiàn, yí ge wǎnshang de gōngzuò dōu bái zuò le.** *I forgot to save my document in the computer. An evening's work all came to nothing.* III ADV for free ■ 世界上没有白吃的午餐。 **Shìjiè shang méiyǒu bái chī de wǔcān.** *There is no free lunch in the world. (→ There's no such thing as a free lunch.)*

báicài 白菜 [modif: 白 white + 菜 vegetable] N cabbage (棵 **kē**) ■ 在中国北方, 白菜是冬天最便宜、最普通的蔬菜。 **Zài Zhōngguó běifāng, báicài shì dōngtiān zuì piányi, zuì pǔtōng de shūcài.** *In Northern China, cabbage is the cheapest, most ordinary vegetable in winter.*

báikāishuǐ 白开水 plain boiled water ■ 感冒了要喝白开水。 **Gǎnmào le yào hē báikāishuǐ.** *You should drink a lot of boiled water when you've got a cold.*

báirén 白人 N white man/woman, white people

báitiān 白天 [modif: 白 white + 天 day] N daytime ■ 春天来了, 白天越来越长了。 **Chūntiān lái le, báitiān yuèláiyuè cháng le.** *Spring has come. Days become longer and longer.* ■ 他家白天一般没有人, 你还是晚上去吧。 **Tā jiā báitiān yìbān méiyǒu rén, nǐ háishì wǎnshang qù ba.** *There is usually nobody at his home during the day. You should go there in the evening.*

bǎi 百 NUM hundred
三百元 sān bǎi yuán three hundred yuan/dollars

NOTE: 百 **bǎi** may have the abstract sense of *a great deal* of and *a multitude of*. This sense can be found in many expressions, e.g. 百闻不如一见 **Bǎi wén bùrú yí jiàn**, which literally means "A hundred sounds are not as good as one sight" and may be translated as "Seeing is believing." Another example is 百忙 **bǎi máng**, meaning *very busy*. For example: ■ 你百忙中来看我，太好了。**Nǐ bǎi máng zhōng lái kàn wǒ, tài hǎo le.** *It's very kind of you to come to see me when you're so busy.*

bǎifēnbǐ 百分比 N percentage

bǎifēndiǎn 百分点 N one percentage

bǎirìké 百日咳 N whooping cough

bǎixìng 百姓 N common people, ordinary people
老百姓 lǎobǎixìng common people, ordinary people

bǎi 摆 TRAD 擺 V put, place, arrange ■ 桌子上摆着一只大花瓶。**Zhuōzi shang bǎizhe yì zhī dà huāpíng.** *On the table is placed a big vase.* ■ 吃饭了，你把碗筷摆好吧! **Chīfàn le, nǐ bǎ wǎnkuài bǎihǎo ba!** *It's mealtime; will you please set the table?*

bǎituō 摆脱 V break away from, shake off

bài 败 TRAD 敗 V be defeated (ANTONYM 胜 **shèng**) ■ 我们球队又败了，得研究一下原因。**Wǒmen qiúduì yòu bài le, děi yánjiū yíxià yuányīn.** *Our (ball) team was defeated again. We've got to look into the reason.*

bàihuài 败坏 V ruin, corrupt
道德败坏 dàodé bàihuài rotten morals

bài 拜 V do obeisance, pay respect to

bàifǎng 拜访 [comp: 拜 pay respect + 访 visit] V pay a visit (to a senior person), make a courtesy call

bài nián 拜年 V pay a New Year's call, wish a Happy New Year

bàituō 拜托 V humbly request (somebody to do something)

bān 班 N **1** class (in school) ■ 我们班有十二个男生，十四个女生。**Wǒmen bān yǒu shí'èr ge nánshēng, shísì ge nǔshēng.** *Our class has twelve male students and fourteen female students.* **2** shift (in a workplace) ■ 这位护士上个星期上白天班，这个星期上夜班。**Zhè wèi hùshi shàng ge xīngqī shàng báitiān bān, zhège xīngqī shàng yèbān.** *This nurse was on day shift last week, and is on night shift this week.* ■ 我妈妈每天九点上班，五点下班。**Wǒ māma měi tiān jiǔ diǎn shàngbān, wǔ diǎn xiàbān.** *My mother goes to work at nine o'clock and leaves work at five o'clock.*
加班 jiābān work overtime / 上班 shàngbān go to work / 下班 xiàbān leave work

bānzhǎng 班长 [modif: 班 class, squad + 长 leader] N leader (of a class in school, a squad in

the army, etc.) ■ 你打算选谁当班长? **Nǐ dǎsuàn xuǎn shéi dāng bānzhǎng?** *Whom are you going to elect as class monitor?*

bān 搬 V move (heavy objects) ■ 我们把这张桌子搬到房间外面去吧。**Wǒmen bǎ zhè zhāng zhuōzi bān dào fángjiān wàimiàn qù ba.** *Let's move this table out of the room.*
搬不动 bān bu dòng cannot move/cannot be moved / 搬得动 bān de dòng can move/can be moved

bānjiā 搬家 V & N move (house); house moving ■ 我们这个周末搬家，有几位朋友来帮忙。**Wǒmen zhège zhōumò bānjiā, yǒu jǐ wèi péngyou lái bāngmáng.** *We're moving house this weekend. Some friends will come to help.*

bān 颁 TRAD 頒 V issue, confer on

bānbù 颁布 [comp: 颁 issue + 布 promulgate] V promulgate, proclaim

bānfā 颁发 [comp: 颁 issue + 发 issue] V issue, distribute
颁发奖状 bānfā jiǎngzhuàng issue a certificate of merit

bān 斑 N spot, speck

bāndiǎn 斑点 N spot, stain

bānwén 斑纹 N bands of striking colors, stripe

bǎn 版 N printing plate

bǎnběn 版本 N edition

bǎn 板 N board (See **hēibǎn** 黑板.)

bàn 办 TRAD 辦 V handle, manage ■ 这件事不容易办。**Zhè jiàn shì bù róngyì bàn.** *This matter is not easy to handle.* ■ 你办事我很放心。**Nǐ bànshì wǒ hěn fàngxīn.** *I feel reassured when you're handling a matter. (→ I have confidence in you when you're in charge.)*

bànfǎ 办法 [modif: 办 handle, manage + 法 method] N way of doing things, method ■ 这些老办法都不行。**Zhèxiē lǎo bànfǎ dōu bùxíng.** *All these old methods won't work.* ■ 你试试我的办法。**Nǐ shìshi wǒ de bànfǎ.** *Do try my method.*
想办法 xiǎng bànfǎ think up a plan/find a way of doing things ■ 我们正在想办法解决这个问题。**Wǒmen zhèngzài xiǎng bànfǎ jiějué zhège wèntí.** *We're trying to find a way to solve this problem.*
有办法 yǒu bànfǎ have a way with …, be resourceful ■ 他对小孩很有办法。**Tā duì xiǎohái hěn yǒu bànfǎ.** *He has a way with children.*
没有办法 méiyǒu bànfǎ there's nothing we can do ■ 飞机票全卖完了，我们明天不能走，没有办法。**Fēijī piào quán màiwán le, wǒmen míngtiān bù néng zǒu, méiyǒu bànfǎ.** *All the air tickets are sold out. We won't be able to leave tomorrow. There's nothing we can do.*

bàngōng 办公 [comp: 办 handle + 公 public, public office] V work (as a white-collar worker, usually in an office) ■ 王经理在办公，你有事可以

给他留个话。**Wáng jīnglǐ zài bàngōng, nǐ yǒushì kěyǐ gěi tā liú ge huà.** *Mr Wang, the manager, is working in his office. You can leave him a message, if you've any business.*

办公时间 bàngōng shíjiān office hours, working hours / 办公大楼 bàngōng dàlóu office building

bàngōngshì 办公室 N office

bànlǐ 办理 [comp: 办 handle, manage + 理 manage, run] v deal with, go through ■ 我正在办理到中国去的签证。**Wǒ zhèngzài bànlǐ dào Zhōngguó qù de qiānzhèng.** *I'm in the process of obtaining a visa for China.*

bàn 半 MEASURE WORD half ■ 我等她等了一个半小时。**Wǒ děng tā děngle yí ge bàn xiǎoshí.** *I waited for her for one and a half hours.*

bàntiān 半天 [modif: 半 half + 天 day] N 1 half a day 2 a period of time felt to be very long, a very long time ■ 我等你等了半天了。**Wǒ děng nǐ děng le bàntiān le.** *I've been waiting for you for a long time.* ■ 那本书我找了半天，还没找到。**Nà běn shū wǒ zhǎo le bàntiān, hái méi zhǎodào.** *I've been looking for the book for a long time but I still haven't found it.*

bàn tú ér fèi 半途而废 v give up halfway

bànyè 半夜 [modif: 半 half + 夜 night] N midnight, at midnight ■ 他经常工作到半夜才睡。**Tā jīngcháng gōngzuò dào bànyè cái shuì.** *He often works till midnight before going to bed.*

bàn 伴 N companion

同伴 tóngbàn companion, mate

bànlǚ 伴侣 [comp: 伴 companion + 侣 companion] N companion (especially husband or wife)

终身伴侣 zhōngshēn bànlǚ life-long companion, husband and wife

bànsuí 伴随 v go along with, keep company

bàn 拌 v mix (See **jiǎobàn** 搅拌.)

bàn 扮 v disguise as

bànyǎn 扮演 v play the role (of a character in a play, a movie, etc.)

bàn 瓣 N 1 (flower) petal 2 (fruit) section

bāng 帮 TRAD 幫 v help, assist ■ 上个周末，很多朋友来帮他搬家。**Shàng ge zhōumò, hěn duō péngyou lái bāng tā bānjiā.** *Last weekend, many friends came to help him move house.* ■ 你能帮我找一下这本书吗？**Nǐ néng bāng wǒ zhǎo yíxià zhè běn shū ma?** *Can you help me find this book?*

NOTE: 帮 **bāng**, 帮忙 **bāngmáng** and 帮助 **bāngzhù** are synonyms. Their differences are: (1) 帮忙 **bāngmáng** is a verb that takes no object, while 帮 **bāng** and 帮助 **bāngzhù** are usually followed by an object. (2) As verbs, 帮 **bāng** and 帮助 **bāngzhù** are interchangeable, but 帮 **bāng** is more colloquial than 帮助 **bāngzhù**. (3) 帮助 **bāngzhù** can also be used as a noun.

bāngmáng 帮忙 v help, help out ■ 上个周末他搬家，很多朋友来帮忙。**Shàng ge zhōumò tā bānjiā, hěnduō péngyou lái bāngmáng.** *Last weekend, he moved house. Many friends came to help.*

NOTE: See note on 帮 **bāng**.

bāngzhù 帮助 [comp: 帮 help + 助 assist] V & N help, assist; help, assistance ■ 李先生帮助我们解决了很多困难。**Lǐ xiānsheng bāngzhù wǒmen jiějué le hěn duō kùnnán.** *Mr Li helped us overcome many difficulties.* ■ 没有你的帮助，我们不可能及时完成任务。**Méiyǒu nǐ de bāngzhù, wǒmen bù kěnéng jíshí wánchéng rènwù.** *Without your help we couldn't have accomplished the task in time.*

NOTE: See note on 帮 **bāng**.

bǎng 绑 TRAD 綁 v tie, bind (with a rope)

bǎngjià 绑架 v kidnap

bǎng 榜 N list of names, honor roll

bǎngyàng 榜样 N (positive) example, role model ■ 我们的老师是美国人，说一口标准中文，真是我们的好榜样！**Wǒmen de lǎoshī shì Měiguórén, shuō yì kǒu biāozhǔn Zhōngwén, zhēn shì wǒmen de hǎo bǎngyàng!** *Our teacher is an American and speaks standard Chinese. He really is a good role model for us.*

bǎng 膀 N upper arm (See **chìbǎng** 翅膀.)

bàng 傍 v be close to

bàngwǎn 傍晚 [modif: 傍 towards, close to + 晚 evening] N dusk ■ 他们傍晚的时候才走出树林，不一会天就黑了。**Tāmen bàngwǎn de shíhòu cái zǒuchū shùlín, bú yìhuì tiān jiù hēi le.** *They came out of the woods at dusk, and soon it was dark.*

bàng 磅 measurement for weight; pound (453.49 grams)

两磅牛肉 liǎng bang niúròu two pounds of beef

bàng 棒[1] N stick, club (根 **gēn**)

铁棒 tiěbàng iron bar

bàng 棒[2] ADJ strong, very good ■ 这个小伙子身体很棒。**Zhège xiǎohuǒzi shēntǐ hěn bàng.** *This young man is very strong.* ■ 他篮球打得真棒。**Tā lánqiú dǎ dé zhēn bàng.** *He really plays basketball very well.* (→ *He is a wonderful basketball player.*)

bāo 包 V & N wrap up; parcel, bag ■ 顾客："请你把这只花瓶好好包起来。" **Gùkè: "Qǐng nǐ bǎ zhè zhī huāpíng hǎohao bāo qǐlai."** *Customer: "Could you please wrap up this vase carefully?"* ■ 他在路边拣到一个包，马上交给警察。**Tā zài lùbiān jiǎn dào yíge bāo, mǎshàng jiāo gěi jǐngchá.** *He picked up a parcel by the roadside and immediately handed it over to the police.*

书包 shūbāo schoolbag / 邮包 yóubāo mailbag, parcel for posting

bāobì 包庇 v cover up (wrongdoing), shield

bāofu 包袱 N a bundle wrapped in a cloth-wrapper

bāoguǒ 包裹 N parcel, package

bāohán 包含 [comp: 包 wrap up + 含 contain]
v contain, have as ingredients

bāokuò 包括 [comp: 包 embrace + 括 include]
v include, embrace ■ 旅行团包括一名翻译一共十五人。 **Lǚxíngtuán bāokuò yì míng fānyì yígòng shíwǔ rén.** *There are fifteen people in the tour group, including an interpreter.*

bāowéi 包围 [comp: 包 wrap up + 围 surround]
v surround, encircle, lay siege

bāozhuāng 包装 **n** package, packaging
包装材料 bāozhuāng cáiliào packaging material

bāozi 包子 [suffix: 包 bun + 子 nominal suffix]
n steamed bun with filling ■ 我早饭吃了两个包子。 **Wǒ zǎofàn chīle liǎng ge bāozi.** *I had two steamed buns for breakfast.*

bāo 胞 **adj** born of the same parents

báo 薄 **adj** thin, flimsy (**antonym** 厚 **hòu**) ■ 天冷了，这条被子太薄，要换一条厚一点儿的。 **Tiān lěng le, zhè tiáo bèizi tài báo, yào huàn yì tiáo hòu yìdiǎnr de.** *It's getting cold. This blanket is too thin. You need a thicker one.*

NOTE: See note on 薄 **bó**.

bǎo 宝 **trad** 寶 **n** treasure

bǎobèi 宝贝 [comp: 宝 treasure + 贝 shellfish] **n** treasured object, treasure
小宝贝 xiǎo bǎobèi (endearment for children) darling, dear

bǎoguì 宝贵 [comp: 宝 precious + 贵 valuable]
adj valuable, precious ■ 世界上什么最宝贵？ **Shìjiè shang shénme zuì bǎoguì?** *What is the most valuable thing in the world?* ■ 我不想浪费你们的宝贵时间，就直话直说了。 **Wǒ bù xiǎng làngfèi nǐmen de bǎoguì shíjiān, jiù zhí huà zhí shuō le.** *I don't want to waste your precious time, and will say what I have to say without mincing words.*

bǎo 保 **v** conserve, protect ■ 这房子用了新材料，特别保暖。 **Zhè fángzi yòngle xīn cáiliào, tèbié bǎo nuǎn.** *This house uses a new material that is particularly good at keeping the house warm.*

bǎo'ān 保安 **n** security guard

bǎochí 保持 [comp: 保 conserve + 持 maintain]
v keep, maintain ■ 他去年在学校运动会上得了长跑冠军，今年能保持吗？ **Tā qùnián zài xuéxiào yùndònghuì shang déle chángpǎo guànjūn, jīnnián néng bǎochí ma?** *He was the champion in long-distance running at the school sports meet last year. Can he maintain it this year? (→ Can he defend his position this year?)*

bǎocún 保存 [comp: 保 conserve + 存 keep]
v keep, save

bǎoguǎn 保管 [comp: 保 conserve + 管 take charge of] **v** take charge of
保管员 bǎoguǎnyuán guardian, custodian

bǎohù 保护 [comp: 保 conserve + 护 protect] **v** protect, safeguard, conserve ■ 这片大森林一定要保护好，不能开发为旅游区。 **Zhè piàn dà sēnlín yídìng yào bǎohù hǎo, bù néng kāifā wéi lǚyóuqū.** *This vast forest must be conserved and mustn't be developed into a tourist area.*

bǎoliú 保留 [comp: 保 conserve + 留 retain] **v** retain, reserve ■ 这张飞机票我们给你保留三天。 **Zhè zhāng fēijī piào wǒmen gěi nǐ bǎoliú sān tiān.** *We'll reserve this air ticket for you for three days.* ■ 你可以保留自己的意见，但是大家的决定不能违反。 **Nǐ kěyǐ bǎoliú zìjǐ de yìjiàn, dànshì dàjiā de juédìng bù néng wéifǎn.** *You can have your own opinions, but the collective decision must not be opposed.*

bǎomì 保密 [v+compl: 保 conserve + 密 secret, confidential] **v** keep … secret
保密文件 bǎomì wénjiàn classified document ■ 这件事一定要保密。 **Zhè jiàn shì yídìng yào bǎomì.** *This matter must be kept secret.*

bǎomǔ 保姆 [modif: 保 protect + 姆 woman]
n (children's) nurse, nanny
当保姆 dāng bǎomǔ work as a nanny

bǎoshǒu 保守 [comp: 保 protect + 守 observe, abide by] **I v** guard, keep ■ 你能保守一个秘密吗？ **Nǐ néng bǎoshǒu yī ge mìmì ma?** *Can you keep a secret?* **II adj** conservative ■ 一个人年纪大了，往往会保守。 **Yí gè rén niánjì dà le, wǎngwǎng huì bǎoshǒu.** *As one gets old, one tends to be conservative.*

bǎowèi 保卫 [comp: 保 protect + 卫 defend] **v** defend ■ 当外敌入侵时，每个人都应该保卫自己的国家。 **Dāng wài dí rùqīn shí, měi ge rén dōu yīnggāi bǎowèi zìjǐ de guójiā.** *When an enemy invades our country, everybody should defend it.*

bǎoxiǎn 保险 [comp: 保 protect + 险 risk] **I adj** safe, risk-free **II v & n** insure; insurance
保险单 bǎoxiǎndān insurance policy / 保险费 bǎoxiǎnfèi insurance premium / 保险公司 bǎoxiǎn gōngsī insurance company

bǎoyǎng 保养 [comp: 保 protect + 养 maintain]
v 1 take good care of one's health **2** maintain (automobiles, machines, etc.), keep in good repair
车辆保养 chēliàng bǎoyǎng vehicle maintenance

bǎozhàng 保障 [comp: 保 protect + 障 defense]
v secure, insure, guarantee
社会保障 shèhuì bǎozhàng social security

bǎozhèng 保证 [comp: 保 protect + 证 evidence]
v & n guarantee, pledge ■ 本公司保证产品质量。 **Běn gōngsī bǎozhèng chǎnpǐn zhìliàng.** *This company guarantees the quality of its products.* ■ 你们能为产品提供保证吗？ **Nǐmen néng wèi chǎnpǐn tígōng bǎozhèng ma?** *Can you provide a guarantee for your products?*
产品保证书 chǎnpǐn bǎozhèng shū (product) quality guarantee

bǎozhòng 保重 **v** take good care of oneself ■ 您退休以后，多多保重身体。 **Nín tuìxiū yǐhòu, duōduō bǎozhòng shēntǐ.** *(I hope) you will take good care of your health after retirement.*

bǎo 饱 TRAD 飽 ADJ having eaten one's fill, full (ANTONYM 饿 è) ■ 谢谢，我饱了。 **Xièxie, wǒ bǎo le.** *Thank you. I'm full.* ■ 您吃饱了吗？ **Nín chī bǎo le ma?** *Have you had (← eaten) enough?* 吃得饱 chī de bǎo have enough to eat / 吃不饱 chī bu bǎo not have enough to eat (→ not have enough food)

NOTE: It is customary for a Chinese host to ask a guest who seems to have finished the meal 您吃饱了吗？ **Nín chī bǎo le ma?** *Have you had (← eaten) enough?* The guest is expected to reply: 吃饱了。多谢。您慢慢吃。 **Chī bǎo le. Duō xiè. Nín màn-man chī.** *Yes, I have. Thank you. Please take your time to eat.*

bǎohé 饱和 ADJ saturated

bǎo jīng cāngsāng 饱经沧桑 IDIOM having witnessed deep blue seas changing into mulberry orchards, having experienced many vicissitudes

bǎo 堡 N fortress, castle

bào 报 TRAD 報 V & N report, respond; newspaper

bàodào 报到 v report for duty, register ■ 学校九月一日开学，学生从八月二十五日起报到。 **Xuéxiào Jiǔyuè yírì kāixué, xuésheng cóng Bāyuè èrshíwǔ rì qǐ bàodào.** *The academic year begins on September 1, and students start registration on August 25.*

bàochóu 报仇 [v+obj: 报 reciprocate + 仇 enmity] v avenge, revenge

bàochou 报酬 [comp: 报 respond + 酬 reward] N renumeration, reward

bàodá 报答 [comp: 报 respond to + 答 reply] v pay a debt of gratitude

bàodào 报道 I v report (news), cover ■ 今天城里各家报纸都报道了昨天的交通事故。 **Jīntiān chéng li gè jiā bàozhǐ dōu bàodàole zuótiān de jiāotōng shìgù.** *Today all the newspapers in the city covered yesterday's road accident.* II N news story ■ 你看了关于昨天交通事故的报道没有？ **Nǐ kànle guānyú zuótiān jiāotōng shìgù de bàodào méiyǒu?** *Have you read the news story about yesterday's road accident?*

bàofu 报复 v retaliate, revenge ■ 谁得罪了她，她一定要报复。 **Shéi dézuì le tā, tā yídìng yào bàofu.** *She will retaliate against whoever has offended her.*

bàogào 报告 V & N report, make known; report ■ 播音员：现在报告新闻。 **Bōyīnyuán: "Xiànzài bàogào xīnwén."** *Newscaster: "Now the news."* ■ 董事会收到了一份重要报告。 **Dǒngshìhuì shōudàole yí fèn zhòngyào bàogào.** *The Board of Directors received an important report.*

bàojǐng 报警 v report (an incident) to the police

bàomíng 报名 v enter one's name, sign up, apply for (a place in school) ■ 我已经向一所大学报名。 **Wǒ yǐjīng xiàng yì suǒ dàxué bàomíng.** *I have applied for a place in a university.* ■ 有六百多人报名参加星期天的长跑 **Yǒu liùbǎi duō rén bàomíng cānjiā Xīngqītiān de chángpǎo.** *Over 600 people have signed up for Sunday's long-distance run.*

bàoshè 报社 [modif: 报 newspaper + 社 association] N newspaper office

bàoxiāo 报销 N & V reimbursement; submit an expense account, get reimbursement

bàozhǐ 报纸 [modif: 报 reporting + 纸 paper] N newspaper (张 zhāng, 份 fèn) ■ 今天报纸上有什么重要消息？ **Jīntiān bàozhǐ shang yǒu shénme zhòngyào xiāoxi?** *What important news is there in today's paper?* ■ 这份报纸广告比新闻多。 **Zhè fèn bàozhǐ guǎnggào bǐ xīnwén duō.** *There are more advertisements than news in this newspaper.*

NOTE: In colloquial Chinese, 报 bào is often used instead of 报纸 bàozhǐ, e.g.: ■ 你看得懂中文报吗？ **Nǐ kàndedǒng Zhōngwén bào ma?** *Can you understand Chinese newspapers?*

bào 抱 v hold … in arms, embrace, hug ■ 妈妈抱着孩子。 **Māma bàozhe háizi.** *The mother is holding her baby in her arms.* ■ 让我抱抱你。 **Ràng wǒ bàobao nǐ.** *Let me hug you.*

bàofù 抱负 N aspiration, ambition

bàoqiàn 抱歉 ADJ apologetic, sorry, regretful ■ 很抱歉，今天我不能加班。 **Hěn bàoqiàn, jīntiān wǒ bù néng jiābān.** *I'm sorry, but I won't be able to work overtime today.* ■ 我忘了昨天的会议，实在抱歉！ **Wǒ wàngle zuótiān de huìyì, shízài bàoqiàn!** *I'm awfully sorry that I forgot the meeting yesterday.*

bàoyuàn 抱怨 v complain, grumble

bào 暴 ADJ fierce and brutal

bàolì 暴力 [modif: 暴 violent + 力 force] N violence, brutal force
暴力电影 bàolì diànyǐng violent movie

bàolù 暴露 [comp: 暴 expose + 露 show, reveal] v expose, lay bare

bàofā 爆发 v erupt, break out
火山爆发 huǒshān bàofā a volcano erupted; volcanic eruption

bàozhà 爆炸 [comp: 爆 explode + 炸 blow up, blast] I v explode II N explosion
自杀炸弹爆炸 zìshā zhàdàn bàozhà the explosion of a suicide bomb

bào 雹 N hail, hailstone

bēi 杯 N cup, mug, glass (只 zhī)

bēizi 杯子 [suffix: 杯 cup + 子 nominal suffix] N cup, mug, glass (只 zhī) ■ 这些杯子要洗一下。 **Zhèxiē bēizi yào xǐ yíxià.** *These cups/mugs/glasses need washing.*
茶杯 chábēi teacup / 酒杯 jiǔbēi wine glass / 一杯茶/酒 yì bēi chá/jiǔ a cup of tea/a glass of wine

NOTE: 杯 bēi may denote either *cup, mug,* or *glass.* 杯 bēi is seldom used alone. It is usually suffixed with 子 zi: 杯子 bēizi, or combined with 茶 chá or 酒 jiǔ: 茶杯 chábēi, 酒杯 jiǔbēi.

bēi 背 TRAD 揹 v carry… on the back ■ 孩子每天高高兴兴背着书包上学校。**Háizi měi tiān gāo-gāo-xìng-xìng bēizhe shūbāo shàng xuéxiào.** *Every day the child goes to school happily, with his schoolbag on his back.*

bēidài 背带 N straps, braces, suspenders

bēi 碑 N stele
纪念碑 jìniànbēi monument

bēi 悲 ADJ grieved

bēi'āi 悲哀 [comp: 悲 grieved + 哀 grieved] ADJ deeply grieved

bēicǎn 悲惨 [comp: 悲 grieved + 惨 miserable] ADJ miserable, tragic

bēiguān 悲观 [comp: 悲 grieved, sad + 观 view] ADJ pessimistic (ANTONYM 乐观 lèguān) ■ 你太悲观了，情况不会这么坏吧。**Nǐ tài bēiguān le, qíngkuàng bú huì zhème huài ba.** *You're too pessimistic. Things can't be that bad.*

bēitòng 悲痛 [comp: 悲 grieved, sad + 痛 agony] ADJ deeply grieved, agonized, with deep sorrow ■ 他在交通事故中失去了妻子、女儿，悲痛极了。**Tā zài jiāotōng shìgù zhōng shīqùle qīzi, nǚ'ér, bēitòng jíle.** *He lost his wife and daughter in a road accident and is deeply grieved.*

bēi 卑 ADJ 1 low and humble 2 mean, contemptible

bēibǐ 卑鄙 [comp: 卑 mean + 鄙 low, despicable] ADJ contemptible, despicable
卑鄙小人 bēibǐ xiǎorén despicable person/people

běi 北 N north, northern ■ 在北半球，刮北风，天就冷。**Zài běi bànqiú, guā běifēng, tiān jiù lěng.** *In the north hemisphere, the weather becomes cold when a north wind blows.*

běibian 北边 [modif: 北 north + 边 side] N north side, to the north, in the north ■ 山的北边是一大片草原。**Shān de běibian shì yí dà piàn cǎoyuán.** *North of the mountains is a vast pasture.* ■ 加拿大在美国的北边。**Jiānádà zài Měiguó de běibian.** *Canada is to the north of the USA.*

běifāng 北方 [modif: 北 north + 方 region] N northern region ■ 中国南方和北方以长江为界。**Zhōngguó nánfāng hé běifāng yǐ Chángjiāng wéi jiè.** *The south and north of China are demarcated by the Yangtze River.*

běijí 北极 [modif: 北 north + 极 pole] N the North Pole
北极星 běijíxīng the North Star, Polaris

běijīng 北京 N Beijing (Peking) (the capital of the People's Republic of China)

běimiàn 北面 N same as 北边 **běibian**

bèi 备 TRAD 備 v prepare

bèifèn 备份 N reserve, spare

bèiwànglù 备忘录 [modif: 备 prepare + 忘 forget + 录 record] N memorandum, memo

bèi 背 I N back (of the body)
背痛 bèitòng backache / 手背 shǒubèi the back of the hand

II v turn away, leave

bèibāo 背包 N backpack

bèijǐng 背景 N background
家庭背景 jiātíng bèijǐng family background

bèipàn 背叛 v betray

bèisòng 背诵 v repeat from memory

bèi 贝 TRAD 貝 N shellfish

bèiké 贝壳 N shell (of shellfish)

bèi 狈 N a kind of wolf with short forelegs

bèi 被 PREP by (introducing the doer of an action) ■ 花瓶被小明打破了。**Huāpíng bèi Xiǎo Míng dǎ pò le.** *The vase was broken by Xiao Ming.* ■ 他被人欺负了。**Tā bèi rén qīfu le.** *He was bullied by somebody.*

bèidòng 被动 ADJ passive
被动式 bèidòngshì (in grammar) the passive voice / 被动吸烟 bèidòng xīyān passive smoking

bèigào(rén) 被告（人） N defendant

bèizi 被子 N quilt, blanket (条 tiáo) ■ 冬天出太阳的时候，很多中国人喜欢晒被子。**Dōngtiān chū tàiyang de shíhou, hěn duō Zhōngguórén xǐhuan shài bèizi.** *Many Chinese like to sun quilts when it's sunny in winter. (→ On sunny winter days, many Chinese like to air their quilts.)*

bèi 倍 MEASURE WORD fold, time ■ 这个学校的学生人数比我们学校多一倍。（这个学校的学生人数是我们学校的两倍。）**Zhège xuéxiào de xuésheng rénshù bǐ wǒmen xuéxiào duō yí bèi. (Zhège xuéxiào de xuésheng rénshù shì wǒmen xuéxiào de liǎng bèi.)** *The student number of this school is twice as big as that of our school. (→ The student population of this school is twice of ours.)*

bèi 辈 N people of the same generation (See zhǎngbèi 长辈.)

bēn 奔 v run fast

bēnbō 奔波 v be busy running about

bēnchí 奔驰 [comp: 奔 run fast + 驰 run, gallop] v (of animals and vehicles) run fast, speed

běn 本¹ N capital, principal
赔本 péi běn lose one's capital in investments or other business dealings

běn 本² MEASURE WORD (for books, magazines, etc.)
一本书 yì běn shū a book

běn 本³ ADJ this one, one's own

NOTE: 本 **běn** in the sense of this one is only used on formal occasions. ■ 本店春节照常营业。**Běn diàn chūnjié zhàocháng yíngyè.** *This store will do business as usual during the Spring Festival. (→ We'll be open during the Chinese New Year.)*

běndì 本地 [modif: 本 this + 地 place] N this locality ■ 我向你介绍一个本地的名菜。**Wǒ xiàng nǐ jièshao yí ge běndì de míngcài.** *I'll recommend you a famous dish of this town.*

běnkē 本科 N undergraduate course
本科生 běnkēshēng an undergraduate

běnlái 本来 ADV originally, at first ■ 这个旅馆本来是一个富商的家。*Zhège lǚguǎn běnlái shì yí ge fù shāng de jiā. This hotel was originally a rich merchant's residence.* ■ 我本来不想去看电影，他一定要我去，我就去了。*Wǒ běnlái bù xiǎng qù kàn diànyǐng, tā yídìng yào wǒ qù, wǒ jiù qù le. At first I did not want to go to see the movie, but he insisted I should go, so I went with him.*

běnlǐng 本领 N skill, ability, capability ■ 他已经二十多岁了，还没有本领独立生活。*Tā yǐjīng èrshí duō suì le, hái méiyǒu běnlǐng dúlì shēnghuó. He is over twenty, but still lacks the skills to live independently.*

běnqián 本钱 N the money with which one makes investments or conducts other business dealings, capital

běnrén 本人 N oneself

他本人 tā běnrén himself / 我本人 wǒ běnrén myself

běnshēn 本身 N itself, in itself

běnshì 本事 N ability, capability ■ 他自以为本事很大，其实什么都做不好。*Tā zì yǐwéi běnshì hěn dà, qíshí shénme dōu zuò bu hǎo. He thinks himself very capable; actually he can't get anything done properly.*

NOTE: 本领 **běnlǐng** and 本事 **běnshì** are synonyms, but 本领 **běnlǐng** emphasizes skills while 本事 **běnshì** has a more general sense of "the ability to get things done" and may be used with negative connotations.

běnzhe 本着 PREP in accordance with, based on

běnzhì 本质 [comp: 本 origin + 质 nature] N innate character, true nature ■ 研究问题我们要透过表面现象看到本质。*Yánjiū wèntí, wǒmen yào tòuguo biǎomiàn xiànxiàng kàndào běnzhì. When studying a problem we should see beyond appearances and get to its essence.*

běnzi 本子 [suffix: 本 a book + 子 nominal suffix] N notebook (本 běn)

bèn 笨 ADJ dumb, stupid ■ 他不善于言词，其实一点都不笨。*Tā bú shànyú yáncí, qíshí yìdiǎn dōu bú bèn. He is not good at expressing himself, but he is by no means stupid.* ■ 千万不能对孩子说"你真笨！"这样的话。*Qiānwàn bù néng duì háizi shuō "Nǐ zhēn bèn!" zhèyàng de huà. Never, ever say to a child such things as "How stupid you are!"*

bènzhuō 笨拙 [comp: 笨 dumb + 拙 clumsy] ADJ clumsy

bēng 崩 V collapse

bēngkuì 崩溃 [comp: 崩 collapse + 溃 decay] V collapse, crumble

béng 甭 ADV (contraction of 不用) don't ■ 甭客气！*Béng kèqi! Don't stand on ceremony! It's OK.*

bèngfā 迸发 V burst out, burst forth

bèng 蹦 V jump

蹦床 bèngchuáng trampoline / 蹦极跳 bèngjí tiào bungee jump

bī 逼 V 1 force, compel 2 get close to, press on towards

bīpò 逼迫 [comp: 逼 force + 迫 force] V force, coerce

bí 鼻 N same as 鼻子 **bízi**

bítì 鼻涕 N nasal mucus

bízi 鼻子 N the nose

bǐ 比 I PREP (introducing the object that is compared with the subject of a sentence), than ■ 今天比昨天冷得多。*Jīntiān bǐ zuótiān lěng de duō. Today is much colder than yesterday.* ■ 我跑得比你快。*Wǒ pǎo de bǐ nǐ kuài. I run faster than you.* II V compete, compare, contrast ■ 你们俩谁跑得快？比一比! *Nǐmen liǎ shuí pǎo de kuài? Bǐ yì bǐ! Of you two, who runs faster? Let's see!*

bǐfang 比方 N example, analogy

打比方 dǎ bǐfang make an analogy, draw an analogy

bǐjiào 比较 V & ADV compare; comparatively, relatively, to some degree ■ 这两种方法哪个好，我们要比较一下。*Zhè liǎng zhǒng fāngfǎ nǎge hǎo, wǒmen yào bǐjiào yíxià. Which of the two approaches is the better one? We need to compare them.* ■ 这两天天气比较好。*Zhè liǎng tiān tiānqì bǐjiào hǎo. The weather these days is not bad.*

和… 比较 hé… bǐjiào compare… with ■ 和农村比较，城市的生活方便得多。*Hé nóngcūn bǐjiào, chéngshì de shēnghuó fāngbiàn de duō. Compared to living in the countryside, city life is much more convenient.*

bǐlì 比例 N percentage ■ 这个学校海外留学生在学生人数中占多少比例？*Zhège xuéxiào hǎiwài liúxuéshēng zài xuésheng rénshù zhōng zhàn duōshǎo bǐlì? What percentage of this school's enrolment are overseas students?*

bǐrú 比如 CONJ for example ■ 今年我们都取得了很大进步，比如约翰，现在已经会用中文写电子邮件了。*Jīnnián wǒmen dōu qǔdéle hěn dà jìnbù, bǐrú Yuēhàn, xiànzài yǐjīng huì yòng Zhōngwén xiě diànzǐ yóujiàn le. We have all made good progress this year. Take John for example, now he can write e-mails in Chinese.*

NOTE: In spoken Chinese you can also use 比如说 **bǐrúshuō**.

bǐsài 比赛 [comp: 比 compare + 赛 compete] V & N compete, have a match; match, game, competition ■ 今天晚上我们和他们比赛篮球。*Jīntiān wǎnshang wǒmen hé tāmen bǐsài lánqiú. This evening we'll have a basketball match with them.* ■ 下个月北京举行中国武术比赛。*Xià ge yuè Běijīng jǔxíng Zhōngguó wǔshù bǐsài. There will be a Chinese martial arts contest in Beijing next month.*

比赛项目 bǐsài xiàngmù event (of a sports meet) / 参加比赛 cānjiā bǐsài participate in a game (or sports event) / 和/跟…比赛 hé/gēn…bǐsài have a match/race with / 看比赛 kàn bǐsài watch a game (or sports event)

bǐyù 比喻 [comp: 比 comparison + 喻 analogy] N metaphor

bǐzhòng 比重 N **1** specific gravity **2** proportion

bǐ 笔¹ TRAD 筆 N writing instrument, pen, pencil (支 zhī) ■ 我可以借用你的笔吗? **Wǒ kěyǐ jièyòng nǐ de bǐ ma?** *May I borrow your pen?*
画笔 huàbǐ paintbrush (for art) / 毛笔 máobǐ Chinese writing brush

bǐ 笔² TRAD 筆 MEASURE WORD (for a sum of money or debt)

bǐjì 笔记 N notes (taken in class or while reading) ■ 我昨天没来上课, 你的笔记能借我看一下吗? **Wǒ zuótiān méi lái shàngkè, nǐ de bǐjì néng jiè wǒ kàn yíxià ma?** *I was absent from class yesterday. Could you let me have a look at your notes?*
记笔记 jì bǐjì take notes (in class, at a lecture, etc.) ■ 老师要求学生上课记笔记。**Lǎoshī yāoqiú xuésheng shàngkè jì bǐjì.** *The teacher requires that students take notes in class.*
做笔记 zuò bǐjì make notes (while reading) ■ 她有边读书边做笔记的好习惯。**Tā yǒu biān dúshū biān zuò bǐjì de hǎo xíguàn.** *She has formed the good habit of making notes while reading.*

bǐjìběn diànnǎo 笔记本电脑 N notebook computer, laptop

bǐcǐ 彼此 [comp: 彼 that + 此 this] PRON each other

bǐ 鄙 ADJ low, despicable

bǐshì 鄙视 [modif: 鄙 low + 视 look at, view] V despise, regard with contempt

bì 币 TRAD 幣 N currency (See huòbì 货币.)

bì 必 ADV inevitably

bìdìng 必定 V be bound to, be sure to, must

bìrán 必然 ADJ inevitable, bound to ■ 他因为骄傲而失败, 这是必然的。**Tā yīnwèi jiāo'ào ér shībài, zhè shì bìrán de.** *He failed because he was conceited. This was inevitable.*

bìxū 必须 [comp: 必 must + 须 need, have to] MODAL V must ■ 每个公民都必须遵守法律。**Měi ge gōngmín dōu bìxū zūnshǒu fǎlǜ.** *Every citizen must abide by the law.* ■ 你要在那个大学学习, 必须在半年前报名。**Nǐ yào zài nàge dàxué xuéxí, bìxū zài bànnián qián bàomíng.** *You must apply for enrolment half a year earlier if you want to study in this university.*

bìyào 必要 [comp: 必 must + 要 require] ADJ necessary ■ 你不必要送这么贵的礼物。**Nǐ bú bìyào sòng zhème guì de lǐwù.** *You don't have to give such an expensive present.* ■ 你外出旅行两天, 带这么多衣服, 必要吗? **Nǐ wàichū lǚxíng liǎngtiān, dài zhème duō yīfu, bìyào ma?** *Is it*

necessary to take so many clothes with you for a trip of two days?

bì 闭 TRAD 閉 V close, shut up ■ 老人看报看累了, 闭上眼睛休息一会。**Lǎorén kàn bào kàn lèi le, bìshang yǎnjing xiūxi yíhuìr.** *The old man was tired from reading the newspapers. He closed his eyes to rest for a while.*

bìmù 闭幕 [v+obj: 闭 close + 幕 curtain] V the curtan falls, (of a theatrical performance, an event, etc.) close
闭幕式 bìmù shì closing ceremony

bìsè 闭塞 [comp: 闭 closed + 塞 blocked] ADJ cut off from the outside world, secluded

bì zuǐ 闭嘴 V shut your mouth, shut up, say no more ■ 她愤怒地喊: "闭嘴!" **Tā fènnù de hǎn: "Bì zuǐ!"** *She shouted angrily, "Shut up!"*

NOTE: 闭嘴! Bìzuǐ! *Shut your mouth!* is a very impolite expression to tell people to stop talking. You can also say 闭上你的嘴! **Bì shang nǐ de zuǐ!** *Shut your mouth!*

bì 碧 ADJ bluish green

bìyù 碧玉 N green jade

bì 弊 N fraud, corrupt practice

bìbìng 弊病 [comp: 弊 corrupt practice + 病 sickness] N malady, shortcoming

bìduān 弊端 N malpractice, disadvantage

bì 蔽 V hide, conceal (See yǐnbì 隐蔽.)

bì 臂 N the arm
手臂 shǒubì the arm

bì 毕 TRAD 畢 V finish

bìjìng 毕竟 ADV after all, anyway

bìyè 毕业 [v+obj: 毕 finish + 业 course of study] V graduate from school ■ 你哪一年毕业? **Nǐ nǎ yì nián bìyè?** *When will you graduate?* ■ 我父亲二十多年前从一所著名大学毕业。**Wǒ fùqin èrshí duō nián qián cóng yì suǒ zhùmíng dàxué bìyè.** *My father graduated from a famous university over twenty years ago.*

bì 痹 N pain or numbness (See mábì 麻痹.)

bì 避 V evade, avoid ■ 很多人在商场里避雨。**Hěn duō rén zài shāngchǎng li bì yǔ.** *Many people are in the shopping mall to shelter from the rain.*

bìmiǎn 避免 [comp: 避 evade + 免 be free from] V avoid, avert ■ 她避免和以前的男朋友见面。**Tā bìmiǎn hé yǐqián de nán péngyou jiànmiàn.** *She avoids meeting her former boyfriend.* ■ 自然灾害是无法避免的。**Zìrán zāihài shì wúfǎ bìmiǎn de.** *Natural disasters cannot be avoided.*

bì 壁 N wall (See gébì 隔壁.)

biān 边 TRAD 邊 N side, border ■ 山的这一边有很多树, 那一边没有树。**Shān de zhè yì biān yǒu hěn duō shù, nà yì biān méiyǒu shù.** *On this side of the hill there are lots of trees, and there are no trees on the other side.*

NOTE: The most frequent use of 边 **biān** is to form "compound location nouns": 东边 **dōngbian** *east side*, 南边 **nánbian** *south side*, 西边 **xībian** *west side*, 北边 **běibian** *north side*, 里边 **lǐbian** *inside*, 外边 **wàibian** *outside*. 边 **biān** in such cases is often pronounced in the neutral tone.

biān … biān 边 … 边 CONJ (used with verbs to indicate simultaneous actions) ■ 他们边走边谈，不一会儿就到了市中心了。**Tāmen biān zǒu biān tán, bùyíhuìr jiù dào shì zhōngxīn le.** *They chatted while walking, and soon reached the city center.*

biānjiāng 边疆 [comp: 边 border + 疆 boundary] **N** border area

biānjiè 边界 [comp: 边 side, border + 界 realm] **N** border (between two countries)

biānjièxiàn 边界线 boundary (between two countries)

biānjìng 边境 [modif: 边 side, border + 境 place] **N** frontier, border

biānyuán 边缘 [comp: 边 side, border + 缘 edge] **N** edge, periphery

边缘状态 **biānyuán zhuàngtài** borderline case

biān 编 TRAD 編 V compile, compose ■ 那本词典是一位有丰富教学经验的老教授编的。**Nà běn cídiǎn shì yí wèi yǒu fēngfù jiàoxué jīngyàn de lǎo jiàoshòu biān de.** *That dictionary was compiled by an old professor with rich teaching experience.*

biānjí 编辑 [comp: 编 compile, compose + 辑 compile] **V & N** edit, compile; editor ■ 报纸编辑每天收到很多读者来信。**Bàozhǐ biānjí měitiān shōudào hěn duō.** *The newspaper editor receives a large number of readers' letters every day.*

biānzhī 编织 [comp: 编 compose + 织 knit] **V** knit

biān 鞭 N whip

鞭子 **biānzi N** whip (条 **tiáo**)

biāncè 鞭策 V spur on, urge on

biānpào 鞭炮 N firecracker

放鞭炮 **fàng biānpào** set off firecrackers

biān 扁 ADJ flat ■ 面包放在这么多食品的下面，都压扁了。**Miànbāo fàng zài zhème duō shípǐn de xiàmiàn, dōu yā biǎn le.** *Placed under so many groceries, the bread was crushed flat.*

biǎn 贬 V reduce, derogate

biǎndī 贬低 [v+compl: 贬 derogate + 低 low] **V** belittle, play down

贬低别人的成绩 **biǎndī biéren de chéngjì** depreciate someone's achievements

biǎnyì 贬义 N derogative meaning

biǎnzhí 贬值 [v+obj: 贬 reduce + 值 value] **V** devalue, depreciate

货币贬值 **huòbì biǎnzhí** currency devaluation

biàn 变 TRAD 變 V transform, change ■ 世界上任何事情都在变。**Shìjiè shang rènhé shìqing dōu zài biàn.** *Everything in the world is changing.*

biànchéng 变成 [v+compl: 变 change + 成 into]

V change into ■ 几年不见，小女孩变成了大姑娘。**Jǐnián bújiàn, xiǎo nǚhái biànchéngle dà gūniang.** *I hadn't seen her for several years and the little girl had changed into a young lady.*

biàngù 变故 N unforeseen event

biànhuà 变化 [comp: 变 change + 化 transform] **V & N** transform, change; transformation, change ■ 情况变化了，不能仍然用老办法。**Qíngkuàng biànhuà le, bùnéng réngrán yòng lǎo bànfǎ.** *Things have changed. We cannot use old ways of doing things as before. (→ We cannot continue doing things the old way.)* ■ 几年没来，我觉得这里变化很明显。**Jǐnián méi lái, wǒ juéde zhèli biànhuà hěn míngxiǎn.** *After a few years' absence, I find obvious changes in this place.*

NOTE: As a verb 变化 **biànhuà** is interchangeable with 变 **biàn**, 变化 **biànhuà** being a little more formal than 变 **biàn**.

biànqiān 变迁 [comp: 变 change + 迁 move] **V** change, evolve

biànzhì 变质 [v+obj: 变 change + 质 quality] **V** change the nature of, deteriorate ■ 这些过期食品变质了。**Zhè xiē guòqī shípǐn biànzhì le.** *These foodstuffs are past their sell-by dates and have gone bad.*

biàn 便 ADJ convenient

biànlì 便利 [comp: 便 convenient + 利 benefit] **ADJ** convenient, easy

biàntiáo 便条 [modif: 便 handy + 条 note] **N** informal written message, note

留便条 **liú biàntiáo** leave a note ■ 老王给我留了一张便条，说他明天下午三点半来看我。**Lǎo Wáng gěi wǒ liúle yì zhāng biàntiáo, shuō tā míngtiān xiàwǔ sān diǎn bàn lái kàn wǒ.** *Lao Wang left a note for me, saying that he would come to see me at 3:30 tomorrow afternoon.*

biànyú 便于 ADJ easy to, convenient to

biàn 遍 MEASURE WORD (used to indicate the frequency of an action done in its complete duration from the beginning to the end) ■ 这本书我看了三遍。**Zhè běn shū wǒ kànle sān biàn.** *I've read this book three times.* ■ 上个月我看了三个电影，其中一个看了两遍。**Shàng ge yuè wǒ kànle sān ge diànyǐng, qízhōng yí ge kànle liǎng biàn.** *I saw three movies last month, one of which I saw twice.*

biànbù 遍布 V spread all over

biàn 辩 TRAD 辯 V argue

biànhù 辩护 [comp: 辩 argue + 护 defend] **V** speak in defense of

辩护律师 **biànhù lǜshī** defense lawyer, defense counsel

biànjiě 辩解 [comp: 辩 argue + 解 explain] **V** try to defend oneself

biànlùn 辩论 [comp: 辩 argue + 论 discuss] **V &**

N debate (场 **chǎng**) ■ 我不想和任何人辩论有关宗教的问题。**Wǒ bùxiǎng he rènhé rén biànlùn yǒuguān zōngjiào de wèntí.** *I don't want to debate with anyone on matters of religion.*
举行一场辩论 jǔxíng yì chǎng biànlùn hold a debate

biànzhèng 辩证 **ADJ** dialectal

biàn 辨 **V** distinguish, recognize

biànrèn 辨认 [comp: 辨 distinguish + 认 recognize] **V** identify, recognize
辨认罪犯 biànrèn zuìfàn identify a criminal

biàn 辫 **TRAD** 辮 **N** braid, pigtail

biànzi 辫子 **N** braid, pigtail (条 **tiáo**)

biāo 标 **TRAD** 標 **V** mark

biāoběn 标本 **N** specimen, sample
采集标本 cǎijí biāoběn collect samples/specimen

biāodiǎn 标点 [comp: 标 mark + 点 point] **N** punctuation mark ■ 你这个标点用得不对。**Nǐ zhège biāodiǎn yòng de bú duì.** *The punctuation mark you used is not correct. (→ You used a wrong punctuation mark.)*

biāojì 标记 **N** sign, mark, symbol

biāotí 标题 [comp: 标 mark + 题 title] **N** title, headline

biāozhì 标志 [comp: 标 mark + 志 record] **N** sign, mark
社会地位的标志 shèhuì dìwèi de biāozhì status symbol

biāozhǔn 标准 [comp: 标 standard + 准 accuracy] **N & ADJ** standard, criterion; up to standard, perfect ■ 外国人说汉语发音不太标准，问题不大；在中国，又有多少人说标准的普通话呢？**Wàiguórén shuō Hànyǔ fāyīn bú tài biāozhǔn, wèntí bú dà; zài Zhōngguó, yòu yǒu duōshǎo rén shuō biāozhǔn de Pǔtōnghuà ne?** *It doesn't matter if a foreigner doesn't speak Chinese with perfect pronunciation. After all, how many Chinese speak perfect Putonghua?*
符合标准 fúhé biāozhǔn conform to the standard ■ 这些产品不符合标准，不能出厂。**Zhèxiē chǎnpǐn bù fúhé biāozhǔn, bù néng chūchǎng.** *These products do not conform to the standard and cannot leave the factory. (→ These products do not meet the standard and cannot be shipped.)*
达到标准 dádào biāozhǔn reach the standard ■ 你们的汉语水平达到什么标准？**Nǐmen de Hànyǔshuǐpíng dádào shénme biāozhǔn?** *What level has your Chinese proficiency reached?*

biāo 飚 **TRAD** 飆 **N** violent storm

biāoshēng 飚升 **V** increase sharply, ascend rapidly

biǎo 表¹ **TRAD** 錶 **N** wrist watch, watch (块 **kuài**, 只 **zhī**) ■ 我的表慢了一点。**Wǒ de biǎo màn le yìdiǎn.** *My watch is a bit slow.* ■ 我的表停了，你的表几点？**Wǒ de biǎo tíng le, nǐ de biǎo jǐ diǎn?** *My watch has stopped. What time is it by your watch?*
戴表 dài biǎo wear a watch ■ 他戴了一块新表。**Tā dàile yí kuài xīn biǎo.** *He wears a new watch.*

男表 nán biǎo men's watch / 女表 nǚbiǎo ladies' watch

biǎo 表² **N** form, table
乘法表 chéngfǎbiǎo multiplication table

biǎogé 表格 form (张 **zhāng**, 份 **fèn**) ■ 这张表格我不会填，你能帮帮我吗？**Zhè zhāng biǎogé wǒ bú huì tián, nǐ néng bāngbang wǒ ma?** *I don't know how to fill in this form. Could you help me?*

biǎo 表³ **V** express one's feelings

biǎodá 表达 [comp: 表 express + 达 reach] **V** express (thoughts or emotions) ■ 你能不能用简单的中文把意思表达清楚？**Nǐ néng bu néng yòng jiǎndān de Zhōngwén bǎ yìsi biǎodá qīngchu?** *Can you express the meaning clearly in simple Chinese?* ■ 我当时的心情很复杂，很难表达清楚。**Wǒ dāngshí de xīnqíng hěn fùzá, hěn nán biǎodá qīngchu.** *I had mixed feelings at that moment; it was difficult to express them clearly.*

biǎojué 表决 **V** decide by vote, vote

biǎomiàn 表面 [modif: 表 surface + 面 face] **N** surface ■ 他表面上很友好，其实完全不是这样。**Tā biǎomiàn shang hěn yǒuhǎo, qíshí wánquán búshì zhèyàng.** *He appears to be very friendly; actually he is not friendly at all.*

biǎomíng 表明 [v+compl: 表 express + 明 clear] **V** make clear, demonstrate ■ 她一直不说话，表明她其实不赞成。**Tā yìzhí bù shuōhuà, biǎomíng tā qíshí bú zànchéng.** *She was silent all the way, showing that actually she disapproved.* ■ 我向他清楚地表明，我们公司完全保证产品质量。**Wǒ xiàng tā qīngchu de biǎomíng, wǒmen gōngsī wánquán bǎozhèng chǎnpǐn zhìliàng.** *I made it very clear to him that our company completely guarantees the quality of our products.*

biǎoqíng 表情 [modif: 表 surface + 情 feelings] **N** facial expression ■ 从她的表情可以看出她内心的感情吗？**Cóng tāde biǎoqíng kěyǐ kànchū tā nèixīn de gǎnqíng ma?** *Can you tell the feelings in her heart from her facial expression?*
一副严肃的表情 yífù yánsù de biǎoqíng with a serious expression

biǎoshì 表示 [comp: 表 show, express + 示 indicate] **V** express, show ■ 一般点头表示同意，摇头表示不同意。**Yìbān diǎntóu biǎoshì tóngyì, yáotóu biǎoshì bù tóngyì.** *Generally, nodding indicates agreement and shaking one's head indicates disagreement.* ■ 他一句话也没说，表示不高兴。**Tā yí jù huà yě méi shuō, biǎoshì bù gāoxìng.** *He did not say a word, showing his displeasure.*

biǎotài 表态 **V** make known one's position or views, declare one's views

biǎoxiàn 表现 [comp: 表 show, express + 现 display] **V** 1 display, show ■ 他表现得很热情。**Tā biǎoxiàn dé hěn rèqíng.** *He showed great enthusiasm.* 2 perform ■ 新工人表现很好，老板决定增加他的工资。**Xīn gōngrén biǎoxiàn hěn**

hǎo, lǎobǎn juédìng zēngjiā tā de gōngzī. *The new worker performed well, and the boss decided to raise his wages.*

biǎoyǎn 表演 [comp: 表 show + 演 act] **v & n** put on (a show), perform, demonstrate; performance, show ■ 他们星期六在这里表演歌舞。**Tāmen Xīngqīliù zài zhèlǐ biǎoyǎn gēwǔ.** *They perform singing and dancing here on Saturday.* ■ 他们的表演很精彩。**Tāmen de biǎoyǎn hěn jīngcǎi.** *Their performance was wonderful.*

biǎoyáng 表扬 [comp: 表 display + 扬 raise, make known] **v & n** praise, commend (**ANTONYM** 批评 **pīpíng**); praise, commendation ■ 他学习进步很大，老师在班上表扬了他。**Tā xuéxí jìnbù hěn dà, lǎoshī zài bān shang biǎoyángle tā.** *He made great progress in his studies and the teacher praised him in class.*

biǎozhāng 表彰 **v** commend, honor

biē 憋 **v** suppress resentment with effort, contain oneself

憋不住 **biē bu zhù** cannot contain oneself, unable to hold oneself back

bié 别 **ADV** don't ■ 别说话了，电影开始了。**Bié shuōhuà le, diànyǐng kāishǐ le.** *Don't talk. (→ Stop talking.) The movie has started.* ■ 你不愿意去，就别去了。**Nǐ bú yuànyì qù, jiù bié qù le.** *If you don't want to go, then don't go.*

NOTE: 别 **bié** is a contraction of 不要 **búyào** in an imperative sentence. It is used colloquially only.

biéde 别的 **PRON** other ■ 他大学毕业以后一直在教书，没有做过别的工作。**Tā dàxué bìyè yǐhòu yìzhí zài jiāoshū, méiyǒu zuòguo biéde gōngzuò.** *He has been teaching since graduating from university and has not held any other job (← done any other work).*

biérén 别人 [modif: 别 other + 人 person, people] **PRON** other people, others ■ 别人怎么说我不管，只要你喜欢就行。**Biérén zěnme shuō wǒ bù guǎn, zhǐyào nǐ xǐhuan jiù xíng.** *I don't mind what others may say. It's OK as long as you like it.*

biéshù 别墅 **n** villa

biézhì 别致 **ADJ** unique, unconventional

biè 别 as in 别扭 **bièniu**

bièniu 别扭 **ADJ** awkward, uncomfortable ■ 我感到挺别扭。**Wǒ gǎndào tǐng bièniu.** *I feel awkward. (or I find the situation uncomfortable.)*

闹别扭 **nào bièniu** be at odds with someone, be difficult with someone, make difficulties.

bīn 宾 **TRAD** 賓 **n** guest

bīnguǎn 宾馆 [modif: 宾 guest + 馆 house] **n** guesthouse ■ 这是政府宾馆，不对外开放。**Zhè shì zhèngfǔ bīnguǎn, bú duì wài kāifàng.** *This is a government guesthouse. It is not open to the public.*

bīn 滨 **TRAD** 濱 **n** waterside

bīnlín 濒临 **v** be close to, be on the verge of

bīng 冰 **n** ice ■ 水到零度就结成冰。**Shuǐ dào líng**

dù jiù jiéchéng bīng. *Water freezes to ice at zero degrees Celsius.*

bīngbáo 冰雹 **n** hailstone, hailstorm

bīngjīlíng 冰激凌 **n** ice cream

bīngqílín 冰淇淋 same as 冰激凌 **bīngjīlíng**

bīngxiāng 冰箱 [modif: 冰 ice + 箱 box] **n** refrigerator ■ 冰箱里没有什么东西，看来得出去吃晚饭了。**Bīngxiāng li méiyǒu shénme dōngxi, kànlái děi chūqu chī wǎnfàn le.** *There isn't much in the fridge. Looks like we'll have to eat dinner out.*

电冰箱 **diàn bīngxiāng** refrigerator

bīng 兵 **n** soldier

当兵 **dāng bīng** be a soldier, serve in the armed forces ■ 她哥哥在部队当兵。**Tā gēge zài bùduì dāng bīng.** *Her brother is serving in the armed forces.*

bǐng 饼 **TRAD** 餅 **n** cake

bǐnggān 饼干 [modif: 饼 cake + 干 dried food] **n** cookie(s), biscuit(s) (片 **piàn**, 包 **bāo**) ■ 他肚子饿了，就吃饼干。**Tā dùzi è le, jiù chī bǐnggān.** *He ate some biscuits when he was hungry.*

bǐng 丙 **n** the third of the "Celestial Stems," the third

bìng 并 **TRAD** 並 **I ADV** (used before a negative word for emphasis) ■ 事情并不象你想象的那么简单。**Shìqing bìng bú xiàng nǐ xiǎngxiàng de nàme jiǎndān.** *Things are not at all as simple as you imagine.* ■ 他并不是没有试过，但是不成功。**Tā bìng bú shì méiyǒu shìguo, dànshi bù chénggōng.** *It was not the case that he never tried, but that he was not successful.* **II CONJ** same as 并且 **bìngqiě.** Used only in written Chinese.

NOTE: 并 **bìng** is used to emphasize the negation. It is not grammatically essential; without 并 **bìng** the sentences still stand. The following is perfectly acceptable: ■ 事情不象你想象的那么简单。**Shìqing bú xiàng nǐ xiǎngxiàng de nàme jiǎndān.** *Things are not as simple as you imagine.*

bìngcún 并存 **v** exist side by side, co-exist

bìngfēi 并非 **ADV** not, not at all

并非如此 **bìngfēi rúcǐ** not like that

bìngliè 并列 **v** stand side by side

bìngqiě 并且 **CONJ** moreover, what's more, and ■ 技术员发现并且解决了问题。**Jìshùyuán fāxiàn bìngqiě jiějuéle wèntí.** *The technician discovered the problem and solved it. (← The technician discovered the problem; what's more, he solved it.)* ■ 他去机场接朋友，并且带他游览市区。**Tā qù jīchǎng jiē péngyou, bìngqiě dài tā yóulǎn shìqū.** *He met his friend at the airport and took him on a sightseeing trip of the city.*

bìng 病 **v & n** fall ill, be ill; illness, disease ■ 他病得很重，得住院。**Tā bìng de hěn zhòng, děi zhùyuàn.** *He is seriously ill and needs to be hospitalized.* ■ 张先生什么病? **Zhāng xiānsheng**

shénme bìng? *What is Mr Zhang ill with?*
(→ What's wrong with Mr Zhang?)
生病 shēng bìng fall ill
bìng jià 病假 **N** sick leave
请病假 qǐng bìngjià ask for/apply for sick leave
■ 她请了三天病假。**Tā qǐngle sāntiān bìngjià.** *She asked for three days' sick leave.*
bìngdú 病毒 [modif: 病 disease + 毒 poison] **N** virus
电脑病毒 diànnǎo bìngdù computer virus
bìngfáng 病房 [modif: 病 sickness + 房 room] **N** (hospital) ward ■ 医生每天上午十点查病房。**Yīshēng měi tiān shàngwǔ shí diǎn chá bìngfáng.** *The doctors make their rounds of the wards at ten o'clock every morning.*
重病房 zhòngbìngfáng intensive care ward
bìngrén 病人 [modif: 病 sick + 人 person] **N** patient ■ 病人要听医生的嘱咐。**Bìngrén yào tīng yīshēng de zhǔfu.** *Patients should take their doctors' advice.*
住院病人 zhùyuàn bìngrén inpatient
bō 波 **N** ripple, wave
bōdòng 波动 **V** fluctuate (like a wave)
情绪波动 qíngxù bōdòng constantly changing moods
bōlàng 波浪 [comp: 波 ripple + 浪 wave] **N** wave
bōtāo 波涛 [comp: 波 wave + 涛 billow] **N** high wave
bōtāo xiōngyǒng 波涛汹涌 **IDIOM** waves surging turbulently, waves running high
bō 玻 **N** as in 玻璃 **bōli**
bōli 玻璃 **N** glass ■ 大楼的正面全部是玻璃。**Dàlóu de zhèngmiàn quánbù shì bōli.** *The front of the big building is all covered by glass.*
玻璃窗 bōli chuāng glass window, window
bō 播 **V** sow
bōfàng 播放 [comp: 播 sow + 放 release] **V** broadcast (radio or TV programmes)
bōzhòng 播种 [comp: 播 sow + 种 plant] **V** sow seeds
bō 剥 **TRAD** 剝 **V** peel, strip
bōxuē 剥削 **V** exploit (people)
bō 拨 **TRAD** 撥 **V** **1** stir with a finger or stick **2** allocate
bōdǎ 拨打 **V** dial to call, press to call
bōkuǎn 拨款 **V** allocate funds, appropriate (money)
bó 伯 **N** same as 伯父 **bófù**
bófù 伯父 **N** father's elder brother ■ 伯父只比爸爸大两岁，但是看来比爸爸老得多。**Bófù zhǐ bǐ bàba dà liǎng suì, dànshì kànlái bǐ bàba lǎo de duō.** *My father's elder brother is only two years older than he is, but looks much older.*

NOTE: 伯父 **bófù** is also a form of address for men older than your father but not old enough to be your grandfather. The colloquialism for 伯父 **bófù** is 伯伯 **bóbo**.

bómǔ 伯母 **N** father's elder brother's wife ■ 我的伯父伯母住在香港。**Wǒ de bófù bómǔ zhù zài Xiānggǎng.** *My uncle (← father's elder brother) and aunt (his wife) live in Hong Kong.*

NOTE: 伯母 **bómǔ** is also a form of address for women older than your mother but not old enough to be your grandmother. It is generally used by well-educated urban Chinese.

bó 脖 **N** neck
bózi 脖子 [suffix: 脖 neck + 子 nominal suffix] **N** neck ■ 我的脖子扭伤了。**Wǒ de bózi niǔ shāng le.** *My neck was sprained.*
bó 博 **ADJ** abundant, extensive
bó dà jīng shēn 博大精深 [博 extensive + 大 big + 精 refined + 深 profound] **ADJ** magnificent and profound
bókè 博客 **V & N** write and post a blog; web log; blog, blogger
bólǎnhuì 博览会 [modif: 博 plentiful, extensive + 览 view + 会 meeting] **N** exposition, exhibition, fair
世界博览会 shìjiè bólǎnhuì World Exposition, World Expo
bóshì 博士 [modif: 博 erudite + 士 scholar] **N** doctor, Ph.D. ■ 张博士是一位中国著名的生物化学家。**Zhāng bóshì shì yīwèi Zhōngguó zhùmíng de shēngwù huàxué jiā.** *Dr Zhang is a well-known biochemist in China.*
博士生 bóshìshēng Ph.D. candidate / 博士生导师 bóshìshēng dǎoshī Ph.D. supervisor / 博士后 bóshìhòu post-doctorate / 博士学位 bóshì xuéwèi Ph.D. degree
bówùguǎn 博物馆 [modif: 博物 natural science + 馆 building] **N** museum
历史博物馆 lìshǐ bówùguǎn historical museum
bó 膊 **N** arm (See **gēbo** 胳膊.)
bó 搏 **V** be engaged in a hand-to-hand combat, fight
bódòu 搏斗 [comp: 搏 fight + 斗 fight] **V** battle, wrestle
bó 薄 **ADJ** meager, small (**ANTONYM** 厚 **hòu**) ■ 请收下这份薄礼。**Qǐng shōu xia zhè fèn bó lǐ.** *Please accept this insignificant gift.*

NOTE: The character 薄 has two pronunciations: **báo** and **bó**. While 薄 **báo** is used to describe material "thinness," 薄 **bó** is used in a figurative sense.

bóruò 薄弱 [comp: 薄 thin + 弱 weak] **ADJ** frail, weak
bó 驳 **TRAD** 駁 **V** refute, retort (See **fǎnbó** 反驳.)
bǔ 捕 **V** catch, arrest
bǔzhuō 捕捉 [comp: 捕 catch + 捉 catch] **V** catch (animals), seize
bǔrǔ 哺乳 **V** breastfeed
bǔrǔ dòngwù 哺乳动物 mammal
bǔ 补 **TRAD** 補 **V** mend, patch

bǔcháng 补偿 [comp: 补 mend + 偿 compensate]
v compensate, make up

bǔchōng 补充 [comp: 补 supplement + 充 fill up]
v make up, supplement: ■ 刚才小李谈了这个问
题，我想补充几句。**Gāngcái Xiǎo Lǐ tánle zhège
wèntí, wǒ xiǎng bǔchōng jǐ jù.** *Just now Xiao Li
spoke of this problem. I'd like to add a few points.*

bǔjiù 补救 [comp: 补 mend + 救 rescue] **v** remedy
补救办法 bǔjiù bànfǎ corrective measure, reme-
dial measure

bǔkè 补课 [v+obj: 补 make up+ 课 lessons] **v**
make up for missed lessons

bǔtiē 补贴 [comp: 补 patch + 贴 paste] **V & N**
subsidize; subsidy

bù 不 **ADV** no, not ■ 今天不冷。**Jīntiān bù lěng.**
It's not cold today. ■ "你是美国人吗？" "不，我是
加拿大人。" **"Nǐ shì Měiguórén ma?" "Bù, wǒ shì
Jiānádàrén."** *"Are you an American?" "No, I'm a
Canadian."*

NOTE: When followed by a syllable in the fourth
(falling) tone, 不 undergoes tone change from the
normal fourth tone to the second (rising) tone, e.g.
不对 **búduì**, 不是 **búshì**.

búyào 不要 **ADV** (used in an imperative sentence
or as advice) do not ■ 你们不要说话了，电影开始
了。**Nǐmen búyào shuōhuà le, diànyǐng kāishǐ le.**
Please don't talk any more. The movie has started.
■ 你不要着急，你孩子的病很快会好的。**Nǐ búyào
zháojí, nǐ háizi de bìng hěnkuài huì hǎo de.** *Don't
you be worried; your child will recover soon.*

Note: See note on 别 **bié.**

bù'ān 不安 [modif: 不 not + 安 peace, peaceful]
ADJ upset, disturbed

búbì 不必 [modif: 不 not + 必 necessary] **ADV**
need not, not have to, unnecessarily ■ 你不必送这么贵
重的礼物。**Nǐ búbì sòng zhème guìzhòng de lǐwù.**
You don't have to give such an expensive gift. ■
孩子会很快恢复健康的，你完全不必担心。**Háizi
huì hěn kuài huīfù jiànkāng de, nǐ wánquán búbì
dānxīn.** *The child will recover very soon. You really don't have to worry.*

búcuò 不错 [modif: 不 not + 错 wrong] **ADJ 1** not
wrong; quite right ■ 你那样考虑一点不错。
Nǐ nàyàng kǎolǜ yìdiǎn bú cuò. *It was quite right
of you to think that way.* **2** not bad, quite good
■ 这个电影不错。**Zhè ge diànyǐng búcuò.** *This
movie is rather good.* ■ 这孩子画得真不错。**Zhè
háizi huà de zhēn búcuò.** *This child really doesn't
draw badly. (→ This child draws quite well.)*

NOTE: ...得不错 **...de búcuò** is ambiguous. It may
mean either *... correctly* or *... rather well.* For example, the sentence 你说得不错。**Nǐ shuō de búcuò.**
may mean either *You spoke correctly. (→ You're
right.)* or *You spoke quite well. (→ Well said.)*

búdà 不大 **ADV** not very, not much ■ 今天不大
热。**Jīntiān búdà rè.** *Today is not very hot.* ■ 我
不大喜欢吃日本菜。**Wǒ búdà xǐhuan chī Rìběn
cài.** *I'm not very fond of Japanese food.*

búdàn ... érqiě 不但 ... 而且 **CONJ** not only ...
but also ... ■ 这家饭店的菜不但好吃，而且好看。
Zhè jiā fàndiàn de cài búdàn hǎochī, érqiě hǎokàn.
*The dishes in this restaurant are not only deli-
cious but also beautiful.* ■ 她不但唱歌唱得好听，
而且跳舞跳得好看。**Tā búdàn chànggē chàng de
hǎotīng, érqiě tiàowǔ tiào de hǎokàn.** *She not only
sings beautifully, but also dances gracefully.*

bùdébù 不得不 **ADV** have to, have no choice but
■ 我做错了题目，不得不重做。**Wǒ zuòcuòle
tímù, bùdebù chóng zuò.** *I did the wrong question
[for a school assignment] and had to do it all
over agian.* ■ 这个星期去上海的飞机票全部卖
完了，我们不得不改到下星期去。**Zhège xīngqī
qù Shànghǎi de fēijī piào quánbù màiwán le,
wǒmen bùdébù gǎi dào xià xīngqī qù.** *This week's
air tickets to Shanghai are sold out, so we have
no choice but change our departure date to next
week.*

bùdéliǎo 不得了 **ADJ 1** horrible, extremely
serious ■ 不得了了，对面房子着火了！**Bùdéliǎo
le, duìmiàn fángzi zháohuǒ le!** *How terrible, the
house opposite is on fire!* ■ 你没有什么不得了的
事，就别麻烦朋友了。**Nǐ méiyǒu shénme bùdéliǎo
de shì, jiù bié máfan péngyou le.** *If it isn't anything
really serious, don't bother your friends.*
2 extremely (used after an adjective and introduced by 得 **de**) ■ 昨天热得不得了。**Zuótiān rè de
bùdéliǎo.** *It was extremely hot yesterday.* ■ 爬那
座雪山危险得不得了，你们非充分准备不可。**Pá
nà zuò xuěshān wēixiǎn de bùdéliǎo, nǐmen fēi
chōngfèn zhǔnbèi bùkě.** *It is extremely dangerous
to climb that snowy mountain. You must be well
prepared.*

bùdéyǐ 不得已 **ADJ** having no alternative but to,
acting against one's will ■ 非到不得已的时候，
不能用这笔钱。**Fēidào bùdéyǐ de shíhou, bú néng
yòng zhè bǐ qián.** *You're not allowed to use this
money, unless you really have to.*

búduàn 不断 [modif: 不 not + 断 interrupt] **ADV**
without interruption, continuously, incessantly
■ 只有不断努力，才能永远进步。**Zhǐyǒu búduàn
nǔlì, cái néng yǒngyuǎn jìnbù.** *Only by continuous
efforts can one make progress forever.*

bùfáng 不妨 **ADV** might as well ■ 你不妨试试针
灸，看看有没有效果。**Nǐ bùfáng shìshi zhēnjiǔ,
kànkan yóuméiyǒu xiàoguǒ.** *You might as well try
acupuncture to see if it is efficacious.*

bùgǎndāng 不敢当 **IDIOM** Thank you, I don't
dare to accept (a polite/modest reply to a compliment) ■ "您中文说得很标准。" "不敢当，
还要不断练习。" **"Nín Zhōngwén shuō de hěn**

biāozhǔn." "Bùgǎndāng, háiyào búduàn liànxí."
"You speak standard Chinese. (→ Your Chinese is perfect.)" "Thank you very much. I still need constant practice." ■ 您对这个问题分析得极其深刻。" "不敢当，您对这个问题有什么看法？" **"Nín duì zhège wèntí fēnxī de jíqí shēnkè." "Bùgǎndāng, nín duì zhège wèntí yǒu shénme kànfǎ?"** *"You've made a penetrating analysis of this problem." "I don't deserve [such praise]. What's your view on this matter?"*

búgù 不顾 [modif: 不 not + 顾 attend to] v disregard, in spite of

bùguǎn 不管 CONJ no matter (what, who, how, etc.) ■ 不管你在哪里看到他，他都带着他的小狗。**Bùguǎn nǐ zài nǎlǐ kàndào tā, tā dōu dàizhe tā de xiǎo gǒu.** *No matter where you see him, he is with his puppy.* ■ 不管他多么忙，他总是每天给妈妈发一份电子邮件。**Bùguǎn tā duōme máng, tā zǒngshì měi tiān gěi māma fā yí fèn diànzǐ yóujiàn.** *No matter how busy he is, he always sends his mother a daily e-mail.*

NOTE: 不管 **bùguǎn** may be replaced by 不论 **búlùn** or 无论 **wúlùn**, but 不管 **bùguǎn** is more colloquial.

búguò 不过 CONJ same as 但是 **dànshì**. Used colloquially.

bù hǎo yìsi 不好意思 IDIOM I'm embarrassed (polite phrase used when you are offering an apology, giving a gift, or receiving a gift or other acts of kindness) ■ 不好意思，我又迟到了。**Bù hǎoyìsi, wǒ yòu chídào le.** *I'm sorry I'm late again.* ■ 这点小礼物，请您收下，不好意思。**Zhè diǎn xiǎo lǐwù, qǐng nín shōuxià, bù hǎoyìsi.** *Please accept this little present.*

NOTE: 不好意思 **bù hǎoyìsi** literally means "I'm embarrassed." It is easy to understand why you say it when you are apologising or receiving a gift. When you are giving a gift, however, you also say it to imply that the gift is so insignificant that you feel embarrassed about it.

bú jiàndé 不见得 ADV not necessarily, unlikely ■ 这位医生的诊断不见得对，你最好再看另一位医生。**Zhè wèi yīshēng de zhěnduàn bùjiàndé duì, nǐ zuìhǎo zài kàn lìng yí wèi yīshēng.** *This doctor's diagnosis is not necessarily correct; you'd better see another one*

bùjīn 不禁 ADV cannot help, cannot refrain from

bùjǐn 不仅 CONJ same as 不但 **búdàn**. Often used in writing.

bùjiǔ 不久 N not long afterwards, near future, soon ■ 他们不久就要回国了。**Tāmen bùjiǔjiù yào huíguó le.** *They're returning to their country soon.*

bùkān 不堪 I v (used before another verb) cannot bear, cannot stand

不堪设想 **bùkān shèxiǎng** (of consequences) cannot be contemplated, too bad even to contemplate

II ADV (used after an adjective) utterly 混乱不堪 **hùnluàn bùkān** in utter chaos

bù kě sīyì 不可思议 ADJ unthinkable, beyond comprehension

búkèqi 不客气 [modif: 不 not + 客气 polite, standing on ceremony] you're welcome, not at all ■ "谢谢你！" "不客气。" **"Xièxie nǐ!" "Búkèqi."** *"Thank you!" "You're welcome."*

búkuì 不愧 [modif: 不 not + 愧 be ashamed] v be worthy of, deserve to be called

búliào 不料 ADV unexpectedly

búlùn 不论 CONJ same as 不管 **bùguǎn**. Used more in writing.

bùmiǎn 不免 ADV would only be natural, unavoidably, inevitably

búnàifán 不耐烦 ADJ impatient

bùrán 不然 CONJ otherwise, or ■ 你别说了，不然我真要生气了。**Nǐ bié shuō le, bùrán wǒ zhēn yào shēngqì le.** *Don't say any more, or I'll really be angry.* ■ 他一定遇到了非常麻烦的事，不然情绪不会这么坏。**Tā yídìng yùdàole fēicháng máfan de shì, bùrán qíngxù bú huì zhème huài.** *He must have gotten into big trouble; otherwise he wouldn't be in such a bad mood.*

NOTE: To be more emphatic, you can use 不然的话 **bùrán de huà** instead of 不然 **bùrán**.

bùrú 不如 v be not as good as, be not as … as ■ 走路不如骑车快。**Zǒulù bùrú qíchē kuài.** *Walking is not as fast as riding a bicycle.* ■ 我体育不如你，但是你功课不如我。**Wǒ tǐyù bùrú nǐ, dànshì nǐ gōngkè bùrú wǒ.** *I'm not as good as you are in sports, but you're not as good as me in academic work.*

bùshǎo 不少 [modif: 不 not + 少 few, little] ADJ quite a few ■ 我在这个城市有不少好朋友。**Wǒ zài zhège chéngshì yǒu bùshǎo hǎo péngyou.** *I have quite a few good friends in this city.* ■ 我做了不少解释，她还是不原谅我。**Wǒ zuòle bùshǎo jiěshì, tā háishì bù yuánliàng wǒ.** *I have done much explanation, but she still won't forgive me.*

bùshí 不时 ADV now and then, from time to time

bùtíng 不停 [modif: 不 not + 停 stop] ADV without let-up, incessantly ■ 雨不停地下了两天。**Yǔ bùtíng de xiàle liǎng tiān.** *It rained for two days without let-up.*

bùtóng 不同 ADJ not the same, different ■ 人和人不同，不能比较。**Rén hé rén bùtóng, bù néng bǐjiào.** *People are different and cannot be compared.* ■ 这两个字发音相同，写法不同，意思也不同。**Zhè liǎng ge zì fāyīn xiāngtóng, xiěfǎ bùtóng, yìsi yě bùtóng.** *These two characters have the*

same pronunciation but they are different in writing and meaning.

…和/跟…不同 … hé/gēn…bùtóng … is/are different from … ■ 我的意见跟他的意见不同。**Wǒ de yìjiàn gēn tā de yìjiàn bùtóng.** *My opinion is different from his.*

bù xī 不惜 [modif: 不 not + 惜 grudge] **v** not hesitate, not spare

不惜工本 bù xī gōngběn spare neither labor or money, spare no expense

bù xiāng shàng xià 不相上下 **IDIOM** equally matched, be same good as

bú xiànghuà 不像话 **ADJ 1** unreasonable, unfair ■ 你这么说，不像话。**Nǐ zhème shuō, bú xiànghuà.** *It's unreasonable of you to say so.* **2** shocking outrageous

bú xiè yí gù 不屑一顾 will not spare a glance for

bùxíng 不行 **v 1** will not do, be not allowed ■ "妈妈，这个周末我带十几个同学来家里玩，行不行？" "不行。" **Māma, zhège zhōumò wǒ dài shí jǐ ge tóngxué lái jiāli wán, xíng bu xíng?** **"Bù xíng."** *"Mom, may I bring a dozen classmates home for a party this weekend?" "No, you may not."* **2** be no good (at something), be poor in ■ 我的中文不行，请你多多帮助。**Wǒ de Zhōngwén bù xíng, qǐng nǐ duōduō bāngzhù.** *My Chinese is not good. Please help me.* ■ 他体育很好，但是功课不行。**Tā tǐyù hěn hǎo, dànshi gōngkè bùxíng.** *He is good at sports, but poor at schoolwork.*

búxìng 不幸 [modif: 不 not + 幸 fortunate] **ADJ** unfortunate ■ 这次交通事故死了一人，伤了三人，真是一件不幸的事。**Zhè cì jiāotōng shìgù sǐle yì rén, shāngle sān rén, zhēn shì yí jiàn búxìng de shì.** *One person died and three were injured in this road accident, which is indeed an unfortunate event.*

Note: 不幸 **búxìng** is used to describe serious events or matters, often involving death. Do not use 不幸 **búxìng** for trivial matters. For example, even though in English it is acceptable to say, "Unfortunately, I haven't seen the film," in Chinese it would be wrong to say 我不幸没有看过那个电影。**Wǒ búxìng méiyǒu kànguo nàge diànyǐng.**

bùxǔ 不许 **v** not permit, not allow ■ 不许逃学。**Bùxǔ táo xué.** *Truancy is not allowed.* ■ 爸爸不许她和那个男孩出去玩。**Bàba bùxǔ tā hé nàge nán hái chūqu wán.** *Father does not allow her to go out with that boy.*

bù yán ér yù 不言而喻 self-evident, it goes without saying

búyàojǐn 不要紧 **ADJ** unimportant, doesn't matter

búyòng 不用 **ADV** no need, there's no need, don't have to ■ 如果你明天不舒服，就不用来了。**Rúguǒ nǐ míngtiān bù shūfu, jiù búyòng lái le.** *If you're not well tomorrow, you don't have to come.* ■ 不用麻烦了，我们一会儿就走。**Búyòng máfan**

le, wǒmen yíhuīr jiù zǒu. *Don't bother. We'll be leaving soon.*

bù yóudé 不由得 **ADV** cannot but, cannot help, in spite of oneself

bù zé shǒuduàn 不择手段 **IDIOM** by fair means or foul, by hook or by crook

bùzhǐ 不止 **ADV** more than, not limited to

bùzú 不足 [modif: 不 not + 足 sufficient] **ADJ** inadequate, insufficient ■ 资金不足 zījīn bùzú *insufficient funds*

bù 布¹ **N** cotton or linen cloth (块 **kuài**, 片 **piàn**) ■ 这块布很好看，做裙子正合适。**Zhè kuài bù hěn hǎokàn, zuò qúnzi zhèng héshì.** *This piece of cotton cloth looks good, just right for a skirt.*

bù 布² **TRAD** 佈 **v** arrange, deploy

bùgào 布告 [comp: 布 deploy + 告 announce] **I v** announce publicly **II N** public announcement, bulletin

bùjú 布局 **N** layout, overall arrangement

bùzhì 布置 **v** decorate ■ 他们马上要结婚了，这几天正在布置新房。**Tāmen mǎshàng yào jiéhūn le, zhè jǐ tiān zhèngzài bùzhì xīnfáng.** *They're getting married soon and are decorating their new home these days.*

bù 步 **N** step ■ 走几步就到了，不用开车。**Zǒu jǐ bù jiù dào le, bú yòng kāi chē.** *It's just a few steps away. There's no need to drive.*

bùfá 步伐 **N** step, pace

bùzhòu 步骤 **N** procedure, steps ■ 她没有按照步骤关电脑，结果死机了。**Tā méiyǒu ànzhào bùzhòu guān diànnǎo, jiéguǒ sǐjī le.** *She didn't follow the procedure to shut down the computer and, as a result, it crashed.*

bù 怖 **v** fear (See **kǒngbù** 恐怖.)

bù 部 **N** part, unit

bùduì 部队 **N** troops, the army ■ 部队是锻炼年轻人的好地方。**Bùduì shì duànliàn niánqīngrén de hǎo dìfang.** *The army is a good place to toughen up young people.*

bùfen 部分 [comp: 部 part + 分 division] **N** portion, part ■ 中国的中学分初中和高中两部分。**Zhōngguó de zhōngxué fēn chūzhōng hé gāozhōng liǎng bùfen.** *Chinese high schools have two parts—junior high and senior high.*

大部分 dà bùfen most of …, the majority of …

bùmén 部门 [comp: 部 department + 门 gate, door] **N** department ■ 他们虽然都在市政府工作，但是在不同的部门，相互不熟悉。**Tāmen suīrán dōu zài shì zhèngfǔ gōngzuò, dànshì zài bùtóng de bùmén, xiānghù bù shúxi.** *Although they both work in the city government, they work at different departments and do not know each other well.*

bùshǔ 部署 **v & N** map out, deploy; plan (for a major operation)

bùwèi 部位 **N** position, location

bùzhǎng 部长 [modif: 部 ministry + 长 chief, the

person in charge] N (government) minister ■ 教育部长对中小学的外语教学很关心。**Jiàoyù Bùzhǎng duì zhōng-xiǎoxué de wàiyǔ jiàoxué hěn guānxīn.** *The Minister of Education is very concerned about foreign language teaching at schools.*

C

cā 擦 V clean or erase by wiping or rubbing ■ 窗户脏了，要擦一下。**Chuānghu zāng le, yào cā yíxià.** *The window is dirty and needs cleaning.* ■ 我的自行车太脏了，我要把它擦干净。**Wǒ de zìxíngchē tài zāng le, wǒ yào bǎ tā cā gānjìng.** *My bike is dirty. I'll wipe it clean.*

cāi 猜 V guess ■ "谁来了？你猜猜看。" "我猜不着。告诉我吧。" **"Shéi lái le? Nǐ cāicai kàn." "Wǒ cāi bu zháo. Gàosu wǒ ba."** *"Guess who's come!" "I can't. Just tell me."*

cái 才¹ TRAD 纔 ADV 1 (before a verb) a short time ago, just ■ 我才来，不知道这件事。**Wǒ cái lái, bù zhīdào zhè jiàn shì.** *I've just arrived and don't know anything about this matter.* ■ 我才认识他，对他还不了解。**Wǒ cái rènshi tā, duì tā hái bù liǎojiě.** *I came to know him not long ago, and I don't know him very well.* 2 (used before a word of time or quantity to indicate that the speaker feels the time is too early, too short or the quantity is too little), only, as early as, as few/little as ■ 我学中文才一年，说得不好。**Wǒ xué Zhōngwén cái yīnián, shuō de bù hǎo.** *I've learned Chinese for only one year, and can't speak it very well.* ■ 这本书才十块钱，太便宜了。**Zhè ben shū cái shí kuài qián, tài piányi le.** *This book is only ten dollars. It's really cheap.* 3 (used after a word of time to indicate that the speaker feels the time is too late or there is too much delay), as late as ■ 这个小孩三岁才会走。**Zhège xiǎo hái sānsuì cái huì zǒu.** *This child learned to walk as late as three years old.* ■ 妈妈等到孩子都回来了才睡觉。**Māma děngdào háizi dōu huílai le, cái shuìjiào.** *Mother did not go to bed until all her children came home.*

cái 才² N talent, remarkable ability

cáigàn 才干 N talent, competence 有才干 **yǒu cáigàn** capable and talented

cái 财 TRAD 財 N wealth, property

cáichǎn 财产 [comp: 财 property, fortune + 产 property] N property, belongings ■ 国家保护合法的个人财产。**Guójiā bǎohù héfǎ de gèrén cáichǎn.** *The state protects legitimate private property.* ■ 这是我的个人财产，你们不能动。**Zhè shì wǒ de gèrén cáichǎn, nǐmen bù néng dòng.** *These are my personal belongings. You can't touch them.*

cáifù 财富 [comp: 财 property, fortune + 富 riches] N wealth, fortune

cáiwù 财务 [modif: 财 finance, wealth + 务 affair] N financial affairs, finance 财务部门 **cáiwù bùmén** department(s) of finance (in a company or institution) / 财务主任 **cáiwù zhǔrèn** director of finance (in a company or institution)

cáizhèng 财政 [modif: 财 finance, wealth + 政 governance] N public finance 财政部 **cáizhèng bù** the Ministry of Finance / 财政年度 **cáizhèng niándù** fiscal year

cái 材 N material

cáiliào 材料 N 1 materials, e.g. steel, timber, plastic ■ 建筑材料越来越贵，房子的造价也就越来越贵。**Jiànzhù cáiliào yuèlaiyuè guì, fángzi de zàojià yě jiù yuèlaiyuè guì.** *As building materials become more and more expensive, building houses also becomes more and more expensive.* 2 data (for a thesis, a report, etc.) ■ 报上提供的材料对我写文章很有帮助。**Bào shang tígòng de cáiliào duì wǒ xiě wénzhāng hěn yǒu bāngzhù.** *The data provided in the newspapers are very helpful to my writing.*

cái 裁 V 1 cut into parts, cut down 2 judge, decide

cáifeng 裁缝 [comp: 裁 cut + 缝 sew] N tailor, dressmaker

cáipàn 裁判 [comp: 裁 arbitrate + 判 judge] I V 1 (in law) adjudicate, judge 2 (in sports) act as referee or umpire II N 1 adjudication, decision made by the court 2 referee, umpire (位 **wèi**, 名 **míng**) 当裁判 **dāng cáipàn** act as a referee ■ 裁判不公平，引起观众不满。**Cáipàn bùgōngpíng, yǐnqǐ guānzhòng bùmǎn.** *The referee was unfair and it made the audience unhappy.* 裁判员 **cáipànyuán** same as 裁判 **cáipàn** II 2

cáiyuán 裁员 [v+obj: 裁 cut down + 员 staff] V cut down staff, lay off

cǎi 采 TRAD 採 V pick, pluck ■ 公园里的花，是给大家看的，任何人都不能采。**Gōngyuán li de huā shì gěi dàjiā kàn de, rènhé rén dōu bù néng cǎi.** *The flowers in the park are for everyone to admire. Nobody is allowed to pick them.*

cǎifǎng 采访 [comp: 采 gather + 访 visit] V (of mass media) interview

cǎigòu 采购 [comp: 采 pick + 购 purchase] V (corporate) purchase, shopping 采购员 **cǎigòuyuán** purchasing agent, (company) buyer

cǎijí 采集 [comp: 采 gather + 集 gather] V gather, collect 采集标本 **cǎijí biāoběn** collect (plant, insect, etc.) specimen

cǎinà 采纳 [comp: 采 gather + 纳 take] V accept, adopt 采纳建议 **cǎinà jiànyì** accept a proposal

cǎiqǔ 采取 [comp: 采 pick + 取 take] V adopt (a policy, a measure, an attitude, etc.) ■ 对这个重大的经济

问题，政府准备采取什么措施？**Duì zhège zhòngdà de jīngjì wèntí, zhèngfǔ zhǔnbèi cǎiqǔ shénme cuòshī?** *What measures is the government ready to adopt to deal with this major ecomonic problem?*

cǎiyòng 采用 [comp: 采 pick + 用 use] v use, employ ■ 采用新技术以后，产品质量有了明显提高。**Cǎiyòng xīn jìshù yǐhòu, chǎnpǐn zhìliàng yǒule míngxiǎn tígāo.** *After adopting the new technique, product quality has improved remarkably.*

cǎi 彩 ADJ colorful

cǎihóng 彩虹 [modif: 彩 multi-colored + 虹 rainbow] N rainbow

cǎipiào 彩票 [modif: 彩 multi-colored + 票 ticket] N lottery, lottery ticket ■ 我赢彩票啦！**Wǒ yíng cǎipiào la!** *I've won the lottery!*

cǎisè 彩色 [modif: 彩 multi-colored + 色 color] ADJ multi-colored

彩色电视机 **cǎisè diànshìjī** color TV set

cǎi 踩 v step on, tread on ■ 你们在花园里玩球，可别踩了花。**Nǐmen zài huāyuán li wán qiú, kě bié cǎile huā.** *When you play ball in the garden, don't step on the flowers.*

cǎi 睬 v pay attention to (See **lǐcǎi 理睬**.)

cài 菜 N 1 vegetables ■ 一个人既要吃肉，又要吃菜，才能健康。**Yí ge rén jì yào chī ròu, yòu yào chī cài, cái néng jiànkāng.** *One should eat both meat and vegetables in order to be in good health.*

种菜 **zhòng cài** grow vegetables ■ 这菜是我们自己种的，你尝尝。**Zhè cài shì wǒmen zìjǐ zhòng de, nǐ chángchang.** *We grew this vegetable ourselves. Do try some.*

2 any non-staple food such as vegetables, meat, fish, eggs, etc.

买菜 **mǎi cài** buy non-staple food, do grocery shopping ■ 妈妈每个星期五都要买很多菜，有鱼、有肉、还有蔬菜。**Māma měi ge Xīngqīwǔ dōu yào mǎi hěn dōu cài, yǒu yú, yǒu ròu, háiyǒu shūcài.** *Every Friday, mother buys lots of food: fish, meat and vegetables.*

3 cooked dish ■ 这个菜又好看又好吃，是谁做的？**Zhège cài yòu hǎokàn yòu hǎochī, shì shuí zuò de?** *This dish is both beautiful and delicious. Who cooked it?* ■ 请别客气，多吃点菜！**Qǐng bié kèqi, duō chī diǎn cài!** *Please don't be too polite. Eat more food!*

点菜 **diǎn cài** order a dish (in a restaurant)

càidān 菜单 N menu

cān 参 TRAD 參 v call, enter

cānguān 参观 [comp: 参 call + 观 watch, see] v visit (a place) ■ 这个古迹十分有名，每天有很多人来参观。**Zhège gǔjì shífēn yǒumíng, měi tiān yǒu hěn duō rén lái cānguān.** *This historical site is well known. Many people come to visit it every day.* ■ 我在中国的时候，参观了很多学校。**Wǒ zài Zhōngguó de shíhou, cānguānle hěn duō xuéxiào.** *I visited many schools when I was in China.*

cānjiā 参加 [v+comp: 参 enter + 加 add] v 1 join ■ 我可以参加中文班吗？**Wǒ kěyǐ cānjiā Zhōngwén bān ma?** *May I join the Chinese class?* ■ 欢迎你参加我们的俱乐部。**Huānyíng nǐ cānjiā wǒmen de jùlèbù.** *You're welcome to join our club.* 2 participate, attend ■ 我们出版社有兴趣参加这个书展。**Wǒmen chūbǎnshè yǒu xìngqù cānjiā zhège shūzhǎn.** *Our publishing house is interested in participating in this book fair.* ■ 欢迎您来参加我们的晚会。**Huānyíng nín lái cānjiā wǒmen de wǎnhuì.** *You're welcome to our evening party.*

cānkǎo 参考 v consult, refer to

仅供参考 **jǐn gōng cānkǎo** For reference only

cānkǎoshū 参考书 N reference book(s)

cānmóu 参谋 [comp: 参 participate + 谋 scheme, plan] I v give advice, suggest II N (army) staff officer

参谋长 **cānmóuzhǎng** chief of staff

cānyú 参与 v participate, involve

cānzhào 参照 v use as reference, refer to

cān 餐 N meal

cāntīng 餐厅 [modif: 餐 meal + 厅 hall] N restaurant ■ 旅馆的餐厅在十二楼。**Lǚguǎn de cāntīng zài shí'èr lóu.** *The restaurant in the hotel is on the twelfth floor.*

cán 残 TRAD 殘 ADJ damaged, savage

cánjí 残疾 [comp: 残 damaged + 疾 disease] ADJ disabled

残疾人 **cánjírén** disabled person

cánkù 残酷 ADJ cruel, brutal

cánliú 残留 v (partly) remain

cánrěn 残忍 ADJ cruel, merciless

cán 惭 TRAD 慚 N shame

cánkuì 惭愧 [comp: 惭 shame + 愧 sense of guilt] ADJ be ashamed ■ 由于我的错误，给你带来了不便，我深感惭愧。**Yóuyú wǒ de cuòwù, gěi nǐ dàiláile búbiàn, wǒ shēn gǎn cánkuì.** *My error has caused you inconvenience. I feel deeply ashamed.*

cǎn 惨 TRAD 慘 ADJ miserable

càn 灿 TRAD 燦 ADJ brilliant

cànlàn 灿烂 ADJ magnificent, splendid

cāng 仓 TRAD 倉 N storage

cāngcù 仓促 ADJ hasty, hurried

仓促离去 **cāngcù líqù** leave in a hurry

cāngkù 仓库 [comp: 仓 storage + 库 warehouse] N warehouse

cāng 苍 TRAD 蒼 N dark green

cāngbái 苍白 [comp: 苍 dark green + 白 white] ADJ pallid, pale

cāngying 苍蝇 N housefly ■ 那里有一只苍蝇，拍死它！**Nàli yǒu yì zhī cāngying, pāi sǐ tā!** *There's a fly; kill it!*

cāng 舱 TRAD 艙 N cabin (in a ship or an airplane)

经济舱 **jīngjì cāng** economy class (cabin) /
商务舱 **shāngwù cāng** business class (cabin) /
头等舱 **tóuděng cāng** first class (cabin)

cāng 沧 TRAD 滄 ADJ (of the sea) dark blue (See **bǎo jīng cāngsāng** 饱经沧桑.)

cānghǎi 沧海 N deep, blue sea

cáng 藏 V hide, conceal ■ 他把玩具藏在床下，不让妈妈看见。**Tā bǎ wánjù cáng zài chuáng xia, bú ràng māma kànjiàn.** *He hid the toy under the bed so his mother wouldn't see.*

cāo 操 N drill, exercise

cāochǎng 操场 [modif: 操 drill, exercise + 场 ground] N sports ground, playground ■ 我们学校的操场很大。**Wǒmen xuéxiào de cānchǎng hěn dà.** *Our school sports ground is very big.* (在) 操场上 (zài) cāochǎng shang on the sports ground ■ 很多学生在操场上玩。**Hěn duō xuésheng zài cāochǎng shang wán.** *Many students are playing on the sports ground.*

cāoláo 操劳 V toil, work very hard

cāoliàn 操练 [comp: 操 drill + 练 practice] V drill, practice, train

cāoxīn 操心 [v+obj: 操 exercise + 心 the heart] V deeply concern, be at pains

cāozòng 操纵 V control, manipulate

cāozuò 操作 [comp: 操 operate + 作 do] V operate ■ 你会操作这台机器吗？**Nǐ huì cāozuò zhè tái jīqì ma?** *Do you know how to operate this machine?* 操作手册 cāozuò shǒucè operating manual / 操作系统 cāozuò xìtǒng operating system

cáo 嘈 ADJ noisy

cáozá 嘈杂 ADJ noisy, clamorous

cǎo 草 N grass, weed (棵 kē) ■ 你们每天给马喂几次草？**Nǐmen měi tiān gěi mǎ wèi jǐ cì cǎo?** *How many times a day do you feed the horses? (← How many times a day do you feed the horses grass?)*

cǎo'àn 草案 [modif: 草 rough + 案 document] N draft (of a plan, proposal, a document, etc.)

cǎodì 草地 [modif: 草 grass + 地 land] N lawn ■ 我家房前有一片草地。**Wǒ jiā fáng qián yǒu yí piàn cǎodì.** *There is a lawn in front of my house.*

cǎoshuài 草率 ADJ careless, sloppy

cǎoyuán 草原 [modif: 草 grass + 原 flat land] N grassland, steppe, pasture ■ "你见过真正的草原吗？" "没有，我一直住在大城市里。" **"Nǐ jiànguo zhēnzhèng de cǎoyuán ma?" "Méiyǒu, wǒ yìzhí zhù zài dà chéngshì li."** *"Have you ever seen real grasslands?" "No. I've been living in a big city all along."*

cè 册 MEASURE WORD (used for books) volume 两千册图书 liǎngqiān cè túshū two thousand [volumes of] books

cè 厕 TRADE 廁 N toilet

cèsuǒ 厕所 N toilet ■ 请问，男厕所在哪里？**Qǐngwèn, nán cèsuǒ zài nǎli?** *Excuse me, where is the men's toilet?* 公共厕所 gōnggòng cèsuǒ public toilet / 男厕所 nán cèsuǒ men's toilet / 女厕所 nǚcèsuǒ women's toilet

NOTE: See note on 洗手间 xǐshǒujiān (in 洗 xǐ).

cè 测 TRAD 測 V measure, gauge

cèliáng 测量 [comp: 测 measure + 量 measure, gauge] V survey, measure

cèyàn 测验 [comp: 测 measure + 验 test] V & N test (in a school), exam; examination ■ 明天数学测验，请同学们好好准备。**Míngtiān shùxué cèyàn, qǐng tóngxuémen hǎohǎo zhǔnbèi.** *There will be a mathematics test tomorrow. Be well prepared, everyone.* ■ 这个学期一共有四次测验。**Zhège xuéqī yígòng yǒu sì cì cèyàn.** *There will be four tests this semester.*

cè 侧 TRAD 側 N side 大楼的右侧 dàlóu de yòucè the right side of the building

cèmiàn 侧面 [comp: 侧 incline + 面 face, side] N side, flank

cè 策 N plan

cèhuà 策划 [comp: 策 plan + 划 plan] V plan (an event, a theatrical performance, etc.) 策划人 cèhuà rén planner

cèlüè 策略 [comp: 策 plan + 略 strategy] N tactics 有策略的 yǒu cèlüè de tactful

céng 层 TRAD 層 MEASURE WORD story (story), level, floor ■ 这座大楼一共有二十层。**Zhè zuò dàlóu yígòng yǒu èrshí céng.** *This building has twenty levels.* ■ "你住在第几层？" "我住在第三层。" **"Nǐ zhù zài dì jǐ céng?" "Wǒ zhù zài dì sān céng."** *"Which floor do you live on?" "I live on the third floor."*

NOTE: See note on 楼 lóu.

céng chū bù qióng 层出不穷 V appear one after another, come out quick and fast

céngcì 层次 N 1 administrative or educational level 2 arrangement of ideas in writing or colors in painting

céng 曾 ADV same as 曾经 **céngjīng**. Used more in writing.

céngjīng 曾经 ADV once, formerly ■ 我曾经在那个城市里住过两年。**Wǒ céngjīng zài nàge chéngshì li zhùguo liǎng nián.** *I lived in that city for two years.* ■ 这位老人曾经是一位著名的科学家。**Zhè wèi lǎorén céngjīng shì yí wèi zhùmíng de kēxuéjiā.** *That old gentleman was once a famous scientist.*

NOTE: 曾经 **céngjīng** is used to emphasize that an action or situation took place in the past.

chā 叉 N fork

chāzi 叉子 N fork (把 bǎ) ■ 这把叉子掉在地上，脏了，请再给我一把。**Zhè bǎ chāzi diào zai dìshang, zāng le, qǐng zài gěi wǒ yì bǎ.** *This fork dropped on the floor and got dirty. Please give me another one.*

chā 差 N difference, discrepancy

chābié 差别 [comp: 差 difference + 别 other] N disparity, gap

城乡差别 chéngxiāng chābié the urban-rural gap

chājù 差距 [comp: 差 difference + 距 distance] N gap, disparity

贫富差距 pín-fù chājù the gap between the rich and poor

chā 插 V insert, stick in ■ 花瓶里要插一些花才好。 **Huāpíng li yào chā yìxiē huā cái hǎo.** *It would be good to have some flowers in the vase.*

chāzuò 插座 N (electric) socket

chá 茶 N tea ■ 茶凉了，快喝吧。 **Chá liáng le, kuài hē ba.** *The tea is no longer hot. Please drink it.*

红茶 hóngchá black tea / 绿茶 lǜchá green tea ■ 您喝红茶还是绿茶？ **Nín hē hóngchá háishì lǜchá?** *Do you drink black tea or green tea?* / 喝茶 hē chá drink tea ■ 经常喝茶，特别是绿茶，对身体很有好处。 **Jīngcháng hē chá, tèbié shì lǜchá, duì shēntǐ hěn yǒu hǎochù.** *Drinking tea regularly, especially green tea, is very beneficial to health.*

chábēi 茶杯 N teacup

cháhú 茶壶 N teapot

chá 查 V check, look up ■ 请你查查，你们学校有没有这个学生。 **Qǐng nǐ chácha, nǐmen xuéxiào yǒu méiyǒu zhège xuésheng.** *Please find out if your school has this student.*

chá cídiǎn 查词典 V look up words in a dictionary ■ 你会查中文词典吗？ **Nǐ huì chá Zhōngwén cídiǎn ma?** *Do you know how to look up words in a Chinese dictionary?*

cháhuò 查获 [comp: 查 investigate + 获 obtain] V hunt down and seize (stolen goods, criminals, etc.)

cházhǎo 查找 V & N search; searching

chá 察 V examine, look over closely (See **guānchá** 观察.)

chà 差 I V be short of, lack in ■ 我还差二十块钱，你可以借给我吗？ **Wǒ hái chà èrshí kuài qián, nǐ kěyǐ jiè gěi wǒ ma?** *I'm still short of twenty dollars. Can you give me a loan?* ■ 现在是十一点差五分。 **Xiànzài shì shíyī diǎn chà wǔ fēn.** *It's five to eleven now.* II ADJ poor, not up to standard ■ 这种电冰箱不但价格贵，而且质量差。 **Zhè zhǒng diànbīngxiāng búdàn jiàgé guì, érqiě zhìliàng chà.** *This refrigerator is not only expensive but also of poor quality.* ■ 他身体很差，经常生病。 **Tā shēntǐ hěn chà, jīngcháng shēngbìng.** *He is in poor health and often falls ill.*

chàbuduō 差不多 ADJ 1 more or less the same ■ 他们俩年龄差不多，经历也差不多，很快成了好朋友。 **Tāmen liǎ niánlíng chàbuduō, jīnglì yě chàbuduō, hěnkuài chéngle hǎo péngyou.** *They were about the same age and had more or less the same experiences, and soon became good friends.* 2 almost ■ "你报告写完了吗？" "差不多了。" **"Nǐ bàogào xiěwánle ma?" "Chàbuduō le."** *"Have*

you finished writing the report?" "Almost." ■ 差不多十二点了，她怎么还不来上班？ **Chàbuduō shí'èr diǎn le, tā zěnme hái bù lái shàngbān?** *It's almost twelve o'clock. Why hasn't she turned up for work?*

chàdiǎnr 差点儿 ADV almost, nearly ■ 今天是妻子的生日，我差点儿忘了。 **Jīntiān shì qīzi de shēngrì, wǒ chàdiǎnr wàngle.** *Today is my wife's birthday. I almost forgot it. (→ I nearly forgot it was my wife's birthday today.)* ■ 去年他几次犯错误，差点儿丢了饭碗。 **Qùnián tā jǐ cì fàn cuòwù, chàdiǎnr diūle fànwǎn.** *Last year he made several mistakes and nearly lost his job.*

chà 岔 I N branching off

岔路 chàlù fork (in a road)

II V change the subject

打岔 dǎchà interrupt and change the subject (of a talk)

chànà 刹那 N a split second, the briefest moment

chà 诧 TRAD 詫 V be surprised

chàyì 诧异 V be surprised, be amazed

chāi 拆 V take apart, demolish ■ 小孩把玩具拆开了，可是不知道怎样再装起来。 **Xiǎohái bǎ wánjù chāikāi le, kěshì bù zhīdào zěnyàng zài zhuāng qǐlai.** *The child took the toy apart, but did not know how to reassemble it.*

chāi 差 N errand (See **chūchāi** 出差.)

chái 柴 N firewood

cháiyóu 柴油 N diesel oil

chān 搀 TRAD 攙 V 1 help by the arm, support with one's hand 2 mix, mingle

chānhuo 搀和 V 1 mix, mingle 2 meddle, interfere 这事你别搀和！ **Zhè shì nǐ bié chānhuo!** *Don't you butt in on this matter!*

chán 馋 TRAD 饞 ADJ too fond of eating, gluttonous 嘴馋 zuǐchán too fond of eating, gluttonous

chán 缠 TRAD 纏 V 1 wind, twine 2 pester, bother ■ 这孩子总缠着我，要我跟他玩。 **Zhè háizi zǒng chánzhe wǒ, yào wǒ gēn tā wán.** *This child keeps pestering me to play with him.*

chánrào 缠绕 V 1 turn twist 2 pester, harrass

chǎn 产 TRAD 產 V produce

chǎnliàng 产量 [modif: 产 product + 量 quantity] N (production) output, yield ■ 仅仅增加产量是没有意义的。 **Jǐnjǐn zēngjiā chǎnliàng shì méiyǒu yìyì de.** *Increasing output alone is meaningless.* ■ 你们工厂去年的产量是多少？ **Nǐmen gōngchǎng qùnián de chǎnliàng shì duōshǎo?** *What was the output of your factory last year?*

chǎnpǐn 产品 [modif: 产 production + 品 goods] N product ■ 我们必须不断研究和开发新产品。 **Wǒmen bìxū búduàn yánjiū hé kāifā xīn chǎnpǐn.** *We must continually research and develop new products.* ■ 产品质量是企业的生命。 **Chǎnpǐn zhìliàng shì qǐyè de shēngmìng.** *The quality of its products is the lifeblood of an enterprise.*

chǎnshēng 产生 [comp: 产 produce + 生 grow] **v** produce, give rise to, lead to ■ 新科技的应用产生了一些新的社会现象。 **Xīn kējì de yìngyòng chǎnshēngle yìxiē xīn de shèhuì xiànxiàng.** *The use of new technology has given rise to some new social phenomena.*

chǎnyè 产业 N property, estate

chǎn 阐 TRAD 闡 v explain

chǎnshù 阐述 [comp: 阐 explain + 述 narrate] **v** elaborate, explain

chàn 颤 v quiver, vibrate

chàndǒu 颤抖 [comp: 颤 qiver + 抖 shake] **v** (of people) tremble, shake

chāng 昌 v prosper

chāngshèng 昌盛 [comp: 昌 prosper + 盛 flourish] **ADJ** prosperous, flourishing

chāng 猖 ADJ ferocious

chāngkuáng 猖狂 [comp: 猖 ferocious + 狂 wild, mad] **ADJ** fierce and unruly, savage

cháng 尝 TRAD 嘗 v taste ■ 这种水果我没有吃过，想尝尝。 **Zhè zhǒng shuǐguǒ wǒ méiyǒu chīguo, xiǎng chángchang.** *I've never eaten this fruit. I'd like to taste it.*

chángshì 尝试 [comp: 尝 taste + 试 try] **v** try, test

cháng 偿 TRAD 償 v make up, compensate

chánghuán 偿还 [comp: 偿 compensate + 还 return] **v** pay back (a debt)

cháng 长 TRAD 長 ADJ long (ANTONYM 短 **duǎn**) ■ 中国的历史很长。 **Zhōngguó de lìshǐ hěn cháng.** *China has a long history.* ■ 你还年轻, 生活道路还长着呢。 **Nǐ hái niánqīng, shēnghuó dàolù hái chángzhe ne.** *You're still young, and have a long way to go in life.*

Chángchéng 长城 N the Great Wall (a historic landmark in Northern China)

Chángjiāng 长江 N the Yangtze River (China's longest river)

chángpǎo 长跑 N long distance running

chángqī 长期 [modif: 长 long + 期 period] **N** a long period of time ■ 他长期研究汉语语法, 发表过很多文章。 **Tā chángqī yánjiū Hànyǔ yǔfǎ, fābiǎoguo hěn duō wénzhāng.** *He has studied Chinese grammar for a long time, and has published many essays.*

chángtú 长途 [modif: 长 long + 途 way] **N** long distance

长途电话 chángtú diànhuà long-distance telephone call / 国际长途电话 guójì chángtú diànhuà international telephone call / 长途汽车 chángtú qìchē long-distance bus, coach

cháng 肠 TRAD 腸 N intestine (See **xiāngcháng** 香肠.)

cháng 常 ADV often ■ 我常去市图书馆借书。 **Wǒ cháng qù shì túshūguǎn jiè shū.** *I often go to the city library to borrow books.*

chángcháng 常常 often ■ 我常常去市图书馆借书。 **Wǒ chángcháng qù shì túshūguǎn jiè shū.** *I often go to the city library to borrow books.* 不常 bù cháng not often, seldom ■ 他住在乡下, 不常进城。 **Tā zhù zài xiāngxia, bù cháng jìn chéng.** *He lives in a village and seldom goes to town.*

NOTE: Colloquially, 常常 **chángcháng** is often used instead of 常 **cháng**.

chángnián 常年 ADV all the year round, year in and year out

chángshí 常识 [modif: 常 common + 识 knowledge] **N 1** common sense ■ 孩子从生活中学会很多常识。 **Háizi cóng shēnghuó zhōng xuéhuì hěn duō chángshí.** *Children learn a lot of common sense from life.* **2** basic knowledge ■ 我不是计算机专家, 我只知道计算机的常识。 **Wǒ bú shì jìsuànjī zhuānjiā, wǒ zhǐ zhīdào jìsuànjī de chángshí.** *I'm not a computer expert; I've only got some basic knowledge.*

chángwù 常务 ADJ in charge of day-to-day business 常务副市长 chángwù fù shìzhǎng executive vice-mayor

chǎng 厂 TRAD 廠 N factory (See **gōngchǎng** 工厂.)

chǎng 场 TRAD 場 I N ground, field 操场 cāochǎng sports ground, playground / 体育场 tǐyùchǎng stadium / 飞机场 fēijīchǎng airport / 市场 shìchǎng market **II MEASURE WORD** (for movies, sport events, etc.) ■ 一场电影 yì chǎng diànyǐng a movie ■ 一场球赛 yì chǎng qiúsài a ball game, a ball match

chǎnghé 场合 N occasion, situation

chǎngmiàn 场面 N scene (in a play, a movie, a novel, etc.)

chǎngsuǒ 场所 N place (for public activity) 公共场所 gōnggòng chǎngsuǒ public place

chǎng 敞 v open

chǎngkāi 敞开 [comp: 敞 open + 开 open] **v** open wide

chàng 畅 TRAD 暢 ADJ uninhibited, unimpeded

chàngtōng 畅通 [comp: 畅 unimpeded + 通 through] **ADJ** unimpeded, flowing freely and smoothly

chàngxiāo 畅销 [modif: 畅 freely + 销 sell] **v** sell well 畅销书 chàngxiāo shū best-seller

chàng 倡 v initiate

chàngdǎo 倡导 v initiate, promote

chàngyì 倡议 [v+obj: 倡 initiate + 议 proposal] **v & N** propose; proposal, suggestion (项 **xiàng**)

chàng 唱 v sing ■ 你会唱中文歌吗？ **Nǐ huì chàng Zhōngwén gē ma?** *Can you sing Chinese songs?*

chànggē 唱歌 [v+obj: 唱 sing + 歌 song] **v** sing songs, sing ■ 你唱歌唱得真好听! **Nǐ chànggē chàng de zhēn hǎotīng!** *You really sing well!*

chāo 抄 v copy by hand ■ 这些数字很重要, 我要

抄下来。**Zhèxiē shùzì hěn zhòngyào, wǒ yào chāo xiàlai.** *These are important numbers. I'll write them down.*

chāoxiě 抄写 v same as 抄 **chāo**

chāo 超 v go beyond, exceed

chāoguò 超过 v 1 overtake ■ 我前面的车开得太慢，我要超过它。**Wǒ qiánmiàn de chē kāi de tài màn, wǒ yào chāoguò tā.** *The car in front of me is moving too slowly. I want to overtake it.* 2 exceed ■ 去年到这个国家的旅游者超过了三百万。**Qùnián dào zhège guójiā de lǚyóuzhě chāoguòle sān bǎiwàn.** *The number of tourists visiting this country last year exceeded three million.*

chāojí 超级 [modif: 超 exceed + 级 grade] ADJ super

chāojí gōnglù 超级公路 N super-highway, motorway

chāo(jí) shì(chǎng) 超(级)市(场) N supermarket (家 **jiā**) ■ 你经常去哪一家超级市场？**Nǐ jīngcháng qù nǎ yì jiā chāojí shìchǎng?** *Which supermarket do you often go to?*

chāoyuè 超越 [comp: 超 exceed + 越 go beyond] v transcend, surpass

chāo 钞 TRAD 鈔 N paper money

现钞 xiànchāo cash, ready money

chāopiàn 钞票 [modif: 钞 paper money + 票 ticket] N paper money, banknotes (张 **zhāng**)

cháo 朝¹ v & PREP face; towards, to ■ 中国人的房子大多朝南。**Zhōngguórén de fángzi dàduō cháo nán.** *Chinese people's houses mostly face the south. (→ Most Chinese houses face south.)* ■ 你一直朝前走十分钟左右，就到公园了。**Nǐ yìzhí cháo qián zǒu shí fēnzhōng zuǒyòu, jiù dào gōngyuán le.** *Walk straight ahead for about ten minutes and you'll reach the park.*

cháo 朝² N dynasty

唐朝 Táng cháo the Tang Dynasty

cháodài 朝代 [comp: 朝 dynasty + 代 generation] N dynasty

cháo 潮 ADJ wet

cháoliú 潮流 N trend, fashion

cháoshī 潮湿 [comp: 潮 wet + 湿 damp] ADJ damp, humid

cháo 嘲 v jeer, mock

cháoxiào 嘲笑 [comp: 嘲 jeer + 笑 laugh] v ridicule, sneer at

cháo 巢 N nest, beehive

cháoxuè 巢穴 [comp: 巢 nest + 穴 cave] N nest, cave, hideout

chǎo 吵 v 1 quarrel ■ 他们夫妻俩又吵了。**Tāmen fūqī liǎ yòu chǎo le.** *The couple quarreled again.* 2 make a big noise, be noisy ■ 这间房面对大街，太吵了。**Zhè jiān fáng miànduì dàjiē, tài chǎo le.** *This room faces a main street. It's too noisy.*

chǎojià 吵架 v & N quarrel

NOTE: For "quarrel," 吵架 **chǎojià** is more commonly used than 吵 **chǎo**, for example: ■ 他们夫妻俩又吵架了。**Tāmen fūqī liǎ yòu chǎojià le.** *The couple quarreled again.*

chǎo 炒 v 1 stir fry, sauté 2 sensationalize, create a commotion

炒股票 chǎo gǔpiào speculate on the stock exchange

chē 车 TRAD 車 N vehicle, traffic (辆 **liàng**) ■ 我的车坏了。**Wǒ de chē huài le.** *My car (or bicycle) has broken down.* ■ 路上车很多。**Lùshang chē hěn duō.** *There is lots of traffic on the road.* ■ 我可以借用你的车吗？**Wǒ kěyǐ jièyòng nǐ de chē ma?** *May I borrow your car (or bicycle)?*

开车 kāi chē drive an automobile / 骑车 qí chē ride a bicycle / 停车场 tíngchēchǎng car park, parking lot / 学车 xué chē learn to drive / 修车 xiū chē repair a car/bicycle / 修车行 xiū chē háng motor vehicle repair and servicing shop

chējiān 车间 N workshop (in a factory) ■ 这个车间有多少工人？**Zhège chējiān yǒu duōshǎo gōngrén?** *How many workers work in this workshop?*

chēkù 车库 [modif: 车 vehicle + 库 storeroom] N garage

chē pái 车牌 N (vehicle) license plate

车牌号 chē pái hào (vehicle) license plate number

chēxiāng 车厢 N carriage (in a train)

chēzhàn 车站 [modif: 车 vehicle + 站 station] N bus stop, coach station, railway station ■ "车站离这里远不远？" "不远，开车只要十分钟。" **"Chēzhàn lí zhèli yuǎn bu yuǎn?" "Bù yuǎn, kāi chē zhǐyào shí fēnzhōng."** *"Is the railway (or bus) station far from here?" "No, it's only ten minutes' drive."* ■ 王先生去车站接朋友了。**Wáng xiānsheng qù chēzhàn jiē péngyou le.** *Mr Wang's gone to the railway (or coach) station to meet a friend.*

长途汽车站 chángtú qìchē zhàn coach station / 出租汽车站 chūzū qìchē zhàn taxi stand / 火车站 huǒchē zhàn railway station

chě 扯 v pull, tear

chè 彻 TRAD 徹 ADJ thorough

chèdǐ 彻底 [comp: 彻 thorough + 底 end, bottom] ADJ thorough, complete ■ 经过彻底调查，确定这个地区没有这种病。**Jīngguò chèdǐ diàochá, quèdìng zhège dìqū méiyǒu zhè zhǒng bìng.** *After a thorough investigation it is confirmed that this region is free from this disease.*

chè 撤 v 1 remove 2 withdraw, retreat

chètuì 撤退 [comp: 撤 withdraw + 退 move back] v retreat, withdraw

chèxiāo 撤销 v cancel, revoke

chén 陈 TRAD 陳 I N a common family name II ADJ old, stale III v display

chénjiù 陈旧 [comp: 陈 old + 旧 old] ADJ old-fashioned, out-dated

chénliè 陈列 [comp: 陈 display + 列 line up] V display, exhibit ■ 商店里陈列着最新的电子产品。 **Shāngdiàn lǐ chénliè zhe zuìxīn de diànzǐ chǎnpǐn.** *Latest electronic products are displayed in the store.*
陈列橱窗 chénliè chúchuāng showcase / 陈列厅 chénliè tīng exhibition hall, show room

chénshù 陈述 V state (one's views, reasons, etc.)

chén 辰 N time (See **dànchén** 诞辰.)

chén 晨 N early morning (See **zǎochén** 早晨.)

chén 沉 I V sink ■ 一公斤铁在水里会沉, 一公斤棉花会沉吗? **Yì gōngjīn tiě zài shuǐ li huì chén, yì gōng jīn miánhuā huì chén ma?** *While a kilogram of iron will sink in water, will a kilogram of cotton?* II ADJ 1 deep, profound 2 heavy

chédiàn 沉淀 N sediment

chénmèn 沉闷 [comp: 沉 heavy + 闷 depressed] ADJ 1 (of weather) depressing, oppressive 2 (of moods) in low spirit 3 (of ambiance, atmosphere) dull, boring

chénmò 沉默 [comp: 沉 deep + 默 silent] ADJ silent, reticent ■ 他总是很沉默, 没人知道他到底在想什么。 **Tā zǒngshì hěn chénmò, méi rén zhīdào tā dàodǐ zài xiǎng shénme.** *He is always reticent, and nobody knows what he is thinking.*

chénsī 沉思 [modif: 沉 deep + 思 think] V ponder, be lost in thought

chéntòng 沉痛 [modif: 沉 heavy + 痛 agonized] ADJ deeply grieved, in deep sorrow

chénzhòng 沉重 [comp: 沉 heavy + 重 heavy] ADJ heavy, serious

chénzhuó 沉着 ADJ cool-headed, composed

chén 臣 N official in a court, minister (See **dàchén** 大臣.)

chén 尘 TRAD 塵 N dust (See **huīchén** 灰尘.)

chèn 衬 TRAD 襯 N lining, underwear

chènshān 衬衫 N shirt (件 **jiàn**) ■ 你去公司上班, 当然要每天换衬衫。 **Nǐ qù gōngsī shàngbān, dāngrán yào měitiān huàn chènshān.** *If you work in a company, of course you should change shirts every day.*

chèntuō 衬托 V set off, make noticeable and attractive

chènyī 衬衣 N shirt or similar underwear (件 **jiàn**) ■ 他拿着干净的衬衣短裤, 进浴室去洗澡。 **Tā názhe gānjìng de chènyī duǎnkù, jìn yùshì qù xǐzǎo.** *Carrying clean underwear, he went into the bathroom to take a bath.*

chèn 趁 PREP taking advantage of, while, when ■ 我想趁这个机会, 向大家说几句话。 **Wǒ xiǎng chèn zhège jīhuì, xiàng dàjiā shuō jǐ jù huà.** *I'd like to take this opportunity to say a few words to you.* ■ 趁王董事长也在这里, 我想报告一下最近的营业情况。 **Chèn Wáng dǒngshìzhǎng yě zài**

zhèli, wǒ xiǎng bàogào yíxià zuìjìn de yíngyè qíngkuàng. *Now that Chairman Wang is here, I'd like to report our recent business situation.*

chèn 称 TRAD 稱 V match, suit

chènxīn 称心 [v+obj: 称 suit + 心 one's heart] ADJ very much to one's liking, find … satisfactory

chèn xīn ru yi 称心如意 ADJ after one's own heart, to one's heart's content

chēng 称 TRAD 稱 V 1 call, be known as, address … as ■ 电脑又称计算机。 **Diànnǎo yòu chēng jìsuànjī.** *"Diannao" is also known as "jisuanji."* ■ 他比我们都大一点, 我们都称他 "李大哥。" **Tā bǐ wǒmen dōu dà yìdiǎn, wǒmen dōu chēng tā "Lǐ dàgē."** *As he is older than we are, we all call him "Elder Brother Li."* 2 weigh ■ 他去飞机场之前, 称了一下行李, 看看有没有超重。 **Tā qù fēijīchǎng zhī qián, chēngle yíxià xíngli, kànkan yǒu méi yǒu chāozhòng.** *He weighed his luggage before leaving for the airport to make sure it was not overweight.*

chēnghào 称号 N honorific title

chēnghu 称呼 [comp: 称 call, name + 呼 call] & N call, address; form of address ■ 我见了你的父母, 该怎么称呼他们? **Wǒjiàn le nǐde fùmǔ, gāi zěnme chēnghu tāmen?** *How should I address your parents when I meet them?* ■ 使用正确的称呼是很重要。 **Shǐyòng zhèngquè de chēnghu shì hěn zhòngyào de.** *The use of correct forms of address is very important.*

chēngzàn 称赞 [comp: 称 praise + 赞 praise] V compliment, praise ■ 老板称赞他工作努力, 成绩优秀。 **Lǎobǎn chēngzàn tā gōngzuò nǔlì, chéngjì yōuxiù.** *The boss praised him as a hardworking high achiever.*

chēng 撑 V support, prop up

chéng 成 V become, turn into ■ 几年没见, 她成了一个漂亮的大姑娘了。 **Jǐnián méi jiàn, tā chéngle yí ge piàoliang de dàguniang le.** *After several years' absence, she had become a pretty young lady.* ■ 他是我小学时的同学, 没想到成了一位大人物。 **Tā shì wǒ xiǎoxué shí de tóngxué, méi xiǎngdào chéngle yí wèi dàrénwù.** *He was my primary school classmate and, unexpectedly, has become a big shot.*

chéngběn 成本 N (in business) cost ■ 生产厂家必须降低成本才能生存。 **Shēngchǎn chǎngjiā bìxū jiàngdī chéngběn cáinéng shēngcún.** *Manufacturers must reduce cost if they are to survive.*
生产成本 shēngchǎn chéngběn production cost

chéngfèn 成分 [comp: 成 percentage + 分 element] N component part, ingredient (种 **zhǒng**) ■ 这种中药有哪些成分? **Zhè zhǒng Zhōngyào yǒu nǎxiē chéngfèn?** *What are the ingredients in this Chinese medicine?*

chénggōng 成功 [v+obj: 成 accomplish + 功 merit, feat] I V succeed ■ 经过无数次的试验, 科

学家们终于成功了。**Jīngguò wúshù cì de shìyàn, kēxuéjiāmen zhōngyú chénggōng le.** *After numerous experiments, the scientists finally succeeded.* ■ 祝你成功! **Zhù nǐ chénggōng!** *I wish you success!* II ADJ successful ■ 在一个成功的男人背后，总有一位好妻子。**Zài yí ge chénggōng de nánrén bèihòu, zǒng yǒu yí wèi hǎo qīzi.** *Behind a successful man, there stands a good wife.* ■ 这次会谈十分成功。**Zhè cì huìtán shífēn chénggōng.** *This formal talk was a success.*

chéngguǒ 成果 [comp: 成 achievement + 果 fruit, good result] N positive result, achievement (项 **xiàng**) ■ 我们中文学习进步这么大，都是老师辛苦工作的成果。**Wǒmen Zhōngwén xuéxí jìnbù zhème dà, dōu shì lǎoshī xīnkǔ gōngzuò de chéngguǒ.** *The rapid progress we have made in our Chinese studies is the result of our teachers' hard work.*

chéngjì 成绩 [comp: 成 achievement + 绩 result] N achievement, examination result ■ 他去年的考试成绩非常好。**Tā qùnián de kǎoshì chéngjì fēicháng hǎo.** *His examination results last year were very good.* ■ 你的工作成绩不理想，必须努力改进。**Nǐ de gōngzuò chéngjì bù lǐxiǎng, bìxū nǔlì gǎijìn.** *Your work results are not good enough. You must work harder to improve them.*

取得成绩 **qǔdé chéngjì** make achievement, get (positive, good) results

chéngjiāo 成交 V strike a bargain, conclude a business deal

chéngjiù 成就 [comp: 成 achievement + 就 achievement] N great achievement (项 **xiàng**) ■ 我们在经济发展方面取得了很大成就。**Wǒmen zài jīngjì fāzhǎn fāngmiàn qǔdéle hěn dà chéngjiù.** *We have won great achievements in economic development.*

chénglì 成立 [comp: 成 accomplish + 立 establish] V establish, set up ■ 你们公司是哪一年成立的？**Nǐmen gōngsī shì nǎ yì nián chénglì de?** *When was your company set up?*

chéngmíng 成名 V become famous ■ 她写了那本小说，几乎一夜成名。**Tā xiěle nà běn xiǎoshuō, jīhū yí yè chéng míng.** *She wrote that novel and became famous almost overnight.*

chéngrén 成人 N adult

成人教育 **chéngrén jiàoyù** adult education/成人电影 **chéngrén diànyǐng** adult movie

chéngshú 成熟 [comp: 成 accomplish + 熟 mature] V & ADJ mature, ripen; mature, ripe ■ 秋天是很多水果成熟的季节。**Qiūtiān shì hěn duō shuǐguǒ chéngshú de jìjié.** *Autumn is the season when many fruits ripen.* ■ 他虽然二十多岁了，但是还不够成熟。**Tā suīrán èrshí duō suì le, dànshì hái bú gòu chéngshú.** *Although he is over twenty, he is not mature enough.*

chéngtiān 成天 ADV all day long

chéngwéi 成为 [comp: 成 become + 为 be] V become ■ 这个小城已经成为著名的大学城。**Zhège xiǎo chéng yǐjīng chéngwéi zhùmíng de dàxué chéng.** *This town has become a well-known university town.* ■ 她想成为一名电影演员。**Tā xiǎng chéngwéi yì míng diànyǐng yǎnyuán.** *She wants to become a film star.*

chéngxiào 成效 N desired effect, beneficial effect

chéngxīn 成心 ADV intentionally, pre-meditatedly

chéngyǔ 成语 N idiom, idiomatic expression, set phrase

chéngyuán 成员 N member (of a family or group)

chéngzhǎng 成长 [comp: 成 become + 长 grow] V grow up ■ 他已经成长为一名优秀青年。**Tā yǐjīng chéngzhǎng wéi yìmíng yōuxiù qīngnián.** *He has grown into a fine young man.*

chéng 诚 TRAD 誠 ADJ sincere

chéngkěn 诚恳 [comp: 诚 sincere + 恳 sincere] ADJ sincere ■ 我们诚恳地希望你提出批评建议。**Wǒmen chéngkěn de xīwàng nǐ tíchū pīpíng jiànyì.** *We sincerely hope you will give us your criticism and suggestions.*

chéngshí 诚实 [comp: 诚 sincere + 实 true] ADJ honest, simple ■ 爸爸从小教育我做人要诚实。**Bàba cóng xiǎo jiàoyù wǒ zuòrén yào chéngshí.** *Since my childhood, my father has taught me to be an honest person.*

chéngzhì 诚挚 ADJ sincere, cordial

chéng 城 N city, town (座 **zuò**)

进城 **jìn chéng** go to town, go to the city center ■ 我今天下午进城，有什么事要我办吗？**Wǒ jīntiān xiàwǔ jìn chéng, yǒu shénme shì yào wǒ bàn ma?** *I'm going to town this afternoon. Is there anything you want me to do for you?*

chéngbǎo 城堡 N castle, citadel (座 **zuò**)

chénglǐ 城里 N in town, downtown

chéngshì 城市 [comp: 城 city wall, city + 市 market] N city, urban area (as opposed to rural area) (座 **zuò**) (ANTONYM 农村 **nóngcūn**) ■ 城市的中心是商业区，东面是工业区。**Chéngshì de zhōngxīn shì shāngyè qū, dōngmiàn shì gōngyè qū.** *The city center is a business district and the east part is an industrial area.* ■ 这个城市不大，但是很漂亮。**Zhège chéngshì bú dà, dànshì hěn piàoliang.** *This city is not big, but it's quite beautiful.*

chéngwài 城外 N out of town, suburban area

chéng 盛 V fill, ladle

chéngfàn 盛饭 V fill (a bowl/plate) with rice

chéng 承 V support, undertake, assume

chéngbàn 承办 [comp: 承 assume + 办 do, manage] V undertake, sponsor, host

chéngbāo 承包 V contract ■ 我们公司承包了这项工程。（or 这项工程承包给我们公司了。）**Wǒmen gōngsī chéngbāo le zhè xiàng gōngchéng.** (or **Zhè xiàng gōngchéng chéngbāo gěi wǒmen gōngsī le.**) *This project is contracted to our company.*

承包商 chéngbāoshāng contractor

chéngdān 承担 [comp: 承 bear + 担 responsibility] v take responsibility for, undertake

chéngnuò 承诺 v & n [comp: 承 assume + 诺 promise] promise, commit; promise, commitment

chéngrèn 承认 v 1 acknowledge, recognize ■ 大家都承认他是一位有成就的科学家。**Dàjiā dōu chéngrèn tā shì yí wèi yǒu chéngjiù de kēxuéjiā.** *Everyone acknowledges that he is a scientist who has made great achievements.* 2 admit (mistakes, errors, etc.) ■ 他错了，还不承认。**Tā cuò le, hái bù chéngrèn.** *He is wrong, but he still doesn't admit it.* ■ 我承认自己不了解情况，批评错了。**Wǒ chéngrèn zìjǐ bù liǎojiě qíngkuàng, pīpíng cuò le.** *I admit that I did not know the situation well and made a wrong criticism.*

chéngshòu 承受 v endure, bear

承受力 chéngshòu lì endurance

chéng 惩 TRAD 懲 v punish

chéngfá 惩罚 [comp: 惩 punish + 罚 penalize] v & n punish, penalize; punishment, penalty

chéng 呈 v appear, show, present

chéngxiàn 呈现 v appear, show

chéng 程 n regulation, procedure

chéngdù 程度 n level, degree ■ 汽车坏到这种程度，已经修不好了。**Qìchē huài dào zhè zhǒng chéngdù, yǐjīng xiū bù hǎo le.** *The car is damaged to such a degree that it cannot be repaired.*

chéngxù 程序 [comp: 程 regulation + 序 order] n 1 procedure

会议程序 huìyì chéngxù agenda of a meeting

2 computer programming

计算机程序 jìsuànjī chéngxù computer program / 应用程序 yìngyòng chéngxù app, application (program)

chéng 乘¹ v use (a means of transport), travel (by car, train, plane, etc.) ■ 爸爸每天乘公共汽车上班。**Bàba měi tiān chéng gōnggòng qìchē shàngbān.** *Father goes to work by bus every day.* ■ 你打算乘火车，还是乘飞机到北京去？**Nǐ dǎsuàn chéng huǒchē, háishì chéng fēijī qù Běijīng?** *Do you plan to go to Beijing by train or by plane?*

chéng 乘² v multiply ■ 二乘三等于六。**Èr chéng sān děngyú liù.** *Two multiplied by three is six. (2 x 3=6)*

chéngzuò 乘坐 v same as 乘¹ chéng

chéng 澄 ADJ (of water) clear, clean

chéngqīng 澄清 v clarify

澄清事实 chéngqīng shìshí clarify a matter

chéng 橙 n orange

chéngzi 橙子 n orange

chèng 秤 n scale, scales

磅秤 bàngchèng bathroom scale

chī 吃 v eat, consume ■ "你吃过早饭没有？" "吃过了。" **"Nǐ chī guo zǎofàn méiyǒu?" "Chī guo le."** *"Have you had breakfast?" "Yes, I have."*

chījīng 吃惊 v be shocked, be startled, be alarmed ■ 股票跌得这么快，王先生很吃惊。**Gǔpiào diē de zhènme kuài, Wáng xiānsheng hěn chījīng.** *Mr Wang was shocked that the share prices fell so quickly.*

大吃一惊 dà chī yì jīng greatly shocked, have the fright of one's life ■ 他回家时，发现家门大开，大吃一惊。**Tā huíjiā shí, fāxiàn jiā mén dà kāi, dà chī yì jīng.** *When he got home, he had the fright of his life when he saw the door wide open.*

chīkǔ 吃苦 [v+obj: 吃 eat + 苦 bitterness] v endure hardships, suffer

吃了很多苦 chī le hěn duō kǔ have suffered a lot

chīkuī 吃亏 [v+obj: 吃 eat + 亏 loss] v suffer losses, be at a disadvantage ■ 不了解市场情况，就要吃亏。**Bù liǎojiě shìchǎng qíngkuàng, jiùyào chīkuī.** *If you don't know the market, you'll suffer losses.*

chīlì 吃力 ADJ making or requiring great efforts

chí 迟 TRAD 遲 ADJ late

chídào 迟到 [modif: 迟 late + 到 arrive] v come late, be late (for work, school, etc.) ■ 对不起，我迟到了。**Duìbuqǐ, wǒ chídào le.** *I'm sorry I'm late.* ■ "你今天迟到了二十分钟，明天不要再迟到了。" "请您原谅，我明天一定不迟到。" **"Nǐ jīntiān chídàole èrshí fēnzhōng, míngtiān bú yào zài chídào le." "Qǐng nín yuánliàng. Wǒ míngtiān yídìng bù chídào."** *"You were late twenty minutes today. Don't be late again tomorrow." "My apologies. I'll definitely not be late tomorrow."*

chídùn 迟钝 [comp: 迟 late + 钝 blunt] ADJ slow, obtuse

chíhuǎn 迟缓 [comp: 迟 late + 缓 delayed] ADJ (of movement) slow, sluggish

chíyí 迟疑 [comp: 迟 late + 疑 doubtful] v hesitate, waver

chízǎo 迟早 [comp: 迟 late + 早 early] ADV sooner or later, eventually

chí 持 v persevere

chíjiǔ 持久 [comp: 持 persevere + 久 a long time] ADJ enduring, lasting

chíxù 持续 [comp: 持 persevere + 续 continue] ADJ continue, sustain, persist

可持续发展 kě chíxù fāzhǎn sustainable development

chí 池 n pool, pond

游泳池 yóuyǒngchí swimming pool

chítáng 池塘 [comp: 池 pool + 塘 pond] n pond

chí 驰 TRAD 馳 v gallop (See **bēnchí** 奔驰.)

chǐ 尺 I n ruler (把 bǎ) ■ 要划直线，就要有一把尺。**Yào huà zhí xiàn, jiù yào yǒu yì bǎ chǐ.** *You need a ruler if you want to draw a straight line.* II MEASURE WORD a traditional Chinese unit of length (equal to 1/3 meter) ■ 三尺等于一公尺，也就是说一尺等于三分之一公尺。**Sān chǐ děngyú yì gōngchǐ, yé jiù shì shuō yì chǐ děngyú sān fēn zhī**

yī gōngchǐ. *Three* chi *make a meter; that is to say, one* chi *is a third of a meter.*

公尺 gōngchǐ meter / 英尺 yīngchǐ foot (as a measurement of length)

chǐcùn 尺寸 size, measurements ■ 你做衣服以前，要量一下尺寸。**Nǐ zuò yīfu yǐqián, yào liáng yíxià chǐcùn.** *Before a garment is made for you, measurements should be taken.*

chǐmǎ 尺码 size (of shoes, shirts, ready-made clothing, etc.) ■ 我们有各种尺码的裙子，保证您满意。**Wǒmen yǒu gè zhǒng chǐmǎ de qúnzi, bǎozhèng nín mǎnyì.** *We have skirts of various sizes. Your satisfaction is guaranteed.*

chǐ 齿 **TRAD** 齒 **N** tooth, teeth

chǐ 耻 **TRAD** 恥 **N** shame

可耻 kěchǐ shameful

chǐrǔ 耻辱 deep shame, great humiliation

chì 赤 **ADJ** red

chìdào 赤道 [modif: 赤 red + 道 zone] **N** the equator

chìzì 赤字 [modif: 赤 red + 字 character, word] **N** the number in red, deficit

chì 翅 **N** wing

chìbǎng 翅膀 **N** wing (of a bird) ■ 这只鸟翅膀受伤了，不能飞了。**Zhè zhī niǎo chìbǎng shòu shāng le, bù néng fēi le.** *This bird's wing is injured; it can't fly.*

chì 斥 **V** upbraid, denounce, scold (See **páichì** 排斥.)

chōng 充 **ADJ** sufficient, full

chōngdāng 充当 **V** act as

chōngdiànqì 充电器 **N** (battery) charger

chōngfèn 充分 **ADJ** abundant, ample, adequate ■ 对明天的会谈双方都作了充分的准备。**Duì míngtiān de huìtán shuāngfāng dōu zuòle chōngfèn de zhǔnbèi.** *Both parties made ample preparations for the talk tomorrow.*

chōngmǎn 充满 [comp: 充 filled + 满 full] **ADJ** full of, filled with ■ 他充满了信心，一定能完成公司的任务。**Tā chōngmǎnle xìnxīn, yídìng néng wánchéng gōngsī de rènwù.** *He is full of confidence that he will complete the task set by the company.*

chōngpèi 充沛 **ADJ** abundant, plentiful

精力充沛 jīnglì chōngpèi full of vigor and vitality, very energetic

chōngshí 充实 **I ADJ** substantial **II V** strengthen, enrich

chōngzú 充足 [comp: 充 filled + 足 enough] **ADJ** sufficient, adequate, enough ■ 我有充足的理由相信，这次试验能成功。**Wǒ yǒu chōngzú de lǐyóu xiāngxìn, zhè cì shìyàn néng chénggōng.** *I have enough reason to believe that the experiment will succeed this time.* ■ 他们有充足的资金研究和开发这项新技术。**Tāmen yǒu chōngzú de zījīn yánjiū hé kāifā zhè xiàng xīn jìshù.** *They have sufficient funds to research and develop this new technology.*

chōng 冲 **TRAD** 衝 **V 1** clash **2** charge, rush, dash

chōngdòng 冲动 **N & ADJ** impulse; impulsive

冲动性购买 chōngdòng xìng gòumǎi impulse buying

chōngjī 冲击 **V 1** pound, lash **2** charge, attack

chōngtū 冲突 **V & N** clash; conflict, clash ■ 警察和抗议者在市政府大楼前发生了冲突。**Jǐngchá hé kàngyìzhě zài shìzhèngfǔ dàlóu qián fāshēng le chōngtū.** *The police and protesters clashed in front of the municipal government building.*

利益冲突 lìyì chōngtū conflict of interest

chóng 虫 **TRAD** 蟲 **N** insect, worm

chóngzi 虫子 [suffix: 虫 insect + 子 nominal suffix] **N** insect, worm (只 zhī) ■ 有一只虫子在你背上爬。**Yǒu yì zhī chóngzi zài nǐ bèi shang pá.** *There's an insect crawling on your back.*

chóng 重 **ADV** again, once again ■ 我在电脑上做的文件没有保存，只好重做。**Wǒ zài diànnǎo shang zuò de wénjiàn méiyǒu bǎocún, zhǐ hǎo chóng zuò.** *I failed to save the file in the computer, and had to redo [the work].*

chóngdié 重叠 **V** overlap

chóngfù 重复 [comp: 重 once again + 复 repeat] **V** repeat ■ 我离家前，妈妈又把话重复了一遍。**Wǒ lí jiā qián, māma yòu bǎ huà chóngfùle yí biàn.** *Before I left home, my mother repeated what she had said.*

chóngxīn 重新 [comp: 重 once again + 新 renew] **ADV** same as 重 **chóng**

Chóngyáng Jié 重阳节 **N** the Double Ninth Festival (the 9th day of the 9th lunar month)

chóng 崇 **ADJ** high, lofty

chóngbài 崇拜 [modif: 崇 lofty + 拜 bow down] **V** worship, adore

chónggāo 崇高 [comp: 崇 high, lofty + 高 high] **ADJ** lofty, sublime ■ 不少人不相信世界上有什么崇高的东西。**Bùshǎo rén bù xiāngxìn shìjiè shang yǒu shénme chónggāo de dōngxi.** *Quite a few people do not believe there is anything lofty in the world.*

chóngjìng 崇敬 [comp: 崇 lofty + 敬 respect] **V** hold in high esteem, revere

chōu 抽 **V** take out (from in between)

chōukòng 抽空 **V** manage to find time (to do something)

chōuti 抽屉 **N** drawer

chōuxiàng 抽象 **ADJ** abstract ■ 这么抽象的道理，有多少人听得懂？**Zhème chōuxiàng de dàolǐ, yǒu duōshǎo rén tīng de dǒng?** *How many people understand such abstract concepts?*

chōuyān 抽烟 [v+obj: 抽 suck + 烟 smoke] **V** smoke a cigarette (cigar), smoke

chóu 绸 **TRAD** 綢 **N** silk fabric, silk (See **sīchóu** 丝绸.)

chóu 愁 **V** worry ■ 你别愁，大伙儿会帮助你的。**Nǐ bié chóu, dàhuǒr huì bāngzhù nǐ de.** *Don't worry. We'll all help you.*

发愁 fā chóu worry over

chóu 稠 ADJ thick, dense

chóumì 稠密 [comp: 稠 dense + 密 dense] ADJ dense

人口稠密 rénkǒu chóumì densely populated

chóu 筹 TRAD 籌 V prepare

chóubèi 筹备 [comp: 筹 prepare + 备 prepare] V prepare (a conference, an event, etc.)

chóuchú 踌躇 V hesitate, be irresolute

chóu 酬 V reward

chóu 仇 N enmity, hatred

chóurén 仇人 N person hated intensely by somebody, sworn enemy

chǒu 丑 TRAD 醜 ADJ ugly

chǒu'è 丑恶 [comp: 丑 ugly + 恶 evil] ADJ hideous, repulsive

chòu 臭 ADJ smelly, stinking (ANTONYM 香 **xiāng**) ■ 他的脚爱出汗，一脱鞋就闻到臭味。**Tā de jiǎo ài chūhàn, yì tuō xié jiù wéndào chòu wèi.** *He has sweaty feet. The moment he takes off his shoes, one scents the foul smell.* ■ 臭豆腐，闻闻臭，吃起来香。**Chòu dòufu, wénwen chòu, chī qǐlai xiāng.** *The preserved beancurd smells bad but tastes delicious.*

chū 出 V emerge from, get out of

出来 chūlai come out ■ 请你出来一下。**Qǐng nǐ chūlai yíxià.** *Would you please step out for a while?*

出去 chūqu go out ■ 请你出去一下。**Qǐng nǐ chūqu yíxià.** *Please go out for a while. (→ Please leave us for a while.)*

chūbǎn 出版 V publish ■ 这本词典由一家国际出版公司出版。**Zhè běn cídiǎn yóu yì jiā guójì chūbǎn gōngsī chūbǎn.** *This dictionary is published by an international publishing house.*

chūchāi 出差 V be on a business trip, leave town on business

chūfā 出发 [comp: 出 depart + 发 discharge] V set off (on a journey), start (a journey) ■ "我们明天什么时候出发？" "早上八点。" **"Wǒmen míngtiān shénme shíhou chūfā?" "Zǎoshang bā diǎn."** *"When do we set off tomorrow?" "Eight o'clock in the morning."*

chūguó 出国 V go abroad, go overseas ■ 我爸爸每年都要出国开会。**Wǒ bàba měi nián dōu yào chūguó kāihuì.** *My father goes abroad for conferences every year.*

chūkǒu 出口 [v+obj: 出 leave + 口 mouth, port] I V export (ANTONYM 进口 **jìnkǒu**) ■ 这个国家出口大量工业品到世界各地。**Zhège guójiā chūkǒu dàliàng gōngyèpǐn dào shìjiè gè dì.** *This country exports large amounts of industrial products to various places in the world.* II N exit ■ 这是停车场的出口，不能从这里进。**Zhè shì tíngchēchǎng de chūkǒu, bù néng cóng zhèlǐ jìn.** *This is the car park exit. You can't enter here.*

出口公司 chūkǒu gōngsī export company / 出口贸易 chūkǒu màoyì export business in foreign trade

chūlù 出路 [modif: 出 out + 路 path] N way out, exit

chūmài 出卖 V 1 sell, be for sale ■ 工厂倒闭以后，出卖机器还债。**Gōngchǎng dǎobì yǐhòu, chūmài jīqì hái zhài.** *After the factory went bankrupt, the machines were sold to pay back debts.* 2 betray, sell out ■ 犹大为了三十块金币出卖耶稣。**Yóudà wèile sānshí kuài jīnbì chūmài Yēsū.** *Judas sold out Jesus for 30 pieces of gold.*

chūsè 出色 ADJ outstanding, remarkable

chūshēn 出身 N family background, (a person's) social origin

chūshén 出神 V be lost in thought, be spellbound

chūshēng 出生 [comp: 出 come out + 生 born] V be born ■ 他出生在1980年。**Tā chūshēng zài yī-jiǔ-bā-líng nián.** *He was born in 1980.* ■ 他于1980年出生在中国。**Tā yú yī-jiǔ-bā-líng nián chūshēng zài Zhōngguó.** *He was born in China in the year 1980.*

出生地 chūshēng dì place of birth / 出生日期 chūshēng rìqī date of birth / 出生证 chūshēng zhèng birth certificate

chūshì 出示 V take out to show, produce

chūxí 出席 V attend (a meeting, a court trial, etc.) ■ 你出席明天的会议吗？**Nǐ chūxí míngtiān de huìyì ma?** *Are you going to attend the meeting tomorrow?*

chūxi 出息 N (a person's) future

有出息 yǒu chūxi (especially of a young person) have a bright future, promising

chūxiàn 出现 [comp: 出 emerge + 现 appear] V come into view, appear, emerge ■ 开车两小时，一座漂亮的小山城出现在我们面前。**Kāichē liǎng xiǎoshí, yí zuò piàoliang de xiǎo shānchéng chūxiàn zài wǒmen miànqián.** *After two hours' drive, a beautiful small mountain town appeared before us.*

chū yángxiàng 出洋相 V make a laughing stock of oneself, be held up for mockery

chūyuàn 出院 V be discharged from hospital ■ 医生，我什么时候可以出院？**Yīshēng, wǒ shénme shíhou kěyǐ chūyuàn?** *When can I be discharged, doctor?*

chūzū 出租 [comp: 出 out + 租 rent] V have … for hire, rent ■ 这家商店出租电视机。**Zhè jiā shāngdiàn chūzū diànshìjī.** *This store has TV sets for hire.*

chūzūchē 出租车 taxi (辆 **liàng**) ■ 我要一辆出租汽车去飞机场。**Wǒ yào yí liàng chūzū qìchē qù fēijīchǎng.** *I want a taxi to go to the airport.*

NOTE: The slang expression 打的 **dǎdī**, which means *to call a taxi* or *to travel by taxi*, is very popular in everyday Chinese.

chū 初 I N beginning

月初 yuèchū at the beginning of a month / 年初 niánchū at the beginning of a year

II ADJ at the beginning, for the first time ■ 我初来贵国，情况还不熟悉。**Wǒ chū lái guì guó, qíngkuàng hái bù shúxi.** *I have just arrived in your country, and do not know much about it.*
III PREF (used for the first ten days of a lunar month), the first

初一 chū yī the first day (of a lunar month)
五月初八 wǔyuè chū bā the eighth day of the fifth lunar month / 年初一 / 大年初一 nián chū yī / dà nián chū yī the first day of the first lunar month (Chinese New Year's Day)

chūbù 初步 [modif: 初 initial + 步 step] ADJ initial, tentative ■ 这仅仅是我们的初步打算。**Zhè jǐnjǐn shì wǒmen de chūbù dǎsuàn.** *This is just our tentative plan.*

chūjí 初级 [modif: 初 initial + 级 grade] ADJ elementary, initial

初级中学 chūjí zhōngxué / 初中 chūzhōng junior high school

chú 除 v get rid of

除草 chú cǎo weed / 除虫 chú chóng kill insects, insecticide

chúfēi 除非 CONJ unless, only if ■ 除非他们正式邀请我，否则我是不会去参加他们的婚礼的。**Chúfēi tāmen zhèngshì yāoqǐng wǒ, fǒuzé wǒ shì bù huì qù cānjiā tāmende hūnlǐ de.** *I'm not going to attend their wedding, unless they send me their formal invitation.*

chúle … (yǐwài) 除了 … （以外） PREP except, besides ■ 这个动物园除了圣诞节每天开放。**Zhège dòngwùyuán chúle Shèngdànjié měi tiān kāifàng.** *This zoo is open to the public all year round except on Christmas Day.* ■ 我除了英文以外，还会说一点儿中文。**Wǒ chúle Yīngwén yǐwài, hái huì shuō yìdiǎnr Zhōngwén.** *Besides English I speak a little Chinese.*

NOTE: (1) While *except* and *besides* are two distinct words in English, 除了 … 以外 , **chúle … yǐwài** may mean either *except* or *besides*, as is shown in the examples. (2) 以外 **yǐwài** may be omitted, i.e. 除了…以外 **chúle … (yǐwài)** and 除了… **chúle** are the same.

chúxī 除夕 N Chinese New Year's Eve

NOTE: In colloquial Chinese, the Chinese New Year's Eve is called 大年夜 **dàniányè**. The dinner on the Chinese New Year's Eve is 年夜饭 **niányèfàn**.

chú 厨 TRAD 廚 N kitchen
chúfáng 厨房 [modif: 厨 kitchen + 房 room] N kitchen ■ 厨房又乱又脏，要收拾一下。**Chúfáng yòu luàn yòu zāng, yào shōushi yíxia.** *The kitchen is dirty and messy. It needs tidying up.* ■ 她在厨房里忙了好久了。**Tā zài chúfáng mángle hǎojiǔ le.** *She has been busy working in the kitchen for a long time.*

chǔ 处 TRAD 處 v handle, deal with

chǔfèn 处分 V & N take disciplinary action; disciplinary action ■ 处分这名学生是为了教育全校所有的学生。**Chǔfèn zhè míng xuésheng shì wèile jiàoyù quán xiào suǒyǒu de xuésheng.** *The purpose of taking disciplinary action against this student is to educate all the students of the school.* ■ 十名官员因接受贵重礼物受到处分。**Shí míng guānyuán yīn jiēshòu guìzhòng lǐwù shòudào chǔfèn.** *Disciplinary action was taken against ten officials who had accepted expensive gifts.*

chǔjìng 处境 N (usually) bad situation, plight
处境危险 chǔjìng wēixiǎn in a dangerous situation

chǔlǐ 处理 v handle, deal with ■ 对于顾客提出的意见，我们都会认真处理。**Duìyú gùkè tíchū de yìjiàn, wǒmen dōu huì rènzhēn chǔlǐ.** *We deal with customers' complaints seriously.* ■ 这种关系很难处理。**Zhè zhǒng guānxi hěn nán chǔlǐ.** *This kind of relationship is difficult to handle.*

chǔzhì 处置 v dispose of, handle, deal with
chǔ 储 TRAD 儲 v store
chǔbèi 储备 [comp: 储 store + 备 prepare] v store away
chǔcún 储存 [comp: 储 store + 存 preserve] v **1** store away, keep in reserve **2** (in computing) save a file
chǔxù 储蓄 [comp: 储 store + 蓄 save up] v save (money), deposit (money)
活期储蓄 huóqī chǔxù checking account
chǔ 础 TRAD 礎 N plinth (See jīchǔ 基础.)
chǔ 楚 ADJ clear, neat (See qīngchu 清楚.)
chù 处 TRAD 處 N **1** place, location ■ 你知道他现在的住处吗？**Nǐ zhīdào tā xiànzài de zhùchù ma?** *Do you know where he lives now?* **2** a government department (bigger than a section 科 and smaller than a bureau 局)
chù 触 TRAD 觸 v touch (See jiēchù 接触.)
chù 畜 N (domestic) animal, beast (See shēngchù 牲畜.)
chùsheng 畜生 N animal (used as a verbal abuse)
chuān 川 N river
chuān liú bù xī 川流不息 IDIOM flowing past in an endless stream, never–ending
chuān 穿 v **1** wear (clothes or shoes), be dressed in ■ 你穿黑衣服去参加中国人的婚礼，不合适。**Nǐ chuān hēi yīfu qù cānjiā Zhōngguórén de hūnlǐ, bù héshì.** *It is not appropriate for you to go to a Chinese wedding in black.* **2** put on (clothes or shoes) ■ 这个小孩会穿衣服了，可是还不会穿鞋子。**Zhège xiǎohái huì chuān yīfu le, kěshì hái bú huì chuān xiézi.** *This child can put on clothes, but still can't put on shoes.*
chuānyuè 穿越 v pass through, cross
chuānzhe 穿着 v be dressed in ■ 那个穿着红衣服的女孩子是我哥哥的女朋友。**Nàge chuānzhe hóng yīfu de nǚháizi shì wǒ gēge de nǚpéngyou.** *The girl in red is my elder brother's girlfriend.*

chuānzhuó 穿着 **N** dress, the way of dressing, attire ■ 他很讲究穿着。**Tā hěn jiǎngjiu chuānzhuó.** *He pays a great deal of attention to his clothes.*

chuán 船 **N** boat, ship

坐船 zuòchuán travel by boat/ship ■ 从香港坐船到上海去，只要两天。**Cóng Xiānggǎng zuòchuán dào Shànghǎi qù, zhǐ yào liǎng tiān.** *It only takes two days to travel from Hong Kong to Shanghai by sea.*

划船 huáchuán row a boat

chuánbó 船舶 [comp: 船 ship + 舶 ship] **N** boats and ships

船舶公司 chuánbó gōngsī shipping company

chuán 传 **TRAD** 傳 **V** 1 pass (something) on ■ 你看完这份文件后，请按照名单传给下一个人。**Nǐ kàn wán zhè fèn wénjiàn hòu, qǐng ànzhào míngdān chuán gěi xià yí ge rén.** *After reading this document, please pass it on to the next person on the list.* 2 spread (news, rumor) ■ 好事不出门，坏事传千里。**Hǎo shì bù chūmén, huài shì chuán qiān lǐ.** *Good news stays at home, but bad news travels far and wide.*

chuánbō 传播 [comp: 传 spread + 播 sow] **V** propagate, disseminate ■ 学校不仅仅是传播知识的地方。**Xuéxiào bù jǐnjǐn shì chuánbō zhīshi de dìfang.** *A school is more than a place to disseminate knowledge.* ■ 这种病传得很快。**Zhè zhǒng bìng chuánbō de hěn kuài.** *This disease spreads fast.*

chuándá 传达 [comp: 传 transmit + 达 arrive] **V** pass on, relay, transmit

传达总公司的指令 chuándá zǒnggōngsī de zhǐlìng pass on instructions from the company HQ

chuándáshì 传达室 **N** reception office (usually in a big institution)

chuándān 传单 **N** leaflet, handbill, flier (张 **zhāng**)

chuánshòu 传授 [comp: 传 transmit + 授 teach] **V** teach, pass on (knowledge, skill, etc.)

chuánshuō 传说 **N** legend, folktale

chuántǒng 传统 **N** tradition ■ 每个民族都有自己的传统。**Měi ge mínzú dōu yǒu zìjǐ de chuántǒng.** *Every ethnic group has its own traditions.* ■ 中医、武术、国画都是中国人的传统文化。**Zhōngyī, wǔshù, guóhuà dōu shì Zhōngguórén de chuántǒng wénhuà.** *Chinese medicine, martial arts and Chinese painting are all part of traditional Chinese culture.*

chuánzhēn 传真 [v+obj: 传 transmit + 真 true] **N** fax ■ 我的传真号码和电话号码是一样的。**Wǒ de chuánzhēn hàomǎ hé diànhuà hàomǎ shì yíyàng de.** *My fax number is the same as my telephone number.* ■ 我发了一份传真给他。**Wǒ fāle yí fèn chuánzhēn gěi tā.** *I sent him a fax.*

chuǎn 喘 **V** breathe with difficulty, pant

chuǎnqì 喘气 **V** gasp, pant

chuàn 串 **I V** string together **II MEASURE WORD** (for a string of things)

一串葡萄 yí chuàn pútao a cluster of grapes

chuāng 窗 **N** window

chuānghu 窗户 [comp: 窗 window + 户 door] **N** window ■ 我房间的窗户朝东。**Wǒ fángjiān de chuānghu cháo dōng.** *The window in my room faces east.* ■ 马上要下雨了，把窗户关上吧。**Mǎshang yào xià yǔ le, bǎ chuānghu guānshang ba.** *It's going to rain soon. Let's close the window.*

打开窗户 dǎkāi chuānghu open a window / 关上窗户 guānshang chuānghu close a window

chuānglián 窗帘 **N** (window) curtain

chuáng 床 **N** bed (张 **zhāng**) ■ 这张床很舒服。**Zhè zhāng chuáng hěn shūfu.** *This bed is very comfortable.* ■ 这个房间很小，放了一张大床，就剩下不多地方了。**Zhè ge fángjiān hěn xiǎo, fàngle yì zhāng dà chuáng, jiù shèngxia bù duō dìfang le.** *This room is small. With a big bed in it, there is not much space left.*

单人床 dānrén chuáng single bed / 双人床 shuāngrén chuáng double bed

chuángdān 床单 **N** bedsheet (条 **tiáo**)

chuàng 创 **TRAD** 創 **V** create

chuànglì 创立 [comp: 创 establish + 立 stand] **V** set up, found

chuàngxīn 创新 **I V** blaze a trail **II ADJ** creative

chuàngyè 创业 [comp: 创 establish + 业 undertaking] **V** start an undertaking

创业精神 chuàngyè jīngshen pioneering spirit, enterprising spirit

chuàngyè gōngsī 创业公司 **N** startup company, startup

chuàngzào 创造 [comp: 创 create + 造 build, make] **V** create ■ 有人说神创造了天地。**Yǒurén shuō shén chuàngzàole tiān-dì.** *Some people say God created the universe.*

chuàngzàoxìng 创造性 **N** creativity ■ 创造性是艺术作品的生命。**Chuàngzàoxìng shì yìshù zuòpǐn de shēngmìng.** *Creativity is the life of a work of art.*

chuàngzuò 创作 [comp: 创 create + 作 make] **V & N** create (works of art and literature); work of art or literature ■ 这位作家创作了反映农民生活的小说。**Zhè wèi zuòjiā chuàngzuòle fǎnyìng nóngmín shēnghuó de xiǎoshuō.** *This author wrote novels about peasant life.* ■ 这位作家的新创作是中国文学的伟大成就。**Zhè wèi zuòjiā de xīn chuàngzuò shì Zhōngguó wénxué de wěidà chéngjiù.** *This author's new work is a great achievement in Chinese literature.*

chuī 吹 **V** blow, puff ■ 风吹草动。**Fēng chuī cǎo dòng.** *Winds blow and the grass stirs. (→ There are signs of disturbance/trouble.)*

chuīniú 吹牛 **V** brag, boast ■ 你别相信他，他在吹

牛。**Nǐ bié xiāngxìn tā, tā zài chuīniú.** *Don't believe him. He's bragging.*

chuīpěng 吹捧 **v** lavish praise on, flatter
相互吹捧 **xiānghù chuīpěng** flatter each other

chuí 垂 **v** hang

chuízhí 垂直 **ADJ** perpendicular, vertical

chuí 锤 **TRAD** 錘 **N** mace

chuízi 锤子 **N** hammer (把 **bǎ**)

chūn 春 **N** spring

chūnjié 春节 [modif: 春 spring + 节 festival]
N the Spring Festival (the Chinese New Year)
■ 春节是中国人最重要的节日。**Chūnjié shì
Zhōngguórén zuì zhòngyào de jiérì.** *The Spring
Festival is the most important festival for the Chinese.* ■ 小明的哥哥、 姐姐都要回家过春节。**Xiǎo
Míng de gēge, jiějie dōu yào huí jiā guò chūnjié.**
*Xiao Ming's elder brothers and sisters will be
coming home for the Spring Festival.*

chūntiān 春天 [modif: 春 spring + 天 days] **N**
spring ■ 春天来了, 花园里的花都开了。**Chūntiān
lái le, huāyuán lǐ de huā dōu kāi le.** *Spring has
come. The flowers in the garden are in full bloom.*
■ 我最喜欢春天, 不太热, 也不太冷。**Wǒ zuì
xǐhuan chūntiān, bú tài rè, yěbú tài lěng.** *I like
spring the best; it's neither too hot nor too cold.*

chún 纯 **TRAD** 純 **ADJ** pure

chúncuì 纯粹 **ADJ** unadulterated, pure ■ 这纯粹
是谎言！**Zhè chúncuì shì huǎngyán!** *This is a lie,
pure and simple!*

chúnjié 纯洁 **ADJ** pure, clean-minded, unselfish

chún 唇 **N** lip (See **zuǐchún** 嘴唇.)

chǔn 蠢 **ADJ** stupid, clumsy

cí 词 **TRAD** 詞 **N** word ■ 现代汉语的词一般是由两个
字组成。**Xiàndài Hànyǔ de cí yìbān shì yóu liǎng
ge zì zǔchéng.** *Modern Chinese words are generally comprised of two characters.* ■ 我没有听说
过这个词。**Wǒ méiyǒu tīngshuōguo zhè ge cí.** *I
haven't heard of this word.*

cídiǎn 词典 **N** dictionary (本 **běn**) ■ 这本词典对我
们很有帮助。**Zhè běn cídiǎn duì wǒmen hěn yǒu
bāngzhù.** *This dictionary is very helpful to us.* ■ 你
看, 我买了一本新词典。**Nǐ kàn, wǒ mǎile yì běn
xīn cídiǎn.** *Look, I've bought a new dictionary.*

cíhuì 词汇 **N** vocabulary, lexicon

cíyǔ 词语 [comp: 词 word + 语 speech] **N** word,
phrase, wording

cí 瓷 **N** porcelain, china

cíqì 瓷器 [modif: 瓷 porcelain + 器 ware] **N** porcelain, chinaware

cí 磁 **N** magnetism

cídài 磁带 [modif: 磁 magnetic + 带 tape] **N** magnetic tape, audio tape ■ 这一盘磁带是我爷爷最喜
欢的, 几乎每天都听。**Zhè yì pán cídài shì wǒ yéye
zuì xǐhuan de, jīhū měi tiān dōu tīng.** *This is my
granddad's favorite tape. He listens to it almost
every day.*

cíkǎ 磁卡 [modif: 磁 magnetic + 卡 card] **N** magnetic card (for making telephone calls, etc.)

cípán 磁盘 [modif: 磁 magnetic + 盘 disc] **N** magnetic disc

cí 雌 **ADJ** (of animals) female (**ANTONYM** 雄 **xióng**)
■ 我不知道家里的狗是雌的还是雄的。**Wǒ bù
zhīdào jiāli de gǒu shì cí de háishì xióng de.** *I don't
know whether our family dog is female or male.*

cí 慈 **ADJ** kind and loving

císhàn 慈善 [comp: 慈 kind and loving + 善
good] **I ADJ** compassionate, charitable **II N** charity
慈善机构 **císhàn jīgòu** institutions of charity,
charities

cíxiáng 慈祥 [comp: 慈 kind and loving + 祥
serene] **ADJ** (of an elderly person's appearance)
kindly

cí 辞 **TRAD** 辭 **v** take leave

cízhí 辞职 [v+obj: 辞 take leave + 职 position] **v**
resign

cǐ 此 **PRON 1** this ■ 此路不通。**Cǐ lù bù tōng.** *This
road is blocked. (→ No through road.)*
此时此地 **cǐshí cǐdì** here and now
2 here ■ 会议到此结束。**Huìyì dào cǐ jiéshù.** *The
meeting ends here/at this point. (→ This is the end
of the meeting.)*

cǐhòu 此后 **CONJ** after this, ever after

cǐkè 此刻 **N** this moment

cǐshí 此时 **N** right now

cǐwài 此外 **CONJ** besides, apart from (that), as
well ■ 他买了一台新电脑, 此外, 还买了一些软
件。**Tā mǎile yì tái xīn diànnǎo, cǐwài, hái mǎile
yìxiē ruǎnjiàn.** *He bought a new computer and
some software as well.*

cì 次[1] **MEASURE WORD** time (expressing frequency of
an act) ■ 我去过他家两次。**Wǒ qùguo tā jiā liǎng
cì.** *I've been to his home twice.* ■ 这是我第一次出
国旅行。**Zhè shì wǒ dì-yī cì chūguó lǚxíng.** *This is
my first trip abroad.*

cì 次[2] **ADJ** inferior

cìpǐn 次品 [modif: 次 inferior + 品 article, product] **N** substandard product

cìyào 次要 **ADJ** next in importance, of secondary
importance

cì 次[3] **N** order, sequence

cìxù 次序 [comp: 次 order + 序 order] **N** order,
sequence

cì 伺 **v** wait on

cìhou 伺候 **v** wait on, serve

cì 刺 **V & N** prick; thorn ■ 花儿很美, 但是会刺
人。**Huār hěn měi, dànshì huì cì rén.** *The flower is
beautiful, but it may prick you.*

cìjī 刺激 [comp: 刺 prick + 激 excite] **V & N 1** irritate; irritation ■ 强烈的阳光刺激我的眼睛, 很
不舒服。**Qiángliè de yángguāng cìjī wǒde yǎnjing,
hěn bù shūfu.** *The strong sunlight irritates my
eyes; it's very uncomfortable.* **2** stimulate, give

incentive to; stimulation, incentive ■ 公司决定增
加加班费，来刺激工人的积极性。**Gōngsī juédìng
zēngjiā jiābānfèi, lái cìjī gōngrén de jījíxìng.** *The
company decided to increase overtime pay in order to arouse workers' enthusiasm.*

cōng 囱 **N** chimney (See **yāncōng** 烟囱.)

cōng 聪 **TRAD** 聰 **ADJ** acute hearing

cōngmíng 聪明 [comp: 聪 acute sense of hearing
+ 明 keen sense of eyesight] adj clever, bright,
intelligent ■ 他不但聪明，而且用功，所以考试总
是第一名。**Tā búdàn cōngmíng, érqiě yònggōng,
suǒyǐ kǎoshì zǒngshi dì-yī míng.** *He is not only
clever, but also hardworking, so he always comes
out first in the exams.*

cōng 匆 **ADJ** hurriedly

cōngcōng 匆匆 **ADJ** hurriedly, in a rush

cōngmáng 匆忙 [comp: 匆 hurriedly + 忙 busy]
ADJ in a hurry, in haste

cōng 葱 **N** onion, scallion
大葱 dàcōng green Chinese onion / 小葱 xiǎocōng
spring onion / 洋葱 yángcōng onion

cóng 从 **TRAD** 從 **PREP** following, from ■ "你从哪
里来?" "我从很远的地方来。" **"Nǐ cóng nǎli
lái?" "Wǒ cóng hěn yuǎn de dìfang lái."** *"Where
do you come from?" "I come from a faraway
place."*
从…出发 cóng…chūfā set out from …

cóngbù 从不 **ADV** never ■ 我从不吸烟。**Wǒ cóngbù xīyān.** *I never smoke.*

cóngcǐ 从此 **CONJ** since then, from then on ■ 我
上次跟他开玩笑，他竟生气了，从此我不跟他开
玩笑了。**Wǒ shàng cì gēn tā kāi wánxiào, tā jìng
shēngqì le, cóngcǐ wǒ bù gēn tā kāi wánxiào le.** *He
got angry when I joked with him the last time.
Since then I have never joked with him.*

cóng … dào … 从 … 到 … **PREP** from … to …,
from … till … ■ 我从上午九点到下午三点都要上
课。**Wǒ cóng shàngwǔ jiǔ diǎn dào xiàwǔ sān diǎn
dōu yào shàngkè.** *I've classes from nine o'clock in
the morning till three o'clock in the afternoon.*
■ 从中国到英国要经过许多国家。**Cóng Zhōngguó
dào Yīngguó yào jīngguò xǔduō guójiā.** *Traveling
from China to England, one has to pass through
many countries.*
从早到晚 cóng-zǎo-dào-wǎn from morning till
night, long hours in a day ■ 夏天他从早到晚都在
农场工作。**Xiàtiān tā cóng-zǎo-dào-wǎn dōu zài
nóngchǎng gōngzuò.** *In summer he works on the
farm from morning till night.*
从古到今 cóng-gǔ-dào-jīn from remote past
till now in history ■ 从古到今，出现过多少英雄
人物！**Cóng-gǔ-dào-jīn, chūxiànguo duōshǎo
yīngxióng rénwù!** *From the remote past till now,
history has produced so many heroes!*

cóng'ér 从而 **CONJ** thus, thereby ■ 我要认真学好
中文，从而了解中华文化。**Wǒ yào rènzhēn xué**
hǎo Zhōngwén, cóng'ér liǎojiě Zhōnghuá wénhuà.
*I will study the Chinese language earnestly, thereby
gaining an understanding of Chinese culture.*

cónglái 从来 **ADV** always, ever
从来不 cónglái bù never ■ 我从来不喝酒。**Wǒ
cónglái bù hē jiǔ.** *I never drink wine.*

cóng … qǐ 从 … 起 **PREP** starting from … ■ 我决
定从明年一月一日起每天早上跑步。**Wǒ juédìng
cóng míngnián Yīyuè yīrì qǐ měi tiān zǎoshang
pǎobù.** *I've decided to jog every morning starting
from January 1 next year.*

cóngqián 从前 **I N** past time, past, in the past
■ 我从前不知道学中文多么有意思。**Wǒ cóngqián
bù zhīdào xué Zhōngwén duōme yǒu yìsi.** *I did not
know how interesting it is to learn Chinese.* **II ADV**
once upon a time (used in story-telling) ■ 从前
有个农民，他 … **Cóngqián yǒu ge nóngmín, tā…**
Once upon a time there was a farmer, who...

cóngróng 从容 **ADJ** unhurried, leisurely

cóngróng bú pò 从容不迫 **ADJ** calm and unhurried, confident and without haste

cóngshì 从事 **V** be engaged in (business, education, law, etc.)

cóngwèi 从未 **ADV** never in the past

cóng 丛 **TRAD** 叢 **N** shrub, thicket

cóngshū 丛书 **N** a series of books on a specific
topic

còu 凑 **V** put together, pool
凑钱 còu qián pool money

còuhe 凑合 **V** make do, make do with

còuqiǎo 凑巧 **ADJ** luckily, as luck would have it

cū 粗 **ADJ** thick (**ANTONYM** 细 xì) ■ 这根绳子太细了，
要粗点儿的。**Zhè gēn shéngzi tài xì le, yào cū diǎn
de.** *This rope is too thin. We need a thicker one.*

cūlǔ 粗鲁 [comp: 粗 crude + 鲁 rash] **ADJ** rude,
boorish

cūxīn 粗心 [modif: 粗 thick + 心 the heart] **ADJ**
careless (**ANTONYM** 细心 xìxīn) ■ 她太粗心了，考试
的时候竟然漏了一道题目。**Tā tài cūxīn le, kǎoshì
de shíhou jìngrán lòu le yí dào tímù.** *She was so
careless that she missed a question in the exam.*

cù 促 **V** urge

cùjìn 促进 [v+obj: 促 promote + 进 progress]
V promote, advance ■ 工会的目的是促进工人
的利益。**Gōnghuì de mùdì shì cùjìn gōngrén
de lìyì.** *The purpose of the trade union is to advance workers' interests.* ■ 让我们为促进友谊努
力。**Ràng wǒmen wèi cùjìn yǒuyì nǔlì.** *Let's work
hard to promote our friendship.*

cù 醋 **N** vinegar ■ 他喜欢吃酸的，什么东西都放
醋。**Tā xǐhuan chī suān de, shénme dōngxi dōu
fàng cù.** *He is fond of sour flavors, and adds vinegar to whatever he eats.*

cuàn 窜 **TRAD** 竄 **V** flee (like a rat)

cuī 催 **V** urge, hurry ■ 他催我还钱。**Tā cuī wǒ
huán qián.** *He urged me to pay him back.* ■ 别催

D

她，时间还早。**Bié cuī tā, shíjiān hái zǎo.** *Don't hurry her. There's enough time.*

cuīcán 摧残 v devastate, wreck

cuì 脆 ADJ crisp (See **gāncuì** 干脆.)

cuìruò 脆弱 [comp: 脆 crispy + 弱 weak] ADJ fragile, frail

cūn 村 N village

cūnzi 村子 [suffix: 村 village + 子 nominal suffix] N village (座 **zuò**) ■ 你们村子有多少户人家？**Nǐmen cūnzi yǒu duōshǎo hù rénjiā?** *How many households are there in your village?*

cún 存 v store, keep ■ 她一有钱就存在银行里。**Tā yì yǒu qián jiù cún zài yínháng lǐ.** *As soon as she gets some money, she deposits it in the bank.* ■ 他出国前把一些东西存在姐姐家。**Tā chū guó qián bǎ yìxiē dōngxi cún zài jiějie jiā.** *Before going abroad he stored some stuff at his sister's home.*

cúnzài 存在 v exist ■ 这家公司存在严重问题。**Zhè jiā gōngsī cúnzài yánzhòng wèntí.** *There are serious problems with this company.*

cùn 寸 MEASURE WORD a traditional Chinese unit of length (equal to ⅓₀ meter)

英寸 yīngcùn inch

cuō 搓 v rub with the hands

cuō 磋 v consult

cuōshāng 磋商 [comp: 磋 consult + 商 discuss] v consult, discuss

cuò 错 TRAD 錯 ADJ wrong (ANTONYM 对 **duì**) ■ 我错了，我不应该那么做。**Wǒ cuò le, wǒ bù yīnggāi nàme zuò.** *I was wrong. I shouldn't have done that.* ■ 你这个字写错了。**Nǐ zhège zì xiě cuò le.** *You've written this character wrong.*

错字 cuòzì a wrong character

cuòwù 错误 [comp: 错 wrong + 误 miss] N & ADJ mistake, error; wrong, mistaken ■ 你这次作业有很多错误。**Nǐ zhè cì zuòyè yǒu hěn duō cuòwù.** *You've made many mistakes in this assignment.* ■ 这是一个错误的决定。**Zhè shì yí ge cuòwù de juédìng.** *This is a wrong decision.*

犯错误 fàn cuòwù make a mistake ■ 人人都会犯错误。**Rénrén dōu huì fàn cuòwù.** *Everybody makes mistakes.*

纠正错误 jiūzhèng cuòwù correct a mistake

cuò 措 v arrange, handle

cuòshī 措施 N measure, step ■ 我们必须迅速采取有效措施。**Wǒmen bìxū xùnsù cǎiqǔ yǒuxiào cuòshī.** *We must take immediate and effective measures.* ■ 由于措施不当，问题更加严重了。**Yóuyú cuòshī bú dàng, wèntí gèngjiā yánzhòng le.** *Owing to inappropriate measures, the problem became even more serious.*

cuò 挫 v frustrate, defeat

受挫 shòucuò be frustrated, be defeated

cuòzhé 挫折 [comp: 挫 frustrate + 折 break] N setback, frustration

dā 答 v same as 答 **dá**

dāying 答应 [comp: 答 reply + 应 respond] v **1** answer, reply ■ 我按了半天门铃，也没人答应。**Wǒ ànle bàntiān ménlíng, yě méi rén dāying.** *I pressed the doorbell for a long time, but nobody answered.* **2** promise ■ 爸爸答应给他买一个新手机。**Bàba dāying gěi tā mǎi yì ge xīn shǒujī.** *His father has promised to buy him a new cell phone.*

dā 搭 v put up, build

dādàng 搭档 v & N work together, co-operate; workmate, partner

dāpèi 搭配 v & N arrange in pairs or groups; pairing, (word) collocation

dá 达 TRAD 達 v reach, attain

dáchéng 达成 v reach (an agreement, an understanding, a business deal, etc.)

dádào 达到 [comp: 达 reach + 到 reach] v reach, achieve ■ 需要学几年才能达到一级汉语水平？**Xūyào xué jǐ nián cái néng dádào yī jí Hànyǔ shuǐpíng?** *How many years do I have to study to reach Level A of the Chinese proficiency standard?* ■ 不能为了达到目的，而不择手段。**Bù néng wèile dádào mùdì, ér bù zé shǒuduàn.** *One shouldn't stop at nothing in order to achieve one's aim. (→ The end doesn't always justify the means.)*

dá 答 v answer, reply ■ 这个问题我不会答。**Zhège wèntí wǒ bú huì dá.** *I can't answer this question.*

dá'àn 答案 [modif: 答 answer + 案 file] N answer (to a list of questions) ■ 测验以后，老师发给学生标准答案。**Cèyàn yǐhòu, lǎoshī fā gěi xuésheng biāozhǔn dá'àn.** *After the test, the teacher distributed standard answers among students.* ■ 关于这个问题，还是没有答案。**Guānyú zhège wèntí, háishi méiyǒu dá'àn.** *There is still no answer to this question.*

dábiàn 答辩 [comp: 答 reply + 辩 argue] v speak in self-defense

论文答辩 lùnwén dábiàn (postgraduate students') oral examination in defense of a thesis

dáfù 答复 v & N (formally) reply

dǎ 打 v **1** strike, hit ■ 不能打人。**Bù néng dǎ rén.** *You can't hit people.* **2** play (certain ball games)

打篮球 dǎ lánqiú play basketball

3 send, dispatch

打电话 dǎ diànhuà make a telephone call

NOTE: While its basic meaning is *strike, hit*, **dǎ** 打 forms many semi-idioms with the words following it, and has multiple meanings in everyday Chinese.

dǎban 打扮 v dress up, make up ■ 新娘打扮得很漂亮。**Xīnniáng dǎban de hěn piàoliang.** *The bride was beautifully dressed.* ■ 她每天要花很多

时间打扮。 **Tā měi tiān yào huā hěn duō shíjiān dǎban.** *Every day she spends lots of time putting on make-up.*

dǎbāo 打包 **v** pack up

dǎchà 打岔 **v** interrupt (somebody's talk), cut in

dǎ chē 打车 **v** call a taxi ■ 时间很紧了，我们得打车。 **Shíjiān hěn jǐn le, wǒmen děi dǎ chē.** *We don't have much time now; we've got to call a taxi.*

dǎdǎo 打倒 [v+compl: 打 strike + 倒 down] **v** strike down, overthrow, down with …

dǎ dī 打的 **v** same as 打车 **dǎ chē**

dǎgōng 打工 **v** work (especially as a manual laborer) ■ 我希望在暑假里有机会打工，付明年的学费。 **Wǒ xīwàng zài shǔjià lǐ yǒu jīhuì dǎgōng, fù míngnián de xuéfèi.** *I hope I'll have an opportunity to work in the summer vacation to pay for my tuition fee next year.*

dǎ guānsi 打官司 **v** go to court, take … to court

dǎjí 打击 [comp: 打 strike + 击 strike] **v** strike a blow against (a crime, a bad tendency, etc.), deal with and punish severely

打击盗版 **dǎjí dàobǎn** attack the crime of piracy (of intellectual products)

dǎjià 打架 **v** fight (between people), come to blows

dǎ jiāodao 打交道 **v** to have dealings with, negotiate with

和各式各样的人打交道 **hé gèshìgèyàng de rén dǎjiāodào** deal with all kinds of people

dǎ kǎ 打卡 **v** punch a card, record presence at work by punching a time clock

dǎ kēshui 打瞌睡 **v** doze, doze off

打一会儿瞌睡 **dǎ yíhuìr kēshuì** have a doze-off

dǎliàng 打量 **v** measure with the eye, size up

dǎliè 打猎 **v & n** hunt; hunting

dǎ pēnti 打喷嚏 **v** sneeze

dǎpò 打破 **v** break

打破花瓶 **dǎpò huāpíng** break a vase / 打破世界纪录 **dǎpò shìjiè jìlù** break a world record

dǎ qiú 打球 **v** play baseball/basketball/volleyball, etc.

dǎrǎo 打扰 **v** disturb, interrupt ■ 爸爸在写一份重要的报告，你别去打扰他。 **Bàba zài xiě yí fèn zhòngyào de bàogào, nǐ bié qù dǎrǎo tā.** *Daddy is working on an important report. Don't disturb him.*

NOTE: When you call on someone, especially at their home, you can say 打扰你们了 **Dǎrǎo nǐmen le** as a polite expression. You can use **dǎjiǎo** 打搅 instead of **dǎrǎo** 打扰, with exactly the same meaning.

dǎsǎo 打扫 **v** clean up ■ 中国人在过春节前，要打扫屋子。 **Zhōngguórén zài guò chūnjié qián, yào dǎsǎo wūzi.** *Before the Spring Festival, Chinese people clean up their houses.*

dǎsuàn 打算 [comp: 打 act + 算 calculate] **v** plan, contemplate ■ 你打算毕业以后做什么？ **Nǐ dǎsuàn bìyè yǐhòu zuò shénme?** *What do you plan to do after graduation?* ■ 我不打算买什么。 **Wǒ bù dǎsuàn mǎi shénme.** *I don't intend to buy anything.*

dǎtīng 打听 **v** inquire, ask ■ 您从北京大学来，我想跟您打听一位教授。 **Nín cóng Běijīng Dàxué lái, wǒ xiǎng gēn nín dǎtīng yí wèi jiàoshòu.** *As you're from Beijing University, I'd like to ask you about a professor.* ■ 你到了那里打听一下就知道了。 **Nǐ dàole nàlǐ dǎtīng yíxià jiù zhīdào le.** *When you're there, just make some inquiries and you'll find out.*

dǎyìnjī 打印机 **n** printer

dǎzhàng 打仗 **v** go to war, fight in battle

dǎ zhāohu 打招呼 **v 1** greet, say hello to **2** let know, notify

dǎzhé 打折 **v** give a discount

dǎzhēn 打针 **v** give (or get) an injection ■ 病人每天要打针吃药。 **Bìngrén měi tiān yào dǎzhēn chīyào.** *The patient must get injections and take medicine every day.*

dǎzì 打字 **v** type ■ 他打字打得又快又好。 **Tā dǎzì dǎ de yòu kuài yòu hǎo.** *He types fast and well. (→ He has excellent keyboard skills.)*

dà 大 **ADJ** big, large (ANTONYM 小 **xiǎo**) ■ 中国实在很大。 **Zhōngguó shízài hěn dà.** *China is indeed big.* ■ 我爷爷种的树都长大了。 **Wǒ yéye zhòng de shù dōu zhǎngdà le.** *The trees that my grandfather planted have all matured.*

dàbuliǎo 大不了 **ADV** if worst comes to worst, at worst

dàchén 大臣 **n** ranking official (in a royal court), minister

dàdǎn 大胆 [modif: 大 big + 胆 gall bladder] **ADJ** bold, courageous ■ 你可以大胆地试验，失败了不要紧。 **Nǐ kěyǐ dàdǎn de shìyàn, shībàile búyàojǐn.** *You can experiment boldly. It doesn't matter if you fail.*

NOTE: The ancient Chinese believed that the gall bladder was the organ of courage—if one had a big gall bladder it meant that the person was endowed with courage and daring, and if one was timid it was because he had a small gall bladder. Therefore, 他胆子很大 **Tā dǎnzi hěn dà** and 他很大胆 **Tā hěn dàdǎn** means *He is bold*; 他胆子很小 **Tā dǎnzi hěn xiǎo** and 他很胆小 **Tā hěn dǎnxiǎo** means *He is timid*.

dàduō 大多 [modif: 大 big + 多 many] **ADV** mostly ■ 这个国家的人大多会说一点儿英文。 **Zhège guójiā de rén dàduō huì shuō yìdiǎnr Yīngwén.** *Most people in this country can speak a little English.* ■ 商场里卖的衣服大多是中国制造的。 **Shāngchǎng lǐ mài de yīfu dàduō shì Zhōngguó zhìzào de.** *Most of the garments sold in shopping malls are made in China.*

dàduōshù 大多数 [modif: 大 big + 多数 majority] N great majority, overwhelming majority ■ 大多数时间这位科学家都在实验室工作。**Dàduōshù shíjiān zhè wèi kēxuéjiā dōu zài shíyànshì gōngzuò.** *Most of the time this scientist works in the lab.*

dàfang 大方 ADJ 1 generous, liberal
出手大方 chūshǒu dàfang spend money freely, very generous
2 elegant and natural
式样大方 shìyàng dàfang elegant style

dàgài 大概 I ADJ general, more or less ■ 他的话我没听清楚，但是大概的意思还是懂的。**Tā de huà wǒ méi tīng qīngchu, dànshì dàgài de yìsi háishì dǒng de.** *I did not catch his words clearly, but I understood the general idea.* II ADV probably ■ 商店大概已经关门了，你明天去吧。**Shāngdiàn dàgài yǐjīng guānmén le, nǐ míngtiān qù ba.** *The shop is probably closed. You should go tomorrow.*

dàhuì 大会 [modif: 大 big + 会 meeting] N assembly, congress, rally ■ 全国人民代表大会每年三月在北京举行会议。**Quánguó Rénmín Dàibiǎo Dàhuì měi nián Sānyuè zài Běijīng jǔxíng huìyì.** *The National People's Congress [of China] holds meetings in Beijing in March every year.*

dàhuǒr 大伙儿 PRON everybody, all the people ■ 大伙儿都说他是个好小伙子。**Dàhuǒr dōu shuō tā shì ge hǎo xiǎohuǒzi.** *Everybody says he is a good lad.* ■ 我们大伙儿一条心，一定能把事办好。**Wǒmen dàhuǒr yìtiáoxīn, yídìng néng bǎ shì bàn hǎo.** *All of us are united and we're sure to do a good job.*

NOTE: 大伙儿 **dàhuǒr** is a very colloquial word. For general use, 大家 **dàjiā** is preferred.

dàjiā 大家 PRON all, everybody ■ 既然大家都赞成这个计划，那么就执行吧。**Jìrán dàjiā dōu zànchéng zhège jìhua, nàme jiù zhíxíng ba.** *As everybody is for this plan, let's carry it out.* ■ 请大家安静一下，我有一件重要的事跟大家说。**Qǐng dàjiā ānjìng yíxià, wǒ yǒu yí jiàn zhòngyào de shì gēn dàjiā shuō.** *Please be quiet, everybody. I've something important to say to you all.*
我们大家 wǒmen dàjiā all of us / 你们大家 nǐmen dàjiā all of you / 他们大家 tāmen dàjiā all of them

dàjiē 大街 [modif: 大 big + 街 street] N main street
逛大街 guàng dàjiē take a stroll in the streets, do window-shopping

dàliàng 大量 ADJ a large amount of, a large number of ■ 每年夏季大量大学毕业生进入人才市场。**Měi nián xiàjì dàliàng dàxué bìyèshēng jìnrù réncái shìchǎng.** *In summer every year, large numbers of graduates enter the labor market.* ■ 人们可以从英特网获取大量信息。**Rénmen kěyǐ cóng yīngtèwǎng huòqǔ dàliàng xìnxī.** *People can obtain a great deal of information from the Internet.*

dàlù 大陆 [modif: 大 big + 陆 land] N continent, mainland ■ 亚洲大陆是世界上人口最多的地方。**Yàzhōu dàlù shì shìjiè shang rénkǒu zuì duō de dìfang.** *The Asian continent is the most populated place in the world.*

dàmǐ 大米 [modif: 大 big + 米 rice] N rice ■ 日本每年消费大量大米。**Rìběn měi nián xiāofèi dàliàng dàmǐ.** *Japan consumes a large quantity of rice every year.*

dàpī 大批 [modif: 大 big + 批 batch] ADJ a large quantity of, lots of ■ 大批农民离开农村，到城市找工作。**Dàpī nóngmín líkāi nóngcūn, dào chéngshì zhǎo gōngzuò.** *Large numbers of peasants leave their villages to seek jobs in cities.*

dàren 大人 [modif: 大 big + 人 person] N adult, grown-up (ANTONYM 小孩儿 xiǎoháir) ■ 小孩儿都希望很快变成大人。**Xiǎoháir dōu xīwàng hěn kuài biànchéng dàren.** *Children all hope to become adults very soon. (→ All children hope to grow up quickly.)* ■ 你已经是大人了，怎么还和孩子一样？**Nǐ yǐjīng shì dàren le, zěnme hái hé háizi yíyàng?** *You're a grown-up. How can you behave like a child?*

NOTE: 大人 **dàren** is a colloquialism. The general word for *adult* is 成年人 **chéngnián rén**.

dà rénwù 大人物 N great personage, big shot, very important person (VIP)

dàshà 大厦 N big, imposing building (座 zuò)

dàshēng 大声 [modif: 大 big + 声 sound, voice] ADJ in a loud voice ■ 请你大声点，我听不清。**Qǐng nǐ dàshēng diǎn, wǒ tīng bu qīng.** *Speak up, please. I can hardly hear you.*

dàshǐ 大使 ambassador
中国驻美国大使 Zhōngguó zhù Měiguó dàshǐ Chinese ambassador to the US

dàshǐguǎn 大使馆 [modif: 大 big + 使 envoy + 馆 house] N embassy ■ 你有英国大使馆的电话号码吗？**Nǐ yǒu Yīngguó dàshǐguǎn de diànhuà hàomǎ ma?** *Do you have the telephone number of the British embassy?*

dàshì 大事 N matter of importance

dàsì 大肆 ADV wantonly, without restraint

dàtǐ 大体 N on the whole, in the main
大体来说 dàtǐ láishuō on the whole

dàxiàng 大象 N elephant (头 tóu) ■ 小孩子都喜欢大象。**Xiǎoháizi dōu xǐhuan dàxiàng.** *Children are all fond of elephants.*

dàxiǎo 大小 [comp: 大 big + 小 small] N size ■ 你知道那间房间的大小吗？**Nǐ zhīdào nà jiān fángjiān de dàxiǎo ma?** *Do you know the size of the room?*

Note: 大 **dà** and 小 **xiǎo** are opposites. Put together, 大小 **dàxiǎo** means *size*. There are other Chinese nouns made up of antonyms, e.g. 高矮 **gāo'ǎi** *height*, 长短 **chángduǎn** *length*, 好坏 **hǎohuài** *quality*.

dàxíng 大型 [modif: 大 big + 型 model] ADJ large-scale, large-sized ■ 今年十月这个城市要举行一个大型汽车展览会。**Jīnnián Shíyuè zhège chéngshì yào jǔxíng yí ge dàxíng qìchē zhǎnlǎnhuì.** *In October this year a large-scale auto show will be held in this city.*

dàxué 大学 [modif: 大 big + 学 school] N university (座 zuò, 所 suǒ) ■ 这座大学很有名。**Zhè zuò dàxué hěn yǒumíng.** *This university is well known.* ■ 你们国家有多少所大学？**Nǐmen guójiā yǒu duōshǎo suǒ dàxué?** *How many universities are there in your country?*

考大学 kǎo dàxué sit for the university entrance examination / 考上大学 kǎo shàng dàxué pass the university entrance examination / 上大学 shàng dàxué go to university, study in a university

dàyángzhōu 大洋洲 [modif: 大 big + 洋 ocean + 洲 continent] N Oceania ■ 新西兰在大洋洲。**Xīnxīlán zài Dàyángzhōu.** *New Zealand is in Oceania.*

dàyī 大衣 [modif: 大 big + 衣 clothes, coat] N overcoat ■ 今天很冷，外出要穿大衣，戴帽子。**Jīntiān hěn lěng, wàichū yào chuān dàyī, dài màozi.** *It's cold today. You need to wear an overcoat and a hat when going out.*

dàyì 大意 [modif: 大 major + 意 meaning] N rough idea, summary

dàyuē 大约 ADV approximately, about, nearly ■ 昨天下午大约四点钟有人给你打电话。**Zuótiān xiàwǔ dàyuē sì diǎnzhōng yǒu rén gěi nǐ dǎ diànhuà.** *Someone telephoned you at about four o'clock yesterday afternoon.*

dàzhì 大致 ADV roughly, generally

dāi 呆 I ADJ foolish, stupid ■ 她很呆，竟会相信这个广告。**Tā hěn dāi, jìng huì xiāngxìn zhège guǎnggào.** *It is foolish of her to believe the commercial.* II V same as 待 **dāi**

dāi 待 V stay ■ 我这次来只待两三天。**Wǒ zhè cì lái zhǐ dāi liǎng-sān tiān.** *For this visit I'll stay only a couple of days.*

dǎi 歹 ADJ bad, evil (ANTONYM 好 **hǎo**)

dǎitú 歹徒 [modif: 歹 bad + 徒 man] N bad guy, criminal

dàifu 大夫 N same as 医生 **yīshēng**, used more as a colloquialism. (位 **wèi**)

dài 代¹ V take the place of, perform on behalf of ■ 这件事你得亲自做，别人不能代你做。**Zhè jiàn shì nǐ děi qīnzì zuò, biérén bù néng dài nǐ zuò.** *You must do it by yourself; nobody can do it on your behalf.*

代课老师 dàikè lǎoshī substitute teacher / 代校长 / 代部长 dài xiàozhǎng / dài bùzhǎng acting principal / acting minister

dài 代² N 1 generation ■ 李家在这个村子里住了好几代了。**Lǐ jiā zài zhège cūnzi li zhùle hǎo jǐ dài le.** *The Lis have been living in this village for generations.* 2 dynasty ■ 唐代中国是当时世界上最强大的国家。**Táng dài Zhōngguó shì dāngshí shìjiè shang zuì qiángdà de guójiā.** *China in the Tang Dynasty was the most powerful country in the world at that time.*

NOTE: The major Chinese dynasties are 秦 **Qín**, 汉 **Hàn**, 唐 **Táng**, 宋 **Sòng**, 元 **Yuán**, 明 **Míng**, 清 **Qīng**.

dàibiǎo 代表 [comp: 代 substitute + 表 manifest] V & N represent, indicate; representative ■ 这只是他个人的意见，不代表公司的立场。**Zhè zhǐ shì tā gèrén de yìjiàn, bú dàibiǎo gōngsī de lìchǎng.** *This is only his personal opinion, which does not represent the view of the company.* ■ 谁是你们的代表？**Shuí shì nǐmen de dàibiǎo?** *Who is your representative?*

dàijià 代价 [modif: 代 substitute + 价 price] N price (for achieving something), cost ■ 她为了实现自己的抱负，付出了很大的代价。**Tā wèile shíxiàn zìjǐ de bàofù, fùchū le hěn dà de dàijià.** *She paid a high price for achieving her ambition.*

dàilǐ 代理 [modif: 代 perform on behalf of + 理 manage] V act on behalf of, act as an agent
代理人 dàilǐrén agent

dàitì 代替 V substitute for, replace, instead of ■ 这次家长会你爸爸妈妈一定要出席，不能请人代替。**Zhè cì jiāzhǎnghuì nǐ bàba māma yídìng yào chūxí, bù néng qǐng rén dàitì.** *Your parents must attend this parents' meeting and nobody can go on their behalf.*

dài 贷 TRAD 貸 V loan

dàikuǎn 贷款 [modif: 贷 loan + 款 fund] V & N loan money to, borrow money from; loan
贷款给一家小企业 dàikuǎn gěi yìjiā xiǎo qǐyè loan money to a small business / 向银行贷款 xiàng yínháng dàikuǎn ask the bank for a loan / 无息贷款 wúxīdàikuǎn interest-free loan

dài 带 TRAD 帶 V bring, take ■ 出去旅游，别忘了照相机。**Chūqù lǚyóu, bié wàngle dài zhàoxiàngjī.** *Don't forget to bring along your camera when you go out sightseeing.* ■ 明天上课的时候，把词典带来。**Míngtiān shàngkè de shíhou, bǎ cídiǎn dàilai.** *Please bring your dictionary with you when you come to class tomorrow.*

带来/带 … 来 dàilai/dài … lái bring … / 带去/带 … 去 dàiqu/dài … qù take … ■ …你不知道图书馆在哪儿？我带你去。**Nǐ bù zhīdào túshūguǎn zài nǎr? Wǒ dài nǐ qù.** *You don't know where the library is? I'll take you there.*

dàilǐng 带领 [comp: 带 lead, head + 领 lead, head] V lead, guide

dài 待 V treat, deal with ■ 他待朋友很热心。**Tā dài péngyou hěn rèxīn.** *He is warmhearted in dealing with friends.* ■ 人家怎么待我，我就怎么待人家。**Rénjiā zěnme dài wǒ, wǒ jiù zěnme dài rénjiā.** *I treat people the way they treat me.*

dàiyù 待遇 **N 1** treatment ■ 代表团受到了贵宾待遇。**Dàibiǎotuán shòudào le guì bīn dàiyù.** *The delegation was given VIP treatment.* **2** remuneration ■ 这个职务责任非常重，但是待遇很好。**Zhège zhíwù zérèn fēicháng zhòng, dànshì dàiyù hěn hǎo.** *This position carries heavy responsibilities, but is highly paid.*

dài 袋 **N** sack, bag ■ 他带了一个大袋子来装书。**Tā dàile yí ge dà dàizi lái zhuāng shū.** *He brought a big bag for books.*
口袋 **kǒudài** pocket

NOTE: 袋 **dài** is seldom used alone. It is either used with the nominal suffix 子 **zi** to form 袋子 **dài zi**, or with another noun to form a compound word, e.g. 口袋 **kǒudài** (pocket).

dài 戴 **V** wear, put on ■ 外面很冷，戴上帽子吧！**Wàimiàn hěn lěng, dàishang màozi ba!** *It's cold outside. Do put on your cap.*
戴手套儿 **dài shǒutàor** wear gloves / 戴眼镜 **dài yǎnjìng** wear spectacles

dài 怠 **ADJ** idle, slack

dàimàn 怠慢 [comp: 怠 slack + 慢 slight] **V** slight, give the cold shoulder to

dài 逮 **V** catch

dàibǔ 逮捕 [comp: 逮 arrest + 捕 capture] **V** arrest, take into custody ■ 已经有两名高级官员因受贿被逮捕。**Yǐjīng yǒu liǎng míng gāojí guānyuán yīn shòuhuì bèi dàibǔ.** *Two senior officials have already been arrested for taking bribes.*

dān 单 **TRAD** 單 **ADJ** single, separate ■ 他不习惯和别人合住，一定要单住一个房间。**Tā bù xíguàn hé biérén hé zhù, yídìng yào dān zhù yí ge fángjiān.** *He is not used to sharing a room with another person and insists on having a room to himself.*

dānchún 单纯 [comp: 单 single + 纯 pure] **ADJ** simple-minded, ingenuous

dāncí 单词 [modif: 单 single + 词 word] **N** word ■ 光学单词用处不大，一定要把单词放在句子中学。**Guāng xué dāncí yòngchu bú dà, yídìng yào bǎ dāncí fàng zài jùzi zhōng xué.** *Learning words in insolation is not very useful. You must learn words in sentences.*

dāndiào 单调 [modif: 单 single + 调 tone] **ADJ** monotonous

dāndú 单独 [comp: 单 single + 独 alone] **ADJ** alone, on one's own ■ 经过半年培训，她能单独工作了。**Jīngguò bànnián péixùn, tā néng dāndú gōngzuò le.** *After six months' training, she can now work all by herself.*

dānqīn jiātíng 单亲家庭 **N** single-parent family

dānrén chuáng 单人床 **N** single bed

dānrén fángjiān 单人房间 **N** (hotel) room for a single person

dānshù 单数 **N** odd number

dānwèi 单位 **N** work unit, e.g. a factory, a school, a government department ■ 你是哪个单位的？**Nǐ shì nǎge dānwèi de?** *Which work unit do you belong to?*

dānyuán 单元 **N** unit (in an apartment house), apartment, flat

dān 担 **TRAD** 擔 **V** carry on the shoulder, take on

dānbǎo 担保 [comp: 担 shoulder + 保 guarantee] **V** gurantee, vouch for
担保人 **dānbǎorén** guarantor

dānrèn 担任 [comp: 担 shoulder + 任 act as] **V** assume the office of, act in the capacity of ■ 今年谁担任我们的中文老师？**Jīnnián shuí dānrèn wǒmen de Zhōngwén lǎoshī?** *Who'll be our Chinese teacher this year?* ■ 政府邀请这位大学校长担任教育部长。**Zhèngfǔ yāoqíng zhè wèi dàxué xiàozhǎng dānrèn jiàoyù bùzhǎng.** *The government has invited this university president to be Minister of Education.*

dānxīn 担心 **V** worry ■ 他担心考试不及格。**Tā dānxīn kǎoshì bù jígé.** *He is worried that he may fail the exam.* ■ 我为爸爸的身体担心。**Wǒ wèi bàba de shēntǐ dānxīn.** *I'm worried about daddy's health.*

dān 耽 **V** delay

dānwù 耽误 [comp: 耽 delay + 误 miss] **V** delay ■ 你们没有按时交货，耽误了我们的生产。**Nǐmen méiyǒu ànshí jiāohuò, dānwùle wǒmen de shēngchǎn.** *Your failure to deliver the goods on time has delayed our production.* ■ 有病得马上看，不要耽误。**Yǒubìng děi mǎshàng kàn, búyào dānwù.** *If you are sick you should go to see a doctor immediately. Don't delay.*

dǎn 胆 **TRAD** 膽 **N 1** gall bladder **2** courage

NOTE: Ancient Chinese believed that the gall bladder determined one's courage and bravery—the bigger the gall bladder, the more courage.

dǎndà 胆大 **ADJ** brave, bold

dǎnliàng 胆量 [modif: 胆 courage + 量 amount] **N** courage, guts
试试他的胆量 **shìshi tāde dǎnliàng** test his courage, see how brave he is.

dǎnqiè 胆怯 **ADJ** timid, coward

dǎnxiǎo 胆小 **ADJ** timid, coward

dǎxiǎo guǐ 胆小鬼 **N** coward

dǎnzi 胆子 **N** courage
胆子大 **dǎnzidà** same as 胆大 **dǎndà** / 胆子小 **dǎnzixiǎo** same as 胆小 **dǎnxiǎo**

dàn 旦 **N** dawn, morning (See **yuándàn** 元旦.)

dàn 但 **CONJ** same as 但是 **dànshì**. Used in writing.

dànshì 但是 **CONJ** but, yet ■ 这种产品价格很低，但是质量不好。**Zhè zhǒng chǎnpǐn jiàgé hěn dī, dànshì zhìliàng bù hǎo.** *This product is cheap but is of low quality.* ■ 这个女孩子长得很漂亮，但是大家都不喜欢她。**Zhège nǚháizi zhǎng de hěn**

piàoliang, dànshì dàjiā dōu bù xǐhuan tā. *This girl is quite pretty, but nobody likes her.*

dàn 淡 ADJ **1** not salty, tasteless, bland ■ 汤太淡了，得放些盐。 **Tāng tài dàn le, děi fàng xie yán.** *The soup is tasteless. Put some salt in it.* **2** weak (of tea, coffee) (ANTONYM 浓 **nóng**) ■ 茶淡一点儿好，我喝浓茶睡不着。 **Chá dàn yìdiǎnr hǎo, wǒ hē nóngchá shuì bu zháo.** *I prefer weak tea. I can't fall asleep after drinking strong tea.*

dànjì 淡季 N slack season

dànshuǐ 淡水 N fresh water, sweet water

dàn 蛋 N egg (especially chicken egg) ■ 他每天早上吃一个蛋。 **Tā měi tiān zǎoshàng chī yí ge dàn.** *He eats an egg every morning.* ■ 鸡蛋营养丰富。 **Jīdàn yíngyǎng fēngfù.** *Eggs are very nutritious.*

dànbáizhì 蛋白质 [modif: 蛋白 egg white + 质 substance] N protein

dàngāo 蛋糕 [modif: 蛋 egg + 糕 cake] N (western-style) cake ■ 你饿吗？先吃点蛋糕当点心吧。 **Nǐ è ma? Xiān chī diǎn dàngāo dàng diǎnxīn ba.** *Are you hungry? Have some cake for a snack.*

dàn 诞 TRAD 誕 V be born

dànchén 诞辰 [modif: 诞 be born + 辰 time] N (of great men and women) birthday ■ 十二月二十五日是耶稣基督的诞辰。 **Shí'èryuè èrshí wǔ rì shì Yēsū Jīdū de dànchén.** *December 25 is the birthday of Jesus Christ.*

dànshēng 诞生 [comp: 诞 be born + 生 be born] V be born

dàn 弹 TRAD 彈 N bullet (See **zǐdàn** 子弹.)

dāng 当¹ TRAD 當 PREP at the time of, when ■ 当他赶到火车站，火车已经开走了。 **Dāng tā gǎndào huǒchēzhàn, huǒchē yǐjīng kāizǒu le.** *When he hurried to the railway station, the train had already left.*

dāng 当² TRAD 當 V work as, serve as ■ "你长大了想当什么？" "我想当医生。" **"Nǐ zhǎngdàle xiǎng dāng shénme?" "Wǒ xiǎng dāng yīshēng."** *"What do you want to be when you grow up?" "I'd like to be a doctor."*

dāng ... de shíhou 当 ... 的时候 CONJ when ... ■ 当我在工作的时候，不希望别人来打扰我。 **Dāng wǒ zài gōngzuò de shíhou, bù xīwàng biérén lái dǎrǎo wǒ.** *When I am working, I don't want to be disturbed.* ■ 当我认识她的时候，她正在一家医院当护士。 **Dāng wǒ rènshi tā de shíhou, tā zhèngzài yì jiā yīyuàn dāng hùshi.** *When I came to know her, she was working as a nurse in a hospital.*

NOTE: 当 **dāng** may be omitted, especially colloquially, e.g. 我在工作的时候，不希望别人来打扰我。 **Wǒ zài gōngzuò de shíhou, bù xīwàng biérén lái dárǎo wǒ.**

dāngchǎng 当场 N on the spot
当场抓获 dāngchǎng zhuāhuò catch red-handed

dāngchū 当初 N originally, at the outset

dāngdài 当代 N contemporary era, present-day

dāngdì 当地 N at the place in question, local
当地人 dāngdì rén a local / 当地时间 dāngdì shíjiān local time

dāngjú 当局 N the authorities

dāngmiàn 当面 ADV to someone's face; in the very presence of
当面撒谎 dāngmiàn sāhuǎng tell a barefaced lie

dāngnián 当年 N in those years, then ■ 想当年，亲戚朋友之间主要靠写信联系。哪有什么电子邮件？ **Xiǎng dāngnián, qīnqi péngyou zhī jiān zhǔyào kào xiě xìn liánxì. Nǎyǒu shénme diànzǐ yóujiàn?** *In those years, relatives and friends mainly relied on letter-writing to keep in touch with each other. How could there be e-mail? (→ There was no such thing as e-mail.)*

dāngqián 当前 N at present, now ■ 王经理向我们介绍了当前市场情况。 **Wáng jīnglǐ xiàng wǒmen jièshàole dāngqián shìchǎng qíngkuàng.** *Mr Wang, the manager, briefed us on the current marketing situation.*

dāngrán 当然 ADJ of course ■ 他们受到这么热情的招待，当然很高兴。 **Tāmen shòudào zhème rèqíng de zhāodài, dāngrán hěn gāoxìng.** *They were of course delighted to be received so warmly.* ■ "你到了北京别忘了给我发一份电子邮件。" "那当然，忘不了。" **"Nǐ dàole Běijīng bié wàngle gěi wǒ fā yí fèn diànzǐ yóujiàn." "Nà dāngrán, wàng bu liǎo."** *"Don't forget to send me an e-mail when you arrive in Beijing." "Of course, I won't forget."*

dāngshí 当时 N at that time, then ■ 当时我没有想到这一点。 **Dāngshí wǒ méiyǒu xiǎngdào zhè yìdiǎn.** *At that time I missed this point.*

dāngshìrén 当事人 N person/people concerned; party (to a lawsuit)

dāngwùzhījí 当务之急 N the most pressing matter of the moment, top priority

dāngxīn 当心 V be cautious, take care

dāngxuǎn 当选 V be elected
当选为代表 dāngxuǎn wéi dàibiǎo be elected a delegate

dǎng 党 TRAD 黨 N political party ■ 他不参加任何党。 **Tā bù cānjiā rènhé dǎng.** *He does not join any party.*

NOTE: 党 **dǎng** in China usually refers to 中国共产党 **Zhōngguó Gòngchǎn Dǎng** the Chinese Communist Party.

dǎngyuán 党员 [modif: 党 party + 员 member] N party member ■ 在中国重要官员几乎都是中国共产党党员。 **Zài Zhōngguó zhòngyào guānyuán jīhū dōu shì Zhōngguó Gòngchǎn Dǎng dǎngyuán.** *In China almost all important officials are members of the Chinese Communist Party.*

dǎng 挡 TRAD 擋 v block, keep off ■ 记者被挡在门外。 *Jìzhě bèi dǎng zài ménwài. The reporters were barred from the house.*

dàng 当 TRAD 當 v 1 treat as, regard as ■ 他非常节省，一块钱当两块钱用。 *Tā fēicháng jiéshěng, yí kuài qián dàng liǎng kuài qián yòng. He is very thrifty and wishes he could make one dollar go twice as far.* 2 think ■ 你中文说得这么好，我还当你是中国人呢！ *Nǐ Zhōngwén shuōde zhème hǎo, wǒ hái dàng nǐ shì Zhōngguórén ne! You speak Chinese so well that I thought you were a Chinese!*

dàngzuò 当做 v treat as, regard as ■ 我一直把他当做好朋友。 *Wǒ yìzhí bǎ tā dàngzuò hǎo péngyou. I always regard him as a good friend.*

dàng 档 TRAD 檔 N shelf

dàng'àn 档案 N archive, file

dàngcì 档次 N grade, class

dàng 荡 TRAD 蕩 v swing, sway (See **dòngdàng** 动荡.)

dāo 刀 N knife (把 **bǎ**) ■ "我可以借用一下你的刀吗？" "可以。" *"Wǒ kěyǐ jièyòng yíxià nǐ de dāo ma?" "Kěyǐ." "May I use your knife?" "Yes."*
铅笔刀 qiānbǐ dāo pencil sharpener / 水果刀 shuǐguǒ dāo penknife

dāozi 刀子 [suffix: 刀 knife + 子 nominal suffix] N same as 刀 **dāo**

dǎo 导 TRAD 導 v lead, guide

dǎodàn 导弹 [modif: 导 guided + 弹 bullet] N guided missile [枚 **méi**]

dǎoháng 导航 [modif: 导 guided + 航 navigation] N navigation (by electronic device)

dǎoxiàng 导向 v lead (to), guide

dǎoyǎn 导演 [modif: 导 guiding + 演 acting] V & N direct (a film or play); director (of films or plays) ■ 这部电影是谁导演的？ *Zhè bù diànyǐng shì shéi dǎoyǎn de? Who directed this movie?*
名导演 míng dǎoyǎn famous director

dǎoyóu 导游 [modif: 导 guide + 游 tourism] N tourist guide

dǎozhì 导致 v lead to, cause

dǎo 岛 TRAD 島 N island ■ 新西兰有两个大岛：南岛和北岛。 *Xīnxīlán yǒu liǎng ge dà dǎo: nán dǎo hé běi dǎo. New Zealand has two big islands: South Island and North Island.*

dǎoyǔ 岛屿 [comp: 岛 island + 屿 small island] N island, islet

dǎo 捣 TRAD 搗 v beat, smash

dǎodàn 捣蛋 v make trouble (in a mischievous way)
故意捣蛋 gùyì dǎodàn be deliberately mischievous

dǎoluàn 捣乱 v make trouble, sabotage
捣乱公共秩序 dǎoluàn gōnggòng zhìxù disrupt public order

dào 悼 v mourn (See **zhuīdào** 追悼.)

dǎo 倒 v fall, topple ■ 风大极了，把很多树都刮倒了。 *Fēng dà jíle, bǎ hěn duō shù dōu guā dǎo le. The winds were so strong that many trees were blown down.*

dǎobì 倒闭 [comp: 倒 go bust + 闭 close down] v go bust, close down

dǎoméi 倒霉 v have bad luck, be out of luck

dào 到 v arrive, come to; up to ■ 北京来的飞机什么时候到？ *Běijīng lái de fēijī shénme shíhou dào? When will the flight from Beijing arrive?* ■ 我们已经学到第十八课了。 *Wǒmen yǐjīng xué dào dìshíbā kè le. We've studied up to Lesson 18.*

dàochù 到处 ADV everywhere ■ 王老师家里到处都是书。 *Wáng lǎoshī jiā li dàochù dōu shì shū. There are books everywhere in Teacher Wang's home.* ■ 他到处游览名胜古迹。 *Tā dàochù yóulǎn míngshèng gǔjì. He visits well-known scenic spots and historical sites everywhere.*

NOTE: 到处 **dàochù** is always placed before a verb phrase, and is often followed by 都 **dōu**.

dàodá 到达 [comp: 到 get to + 达 reach] v arrive, reach ■ 张部长乘坐的飞机将在晚上六点三刻到达北京机场。 *Zhāng bùzhǎng chéngzuò de fēijī jiāng zài wǎnshang liù diǎn sān kè dàodá Běijīng jīchǎng. The airplane Minister Zhang is traveling in will arrive at Beijing Airport at 6:45.*

dàodǐ 到底 [v+obj: 到 get to + 底 bottom] ADV 1 in the end, finally ■ 她到底还是找到了理想的丈夫。 *Tā dàodǐ háishì zhǎodàole lǐxiǎng de zhàngfu. Finally she found her ideal husband.* 2 after all (used in a question) ■ 你到底去不去啊？ *Nǐ dàodǐ qù bu qù a? Are you going or not?* ■ 他到底想要什么？ *Tā dàodǐ xiǎng yào shénme? What does he want after all?*

dào 倒[1] v 1 put upside down ■ 他把画挂倒了。 *Tā bǎ huà guà dào le. He hung the picture upside down.* 2 pour (water), make (tea) ■ 她给客人倒了一杯水。 *Tā gěi kèrén dàole yì bēi shuǐ. She gave the visitor a glass of water.*

dào 倒[2] ADV contrary to what may be expected (used before a verb or an adjective to indicate an unexpected action or state) ■ 弟弟倒比哥哥高。 *Dìdi dào bǐ gēge gāo. The younger brother is unexpectedly taller than his elder brother.* ■ 用了电脑人们倒好象更忙了。 *Yòngle diànnǎo rénmen dào hǎoxiàng gèng máng le. With the use of computers people seem to be busier.*

dào 盗 N robber, bandit

dàoqiè 盗窃 [comp: 盗 rob + 窃 steal] v steal, embezzle, commit larceny
盗窃犯 dàoqièfàn thief, larcener

dào 道[1] N way, path

dàodé 道德 [modif: 道 the way + 德 virtue] N moral, ethics ■ 赚钱也要讲道德。 *Zhuànqián yě yào jiǎng dàodé. When making money you should also pay attention to ethics.*

不道德 bú dàodé immoral ■ 这样做是不道德
的。**Zhèyàng zuò shì bú dàodé de.** *Such conduct
is immoral.*

dàolǐ 道理 [comp: 道 way, principle + 理 pattern,
reason] **N** principle, reason, hows and whys ■ 这
个道理人人都懂。**Zhège dàolǐ rénrén dōu dǒng.**
*Everybody understands this principle. (→ Every-
body understands why this is true/correct.)*

讲道理 jiǎng dàolǐ (of a person) reasonable ■ 他这
个人很不讲道理。**Tā zhège rén hěn bù jiǎng dàolǐ.**
This man is very unreasonable.

有道理 yǒu dàolǐ reasonable, true ■ 你说的话很
有道理。**Nǐ shuō de huà hěn yǒu dàolǐ.** *What you
said is reasonable/true.* ■ 他说得很好听，其实
没有什么道理。**Tā shuō de hěn hǎotīng, qíshí
méiyǒu shénme dàolǐ.** *He mouthed fine words but
in fact was not quite right.*

NOTE: 道 **dào** and 理 **lǐ** are two important concepts in
Chinese thought. The original meaning of 道 **dào** is
path, way. By extension it denotes *the fundamental
principle of the universe.* 理 **lǐ** originally meant *the
grain of a piece of jade* and came to mean *the un-
derlying logic of things.*

dàolù 道路 [comp: 道 way + 路 road] **N** road, path
■ 盖房子以前，先要修道路。**Gài fángzi yǐqián,
xiān yào xiū dàolù.** *Before putting up houses,
roads must be built.* ■ 车辆把前面的道路堵住
了。**Chēliàng bǎ qiánmiàn de dàolù dǔzhù le.**
Traffic has blocked the road ahead.

dào 道² **V** same as 说 **shuō**, used only in old-fashioned writing

dàoqiàn 道歉 [v+obj: 道 say + 歉 apology] **V & N**
apologize, say sorry; apology ■ 你应该向他们道
歉。**Nǐ yīnggāi xiàng tāmen dàoqiàn.** *You should
apologize to them.*

dào 道³ **MEASURE WORD 1** (for things in the shape of
a line)

一道光线 yí dào guāngxiàn a ray of sunshine
2 (for questions in school exercises, examinations,
etc.)

两道难题 liǎng dào nántí two difficult questions
dào 稻 **N** rice, paddy
dàogǔ 稻谷 **N** seeds of rice with husk on
dé 得 **V** get, obtain ■ 她去年英文考试得了A。**Tā
qùnián Yīngwén kǎoshì déle A.** *She got A for the
English examination last year.*

dé bù cháng shī 得不偿失 **IDIOM** the loss out-
weighing the gain, not worth power and shot

dédào 得到 **V** succeed in getting/obtaining ■ 他
得到一个去中国学汉语的机会。**Tā dédào yí ge qù
Zhōngguó xué Hànyǔ de jīhuì.** *He got a chance
to go to China to study Chinese.* ■ 我得到他们很
大帮助。**Wǒ dédào tāmen hěn dà bāngzhù.** *I was
greatly helped by them.*

NOTE: The verb 得 **dé** is seldom used alone. It is
often followed by 到 **dào**, grammatically a complement, to mean *get* or *obtain.*

délì 得力 **ADJ** competent and efficient, very capable

得力助手 délì zhùshǒu very capable assistant,
indispensable right-hand person

dé tiān dú hòu 得天独厚 **IDIOM** richly endowed
by nature

déyì 得意 **ADJ** complacent, deeply pleased with
oneself

得意忘形 déyì wàng xíng be dizzy with success /
得意洋洋 déyì yángyáng show extreme self-com-
placency; be elated

dézuì 得罪 **V** offend, incur displeasure

得罪不起 dézuì bùqǐ can't afford to offend

dé 德 **TRAD** 德 **N** virtue, morality (See **pǐndé** 品德,
dàodé 道德)

Déguó 德国 **N** Germany

Déwén 德文 **N** the German language (especially
the writing)

Déyǔ 德语 **N** the German language

de 的 **PARTICLE** (attached to a word or phrase to
indicate that it is an attribute. 的 **de** is normally
followed by a noun.)

我的电脑 Wǒ de diànnǎo my computer / 最新型的
电脑 zuì xīnxíng de diànnǎo the latest model computer / 学校刚买来的电脑 xuéxiào gāng mǎilai de
diànnǎo the computer that the school just bought

NOTE: 的, 得, 地 have different functions and are
three distinct words. However, as they are pronounced the same **(de)** in everyday speech, some
Chinese speakers do not distinguish them.

…**de huà**… 的话 **CONJ** if ■ 明天下雨的话，会
议就改期举行。**Míngtiān xià yǔ de huà, huìyì jiù
gǎiqī jǔxíng.** *If it rains tomorrow, we'll change the
date for the meeting.*

NOTE: See note on 要是 **yàoshì.**

de 得 **PARTICLE** (introducing a word, phrase or
clause to indicate that it is a complement. 得 **de** is
normally preceded by a verb or an adjective.)

来得很早 lái de hěn zǎo come early / 说得大家
都笑了起来 shuō de dàjiā dōu xiàole qǐlái talk in
such a way that everybody starts laughing / 贵得
很贵 guì de hěn very expensive

NOTE: See note on 的 **de.**

de 地 **PARTICLE** (attached to a word or phrase to
indicate that it is an adverbial. 地 **de** is normally
followed by a verb or an adjective.)

慢慢地说 mànman de shuō speak slowly / 愉快地
旅行 yúkuài de lǚxíng travel pleasantly

NOTE: See note on 的 **de**.

děi 得 MODAL V have to, has to ■ 时间不早了，我们得走了。**Shíjiān bù zǎo le, wǒmen děi zǒu le.** *It's quite late. We've got to go.* ■ 这件事怎么办，我们还得想个办法。**Zhè jiàn shì zěnme bàn, wǒmen hái děi xiǎng ge bànfǎ.** *We've got to find a way of dealing with this matter.*

dēng 灯 TRAD 燈 N lamp, lighting ■ 这个房间的灯坏了。**Zhège fángjiān de dēng huài le.** *The light in this room is out of order.* ■ 最后一个离开办公室的人，别忘了关灯。**Zuìhòu yí ge líkāi bàngōngshì de rén, bié wàngle guān dēng.** *The last one to leave the office, please turn off the light.*

电灯 diàndēng light, electric light / 关灯 guān dēng turn off the light / 开灯 kāi dēng turn on the light / 日光灯 rìguāng dēng fluorescent lamp / 台灯 táidēng desk lamp

dēnglóng 灯笼 N lantern

dēng 登 V publish (in a newspaper, a journal, etc.) ■ 今天各大报纸都登了这条新闻。**Jīntiān gè dà bàozhǐ dōu dēngle zhè tiáo xīnwén.** *This news is published in all the major newspapers today.*

dēngjīpái 登机牌 N boarding card

dēngjì 登记 V register, check in ■ 在旅馆里住，都要登记。**Zài lǚguǎn li zhù, dōu yào dēngjì.** *To stay in a hotel, one has to register.*

dēnglù 登陆 [v+obj: 登 go up + 陆 land] V land (from waters, especially by troops)

dēnglù 登录 V same as 登记 **dēngjì**

dēng 蹬 V pedal, treadle

děng 等¹ V wait, wait for ■ 她在等一个重要的电话。**Tā zài děng yí ge zhòngyào de diànhuà.** *She is waiting for an important telephone call.* ■ 我昨天等你等了半小时。**Wǒ zuótiān děng nǐ děngle bàn xiǎoshí.** *I waited for you for half an hour yesterday.*

děngdài 等待 [comp: 等 wait + 待 await, anticipate] V wait (usually used in writing) ■ 你不能总是等待机会，要主动寻找机会。**Nǐ bù néng zǒngshì děngdài jīhuì, yào zhǔdòng xúnzhǎo jīhuì.** *You mustn't always wait for an opportunity; you should proactively search for it.*

děng yíxià 等一下 wait a minute ■ 等一下，我马上就来。**Děng yíxià, wǒ mǎshang jiù lái.** *Wait a minute, I'll come soon.*

děng 等² N grade, rank, class ■ 我们商店只卖一等品。**Wǒmen shāngdiàn zhǐ mài yī-děng pǐn.** *Our store sells first class goods only.* (→ *We sell only the best here.*)

děngyú 等于 V be equal to, equal ■ 一加二等于三。**Yī jiā èr děngyú sān.** *One plus two equals three.*

děng 等³ PARTICLE **1** and so on and so forth, et cetera ■ 我们在中国参观了北京、上海、西安等地。**Wǒmen zài Zhōngguó cānguānle Běijīng, Shànghǎi, Xī'ān děng dì.** *In China we visited Bei-jing, Shanghai, Xi'an and other places.* **2** (used at the end of an enumeration) ■ 我们在中国游览了北京、上海、西安等三个大城市。**Wǒmen zài Zhōngguó yóulǎn le Běijīng, Shànghǎi, Xī'ān děng sānge dà chéngshì.** *We toured the three major cit-ies of Beijing, Shanghai and Xi'an.*

dī 低 ADJ & V low (ANTONYM 高 **gāo**); lower ■ 这把椅子太低了，坐着不舒服。**Zhè ba yǐzi tài dī le, zuòzhe bù shūfu.** *This chair is too low; it's un-comfortable to sit in.* ■ 他低着头，离开校长办公室。**Tā dīzhe tóu, líkāi xiàozhǎng bàngōngshì.** *He left the principal's office with his head hung low.*

dī 滴 MEASURE WORD drop (used with liquids) ■ 节约每一滴水。**Jiéyuē měi yì dī shuǐ.** *Save every drop of water.*

dī 堤 N dyke, embankment

dībà 堤坝 N dyke, embankment

díquè 的确 ADV really, truly ■ 这个名胜的确美丽。**Zhège míngshèng díquè měilì.** *This well-known scenic spot is truly beautiful.*

dí 敌 TRAD 敵 N enemy

dírén 敌人 [modif: 敌 enemy + 人 person, people] N enemy ■ 我想我在公司里没有敌人。**Wǒ xiǎng wǒ zài gōngsī li méiyǒu dírén.** *I don't think I have any enemies in the company.* ■ 吸烟是健康的敌人。**Xīyān shì jiànkāng de dírén.** *Smoking is an enemy of health.*

díshì 敌视 [modif: 敌 enemy + 视 view] V be hos-tile to

dǐ 底 N base, bottom

dǐxia 底下 [comp: 底 bottom + 下 under] N under-neath, under ■ 床底下有一双拖鞋。**Chuáng dǐxia yǒu yì shuāng tuōxié.** *There's a pair of slippers un-der the bed.* ■ 孩子躲在桌子底下。**Háizi duǒ zài zhuōzi dǐxia.** *The child hid under the table.*

dǐ 抵 V **1** arrive **2** resist

dǐdá 抵达 [comp: 抵 arrive + 达 reach] V arrive at

dǐkàng 抵抗 [comp: 抵 arrive + 抗 resist] V resist

dǐzhì 抵制 V boycott, reject

dì 地 N earth, ground

dìbù 地步 N **1** extent **2** (poor) condition

dìdào 地道 [modif: 地 ground + 道 way] N tunnel, underpass (条 tiáo) ■ 请走地道 **Qǐng zǒu dìdào** *Please use the underpass.*

dìdiǎn 地点 [comp: 地 place + 点 point] N the place of an event or activity, venue ■ 会议的地点还没有定。**Huìyì de dìdiǎn hái méiyǒu dìng.** *The venue of the meeting has not been decided on.*

dìfang 地方 [comp: 地 earth + 方 place] N **1** place, location, area (个 gè) ■ 你住在什么地方？**Nǐ zhù zài shénme dìfang?** *Where do you live?* ■ 他们正在找开会的地方。**Tāmen zhèngzài zhǎo kāihuì de dìfang.** *They're looking for a venue for their con-ference.* **2** part of, aspect ■ 这本书我有些地方不大明白。**Zhè běn shū wǒ yǒuxie dìfang búdà míng-bai.** *I'm not quite clear about parts of the book.*

NOTE: 地方 **dìfang** is a word of wide application. It has both concrete, specific senses and abstract, general senses, as in the following examples: ■ 医生：你什么地方不舒服？**Yīshēng: Nǐ shénme dìfang bù shūfu?** *Doctor: What spot ails you? (→ What's wrong with you?)* ■ 照顾不到的地方，请多多原谅。**Zhàogù búdào de dìfang, qǐng duōduō yuánliàng.** *If there's anything not well attended to, please accept my sincere apology.*

dìlǐ 地理 **N** geography
国家地理学会 Guójiā Dìlǐ Xuéhuì **National Geographic Society** / 地理学 dìlǐxué **geography** / 地理学家 dìlǐxué jiā **geographer**

dìmiàn 地面 **N** the earth's surface ■ 这里的地面比海平面高出二百公尺。**Zhèli de dìmiàn bǐ hǎipíngmiàn gāochū èrbǎi gōngchǐ.** *The ground here is 200 meters above sea level.*

dìqiú 地球 [modif: 地 ground + 球 ball] **N** the earth ■ 人类只有一个家园 — 地球。**Rénlèi zhǐ yǒu yí ge jiāyuán – dìqiú.** *Mankind has only one home—the earth.*

dìqū 地区 [modif: 地 place + 区 region] **N** region, area ■ 这个国家东部地区比西部地区发达。**Zhège guójiā dōngbù dìqū bǐ xībù dìqū fādá.** *In this country, the eastern regions are more developed than the western regions.*

dìshì 地势 **N** physical feature of a place, terrain

dìtǎn 地毯 [modif: 地 ground + 毯 blanket] **N** carpet (张 zhāng)

dìtiě 地铁 **N** underground railway, subway

dìtú 地图 **N** map (张 zhāng) ■ 这张地图太旧了，没多大用处。**Zhè zhāng dìtú tài jiù le, méi duō dà yòngchu.** *This map is too old and is not of much use.*

dìtúcè 地图册 **N** atlas

dìwèi 地位 [comp: 地 place + 位 seat] **N** status, position ■ 他在公司里有很高的地位。**Tā zài gōngsī li yǒu hěn gāo de dìwèi.** *He holds a high position in the company.*

dìxià 地下 [modif: 地 ground + 下 under] **N** underground
地下商场 dìxià shāngchǎng **underground shopping center** / 地下铁路（地铁）dìxià tiělù (dìtiě) **underground railway, subway** / 地下停车场 dìxià tíngchēchǎng **parking garage, underground car park**

dìzhèn 地震 [modif: 地 earth + 震 quake] **N** earthquake, seism (场 cháng) ■ 在南太平洋发生了里氏六级地震。**Zài nán Tàipíngyáng fāshēng le Lǐ shì liù jí dìzhèn.** *An earthquake, measured as 6 on the Richter scale, occurred in the South Pacific Ocean.*

dìzhǐ 地址 **N** address ■ 这是我的地址和电话号码，请你记一下。**Zhè shi wǒ de dìzhǐ he diànhuà hàomǎ, qǐng nǐ jì yíxia.** *Here are my address and telephone number. Please write them down.*

dìzhì 地质 **N** geology
地质调查 dìzhìdiàochá **geological survey** / 地质学 dìzhìxué **geology** / 地质学家 dìzhìxuéjiā **geologist**

dì 弟 **N** younger brother

dìdi 弟弟 **N** younger brother ■ 我弟弟比我小两岁。**Wǒ dìdi bǐ wǒ xiǎo liǎng suì.** *My younger brother is two years younger than me.* ■ "你有没有弟弟？" "没有，我只有一个哥哥。**"Nǐ yǒu méiyǒu dìdi?" "Méiyǒu, wǒ zhǐ yǒu yī ge gēge."** *"Do you have a younger brother?" "No, I only have an older brother."*

dì 递 **TRAD** 遞 **V** hand over, pass on ■ 请你把那本词典递给我。**Qǐng nǐ bǎ nà běn cídiǎn dì gěi wǒ.** *Please pass me that dictionary.*
快递 kuàidì **fast delivery (of mail)** / 快递服务 kuàidì fúwù **fast delivery service**

dìzēng 递增 **V** increase progressively

dì 帝 **N** the Supreme Being (See huángdì 皇帝.)

dì 第 **PREF** (used before a number to form an ordinal numeral)
第一 dì-yī **the first** / 第一天 dì-yī tiān **the first day** / 第十 dì-shí **the tenth** / 第十课 dì-shí kè **the tenth lesson, Lesson 10**

diān 颠 **TRAD** 顛 **V** bump, jolt

diānbǒ 颠簸 [comp: 颠 bump + 簸 jerk] **V** bump, bump along

diāndǎo 颠倒 **V** turn upside down, reverse
颠倒黑白 diāndǎo hēibái **confound black and white, confuse right and wrong**

diǎn 点¹ **TRAD** 點 **N 1** drop, point, dot ■ 雨点打在窗户上。**Yǔdiǎn dǎ zài chuānghu shang.** *Raindrops beat on the windowpane.* ■ "点" 字下面有四点。**"Diǎn" zì xiàmian yǒu sì diǎn.** *There're four dots at the bottom of the character 点.*
墨点 mò diǎn **ink stain** / 水点 shuǐ diǎn **water stain** **2** (indicating decimal)
三点四 sān diǎn sì **3.4 (three point four)** / 十二点三五 shí'èr diǎn sān wǔ **12.35 (twelve point three five)**

diǎn 点² **TRAD** 點 **V** drip, put a dot, touch ■ 你给我点眼药水，行吗？**Nǐ gěi wǒ diǎn yǎnyàoshuǐ, xíng ma?** *Could you please put my eye drops in for me?*

diǎn 点³ **TRAD** 點 **MEASURE WORD** a little, a bit ■ 他喜欢在睡觉前喝一点儿酒。**Tā xǐhuan zài shuìjiào qián hē yìdiǎnr jiǔ.** *He likes to drink a little wine before going to bed.*
有（一）点儿… yǒu (yì) diǎnr… **a bit…, a little…** (used before nouns and adjectives) ■ 我有一点儿累，想休息一会儿。**Wǒ yǒu yìdiǎn lèi, xiǎng xiūxi yíhuìr.** *I'm a bit tired. I want to take a little break.*

diǎnxīn 点心 **N** snack, light refreshments ■ 有点儿饿了吧？吃一点儿点心吧。**Yǒu diǎnr è le ba? Chī yìdiǎnr diǎnxīn ba.** *Aren't you a bit hungry? Have a snack!*

NOTE: The Cantonese pronunciation of 点心 is "dim sum." Many Chinese restaurants overseas sell Cantonese-style refreshments or snack known as "dim sum." To have such refreshments for a meal is "yum cha," the Cantonese pronunciation of 饮茶 **yǐnchá**, which literally means *drink tea*.

diǎnzhōng 点钟 N o'clock ■ "现在几点钟？" "三点钟。" **"Xiànzài jǐ diǎnzhōng?" "Sān diǎnzhōng."** *"What time is it?" "Three o'clock."*

NOTE: In colloquial Chinese 点钟 **diǎnzhōng** can be shortened to 点 **diǎn**, e.g.: ■ "现在几点？" "三点。" **"Xiànzài jǐ diǎn?" "Sān diǎn."** *"What time is it?" "Three o'clock."*

diǎnzhuì 点缀 [comp: 点 touch + 缀 decorate] V embellish, decorate

diǎn 典 N standard, law

diǎnlǐ 典礼 [modif: 典 standard + 礼 rite] N ceremony 毕业典礼 bìyè diǎnlǐ graduation ceremonry, commencement / 结婚典礼 jiéhūn diǎnlǐ wedding ceremony

diǎnxíng 典型 ADJ typical, representative 典型事例 diǎnxíng shìlì typical case

diàn 电 TRAD 電 N electricity, power; electronics ■ 我们这里电比较便宜。 **Wǒmen zhèlǐ diàn bǐjiào piányì.** *Power is rather cheap here.* ■ 今天停电。 **Jīntiān tíng diàn.** *No power today.* (→ *There's a power outage today.*)

diànbào 电报 [modif: 电 electric + 报 report] N telegram, cable (份 **fèn**) ■ 现在还有人打电报吗？ **Xiànzài háiyǒu rén dǎ diànbào ma?** *Do people still send telegrams?*

diànchē 电车 [modif: 电 electricity + 车 vehicle] N trolley bus, streetcar (辆 **liàng**) ■ 这辆电车去哪儿？ **Zhè liàng diànchē qù nǎr?** *Where does this trolley bus go?* ■ 他每天坐电车上班。 **Tā měi tiān zuò diànchē shàngbān.** *He goes to work by trolley bus every day.*

diànchí 电池 [comp: 电 electricity + 池 pool] N battery, electrical cell (节 **jié**) 可充电电池 kě chōngdiàn diànchí rechargeable battery

diàndēng 电灯 [modif: 电 electricity + 灯 lamp] N electric light (个 **gè**) ■ 这个房间的电灯坏了。 **Zhège fángjiān de diàndēng huài le.** *The lights in this room are out of order.* ■ 你会装电灯吗？ **Nǐ huì zhuāng diàndēng ma?** *Do you know how to install an electric light?* 开电灯 kāi diàndēng turn on the light / 关电灯 guān diàndēng turn off the light

diànhuà 电话 [modif: 电 electricity + 话 speech] N telephone, telephone call (个 **gè**) ■ "我可以用一下你的电话吗？" "当然可以。" **"Wǒ kěyǐ yòng yíxià nǐ de diànhuà ma?" "Dāngrán kěyǐ."** *"May I use your telephone?" "Sure."*

打电话 dǎ diànhuà use the telephone, be on the phone / 给 … 打电话 gěi … dǎ diànhuà call … on the telephone, ring … / 听电话 tīng diànhuà answer a telephone call

diànnǎo 电脑 [modif: 电 electricity + 脑 brain] N computer (台 **tái**) ■ 我会用电脑写汉字。 **Wǒ huì yòng diànnǎo xiě Hànzì.** *I can write Chinese characters on a computer.* ■ 这个机器是由电脑控制的。 **Zhège jīqì shì yóu diànnǎo kòngzhì de.** *This machine is controlled by a computer.*

diànshàn 电扇 [modif: 电 electricity + 扇 fan] N electric fan ■ 夜里热极了，我得开着电扇睡觉。 **Yèlǐ rè jíle, wǒ děi kāizhe diànshàn shuìjiào.** *It's so hot at night that I have to sleep with the electric fan on.*

diànshì 电视 [modif: 电 electricity + 视 view] N television ■ "今天晚上的电视有没有好节目？" "没有。" **"Jīntiān wǎnshang de diànshì yǒu méiyǒu hǎo jiémù?" "Méiyǒu."** *"Are there any good programs on TV tonight?" "No."* 看电视 kàn diànshì watch TV / 电视机 diànshì jī TV set / 电视台 diànshì tái TV station

diàntái 电台 [modif: 电 electricity + 台 station] N radio station ■ 我常常听这个电台。 **Wǒ chángcháng tīng zhège diàntái.** *I often listen to this radio station.*

diàntī 电梯 [modif: 电 electricity + 梯 stairs] N elevator, lift ■ 大楼着火的时候，千万不能用电梯。 **Dàlóu zháohuǒ de shíhou, qiānwàn bù néng yòng diàntī.** *Do not use the elevator when there is a fire in the building.* 乘电梯 chéng diàntī go up/down by elevator

diànyǐng 电影 [modif: 电 electricity + 影 shadow] N film, movie (场 **chǎng**, 个 **gè**) ■ 我昨天看的电影很有意思。 **Wǒ zuótiān kàn de diànyǐng hěn yǒu yìsi.** *The film I saw yesterday was very interesting.* 看电影 kàn diànyǐng see a film, go to the movies. ■ 他常常和女朋友一起看电影。 **Tā chángcháng hé nǚpéngyou yìqǐ kàn diànyǐng.** *He often goes to the movies with his girlfriend.* 电影票 diànyǐng piào film ticket

diànyǐngyuàn 电影院 [modif: 电影 film, movie + 院 place (for certain activities)] N cinema, cinema complex, movie theater (座 **zuò**) ■ 这座新建的电影院有五个电影场。 **Zhè zuo xīn jiàn de diànyǐngyuàn yǒu wǔ ge diànyǐngchǎng.** *This newly-built cinema complex has five cinemas.*

diànyuán 电源 [modif: 电 power + 源 source] N power supply; mains

diànzǐ 电子 [suffix: 电 electricity, electron + 子 nominal suffix] N electron 电子工业 diànzǐ gōngyè electronics industry / 电子贺卡 diànzǐ hèkǎ e-card / 电子游戏 diànzǐ yóuxì electronic game

diànzǐ yóujiàn 电子邮件 N e-mail

收到电子邮件 shōu dào diànzǐ yóujiàn receive e-mail / 发电子邮件 fā diànzǐ yóujiàn send e-mail

diàn 垫 TRAD 墊 V & N put something under something else to raise it or make it level; mat, pad, cushion
垫子 diànzi mat, pad, cushion

diàn 店 N same as 商店 **shāngdiàn**

diàn 掂 V keep thinking about, remember with concern

diànjì 惦记 [comp: 惦 keep thinking about + 记 remember] V keep thinking about, remember with concern

diàn 奠 V establish

diàndìng 奠定 V establish, lay the foundation of

diāo 叼 V hold in the mouth

diāo 雕 V carve
浮雕 fúdiāo relief (sculpture) / 石雕 shídiāo stone carving

diāokè 雕刻 [comp: 雕 carve + 刻 carve] V carve, engrave (a work of art)

diāosù 雕塑 N sculpture

diào 掉 V fall, drop ■ 杯子从桌子上掉到地上。 Bēizi cóng zhuōzi shang diàodao dì shang. The cup fell from the table to the floor.

NOTE: 掉 **diào** is often used after a verb, as a complement to mean "finish [doing …]," e.g.
吃掉 chīdiao eat up ■ 水果都吃掉了。 Shuǐguǒ dōu chīdiao le. The fruit is all eaten up.
卖掉 màidiao sell out ■ 那些书还没有卖掉。 Nà xiē shū hái méiyǒu màidiao. Those books aren't sold out yet.
扔掉 rēngdiao throw away, discard ■ 这件衣服太小了，不能穿了，你扔掉吧！ Zhè jiàn yīfu tài xiǎo le, bù néng chuān le, nǐ rēngdiao ba! This dress is too small for you. You'd better throw it away.
忘掉 wàngdiao forget ■ 这件事我怎么也忘不掉。 Zhè jiàn shì wǒ zěnme yě wàng bu diao. I can't forget this incident, no matter how hard I try.
用掉 yòngdiao use up ■ 我上个月用掉了一千块钱。 Wǒ shàng ge yuè yòngdiaole yìqiān kuài qián. I used up one thousand dollars last month. (→ I spent a thousand dollars last month.)

diào 钓 TRAD 釣 V angle ■ 你钓到几条鱼？ Nǐ diào-dao jǐ tiáo yú? How many fish have you caught [with hook and line]?

diào 调 TRAD 調 V 1 exchange, swap ■ 你想和我调一下座位吗？ Nǐ xiǎng hé wǒ diào yíxià zuòwèi ma? Would you like to swap seats with me? 2 transfer ■ 他调到总公司去工作了。 Tā diàodào zǒnggōngsī qù gōngzuò le. He has been transferred to the company headquarters.

diàochá 调查 V & N investigate; investigation ■ 政府有关部门正在调查这家公司的商业活动。 Zhèngfǔ yǒuguān bùmén zhèngzài diàochá zhè jiā gōngsī de shāngyè huódòng. The relevant government departments are investigating this

company's commercial activities. ■ 关于这个事件，警察正在进行调查。 Guānyú zhège shìjiàn, jǐngchá zhèngzài jìnxíng diàochá. The police are conducting an investigation of this incident.

diàodòng 调动 V transfer to another post
申请调动工作 shēnqǐng diàodòng gōngzuò apply for a job transfer

diào 吊 V hang, suspend
上吊 shàngdiào hang oneself (to commit suicide)

diē 跌 V 1 fall, tumble ■ 老人跌了一交，摔断了左腿。 Lǎorén diē le yì jiāo, shuāiduànle zuǒ tuǐ. The old man (or woman) fell down and broke his (or her) left leg. 2 (prices) fall, drop ■ 昨天股票跌了，还是升了？ Zuótiān gǔpiào diē le, háishì shēng le? Did the shares fall or rise yesterday?

dié 叠 V lap, overlap (See chóngdié 重叠.)

dié 碟 N disk (See guāngdié 光碟.)

dié 蝶 N butterfly (See húdié 蝴蝶.)

dié 谍 TRAD 諜 N spy (See jiàndié 间谍.)

dīng 丁 N small cube
肉丁 ròudīng diced meat

dīng 叮 V 1 (of mosquitoes) bite 2 remind repeatedly

dīngzhǔ 叮嘱 V urge repeatedly, exhort

dīng 盯 V gaze, stare ■ 你别老盯着人家看，多不礼貌！ Nǐ bié lǎo dīngzhe rénjiā kàn, duō bù lǐmào! You shouldn't stare at people. How rude!

dīng 钉 TRAD 釘 N nail

dīngzi 钉子 N nail

dǐng 顶 TRAD 頂 1 N top (of the head), peak, summit
山顶 shāndǐng peak / 头顶 tóudǐng crown of the head / 屋顶 wūdǐng roof
2 V carry on the head, hit with the head ■ 九号队员顶球入门。 Jiǔhào duìyuán dǐng qiú rù mén. Number Nine headed the ball into the goal.

dìng 定 V fix, set, decide ■ 你去北京的日期定了吗？ Nǐ qù Běijīng de rìqī dìng le ma? Have you decided on the date to leave for Beijing?

dìngqī 定期 [modif: 定 fixed + 期 period] ADV at regular intervals
定期维修车辆 dìngqī wéixiū chēliàng regular maintenance of vehicles

dìngyì 定义 [modif: 定 fixed + 义 meaning] N definition
下定义 xià dìngyì give a definition

dìng 订 TRAD 訂 V book
订房间 dìng fángjiān reserve a hotel/motel room, book a table/a seat ■ 我想订一个双人房间。 Wǒ xiǎng dìng yí ge shuāngrén fángjiān. I'd like to book a double room.
订票 dìng piào book a ticket ■ 我现在在订机票，万一有事能退吗？ Wó xiànzài dìng jī piào, wànyī yǒushì néng tuì ma? If I book an air ticket now, can I cancel it in case of emergency?
订座 dìng zuò book a table (at a restaurant), book a seat (in a theater)

diū 丢 v lose, throw away ■ 我的表丢了。**Wǒ de biǎo diū le.** *I've lost my watch.*

diūrén 丢人 lose face, be disgraced ■ 他考试门门不及格，真丢人! **Tā kǎoshì ménmén bù jígé, zhēn diūrén!** *It was disgraceful for him to fail every subject in the exam.*

diū sān là sì 丢三落四 IDIOM be forgetful, be scatter-brained ■ 年纪大了，容易丢三落四的。**Niánjì dà le, róngyì diū sān là sì de.** *When one gets old, one tends to be more forgetful.*

NOTE: 落 here is pronounced as **là**, not its usual **luò**.

dōng 东 TRAD 東 N east; eastern ■ 一直往东走，就是我们的学校。**Yìzhí wǎng dōng zǒu, jiùshì wǒmen de xuéxiào.** *Walk straight towards the east and you'll come to our school.* ■ 我在体育馆东门等你。**Wǒ zài tǐyùguǎn dōng mén děng nǐ.** *I'll be waiting for you at the east gate of the gymnasium.*

dōngběi 东北 [comp: 东 east + 北 north] N northeast, the Northeast ■ 中国东北天气非常冷。**Zhōngguó Dōngběi tiānqì fēicháng lěng.** *It's very cold in Northeast China.*

NOTE: 东北 **dōngběi** as a specific geographical term refers to *the northeastern part of China*, which used to be known in the West as Manchuria.

dōngbian 东边 N the east side, to the east, in the east ■ 我们学校的东边是一座公园。**Wǒmen xuéxiào de dōngbian shì yí zuò gōngyuán.** *To the east of our school is a park.* ■ 日本在中国的东边。**Rìběn zài Zhōngguó de dōngbian.** *Japan lies to the east of China.*

dōngdào 东道 N host

东道国 dōngdàoguó host country / 东道主 dōngdàozhǔ host (usually for an official function)

dōngfāng 东方 [modif: 东 east + 方 direction, part] N the East, the Orient

东方文化 Dōngfāng wénhuà the cultures of the East

dōngmiàn 东面 N same as 东边 **dōngbian**

dōngnán 东南 [comp: 东 east + 南 south] N southeast ■ 中国东南地区经济发达，人口很多。**Zhōngguó dōngnán dìqū jīngjì fādá, rénkǒu hěn duō.** *The southeastern regions in China are economically well-developed and densely populated.*

dōngxi 东西 N 1 thing, things (个 gè, 件 jiàn, 种 zhǒng) ■ 这些东西都是小明的。**Zhèxiē dōngxi dōu shì Xiǎo Míng de.** *All these things are Xiao Ming's.* ■ 我没有看到过这种东西。**Wǒ méiyǒu kàndàoguo zhè zhǒng dōngxi.** *I've never seen such a thing.* 2 a person or animal (used affectionately or disapprovingly in colloquial Chinese) ■ 这小东西真可爱。**Zhè xiǎo dōngxi zhēn kě'ài.** *What a cute little thing.* (referring to a baby or kitten)

■ 你这个坏东西又在骗人了。**Nǐ zhè ge huài dōngxi yòu zài piànrén le.** *You rascal! You're trying to deceive me again.*

NOTE: 东西 **dōngxi**, which literally means *east and west*, is an extremely common "all-purpose" noun that can denote any object or objects in Chinese. More examples: ■ 妈妈出去买东西了。**Māma chūqu mǎi dōngxi le.** *Mother's gone shopping.* ■ 图书馆里不能吃东西。**Túshūguǎn lǐ bù néng chī dōngxi.** *No food in the library.* ■ 我想喝点儿东西。**Wǒ xiǎng hē diǎnr dōngxi.** *I'd like to have a drink.*

dōng zhāng xī wàng 东张西望 v look around

dōng 冬 N winter

dōngtiān 冬天 [modif: 冬 winter + 天 days] N winter ■ 今年的冬天比去年冷。**Jīnnián de dōngtiān bǐ qùnián lěng.** *This year's winter is colder than last year's.* ■ 这一对老人喜欢在暖和的地方过冬天。**Zhè yí duì lǎorén xǐhuan zài nuǎnhuo de dìfang guò dōngtiān.** *This old couple likes to spend winter in a warm region.*

dǒng 懂 v comprehend, understand ■ 我不懂你的意思。**Wǒ bù dǒng nǐ de yìsi.** *I don't understand what you mean.* ■ 我听得懂一些简单的中文。**Wǒ tīng de dǒng yìxiē jiǎndān de Zhōngwén.** *I can understand a little simple spoken Chinese.*

读懂 dúdǒng read and understand ■ 这本书我读了两遍才读懂。**Zhè běn shū wǒ dúle liǎng biàn cái dúdǒng.** *I understood this book only after reading it twice.* / 看懂 kàndǒng see (or read) and understand ■ 这个电影我没有看懂。**Zhège diànyǐng wǒ méiyǒu kàndǒng.** *I didn't understand that movie.* / 听懂 tīngdǒng listen and understand

dǒngshìzhǎng 董事长 [modif: 董事 in charge + 长 chief] N chairman of the board of directors ■ 大华公司王董事长在记者招待会上宣布了重大消息。**Dàhuá Gōngsī Wáng dǒngshìzhǎng zài jìzhě zhāodàihuì shang xuānbùle zhòngdà xiāoxi.** *Mr Wang, chairman of the board of Da Hua Company, announced important news at the press conference.*

dòng 动 TRAD 動 v move ■ 别动，我给你照张像。**Bié dòng, wǒ gěi nǐ zhào zhāng xiàng.** *Stay put, I'll take your picture.*

dòngdàng 动荡 N turbulence, upheaval

dònggōng 动工 v begin construction

dònghuà piàn 动画片 N animated cartoon, cartoons (部 bù)

dòngjī 动机 N motive, intention ■ 他的动机是好的，可惜效果不那么好。**Tāde dòngjī shì hǎo de, kěxī xiàoguǒ bù nàme hǎo.** *His intention was good; it's a shame the effect was not so good.*

动机不纯 dòngjī bùchún with hidden motives

dòngjìng 动静 [comp: 动 movement + 静 quietness] N sign of activity

dònglì 动力 [modif: 动 movement + 力 power] N

1 source of power, power **2** driving force (to do something), motivation

dòngmài 动脉 [modif: 动 movement + 脉 artery] **N** artery

主动脉 zhǔ dòngmài main artery, aorta

dòngrén 动人 [modif: 动 moving + 人 people] **ADJ** moving, touching ■ 这个电影的故事十分动人。 *Zhège diànyǐng de gùshi shífēn dòngrén. This film has a moving story line.*

dòngshēn 动身 [v+obj: 动 act + 身 the body] **V** start (a journey), set off (on a journey) ■ 你如果要在天黑前到达，就得早上动身。 *Nǐ rúguǒ yào zài tiān hēi qián dàodá, jiù děi zǎoshang dòngshēn. If you want to arrive before dark, you've got to set off early in the morning.*

dòngshǒu 动手 [v+obj: 动 act + 手 hand] **V** start work ■ 我们现在动手，一定能在七点前完成任务。 *Wǒmen xiànzài dòngshǒu, yídìng néng zài qī diǎn qián wánchéng rènwù. If we start work now, we're sure to be able to finish the job before seven o'clock.*

dòngtài 动态 [modif: 动 movement + 态 condition] **N** general tendency of affairs, developments

科技动态 kējì dòngtài developments in science and technology, what's new in science and technology

dòngwù 动物 [modif: 动 moving + 物 object] **N** animal (只 zhī) ■ 这些小动物真可爱！ *Zhèxiē xiǎo dòngwù zhēn kě'ài! These little animals are really lovable!* ■ 小孩子特别喜欢动物。 *Xiǎo háizi tèbié xǐhuan dòngwù. Children are particularly fond of animals.*

dòngwùxué 动物学 N zoology

dòngwùyuán 动物园 N zoo ■ 下星期五我们班参观动物园。 *Xià Xīngqīwǔ wǒmen bān cānguān dòngwùyuán. Our class will visit the zoo next Friday afternoon.*

dòngyuán 动员 [v+obj: 动 move + 员 staff, people] **V** mobilize

dòngzuò 动作 [comp: 动 act + 作 do] **N** movement (of the body) ■ 你跳舞的动作真优美！ *Nǐ tiàowǔ de dòngzuò zhēn yōuměi! The movements of your dance are really beautiful! (→ You're a graceful dancer!)*

dòng 冻 TRAD 凍 V freeze ■ 天这么冷，我真冻坏了。 *Tiān zhème lěng, wǒ zhēn dòng huài le. It's so cold. I'm frozen to death.*

冻肉 dòngròu frozen meat / 肉冻 ròudòng jellied meat / 水果冻 shuǐguǒ dòng fruit jelly

dòngjié 冻结 V freeze, congeal

工资冻结 gōngzī dòngjié wage freeze

dòng 栋 TRAD 棟 MEASURE WORD (for buildings)

一栋古典风格的小楼 yídòng gǔdiǎn fēnggé de xiǎo lóu a nice house in classical style

dòng 洞 N hole, cave, cavity ■ 你敢进这个山洞吗？ *Nǐ gǎn jìn zhège shāndòng ma? Do you dare*

to enter this mountain cave?

dòngxué 洞穴 N cave (for hiding), cavern

dōu 都 ADV all, both, without exception ■ 我每天都跑步。 *Wǒ měi tiān dōu pǎobù. I jog every day.* ■ 我所有的朋友都来了。 *Wǒ suǒyǒu de péngyou dōu lái le. All my friends have come.*

NOTE: When words like 每天 **měi tiān** (every day), 每个 **měi ge** (every one), 大家 **dàjiā** (everybody) or 所有的 **suǒyǒu de** (all) are used, they usually occur with the adverb 都 **dōu**.

dǒu 陡 ADJ steep, precipitous

dǒuqiào 陡峭 ADJ steep, precipitous

dǒu 抖 V tremble, shiver (See fādǒu 发抖.)

dòu 斗 TRAD 鬥 V fight

dòuzhēng 斗争 [comp: 斗 fight + 争 strive] **I V** struggle, fight ■ 为世界和平而斗争！ *Wèi shìjiè hépíng ér dòuzhēng! Struggle for world peace!* **II N** struggle, fight ■ 你们的斗争一定会胜利。 *Nǐmen de dòuzhēng yídìng huì shènglì. Your struggle will definitely be victorious.*

dòu 豆 N bean, pea

dòufu 豆腐 [modif: 豆 soybean + 腐 curd] **N** bean curd, tofu ■ 豆腐价格便宜，营养丰富。 *Dòufu jiàgé piányì, yíngyǎng fēngfù. Bean curd is cheap and nutritious.*

dòu 逗 V play with, tease ■ 他下班以后，最爱逗孩子玩。 *Tā xiàbān yǐhòu, zuì ài dòu háizi wán. After work, the thing he likes to do best is play with the baby.*

dū 督 V supervise

dūcù 督促 [comp: 督 supervise + 促 urge] **V** supervise and urge

dū 都 N capital city, metropolis

dūshì 都市 N metropolis, big city

dú 独 TRAD 獨 ADJ solitary, alone

dúcái 独裁 V & N establish a dictatorship, rule arbitrarily; dictatorship

独裁者 dúcáizhě dictator / 独裁政权 dúcái zhèngquán dictatorial regime

dúlì 独立 [modif: 独 solitary + 立 stand] **V** be independent ■ 孩子大了都想独立，父母不用太担心。 *Háizi dàle dōu xiǎng dúlì, fùmǔ búyòng tài dānxīn. When children grow up, they all want to be independent. Parents should not be too worried.*

dútè 独特 [comp: 独 solitary + 特 unique] **ADJ** unique, distinctive

独特的风格 dú tè de fēnggé unique style

dú 读 TRAD 讀 V 1 read, read aloud ■ 他正在读一份重要文件。 *Tā zhèng zài dú yí fèn zhòngyào wénjiàn. He is reading an important document.* **2** attend (a school), study (in a school) ■ 他们的大儿子在读中学，小女儿在读小学。 *Tāmen de dà érzi zài dú zhōngxué, xiǎo nǚ'er zài dú xiǎoxué. Their elder son is studying in a high school and their young daughter is studying in a primary school.*

读小学/中学/大学 dú xiǎoxué/zhōngxué/dàxué attend a primary school/high school/university.

NOTE: (1) In colloquial Chinese, 读 **dú** may be replaced by 看 **kàn** when used in the sense of "read," e.g. 看书 **kàn shū**, 看报 **kàn bào**. (2) When used in the sense of "attend (school)" or "study (in a school)" 读 **dú** may be replaced by 念 **niàn** to become 念小学/中学/大学 **niàn xiǎoxué/zhōngxué/dàxué**, which is more colloquial.

dúshū 读书 [v+obj: 读 read + 书 book] **v 1** read ■ 这孩子喜欢读书，他爸爸妈妈看了真高兴。**Zhè háizi xǐhuan dúshū, tā bàba māma kànle zhēn gāoxìng.** *The child likes reading, much to the delight of his parents.* **2** be a student, study (in a school) ■ 我姐姐工作了，可是我妹妹还在读书。**Wǒ jiějie gōngzuò le, kěshì wó mèimei háizài dúshū.** *My elder sister is working but my younger sister is still a student.*

dúzhě 读者 [suffix: 读 read + 者 nominal suffix] **N** reader ■ 今天报上登了很多读者来信，对这个问题发表意见。**Jīntiān bào shang dēng le hěn duō dúzhě láixìn, duì zhège wèntí fābiǎo yìjian.** *Today's newspaper publishes many readers' letters airing views on this issue.*

dú 毒 N 1 poison, toxin 毒蛇 dúshé poisonous snake / 蛇毒 shé dú venom of a snake / 有毒 yǒudú poisonous **2** same as 毒品 **dúpǐn** 贩毒 fàndú drug trafficking / 吸毒 xīdú drug taking, on drugs

dúpǐn 毒品 N illegal substance taken for pleasure (e.g. heroin, cocaine, etc.), drugs

dǔ 堵 v block ■ 什么东西堵住了下水道。**Shénme dōngxi dǔzhùle xiàshuǐdào.** *Something is blocking the sewer.*

dǔchē 堵车 N traffic jam

dǔsè 堵塞 [comp: 堵 block + 塞 block] **v** block 交通堵塞 jiāotōng dǔsè traffic jam. ■ 水管堵塞了。**Shuǐguǎn dǔsè le.** *There is a blockage in the water pipe.*

dǔ 赌 TRAD 賭 **v** gamble

dǔbó 赌博 [comp: 赌 gamble + 博 gamble] **v** gamble

dǔ 睹 v see, witness (See **mùdǔ 目睹**.)

dù 肚 N stomach

dùzi 肚子 [suffix: 肚 stomach + 子 nominal suffix] **N** abdomen, stomach, belly ■ 我肚子痛。**Wǒ dùzi tòng.** *I have a stomachache. (← My stomach hurts.)*

dù 度 I N limit, extent 难度 nándù degree of difficulty ■ 这篇课文难度太高。**Zhè piān kèwén nándù tài gāo.** *This text is too difficult.* **II** MEASURE WORD degree (of temperature, longitude, latitude, etc.) ■ 今天最高气温是二十五

度。**Jīntiān zuì gāo qìwēn shì èrshíwǔ dù.** *The highest temperature today is 25 degrees.*

dùguò 度过 v spend (a period of time) ■ 孩子们在爷爷奶奶家度过了愉快的暑假。**Háizimen zài yéye nǎinai jiā dùguòle yí ge yúkuài de shǔjià.** *The children spent a pleasant summer vacation with their grandpa and grandma.*

dù 渡 v cross (a body of water, e.g. a river, a strait, etc.) ■ 我们怎么渡江呢？**Wǒmen zěnme dù jiāng ne?** *How are we going to cross the river?*

dùlún 渡轮 N ferryboat (艘 sǒu)

dù 杜 v shut out, prevent

dùjué 杜绝 v put an end to (wrongdoings)

dù 妒 v be jealous

dùjì 妒忌 v be jealous, envy

duān 端 v carry ... level with one or both hands ■ 她端了一大盘水果走了进来。**Tā duānle yí dà pán shuǐguǒ zǒule jìnlai.** *She came in, carrying a big plate of fruit.*

Duānwǔ Jié 端午节 N the Dragon Boat Festival (the 5th day of the 5th lunar month)

duānzhèng 端正 ADJ upright, proper

duǎn 短 ADJ (of length, time) short (ANTONYM 长 cháng) ■ 这条街很短，只有十几座房子。**Zhè tiáo jiē hěn duǎn, zhǐ yǒu shíjǐ zuò fángzi.** *This is a short street, with only a dozen houses.* ■ 我在上海的时间很短，没有好好玩。**Wǒ zài Shànghǎi de shíjiān hěn duǎn, méiyǒu hǎohǎo wán.** *I only stayed in Shanghai for a short time and did not have much time for fun (e.g. sightseeing, window-shopping, dining in restaurants).*

duǎncù 短促 [comp: 短 short + 促 hurried] **ADJ** very brief

duǎnqī 短期 [modif: 短 short + 期 period] **N** short-term ■ 她要去北京参加一个短期汉语口语训练班。**Tā yào qù Běijīng cānjiā yí ge duǎnqī Hànyǔ kǒuyǔ xùnliàn bān.** *She is going to Beijing to attend a short training course in spoken Chinese.* ■ 这个目标不可能在短期内达到。**Zhège mùbiāo bù kěnéng zài duǎnqī nèi dádào.** *This goal cannot be reached in a short time.*

duǎnxìn 短信 [modif: 短 short + 信 letter] **N** text message (by cell phone), text ■ 我昨天收到他发来的两条短信。**Wǒ zuótiān shōudao tā fālai de liǎng tiáo duǎnxìn.** *I received two text messages from him yesterday.*

duàn 段 MEASURE WORD section (of something long) ■ 这段路不平，开车要特别小心。**Zhè duàn lù bù píng, kāi chē yào tèbié xiǎoxīn.** *This section of the road is quite rough. One should be particularly careful when driving.* 一段路 yí duàn lù a section of a road/street, part of a journey / 一段时间 yí duàn shíjiān a period of time / 一段经历 yí duàn jīnglì an experience (in life)

duàn 断 TRAD 斷 **v 1** break, snap ■ 把电线剪

断。**Bǎ diànxiàn jiǎn duàn.** *Cut the electric wire.* ■ 我和她的联系断了，我不知道她在哪里。**Wǒ hé tā de liánxì duàn le, wǒ bù zhīdào tā zài nǎli.** *I have lost contact with her. I do not know where she is.* **2** break off, cut off

断电 **duàn diàn** cut off electricity, electricity outage / 断水 **duàn shuǐ** cut off water supply

duàndìng 断定 **v** conclude, come to an conclusion

duàn duàn xù xù 断断续续 **ADJ** intermittent, sporadic, off and on

duànjué 断绝 **v** break off, sever

断绝贸易关系 **duànjué màoyì guānxi** break off trade relation

duàn nǎi 断奶 **N** wean (a child)

duàn 锻 **TRAD** 鍛 **v** forge, shape metal

duànliàn 锻炼 [comp: 锻 shape metal + 炼 smelt] **v** undergo physical training, do physical exercises ■ 你要成为一名好运动员，就得天天锻炼。**Nǐ yào chéngwéi yì míng hǎo yùndòngyuán, jiù děi tiāntiān duànliàn.** *If you want to become a good athlete, you have to train every day.*

duī 堆 **v** heap up, pile up

duījī 堆积 **v** pile up

duì 对¹ **TRAD** 對 **v 1** treat, deal with ■ 她对我很好。**Tā duì wǒ hěn hǎo.** *She treats me well.* (→ *She is nice to me.*) ■ 我的批评是对事不对人。**Wǒ de pīpíng shì duì shì bú duì rén.** *My criticism concerns the issue, not the person.* **2** same as 对于 **duìyú**

duì 对² **TRAD** 對 **ADJ** correct, true (**ANTONYM** 错 **cuò**) ■ 你的话很对。**Nǐ de huà hěn duì.** *Your words are correct.* (→ *You're right.*) ■ 你说得很对。**Nǐ shuō de hěn duì.** *You spoke correctly.* (→ *You're right.*)

NOTE: 对不对 **duì bu duì** is used at the end of a sentence to form a question, e.g. ■ 他回答得对不对？**Tā huídá de duì bu duì?** *Did he answer correctly?* ■ 你是英国人，对不对？**Nǐ shì Yīngguórén, duì bu duì?** *You're from the UK, aren't you?* ■ 中华文明是世界上最古老的文明，对不对？**Zhōnghuá wénmíng shì shìjiè shang zuì gǔlǎo de wénmíng, duì bu duì?** *Chinese civilization is the oldest in the world, isn't it?*

duì 对³ **TRAD** 對 **MEASURE WORD** pair, two (matching people or things)

一对花瓶 **yí duì huāpíng** two matching vases / 一对夫妻 **yí duì fūqī** a couple (husband and wife)

duìbǐ 对比 [comp: 对 check + 比 compare, contrast] **v** compare and contrast ■ 你对比一下中文和英文，就会发现很多有趣的问题。**Nǐ duìbǐ yíxià Zhōngwén hé Yīngwén, jiù huì fāxiàn hěn duō yǒuqù de wèntí.** *If you compare and contrast Chinese and English, you will find many interesting issues.*

duìbuqǐ 对不起 **IDIOM** I'm sorry, I beg your pardon ■ 对不起，我迟到了。**Duìbuqǐ, wǒ chídào le.**

Sorry, I'm late. ■ 对不起，我没听清楚，请你再说一遍。**Duìbuqǐ, wǒ méi tīng qīngchu, qǐng nǐ zài shuō yíbiàn.** *I'm sorry, I didn't catch it. Could you please say it again?*

NOTE: 对不起 **duìbuqǐ** is a very useful idiomatic expression in colloquial Chinese. It is used when you've done something wrong or caused some inconvenience to others. For more formal occasions, use 请原谅 **qǐng yuánliàng** *please forgive me* or *my apologies.*

duìcè 对策 [modif: 对 deal with + 策 strategy] **N** counter measure

duìchèn 对称 **N & ADJ** symmetry; symmetrical

不对称 **búduìchèn** asymmetrical

duìdài 对待 [comp: 对 deal with + 待 treat] **v** treat (people), approach (matters)

duìfāng 对方 [modif: 对 the opposite side + 方 side] **N** the other side, the other party ■ 你必须清楚地了解对方的企图。**Nǐ bìxū qīngchu de liǎojiě duìfāng de qǐtú.** *You must have a clear idea of the other party's intention.*

duìfu 对付 **v** cope with, deal with ■ 这种不讲道理的人，实在难对付。**Zhè zhǒng bù jiǎng dàolǐ de rén, shízài nán duìfu.** *It is indeed difficult to deal with such unreasonable people.* ■ 我不知道怎么样对付这种情况。**Wǒ bù zhīdào zěnmeyàng duìfu zhè zhǒng qíngkuàng.** *I don't know how to cope with such a situation.*

duìhuà 对话 **V & N** have a dialogue; dialogue ■ 他能够流利地用中文对话。**Tā nénggòu liúlì de yòng Zhōngwén duìhuà.** *He is able to have a dialogue in fluent Chinese.*

duìkàng 对抗 [comp: 对 opposite + 抗 resist] **v** antagonize, oppose vigorously

duìlì 对立 [modif: 对 opposite + 立 stand] **v** oppose, be hostile

duìlián 对联 **N** antithetical couplet written on scrolls

duìmiàn 对面 **N** opposite, the opposite side ■ 学校的对面是一座公园。**Xuéxiào de duìmiàn shì yí zuò gōngyuán.** *Opposite the school is a park.*

duìshǒu 对手 [modif: 对 opposite + 手 hand] **N** opponent

竞争对手 **jìngzhēng duìshǒu** opponent in a competition, rival

duìxiàng 对象 **N 1** person or thing to which an action or a feeling is directed, object ■ 她研究的对象是学前儿童。**Tā yánjiū de duìxiàng shì xuéqián értóng.** *Preschool children are the object of her study.* **2** marriage partner, fiancé(e) ■ 他已经三十多岁了，还没有对象。**Tā yǐjīng sānshí duō suì le, hái méiyǒu duìxiàng.** *He is over thirty, but still has no fiancée.*

找对象 **zhǎo duìxiàng** look for a marriage partner

duìyìng 对应 **ADJ** corresponding

duìyìng cí 对应词 N corresponding word ■ 这个英文词在中文里几乎没有对应词。**Zhège Yīngwén cí zài Zhōngwén lǐ jīhū méiyǒu duìyìng cí.** *You can hardly find a word in Chinese that corresponds to this English word.*

duìyú 对于 PREP **1** (introducing the object of an action), regarding ■ 我对于这个理论还没有完全理解。**Wǒ duìyú zhège lǐlùn hái méiyǒu wánquán lǐjiě.** *I still haven't understood this theory completely.* **2** (indicating a certain relationship), to, towards ■ 学习中文对于了解中国人和中国文化很有帮助。**Xuéxí Zhōngwén duìyú liǎojiě Zhōngguórén hé Zhōngguó wénhuà hěn yǒu bāngzhù.** *Learning Chinese is very helpful to understanding the Chinese people and Chinese culture.*

duìzhào 对照 V contrast and compare, refer to

duì 队 TRAD 隊 N team

队员 duìyuán member of a team / 篮球队 lánqiú duì basketball team / 足球队 zúqiú duì soccer team

duìwu 队伍 N troops ■ 队伍天黑后进了村。**Duìwu tiānhēi hòu jìnle cūn.** *The troops entered the village after dark.*

duìzhǎng 队长 [modif: 队 team + 长 chief] N team leader ■ 队员都服从队长。**Duìyuán dōu fúcóng duìzhǎng.** *All the team members submit to the team leader.*

duì 兑 V exchange, convert

duìhuàn 兑换 [comp: 兑 convert + 换 exchange] V (of currency) exchange, convert ■ 把1,000美元兑换成人民币 **bǎ yìqiān Měiyuán duìhuàn chéng Rénmínbì** *convert 1,000 US dollars to Renminbi (Chinese yuan).*

兑换率 duìhuànlǜ exchange rate

duìxiàn 兑现 V **1** cash (a check) **2** honor a promise

dūn 吨 TRAD 噸 MEASURE WORD ton ■ 一吨等于一千公斤。**Yìdūn děngyú yìqiān gōngjīn.** *One ton equals 1,000 kilograms.*

dūn 蹲 V squat

dùn 盾 N shield (See **máodùn 矛盾**.)

dùn 顿 TRAD 頓 MEASURE WORD (for meals) ■ 我们一天吃三顿饭：早饭、午饭、晚饭。**Wǒmen yì tiān chī sān dùn fàn: zǎofàn, wǔfàn, wǎnfàn.** *We have three meals a day: breakfast, lunch and supper (or dinner).* ■ 她好好地吃了一顿晚饭。**Tā hǎohǎo de chīle yí dùn wǎnfàn.** *She had a good meal for supper. (→ She had a good supper.)*

dùnshí 顿时 ADV immediately, at once

duō 多 I ADJ many, much (ANTONYM 少 shǎo) ■ 今天的作业不多。**Jīntiān de zuòyè bù duō.** *There isn't much homework today.* ■ 他昨天酒喝得太多，今天头疼。**Tā zuótiān jiǔ hē de tài duō, jīntiān tóu téng.** *He drank too much last night. Today he has a headache.*

比 … 得多 bǐ … de duō much more … than ■ 今天比昨天热得多。**Jīntiān bǐ zuótiān rè de**

duō. *Today is much hotter than yesterday.* II NUMERAL more, over ■ 我们学了五百多个汉字。**Wǒmen xuéle wǔbǎi duō ge Hànzì.** *We've learned more than five hundred Chinese characters.* ■ 他在台湾住了八个多月。**Tā zài Táiwān zhùle bā ge duō yuè.** *He lived in Taiwan for over eight months.* III ADV **1** how ...! ■ 要是我能去北京学中文，多好啊！**Yàoshì wǒ néng qù Běijīng xué Zhōngwén, duō hǎo a!** *How nice it would be if I could go to Beijing to study Chinese!* **2** how ...? ■ 老先生，您多大了？**Lǎo xiānsheng, nín duō dà le?** *How old are you, sir? (to an elderly man)*

duōkuī 多亏 ADV luckily, fortunately

duōme 多么 ADV same as **duō 多** III **1**

duōshǎo 多少 [comp: 多 many, much + 少 few, little] PRON how many, how much ■ 你们班多少人学中文？**Nǐmen bān duōshǎo rén xué Zhōngwén?** *How many in your class are studying Chinese?*

多少钱… duōshǎo qián … How much is ...? ■ 这本书多少钱？**Zhè běn shū duōshǎo qián?** *How much is this book?*

没有多少 méiyǒu duōshǎo not many, not much ■ 他没有多少钱，可是要装出很有钱的样子。**Tā méiyǒu duōshǎo qián, kěshì yào zhuāngchū hěn yǒuqián de yàngzi.** *He hasn't got much money, but he pretends to be rich.*

NOTE: See note on 几 **jǐ**.

duōshù 多数 [modif: 多 many + 数 number] N majority

duōyú 多余 [comp: 多 more + 余 spare] ADJ surplus

duōyuánhuà 多元化 N pluralism

duōyuán wénhuà 多元文化 N multiculturalism

duō 哆 as in 哆嗦 **duōsuo**

duōsuo 哆嗦 V tremble, shiver

duó 夺 TRAD 奪 V take by force, win ■ 我们队夺得了冠军。**Wǒmen duì duódéle guànjūn.** *Our team has won the championship.*

duǒ 朵 MEASURE WORD (for flowers) ■ 送给你一朵花。**Sòng gěi nǐ yì duǒ huā.** *Here's a flower for you.*

duǒ 躲 V hide (oneself) ■ 他躲在门背后。**Tā duǒ zài mén bèihòu.** *He hid behind the door.*

duǒbì 躲避 [comp: 躲 hide + 避 avoid] V hide, avoid, keep away from

躲避债主 duǒbì zhàizhǔ hide from the creditor

duǒcáng 躲藏 [comp: 躲 hide + 藏 hide] V go into hiding

duò 堕 TRAD 墮 V fall

duòluò 堕落 [comp: 堕 fall + 落 fall] V (of one's morals or behavior) become worse, degenerate

E

é 额 TRAD 額 N the forehead
额头 étóu the forehead
éwài 额外 ADJ additional, extra
额外的开支 éwài de kāizhī extra expenditure
é 俄 N (a shortened form of Russia or Russian)
Éguó 俄国 N Russia, the state of Russia
Éluósī 俄罗斯 N Russia
俄罗斯人 Éluósī rén a Russian person, the Russian people
Éwén 俄文 [comp: 俄 Russian + 文 writing] N the Russian language (especially the writing)
Éyǔ 俄语 [comp: 俄 Russia + 语 speech] N the Russian language
é 鹅 TRAD 鵝 N goose (只 zhī)
天鹅 tiān'é swan
ě 恶 TRAD 惡 V vomit
ěxīn 恶心 V 1 feel sick, be sickened ■ 我看到那种食物，就感到恶心。**Wǒkàn dào nà zhǒng shíwù, jiù gǎndào ěxīn.** *I feel sick at the sight of the food.* 2 feel disgusted, be nauseated ■ 她拍老板马屁的样子，真叫人恶心！**Tā pāi lǎobǎn mǎpì de yàngzi, zhēnjiào rén ěxīn!** *The way she fawns over the boss is really nauseating!*
è 饿 TRAD 餓 ADJ hungry (ANTONYM 饱 bǎo) ■ 我饿了，我们去吃饭吧。**Wǒ è le, wǒmen qù chī fàn ba!** *I'm hungry. Let's go and eat.* ■ 看到这么多好吃的东西，我感到饿了。**Kàndào zhème duō hǎochī de dōngxi, wǒ gǎndào è le.** *At the sight of so much delicious food, I feel hungry.*
è 恶 TRAD 惡 ADJ bad, wicked (ANTONYM 善 shàn) ■ 人性是善，还是恶？**Rénxìng shì shàn, háishi è?** *Is human nature good or bad?*
èdú 恶毒 [comp: 恶 evil + 毒 poisonous] ADJ vicious, malicious
èhuà 恶化 V get worse, aggravate
èliè 恶劣 [comp: 恶 bad + 劣 inferior] ADJ very bad, abominable
è 遏 V check, hold back
èzhì 遏制 V restrain, control
ēn 恩 N kindness, grace
ēnyuàn 恩怨 N gratitude and resentment, personal emotional entanglement
ér 儿 TRAD 兒 N child, son
értóng 儿童 [comp: 儿 child + 童 child] N child, children ■ 这种电影不适合儿童看。**Zhè zhǒng diànyǐng búshìhé értóng kàn.** *This kind of film is not suitable for children.*
儿童时代 értóng shídài childhood
érzi 儿子 [suffix: 儿 son + 子 nominal suffix] N son (个 gè) ■ 他们有两个儿子，大儿子工作了，小儿子还在念大学。**Tāmen yǒu liǎng ge érzi, dà érzi gōngzuò le, xiǎo érzi háizài niàn dàxué.** *They have two sons. While the elder son has started working, the younger son is still studying in a university.*

ér 而 CONJ (indicating a contrast) but, yet, on the other hand ■ 学而不用，等于没学。**Xué ér bú yòng, děngyú méi xué.** *If you learn skills but do not use them, it is tantamount to not having learnt them at all.* ■ 他姐姐功课很好，而他呢，去年考试三门不及格。**Tā jiějie gōngkè hěn hǎo, ér tā ne, qùnián kǎoshì sān mén bù jígé.** *His sister's schoolwork is excellent, but he failed in three subjects last year.*
érqiě 而且 CONJ moreover, what's more ■ 这件衣服大了一点儿，而且比较贵，还是不买吧。**Zhè jiàn yīfu dàle yìdiǎnr, érqiě bǐjiào guì, háishì bù mǎi ba.** *This dress is a bit too big and also expensive. You shouldn't buy it.*
不但 …, 而且 … búdàn …, érqiě … not only …, but also … ■ 我爸爸不但会开车，而且会修车。**Wǒ bàba búdàn huì kāi chē, érqiě huì xiū chē.** *My daddy can not only drive but also fix cars.* ■ 这个电脑游戏不但小孩爱玩，而且大人也爱玩。**Zhège diànnǎo yóuxì búdàn xiǎohái ài wán, érqiě dàren yě ài wán.** *Not only children but also grownups like to play this electronic game.*
ěryǐ 而已 PARTICLE nothing but, only
ěr 耳 N the ear
ěrduo 耳朵 N the ear (只 zhī) ■ 人有两只耳朵，就说明应该听不同的声音。**Rén yǒu liǎng zhī ěrduo, jiù shuōmíng yīnggāi tīng bùtóng de shēngyīn.** *A man has two ears, which means he should listen to different voices. (→ A man has two ears, which means he should hear out different opinions.)*
ěrhuán 耳环 N earrings (付 fù)
戴耳环 dài ěrhuán wear earrings
èr 二 NUMERAL second, two ■ 二千二百二十
二 èrqiān èrbǎi èrshí'èr two thousand and two hundred and twenty-two ■ 我二哥去年结婚了。**Wǒ èrgē qùnián jiéhūn le.** *My second elder brother got married last year.*

NOTE: See note on 两 **liǎng**.

èr yǎng huà tàn 二氧化碳 N carbon dioxide, CO_2

F

fā 发 TRAD 發 V 1 send out, release ■ 我上个星期给他发了一封信，今天上午又发了一个传真。**Wǒ shàng ge xīngqī gěi tā fāle yì fēng xìn, jīntiān shàngwǔ yòu fāle yí ge chuánzhēn.** *I sent him a letter last week and sent him a fax this morning.* 2 develop (into a state)
发传真 fā chuánzhēn send a fax / 发电子邮件 fā diànzǐ yóujiàn send an e-mail message / 发（手机）短信 fā (shǒujī) duǎnxìn send a text message (by cell phone)

fābiǎo 发表 [comp: 发 release + 表 express] v publicize, make known, publish ■ 请您发表对目前经济形势的看法。 **Qǐng nín fābiǎo duì mùqián jīngjì xíngshì de kànfǎ.** *Please express your views on the current economic situation.*

fābù 发布 v release, issue
发布通告 **fābù tōnggào** release an announcement / 发布新闻 **fābù xīnwén** release news

fācái 发财 [v+obj: 发 develop + 财 wealth] v make a fortune, become prosperous

fāchóu 发愁 [v+obj: 发 develop + 愁 worry] v get worried, fret

fāchū 发出 [comp: 发 release + 出 out] v 1 produce, emit, give off ■ 水果成熟会发出特殊的香味。 **Shuǐguǒ chéngshú huì fāchū tèshū de xiāngwèi.** *Ripe fruit gives off a special fragrance.* 2 send out ■ 学校已经向新生发出通知。 **Xuéxiào yǐjīng xiàng xīnshēng fāchū tōngzhī.** *The school has sent out notifications to the new students.*

fādá 发达 ADJ developed, well-developed ■ 这个国家制造业很发达。 **Zhège guójiā zhìzàoyè hěn fādá.** *This country has a well-developed manufacturing industry.*

fādāi 发呆 v be dazed, in a daze

fādòng 发动 v launch (a massive campaign)

fādǒu 发抖 v tremble ■ 她冷得发抖。 **Tā lěng de fādǒu.** *She trembled with cold.*

fāhuī 发挥 v allow display, give free rein to ■ 这项工作能够充分发挥他在这方面的能力。 **Zhè xiàng gōngzuò nénggòu chōngfèn fāhuī tā zài zhè fāngmiàn de nénglì.** *This job allows him to display his ability in this area fully.*

fāhuǒ 发火 [v+obj: 发 release + 火 fire] v lose one's temper, flare up

fājué 发觉 v find, find out, become aware of

fāmíng 发明 v & N invent; invention (项 xiàng) ■ 飞机是谁发明的？ **Fēijī shì shuí fāmíng de?** *Who invented the airplane?* ■ 这项新发明会给公司带来巨大的利益。 **Zhè xiàng xīn fāmíng huì gāi gōngsī dàilái jùdà de lìyì.** *This new invention will bring tremendous benefit to the company.*

fāpiào 发票 N receipt (张 zhāng)

fāshāo 发烧 [v+obj: 发 develop + 烧 burning, fever] v run a fever ■ 她昨天着凉了，夜里就发烧了。 **Tā zuótiān zháoliáng le, yèlǐ jiù fāshāo le.** *She caught a cold yesterday and began to run a fever at night.*

fāshè 发射 [comp: 发 send out + 射 shoot] v shoot, launch
发射嫦娥一号探月卫星 **fāshè Cháng'é yīhào tànyuè wèixīng** launch Cháng'é No. 1 Lunar Orbiting Spacecraft

fāshēng 发生 [comp: 发 develop + 生 grow] v take place, happen ■ 这里发生了什么事？ **Zhèlǐ fāshēngle shénme shì?** *What happened here?* ■ 前面发生了交通事故，车辆必须绕道。 **Qiánmiàn**

fāshēngle jiāotōng shìgù, chēliàng bìxū ràodào. *A road accident happened up ahead. Traffic must detour.*

fāshì 发誓 v pledge, vow
发誓不再抽烟 **fāshì búzài chōuyān** vow not to smoke again

fāxiàn 发现 [comp: 发 develop + 现 show] v discover, find, find out ■ 谁先发现新西兰的？ **Shuí xiān fāxiàn Xīnxīlán de?** *Who first discovered New Zealand?* ■ 我发现他爱打扮了，是不是有了女朋友？ **Wǒ fāxiàn tā ài dǎbàn le, shì bu shì yǒule nǚpéngyou?** *I notice that he is paying more attention to his grooming. Has he gotten a girlfriend?*

fāxíng 发行 v issue (books, stamps, etc.), publish

fāyán 发言 [v+obj: 发 release + 言 words] v & N speak (at a meeting), make a speech; speech, talk ■ 代表们在会上纷纷发言。 **Dàibiǎomen zài huìshang fēnfēn fāyán.** *The delegates spoke at the meeting, one after another.* ■ 他在会上的发言引起了代表们的争论。 **Tā zài huìshang de fāyán yǐnqǐle dàibiǎomen de zhēnglùn.** *His speech at the meeting gave rise to a debate among the delegates.*

fāyánrén 发言人 N spokesperson

fāyán 发炎 [v+obj: 发 develop + 炎 inflammation] v become inflamed

fāyáng 发扬 [comp: 发 develop + 扬 unfold] v develop, carry forward ■ 希望你发扬优点，克服缺点。 **Xīwàng nǐ fāyáng yōudiǎn, kèfú quēdiǎn.** *I hope you will develop your strong points and overcome your shortcomings.*

fāyīn 发音 [v+obj: 发 send out + 音 sound] N pronunciation ■ 我这个字发音对不对？ **Wǒ zhège zì fāyīn duì bu duì?** *Did I pronounce this character correctly?* ■ 他中文说得很流利，虽然发音不太好。 **Tā Zhōngwén shuō de hěn liúlì, suīrán fāyīn bú tài hǎo.** *He speaks Chinese fluently, though his pronunciation is not too good.*

fāyù 发育 [comp: 发 develop + 育 cultivate] v (of humans) develop physically

fāzhǎn 发展 [comp: 发 develop + 展 unfold] v develop ■ 经济要发展，政治要民主。 **Jīngjì yào fāzhǎn, zhèngzhì yào mínzhǔ.** *The economy should be developed, and politics should be democratized.* ■ 公司决定发展在这个地区的业务。 **Gōngsī juédìng fāzhǎn zài zhè ge dìqū de yèwù.** *The company has decided to develop its business in this region.*
发展中国家 **fāzhǎnzhōng guójiā** developing country

fá 乏 v lack (See quēfá 缺乏.)

fá 罚 TRAD 罰 v punish, penalize ■ 他因为超速驾车，被罚了两百块。 **Tā yīnwéi chāosù jiàchē, bèi fá le liǎng bǎi kuài.** *He was fined 200 yuan for speeding.*

fákuǎn 罚款 v & N fine, impose a fine; fine ■ 超速要罚款。 **Chāosù yào fákuǎn.** *Speeding will be fined.*

罚款单 fákuǎndān fine notice / 缴罚款 jiāo fákuǎn pay for a fine

fǎ 法 **N** method, law

Fǎguó 法国 [modif: 法 France + 国 state, country] **N** France ■ 法国是一个重要的国家。 **Fǎguó shì yí ge zhòngyào de guójiā.** *France is an important country.*

fǎlǜ 法律 [comp: 法 law + 律 rule] **N** law ■ 他哥哥在读法律，他想当律师。 **Tā gēge zài dú fǎlǜ, tā xiǎng dāng lǜshī.** *His brother is studying law; he wants to be a lawyer.* ■ 每一个公民都必须遵守法律。 **Měi yí ge gōngmín dōu bìxū zūnshǒu fǎlǜ.** *Every citizen must obey the law.*

违反法律 wéifǎn fǎlǜ violate the law / 修改法律 xiūgǎi fǎlǜ amend a law

fǎrén 法人 [modif: 法 legal + 人 person] **N** legal person

Fǎwén 法文 [comp: 法 France + 文 writing] **N** the French language (especially the writing)

Fǎyǔ 法语 [comp: 法 France + 语 speech] **N** the French language ■ 她法语说得很漂亮。 **Tā Fǎyǔ shuō de hěn piàoliang.** *She speaks French beautifully.*

fǎyuàn 法院 [modif: 法 law + 院 house] **N** law court, court

高级人民法院 gāojí rénmín fǎyuàn Supreme People's Court / 中级人民法院 zhōngjí rénmín fǎyuàn Intermediate People's Court

fān 番¹ **ADJ** foreign, outlandish

fānqié 番茄 [modif: 番 foreign + 茄 eggplant] **N** tomato (只 **zhī**)

fān 番² **MEASURE WORD** time

三番五次 sān fān wǔ cì time and again

fān 翻 **V** turn, turn over ■ 请把书翻到二十页。 **Qǐng bǎ shū fāndào èrshí yè.** *Please turn your books to page twenty.*

fānyì 翻译 **V & N** translate, interpret; translator, interpreter ■ 这位翻译中文英文都好极了。 **Zhè wèi fānyì Zhōngwén Yīngwén dōu hǎo jíle.** *This translator (or interpreter) has very good command of both Chinese and English.*

把 ... 翻译成 ... bǎ ... fānyì chéng ... translate ... into ... ■ 你能不能把这封信翻译成中文？ **Nǐ néng bu néng bǎ zhè fēng xìn fānyì chéng Zhōngwén?** *Can you translate this letter into Chinese?*

当翻译 dāng fānyì to work as a translator (or interpreter) ■ 明天有中国朋友来参观我们工厂，请你当翻译。 **Míngtiān yǒu Zhōngguó péngyou lái cānguān wǒmen gōngchǎng, qǐng nǐ dāng fānyì.** *Tomorrow some Chinese friends will come to visit our factory. I'll ask you to act as interpreter.*

fān 帆 **N** sail

fānchuán 帆船 **N** sailboat (艘 **sōu**)

fán 凡 **ADV** every

fánshì 凡是 **ADV** every, all ■ 凡是我姐姐的朋友，

我都认识。 **Fánshì wǒ jiějie de péngyou, wǒ dōu rènshi.** *I know every one of my sister's friends.* ■ 凡是违反法律的事，都不能做。 **Fánshì wéifǎn fǎlǜ de shì, dōu bù néng zuò.** *You must not do anything that violates the law.*

NOTE: 凡是 **fánshì** is used before a noun phrase to emphasize that what is referred to is all-embracing, without a single exception. The phrase introduced by 凡是 **fánshì** usually occurs at the beginning of a sentence, and 都 **dōu** is used in the second half of the sentence.

fán 烦 **TRAD** 煩 **ADJ** annoyed

fánmèn 烦闷 [comp: 烦 annoyed + 闷 stuffy] **ADJ** worried and unhappy

fánnǎo 烦恼 [comp: 烦 annoyed + 恼 angry] **ADJ** annoyed and angry, vexed

fán 繁 **ADJ** numerous, abundant

fánhuá 繁华 **ADJ** flourishing, prosperous-looking

fánmáng 繁忙 **ADJ** busy, fully occupied

fánróng 繁荣 [comp: 繁 abundant + 荣 flourishing] **ADJ** prosperous, thriving ■ 由于经济繁荣，人民的生活水平不断提高。 **Yóuyú jīngjì fánróng, rénmín de shēnghuó shuǐpíng búduàn tígāo.** *With a prosperous economy, the people's standard of living keeps rising.*

fántǐ zì 繁体字 [modif: 繁 complicated + 体 style + 字 character] **N** unsimplified Chinese character, e.g. 門 for 门.

NOTE: As 繁体字 literally means *complicated style character*, some people don't like the negative implication, and prefer to use the term 正体字 **zhèngtǐ zì** *orthographic characters* or 传统字 **chuántǒng zì** *traditional characters*. 繁体字 are used in Taiwan, Hong Kong and overseas Chinese communities.

fánzhí 繁殖 **V** reproduce, breed

fǎn 反 **ADJ** reverse, opposite (**ANTONYM** 正 **zhèng**) ■ 请看反面。 **Qǐng kàn fǎnmiàn.** *Please read the reverse side.*

fǎnbó 反驳 [comp: 反 oppose + 驳 refute] **V** argue against, refute, retort

fǎncháng 反常 [modif: 反 reverse + 常 normal] **ADJ** abnormal, unusual ■ 情况反常。 **Qíngkuàng fǎncháng.** *We have an unusual situation here.*

fǎndào 反倒 **ADV** on the contrary, instead

fǎndòng 反动 [modif: 反 reverse + 动 action] **ADJ** reactionary

fǎnduì 反对 [modif: 反 opposing + 对 deal with] **V** oppose, object (**ANTONYM** 同意 **tóngyì**) ■ 我不反对你的计划，但是我觉得很难做到。 **Wǒ bù fǎnduì nǐ de jìhuà, dànshì wǒ juéde hěn nán zuòdào.** *I don't object to your plan, but I think it'll be difficult to implement.*

反对意见 fǎnduì yìjiàn opposing opinion
反对党 fǎnduì dǎng the Opposition [party]

fǎn'ér 反而 ADV contrary to expectations, instead ■ 他吃了药，病情反而恶化了。**Tā chī le yào, bìngqíng fǎn'ér èhuà le.** *Contrary to expectations his conditions worsened after he took the medicine.*

fǎnfù 反复 [comp: 反 reverse + 复 duplicate] ADV repeatedly, over and over again ■ 董事长反复强调市场调查的重要性。**Dǒngshìzhǎng fǎnfù qiángdiào shìchǎng diàochá de zhòngyàoxìng.** *The chairman of the board emphasized over and over again the importance of market surveys.*

fǎngǎn 反感 [modif: 反 oppose + 感 feelings] V feel disgusted, be aversed to 对他的行为很反感 duì tāde xíngwéi hěn fǎngǎn feel disgusted with his behavior

fǎnkàng 反抗 [comp: 反 oppose + 抗 resist] V resist, fight back, rebel ■ 当父母的如果管得太多，孩子会反抗。**Dāng fùmǔ de rúguǒ guǎn de tài duō, háizi huì fǎnkàng.** *If a parent is too bossy, the child will rebel.*

fǎnkuì 反馈 [modif: 反 reverse + 馈 feed] N feedback

fǎnmiàn 反面 [modif: 反 reverse + 面 face, side] N the opposite side, the reverse

fǎnshè 反射 [modif: 反 reverse + 射 shoot] V reflect 条件反射 tiáojiàn fǎnshè conditional reflection

fǎnsī 反思 [modif: 反 reverse + 思 think] V think from a new angle, reflect on

fǎnwèn 反问 [modif: 反 reverse + 问 ask] V ask a question as a reply ■ 她反问我："你说呢？" **Tā fǎnwèn wǒ: "Nǐ shuō ne?"** *She replied,"What do you think?"*

fǎnwèn jù 反问句 N rhetorical question (e.g. 你难道不知道吗？ **Nǐ nándào bùzhīdào ma?** *Don't you know?*)

fǎnyìng 反应 [comp: 反 opposite + 应 reply, respond] N response, reaction ■ 病人还在昏迷中，医生问他话，没有反应。**Bìngrén háizài hūnmí zhōng, yīshēng wèn tā huà, méiyǒu fǎnyìng.** *The patient is still in coma and gives no response to the doctor's questions.* ■ 对于这个新产品，市场反应非常好。**Duìyú zhège xīn chǎnpǐn, shìchǎng fǎnyìng fēicháng hǎo.** *There is excellent market response to this new product.*

fǎnyìng 反映 V 1 reflect, mirror ■ 这篇小说反映了当代大学生的生活。**Zhè piān xiǎoshuō fǎnyìng le dāngdài dàxuéshēng de shēnghuó.** *This novel reflects the life of contemporary university students.* 2 report, make known, convey ■ 我要把你们的意见反映给领导。**Wǒ yào bǎ nǐmen de yìjiàn fǎnyìng gěi lǐngdǎo.** *I will convey your views to the leadership.*

fǎnzheng 反正 [comp: 反 reverse + 正 front] ADV anyway, at any rate ■ 你同意也好，不同意也好，我反正决定这么办了。**Nǐ tóngyì yěhǎo, bùtóngyì yěhǎo, wǒ fǎnzheng juédìng zhème bàn**

le. *Whether you approve or not, I have decided to do it anyway.*

fǎnzhī 反之 ADV otherwise, on the contrary

fǎn 返 V return (See **wǎngfǎn** 往返.)

fàn 犯 V violate, offend ■ 他犯了一个严重错误，心里很难过。**Tā fànle yí ge yánzhòng cuòwù, xīnli hěn nánguò.** *He is very sad that he made a serious mistake.*

fàn fǎ 犯法 V violate the law

fàn guī 犯规 V foul (in sports), break a rule

fàn zuì 犯罪 V commit a crime, break the law 犯罪分子 fàn zuì fènzi a criminal

fàn 饭 TRAD 飯 N 1 cooked rice ■ 小王每顿吃两碗饭。**Xiǎo Wáng měi dùn chī liǎng wǎn fàn.** *Xiao Wang eats two bowls of rice every meal.* ■ 他是南方人，爱吃米饭，不爱吃馒头和面条儿。**Tā shì nánfāngrén, ài chī mǐfàn, bú ài chī mántou hé miàntiáor.** *He is a Southerner. He loves rice and doesn't like steamed buns or noodles.* 2 meal (顿 dùn) ■ 他们常常在外面吃饭。**Tāmen chángcháng zài wàimiàn chīfàn.** *They often have their meals outside. (→ They often dine out.)* ■ 我请你吃饭。**Wǒ qǐng nǐ chīfàn.** *I'll treat you to a meal.*

fàndiàn 饭店 [modif: 饭 meal + 店 shop, store] N 1 restaurant (家 jiā) ■ 这家饭店饭菜好吃，价钱也便宜。**Zhè jia fàndiàn fàncài hǎochī, jiàqián yěpiányì.** *The dishes in this restaurant are delicious and affordable.* ■ 市中心新开了一家饭店，都说不错。**Shìzhōngxīn xīn kāile yì jiā fàndiàn, dōu shuō búcuò.** *A new restaurant opened downtown recently, and everyone says it's good.* 2 hotel (家 jiā) ■ 他住在一家五星饭店里。**Tā zhù zài yì jiā wǔxīng fàndiàn lǐ.** *He lives in a five-star hotel.*

NOTE: The original meaning of 饭店 **fàndiàn** is *restaurant*, but it is also used to denote *a hotel*. For example, 北京饭店 **Běijīng fàndiàn** may mean *Beijing Restaurant* or *Beijing Hotel*.

fànwǎn 饭碗 rice bowl; way of making a living, job

fàn 范 TRAD 範 N 1 model 2 border

fànchóu 范畴 N category, domain

fànwéi 范围 [comp: 范 border + 围 boundary] N scope, range, limits ■ 这不属于我的工作范围。**Zhè bù shǔyú wǒ de gōngzuò fànwéi.** *This is outside my job description.* ■ 这家公司的营业范围很广。**Zhè jiā gōngsī de yíngyè fànwéi hěn guǎng.** *The business range of this company is very wide.*

fàn 贩 TRAD 販 V buy to resell

fànmài 贩卖 [comp: 贩 buy + 卖 sell] V buy and sell for a profit (usually in an illegal way) 贩卖毒品 fànmài dúpǐn drug trafficking / 贩卖人口 fànmài rénkǒu human trafficking

fàn 泛 I V float II ADJ general, extensive

fànlàn 泛滥 [comp: 泛 float + 滥 flood] V overflow, flood; go rampant ■ 假货泛滥市场。**Jiǎhuò**

fànlàn shìchǎng. *The market is flooded with counterfeit goods.*

fāng 方 ADJ square ■ 中国人传统在方桌或者圆桌上吃饭，不用长桌吃饭。**Zhōngguórén chuántǒng zài fāngzhuō huòzhě yuánzhuō shang chīfàn, bú yòng chángzhuō chīfàn.** *Traditionally, the Chinese dine at a square or round table, not at an oblong one.*

fāng'àn 方案 [comp: 方 method + 案 file] N plan, program (for a major project) ■ 经过反复讨论，委员会通过了这个方案。**Jīngguò fǎnfù tǎolùn, wěiyuánhuì tōngguòle zhège fāng'àn.** *After repeated discussions the committee approved the program.*

fāngbiàn 方便 ADJ convenient, handy (ANTONYM 麻烦 máfan) ■ 住在城里买东西很方便。**Zhù zài chéngli mǎi dōngxi hěn fāngbiàn.** *With city living, shopping is convenient.* ■ 你方便的话，请帮我找一下这本书。**Nǐ fāngbiàn de huà, qǐng bāng wǒ zhǎo yíxià zhè běn shū.** *If it's not too much trouble, please help me locate this book.*

NOTE: A euphemism for "going to the toilet" is 方便一下 **fāngbiàn yíxià**, e.g. ■ 我要方便一下。**Wǒ yào fāngbiàn yíxià.** *I'm going to use the restroom.*

fāngbiàn miàn 方便面 N instant noodles

fāngfǎ 方法 [comp: 方 method, way of doing things + 法 method] N method ■ 这个方法不行，要另想办法。**Zhège fāngfǎ bùxíng, yào lìng xiǎng bànfǎ.** *This method won't do. We'll have to find another way.* ■ 学中文有没有什么好方法？**Xué Zhōngwén yǒu méiyǒu shénme hǎo fāngfǎ?** *Are there any good methods of learning Chinese?*

fāngmiàn 方面 [comp: 方 side + 面 face, surface] N side, aspect ■ 政府应该考虑社会各方面的意见。**Zhèngfǔ yīnggāi kǎolǜ shèhuì gè fāngmiàn de yìjiàn.** *The government should consider viewpoints from various aspects of society.* ■ 大量生产这种产品，在技术方面还有些问题。**Dàliàng shēngchǎn zhèzhǒng chǎnpǐn, zài jìshù fāngmiàn hái yǒu xiē wèntí.** *There are still some technological problems if this new product is to be mass-produced.*

fāngshì 方式 [comp: 方 method + 式 manner] N manner, way ■ 说话的内容很重要，说话的方式同样重要。**Shuōhuà de nèiróng hěn zhòngyào, shuōhuà de fāngshì tóngyàng zhòngyào.** *What you say is important, and how you say it is equally important.*

生活方式 shēnghuó fāngshì way of life, lifestyle

fāngwèi 方位 N points of the compass, directions

fāngxiàng 方向 N direction, orientation ■ 你的方向错了。**Nǐ de fāngxiàng cuò le.** *You're in the wrong direction.* ■ 汽车朝飞机场方向开去。**Qìchē cháo fēijīchǎng fāngxiàng kāiqu.** *The car headed in the direction of the airport.*

fāngyán 方言 N dialect

fāngzhēn 方针 N guiding principle, policy ■ 你们国家的教育方针是什么？**Nǐmen guójiā de jiàoyù fāngzhēn shì shénme?** *What are the guiding principles of education in your country?*

fáng 防 V prevent, guard against ■ 防火比救火重要，防病比治病重要。**Fánghuǒ bǐ jiùhuǒ zhòngyào, fángbìng bǐ zhìbìng zhòngyào.** *Preventing fires is more important than fire fighting; preventing diseases is more important than curing diseases.*

防火 fánghuǒ fire prevention / 防病 fángbìng disease prevention / 防盗 fángdào anti-burglary measures

fángshǒu 防守 [comp: 防 prevent + 守 defend] V defend, guard

fángyì 防疫 V epidemic prevention

防疫针 fángyìzhēn inoculation

fángyù 防御 [comp: 防 prevent + 御 defend] V defend (usually in war)

fángzhǐ 防止 [comp: 防 prevent + 止 stop] V prevent, guard against ■ 政府将采取措施防止人才外流。**Zhèngfǔ jiāng cǎiqǔ cuòshī fángzhǐ réncái wàiliú.** *The government will adopt measures to prevent brain drain.*

fángzhì 防治 [comp: 防 prevent + 治 treat] V prevent and treat (diseases)

防治病虫害 fángzhì bìngchónghài prevention and treatment of plant diseases and elimination of pests

fáng'ài 妨碍 [comp: 妨 prevent + 碍 hinder] V hinder, hamper, disturb ■ 你们把车停在这里，会妨碍交通。**Nǐmen bǎ chē tíng zài zhèli, huì fáng'ài jiāotōng.** *If you park your car here, it will block traffic.*

fáng 房 N 1 house ■ 他们现在租房住，打算明年买房。**Tāmen xiànzài zū fáng zhù, dǎsuàn míngnián mǎi fáng.** *They now live in a rented house and are planning to buy a house next year.*

草房 cǎofáng thatched cottage / 楼房 lóufáng house of two or more levels / 平房 píngfáng single-story house, bungalow

2 room (间 jiān) ■ 楼上有三间房。**Lóu shang yǒu sān jiān fáng.** *There are three bedrooms upstairs.*

病房 bìngfáng sick room, ward / 客房 kèfáng guest room

fángdōng 房东 N landlord, landlady

fángjiān 房间 [comp: 房 room, home + 间 space] N room (间 jiān) ■ 这间房间不大，但是挺舒服。**Zhè jiān fángjiān bú dà, dànshì tǐng shūfu.** *This room is not big, but it's very comfortable.*

fángzi 房子 [suffix: 房 house + 子 nominal suffix] N house, housing ■ 他们有了钱就买房子。**Tāmen yǒule qián jiù mǎi fángzi.** *They will buy a house once they have the money.*

fǎng 仿 V imitate

fǎngfú 仿佛 V be like, be alike ■ 他们俩年龄相仿佛，经历也差不多。**Tāmen liǎ niánlíng xiāng fǎngfú, jīnglì yě chàbuduō.** *The two of them are of similar age and share similar life experiences.*

fǎng 纺 TRAD 紡 V spin (into thread/yarn)

fǎngzhī 纺织 [comp: 纺 spin + 织 weave] v spin and weave ■ 在这个山村里，还有老人会纺织土布。**Zài zhège shāncūn li háiyǒu lǎorén huì fǎngzhī tǔbù.** *In this mountain village there are old people who still make homespun cloth.*
纺织工业 fǎngzhī gōngyè textile industry / 纺织品 fǎngzhīpǐn textile goods

fǎng 访 TRAD 訪 v visit

fǎngwèn 访问 [comp: 访 visit + 问 ask, ask after] v visit, interview ■ 已经有一百多万人访问过这个网站。**Yǐjīng yǒu yìbǎi duō wàn rén fǎngwènguo zhège wǎngzhàn.** *Over a million people have visited this website.*

fàng 放 v put, put in ■ 请你不要把你的书放在我的桌子上。**Qǐng nǐ bú yào bǎ nǐ de shū fàng zài wǒ de zhuōzi shang.** *Please don't put your books on my desk.* ■ 你的咖啡里要不要放糖？**Nǐ de kāfēi li yào bú yào fàng táng?** *Shall I put sugar in your coffee?*

fàngdà 放大 [comp: 放 expand + 大 large] v enlarge ■ 这张照片请放大。**Zhè zhāng zhàopiàn qǐng fàngdà.** *Please enlarge this photo.*
放大镜 fàngdàjìng magnifying glass

fàngjià 放假 [v+obj: 放 release + 假 holiday] v be on holiday, have the day off ■ 我们学校从十二月十五日到一月二十日放假。**Wǒmen xuéxiào cóng Shí'èr yuè shíwǔ rì dào Yīyuè èrshí rì fàngjià.** *We have school holidays from December 15 to January 20.* ■ 明日停电，学校放假一天。**Míngrì tíngdiàn, xuéxiào fàngjià yìtiān.** *School's closed tomorrow due to a power cut.*

fàngqì 放弃 [comp: 放 release + 弃 abandon] v abandon, give up ■ 这个机会十分难得，你不要放弃。**Zhège jīhuì shífēn nándé, nǐ bú yào fàngqì.** *This is a very rare opportunity. Don't pass it up.* ■ 我们已经放弃了原来的计划。**Wǒmen yǐjīng fàngqìle yuánlái de jìhuà.** *We have abandoned our original plan.*

fàngshè 放射 v radiate
放射科 fàngshèkē department of radiology (in a hospital) / 放射治疗 fàngshè zhìliáo radiotherapy

fàngshǒu 放手 [v+obj: 放 release + 手 the hand] let go one's hold, let go

fàngsōng 放松 [comp: 放 release + 松 loose] v relax, rest and relax ■ 这星期工作太紧张了，周末我要好好放松放松。**Zhè xīngqī gōngzuò tài jǐnzhāng le, zhōumò wǒ yào hǎohǎo fàngsōng fàngsōng.** *This week I've been really stressed out with work; I'll rest and relax over the weekend.*

fàngxīn 放心 [v+obj: 放 set in place + 心 the heart] v set one's mind at ease, be at ease (ANTONYM 担心 dānxīn) ■ 你办事，我放心。**Nǐ bànshì, wǒ fàngxīn.** *With you in charge, my mind's at ease.* ■ 才十几岁的孩子出国留学，父母怎么会放心呢？**Cái shí jǐ suì de háizi chūguó liúxué, fùmǔ zénme huì fàngxīn ne?** *How can parents not worry when their teenage children go overseas to study?*

fēi 飞 TRAD 飛 v fly ■ 小鸟飞走了。**Xiǎo niǎo fēi zǒu le.** *The little bird flew away.*

fēijī 飞机 [modif: 飞 flying + 机 machine] N airplane ■ 从北京来的飞机什么时候到？**Cóng Běijīng lái de fēijī shénme shíhou dào?** *When does the plane from Beijing arrive?*
坐/乘飞机 zuò/chéng fēijī travel by plane ■ 我们全家明天坐飞机去上海。**Wǒmen quán jiā míngtiān zuò fēijī qù Shànghǎi.** *My family will go to Shanghai tomorrow by air.*
飞机票 fēijī piào air ticket / 飞机场 fēijī chǎng airport / 开飞机 kāi fēijī pilot a plane

fēi qín zǒu shòu 飞禽走兽 IDIOM flying fowls and running beasts, birds and beasts of all kinds

fēixiáng 飞翔 [comp: 飞 fly + 翔 fly] v circle in the air (like an eagle), hover

fēiyuè 飞跃 [comp: 飞 fly + 跃 leap] I v go forward in leaps and bounds II N sudden and rapid development

fēi 非 ADV not, do not

fēi … bùkē 非 … 不可 ADV have no choice but to …, simply must … ■ 我今天非写完这个报告不可。**Wǒ jīntiān fēi xiěwán zhège bàogào bùkě.** *I simply must finish writing this report today.*

NOTE: 非...不 … **fēi … bùkě** is used to emphasize the verb after 非 **fēi**. 不可 **bùkě** may be omitted, e.g. 我今天非写完这个报告。**Wǒ jīntiān fēi xiěwán zhège bàogào.** *I simply must finish writing this report today.*

fēicháng 非常 [modif: 非 not + 常 usual] ADV unusually, very ■ 中国非常大。**Zhōngguó fēicháng dà.** *China is very big.* ■ 我非常想去新加坡旅行。**Wǒ fēicháng xiǎng qù Xīnjiāpō lǚxíng.** *I very much want to take a trip to Singapore.*

fēifǎ 非法 [modif: 非 not + 法 legal] ADJ illegal, unlawful
非法收入 fēifǎ shōurù illegal income

Fēizhōu 非洲 [modif: 非 Africa + 洲 continent] N Africa

féi 肥 ADJ fat, fattened ■ 这头猪真肥！**Zhè tóu zhū zhēn féi!** *What a fat pig!*

NOTE: 肥 **féi** is normally used to describe animals. It is insulting to use it to describe humans.

féiliào 肥料 [modif: 肥 fat, fatten + 料 material] N fertilizer
有机肥料 yǒujī féiliào organic fertilizer

féiwò 肥沃 [comp: 肥 fat + 沃 fertile] ADJ (of soil) fertile

féizào 肥皂 N soap (块 kuài)
肥皂粉 féizàofěn detergent powder

fěi 诽 TRAD 誹 v slander

fěibàng 诽谤 [comp: 诽 slander + 谤 slander] v slander, libel

fěi 匪 N bandit

fěitú 匪徒 N bandit, brigand, criminal thug

fèi 肺 N the lungs ■ 吸烟伤害肺。**Xīyān shānghài fèi.** *Smoking harms the lungs.*

fèi 费 TRAD 費 1 N fee, charge ■ 我一个月要花很多钱交各种各样的费。**Wǒ yí ge yuè yào huā hěn duō qián jiāo gè-zhǒng-gè-yàng de fèi.** *I spend a lot of money on various fees every month.*

管理费 guǎnlǐ fèi administration charge / 机场费 jīchǎng fèi airport tax / 交费 jiāo fèi pay fees, a charge, etc. / 水电费 shuǐdiàn fèi water and electricity bill / 学费 xué fèi tuition fee

2 V cost, spend ■ 他费了很多钱才把车修好。**Tā fèi le hěn duō qián cái bǎ chē xiūhǎo.** *Only after spending a small fortune did he get his car repaired.*

费了九牛二虎之力 fèi le jiǔ-niú-èr-hǔ zhī lì spend the strength of nine bulls and two tigers, make tremendous efforts ■ 我费了九牛二虎之力才完成这个任务。**Wǒ fèi le jiǔ-niú-èr-hǔ zhī lì cái wánchéng zhège rènwù.** *It was with tremendous effort that I accomplished the task.*

fèiyòng 费用 N expense, cost ■ 在这个国家念大学，一年的费用是多少？**Zài zhège guójiā niàn dàxué, yìnián de fèi yòng shì duōshǎo?** *How much is the annual cost of studying in a university in this country?*

生活费用 shēnghuó fèiyòng living expenses, cost of living / 办公费用 bàngōng fèiyòng administration cost, overheads

fèi 废 TRAD 廢 ADJ useless

fèichú 废除 V abolish, abrogate

fèihuà 废话 [modif: 废 useless + 话 words] N nonsense, rubbish

fèipǐn 废品 [modif: 废 useless + 品 article] N junk, reject, useless product

废品回收 fèipǐn huíshōu collecting junk, waste recycling

fèiqì 废气 N waste gas

减少废气排放 jiǎnshǎo fèiqì páifàng reduce waste gas emission

fèi qǐn wàng shí 废寝忘食 V (so absorbed or occupied as to) forget food and sleep

fèiwù 废物 [modif: 废 useless + 物 object] N 1 waste material ■ 这些录音带、录像带都是废物了。**Zhè xiē lùyīndài, lùxiàngdài dōu shì fèiwù le.** *All these audiotapes and video tapes are waste materials now.* **2** good-for-nothing ■ 她连这么简单的事都做不好，真是个废物！**Tā lián zhème jiǎndān de shì dōu zuòbuhǎo, zhēnshì ge fèiwù!** *She can't even do well such simple jobs. What a good-for-nothing!*

fèixū 废墟 N ruins, debris

fèi 沸 V boil

fèiténg 沸腾 [comp: 沸 boil + 腾 gallop] V 1 boil **2** seethe with excitement

fēn 分 I V divide ■ 今天是你的生日，你来分生日蛋糕。**Jīntiān shì nǐ de shēngrì, nǐ lái fēn shēngrì dàngāo.** *Today's your birthday, come and cut your birthday cake.*

分享 fēnxiǎng share (joy, benefits, etc.)

II N point, mark ■ 你去年中文考试得了多少分？**Nǐ qùnián Zhōngwén kǎoshì dé le duōshǎo fēn?** *What marks did you get for the Chinese examination last year?* **III** N minute ■ 现在是十点二十分。**Xiànzài shì shí diǎn èrshí fēn.** *It's ten twenty now.* **IV** MEASURE WORD (Chinese currency; 1 分 **fēn** = 0.1 角 **jiǎo** = 0.01 元 **yuán**), cent

fēnbiàn 分辨 [comp: 分 divide + 辨 distinguish] V distinguish, differentiate

分辨不同的声调 fēnbiàn bùtóng de shēngdiào differentiate different tones (of Chinese syllables)

fēnbié 分别 V 1 part with, be separated from ■ 我和姐姐分别三年了，今天见面，多高兴啊！**Wǒ hé jiějie fēnbié sānnián le, jīntiān jiànmiàn, duō gāoxìng a!** *I'm meeting my older sister today after three years' separation. How happy I am!* **2** distinguish ■ 对于犯错误的人，我们要分别情况，不同对待。**Duìyú fàn cuòwù de rén, wǒmen yào fēnbié qíngkuàng, bùtóng duìdài.** *Regarding those who have made mistakes, we should distinguish between circumstances and deal with them accordingly.*

fēnbù 分布 V & N be distributed (over an area); distribution ■ 这家连锁餐馆分布在全国各地。**Zhè jiā liánsuǒ cānguǎn fēnbù zài quánguó gèdì.** *This chain restaurants are distributed in various cities of the country.*

fēncùn 分寸 [comp: 分 point + 寸 inch] N proper limits of speech and action, sense of propriety

fēnhóng 分红 V pay or receive dividends

fēnjiě 分解 V decompose, break down

fēnliè 分裂 [comp: 分 divide + 裂 break up] V split, break up

fēnmì 分泌 V secrete

分泌胃液 fēnmì wèiyè secrete gastric juice

fēnmíng 分明 ADJ sharply contoured, distinct ■ 我家乡四季分明。**Wǒ jiāxiāng sìjì fēnmíng.** *My hometown has four distinct seasons.*

fēnpèi 分配 [comp: 分 divide + 配 ration] V distribute, allocate ■ 根据各人的能力，分配不同的工作。**Gēnjù gèrén de nénglì, fēnpèi bùtóng de gōngzuò.** *Different jobs are allocated according to people's abilities.*

fēnqí 分歧 N difference (in opinions), divergence

消除分歧 xiāochú fēnqí settle differences

fēnsàn 分散 I V disperse, scatter

分散投资 fēnsàn tóuzī diversify one's investments

II ADJ scattered

fēn shǒu 分手 V part company, say goodbye to

fēnshù 分数 N number recorded when grading, mark, grade

fēnxī 分析 [comp: 分 divide + 析 analyze] V & N

analyze; analysis ■ 我们要仔细分析这两件事之间的关系。**Wǒmen yào zǐxì fēnxī zhè liǎng jiàn shì zhī jiān de guānxi.** *We should analyze the relationship between these two events carefully.* ■ 经过分析他们知道了这个药的化学成分。**Jīngguò fēnxī tāmen zhīdào le zhège yào de huàxué chéngfèn.** *After an analysis, they learned the drug's chemical components.*

... **fēnzhī** ... ... 分之 ... NUMERAL (indicating fraction)
三分之二 sān fēnzhī èr two thirds / 八分之一 bā fēnzhī yī one eighth / ... 百分之 ... bǎi fēnzhī ... percent / 百分之七十 bǎi fēnzhī qīshí seventy percent (70%) / 百分之四十五点三 bǎi fēnzhī sìshíwǔ diǎn sān forty-five point three percent (45.3%)

fēnzhōng 分钟 N minute (of an hour) ■ 我等你等了四十多分钟。**Wǒ děng nǐ děngle sìshí duō fēnzhōng.** *I waited for you for over forty minutes.* ■ 打长途电话，以每分钟计费。**Dǎ chángtú diànhuà, yǐ měi fēnzhōng jìfèi.** *The cost of long-distance telephone calls is calculated by the minute.*

fēn 吩 V instruct

fēnfù 吩咐 V instruct, tell (what to do) ■ 她吩咐旅馆服务员把晚饭送到房间来。**Tā fēnfù lǚguǎn fúwùyuán bǎ wǎnfàn sòngdào fángjiān lái.** *She instructed the hotel attendant to deliver the dinner to her room.*

fēn 纷 TRAD 紛 ADJ numerous, varied

fēnfēn 纷纷 ADJ numerous and disorderly ■ 对于这个处分，大家议论纷纷，有人说太重，有人说太轻。**Duìyú zhège chǔfèn, dàjiā yìlùn fēnfēn, yǒurén shuō tài zhòng, yǒurén shuō tài qīng.** *There is great controversy over this disciplinary action; some say it is too severe, others say it is too light.*

fēn 氛 N atmosphere

fén 坟 N tomb

fénmù 坟墓 [comp: 坟 tomb + 墓 graveyard] N grave, tomb (座 zuò)

fěn 粉 N powder

fěnbǐ 粉笔 [modif: 粉 powder + 笔 pen] N chalk (支 zhī) ■ 约翰，请你到办公室去给我拿几支粉笔来。**Yuēhàn, qǐng nǐ dào bàngōngshì qu gěi wǒ ná jǐ zhī fěnbǐ lái.** *John, please go to the office and get me a few pieces of chalk.*

fěnmò 粉末 N powder, dust

fěnsè 粉色 N pink

fěnsuì 粉碎 V smash, crush

fèn 分 N component
糖分 tángfèn sugar content

fènliàng 分量 N weight ■ 你们这批货物分量不足。**Nǐmen zhè pī huòwù fènliàng bù zú.** *This batch of your goods is short weight.* ■ 他在公司里工作了二十多年了，说话很有分量。**Tā zài gōngsī li gōngzuòle èrshí duō nián le, shuōhuà hěn yǒu fènliàng.** *He has been working in the company for*

over twenty years and what he says carries a lot of weight.

fèn 份 MEASURE WORD (for a set of things or newspapers, documents, etc.)
一份礼物 yí fèn lǐwù a present / 一份报告 yí fèn bàogào a report

fèn 奋 TRAD 奮 V exert oneself

fèndòu 奋斗 [modif: 奋 exert oneself + 斗 fight] V fight, struggle, strive ■ 要成功就要奋斗。**Yào chénggōng jiù yào fèndòu.** *If you want to succeed, you must fight for it.*

fèn 愤 TRAD 憤 N anger

fènnù 愤怒 [comp: 愤 angry + 怒 enraged] ADJ enraged, angry ■ 她发现又受了欺骗，十分愤怒。**Tā fāxiàn yòu shòule qīpiàn, shífēn fènnù.** *She was enraged to discover that she had been cheated again.*

fēng 丰 TRAD 豐 ADJ abundant

fēngfù 丰富 [comp: 丰 abundance + 富 wealth] ADJ abundant, rich, plenty ■ 这位老师有丰富的经验。**Zhè wèi lǎoshī yǒu fēngfù de jīngyàn.** *This teacher has rich experience.* ■ 这本书的内容非常丰富，值得反复阅读。**Zhè běn shū de nèiróng fēicháng fēngfù, zhídé fǎnfù yuèdú.** *This book has very rich content and is worth repeated reading.*

fēngmǎn 丰满 [comp: 丰 plentiful + 满 full] ADJ
1 plump
身材丰满 shēncái fēngmǎn with a full (and attractive) figure
2 plentiful
羽毛丰满 yǔmáo fēngmǎn full-fledged, developed well enough to be independent

fēngshèng 丰盛 ADJ sumptuous, rich

fēngshōu 丰收 [modif: 丰 abundant + 收 harvest] N bumper harvest

fēng 风 TRAD 風 N wind ■ 今天风很大。**Jīntiān fēng hěn dà.** *It's very windy today.* ■ 冬天中国常常刮西北风。**Dōngtiān Zhōngguó chángcháng guā xīběi fēng.** *In winter a northwestern wind prevails in China.*

fēngbào 风暴 N windstorm (场 chǎng)

fēngdù 风度 N demeanor, bearing, (elegant) demeanor
很有风度 hěn yǒu fēngdù with elegant demeanor

fēnggé 风格 N style (of doing things)
管理风格 guǎnlǐ fēnggé managerial style / 建筑风格 jiànzhù fēnggé architectural style

fēngguāng 风光 N scenery, sight

fēngjǐng 风景 N landscape, scenery ■ 山顶上的风景特别优美。**Shāndǐng shang de fēngjǐng tèbié yōuměi.** *The scenery on top of the mountain is particularly beautiful.*

fēnglì 风力 [modif: 风 wind + 力 force] N wind force, wind power ■ 今天风力很大，不能划船。**Jīntiān fēnglì hěn dà, bù néng huáchuán.** *Today the wind is too strong for us to go boating.*

fēngqì 风气 [comp: 风 winds + 气 atmosphere] **N** general mood and common practice (of a society, a locality or an organization)

fēngqù 风趣 **N** humor, wit

有风趣 yǒu fēngqù witty, humorous

fēngsú 风俗 **N** custom, social customs ■ 他每到一个地方就了解当地的风俗。**Tā měi dào yí ge dìfang jiù liǎojiědāngdì de fēngsú.** *Wherever he goes he will learn the local customs.* ■ 有些旧风俗正在渐渐消失。**Yǒuxiē jiù fēngsú zhèngzài jiànjiàn xiāoshī.** *Some old customs are gradually disappearing.*

fēng tǔ rén qíng 风土人情 **N** local conditions and customs

fēngwèi 风味 **N** special flavor, local color

fēngxiǎn 风险 **N** risk

冒风险 mào fēngxiǎn run a risk, take a chance, risk-taking

fēngxiàng 风向 **N** wind direction

fēng 疯 **TRAD** 瘋 **ADJ** insane, crazy ■ 你疯啦？**Nǐ fēng la?** *Are you crazy?*

fēngkuáng 疯狂 [comp: 疯 insane + 狂 mad] **ADJ** insane, frenzied

fēng 封 **I MEASURE WORD** (for letters) ■ 王先生，有你一封信。**Wáng xiānsheng, yǒu nǐ yì fēng xìn.** *Mr Wang, here's a letter for you.* **II v** close, seal up

fēngbì 封闭 [comp: 封 seal + 闭 close] **v** close, seal

fēngjiàn 封建 **ADJ** 1 feudal 2 traditional (in a bad sense)

fēngsuǒ 封锁 [comp: 封 seal + 锁 lock] **v** block, seal off

封锁消息 fēngsuǒ xiāoxī news blackout

fēng 蜂 **N** wasp (See **mìfēng** 蜜蜂.)

fēng 锋 **TRAD** 鋒 **N** sharp point of a knife

fēnglì 锋利 **ADJ** sharp

féng 逢 **v** come upon, meet ■ 每逢结婚纪念日，他们夫妻总要庆祝一下。**Měi féng jiéhūn jìniànrì, tāmen fūqī zǒngyào qìngzhù yíxià.** *Every time their wedding anniversary comes around, that couple will celebrate it.*

féng nián guò jié 逢年过节 **IDIOM** on festival days and the New Year's Day, on festive occasions

féng 缝 **TRAD** 縫 **v** sew ■ 现在很少人自己缝衣服了。**Xiànzài hěn shǎo rén zìjǐ féng yīfu le.** *Very few people sew their own clothes nowadays.*

fěng 讽 **TRAD** 諷 **v** satirize

fěngcì 讽刺 [comp: 讽 mock + 刺 prick] **v & N** satirize, ridicule, mock; satire

fèng 奉 **v** offer; obey; believe in

fèngxiàn 奉献 [comp: 奉 offer + 献 offer] **v** offer as a tribute; present with respect

fèng 缝 **N** seam, chink, slit

fó 佛 **N** Buddha

fójiào 佛教 **N** Buddhism

fǒu 否 **v** negate

fǒudìng 否定 **v** negate, deny (**ANTONYM** 肯定 **kěndìng**) ■ 我不想否定你们的成绩。**Wǒ bù xiǎng fǒudìng nǐmen de chéngjì.** *I don't want to deny your achievements.*

fǒujué 否决 [modif: 否 negative + 决 decide] **v** vote down, veto, overrule

fǒurèn 否认 **v** deny, repudiate (**ANTONYM** 承认 **chéngrèn**)

fǒuzé 否则 **CONJ** otherwise, or ■ 这个问题必须尽快解决，否则会危害整个工程。**Zhège wèntí bìxū jìnkuài jiějué, fǒuzé huì wēihài zhěngge gōngchéng.** *This problem must be solved as soon as possible, otherwise it will jeopardize the entire project.* ■ 你们一定要在十天内付清电费，否则要断电。**Nǐmen yídìng yào zài shí tiān nèi fùqīng diànfèi, fǒuzé yào duàndiàn.** *You must pay the electricity bill in ten days or you'll face an electricity cutoff.*

fū 夫 **N** man

fūfù 夫妇 [comp: 夫 man + 妇 woman] same as 夫妻 **fūqī**

fūqī 夫妻 [comp: 夫 husband + 妻 wife] **N** husband and wife

夫妻关系 fūqī guānxi marital relationship

fūrén 夫人 **N** (formal term for another person's) wife ■ 王董事长和夫人将出席宴会。**Wáng dǒngshìzhǎng hé fūrén jiāng chūxí yànhuì.** *Chairman Wang and his wife will attend the dinner party.*

fū 肤 **TRAD** 膚 **N** skin (See **pífū** 皮肤.)

fū 敷 **v** apply

敷药 fū yào apply medicine (to a wound)

fūyǎn 敷衍 **v** go through the motions, be perfunctory

fú 服 **I v** obey **II N** clothes

fúcóng 服从 [comp: 服 obey + 从 follow] **v** obey, submit to ■ 少数服从多数。**Shǎoshù fúcóng duōshù.** *The minority submits to the majority.* ■ 我服从总公司的决定。**Wǒ fúcóng zǒnggōngsī de juédìng.** *I will defer to the decision of the company headquarters.*

fúqì 服气 **v** be convinced

fúwù 服务 [comp: 服 obey + 务 work] **v** serve, work for

为 … 服务 wèi … fúwù serve …, work for … ■ 我能为大家服务，感到很高兴。**Wǒ néng wèi dàjiā fúwù, gǎndào hěn gāoxìng.** *I'm happy to be able to serve you all.*

fúwù qì 服务器 **N** server (for computers)

fúwù yè 服务业 **N** service industry

fúwù yuán 服务员 [suffix: 服务 serve + 员 person] **N** attendant, waiter/waitress ■ 这位服务员态度不大好。**Zhè wèi fúwùyuán tàidu bú dà hǎo.** *This attendant's work attitude is not very good.* ■ 要付服务员小费吗？**Yào fù fúwùyuán xiǎofèi ma?** *Do we tip the attendants?*

fúzhuāng 服装 N clothes, garments, apparel
服装商店 fúzhuāngshāngdiàn clothes store

fú 扶 v support with the hand
扶着老人过马路 fúzhe lǎorén guò mǎlù help an old person walk across the street

fú 浮 v float

fú 幅 MEASURE WORD (for pictures, posters, maps, etc.)
一幅中国画 yì fú Zhōngguó huà a Chinese painting

fúdù 幅度 N range, extent

fú 辐 TRAD 輻 N spoke (of a wheel)

fúshè 辐射 v & N radiate, radiation

fú 福 N blessing, happiness

fúlì 福利 [comp: 福 blessing + 利 benefit] N welfare, well-being
为职工谋福利 wéi zhígōng móu fúlì work for the welfare of the staff

fúqi 福气 N good fortune
有福气 yǒu fúqi have good fortune, be very lucky

fú 俘 v capture
战俘 zhànfú prisoner of war

fúlǔ 俘虏 N captive, prisoner of war

fú 伏 v bend over, lean on (See **máifu** 埋伏.)

fú 袱 N cloth-wrapper (See **bāofu** 包袱.)

fú 符 v be in accord

fúhào 符号 N symbol, mark

fúhé 符合 [comp: 符 conform to + 合 accord with] v conform to, accord with ■ 这种产品的质量不符合要求。**Zhè zhǒng chǎnpǐn de zhìliàng bù fúhé yāoqiú.** *The quality of this product does not meet the requirements.*

fǔ 府 N government office (See **zhèngfǔ** 政府.)

fǔ 俯 v bow one's head, bend down

fǔshì 俯视 v look down at, overlook

fǔyǎng 俯仰 v bend and lift one's head

fǔ 腐 ADJ rotten

fǔbài 腐败 [comp: 腐 rotten + 败 collapse] I ADJ 1 badly decayed, spoiled
腐败食品 fǔbài shípǐn food that has spoiled 2 corrupt ■ 腐败的官员人人恨。**Fǔbài de guānyuán rénrén hèn.** *Everyone hates corrupt officials.* II N corruption

fǔlàn 腐烂 [comp: 腐 corrupt + 烂 rotten] v & ADJ decompose, rot; decomposed, putrid

fǔshí 腐蚀 v 1 corrode, etch 2 make (people) corrupt

fǔxiǔ 腐朽 [comp: 腐 decomposed + 朽 decayed] ADJ decayed, rotten

fǔ 辅 TRAD 輔 N assistance, supplement

fǔdǎo 辅导 v coach, tutor ■ 王小姐辅导我们学中文。**Wáng xiǎojiě fǔdǎo wǒmen xué Zhōngwén.** *Miss Wang tutors us in Chinese.* ■ 王老师，您的辅导对我们很有帮助。**Wáng lǎoshī, nín de fǔdǎo duì wǒmen hěn yǒu bāngzhù.** *Teacher Wang, your tutorial is helpful to us.*
辅导课 fǔdǎo kè tutorial class, tutorial / 辅导老师

fǔdǎo lǎoshī tutor, teaching assistant

fǔzhù 辅助 [comp: 辅 assist + 助 help] v assist, play an auxiliary role

fǔ 抚 TRAD 撫 v 1 touch softly 2 foster (a child)

fǔmō 抚摸 same as 抚摩 **fǔmó**

fǔmó 抚摩 v stroke, caress

fǔyǎng 抚养 [comp: 抚 foster + 养 provide for] v bring up (a child), provide for (a child)

fù 父 N father

fùqin 父亲 [modif: 父 father + 亲 parent] N father ■ 您父亲做什么工作？**Nín fùqin zuò shénme gōngzuò?** *What does your father do?* ■ 我爱我父亲。**Wǒ ài wǒ fùqin.** *I love my father.*

NOTE: 爸爸 **bàba** and 父亲 **fùqin** denote the same person. While 爸爸 **bàba** is colloquial, like "daddy," 父亲 **fùqin** is formal, equivalent to "father." When referring to another person's father, 父亲 **fùqin** is preferred. As a form of address to your own father, only 爸爸 **bàba** is normally used.

fù 付 v pay ■ 提供服务后请立即付费。**Tígòng fúwù hòu qǐng lìjí fù fèi.** *You are expected to pay as soon as a service is provided. (→ Pay promptly for services rendered.)* ■ 我已经付给眼镜店百分之二十的定金。**Wǒ yǐjīng fù gěi yǎnjìngdiàn bǎifēn zhī èrshí de dìngjīn.** *I have paid the optician a deposit of twenty percent.*

fùchù 付出 [v+compl: 付 pay + 出 out] v pay out, contribute

fùkuǎn 付款 [v+obj: 付 pay + 款 fund] N & v pay a sum of money, make a payment ■ 收到货后请马上付款。**Shōudào huò hòu qǐng mǎshàng fùkuǎn.** *Please pay promptly after receiving the goods.*

fù 负 TRAD 負 v carry on the back

fùdān 负担 [comp: 负 carry on the back + 担 carry on the shoulder] v & N bear (costs); burden, financial burden
负担旅费 fùdān lǚfèi bear travel expenses

fùzé 负责 [v+obj: 负 carry on back + 责 responsibility] v be responsible, be in charge ■ 这件事我负责。**Zhè jiàn shì wǒ fùzé.** *I'm responsible for this matter. (or I'm in charge of this matter.)* ■ 他做事非常负责。**Tā zuòshì fēicháng fùzé.** *He has a strong sense of responsibility.*

fùzérén 负责人 N the person in charge ■ 我很不满意，我要见你们的负责人。**Wǒ hěn bù mǎnyì, wǒ yào jiàn nǐmen de fùzérén.** *I'm very dissatisfied (or disappointed). I want to see the person in charge here.*

fù zérèn 负责任 same as 负责 **fùzé**

fù 妇 TRAD 婦 N woman

fùnǚ 妇女 [comp: 妇 woman + 女 woman] N woman, womankind ■ 妇女的地位有了很大提高。**Fùnǚ de dìwèi yǒule hěn dà tígāo.** *The social status of women has risen remarkably.*

fù 附 v 1 be close to 2 attach, add

fùhé 附和 v chime in with, echo

fùjiàn 附件 N 1 appendix, side document 2 spare part, accessory

fùjìn 附近 [comp: 附 close to + 近 close by] N the area nearby ■ 附近有没有邮局？ **Fùjìn yǒu méiyǒu yóujú?** *Is there a post office nearby?* ■ 李先生就住在附近。**Lǐ xiānsheng jiù zhù zài fùjìn.** *Mr Li lives near here.*

fùshǔ 附属 [comp: 附 attach + 属 belong to] v attach, affiliate

北京师范大学附属中学 Běijīng Shīfàn Dàxué Fùshǔ Zhōngxué Middle School affiliated to Beijing Normal University

fù 附 v instruct (See **fēnfù** 吩附, **zhǔfu** 嘱附.)

fù 复 TRAD 復 V & N repeat; compound

fùhuó 复活 V & N resurrect, resurrection

fùhuó jié 复活节 [modif: 复活 resurrection + 节 festival, day] Easter

fùshù 复述 [modif: 复 repeat + 述 narrate] v retell, repeat ■ 请你把她的话一个一个字地复述一下。**Qǐng nǐ bǎ tā de huà yí ge yí ge zì de fùshù yíxia.** *Please repeat what she says verbatim.*

fùxí 复习 [modif: 复 repeat + 习 study] v review (one's lesson) ■ 下星期要考试，这几天我在复习。**Xià xīngqī yào kǎoshì, zhè jǐ tiān wǒ zài fùxí.** *I'll be having an examination next week. I'm reviewing my lesson these days.*

fùxìng 复兴 [comp: 复 revive + 兴 flourish] v revive, rejuvenate

fùyìn 复印 v make a photocopy of, photocopy

fùyìnjī 复印机 N photocopier

fùyìnjiàn 复印件 N a photocopy

fùzá 复杂 [comp: 复 multiple + 杂 miscellaneous] ADJ complicated, complex (ANTONYM 简单 **jiǎndān**) ■ 这件事很复杂，我说不清楚。**Zhè jiàn shì hěn fùzá, wǒ shuō bu qīngchu.** *This is a complicated matter. I can't explain it clearly.* ■ 这么复杂的中文句子，我不会说。**Zhème fùzá de Zhōngwén jùzi, wǒ bú huì shuō.** *I can't say such a complicated sentence in Chinese.*

fùzhì 复制 [modif: 复 double + 制 make] v copy, clone

fù 腹 N abdomen, belly

fùxiè 腹泻 N diarrhoea

fù 覆 v cover

fùgài 覆盖 v cover, cover up

fù 赋 v bestow on, grant

fùyú 赋予 v give, entrust

fù 副 I MEASURE WORD (for objects in pairs or sets) pair, set

一副手套 yí fù shǒutào a pair of gloves / 一副眼镜 yí fù yǎnjìng a pair of spectacles

II ADJ deputy, vice-…

副校长 fù xiàozhǎng deputy principal

fù zuòyòng 副作用 N side effect

fù 富 ADJ rich, wealthy (ANTONYM 穷 **qióng**) ■ 这个地区很富，房子都很漂亮。**Zhège dìqū hěn fù, fángzi dōu hěn piàoliang.** *This is a wealthy area with beautiful houses.*

富人 fùrén rich person, rich people

NOTE: In everyday Chinese, 富 **fù** is not used as much as 有钱 **yǒuqián** to mean *rich*.

fùyù 富裕 [comp: 富 rich + 裕 abundant] ADJ rich, well-to-do

fù 傅 N teacher, advisor (See **shīfu** 师傅.)

fù 缚 TRAD 縛 v tie up (See **shùfù** 束缚.)

fù 赴 v go to, attend

G

gāi 该[1] TRAD 該 I MODAL V should, ought to ■ 你不该常常迟到。**Nǐ bù gāi chángcháng chídào.** *You shouldn't be late so often.* ■ 他不该答应了你，又不去办。**Tā bù gāi dāyìngle nǐ, yòu bú qù bàn.** *He shouldn't have made you a promise and then done nothing.* II v be somebody's turn to do something ■ 今天该你洗碗。**Jīntiān gāi nǐ xǐ wǎn.** *It's your turn to wash dishes today.*

gāi 该[2] TRAD 該 PRON that, the said, the above mentioned ■ 该校学生人数在五年内增加一倍。**Gāi xiào xuésheng rénshù zài wǔ nián nèi zēngjiā yí bèi.** *The student population of that school has doubled in five years.*

NOTE: 该 **gāi** in this sense is used only in formal writing.

gǎi 改 v alter, change, correct ■ 你这个字写错了，要改一下。**Nǐ zhège zì xiěcuò le, yào gǎi yíxià.** *You've written a wrong character. You should correct it.* ■ 你这个坏习惯一定要改。**Nǐ zhège huài xíguàn yídìng yào gǎi.** *You must break this bad habit.*

gǎibiàn 改变 [comp: 改 alter + 变 change] V & N transform, change; transformation, change ■ 我想改变一下我们的旅行路线。**Wǒ xiǎng gǎibiàn yíxià wǒmende lǚxíng lùxiàn.** *I'd like to change our itinerary.* ■ 你明年的计划有没有什么改变？**Nǐ míngnián de jìhuà yǒu méiyǒu shénme gǎibiàn?** *Are there any changes in your plan for the next year?*

gǎigé 改革 [comp: 改 change + 革 remove] V & N reform ■ 只有不断改革，才能跟上时代。**Zhǐyǒu búduàn gǎigé, cáinéng gēnshàng shídài.** *Only by constant reform can we keep abreast with the times.* ■ 改革开放是中国八十年代以来的两项重大政策。**Gǎigé, kāifàng shì Zhōngguó bāshí niándài yǐlai de liǎng xiàng zhòngdà zhèngcè.** *Reform and opening-up have been two major policies in China since the 80s.*

gǎiháng 改行 v change one's profession (or trade)

gǎijìn 改进 [v+comp: 改 change + 进 progress] **V & N** make ... more advanced/sophisticated, improve; improvement (项 **xiàng**) ■ 怎么样改进我们的服务？请您多提意见。**Zěnmeyàng gǎijìn wǒmen de fúwù? Qǐng nín duō tí yìjiàn.** *What should we do to improve our service? Please feel free to make suggestions.* ■ 这项技术改进使产量大大增加。**Zhè xiàng jìshù gǎijìn shǐ chǎnliàng dàdà zēngjiā.** *This technological improvement greatly increased production.*

gǎiliáng 改良 [v+compl: 改 change + 良 better] **v** improve, reform

gǎiqī 改期 **v** change a scheduled time, change the date (of an event)

gǎishàn 改善 [v+comp: 改 change + 善 good] **V & N** make ... better/more favorable, ameliorate; improvement, amelioration ■ 人人都想改善生活条件。**Rénrén dōu xiǎng gǎishàn shēnghuó tiáojiàn.** *Everybody wants to improve their living conditions.* ■ 人们的居住条件得到了改善。**Rénmen de jūzhù tiáojiàn dédàole gǎishàn.** *People's housing conditions have been improved.*

gǎizào 改造 [comp: 改 change + 造 build up] **V & N** remold, rebuild; remolding, rebuilding ■ 这个城区要全面改造。**Zhège chéngqū yào quánmiàn gǎizào.** *This urban district will undergo comprehensive rebuilding.* ■ 这个城区的改造需要大量资金。**Zhège chéngqū de gǎizào xūyào dàliàng zījīn.** *The rebuilding of this urban district needs a large amount of funding.*

gǎizhèng 改正 [v+comp: 改 change + 正 correct] **v** put ... right, rectify ■ 改正下面句子中的错误。**Gǎizhèng xiàmiàn jùzi zhōng de cuòwù.** *Correct the errors in the following sentences (as in a test).*

gài 盖¹ **TRAD** 蓋 **v 1** build ■ 我们学校明年要盖一座电脑中心。**Wǒmen xuéxiào míngnián yào gài yí zuò diànnǎo zhōngxīn.** *Our school is going to build a computer center next year.* **2** affix a seal 盖章 **gài zhāng** affix a seal, stamp

gài 盖² **TRAD** 蓋 **N** cover, lid,, top 锅盖 **guōgài** pot lid / 盖子 **gàizi** cover, lid

gài 概 **ADV** totally

gàikuò 概括 [comp: 概 total + 括 include] **v** summarize ■ 你能不能把这份报告概括成五百个字左右的短文。**Nǐ néng bu néng bǎ zhè fèn bàogào gàikuò chéng wǔbǎi ge zì zuǒyòu de duǎn wén.** *Can you summarize this report in about 500 Chinese characters?*

gàiniàn 概念 [modif: 概 total + 念 idea] **N** concept, notion ■ 你用老概念解释不了新现象。**Nǐ yòng lǎo gàiniàn jiěshì bù liǎo xīn xiànxiàng.** *You cannot explain fresh phenomena with outdated concepts.*

gài 钙 **TRAD** 鈣 **N** calcium 钙片 **gàipiàn** calcium tablet

gān 干¹ **TRAD** 乾 **ADJ** dry ■ 衣服干了，收进来吧。**Yīfu gān le, shōu jìnlái ba.** *The clothes are dry. Let's take them in.*

gānbēi 干杯 [v+obj: 干 to dry + 杯 cup] **v** drink a toast, "Bottoms up!" ■ 为我们的友谊，干杯！**Wèi wǒmen de yǒuyì, gānbēi!** *To our friendship!*

gāncuì 干脆 [comp: 干 dry + 脆 crisp] **I ADJ** decisive, not hesitant, straight to the point ■ 做事要干脆，别犹犹豫豫。**Zuò shì yào gāncuì, bié yóu-yóu-yù-yù.** *Be decisive in action; don't be hesitant.* ■ 行就行，不行就不行，就干脆地说吧！**Xíng jiù xíng, bù xíng jiù bù xíng, jiù gāncuì de shuō ba!** *Whether it's OK or not, just say it directly without mincing words.* **II ADV** just, simply ■ 你既然这么讨厌男朋友，干脆不要他了！**Nǐ jìrán zhème tǎoyàn nánpéngyou, gāncuì bú yào tā le!** *Since you dislike your boyfriend so much, just dump him!*

gānhàn 干旱 [comp: 干 dry + 旱 drought] **ADJ** arid, very dry

gānjing 干净 [comp: 干 dry + 净 clean] **ADJ** clean (**ANTONYM** 脏 **zāng**) ■ 这件衣服洗不干净了。**Zhè jiàn yīfu xǐ bu gānjing le.** *This dress cannot be washed clean.*

gānzào 干燥 [comp: 干 dry + 燥 arid] **ADJ** dry, arid ■ 沙漠天气干燥。**Shāmò tiānqì gānzào.** *In the desert, the weather is dry.*

gān 干² **v** be concerned with, interfere

gānrǎo 干扰 **v** disturb, interfere

gānshè 干涉 **v** intervene, interfere 干涉内政 **gānshè nèizhèng** interfere with the internal affairs (of a country)

gānyù 干预 **v** intervene, meddle with 干预子女的婚姻 **gānyù zǐnǚ de hūnyīn** meddle in the marriage of (one's adult child)

gān 杆 **N** pole

gān 肝 **N** the liver ■ 他有肝病，不能喝酒。**Tā yǒu gān bìng, bù néng hē jiǔ.** *He has liver trouble and cannot drink alcohol.*

gāngà 尴尬 **ADJ** awkward, embarrassing, embarrassed

gānxīn 甘心 **v** do something willingly

gǎn 赶 **TRAD** 趕 **v 1** catch up with ■ 他跑得这么快，我怎么赶得上？**Tā pǎo de zhème kuài, wǒ zénme gǎn de shàng?** *How can I catch up with him when he is running so fast?* **2** hurry up, rush for, try to catch ■ 我得马上走，去赶最后一辆公共汽车。**Wǒ děi mǎshàng zǒu, qù gǎn zuì hòu yìbān gōnggòng qìchē.** *I've got to go right now to catch the last bus.* 赶得上 **gǎn de shàng** can catch up / 赶不上 **gǎn bu shàng** cannot catch up / 赶上 **gǎn shàng** succeed in catching up / 没赶上 **méi gǎn shàng** fail to catch up

gǎnjǐn 赶紧 **ADV** hasten (to do something) ■ 他母亲生重病住院了，他得赶紧回家。**Tā**

mǔqin shēng zhòngbìng zhùyuàn le, tā děi gǎnjǐn huíjiā. *His mother is hospitalized owing to severe illness and he has to rush back home.*

gǎnkuài 赶快 ADV same as 赶紧 **gǎnjǐn**

gǎn 敢 MODAL V dare ■ 这么多人，我不敢讲话。**Zhè me duō rén, wǒ bù gǎn jiǎnghuà.** *There're so many people here; I don't dare to speak.*

gǎn 感 V feel

gǎndào 感到 [v+comp: 感 feel + 到 arrive (as a complement)] V feel ■ 我有机会访问你们的国家，感到很高兴。**Wǒ yǒu jīhuì fǎngwèn nǐmen de guójiā, gǎndào hěn gāoxìng.** *I feel very happy to have the opportunity to visit your country.* ■ 听了他的不幸经历，我感到很难过。**Tīngle tā de búxìng jīnglì, wǒ gǎndào hěn nánguò.** *After hearing his unfortunate experience, I felt very sad.*

gǎndòng 感动 [comp: 感 feel + 动 move] V move, touch emotionally ■ 这个电影很感动人，不少观众感动得哭了。**Zhège diànyǐng hěn gǎndòng rén, bùshǎo guānzhòng gǎndòng de kū le.** *This film was so moving that many in the audience wept.*

gǎnjī 感激 [comp: 感 feel + 激 excite] V feel deeply grateful ■ 你在我最困难的时候帮助我，我十分感激。**Nǐ zài wǒ zuì kùnnán de shíhou bāngzhù wǒ, wǒ shífēn gǎnjī.** *I'm very grateful to you as you helped me in my most difficult times.*

gǎnjué 感觉 [comp: 感 feel + 觉 be conscious of] V & N feel; feeling, impression ■ 我感觉他对我们不大友好。**Wǒ gǎnjué tā duì wǒmen bú dà yǒuhǎo.** *I feel that he is not very friendly to us.* ■ 她相信自己的感觉，常常跟着感觉走。**Tā xiāngxìn zìjǐ de gǎnjué, chángcháng gēnzhe gǎnjué zǒu.** *She believes her instinct and often follows it.*

gǎnkǎi 感慨 V sigh with deep inner feelings (over a revelation, an experience, etc.)

gǎnmào 感冒 V & N catch a cold; cold, flu ■ 突然变冷，很多人感冒了。**Tūrán biàn lěng, hěn duō rén gǎnmào le.** *It suddenly became cold, so quite a few people caught colds.* ■ 穿上衣服吧，当心感冒！**Chuān shang yīfu ba, dāngxīn gǎnmào!** *Put on your clothes. Take care not to catch a cold.*

gǎnqíng 感情 [comp: 感 feeling + 情 emotion, affection] N 1 feelings, emotion ■ 你要理解她的感情。**Nǐ yào lǐjiě tā de gǎnqíng.** *You should understand her feelings.* 2 affection, love ■ 他们在一起工作多年，渐渐产生了感情。**Tāmen zài yìqǐ gōngzuò duō nián, jiànjiàn chǎnshēng le gǎnqíng.** *Having worked together for quite a few years, they have gradually become fond of each other.*

gǎnrǎn 感染 V 1 (of a wound) become infected 2 (of a movie, a story, music, etc.) affect, appeal

gǎnshòu 感受 N impression or lesson learned from personal experiences

gǎnxiǎng 感想 [comp: 感 feeling + 想 thoughts]

N impressions, reflections ■ 请问，您参观了这个学校，有什么感想？**Qǐngwèn, nín cānguānle zhège xuéxiào, yǒu shénme gǎnxiǎng?** *Could you please tell us your impressions of the school you've just visited?*

gǎnxiè 感谢 [v+obj: 感 feel + 谢 grateful] V be grateful, thank ■ 我感谢你对我的帮助。**Wǒ gǎnxiè nǐ duì wǒ de bāngzhù.** *I'm grateful for your help.* ■ 我真不知道怎么样感谢你才好。**Wǒ zhēn bù zhīdào zénmeyàng gǎnxiè nǐ cái hǎo.** *I really don't know how to thank you enough.*

gǎn xìngqù 感兴趣 V be interested (in) ■ 我对小说不感兴趣。**Wǒ duì xiǎoshuō bù gǎn xìngqù.** *I'm not interested in fiction.*

gǎn 杆 TRAD 桿 N shaft (See **gànggǎn** 杠杆.)

gàn 干 TRAD 幹 V do, work ■ 你干了一下午了，该休息休息了。**Nǐ gànle yíxiàwǔ le, gāi xiūxi xiūxi le.** *You've been working for the entire afternoon. You should take a break.* ■ 这活儿我干不了。**Zhè huór wǒ gàn bu liǎo.** *I can't do this job.*

gànbù 干部 N cadre, official (位 **wèi**)

NOTE: 干部 **gànbù** is a communist party term, denoting *party (or government) officials*. It is not commonly used today. In its stead, 官员 **guānyuán** is the word for *government officials*.

gàn huór 干活儿 V work (especially manually)

gànjìn 干劲 N drive and enthusiasm (for a job) 干劲不足 **gànjìn bùzú** lack of enthusiasm / 干劲十足 **gànjìn shízú** with enormous enthusiasm

gāng 刚 TRAD 剛 ADV just, barely ■ 他去年考试刚及格。**Tā qùnián kǎoshì gāng jígé.** *He barely passed the exam last year.*

gāngcái 刚才 [comp: 刚 just + 才 only] N a short while ago, just ■ 刚才王先生来电话，说明天的会见要改期。**Gāngcái Wáng xiānsheng lái diànhuà, shuō míngtiān de huìjiàn yào gǎiqī.** *Mr Wang called just now, saying that tomorrow's meeting would be rescheduled.* ■ 我刚才看见小明到图书馆去，你去那儿一定能找到他。**Wǒ gāngcái kànjiàn Xiǎo Míng dào túshūguǎn qù, nǐ qù nàr yídìng néng zhǎodào tā.** *I saw Xiao Ming going to the library a short while ago. You're sure to find him there.*

gānggāng 刚刚 ADV same as 刚 **gāng**, but more emphatic.

gāng 钢 TRAD 鋼 N steel

gāngbǐ 钢笔 [modif: 钢 steel + 笔 pen] N fountain pen (支 **zhī**) ■ 现在有各种各样的笔，很少人用钢笔。**Xiànzài yǒu gè-zhǒng-gè-yàng de bǐ, hěn shǎo rén yòng gāngbǐ.** *Now there are many varieties of pens. Very few people use fountain pens.*

gāngtiě 钢铁 [comp: 钢 steel + 铁 iron] N iron and steel, steel ■ 钢铁制造是基础工业。**Gāngtiě zhìzào shì jīchǔ gōngyè.** *Steel and iron manufacturing is a basic (or primary) industry.*

gāng 纲 TRAD 綱 N guiding principle; outline

gānglǐng 纲领 N guideline, fundamental principle

gǎng 岗 TRAD 崗 N sentry post

gǎngwèi 岗位 [comp: 岗 sentry post + 位 seat] N post (as a job)
脱离工作岗位 tuōlí gōngzuò gǎngwèi leave one's job

gàng 杠 N big and thick stick; bar

gànggǎn 杠杆 N lever

gǎng 港 N port, harbor

gǎngkǒu 港口 N port, harbor

gǎngwān 港湾 N harbor

gāo 高 ADJ tall, high (ANTONYM 矮 ǎi, 低 dī) ■ 我哥哥比我高。**Wǒ gēge bǐ wǒ gāo.** *My elder brother is taller than I am.* ■ 那座高高的楼房是一座新医院。**Nà zuò gāogāo de lóufáng shì yí zuò xīn yīyuàn.** *That tall building is a new hospital.*

gāochāo 高超 [comp: 高 superior + 超 super] ADJ (of skills) superior, consummate

gāocháo 高潮 [modif: 高 high + 潮 tide] N high tide, high water

gāodà 高大 ADJ tall and big (ANTONYM 矮小 ǎixiǎo) ■ 他们有三个儿子，都长得很高大。**Tāmen yǒu sān ge érzi, dōu zhǎng de hěn gāodà.** *They have three sons who are all tall and big.*

gāodàng 高档 [modif: 高 high + 档 grade] ADJ top grade, high quality
高档家具 gāodàng jiājù fine furniture

gāodù 高度 [comp: 高 high + 度 degree] I N altitude, height ■ 从三十公尺的高度往下跳，当然很危险。**Cóng sānshí gōngchǐ de gāodù wàng xià tiào, dāngrán hěn wēixiǎn.** *Jumping from a height of thirty meters is certainly very risky.* II ADJ with a high degree
高度赞扬 gāodù zànyáng praise highly

gāofēng 高峰 [modif: 高 high + 峰 peak] N peak, summit
高峰会议 gāofēng huìyì summit meeting

gāojí 高级 [modif: 高 advanced, senior + 级 grade] ADJ advanced, high-level
高级中学（高中）gāojí zhōngxué (gāozhōng) senior high school

gāokǎo 高考 N abbreviation for 高等院校入学考试 **gāoděng yuànxiào rùxué kǎoshì** Entrance Examination for Institutions of Higher Education

gāomíng 高明 [comp: 高 advanced + 明 enlightened] ADJ (of ideas or skills) brilliant, consummate

gāoshàng 高尚 ADJ (of moral quality, behavior, etc.) noble, lofty

gāosù 高速 [modif: 高 high + 速 speed] ADJ of high speed
高速公路 gāosù gōnglù superhighway, motorway / 高速铁路 gāosù tiělù high speed railroad

gāoxìng 高兴 [comp: 高 high + 兴 excited] ADJ joyful, delighted, willing ■ 见到你，我很高兴。**Jiàndào nǐ, wǒ hěn gāoxìng.** *I'm delighted to see*

you. ■ 我可不高兴给他送什么生日贺卡。**Wǒ kě bù gāoxìng gěi tā sòng shénme shēngrì hèkǎ.** *I'm unwilling to send him any kind of birthday card.*

gāoyuán 高原 [modif: 高 high + 原 plain] N highland, plateau ■ 高原的阳光特别强烈。**Gāoyuán de yángguāng tèbié qiángliè.** *Sunshine is particularly intense on a plateau.*

gāozhàng 高涨 V upsurge, rise

gāo 膏 N paste, ointment (See yágāo 牙膏.)

gāo 糕 N cake

gāodiǎn 糕点 N cakes and pastries

gǎo 搞 V 1 do, be engaged in, carry on ■ "你父亲搞什么工作？" "他搞软件设计。" **"Nǐ fùqin gǎo shénme gōngzuò?" "Tā gǎo ruǎnjiàn shèjì."** *"What does your father do?" "He's engaged in software design."* 2 get hold of, fetch

gǎo guǐ 搞鬼 V play tricks, get up to mischief

gǎo 稿 N draft (of an essay, a painting, etc.)
初稿 chūgǎo initial draft

gǎojiàn 稿件 N manuscript, contribution (to a magazine, a publisher, etc.)

gǎozi 稿子 N draft, sketch, manuscript
打稿子 dǎgǎozi draw up a draft

gào 告 V 1 tell, inform ■ 我告你一件事，你别对别人说。**Wǒ gào nǐ yí jiàn shì, nǐ bié duì biérén shuō.** *I'll tell you something. Don't tell others.* 2 sue, bring a legal action against ■ 有人告他偷东西。**Yǒurén gào tā tōu dōngxi.** *He was sued for theft.*

gàobié 告别 V bid farewell to, part with ■ 我告别父母到中国来学汉语，已经八个月了。**Wǒ gàobié fùmǔ dào Zhōngguó lái xué Hànyǔ, yǐjīng bā ge yuè le.** *It is eight months since I bade my parents farewell and came to China to study Chinese.*

gàocí 告辞 V bid farewell formally

gàojiè 告诫 V warn sternly, exhort

gàosu 告诉 [comp: 告 tell + 诉 inform] V tell, inform ■ 他告诉我一个重要消息。**Tā gàosu wǒ yí ge zhòngyào xiāoxi.** *He told me an important piece of news.* ■ 这件事千万别告诉他。**Zhè jiàn shì qiānwàn bié gàosu tā.** *You mustn't tell him about this matter.*

gē 哥 N elder brother

gēge 哥哥 N elder brother ■ 她把哥哥介绍给自己最好的朋友。**Tā bǎ gēge jièshào gěi zìjǐ zuìhǎo de péngyou.** *She introduced her elder brother to her best friend.*

gē 胳 N arm

gēbo 胳膊 N the arm (只 zhī) ■ 这位举重运动员胳膊特别粗。**Zhè wèi jǔzhòng yùndòngyuán gēbo tèbié cū.** *This weightlifter has unusually thick arms.*

gē 割 V cut ■ 夏天割草，冬天可以喂牛羊。**Xiàtiān gē cǎo, dōngtiān kěyǐ wèi niúyáng.** *Grass is cut in summer to feed cattle and sheep in winter.*

gē 歌 N song ■ 这个歌很好听，我想再听一遍。

Zhè ge gē hěn hǎotīng, wǒ xiǎng zài tīng yí biàn. *This song is beautiful. I want to hear it once more.* ■ 你会唱中文歌吗？**Nǐ huì chàng Zhōngwén gē ma?** *Can you sing Chinese songs?*

gēcí 歌词 N words of a song

gēshǒu 歌手 N (professional) singer

gēsòng 歌颂 [歌 sing + 颂 praise] V sing the praise of; eulogize

gē 搁 TRAD 擱 V put, place ■ 你先把脏衣服搁在洗衣机里。**Nǐ xiān bǎ zāng yīfu gē zài xǐyījī li.** *You put the dirty clothes in the washing machine first.*

gēda 疙瘩 N knot in one's heart, hang-up

gē 鸽 TRAD 鴿 N dove

gēzi 鸽子 N dove (只 **zhī**)

gé 革 V expel

gémìng 革命 N revolution (场 **chǎng**) ■ 在那场革命中牺牲了很多人。**Zài nà chǎng gémìng zhōng xīshēngle hěn duō rén.** *Many people died in that revolution.*

gé 格 N pattern, standard

géjú 格局 [comp: 格 pattern + 局 situation] N arrangement pattern, layout

géshì 格式 [comp: 格 pattern + 式 manner] N format, form

géwài 格外 ADV exceptionally, unusually

gé 隔 V separate, partition ■ 隔一条江就是另一个国家。**Gé yì tiáo jiāng jiù shì lìng yí ge guójiā.** *Beyond the river is another country.*

gébì 隔壁 N next door ■ 我们家隔壁住着一对老夫妻。**Wǒmen jiā gébì zhùzhe yí duì lǎo fūqī.** *Next door to our home lives an old couple.*

géhé 隔阂 N feelings of alienation or estrangement, often caused by misunderstanding

消除隔阂 xiāochú géhé banish feelings of estrangement by clearing up a misunderstanding

gélí 隔离 V isolate (a patient, a criminal), quarantine, separate

隔离病房 gélí bìngfáng isolation ward

gè 个 TRAD 個 MEASURE WORD (the most commonly used measure word, used in default of any other measure word; normally pronounced in the neutral tone)

一个人 yí ge rén a person / 两个苹果 liǎng ge píngguǒ two apples / 三个工厂 sān ge gōngchǎng three factories

gèbié 个别 ADJ 1 very few, exceptional ■ 这是个别现象。**Zhè shì gèbié xiànxiàng.** *This is an isolated case.* 2 individual, one-to-one ■ 对学习特别困难的学生，老师个别辅导。**Duì xuéxí tèbié kùnnán de xuésheng, lǎoshī gèbié fǔdǎo.** *The teacher gives individual tutoring to students with special difficulties.*

gèrén 个人 [modif: 个 individual + 人 person] N individual (ANTONYM 集体 **jítǐ**) ■ 个人利益和集体利益产生矛盾时，怎么处理？**Gèrén lìyì hé jítǐ lìyì chǎnshēng máodùn shí, zénme chǔlǐ?** *How should we handle cases where there is a conflict between an individual's interest and the collective interest?* ■ 这是我个人的意见，不代表公司。**Zhè shì wǒ gèrén de yìjiàn, bù dàibiǎo gōngsī.** *This is my personal opinion and it does not represent that of the company.*

gètǐ 个体 N individual

gèxìng 个性 [modif: 个 personal + 性 nature] N personality

个性开朗 gèxìng kāilǎng an outgoing personality

gèzi 个子 N height and size (of a person), build ■ 他因为营养不良，个子很小。**Tā yīnwèi yíngyǎng bùliáng, gèzi hěn xiǎo.** *Due to malnutrition, he is of small build.*

gè 各 PRON each, every ■ 各人的事，各人自己负责。**Gè rén de shì, gè rén zìjǐ fùzé.** *Everyone should be responsible for his own affairs.* ■ 爸爸妈妈各有主张，他不知道该听谁的。**Bàba māma gè yǒu zhǔzhāng, tā bù zhīdào gāi tīng shuí de.** *Dad and mom each have their own views. He doesn't know whom to listen to.*

各种 gè zhǒng all kinds of ■ 我各种水果都喜欢吃。**Wǒ gè zhǒng shuǐguǒ dōu xǐhuan chī.** *I like to eat all kinds of fruit.*

gè shū jǐ jiàn 各抒己见 IDIOM Each airs his own views.

gèzì 各自 PRON by oneself

各自为政 gè zì wéi zhèng each doing things in his/her/their own way, administer autonomously

gěi 给 TRAD 給 I V give, provide ■ 妈妈每两个星期给小明五十块钱。**Māma měi liǎng ge xīngqī gěi Xiǎo Míng wǔshí kuài qián.** *Mom gives Xiao Ming fifty yuan every fortnight.* ■ 在我写论文的过程中，王老师给了我很多指导。**Zài wǒ xiělùnwén de guòchéng zhōng, Wáng lǎoshī gěile wǒ hěn duō zhídǎo.** *In the course of writing this thesis, Teacher Wang gave me a great deal of guidance.* II PREP for, to ■ 她给我们做了一顿很好吃的中国饭。**Tā gěi wǒmen zuòle yí dùn hěn hǎochī de Zhōngguó fàn.** *She cooked us a delicious Chinese meal.* ■ 今天晚上你们去看电影吧，我给你们照顾孩子。**Jīntiān wǎnshang nǐmen qù kàn diànyǐng ba, wǒ gěi nǐmen zhàogù háizi.** *You go and watch the film tonight. I'll take care of your child for you (→ I'll baby-sit your child).*

gēn 根 I N root ■ 这棵树非常大，根一定很深。**Zhè kē shù fēicháng dà, gēn yídìng hěn shēn.** *This tree is very big. Its roots must be deep.* II MEASURE WORD (for long, thin things)

一根筷子 yì gēn kuàizi a chopstick

gēnběn 根本 [comp: 根 root + 本 root] N & ADJ essence, what is fundamental; essential, fundamental, basic ■ 问题的根本在于产品的质量不合格。**Wèntí de gēnběn zàiyú chǎnpǐn de zhìliàng bù hégé.** *The essence of the problem is that product quality is not up to standard.* ■ 我们不能头痛医

头，脚痛医脚，而必须找到一个根本的解决方法。**Wǒmen bù néng tóutòng yī tóu, jiǎotòng yī jiǎo, ér bìxū zhǎodào yí ge gēnběn de jiějué fāngfǎ.** *We cannot just take temporary and cosmetic measures, but must find a fundamental solution.*

gēnjù 根据 I v do according to, on the basis of ■ 我们根据最新情况，对计划作了修改。**Wǒmen gēnjù zuìxīn qíngkuàng, duì jìhuà zuòle xiūgǎi.** *We have amended our plan according to the latest situation.* **II** N grounds, basis ■ 你对我的批评没有根据。**Nǐ duì wǒ de pīpíng méiyǒu gēnjù.** *Your criticism of me is groundless.*

gēn shēn dì gù 根深蒂固 ADJ deep-rooted, deeply entrenched
根深蒂固的种族偏见 gēnshēn dìgùde zhǒngzú piānjiàn deep-rooted racial prejudice

gēnyuán 根源 [comp: 根 root + 源 source] N root cause, origin
宗教的根源 zōngjiào de gēnyuán the root cause of religion

gēn 跟 I v follow ■ 我在前面走，我的小狗在后面跟。**Wǒ zài qiánmiàn zǒu, wǒ de xiǎogǒu zài hòumiàn gēn.** *I walked in front and my puppy followed behind.* **II** PREP with ■ 老师："请大家跟我念。" **Lǎoshī: "Qǐng dàjiā gēn wǒ niàn."** *Teacher: "Read after me, please."*
跟上 gēnshàng catch up with, keep abreast with / 跟 … 一起 gēn … yìqǐ together with ... / 跟爸爸一起去看足球赛 gēn bàba yìqǐ qù kàn zúqiú sài watch soccer games together with my father

gēnqián 跟前 N near, nearby

gēnsuí 跟随 v same as 跟 **gēn**

gēnzōng 跟踪 [v+obj: 跟 follow + 踪 trace] v follow the track of, trail, shadow, stalk
发现被人跟踪 fāxiàn bèi rén gēnzōng find oneself being followed

gēng 更 v change

gēngxīn 更新 [v+compl: 更 change + 新 new] v renew, replace
设备更新 shèbèi gēngxīn renewal of equipment

gēngzhèng 更正 [v+compl: 更 change + 正 correct] v make corrections, correct
更正错误的数据 gēngzhèng cuòwù de shùjù correct wrong data

gēng 耕 v plough

gēngdì 耕地 [v+obj: 耕 plough + 地 land] V & N plough the field; farmland
可耕地 kěgēngdì arable land

gèng 更 ADV still more, even more ■ 美国很大，加拿大更大。**Měiguó hěn dà, Jiānádà gèng dà.** *America is big and Canada is even bigger.* ■ 我爱我的老师，但我更爱真理。**Wǒ ài wǒ de lǎoshī, dàn wǒ gèng ài zhēnlǐ.** *I love my teacher, but I love truth more.*

gèngjiā 更加 ADV same as 更 **gèng**

gōng 工 N work

gōngchǎng 工厂 [modif: 工 work + 厂 factory] N factory, works (座 **zuò**, 家 **jiā**) ■ 这座工厂生产什么？**Zhè zuò gōngchǎng shēngchǎn shénme?** *What does this factory make?* ■ 他在中国参观了三家工厂。**Tā zài Zhōngguó cānguānle sān jiā gōngchǎng.** *He visited three factories in China.*
办工厂 bàn gōngchǎng run a factory / 建工厂 jiàn gōngchǎng build a factory / 开工厂 kāi gōngchǎng set up a factory

gōngchéng 工程 [modif: 工 work + 程 course] N project, construction work, engineering ■ 这个工程从设计、施工到完成一共花了三年半时间。**Zhège gōngchéng cóng shèjì, shīgōng dào wánchéng yígòng huāle sānnián bàn shíjiān.** *From design, construction till completion, this project took three and a half years.*
土木工程 tǔmù gōngchéng civil engineering / 水利工程 shuǐlì gōngchéng water conservancy project

gōngchéngshī 工程师 [modif: 工程 engineering + 师 master] N engineer (位 **wèi**) ■ 这座著名的大学培养了大批工程师。**Zhè zuò zhùmíng de dàxué péiyǎngle dàpī gōngchéngshī.** *This well-known university has trained a large number of engineers.*
总工程师 zǒng gōngchéngshī chief engineer

gōngfu 工夫 N 1 time ■ 他用了一个晚上的工夫把报告修改了一遍。**Tā yòngle yí ge wǎnshang de gōngfu bǎ bàogào xiūgǎile yí biàn.** *He spent an entire evening revising this report.* 2 efforts ■ 王老师每天花很大工夫备课。**Wáng lǎoshī měi tiān huā hěn dà gōngfu bèikè.** *Teacher Wang makes great efforts to prepare his lessons every day.*

gōnghuì 工会 [modif: 工 workers + 会 association] N labor union, trade union

gōngjù 工具 [modif: 工 work + 具 implement] N tool ■ 没有合适的工具，这活儿没法干。**Méiyǒu héshì de gōngjù, zhè huór méifǎ gàn.** *This job can't be done without the proper tools.*

gōngrén 工人 [modif: 工 work + 人 person] N workman, worker

gōngyè 工业 [modif: 工 work + 业 industry] N (manufacturing) industry ■ 工业发展了，国家才能富。**Gōngyè fāzhǎn le, guójiā cái néng fù.** *Only when industry is developed, can a country be rich.*

gōngyìpǐn 工艺品 [modif: 工艺 craft + 品 article] N handicraft ■ 约翰打算买一些中国工艺品带回国送人。**Yuēhàn dǎsuàn mǎi yìxiē Zhōngguó gōngyìpǐn dàihuí guó sòng rén.** *John planned to buy some Chinese handicrafts and bring them home as gifts.*

gōngzī 工资 [modif: 工 work + 资 fund] N wages, salary ■ 你们是每月发工资，还是每两个星期发工资？**Nǐmen shì měi yuè fā gōngzī, háishì měi liǎng ge xīngqī fā gōngzī?** *Do you pay wages every month or every fortnight?*

gōngzuò 工作 [comp: 工 work + 作 do] **V & N** work; work, job (件 **jiàn**) ■ 我们一星期工作五天。 **Wǒmen yì xīngqī gōngzuò wǔ tiān.** *We work five days in a week.* ■ 他找工作找了两个月了。 **Tā zhǎo gōngzuò zhǎole liǎng ge yuè le.** *He's been looking for a job for two months.*

gōng 公[1] **ADJ** male (of certain animals) (**ANTONYM** 母 **mǔ**) ■ 公牛脾气很大，你千万别惹它。 **Gōngniú píqì hěn dà. Nǐ qiānwàn bié rě tā.** *Bulls have a fierce temper. Never provoke one.*

gōng 公[2] **ADJ** 1 public (**ANTONYM** 私 **sī**) ■ 天下为公。 **Tiānxià wéi gōng.** *The world is for public interests.* (→ *The world is for the people.*) 2 open 3 fair

gōng'ān 公安 [modif: 公 public + 安 security] **N** public security

gōng'ān jú 公安局 **N** public security bureau (police bureau)

gōng'ān rényuán 公安人员 public security personnel, policeman

NOTE: See note on 警察 **jǐngchá**.

gōngbù 公布 **V** make a public announcement, publish

gōngchǐ 公尺 [modif: 公 metric + 尺 a traditional Chinese measurement of length] **MEASURE WORD** meter ■ 这个游泳池长二十五公尺，宽十公尺。 **Zhàge yóuyǒngchí cháng èrshíwǔ gōngchǐ, kuān shí gōngchǐ.** *This swimming pool is 25 by 10 meters.*

gōngdào 公道 [comp: 公 fair + 道 reasonable] **ADJ** fair, just, impartial

gōngfèi 公费 [modif: 公 public + 费 expenditure] **N** public expense, at public expense

公费医疗 gōngfèi yīliáo public medical system

gōngfēn 公分 [modif: 公 metric + 分 a traditional Chinese measurement of length] **MEASURE WORD** centimeter

gōnggào 公告 [modif: 公 public + 告 announcement] **V & N** announcement (by a government agency), public announcement

gōnggòng 公共 [comp: 公 public + 共 shared] **ADJ** public ■ 这是一座公共图书馆，任何人都可以进去看书。 **Zhè shì yí zuò gōnggòng túshūguǎn, rènhé rén dōu kěyǐ jìnqù kàn shū.** *This is a public library. Anybody can go in and read.*

gōnggòng qìchē 公共汽车 **N** bus ■ 我的车卖了，我现在坐公共汽车上班。 **Wǒ de chē mài le, wǒ xiànzài zuò gōnggòng qìchē shàngbān.** *I've sold my car. Now I go to work by bus.*

NOTE: The word for *bus* in Taiwan is 公车 **gōngchē**. In Hong Kong, the word for *bus* is 巴士 **bāshì**, obviously a transliteration of the English word *bus*.

gōnggòng guānxi 公共关系 **N** public relations

gōngguān 公关 **N** shortening of 公共关系 **gōnggòng guānxi**, PR

gōngjīn 公斤 [modif: 公 metric + 斤 a traditional Chinese measurement of weight] **MEASURE WORD** kilogram ■ 这里有五公斤苹果，我送给你。 **Zhèli yǒu wǔ gōngjīn píngguǒ, wǒ sòng gěi nǐ.** *Here are five kilograms of apples, my gift to you.*

gōngkāi 公开 [comp: 公 public + 开 open] **ADJ & V** open, public (**ANTONYM** 秘密 **mìmì**); make public, reveal ■ 他发表公开谈话，反对政府的计划。 **Tā fābiǎo gōngkāi tánhuà, fǎnduì zhèngfǔ de jìhuà.** *He gave a public talk opposing the government plan.* ■ 希望你能公开自己的观点。 **Xīwàng nǐ néng gōngkāi zìjǐ de guāndiǎn.** *I hope you will make your views known.*

gōnglǐ 公里 [modif: 公 metric + 里 a traditional Chinese measurement of distance] **N** kilometer ■ 从城里到飞机场大概有十公里。 **Cóng chéngli dào fēijīchǎng dàgài yǒu shí gōnglǐ.** *It's about ten kilometers from town to the airport.*

gōnglù 公路 [modif: 公 public + 路 road] **N** public road, highway (条 **tiáo**) ■ 全国公路四通八达。 **Quán guó gōnglù sì-tōng-bā-dá.** *Public roads reach every corner of the country.*

高速公路 gāosù gōnglù motorway, expressway

gōngmín 公民 [modif: 公 public + 民 people, person] **N** citizen ■ 你拿哪个国家的护照，你就是哪个国家的公民。 **Nǐ ná nǎge guójiā de hùzhào, nǐ jiù shì nǎge guójiā de gōngmín.** *You are a citizen of the country whose passport you hold.*

gōngpíng 公平 [comp: 公 fair + 平 equal] **ADJ** fair, impartial

买卖公平 mǎimài gōngpíng fair trade

gōngpó 公婆 **N** husband's parents

gōngrán 公然 **ADV** brazenly, openly

公然撒谎 gōngrán sāhuǎng tell a bare-faced lie

gōngrèn 公认 [modif: 公 publicly + 认 acknowledge] **V** generally acknowledge, universally accept

gōngshì 公式 **N** formula

数学公式 shùxué gōngshì mathematics formula

gōngsī 公司 **N** commercial firm, company, corporation ■ 我们公司的营业范围很广泛。 **Wǒmen gōngsī de yíngyè fànwéi hěn guǎngfàn.** *Our company has an extensive range of business activities.* ■ 贵公司是哪一年成立的？ **Guì gōngsī shì nǎ yì nián chénglì de?** *In which year was your company founded?*

总公司 zǒng gōngsī company headquarters / 分公司 fēn gōngsī branch of a company

gōngwù 公务 **N** public affair, official duty

gōngwùyuán 公务员 [suffix: 公务 public affair + 员 personal nominal suffix] **N** civil servant, government functionary

gōngyòng diànhuà 公用电话 [modif: 公用 public use + 电话 telephone] **N** public telephone, payphone ■ 现在很多人都有手机，公用电话不象从前那样重要了。 **Xiànzài hěn duō rén dōu yǒu shǒujī, gōngyòng diànhuà búxiàng yǐqián nàyàng**

zhòngyào le. *Nowadays many people have cell phones, so public telephones are not as important as before.*

gōngyù 公寓 N apartment house, housing complex 一套公寓 yítào gōngyù a flat, a unit of housing / 一幢公寓 yízhuàng gōngyù an apartment house, a housing complex

gōngyuán 公元 N of the Christian/common era, AD (anno Domini) ■ 他生于公元前二十五年，死于公元三十一年。**Tā shēng yú gōngyuán qián èrshíwǔ nián, sǐ yú gōngyuán sānshíyī nián.** *He was born in 25 BC and died in AD 31.*
公元前 gōngyuán qián BC (before Christ), BCE (before the Christian/common era)

gōngyuán 公园 [modif: 公 public + 园 garden] N public garden, park (座 zuò) ■ 这个公园春天特别美。**Zhège gōngyuán chūntiān tèbié měi.** *This park is especially beautiful in spring.* ■ 早上很多人在公园里跑步。**Zǎoshang hěn duō rén zài gōngyuán li pǎobù.** *Many people jog in the park early in the morning.*

gōngzhèng 公正 ADJ just, upright

gōngzhèng 公证 [modif: 公 public + 证 testify] V notarize
公证处 gōngzhèngchù notary office / 公证人 gōngzhèngrén notary public, notary

gōngzhǔ 公主 N princess (位 wèi)

gōng 功 N skill

gōngfu 功夫 N 1 same as 工夫 gōngfu 2 martial arts 练功夫 liàn gōngfu practice martial arts ■ 每天一大早他就起来练功夫。**Měitiān yí dà zǎo tā jiù qǐlai liàn gōngfu.** *Every day he gets up in the early morning and practices the martial arts.*

gōngfu piàn 功夫片 martial arts film

gōngkè 功课 N schoolwork, homework ■ 他功课不错，考试成绩总是很好。**Tā gōngkè búcuò, kǎoshì chéngjì zǒngshì hěn hǎo.** *His schoolwork is quite good, and his examination results are always very good.*

gōngláo 功劳 [comp: 功 merit + 劳 labor] N contribution, credit ■ 没有功劳，也有苦劳。**Méiyǒu gōngláo, yě yǒu kǔláo.** *I've worked hard, even if my contributions are not great.*

gōngnéng 功能 N function
功能键 gōngnéng jiàn function key(s)

gōngxiào 功效 N effect, efficacy

gōng 恭 ADJ deferential

gōngjìng 恭敬 [comp: 恭 deferential + 敬 respectful] ADJ very respectful, deferential

gōngxǐ 恭喜 V & N congratulate, congratulation 恭喜发财 gōngxǐn fācái Happy new year and may you prosper! (greeting on Chinese New Year's Day)

gōng 攻 V attack

gōngjī 攻击 V attack

gōngkè 攻克 V attack and capture (a city, a fortress, etc.)

gōng 供 V supply ■ 大风期间，城市供水供电正常。**Dàfēng qījiān, chéngshì gōngshuǐ gōngdiàn zhèngcháng.** *During the storm, the city's water and electricity supply was maintained.* ■ 供大于求。**Gōng dà yú qiú.** *Supply exceeds demand.*

gōng bù yìng qiú 供不应求 IDIOM Supply falls short of demand.

gōngjǐ 供给 [comp: 供 supply + 给 provide] V supply, provide ■ 对于经济特别困难的学生，政府供给生活费。**Duìyú jīngjì tèbié kùnnan de xuésheng, zhèngfǔ gōngjǐ shēnghuófèi.** *The government provided a living stipend to students with special financial difficulties.*

gōng 宫 TRAD 宮 N palace
皇宫 huánggōng royal palace (for an emperor) / 王宫 wánggōng royal palace (for a king)

gōngdiàn 宫殿 N palace

gōng 躬 V bow (See jūgōng 鞠躬.)

gǒng 巩 TRAD 鞏 V consolidate

gǒnggù 巩固 [comp: 巩 consolidate + 固 reinforce] V & ADJ consolidate, strengthen; solid, firm ■ 我们这次会谈是为了巩固和发展我们之间的合作关系。**Wǒmen zhè cì huìtán shì wèile gǒnggù hé fāzhǎn wǒmen zhījiān de hézuò guānxi.** *The purpose of our talks is to strengthen and develop cooperation.* ■ 他们夫妻之间关系很巩固。**Tāmen fūqī zhī jiān guānxi hěn gǒnggù.** *Their marital relationship has a solid foundation.*

gòng 共 ADV 1 altogether, in total ■ 那座大学共有学生一万三千五百四十名。**Nà zuò dàxué gòng yǒu xuésheng yíwàn sānqiān wǔbǎi sìshí míng.** *That university has a total student population of 13,540.* 2 jointly, together (used only in writing) ■ 两家公司的董事长将共进午餐。**Liǎng jiā gōngsī de dǒngshìzhǎng jiāng gòngjìn wǔcān.** *The chairmen of the two companies will have luncheon together.*

gòngchǎndǎng 共产党 [modif: 共 to share + 产 property + 党 party] N communist party
中国共产党 Zhōngguó Gòngchǎndǎng the Chinese Communist Party

gònghéguó 共和国 N republic ■ 中国的全称是中华人民共和国。**Zhōngguó de quánchēng shì Zhōnghuá Rénmín Gònghéguó.** *China's full name is the People's Republic of China.*

gòngjì 共计 [modif: 共 total + 计 calculate] V total, add up to

gòngmíng 共鸣 [modif: 共 jointly + 鸣 chirp] N 1 resonance 2 sympathetic response, sympathy 引起共鸣 yǐnqǐ gòngmíng find a ready echo

Gòngqīngtuán 共青团 N abbreviation for 中国共产主义青年团 Zhōngguó Gòngchǎn zhǔyì Qīngniántuán the Chinese Communist Youth League

gòngshí 共识 [modif: 共 shared + 识 understanding] N common understanding, consensus

达成共识 dáchéng gòngshí achieve common understanding, reach a cosensus

gòngtóng 共同 [comp: 共 together + 同 shared] **ADJ** common, shared ■ 我们共同努力，保护我们共同的家园－地球。**Wǒmen gòngtóng nǔlì, bǎohù wǒmen gòngtóng de jiāyuán – dìqiú.** *Let's work together to protect our common homeland—the Earth.* ■ 我们之间缺乏共同语言，就不必多谈了。**Wǒmen zhī jiān quēfá gòngtóng yǔyán, jiù bú bì duō tán le.** *As we do not have a common language, there is no need for further conversation.*

gòngxiàn 贡献 [comp: 贡 tribute + 献 offer] **V** contribute, dedicate ■ 这位科学家为环境保护贡献了自己的一生。**Zhè wèi kēxuéjiā wèi huánjìng bǎohù gòngxiàn le zìjǐ de yìshēng.** *This scientist dedicated his life to environment protection.* ■ 在过去的一年中全体职工为公司的繁荣作出了贡献。**Zài guòqù de yì nián zhōng quántǐ zhígōng wèi gōngsī de fánróng zuòchu le gòngxiàn.** *In the past year, all the staff have contributed to the prosperity of the company.*
为…作出贡献 wèi … zuòchu gòngxiàn make a contribution to ...

gōu 勾 **V 1** strike out with a pen **2** induce
gōujié 勾结 **V** collude with, gang up with
gōu 沟 **TRAD** 溝 **N** ditch, trench (条 tiáo)
gōutōng 沟通 **V** link up, connect
沟通意见 gōutōng yìjiàn exchange ideas
gōu 钩 **TRAD** 鉤 **N** hook
gōuzi 钩子 **N** hook (只 zhī)
gǒu 狗 **N** dog (只 zhī, 条 tiáo) ■ 我喜欢狗，但是不会像有些人那样让狗睡在我的床上。**Wǒ xǐhuan gǒu, dànshì bú huì xiàng yǒuxiē rén nàyàng ràng gǒu shuì zai wǒ de chuáng shang.** *I like dogs but, unlike some people, I won't let a dog sleep on my bed.*
母狗 mǔ gǒu bitch / 小狗 xiǎo gǒu puppy
gòu 构 **TRAD** 構 **V** construct, form
gòuchéng 构成 **V** make up, form ■ 远山近水构成了美丽的风景。**Yuǎn-shān-jìn-shuǐ gòngchéngle měilì de fēngjǐng.** *Hills in the background and a lake in the foreground make up a beautiful landscape.*
gòusī 构思 [v+obj: 构 consctruct + 思 thoughts] **V** (of writers or artists) work out the plot of a story or composition of a picture
gòuzào 构造 **N** structure ■ 小小的手机构造极其复杂。**Xiǎoxiǎo de shǒujī gòuzào jíqí fùzá.** *The cell phone, small as it is, has an extremely complex structure.*
gòu 购 **TRAD** 購 **V** purchase, buy
gòumǎi 购买 [comp: 购 purchase + 买 buy] **V** purchase
购买采矿设备 gòumǎi cǎi kuàng shèbèi purchase mining equipment / 购买力 gòumǎilì purchasing power
gòuwù 购物 [v+obj: 购 buy + 物 things] **V & N** shop; shopping

购物单 gòuwù dān shopping list
gòu 够 **TRAD** 夠 **ADJ** enough, sufficient ■ 够了，够了，谢谢你！**Gòu le, gòu le, xièxie nǐ!** *That's enough. Thank you!* ■ 我们的汽油不够了，得加满才能开到目的地。**Wǒmen de qìyóu bú gòu le, děi jiā mǎn cái néng kāi dào mùdìdì.** *Our petrol is not enough. We've got to fill up to reach our destination.*

gū 孤 **ADJ** lonely
gūdú 孤独 [modif: 孤 lonely + 独 one, alone] **ADJ** lonely
gū'ér 孤儿 [modif: 孤 lonely + 儿 child] **N** orphan
孤儿院 gū'éryuàn orphanage
gūlì 孤立 [modif: 孤 lonely + 立 stand] **ADJ** isolated, without support or sympathy
gū 估 **V** estimate
gūjì 估计 [comp: 估 estimate + 计 calculate] **V & N** estimate, reckon, size up; estimate, approximate calculation, appraisal ■ 我估计整个工程要花三百万元。**Wǒ gūjì zhěngge gōngchéng yào huā sānbǎiwàn yuán.** *I estimate the entire project will cost three million yuan.* ■ 根据专家估计，今年经济增长可达百分之五。**Gēnjù zhuānjiā gūjì, jīnnián jīngjì zēngzhǎng kě dá bǎifēn zhī wǔ.** *According to expert estimates, economic growth will reach five percent this year.*
gū 姑 **N** aunt, woman
gūgu 姑姑 **N** one's father's sister, aunt ■ 我姑姑一直没有结婚，把我当做自己的孩子。**Wǒ gūgu yìzhí méiyǒu jiéhūn, bǎ wǒ dāngzuo zìjǐ de háizi.** *My father's sister never married and treats me as her own child.*
gūniang 姑娘 **N** unmarried young woman, girl, lass ■ 那个姑娘是谁家的孩子？**Nàge gūniang shì shuí jiā de háizi?** *Whose child is that girl?*
小姑娘 xiǎo gūniang little girl / 大姑娘 dàgūniang young woman (usually unmarried), lass

NOTE: 姑娘 **gūniang** is a colloquial word. When used to mean *unmarried young lady*, 姑娘 **gūniang** is used together with the word 小伙子 **xiǎohuǒzi** (young man), e.g. ■ 姑娘小伙子都爱热闹。**Gūniang xiǎohuǒzi dōu ài rènao.** *Young people all like having fun.*

gūqiě 姑且 **ADV** tentatively, for the time being
gū 辜 **V** as in 辜负 **gūfù**
gūfù 辜负 **V** fail to live up to, let down
辜负父母的期望 gūfù fùmǔ de qīwàng fail to live up to parents' expectations
gǔ 古 **ADJ** ancient ■ 中国是一个文明古国，有很多古建筑。**Zhōngguó shì yí ge wénmíng gǔguó, yǒu hěnduō gǔ jiànzhù.** *China is a country of ancient civilization and boasts a large number of ancient buildings.*
gǔdài 古代 [modif: 古 ancient + 代 generation, time] **N** ancient times ■ 古代中国创造了伟大的文

明。**Gǔdài Zhōngguó chuàngzàole wěidà de wénmíng.** *Ancient China created a great civilization.*

gǔdiǎn 古典 **ADJ** classic
古典音乐 gǔdiǎn yīnyuè classical music

gǔdǒng 古董 **N** antique, old curio (件 **jiàn**)

gǔguài 古怪 **ADJ** weird, queer
行为古怪 xíngwéi gǔguài behave strangely

gǔjì 古迹 [modif: 古 ancient + 迹 footprints] **N** historic site, place of historic interest ■ 这个古迹每年吸引几万人参观。**Zhège gǔjì měi nián xīyǐn jǐ wàn rén cānguān.** *This historic site attracts tens of thousands of visitors every year.* ■ 有些古迹没有得到有效保护，多么可惜！**Yǒuxiē gǔjì méiyǒu dédào yǒuxiào bǎohù, duōme kěxī!** *What a shame it is that some places of historic interest have not been protected effectively.*

gǔlǎo 古老 [comp: 古 ancient + 老 old] **ADJ** ancient, time-honored ■ 中国的苏州有两千五百多年的历史，真是一座古老的城市。**Zhōngguó de Sūzhōu yǒu liǎngqiān wǔbǎi duō nián de lìshǐ, zhēn shì yí zuò gǔlǎo de chéngshì.** *The city of Suzhou in China has a history of over 2,500 years. It is indeed an ancient city.*

gǔ 鼓 **N** drum

gǔdòng 鼓动 **V** agitate, arouse

gǔlì 鼓励 **V** encourage ■ 新加坡政府鼓励华人说华语。**Xīnjiāpō zhèngfǔ gǔlì Huárén shuō Huáyǔ.** *The Singapore government encourages ethnic Chinese people to speak Mandarin.*
物质鼓励 wùzhì gǔlì material incentive
精神鼓励 jīngshén gǔlì moral incentive, moral encouragement

gǔwǔ 鼓舞 [comp: 鼓 drum up + 舞 dance] **V** inspire, fire up … with enthusiasm, hearten ■ 这个消息真是鼓舞人心！**Zhège xiāoxi zhēn shì gǔwǔ rénxīn.** *This news is really inspiring!*

gǔzhǎng 鼓掌 [v+obj: 鼓 drum + 掌 palm] **V** clap one's hands, applaud ■ 小明要给大家唱一首中国歌曲，让我们鼓掌欢迎。**Xiǎo Míng yào gěi dàjiā chàng yì shǒu Zhōngguó gēqǔ, ràng wǒmen gǔzhǎng huānyíng.** *Xiao Ming is going to sing us a Chinese song. Let's give him a big hand.*

gǔ 骨 **N** bone

gǔgàn 骨干 **N** core member, backbone, mainstay
公司的骨干 gōngsī de gǔgàn the backbone (most important staff) of a company

gǔtou 骨头 **N** bone (根 **gēn**) ■ 他扔给小狗一根骨头。**Tā rēng gěi xiǎogǒu yì gēn gǔtou.** *He threw the puppy a bone.*

gǔ 股 **N** share

gǔdōng 股东 **N** shareholder, stockholder

gǔfèn 股份 **N** share, stock

gǔpiào 股票 [modif: 股 share + 票 ticket] **N** share ■ 他上个月买了这家公司十万股票。**Tā shàngge yuè mǎile zhè jiā gōngsī shíwàn gǔpiào.** *He bought 100,000 shares of the company last month.*

gǔ 谷[1] **TRAD** 穀 **N** cereal, grain (See **dàogǔ** 稻谷.)

gǔ 谷[2] **N** valley
山谷 shāngǔ mountain valley, ravine

gù 固 **ADJ & V** secure, solid; secure, consolidate

gùdìng 固定 [comp: 固 secure + 定 fix] **V** fix, make immovable
固定资产 gùdìng zīchǎn fixed assets

gùrán 固然 **ADV** true

gùtǐ 固体 **N** solid matter, solid

gùyǒu 固有 **ADJ** inherent, innate

gùzhi 固执 **ADJ** obstinate, stubborn
固执己见 gù zhí jǐ jiàn stubbornly stick to one's opinions; pigheaded

gù 故 **ADJ** old, former

gùshi 故事 [modif: 故 old, past + 事 happening, event] **N** story, tale ■ 这是一个真实的故事。**Zhè shì yí ge zhēnshí de gùshi.** *This is a true story.* ■ 他每天晚上都给孩子讲一个故事。**Tā měi tiān wǎnshang dōu gěi háizi jiǎng yí ge gùshi.** *He tells his child a story every evening.*
讲故事 jiǎng gùshi tell a story / 听故事 tīng gùshi listen to a story

gùxiāng 故乡 [modif: 故 former years + 乡 village, homeland] **N** native place, hometown, home village ■ 他退休以后，要回故乡定居。**Tā tuìxiū yǐhòu yào huí gùxiāng dìngjū.** *After retirement he will return to his hometown to live.*

gùyì 故意 [modif: 故 on purpose + 意 intention] **ADJ** deliberate, intentional, on purpose (**ANTONYM** 无意 **wúyì**) ■ 他犯的错误是无意的，不是故意的。**Tā fàn de cuòwù shì wúyì de, búshì gùyì de.** *He did not commit this mistake deliberately, but by accident.*

gùzhàng 故障 **N** (mechanical) breakdown, trouble (of a machine)
排除故障 páichú gùzhàng fix a breakdown, troubleshooting

gù 顾 **TRAD** 顧 **V** attend to, care for ■ 你不能只顾自己，不管别人。**Nǐ bù néng zhǐ gù zìjǐ, bù guǎn biérén.** *You shouldn't care for only yourself and nobody else.* ■ 他忙得顾不上吃饭。**Tā máng de gù bu shàng chīfàn.** *He was so busy that he did not have time for meals.*

gùkè 顾客 **N** customer, client (位 **wèi**) ■ 我们尽量满足顾客的要求。**Wǒmen jìnliàng mǎnzú gùkè de yāoqiú.** *We try our best to meet customers' demands.*

gùlǜ 顾虑 **V** have misgivings, worry
顾虑重重 gùlǜ chóngchóng be filled with misgivings

gùwèn 顾问 **N** advisor, consultant (位 **wèi**)

gù 雇 **TRAD** 僱 **V** employ, hire

gùyòng 雇佣 **V** hire, employ

NOTE: 雇佣 **gùyòng** is used when hiring low-rank employees, e.g. unskilled workers. To employ a professional, the verb to use is 聘用 **pìnyòng**.

guā 瓜 N melon, gourd (See **huángguā** 黄瓜, **xīguā** 西瓜.)

guā 刮 v (of a wind) blow ■ 这儿冬天经常刮西北风。**Zhèr dōngtiān jīngcháng guā xīběi fēng.** *A northwestern wind often blows here in winter.*

guā fēng 刮风 v (of wind) blows, be windy

guà 挂 TRAD 掛 v hang up ■ 墙上挂着一幅世界地图。**Qiáng shang guàzhe yì fú shìjiè dìtú.** *A map of the world hung on the wall.*

guàhào 挂号 v register (at a hospital) ■ 在中国看病的第一件事就是挂号。**Zài Zhōngguó kànbìng de dì-yī jiàn shì jiù shì guàhào.** *In China, when you go to see a doctor, the first thing to do is to register.*
挂号费 guàhào fèi registration fee, doctor's consultation fee / 挂号处 guàhào chù registration office

NOTE: In China if you are sick, you go to a hospital where doctors work in their specialist departments, e.g. internal medicine, gynecology and dermatology. 挂号 **guàhào** means *to tell a receptionist which department you want to go to and pay the consultation fee.* Dentistry is usually one of the departments and a dentist is generally considered just another doctor.

guāi 乖 ADJ (of children) be good, be well-behaved
乖孩子 guāi háizi a well-behaved child

guǎi 拐 v turn, make a turn ■ 往前走，再向左拐，就是火车站。**Wǎng qián zǒu, zài xiàng zuǒ guǎi, jiù shì huǒchēzhàn.** *Walk straight on, then turn left, and you will find the railway station.*

guǎiwān 拐弯 v turn a corner

guǎizhang 拐杖 N walking stick

guài 怪¹ ADJ strange, odd, queer ■ 我刚才放在这儿的书怎么一会儿就不见了，真怪！**Wǒ gāngcái fàng zài zhèr de shū zěnme yíhuìr jiù bú jiàn le, zhēn guài!** *I left a book here just now and it's vanished. How odd!* ■ 昨天我碰到了怪事。**Zuótiān wǒ pèngdàole guài shì.** *Something strange happened to me yesterday.*

guài 怪² v blame ■ 都怪我，没讲清楚。**Dōu guài wǒ, méi jiǎng qīngchu.** *It was all my fault. I did not make it clear.* ■ 你们别怪来怪去的，看看该怎么办吧。**Nǐmen bié guài-lái-guài-qù de, kànkan gāi zénme bàn ba.** *Don't blame each other. Try to find out what should be done.*

guàibudé 怪不得 ADV no wonder, so that's why

guān 关 TRAD 關 v close; turn off ■ 你离开的时候，请把灯关掉，把门关上。**Nǐ líkāi de shíhou, qǐng bǎ dēng guāndiào, bǎ mén guānshàng.** *When you leave, please turn off the lights and close the door.* ■ 学校晚上十一点半关大门。**Xuéxiào wǎnshang shíyī diǎn bàn guān dàmén.** *The school gate is closed at 11:30 p.m.*
把电灯/电视机/录音机/机器关掉 bǎ diàndēng/diànshì jī/lùyīn jī/jīqì guāndiào turn off the lights/

TV/recorder/machine / 把门/窗关上 bǎ mén/chuāng guānshang close the door/window

guānbì 关闭 [comp: 关 close + 闭 close] v close down, shut down
关闭机场 guānbì jīchǎng shut down the airport

guānhuái 关怀 v be kindly concerned about, show loving care to

guānjiàn 关键 [comp: 关 pass + 键 key] N what is crucial or critical ■ 一家公司的成功，关键在于人力资源。**Yì jiā gōngsī de chénggōng, guānjiàn zàiyú rénlì zīyuán.** *The success of a company lies in its human resources.* ■ 他踢进了关键的一球。**Tā tījìnle guānjiàn de yì qiú.** *He scored the crucial goal.*

guānxi 关系 [comp: 关 related + 系 connected] I N connection, relation ■ 这两件事有没有关系？**Zhè liǎng jiàn shì yǒu méiyǒu guānxi?** *Is there any connection between these two matters?* (→ *Are these two matters related?*) ■ 我和他只是一般朋友关系。我希望保持这种关系。**Wǒ hé tā zhǐ shì yìbān péngyou guānxi. Wǒ xīwàng bǎochí zhè zhǒng guānxi.** *He and I are merely ordinary friends, and I intend to keep it that way.* II v affect, have bearing on ■ 睡得好不好，关系到你的健康。**Shuì de hǎo bù hǎo, guānxi dào nǐ de jiànkāng.** *Whether you sleep well or not affects your health.* ■ "对不起。" "没关系。" **"Duìbuqǐ." "Méiguānxi."** *[when you have unintentionally hurt somebody] "I'm sorry." "It's OK."*

guānxīn 关心 [v + obj: 关 connected + 心 the heart] v be concerned about, care for ■ 妈妈总是关心孩子的健康。**Māma zǒngshì guānxīn háizi de jiànkāng.** *Mothers are always concerned about their children's health.* ■ 对公司的业务情况，每个职工都很关心。**Duì gōngsī de yèwù qíngkuàng, měi ge zhígōng dōu hěn guānxīn.** *Every employee is deeply concerned about the business of the company.*

guānyú 关于 PREP about, on ■ 我很久没有听到关于他的消息了。**Wǒ hěn jiǔ méiyǒu tīngdào guānyú tā de xiāoxi le.** *I haven't heard about him for a long time.* ■ 关于这个月的营业情况，你得问王经理。**Guānyú zhège yuè de yíngyè qíngkuàng, nǐ děi wèn Wáng jīnglǐ.** *You should ask Mr Wang, the manager, about business this month.*

guānzhào 关照 [comp: 关 concerned + 照 look after] v 1 look after, take care of ■ 这里的工作请你关照一下。**Zhèli de gōngzuò qǐng nǐ guānzhào yíxià.** *Please keep an eye on the work here.* 2 notify, inform ■ 我已经关照服务员叫出租汽车了。**Wǒ yǐjīng guānzhào fúwùyuán jiào chūzū qìchē le.** *I've already asked the attendant to call a taxi.*

guān 观 TRAD 觀 v look at, observe

guānchá 观察 [comp: 观 see + 察 examine] v observe, watch ■ 这个人是否可靠，还需进一

步观察。**Zhège rén shìfǒu kěkào, hái xū jìnyíbù guānchá.** *Further observation is needed to determine whether this person is reliable or not.* ■ 对于市场情况，他观察得很仔细。**Duìyú shìchǎng qíngkuàng, tā guānchá de hěn zǐxì.** *He watches the market very carefully.*

观察员 guāncháyuán observer (at a conference, especially an international conference)

guāndiǎn 观点 [modif: 观 observe + 点 point] **N** viewpoint, view ■ 对问题有不同的观点，是很正常的。**Duì wèntí yǒu bù tóng de guāndiǎn, shì hěn zhèngcháng de.** *It is normal to have different views on an issue.*

guānguāng 观光 [v+obj: 观 observe + 光 view] **v** go sightseeing, visit and observe

guānniàn 观念 **N** concept, sense
是非观念 shìfēi guānniàn the sense of what is right and what is wrong

guānzhòng 观众 [modif: 观 watch + 众 crowd] **N** audience (in a theater, of TV, etc.), spectator ■ 观众对这个戏反映很好。**Guānzhòng duì zhège xì fǎnyìng hěn hǎo.** *The audience responded very well to this play.*

guān 官 **N** (government) official ■ 很多中国人想当官。**Hěn duō Zhōngguórén xiǎng dāng guān.** *Many Chinese want to be officials.*

NOTE: 官 **guān** is a colloquial word. For more formal occasions, use 官员 **guānyuán.**

guānfāng 官方 [modif: 官 official + 方 side] **ADJ** official
官方消息 guānfāng xiāoxi official news, news released by the authorities

guānyuán 官员 [suffix: 官 official + 员 nominal suffix] **N** official (位 **wèi**) ■ 这位官员很负责任。**Zhè wèi guānyuán hěn fùzérèn.** *This official has a strong sense of responsibility.* ■ 我想见一下这里的负责官员。**Wǒ xiǎng jiàn yíxià zhèli de fùzé guānyuán.** *I want to see the official in charge here.*

NOTE: See note on 干部 **gànbù.**

guǎn 管 **v** be in charge, take care (of) ■ 王老师管一年级的教学。**Wáng lǎoshī guǎn yī-niánjí de jiàoxué.** *Teacher Wang is in charge of the first-year courses.* ■ 别管我！**Bié guǎn wǒ!** *Leave me alone!*

guǎndào 管道 [comp: 管 pipe + 道 path] **N** pipeline, conduit

guǎnlǐ 管理 [comp: 管 be in charge + 理 put in order] **v & N** manage, administer; management, administration ■ 他管理工厂很有办法。**Tā guǎnlǐ gōngchǎng hěn yǒu bànfǎ.** *He is resourceful and efficient in managing the factory.*
商业管理 shāngyè guǎnlǐ business administration

guǎnxiá 管辖 **v** have jurisdiction over

guǎn 馆 **TRAD** 館 **N** building (for a specific purpose)
饭馆 fànguǎn restaurant / 馆子 guǎnzi restaurant (colloquial) / 体育馆 tǐyùguǎn gymnasium / 图书馆 túshūguǎn library

guàn 贯 **TRAD** 貫 **v** pass through

guànchè 贯彻 **v** implement, carry out ■ 贯彻这项新政策，大约要半年时间。**Guànchè zhè xiàng xīn zhèngcè, dàyuē yào bànnián shíjiān.** *Implementing the new policy will take about half a year.*

guàn 冠 **N** the best

guànjūn 冠军 **N** champion, championship ■ 我们学校获得了全市中学生篮球邀请赛冠军。**Wǒmen xuéxiào huòdéle quán shì zhōngxuéshēng lánqiú yāoqǐngsài guànjūn.** *Our school has won the championship of the city high school basketball invitational tournament.*

guàn 惯 **TRAD** 慣 **ADJ** accustomed to

guànlì 惯例 **N** usual practice, convention
打破惯例 dǎpò guànlì break with convention

guàn 灌 **v** fill (water, air), pour

guàngài 灌溉 **v & N** irrigate; irrigation

guàn 罐 **N** tin, jar

guàntou 罐头 [suffix: 罐 tin, can + 头 nominal suffix] **N** can, tin ■ 这个罐头里面是什么呀？**Zhège guàntou lǐmiàn shì shénme ya?** *What's in this can?*
罐头食品 guàntou shípǐn canned food

guāng 光[1] **N** light ■ 发光的不一定是金子。**Fā guāng de bù yídìng shì jīnzi.** *All that glitters is not gold.*
灯光 dēngguāng lamplight / 阳光 yángguāng sunlight / 月光 yuèguāng moonlight

guāngcǎi 光彩 **I N** color and luster **II ADJ** glorious

guāngdié 光碟 [modif: 光 light, laser + 碟 disc] same as 光盘 **guāngpán**

guānghuá 光滑 [comp: 光 smooth + 滑 smooth] **ADJ** smooth, glossy

guānghuī 光辉 [comp: 光 light + 辉 splendor] **N & ADJ** brilliance, radiance; brilliant, splendid ■ 云挡不住太阳的光辉。**Yún dǎng bu zhù tàiyang de guānghuī.** *The clouds cannot shut out the brilliance of the sunshine.* ■ 他在医学研究上取得了光辉的成绩。**Tāzài yīxué yánjiū shang qǔdé le guānghuī de chéngjì.** *He achieved brilliant results in medical research.*

guānglín 光临 **v** (a polite expression) be present, come ■ 欢迎光临！**Huānyíng guānglín!** *You're cordially welcome! We welcome you.*

guāngmáng 光芒 **N** rays of light

guāngmíng 光明 [comp: 光 light + 明 bright] **ADJ** bright, promising ■ 只要努力就会有光明的前途。**Zhǐyào nǔlì jiùhuì yǒu guāngmíng de qiántú.** *If only you work hard, you will have a bright future.*

guāngpán 光盘 **N** compact disc (CD)
刻录光盘 kèlùguāngpán burn a CD

guāngróng 光荣 [comp: 光 light + 荣 glory] **ADJ** glorious, honorable ∎ 他代表全校参加这次比赛，是很光荣的。 **Tā dàibiǎo quánxiào cānjiā zhè cì bǐsài, shì hěn guāngróng de.** *He represented the school in the competition, which was a great honor.*

guāngxiàn 光线 [comp: 光 light + 线 string] **N** light, ray (道 dào) ∎ 这个房间光线太暗。 **Zhège fángjiān guāngxiàn tài àn.** *This room is not bright enough.*

guāng 光² **ADV** only, sole ∎ 光有钱就能幸福吗？ **Guāng yǒu qián jiù néng xìngfú ma?** *Can money alone make you happy?* ∎ 她光练口语，不写汉字，可不行。 **Tā guāng liàn kǒuyǔ, bù xiě Hànzì, kě bù xíng.** *She only practices oral Chinese and does not write characters. This won't do.*

guǎng 广 **TRAD** 廣 **ADJ** extensive, wide

guǎngbō 广播 [modif: 广 extensive, wide + 播 sow, spread] **I V** broadcast ∎ 今天早上广播了一条重要新闻。 **Jīntiān zǎoshang guǎngbōle yì tiáo zhòngyào xīnwén.** *A piece of important news was broadcast early this morning.* **II N** broadcasting ∎ 这位老人每天都听新闻广播。 **Zhè wèi lǎorén měi tiān dōu tīng xīnwén guǎngbō.** *This old man listens to the news broadcast every day.* 广播电台 **guǎngbō diàntái** radio station / 广播公司 **guǎngbō gōngsī** broadcasting company

guǎngchǎng 广场 [modif: 广 broad + 场 ground] **N** square, plaza ∎ 中国最著名的广场是天安门广场。 **Zhōngguó zuì zhùmíng de guǎngchǎng shì Tiān'ānmén Guǎngchǎng.** *The best-known square in China is Tiananmen Square.*

guǎngdà 广大 [comp: 广 broad + 大 big] **ADJ** vast, extensive ∎ 中国西北广大地区还没有充分开发。 **Zhōngguó xīběi guǎngdà dìqū hái méiyǒu chōngfèn kāifā.** *The vast area of China's Northwest is yet to be fully developed.*

guǎngfàn 广泛 [comp: 广 broad + 泛 extensive] **ADJ** widespread, wide-ranging, extensive ∎ 他们对市场进行了广泛的调查。 **Tāmen duì shìchǎng jìnxíng guǎngfàn de diàochá.** *They conducted an extensive market investigation.*

guǎnggào 广告 [modif: 广 broad + 告 inform] **N** advertisement ∎ 一般电视观众都讨厌电视广告。 **Yìbān diànshì guānzhòng dōu tǎoyàn diànshì guǎnggào.** *TV viewers generally hate commercials.* ∎ 开店以前，他们先在报上登了大广告。 **Kāidiàn yǐqián, tāmen xiān zài bào shang dēngle dà guǎnggào.** *Before the store opened, they ran a huge advertisement in the newspaper.*

guǎngkuò 广阔 [comp: 广 broad + 阔 wide] **ADJ** vast, wide ∎ 中国东北有一片广阔的平原。 **Zhōngguó dōngběi yǒu yípiàn guǎngkuò de píngyuán.** *China's Northeast boasts a vast plain.*

guàng 逛 **V** stroll, take a random walk ∎ 我这么忙，哪有时间陪你逛街？ **Wǒ zhème máng, nǎ yǒu**

shíjiān péi nǐ guàng jiē? *I'm so busy. How can I find time to go window-shopping with you?* 逛公园 **guàng gōngyuán** stroll in the park / 逛街 **guàng jiē** stroll around the streets, do window shopping

guī 规 **TRAD** 規 **N** regulation, rule

guīdìng 规定 [comp: 规 stipulate + 定 decide] **V & N** stipulate, regulate, specify; stipulation, regulation, provision, ∎ 政府规定，珍贵文物不能带出国。 **Zhèngfǔ guīdìng, zhēnguì wénwù bù néng dàichū guó.** *The government stipulates that precious cultural relics may not be taken out of the country.* ∎ 必须遵守海关的规定。 **Bìxū zūnshǒu hǎiguān de guīdìng.** *Customs regulations must be obeyed.*

guīfàn 规范 **N** standard, norm 符合规范 **fúhé guīfàn** meet the standard

guīgé 规格 **N** specifications (of a product), norm

guīhuà 规划 **N & V** long-term program; draw up a long-term program 五年发展规划 **wǔ nián fāzhǎn guīhuà** five-year development plan

guīju 规矩 [comp: 规 compass + 矩 ruler] **I N** rule, established practice 老规矩 **lǎoguīju** well-established practice **II ADJ** well behaved, behaving within the norm

guīlǜ 规律 [comp: 规 regulation + 律 law] **N** law, regular pattern ∎ 经济活动十分复杂，但是还是有规律的。 **Jīngjì huódòng shífēn fùzá, dànshì háishì yǒu guīlǜ de.** *Economic activities are very complicated, but they also follow regular patterns.*

guīmó 规模 **N** scale ∎ 这次航空展览会规模很大。 **Zhè cì hángkōng zhǎnlǎnhuì guīmó hěn dà.** *This is a large-scale air show.*

guīzé 规则 **N** rule, law, regulation 交通规则 **jiāotōng guīzé** traffic regulations / 游戏规则 **yóuxì guīzé** rules of a game

guīzhāng 规章 **N** rules and regulations

guī 归 **TRAD** 歸 **V** return, go back to

guī gēn jié dǐ 归根结底 **IDIOM** in the final analysis, ultimately

guīhuán 归还 [comp: 归 return + 还 return] **V** return 归还原主 **guīhuán yuánzhǔ** be returned to the original owner

guīnà 归纳 **V & N** sum up, induce; summing-up, induction 归纳法 **guīnàfǎ** inductive method

guī 硅 **N** silicium, silicon (Si) 硅谷 **guīgǔ** silicon valley

guǐ 鬼 **N** ghost ∎ "你怕鬼吗？" "不怕，我根本不相信有鬼。" **"Nǐ pà guǐ ma?" "Bú pà, wǒ gēnběn bù xiāngxìn yǒu guǐ."** *"Are you afraid of ghosts?" "No, I don't believe in ghosts at all."* 鬼故事 **guǐ gùshi** ghost story 鬼屋 **guǐ wū** haunted house

guǐ 轨 **TRAD** 軌 **N** rail 出轨 **chūguǐ** (of a train) derail

guǐdào 轨道 N track; orbit

上了轨道 shàng le guǐdào settle into normal routine

guì 贵 TRAD 貴 ADJ expensive, of great value (ANTONYM 便宜 **piányi**) ■ 这家商店的东西很贵。**Zhè jiā shāngdiàn de dōngxi hěn guì.** *The goods in this shop are all very expensive.* ■ 什么？要一千块钱？太贵了！**Shénme? Yào yìqiān kuài qián? Tài guì le.** *What? One thousand dollars? It's too expensive.*

guìxìng 贵姓 [modif: 贵 valuable + 姓 family name] IDIOM your family name ■ "请问，您贵姓？" "我姓王。" **"Qǐngwèn, nín guìxìng?" "Wǒ xìng Wáng."** *"What's your family name?" "Wang."* ■ "您大名是…？" "我叫宝华。" **"Nín dàmíng shì…?" "Wǒ jiào Bǎohuá."** *"And your given name is…?" "It's Baohua."* ■ "您是王宝华先生？" "是，是。" **"Nín shì Wáng Bǎohuá xiānsheng?" "Shì, shì."** *"Oh, you're Mr Wang Baohua?" "That's right."*

NOTE: (1) While 贵姓 **guìxìng** is the polite form when asking about somebody's *family name*, the polite way to ask somebody's given name is 请问，您大名是…? **Qǐngwèn, nín dàmíng shì…?** *And your (honorific) name is …*大名 literally means *big name*. The answer to this question is 我叫XX. **Wǒ jiào XX.** *I am …* (2) The word 贵 **guì** in the sense of *valuable* is added to certain nouns to mean *your…*, e.g. 贵姓 **guìxìng** *your family name*, 贵国 **guìguó** *your country*, 贵校 **guìxiào** *your school*. They are only used in formal and polite contexts.

guìzú 贵族 N aristocrat, aristocracy

guì 跪 V kneel

跪下去 guìxià qù kneel down

guì 柜 TRAD 櫃 N cupboard, cabinet

书柜 shūguì bookcase

guìtái 柜台 N counter, bar

guìzi 柜子 N cupboard, cabinet

gǔn 滚 V roll ■ 球滚到沙发下面去了。**Qiú gǔn dào shāfā xiàmiàn qu le.** *The ball rolled under the armchair.*

NOTE: 滚 **gǔn** is used to tell somebody "get out of here" or "beat it," e.g. ■ 滚！滚出去！**Gǔn! Gǔn chūqu!** *Get lost! Get out of here!* ■ 滚开！**Gǔn kāi!** *Beat it!* These are highly offensive.

gùn 棍 N stick, rod

棍棒 gùnbàng N club, cudgel, bludgeon (根 **gēn**)

guō 锅 TRAD 鍋 N pot, pan, wok

guó 国 TRAD 國 N country, state, nation ■ 国与国之间应该是平等的。**Guó yú guó zhī jiān yīnggāi shì píngděng de.** *There should be equality among nations.*

德国 Déguó Germany / 俄国 Éguó Russia / 法国 Fǎguó France / 美国 Měiguó the United States of America / 英国 Yīngguó the United Kingdom

guófáng 国防 [modif 国 nation + 防 defense] N national defense

国防部 guófángbù Ministry of National Defense

guójí 国籍 N nationality, citizenship

加入加拿大国籍 jiārù Jiānádà guójí obtain Canadian citizenship, be naturalized as a Canadian citizen

guójì 国际 ADJ concerning two or more nations, international ■ 反对恐怖活动已经成为一个国际问题。**Fǎnduì kǒngbù huódòng yǐjīng chéngwéi yí ge guójì wèntí.** *Anti-terrorism has become an international issue.* ■ 打国际长途电话越来越便宜了。**Dǎ guójì chángtú diànhuà yuèláiyuè piányì le.** *International long-distance calls have become less and less expensive.*

国际法 guójì fǎ international law / 国际会议 guójì huìyì international conference

guójiā 国家 [comp: 国 country + 家 family] N country, state, nation ■ 他代表国家参加运动会。**Tā dàibiǎo guójiā cānjiā yùndònghuì.** *He represented his country in the sports meet.* ■ "你去过几个国家？" **"Nǐ qùguo jǐ ge guójiā?"** *"How many countries have you been to?"*

NOTE: It is significant that the Chinese word meaning *country*—国家 **guójiā**—is composed of the word 国 **guó** (country) and the word 家 **jiā** (family). In traditional Chinese thought, China was one big family and the country was ruled as such, with the emperor as the patriarch.

Guómíndǎng 国民党 N the Kuomintang (KMT, the political party which ruled China before 1949 and is now a major party in Taiwan.)

Guóqìngjié 国庆节 [modif: 国 nation + 庆 celebration + 节 fesitival] N National Day (October 1 in the People's Republic of China)

guówáng 国王 [modif: 国 country + 王 king] N king, monarch (位 **wèi**)

guówùyuàn 国务院 [modif: 国 state + 务 affairs + 院 institution] N (Chinese) State Council, (the US) State Department

guǒ 果 N fruit

guǒduàn 果断 ADJ resolute

采取果断措施 cǎiqǔ guǒduàn cuòshī take decisive measures

guǒrán 果然 ADV sure enough, as expected

guǒshí 果实 N fruit, fruits

guǒzhī 果汁 N fruit juice

guǒ 裹 V wrap, bind (See **bāoguǒ** 包裹.)

guò 过¹ TRAD 過 V 1 pass, cross ■ 过马路，一定要小心。**Guò mǎlù, yídìng yào xiǎoxīn.** *You must be very careful when crossing the street.*

过来 guòlai come over, come across (towards the speaker) ■ 他正从马路那边过来。**Tā zhèng cóng mǎlù nàbian guòlai.** *He's coming over from the other*

side of the street. ■ 公共汽车开过来了。**Gōnggòng qìchē kāi guòlái le.** *A bus is coming over.*

过去 guòqu go over, go across (away from the speaker) ■ 街上车太多，很难过去。**Jiē shang chē tài duō, hěn nán guòqu.** *Traffic in the street is too heavy. It's very difficult to go across.* ■ 河水很急，我游不过去。**Héshuǐ hěn jí, wǒ yóu bù guòqu.** *The river runs swiftly. I can't swim across it.*
2 spend (time), live (a life), observe (a festival) ■ 他在国外过了这么多年，生活习惯有些改变了。**Tā zài guówài guòle zhème duō nián, shēnghuó xíguàn yǒu xiē gǎibiàn le.** *He has spent so many years overseas that some of his habits have changed.* ■ 从此以后，他们俩过得很幸福。**Cóngcǐ yǐhòu, tāmen liǎ guò de hěn xìngfú.** *They lived happily ever after.*

过日子 guò rìzi live a life / 过年 guò nián observe New Year's Day / 过节 guò jié observe a festival
guòchéng 过程 **N** process, course ■ 从葡萄变成酒，是一个又长又复杂的过程。**Cóng pútao biànchéng jiǔ, shì yí ge yòu cháng yòu fùzá de guòchéng.** *The process by which grapes become wine is a long and complicated one.*

guòdù 过渡 [comp: 过 cross + 渡 ferry] **N** transition
guòlǜ 过滤 **V** filter
guònián 过年 **V** observe the (Chinese) New Year's Day ■ 小孩子最喜欢过年。**Xiǎoháizi zuì xǐhuan guònián.** *Children are most enthusiastic about celebrating New Year's Day.*
guòqī 过期 [v+obj: 过 pass + 期 period] **ADJ** invalid after the expiry date, past the sell-by date
guòqù 过去 [comp: 过 pass + 去 gone] **N** (something) in the past ■ 过去的事，不要多想了。**Guòqù de shì, bú yào duō xiǎng le.** *Don't keep thinking about what's past. (→ Let bygones be bygones.)* ■ 他过去常常生病，现在身体好多了。**Tā guòqù chángcháng shēngbìng, xiànzài shēntǐ hǎo duō le.** *He was often sick in the past. Now he is in much better health.*
guò 过[2] **TRAD** 過 **ADJ** excess, excessive
guòdù 过度 **ADJ** excessive, over
饮酒过度 yǐnjiǔ guò dù drink excessively
guòfèn 过分 [v+obj: 过 pass + 分 limit] **ADJ** excessive, going too far
过分的要求 guòfèn de yāoqiú excess demands
guòjiǎng 过奖 **V & N** overpraise; undeserved compliment ■ 您过奖了！**Nín guòjiǎng le!** *You flatter me. Thank you very much (for your compliment)!*
guòmǐn 过敏 **ADJ** [modif: 过 excessive + 敏 sensitive] over-sensitive, allergic ■ 我对这种药过敏。**Wǒ duì zhè zhong yào guòmǐn.** *I'm allergic to this medicine.*
guòshī 过失 **N** fault, error
guòwèn 过问 **V** take an interest in, concern oneself with

guòyú 过于 **ADV** too, excessively
guo 过[3] **TRAD** 過 **PARTICLE** (used after a verb or adjective to emphasize a past experience) ■ "你去过中国没有？" "去过，我去过中国很多地方。" **"Nǐ qùguo Zhōngguó méiyǒu?" "Qùguo, wǒ qùguo Zhōngguó hěn duō dìfang."** *"Have you been to China?" "Yes, I've been to many parts of China."*

H

hā 哈 **ONOMATOPOEIA** (sound of loud laughter)
hāhā 哈哈 **ONOMATOPOEIA** (representing loud laughter) ■ 听了孩子天真的话，老人哈哈大笑起来。**Tíngle háizi tiānzhēn de huà, lǎorén hāhā dàxiào qǐlai.** *Hearing the child's naïve words, the old man burst into laughter.*
hái 还 **TRAD** 還 **ADV** still, as before ■ 时间还早，我想看一会儿书再睡。**Shíjiān hái zǎo, wǒ xiǎng kàn yíhuìr shū zài shuì.** *It's still early. I want to do a little reading before going to bed.* ■ 已经上午十点钟了，我还没有吃早饭呢。**Yǐjīng shàngwǔ shí diǎnzhōng le, wǒ hái méiyǒu chī zǎofàn ne.** *It's already ten o'clock, and I still haven't had my breakfast.*
háishì 还是[1] **ADV** still, as before ■ 老师说了两遍，我还是不大懂。**Lǎoshī shuō le liǎng biàn, wǒ háishì bú dà dǒng.** *The teacher has explained twice, but I still don't quite understand.*
háishì 还是[2] **CONJ** or ■ 你喝茶还是喝咖啡？**Nǐ hē chá háishì hē kāfēi?** *Would you like tea or coffee?* ■ 我们今天去看电影还是明天去？**Wǒmen jīntiān qù kàn diànyǐng háishì míngtiān qù?** *Shall we go and see the movie today or tomorrow?*
hái 孩 **N** child
háizi 孩子 [suffix: 孩 child + 子 nominal suffix] **N** child, children ■ 这个孩子真聪明！**Zhège háizi zhēn cōngmíng!** *This child is really smart! (→ What a bright child!)*
男孩子 nán háizi boy, son / 女孩子 nǚ háizi girl, daughter ■ 他们有三个孩子——一个男孩子，两个女孩子。**Tāmen yǒu sān ge háizi—yí ge nán háizi, liǎng ge nǚ háizi.** *They have three chidren – a son and two daughters.*
hǎi 海 **N** sea ■ 没有风，海很平静。**Méiyǒu fēng, hǎi hěn píngjìng.** *There's no wind. The sea is calm.* ■ 这个国家任何地方都离海很近。**Zhège guójiā rènhé dìfang dōu lí hǎi hěn jìn.** *Anywhere in this country is close to the sea.*
hǎibá 海拔 **N** height from sea level, elevation
海拔一百米 hǎibá yībǎi mǐ 100 meters from sea level
hǎibīn 海滨 **N** seaside
hǎigǎng 海港 **N** seaport ■ 上海港是中国最重要的海港之一。**Shànghǎi gǎng shì Zhōngguó zuì**

zhòngyào de hǎigǎng zhī yī. *The Port of Shanghai is one of the most important seaports in China.*

hǎiguān 海关 [modif: 海 sea + 关 pass] N customs, customs house ■ 通过海关的时候，要检查护照。 **Tōngguò hǎiguān de shíhou, yào jiǎnchá hùzhào.** *Your passport will be examined when you pass through customs.*

海关检查 hǎiguān jiǎnchá customs inspection, customs examination / 海关手续 hǎiguān shǒuxù customs formalities / 海关人员 hǎiguān rényuán customs officer

hǎixiān 海鲜 seafood

海鲜馆 hǎixiān guǎn seafood restaurant

hǎiyáng 海洋 [comp: 海 sea + 洋 ocean] N sea, ocean, seas and oceans ■ 地球表面十分之七是海洋。 **Dìqiú biǎomiàn shí fēnzhī qī shì hǎiyáng.** *Seven-tenths of the Earth's surface is covered by seas and oceans.*

海洋生物 hǎiyáng shēngwù sea life / 海洋权 hǎiyáng quán maritime rights

hài 害 V harm, cause harm to ■ 吸烟不但害自己，而且害别人。 **Xīyān búdàn hài zìjǐ, érqiě hài biérén.** *Smoking not only harms the smoker; it harms others too.*

有害 yǒuhài harmful

hàichóng 害虫 N pest (insect)

hàichu 害处 [modif: 害 harmful + 处 place] N harm (ANTONYM 好处 hǎochu) ■ 大家都知道吸烟的害处。 **Dàjiā dōu zhīdào xīyān de hàichu.** *Everybody knows the harm that smoking causes.* ■ 对孩子严格一点，只有好处，没有害处。 **Duì háizi yángé yìdiǎn, zhǐyǒu hǎochu, méiyǒu hàichu.** *To be strict with children has only benefits, and will cause no harm.*

hàipà 害怕 V fear, be fearful ■ 她夜里一个人走回家，心里有点害怕。 **Tā yèli yí ge rén zǒu huí jiā, xīnli yǒudiǎn hàipà.** *She was fearful walking home alone at night.*

hàixiū 害羞 ADJ be bashful, be shy

hán 含 V hold in the mouth, contain, have ... as ingredients ■ 孩子嘴里含着一块糖，说不清话。 **Háizi zuǐ li hánzhe yí kuài táng, shuō bu qīng huà.** *The child had a piece of candy in his (or her) mouth and couldn't speak clearly.*

hánhu 含糊 ADJ vague, ambiguous

hányì 含义 N implied meaning, meaning

hán 寒 ADJ cold

hánjià 寒假 [modif: 寒 cold + 假 holiday] N winter vacation ■ 中国的学校一般在一月开始放寒假。 **Zhōngguó de xuéxiào yìbān zài Yīyuè kāishǐ fàng hánjià.** *In China, schools generally begin their winter holidays in January.*

hánlěng 寒冷 [comp: 寒 freezing + 冷 cold] ADJ freezing cold ■ 加拿大北部天气寒冷，一年中有半年多下雪。 **Jiānádà běibù tiānqì hánlěng, yì nián zhōng yǒu bànnián duō xià xuě.** *North Cana-*

da is very cold; it snows over six months in a year.

hánxuān 寒暄 V exchange greetings (at the beginning of a meeting)

hǎn 喊 V shout ■ 有人在外面喊你。 **Yǒu rén zài wàimiàn hǎn nǐ.** *Someone is calling for you outside.*

hàn 汗 N sweat, perspiration

出汗 chūhàn sweat, perspire ■ 这个房间热得我出汗。 **Zhège fángjiān rè de wǒ chūhàn.** *The room was so hot that I perspired.*

Hàn 汉 TRAD 漢 N the Han people

Hànyǔ 汉语 [modif: 汉 the Han people + 语 speech] N the language of the Han people, the Chinese language ■ 你学了几年汉语了？ **Nǐ xuéle jǐ nián Hànyǔ le?** *How many years have you been learning Chinese?* ■ 我会说一点汉语。 **Wǒ huì shuō yìdiǎn Hànyǔ.** *I speak a little Chinese.*

NOTE: In Chinese there are a number of words denoting the *Chinese language*. 汉语 **Hànyǔ** literally means the language of the Han Chinese people, in contrast with the languages of the non-Han peoples in China. 汉语 **Hànyǔ** is therefore the accurate, scientific term for the language. However, the most popular term for the *Chinese language* is 中文 **Zhōngwén**. In Singapore and other Southeast Asian countries, the standard Chinese language is often referred to as 华语 **Huáyǔ** in contrast to the various Chinese dialects spoken there. Also see note on 普通话 **Pǔtōnghuà.**

Hànzì 汉字 [modif: 汉 the Han people + 字 word, character] N Chinese character ■ 这个汉字我不认识。 **Zhège Hànzì wǒ bú rènshi.** *I don't know this Chinese character.* ■ 你会写多少汉字？ **Nǐ huì xiě duōshǎo Hànzì?** *How many Chinese characters can you write?*

hàn 捍 V defend, guard

hànwèi 捍卫 [modif: 捍 defend + 卫 defend] V defend, protect

hàn 旱 ADJ dry spell, drought (See gānhàn 干旱.)

hàn 憾 N regret (See yíhàn 遗憾.)

hǎn 罕 ADJ rare

hǎnjiàn 罕见 [modif: 罕 seldom + 见 seen] ADJ rare

háng 行 MEASURE WORD line, row, queue (used with nouns that are formed in lines) ■ 第四页第二行 **dì-sì yè dì-èr háng** *line two on page four*

hángliè 行列 N rows or ranks, rank and file

hángqíng 行情 N price quotations ■ 黄金的行情看涨。 **Huángjīn de hángqíng kànzhǎng.** *The price for gold is expected to rise.*

hángyè 行业 [comp: 行 line, occupation + 业 industry] N trade and profession, industry

各行各业 gèháng gèyè every trade and profession

háng 航 V navigate

hángbān 航班 N flight, flight number

飞往广州的航班 fēiwǎng Guǎngzhōu de hángbān a flight to Guangzhou

hángkōng 航空 **N** aviation
航空公司 hángkōng gōngsī aviation company, airline / 航空学校 hángkōng xuéxiào aviation school

hángtiān 航天 **N** spaceflight
航天飞机 hángtiān fēijī space shuttle, spaceship

hángxíng 航行 **v** (of a ship) sail, (of an aircraft) fly

háo 毫 **N** fine long hair

háo bù 毫不 **ADV** not in the least, not at all ■ 他读书不用功，考试成绩不好毫不奇怪。**Tā dúshū bú yònggōng, kǎoshì chéngjì bù hǎo háo bù qíguài.** *He didn't study hard, so it's no wonder he got very poor grades at the exams.*

NOTE: 毫不 **háo bù** is an adjective used before an adjective of two or more syllables. For example, you can say 毫不奇怪 **háo bù qíguài** *not at all strange,* but you cannot say 毫不怪 **háo bú guài.**

háomǐ 毫米 **N** millimeter

háo wú 毫无 **v** have no … at all, be in total absence of ■ 他心很硬，对不幸的人毫无同情心。**Tā xīn hěn yìng, duì búxìng de rén háo wú tóngqíngxīn.** *He is hardhearted, and has no sympathy at all for less fortunate people.*

NOTE: The object 毫无 **háo wú** usually takes a word of two or more syllables. The object usually refers to something abstract, like 同情心 **tóngqíngxīn** *sympathy.*

háo 豪 **ADJ** bold and unrestrained

háohuá 豪华 [comp: 豪 bold and unrestrained + 华 brilliant] **ADJ** luxurious, sumptuous

háomài 豪迈 **ADJ** heroic, bold and generous

hǎo 好¹ **ADJ** good, all right (ANTONYMS 坏 huài, 差 chà) ■ 他总是愿意帮助学生，他是个好老师。**Tā zǒngshì yuànyì bāngzhù xuésheng, tā shì ge hǎo lǎoshī.** *He is always ready to help his students. He is a good teacher.* ■ 你中文说得很好。**Nǐ Zhōngwén shuō de hěn hǎo.** *You speak Chinese very well.*

hǎochu 好处 **N** benefit, being beneficial (ANTONYMS 坏处 huàichu, 害处 hàichu) ■ 你惹爸爸生气，有什么好处呢？**Nǐ rě bàba shēngqì, yǒu shénme hǎochu ne?** *What is the good of offending daddy?* 对 … 有好处 duì … yǒu hǎochu be beneficial to ■ 经常锻炼对身体有很多好处。**Jīngcháng duànliàn duì shēntǐ yǒu hěn duō hǎochu.** *Regular physical exercise is very beneficial to health.*

hǎoxīn 好心 **ADJ** kind-hearted, with good intention ■ 她是个好心人。**Tā shì ge hǎoxīn rén.** *She is a kind-hearted person.*

hǎo 好² **ADV** very, very much ■ 你这件新衣服好漂亮！**Nǐ zhè jiàn xīn yīfu hǎo piàoliang!** *Your new dress is very pretty indeed!*

hǎochī 好吃 **ADJ** delicious ■ 这种水果我没有尝过，好吃不好吃？**Zhè zhǒng shuǐguǒ wǒ méiyǒu chángguo, hǎochī bu hǎochī?** *I've never tried this fruit before. Is it good?* ■ 王太太做的这个菜，好吃极了！**Wáng tàitai zuò de zhège cài, hǎochī jíle!** *This dish cooked by Mrs Wang is really delicious!*

hǎo duō 好多 **ADJ** a good many, many, much ■ 我生日那天，收到好多贺卡和礼物。**Wǒ shēngrì nà tiān, shōudào hǎo duō hèkǎ hé lǐwù.** *On my birthday I got lots of cards and gifts.*

hǎohǎor 好好儿 **ADJ** normal, nothing wrong ■ 她昨天还好好儿的，今天怎么病了呢？**Tā zuótiān hái hǎohǎor de, jīntiān zěnme bìng le ne?** *She was quite well yesterday. How come she should fall ill today?*

hǎojiǔ 好久 **ADV** a long time ■ 我好久没玩得这么痛快了。**Wǒ hǎojiǔ méi wán de zhème tòngkuai le.** *I haven't had such fun for a long time.* ■ 他等了她好久，她才来。**Tā děngle tā hǎojiǔ, tā cái lái.** *He waited for her for a long time before she came.*

hǎokàn 好看 **ADJ** **1** pleasant to the eye, good-looking, pretty (ANTONYM 难看 nánkàn) ■ 她妈妈年轻的时候很好看。**Tā māma niánqīng de shíhou hěn hǎokàn.** *Her mother was beautiful when young.* **2** (of a book, movie, etc.) interesting, absorbing ■ 这本小说好看不好看？**Zhè běn xiǎoshuō hǎokàn bu hǎokàn?** *Is this novel interesting?*

hǎo róngyì 好容易 **ADV** with great difficulty ■ 我好容易找到他家，他偏不在。**Wǒ hǎo róngyì zhǎodào tā jiā, tā piān bú zài.** *I found his home with great difficulty, and he had to be out.*

NOTE: 好容易 **hǎo róngyì** is an idiomatic expression. You can also say 好不容易 **hǎo bù róngyì**, with exactly the same meaning, e.g. ■ 我好不容易找到他家，他偏不在。**Wǒ hǎo bù róngyì zhǎodào tā jiā, tā piān bú zài.** *I found his home with great difficulty, and he must be out.*

hǎotīng 好听 **ADJ** pleasant to the ear, melodious (ANTONYM 难听 nántīng) ■ 这首歌真好听，我越听越想听。**Zhè shǒu gē zhēn hǎotīng, wǒ yuè tīng yuè xiǎng tīng.** *This song is beautiful. The more I listen, the more I want to hear it.* ■ 他说话的声音很好听。**Tā shuōhuà de shēngyīn hěn hǎotīng.** *The voice he speaks in is pleasant. (→ He has a pleasant voice.)*

hǎowánr 好玩儿 **ADJ** great fun ■ 这个游戏很好玩儿。**Zhège yóuxì hěn hǎowánr.** *This game is great fun.*

hǎoxiàng 好像 **v** be like, be similar to ■ 天边的白云好像一座雪山。**Tiānbiān de bái yún hǎoxiàng yí zuò xuěshān.** *The white cloud on the horizon looks like a snow mountain.* ■ 他今天好像不大高兴，你知道为什么吗？**Tā jīntiān hǎoxiàng bú dà gāoxìng, nǐ zhīdào wèishénme ma?** *He looks unhappy today. Do you know why?*

hǎoxiē 好些 **ADJ** a good many, a large number of, lots of ■ 我有好些日子没见到他了。 **Wǒ yǒu hǎoxiē rìzi méi jiàndào tā le.** *I haven't seen him for a long time.*

NOTE: 好些 **hǎoxiē** is a colloquial word, only used in casual, familiar styles.

hào 好 **V** be fond of ■ 这个学生虚心好学，进步很快。 **Zhège xuésheng xūxīn hào xué, jìnbù hěn kuài.** *This student is modest and fond of learning. He is making rapid progress.*

hào chī 好吃 **V** be fond of eating, be gluttonous

hào kè 好客 [v+obj: 好 be fond of + 客 guest] **ADJ** hospitable

热情好客 rèqíng hàokè warm and hospitable

hào qí 好奇 **ADJ** curious ■ 这个孩子对什么都好奇。 **Zhège háizi duì shénme dōu hàoqí.** *This child is curious about everything.*

hào sè 好色 **ADJ** oversexed, lewd

hào xué 好学 **ADJ** fond of learning, thirsty for knowledge

hào 号 **TRAD** 號 **N 1** order of sequence ■ 小王住在三号楼五号房间。 **Xiǎo Wáng zhù zài sān hào lóu, wǔ hào fángjiān.** *Xiao Wang lives in Building 3, Room 5.* **2** date of month ■ "今天几号？" "今天二十号，九月二十号。" **"Jīntiān jǐ hào?"** **"Jīntiān èrshí hào, Jiǔyuè èrshí hào."** *"What is the date today?" "It's the 20th, September 20th."*

NOTE: See note on 日 **rì.**

hàomǎ 号码 [comp: 号 order of sequence + 码 size] **N 1** serial number ■ 你知道张先生的手机号码吗？ **Nǐ zhīdào Zhāng xiānsheng de shǒujī hàomǎ ma?** *Do you know Mr Zhang's cell phone number?* **2** size ■ "你穿多大号码的衬衫？" "我穿四十码。" **"Nǐ chuān duō dà hàomǎ de chènshān?" "Wǒ chuān sìshí mǎ."** *"What size shirt do you wear?" "Size 40."*

hàozhào 号召 **V** call upon, appeal

hào 耗 **V** consume

hàofèi 耗费 [comp: 耗 consume + 费 cost] **V** consume (especially in a wasteful way), cost (a large amount of money, time, etc.)

hē 喝 **V** drink ■ 我口渴，我想喝点水。 **Wǒ kǒu kě, wǒ xiǎng hē diǎn shuǐ.** *I'm thirsty. I'd like to drink some water.*

NOTE: 喝 **hē** (drink) and 渴 **kě** (thirsty) look similar. Be careful not to confuse the two characters.

hē 呵 **V** blow a puff of breath, exhale through the mouth

hé 合 **V** close ■ 他太累了，一合上眼就睡着了。 **Tā tài lèi le, yì hé shang yǎn jiù shuìzháo le.** *He was so tired that he fell asleep the moment he closed his eyes.*

hébìng 合并 **V & N** merge; merger

héchéng 合成 **V 1** compose, compound **2** synthesize

合成纤维 héchéng xiānwéi synthetic fiber

héfǎ 合法 [v+obj: 合 conform to + 法 the law] **ADJ** legal, legitimate

hégé 合格 [v+obj: 合 conform to + 格 standard] **ADJ** qualified, up to standard

héhu 合乎 **V** conform with, correspond to

héhuǒ 合伙 **V** form a partnership, work in a partnership

和老同学合伙开公司 hé lǎo tóngxué héhuǒ kāi gōngsī set up a company in partnership with an old classmate

hélǐ 合理 [v+obj: 合 conform to + 理 reason] **ADJ** conforming to reason, reasonable, logical ■ 你这个建议十分合理。 **Nǐ zhège jiànyì shífēn hélǐ.** *Your proposal is very reasonable.* ■ 对于你们的合理要求，我们会尽力满足。 **Duìyú nǐmen de hélǐ yāoqiú, wǒmen huì jìnlì mǎnzú.** *We will do our best to meet your reasonable demands.*

héshēn 合身 **V** (of clothes) have the proper size and shape for a figure, fit well

héshì 合适 [comp: 合 harmony + 适 fit] **ADJ** suitable, appropriate ■ 他做这个工作非常合适。 **Tā zuò zhège gōngzuò fēicháng héshì.** *He is very suitable to do this job.* ■ 他比你年纪大，你叫他小张不合适。 **Tā bǐ nǐ niánjì dà, nǐ jiào tā Xiǎo Zhāng bù héshì.** *He is older than you. It's inappropriate for you to call him "Little Zhang."*

hésuàn 合算 **ADJ** worthwhile, paying ■ 这笔生意做得不合算。 **Zhè bǐ shēngyì zuò dè bù hésuàn.** *This business deal didn't pay.*

hétóng 合同 **N** contract, agreement (份 **fèn**)

签订合同 qiāndìng hétóng sign a contract

héyǐng 合影 **N** group photo (张 **zhāng**)

hézuò 合作 [modif: 合 jointly + 作 operate] **V & N** cooperate; cooperation ■ 我们非常高兴和你们合作。 **Wǒmen fēicháng gāoxìng hé nǐmen hézuò.** *We're very happy to cooperate with you.* ■ 我们应该加强合作。 **Wǒmen yīnggāi jiāqiáng hézuò.** *We should strengthen our cooperation.*

hé 何 **PRON** which, what

hébì 何必 **ADV** there is no need, why

hékuàng 何况 **CONJ 1** what's more, moreover **2** let alone

hé 河 **N** river ■ 这条河太宽，我游不过去。 **Zhè tiáo hé tài kuān, wǒ yóu bu guòqu.** *This river is too broad. I can't swim across it.*

NOTE: In modern Chinese, 江 **jiāng** and 河 **hé** both mean *river*. Usually (not always) rivers in the south are known as 江 **jiāng** and rivers in the north are 河 **hé**.

hé 和¹ **ADJ 1** gentle, mild, harmonious **2** peaceful

hé'ǎi 和蔼 **ADJ** affable and gentle

héjiě 和解 **V** become reconciled

hémù 和睦 **ADJ** harmonious, amiable

hépíng 和平 N peace

héqì 和气 ADJ gentle and friendly

héxié 和谐 ADJ & N harmonious; harmony

hé 和[2] I CONJ and ■ 我和你都在学中文。**Wǒ hé nǐ dōu zài xué Zhōngwén.** *You and I are both learning Chinese.* II PREP with ■ 我想和你谈谈。**Wǒ xiǎng hé nǐ tántan.** *I'd like to have a word with you.* 和…一起 **hé … yìqǐ** together with… ■ 昨天我和朋友一起吃中饭。**Zuótiān wǒ hé péngyou yìqǐ chī zhōngfàn.** *Yesterday I had lunch with a friend of mine.*

hé 盒 N box

hézi 盒子 [suffix: 盒 box + 子 nominal suffix] N box (只 **zhī**) ■ 她的铅笔盒子里有四支铅笔。**Tāde qiānbǐ hé li yǒu sì zhī qiānbǐ.** *There are four pencils in her pencil box.*

hé 核 N kernel, core, nuclear

hédiànzhàn 核电站 N nuclear power plant

héwǔqì 核武器 N nuclear weapon

héxīn 核心 [comp: 核 core + 心 the heart] N core, kernel

hè 贺 TRAD 賀 V congratulate

hèkǎ 贺卡 [modif: 贺 greeting + 卡 card] N greeting card (张 **zhāng**) ■ 去年圣诞节你收到多少贺卡? **Qùnián Shèngdànjié nǐ shōudào duōshǎo hèkǎ?** *How many cards did you get last Christmas?* ■ 明天是小王生日，我们送他一张生日贺卡吧。**Míngtiān shì Xiǎo Wáng shēngrì, wǒmen sòng tā yì zhāng hèkǎ ba.** *Tomorrow is Xiao Wang's birthday. Let's give him a card.*

电子贺卡 **diànzǐ hèkǎ** e-card / 圣诞贺卡 **Shèngdàn hèkǎ** Christmas card / 生日贺卡 **shēngrì hèkǎ** birthday card / 新年贺卡 **Xīnnián hèkǎ** New Year's Day card

hēi 黑 ADJ black, dark ■ 我不喜欢穿黑颜色的衣服。**Wǒ bù xǐhuan chuān hēi yánsè de yīfu.** *I don't like to wear black.* ■ 天快黑了，他们还在踢球。**Tiān kuài hēi le, tāmen hái zài tīqiú.** *It's almost dark, but they're still playing soccer.*

hēi'àn 黑暗 [comp: 黑 black, dark + 暗 dim] ADJ dark (ANTONYM 光明 **guāngmíng**) ■ 他很天真，不知道社会的黑暗面。**Tā hěn tiānzhēn, bù zhīdào shèhuì de hēi'àn miàn.** *He is naive, unaware of the seamy side of society.*

hēibǎn 黑板 N blackboard ■ 我们现在不用黑板，用白板。**Wǒmen xiànzài bú yòng hēibǎn, yòng báibǎn.** *Now we don't use the blackboard; we use the whiteboard.*

hēikè 黑客 N hacker

hēi 嘿 INTERJ 1 (used to attract someone's attention in a casual or impolite manner) ■ 嘿，这里不准吸烟。**Hēi, zhèli bùzhǔn xīyān.** *Hey! You can't smoke here.* 2 (used to indicate admiration) ■ 嘿，昨天的球赛咱们队打得真棒! **Hēi, zuótiān de qiúsài zánmen duì dǎ de zhēn bàng!** *Hey, our team played marvelously in yesterday's match!*

hén 痕 N trace

伤痕 **shānghén** scar

hénjì 痕迹 N stain, trace

hěn 很 ADV very ■ 见到你，我很高兴。**Jiàndào nǐ, wǒ hěn gāoxìng.** *I'm glad to meet you.* ■ 我很讨厌下雨天。**Wǒ hěn tǎoyàn xià yǔ tiān.** *I hate rainy days.*

NOTE: When used as predicates, Chinese adjectives normally require an adverb. For example, 我高兴 **Wǒ gāoxìng** sounds unnatural, while 我很高兴 **Wǒ hěn gāoxìng** *(I'm [very] happy)*, 我不高兴 **Wǒ bù gāoxìng** *(I'm not happy)* or 我非常高兴 **Wǒ fēicháng gāoxìng** *(I'm very happy)* are normal sentences. The adverb 很 **hěn** is often used as a default adverb before an adjective. In such cases the meaning of 很 **hěn** is very weak.

hěn 狠 ADJ 1 cruel, relentless

心毒手狠 **xīndú shǒuhěn** with a vicious mind and cruel means

2 severe, stern

狠狠地批评 **hěnhěnde pīpíng** criticize severely

hěndú 狠毒 [comp: 狠 cruel + 毒 poisonous] ADJ cruel and vicious

hěnxīn 狠心 I ADJ ruthless II N strong determination 下狠心 **xià hěnxīn** make a tough decision resolutely

hèn 恨 V 1 hate, be angry with (ANTONYM 爱 **ài**) ■ 她恨男朋友欺骗了她。**Tā hèn nán péngyou qīpiàn le tā.** *She hates her boyfriend for cheating on her.* 2 regret deeply ■ 他恨自己念书不用功，但是太晚了。**Tā hèn zìjǐ niànshū bú yònggōng, dànshì tài wǎn le.** *He deeply regrets not having studied hard, but it's too late.*

hènbude 恨不得 ADV how … wish to ■ 他恨不得马上回家过年。**Hā hènbude mǎshàng huíjiā guònián.** *How he wished he could go home right now for the Spring Festival.*

NOTE: We use 恨不得 to express a wish that is very strong but cannot be fulfilled. If we say 他恨不得马上回家过年。**Tā hènbude mǎshàng huíjiā guònián,** it means it is quite impossible for him to go back home right now.

hēng 哼 V 1 snort ■ 他哼了一声，翻过身去，又睡了。**Tā hēngle yìshēng, fānguo shēn qù, yòu shuì le.** *He gave a snort, turned over and fell asleep again.* 2 hum ■ 她一边做饭，一边哼着歌。**Tā yìbiān zuòfàn, yìbiān hēngzhe gē.** *While she cooked, she hummed a song.*

héng 横 ADJ horizontal (See **zònghéng** 纵横.)

héng 恒 ADJ permanent (See **yǒnghéng** 永恒.)

hōng 轰 TRAD 轟 V rumble, explode

hōngdòng 轰动 [comp: 轰 rumble + 动 move] V cause a sensation, be sensensational

hōngzhà 轰炸 V drop bombs, attack with bombs

hōng 烘 V dry or warm by the fire, roast

hōnggānjī 烘干机 **N** (clothes) dryer

hóng 洪 **ADJ** big

hóngshuǐ 洪水 **N** flood

hóng 红 **TRAD** 紅 **ADJ** red ■ 中国人传统上喜欢红颜色。**Zhōngguórén chuántǒng shang xǐhuan hóng yánsè.** *Traditionally the Chinese love the color red.* ■ 红花绿树，你的花园真好看。**Hóng huā, lǜ shù, nǐ de huāyuán zhēn hǎokàn.** *With red flowers and green trees, your garden is really beautiful.*

hóngbāo 红包 a red envelope (containing money), bribe or gift for children on Chinese New Year's Day ■ 在那里办事，要送红包。**Zài nàli bànshì, yào sòng hóngbāo.** *To get things done there, bribes must be given.*

hóngchá 红茶 [modif: 红 red + 茶 tea] **N** black tea ■ 中国人喝红茶，不放糖和牛奶。**Zhōngguórén hē hóngchá, bú fàng táng hé niúnǎi.** *The Chinese don't put sugar or milk in their black tea.*

hónglǜdēng 红绿灯 **N** traffic lights, stoplights

hóng 虹 **N** rainbow (See **cǎihóng** 彩虹.)

hóng 宏 **ADJ** grand, magnificent

hóngguān 宏观 **ADJ** macroscopic, macro- 宏观经济学 **hóngguān jīngjìxué** macroeconomics

hóngwěi 宏伟 **ADJ** magnificent, grand

hǒng 哄 **V 1** coax **2** cheat, hoodwink

hǒngpiàn 哄骗 [comp: 哄 cheat + 骗 deceive] **V** lie in order to cheat

hóu 猴 **N** monkey

hóuzi 猴子 [suffix: 猴 monkey + 子 nominal suffix] **N** monkey (只 **zhī**) ■ 动物园里的猴子每天吸引很多小朋友。**Dòngwùyuán li de hóuzi měi tiān xīyǐn hěn duō xiǎo péngyou.** *The monkeys in the zoo attract many children every day.*

hóu 喉 **N** throat

hóulóng 喉咙 **N** throat, larynx 喉咙疼 **hóulóng téng** have a sore throat

hǒu 吼 **V** roar, howl

hòu 后 **TRAD** 後 **N** back, rear (**ANTONYMS** 前 **qián**, 先 **xiān**) ■ 请用后门。**Qǐng yòng hòumén.** *Please use the back door.*

hòubèi 后背 **N** the back (of the body)

hòubian 后边 [modif: 后 back, rear + 边 side] **N** back, rear (**ANTONYM** 前边 **qiánbian**) ■ 我家的后边有一条小河。**Wǒ jiā de hòubian yǒu yì tiáo xiǎo hé.** *There is a stream behind my house.* ■ 听课的时候我喜欢坐在前边，不喜欢坐在后边。**Tīng kè de shíhou, wǒ xǐhuān zuò zài qiánbian, bù xǐhuan zuò zài hòubian.** *When attending lectures, I like to sit in the front row, not the back row.*

hòudài 后代 [modif: 后 rear + 代 generation] **N** succeeding generations, posterity

hòu gù zhī yōu 后顾之忧 **IDIOM** trouble back at home, fear of disturbance at the rear

hòuguǒ 后果 [modif: 后 later + 果 result] **N** consequences ■ 你愿意承受这一行动的后果吗？**Nǐ yuànyì chéngshòu zhè yī xíngdòng de hòuguǒ ma?** *Are you willing to bear the consequences of this action?*

hòuhuǐ 后悔 [modif: 后 afterwards + 悔 regret, repent] **V** regret, feel sorry (for having done something) ■ 你放弃这么好的机会，以后会后悔的。**Nǐ fàngqì zhème hǎo de jīhuì, yǐhòu huì hòuhuǐ de.** *You'll regret giving up such a good opportunity.*

hòulái 后来 [modif: 后 late + 来 come] **N** afterwards, later on ■ 他刚到北京的时候，不爱吃中国菜，后来就慢慢习惯了。**Tā gāng dào Běijīng de shíhou, bú ài chī Zhōngguó cài, hòulái mànman xíguàn le.** *When he first came to Beijing he did not like Chinese food, but later on he gradually got used to it.*

hòumiàn 后面 **N** same as 后边 **hòubian**

hòunián 后年 [modif: 后 late + 年 year] **N** the year after next ■ 我今年十九岁，后年就二十一岁了。**Wǒ jīnnián shíjiǔ suì, hòunián jiù èrshíyī suì le.** *I'm nineteen this year, and I'll be twenty-one the year after next.*

hòuqín 后勤 **N** logistics, support services

hòutiān 后天 [modif: 后 late + 天 day] **N** the day after tomorrow ■ 今天刚星期三，后天才星期五呢。**Jīntiān gāng Xīngqīsān, hòutiān cái Xīngqīwǔ ne.** *It's only Wednesday today. Friday will be the day after tomorrow.*

hòu 厚 **ADJ** thick (**ANTONYM** 薄 **báo**) ■ 这么厚的小说，她两天就看完了。**Zhème hòu de xiǎoshuō, tā liǎng tiān jiù kànwán le.** *It took her only two days to finish reading such a thick novel.*

hòu 候 **V** wait

hòuxuǎnrén 候选人 **N** candidate (for an election or selection)

hū 乎 **PARTICLE** (added to another word to express strong emotions) (See **jīhū** 几乎, **sìhū** 似乎.)

hū 呼 **V** exhale

hūhuàn 呼唤 **V** call, shout to

hūxī 呼吸 [comp: 呼 exhale + 吸 inhale] **V** breathe ■ 我刚才不大舒服，在花园里呼吸了新鲜空气，感到好多了。**Wǒ gāngcái búdà shūfu, zài huāyuán li hūxīle xīnxiān kōngqì, gǎndào hǎo duō le.** *I didn't feel well just now. I'm feeling much better now that I've had some fresh air in the garden.*

hūyù 呼吁 **V** appeal, call on

hū 忽 **ADV** suddenly

hūlüè 忽略 **V** neglect, overlook

hūrán 忽然 **ADV** suddenly ■ 刚才天气还好好儿的，忽然下起大雨来了。**Gāngcái tiānqì hái hǎohǎor de, hūrán xià qǐ dà yǔ lái le.** *Just now the weather was still fine. Suddenly it's raining hard.*

hūshì 忽视 **V** overlook, negelect ■ 他们忽视了一个细节，使计划失败。**Tāmen hūshì le yí ge xìjié, shǐ jìhuà shībài.** *They overlooked a detail, which doomed the plan.*

hú 胡[1] ADJ reckless, wantonly

húluàn 胡乱 ADV rashly, carelessly

húshuō 胡说 [modif: 胡 foreign + 说 talking] V & N talk nonsense; nonsense ■ 你别胡说，我和她只是朋友关系。**Nǐ bié húshuō, wǒ hé tā zhǐ shì péngyou guānxi.** *Don't talk nonsense; she and I are only friends.*

hú shuō bā dào 胡说八道 IDIOM pure nonsense, drivel

hú 胡[2] TRAD 鬍 N beard, mustache

húxū 胡须 N beard, mustache

húzi 胡子 [suffix: 胡 beard, whiskers + 子 nominal suffix] N beard, whiskers ■ 你的胡子长了，要刮一下。**Nǐ de húzi cháng le, yào guā yíxià.** *You've grown quite a beard. You need a shave.*

刮胡子 guā húzi shave (beard, whiskers)

hú 壶 TRAD 壺 N kettle (把 bǎ) ■ 壶里还有水吗？**Hú li hái yǒu shuǐ ma?** *Is there any water left in the kettle?*

水壶 shuǐhú kettle

hú 糊 V paste

hútu 糊涂 [comp: 糊 muddled + 涂 mire] ADJ muddle-headed, muddled, confused ■ 你真糊涂，怎么又忘了把钥匙放在哪儿了？**Nǐ zhēn hútu, zěnme yòu wàngle bǎ yàoshi fàng zài nǎ'er le?** *You're really muddle-headed. How is it that you've forgotten where you've left the keys again?* ■ 你越解释，我越糊涂，还是让我自己再看一遍书吧。**Nǐ yuè jiěshì, wǒ yuè hútu, háishì ràng wǒ zìjǐ zài kàn yí biàn shū ba.** *The more you explain, the more confused I am. I'd better read the book once more by myself.*

hútu chóng 糊涂虫 [modif: 糊涂 muddle-headed + 虫 bug] N muddle-headed person, bungler

hú 蝴 as in 蝴蝶 húdié

húdié 蝴蝶 N butterfly

hú 湖 N lake ■ 中国最大的湖是青海省的青海湖。**Zhōngguó zuì dà de hú shì Qīnghǎi Shěng de Qīnghǎi Hú.** *China's biggest lake is Qinghai Lake in Qinghai Province.*

湖边 húbiān lakeside

húpō 湖泊 N lakes

hǔ 虎 N tiger (See lǎohǔ 老虎.)

hù 互 ADJ reciprocal

hùliánwǎng 互联网 [modif: 互 each other + 联 link + 网 net] N the Internet, the World Wide Web ■ 有了互联网，信息交流方便多了。**Yǒule hùliánwǎng, xìnxī jiāoliú fāngbiàn duōle.** *With the Internet, information exchange is so much more convenient.* ■ 我每天都上互联网，看新闻，找资料。**Wǒ měitiān dōu shàng hùliánwǎng, kàn xīnwén, zhǎo zīliào.** *I get on the Internet every day to read news or search for data.*

hùxiāng 互相 ADV each other, one another ■ 我们是好朋友，应当互相关心，互相帮助。**Wǒmen shì hǎo péngyou, yīngdāng hùxiāng guānxīn, hùxiāng bāngzhù.** *We're good friends, so we should care for each other and help each other.*

hù 户 MEASURE WORD (used with nouns denoting households and families) ■ 这条街上有三十几户人家。**Zhè tiáo jiē shang yǒu sānshí jǐ hù rénjiā.** *There are over thirty households [living] along this street.*

hù 护 TRAD 護 V protect

hùshi 护士 N nurse ■ 护士按照医生的嘱咐给病人吃药。**Hùshi ànzhào yīshēng de zhǔfu gěi bìngrén chī yào.** *Nurses administer medicine to patients according to doctors' instructions.*

NOTE: In China nurses are almost exclusively women. To address a nurse politely, use 护士小姐 **hùshì xiǎojiě**, e.g. ■ 护士小姐，我还需要吃这个药吗？ **Hùshì xiǎojiě, wǒ hái xūyào chī zhè ge yào ma?** *Nurse, do I still need to take this medicine?* or you can put her family name before 护士 **hùshì**, e.g. 张护士 **Zhāng hùshì**, 李护士 **Lǐ hùshì**.

hùzhào 护照 N passport ■ 约翰在北京旅行的时候，发现护照丢了，就马上和大使馆联系。**Yuēhàn zài Běijīng lǚxíng de shíhou, fāxiàn hùzhào diū le, jiù mǎshang hé dàshǐguǎn liánxì.** *While traveling in Beijing, John found that he had lost his passport and immediately contacted the embassy.*

huā 花[1] N flower (朵 duǒ) ■ 花瓶里插了几朵美丽的花。**Huāpíng li chāle jǐ duǒ měilì de huā.** *Some beautiful flowers were placed in the vase.* ■ 去医院看病人，可以带一些花。**Qù yīyuàn kàn bìngrén, kěyǐ dài yìxiē huā.** *You can take some flowers with you when you visit a patient in the hospital.*

种花 zhòng huā plant flowers, do gardening

huābàn 花瓣 N (flower) petal

huālěi 花蕾 N bud

huāpíng 花瓶 N vase

huār 花儿 ADJ full of colors, mottled, loud ■ 这条裙子太花儿了，你穿不合适。**Zhè tiáo qúnzi tài huār le, nǐ chuān bù héshì.** *This skirt is too flashy. It's unsuitable for you to wear.*

huāshēng 花生 N peanut

花生酱 huāshēngjiàng peanut butter

huāyuán 花园 [modif: 花 flower + 园 garden] N garden (座 zuò) ■ 这里几乎每座房子都有一个小花园。**Zhèli jīhū měi zuò fángzi dōu yǒu yí ge xiǎo huāyuán.** *Almost every house here has a small garden.*

huā 花[2] V 1 spend ■ 去年我花了两百元买书。**Qùnián wǒ huāle liǎngbǎi yuán mǎi shū.** *Last year I spent 200 yuan on books.* ■ 你每天花多少时间做作业？**Nǐ měitiān huā duōshǎo shíjiān zuò zuòyè?** *How much time do you spend on assignments every day?* 2 cost (money) ■ 这次旅行花了我三千块钱。**Zhè cì lǚxíng huāle wǒ sānqiān kuài qián.** *This trip cost me 3,000 yuan.* ■ 在英国

留学一年要花多少钱？ **Zài Yīngguó liúxué yì nián yào huā duōshǎo qián?** *How much would it cost to study in the UK for a year?* **3** take (time) ■ 写这篇文章花了我整整两天。 **Xiě zhè piān wénzhāng huāle wǒ zhěngzhěng liǎng tiān.** *It took me two full days to write this essay.*

NOTE: In writing, the character 化 **huà** can be used instead of 花 **huā** as a verb meaning *spend, cost,* etc.

huá 华 TRAD 華 I N China
华人 **Huárén** foreign citizen of Chinese descent, ethnic Chinese
II ADJ magnificent, gorgeous
huálì 华丽 [comp: 华 magnificent + 丽 beautiful] ADJ gorgeous, magnificent
Huáqiáo 华侨 N overseas Chinese
Huáyì 华裔 N person of Chinese descent
huá 划 TRAD 劃 V scratch or scrape with a sharp object ■ 我的手划破了，不能在花园里干活了。 **Wǒ de shǒu huá pò le, bù néng zài huāyuán li gànhuó le.** *I've scratched my hand. I can't work in the garden any more.*
huá 滑 ADJ slippery ■ 下雪以后，路上很滑。 **Xià xuě yǐhòu, lù shang hěn huá.** *After a snowfall, roads are slippery.*
huábīng 滑冰 V & N skate; ice-skating
huáxuě 滑雪 V & N ski; skiing
huà 化 V melt ■ 太阳出来，雪很快化了。 **Tàiyang chūlai, xuě hěn kuài huà le.** *When the sun came out, the snow melted very quickly.*
huàféi 化肥 [modif: 化 chemical + 肥 fertilizer] N chemical fertilizer
huàgōng 化工 N shortened form of 化学工业 **huàxué gōngyè** (chemical industry)
化工厂 **huàgōngchǎng** chemical plant
huàshí 化石 N fossil
huàxué 化学 [modif: 化 change, transform + 学 study] N chemistry ■ 他对化学感兴趣，以后想当化学工程师。 **Tā duì huàxué gǎn xìngqu, yǐhòu xiǎng dāng huàxué gōngchéngshī.** *He is interested in chemistry, and hopes to become a chemical engineer.*
化学工业 **huàxué gōngyè** chemical industry
huàyàn 化验 [modif: 化 chemical + 验 test] N chemical test, laboratory test ■ 你必须化验一下血。 **Nǐ bìxū huàyàn yíxià xuè.** *You must have your blood tested.*
化验报告 **huàyàn bàogào** laboratory test report / 化验单 **huàyàndān** laboratory test application (a form signed by a doctor for the patient to have a test done in a laboratory) / 化验室 **huàyànshì** laboratory / 化验员 **huàyànyuán** laboratory assistant, laboratory technician
huàzhuāng 化妆 V put on make-up
化妆品 **huàzhuāngpǐn** cosmetics
huà 划 TRAD 劃 V **1** plan **2** delimit
huàfēn 划分 V divide, differentiate, classify

huà 画 TRAD 畫 V draw, paint ■ 这个小孩喜欢画各种动物，而且画得挺好。 **Zhège xiǎohái xǐhuan huà gè zhǒng dòngwù, érqiě huà de tǐng hǎo.** *This child likes to draw animals, and is very good at it.*
铅笔画 **qiānbǐ huà** pencil drawing / 水彩画 **shuǐcǎi huà** watercolor (painting) / 油画 **yóuhuà** oil painting
huàbào 画报 [modif: 画 picture + 报 paper] N illustrated magazine, pictorial (份 **fèn**, 本 **běn**) ■ 星期天的报纸大多有一份画报。 **Xīngqītiān de bàozhǐ dàduō yǒu yí fèn huàbào.** *Most Sunday newspapers carry a pictorial (or color) supplement.*
huàjiā 画家 [suffix: 画 paint + 家 nominal suffix denoting an expert] N painter, artist (位 **wèi**) ■ 这位画家画风景特别好。 **Zhè wèi huàjiā huà fēngjǐng tèbié hǎo.** *This artist is particularly good at landscapes.*
huàr 画儿 N picture, drawing (张 **zhāng**, 幅 **fú**) ■ 这张画儿画得真好！ **Zhè zhāng huàr huà de zhēn hǎo!** *This picture is so well done!*

NOTE: You can use 画 **huà** instead of 画儿 **huàr**, e.g. ■ 这张画画得真好！ **Zhè zhāng huà huà de zhēn hǎo!** *This picture is so well done!*

huà shé tiān zú 画蛇添足 IDIOM add legs to a snake (→ do superfluous things, thus causing damage or attracting ridicule)
huà 话 TRAD 話 N speech, what is said, words (句 **jù**) ■ 你这句话很有道理。 **Nǐ zhè jù huà hěn yǒu dàolǐ.** *Your words are very reasonable. (→ You're quite right there.)* ■ 别忘了我的话。 **Bié wàngle wǒ de huà.** *Don't forget what I said.*
huàtí 话题 [modif: 话 speech + 题 theme] N topic of conversation, subject of a talk, theme
huàtǒng 话筒 N microphone
huái 怀 N TRAD 懷 bosom
huáiniàn 怀念 [comp: 怀 miss + 念 think of] V cherish the memory of, think of tenderly
huáiyí 怀疑 [v+obj: 怀 harbor + 疑 doubt] V **1** disbelieve, doubt ■ 我怀疑他说的话是不是真的。 **Wǒ huáiyí tā shuōde huà shìbushì zhēn de.** *I doubt if he was telling the truth.* **2** think something is likely, suspect: ■ 我怀疑他在撒谎。 **Wǒ huáiyí tā zài sāhuǎng.** *I suspect that he was lying.*

NOTE: 怀疑 **huáiyí** has two seemingly contradictory meanings – *disbelieve* and *think something is likely*, but the context will make the meaning clear.

huáiyùn 怀孕 V be pregnant
huài 坏 TRAD 壊 I ADJ bad (ANTONYM 好 **hǎo**) ■ 小孩子看电影，总爱问谁是好人，谁是坏人。 **Xiǎoháizi kàn diànyǐng, zǒng ài wèn shéi shì hǎorén, shéi shì huàirén.** *When children watch movies, they like to ask who is the good guy and who is the bad guy.* II V break down, be out of order ■ 这台电脑已经用坏了，得买台新的。 **Zhè**

tái diànnǎo yǐjīng yòng huài le, děi mǎi yì tái xīn de. *This computer has already broken down; you need to buy a new one.* ■ 他们的车半路上坏了。 **Tāmen de chē bànlù shang huài le.** *Their car broke down halfway.*

huàichu 坏处 [modif: 坏 bad + 处 place] **N** negative effect, disadvantage (ANTONYM 好处 **hǎochu**) ■ 这样做好处很多，但是也有不少坏处。 **Zhèyàng zuò hǎochu hěn duō, dànshì yě yǒu bù shǎo huàichu.** *This way of doing things has many advantages, but it also has quite a few disadvantages.*

NOTE: 坏处 **huàichu** and 害处 **hàichu** both refer to the undesirable effects of an action or actions. 坏处 **huàichu** connotes general negativity while 害处 **hàichu** emphasizes the harm that results.

huān 欢 TRAD 歡 ADJ joyful

huānlè 欢乐 [comp: 欢 joyful + 乐 happy] ADJ joyful, happy

huānsòng 欢送 [modif: 欢 joyfully + 送 send off] **v** send off ■ 我们明天到机场去欢送中国公司的代表。 **Wǒmen míngtiān dào jīchǎng qù huānsòng Zhōngguó gōngsī de dàibiǎo.** *We're going to the airport tomorrow to send off the representative from the Chinese company.*

欢送会 **huānsònghuì** a send-off party (e.g. a farewell tea party)

huānyíng 欢迎 [modif: 欢 joyfully + 迎 meet] **v** welcome ■ 热烈欢迎您！ **Rèliè huānyíng nín!** *A warm welcome to you!* ■ 怎样改进我们的服务？欢迎顾客们提建议。 **Zěnyàng gǎijìn wǒmen de fúwù? Huānyíng gùkèmen tí jiànyì.** *What can we do to improve our service? Customers are welcome to give us their suggestions.*

huán 还 TRAD 還 **v** return, pay back ■ 他向银行借了十万元，要在五年内还清。 **Tā xiàng yínháng jièle shíwàn yuán, yào zài wǔ nián nèi huán qīng.** *He borrowed 100,000 yuan from a bank and must repay the loan within five years.* ■ 有借有还，再借不难。 **Yǒu jiè yǒu huán, zài jiè bù nán.** *Return what you borrowed, and it won't be difficult to borrow again.*

huányuán 还原 [v+obj: 还 return to + 原 the original] **v** return to the original, restore

huán 环 TRAD 環 **N** circle

huánjié 环节 **N** link

重要环节 **zhòngyào huánjié** important link

huánjìng 环境 [comp: 环 surroundings + 境 boundary, area] **N** environment ■ 这家造纸厂污染环境，引起当地居民的强烈不满。 **Zhè jiā zàozhǐ chǎng wūrǎn huánjìng, yǐnqǐ dāngdì jūmín de qiángliè bùmǎn.** *This paper mill pollutes the environment, arousing the local people's great displeasure.*

huǎn 缓 TRAD 緩 ADJ leisurely

huǎnjiě 缓解 **v** alleviate, relieve

huǎnhé 缓和 **I v** ease up, alleviate (ANTONYM 紧张 **jǐnzhāng**) ■ 他说了一个笑话，让会场上的紧张气氛缓和下来。 **Tā shuō le yí ge xiàohua, ràng huìchǎng shàng de jǐnzhāng qìfen huǎnhé xiàlai.** *She told a joke, which defused tension at the meeting.* **II** ADJ relaxed, gentle

口气缓和 **kǒuqì huǎnhé** with a gentle, mild tone

huàn 换 TRAD 換 **v** change, replace ■ 她的地址换了，我不知道她的新地址。 **Tā de dìzhǐ huàn le, wǒ bù zhīdào tā de xīn dìzhǐ.** *She has changed her address. I don't have her new one.* ■ 这双鞋太小了，我想换大一号的。 **Zhè shuāng xié tài xiǎo le, wǒ xiǎng huàn dà yí hào de.** *This pair of shoes is too small. I'd like to replace it with a bigger size.*

huàn 患 **v** suffer (from a disease)

huànzhě 患者 **N** patient

精神病患者 **jīngshénbìng huànzhě** one who suffers from mental disorder, psychiatric patient

huàn 幻 ADJ illusionary

huànxiǎng 幻想 [modif: 幻 illusionary + 想 think] **v & N** fantasize, have an illusion; fantasy, illusion

huāng 荒 **I** ADJ barren, desolate **II N** crop failure, famine

huāngliáng 荒凉 [comp: 荒 barren + 凉 cold] ADJ bleak, desolate

huāngmiù 荒谬 ADJ absurd, preposterous

荒谬至极 **huāngmiù zhìjí** absolutely absurd

huāngtáng 荒唐 ADJ preposterous, way off the mark

荒唐透顶 **huāngtáng tòudǐng** incredibly silly, totally unreasonable

huāng 慌 **v** be flustered, panic ■ 他考试要迟到了，慌得坐错了车。 **Tā kǎoshì yào chídào le, huāng de zuòcuòle chē.** *As he was about to be late for the examination, he was so flustered that he took the wrong bus.*

慌了手脚 **huāngle shǒu jiǎo** be so flustered as to not know what to do

huāngmáng 慌忙 ADJ hurried and confused, in a great rush

huāngzhāng 慌张 ADJ in frantic haste, flustered, flurried

huáng 皇 **N** emperor

huángdì 皇帝 **N** emperor ■ 中国历史上第一个皇帝是秦始皇帝。 **Zhōngguó lìshǐ shang dì yī ge huángdì shì Qín Shǐ Huángdì.** *The first emperor in Chinese history was Qin Shi Huangdi.*

huánghòu 皇后 **N** wife of an emperor, empress

huáng 黄 TRAD 黃 ADJ yellow

huángguā 黄瓜 **N** cucumber (根 **gēn**) ■ 我夏天爱吃新鲜黄瓜。 **Wǒ xiàtiān ài chī xīnxiān huángguā.** *I love to eat fresh cucumber in summer.*

Huánghé 黄河 **N** the Yellow River

huánghūn 黄昏 **N** dusk, twilight

huángjīn 黄金 **N 1** gold **2** something that is precious

黄金地段 huángjīn dìduàn golden section (of property)

huángsè 黄色 **N & ADJ 1** yellow **2** pornography; pornographic

黄色电影 huángsè diànyǐng pornographic movie / 黄色杂志 huángsè zázhì pornographic magazine

huángyóu 黄油 **N** butter ■ 在新鲜面包上涂一层黄油，可好吃了！**Zài xīnxiān miànbāo shang tú yì céng huángyóu, kě hǎo chī le!** *If you spread a thin layer of butter on freshly baked bread, how delicious it is!*

huǎng rán dà wù 恍然大悟 **IDIOM** suddenly see the light, suddenly realize what has happened

huǎng 谎 **TRAD** 謊 **N** lie, falsehood

huǎngyán 谎言 **N** lie, falsehood

huàng 晃 **V** sway, shake (See **yáohuàng** 摇晃.)

huī 灰 **ADJ** gray ■ 这个城市污染很严重，天空总是灰灰的。**Zhège chéngshì wūrǎn hěn yánzhòng, tiānkōng zǒng shì huīhuī de.** *This city has a serious pollution problem. Its sky is always gray.*

huīchén 灰尘 **N** dust

huīxīn 灰心 **ADJ** disheartened, discouraged ■ 他虽然遭到失败，但是没有灰心。**Tā suīrán zāodào shībài, dànshì méiyǒu huīxīn.** *Although he failed, he was not disheartened.*

huī 恢 **ADJ** extensive, vast

huīfù 恢复 **V** recover, restore ■ 祝你早日恢复健康！**Zhù nǐ zǎorì huīfù jiànkāng!** *I wish you a speedy recovery of health!* ■ 经过十几天的圣诞和新年假期，城市生活又恢复正常了。**Jīngguò shí jǐ tiān de Shèngdàn hé Xīnnián jiàqī, chéngshì shēnghuó yòu huīfù zhèngcháng le.** *After a dozen days of Christmas and New Year holidays, city life returned to normal.*

huī 挥 **TRAD** 揮 **V** wave

huīhuò 挥霍 **V** spend money carelessly, be a spendthrift, squander

huī 辉 **TRAD** 輝 **N** splendor

huīhuáng 辉煌 [comp: 辉 splendid + 煌 bright] **ADJ** brilliant, splendid

huí 回¹ **V** return (to a place), go back ■ 时间不早了，我们回家吧。**Shíjiān bù zǎo le, wǒmen huí jiā ba.** *It's quite late. Let's go back home.* ■ 小陈在英国大学毕业以后，就回中国找工作。**Xiǎo Chén zài Yīngguó dàxué bìyè yǐhòu, jiù huí Zhōngguó zhǎo gōngzuò.** *After graduating from university in the UK, Xiao Chen returned to China to look for a job.*

回来 huílai return to a place (coming towards the speaker) ■ 哥哥要从国外回来过圣诞节。**Gēge yào cóng guówài huílai guò Shèngdànjié.** *My elder brother is coming home from abroad for Christmas.* ■ 妈，我回来了！**Mā, wǒ huílai le!** *Mom, I'm home!*

回去 huíqu return to a place (away from the speaker) ■ 你回去以后，要常常给我们发电子邮件，保持联系。**Nǐ huíqu yǐhòu, yào chángcháng**

gěi wǒmen fā diànzǐ yóujiàn, bǎochí liánxì. *After you've returned home, you should send us e-mail often to keep in touch.*

huíbào 回报 **V 1** report back **2** reward, requite

huíbì 回避 **V** evade, dodge

回避问题 huíbì wèntí evade a question

huídá 回答 [comp: 回 reply + 答 answer] **V** reply, answer ■ 警察说：“我问你几个问题，你要老实回答。”**"Jǐngchá shuō: "Wǒ wèn nǐ jǐ ge wèntí, nǐ yào lǎoshí huídá."** *The policeman said, "I'm going to ask you some questions. You must answer truthfully."* ■ 他上个周末向女朋友求婚，女朋友说要考虑考虑再回答。**Tā shàng ge zhōumò xiàng nǚpéngyǒu qiúhūn, nǚpéngyǒu shuō yào kǎolù kǎolù zài huídá.** *Last weekend he asked his girlfriend to marry him, but she said she needed to think it over before replying.*

huíguó 回国 **V** return to one's home country ■ 每年在美国的留学生大学毕业后，有多少人回国？**Měi nián zài Měiguó de liúxuéshēng dàxué bìyè hòu, yǒu duōshǎo rén huí guó?** *How many foreign students in the USA return to their home countries after graduation every year?*

huíshōu 回收 **V** reclaim, recover

废品回收 fèipǐn huíshōu collect junk for recycling

huítóu 回头 **ADV** later ■ 回头见！**Huítóu jiàn!** *See you later!* ■ 回头再说。**Huítóu zài shuō.** *I'll talk to you later.*

NOTE: 回头 **huítóu** is a colloquialism, used only in very informal styles.

huíxìn 回信 [modif: 回 reply + 信 message] **V & N** write back, write in reply; letter in reply ■ 我们上个月送去了报价，还没有收到他们回信。**Wǒmen shàng ge yuè sòngqule bàojià, hái méiyǒu shōudào tāmen huíxìn.** *We sent them quotations last month, and still haven't gotten a reply from them.*

huíyì 回忆 **V & N** recall, recollect; recollection, memory ■ 你回忆一下，最后一次是在哪里用那把钥匙的。**Nǐ huíyì yíxià, zuìhòu yí cì shì zài nǎli yòng nà bǎ yàoshi de.** *Try to remember where you used that key for the last time.* ■ 根据被害人的回忆，事故发生在夜里十一点钟左右。**Gēnjù bèihàirén de huíyì, shìgù fāshēng zài yèlǐ shíyī diǎnzhōng zuǒyòu.** *According to the victim's recollection, the accident took place around eleven o'clock at night.*

huí 回² **MEASURE WORD** number of times (of doing something) ■ 我去看了他们两回了，他们一次都没有来过。**Wǒ qù kànle tāmen liǎng huí le, tāmen yí cì dōu méiyǒu láiguo.** *I've visited them twice, but they haven't come to see me even once.*

huǐ 悔 **V** regret

huǐhèn 悔恨 [comp: 悔 regret + 恨 hate] **V** repent bitterly

huǐ 毁 **V** destroy

huǐmiè 毁灭 [comp: 毁 destroy + 灭 annihilate] v exterminate, destroy

毁灭罪证 huǐmiè zuìzhèng destroy incriminating evidence

huì 贿 TRAD 賄 v bribe

受贿 shòu huì take bribes

huìlù 贿赂 v & N give bribes; bribe, bribery ■ 在这个国家，贿赂官员是常见的事吗？ **Zài zhège guójiā, huìlù guānyuán shì chángjiàn de shì ma?** *Is it commonplace to bribe officials in this country?* ■ 这家公司通过贿赂和政府部门保持良好关系。 **Zhè jiā gōngsī tōngguò huìlù hé zhèngfǔ bùmén bǎochí liánghǎo guānxi.** *This company maintains good relationships with government departments by bribery.*

huì 会¹ TRAD 會 I MODAL v 1 know how to, can ■ 我会游泳，但是今天不能去游泳，因为我感冒了。 **Wǒ huì yóuyǒng, dànshì jīntiān bù néng qù yóuyǒng, yīnwèi wǒ gǎnmào le.** *I can swim, but I'm not able to today because I've got a cold.* 2 probably, will ■ 我看夜里会下雨。 **Wǒ kàn yèlǐ huì xiàyǔ.** *I think it will rain tonight.* ■ 只要努力工作，就会取得满意的成绩。 **Zhǐyào nǔlì gōngzuò, jiù huì qǔdé mǎnyì de chéngjì.** *Provided you work hard, you will achieve satisfactory results.* II v have the ability or knowledge, can (do), understand ■ 你会日文吗？ **Nǐ huì Rìwén ma?** *Do you speak (or write) Japanese?* ■ 这道题目我不会。 **Zhè dào tímù wǒ bú huì.** *I don't know how to do this question.*

NOTE: 会 **huì** as a full verb meaning *have the ability or knowledge* is used with a limited range of nouns, such as nouns denoting languages. Using 会 **huì** in this way is colloquial.

huì 会² TRAD 會 N meeting, conference ■ 我去开会了，这里请你照顾一下。 **Wǒ qù kāi huìle, zhèlǐ qǐng nǐ zhàogù yíxià.** *I'm going to a meeting. Please keep an eye on things here.* ■ 明天的会非常重要，请您一定参加。 **Míngtiān de huì fēicháng zhòngyào, qǐng nín yídìng cānjiā.** *The meeting tomorrow is very important. Please be sure to attend it.*

大会 dàhuì an assembly, a rally / 开会 kāi huì have a meeting

huìchǎng 会场 [modif: 会 meeting, conference + 场 venue] N venue for a meeting, conference, assembly or rally ■ 大会会场布置得很庄严。 **Dàhuì huìchǎng bùzhì de hěn zhuāngyán.** *The assembly hall was solemnly decorated.*

huìhuà 会话 v & N talk, hold a conversation; conversation ■ 我和她一天用中文会话，一天用英文会话。 **Wǒ hé tā yìtiān yòng Zhōngwén huìhuà, yìtiān yòng Yīngwén huìhuà.** *She and I talk in Chinese one day, and in English the next day.* ■ 中文会话不太难，难的是写汉字。 **Zhōngwén huìhuà bú tài nán, nán de shì xiě hànzì.** *Chinese conversa-

tion is not too difficult. What is difficult is writing Chinese characters.*

huìjiàn 会见 [comp: 会 meet + 见 see] v (formal) meet, receive ■ 明天上午商业部长会见我们公司的王董事长。 **Míngtiān shàngwǔ Shāngyè Bùzhǎng huìjiàn wǒmen gōngsī de Wáng dǒngshìzhǎng.** *The Minister of Commerce will meet Chairman Wang from our company tomorrow morning.*

huìkè 会客 [v+obj: 会 meet + 客 guest] v receive visitors ■ 今天市长有重要会议，不能会客。 **Jīntiān shìzhǎng yǒu zhòngyào huìyì, bù néng huì kè.** *Today the mayor is at an important conference and is not able to receive visitors.*

huìtán 会谈 [comp: 会 meet + 谈 talk] v (formal) talk ■ 两个大学的校长将举行会谈，讨论怎样加强合作。 **Liǎng ge dàxué de xiàozhǎng jiāng jǔxíng huìtán, tǎolùn zěnyàng jiāqiáng hézuò.** *The presidents of the two universities will hold a talk to discuss how to strengthen cooperation.*

huìwù 会晤 [comp: 会 meet + 晤 meet] v meet (formally)

huìyì 会议 [comp: 会 meet + 议 discuss] N meeting, conference ■ 这次会议讨论什么问题？ **Zhè cì huìyì tǎolùn shénme wèntí?** *What questions will be discussed at the conference? (→ What is on the conference agenda?)*

参加会议 cānjiā huìyì participate in a meeting or conference ■ 参加会议的还有全国各地的中学校长代表。 **Cānjiā huìyì de háiyǒu quán guó gè dì de zhōngxué xiàozhǎng dàibiǎo.** *Representatives of high school principals from various parts of the country also attended the conference.*

出席会议 chūxí huìyì attend a meeting or conference ■ 教育部长和几位重要人物出席了会议。 **Jiàoyù bùzhǎng hé jǐ wèi zhòngyào rénwù chūxíle huìyì.** *The Minister of Education and several other VIPs attended this conference.*

举行会议 jǔxíng huìyì hold a meeting or conference ■ 下个月这个城市要举行一个国际会议。 **Xià ge yuè zhège chéngshì yào jǔxíng yí ge guójì huìyì.** *An international conference will be held in this city next month.*

取消会议 qǔxiāo huìyì cancel a meeting or conference ■ 你知道为什么取消这次会议吗？ **Nǐ zhīdào wèishénme qǔxiāo zhè cì huìyì ma?** *Do you know why this meeting was canceled?*

召开会议 zhàokāi huìyì convene a meeting or conference ■ 校长召开全体教师会议，讨论学生纪律问题。 **Xiàozhǎng zhàokāi quántǐ jiàoshī huìyì, tǎolùn xuésheng jìlǜ wèntí.** *The principal convened a teachers' meeting to discuss the issue of student discipline.*

huì 汇 TRAD 匯 v 1 converge, gather 2 remit

huìbào 汇报 v report (to one's superior)

huìkuǎn 汇款 [v+obj: 汇 remit + 款 money] v & N remit money, send remittance; remittance

huìlǜ 汇率 N (currency) exchange rate

huì 慧 ADJ intelligent (See **zhìhuì** 智慧.)

huì 惠 N kindness, favor (See **shíhuì** 实惠.)

hūn 荤 TRAD 葷 N meat food (animal, fowl, fish meat) (ANTONYM 素 **sù**)

hūncài 荤菜 N meat dish (animal, fowl, fish meat) (ANTONYM 素菜 **sùcài**)

hūn 昏 V faint

hūnmí 昏迷 [comp: 昏 faint + 迷 coma] V fall into a coma ■ 他在交通事故中受伤，昏迷了一天一夜 才醒来。 **Tā zài jiāotōng shìgù zhōng shòule shāng, hūnmíle yì-tiān-yí-yè cái xǐnglai.** *He was injured in an traffic accident and was unconscious for twenty-four hours.*

hūn 婚 V marry

hūnlǐ 婚礼 N wedding ceremony

hūnyīn 婚姻 [comp: 婚 marriage + 姻 marriage] N marriage ■ 婚姻是人生大事。 **Hūnyīn shì rénshēng dà shì.** *Marriage is an important event in one's life.*

hún 浑 TRAD 渾 ADJ **1** muddy **2** whole, all over

húnshēn 浑身 [modif: 浑 all over + 身 body] ADJ from head to foot, all over the body

浑身疼痛 húnshēn téngtòng ache all over

hùn 混 V mix up ■ 这两个词发音相同，意思不 同，你别把它们混起来。 **Zhè liǎng ge cí fāyīn xiāngtóng, yìsi bù tóng, nǐ bié bǎ tāmen hùn qǐlai.** *These two words have the same pronunciation, but different meanings. Do not mix them up.*

hùnhé 混合 [comp: 混 mix up + 合 combine] V mix, blend, mingle

hùnluàn 混乱 [comp: 混 mix up + 乱 chaos] ADJ chaotic, confused

hùn wéi yì tán 混为一谈 IDIOM lump different things together, fail to make distinction between different things

hùnxiáo 混淆 V confuse, eliminate differences in order to confuse

混淆是非 hùnxiáo shìfēi confuse right and wrong

hùnzhuó 混浊 ADJ muddy, turbid

huó 活 V be alive ■ 很多中国人只吃活鱼，不吃 死鱼。 **Hěn duō Zhōngguórén zhǐ chī huó yú, bù chī sǐ yú.** *Many Chinese only eat live (→ freshly caught) fish, not dead ones.*

huódòng 活动 [comp: 活 alive + 动 move] V & N do physical exercise, move about; activity, purposeful action ■ 他每天起床后，先在花园里活动 活动，再吃早饭。 **Tā měi tiān qǐchuáng hòu, xiān zài huāyuán li huódòng huódòng, zài chī zǎofàn.** *Every day after getting up he does a bit of exercise in the garden before having breakfast.*

参加活动 cānjiā huódòng participate in an activity

huógāi 活该 IDIOM serve one right

huólì 活力 [comp: 活 alive + 力 force] N vitality, vigor

huópo 活泼 ADJ lively, vivacious ■ 她性格活泼，

爱交朋友，到处受欢迎。 **Tā xìnggé huópo, ài jiāo péngyou, dàochù shòu huānyíng.** *She is vivacious by nature and likes to make friends, so she is popular wherever she goes.*

huór 活儿 N work, job ■ 这活儿不容易，你干得 了吗？ **Zhè huór bù róngyì, nǐ gàn de liǎo ma?** *This job is not easy. Can you manage it?* ■ 没有适当的 工具，这活儿没法干。 **Méiyǒu shìdàng de gōngjù, zhè huór méi fǎ gàn.** *This job can't be done without the proper tools.*

干活儿 gàn huór work, do a job

NOTE: 活儿 **huór** and 干活儿 **gàn huór** are very colloquial, and usually refer to *manual work*.

huóyuè 活跃 [comp: 活 alive + 跃 leap, jump] ADJ active, brisk ■ 这两天股票市场十分活跃。 **Zhè liǎng tiān gǔpiào shìchǎng shífēn huóyuè.** *The share market is very brisk these days.*

huǒ 火 N fire ■ 生了火，房间里就暖和了。 **Shēngle huǒ, fángjiān li jiù nuǎnhuo le.** *After a fire was lit, the room became warm.*

着火 zháo huǒ catch fire, be caught on fire ■ 着 火了！着火了！ **Zháo huǒ le! Zháo huǒ le!** *Fire! Fire!*

huǒchái 火柴 [modif: 火 fire + 柴 wood] N match (根 **gēn**, 盒 **hé**) ■ "你有火柴吗？" "没有，我有 打火机。" **"Nǐ yǒu huǒchái ma?" "Méiyǒu, wǒ yǒu dǎhuǒjī."** *"Have you got a match?" "No, but I've got a cigarette lighter."*

划火柴 huá huǒchái strike a match / 火柴盒 huǒchái hé a matchbox

huǒchē 火车 [modif: 火 fire + 车 vehicle] N train (辆 **liàng**, 列 **liè**) ■ 我们坐火车到北京去。 **Wǒmen zuò huǒchē dào Běijīng qù.** *We'll go to Beijing by train.* ■ 上海来的火车晚上八点二十五分到 达。 **Shànghǎi lái de huǒchē wǎnshang bā diǎn èrshíwǔ fēn dàodá.** *The train from Shanghai arrives at 8:25 in the evening.*

火车站 huǒchē zhàn railway station / 火车票 huǒchē piào train ticket / 火车时刻表 huǒchē shíkè biǎo railway timetable

huǒjiàn 火箭 [modif: 火 fire + 箭 arrow] N rocket (枚 **méi**)

发射火箭 fāshè huǒjiàn launch a rocket

huǒshān 火山 [modif: 火 fire + 山 mountain] N volcano (座 **zuò**)

火山爆发 huǒshān bàofā the eruption of a volcano / 活火山 huó huǒshān active volcano / 死火 山 sǐ huǒshān dormant volcano

huǒyàn 火焰 N flame

熊熊火焰 xióngxióng huǒyàn raging flames

huǒyào 火药 [modif: 火 fire + 药 drug] N gunpowder, explosive

huǒzāi 火灾 [modif: 火 fire + 灾 disaster] N fire disaster, fire (场 **cháng**)

huǒ 伙 TRAD 夥 N partner

huǒbàn 伙伴 [comp: 伙 partner + 伴 companion] **N** partner, mate

huǒshí 伙食 **N** meals (provided by a school, a factory, etc.) ■ 大学里的伙食很好。**Dàxué li de huǒshí hěn hǎo.** *The university canteens provide good meals.*

huò 或 **CONJ** same as 或者 **huòzhě.** Used more in writing.

huòxǔ 或许 **ADV** perhaps, maybe ■ 你明天来，或许王市长能会见你。**Nǐ míngtiān lái, huòxǔ Wáng shìzhǎng néng huìjiàn nǐ.** *If you come tomorrow, perhaps Mayor Wang will be able to see you.*

huòzhě 或者 **CONJ** or ■ 你们去北京，可以乘飞机，或者坐高铁。**Nǐmen qù Běijīng, kěyǐ chéng fēijī, huòzhě zuò gāotiě.** *You may fly to Beijing, or go by the high speed train.*

huò 货 **TRAD** 貨 **N** goods ■ 暂时没有货，过两天再来问吧。**Zànshí méiyǒu huò, guò liǎng tiān zài lái wèn ba.** *It's out of stock for the time being. Do come and inquire after a couple of days.*

huòbì 货币 **N** currency

货币贬值 huòbì biǎnzhí currency devaluation / 货币升值 huòbì shēngzhí currency appreciation

huò 获 **TRAD** 獲 **V** gain, win

huòdé 获得 [comp: 获 gain, win + 得 get] **V** win, obtain, get ■ 他工作努力，获得了优秀成绩。**Tā gōngzuò nǔlì, huòdéle yōuxiù chéngjì.** *He works hard and has won excellent achievements.*

huò 惑 **V** be puzzled (See yíhuò 疑惑.)

huò 祸 **TRAD** 禍 **N** disaster

车祸 chēhuò car accident, traffic accident

J

jī 几 **TRAD** 幾 **ADV** nearly

jīhū 几乎 **ADV** almost, nearly ■ 这个国家的人几乎都会说一点英语。**Zhège guójiā de rén jīhū dōu huì shuō yìdiǎn Yīngyǔ.** *Almost everyone in this country speaks some English.* ■ 她的工资几乎全用来买新衣服。**Tā de gōngzī jīhū quán yònglai mǎi xīn yīfu.** *She spends nearly all her salary on new clothes.*

jī 机 **TRAD** 機 **N** machine

jīchǎng 机场 [modif: 机 airplane + 场 ground, field] **N** airport ■ "机场离这里远不远？" "不远，大概十公里。" **"Jīchǎng lí zhèli yuǎn bu yuǎn?" "Bù yuǎn, dàgài shí gōnglǐ."** *"Is the airport far from here?" "Not very far. About ten kilometers."*

机场安全检查 jīchǎng ānquán jiǎnchá airport security check / 机场费 jīchǎng fèi airport tax

jīchuáng 机床 **N** machine tool (台 **tái**)

jīdòng 机动 **ADJ** 1 flexible

机动资金 jīdòng zījīn emergency fund, reserve fund **2** motorize, machine-powdered

jīdòngchē 机动车 jīdòngchē motorized vehicle (e.g. automobiles, motorcycles)

jīgòu 机构 **N** government agency, organization

jīguān 机关 **N** government office, state organ ■ 这一地区有很多重要的政府机关。**Zhè yí dìqū yǒu hěn duō zhòngyào de zhèngfǔ jīguān.** *There are many important government offices in this district.*

jīhuì 机会 [comp: 机 situation, opportunity + 会 by chance] **N** opportunity, chance ■ 这个机会很难得，不要错过。**Zhège jīhuì hěn nándé, bú yào cuòguo.** *This is a rare opportunity. Don't miss it.* ■ 你有没有机会去北京学中文？**Nǐ yǒu méiyǒu jīhuì qù Běijīng xué Zhōngwén?** *Do you have any chance of going to Beijing to learn Chinese?*

放弃机会 fàngqì jīhuì give up an opportunity / 抓住机会 zhuāzhù jīhuì grasp an opportunity

jīling 机灵 **ADJ** quick-witted

jīqì 机器 [comp: 机 device, machine + 器 utensil] **N** machine (台 **tái**) ■ 这种机器很有用。**Zhè zhǒng jīqì hěn yǒuyòng.** *This kind of machine is very useful.* ■ 你会不会使用这台机器？**Nǐ huì bu huì shǐyòng zhè tái jīqì?** *Do you know how to use this machine?*

使用机器 shǐyòng jīqì operate a machine / 修理机器 xiūlǐ jīqì repair a machine / 机器人 jīqì rén automaton, robot

jītǐ 机体 **N** organism

jīxiè 机械 [comp: 机 machinery + 械 tool] **N** machines, machinery ■ 建筑机械已经进入工地，马上要开工了。**Jiànzhù jīxiè yǐjīng jìnrù gōngdì, mǎshàng yào kāigōng le.** *Construction machinery has entered the construction site. (→ Construction machinery is on the site now.) Work will begin soon.*

jīyù 机遇 **N** (rare) opportunity

jīzhì 机智 **N & ADJ** wit; sharp-witted

jī 饥 **TRAD** 飢 **ADJ** starved

jī'è 饥饿 [comp: 饥 starved + 饿 hungry] **ADJ** starved, hungry

jī 讥 **TRAD** 譏 **V** sneer

jīxiào 讥笑 [comp: 讥 sneer + 笑 laugh] **V** sneer at, laugh at, ridicule

jī 鸡 **TRAD** 雞 **N** chicken, hen, rooster (只 **zhī**)

公鸡 gōngjī rooster / 母鸡 mǔjī hen / 小鸡 xiǎojī chick

> NOTE: 鸡 **jī** may denote either *a hen, a rooster* or *chick,* though they may be specified by 公鸡 **gōngjī** *cock,* 母鸡 **mǔjī** *hen* and 小鸡 **xiǎojī** *chicken.* As food, it is always 鸡 **jī.**

jīdàn 鸡蛋 [modif: 鸡 hen + 蛋 egg] **N** hen's egg (只 **zhī,** 个 **gè**) ■ 新鲜鸡蛋营养丰富。**Xīnxiān jīdàn yíngyǎng fēngfù.** *Fresh eggs are very nutritious.*

jī 肌 **N** muscle

jīròu 肌肉 [comp: 肌 muscle + 肉 flesh] N muscle

jī 圾 N garbage (See **lājī** 垃圾.)

jī 积 TRAD 積 V accumulate

jījí 积极 ADJ (ANTONYM 消极 **xiāojí**) **1** enthusiastic, active ■ 我对这件事不积极；我觉得没多大意思。**Wǒ duì zhè jiàn shì bù jījí; wǒ juéde méi duōdà yìsi.** *I'm not enthusiastic about this matter; I don't think it makes much sense.* **2** positive ■ 对于困难，我们应该争取采取积极的态度。**Duìyú kùn-nán, wǒmen yīnggāi cǎiqǔ jījí de tàidu.** *We should adopt a positive attitude towards difficulties.*

jījíxìng 积极性 N initiative, enthusiasm, zeal ■ 要使我们的公司成功，每一名职工必须发挥积极性。**Yào shǐ wǒmen de gōngsī chénggōng, měi yì míng zhígōng bìxū fāhuī jījíxìng.** *To make our company a success, every staff member must exercise initiative.*

jīlěi 积累 [comp: 积 accumulate + 累 pile up] V accumulate, build up ■ 他在三十年工作中积累了丰富的经验。**Tā zài sānshí nián gōngzuò zhōng jīlěile fēngfù de jīngyàn.** *He accumulated rich experience in the course of his career of over thirty years.*

jī 基 N (earthen) foundation

jīběn 基本 [comp: 基 (earthen) foundation + 本 root] ADJ fundamental, basic ■ 这件事的基本情况我已经知道了。**Zhè jiàn shì de jīběn qíngkuàng wǒ yǐjīng zhīdào le.** *I've learned the basic facts of this matter (or event).*

基本上 **jīběn shang** basically, on the whole ■ 我基本上同意你的计划。**Wǒ jīběn shang tóngyì nǐ de jìhuà.** *I basically approve of your plan.*

jīchǔ 基础 [comp: 基 foundation + 础 plinth, base] N foundation, base ■ 你想建高楼，就要先打好基础。**Nǐ xiǎng jiàn gāolóu, jiù yào xiān dǎhao jīchǔ.** *If you want to erect a high building, you must first of all lay a good foundation.* ■ 学中文，第一年是打基础。**Xué Zhōngwén, dì-yī nián shì dǎ jīchǔ.** *The first year of your Chinese studies lays the foundation.*

jīdì 基地 [modif: 基 base + 地 place] N base

jījīn 基金 [modif: 基 foundation + 金 money] N stock of money (for special purposes), fund, foundation

教育基金 **jiàoyù jījīn** education fund

jīyīn 基因 [comp: 基 base + 因 cause] N gene

基因工程 **jīyīn gōngchéng** genetic engineering

jī 激 V arouse, excite

jīdòng 激动 [comp: 激 arouse emotion + 动 move] ADJ exciting, excited ■ 比赛结束前两分钟，他踢进一球，真是激动人心！**Bǐsài jiéshù qián liǎng fēnzhōng, tā tījìn yì qiú, zhēnshì jīdòng rénxīn!** *Two minutes before the end of the match he scored a goal. How exciting!* ■ 我妹妹听了这个消息激动得一夜没睡。**Wǒ mèimei tīngle zhège xiāoxi jīdòng de yíyè méi shuì.** *After hearing the news my sister was so excited that she didn't sleep the entire night.*

jīfā 激发 [comp: 激 excite + 发 release] V arouse, stir up

激发爱国主义 **jīfā àiguózhǔyì** arouse patriotism

jīlì 激励 [comp: 激 excite + 励 encourage] V excite and urge, strongly encourage

jīliè 激烈 [comp: 激 exciting + 烈 fierce] ADJ fierce, intense ■ 运动会上运动员之间的竞赛十分激烈。**Yùndònghuì shang yùndòngyuán zhī jiān de jìngsài shífēn jīliè.** *At the sports meet competition between athletes was very fierce.*

jīqíng 激情 [modif: 激 exciting + 情 emotion] N intense emotion, passion

jī 击 TRAD 擊 V beat, hit, strike

拳击 **quánjī** boxing

jí 及 CONJ and, with ■ 他父亲、伯父，及祖父都是商人。**Tā fùqin, bófù, jí zǔfù dōu shì shāngrén.** *His father, uncle and grandfather were all businessmen.*

jígé 及格 [comp: 及 reach + 格 grade] V pass (a test, an examination, etc.) ■ "王老师，我这次测验及格吗？" "你不但及格，而且取得优秀成绩。" **"Wáng lǎoshī, wǒ zhè cì cèyàn jígé ma?" "Nǐ búdàn jígé, érqiě qǔdé yōuxiù chéngjì."** *"Teacher Wang, did I pass the test?" "Yes, you did, and you also got an excellent grade."*

jíshí 及时 [v+obj: 及 reach + 时 time] ADJ **1** timely, at the proper time ■ 这场雨下得真及时，农民高兴极了。**Zhè chǎng yǔ xià de zhēn jíshí, nóngmín gāoxìng jíle.** *This rain came at the right time. Farmers are delighted.* **2** immediately, promptly, without delay ■ 感谢您及时回复我们的信。**Gǎnxiè nín jíshí huífù wǒmen de xìn.** *Thank you for replying promptly to our letter.*

jízǎo 及早 ADJ as soon as possible, prompt

jí 级 TRAD 級 N **1** grade, rank ■ 他是一级教师。**Tā shì yī-jí jiàoshī.** *He is a first-class teacher.* **2** school grade

一年级 **yī-niánjí** Grade One, first year of study / 一年级学生 **yī-niánjí xuésheng** grade one student, first-year student

jíbié 级别 N grade, scale

工资级别 **gōngzījíbié** wage/salary scale

jí 极 TRAD 極 ADV extremely, highly ■ 今天天气极好。**Jīntiān tiānqì jí hǎo.** *The weather is extremely good today.*

jíduān 极端 [comp: 极 extreme + 端 extreme] ADV extremely

走极端 **zǒu jíduān** go to extremes

jíle 极了 ADV extremely, very ■ 这两天我忙极了。**Zhè liǎng tiān wǒ máng jíle.** *I'm extremely busy these days.*

NOTE: 极了 **jíle** is used after adjectives or some verbs to mean *extremely ...* or *very ...* For example: ■ 高兴极了 **gāoxìng jíle** *very happy, delighted*

jíqí 极其 ADV extremely, highly ■ 我们极其重视产品质量。**Wǒmen jíqí zhòngshì chǎnpǐn zhìliàng.** *We attach great importance to the quality of our products.* ■ 顾客对这样的服务态度极其不满。**Gùkè duì zhèyàng de fúwù tàidu jíqí bùmǎn.** *Customers are extremely unhappy with such service.*

jíxiàn 极限 [comp: 极 extreme + 限 limit] N the ultimate, the limit

jí 即 V be, mean
非此即彼 **fēi cǐ jí bǐ** If it is not this one, it must be that one.

jíbiàn 即便 CONJ even if, even though

jíjiāng 即将 ADV will soon

jíshǐ 即使 CONJ even if, even though ■ 他即使非常忙，也要抽工夫学中文。**Tā jíshǐ fēicháng máng, yě yào chōu gōngfu xué Zhōngwén.** *Even though he is very busy, he will try and find time to learn Chinese.*

jí 籍 N 1 registration 2 membership
国籍 **guójí** nationality / 会籍 **huìjí** membership of an association

jíguàn 籍贯 N place of one's birth or origin

jí 急 ADJ 1 anxious ■ 他心里很急。**Tā xīnlǐ hěn jí.** *He's very anxious.* 2 urgent ■ 这件事很急。**Zhè jiàn shì hěn jí.** *This is an urgent matter.* ■ 他家里有急事，今天没来上班。**Tā jiāli yǒu jíshì, jīntiān méi lái shàngbān.** *He has an urgent family matter [to attend to] and did not come to work today.*

jí gōng jìn lì 急功近利 IDIOM eager for instant success and benefit

jíjù 急剧 ADV sudden and intense, abrupt

jímáng 急忙 [comp: 急 hurried + 忙 hastened] ADJ hurried, hasty ■ 听说孩子病了，她急忙赶回家。**Tīngshuō háizi bìng le, tā jímáng gǎn huíjiā.** *Hearing that her child was sick, she rushed back home.*

jíqiè 急切 ADJ eager and impatient, urgent

jíxìng 急性 ADJ acute (disease) (ANTONYM 慢性 **mànxìng**)

jíxìngzi 急性子 N an impatient or impetuous person ■ 我妈妈是个急性子，爸爸是个慢性子，但是他们俩好像很合得来。**Wǒ māma shì ge jíxìngzi, bàba shì ge mànxìngzi, dànshì tāmen liǎ hǎoxiàng hěn hé de lái.** *My mother is an impatient person while my father moves slowly. However, they seem to get along quite well.*

jí yú qiú chéng 急于求成 IDIOM eager to have an immediate success

jízào 急躁 [comp: 急 hurried + 躁 dry] ADJ impetuous, impatient ■ 他有一个缺点，就是性情急躁。**Tā yǒu yí ge quēdiǎn, jiùshì xìngqíng jízào.** *He has a shortcoming; that is, he is rather impatient.*

jízhěn 急诊 N medical emergency
急诊室 **jízhěnshì** emergency room

jí 疾 N disease

jíbìng 疾病 [comp: 疾 disease + 病 illness] N disease, illness

jí 嫉 V be jealous

jídù 嫉妒 [comp: 嫉 be jealous + 妒 be jealous] V be jealous ■ 她嫉妒她妹妹的美貌。**Tā jídù tā mèimei de měimào.** *She is jealous of her sister's beauty.*

jí 吉 ADJ lucky, fortunate

jíxiáng 吉祥 [comp: 吉 lucky + 祥 auspicious] ADJ lucky, auspicious

jíxiángwù 吉祥物 [modif: 吉祥 lucky + 物 thing] N mascot

jí 集 V gather

jíhé 集合 [comp: 集 assemble + 合 combine] V gather together, assemble ■ 我们明天上午十点钟在火车站集合。**Wǒmen míngtiān shàngwǔ shí diǎnzhōng zài huǒchēzhàn jíhé.** *We'll assemble at the railway station at ten o'clock tomorrow morning.*

jítǐ 集体 [modif: 集 collective + 体 body] N collective (ANTONYM 个人 **gèrén**) ■ 这是董事会集体的决定。**Zhè shì dǒngshìhuì jítǐ de juédìng.** *This is the collective decision of the board of directors.*

jítuán 集团 N group, grouping

jízhōng 集中 V & ADJ concentrate, focus; concentrated, focused ■ 我要集中精力，学好中文。**Wǒ yào jízhōng jīnglì, xuéhǎo Zhōngwén.** *I will concentrate my energy on gaining a good command of the Chinese language.* ■ 这个学生上课时注意力不集中。**Zhège xuéshng shàngkè shí zhùyìlì bù jízhōng.** *This student's attention is not focused in class. (→ This student doesn't pay attention in class.)*

jǐ 几 TRAD 幾 PRON 1 several, some ■ 我上星期买了几本书。**Wǒ shàng xīngqī mǎi le jǐ běn shū.** *I bought several books last week.* 2 how many ■ 你上星期买了几本书？**Nǐ shàng xīngqī mǎi le jǐ běn shū?** *How many books did you buy last week?*

NOTE: When 几 **jǐ** is used in a question to mean *how many*, it is presumed that the answer will be a number less than ten. Otherwise 多少 **duōshǎo** should be used instead. Compare: ■ 你有几个哥哥？**Nǐ yǒu jǐ ge gēge?** *How many elder brothers do you have?* ■ 你们学校有多少学生？**Nǐmen xuéxiào yǒu duōshǎo xuéshng?** *How many students are there in your school?*

jǐ 己 pron self (See **zìjǐ** 自己.)

jǐ 挤 TRAD 擠 I V squeeze, crowd ■ 他再忙也要挤出时间和孩子玩玩。**Tā zài máng yě yào jǐchu shíjiān hé háizi wánwan.** *No matter how busy he is, he always finds time to play with his children.* ■ 这间房间挤不下这么多人。**Zhè jiān fángjiān jǐ bú xià zhème duō rén.** *It is impossible to pack so many people in this room.* II ADJ crowded ■ 春节前几天商店很挤。**Chūnjié qián jǐ tiān shāngdiàn**

hěn jǐ. *Stores are crowded days before the Spring Festival.*

jǐ 给 v provide, give

jǐyú 给予 v provide, give

jì 计 TRAD 計 v plan

jìhuà 计划 [comp: 计 plan + 划 plan] v & N plan ■ 我计划明年去美国旅游。**Wǒ jìhuà míngnián qù Měiguó lǚyóu.** *I plan to tour the States next year.* ■ 这个计划不可行。**Zhè ge jìhuà bù kěxíng.** *This plan is not feasible.*

制定计划 zhìdìng jìhuà draw up a plan / 执行计划 zhíxíng jìhuà implement a plan

jìjiào 计较 [comp: 计 calculate + 较 compare] v be fuzzy, haggle over

斤斤计较 jīnjīn jìjiào haggle over insignificant things

jìsuàn 计算 [comp: 计 calculate + 算 calculate] v calculate ■ 请你计算一下这个班去年考试的平均成绩。**Qǐng nǐ jìsuàn yíxià zhège bān qùnián kǎoshì de píngjūn chéngjì.** *Please calculate the average marks of this class for last year's examination.*

jìsuànjī 计算机 same as 电脑 **diànnǎo.** Used as a more formal term.

jì 记 TRAD 記 v 1 remember, recall ■ 那条街叫什么，我记不清了。**Nà tiáo jiē jiào shénme, wǒ jì bu qīng le.** *I don't remember clearly the name of that street. (→ I can't quite recall the name of that street.)* ■ 我们第一次是在什么地方见面的，你还记得吗？**Wǒmen dì-yī cì shì zài shénme dìfang jiànmiàn de, nǐ hái jìdé ma?** *Do you still remember where we first met?* 2 bear in mind ■ 你要记住我的话，别忘了！**Nǐ yào jìzhù wǒ de huà, bié wàng le!** *You should bear in mind what I said. Don't forget it.* 3 record (usually by writing down) ■ 你说得慢一点儿，我把它记下来。**Nǐ shuō de màn yìdiǎnr, wǒ bǎ tā jì xiàlai.** *Speak slowly. I'll write it down.*

记得 jìdé can remember, can recall / 记不得 jì bu dé cannot remember, cannot recall / 记住 jìzhù learn by heart, bear in mind

jìlù 记录 [comp: 记 record + 录 record] v & N record ■ 护士把病人的体温记录下来。**Hùshi bǎ bìngrén de tǐwēn jìlù xiàlai.** *The nurse recorded the patient's temperature.* ■ 这位运动员打破了世界记录。**Zhè wèi yùndòngyuán dǎpòle shìjiè jìlù.** *This athlete broke the world record.*

会议记录 huìyì jìlù minutes (of a meeting)

jìxìng 记性 N ability to memorize things, memory ■ 我弟弟记性很好。**Wǒ dìdi jìxìng hěn hǎo.** *My younger bother has a very good memory.*

jìyì 记忆 [comp: 记 remember + 忆 recall] v & N remember, memorize; memory ■ 童年的经历老人还记忆犹新。**Tóngnián de jīnglì lǎorén hái jìyì yóuxīn.** *The old man still vividly remembers his childhood experiences.* ■ 他们俩在海边共度的夏

天，成了他难忘的记忆。**Tāmen liǎ zài hǎibiān gòngdù de xiàtiān, chéngle tā nánwàng de jìyì.** *The summer they spent together by the seaside has become an indelible memory for him.*

jìzài 记载 v & N record; written record

jìzhě 记者 [suffix: 记 record + 者 nominal suffix] N news reporter, correspondent ■ 记者及时报导了那次交通事故。**Jìzhě jíshí bàodǎole nà cì jiāotōng shìgù.** *Journalists reported the road accident promptly.*

新闻记者 xīnwén jìzhě journalist, news reporter

jì 纪[1] TRAD 紀 N discipline

jìlǜ 纪律 [comp: 纪 discipline + 律 rule] N discipline (条 tiáo) ■ 军队的纪律很严格。**Jūnduì de jìlǜ hěn yángé.** *Discipline in the army is very strict.* ■ 他违反学校纪律，受到了批评。**Tā wéifǎn xuéxiào jìlǜ, shòudàole pīpíng.** *He violated school discipline and was reprimanded.*

jì 纪[2] TRAD 紀 v record, memory

jìniàn 纪念 [comp: 纪 record + 念 remember] v commemorate ■ 端午节纪念伟大的爱国诗人屈原。**Duānwǔ jié jìniàn wěidà de àiguó shīrén Qū Yuán.** *The Dragon Boat Festival commemorates the great patriotic poet Qu Yuan.*

jìyào 纪要 N summary of minutes, major points

jì 寂 ADJ lonely

jìjìng 寂静 [comp: 寂 lonely + 静 silent] ADJ peaceful and quiet, still

jìmò 寂寞 ADJ lonely

jì 技 N skill

jìnéng 技能 N technical ability

jìqiǎo 技巧 N skill, craftsmanship

写作技巧 xiězuòjìqiǎo writing skills

jìshù 技术 [comp: 技 skill + 术 craft] N technique, technology, skill ■ 由于新技术的应用，产品质量有了很大提高。**Yóuyú xīn jìshù de yìngyòng, chǎnpǐn zhìliàng yǒule hěn dà tígāo.** *Thanks to the application of the new technology, the product quality has been greatly improved.* ■ 你得学点技术，走到哪儿都有用。**Nǐ děi xué diǎn jìshù, zǒu dào nǎr dōu yǒuyòng.** *You've got to learn some skills, which will be useful wherever you go.*

技术工人 jìshù gōngrén skilled worker

jìshùyuán 技术员 [modif: 技术 technique, technology + 员 person] N technician (位 wèi) ■ 车床出问题了，要请技术员来看一下。**Chēchuáng chū wèntí le, yào qǐng jìshùyuán lái kàn yíxià.** *Something has gone wrong with the machine tool. Please send for the technician.*

jì 际 TRAD 際 N boundary, border (See guójì 国际, shíjì 实际.)

jì 季 N season

jìdù 季度 N quarter (of a year)

jìjié 季节 [comp: 季 season + 节 solar term] N season ■ 春夏秋冬，你最喜欢哪个季节？**Chūnxià-qiū-dōng, nǐ zuì xǐhuan nǎge jìjié?** *Spring,*

summer, autumn and winter—which season do you like the best?

jìjūn 季军 N third place winner in a sport competition

jì 系 v fasten, tie

系领带 jì lǐngdài knot a necktie, tie a tie

jì 济 TRAD 濟 v aid (See **jīngjì** 经济.)

jì 剂 TRAD 劑 N a pharmaceutical and other chemical preparation

jìliàng 剂量 N dosage

jì 迹 TRAD 跡 N remains, trace

jìxiàng 迹象 N sign, indication

地震的迹象 dìzhèn de jìxiàng signs of a (forthcoming) earthquake

jì 既 CONJ 1 both ... and ...

既 ... 又 ... jì ... yòu ... both ... and ... / 既 ... 也 ... jì ... yě ... both ... and ... ■ 她既要上班, 又要管孩子。**Tā jì yào shàngbān, yòu yào guǎn háizi.** *She has to both work and care for the children.* ■ 你既要看到一个人的优点, 也要看到一个人的缺点。**Nǐ jì yào kàndào yí ge rén de yōudiǎn, yěyào kàndào yí ge rén de quēdiǎn.** *You should see both the merits and shortcomings of a person.* **2** same as 既然 **jìrán.** Used more in writing.

jìrán 既然 CONJ now that, since, as ■ 他既然已经决定, 你就不必多说了。**Tā jìrán yǐjīng juédìng, nǐ jiù búbì duō shuō le.** *Now that he's made up his mind, you needn't say anything more.* 既然你不喜欢他, 为什么还要和他一起出去玩呢? **Jìrán nǐ bù xǐhuan tā, wèishénme háiyào hé tā yìqǐ chūqu wán ne?** *Since you don't like him, why do you still go out with him?*

jì 绩 TRAD 績 N accomplishment (See **chéngjì** 成绩.)

jì 继 TRAD 繼 v continue

jìchéng 继承 [comp: 继 continue + 承 inherit] v inherit, carry on

jìchéngrén 继承人 [modif: 继承 inherit + 人 person] N heir, heiress, successor

jì wǎng kāi lái 继往开来 IDIOM carry forward the cause of the predecessors and forge ahead into the future

jìxù 继续 [comp: 继 continue + 续 keep on] v continue ■ 我们吃午饭吧, 下午继续开会。**Wǒmen chī wǔfàn ba, xiàwǔ jìxù kāihuì.** *Let's have lunch. The meeting will continue in the afternoon.* ■ 这种情况不能再继续下去了。**Zhè zhǒng qíngkuàng bùnéng zài jìxù xiàqu le.** *This situation must not be allowed to go on.*

jì 寄 v send by mail, post ■ 请你马上把这些书寄给王先生。**Qǐng nǐ mǎshàng bǎ zhèxiē shū jìgei Wáng xiānsheng.** *Please post these books to Mr Wang immediately.*

jìtuō 寄托 v entrust

寄托希望 jìtuō xīwàng place one's hope on

jì 忌 v avoid, shun

忌酒 jìjiǔ avoid wine, refrain from drinking wines

jìdu 忌妒 same as 嫉妒 **jídù**

jìhuì 忌讳 N taboo

jiā 加 v add, plus ■ 一加二等于三。**Yì jiā èr děngyú sān.** *One plus two equals three.*

jiābān 加班 [modif: 加 add + 班 shift] v work overtime

加班费 jiābān fèi overtime pay

jiāgōng 加工 [v+obj: 加 add + 工 work] v process (unfinished products) ■ 这个工厂主要做来料加工。**Zhège gōngchǎng zhǔyào zuò láiliào jiāgōng.** *This factory mainly processes supplied materials.*

来料加工 láiliào jiāgōng processing of supplied materials / 食品加工 shípǐn jiāgōng food processing

jiājù 加剧 v aggravate, exacerbate

Jiānádà 加拿大 N Canada

jiāqiáng 加强 [comp: 加 add + 强 strong] v strengthen, reinforce ■ 我们要加强研究开发工作。**Wǒmen yào jiāqiáng yánjiū kāifā gōngzuò.** *We should strengthen research and development work.*

jiāyǐ 加以 I v (used before a verb to indicate what should be done) ■ 这个问题应及时加以解决。**Zhège wèntí yīng jíshí jiāyǐ jiějué.** *This problem should be solved promptly.* ■ 对违反纪律的学生必须加以严肃处理。**Duì wéifǎn jìlǜ de xuésheng bìxū jiāyǐ yánsù chǔlǐ.** *Students who have violated disciplines must be dealt with seriously.* II CONJ in addition, moreover ■ 他身体很差, 加以工作太辛苦, 终于病倒在床上。**Tā shēntǐ hěn chà, jiāyǐ gōngzuò tài xīnkǔ, zhōngyú bìngdǎo zài chuáng shang.** *He was in poor health; moreover, he worked too hard and was finally bedridden with illness.*

NOTE: 加以 **jiāyǐ** as a verb smacks of officialese and is chiefly used in writing. The sentence still stands when 加以 **jiāyǐ** is omitted, e.g. ■ 这个问题应及时解决。**Zhège wèntí yīng jíshí jiějué.** *This problem should be solved promptly.*

jiāyóu 加油 v 1 add fuel, fuel up 2 make extra efforts

加油干 jiāyóugàn double one's efforts, put more efforts into work

NOTE: 加油 **jiāyóu** is the colloquial expression used to cheer on a sportsperson or a sporting team in competition, equivalent to *Come on!,* or *Go! Go!*

jiāyóuzhàn 加油站 N gas station, service station

jiā 嘉 ADJ good, fine

jiābīn 嘉宾 N honored guest

jiā 佳 ADJ good, fine, beautiful

jiājié 佳节 N joyous festival

jiāyáo 佳肴 N delicious dish, delicacies

jiā 夹 v pinch, squeeze, wedge between, sandwich ■ 你会不会用筷子夹一个蛋? **Nǐ huì bu huì yòng**

kuàizi jiā yí ge dàn? *Can you use chopsticks to pick up an egg?*

jiākè 夹克 N same as 夹克衫 **jiākèshān**
皮夹克 píjiākè leather jacket

jiākèshān 夹克衫 jacket (件 **jiàn**)

jiāzá 夹杂 v be mixed up with

jiāzi 夹子 N tongs, clip
衣服夹子 yīfu jiāzi clothes pin

jiā 家 I N 1 family, household ■ 我家有四口人：父亲、母亲、姐姐和我。**Wǒ jiā yǒu sì kǒu rén: fùqin, múqin, jiějie hé wǒ.** *There're four people in my family: my father, my mother, my sister and I.* 2 home ■ 下课以后我就回家。**Xià kè yǐhòu wǒ jiù huíjiā.** *I go home as soon as school is over.* II MEASURE WORD (for families or businesses)
四家人家 sì jiā rénjiā four families / 一家商店 yì jiā shāngdiàn a store / 两家工厂 liǎng jiā gōngchǎng two factories
III SUFFIX (denoting an accomplished expert)
画家 huàjiā painter, artist / 科学家 kēxuéjiā scientist

jiācháng 家常 ADJ everyday life, commonplace
谈家常 tán jiācháng have a chitchat / 家常便饭 jiācháng biànfàn simple, home-cooked meal

jiājù 家具 [modif: 家 home + 具 implements] N furniture (套 **tào**, 件 **jiàn**) ■ 他们结婚时买了一套漂亮而实用的家具，后来又添了几件小家具。**Tāmen jiéhūn shí mǎile yí tào piàoliang ér shíyòng de jiājù, hóulái yòu tiānle jǐ jiàn xiǎo jiājù.** *When they got married, they bought a beautiful and practical set of household furniture, and later on added several pieces of occasional furniture.*

jiāshǔ 家属 N family member, one's dependent (名 **míng**)

jiātíng 家庭 [comp: 家 home, family + 庭 courtyard] N family (个 **gè**) ■ 他的家庭很幸福。**Tā de jiātíng hěn xìngfú.** *He has a happy family.* ■ 中国人比较重视家庭。**Zhōngguórén bǐjiào zhòngshì jiātíng.** *The Chinese attach much importance to the family.*

NOTE: 家 **jiā** has more meanings than 家庭 **jiātíng**. While 家庭 **jiātíng** means only *family*, 家 **jiā** may mean *family*, *household* or *home*.

jiāwù 家务 [modif: 家 family, home + 务 work, duty] N household chores, housework (件 **jiàn**) ■ 你帮太太做家务吗？**Nǐ bāng tàitai zuò jiāwù ma?** *Do you help your wife with household chores?*

jiāxiāng 家乡 [modif: 家 home + 乡 village] N hometown, home village ■ 这几年家乡发生了巨大变化。**Zhè jǐ nián, jiāxiāng fāshēngle jùdà biànhuà.** *In the past few years great changes have taken place in my hometown.*

jiā yù hù xiǎo 家喻户晓 IDIOM be a household name, widely known

jiǎ 假 ADJ false, untrue, fake (ANTONYM 真 **zhēn**)

■ 他说的这些话都是假的。**Tā shuō de zhèxiē huà dōu shì jiǎ de.** *All he said was untrue.*

jiǎhuà 假话 N lie, falsehood

jiǎhuò 假货 N fake (goods), forgery

jiǎrú 假如 CONJ supposing, if

jiǎshè 假设 v suppose, assume

jiǎshǐ 假使 CONJ if, in case

jiǎtuǐ 假腿 N artificial leg

jiǎyá 假牙 N dentures

jiǎzhuāng 假装 [comp: 假 false + 装 disguise] v pretend, feign

jiǎ 甲¹ N first

jiǎ 甲² N shell, nail
指甲 zhǐjia finger nail

jià 价 TRAD 價 N price

jiàgé 价格 N price ■ 新汽车价格合理，卖得很快。**Xīn qìchē jiàgé hélǐ, màide hěn kuài.** *The new car is reasonably priced and sells quickly.*

jiàqián 价钱 [comp: 价 price + 钱 money] N price ■ 价钱太贵，还是不要买吧！**Jiàqián tài guì, háishì bú yào mǎi ba.** *The price is too high. Don't buy it.* ■ 他只是问一下价钱，没打算买。**Tā zhǐshì wèn yíxià jiàqián, méi dǎsuàn mǎi.** *He only asked the price and didn't intend to buy it.*

jiàzhí 价值 [comp: 价 price + 值 worth] N value ■ 这些书太旧了，没有多大价值。**Zhèxiē shū tài jiù le, méiyǒu duō dà jiàzhí.** *These books are too old and do not have much value.*

jiàzhíguān 价值观 N values ■ 对不起，我的价值观和你不一样。**Duìbuqǐ, wǒ de jiàzhíguān hé nǐ bù yíyàng.** *Sorry, my values are different from yours.*
核心价值观 héxīn jiàzhíguān core values

jià 驾 TRAD 駕 v drive, pilot

jiàshǐ 驾驶 v drive, pilot
驾驶轮船 jiàshǐ lúnchuan pilot a ship / 驾驶飞机 jiàshǐ fēijī pilot a plane / 驾驶汽车 jiàshǐ qìchē drive an automobile

jiàshǐyuán 驾驶员 [suffix: 驾驶 drive, pilot + 员 nominal suffix] N driver, pilot

jià 架 MEASURE WORD (used for machines, aircraft, etc.)
一架客机 yí jià kèjī a passenger plane

jià 嫁 v (of a woman) marry ■ 他们的女儿嫁给了一个美国人。**Tāmen de nǚér jiàgeile yí ge Měiguórén.** *Their daughter married an American.* ■ 嫁鸡随鸡，嫁狗随狗。**Jià jī suí jī, jià gǒu suí gǒu.** *Marry a rooster and you follow a rooster; marry a dog and you follow a dog. (An old saying meaning that a woman complies with whoever she marries.)*

jià 稼 v sow (grain seeds) (See zhuāngjia 庄稼.)

jià 假 N leave of absence, holiday, vacation

jiàqī 假期 [modif: 假 holiday + 期 period] N holiday period, leave ■ 假期你打算做什么？**Jiàqī nǐ dǎsuàn zuò shénme?** *What do you plan to do during the holidays?* ■ 假期的时候，火车飞机都很挤。**Jiàqī**

de shíhou, huǒchē fēijī dōu hěn jǐ. *During the holiday period, trains and planes are all crowded.*

jiàtiáo 假条 [comp: 假 leave + 条 slip] **N** an application for leave, a leave form ■ 明天家里有重要的事不能来上课，这是假条。**Míngtiān jiāli yǒu zhòngyào de shì, bù néng lái shàngkè, zhè shì jiàtiáo.** *I can't come to class tomorrow as there's important family business to attend to. Here's my leave application.*

病假条 **bìngjiàtiáo** an application for sick leave, a doctor's certificate of illness, a medical certificate ■ 医生给他开了病假条。**Yīshēng gěi tā kāile bìngjiàtiáo.** *The doctor gave me a medical certificate.*

jiān 尖 **ADJ** sharp, pointed ■ 这孩子耳朵尖，我们这么小声说话她都听见了。**Zhè háizi ěrduo jiān, wǒmen zhème xiǎoshēng shuōhuà tā dōu tīngjiànle.** *This child has sharp ears. We talked in such low voices but she heard us.*

jiānduān 尖端 [modif: 尖 sharp, pointed + 端 end] **ADJ 1** pointed end **2** sophisticated

尖端产品 **jiānduān chǎnpǐn** technologically advanced product / 尖端科学 **jiāoduān kēxué** sophisticated science / 尖端技术 **jiānduān jìshù** most advanced technology

jiānruì 尖锐 [comp: 尖 pointed + 锐 sharp] **ADJ 1** very sharp, penetrating ■ 多家报纸对政府提出尖锐批评。**Duō jiā bàozhǐ duì zhèngfǔ tíchū jiānruì pīpíng.** *Several newspapers made biting criticism of the government.* **2** fierce, uncompromising ■ 他们之间的矛盾很尖锐。**Tāmen zhī jiān de máodùn hěn jiānruì.** *There is bitter conflict between them.*

jiān 坚 **TRAD** 堅 **ADJ** hard, firm

jiānchí 坚持 [modif: 坚 firm, firmly + 持 hold] **V** uphold, persist (in) ■ 不管刮风下雨，他坚持每天跑步。**Bùguǎn guāfēng xià yǔ, tā jiānchí měi tiān pǎobù.** *He persists in jogging every day no matter how wet or windy it is.* ■ 尽管大家都不同意，他仍然坚持自己的观点。**Jìnguǎn dàjiā dōu bù tóngyì, tā réngrán jiānchí zìjǐ de guāndiǎn.** *Despite everyone's disagreement, he still holds on to his views.*

jiāndìng 坚定 [comp: 坚 solid + 定 fixed] **ADJ** firm ■ 我坚定地相信公司的决定是正确的。**Wǒ jiāndìng de xiāngxìn gōngsī de juédìng shì zhèngquè de.** *I'm firmly convinced that the company's decision is correct.*

jiāngù 坚固 [comp: 坚 solid + 固 solid] **ADJ** solid, sturdy

jiānjué 坚决 [comp: 坚 solid + 决 determined] **ADJ** resolute, determined ■ 我坚决执行公司的决定。**Wǒ jiānjué zhíxíng gōngsī de juédìng.** *I will resolutely carry out the company's decision.*

jiānqiáng 坚强 [comp: 坚 solid + 强 strong] **ADJ** strong, staunch

性格坚强 **xìnggé jiānqiáng** strong character

jiānrèn 坚韧 [comp: 坚 solid + 韧 resilient] **ADJ** tough and tenacious

jiānshí 坚实 [comp: 坚 solid + 实 substantial] **ADJ** solid, substantial

打下坚实的基础 **dǎxià jiānshí de jīchǔ** lay a solid foundation

jiānyìng 坚硬 [comp: 坚 solid + 硬 hard] **ADJ** solid and hard ■ 大门是用坚硬的木头做的。**Dàmén shì yòng jiānyìng de mùtou zuò de.** *The gate is made from very hard timber.*

jiān 间 **TRAD** 間 **I MEASURE WORD** (for rooms)

一间教室 **yì jiān jiàoshì** a classroom / 两间办公室 **liǎng jiān bàngōngshì** two offices

II N room (for a special purpose)

洗澡间 **xǐzǎo jiān** bathroom / 手术间 **shǒushù jiān** operating room, surgical room

jiān 肩 **N** the shoulder ■ 我左肩疼。**Wǒ zuǒ jiān téng.** *My left shoulder hurts.*

jiānbǎng 肩膀 **N** shoulder

jiān 艰 **TRAD** 艱 **ADJ** difficult

jiānjù 艰巨 [comp: 艰 difficult + 巨 gigantic] **ADJ** (of a big and important task) very difficult, strenuous ■ 他们要到外国去开辟市场，这是一项艰巨的任务。**Tāmen yào dào wàiguó qù kāipì shìchǎng, zhè shì yí xiàng jiānjù de rènwù.** *They are going overseas to open up a new market, which is a difficult and immense undertaking.*

jiānkǔ 艰苦 [comp: 艰 difficult + 苦 bitter, harsh] **ADJ** difficult, hard, tough ■ 城里人往往不了解很多农民的艰苦生活。**Chénglirén wǎngwǎng bù liáojiě hěnduō nóngmín de jiānkǔ shēnghuó.** *People in the city usually do not know the hard life many peasants live.*

jiānnán 艰难 [comp: 艰 difficult + 难 difficult] **ADJ** arduous, hard

艰难的任务 **jiānnán de rènwu** arduous task

jiān 监 **TRAD** 監 **V** supervise, inspect

jiāndū 监督 [comp: 监 supervise + 督 superintend] **V 1** supervise, superintend **2** have under surveillance, watch over

jiānshì 监视 [comp: 监 supervise + 视 view] **V** keep under surveillance, monitor ■ 在入口处安装了摄像机，来监视进出人员。**Zài rùkǒuchù ānzhuāng le shèxiàngjī, lái jiānshì jìnchū rényuán.** *A camera has been installed at the entrance to keep a watch on the people coming and going.*

jiānyù 监狱 **N** prison (座 **zuò**)

jiān 兼 **V** act concurrently ■ 他是这家公司的董事长兼总经理。**Tā shì zhè jiā gōngsī de dǒngshìzhǎng jiān zǒngjīnglǐ.** *He is chairman of the board and currently CEO of the company.*

jiānzhí 兼职 **V & N** (hold) concurrent post, (do) part-time job

jiān 煎 **V** fry, shallow-fry

jiǎn 拣 **TRAD** 揀 **V** choose, select ■ 这么多漂亮衣

服，她不知道拣哪一件好。**Zhème duō piàoliang yīfu, tā bù zhīdào jiǎn nǎ yí jiàn hǎo.** *There were so many pretty dresses; she did not know which to choose.*

jiǎn 剪 v cut (with scissors), shear ■ 剪羊毛是很辛苦的，不过工资挺高。**Jiǎn yángmáo shì hěn xīnkǔ de, búguò gōngzī tǐng gāo.** *Sheep shearing is a hard job, but it is well paid.*

jiǎncǎi 剪彩 v cut the ribbon of an opening ceremony

jiǎndāo 剪刀 N scissors, shears (把 **bǎ**)

jiǎn 减 v subtract, deduct ■ 三百六十七减二百八十六是多少？**Sānbǎi liùshíqī jiǎn èrbǎi bāshíliù shì duōshǎo?** *How much is 367 minus 286?*

减数 **jiǎnshù** subtrahend (e.g. 286 in the example) / 被减数 **bèi jiǎnshù** minuend (e.g. 367 in the example)

jiǎnféi 减肥 v reduce weight

jiǎnqīng 减轻 [v+compl: 减 subtract + 轻 light] v lighten, alleviate ■ 使用电脑以后，人们的工作量并没有减轻。**Shǐyòng diànnǎo yǐhòu, rénmen de gōngzuò liàng bìng méiyǒu jiǎnqīng.** *After the employment [i.e use] of computers, people's workload has not in fact been lightened.*

jiǎnshǎo 减少 [v+compl: 减 subtract + 少 few, little] v make fewer, make less, reduce ■ 在过去三年中，这个学校的学生人数减少了百分之二十。**Zài guòqù sān nián zhōng, zhège xuéxiào de xuésheng rénshù jiǎnshǎo le bǎifēn zhī èrshí.** *In the past three years, the student population of this school has been reduced by twenty percent.*

jiǎn 检 TRAD 檢 v examine

jiǎnchá 检查 [comp: 检 examine + 查 inspect, check] v examine, inspect, check ■ 先生，我要检查一下你的行李。**Xiānsheng, wǒ yào jiǎnchá yíxià nǐ de xíngli.** *I need to inspect your luggage, sir.* ■ 下个月总公司要派人来检查我们的工作。**Xià ge yuè zǒnggōngsī yào pài rén lái jiǎnchá wǒmen de gōngzuò.** *Next month the head office will dispatch people to inspect our work.*

jiǎntǎo 检讨 v & N 1 make a self-criticism; self-criticism 2 review

书面检讨 **shūmiàn jiǎntǎo** written self-criticism / 做检讨 **zuò jiǎntǎo** make a self-criticism

jiǎnxiū 检修 [comp: 检 examine + 修 repair] v examine and repair (a machine), maintain

大检修 **dàjiǎnxiū** overhaul / 汽车检修工 **qìchē jiǎnxiū gōng** car mechanic

jiǎnyàn 检验 [comp: 检 examine + 验 test] v & N examine, test; examination, testing

质量检验 **zhìliàng jiěyàn** quality control.

jiǎn 捡 TRAD 撿 v pick up

把垃圾捡起来 **bǎ lājī jiǎn qǐlai** pick up the litter

jiǎn 俭 TRAD 儉 ADJ thrifty, frugal

jiǎn pǔ 俭朴 ADJ thrifty and simple

生活俭朴 **shēnghuó jiǎn pǔ** lead a thrifty and simple life

jiǎn 简 TRAD 簡 ADJ simple

jiǎndān 简单 [comp: 简 simple + 单 single] ADJ simple (ANTONYM 复杂 **fùzá**) ■ 这个问题不简单，要好好想一想。**Zhège wèntí bù jiǎndān, yào hǎohǎo xiǎng yi xiǎng.** *This question is not a simple one. It needs careful consideration.* ■ 中饭吃得简单些，不要搞这么多菜。**Zhōngfàn chī de jiǎndān xie, búyào gǎo zhème duō cài.** *Let's just have a simple lunch and not have so many dishes.*

jiǎnhuà 简化 [suffix: 简 simple + 化 verb suffix] v simplify

简化手续 **jiǎnhuà shǒuxù** simplify formalities

jiǎnlì 简历 [modif: 简 simple + 历 history] résumé, curriculum vitae

jiǎnlòu 简陋 ADJ simple and crude

jiǎntǐzì 简体字 [modif: 简 simple + 体 style + 字 character] N simplified Chinese character

NOTE: See note on 繁体字 **fántǐzì**.

jiǎnyào 简要 ADJ brief and to the point

简要提纲 **jiǎnyào tígāng** brief outline

jiǎnzhí 简直 ADV simply, virtually

简直叫人不敢相信 **jiǎnzhí jiào rén bùgǎn xiāngxìn** simply unbelievable

jiàn 件 MEASURE WORD (for things, affairs, clothes or furniture)

一件东西 **yí jiàn dōngxi** a thing, something ■ 我有一件东西忘在机场了。**Wǒ yǒu yí jiàn dōngxi wàng zài jīchǎng le.** *I've [inadvertently] left something in the airport.*

一件事情 **yí jiàn shìqing** a matter ■ 我有几件事情要跟你说。**Wǒ yǒu jǐ jiàn shìqing yào gēn nǐ shuō.** *I've something to discuss with you.*

一件衣服 **yí jiàn yīfu** a piece of clothing (e.g. a jacket, dress) ■ 他上星期买了三件衣服。**Tā shàng xīngqī mǎile sān jiàn yīfu.** *He bought three pieces of clothing last week.*

jiàn 见 TRAD 見 v see, perceive ■ 我能不能见一下王先生？**Wǒ néng bu néng jiàn yíxià Wáng xiānsheng?** *May I see Mr Wang?* ■ 经理，有一位小姐要见你。**Jīnglǐ, yǒu yí wèi xiǎojiě yào jiàn nǐ.** *There's a young lady here who wants to see you, sir (← manager).*

jiàn duō shí guǎng 见多识广 IDIOM widely experienced and knowledgeable

jiànjiě 见解 N opinion, view

提出见解 **tíchū jiànjiě** voice one's opinion

jiànmiàn 见面 [v+obj: 见 see + 面 face] v meet, see (a person) ■ "我们以前见过面吗？" "见过一次。" **"Wǒmen yǐqián jiànguo miàn ma?" "Jiànguo yí cì."** *"Have we met before?" "Yes, once."* ■ 这个周末她要带男朋友回家和父母见面。**Zhège zhōumò tā yào dài nánpéngyou huíjiā hé fùmǔ jiànmiàn.** *This weekend she will bring her boyfriend home to meet her parents.*

jiànshi 见识 N knowledge, experience

jiànwén 见闻 N what is seen and heard, experiences

jiàn yì yǒng wéi 见义勇为 IDIOM be ready to do whatever one sees right, be ready to take up the cudgel for a just cause

jiàn 舰 TRAD 艦 N warship
军舰 jūn jiàn warship (艘 **sōu**)

jiànduì 舰队 N fleet, naval force

jiàntǐng 舰艇 N naval vessels

jiàn 建 V **1** build, construct ■ 在新区里要建两座学校。**Zài xīnqū li yào jiàn liǎng zuò xuéxiào.** *Two schools will be built in the new district.* **2** found, set up ■ 这座大学建于1950年。**Zhè zuò dàxué jiàn yu yī-jiǔ-wǔ-líng nián.** *This university was founded in 1950.*

jiànlì 建立 [comp: 建 found + 立 establish] V **1** establish, set up ■ 我们希望和你们建立友好合作关系。**Wǒmen xīwàng hé nǐmen jiànlì yǒuhǎo hézuò guānxi.** *We hope to establish a relationship of friendly cooperation with you.* **2** same as 建 **jiàn**

jiànshè 建设 [comp: 建 build + 设 install] V build, construct ■ 我们努力工作，建设自己的国家。**Wǒmen nǔlì gōngzuò, jiànshèqì zìjǐ de guójiā.** *We work hard to build our country.* ■ 真难想象，在一片沙漠上建设起这样一座城市。**Zhēn nán xiǎngxiàng, zài yí piàn shāmò shang jiànshèqi zhèyàng yí zuò chéngshì.** *It's hard to imagine that such a city could have been built in the desert.*

jiànyì 建议 V & N suggest, propose; suggestion, proposal ■ 他建议用电脑系统控制生产过程。**Tā jiànyì yòng diànnǎo xìtǒng kòngzhì shēngchǎn guòchéng.** *He suggests that the production process be controlled by a computer system.* ■ 他的建议没有被采用，甚至没有被考虑。**Tā de jiànyì méiyǒu bèi cǎiyòng, shènzhì méiyǒu bèi kǎolǜ.** *His suggestion was not adopted; it was not even considered.*

jiànzhù 建筑 [comp: 建 build + 筑 build] V & N build, erect; building, edifice (座 **zuò**) ■ 他们想建筑世界上最高的大楼。**Tāmen xiǎng jiànzhù shìjiè shang zuì gāo de dàlóu.** *They want to build the tallest building in the world.* ■ 这座古代建筑具有很高的艺术价值。**Zhè zuò gǔdài jiànzhù jùyǒu hěn gāo de yìshù jiàzhí.** *This ancient building has high artistic value.*

jiànzhùxué 建筑学 N (the discipline of) architecture

jiànzhùshī 建筑师 N architect

jiàn 荐 TRAD 薦 V recommend (See tuījiàn 推荐.)

jiàn 健 ADJ strong

jiànkāng 健康 [comp: 健 energetic + 康 good health] N & ADJ health; healthy, in good health ■ 生了病才知道健康多么宝贵。**Shēngle bìng cái zhīdào jiànkāng duōme bǎoguì.** *You don't know how precious good health is until you are ill.* ■ 祝您健康！/祝您身体健康！**Zhù nín jiànkāng! / Zhù nín shēntǐ jiànkāng!** *I wish you good health.*

jiànquán 健全 [comp: 健 healthy + 全 whole] ADJ & V sound, perfect; make perfect, improve
身心健全 shēn-xīn jiànquán a healthy body and a sound mind / 健全的税收制度 jiànquán de shuìshōu zhìdù a sound tax system

jiànshēn 健身 [v+obj: 健 invigorate + 身 the body] V do physical exercises, have a work-out
健身房 jiànshēnfáng gymnasium, health club

jiàn 键 TRAD 鍵 N key

jiànpán 键盘 N keyboard

jiàn 渐 TRAD 漸 ADV same as 渐渐 **jiànjiàn**

jiànjiàn 渐渐 ADV gradually, by and by ■ 他渐渐习惯了那里的生活。**Tā jiànjiàn xíguànle nàli de shēnghuó.** *He gradually grew accustomed to the life there.*

jiàn 践 TRAD 踐 V trample

jiàntà 践踏 [comp: 践 trample + 踏 step on] V trample
践踏公民权利 jiàntà gōngmín quánlì trample civil rights

jiàn 溅 TRAD 濺 V splash, spatter

jiàn 鉴 TRAD 鑒 N mirror
以史为鉴 yǐ shǐ wéi jiàn take history as a mirror (→ learn from history)

jiànbié 鉴别 V distinguish, discern
鉴别古画 jiànbié gǔ huà appraise an ancient painting, study an ancient painting to determine its authenticity and/or value

jiàndìng 鉴定 V & N **1** appraise; appraisal **2** determine the authencity, quality, etc.

jiànyú 鉴于 PREP in view of, considering

jiàn 箭 N arrow ■ 你会射箭吗？**Nǐ huì shè jiàn ma?** *Do you know how to shoot an arrow?*

jiàn 间 TRAD 間 V separate

jiàndié 间谍 N spy
间谍活动 jiàndié huódòng espionage

jiàngé 间隔 [comp: 间 separate + 隔 separate] V & N separate, cut off, isolate; interval, intermission, space between

jiànjiē 间接 ADJ indirect

jiàn 剑 TRAD 劍 N sword, sabre (把 **bǎ**)

jiāng 江 N river (条 **tiáo**) ■ 这条江从西向东流。**Zhè tiáo jiāng cóng xī xiàng dōng liú.** *This river flows from west to east.* ■ 你能游过江吗？**Nǐ néng yóuguo jiāng ma?** *Can you swim across the river?*

NOTE: The most famous 江 **jiāng** in China is 长江 **Chángjiāng**, the longest river in China. 长江 **Chángjiāng**, which literally means *the long river*, is also known as the Yangtze River. See note on 河 **hé**.

jiāng 将¹ TRAD 將 PREP same as 把 **bǎ**. Only used in writing.

jiāng 将² TRAD 將 ADV will, shall, be going to, be about to ■ 张部长将在下周二出席会议，并发表重要讲话。**Zhāng bùzhǎng jiāng zài xià zhōuèr chūxí huìyì, bìng fābiǎo zhòngyào jiǎnghuà.** *Minis-*

ter Zhang will attend the conference next Tuesday and deliver an important speech.

jiāngjìn 将近 **ADV** be close to, near

jiāngjiu 将就 **V** make do with, put up with

jiāngjūn 将军 **N** (armed forces) general

jiānglái 将来 [modif: 将 shall, will + 来 come] **N** future ■ 我现在看不懂中文报纸，将来一定看得懂。**Wǒ xiànzài kàn bu dǒng Zhōngwén bàozhǐ, jiānglái yídìng kàn de dǒng.** *I can't read Chinese newspapers now, but I'll certainly be able to in the future.* ■ 将来的世界会怎么样？谁也不知道。**Jiānglái de shìjiè huì zěnmeyàng? Shéi yě bù zhīdào.** *What will the world be like in the future? Nobody knows.*

jiāngyào 将要 **ADV** same as 将² **jiāng ADV**

jiāng 僵 **ADJ** stiff and numb, deadlocked 冻僵 **dòngjiāng** frozen stiff

jiāngyìng 僵硬 **ADJ 1** (of limbs) stiff, stark **2** rigid, inflexible

jiāng 疆 **N** boundary, border (See **biānjiāng** 边疆.)

jiǎng 讲 **TRAD** 講 **V** talk ■ 别讲了，这些事我知道。**Bié jiǎng le, zhè xiē shì wǒ zhīdào.** *Say no more. I know all about these matters.* ■ 他讲得多，做得少。**Tā jiǎng de duō, zuò de shǎo.** *He talks a lot but does little.*

讲道理 **jiǎng dàolǐ** See **dàolǐ** 道理. / 讲故事 **jiǎng gùshi** See **gùshi** 故事.

jiǎnghuà 讲话 [comp: 讲 speak + 话 speak] **N** speech, talk ■ 我的讲话只是代表我个人的意见，不代表公司立场。**Wǒ de jiǎnghuà zhǐshì dàibiǎo wǒ gèrén de yìjiàn, bú dàibiǎo gōngsī lìchǎng.** *My talk expresses only my personal opinion, and does not reflect the stand of the company.*

jiǎngjiu 讲究 **I V** be particular about, pay much attention to ■ 她十分讲究穿着。**Tā shífēn jiǎngjiu chuānzhuó.** *She pays much attention to clothes.* **II ADJ** exquisite, of very high standard 做工讲究 **zuògōng jiǎngjiu** exquisite workmanship

jiǎngzuò 讲座 **N** lecture, course of lectures 当代中国经济讲座 **dāngdài Zhōngguó jīngjì jiǎngzuò** lecture(s) on Contemporary Chinese Economy

jiǎng 奖 **TRAD** 獎 **V & N** award; prize, award ■ 这首诗怎么翻译成中文？谁翻得好，就奖给谁一本词典。**Zhè shǒu shī zěnme fānyì chéng Zhōngwén? Shéi fānde hǎo, jiù jiǎnggei shéi yì běn cídiǎn.** *How may this poem be translated into Chinese? Whoever gives the best translation will be awarded a dictionary.* ■ 这个电影得过奖，不过一点也不好看。**Zhège diànyǐng déguo jiǎng, búguò yìdiǎn yě bù hǎokàn.** *This film has won an award, but isn't at all interesting.*

奖杯 **jiǎngbēi** trophy, cup (given as a prize) / 奖金 **jiǎngjīn** prize money, bonus, award

jiǎnglì 奖励 [comp: 奖 reward + 励 encourage] **V** reward in order to encourage

奖励助人为乐者 **jiǎnglì zhù-rén-wéi-lè zhě** reward and encourage a good Samaritan

jiǎngshǎng 奖赏 **V** award, reward

jiǎngxuéjīn 奖学金 [modif: 奖 award + 学 study + 金 gold, money] **N** scholarship ■ 他获得了教育部奖学金，去英国进修一年。**Tā huòdéle jiàoyùbù jiǎngxuéjīn, qù Yīngguó jìnxiū yì nián.** *He was granted a Ministry of Education scholarship for a year of advanced studies in the UK.*

jiǎng 桨 **TRAD** 槳 **N** oar (把 **bǎ**)

jiàng 降 **V** fall, lower (**ANTONYM** 升 **shēng**) ■ 一天中气温降了十度。**Yì tiān zhōng qìwēn jiàngle shí dù.** *The temperature fell by ten degrees within a day.*

jiàngdī 降低 [comp: 降 fall + 低 lower] (**ANTONYM** 升高 **shēnggāo**) **V** lower, cut, reduce ■ 顾客很少，他们只能降低价格。**Gùkè hěn shǎo, tāmen zhǐnéng jiàngdī jiàgé.** *As there were few customers, they had to reduce prices.* ■ 很多老年人觉得社会道德水平降低了。**Hěn duō lǎoniánrén juéde shèhuì dàodé shuǐpíng jiàngdī le.** *Quite a few elderly people feel that the level of morality in society has declined.*

jiànglín 降临 **V** befall, arrive

jiàngluò 降落 **V** descend, land 降落伞 **jiàngluòsǎn** parachute

jiàng 酱 **TRAD** 醬 **N** soy paste

jiàngyóu 酱油 [comp: 酱 soybean + 油 oil, sauce] **N** soy sauce ■ 做中国菜怎么少得了酱油呢？**Zuò Zhōngguó cài zěnme shǎodeliǎo jiàngyóu ne?** *How can one cook Chinese dishes without soy sauce?*

jiāo 交 **V** hand over, pay (bills, fees) ■ 这件事交给我办吧。**Zhè jiàn shì jiāogei wǒ bàn ba.** *Hand this matter over for me to deal with.* ■ 这个月的电费你交了吗？**Zhè ge yuè de diànfèi nǐ jiāole ma?** *Have you paid this month's electricity bill?*

jiāochā 交叉 **V** intersect, cross 交叉点 **jiāochādiǎn** Same as 交点 **jiāodiǎn**

jiāodài 交代 **V 1** leave word, hand over 交代任务 **jiāo dài rènwu** give information about a job, brief on a task **2** confess (a wrongdoing)

jiāohuàn 交换 [comp: 交 transfer + 换 exchange] **V** exchange ■ 主客交换了礼物。**Zhǔkè jiāohuànle lǐwù.** *The host and the guest exchanged gifts.* ■ 这两个大学每年交换五名学生。**Zhè liǎng ge dàxué měi nián jiāohuàn wǔmíng xuésheng.** *The two universities exchange five students every year.*

jiāojì 交际 **V & N** make social contacts; social contact, social intercourse, communication ■ 他善于交际，朋友很多。**Tā shànyú jiāojì, péngyou hěn duō.** *He is good at making social contacts and has numerous friends.* ■ 和不同的人交际要用不同的方法。**Hé bùtóng de rén jiāojì yào yòng bùtóng de fāngfǎ.** *You should use different ways to maintain social contact with different people.*

jiāojìfèi 交际费 **N** entertainment expense

jiāojìhuā 交际花 N social butterfly

jiāojìwǔ 交际舞 N ballroom dancing

jiāoliú 交流 [comp: 交 associate with + 流 flow] v exchange, communicate ■ 老师们常常在一起交流教学经验。 **Lǎoshīmen chángcháng zài yìqǐ jiāoliú jiàoxué jīngyàn.** *Teachers often get together to exchange teaching experiences.*

jiāoshè 交涉 v negotiate

jiāotōng 交通 [comp: 交 transfer + 通 open, through] N transport, transportation, traffic ■ 火车仍然是中国最主要的交通工具。 **Huǒchē réngrán shì Zhōngguó zuì zhǔyào de jiāotōng gōngjù.** *The railway remains China's chief means of transport.* ■ 住在市中心，交通很方便。 **Zhù zài shìzhōngxīn, jiāotōng hěn fāngbiàn.** *Transportation is convenient for those living in the city center.*

交通事故 jiāotōng shìgù traffic accident, road accident / 交通警察 jiāotōng jǐngchá traffic policeman, traffic police

jiāowǎng 交往 v associate with, be in contact with

jiāoyì 交易 N business transaction, business deal (笔 **bǐ**)

做一笔交易 zuò yì bǐ jiāoyì do a business deal

jiāoqū 郊区 N suburbs, outskirts (of a city)

jiāo 教 v teach ■ 张小姐教我们中文。 **Zhāng xiǎojiě jiāo wǒmen Zhōngwén.** *Miss Zhang teaches us Chinese.*

jiāoshū 教书 v teach in school, be a teacher

jiāo 骄 TRAD 驕 ADJ conceited

jiāo'ào 骄傲 [comp: 骄 conceited, proud + 傲 arrogant] ADJ proud, conceited, arrogant ■ 他为自己的孩子感到骄傲。 **Tā wèi zìjǐ de háizi gǎndào jiāo'ào.** *He is proud of his children.* ■ 你能力很强，但也不能骄傲啊！ **Nǐ nénglì hěn qiáng, dàn yě bù néng jiāo'ào a!** *You're very capable, but you mustn't be conceited.*

jiāo 娇 TRAD 嬌 ADJ 1 tender and beautiful 2 same as 娇气 **jiāoqì**

jiāoqì 娇气 ADJ delicate, squeamish, fragile

jiāo 焦 ADJ scorched, burnt

jiāodiǎn 焦点 N focus

jiāojí 焦急 ADJ anxious, very worried

焦急地等待 jiāojí de děngdài wait anxiously

jiāo 蕉 N banana (See **xiāngjiāo** 香蕉)

jiāo 椒 N hot spice plant

花椒 huājiāo Chinese prickly ash

jiāo 浇 TRAD 澆 v water

浇花 jiāohuā water flowers / 浇水 jiāoshuǐ supply water to plants or crops

jiāoguàn 浇灌 v irrigate, water

jiāo 胶 TRAD 膠 N rubber

jiāoshuǐ 胶水 N glue, mucilage

jiáo 嚼 v chew, munch, masticate ■ 这块牛肉太老了，嚼不动。 **Zhè kuài niúròu tài lǎo le, jiáo bú dòng.** *This beef is too tough; I can't chew it up.*

jiǎo 角¹ N corner ■ 不少人常常在公园的一角练习英语口语，那地点就成 "英语角。" **Bùshǎo rén chángcháng zài gōngyuán de yì jiǎo liànxí Yīngyǔ kǒuyǔ, nà dìdiǎn jiù chéngle "Yīngyǔ Jiǎo."** *Many people often practice oral English in a corner of the park, and that spot becomes the "English Corner."*

jiǎo 角² N angle

jiǎodù 角度 N angle, point of view

jiǎoluò 角落 N corner, nook

jiǎo 角³ MEASURE WORD (Chinese currency: 1 角 **jiǎo** = 0.1 元 **yuán** = 10 分 **fēn**) ten cents, a dime ■ 两角钱 **liǎng jiǎo qián** *two jiao; twenty cents* ■ 八块九角五分 **bā kuài jiǔ jiǎo wǔ fēn** *eight yuan nine jiao and five fen; eight dollars and ninety-five cents*

NOTE: In colloquial Chinese 毛 **máo** is often used instead of 角 **jiǎo**, e.g. 两毛钱 **liǎng máo qián** *two mao; twenty cents*

jiǎo 饺 TRAD 餃 N same as 饺子 **jiǎozi**

jiǎozi 饺子 [suffix: 饺 dumpling + 子 nominal suffix] N stuffed dumpling, jiaozi ■ 你晚饭吃了多少个饺子？ **Nǐ wǎnfàn chīle duōshǎo ge jiǎozi?** *How many dumplings did you eat for supper?*

包饺子 bāo jiǎozi wrap *jiaozi*, make *jiaozi*

jiǎo 脚 N foot (只 **zhī**) ■ 我的脚很大，穿不下这双鞋。 **Wǒ de jiǎo hěn dà, chuān bú xià zhè shuāng xié.** *My feet are big. This pair of shoes doesn't fit.* ■ 他的左脚受伤了。 **Tā de zuǒ jiǎo shòushāng le.** *His left foot is injured.*

jiǎo 狡 ADJ sly, cunning

jiǎohuá 狡猾 [comp: 狡 sly, cunning + 猾 sleek] ADJ cunning, crafty

jiǎo 搅 TRAD 攪 v 1 mix 2 confuse, disturb

jiǎobàn 搅拌 v mix and stir

jiǎo 缴 TRAD 繳 v pay

jiǎonà 缴纳 v pay, hand in

缴纳罚款 jiǎonà fákuǎn pay a fine

jiǎo 侥 TRAD 僥 v as in 侥幸 **jiǎoxìng**

jiǎoxìng 侥幸 v avoid disaster by chance

jiào 叫¹ v call, address, shout, cry out ■ 大家都叫他小王。 **Dàjiā dōu jiào tā Xiǎo Wáng.** *Everybody calls him Xiao Wang.* ■ 我见了你的父母，应该叫什么？ **Wǒ jiànle nǐ de fùmǔ, yīnggāi jiào shénme?** *How should I address your parents when I meet them?*

jiào 叫² PREP same as 被 **bèi**. Used more in colloquialisms.

jiàozuò 叫做 v be called, be known as, be referred to as ■ 这种病叫做百日咳。 **Zhè zhǒng bìng jiàozuò bǎirìké.** *This illness is called the "hundred-day cough (or whooping cough)."*

jiào 教 N teaching

jiàocái 教材 [modif: 教 teaching + 材 material] N teaching material, textbook, coursebook (份 **fèn**, 本 **běn**) ■ "你们上中文课用什么教材？" "用我们

老师自己编的教材。"**"Nǐmen shàng Zhōngwén kè yòng shénme jiàocái?" "Yòng wǒmen lǎoshī zìjǐ biān de jiàocái."** *What textbook do you use for Chinese?" "The one written by our teacher."*

jiàoliàn 教练 [comp: 教 teach + 练 train] **N** (sports) coach

jiàoshī 教师 [modif: 教 teaching + 师 teacher, master] **N** teacher (位 **wèi**, 名 **míng**) ■ 在中国人的传统中，严格的教师才是好教师。**Zài Zhōngguórén de chuántǒng zhōng, yángé de jiàoshī cái shì hǎo jiàoshī.** *In the Chinese tradition, only a strict teacher was a good teacher.*

jiàoshì 教室 [modif: 教 teaching + 室 room] **N** classroom (间 **jiān**) ■ "你们的教室在哪里？" "在二楼，二二三房间。" **"Nǐmen de jiàoshì zài nǎli?" "Zài èrlóu, èr-èr-sān fángjiān."** *"Where is your classroom?" "It's on the second floor, Room 223."*

教室大楼 jiàoshì dàlóu classroom building

jiàoshòu 教授 [comp: 教 teach + 授 teach] **N** university professor ■ 李教授既要教学，又要研究。**Lǐ jiàoshòu jìyào jiàoxué, yòu yào yánjiū.** *Professor Li is engaged in both teaching and research.*

jiàoxué 教学 **N** teaching ■ 老师们每月开会，讨论教学中出现的问题。**Lǎoshīmen měi yuè kāihuì, tǎolùn jiàoxué zhong chūxiàn de wèntí.** *The teachers have a monthly meeting to discuss problems emerging in teaching.*

jiàoxùn 教训 [comp: 教 teach + 训 lecture] **I v** lecture, talk down to ■ 你可以不同意别人的意见，可别老是教训别人。**Nǐ kěyǐ bù tóngyì biérén de yìjiàn, kě bié lǎoshì jiàoxùn biérén.** *You may hold different opinions from others, but you shouldn't always talk down to people.* **II N** lesson (learnt from mistakes or experience) ■ 犯错误不要紧，重要的是接受教训。**Fàn cuòwù bú yàojǐn, zhòngyào de shì jiēshòu jiàoxùn.** *Making mistakes doesn't matter; what's important is to learn your lesson.*

jiàoyǎng 教养 **N** upbringing, education

有教养 yǒu jiàoyǎng well brought up, well-bred

jiàoyù 教育 [modif: 教 teach + 育 nurture] **V & N** educate, teach; education ■ 父母应该教育自己的孩子。**Fùmǔ yīnggāi jiàoyù zìjǐ de háizi.** *Parents should educate their children.* ■ 教育关系到国家的将来。**Jiàoyù guānxi dào guójiā de jiānglái.** *Education has an important bearing on the future of a country.*

jiàoyuán 教员 [modif: 教 teaching + 员 staff] **N** teacher (in a particular school) ■ 这个学校有二十四名教员。**Zhège xuéxiào yǒu èrshísì míng jiàoyuán.** *This school has twenty-four teachers.*

jiào 较 **TRAD** 較 **I PREP** same as **bǐ** 比 **I PREP.** Used only in writing. **II ADV** comparatively, relatively. Used only in writing.

jiàoliàng 较量 **V** test the strength of, compete

jiē 阶 **TRAD** 階 **N** steps, grade

jiēcéng 阶层 **N** social stratum

jiēduàn 阶段 [comp: 阶 steps, stair + 段 section] **N** period, stage ■ 这项工程正处在开始阶段。**Zhè xiàng gōngchéng zhèng chù zài kāishǐ jiēduàn.** *This project is just at an initial stage.*

jiējí 阶级 [comp: 阶 steps, stair + 级 grade] **N** social class

jiē 揭 **V** take off, reveal

jiēfā 揭发 **V** expose (wrongdoing), bring to light

jiēlù 揭露 **V** uncover, expose

揭露阴谋 jiēlù yīnmóu uncover a conspiracy

jiē 结 **TRAD** 結 **V** bear (fruit)

jiēshi 结实 **ADJ** sturdy, strong, robust ■ 他们做的家具都很结实。**Tāmen zuò de jiājù dōu hěn jiēshi.** *The furniture they make is very sturdy.* ■ 他身体很结实。**Tā shēntǐ hěn jiēshi.** *He has a robust body.*

jiē 皆 **PRON** all, both

人人皆知 Rénrén jiē zhī Everyone knows

jiē 接 **V 1** receive (a letter, a telephone call) 我昨天接到一封信，两个传真和八个电子邮件。**Wǒ zuótiān jiēdào yì fēng xìn, liǎng ge chuánzhēn hé bā ge diànzǐ yóujiàn.** *Yesterday I received a letter, two faxes and eight e-mail messages.* ■ 我要休息一会儿，谁的电话都不接。**Wǒ yào xiūxi yíhuìr, shuí de diànhuà dōu bù jiē.** *I'll have a rest and take no calls.* **2** meet and greet (a visitor) ■ 王先生是第一次到这里来，你应该去机场接他。**Wáng xiānsheng shì dì-yī cì dào zhèli lái, nǐ yīnggāi qù jīchǎng jiē tā.** *This is the first time that Mr Wang's coming here. You should go and meet him at the airport.*

jiēchù 接触 [comp: 接 join + 触 touch] **V** get in touch (with) ■ 我先和他们初步接触一下，了解他们的想法。**Wǒ xiān hé tāmen chūbù jiēchù yíxià, liǎojiě tāmen de xiǎngfǎ.** *I'll first get in touch with them tentatively to find out their thoughts.*

jiēdài 接待 [comp: 接 receive + 待 entertain] **V** receive (a visitor) ■ 今天市长不接待。**Jīntiān shìzhǎng bù jiēdài.** *The mayor is not receiving visitors today.*

jiēdào 接到 [v+compl: 接 receive + 到 arrive] **V** have received ■ 我还没有接到会议邀请信。**Wǒ hái méiyǒu jiēdào huìyì yāoqǐngxìn.** *I have not yet received a letter of invitation to the conference.*

jiējiàn 接见 [comp: 接 receive + 见 see] **V** receive (somebody), meet (somebody), give an audience ■ 教育部长昨天接见了中学教师代表。**Jiàoyù bùzhǎng zuótiān jiējiànle zhōngxué jiàoshī dàibiǎo.** *The Minister of Education received representatives of secondary school teachers yesterday.*

jiējìn 接近 **V** be close to, be near ■ 她接近董事会，很了解内情。**Tā jiējìn dǒngshìhuì, hěn liǎojiě nèiqíng.** *She is close to the board of directors and knows the inside information.* ■ 已经接近下班时间了，工作只做了一半。**Yǐjīng jiējìn xiàbān shíjiān le, gōngzuò zhǐ zuòle yí bàn.** *It is close to*

the time to get off work, but the job is only half
done.

jiēlián 接连 **ADV** one after another, in succession

jiēshòu 接受 [comp: 接 receive + 受 accept] **V** accept ■ 我们不接受礼物。**Wǒmen bù jiēshòu lǐwù.**
We do not accept gifts.

jiēzhe 接着 **CONJ** and immediately, then, at the
heels of (a previous action or event) ■ 我先听到
有人叫我，接着小王跑了进来。　**Wǒ xiān tīngdào
yǒu rén jiào wǒ, jiēzhe Xiǎo Wáng pǎole jìnlai.**
*I first heard someone calling me, and then Xiao
Wang ran into the room.*

jiē 街 **N** street (条 tiáo) ■ 我家前边的那条街总是很安
静。　**Wǒ jiā qiánbian de nà tiáo jiē zǒngshì hén ānjìng.**
The street in front of my home is always quiet.

街上 jiē shang on the street ■ 街上人很多。**Jiē
shang rén hěn duō.** *There are many people in the
street.*

步行街 bùxíng jiē pedestrian street / 逛大街 guàng
dàjiē stroll the streets, do window shopping

jiēdào 街道 [comp: 街 street + 道 way] **N** street
(条 tiáo) ■ 这里的街道很安静。**Zhèli de jiēdào
hěn ānjìng.** *The streets in this area are quiet.*

jié 节¹ **TRAD** 節 **N** festival ■ 这个节我过得很愉
快。**Zhège jié wǒ guò de hěn yúkuài.** *I had a
very happy festival.* ■ 这个地方一年有好几
个节。**Zhège dìfang yì nián yǒu hǎo jǐ ge jié.**
There're quite a number of festivals in this area.

过节 guò jié observe a festival, celebrate a festival

jié 节² **TRAD** 節 **MEASURE WORD** a period of time
一节课 yì jié kè a period of class

jiémù 节目 [comp: 节 section + 目 item] **N** TV
program, item in a theatrical performance ■ 昨天
的电视节目很精彩。**Zuótiān de diànshì jiémù hěn
jīngcǎi.** *The TV program yesterday was wonderful!* ■ 这个节目是谁编的？谁演的？**Zhège jiémù
shì shuí biān de? Shuí yǎn de?** *Who wrote this program? Who acted it?*

儿童节目 értóng jiémù children's program / 体育
节目 tǐyù jiémù sports program / 文艺节目 wényì
jiémù theatrical program / 新闻节目 xīnwén jiémù
news program (on TV or radio)

jiérì 节日 [modif: 节 festival + 日 day] **N** festival
day ■ 中国人最重要的节日是春节，也就是中国
人的新年。**Zhōngguórén zuì zhòngyào de jiérì
shì chūnjié, yě jiùshì Zhōngguórén de xīnnián.**
*The most important festival for the Chinese is the
Spring Festival, which is the Chinese New Year.*

jiéshěng 节省 **V** save, be frugal with (**ANTONYM** 浪
费 làngfèi) ■ 你平时节省一点钱，几年下来就可
能有一大笔钱。**Nǐ píngshí jiéshěng yìdiǎn qián, jǐ
nián xiàlai jiù kěnéng yǒu yídà bǐ qián.** *If you save
a little money routinely, after several years you
may have a substantial sum of money.*

jiéyuē 节约 **V** economize, save, practice thrift
(**ANTONYM** 浪费 làngfèi) ■ 我们应当节约用电，节

约用水。**Wǒmen yīngdāng jiéyuē yòngdiàn, jiéyuē
yòngshuǐ.** *We should cut down electricity and water consumption.*

jiézhì 节制 **V** control, be moderate in
节制生育（节育）jié zhì shēng yù (jiéyù) birth
control, family planning

jiézòu 节奏 **N** rhythm, tempo

jié 杰 **ADJ** outstanding, excellent

jiéchū 杰出 [comp: 杰 excellent + 出 out] **ADJ**
outstanding, distinguished

jié 竭 **V** exhaust

jié jìn quán lì 竭尽全力 **IDIOM** do one's very best,
pull out all stops

jiélì 竭力 [v+obj: 竭 exhaust + 力 strength, power]
V do one's utmost, do everything within one's
power

竭力满足顾客 jiélì mǎnzú gùkè do all one can to
satisfy customers

jié 结 **TRAD** 結 **N** knot

jiégòu 结构 **N** structure, construction ■ 这座古
代建筑是木结构的。**Zhèzuò gǔdài jiànzhù shì
mù jiégòu de.** *This ancient building is a timber
structure.*

jiéguǒ 结果 [v+obj: 结 bear + 果 fruit] **I N** result,
consequence ■ 这次试验的结果很鼓舞人心。**Zhè
cì shìyàn de jiéguǒ hěn gǔwǔ rénxīn.** *The result of
this test is heartening.* **II CONJ** as a result, consequently, finally ■ 他们讨论了半天，结果取得了
一致意见。**Tāmen tǎolùnle bàntiān, jiéguǒ qǔdéle
yízhì yìjiàn.** *They discussed it for a long time, and
finally reached a unanimous agreement.* ■ 技术员
连续工作二十小时，结果解决了问题。**Jìshùyuán
liánxù gōngzuò èrshí xiǎoshí, jiéguǒ jiějuéle wèntí.**
Technicians worked for twenty hours continuously, and finally solved the problem.

jiéhé 结合 [comp: 结 tie + 合 merge] **V** combine,
integrate ■ 热情的态度要和冷静的头脑相结合。
**Rèqíng de tàidu yào hé lěngjìng de tóunǎo xiāng
jiéhé.** *Enthusiasm should be combined with a cool
head.* ■ 他们俩终于结合为一对幸福的夫妻。
Tāmen liǎ zhōngyú jiéhéwéi yí duì xìngfú de fūqī.
*They were finally joined as happy husband and
wife.*

jiéhūn 结婚 [v+obj: 结 tie + 婚 marriage] **V** marry
(**ANTONYM** 离婚 líhūn) ■ 他和中学时的女朋友结婚
了。**Tā hé zhōngxué shí de nǚpéngyou jiéhūn le.**
He married his high school sweetheart.

jiéjīng 结晶 **N 1** crystallization **2** fruit, result
多年努力的结晶 duōnián nǔlì de jiéjīng the fruit
of many years' painstaking efforts

jiéjú 结局 **N** outcome, final result

jiélùn 结论 [modif: 结 end + 论 view, treatise] **N**
verdict, conclusion ■ 经过调查，我们的结论如
下。**Jīngguò diàochá, wǒmen de jiélùn rú xià.** *As a
result of the investigation, our conclusions are as
follows.* ■ 我不同意你的结论。**Wǒ bù tóngyì nǐ de**

jiélùn. *I don't agree with your conclusion.*

jiéshù 结束 [comp: 结 tie + 束 knot] **v** end, terminate (**ANTONYM** 开始 **kāishǐ**) ■ 电影什么时候结束？ **Diànyǐng shénme shíhou jiéshù?** *When does the movie end?* ■ 第二次世界大战是哪一年开始，哪一年结束的？ **Dì-èr ci shìjiè dàzhàn shì nǎ yì nián kāishǐ, nǎ yì nián jiéshǔ de?** *In which year did World War II begin, and in which year did it end?*

jiésuàn 结算 [modif: 结 tie + 算 calculation] **v** settle an account, close an account

jiézhàng 结账 **v** settle accounts, balance the books

jié 洁 **ADJ** clean (See **qīngjié** 清洁.)

jié 截 **v** intercept, stop

jiézhǐ 截止 **v** end, up to ■ 招标日期本星期五截止。 **Zhāo biāo rìqī běn Xīngqīwǔ jiézhǐ.** *Invitation to public bidding will end by this Friday.*

jiézhì 截至 **PREP** by, up to

jié 捷 **ADJ** prompt, nimble, quick (See **mǐnjié** 敏捷.)

jiě 姐 **N** same as 姐姐 **jiějie**

jiějie 姐姐 **N** elder sister ■ 我姐姐对我很好。 **Wǒ jiějie duì wǒ hěn hǎo.** *My elder sister is very nice to me.* ■ 你有没有姐姐？ **Nǐ yǒu méiyǒu jiějie?** *Do you have an elder sister?*

jiě 解 **v** untie, undo ■ 医生：请你把上衣解开，我要听听你的心肺。 **Yīshēng: Qǐng nǐ bǎ shàngyī jiě kāi, wǒ yào tīngting nǐ de xīnfèi.** *Doctor: Please undo your jacket. I want to listen to your heart and lungs.*

jiěchú 解除 **v** remove, relieve

解除职务 jiěchú zhíwù remove someone of his/her post

jiědá 解答 [comp: 解 untie + 答 reply] **v** provide an answer, give an explanation ■ 这个问题谁会解答？ **Zhè ge wèntí shuí huì jiědá?** *Who can answer this question?*

jiěfàng 解放 [comp: 解 untie + 放 release] **v** set free, liberate, emancipate ■ 美国南北战争解放了南方的黑人。 **Měiguó nánběi zhànzhēng jiěfàngle nánfāng de hēirén.** *The American South-North War (→ the American Civil War) emancipated Black people in the South.*

jiěgù 解雇 [v+obj: 解 release + 雇 employment] **v** dismiss (an employee), discharge

jiějué 解决 [comp: 解 dissect + 决 finalize] **v** solve (a problem), settle (an issue) ■ 这个问题还没有解决。 **Zhè ge wèntí hái méiyǒu jiějué.** *This problem has not been resolved.* ■ 要解决目前的困难，必须和各方面合作。 **Yào jiějué mùqián de kùnnán, bìxū hé gè fāngmiàn hézuò.** *We must cooperate with all parties if the present difficulties are to be overcome.*

jiěpōu 解剖 [comp: 解 dissect + 剖 cut open] **v** **1** dissect **2** analyze, probe

jiěsàn 解散 **v** dismiss, disband

jiěshì 解释 [comp: 解 untie + 释 clarify] **V & N** explain, account for; explanation, interpretationn ■ 请你解释一下这个句子。 **Qǐng nǐ jiěshì yíxià zhè ge jùzi.** *Please explain this sentence to me.* ■ 对这种现象，我有一个解释。 **Duì zhè zhǒng xiànxiàng, wǒ yǒu yí ge jiěshì.** *I have an explanation for this phenomenon.*

jiětǐ 解体 **v** disintegrate, fall apart

jiè 介 **v** intervene

jièshào 介绍 [comp: 介 intervene + 绍 connect] **v** introduce ■ 我来介绍一下，这位是李先生，这位是王小姐。 **Wǒ lái jièshào yíxià, zhè wèi shì Lǐ xiānsheng, zhè wèi shì Wáng xiǎojiě.** *Let me introduce [the people here]. This is Mr Li. This is Miss Wang.* ■ 你刚从中国回来，请你介绍一下中国的情况。 **Nǐ gāng cóng Zhōngguó huílai, qǐng nǐ jièshao yíxià Zhōngguó de qíngkuàng.** *As you've just come back from China, please tell us something about the current situation in China.*

jièshào rén 介绍人 **N** **1** matchmaker, go-between **2** sponsor (for membership in a club, a political party, an association etc.)

jiè 届 **MEASURE WORD** (used for a conference or congress held at regular intervals, for graduating classes) ■ 我是那个中学九九届的毕业生。 **Wǒ shì nà ge zhōngxué jiǔjiǔ jiè de bìyèshēng.** *I was a graduate of the class of '99 of that high school.* ■ 第十届国际生物学大会将于十二月在新加坡举行。 **Dì-shí jiè guójì shēngwùxué dàhuì jiāng yú Shí'èr yuè zài Xīnjiāpō jǔxíng.** *The 10th International Conference on Biology will be held in Singapore in December.*

jiè 界 **N** realm (See **shìjiè** 世界.)

jièxiàn 界限 [comp: 界 boundary + 限 limit] **N** dividing line, limits

jiè 戒 **v** guard against

jièbèi 戒备 [comp: 戒 guard + 备 prepare] **v** take precaution, be on alert

jièzhi 戒指 **N** (finger) ring

jiè 借 **v** borrow, lend

NOTE: This verb may mean either *borrow* or *lend*, depending on the patterns in which it occurs:
A 借给 B ... **A jiègei B ...** *A lends B ...*, e.g.
■ 他借给我一百元。 **Tā jiègei wǒ yìbǎi yuán.** *He lent me one hundred dollars.*
A 向 B 借... **A xiàng B jiè...** *A borrows ... from B*
■ 我向他借了一百元。 **Wǒ xiàng tā jièle yìbǎi yuán.** *I borrowed one hundred dollars from him.*

jièjiàn 借鉴 [v+obj: 借 borrow + 鉴 mirror] **v** use for reference, learn (lessons) from

jièkòu 借口 [v+obj: 借 borrow + 口 mouth] **V & N** use as an excuse; excuse, pretext

借口身体不好不上班 jièkòu shēntǐ bùhǎo bú shàngbān use poor health as an excuse for not going to work / 找借口 zhǎo jièkǒu make up an excuse, invent an excuse

jièzhù 借助 [v+obj: 借 borrow + 助 help] v have the aid of, make use of

jīn 巾 N towel (See **máojīn** 毛巾.)

jīn 今 N now, the present

jīnhòu 今后 N from today, from now on ■ 我保证今后不迟到，不早退。**Wǒ bǎozhèng jīnhòu bù chídào, bù zǎotuì.** *I assure you that from now on I will not be late for work or leave work earlier than is allowed.*

jīnnián 今年 [modif: 今 now + 年 year] N this year

jīntiān 今天 [modif: 今 now + 天 day] N today ■ 今天天气很好。**Jīntiān tiānqì hěn hǎo.** *The weather's fine today.* ■ 我今天要上五节课。**Wǒ jīntiān yào shàng wǔ jié kè.** *I have five classes today.*

jīn 斤 MEASURE WORD *jin* (a traditional Chinese unit of weight equal to half a kilogram) ■ 这条鱼重八斤。**Zhè tiáo yú zhòng bā jīn.** *This fish weighs eight* jin. ■ 妈妈买了两斤肉。**Māma mǎile liǎng jīn ròu.** *Mom bought two* jin *of meat.*

jīn 金 N 1 gold (两 **liǎng**, ounce) ■ 这块金表价值极高，你要好好保存。**Zhè kuài jīn biǎo jiàzhí jí gāo, nǐ yào hǎohǎo bǎocún.** *This gold watch is very valuable. You must keep it well.* 2 money 奖学金 jiǎngxuéjīn scholarship / 奖金 jiǎngjīn bonus, prize money / 退休金 tuìxiū jīn superannuation, pension

jīnqián 金钱 N money, currency

jīnróng 金融 N finance 国际金融中心 guójì jīnróng zhōngxīn an international financial center

jīnshǔ 金属 N metal ■ 金、银、铜、铁都是金属。**Jīn, yín, tóng, tiě dōu shì jīnshǔ.** *Gold, silver, copper and iron are all metals.*

jīnzi 金子 N gold

jīn 津 N saliva

jīn jīn yǒu wèi 津津有味 IDIOM (eat, read or watch) with relish, with keen pleasure

jīn 筋 N muscle, tendon, sinew

jīndǒu 筋斗 N somersault 翻筋斗 fān jīndǒu turn/do a somersault

jīn pí lì jìn 筋疲力尽 IDIOM exhausted, dog tired

jǐn 仅 TRAD 僅 ADV only, merely ■ 她一个月的工资仅够付房租和吃饭。**Tā yí ge yuè de gōngzī jǐn gòu fù fángzū hé chīfàn.** *Her monthly wages are only enough for rent and food.*

jǐnjǐn 仅仅 ADV same as 仅 **jǐn,** but more emphatic

jǐn 锦 TRAD 錦 N brocade

jǐn shàng tiān huā 锦上添花 IDIOM add flowers to the brocade, make what is good even better

jǐn xiù qiánchéng 锦绣前程 IDIOM glorious future, great future

jǐn 尽 TRAD 盡 v to the greatest extent

jǐnguǎn 尽管 I ADV feel free to, not hesitate ■ 有什么问题，尽管和我联系。**Yǒu shénme wèntí, jǐnguǎn hé wǒ liánxì.** *If you have any questions, do not hesitate to contact us.* ■ 你尽管吃，菜还多着呢！**Nǐ jǐnguǎn chī, cài hái duōzhe ne!** *Eat to your heart's content. More dishes are coming.* II CONJ even though ■ 尽管她很聪明，但是念书不用功，结果成绩不好。**Jǐnguǎn tā hěn cōngmíng, dànshì niànshū bú yònggōng, jiēguǒ chéngjì bùhǎo.** *Even though she is quite intelligent, she does not study hard and consequently fails to get good results in exams.*

jǐn kuài 尽快 ADV as soon as possible, as fast as possible ■ 这事要尽快办。**Zhè shì yào jǐn kuài bàn.** *This matter must be handled as soon as possible.*

jǐnliàng 尽量 ADV as far as possible, to the best of one's ability ■ 对孩子你要尽量耐心一点。**Duì háizi nǐ yào jǐnliàng nàixīn yìdiǎn.** *In dealing with children you should try your best to be patient.*

jǐn 紧 TRAD 緊 ADJ tight, taut ■ 今天的活动安排得比较紧。**Jīntiān de huódòng ānpái de bǐjiào jǐn.** *Today's activities are scheduled rather tightly.* ■ 这件上衣肩部紧了一点。**Zhè jiàn shàngyī jiānbù jǐnle yìdiǎn.** *The shoulders of the coat are a bit tight.*

jǐnjí 紧急 [comp: 紧 pressing + 急 urgent] ADJ urgent, pressing 紧急任务 jǐnjí rènwù urgent task / 紧急状况 jǐnjí zhuàngkuàng emergency situation, contingency

jǐnmì 紧密 ADJ close together, inseparable

jǐnpò 紧迫 ADJ pressing, urgent

jǐnzhāng 紧张 [comp: 紧 tight + 张 tense] ADJ tense, nervous ■ 明天要考试了，我没有很好准备，心里很紧张。**Míngtiān yào kǎoshì le, wǒ méiyǒu hěn hǎo zhǔnbèi, xīnli hěn jǐnzhāng.** *We're having an examination tomorrow. I'm not well prepared, and feel really nervous.* ■ 这个电影很紧张，看得我心直跳。**Zhège diànyǐng hěn jǐnzhāng, kàn de wǒ xīn zhí tiào.** *This film was so nerve-racking that my heart beat violently.*

jǐn 谨 TRAD 謹 ADJ cautious

jǐnshèn 谨慎 [comp: 谨 cautious + 慎 cautious] ADJ cautious, careful 谨慎驾驶 jǐnshèn jiàshǐ drive carefully

jìn 尽 TRAD 盡 v exhaust ■ 我已经尽了自己的责任。**Wǒ yǐjīng jìnle zìjǐ de zérèn.** *I've done all I can to fulfill my responsibilities.*

jìnlì 尽力 v do all one can, do one's utmost

jìn 进 TRAD 進 v move forward, enter ■ 请进！**Qǐng jìn!** *Please come in! (or Please go in!)* 进来 jìnlai come in, come into ■ 进来吧，我们在等你呢！**Jìnlai ba, wǒmen zài děng nǐ ne!** *Please come in. We've been waiting for you.* 进去 jìnqu go in, go into ■ 他们在开会，请不要进去。**Tāmen zài kāihuì, qǐng bú yào jìnqu.** *They're having a meeting. Please don't go in.*

jìnbù 进步 N & ADJ progress, progressive (ANTONYM 落后 luòhòu) ■ 你们的中文学习有了很大进步。**Nǐmen de Zhōngwén xuéxí yǒule hěn dà**

jìnbù. *You have made very good progress in your Chinese studies.* ■ 社会上的进步力量一定会取胜。**Shèhuì shang de jìnbù lìliàng yídìng huì qǔshèng.** *The progressive forces in society will surely prevail.*

jìn'ér 进而 ADV and then, subsequently

jìngōng 进攻 [comp: 进 advance + 攻 attack] V advance and attack, attack ■ 部队出发进攻敌人。**Bùduì chūfā jìngōng dírén.** *The troops set out to attack the enemy forces.*

jìnhuà 进化 [comp: 进 advance + 化 change, transform] V evolve, develop ■ 人是从猴子进化来的，你信不信？**Rén shì cóng hóuzi jìnhuà lái de, nǐ xìn bú xìn?** *Man evolved from the monkey. Do you believe this?*

进化论 jìnhuàlùn (Charles Darwin's) theory of evolution

jìnkǒu 进口 [v+obj: 进 enter + 口 the mouth] V import (ANTONYM 出口 chūkǒu) ■ 这台机床是从德国进口的。**Zhè tái jīchuáng shì cóng Déguó jìnkǒu de.** *This machine tool was imported from Germany.* ■ 这个国家每年进口大量农产品。**Zhège guójiā měi nián jìnkǒu dàliàng nóngchǎnpǐn.** *This country imports large quantities of farm produce every year.*

jìnrù 进入 [comp: 进 enter + 入 enter] V enter, enter into ■ 狗不得进入商场。**Gǒu bùdé jìnrù shāngchǎng.** *Dogs are not allowed to enter the shopping center. (→ No Dogs in the Mall.)* ■ 工程进入最后阶段。**Gōngchéng jìnrùle zuìhòu jiēduàn.** *The project has entered into the last stage.*

jìnxíng 进行 [comp: 进 enter + 行 walk] V conduct, carry out ■ 孩子做错了事，应该进行教育。**Háizi zuò cuòle shì, yīnggāi jìnxíng jiàoyù.** *When a child makes a mistake, he should be educated.*

NOTE: The object that 进行 **jìnxíng** takes must be a noun of two or more syllables. 进行 **jìnxíng** is used only in formal Chinese.

jìnxiū 进修 V do advanced studies, undergo in-service advanced training ■ 我们的中文老师要去北京进修半年。**Wǒmen de Zhōngwén lǎoshī yào qù Běijīng jìnxiū bànnián.** *Our Chinese teacher will go to Beijing for half a year's advanced studies.*

jìnyíbù 进一步 [v+obj: 进 advance + 一步 one (more) step] ADV advancing a step further, further, more deeply ■ 对于这个问题，我们还要进一步研究。**Duìyú zhège wèntí, wǒmen hái yào jìnyíbù yánjiū.** *We need to study this problem further.*

jìnzhǎn 进展 V make progress, make headway

jìn 晋 V go forward, advance

jìnshēng 晋升 [comp: 晋 advance + 升 rise] V promote (to a higher position)

晋升为地区经理 jìnshēng wéi dìqū jīnglǐ be promoted to area manager

jìn 近 ADJ close to, close by (ANTONYM 远 yuǎn) ■ 商店很近，不用开车去。**Shāngdiàn hěn jìn, búyòng kāichē qù.** *The store is close by. There is no need to drive.*

离 … 近 lí … jìn be close to ■ 爸爸的办公室离家很近。**Bàba de bàngōngshì lí jiā hěn jìn.** *My father's office is close to home.*

jìndài 近代 [modif: 近 close to + 代 generations] N modern times (usually from the year 1840)

jìnlái 近来 N recently, nowadays, these days ■ 他近来好事连连。**Tā jìnlái hǎoshì liánlián.** *These days good things are happening to him, one after another.* ■ 近来天气反常。**Jìnlái tiānqì fǎncháng.** *The weather has been rather abnormal recently.*

jìnshì 近视 N myopia, near-sightedness, short-sightedness ■ 我是近视眼。**Wǒ shì jìnshì yǎn.** *I'm myopic.*

jìn 劲 TRAD 勁 N physical strength ■ 这位举重运动员真有劲！**Zhè wèi jǔzhòng yùndòngyuán zhēn yǒu jìn!** *This weight lifter is really powerful!*

没劲 méijìn dull, boring, bored ■ 这日子过得真没劲！**Zhè rìzi guòde zhēn méijìn!** *Life is so boring!*

jìn 禁 V forbid

jìnzhǐ 禁止 [comp: 禁 forbid + 止 stop] V forbid, prohibit ■ 电影院内严格禁止使用手机。**Diànyǐngyuàn nèi yángé jìnzhǐ shǐyòng shǒujī.** *Using the cell phone is strictly prohibited in the cinema.*

jìn 浸 V soak

jìnpào 浸泡 V soak, immerse

jīng 茎 TRAD 莖 N stem or stalk (of a plant)

jīng 经 TRAD 經 V pass through, experience

jīngcháng 经常 [comp: 经 constant + 常 often] ADV often ■ 你经常迟到，这样不好。**Nǐ jīngcháng chídào, zhèyàng bù hǎo.** *You're often late, which is not good.*

jīngdiǎn 经典 N classics, classical works

jīngfèi 经费 N outlay, fund (for a specific purpose or the regular running of an organization)

jīngguò 经过 [comp: 经 go through + 过 pass] I V go through, pass ■ 我去学校的路上，要经过一座公园。**Wǒ qù xuéxiào de lùshang, yào jīngguò yí zuò gōngyuán.** *I pass by a park on my way to school.* ■ 没有亲自经过，就不知道多难。**Méiyǒu qīnzì jīngguò, jiù bù zhīdào duō nán.** *Without experiencing it personally, you wouldn't know how difficult it is.* II PREP through, after ■ 经过这件事，他变得聪明了。**Jīngguò zhè jiàn shì, tā biàn de cōngmíng le.** *He was more sensible after this incident.*

jīngjì 经济 [comp: 经 govern + 济 bring relief to] N economy ■ 这个国家的经济不太好。**Zhège guójiā de jīngjì bú tài hǎo.** *This country's economy is not in very good shape.* ■ 每个国家都在发展自己的经济。**Měi ge guójiā dōu zài fāzhǎn zìjǐ de jīngjì.** *Every country is working hard to develop its economy.*

经济学 jīngjìxué economics / 经济学家 jīngjìxué jiā economist / 市场经济 shìchǎng jīngjì market economy

jīnglǐ 经理 [comp: 经 manage + 理 administrate] **N** manager (位 wèi) ■ 他是管人力资源的经理。**Tā shì guǎn rénlì zīyuán de jīnglǐ.** *He is the manager in charge of human resources.*

副经理 fù jīnglǐ deputy manager / 市场经理 shìchǎng jīnglǐ marketing manager / 总经理 zǒng jīnglǐ general manager, chief executive officer (CEO)

jīnglì 经历 **V & N** experience, undergo; personal experience ■ 这位老人经历了很多困难，才获得幸福的晚年。**Zhè wèi lǎorén jīnglìle hěn duō kùnnan, cái huòdé xìngfú de wǎnnián.** *This old man has experienced many troubles before enjoying blissful old age.* ■ 请你谈谈在美国学习和工作的经历。**Qǐng nǐ tántan zài Měiguó xuéxí hé gōngzuò de jīnglì.** *Please tell us about your experience studying and working in the States.*

jīngshāng 经商 **V** engage in business, be a businessman

jīngyàn 经验 [comp: 经 go through + 验 test] **N** experience, lesson (learnt from experiences) ■ 这个经验对我很有价值。**Zhège jīngyàn duì wǒ hěn yǒu jiàzhí.** *This experience is very valuable to me.*

取得经验 qǔdé jīngyàn acquire experience / 有经验 yǒu jīngyàn experienced ■ 她是一位有经验的老师。**Tā shì yí wèi yǒu jīngyàn de lǎoshī.** *She's an experienced teacher.*

jīngyíng 经营 **V** operate (a business)

jīng 惊 TRAD 驚 **V** be startled

jīngdòng 惊动 [v+compl: 惊 startle + 动 move] **V** disturb, alarm

jīnghuāng 惊慌 [comp: 惊 be startled + 慌 confused] **V** panick

惊慌失措 jīnghuāng shīcuò be panic-stricken and at a loss what to do

jīngqí 惊奇 **V** be surprised and incredulous, be amazed

jīngyà 惊讶 **V** be astonished, be surprised

jīng 睛 **N** eyeball, the pupil of the eye (See yǎnjing 眼睛.)

jīng 精 **ADJ** choice

jīngcǎi 精彩 [comp: 精 choice + 彩 colorful, brilliant] **ADJ** (of a theatrical performance or sports event) brilliant, thrilling, wonderful ■ 昨天的足球比赛真精彩啊！**Zuótiān de zúqiú bǐsài zhēn jīngcǎi a!** *The football match yesterday was really wonderful!* ■ 他在会上的发言十分精彩，赢得了热烈的掌声。**Tā zài huì shang de fāyán shífēn jīngcǎi, yíngdéle rèliè de zhǎngshēng.** *He made a stirring speech at the meeting and earned warm applause.*

jīng dǎ xì suàn 精打细算 IDIOM be very careful in budgeting to save every cent

jīnghuá 精华 **N** the cream of the crop, the very best

jīngjiǎn 精简 **V** trim and prune (an organization), reduce staffing

jīnglì 精力 [comp: 精 energy + 力 strength] **N** energy, vigor ■ 我父亲年纪大了，精力不如以前了。**Wǒ fùqin niánjì dà le, jīnglì bùrú yǐqián le.** *My father is getting old and is not so energetic as before.*

jīngmì 精密 **ADJ** precise, accurate
精密仪器 jīngmì yíqì precision instrument

jīngquè 精确 **ADJ** accurate, exact

jīngshén 精神 [comp: 精 essence + 神 spirit] **N** vigor, vitality ■ 这位老人八十多岁了，但是精神很好。**Zhè wèi lǎorén bāshí duō suì le, dànshì jīngshén hěn hǎo.** *This old man (or woman) is over eighty, but is energetic and alert.* ■ 不知道为什么，我今天没有精神。**Bù zhīdào wèishénme, wǒ jīntiān méiyǒu jīngshén.** *I don't know why, but I'm in low spirits today.*

jīngshén bìng 精神病 **N** mental illness, psychosis
精神病医生 jīngshén bìng yīshēng psychiatrist / 精神病医院 jīngshén bìng yīyuàn mental hospital

jīngtōng 精通 **ADJ** having great proficiency in, be master of

jīngxīn 精心 **ADJ** meticulous, painstaking

jīng yì qiú jīng 精益求精 **V** seek perfection

jīngzhì 精致 **ADJ** exquisite, fine

jīng 兢 only used in 兢兢业业 jīng jīng yè yè

jīng jīng yè yè 兢兢业业 IDIOM cautious and conscientious

jīng 京 **N** capital city

jīngjù 京剧 [modif: 京 Beijing (Peking) + 剧 opera] **N** Beijing (Peking) opera ■ 京剧有歌有舞，还有武术，真精彩！**Jīngjù yǒu gē yǒu wǔ, háiyǒu wǔshù, zhēn jīngcǎi!** *Beijing opera contains singing, dancing and martial arts as well. It's really brilliant!*

jīng 景 **N** view, scenery

jǐngsè 景色 [comp: 景 view + 色 color] **N** view, scenery

jǐng 警 **V** warn

jǐngchá 警察 **N** policeman, police ■ 这里发生了交通事故，快叫警察！**Zhèli fāshēngle jiāotōng shìgù, kuài jiào jǐngchá!** *A traffic accident has happened here. Call the police quickly!*

NOTE: In China the police bureau is called 公安局 gōng'ānjú *Public Security Bureau*, which should be distinguished from 国安局 guó'ānjú *Bureau of National Security*.

jǐnggào 警告 [comp: 警 warn + 告 tell] **V & N** warn; warning, caution ■ 路旁有牌子警告，前面是弯曲山路，必须减速。**Lùpáng yǒu páizi jǐnggào, qiánmian shì wānqū shānlù, bìxū jiǎnsù.** *A poster by the roadside warns motorists to reduce speed as the road ahead is zigzagging and hilly.*

jǐngtì 警惕 **V** be vigilant

jǐngwèi 警卫 v guard and defend (a military installation, a VIP, etc.)

jǐng 井 N well, (water) well
水井 shuǐjǐng water well / 油井 yóujǐng oil well

jǐng 颈 TRAD 頸 N neck
头颈 tóujǐng the neck / 长颈鹿 chángjǐnglù giraffe (long-necked-deer)

jǐngzhuī 颈椎 N cervical vertabra

jìng 净 ADJ clean (See gānjing 干净.)

jìng 竞 TRAD 競 v compete

jìngsài 竞赛 [comp: 竞 compete + 赛 contest] v compete; contest ■ 他们兄弟俩一直竞赛，看谁学习成绩好。 **Tāmen xiōngdì liǎ yìzhí jìngsài, kàn shuí xuéxí chéngjì hǎo.** *The two brothers have always been competing with each other to see who is the better student.*

jìngxuǎn 竞选 [v+obj: 竞 compete + 选 election] v run for office

jìngzhēng 竞争 [comp: 竞 compete + 争 strive] v & N compete; competition ■ 在这个市场上有好几个公司和我们竞争。 **Zài zhège shìchǎngshang yǒu hǎo jǐ gè gōngsī hé wǒmen jìngzhēng.** *Quite a few companies are competing with us in this market.* ■ 我们相信公平竞争。 **Wǒmen xiāng xìn gōngping jìngzhēng.** *We believe in fair competition.*

jìng 竟 ADV unexpectedly

jìngrán 竟然 ADV unexpectedly, contrary to expectation ■ 这个小孩下棋竟然胜了他爸爸。 **Zhège xiǎohái xiàqí jìngrán shèng le tā bàba.** *Quite unexpectedly the child should beat his father in chess.*

jìng 敬 v respect

jìng'ài 敬爱 [comp: 敬 respect + 爱 love] v respect and love ■ 有多少孩子敬爱自己的父母？ **Yǒu duōshǎo háizi jìng'ài zìjǐ de fùmǔ?** *How many children respect and love their parents?*

jìngjiǔ 敬酒 v propose a toast ■ 我提议向我们的主人敬酒。 **Wǒ tíyì xiàng wǒmen de zhǔrén jìngjiǔ.** *I'd like to propose a toast to our host.*

jìnglǐ 敬礼 v salute

jìngyè 敬业 v work with dedication, be dedicated to one's work

jìng 境 N boundary, place

jìngjiè 境界 N 1 geographical boundary 2 spiritual extent, mental state

jìng 静 ADJ quiet, peaceful, silent ■ 阅览室里很静，针掉在地上都听得见。 **Yuèlǎnshì li hěn jìng, zhēn diào zài dìshang dōu tīng de jiàn.** *The reading room is so quiet that one can hear a pin drop.* ■ 请大家静一静，我要宣布一件事。 **Qǐng dàjiā jìng yi jìng, wǒ yào xuānbù yí jiàn shì.** *Be quiet, everybody. I have an announcement to make.*

jìng 镜 TRAD 鏡 N mirror

jìngtóu 镜头 N 1 camera lens 2 shot or scene in photography or cinematography

jìngzi 镜子 [suffix: 镜 mirror + 子 nominal suffix] N mirror (面 miàn)

照镜子 zhào jìngzi look at oneself in a mirror

jiū 究 v investigate

jiūjìng 究竟 ADV same as 到底 dàodǐ

jiū 纠 TRAD 糾 v rectify

jiūfēn 纠纷 N dispute

jiūzhèng 纠正 [v+compl: 纠 rectify + 正 correct] v rectify, correct ■ 我们应该及时纠正错误。 **Wǒmen yīnggāi jíshí jiūzhèng cuòwù.** *We should rectify our mistakes promptly.*

jiǔ 九 NUMERAL nine
九一一 jiǔ-yāo-yāo 9/11, September 11 / 九千九百九十九 jiǔqiān jiǔbǎi jiǔshíjiǔ 9,999 / 九九八十一 jiǔjiǔ bāshíyī Nine times nine is eighty-one.

NOTE: See note on 一 **yī** regarding pronunciation of 一 as **yāo**.

jiǔ 久 ADJ for a long time ■ 我等你等了很久了。 **Wǒ děng nǐ děngle hěn jiǔ le.** *I've been waiting for you for a long time.* ■ 日久见人心。 **Rì jiǔ jiàn rén xīn.** *As time goes on, you will know a person's nature.*

jiǔ 灸 N moxibustion (See zhēnjiǔ 针灸.)

jiǔ 酒 N alcoholic beverage (种 zhǒng, 瓶 píng) ■ 这种酒，我不喜欢喝。 **Zhè zhǒng jiǔ, wǒ bù xǐhuan hē.** *I don't like this kind of alcoholic drink.* ■ 我不喝酒，我还要开车。 **Wǒ bù hē jiǔ, wǒ háiyào kāichē.** *No alcoholic drinks for me. I'll be driving.*
白酒 báijiǔ colorless spirit distilled from grains / 黄酒 huángjiǔ yellow rice wine

jiǔbā 酒吧 N (wine) bar, pub

jiǔdiàn 酒店 N 1 wine shop, restaurant 2 hotel

jiǔhuì 酒会 N cocktail party, reception

jiǔjīng 酒精 N alcohol

jiù 旧 TRAD 舊 ADJ (of things) old, second-hand (ANTONYM 新 xīn) ■ 这件衣服不太旧，还可以穿。 **Zhè jiàn yīfu bú tài jiù, hái kěyǐ chuān.** *This jacket is not too old. It can still be worn.* ■ 旧的不去，新的不来。 **Jiù de bú qù, xīn de bù lái.** *If the old doesn't go, the new won't come. (→ If you don't discard old stuff, you won't have new things.)*

jiù 舅 N mother's brother, uncle

jiùfù 舅父 mother's brother, uncle

jiùjiu 舅舅 same as 舅父 **jiùfù,** used as a form of address

jiùmā 舅妈 same as 舅母 **jiùmǔ,** used as a form of address

jiùmǔ 舅母 mother's brother's wife, aunt

jiù 救 v save ■ 王医生及时动手术，救了他的命。 **Wáng yīshēng jíshí dòng shǒushù, jiùle tā de mìng.** *Dr Wang operated on him immediately and saved his life.* ■ 他在河中大叫，"救命！救命！" **Tā zài hé zhong dà jiào, "Jiù mìng! Jiù mìng!"** *He cried out in the river, "Help! Help!"*

jiùhù 救护 v give first aid, rescue

救护车 jiùhùchē ambulance / 救护人员 jiùhù rényuán rescue personnel, rescue team

jiùhuŏ 救火 v put out a fire, fire fighting
救火车 jiùhuŏchē fire engine

jiùjì 救济 v provide relief
救济物资 jiùjì wùzī relief supplies

jiù 就¹ PREP 1 with regard to, concerning ■ 商业部长就物价问题发表谈话。**Shāngyè bùzhăng jiù wùjià wèntí fābiăo tánhuà.** *The Minister of Commerce delivered a talk on prices.* **2** as far as ... is concerned, in terms of ■ 就人口来说，中国是世界上第一大国。**Jiù rénkŏu láishuō, Zhōngguó shì shìjiè shang dì-yī dà guó.** *In terms of population, China is the biggest country in the world.*

jiù 就² ADV as early as ..., as soon as ... (used before a verb to emphasize that the action takes place very early, very quickly or only for a very short period of time) ■ 他今天早上六点钟就起床了。**Tā jīntiān zăoshang liù diănzhōng jiù qĭchuáng le.** *He got up as early as six o'clock this morning.* ■ 我马上就来。**Wŏ măshàng jiù lái.** *I'll come immediately. (→ I'm coming.)*
一… 就 … yī … jiù … as soon as ... ■ 妈妈一下班就做晚饭。**Māma yí xiàbān jiù zuò wănfàn.** *Mom prepared supper as soon as she got off work.*

jiùjìn 就近 ADV nearby

jiùshì 就是 CONJ even if ■ 我就是不睡觉，也要做完这个作业。**Wŏ jiùshì bú shuìjiào, yě yào zuòwán zhège zuòyè.** *Even if I don't sleep, I must finish this assignment.* ■ 他们就是借钱，也要供儿子上大学。**Tāmen jiùshì jièqián, yě yào gòng érzi shàng dàxué.** *They are determined to put their son through university even if they have to borrow money.*

jiùyè 就业 v obtain employment

jiùzhí 就职 v take office

jū 居 v occupy, dwell

jūmín 居民 [modif: 居 occupy + 民 people] N resident, inhabitant

jūrán 居然 ADV unexpectedly, shockingly

jūzhù 居住 [comp: 居 occupy + 住 live] V & N reside; residency

jū 拘 v detain, arrest

jūliú 拘留 v hold in custody (for a given period of time)

jūshù 拘束 [comp: 拘 limit + 束 restrain] ADJ restrained, ill at ease

jú 局 N office

júbù 局部 ADJ part (not whole), local ■ 今天本市局部停电。**Jīntiān běnshì júbù tíngdiàn.** *Today parts of this city will not have power supply.*

júmiàn 局面 N situation, phase
打开局面 dăkāi júmiàn usher in a new phase, make a breakthrough

júshì 局势 N situation

júxiàn 局限 N limit

júzhăng 局长 [modif: 局 bureau + 长 chief] N director/chief of a bureau ■ 一个部下面有几个局，所以一位部长下面有几位局长。**Yí ge bù xiàmian yŏu jǐ ge jú, suŏyǐ yí wèi bùzhăng xiàmian yŏu jǐ wèi júzhăng.** *As there are several bureaus under a ministry, there are several bureau chiefs under a minister.*

jú 橘 N tangerine

júzi 橘子 [suffix: 橘 tangerine + 子 nominal suffix] N tangerine (只 zhī) ■ 苹果、香蕉、橘子，我都爱吃。**Píngguŏ, xiāngjiāo, júzi, wŏ dōu ài chī.** *I like apples, bananas and tangerines.*

NOTE: 橘子 **júzi** can also be written 桔子 **júzi**.

jū 鞠 v as in 鞠躬 **jūgōng**

jūgōng 鞠躬 v bow, take a bow

jǔ 举 TRAD 舉 v hold high, raise, lift ■ 谁同意，请举手！**Shuí tóngyì, qǐng jǔ shŏu!** *Those in favor [of the motion], please raise your hands.* ■ 举头望明月，低头思故乡 (李白) **Jǔ tóu wàng míng yuè, dī tóu sī gùxiāng (Lí Bái)** *I raise my head to gaze at the bright moon and hang my head yearning for my hometown (Li Bai) (lines from a poem by Li Bai)*

jǔbàn 举办 v host (an event, a conference, etc.)

jǔdòng 举动 N (body) movement, act
一举一动 yì jǔ yí dòng every movement (of a person)

jǔshì wénmíng 举世闻名 ADJ famous all over the world

jǔshì zhǔmù 举世瞩目 ADJ attracting worldwide attention

jǔxíng 举行 v hold (a meeting, a ceremony) ■ 下个月将举行国际会议，讨论这个问题。**Xiàge yuè jiāng jǔxíng guójì huìyì, tăolùn zhège wèntí.** *An international conference will be held next month to discuss this issue.*

jǔ zú qīng zhòng 举足轻重 IDIOM hold the balance, be decisive to the whole situation

jǔjué 咀嚼 v chew, masticate

jǔ 沮 as in 沮丧 jǔsàng

jǔsàng 沮丧 ADJ dejected, depressed

jù 巨 ADJ gigantic

jùdà 巨大 [comp: 巨 gigantic + 大 big] ADJ huge, gigantic, tremendous ■ 我们国家的经济发展取得了巨大的成绩。**Wŏmen guójiā de jīngjì fāzhăn qǔdéle jùdà de chéngjì.** *Our country has made tremendous achievements in economic development.*

jù 句 MEASURE WORD (for sentences)
一句话 yí jù huà one sentence / 这句话 zhè jù huà this sentence

jùzi 句子 [suffix: 句 sentence + 子 nominal suffix] N sentence (句 jù, 个 gè) ■ 张老师，这句句子什么意思？我看不懂。**Zhāng lăoshī, zhè jù jùzi shénme yìsi? Wŏ kàn bu dŏng.** *Teacher Zhang, what is the meaning of this sentence? I don't understand it.* ■ 这句句子语法不对。**Zhè jù jùzi yǔfă bú duì.** *The grammar of this sentence is wrong.*

jù 拒 v resist

jùjué 拒绝 v refuse, reject ■ 她拒绝了他的邀请。**Tā jùjuéle tā de yāoqǐng.** *She turned down his invitation.* ■ 他拒绝承认错误。**Tā jùjué chéngrèn cuòwù.** *He refused to admit to any wrongdoing.*

jù 具 v own, possess

jùbèi 具备 v possess, be provided with ■ 这个小城市不具备建立大学的条件。**Zhège xiǎo chéngshì bú jùbèi jiànlì dàxué de tiáojiàn.** *This small city does not possess the conditions necessary for establishing a university.*

jùtǐ 具体 ADV specific, concrete ■ 你说他这个人不好，能不能说得具体些？**Nǐ shuō tā zhège rén bù hǎo, néng bù néng shuōde jùtǐ xiē?** *You say he is not a good man. Can you be more specific?* ■ 请你举两三个具体的例子。**Qǐng nǐ jǔ liǎng-sān ge jùtǐ de lìzi.** *Please give two or three concrete examples.*

jùyǒu 具有 v have, possess, be provided with ■ 这一事件具有重大的历史意义。**Zhè yí shìjiàn jùyǒu zhòngdà de lìshǐ yìyì.** *This incident has major historic significance.* ■ 中国文化具有哪些特点？**Zhōngguó wénhuà jùyǒu nǎxiē tèdiǎn?** *What characteristic features does Chinese culture have?*

jù 俱 ADV together

jùlèbù 俱乐部 [modif: 俱 together + 乐 joy + 部 department] N club ■ 这个俱乐部每年要交多少会费？**Zhège jùlèbù měi nián yào jiāo duōshǎo huìfèi?** *What are the annual dues of this club?*

jù 惧 TRAD 懼 v fear (See **kǒngjù 恐惧**.)

jù 剧 TRAD 劇 N drama

jùběn 剧本 [modif: 剧 play + 本 book] N script of a play

电影剧本 **diànyǐng jùběn** script of a film, scenario

jùchǎng 剧场 [modif: 剧 drama + 场 site] N theater (座 **zuò**) ■ 今晚在剧场里有精彩演出。**Jīnwǎn zài jùchǎng li yǒu jīngcǎi yǎnchū.** *There will be a wonderful performance in the theater this evening.*

jùliè 剧烈 ADJ fierce, acute

剧烈的疼痛 **jùliè de téngtòng** acute pain

jù 据 TRAD 據 PREP according to

jùshuō 据说 v it is said, they say, rumor has it ■ 据说王小姐有很多男朋友。**Jùshuō Wáng xiǎojiě yǒu hěn duō nán péngyou.** *It is said that Miss Wang has many boyfirends.* ■ 据说，一家外国公司就要买下我们工厂了。**Jùshuō, yì jiā wàiguó gōngsī jiù yào mǎixia wǒmen gōngchǎng le.** *Rumor has it that a foreign company is going to buy our factory.*

jùxī 据悉 v it is reported that

jù 距 PREP (stretch of distance) from

jùlí 距离 N distance ■ 两地之间的距离有一百多公里。**Liǎngdì zhī jiān de jùlí yǒu yìbǎi duō gōnglǐ.** *The distance between the two places is over a hundred kilometers.* ■ 她和谁都保持一定距离。**Tā hé shuí dōu bǎochí yídìng jùlí.** *She keeps a distance from everybody. (→ She gives everyone a wide berth.)*

jù 聚 v assemble, get together

jùhuì 聚会 [comp: 聚 get together + 会 meet] N social gathering, (social) party

举行生日聚会 **jǔxíng shēngrì jùhuì** throw a birthday party

jù jīng huì shén 聚精会神 IDIOM give undivided attention to

juān 捐 v donate

juānkuǎi 捐款 [v+obj: 捐 donate + 款 fund] V & N contribute money, make a cash donation; cash donation, financial donation

juānxiàn 捐献 [comp: 捐 donate + 献 offer] v donate (something of considerable value)

juǎn 卷 v roll up ■ 他把地图卷起来，放在书架上。**Tā bǎ dìtú juǎn qǐlai, fàng zài shūjià shang.** *He rolled the map up and placed it on the bookshelf.*

juàn 倦 ADJ tired, fed up (See **píjuàn 疲倦**.)

juàn 绢 TRAD 絹 N silk (See **shǒujuàn 手绢**.)

jué 决 ADV definitely, under any circumstance (used before a negative word, e.g. 不 **bù**) ■ 我决不做任何对社会有害的事。**Wǒ jué bù zuò rènhé duì shèhuì yǒuhài de shì.** *I would never, ever, do anything that is harmful to society.*

juécè 决策 [v+obj: 决 decide + 策 policy] V & N decide on a policy, formulate strategy; policy decision, strategic decision (项 **xiàng**)

juédìng 决定 [comp: 决 determine + 定 decide] v & N decide, make up one's mind; decision ■ 你有没有决定买哪一辆汽车？**Nǐ yǒu méiyǒu juédìng mǎi nǎ yí liàng qìchē?** *Have you decided which car to buy?* ■ 我希望你改变这个决定。**Wǒ xīwàng nǐ gǎibiàn zhège juédìng.** *I hope you will change this decision.*

做决定 **zuò juédìng** make a decision ■ 买哪一座房子，他们还没有做决定。**Mǎi nǎ yí zuò fángzi, tāmen hái méiyǒu zuò juédìng.** *They haven't decided which house to buy.*

juésài 决赛 [modif: 决 decisive + 赛 match] N final game (of a match), final round, finals

juéxīn 决心 [modif: 决 determined + 心 heart] V & N be determined, make up one's mind; determination ■ 我们决心按时完成计划。**Wǒmen juéxīn ànshí wánchéng jìhuà.** *We are determined to fulfill the plan according to schedule.* ■ 我们有决心，有信心，一定按时完成计划。**Wǒmen yǒu juéxīn, yǒu xìnxīn, yídìng ànshí wánchéng jìhuà.** *We are determined, and we are confident, that we will fulfill the plan according to schedule.*

jué 觉 TRAD 覺 v feel

juéde 觉得 v feel, find, think ■ 我觉得你说的话很有道理。**Wǒ juéde nǐ shuō de huà hěn yǒu dàolǐ.** *I think what you said is quite true (or reasonable).* ■ 你觉得他的想法行不行？**Nǐ juéde tā de xiǎngfǎ xíng bu xíng?** *Do you think his idea will work?*

juéwù 觉悟 [comp: 觉 feel + 悟 realize] **v** gain understanding, become aware of

juéxǐng 觉醒 [觉 feel + 醒 awake] **v** be awakened (to truth, reality, etc.)

jué 绝 TRAD 絕 ADJ absolute

juéduì 绝对 ADJ absolute ■ 我告诉你的消息绝对正确。**Wǒ gàosù nǐ de xiāoxi juéduì zhèngquè.** *The news I told you is absolutely correct.*

绝对多数 juéduì duōshù absolute majority

jué 角 **N** role, part

juésè 角色 **N** role, part

jué 倔 ADJ as in 倔强 **juéjiàng**

juéjiàng 倔强 ADJ stubborn, unbending

jué 掘 **v** dig (See wājué 挖掘.)

jué 嚼 **v** same as 嚼 **jiáo** (See jǔjué 咀嚼.)

NOTE: **jué** 嚼 is pronounced as **jué** only in **jǔjué** 咀嚼, which is a medical term. In everyday Chinese 嚼 is pronounced as **jiáo**. See **jiáo** 嚼.

jūn 军 TRAD 軍 **N** army, armed forces

中国人民解放军 Zhōngguó Rénmín Jiěfàng Jūn the Chinese People's Liberation Army (PLA) / 海军 hǎijūn navy / 空军 kōngjūn air force / 陆军 lùjūn army

jūnduì 军队 [modif: 军 army + 队 rows of people] **N** armed forces, troops

jūnhuǒ 军火 **N** arms and ammunition

jūnrén 军人 **N** soldier (名 **míng**)

jūnshì 军事 [modif: 军 army + 事 affair] **N** military affairs ■ 军事上的事，我不大懂。**Jūnshì shang de shì, wǒ bú dà dǒng.** *I don't know much about military affairs.*

jūnzhuāng 军装 **N** army uniform (套 **tào**)

jūn 均 ADJ equal

jūnyún 均匀 ADJ well distributed, evenly applied

jūn 君 **N 1** monarch **2** gentleman

jūnzhǔ 君主 **N** monarch

君主立宪 jūnzhǔ lìxiàn constitutional monarchy

jūnzǐ 君子 **N** cultured and honorable man, gentleman (ANTONYM 小人 **xiǎorén**)

NOTE: In Confucianism 君子 **jūnzǐ** refers to a *cultured gentleman* and *a man of virtue*. 君子 **jūnzǐ** is in contrast with 小人 **xiǎorén** *a mean person* or *an inferior being.*

jūn 菌 **N** fungus, bacterium (See xìjūn 细菌.)

jùn 俊 ADJ handsome (See yīngjùn 英俊.)

K

kāfēi 咖啡 **N** coffee (杯 **bēi**) ■ 这种咖啡很好喝。**Zhè zhǒng kāfēi hěn hǎohē.** *This kind of coffee tastes good.* ■ 从厨房飘来咖啡的香味。**Cóng chúfáng piāolai kāfēi de xiāngwèi.** *The aroma of coffee floated in from the kitchen.*

冲咖啡 chōng kāfēi make (instant) coffee / 煮咖啡 zhǔ kāfēi brew coffee

NOTE: 咖啡 **kāfēi** is one of the few transliterations (音译词 **yīnyìcí**) in Chinese vocabulary, as it represents more or less the sound of "coffee."

kǎ 卡 **N** card (张 **zhāng**) ■ 这张卡很重要，你要放好了。**Zhè zhāng kǎ hěn zhòngyào, nǐ yào fànghǎo le.** *This is a very important card. Keep it safely.*

贺卡 hèkǎ greeting card / 信用卡 xìnyòng kǎ credit card / 银行卡 yínháng kǎ banking card

kǎchē 卡车 **N** lorry, truck (辆 **liàng**) ■ 开过来一辆卡车。**Kāi guòlái yí liàng kǎchē.** *A truck is coming.* ■ 我叔叔是个卡车司机。**Wǒ shūshu shì ge kǎchē sījī.** *My uncle is a truck driver.*

NOTE: The composition of 卡车 **kǎchē** is semi-transliteration (半音译词 **bàn yīnyìcí**): 卡 **kǎ** represents the sound of the English word "car" and 车 **chē** means *vehicle*. See 咖啡 **kāfēi** for an example of transliteration.

kǎtōng 卡通 **N** cartoon, caricature

kāi 开 TRAD 開 **v 1** open, open up (ANTONYM 关 **guān**) ■ 开开门！**Kāikai mén!** *Open the door, please!* **2** turn on, switch on (ANTONYM 关 **guān**) ■ 天黑了，开灯吧。**Tiān hēi le, kāi dēng ba.** *It's dark. Let's turn on the light.* **3** drive (a vehicle), pilot (a plane) ■ 我会开汽车，不会开飞机。**Wǒ huì kāi qìchē, bú huì kāi fēijī.** *I can drive a car, but I can't pilot a plane.*

kāicǎi 开采 **v** mine, excavate

kāichú 开除 **v** expel

被学校开除 bèi xuéxiào kāichú be expelled from the school

kāifā 开发 [comp: 开 open + 发 develop] **v** develop (resources, products, etc.), open up and exploit ■ 这个地区资源丰富，经济落后，需要开发。**Zhège dìqū zīyuán fēngfù, jīngjì luòhòu, xūyào kāifā.** *This region is rich in natural resources but is backward economically. It needs developing.* ■ 我们公司花大量资金研究开发新产品。**Wǒmen gōngsī huā dàliàng zījīn yánjiū kāifā xīn chǎnpǐn.** *Our company spends large amounts of funds on researching and developing new products.*

kāifàng 开放 [comp: 开 open + 放 release] **v** open, open up ■ 这个展览会从下周起对外开放。**Zhège zhǎnlǎnhuì cóng xià zhōu qǐ duìwài kāifàng.** *This exhibition will open to the public next week.*

kāiguān 开关 **N** switch ■ 这个机器的开关坏了。**Zhège jīqì de kāiguān huài le.** *The switch of this machine is out of order.*

kāihuì 开会 [v+obj: 开 open up + 会 meeting] **v** attend a meeting, hold a meeting ■ 我们最好开个会，讨论一下这个问题。**Wǒmen zuìhǎo kāi ge huì, tǎolùn yíxià zhège wèntí.** *We'd best have a meeting to discuss this issue.*

kāikuò 开阔 [comp: 开 open + 阔 wide] ADJ open and wide, expansive, spacious

kāilǎng 开朗 ADJ broad-minded and outspoken, always cheerful

性格开朗 xìnggé kāilǎng of cheerful disposition

kāimén 开门 N open for business ■ "这里的商店什么时候开门？" "九点钟开门。" **"Zhèli de shāngdiàn shénme shíhou kāimén?" "Jiǔ diǎnzhōng kāimén."** *"When do stores here open for business?" "Nine o'clock."*

kāimíng 开明 ADJ civilized, enlightened

kāimù 开幕 [v+obj: 开 open + 幕 curtain] V (of a play, a ceremony, conference, etc.) open, start

kāimù shì 开幕式 N opening ceremony

kāipì 开辟 [comp: 开 open up + 辟 open up] V open up, start ■ 这里要开辟成特别经济区。**Zhèli yào kāipì chéng tèbié jīngjìqū.** *A special economic zone will be started here.*

kāishǐ 开始 [comp: 开 open + 始 begin] V & N begin, commence (ANTONYM 结束 jiéshù); beginning, start ■ 我从明年一月一日开始每天跑步半小时。**Wǒ cóng míngnián Yíyuè yírì kāishǐ měi tiān pǎobù bàn xiǎoshí.** *I'll begin jogging half an hour every day from January 1 next year.* ■ 开始我觉得中文非常难，现在觉得不太难了。**Kāishǐ wǒ juéde Zhōngwén fēicháng nán, xiànzài juéde bú tài nán le.** *At the beginning I found Chinese very difficult, but now I think it's not too difficult.*

kāishuǐ 开水 N boiled water

kāituò 开拓 V open up

kāi wánxiào 开玩笑 V joke ■ 别开玩笑了！**Bié kāi wánxiào le!** *Stop kidding!* ■ 这是很严肃的事，你不要开玩笑。**Zhè shì hěn yánsù de shì, nǐ bú yào kāi wánxiào.** *This is a very serious matter. Don't joke about it. (→ This is no laughing matter.)*

跟/和 … 开玩笑 gēn/hé … kāi wánxiào joke with …, make fun of … ■ 他常常跟妹妹开玩笑。**Tā chángcháng gēn mèimei kāi wánxiào.** *He often jokes with his younger sister.*

kāi yèchē 开夜车 burn the midnight oil ■ 明天要交作业，今天晚上我得开夜车。**Míngtiān yào jiāo zuòyè, jīntiān wǎnshang wǒ děi kāi yèchē.** *I must hand in my assignment tomorrow. I'll have to burn the midnight oil tonight.*

kāixué 开学 [v+obj: 开 open + 学 school] V start (school) ■ 中国的学校一般九月一日开学。你们国家的学校哪一天开学？**Zhōngguó de xuéxiào yìbān Jiǔyuè yírì kāixué. Nǐmen guójiā de xuéxiào nǎ yì tiān kāixué?** *Schools in China usually start on September 1. On which day does school begin in your country?*

kāiyǎn 开演 [v+obj: 开 open + 演 performance] V start (a performance, a film, etc.) ■ 电影什么候开演？**Diànyǐng shénme shíhou kāiyǎn?** *When does the film start?*

kāizhǎn 开展 [comp: 开 open up + 展 fold] V launch, develop, expand ■ 他一当上经理，就积极开展业务。**Tā yì dāngshang jīnglǐ, jiù jījí kāizhǎn yèwù.** *As soon as he became manager, he actively expanded the business.*

kāizhī 开支 I V pay II N expenditure, expenses 日常家用开支 rìcháng jiāyòng kāizhī daily household expenses

kān 刊 V publish

kāndēng 刊登 V publish (in a newspaper, magazine, etc.)

kānwù 刊物 [modif: 刊 publish + 物 things] N periodical, journal, magazine

kān 勘 V survey

kāntàn 勘探 V & N explore, prospect (for mineral resouces); prospecting, exploration 石油勘探队 shíyóu kāntànduì oil prospecting team

kǎn kǎn ér tán 侃侃而谈 IDIOM speak with great ease and confidence

kǎn 砍 V chop, hack ■ 这棵树要砍掉。**Zhè kē shù yào kǎndiào.** *This tree should be chopped down.*

kǎnfá 砍伐 V fell trees, limber

kàn 看 V 1 look, see ■ 我看看你的新衣服。**Wǒ kànkan nǐ de xīn yīfu.** *Let me have a look at your new dress.* 2 watch (TV, a movie, etc.) 3 read ■ "你每天看报吗？" "我不每天看报。" **"Nǐ měi tiān kàn bào ma?" "Wǒ bù měi tiān kàn bào."** *"Do you read newspapers every day?" "No."* 看电视 kàn diànshì watch TV / 看电影 kàn diànyǐng watch a film / 看体育比赛 kàn tǐyù bǐsài watch a sport event

NOTE: See note on 看见 **kànjiàn**.

kànbìng 看病 [v+obj: 看 see + 病 illness] V see a doctor ■ 我下午要请半天假，去看病。**Wǒ xiàwǔ yào qǐng bàn tiān jià, qù kànbìng.** *I'll ask for half-day leave to see a doctor this afternoon.*

kànbuqǐ 看不起 V look down upon, despise ■ 我看不起这种不老实的人。**Wǒ kànbuqǐ zhè zhǒng bù lǎoshí de rén.** *I despise such dishonest people.* 看得起 kàndeqǐ respect, hold in esteem

kàndài 看待 V look on, regard, treat

kànfǎ 看法 [modif: 看 view + 法 way, method] N 1 way of looking at things, view ■ 你的看法不一定对。**Nǐ de kànfǎ bù yídìng duì.** *Your view is not necessarily correct.* 2 negative opinion ■ 他对我有看法。**Tā duì wǒ yǒu kànfǎ.** *He has a negative opinion of me.*

kànjiàn 看见 [v+compl: 看 look + 见 see] V see, get sight of ■ 我朝山上看了很久，才看见一个人在爬山。**Wǒ cháo shān shang kànle hěn jiǔ, cái kànjiàn yí ge rén zài pá shān.** *I looked at the hill for a long time before I saw a man climbing.* 看不见 kàn bu jiàn cannot see / 看得见 kàn de jiàn can see ■ "山上的人，你看得见吗？" "看不见。" **"Shān shang de rén, nǐ kàn de jiàn**

ma?" **"Kàn bu jiàn."** *"Can you see the man (or people) on the hill?" "No, I can't."* / 没看见 méi kànjiàn fail to see ■ 我没看见他在图书馆里。**Wǒ méi kànjiàn tā zài túshūguǎn li.** *I did not see him in the library.*

NOTE: While 看 **kàn** is *to look* or *to look at*, 看见 **kànjiàn** is *to see* or *to catch sight* of. For example: ■ 我朝窗外看，没有看见什么。**Wǒ cháo chuāng wài kàn, méiyǒu kànjiàn shénme.** *I looked out of the window and did not see anything.*

kànlái 看来 ADV it looks as if, it seems as if ■ 看来要下大雨了。**Kànlái yào xià dà yǔ le.** *It seems that a downpour is coming our way.* ■ 他看来很能干。**Tā kànlái hěn nénggàn.** *He looks like a very able man.*

kànwàng 看望 [comp: 看 see + 望 look] V call on, pay a visit to ■ 我每年过年都要看望中学时的老师。**Wǒ měi nián guònián dōu yào kànwàng zhōngxué shí de lǎoshī.** *I pay a visit to my high school teacher every New Year's Day.*

kànyàngzi 看样子 ADV same as 看来 **kànlái**

kāng 康 N good health (See **jiànkāng** 健康.)

kāngkǎi 慷慨 ADJ generous, liberal

káng 扛 V carry on the shoulder

kàng 抗 V resist

kàngyì 抗议 V & N protest ■ 许多居民抗议建造新机场。**Xǔduō jūmín kàngyì jiànzào xīn jīchǎng.** *Many residents protested against the building of a new airport.*

kǎo 考 V examine, test ■ 下星期二考中文。**Xià Xīngqī'èr kǎo Zhōngwén.** *There will be an examination on Chinese next Tuesday.* ■ 他不是不知道怎么回答，而是要考考你。**Tā bú shì bù zhīdào zěnme huídá, érshì yào kǎokao nǐ.** *It is not that he did not know how to answer the question, but that he wanted to test you.*

考得好 kǎo de hǎo do well in an examination / 考得不好 kǎo de bù hǎo do poorly in an examination

kǎochá 考察 [comp: 考 examine + 察 investigate] V inspect, make a on-the-spot investigation, test and judge (a person)

kǎogǔ 考古 [V+OBJ: 考 examine + 古 ancient] V do archaeological studies

考古学 kǎogǔxué archaeology / 考古学家 kǎogǔxué jiā archaeologist

kǎohé 考核 [comp: 考 examine + 核 check] V appraise, check, assess

年终考核 niánzhōng kǎohé annual (staff) performance review

kǎolǜ 考虑 V think over carefully, consider, contemplate ■ 我要好好考虑一下你的建议，明天给你回答。**Wǒ yào hǎohǎo kǎolǜ yíxià nǐ de jiànyì, míngtiān gěi nǐ huídá.** *I need to consider your suggestion carefully. I will give you a reply tomorrow.*

■ 他正在考虑转到另一个学校去。**Tā zhèngzài kǎolǜ zhuǎndào lìng yí ge xuéxiào qu.** *He is contemplating transferring to another school.*

kǎoshì 考试 [comp: 考 examine, inquire + 试 test] V & N examine, test; examination, test (次 cì) ■ 我们明天考试。**Wǒmen míngtiān kǎoshì.** *We're having an examination tomorrow.* ■ 这次考试太难了！**Zhè cì kǎoshì tài nán le!** *This test was really difficult!*

汉语水平考试 Hànyǔ Shuǐpíng Kǎoshì (HSK) Chinese Proficiency Test

kǎoyàn 考验 [comp: 考 test + 验 examine] V & N test, put through rigorous testing; testing

kǎo 烤 V bake, roast ■ 中国人很少吃烤牛肉。**Zhōngguórén hěn shǎo chī kǎo niúròu.** *The Chinese rarely eat roast beef.*

kǎo yā 烤鸭 N roast duck

kào 靠 V rely on, depend on ■ 这事全靠你了。**Zhè shì quán kào nǐ le.** *This matter depends entirely on you.* ■ 做事不能靠运气。**Zuòshì bù néng kào yùnqi.** *You cannot rely on luck to get things done.*

靠得住 kàodezhù trustworthy, reliable / 靠不住 kàobuzhù untrustworthy, unreliable

kàolǒng 靠拢 V draw close, close up

kē 科 N classification

kēmù 科目 N (school) subject, course

kēxué 科学 [modif: 科 classification + 学 study] N science ■ 科学能解决世界上所有的问题吗？**Kēxué néng jiějué shìjiè shang suǒyǒu de wèntí ma?** *Can science solve all the problems in the world?* ■ 我丈夫学科学，我学语言。**Wǒ zhàngfu xué kēxué, wǒ xué yǔyán.** *My husband studies science, and I study languages.*

科学研究（科研）kēxué yánjiū (kēyán) scientific research / 科学院 kēxué yuàn academy of sciences / 中国科学院 Zhōngguó Kēxué Yuàn Chinese Academy of Sciences

kēxuéjiā 科学家 [modif: 科学 science + 家 nominal suffix] N scientist (位 wèi) ■ 这座大学有几位世界著名的科学家。**Zhè zuò dàxué yǒu jǐ wèi shìjiè zhùmíng de kēxuéjiā.** *This university has several world-renowned scientists.*

kē 棵 MEASURE WORD (for plants) 三棵树 sān kē shù three trees / 一棵草 yì kē cǎo a blade of grass

kē 颗 MEASURE WORD (for beans, pearls, etc.) 一颗黄豆 yìkē huángdòu a soybean

kēlì 颗粒 N 1 pellet 2 grain

kē 磕 V knock (against something hard)

ké 咳 V cough

késou 咳嗽 [comp: 咳 cough + 嗽 cough up] V cough ■ 这个病人每天夜里都咳嗽。**Zhège bìngrén měi tiān yèli dōu késou.** *The patient coughs every night.* ■ 你咳嗽得厉害，得去看病。**Nǐ késou hěn lìhai, děi qù kànbìng.** *You've got a bad cough. You need to see a doctor.*

咳嗽药水 késou yàoshuǐ cough syrup

késoutáng 咳嗽糖 N cough lozenge

ké 壳 TRAD 殼 N shell (See **bèiké** 贝壳.)

kě 可[1] ADV 1 indeed (used before an adjective for emphasis) ■ 当父母可不容易呢！Dāng fùmǔ kě bù róngyì ne! *Being a parent is indeed no easy job!* ■ 她跳舞跳得可美啦。Tā tiàowǔ tiào de kě měi la. *She dances really beautifully!* 2 after all (used before a verb for emphasis) ■ 我可找到你了！Wǒ kě zhǎodào nǐ le! *I've found you after all.* ■ 他可出院了。Tā kě chūyuàn le. *He was discharged from the hospital after all.* 3 be sure to (used in an imperative sentence for emphasis) ■ 可别忘了给他发一份电子邮件。Kě bié wàngle gěi tā fā yí fèn diànzǐ yóujiàn! *Be sure not to forget to send him an e-mail. (→ Be sure to send him an e-mail.)* ■ 考试的时候可要看懂题目。Kǎoshì de shíhou kě yào kàndǒng tímù. *During an examination, make sure that you understand the questions.*

NOTE: 可 kě is only used colloquially. When using 可 kě to emphasize an adjective or a verb, 啦 la, 呢 ne or 了 le is often used at the end of the sentence.

kě 可[2] CONJ same as 可是 **kěshì**

kě'ài 可爱 ADJ lovable, lovely

kěguān 可观 ADJ considerable, sizeable

一笔可观的现金 yìbǐ kěguān de xiànjīn a considerable sum of cash

kějiàn 可见 CONJ it can be seen, it is thus clear

kěkào 可靠 V reliable, trustworthy ■ 很难找到可靠的人来管理秘密文件。Hěn nán zhǎodào kěkào de rén lái guǎnlǐ mìmìwénjiàn. *It is difficult to find a trustworthy person to take care of confidential documents.* ■ 你这个消息可靠吗？Nǐ zhège xiāoxi kěkào ma? *Is your news reliable?*

kěkǒu 可口 ADJ palatable, tasty

kělián 可怜 ADJ pitiful, pitiable ■ 这小孩的父母在交通事故中死了，真可怜！Zhè xiǎohái de fùmǔ zài jiāotōng shìgù zhong sǐ le, zhēn kělián! *Both his parents died in a road accident, the poor child!*

kěnéng 可能 [comp: 可 may + 能 can] I MODAL V may, possible, possibly ■ 他两天没来上课，可能病了。Tā liǎng tiān méi lái shàngkè, kěnéng bìng le. *He's been absent from class for two days. He may be ill.* II N possibility ■ 这种可能是有的。Zhè zhǒng kěnéng shì yǒu de. *This is possible.* (没)有可能 (méi) yǒu kěnéng (im)possible, (im-)possibly ■ "这件事有解决的可能吗？""有可能。" "Zhè jiàn shì yǒu jiějué de kěnéng ma?" "Yǒu kěnéng." *"Is it possible to solve this matter?" "Yes."*

kěkǒukělè 可口可乐 N Coca-Cola (瓶 **píng**)

百事可乐 bǎishìkělè Pepsi[-Cola]

NOTE: 可口可乐 kěkǒukělè is a transliteration of "Coca-Cola." It can be shortened into 可乐 kělè.

kěpà 可怕 ADJ fearsome, frightening ■ 这种病很可怕，还没有药治。Zhè zhǒng bìng hěn kěpà, hái méiyǒu yào zhì. *This disease is frightening, as there is still no medicine for it.*

kěshì 可是 CONJ same as 但是 **dànshì**.

kěwù 可恶 ADJ detestable, hateful

kěxī 可惜 ADJ be a pity, be a shame ■ 真可惜！Zhēn kěxī! *What a shame!*

kěxiào 可笑 ADJ laughable, ridiculous

kěxíng 可行 ADJ can be done, feasible

可行性 kěxíngxìng feasibility / 可行性报告 kěxíngxìng bàogào feasibility report

kěyǐ 可以 MODAL V giving permission, may, can, be allowed ■ "我可以走了吗？" "可以。" "Wǒ kěyǐ zǒu le ma?" "Kěyǐ." *"May I leave now?" "Yes, you may."* ■ 你不可以把阅览室的书带回家。Nǐ bù kěyǐ bǎ yuèlǎnshì de shū dàihuí jiā. *You are not allowed to take books home from the reading room.*

kě 渴 ADJ thirsty ■ 我渴了，请给我一杯水。Wǒ kě le, qǐng gěi wǒ yì bēi shuǐ. *I'm thirsty. Please give me a glass of water.*

口渴 kǒukě thirsty ■ 你口渴吗？这里有水。Nǐ kǒu kě ma? Zhèli yǒu shuǐ. *Are you thirsty? Here's some water.*

NOTE: See note on 喝 **hē**.

kěwàng 渴望 [comp: 渴 thirsty + 望 hope] V thirst for, long for

kè 克 MEASURE WORD gram

五百克 wǔbǎi kè 500 grams

kèfú 克服 V overcome, conquer ■ 我相信一定能克服这些暂时的困难。Wǒ xiāngxìn yídìng néng kèfú zhèxiē zànshí de kùnnan. *I am convinced that we are surely able to overcome these temporary difficulties.*

kèzhì 克制 V restrain, exercise restraint

kè 刻[1] V carve ■ 他在石头上刻上自己的名字。Tā zài shítou shang kè shang zìjǐ de míngzi. *He carved his name on the rock.*

kè 刻[2] MEASURE WORD quarter of an hour

一刻钟 yí kè zhōng a quarter of an hour; 15 minutes / 三点一刻 sān diǎn yí kè a quarter past three

kè bu róng huǎn 刻不容缓 IDIOM demand immediate action, of extreme urgency

kèkǔ 刻苦 ADJ hardworking, assiduous, painstaking ■ 这位科学家刻苦研究十几年，终于找到了答案。Zhè wèi kēxuéjiā kèkǔ yánjiū shí jǐ nián, zhōngyú zhǎodào le dá'àn. *The scientist researched arduously for a dozen years and finally found the answer.*

kè 客 N guest

kèguān 客观 ADJ 1 objective 2 impartial, without bias

kèhù 客户 N client, customer, buyer

kèqi 客气 [modif: 客 guest + 气 manner] ADJ 1 polite, stand on ceremony ■ 您跟我们一起吃午饭

吧，别客气。**Nín gēn wǒmen yìqǐ chī wǔfàn ba, bié kèqi.** *Have lunch with us. Don't stand on ceremony.*
2 modest ■ 你唱歌唱得这么好，还说不好，太客气了。**Nǐ chànggē chàng de zhème hào, hái shuō bù hǎo, tài kèqi le.** *You sing so well but you still say you don't sing well. You're too modest.*

kèren 客人 N guest, visitor ■ 宴会八点钟开始，七点三刻客人陆续到来。**Yànhuì bā diǎnzhōng kāishǐ, qī diǎn sān kè kèren lùxù dàolai.** *The banquet began at eight o'clock; guests arrived one after another at a quarter to eight.*

kètīng 客厅 [modif: 客 guest + 厅 hall] **N** living room, sitting room

kè 课 TRAD 課 N lesson, class, lecture ■ 今天的课你听懂没有？**Jīntiān de kè nǐ tīngdǒng méiyǒu?** *Do you understand today's lesson?*
上课 shàng kè go to class / 下课 xià kè finish class

kèběn 课本 [modif: 课 lesson + 本 book] **N** textbook, course book (本 **běn**) ■ 王老师打算编一本适合日本学生学中文的课本。**Wáng lǎoshī dǎsuàn biān yì běn shìhé Rìběn xuésheng xué Zhōngwén de kèběn.** *Teacher Wang plans to compile a textbook suitable for Japanese students of Chinese.*

kèchéng 课程 [modif: 课 lesson + 程 course] **N** course, a program of study ■ 医学课程花的时间比其他课程长。**Yīxué kèchéng huā de shíjiān bǐ qítā kèchéng cháng.** *A course in medicine takes more time than other courses.* ■ 我们的课程排得很满，没有多少时间搞课外活动。**Wǒmen de kèchéng pái de hěn mǎn, méiyǒu duōshǎo shíjiān gǎo kèwài huódòng.** *Our timetable is very crowded and leaves little time for extracurricular activities.*

kètí 课题 N research topic

kèwén 课文 [modif: 课 lesson + 文 writing] **N** text (篇 **piān**) ■ 我要多念几遍课文。**Wǒ yào duō niàn jǐ biàn kèwén.** *I should read the text a few more times.*

kěn 肯 MODAL V be willing to ■ 你肯不肯帮我做一件事？**Nǐ kěn bu kěn bāng wǒ zuò yí jiàn shì?** *Are you willing to do something for me? (→ Would you do me a favor?)* ■ 中国的父母一般肯为孩子作出牺牲。**Zhōngguó de fù-mǔ yìbān kěn wèi háizi zuòchu xīshēng.** *Generally speaking, Chinese parents are willing to make sacrifices for their children.*

kěndìng 肯定 V & ADJ confirm, acknowledge; affirmative, positive, definite (ANTONYM 否定 **fǒudìng**) ■ 总公司充分肯定你们的成绩。**Zǒnggōngsī chōngfèn kěndìng nǐmen de chéngjì.** *The company's head office fully acknowledges your achievements.* ■ 很抱歉，我不能给你一个肯定的回答。**Hěn bàoqiàn, wǒ bù néng gěi nǐ yí ge kěndìng de huídá.** *I'm sorry, but I'm not in a position to give you a definite reply.*

kěn 啃 V gnaw, nibble

kěn 恳 TRAD 懇 ADJ sincere

kěnqiè 恳切 ADJ earnest, sincere

kēng 坑 N pit, hollow

kōng 空 ADJ empty ■ 箱子是空的，里面什么也没有。**Xiāngzi shì kōng de, lǐmiàn shénme yě méiyǒu.** *The suitcase is empty; there's nothing in it.*

kōngdòng 空洞 [modif: 空 empty + 洞 cave] **ADJ** hollow, devoid of content
空洞的承诺 kōngdòng de chéngnuò hallow promise

kōngjiān 空间 N space, room ■ 要给孩子留一些空间，让他做自己喜欢做的事。**Yào gěi háizi liú yìxiē kōngjiān, ràng tā zuò zìjǐ xǐhuan zuò de shì.** *Leave a child room (or time) to let him do what he enjoys doing.*

kōngqì 空气 [modif: 空 empty + 气 vapor] **N** air ■ 这里的空气真好！**Zhèli de kōngqì zhēn hǎo!** *The air here is really fresh.* ■ 空气是由什么组成的？**Kōngqì shì yóu shénme zǔchéng de?** *What is air composed of?*

kōngqián 空前 ADJ unprecedented ■ 这种经济增长的速度是空前的。**Zhè zhǒng jīngjì zēngzhǎng de sùdù shì kōngqián de.** *This kind of economic growth rate is unprecedented.*

kōng qián jué hòu 空前绝后 IDIOM unprecedented and unrepeatable

kōngtiáo 空调 N air conditioning
有空调的房间 yǒu kōngtiáo de fángjiān air conditioned room

kōngtiáojī 空调机 N air conditioner

kōngxiǎng 空想 [modif: 空 empty + 想 thinking] **N** pipe-dream, fantasy

kōngxū 空虚 [comp: 空 empty + 虚 void] **ADJ** void, empty
生活空虚 shēnghuó kōngxū live a life devoid of any meaning

kōngzhōng 空中 N in the sky, in the air ■ 他们在表演空中飞人的节目。**Tāmen zài biǎoyǎn kōngzhōng fēirén de jiémù.** *They are performing on the flying trapeze.*

kǒng 孔 N aperture, hole ■ 这座桥有三个孔。**Zhè zuò qiáo yǒu sān ge kǒng.** *The bridge has three arches.*

kǒngbù 恐 V fear

kǒngbù 恐怖 [comp: 恐 fear, dread + 怖 terrifying] **ADJ** horrible, terrifying ■ 这个电影太恐怖了，小孩子不能看。**Zhège diànyǐng tài kǒngbù le, xiǎo háizi bù néng kàn.** *This film is too frightening for children to see.*
恐怖电影 kǒngbù diànyǐng horror movie / 恐怖分子 kǒngbù fènzǐ terrorist / 恐怖主义 kǒngbù zhǔyì terrorism

kǒnghè 恐吓 V intimidate, bluster by threats

kǒngjù 恐惧 [comp: 恐 fear + 惧 fear] **V** be in great fear of, dread

kǒngpà 恐怕 [comp: 恐 fear, dread + 怕 fear] **ADV** I'm afraid, perhaps ■ 他的病恐怕两三天好不了。**Tā de bìng kǒngpà liǎng-sān tiān hǎobuliǎo.** *I'm afraid he won't recover in a couple of days.*

NOTE: 恐怕 **kǒngpà** and 也许 **yěxǔ** may both mean *perhaps,* but 恐怕 **kǒngpà** implies that what will perhaps happen is undesirable.

kòng 控 v control

kòngzhì 控制 v control ■ 我们要控制人口的增长，提高人口的质量。 **Wǒmen yào kòngzhì rénkǒu de zēngzhǎng, tígāo rénkǒu de zhìliàng.** *We should control population growth and raise population quality.* ■ 她控制不住自己的感情，大哭起来。 **Tā kòngzhì bú zhù zìjǐ de gǎnqíng, dàkū qǐlai.** *She couldn't control her emotions and began to cry loudly.*

kòng 空 I v leave empty or blank II N free time, unoccupied space ■ "你今天晚上有空吗？" "我今天晚上没有空，明天晚上有空。" **"Nǐ jīntiān wǎnshang yǒukòng ma?" "Wǒ jīntiān wǎnshang méiyǒu kòng, míngtiān wǎnshang yǒu kòng."** *"Are you free this evening?" "No, I'm not. I'll be free tomorrow evening."* ■ 你有空常来玩。 **Nǐ yǒu kòng cháng lái wán.** *Do come to visit us when you have time.*

kòngbái 空白 [comp: 空 vacant + 白 white] N blank space

kòngxì 空隙 [comp: 空 vacant + 隙 crack] N narrow gap, brief interval

kòngxián 空闲 ADJ & N be free, not occupied; free time, leisure

kǒu 口 I N mouth ■ 病从口入。 **Bìng cóng kǒu rù.** *Disease enters your body by the mouth. (→ Bad food causes disease.)* II MEASURE WORD (for members of a family) ■ 我家有四口人。 **Wǒ jiā yǒu sì kǒu rén.** *There're four people in my family.*

kǒuchī 口吃 v stammer, stutter

kǒudài 口袋 N pocket (只 **zhī**) ■ 他喜欢把手插在口袋里。 **Tā xǐhuan bǎ shǒu chā zài kǒudài li.** *He likes to put his hands in his pockets.*

kǒuhào 口号 N slogan (条 **tiáo**) ■ 这种政治口号已经没有人喊了。 **Zhè zhǒng zhèngzhì kǒuhào yǐjīng méiyǒu rén hǎn le.** *Nobody shouts such political slogans any more.*

kǒuqì 口气 N 1 tone (of speech) 温和的口气 **wēnhé de kǒuqì** gentle tone 2 manner of speaking 听他的口气 **tīng tāde kǒuqì** judging by the way he spoke

kǒuqiāng 口腔 N oral cavity

kǒutóu 口头 ADJ oral, spoken 口头协议 **kǒutóu xiéyì** verbal agreement

kǒuwèi 口味 N 1 flavor or taste of food 2 one's taste ■ 各人的口味不一样。 **Gè rén de kǒuwèi bù yíyàng.** *Tastes differ.*

kǒuyīn 口音 N accent

kǒuyǔ 口语 [modif: 口 the mouth + 语 speech] N spoken language, speech ■ 我中文口语不行，很多话不会说。 **Wǒ Zhōngwén kǒuyǔ bù xíng, hěn duō huà bú huì shuō.** *My oral Chinese is rather*

poor. There are many things I can't express. ■ 他喜欢找中国人说话练口语。 **Tā xǐhuan zhǎo Zhōngguórén shuōhuà liàn kǒuyǔ.** *He likes to talk with Chinese to practice his oral Chinese.*

kòu 扣 v buckle, fasten up

kòuyā 扣押 v detain, hold in custody

kū 哭 v cry, weep, sob (ANTONYM 笑 **xiào**) ■ 别哭了，有话好好说。 **Bié kū le, yǒu huà hǎohǎo shuō.** *Don't cry. Speak up if you have something to say.* ■ 她难过得哭起来。 **Tā nánguò de kū qǐlai.** *She was so sad that she cried.*

kūqì 哭泣 v sob, cry softly

kū xiào bu dé 哭笑不得 IDIOM not know whether to laugh or cry, find something both funny and annoying

kū 枯 ADJ withered

kūjié 枯竭 ADJ dry up, exhausted

kūwěi 枯萎 ADJ withered

kūzào 枯燥 [comp: 枯 withered + 燥 dry] ADJ dull and dry 枯燥乏味 **kūzào fáwèi** dull and insipid

kǔ 苦 ADJ 1 (of food) bitter ■ 这杯咖啡太苦了，要放点儿糖。 **Zhè bēi kāfēi tài kǔ le, yào fàng diǎnr táng.** *This coffee is too bitter. Put a bit of sugar in it.* 2 (of life) hard, suffering, miserable ■ 经济不好，不少人生活很苦。 **Jīngjì bù hǎo, bù shǎo rén shēnghuó hěn kǔ.** *As the economy is not in good shape, many people's lives are very hard.* 吃苦 **chīkǔ** suffer hardships, endure hardships

kǔ jìn gān lái 苦尽甘来 IDIOM after suffering comes happiness

kǔsè 苦涩 ADJ 1 (of taste) bitter and astringent 2 (of emotion) pained, agonized

kù 裤 TRAD 褲 N trousers

kùzi 裤子 [suffix: 裤 trousers + 子 nominal suffix] N trousers (条 **tiáo**) ■ 这条裤子短了一点儿。 **Zhè tiáo kùzi duǎnle yìdiǎnr.** *This pair of trousers is a bit too short.* ■ 这个小孩会脱裤子，但还不会穿裤子。 **Zhège xiǎohái huì tuō kùzi, dàn hái bú huì chuān kùzi.** *This child can take off his trousers, but still can't put them on.*

kù 酷[1] ADJ cruel (See **cánkù** 残酷.)

kù 酷[2] ADJ cool, relaxed and fashionable, attractive

kù 库 N warehouse (See **cāngkù** 仓库.)

kuā 夸 v 1 exaggerate, boast 2 praise

kuāzhāng 夸张 v exaggerate

kuà 跨 v take big strides ■ 他再向前跨一步，就要滚下楼梯了。 **Tā zài xiàngqián kuà yí bù, jiùyào gǔnxia lóutī le.** *If he took another step forward, he would tumble down the staircase.* 跨国公司 **kuàguó gōngsī** multinational company

kuà 挎 v carry on the arm or over one's shoulder

kuài 快 ADJ quick, fast (ANTONYM 慢 **màn**) ■ 快，公共汽车来了！ **Kuài, gōnggòng qìchē lái le!** *Quick, the bus is coming!* ■ 他跑得很快。 **Tā pǎo de hěn kuài.** *He runs very fast.*

kuàihuo 快活 **ADJ** merry, cheerful

kuàilè 快乐 **ADJ** joyful, happy ■ 祝你生日快乐！ *Zhù nǐ shēngrì kuàilè! Happy birthday!* ■ 在这个快乐的节日里，人们暂时忘了生活中种种不愉快的事。 *Zài zhège kuàilè de jiérì li, rénmen zànshí wàngle shēnghuó zhōng zhǒngzhǒng bù yúkuài de shì. At this happy festival, people forget for the time being unpleasant things in life.*

kuài 块 **TRAD** 塊 **MEASURE WORD 1** (for things that can be broken into lumps or chunks)

一块蛋糕 yí kuài dàngāo a piece/slice of cake / 两块面包 liǎng kuài miànbāo two pieces of bread **2** (for money) yuan, dollar (only in spoken Chinese)

三块钱 sān kuài qián three yuan (or dollars)

NOTE: See note on 元 **yuán**.

kuài 筷 **N** chopstick

kuàizi 筷子 [suffix: 筷 chopstick + 子 nominal suffix] **N** chopsticks (双 **shuāng** a pair) ■ 你会用筷子吗？ *Nǐ huì yòng kuàizi ma? Can you eat with chopsticks?*

kuài 会 **TRAD** 會 as in 会计 **kuàijì**

kuàijì 会计 **N 1** accounting

会计年度 kuàijì niándù fiscal year **2** accountant

会计主任 kuàijì zhǔrèn chief accountant

kuān 宽 **TRAD** 寬 **ADJ** wide ■ 江面很宽，我游不过去。 *Jiāngmiàn hěn kuān, wǒ yóu bu guòqu. The river is too wide for me to swim across.*

kuānchang 宽敞 [comp: 宽 wide + 敞 open] **ADJ** spacious

kuāndài 宽带 **N** broadband

kuānróng 宽容 **ADJ** tolerant, lenient

kuǎn 款 **N** sum of money (笔 **bǐ**) ■ 你可以用这张卡取款，或者存款。 *Nǐ kěyǐ yòng zhè zhāng kǎ qǔ kuǎn, huòzhě cún kuǎn. You can withdraw or deposit money with this card.*

kuǎndài 款待 **V** entertain hospitably

kuǎnshì 款式 **N** design, style

kuáng 狂 **ADJ** mad, crazy (See **fēngkuáng** 疯狂.)

kuàng 况 **N** situation (See **qíngkuàng** 情况, **zhuàngkuàng** 状况.)

kuàngqiě 况且 **CONJ** moreover, besides

kuàng 矿 **TRAD** 礦 **N** (coal, gold, etc.) mine (座 **zuò**) ■ 这座矿已经开了一百多年了。 *Zhè zuò kuàng yǐjīng kāile yìbǎi duō nián le. This coal mine has been mined for over a century.*

金矿 jīnkuàng gold mine / 煤矿 méikuàng coal mine / 油矿 méikuàng oilfield

kuàngchǎn 矿产 [modif: 矿 mineral + 产 product] **N** mineral products

kuànggōng 矿工 [modif: 矿 mine + 工 worker] **N** miner

kuàngquánshuǐ 矿泉水 [modif: 矿 mine + 泉 spring + 水 water] **N** mineral water

kuàng 旷 **TRAD** 曠 **ADJ** free from worries

kuànggōng 旷工 **V** absent from work without leave

kuàngkè 旷课 **V** absent from school without leave

kuàng 框 **N** door/window frame

kuàngjià 框架 **N** framework

kuī 亏 **TRAD** 虧 **V & N** lose, be deficient; loss (**ANTONYM** 盈 **yíng**)

转亏为盈 zhuǎn kuī wéi yíng turn loss into gain

kuīdài 亏待 **V** treat shabbily

kuīsǔn 亏损 [comp: 亏 loss + 损 loss] **N** loss, deficiency

kuì 愧 **ADJ** ashamed (See **cánkuì** 惭愧.)

kūn 昆 as in 昆虫 **kūnchóng**

kūnchóng 昆虫 **N** insect (只 **zhī**)

kǔn 捆 **V** tie, bind

kǔnbǎng 捆绑 **V** tie up (a person)

kùn 困 **V** be stranded, be in a tough spot ■ 由于突然发大水，人们被困在那个小山村。 *Yóuyú tūrán fā dàshuǐ, rénmen bèi kùn zài nàge xiǎo shāncūn. Because of a sudden flood, people were stranded in the small mountain village.*

kùnnan 困难 [comp: 困 be stranded + 难 difficult] **N & ADJ** difficulty; difficult ■ 你不要怕困难，要想一想怎么办。 *Nǐ bú yào pà kùnnan, yào xiǎng yi xiǎng zěnme bàn. You mustn't be afraid of difficulties. You should think of what to do.* ■ 我们现在的情况比较困难。 *Wǒmen xiànzài de qíngkuàng bǐjiào kùnnan. Our situation is rather difficult.*

克服困难 kèfú kùnnan overcome difficulty

kuò 扩 **TRAD** 擴 **V** spread out

kuòchōng 扩充 **V** strengthen, reinforce

kuòdà 扩大 **V** expand, enlarge ■ 他们打算扩大生产规模。 *Tāmen dǎsuàn kuòdà shēngchǎn guīmó. They plan to expand the scale of production.*

kuòsàn 扩散 **V** spread, proliferate

kuòzhāng 扩张 **V** expand, extend

kuò 括 **V** include, embrace (See **gàikuò** 概括.)

kuò 阔 **TRAD** 闊 **ADJ** wide (See **guǎngkuò** 广阔.)

L

lā 拉 **V** pull ■ 请你拉这个门，别推这个门。 *Qǐng nǐ lā zhège mén, bié tuī zhège mén. Please pull this door; not push it.*

lājī 垃圾 **N** rubbish, garbage ■ 请不要乱扔垃圾。 *Qǐng bú yào luàn rēng lājī. Please do not litter.*

lājī chǔlǐ 垃圾处理 **N** rubbish disposal

lājī dài 垃圾袋 **N** rubbish bag

lājī xiāng 垃圾箱 **N** rubbish bin

lāsuǒ 拉锁 **N** zipper, zip fastener

lǎba 喇叭 **N 1** horn, trumpet

吹喇叭 chuī lǎba blow the horn, play the trumpet **2** loudspeaker

là 蜡 **TRAD** 蠟 **N** wax

làzhú 蜡烛 **N** candle (支 **zhī**)
点蜡烛 diǎn làzhú light a candle

là 辣 **ADJ** spicy hot, peppery

làjiāo 辣椒 **N** hot pepper

la 啦 **PARTICLE** (an exclamation indicating completion of an action and/or emergence of a new situation; 了 **le** + 啊 **a**) ■ 我们赢啦！**Wǒmen yíng la!** *We've won!* ■ 我做完作业啦！**Wǒ zuòwán zuòyè la!** *I've finished my assignment!*

NOTE: 啦 **la** is the combination of 了 **le** and 啊 **a**. It is only used at the end of a sentence. You can replace 啦 **la** with 了 **le** but then the strong emotive coloring of 啊 **a** is lost. Compare: 我赢啦! **Wǒ yíng la!** *I won!* and 我赢了。**Wǒ yíng le** *I won*.

lái 来[1] **TRAD** 來 **V** come, come to; move toward the speaker (**ANTONYM** 去 **qù**) ■ 王先生来了没有？**Wáng xiānsheng láile méiyǒu?** *Has Mr Wang come?*

láibují 来不及 **V** not enough time (to do something) ■ 到那时候，哭都来不及。**Dào nà shíhou, kū dōu láibují.** *Should such a moment come, there would even be no time to cry (→ it would be too late to regret).* ■ 来不及吃早饭了。**Láibují chī zǎofàn le.** *There is no time for breakfast.*

NOTE: The opposite is 来得及 **láidejí**, e.g. ■ 还来得及吃早饭。**Hái láidejí chī zǎofàn.** *There is still enough time to have breakfast.*

láilì 来历 **N** origin, background
来历不明 láilì bùmíng of uncertain origin, of dubious background

láixìn 来信 [modif: 来 arriving + 信 letter] **N** letter received, incoming letter ■ 来信早已收到。**Láixìn zǎo yǐ shōudào.** *I received your letter long ago.*

láiyuán 来源 **N** source, origin
消息来源 xiāoxi láiyuán source of the news

láizì 来自 **V** come from ■ 这个中文班的学生来自世界各国。**Zhège Zhōngwén bān de xuésheng láizì shìjiè gè guó.** *The students of this Chinese class came from all over the world.*

lái 来[2] **TRAD** 來 **NUMERAL** approximately, more or less, close to (used after the number 10 or a multiple of 10 to indicate approximation)
十来辆车 shí lái liàng chē about ten cars / 五十来个学生 wǔshí lái ge xuésheng approximately fifty students / 三百四十来块钱 sānbǎi sìshí lái kuài qián about 340 yuan

lài 赖 **TRAD** 賴 **V** rely on (See yīlài 依赖.)

lán 兰 **TRAD** 蘭 **N** orchid

lánhuā 兰花 **N** orchid

lán 拦 **TRAD** 攔 **V** stop, block, hold back ■ 你要去就去，没人拦你。**Nǐ yào qù jiù qù, méi rén lán nǐ.** *If you want to go, go ahead. Nobody is trying to stop you.*

lán 栏 **TRAD** 欄 **N** railing, fence

lánmù 栏目 **N** (newspaper or magazine) column

lán 蓝 **TRAD** 藍 **ADJ** blue ■ 天很蓝，因为空气很干净。**Tiān hěn lán, yīnwèi kōngqì hěn gānjing.** *The sky is blue because the air is clean.* ■ 蓝蓝的天上白云飘，多好看啊！**Lánlán de tiān shang báiyún piāo, duō hǎokàn a!** *White clouds float in the blue sky. How beautiful!*

lán 篮 **TRAD** 籃 **N** basket

lánqiú 篮球 [modif: 篮 basket + 球 ball] **N** basketball
打篮球 dǎ lánqiú play basketball ■ 他们在打篮球。**Tāmen zài dǎ lánqiú.** *They're playing basketball.*

lánzi 篮子 **N** basket

lǎn 览 **TRAD** 覽 **V** view (See yóulǎn 游览, zhǎnlǎn 展览 etc.)

lǎn 懒 **TRAD** 懶 **ADJ** lazy, indolent ■ 你真太懒了，收到他来信两个星期了，还不回信。**Nǐ zhēn tài lǎn le, shōudào tā láixìn liǎng ge xīngqī le, hái bù huíxìn.** *You're really lazy. It's two weeks since you received his letter and you still haven't replied.*
好吃懒做 hào chī lǎn zuò like eating but hate working, be gluttonous and lazy

lǎnduò 懒惰 [comp: 懒 lazy + 惰 inertia] **ADJ** lazy

làn 烂 **TRAD** 爛 **V & ADJ** go rotten, go bad; rotten ■ 水果容易烂，运输是个问题。**Shuǐguǒ róngyì làn, yùnshū shì ge wèntí.** *Fruit rots easily, and its transport is a problem.* ■ 这个苹果烂了，扔了吧。**Zhège píngguǒ làn le, rēng le ba.** *This apple is rotten. Throw it away.*

láng 狼 **N** wolf (只 **zhī**) ■ 狼是羊群的大敌。**Láng shì yángqún de dàdí.** *Wolves are the great enemies of the sheep flock.*
披着羊皮的狼 pīzhe yángpí de láng a wolf in sheep's clothing
一群狼 yì qún láng a pack of wolves

lángbèi 狼狈 **ADJ** in an awkward position, cutting a sorry figure of oneself

lángbèi wéijiān 狼狈为奸 **V** act in collusion with each other, be in cahoots with

láng tūn hǔ yàn 狼吞虎咽 **IDIOM** wolf down (food), devour ravenously

lǎng 朗 **ADJ** loud and clear

lǎngdú 朗读 [modif: 朗 loud and clear + 读 read] **V** read in a loud and clear voice ■ 学外语，一定要朗读课文。**Xué wàiyǔ, yídìng yào lǎngdú kèwén.** *To learn a foreign language, one should read texts aloud.*

làng 浪 **N** wave ■ 风急浪高，不能出海。**Fēng jí làng gāo, bù néng chūhǎi.** *The winds are strong and the waves high. We can't go out to sea.*

làngfèi 浪费 **V** waste ■ 浪费时间就是浪费生命。**Làngfèi shíjiān jiùshì làngfèi shēngmìng.** *To waste time is to waste life.*

làngmàn 浪漫 **ADJ** romantic

lāo 捞 **TRAD** 撈 **V** pull or drag out of water ■ 孩子们在小河里捞什么呢？**Háizimen zài xiǎo hé li lāo**

shénme ne? *What are the children trying to scoop out of the stream?*
打捞 dǎlāo salvage (a sunken ship, etc.)
láo 劳 TRAD 勞 V toil
láodòng 劳动 [comp: 劳 toil + 动 move] V do manual labor ■ 他夏天在父亲的农场劳动。**Tā xiàtiān zài fùqin de nóngchǎng láodòng.** *In summer he works on his father's farm.*
脑力劳动 nǎolì láodòng mental work / 体力劳动 tǐlì láodòng physical (manual) labor
Láodòng Jié 劳动节 Labor Day (on May 1)
láojià 劳驾 IDIOM May I trouble you to ..., Would you mind (doing ... for me) ■ 劳驾，请您让一下。**Láojià, qǐng nín ràng yíxià.** *Excuse me, would you please make way?*

NOTE: 劳驾 **láojià** is a Northern dialect expression. 对不起 **duibuqǐ** is more widely used.

láodao 唠叨 ADJ be garrulous
唠唠叨叨说个没完 láoláo dāodāo shuō gè méiwán chatter on and on
láo 牢[1] ADJ firm, fast
láogù 牢固 [comp: 牢 firm + 固 solid] ADJ firm, solid
láosāo 牢骚 N complaint, grumbling
发牢骚 fāláosāo grumble
láo 牢[2] N shortening for **láofáng** 牢房
坐牢 zuòláo serve jail term
láofáng 牢房 N prison, jail
lǎo 老 ADJ 1 old, elderly ■ 爸爸老了，不能在农场劳动了。**Bàba lǎo le, bù néng zài nóngchǎng láodòng le.** *My father is old and can't work on the farm any more.* 2 long-standing ■ 这个老问题一直没有办法解决。**Zhè ge lǎo wèntí yìzhí méiyǒu bànfǎ jiějué.** *This perennial problem has remained unsolved for a long time.*
老朋友 lǎo péngyou long-standing friend ■ 我们在小学的时候就认识了，是老朋友。**Wǒmen zài xiǎoxué de shíhou jiù rènshi le, shì lǎo péngyou.** *We've known each other since primary school. We're old friends.*
3 PREFIX (added to numerals to indicate seniority among siblings)
老大 lǎo dà the eldest child / 老二 lǎo èr the second child

NOTE: Chinese tradition values and respects old age. Today, people still attach 老 **lǎo** to a family name as a form of address to show respect and friendliness to an older person, e.g. 老李 **Lǎo Lǐ**, 老王 **Lǎo Wáng**. See note on 小 **xiǎo**.

lǎobǎixìng 老百姓 [modif: 老 old + 百 hundred + 姓 family names] N common people, ordinary folk ■ 老百姓对当官的有意见，怎么办呢？**Lǎobǎixìng duì dāngguānde yǒu yìjiàn, zěnme bàn ne?** *What should common people do when they have a complaint against an official?*

lǎobǎn 老板 N 1 boss, one in charge ■ 他是我的老板，他要我做什么我就做什么。**Tā shì wǒ de lǎobǎn, tā yào wǒ zuò shénme wǒ jiù zuò shénme.** *He is my boss; I do what he tells me to do.* 2 owner of a store, a business, etc. ■ 老板不在，没人可以作主。**Lǎobǎn bú zài, méi rén kěyǐ zuòzhǔ.** *As the owner is away, nobody can make a decision.*
lǎodàniáng 老大娘 N (a respectful form of address or reference to an old woman) (位 **wèi**) ■ 他把座位让给一位老大娘。**Tā bǎ zuòwèi rànggěi yí wèi lǎodàniáng.** *He offered his seat to an old woman.* ■ 老大娘，您找谁？**Lǎodàniáng, nín zhǎo shuí?** *Who are you looking for, ma'am?*

NOTE: 老大娘 **lǎodàniáng** has a rustic flavor. It is normally not used in cities or among better-educated people. 老太太 **lǎotàitai** is a more appropriate word.

lǎodàye 老大爷 N (a respectful form of addresses or reference to an old man) (位 **wèi**) ■ 老大爷，请您让我看看您的票子。**Lǎodàye, qǐng nín ràng wǒ kànkan nín de piàozi.** *Please show me your ticket, sir.*

NOTE: 老大爷 **lǎodàye** has a rustic flavor. It is normally not used in cities or among better-educated people. 老先生 **lǎoxiānsheng** is a more appropriate word.

lǎohǔ 老虎 [prefix: 老 nominal prefix + 虎 tiger] N tiger (头 **tóu**, 只 **zhī**) ■ 动物园里的老虎逃跑了！**Dòngwùyuán li de lǎohǔ táopǎo le!** *A tiger has escaped from the zoo!*
lǎolao 姥姥 N (maternal) granny
lǎopó 老婆 N (vulgarism) wife, old girl
lǎorén 老人 [modif: 老 old + 人 person] N old person, elderly person (位 **wèi**) ■ 这位老人人老心不老，还在学中文和武术。**Zhè wèi lǎorén rén lǎo xīn bù lǎo, háizài xué Zhōngwén hé wǔshù.** *This old person is young at heart. He (or She) is still learning Chinese and martial arts.*
lǎoshī 老师 [modif: 老 aged + 师 teacher, master] N teacher (位 **wèi**) ■ 我的中文老师是北京人。**Wǒ de Zhōngwén lǎoshī shì Běijīngrén.** *My Chinese teacher is from Beijing.* ■ 我要问老师几个问题。**Wǒ yào wèn lǎoshī jǐ ge wèntí.** *I want to ask the teacher some questions.*

NOTE: 老师 **lǎoshī,** usually prefixed by a family name, is the standard form of address to a teacher, e.g. 王老师 **Wáng Lǎoshī.** There is no equivalent of 王老师 **Wáng Lǎoshī** in English. This dictionary uses the literal translation Teacher Wang.

lǎoshi 老是 ADV always, constantly ■ 你怎么老是这么晚回家？**Nǐ zěnme lǎoshi zhème wǎn huíjiā?** *Why do you always come home so late?* ■ 他老是写错这个字。**Tā lǎoshi xiěcuò zhège zì.** *He always writes this character wrongly.*
lǎoshi 老实 ADJ 1 honest to goodness, faithful

■ 说老实话，做老实人。**Shuō lǎoshi huà, zuò lǎoshi rén.** *Speak the truth and be an honest person.* **2** simple-minded, naive ■ 他太老实，容易受人欺骗。**Tā tài lǎoshi, róngyì shòurén qīpiàn.** *He is too honest and is prone to be deceived.*

老实说 lǎoshi shuō to be frank, to tell the truth ■ 老实说，你这种做法我并不赞成。**Lǎoshi shuō, nǐ zhè zhǒng zuòfǎ wǒ bìng bù zànchéng.** *To tell the truth, I don't approve of your way of doing things.*

lǎoshihuà 老实话 **N** plain truth

lǎoshi rén 老实人 **N** honest person, simple-minded person, gullible person

lǎoshǔ 老鼠 **N** mouse, mice, rat, rats (只 **zhī**)

lǎotàitai 老太太 **N** (a respectful form of address or reference to an old woman) (位 **wèi**) ■ 老太太，您找谁？**Lǎotàitai, nín zhǎo shuí?** *Who are you looking for, ma'am?* ■ 他把座位让给一位老太太。**Tā bǎ zuòwèi rànggěi yí wèi lǎotàitai.** *He offered his seat to an old lady.*

lǎotóur 老头儿 **N** old man (个 **gè**) ■ 几个老头儿在树下打牌。**Jǐ ge lǎotóur zài shù xia dǎpái.** *Some old men were playing cards under the tree.*

NOTE: (1) **lǎotóur** 老头儿 is an impolite way of referring to an old man. As a form of address, **lǎotóur** 老头儿 is very rude. Instead, use the neutral term **lǎorén** 老人 or the polite terms **lǎoxiānsheng** 老先生 or **lǎodàye** 老大爷. (2) The corresponding impolite word for *an old woman* is **lǎotàipó** 老太婆. Use **lǎotàitai** 老太太 or **lǎodàniáng** 老大娘 instead.

lǎoxiānsheng 老先生 [modif: 老 old, elderly + 先生 gentleman] **N** (a respectful form of address or reference to an old man) (位 **wèi**) ■ 老先生，请您让我看看您的票子。**Lǎoxiānsheng, qǐng nín ràng wǒ kànkan nín de piàozi.** *Please show me your ticket, sir.*

lè 乐 TRAD 樂 **ADJ** happy

lèguān 乐观 [modif: 乐 happy + 观 view] **ADJ** optimistic (ANTONYM 悲观 **bēiguān**) ■ 他很乐观，相信世界会越变越好。**Tā hěn lèguān, xiāngxìn shìjiè huì yuè biàn yuè hǎo.** *He is optimistic, believing that the world is getting ever better.* ■ 根据乐观的估计，今年经济增长可以达到百分之五。**Gēnjù lèguān de gūjì, jīnnián jīngjì zēngzhǎng kěyǐ dádào bǎifēn zhī wǔ.** *According to an optimistic estimate, the economy will grow by five percent this year.*

lèqù 乐趣 [comp: 乐 joy + 趣 interest] **N** pleasure, joy

lèyì 乐意 [modif: 乐 happy + 意 will] **ADJ** be happy to, be willing to

le 了 PARTICLE **1** (used after a verb to indicate the completion of an action) ■ 我昨天写了三封信。**Wǒ zuótiān xiěle sān fēng xìn.** *I wrote three letters yesterday.* ■ 他吃了晚饭就上网玩游戏。**Tā**

chīle wǎnfàn jiù shàngwǎng wán yóuxì. *As soon as he had eaten supper, he went online to play games.* **2** (used at the end of a sentence to indicate the emergence of a new situation) ■ 秋天来了，树叶黄了。**Qiūtiān lái le, shùyè huáng le.** *Autumn has come and leaves have turned yellow.* ■ 我会说一点儿中文了。**Wǒ huì shuō yidiǎnr Zhōngwén le.** *I can speak a bit of Chinese now.*

léi 雷 **N** thunder ■ 昨天又打雷，又闪电，挺吓人的。**Zuótiān yòu dǎ léi, yòu shǎndiàn, tǐng xiàrén de.** *There was thunder and lightning yesterday. It was rather frightening.*

打雷 dǎ léi thunder

léidá 雷达 **N** radar

léiyǔ 雷雨 [comp: 雷 thunder + 雨 rain] **N** thunderstorm

lèi 泪 TRAD 淚 **N** teardrop, tear (See **yǎnlèi** 眼泪.)

lèi 类 TRAD 類 **N** kind, category, class ■ 这两类不同的情况，不要混为一谈。**Zhè liǎng lèi bùtóng de qíngkuàng, bú yào hùnwéi yìtán.** *These are two different situations. Don't lump them together.*

lèisì 类似 **ADJ** similar

lèixíng 类型 [comp: 类 category + 型 type] **N** type (种 **zhǒng**)

lèi 累 **ADJ** exhausted, tired ■ "你劳动了半天，累不累？""不累，一点都不累。"**"Nǐ láodòngle bàntiān, lèi bu lèi?" "Bú lèi, yìdiǎn dōu bú lèi."** *"Are you tired after doing manual labor for such a long time?" "No, I'm not the least tired."*

lěng 冷 **ADJ** cold (ANTONYM 热 **rè**) ■ 今天很冷。**Jīntiān hěn lěng.** *It's cold today.* ■ 他每天都洗冷水澡。**Tā měi tiān dōu xǐ lěngshuǐ zǎo.** *He takes a cold bath every day.*

lěngdàn 冷淡 [comp: 冷 cold + 淡 bland] **ADJ** cold, indifferent, apathetic ■ 商业界对政府的新政策很冷淡。**Shāngyè jiè duì zhèngfǔ de xīn zhèngcè hěn lěngdàn.** *The business circle is indifferent to the new policies of the government.*

lěngjìng 冷静 [comp: 冷 cold + 静 quiet] **ADJ** cool-headed, calm, sober ■ 你冷静一些，别这么激动。**Nǐ lěngjìng yìxiē, bié zhème jīdòng.** *Calm down; don't be so agitated.*

lěngluò 冷落 **I V** treat coldly, cold-shoulder **II ADJ** unfrequented, desolate

lěngkù 冷酷 **ADJ** unfeeling, cold-blooded

lěngquè 冷却 **V & N** cool; cooling

lěngquèjì 冷却剂 **N** coolant, cooler

lèng 楞 **ADJ** stupefied, blank

发愣 fālèng look stupefied, stare blankly

lí 厘 MEASURE WORD one hundredth

límǐ 厘米 MEASURE WORD one hundredth of a meter, centimeter ■ 他身高178厘米。**Tā shēngāo yìbǎi qīshí bā límǐ.** *He is 178 centimeters tall.*

lí 离 TRAD 離 **I V** depart, leave ■ 他每天很早就离家，很晚才回家。**Tā měi tiān hěn zǎo jiù lí jiā, hěn wǎn cái huí jiā.** *He leaves home early and*

returns late every day. **II** PREP (indicating distance in space or time) away from, from ■ 现在离寒假只有两个星期了。 **Xiànzài lí jiàqī zhǐyǒu liǎngge xīngqī le.** *There are only two weeks before the winter holiday.*

离 … 近 lí … jìn close to / 离 … 远 lí … yuǎn far away from ■ 加拿大离英国很远，离美国很近。 **Jiānádà lí Yīngguó hěn yuǎn, lí Měiguó hěn jìn.** *Canada is far away from Britain, and close to the USA.*

líhūn 离婚 [v+obj: 离 separate + 婚 marriage] v divorce ■ 她和丈夫离婚了。 **Tā hé zhàngfu líhūn le.** *She and her husband are divorced.*

líkāi 离开 [comp: 离 leave + 开 away from] v depart, leave ■ 他十八岁的时候离开父母，到美国去念书。 **Tā shíbā suì de shíhou líkāi fùmǔ, dào Měiguó qù niànshū.** *When he was eighteen, he left his parents and went to America to study.* ■ 我离开一会儿，马上就回来。 **Wǒ líkāi yíhuìr, mǎshàng jiù huílai.** *Excuse me for a minute. I'll be back soon.*

离不开 líbukāi cannot do without ■ 孩子还小，离不开妈。 **Háizi hái xiǎo, líbukāi mā.** *The child is too young to be without his mother.*

lí 梨 N pear (只 **zhī**) ■ 这梨很甜，你尝尝。 **Zhè lí hěn tián, nǐ chángchang.** *This pear is very sweet. Try it.*

límíng 黎明 N dawn, daybreak

Lǐ 李 N (a family name)

NOTE: According to the latest census, 李 **Lǐ** is the most common family name in China.

lǐ 礼 TRAD 禮 N rite

lǐbàitiān 礼拜天 [modif: 礼拜 worship + 天 day] N same as 星期天 **Xīngqītiān.** (A rather old-fashioned word.)

lǐjié 礼节 N etiquette, protocol

lǐmào 礼貌 ADJ polite, courteous ■ 礼貌待客。 **Lǐmào dài kè.** *Treat guests/customers with courtesy.* ■ 盯着人家看，是不礼貌的。 **Dīngzhe rénjiā kàn, shì bù lǐmào de.** *It is impolite to stare at people.*

lǐ shàng wǎng lái 礼尚往来 IDIOM courtesy demands reciprocity, pay a man in his own coin

lǐtáng 礼堂 [modif: 礼 ceremony, ritual + 堂 hall] N auditorium, assembly hall (座 **zuò**) ■ 礼堂里正在举行一个大会。 **Lǐtáng li zhèngzài jǔxíng yí ge dàhuì.** *A rally is being held in the auditorium.*

lǐwù 礼物 [modif: 礼 gift + 物 thing] N gift, present (件 **jiàn**) ■ 这件小小的礼物，请您收下。 **Zhè jiàn xiǎoxiǎo de lǐwù, qǐng nín shōuxia.** *Please accept this small present.* ■ 今天是你的生日，我送你一件小礼物。 **Jīntiān shì nǐ de shēngrì, wǒ sòng nǐ yí jiàn xiǎo lǐwù.** *Today's your birthday. I'll give you a little gift.*

结婚礼物 jiéhūn lǐwù wedding present / 生日礼物 shēngrì lǐwù birthday present / 新年礼物 xīnnián lǐwù New Year present

NOTE: Chinese modesty requires that you belittle your present, describing it as 一件小礼物 **yí jiàn xiǎo lǐwù** *a small/insignificant gift.* Upon receiving a present, it is bad manners to open it immediately. The recipient is first supposed to say 不用不用 **búyòng búyòng** *You didn't have to* and then express thanks for the gift, describing it as 这么好的礼物 **Zhème hǎo de lǐwù** *such a nice gift,* e.g. ■ 谢谢你送给我这么好的礼物。 **Xièxie nǐ sònggei wǒ zhème hǎo de lǐwù.** *Thank you for giving me such a nice gift.*

lǐ 里¹ TRAD 裡 N inside (ANTONYM 外 **wài**) ■ 房间里没有人。 **Fángjiān li méiyǒu rén.** *There is nobody in the room.* ■ 生活里总会出现种种麻烦。 **Shēnghuó li zǒng huì chūxiàn zhǒng-zhǒng máfan.** *You are bound to encounter various troublesome situations in life.*

lǐ 里² MEASURE WORD a traditional Chinese unit of distance equivalent to half a kilometer ■ 从市中心到飞机场有二十里，也就是十公里。 **Cóng shìzhōngxīn dào fēijīchǎng yǒu èrshí lǐ, yě jiù shì shí gōnglǐ.** *From the city center to the airport it's twenty li, or ten kilometers.*

lǐbian 里边 [modif: 里 inner + 边 side] N inside, in (ANTONYM 外边 **wàibian**) ■ 房子外边不好看，里边很舒服。 **Fángzi wàibian bù hǎokàn, lǐbian hěn shūfu.** *The outside of the house is not very attractive, but inside is quite comfortable.* ■ 箱子里边有什么？ **Xiāngzi lǐbian yǒu shénme?** *What's inside the box?*

lǐchéng bēi 里程碑 N milestone

lǐmiàn 里面 N same as 里边 **lǐbian**

lǐ 理 I N pattern, reason II v 1 manage 2 same as 理睬 **lǐcǎi**

lǐcái 理财 V & N manage financial affairs; fund managing

lǐcǎi 理睬 v pay attention to, show interest in

NOTE: This word is used in a negative sentence only. e.g. 别理睬他。 **Bié lǐcǎi tā.** *Don't pay him any attention. (Just ignore him.)*

lǐfà 理发 [v+obj: 理 tidy up + 发 hair] v have a haircut and shampoo, have one's hair done ■ 我半个月理一次发。 **Wǒ bàn ge yuè lǐ yí cì fà.** *I have a haircut every half a month.*

lǐfàdiàn 理发店 barbershop, hair salon

NOTE: Instead of the straightforward word 理发店 **lǐfàdiàn,** many hair salons now give themselves fanciful names such as 美发厅 **měifàtīng.**

lǐfàshī 理发师 barber, hairdresser, hairstylist

lǐjiě 理解 [comp: 理 reason + 解 understand] v understand, comprehend ■ 这首古诗我不理解。 **Zhè shǒu gǔ shī wǒ bù lǐjiě.** *I don't understand this classic poem.* ■ 我理解你的心情。 **Wǒ lǐjiě nǐ de xīnqíng.** *I understand how you feel.*

lǐlùn 理论 [comp: 理 reason + 论 theory] **N** theory ■ 你用什么理论来解释这一现象？**Nǐ yòng shénme lǐlùn lái jiěshì zhè yí xiànxiàng?** *What theory are you going to apply to interpret this phenomenon?*

lǐ suǒ dāngrán 理所当然 **ADJ** naturally, as should be expected

lǐxiǎng 理想 [comp: 理 reason + 想 thought, wish] **N** ideal, aspiration ■ 我小时候的理想是当个旅行家。**Wǒ xiǎoshíhou de lǐxiǎng shì dāng ge lǚxíngjiā.** *When I was a child, I dreamed of being a traveler.* 实现理想 shíxiàn lǐxiǎng realize an ideal

lǐyóu 理由 [comp: 理 reason + 由 origin, cause] **N** reason, justification, ground ■ 我们有充分的理由处分他。**Wǒmen yǒu chōngfèn de lǐyóu chǔfèn tā.** *We have sufficient reason to discipline him.* ■ 你有什么理由不来上班？**Nǐ yǒu shénme lǐyóu bù lái shàngbān?** *What reason can you give for being absent from work?*

lǐ zhí qì zhuàng 理直气壮 **IDIOM** speak with absolute assurance, bold and assured that justice is on one's side

lǐzhì 理智 [comp: 理 reason + 智 wisdom] **N** reason and intellect, ability to use sound reasoning

lì 力 **N** strength, force, might ■ 他提出的理由很有力。**Tā tíchū de lǐyóu hěn yǒulì.** *He put forward forceful arguments.* ■ 我全身无力，恐怕生病了。**Wǒ quánshēn wú lì, kǒngpà shēngbìng le.** *I feel weak all over; I'm afraid I'm ill.*

lìliàng 力量 **N 1** strength ■ 人多力量大。**Rén duō lìliàng dà.** *Strength lies in numbers.* **2** efforts, ability ■ 我们尽最大的力量克服当前的困难。**Wǒmen jìn zuì dà de lìliàng kèfú dāngqián de kùnnan.** *We are making maximum efforts to overcome the present difficulties.*

lìqi 力气 **V** physical strength ■ 没想到这个孩子力气这么大。**Méi xiǎngdào zhège háizi lìqi zhème dà.** *I did not expect this child to be so strong.*

lìqiú 力求 **V** strive for, do one's best for 力求完美 lìqiú wánměi strive for perfection

lì suǒ néng jí 力所能及 **IDIOM** (do something) within one's ability, in one's power

lìtú 力图 **V** try hard to, strive to

lìzhēng 力争 **V** work hard for, do all one can to

lì 历 **TRAD** 歷 **N** past experience

lìdài 历代 **N** successive dynasties

lìlái 历来 **ADV** all through the ages, always, ever since

lìshǐ 历史 [comp: 历 past experience + 史 recording] **N** history ■ 你知道这个城市的历史吗？**Nǐ zhīdào zhège chéngshì de lìshǐ ma?** *Do you know the history of this city?*

lìshǐxuéjiā 历史学家 **N** historian

lì 立 **V** stand ■ 你立在门口干什么？**Nǐ lì zài ménkǒu gàn shénme?** *Why are you standing by the door?*

坐立不安 zuò lì bù ān **IDIOM** on pins and needles, on tenterhooks, anxious

lìchǎng 立场 **N** position, standpoint ■ 站在公司

的立场上，你就会同意这个措施是必要的。**Zhàn zài gōngsī de lìchǎng shang, nǐ jiù huì tóngyì zhège cuòshī shì bìyào de.** *From the company's standpoint, you would agree that this measure is necessary.*

lìfāng 立方 **MEASURE WORD** (mathematics) cube 三立方米/公尺 sān lìfāng mǐ/gōngchǐ 3 cubic meters

lìjí 立即 **ADV** immediately, without delay ■ 王董事长要我立即飞往上海处理一件事。**Wáng dǒngshìzhǎng yào wǒ lìjí fēiwǎng Shànghǎi chǔlǐ yí jiàn shì.** *Chairman Wang wants me to fly to Shanghai immediately to handle an emergency.*

lìjiāoqiáo 立交桥 **N** flypast, flyover (座 zuò)

lìkè 立刻 [comp: 立 immediately + 刻 a brief time] **ADV** at once, immediately ■ 我接到你的电话，立刻就来了。**Wǒ jiēdào nǐ de diànhuà, lìkè jiù lái le.** *I came immediately after getting your call.* ■ 你要我立刻拿出这么多钱，办不到。**Nǐ yào wǒ lìkè náchū zhème duō qián, bàn bú dào.** *You want me to produce such a large amount of money right away. I can't do it.*

lìtǐ 立体 **ADJ** three-dimensional

lìzú 立足 **V** find a home/foothold

lì 厉 **TRAD** 厲 **ADJ** severe, strict

lìhai 厉害 **ADJ** severe, formidable, redoubtable ■ 这个人说话很厉害。**Zhège rén shuōhuà hěn lìhai.** *This person has a sharp tongue.* ■ 她看样子厉害，其实没有用。**Tā kànyàngzi lìhai, qíshí méiyǒuyòng.** *She looks formidable but actually is rather useless.*

NOTE: 厉害 **lìhai** may be written as 利害. It is often used with 得 de to indicate a very high degree, e.g. ■ 这两天热得厉害。**Zhèliǎngtiān rède lìhai.** *These days are terribly hot.* ■ 情人节花儿贵得厉害。**Qíngrénjié huār guìde lìhai.** *Flowers are terribly expensive on Valentine's Day.*

lì 丽 **TRAD** 麗 **ADJ** beautiful (See měilì 美丽.)

lì 励 **TRAD** 勵 **V** encourage (See gǔlì 鼓励.)

lì 利 **N** benefit

lìbì 利弊 [comp: 利 advantage + 弊 disadvantage] **N** pros and cons

lìhai 利害 same as 厉害 **lìhai**

lìlǜ 利率 **N** interest rate ■ 你看银行会在最近提高利率吗？**Nǐ kàn yínháng huì zài zuìjìn tígāo lìlǜ ma?** *Do you think the banks will raise interest rates soon?*

lìrùn 利润 **N** profit ■ 这家公司今年第一季度的利润下降了百分之十二。**Zhè jiā gōngsī jīnnián dìyī jìdù de lìrùn xiàjiàng le bǎifēnzhī shí'èr.** *The company profits decreased by 12 percent in the first quarter this year.*

lìxī 利息 **N** interest (on a loan)

lìyì 利益 [comp: 利 benefit + 益 benefit] **N** benefit, interest ■ 每个人都为了个人利益而工作，但也

要考虑社会的利益。**Měi gè rén dōu wèile gèrén de lìyì ér gōngzuò, dàn yě yào kǎolǜ shèhuì de lìyì.** *Everybody works to their personal interest, but should also take into consideration the interests of society.*

lìyòng 利用 [comp: 利 benefit + 用 use] **v** make use of, benefit from ■ 你应该好好利用时间。**Nǐ yīnggāi hǎohǎo lìyòng shíjiān.** *You should make good use of your time.* ■ 我们要合理地利用自然资源。**Wǒmen yào hélǐ de lìyòng zìrán zīyuán.** *We should make use of natural resources in a rational way.*

lì 例 **N** example

lìrú 例如 [comp: 例 example + 如 same as] **CONJ** for example, such as ■ 有些汉字，例如 "日"、"月"、"山"，是从图画变来的。**Yǒuxiē hànzì, lìrú "rì," "yuè," "shān," shì cóng túhuà biànlai de.** *Some Chinese characters, such as* 日, 月, 山, *are derived from pictures.*

lìwài 例外 **N** exception

lìzi 例子 [suffix: 例 example + 子 nominal suffix] **N** example (个 gè) ■ 王老师举了很多例子，说明这个词的用法。**Wáng lǎoshī jǔle hěn duō lìzi, shuōmíng zhège cí de yòngfǎ.** *Teacher Wang gave many examples to illustrate the way this word is used.*

举例子 jǔ lìzi give an example

lì 粒 **MEASURE WORD** (for rice, pearls, etc.)
一粒米 yí lì mǐ a grain of rice

liǎ 俩 **TRAD** 倆 **NUMERAL** two people ■ 他们俩是好朋友，经常在一起玩。**Tāmen liǎ shì hǎo péngyou, jīngcháng zài yìqǐ wán.** *The two of them are good friends. They often play together.* ■ 这件事你们夫妻俩好好商量一下。**Zhè jiàn shì nǐmen fùqī liǎ hǎohǎo shāngliang yíxià.** *(To a couple) I hope you two will discuss this matter properly.*

lián 连 **TRAD** 連 **I v** connect, join ■ 海洋把世界连成一片。**Hǎiyáng bǎ shìjiè lián chéng yípiàn.** *Oceans and seas connect the entire world.* **II ADV** in succession, repeated ■ 我连发了三份电子邮件给他，他都没有回。**Wǒ lián fāle sān fèn diànzǐ yóujiàn gěi tā, tā dōu méiyǒu huí.** *I sent him three e-mail messages in succession but there has been no reply.*

lián ... dōu ... 连 ... 都 ... **IDIOM** even ■ 连三岁小孩都知道。**Lián sān suì xiǎohái dōu zhīdào.** *Even a toddler (← a three-year-old) knows this.* ■ 你连中文报纸都会看了！**Nǐ lián Zhōngwén bàozhǐ dōu huì kàn le!** *You can even read Chinese language newspapers!*

NOTE: (1) 连 ... 都 ... **lián ... dōu ...** is an emphatic expression, stressing the word after 连 **lián**. (2) 都 **dōu** may be replaced by 也 **yě**, i.e. 连 ... 也 ... **lián ... yě...** is the same as 连 ... 都 ... **lián ... dōu ...**, for example:■ 连三岁小孩也知道。**Lián sān suì xiǎohái yě zhīdào.** *Even a toddler knows this.*

liánmáng 连忙 **ADV** make haste, hasten without the slightest delay ■ 他踩了一位小姐的脚，连忙说 "对不起，对不起。" **Tā cǎile yí wèi xiǎojiě de jiǎo, liánmáng shuō "duìbuqǐ, duìbuqǐ."** *Stepping on a young lady's toes, he hastened to say, "I'm sorry, I'm sorry."* ■ 她听说老父亲跌倒了，连忙回家。**Tā tīngshuō lǎo fùqin diēdǎo le, liángmáng huíjiā.** *Hearing that her old father had had a fall, she hastened back home.*

liánnián 连年 **ADV** in successive years

liánsuǒ 连锁 **ADJ** linked together like a chain

liánsuǒ diàn 连锁店 **N** chain stores

liántóng 连同 **CONJ** together with

liánxù 连续 **v** in succession, in a row ■ 他连续两天开夜车。**Tā liánxù liǎng tiān kāi yèchē.** *He burned the midnight oil for two consecutive nights.* ■ 他连续喝了八瓶啤酒，终于醉倒了。**Tā liánxù hēle bā píng píjiǔ, zhōngyú zuìdǎo le.** *He drank eight bottles of beer in succession and finally became drunk.*

lián 怜 **TRAD** 憐 **v** pity (See **kělián** 可怜.)

lián 联 **TRAD** 聯 **v** connect

liánhé 联合 [comp: 联 join + 合 merge] **v** unite, get together (to do something) ■ 两国要联合开发海洋资源。**Liǎng guó yào liánhé kāifā hǎiyáng zīyuán.** *The two countries will jointly develop their ocean resources.*

Liánhéguó 联合国 **N** the United Nations Organization

liánhuān 联欢 [modif: 联 jointly + 欢 have a good time] **v** have a get-together, have a gala/party ■ 明天中外学生联欢，你表演什么节目？**Míngtiān zhōngwài xuésheng liánhuān, nǐ biǎoyǎn shénme jiémù?** *At the gala for Chinese and overseas students tomorrow, what item will you be performing?*

liánluò 联络 **v** contact, keep in contact

liánluò yuán 联络员 **N** contact person, liaison person

liánméng 联盟 **N** alliance, union

liánxì 联系 [comp: 联 connect + 系 tie, knot] **v & N** get in touch, contact; connection, being related ■ 如感兴趣，请与陈先生联系。**Rú gǎn xìngqù, qǐng yǔ Chén xiānsheng liánxì.** *If interested, please contact Mr Chen.* ■ 这两件事有什么联系？**Zhè liǎng jiàn shì yǒu shénme liánxì?** *What do these two matters have to do with each other?*

liánxì rén 联系人 **N** contact (person)

liánxiǎng 联想 **v** form mental association, connect with mentally

lián 廉 **ADJ 1** inexpensive, cheap **2** morally clean

liánjià 廉价 **ADJ** low-priced, inexpensive
廉价出售 liánjià chūshòu sell at a low price

liánjié 廉洁 [comp: 廉 morally clean + 洁 clean] **ADJ** (of officials) honest and clean, not corrupt

lián 帘 **N** curtain (See **chuānglián** 窗帘.)

liǎn 脸 TRAD 臉 N face (张 **zhāng**) ■ 我每天早上用冷水洗脸。**Wǒ měi tiān zǎoshang yòng lěngshuǐ xǐ liǎn.** *I wash my face in cold water every morning.* ■ 顾客来了，她总是笑脸相迎。**Gùkè lái le, tā zǒngshì xiào liǎn xiāngyíng.** *When a customer comes, she always smiles a welcome.*

丢脸 **diūliǎn** be disgraced, lose face

liàn 练 TRAD 練 V practice ■ 他早晨五点起床，先练武术，再练中文口语。**Tā zǎochén wǔ diǎn qǐchuáng, xiān liàn wǔshù, zài liàn Zhōngwén kǒuyǔ.** *He gets up at five o'clock every morning, practices martial arts first and then oral Chinese.*

liànxí 练习 [comp: 练 drill, train + 习 practice] V & N exercise, train, drill ■ 你常常练习汉语口语吗？**Nǐ chángcháng liànxí Hànyǔ kǒuyǔ ma?** *Do you often practice oral Chinese?* ■ 我数学练习做好了，还有三道英文练习没有做。**Wǒ shùxué liànxí zuò hǎo le, hái yǒu sān dào Yīngwén liànxí méiyǒu zuò.** *I've finished my mathematics exercises. I haven't done the three English exercises.*

liàn 炼 TRAD 煉 V smelt (See **duànliàn** 锻炼, **tí-liàn** 提炼.)

liàn 恋 TRAD 戀 N infatuation

liàn'ài 恋爱 [comp: 恋 infatuate + 爱 love] V & N be in romantic love, be courting; romantic love ■ 他们俩恋爱了两年，在上个月结婚了。**Tāmen liǎ liàn'ài le liǎngnián, zài shàng ge yuè jiéhūn le.** *They courted for two years and got married last month.* ■ 恋爱、婚姻是青年人的大事。**Liàn'ài, hūnyīn shì qīngniánrén de dàshì.** *Falling in love and marriage are major events for young people.*

谈恋爱 **tán liàn'ài** in courtship, in love

liáng 良 ADJ good

liánghǎo 良好 [comp: 良 good + 好 good] ADJ good, fine, commendable ■ 这种药经过试验，证明效果良好。**Zhè zhǒng yào jīngguò shìyàn, zhèngmíng xiàoguǒ liánghǎo.** *After testing, this medicine proved to have good effects.*

liángxīn 良心 [modif: 良 good + 心 heart] N conscience

liáng 凉 ADJ cool, chilly ■ 尽管中午很热，早上和夜里还是挺凉的。**Jìnguǎn zhōngwǔ hěn rè, zǎoshang hé yèli háishì tǐng liáng de.** *Even though it is hot at noon, it is still cool in the early morning and at night.*

liángkuai 凉快 [comp: 凉 cool + 快 pleasant] ADJ pleasantly cool ■ 今天很热，但是树下挺凉快。**Jīntiān hěn rè, dànshì shù xià tǐng liángkuai.** *It's hot today but it's rather cool under the tree.*

liáng 量 V measure, take measurements ■ 你量一量，这个房间有多大。**Nǐ liáng yi liáng, zhège fángjiān yǒu duō dà.** *Measure the room; find out how big it is.*

liáng 粮 TRAD 糧 N grain

liángshí 粮食 [comp: 粮 grain + 食 food] N grain, cereal, staple food ■ 大米和小麦是中国的主要粮食。**Dàmǐ hé xiǎomài shì Zhōngguó de zhǔyào liángshí.** *Rice and wheat are China's staple food.*

liáng 梁 TRAD 樑 N beam (in structure) (See 桥梁 **qiáoliáng**.)

liǎng 两 [1] MEASURE WORD (a traditional Chinese unit of weight equivalent to 50 grams), ounce ■ 我买二两茶叶。**Wǒ mǎi èr liǎng cháyè.** *I want two liang of tea.*

liǎng 两 [2] NUMERAL 1 two ■ 两个人 **liǎng ge rén** *two people* ■ 两本书 **liǎng běn shū** *two books* 2 (as an approximation) a couple of, a few ■ 我来说两句话。**Wǒ lái shuō liǎng jù huà.** *Let me say a few words.*

NOTE: Both 两 **liǎng** and 二 **èr** may mean *two*, but are used differently. 二 **èr** must be used in mathematics or when saying the number 2 in isolation, e.g.: ■ 一、二、三、四 ...**yī, èr, sān, sì** ... *1, 2, 3, 4* ... ■ 二加三是五。**Èr jiā sān shì wǔ.** *2 plus 3 is 5.* Use 两 **liǎng** when referring to *two something*, e.g.: ■ 两张桌子 **liǎng zhāng zhuōzi** *two tables* ■ 两个小时 **liǎng ge xiǎoshí** *two hours* The ordinal number second is 第二 **dì-èr**.

liàng 亮 ADJ bright ■ 天亮了！**Tiān liàng le!** *Day is breaking!* ■ 这个灯不太亮。**Zhège dēng bú tài liàng.** *This lamp is not very bright.*

liàng 谅 TRAD 諒 V forgive

liàngjiě 谅解 [comp: 谅 forgive + 解 understand] V understand and forgive, make allowance for

liàng 晾 V dry in the air, air dry

liàng 辆 TRAD 輛 MEASURE WORD (for vehicles) 一辆汽车 **yí liàng qìchē** a car / 两辆自行车 **liǎng liàng zìxíngchē** two bicycles

liàng 量 N quantity (See **chǎnliàng** 产量, **dàliàng** 大量, **fènliàng** 分量, **jìnliàng** 尽量, **lìliàng** 力量, **zhìliàng** 质量, **zhòngliàng** 重量.)

liáo 聊 V chat

liáotiān 聊天 V chat ■ 奶奶常去邻居家聊天。**Nǎinai cháng qù línjū jiā liáotiān.** *My granny often goes to her neighbor's home for a chat.* ■ 我没空陪你聊天。**Wǒ méi kòng péi nǐ liáotiān.** *I don't have the time to chat with you.*

liáo 辽 TRAD 遼 ADJ vast

liáokuò 辽阔 ADJ vast, extensive

liáo 疗 V treat, cure (See **zhìliáo** 治疗.)

liǎo 了 V finish, be done with ■ 这么多工作，一星期也做不了。**Zhème duō gōngzuò, yì xīngqī yě zuò bu liǎo.** *So much work can't be finished even in a week.*

NOTE: 了 **liǎo**, together with 得 **de** or 不 **bu**, is often used after a verb as a complement to mean *can ... or cannot ...* For example: ■ 这件事我干得了，那件事我干不了。**Zhè jiàn shì wǒ gàn de liǎo, nà jiàn shì wǒ gàn bu liǎo.** *I can do this job, but I can't do that job.*

liǎobuqǐ 了不起 **ADJ** wonderful, terrific ■ 这个孩子门门功课第一名，真了不起！**Zhège háizi mén-mén gōngkè dì-yī míng, zhēn liǎobuqǐ!** *This child came out the first in all the subjects. How wonderful!* ■ 你别自以为了不起。**Nǐ bié zì yǐwéi liǎobuqǐ.** *Don't think yourself so terrific. (→ Don't think you're so hot.)*

liǎojiě 了解 [comp: 了 see through + 解 analyze, comprehend] **v** know, understand, find out ■ 我和他是老朋友，我很了解他。**Wǒ hé tā shì lǎo péngyou, wǒ hěn liǎojiě tā.** *He and I are old friends. I know him very well.* ■ 我来是要了解这一地区的市场情况。**Wó lái shì yào liǎojiě zhè yí dìqū de shìchǎng qíngkuàng.** *I've come to find out the marketing situation in this region.*

liào 料[1] **N** material (See **cáiliào** 材料, **sùliào** 塑料, etc.)

liào 料[2] **v** anticipate (See **yìliào** 意料.)

liè 列 **MEASURE WORD** (for trains)
一列火车 yí liè huǒchē a train (consisting of several carriages)

lièchē 列车 **N** train
20 次列车 èrshí cì lièchē train No 20

lièchē yuán 列车员 **N** train attendant

lièjǔ 列举 **v** enumerate, list

liè 烈 **ADJ** intense (See **jīliè** 激烈, **rèliè** 热烈.)

liè 猎 **TRAD** 獵 **v** hunt

lièrén 猎人 **N** hunter

liè 劣 **ADJ** inferior, of low quality (See **èliè** 恶劣.)

lín 邻 **TRAD** 鄰 **N** neighbor

línjū 邻居 [modif: 邻 neighboring + 居 residents] **N** neighbor ■ 和邻居保持良好的关系，很重要。**Hé línjū bǎochí liánghǎo de guānxi, hěn zhòngyào.** *It is important to maintain good relations with the neighbors.* ■ 我家左面的邻居是一对老夫妻。**Wǒ jiā zuǒmiàn de línjū shì yí duì lǎo fūqī.** *My neighbors on the left are an old couple.*

lín 林 **N** wood, woods (See **sēnlín** 森林, **shùlín** 树林.)

lín 淋 **v** drench, pour

línyù 淋浴 **N** shower (bath)
洗淋浴 xǐ línyù take a shower

lín 临 **TRAD** 臨 **v** arrive

línchuáng 临床 **N** (medical) diagnosis and treatment, clinical work

línshí 临时 **ADJ** tentative, provisional ■ 这是临时措施，正式办法还要研究制定。**Zhè shì línshí cuòshī, zhèngshì bànfǎ hái yào yánjiū zhìdìng.** *This is only a tentative measure. We need to study and devise formal measures.*

lìn 吝 **ADJ** misery, stingy

lìnsè 吝啬 **ADJ** misery, stingy, mean

lìnsèguǐ 吝啬鬼 **N** miser

líng 灵 **TRAD** 靈 **I N** spirit, soul **II ADJ** agile, quick

línggǎn 灵感 **N** sudden creative relevation, inspiration

línghún 灵魂 [comp: 灵 spirit + 魂 soul] **N** soul, spirit

língmǐn 灵敏 **ADJ** very sensitive, reacting promptly

líng 零 **NUMERAL** zero
一百零二 yìbǎi líng èr 102 / 四千零五 sìqiān líng wǔ 4005

NOTE: (1) No matter how many zeros there are between digits, only one 零 líng is used. For example, 4005 is 四千零五 sìqiān líng wǔ, not 四千零零五 sìqiān líng líng wǔ. (2) 零 líng can also be written as 0, e.g 一百0五 yìbǎi líng wǔ 105.

língjiàn 零件 **N** part, spare part

língqián 零钱 [modif: 零 parts + 钱 money] **N** allowance, pocket money, small change ■ 我身上没有零钱。**Wǒ shēnshang méiyǒu língqián.** *I don't have small change on me.*

língshí 零食 [modif: 零 parts + 食 food] **N** between-meal nibbles

língshòu 零售 **v** retail, sell retail (**ANTONYM** 批发 **pīfā**)

língxīng 零星 **ADJ** fragmentary, odd

líng 铃 **TRAD** 鈴 **N** bell ■ 门铃响了，看看是谁来了。**Mén líng xiǎng le, kànkan shì shéi lái le.** *The doorbell is ringing. Go and see who's there.* ■ 上课铃响了，学生们陆续走进教室。**Shàngkè líng xiǎng le, xuéshengmen lùxù zǒujìn jiàoshì.** *The bell rang for class and students entered the classroom one after another.*

línglì 伶俐 **ADJ** quick-witted, smart, clever

líng 凌 **v** approach

língchén 凌晨 **N** the time before dawn

líng 龄 **TRAD** 齡 **N** age (See **niánlíng** 年龄.)

líng 领 **TRAD** 領 **v** lead, take ■ 服务员领客人到他们预订的桌子。**Fúwùyuán lǐng kèrén dào tāmen yùdìng de zhuōzi.** *The waiter led the customers to the table they had reserved.*

lǐngdài 领带 **N** necktie, tie (条 **tiáo**)
戴领带 dài lǐngdài wear a tie

lǐngdǎo 领导 [comp: 领 lead + 导 guide] **v & N** lead, exercise leadership; leader, the person in charge, leadership ■ 政府领导人民发展经济。**Zhèngfǔ lǐngdǎo rénmín fāzhǎn jīngjì.** *The government provides leadership for the people to develop the economy.* ■ 领导不在，你有什么事情请跟我说。**Lǐngdǎo bú zài, nǐ yǒu shénme shìqíng qǐng gēn wǒ shuō.** *The person in charge is not in. Please talk to me if you've any business.*

NOTE: (1) 领导 **lǐngdǎo** as a verb is somewhat pompous, appropriate only for grand occasions. (2) As a noun 领导 **lǐngdǎo** is no longer very popular in China and has never been very popular in other Chinese-speaking communities. To refer to the person in charge, many Chinese use 老板 **lǎobǎn** (boss)

or specific terms such as 厂长 **chǎngzhǎng** (factory manager) or 校长 **xiàozhǎng** (headmaster, school principal, university president).

lǐnghuì 领会 v understand, grasp

lǐngshì 领事 N (diplomatic) consul

lǐngshìguǎn 领事馆 N consulate
美国驻上海领事馆 Měiguó zhù Shànghǎi lǐngshìguǎn the US consulate in Shanghai

lǐngtǔ 领土 N territory (of a country)

lǐngwù 领悟 v comprehend, see the light

lǐngxiù 领袖 N leader (of a country, a political party, etc.) (位 **wèi**) ■ 他是这个国家的一位重要政治领袖。**Tā shì zhège guójiā de yí wèi zhòngyào zhèngzhì lǐngxiù.** *He is an important political leader of this country.*

lǐngyù 领域 N 1 territory, domain 2 field (of activity or thinking)

lìng 令 v command, cause (See **mìnglìng** 命令.)

lìng 另 ADJ same as 另外 **lìngwài**. Used before a monosyllabic verb.

lìngwài 另外 ADJ other, another ■ 这个方法不行，得另外想办法。**Zhège fāngfǎ bù xíng, děi lìngwài xiǎng bànfǎ.** *This method doesn't work. We've got to find another way.* ■ 除了小王以外，另外有没有人会用这台机器？**Chúle Xiǎo Wáng yǐwài, lìngwài yǒu méiyǒu rén huì yòng zhè tái jīqì?** *Is there anybody other than Xiao Wang who can operate this machine?*

liū 溜 v 1 slide, glide 2 sneak, slip away

liú 流 v flow ■ 河水慢慢地向东流去。**Hé shuǐ mànmàn de xiàng dōng liúqù.** *The river flows slowly to the east.*

liúchuán 流传 v circulate, spread

liúlàng 流浪 v lead a vagrant's life, wander, roam about

liúlèi 流泪 v shed tears

liúlì 流利 ADJ fluent ■ 我什么时候才能流利地说中文呢？**Wǒ shénme shíhou cái néng liúlì de shuō Zhōngwén ne?** *When will I be able to speak Chinese fluently?*

liúlù 流露 v show unintentionally, reveal

liúmáng 流氓 N rogue, hooligan, ruffian

liútōng 流通 v & N (of air current, commodities or currencies) circulate, flow; circulation

liúxíng 流行 v be fashionable, be popular ■ 今年流行绿色。**Jīnnián liúxíng lǜsè.** *The green color is in fashion this year.*
流行歌手 liúxíng gēshǒu pop singer / 流行音乐 liúxíng yīnyuè pop music

liúxíngbìng 流行病 N epidemic

liúxíngxìng gǎnmào (liúgǎn) 流行性感冒（流感）N influenza, flu

liú 留 v remain (in the same place), stay behind ■ 你们先回家吧，我再留一会儿做完这件事。**Nǐmen xiān huíjiā ba, wǒ zài liú yíhuìr zuòwán zhè**

jiàn shì. *You go home first. I'll stay behind for a while to finish this job.* ■ 我留他吃饭，他说有事要办，就走了。**Wǒ liú tā chī fàn, tā shuō yǒu shì yào bàn, jiù zǒu le.** *I asked him to stay for a meal, but he said he had something to attend to, and left.*

liúliàn 留恋 v be reluctant to leave, unable to tear away

liúniàn 留念 v accept or keep as a memento or keepsake
合影留念 héyǐng liúniàn take a group photo as a memento

liúshén 留神 v take precaution, look out for

liúxué 留学 [comp: 留 stay + 学 study] v study abroad ■ 很多亚洲学生在美国留学。**Hěn duō Yàzhōu xuéshēng zài Měiguó liúxué.** *Many Asian students are studying in America.*

liúxuéshēng 留学生 international students (especially in a university) ■ 不少留学生星期日也在图书馆学习。**Bùshǎo liúxuéshēng Xīnqīrì yě zài túshūguǎn xuéxí.** *Even on Sundays quite a few international students study in the library.*

liú 瘤 N tumor (See **zhǒngliú** 肿瘤.)

liú 浏 TRAD 瀏 as in 浏览 **liúlǎn**

liúlǎn 浏览 v browse
浏览器 liúlǎnqì (computer) browser

liù 六 NUMERAL six
六十六 liùshí liù sixty-six / 六十五岁 liùshí wǔ suì sixty-five years of age

lóng 龙 TRAD 龍 N dragon (条 **tiáo**) ■ 中国人把自己称作"龙的传人"。**Zhōngguórén bǎ zìjǐ chēngzuò "lóng de chuánrén."** *The Chinese call themselves "descendants of the dragon."*

lóng 聋 TRAD 聾 ADJ deaf, hard of hearing
聋子 lóngzi deaf person

lóngyǎrén 聋哑人 N deaf and dumb person, deaf-mute

lóng 隆 ADJ grand

lóngzhòng 隆重 ADJ ceremonious, in a grand style

lóng 笼 TRAD 籠 N cage
笼子 lóngzi cage / 鸟笼 niǎolóng bird cage

lǒngzhào 笼罩 v shroud, envelope

lǒng 垄 TRAD 壟 N ridge

lǒngduàn 垄断 N monopoly

lóu 楼 TRAD 樓 N 1 building with two or more stories (座 **zuò**) ■ 这座楼是去年建的。**Zhè zuò lóu shì qùnián jiàn de.** *This building was built last year.* 2 floor (层 **céng**) ■ 老师的办公室在三楼。**Lǎoshī de bàngōngshì zài sān-lóu.** *Teachers' offices are on the third floor.*
大楼 dàlóu a big building (especially a high-rise building) / 高楼 gāo lóu high-rise

NOTE: In naming floors, the Chinese system is the same as the American system and different from the British one, i.e. 一楼 **yī-lóu** is the *American first floor*, and the *British ground floor*.

lóu fáng 楼房 N multi-storied building (contrast with 平房 **píngfáng** one-story building, bungalow)

lóu shang 楼上 N upstairs

lóutī 楼梯 [modif: 楼 floor, story + 梯 steps] N stairs, stairway, staircase ■ 别站在楼梯上讲话，会妨碍别人上下。 **Bié zhàn zài lóutī shang jiǎnghuà, huì fáng'ài biérén shàng-xià.** *Do not stand talking on the stairs. It'll obstruct people going up and down.*

lóu xia 楼下 N downstairs

lǒu 搂 TRAD 摟 V embrace, hold in arms

lòu 漏 V leak ■ 屋顶漏了，要找人修理。 **Wūdǐng lòu le, yào zhǎo rén xiūlǐ.** *The roof leaks. We'll have to find someone to fix it.*

lú 炉 TRAD 爐 N stove, furnace

lúzào 炉灶 N stove, furnace

lù 陆 TRAD 陸 N land

lùdì 陆地 N dry land, land

lùxù 陆续 ADV one after another, in succession ■ 开会的代表陆续到达。 **Kāihuì de dàibiǎo lùxù dàodá.** *Congress delegates arrived one after another.*

lù 录 TRAD 錄 V record

lùqǔ 录取 V enroll (students), appoint (job applicants)

lùxiàng 录像 [v+obj: 录 record + 像 image] V record with a video camera or video recorder ■ 他们的婚礼全录像了。 **Tāmen de hūnlǐ quán lùxiàng le.** *Their wedding ceremony was videotaped.*

lùxiàngjī 录像机 N video recorder

lùyīn 录音 [v+obj: 录 record + 音 sound] V make a recording of sounds (e.g. music, reading) ■ 这里在录音，请安静！ **Zhèlǐ zài lùyīn, qǐng ānjìng!** *Recording is in progress. Please be quiet.* ■ 你有没有听过王老师读这篇课文的录音？ **Nǐ yǒu méiyǒu tīngguo Wáng lǎoshī dú zhè piān kèwén de lùyīn?** *Have you listened to the recording of Teacher Wang's reading of this text?*

lùyīnjī 录音机 N audio recorder, sound recorder

lù 路 N road, path, way (条 **tiáo**) ■ 这条路很长，一直通到山里。 **Zhè tiáo lù hěn cháng, yìzhí tōngdào shān li.** *This road is very long and leads all the way into the hills.* ■ 你认识去大学的路吗？ **Nǐ rènshì qù dàxué de lù ma?** *Do you know the way to the university?*

马路 **mǎlù** road (in a city)

lùshang 路上 N **1** on one's way (to) ■ 她去学校的路上，要经过一座公园。 **Tā qù xuéxiào de lùshàng, yào jīngguò yí zuò gōngyuán.** *On her way to school, she passes by a park.* **2** on the road ■ 路上车辆很多。 **Lùshang chēliàng hěn duō.** *There is lots of traffic on the road.*

lùxiàn 路线 [modif: 路 road + 线 line] N route, itinerary ■ 这是不是去那里最近的路线？ **Zhè shì bu shì qù nàli zuì jìn de lùxiàn?** *Is this the shortest route to that place?*

lù 露 V show, reveal ■ 她笑的时候，露出雪白的牙齿。 **Tā xiào de shíhou, lùchū xuěbái de yáchǐ.** *When she smiles, white teeth show.*

lǚ 旅 V travel

lǚguǎn 旅馆 [modif: 旅 travel + 馆 house] N hotel (座 **zuò**, 家 **jiā**) ■ 我上个月在那家旅馆订了房间。 **Wǒ shàng ge yuè zài nà jiā lǚguǎn dìngle fángjiān.** *I booked a room in that hotel last month.*

汽车旅馆 **qìchē lǚguǎn** motel / 五星旅馆 **wǔxīng lǚguǎn** five-star hotel

lǚkè 旅客 [modif: 旅 traveling + 客 guest] N hotel guest, passenger (of coach, train, plane, etc.) ■ 航空公司尽力保证旅客的安全。 **Hángkōng gōngsī jìnlì bǎozhèng lǚkè de ānquán.** *The airline does all it can to guarantee the safety of the traveling public.* ■ 旅客们，欢迎你们乘坐本次列车。 **Lǚkèmen, huānyíng chéngzuò běn cì lièchē.** *Welcome aboard this train, everyone!*

lǚtú 旅途 [modif: 旅 travel + 途 journey] N journey, travel ■ 祝你旅途愉快！ **Zhù nǐ lǚtú yúkuài!** *Have a pleasant journey!* ■ 他把旅途看到，听到的都写下来。 **Tā bǎ lǚtú kàndào, tīngdào de dōu xiě xiàlái.** *He wrote down all he saw and heard on his travels.*

lǚxíng 旅行 [comp: 旅 travel + 行 walk, go] V travel, journey, tour ■ 我在中国旅行的时候，学到不少知识。 **Wǒ zài Zhōngguó lǚxíng de shíhou, xuédào bùshǎo zhīshi.** *I gained a lot of knowledge when I traveled in China.* ■ 一个人在外国旅行，千万要注意安全。 **Yígerén zài wàiguó lǚxíng, qiānwàn yào zhùyì ānquán.** *When you are traveling alone in a foreign country, you must always be mindful of personal safety.*

旅行社 **lǚxíngshè** travel agency, travel service

lǚyóu 旅游 [comp: 旅 travel + 游 play, holiday] V travel for pleasure, tour, go sight-seeing ■ 我有了钱，就到国外去旅游。 **Wǒ yǒule qián, jiù dào guówài qù lǚyóu.** *I'll go overseas for a holiday when I've got the money.*

旅游车 **lǚyóuchē** tour bus / 旅游公司 **lǚyóu gōngsī** tourist company / 旅游路线 **lǚyóu lùxiàn** tour itinerary / 旅游团 **lǚyóutuán** tour group / 旅游者 **lǚyóuzhě** tourist, holiday-maker

lǚ 履 N shoe

lǚlì 履历 N résumé

lǚxíng 履行 V fulfill (one's promise), perform (one's obligation)

lǚ 屡 TRAD 屢 ADV repeatedly

lǚcì 屡次 ADV repeatedly, time and again

lǚ 侣 N companion (See **bànlǚ** 伴侣.)

lǜ 虑 V consider, ponder (See **kǎolǜ** 考虑.)

lǜ 滤 V filter (See **guòlǜ** 过滤.)

lǜ 率 N rate (See **xiàolǜ** 效率.)

lǜ 绿 TRAD 綠 ADJ green ■ 春天到了，树木都绿了。 **Chūntiān dào le, shùmù dōu lǜ le.** *Spring has come; the trees are all green.* ■ 红花绿树，美极了。 **Hónghuā lǜshù, měi jíle.** *Red flowers and green trees—they're so beautiful!*

lùdǎng 绿党 N the Green Party

lùkǎ 绿卡 N green card (permanent residency permit in the USA and some other countries)

lǜ 律 N law

lǜshī 律师 [modif: 律 law + 师 master] N lawyer, solicitor, barrister

律师事务所 lǜshī shìwùsuǒ law firm

luàn 乱 TRAD 亂 ADJ **1** disorderly, chaotic (ANTONYM 整齐 zhěngqí) ■ 我的房间很乱，要收拾一下。**Wǒ de fángjiān hěn luàn, yào shōushi yíxià.** *My room is in a mess and needs tidying up.* **2** at will, random ■ 他总是乱花钱。**Tā zǒngshì luàn huā qián.** *He always spends money unwisely. (→ He always wastes his money.)* ■ 你别乱说。**Nǐ bié luànshuō.** *Do not talk irresponsibly.*

lüè 掠 V plunder

lüèduó 掠夺 [comp: 掠 plunder + 夺 grab] V plunder, rob

lüè 略 V capture

lüèwēi 略微 ADJ slightly, a little, somewhat

lún 轮 TRAD 輪 N wheel

lúnchuán 轮船 [modif: 轮 wheel + 船 boat, ship] N steamship, ship ■ 现在很少人坐轮船旅行。**Xiànzài hěn shǎo rén zuò lúnchuán lǚxíng.** *Few people travel by ship now.*

lúnkuò 轮廓 N outline, contour

lúnliú 轮流 V take turns

轮流值班 lúnliú zhíbān be on duty by turns

lúntāi 轮胎 N tyre

lùn 论 TRAD 論 V discuss

lùntán 论坛 N forum

lùnwén 论文 [comp: 论 treatise + 文 essay] N dissertation, thesis, essay (篇 piān) ■ 张教授发表了多篇关于中国历史的论文。**Zhāng jiàoshòu fābiǎole duō piān guānyú Zhōngguó lìshǐ de lùnwén.** *Professor Zhang has published several theses on Chinese history.*

lùnzhèng 论证 [comp: 论 argue + 证 prove] V prove (an argument), demonstrate, discuss

luō 啰 TRAD 囉 as in 啰唆 luōsuō

luōsuō 啰唆 ADJ long-winded, wordy, verbose

luó 逻 TRAD 邏 V patrol (See xúnluó 巡逻.)

luójí 逻辑 N logic

不合逻辑 bù hé luójì illogical / 合乎逻辑 héhu luójì logical

NOTE: **luójì** 逻辑 is a transliteration from the English word "logic." See note on 咖啡 **kāfēi**.

luósīdīng 螺丝钉 N screw

luó 萝 TRAD 蘿 N trailing plant

luóbo 萝卜 N turnip, radish, carrot (根 gēn, 个 gè) ■ 咱们做个萝卜汤吧。**Zánmen zuò ge luóbo tāng ba.** *Let's prepare turnip soup.*

白萝卜 bái luóbo turnip / 红萝卜 hóng luóbo radish / 胡萝卜 hú luóbo carrot

luò 络 TRAD 絡 N net

luòyì bù jué 络绎不绝 V in an endless stream, endless

luò 落 V fall, drop ■ 秋天，树叶落了。**Qiūtiān, shùyè luò le.** *In autumn, leaves fall.*

luòchéng 落成 V (of a building or engineering project) be completed

luòhòu 落后 ADJ backward, outdated ■ 你这种观点太落后了。**Nǐ zhè zhǒng guāndiǎn tài luòhòu le.** *Your views are outdated.*

luòshí 落实 V (of a policy or idea) be implemented, be fulfilled

M

mā 妈 TRAD 媽 N ma, mom

māma 妈妈 N mom, mommy ■ 妈妈在辅导妹妹做作业。**Māma zài fúdǎo mèimei zuò zuòyè.** *Mom is tutoring my younger sister in her homework.* ■ 我想每个人都爱自己的妈妈。**Wǒ xiǎng měi ge rén dōu ài zìjǐ de māma.** *I think everyone loves their mom.*

má 麻[1] N hemp

má 麻[2] ADJ numb

mábì 麻痹 I V lull II N paralysis ■ 小儿麻痹症 xiǎoér mábìzhèng *infantile paralysis*

máfan 麻烦 [IDIOM] I V put somebody to trouble, bother ■ 麻烦你把这封信交给王经理。**Máfan nǐ bǎ zhè fēng xìn jiāo gei Wáng jīnglǐ.** *Would you mind delivering this letter to Mr Wang, the manager?* II ADJ troublesome, knotty ■ 这件事很麻烦，我不一定能做好。**Zhè jiàn shì hěn máfan, wǒ bù yídìng néng zuò hǎo.** *This matter is complicated. I'm not sure I can get it done well.*

NOTE: 麻烦您 **máfan nín** is a polite expression to request somebody's service or to ask a favor. More examples: ■ 麻烦您把盐递给我。 **Máfan nín bǎ yán dì gei wǒ.** *Please pass the salt [to me].* ■ 麻烦您查一下他的电话号码。 **Máfan nín chá yíxià tā de diànhuà hàomǎ.** *Would you mind finding out his telephone number for me?*

májiàng 麻将 N the game of mahjong, mahjong

打麻将 dǎmájiàng play mahjong

mámù 麻木 [comp: 麻 numb + 木 wooden] ADJ unable to feel anything, numb

mázuì 麻醉 [comp: 麻 numb + 醉 drunk] V & N anaesthetize; anaesthesia

局部麻醉 júbù mázuì local anaesthesia / 全身麻醉 quánshēn mázuì general anaesthesia

mázuì shī 麻醉师 N anaesthetist

mǎ 马 TRAD 馬 N horse (匹 pī) ■ 你会骑马吗？**Nǐ huì qí mǎ ma?** *Can you ride a horse?*

mǎhu 马虎 IDIOM sloppy, careless ■ 你这个作业做得太马虎了。**Nǐ zhège zuòyè zuò de tài mǎhu le.** *You did this assignment carelessly.*

mǎlù 马路 [modif: 马 horse + 路 road] N street,

avenue (条 **tiáo**) ■ 这条马路从早到晚车很多。 **Zhè tiáo mǎlù cóng-zǎo-dào-wǎn chē hěn duō.** *This street has lots of traffic from morning till night.* 马路上 mǎlù shang in the street, on the road ■ 你不能把车停在马路上。 **Ní bù néng bǎ chē tíng zài mǎlù shang.** *You can't park the car in the street.* 过马路 guò mǎlù walk across a street ■ 过马路要特别小心。 **Guò mǎlù yào tèbié xiǎoxīn.** *One should be especially careful when crossing the street.*

mǎ mǎ hū hū 马马虎虎 IDIOM **1** so-so, not too bad, just managing ■ "去年你考试成绩怎么样？" "马马虎虎。" **"Qùnián nǐ kǎoshì chéngjì zěnmeyàng?" "Mǎ-mǎ-hū-hū."** *"How did you do in the exams last year?" "So-so."* **2** careless, sloppy

mǎshàng 马上 ADV at once, immediately ■ 好，我马上来！ **Hǎo, wǒ mǎshàng lái!** *OK, I'm coming!* ■ 他要我们马上去医院。 **Tā yào wǒmen mǎshàng qù yīyuàn.** *He told us to go to the hospital immediately.*

mǎ 码 TRAD 碼 V stack

mǎtóu 码头 N dock, wharf ■ 船马上要靠码头了。 **Chuán mǎshàng yào kào mǎtóu le.** *The ship will soon anchor at the dock.*

mǎ 蚂 TRAD 螞 as in 蚂蚁 **mǎyǐ**

mǎyǐ 蚂蚁 N ant (只 **zhī**)

mà 骂 TRAD 罵 V curse, swear ■ 你怎么骂人？ **Nǐ zěnme mà rén?** *How can you swear at people?*

ma 嘛 PARTICLE surely, that goes without saying (used at the end of a sentence to indicate that the truth of the statement is obvious) ■ 农村的空气就是比城市干净嘛！ **Nóngcūn de kōngqì jiùshì bǐ chéngshì gānjing ma!** *The air in rural areas is surely cleaner than that in cities.*

ma 吗 TRAD 嗎 PARTICLE (used at the end of a sentence to turn it into a yes-or-no question) ■ 你会说中文吗？ **Nǐ huì shuō Zhōngwén ma?** *Do you speak Chinese?* ■ 这么简单的题目，你也不会做吗？ **Zhème jiǎndān de tímù, nǐ yě bú huì zuò ma?** *Can't you do such a simple question?*

mái 埋 V bury ■ 他把死狗埋在树下。 **Tā bǎ sǐ gǒu mái zài shù xia.** *He buried his dead dog under the tree.*

máifu 埋伏 V lie in ambush, ambush

máimò 埋没 [comp: 埋 bury + 没 annul] V stifle (talent)

máizàng 埋葬 V bury (a dead person)

mǎi 买 TRAD 買 V buy ■ 我要买一双鞋。 **Wǒ yào mǎi yì shuāng xié.** *I want to buy a pair of shoes.* ■ 你这本书在哪儿买的？ **Nǐ zhè běn shū zài nǎr mǎi de?** *Where did you buy this book?*

mǎimài 买卖 [comp: 买 buy + 卖 sell] N trade, business ■ 最近店里的买卖怎么样？ **Zuìjìn diànli de mǎimài zěnmeyàng?** *How is business at your shop recently?* ■ 他在城里有个小买卖。 **Tā zài**

chénglǐ yǒu ge xiǎo mǎimài. *He has a small business in town.*

做买卖 zuò mǎimài do business, be engaged in business ■ 几乎每一家大公司都想跟中国做买卖。 **Jīhū měi yì jiā dà gōngsī dòu xiǎng gēn Zhōngguó zuò mǎimài.** *Almost every corporation wants to do business with China.* ■ 他很会做买卖，几年工夫就发财了。 **Tā hěn huì zuò mǎimài, jǐ nián gōngfu jiù fācái le.** *He is very good at doing business, and has become prosperous just in a few years.*

mài 迈 TRAD 邁 V step forward

mài 麦 TRAD 麥 N wheat

大麦 dàmài barley / 荞麦 qiáomài buckwheat / 小麦 xiǎomài wheat / 燕麦 yànmài oats

màikèfēng 麦克风 N microphone

mài 卖 TRAD 賣 V sell ■ 他把汽车卖了。 **Tā bǎ qìchē mài le.** *He sold his car.* ■ 你们这里卖水果吗？ **Nǐmen zhèlǐ mài shuǐguǒ ma?** *Do you sell fruit here?*

mài 脉 TRAD 脈 N blood vessel

màibó 脉搏 N pulse

量脉搏 liáng màibó take one's pulse

mán 瞒 V conceal truth from ■ 这件事你不该瞒我。 **Zhè jiàn shì nǐ bù gāi mán wǒ.** *You shouldn't have hidden this matter from me.*

mán 馒 TRAD 饅 as in 馒头 **mántou**

mántou 馒头 [suffix: 馒 steamed bun + 头 nominal suffix] N steamed bun ■ 我早饭吃了两个馒头。 **Wǒ zǎofàn chīle liǎng ge mántou.** *I ate two steamed buns for breakfast.*

mán 埋 as in 埋怨 **mányuàn**

mányuàn 埋怨 V blame, complain

mán 蛮 TRAD 蠻 ADJ rough, churlish, crude (See 野蛮 **yěmán**.)

mán 瞒 TRAD 瞞 V hide the truth from (See 隐瞒 **yǐnmán**.)

mǎn 满 ADJ full, full to the brim ■ 碗里的水满了。 **Wǎn li de shuǐ mǎn le.** *The bowl is full of water.* ■ 房间里挤得满满的。 **Fángjiān li jǐ de mǎnmǎn de.** *The room is packed.*

mǎnyì 满意 [v+obj: 满 make full + 意 wish, desire] ADJ satisfied, satisfactory ■ 我们要让顾客高兴地来，满意地走。 **Wǒmen yào ràng gùkè gāoxìng de lái, mǎnyì de zǒu.** *We should make customers arrive happy and leave satisfied.*

对 … 满意 duì … mǎnyì be satisfied with ■ 我对你们的服务很不满意。 **Wǒ duì nǐmen de fúwù hěn bù mǎnyì.** *I'm very dissatisfied with your service.*

mǎnzú 满足 V meet the needs of, satisfy ■ 老师尽量满足学生的要求。 **Lǎoshī jìnliàng mǎnzú xuésheng de yāoqiú.** *The teacher tries his best to meet the demands of his students.* ■ 我们要增加产量，满足市场的需要。 **Wǒmen yào zēngjiā chǎnliàng, mǎnzú shìchǎng de xūyào.** *We should increase output to satisfy the needs of the market.*

màn 慢 ADJ slow (ANTONYM 快 **kuài**) ■ 别着急，慢慢地走。**Bié zháojí, mànman de zǒu.** *Don't be impatient. Walk slowly.* ■ 你说得慢，我就听得懂。**Nǐ shuō de màn, wǒ jiù tīng de dǒng.** *If you speak slowly, I can understand you.*

mànxìng 慢性 ADJ chronic (disease)

mànxìngzi 慢性子 N slow or indolent person, slow coach

màn 漫 V overflow

màncháng 漫长 ADJ long, endless

mànhuà 漫画 N cartoon, caricature

màn 蔓 as in 蔓延 **mànyán**

mànyán 蔓延 V spread, extend

máng 忙 ADJ busy ■ 我最近很忙，没有空儿跟你去看电影。**Wǒ zuìjìn hěn máng, méiyǒu kòngr gēn nǐ qù kàn diànyǐng.** *I'm busy these days, and don't have time to go to the movies with you.* ■ 你在忙什么？**Nǐ zài máng shénme?** *What are you busy with?*

NOTE: When friends meet in China, a common conversation opener is 你最近忙吗？**Nǐ zuìjìn máng ma?** *Have you been busy lately?*

mánglù 忙碌 ADJ busy ■ 忙忙碌碌 **mángmang lùlù** *very busy, always engaged in doing something*

máng 盲 ADJ blind

mángmù 盲目 ADJ blind, doing something without awareness

mángrén 盲人 [modif: 盲 blind + 人 person] N blind person

盲人学校 **mángrén xuéxiào** school for the blind

máng 茫 ADJ boundless and indistinct

mángmáng 茫茫 ADJ boundless and blurred, vast

mángrán 茫然 ADJ knowing nothing about, ignorant, in the dark

māo 猫 TRAD 貓 N cat (只 **zhī**) ■ 我家有一只小白猫。**Wǒ jiā yǒu yì zhī xiǎo bái māo.** *We keep a white kitten at home.*

máo 毛¹ N hair
羊毛 **yángmáo** wool

máo 毛² MEASURE WORD same as 角² **jiǎo** MEASURE WORD. Used colloquially.

máobìng 毛病 N 1 illness ■ 我什么毛病也没有，身体健康得很。**Wǒ shénme máobìng yě méiyǒu, shēntǐ jiànkāng de hěn.** *I have no complaints at all; I am in excellent health.* 2 trouble, breakdown ■ 洗衣机出毛病了。**Xǐyījī chū máobìng le.** *The washing machine is out of order.*

máojīn 毛巾 N towel (条 **tiáo**) ■ 他拿着一条大毛巾进浴室洗澡。**Tā názhe yì tiáo dà máojīn jìn yùshì xǐzǎo.** *He went into the bathroom with a big towel to take a bath.*

máoxiàn 毛线 N knitting wool, woolen yarn

máoyī 毛衣 [modif: 毛 woolen + 衣 clothing] N woolen sweater, woolen pullover (件 **jiàn**) ■ 她给对象织了一件毛衣。**Tā gěi duìxiàng zhīle yí jiàn máoyī.** *She knitted a woolen sweater for her fiancé.*

máo 矛 N spear

máodùn 矛盾 [comp: 矛 spear + 盾 shield] N & ADJ contradiction, disunity; contradictory, inconsistent ■ 他们之间有很大的矛盾。**Tāmen zhījiān yǒu hěn dà de máodùn.** *There is a big rift between them.* 自相矛盾 **zìxiāng máodùn** self-contradictory, inconsistent ■ 这篇文章前后自相矛盾。**Zhè piān wénzhāng qiánhòu zìxiāng máodùn.** *This article is inconsistent in its argument.*

NOTE: 矛盾 **máodùn** is a colorful word derived from an ancient Chinese fable. A man who sold spears (矛 **máo**) and shields (盾 **dùn**) boasted that his spears were so sharp that they could penetrate any shield, and that his shields were so strong that no spear could ever penetrate them. As there seemed to be a contradiction there, 矛盾 **máodùn** came to mean *inconsistency* or *contradiction*.

mào 冒 V 1 emit, send forth, give off ■ 开水冒着热气。**Kāishuǐ màozhe rè qì.** *Boiling water gives off steam.* 2 risk 3 make false claims

màochōng 冒充 V pass off as genuine

màofàn 冒犯 V offend, tread on the toe

màopái 冒牌 [v+obj: 冒 falsely claim + 牌 brand] V counterfeit, forge
冒牌货 **màopáihuò** counterfeit, fake, forgery

màoxiǎn 冒险 [v+obj: 冒 risk + 险 danger] V risk, take a risk

mào 帽 N hat, cap

màozi 帽子 [suffix: 帽 hat, cap + 子 nominal suffix] N hat, cap ■ 今天外面很冷，你要戴帽子。**Jīntiān wàimiàn hěn lěng. Nǐ yào dài màozi.** *It's very cold outside. You'd better wear a hat.*
戴帽子 **dài màozi** put on/wear a hat (or a cap) / 脱帽子 **tuō màozi** take off a hat (or a cap)

mào 贸 TRAD 貿 N transaction

màoyì 贸易 [comp: 贸 transaction + 易 exchange] N trade, exchange ■ 搞制造和搞贸易，哪个更赚钱？**Gǎo zhìzào hé gǎo màoyì, nǎge gèng zhuànqián?** *Manufacturing or trade, which is more profitable?*
对外贸易 **duìwài màoyì** foreign trade / 国际贸易 **guójì màoyì** international trade / 贸易公司 **màoyì gōngsī** trading company

mào 茂 ADJ luxuriant

màoshèng 茂盛 [comp: 茂 luxuriant + 盛 thriving] ADJ (of vegetation) luxuriant, lush

mào 貌 N appearance (See **lǐmào** 礼貌, **miànmào** 面貌.)

me 么 TRAD 麼 PARTICLE (used to form certain words) (See **duōme** 多么, **nàme** 那么, **shénme** 什么, **wèishénme** 为什么, **zěnme** 怎么, **zěnmeyàng** 怎么样, **zhème** 这么.)

méi 没 ADJ same as 没有 **méiyǒu**
没关系 **méi guānxi** (See **guānxi** 关系.)

没意思 méi yìsi (See **yìsi** 意思.)

méishénme 没什么 **IDIOM** nothing serious, it doesn't matter ■ "你不舒服吗？" "没什么，就是有点儿头疼。" **"Nǐ bù shūfu ma?" "Méishénme, jiùshì yǒudiǎnr tóuténg."** *"Aren't you feeling well?" "Nothing serious, just a bit of headache."* ■ "对不起，我这么晚打电话给你。" "没什么，有什么事吗？" **"Duìbuqǐ, wǒ zhème wǎn dǎ diànhuà gei nǐ." "Méishénme, yǒu shénme shì ma?"** *"I'm sorry for ringing you so late." "It doesn't matter. What can I do for you?"*

méiyòng 没用 **ADJ** useless ■ 那本词典太旧，没用了。 **Nà běn cídiǎn tài jiù, méiyòng le.** *That dictionary is too old and no longer useful.* ■ 他这个人太没用了，连一个小孩都对付不了。 **Tā zhège rén tài méiyòng le, lián yí ge xiǎohái dōu duìfu bù liǎo.** *That man is really useless. He can't even deal with a child.*

méiyǒu 没有 **V 1** do not have ■ 我没有这么多钱。 **Wǒ méiyǒu zhème duō qián.** *I don't have that much money.* ■ 他没有兄弟，只有一个姐姐。 **Tā méiyǒu xiōngdì, zhǐyǒu yí ge jiějie.** *He has no brothers, only an elder sister.* **2** there is/are no ■ 房间里没有人。 **Fángjiān li méiyǒu rén.** *There is nobody in the room.* ■ 这条街上没有饭店。 **Zhè tiáo jiē shang méiyǒu fàndiàn.** *There is no restaurant on this street.* **3** did not, have not (indicating negation of past experiences, usually used before a verb or at the end of a question) ■ 我没有学过这个字。 **Wǒ méiyǒu xuéguo zhège zì.** *I haven't learnt this Chinese character.* ■ "你去过中国没有？" "还没有。" **"Nǐ qùguo Zhōngguó méiyǒu?" "Hái méiyǒu."** *"Have you ever been to China?" "Not yet."*

还没有 hái méiyǒu not yet

NOTE: In spoken Chinese, 没有 **méiyǒu** is often shortened 没 **méi**. However, when 没有 **méiyǒu** is used at the end of a question, as in ■ 你去过中国没有？ **Nǐ qùguo Zhōngguó méiyǒu?** *Have you ever been to China?* it cannot be replaced by 没 **méi**.

méizhé 没辙 **V** be at a loss what to do, be at one's wit's end

méi 枚 **MEASURE WORD** (for small objects, such a coin) 一枚硬币 yìméi yìngbì a coin

méi 煤 **V** coal ■ 这个国家不产煤。 **Zhège guójiā bù chǎn méi.** *This country does not produce coal.*

méikuàng 煤矿 **N** coal mine

méikuànggōng 煤矿工 **N** coal miner, collier

méiqì 煤气 **N** coal gas

méitàn 煤炭 same as **méi** 煤

méitián 煤田 **N** coalfield

méi 媒 **N** matchmaking 做媒 zuòméi be a matchmaker

méijiè 媒介 **N** medium

méiren 媒人 **N** matchmaker

méitǐ 媒体 **N** medium, media

大众媒体 dàzhòng méitǐ mass media

méi 眉 **N** eyebrow

méimao 眉毛 **N** eyebrow

méi 霉 **N** mildew, mould

méijūn 霉菌 **N** mould

měi 每 **I ADV** every, each ■ 我每隔三天游一次泳。 **Wǒ měi gé sān tiān yóu yí cì yǒng.** *I swim once every three days.* ■ 卡车司机每工作两天，休息一天。 **Kǎchē sījī měi gōngzuò liǎng tiān, xiūxi yì tiān.** *The truck drivers have a day off after working for two days.* **II PRON** every, each ■ 你每天都看电视新闻吗？ **Nǐ měi tiān dōu kàn diànshì xīnwén ma?** *Do you watch TV news every day?* ■ 这条街每座房子都不一样。 **Zhè tiáo jiē měi zuò fángzi dōu bù yíyàng.** *Every house on this street is different from the other.*

NOTE: Usage in Chinese requires that when 每 **měi** is used as a pronoun to mean *every* or *each*, it should be followed by 都 **dōu** *all*, without exception.

měi 美 **ADJ** beautiful ■ 这里的风景真美！ **Zhèlǐ de fēngjǐng zhēn měi!** *The scenery here is truly beautiful!* ■ 她从小就是个美人儿。 **Tā cóngxiǎo jiù shì ge měirénr.** *She has been a beauty since childhood.*

měiguān 美观 [modif: 美 beautiful + 观 looking] **ADJ** pleasing to the eye

Měiguó 美国 **N** the USA, America

měihǎo 美好 [comp: 美 beautiful + 好 fine] **ADJ** (of abstract things) fine, beautiful ■ 我有一个美好的愿望。 **Wǒ yǒu yí ge měihǎo de yuànwàng.** *I have a beautiful aspiration.* ■ 世界上的事物并不都象人们希望的那样美好。 **Shìjiè shang de shìwù bìng bù dōu xiàng rénmen xīwàng de nàyàng měihǎo.** *Things in the world are not all as fine as people wish them to be.*

měilì 美丽 [comp: 美 beautiful + 丽 beautiful] **ADJ** beautiful ■ 春天各种颜色的花儿都开放了，花园真美丽。 **Chūntiān gè zhǒng yánsè de huār dōu kāifàng le, huāyuán zhēn měilì.** *In spring with flowers of all colors in full bloom, the garden is beautiful.*

měimǎn 美满 [comp: 美 beautiful + 满 full, totally satisfied] **ADJ** (of marriage, family, etc.) totally satisfactory, happy ■ 她有美满的家庭、成功的事业，真是太幸福了。 **Tā yǒu měimǎn de jiātíng, chénggōng de shìyè, zhēnshì tài xìngfú le.** *She has a happy family and a successful career. What a fortunate woman!*

měimiào 美妙 [comp: 美 beautiful + 妙 wonderful] **ADJ** wonderful, splendid

měishù 美术 [modif: 美 beautiful + 术 craft] **N** fine arts ■ 她对美术非常感兴趣。 **Tā duì měishù fēicháng gǎn xìngqù.** *She has a great interest in the fine arts.*

měishùguǎn 美术馆 **N** gallery, art museum

měishùjiā 美术家 **N** fine arts specialist, artist

Měiyuán 美元 [modif: 美 American + 元 dollar] **N** US dollar, greenback ■ 我想换一些美元。 **Wǒ xiǎng huàn yìxiē Měiyuán.** *I want to change some money into American dollars.*

Měizhōu 美洲 [modif: 美 America + 洲 continent] **N** (the continent of) Americas
北美洲 Běi-Měizhōu North America / 南美洲 Nán-Měizhōu South America / 中美洲 Zhōng-Měizhōu Central America

mèi 妹 **N** younger sister

mèimei 妹妹 **N** younger sister ■ 我妹妹还在念小学呢。 **Wǒ mèimei háizài niàn xiǎoxué ne.** *My younger sister is still in primary school.*

mèi 魅 **N** evil spirit

mèilì 魅力 **N** charm, enchantment

mēn 闷 **TRAD** 悶 **ADJ** stuffy, uncomfortable

mēnrè 闷热 **ADJ** hot and stifling, muggy, sultry

mén 门¹ **TRAD** 門 **N** door, gate (道 dào) ■ 我们学校的大门正对汽车站。 **Wǒmen xuéxiào de dàmén zhèng duì qìchē zhàn.** *There is a bus stop directly opposite the gate of our school.*
门口 ménkǒu doorway, by the door, by the gate ■ 他站在门口等一个朋友。 **Tā zhàn zài ménkǒu děng yí ge péngyou.** *He's standing by the door, waiting for a friend.*
大门 dàmén gate

mén 门² **TRAD** 門 **MEASURE WORD** (for school subjects, languages, etc.) ■ 你今年念几门课？ **Nǐ jīnnián niàn jǐ mén kè?** *How many subjects do you study this year?* ■ 要学会一门语言，非下功夫不可。 **Yào xuéhuì yì mén yǔyán, fēi xià gōngfu bùkě.** *To learn a language, you simply must make great efforts.*

ménzhěn 门诊 **N** outpatient service

men 们 **TRAD** 們 **SUFFIX** (indicating plural number) ■ 学生们都很喜欢这位新老师。 **Xuéshengmen dōu hěn xǐhuan zhè wèi xīn lǎoshī.** *All the students like this new teacher.*

NOTE: As a plural number marker, 们 **men** is only used with nouns denoting people. It is not used when there are words indicating plurality, such as numerals or words like 一些 **yìxiē**, 很多 **hěn duō**. In many cases, the plural number of a personal noun is implicit without the use of 们 **men**. In the example sentence, 们 **men** is not obligatory, i.e. 学生都很喜欢这位新老师。 **Xuésheng dōu hěn xǐhuan zhè wèi xīn lǎoshī.** *All the students like this new teacher.* is correct and idiomatic.

mēng 蒙 **V 1** cover **2** cheat, deceive

méng 萌 **V** sprout

méngyá 萌芽 **N** sprout, bud, shoot

měng 猛 **ADJ** fierce, violent

měngliè 猛烈 **ADJ** fierce, furious

mèng 梦 **TRAD** 夢 **N** dream ■ 我昨天夜里做了一个奇怪的梦。 **Wǒ zuótiān yèli zuòle yí ge qíguài de mèng.** *I had a strange dream last night.*

做梦 zuòmèng have a dream

mèngxiǎng 梦想 [comp: 梦 dream + 想 think] **V** dream of, have a pipe dream

mī 眯 **V** narrow one's eyes

mí 迷 **V** be lost

míhuò 迷惑 **V 1** puzzle, be puzzled **2** delude, be deluded

mílù 迷路 **V** lose one's way, get lost

mírén 迷人 **ADJ** charming, alluring

míshī 迷失 **V** lose (one's way), take a wrong turning

míxìn 迷信 **N** superstition

mí 谜 **TRAD** 謎 **N** riddle

míyǔ 谜语 **N** riddle
猜谜语 (猜谜) cāi míyǔ (cāi mí) guess a riddle ■ 我给你猜一个谜语。 **Wǒ gěi nǐ cāi yí ge míyǔ.** *Can you guess my riddle?*

mí 弥 **TRAD** 彌 **ADJ** full

míbǔ 弥补 **V** make up, remedy

mímàn 弥漫 **V** fill (the air) with

mǐ 米¹ **MEASURE WORD** meter (colloquial)
一米 yì mǐ one meter / 三米半 sān mǐ bàn three and half meters

NOTE: The formal word for *meter* is 公尺 **gōngchǐ**.

mǐ 米² **N** rice, paddy rice (粒 lì) ■ 在中国南方，很多农民种米。 **Zài Zhōngguó nánfāng, hěn duō nóngmín zhòng mǐ.** *In the south of China many farmers grow rice.*
米酒 mǐjiǔ rice wine

mǐfàn 米饭 [comp: 米 rice + 饭 meal] **N** cooked rice (碗 wǎn) ■ 米饭煮好了，菜还没有做好。 **Mǐfàn zhǔ hǎo le, cài hái méiyǒu zuò hǎo.** *The rice is cooked, but the dishes are not ready yet.* ■ 王家是南方人，每天都吃米饭。 **Wáng jiā shì nánfāngrén, měi tiān dōu chī mǐfàn.** *The Wangs are southerners. They eat rice every day.*

NOTE: The staple food for southern Chinese (Chinese living south of the Yangtze River) is 米饭 **mǐfàn**, while northern Chinese mainly eat 面食 **miànshí** (food made of wheat flour), such as 面条儿 **miàntiáor** (noodles) and 馒头 **mántou** (steamed buns).

mì 秘 **ADJ** secret

mìmì 秘密 [comp: 秘 secret + 密 confidential] **N & ADJ** secret; secret, confidential ■ "我告诉你一个秘密。" "要是你能告诉我，那就不是秘密。" **"Wǒ gàosù nǐ yí ge mìmì." "Yàoshì nǐ néng gàosù wǒ, nà jiù bú shì mìmì."** *"I'll tell you a secret." "If you can tell me, then it's not really a secret."* ■ 她有一个秘密信箱。 **Tā yǒu yí ge mìmì xìnxiāng.** *She has a secret post office box.*
秘密警察 mìmì jǐngchá secret police / 秘密文件 mìmì wénjiàn classified document

mìshu 秘书 **N** secretary ■ 他要秘书通知小王马上来见他。 **Tā yào mìshu tōngzhī Xiǎo Wáng mǎshàng lái jiàn tā.** *He wants his secretary to*

inform Xiao Wang to come and see him immediately.

私人秘书 sīrén mìshu private secretary

mì 密 ADJ **1** close, intimate **2** secret, confidential

mìdù 密度 [modif: 密 dense + 度 degree] N density, thickness

mìfēng 密封 [modif: 密 dense + 封 seal] V seal, seal up

mìmǎ 密码 N (computing) password, secret code, cipher code

输入密码 shūrù mìmǎ key in the password

mìqiè 密切 [comp: 密 close + 切 intimate] ADJ close, intimate ■ 这家人家的兄弟姐妹关系很密切。**Zhè jiā rénjiā de xiōng-dì-jiě-mèi guānxi hěn mìqiè.** *The siblings in this family are very close to each other.* ■ 公司各部门要密切配合，不能自行其是。**Gōngsī gè bùmén yào mìqiè pèihé, bù néng zì xíng qí shì.** *The departments in a company should be closely coordinated, and not act as they think fit.*

mì 蜜 N honey

mìfēng 蜜蜂 [modif: 蜜 honey + 蜂 wasp] N bee (只 zhī) ■ 他养蜜蜂为生。**Tā yǎng mìfēng wéishēng.** *He makes a living by beekeeping.*

mián 棉 N cotton

miánhuā 棉花 [modif: 棉 cotton + 花 bloom] N cotton ■ 中国是棉花进口国，还是棉花出口国？**Zhōngguó shì miánhuā jìnkǒuguó, háishì miánhuā chūkǒuguó?** *Is China a cotton importer or cotton exporter?*

mián 眠 V sleep (See **shīmián** 失眠.)

miǎn 免 V avoid

miǎnde 免得 CONJ so as not to, lest ■ 你要早作准备，免得临时匆忙。**Nǐ yào zǎo zuò zhǔnbèi, miǎnde línshí cōngmáng.** *You should start preparing early, so as not to be in a hurry when the time comes.*

miǎnfèi 免费 [v+obj: 免 do without + 费 fee, payment] ADJ free of charge

miǎnyì 免疫 [v+obj: 免 avoid + 疫 disease] N immunity (from disease)

miǎn 勉 V strive

miǎnlì 勉励 V encourage, urge

miǎnqiǎng 勉强 **1** ADJ grudgingly, barely ■ 他勉强答应了我的要求。**Tā miǎnqiǎng dāyìngle wǒ de yāoqiú.** *He yielded to my demand grudgingly.* **2** V force to do ■ 他不愿去，你就别勉强他。**Tā bú yuàn qù, nǐ jiù bié miǎnqiǎng tā.** *If he's unwilling to go, don't force him to.*

miàn 面¹ N face ■ 你们俩有矛盾，还是面对面地谈一下吧。**Nǐmen liǎ yǒu máodùn, háishì miàn-duì-miàn de tán yíxià ba.** *If there is conflict between the two of you, you'd better discuss it face to face.*

miànduì 面对 V be faced with

面对一个复杂的问题 miànduì yí ge fùzá de wèn

tí be faced with a complicated problem

miànjī 面积 N (mathematics) area ■ 这个房间的面积是二十平方公尺。**Zhège fángjiān de miànjī shì èrshí píngfāng gōngchǐ.** *This room has an area of 20 square meters.*

miànlín 面临 V be faced with, be up against

面临新的挑战 miànlín xīn de tiǎozhàn be up against a new challenge

miànmào 面貌 [comp: 面 face + 貌 looks, appearance] N appearance, state (of things)

miànqián 面前 N in face of, in front of, before ■ 在我们面前摆着两种选择。**Zài wǒmen miànqián bǎizhe liǎng zhǒng xuǎnzé.** *We are faced with two choices.*

miànzi 面子 N face, honor

爱面子 ài miànzi be keen on face-saving / 丢面子 diū miànzi lose face / 给… 留面子 gěi … liú miànzi save face (for somebody)

miàn 面² TRAD 麵 N **1** (面条儿 **miàntiáor**) noodle

方便面 fāngbiàn miàn instant noodles

2 wheat flour

miànbāo 面包 [modif: 面 wheat flour + 包 lump] N bread (只 zhī, 条 tiáo) ■ 新做的面包特别香。**Xīn zuò de miànbāo tèbié xiāng.** *Freshly baked bread smells particularly good.*

一片面包 yípiàn miànbāo a slice of bread

miànbāochē 面包车 [modif: 面包 a loaf of bread + 车 vehicle] N minibus, van (辆 liàng)

miànbāo fáng 面包房 bakery

miànfěn 面粉 N flour

miàntiáor 面条儿 N noodles (碗 wǎn) ■ 面条儿要热的才好吃。**Miàntiáor yào rè de cái hǎochī.** *Noodles must be eaten hot.* ■ 她是北方人，面条儿做得好，米饭做得不好。**Tā shì běifāngrén, miàntiáor zuò de hǎo, mǐfàn zuò de bù hǎo.** *She's a northerner. She makes good noodle meals, but doesn't cook rice well.* ■ 简单点，做碗面条儿就行。**Jiǎndān diǎn, zuò wǎn miàntiáor jiù xíng.** *Let's keep it simple. Making a bowl of noodles is good enough.*

miàn 面³ MEASURE WORD (for flat objects)

一面镜子 yí miàn jìngzi a mirror / 两面旗子 liǎng miàn qízi two flags

miáo 苗 N seedling

miáotiáo 苗条 ADJ slender, slim

miáo 描 V trace, copy

miáohuì 描绘 [comp: 描 trace + 绘 paint] V depict, describe

miáoxiě 描写 V describe (in writing) ■ 她在信中描写了那里的美丽风景。**Tā zài xìn zhōng miáoxiěle nàli de měilì fēngjǐng.** *In her letter she gives a description of the beautiful landscape there.*

miáo 瞄 V fix one's gaze on

miáozhǔn 瞄准 V take aim, aim at

miáo 渺 ADJ distant and indistinct

miáoxiǎo 渺小 **ADJ** tiny, negligible

miǎo 秒 **MEASURE WORD** (of time) second ■ 我跑一百公尺要十四秒，你呢？ *Wǒ pǎo yìbǎi gōngchǐ yào shísì miǎo, nǐ ne? It takes me 14 seconds to run 100 meters. How about you?*

miǎo 藐 **ADJ** small, petty

miǎoshì 藐视 **V** despise, slight

miào 妙 **ADJ** wonderful, ingenious ■ 你的主意真妙！ *Nǐ de zhǔyi zhēn miào! What a wonderful idea!*
不妙 búmiào not good, unpromising ■ 这两天情况不妙。 *Zhè liǎngtian qíngkuàng búmiào. Things are not good these days.*

miào 庙 **TRAD** 廟 **N** temple (座 zuò) ■ 在中国的名胜，常常有一座古庙。 *Zài Zhōngguó de míngshèng, chángcháng yǒu yí zuò gǔ miào. In scenic spots in China, there is often an ancient temple.*

miè 灭 **TRAD** 滅 **V** extinguish, put out, go out ■ 火灭了。 *Huǒ miè le. The fire was extinguished.*
灭火器 mièhuǒqì fire extinguisher

mièwáng 灭亡 **V** exterminate, be exterminated

miè 蔑 **V** disdain, smear

mièshì 蔑视 **V** look upon with contempt

mín 民 **N** people

mínjiān 民间 **N 1** among common folks
民间故事 mínjiān gùshi folk tale
2 people-to-people
民间往来 mínjiān wǎnglái people-to-people exchange

mínyòng 民用 **ADJ** for civil use, civil

mínzhǔ 民主 **N & ADJ** democracy; democratic
实行政治民主 shíxíng zhèngzhì mínzhǔ practice political democracy / 民主管理 mínzhǔ guǎnlǐ democratic governance

mínzú 民族 [comp: 民 people + 族 clan] **N** ethnic group, nationality (个 gè) ■ 汉民族是中国最大的民族。 *Hàn mínzú shì Zhōngguó zuì dà de mínzú. The Hans are the biggest ethnic group in China.*
少数民族 shǎoshù mínzú minority ethnic group

mǐn 敏 **ADJ** clever, quick-witted

mǐn'gǎn 敏感 **ADJ** sensitive

mǐnjié 敏捷 **ADJ** agile, nimble

mǐnruì 敏锐 [comp: 敏 quick + 锐 sharp] **ADJ** alert, sharp-witted

míng 名 **I N** name, (personal) given name ■ 他们要给新生儿取个名。 *Tāmen yào gěi xīnshēngér qǔ ge míng. They're going to name their newborn baby.* **II MEASURE WORD** (used for people, especially those with a specific position or occupation)
一名军人 yì míng jūnrén a soldier / 两名学生 liǎng míng xuésheng two students

míngcì 名次 **N** place in a competition, position in a name list

míng'é 名额 **N** the number of people assigned or allowed for a particular purpose, quota of
大学招生名额 dàxué zhāoshēng míng'é university enrolment quota

míng fù qí shí 名副其实 **IDIOM** be worthy of the name
名副其实的好老师 míngfùqíshí de hǎo lǎoshī a good teacher in every sense of the word

míngpái 名牌 **N** famous brand, name brand

míngpiàn 名片 **N** name card, visiting card (张 zhāng)

míngshèng 名胜 **N** famous scenic spot ■ 这个地区有很多名胜，每年吸引大批旅游者。 *Zhège dìqū yǒu hěn duō míngshèng, měi nián xīyǐn dàpī lǚyóuzhě. The area boasts many famous scenic spots and attracts large numbers of tourists every year.*

míngshèng gǔjī 名胜古迹 **IDIOM** famous scenic spots and cultural relics

míngyù 名誉 **N** reputation, honor
名誉博士 míngyù bóshì honorary doctorate / 恢复名誉 huīfù míngyù restore honor

míngzi 名字 [comp: 名 given name + 字 courtesy name] **N** name, given name ■ 我的名字叫王小明。 *Wǒ de míngzi jiào Wáng Xiǎo Míng. My name is Wang Xiaoming.* ■ "你知道他的名字吗？" "不知道。" *"Nǐ zhīdào tā de míngzi ma?" "Bù zhīdào." Do you know his name?" "No."*

NOTE: To be exact, 名字 **míngzi** only means *given name,* but informally 名字 **míngzi** may also mean *full name (family name + given name).* The formal word for *full name* is 姓名 **xìngmíng**. See 姓 **xìng**.

míng 明 **ADJ** bright

míngbai 明白 [comp: 明 bright + 白 white] **1 ADJ** clear, obvious ■ 对不起，我没有说明白。 *Duìbuqǐ, wǒ méiyǒu shuō míngbai. Sorry, I didn't make it very clear.* **2 V** understand, see the point ■ 老师又解释了一遍，我才明白了。 *Lǎoshī yòu jiěshì yí biàn, wǒ cái míngbai le. I only understood after the teacher explained it again.* ■ 我还不明白，能不能再说一遍？ *Wǒ hái bù míngbai, néng bu néng zài shuō yí biàn? I still don't understand. Could you say it again?*

míngliàng 明亮 [comp: 明 bright + 亮 bright] **ADJ** bright, well-lit ■ 这间房间很明亮，我很喜欢。 *Zhè jiān fángjiān hěn míngliàng, wǒ hěn xǐhuan. This room is very bright. I like it.*

míngmíng 明明 **ADV** clearly, obviously, as clear as day ■ 你明明知道，为什么要说不知道？ *Nǐ míngmíng zhīdào, wèishénme yàoshuō bùzhīdào? You obviously knew it; why did you say you didn't?*

míngnián 明年 [modif: 明 (in this context) next + 年 year] **N** next year ■ 明年我二十一岁了！ *Míngnián wǒ èrshíyī suì le! I'll be twenty-one next year!*

NOTE: 明年 **míngnián** is next year only to this year 今年 **jīnnián**. For the year after another year, we use 第二年 **dì-èr nián** or 下一年 **xià yì nián**. For example:

■ 他们在2012年结婚，第二年生了一个儿子。**Tāmen zài èr-líng-yī-èr nián jiéhūn, dì-èr nián shēngle yí ge érzi.** *They married in 2012 and had a son the following year.* It would be wrong to use 明年 **míngnián** in this example.

míngquè 明确 [comp: 明 clear + 确 definite, specific] **ADJ & V** definite and explicit; make definite and explicit ■ 他说得很明确，本月十五日下午三点二十五分到达北京机场。**Tā shuō de hěn míngquè, běnyuè shíwǔ rì xiàwǔ sān diǎn èrshíwǔ fēn dàodá Běijīng jīchǎng.** *He made it very clear—he will be arriving at Beijing Airport at 3:25 p.m. on the fifteenth of this month.* ■ 请你明确一下品种、数量和交货日期。**Qǐng nǐ míngquè yíxià pǐnzhǒng, shùliàng hé jiāohuò rìqī.** *Please be definite about the product specifications, quantity and date of shipment.*

míngtiān 明天 [modif: 明 (in this context) next + 天 day] **N** tomorrow ■ "明天是几月几号？" "明天是六月二十一日。" **"Míngtiān shì jǐ yuè jǐ hào?" "Míngtiān shì Liùyuè èrshíyī rì."** *"What date is tomorrow?" "It's June 21."* ■ 我想睡觉了，这些作业明天再做吧。**Wǒ xiǎng shuìjiào le, zhèxiē zuòyè míngtiān zài zuò ba.** *I want to go to bed. I'll do these assignments tomorrow.*

míngxiǎn 明显 [comp: 明 clear + 显 showing] **ADJ** obvious, apparent, evident ■ 你明显瘦了。**Nǐ míngxiǎn shòu le.** *You've obviously lost weight.* ■ 价格没有明显变化。**Jiàgé méiyǒu míngxiǎn biànhuà.** *There has been no apparent change in prices.*

míngxīng 明星 **N** movie star, star
体育明星 **tǐyù míngxīng** sports star

míngzhì 明智 **ADJ** wise, sensible

mìng 命 **N** life

mìnglìng 命令 **V & N** order, command ■ 公司总部命令分公司立即关闭。**Gōngsī zǒngbù mìnglìng fēngōngsī lìjí guānbì.** *The company's head office ordered immediate closure of the branch.* ■ 军人必须服从命令。**Jūnrén bìxū fúcóng mìnglìng.** *A soldier must obey orders.*

mìngmíng 命名 **V** give a name to, name

mìngyùn 命运 [comp: 命 destiny + 运 luck] **N** fate, destiny ■ 他总是怪自己命运不好。**Tā zǒngshì guài zìjǐ mìngyùn bù hǎo.** *He always blames his bad luck (← poor fate).* ■ 有些传统的中国人相信出生的年、月、日、时决定一个人的命运。**Yǒuxiē chuántǒng de Zhōngguórén xiāngxìn chūshēng de nián, yuè, rì, shí juédìng yí ge rén de mìngyùn.** *Some traditional Chinese believe that the year, month, date and hour of birth determines a person's fate.*

miù 谬 **ADJ** wrong, false

miùwù 谬误 **N** error, mistake

mō 摸 **V** touch ■ 请不要摸展览品。**Qǐng bú yào mō zhǎnlǎnpǐn.** *Please do not touch the exhibits.*

mōsuǒ 摸索 [comp: 摸 grope + 索 search] **V** grope, search for, explore

mó 模 **N** mould

mófàn 模范 **N** good example, role model

mófǎng 模仿 [comp: 模 mould + 仿 simulate] **V** imitate, ape, be a copycat ■ 小明喜欢模仿爸爸讲话，而且模仿得很像。**Xiǎo Míng xǐhuan mófǎng bàba jiǎnghuà, érqiě mófǎng de hěn xiàng.** *Xiao Ming likes to mimic his daddy, and he does it well.*

móhú 模糊 **ADJ** fuzzy, blurred

móshì 模式 **N** pattern, model

mótè 模特 **N** a person posing for artists, photographers, fashion designers, etc., model
人体模特 **réntǐ mótè** artistic model / 时装模特 **shízhuāng mótè** fashion model

móxíng 模型 **N** copy, model
飞机模型 **fēijī móxíng** airplane models

mó 膜 **N** membrane
塑料薄膜 **sùliào bómó** plastic film

mó 摩 **V** rub, scrape

mócā 摩擦 [comp: 摩 rub + 擦 wipe] **V & N** rub; friction, clash
和同事发生摩擦 **hé tóngshì fāshēng mócā** generate friction among colleagues

mótuōchē 摩托车 **N** motorcycle (辆 **liàng**) ■ 开摩托车千万要小心，别开得太快。**Kāi mótuōchē qiānwàn yào xiǎoxīn, bié kāi de tài kuài.** *You should be very, very careful when riding a motorcycle. Don't ride too fast.*

mó 磨 **V 1** grind
磨刀 **módāo** sharpen a knife
2 waste (time)
磨时间 **móshíjiān** stall, kill time

móhé 磨合 **V** break in, grind in, wear in

mó 魔 **N & ADJ** demon, monster; magic

móguǐ 魔鬼 [comp: 魔 monster + 鬼 ghost] **N** monster, demon (个 **gè**)

móshù 魔术 [modif: 魔 magic + 术 craft] **N** magic
变魔术 **biàn móshù** do magic (as entertainment)

móshùshī 魔术师 **N** magician

mò 末 **N** end (See **zhōumò** 周末.)

mǒ 抹 **V** apply by smearing

mǒshā 抹杀 **V** totally ignore (a fact), deny

mò 莫 **V** don't

mò míng qí miào 莫名其妙 **IDIOM** (something is so strange that) no one can understand it, be unable to make head or tail of something, utterly baffled/baffling

mò 漠 **N** desert (See **shāmò** 沙漠.)

mò 墨 **N** ink

mòshuǐ 墨水 [modif: 墨 ink + 水 water] **N** ink ■ 电脑打字很费墨水。**Diànnǎo dǎzì hěn fèi mòshuǐ.** *Computer printing takes lots of ink.*

mò 默 **ADJ** silent

mòmò 默默 **ADV** quietly, silently

mò 陌 **N** path

mòshēng 陌生 **ADJ** unfamiliar

mòshēng rén 陌生人 **N** stranger

móu 谋 **TRAD** 謀 **V** plot, plan

móuhài 谋害 **V** plot for murder

móuqiú 谋求 [comp: 谋 plot + 求 seek] **V** seek, be in quest of
谋求最大利润 móuqiú zuìdà lìrùn seek the maximum profits

mǒu 某 **PRON** certain (used to denote an indefinite person or thing, usually in writing) ■ 在该国某地发生森林大火。 **Zài gāiguó mǒu dì fāshēng sēnlín dàhuǒ.** *At a certain place in that country a forest fire broke out.*

mú 模 **N** mould, matrix

múyàng 模样 **I N** appearance, look **II ADV** approximately, about

mǔ 母 **ADJ 1** maternal, of a mother ■ 孩子需要母爱。 **Háizi xūyào mǔ'ài.** *Children need maternal love.* **2** female (of certain animals) (**ANTONYM** 公 **gōng**) ■ 他们养了八只公鸡，二十多只母鸡。 **Tāmen yǎngle bā zhī gōngjī, èrshí duō zhī mǔ jī.** *They keep eight roosters and over twenty hens.*

mǔqin 母亲 [modif: 母 mother + 亲 parent] **N** mother ■ 母亲在家照顾孩子。 **Mǔqin zài jiā zhàogù háizi.** *The mother takes care of her children at home.* ■ 你常常给母亲打电话吗？ **Nǐ chángcháng gěi mǔqin dǎ diànhuà ma?** *Do you often give your mother a call?*
母亲节 mǔqin jié Mother's Day

mǔxìng 母性 **N** maternal instinct, maternity

mǔyǔ 母语 **N** mother tongue ■ 她英语说得这么好，真让人不相信英语不是她的母语。 **Tā Yīngyǔ shuō de zhème hǎo, zhēn ràng rén bù xiāngxìn Yīngyǔ bú shì tā de mǔyǔ.** *She speaks English so well that it's hard to believe that it isn't her mother tongue.*

mǔ 亩 **TRAD** 畝 **MEASURE WORD** (a traditional Chinese unit of area, especially in farming; 1 mu is equivalent to 1/15 hectare, about 667 square meters)
十亩地 (田) shí mǔ dì (tián) 10 *mu* of ground (paddy fields/farmland)

mù 木 **N 1** same as 木头 **mùtou 2** tree ■ 独木不成林。 **Dú mù bù chéng lín.** *A single tree does not make a forest. (→ One swallow doesn't make a summer.)*

mùtou 木头 [suffix: 木 wood + 头 nominal suffix] **N** wood, timber ■ 我喜欢木头家具。 **Wǒ xǐhuan mùtou jiājù.** *I like wooden furniture.*

mù 沐 **V** wash one's hair

mùyù 沐浴 **V** take a bath

mù 目 **N** the eye

mùbiāo 目标 **N** target, objective, goal ■ 她的目标是五年内存十万元。 **Tā de mùbiāo shì wǔ nián nèi cún shíwàn yuán.** *Her goal is to save a hundred thousand yuan in five years.*

mùdì 目的 **N** aim, purpose ■ 我们做市场调查的目的是更好地为顾客服务。 **Wǒmen zuò shìchǎng** diàochá de mùdì shì gèng hǎo de wèi gùkè fúwù. *The purpose of our market investigation is to serve our customers more satisfactorily.*

mùdǔ 目睹 **V** see with one's own eyes; witness

mùguāng 目光 **N** sight, vision
目光远大 mùguāng yuǎndà farseeing, farsighted and ambitious

mùlù 目录 **N 1** catalog
产品目录 chǎnpǐn mùlù product catalog / 图书目录 tú shū mù lù library catalog
2 table of contents

mùqián 目前 **N** at present ■ 目前的困难是暂时的。 **Mùqián de kùnnan shì zànshí de.** *The present difficulties are only temporary.*

mù 慕 **V** admire (See xiànmù 羡慕.)

mù 牧 **V** herd, tend (sheep, cattle, etc.)

mùmín 牧民 **N** herdsman

mùqū 牧区 **N** pastureland, pastoral area

N

ná 拿 **V** hold, carry in hand ■ 我手里拿着很多书，不能开门，请你帮帮我。 **Wǒ shǒu li názhe hěn duō shū, bù néng kāi mén, qǐng nǐ bāngbang wǒ.** *I'm holding lots of books and can't open the door. Please help me.*
拿主意 ná zhǔyi make a decision ■ 这件事你得自己拿主意。 **Zhè jiàn shì nǐ děi zìjǐ ná zhǔyi.** *You've got to make a decision about this matter by yourself.*
拿走 ná zǒu take away, remove ■ 他已经不在这个办公室工作了，不过东西还没有拿走。 **Tā yǐjīng bú zài zhège bàngōngshì gōngzuò le, búguò dōngxi hái méiyǒu názǒu.** *He no longer works in this office, but he has not removed his things.*

náshǒu 拿手 **ADJ** very good at, adept at
拿手好戏 náshǒu hǎoxì something that one is adept at, one's favorite game

nǎ 哪 **PRON 1** which ■ 哪辆自行车是你的？ **Nǎ liàng zìxíngchē shì nǐ de?** *Which bicycle is yours?* ■ 这么多新车，你说哪辆最漂亮？ **Zhème duō xīn chē, nǐ shuō nǎ liàng zuì piàoliang?** *Of so many new cars, which do you think is the most attractive?* **2** whatever, whichever ■ 这些鞋子，我哪双都不喜欢。 **Zhèxiē xiézi, wǒ nǎ shuāng dōu bù xǐhuan.** *I don't like any of these shoes.* ■ 下星期我都在家，你哪天来都可以。 **Xià xīngqī wǒ dōu zài jiā, nǐ nǎ tiān lái dōu kěyǐ.** *I'll be home all next week. You may come any day.*

nǎli 哪里 [modif: 哪 which + 里 place] **PRON** where ■ 你住在哪里？ **Nǐ zhù zài nǎli?** *Where do you live?*

NOTE: 哪里哪里 **nǎli nǎli** is an idiomatic expression used as a modest reply to a compliment, e.g. ■ "你汉字写得真漂亮。" "哪里哪里。" **"Nǐ Hànzì xiě de zhēn piàoliang." "Nǎli, nǎli."** *"You write beautiful Chinese characters." "Thank you."*

nǎpà 哪怕 CONJ even if, even though ■ 哪怕卖掉房子，王先生和王太太也要让孩子念大学。**Nǎpà màidiào fángzi, Wáng xiānsheng hé Wáng tàitai yěyào ràng háizi niàn dàxué.** *Even if they have to sell the house, Mr and Mrs Wang will put their son through university.* ■ 他总是完成每天的工作，哪怕要开夜车。**Tā zǒngshì wánchéng měi tiān de gōngzuò, nǎpà yào kāi yèchē.** *He always finishes the day's work, even when he has to burn the midnight oil.*

NOTE: 哪怕 **nǎpà** introduces an exaggerated, rather unlikely situation to emphasize the statement of the sentence.

nǎr 哪儿 PRON same as 哪里 **nǎli.** Used colloquially.

nǎxiē 哪些 PRON the plural form of 哪 **nǎ** ■ 你想看哪些书？**Nǐ xiǎng kàn nǎxiē shū?** *Which books do you want to read?*

nà 那 PRON 1 that ■ 这辆自行车是我的，那辆自行车是我弟弟的。**Zhè liàng zìxíngchē shì wǒ de, nà liàng zìxíngchē shì wǒ dìdi de.** *This bike is mine. That one is my younger brother's.* ■ "麻烦你帮我租一套房子。" "那不难。" **"Máfan nǐ bāng wǒ zū yí tào fángzi." "Nà bù nán."** *"Would you mind renting a house for me?" "That won't be a problem."* 2 same as 那么 **nàme** II conjunction

nàge 那个 [modif: 那 that + 个 one] PRON that one ■ 那个不是我的，我的在这里。**Nàge bú shì wǒ de, wǒ de zài zhèli.** *That one is not mine. Mine's here.*

nàli 那里 [modif: 那 that + 里 place] PRON there, over there ■ 他在那里工作。**Tā zài nàli gōngzuò.** *He works there.* ■ 那里就是图书馆。**Nàli jiù shì túshūguǎn.** *Over there is the library.*

NOTES: (1) 那里 **nàli** is used after a personal noun or pronoun to make it a place word, as a personal noun or pronoun it cannot be used immediately after a preposition. For example, 我从张小姐听到这个消息。**Wǒ cóng Zhāng xiǎojiě tīngdào zhège xiāoxi.** is incorrect. 那里 **nàli** must be added after 张小姐 **Zhāng xiǎojiě** (Miss Zhang): 我从张小姐那里听到这个消息。**Wǒ cóng Zhāng xiǎojiě nàli tīngdào zhège xiāoxi.** *I learnt the news from Miss Zhang.* In this case 张小姐那里 **Zhāng xiǎojiě nàli** becomes a place word which can occur after the preposition 从 **cóng.** (2) Colloquially, 那儿 **nàr** may replace 那里 **nàli.**

nàme 那么 I PRON like that ■ 上海没有北京那么冷。**Shànghǎi méiyǒu Běijīng nàme lěng.** *Shanghai is not as cold as Beijing.* ■ 你那么做，她会不高兴。**Nǐ nàme zuò, tā huì bù gāoxìng.** *If you behave like that, she'll be unhappy.* II CONJ in that case, then ■ 你不喜欢吃米饭，那么吃面包吧。**Nǐ bù xǐhuan chī mǐfàn, nàme chī miànbāo ba.** *You don't like rice; in that case eat bread. (→ Since you don't like rice, have bread instead.)* ■ "去北

京的飞机票全卖完了。" "那么，我们就乘火车去吧。" **"Qù Běijīng de fēijī piào quán màiwán le." "Nàme, wǒmen jiù chéng huǒchē qù ba."** *"The air tickets to Beijing are sold out." "In that case, let's go by train."*

NOTE: Although 那么 **nàme** as a conjunction is glossed as *in that case, then,* Chinese speakers tend to use it much more than English speakers use "in that case" or "then." In colloquial Chinese 那么 **nàme** is often shortened to 那 **nà,** e.g. ■ 你不喜欢吃米饭，那吃面包吧。**Nǐ bù xǐhuan chī mǐfàn, nà chī miànbāo ba.** *You don't like rice; in that case eat bread.*

nàr 那儿 PRON same as 那里 **nàli.** Used colloquially.

nàxiē 那些 PRON those ■ 这些是中文书，那些是英文书。**Zhèxiē shì Zhōngwén shū, nàxiē shì Yīngwén shū.** *These are Chinese books. Those are English books.*

nàyàng 那样 PRON same as 那么 **nàme** I PRON

nà 纳 V pay, offer

nàmènr 纳闷儿 V be wondering why (what, who, how, etc.), be puzzled

nàshuì 纳税 V pay taxes

纳税人 **nàshuìrén** tax-payer

nǎi 奶 N milk

nǎinai 奶奶 N paternal grandmother, granny ■ 奶奶，我上学去了！**Nǎinai, wǒ shàngxué qù le!** *Granny, I'm going to school!*

NOTE: The formal word for *paternal grandmother* is 祖母 **zǔmǔ** and that for *maternal grandmother* is 外祖母 **wàizǔmǔ.** While 奶奶 **nǎinai** is the colloquialism for 祖母 **zǔmǔ,** that for 外祖母 **wàizǔmǔ** is 姥姥 **lǎolao,** or 外婆 **wàipó.**

nài 耐 V able to endure

nàifán 耐烦 [v+obj: 耐 tolerate + 烦 irritation] ADJ patient ■ 尽管顾客东挑西拣，营业员也不能露出不耐烦的样子。**Jìnguǎn gùkè dōng-tiāo-xī-jiǎn, yíngyèyuán yě bù néng lùchū bú nàifán de yàngzi.** *Even if the customer is very choosy, the shop assistant mustn't appear impatient.*

NOTE: 耐烦 **nàifán** is only used in its negative form, 不耐烦 **bú nàifán.**

nàixīn 耐心 [modif: 耐 tolerate + 心 heart] ADJ & N patient; patience ■ 除了耐心地等待，没有别的办法。**Chúle nàixīn de děngdài, méiyǒu biéde bànfǎ.** *There is nothing you can do except wait patiently.* ■ 我看他快要没有耐心了。**Wǒ kàn tā kuài yào méiyǒu nàixīn le.** *I think he will soon run out of patience.*

nàiyòng 耐用 ADJ durable ■ 我们的产品很耐用。**Wǒmen de chǎnpǐn hěn nàiyòng.** *Our products are durable.* ■ 这种牌子的手表很便宜，但是

不耐用。**Zhè zhǒng páizi de shǒubiǎo hěn piányi, dànshì bú nàiyòng.** *Watches of this brand are cheap but don't last long.*

nán 男 ADJ (of humans) male (ANTONYM 女 **nǚ**)

nán háizi 男孩子 N boy

nán qīngnián 男青年 N young man

nánrén 男人 N man, men ■ 男人能做的事，女人也能做。**Nánrén néng zuò de shì, nǚrén yě néng zuò.** *What men can do, women also can.*

nánshēng 男生 N male student/pupil

nánzihàn 男子汉 N a true man, true men

nán 南 N south, southern ■ 很多老年人喜欢住在南方。**Hěn duō lǎoniánrén xǐhuan zhù zài nánfāng.** *Many old people like to live in the south.*

nánbian 南边 [modif: 南 south + 边 side] N south side, to the south, in the south ■ "新西兰的南边还有什么国家吗？" "没有了。" **"Xīnxīlán de nánbian hái yǒu shénme guójiā ma?" "Méiyǒu le."** *"Is there any country to the south of New Zealand?" "No, there isn't."*

nánfāng 南方 N the southern part, the south of a country ■ 中国的南方夏天一般很热。**Zhōngguó de nánfāng xiàtiān yìbān hěn rè.** *In southern China, summer is generally very hot.*

nánfāngrén 南方人 N southerner

nánmiàn 南面 N same as 南边 **nánbian**

nán yuán běi zhé 南辕北辙 IDIOM act in opposite to one's goal, self-defeating

nán 难 TRAD 難 ADJ difficult (ANTONYM 容易 **róngyì**) ■ 这道练习太难了，我不会做。**Zhè dào liànxí tài nán le, wǒ bú huì zuò.** *This exercise is too difficult. I can't do it.* ■ 在这个政府部门，人难见，事难办。**Zài zhège zhèngfǔ bùmén, rén nán jiàn, shì nán bàn.** *In this government department, it is difficult to meet any officials or to get things done.*

nándào 难道 ADV (used at the beginning of a sentence or before a verb to make it a rhetorical question). ■ 难道你不知道吗？**Nándào nǐ bù zhīdào ma?** *Didn't you know?* ■ 他连旧车都买不起，难道还买得起新车吗？**Tā lián jiù chē dōu mǎi bu qǐ, nándào hái mǎi de qǐ xīn chē ma?** *He even can't afford a second-hand car. How can he afford a new car?*

nándé 难得 ADJ hard to come by, rare ■ 这个机会很难得，你别错过。**Zhège jīhuì hěn nán dé, nǐ bié cuòguò.** *This is a rare opportunity; don't you miss it.*

nánguài 难怪 ADV no wonder

nánguò 难过 ADJ sad, grieved (ANTONYM 高兴 **gāoxìng**) ■ 听到这个不幸的消息，我们非常难过。**Tīngdào zhège búxìng de xiāoxi, wǒmen fēicháng nánguò.** *Hearing this unfortunate news, we were all very sad.*

NOTE: 难过 **nánguò** is usually used as a predicate, and seldom as an attribute.

nánkān 难堪 ADJ embarrassed, embarrassing 难堪的局面 **nánkān de júmiàn** embarrassing situation, awkward plight

nánkàn 难看 ADJ ugly (ANTONYM 好看 **hǎokàn**) ■ 他穿这件衣服真难看。**Tā chuān zhè jiàn yīfu zhēn nánkàn.** *He really looks ugly in that suit.*

nánmiǎn 难免 ADJ hardly avoidable, almost inevitable

nán néng kě guì 难能可贵 IDIOM deserving praise for a rare achievement, highly commendable

nánshòu 难受 ADJ 1 feel ill, uncomfortable ■ 他昨天晚上酒喝得太多，今天早上头疼难受。**Tā zuótiān wǎnshang jiǔ hē de tài duō, jīntiān zǎoshang tóuténg nánshòu.** *He drank too much last night. This morning he had a headache and felt terrible (→ had a hangover).* ■ 这双新鞋小了点儿，穿着难受。**Zhè shuāng xīn xié xiǎole diǎnr, chuānzhe nánshòu.** *The new shoes are too small, and are uncomfortable to wear.* 2 feel sorry, feel bad, sad ■ 我的错误给公司带来损失，我心里很难受。**Wǒ de cuòwù gěi gōngsī dàilái sǔnshī, wǒ xīnli hěn nánshòu.** *I feel bad that my mistake has caused loss to the company.*

náo 挠 TRAD 撓 V 1 gently scratch with one's fingers 挠痒痒 **náo yǎngyang** scratch an itch 2 obstruct, make trouble (See **zǔnáo** 阻挠.)

nǎo 恼 ADJ irritated, vexed

nǎohuǒ 恼火 ADJ annoyed, angry

nǎo 脑 TRAD 腦 N brain

nǎodai 脑袋 [modif: 脑 brain + 袋 bag] N same as 头 **tóu.** Used only colloquially and in a derogative sense.

nǎozi 脑子 [suffix: 脑 brain + 子 nominal suffix] N brain, mind ■ 他怎么会有这种想法？脑子出问题了吧？**Tā zěnmehuì yǒu zhè zhǒng xiǎngfǎ? Nǎozi chū wèntí le ba?** *How come he has such ideas? Something wrong with his mind? (or He must be out of his mind./He must be crazy.)* 动脑子 **dòng nǎozi** use brains ■ 遇到难题，要多动脑子，总会找到解决的办法。**Yùdào nántí, yào duō dòng nǎozi, zǒnghuì zhǎodào jiějué de bànfǎ.** *When confronted with difficulties, use your brains and you will always find a solution.*

nào 闹 TRAD 鬧 V make trouble, create a disturbance ■ 这几个孩子闹得我根本看不进书。**Zhè jǐ ge háizi nào de wǒ gēnběn kànbujìn shū.** *These kids raised such a ruckus that I could not concentrate on reading at all.* ■ 别闹了，邻居该来提意见了。**Bié nào le, línjū gāilái tí yìjiàn le.** *Stop making such a noise. The neighbors will come to complain.*

闹笑话 **nào xiàohua** make a fool of oneself, cut a ridiculous figure / 闹脾气 **nào píqi** throw a tantrum

ne 呢 PARTICLE 1 (used at the end of a question to soften the tone of enquiry) ■ 你打算明年做什么

呢？ **Nǐ dǎsuàn míngnián zuò shénme ne?** *What do you intend to do next year?* **2** How about…? Where is (are)…? ■ 你们明天出去旅游，孩子呢？ **Nǐmen míngtiān chūqu lǚyóu, háizi ne?** *You're going on holiday tomorrow. How about the kids?* ■ "小明，你妈呢？" **"Xiǎo Míng, nǐ mā ne?"** *"Xiao Ming, where is your mom?"*

nèi 那 same as 那 **nà**. Used colloquially.

nèi 内 N inside, within (ANTONYM 外 **wài**) ■ 房间内外都很干净。 **Fángjiān nèi wài dōu hěn gānjìng.** *The home is clean both inside and out.* ■ 我一定在十天内还清借款。 **Wǒ yídìng zài shí tiān nèi huánqīng jièkuǎn.** *I will pay off the debt within ten days.*

nèibù 内部 N interior, inside ■ 展览会内部整理，暂停对外开放。 **Zhǎnlǎnhuì nèibù zhěnglǐ, zàntíng duìwài kāifàng.** *The exhibition is temporarily closed for reorganization.*

内部资料 **nèibù zīliào** document for internal circulation (e.g. within a government department)

nèicún 内存 N RAM, memory

nèihán 内涵 N **1** intention, connotation **2** self-cultivation

nèikē 内科 [modif: 内 inside + 科 department] N department of internal medicine (in a hospital)

nèimù 内幕 N inside story

nèiróng 内容 [modif: 内 inside + 容 contain] N content, substance ■ 这本书的内容很丰富。 **Zhè běn shū de nèiróng hěn fēngfù.** *The book is rich in content.* ■ 王董事长讲话的主要内容是什么？ **Wáng dǒngshìzhǎng jiǎnghuà de zhǔyào nèiróng shì shénme?** *What is the main idea of Chairman Wang's talk?*

nèizài 内在 [modif: 内 inner + 在 being] ADJ inherent, intrinsic (ANTONYM 外在 **wàizài**)

nèn 嫩 ADJ young and tender, tender ■ 请你把牛肉做得嫩一点。 **Qǐng nǐ bǎ niúròu zuò de nèn yìdiǎn.** *Please make the beef tender. (→ Don't overcook the beef.)*

néng 能 MODAL V can, be able to ■ 我今天不舒服，不能去上班。 **Wǒ jīntiān bù shūfu, bù néng qù shàngbān.** *I'm unwell today and won't be able to go to work.* ■ 这辆车加满汽油，能跑多少公里？ **Zhè liàng chē jiā mǎn qìyóu, néng pǎo duōshǎo gōnglǐ?** *How many kilometers can this car run on a full tank?*

NOTE: See note on 会 **huì** modal verb.

nénggàn 能干 ADJ (of people) able, capable, efficient ■ 他非常能干，别人一星期做的工作，他三天就完成了。 **Tā fēicháng nénggàn, biérén yì xīngqī zuò de gōngzuò, tā sān tiān jiù wánchéng le.** *He is very efficient. He can finish in three days what takes others a week to do.*

nénggòu 能够 MODAL V same as 能 **néng**

nénglì 能力 [comp: 能 ability + 力 strength] N abili-

ty ■ 他能力比一般人强，但是太骄傲了。 **Tā nénglì bǐ yìbān rén qiáng, dànshì tài jiāo'ào le.** *He is more capable than most people, but he is too conceited.* ■ 我们要求职工有使用电脑的能力。 **Wǒmen yāoqiú zhígōng yǒu shǐyòng diànnǎo de nénglì.** *We require that our staff have computer competence.*

néngliàng 能量 [modif: 能 ability + 量 amount] N energy, capabilities

néngyuán 能源 [modif: 能 energy + 源 source, resource] N energy resources ■ 石油和煤总有用完的一天，人类必须开发新能源。 **Shíyóu hé méi zǒngyǒu yòngwán de yìtiān, rénlèi bìxū kāifā xīn néngyuán.** *There will be a day when oil and coal are exhausted. Mankind must develop new energy resources.*

ng 嗯 INTERJ (used after a question to reinforce questioning) ■ 你把自行车借给谁了，嗯？ **Nǐ bǎ zìxíngchē jiègei shuí le, ng?** *Who did you lend your bicycle to, eh?*

ní 泥 N mud ■ 他们在下雨天踢球，搞得身上都是泥。 **Tāmen zài xiàyǔtiān tīqiú, gǎode shēnshang dōushì ní.** *They played soccer in the rain and got themselves all covered with mud.*

nǐ 你 PRON you (singular) ■ 你是谁？ **Nǐ shì shuí?** *Who're you?* ■ 我不认识你。 **Wǒ bú rènshi nǐ.** *I don't know you.*

nǐmen 你们 [suffix: 你 you (singular) + 们 suffix denoting a plural number] PRON you (plural) ■ 你们都是我的朋友。 **Nǐmen dōu shì wǒ de péngyou.** *You all are my friends.* ■ 我告诉你们一个好消息。 **Wǒ gàosu nǐmen yí ge hǎo xiāoxi.** *I'll tell you a piece of good news.*

nǐ 拟 TRAD 擬 V draw up, draft

nǐdìng 拟定 V draw up, work out

拟定计划 **nǐdìng jìhuà** draw up a plan

nì 逆 ADJ contrary, counter

nìxíng 逆行 V go in the wrong direction

nì 腻 ADJ **1** greasy (See **yóunì 油腻**.) **2** fed up with

nián 年 N year (no measure word required) ■ 一年有十二个月。 **Yì nián yǒu shí'èr ge yuè.** *There're twelve months in a year.* ■ 我在美国住了两年。 **Wǒ zài Měiguó zhùle liǎng nián.** *I lived in the States for two years.*

今年 **jīnnián** this year / 明年 **míngnián** next year / 去年 **qùnián** last year

NOTE: No measure word is used with 年 **nián**, e.g. 一年 **yì nián** (one year), 两年 **liǎng nián** (two years), 三年 **sān nián** (three years).

niándài 年代 [comp: 年 year + 代 age] N a decade of a century ■ 我爸爸妈妈喜欢听(二十世纪)八十年代的歌。 **Wǒ bàba māma xǐhuan tīng (èrshí shìjì) bāshí niándài de gē.** *My dad and mom enjoy listening to songs of the eighties (of the twentieth century).*

niándù 年度 **I N** year

财务年度 cáiwù niándù fiscal year

II ADJ annual

年度报告 niándù bàogào annual report

niánjí 年级 [comp: 年 year + 级 grade] **N** grade (in school) ■ 这个年级有多少学生？ **Zhège niánjí yǒu duōshǎo xuésheng?** *How many students are there in this grade?* ■ 他们的女儿刚念一年级。 **Tāmen de nǚ'ér gāng niàn yì niánjí.** *Their daughter is only a first grade pupil.*

niánjì 年纪 [comp: 年 year + 纪 number] **N** age ■ 他虽然年纪小，但是很懂事。 **Tā suīrán niánjì xiǎo, dànshì hěn dǒngshì.** *Although he's very young, he's quite sensible.* ■ "老先生，您多大年纪了？" "七十了。" **"Lǎo xiānsheng, nín duōdà niánjì le?" "Qīshí le."** *"How old are you, sir?" "Seventy."*

NOTE: 您多大年纪了？ **Nín duōdà niánjì le?** is an appropriate way to ask the age of an elderly person. To ask a young child his/her age, the question should be 你几岁了？ **Nǐ jǐ suì le?** For people who are neither children nor elderly, the question to use is 你多大岁数？ **Nǐ duō dà suìshu?**

niánlíng 年龄 [comp: 年 year + 龄 age] **N** age (of a person or other living things) ■ 你别问别人的年龄，尤其别问女士的年龄。 **Nǐ bié wèn biérén de niánlíng, yóuqí bié wèn nǚshì de niánlíng.** *Do not ask about somebody's age, especially a lady's age.* ■ 这棵树的年龄比我爷爷还大。 **Zhè kē shù de niánlíng bǐ wǒ yéye hái dà.** *This tree is older than my grandpa.*

niánqīng 年轻 [modif: 年 age + 轻 light] **ADJ** young ■ 你还年轻，有些事你还不大懂。 **Nǐ hái niánqīng, yǒuxiē shì nǐ hái bú dà dǒng.** *You're still too young to understand some matters.* ■ 他年轻的时候可能干了！ **Tā niánqīng de shíhou, kě nénggàn le!** *He was a very capable man when he was young.*

niánqīngrén 年轻人 **N** young person, young people

niàn 念 **v 1** read, read aloud ■ 你每天念中文课文吗？ **Nǐ měi tiān niàn Zhōngwén kèwén ma?** *Do you read your Chinese lessons every day?* **2** study (in a school) ■ 他们的大儿子在英国念大学，他念数学。 **Tāmen de dà érzi zài Yīngguó niàn dàxué, tā niàn shùxué.** *Their eldest son is studying in a university in the UK; he studies mathematics.*

NOTE: See note on 读 **dú.**

niáng 娘 **N 1** girl (See **gūniang** 姑娘.) **2** mother

niàng 酿 **v** make (wine), brew (beer)

酿酒 niàngjiǔ make wine

niǎo 鸟 **TRAD** 鳥 **N** bird (只 **zhī**) ■ 两只鸟在花园里飞来飞去。 **Liǎng zhī niǎo zài huāyuán li fēi-lái-fēi-qù.** *Two birds darted here and there in the garden.*

niē 捏 **v** mold

niēzào 捏造 [comp: 捏 mold + 造 make] **v** fabricate, make up

nín 您 **PRON** you (honorific)

NOTE: 您 **nín** is the honorific form of 你 **nǐ.** Use 您 **nín** when respect or deference is called for. Normally, 您 **nín** does not have a plural form. 您们 **nínmen** is absolutely unacceptable in spoken Chinese, and only marginally so in written Chinese. To address more than one person politely, you can say 您两位 **nín liǎng wèi** (two people), 您三位 **nín sān wèi** (three people), or 您几位 **nín jǐ wèi** (several people).

níng 凝 **v** freeze, coagulate

nínggù 凝固 **v** solidify

níngjié 凝结 [comp: 凝 freeze + 结 coagulate] **v** (of gas or hot air) becomes liquid, condense

níngshì 凝视 [modif: 凝 freeze + 视 look] **v** look at steadily and for a long time, gaze

níng 宁 **TRAD** 寧 **ADJ** peaceful, tranquil

níngjìng 宁静 **ADJ** tranquil, quiet

níng 拧 **TRAD** 擰 **v** wring, twist

拧毛巾 níng máojīn wring a towel

nǐng 拧 **TRAD** 擰 **v** screw, wrench

拧螺丝 nǐng luósī turn a screw (to tighten or loosen)

nìng 宁 **TRAD** 寧 **MODAL v** would rather

宁死不屈 nìng sǐ bù qū would rather die than succumb

nìngkě 宁可 **MODAL v** same as 宁肯 **nìngkěn**

nìngkěn 宁肯 **MODAL v** would rather ■ 她宁肯走去，也不搭他的车。 **Tā nìngkěn zǒuqù, yě bù dā tāde chē.** *She would rather walk there than go in his car.*

NOTE: As is shown in the example sentence, 宁肯 **nìngkěn** is often used alongside with 也 **yě:** 宁肯 …也 … **nìngkěn … yě …**

nìngyuàn 宁愿 **MODAL v** same as 宁肯 **nìngkěn**

niú 牛 **v** cattle, ox, cow, calf, buffalo (头 **tóu**) ■ 牛在草地上吃草。 **Niú zài cǎodì shang chī cǎo.** *The cattle are grazing in the field.* ■ 西方人用狗放羊放牛，所以他们说狗是人最好的朋友。 **Xīfāngrén yòng gǒu fàng yáng fàng niú, suǒyǐ tāmen shuō gǒu shì rén zuì hǎo de péngyou.** *People in the West use dogs to herd cattle and sheep; that's why they say the dog is man's best friend.*

公牛 gōng niú bull / 黄牛 huángniú ox / 奶牛 nǎiniú cow / 水牛 shuǐniú water buffalo / 小牛 xiǎo niú calf

NOTE: In the Chinese context, the ox (黄牛 **huángniú**) and the water buffalo (水牛 **shuǐniú**) are more important than the milk cow (奶牛 **nǎiniú**).

niúnǎi 牛奶 **N** cow's milk, milk

niúròu 牛肉 **N** beef

烤牛肉 kǎo niúròu roast beef

niúzǎi kù 牛仔裤 **N** jeans

niǔ 扭 **V** turn (one's head, back, etc.)

niǔzhuǎn 扭转 **V** turn around, reverse

niǔ 纽 **TRAD** 紐 **N** knob, button

niǔkòur 纽扣儿 **N** button (颗 **kē**, 个 **gè**)

nóng 农 **TRAD** 農 **N** farming

nóngchǎng 农场 [modif: 农 farming + 场 field, ground] **N** farm ■ 这个农场真大！ **Zhège nóngchǎng zhēn dà!** *How big this farm is!* ■ 外国人可以在这里买农场吗？ **Wàiguórén kěyǐ zài zhèlǐ mǎi nóngchǎng ma?** *Can a foreigner buy a farm here?*

nóngchǎngzhǔ 农场主 **N** one who owns a farm, farmer

nóngcūn 农村 [modif: 农 farming + 村 village] **N** farming area, rural area, countryside (ANTONYM 城市 **chéngshì**) ■ 农村人口比较少，生活不太方便。 **Nóngcūn rénkǒu bǐjiào shǎo, shēnghuó bú tài fāngbiàn.** *In rural areas, the population is small and life is not very convenient.*

nónglì 农历 **N** Chinese lunar calendar

nóngmín 农民 [modif: 农 farming + 民 people] **N** peasant, farmer ■ 农民都很关心天气。 **Nóngmín dōu hěn guānxīn tiānqì.** *Farmers are all concerned about the weather.* ■ 她十年前和一位农民结婚，以后一直住在农村。 **Tā shí nián qián hé yí wèi nóngmín jiéhūn, yǐhòu yìzhí zhù zài nóngcūn.** *She married a farmer ten years ago and has since lived in the countryside.*

nóngyè 农业 [modif: 农 farming + 业 industry] **N** agriculture ■ 我们必须努力发展农业。 **Wǒmen bìxū nǔlì fāzhǎn nóngyè.** *We must work hard to develop agriculture.*

nóng 浓 **TRAD** 濃 **ADJ** (of gas or liquid) thick, dense (ANTONYM 淡 **dàn**)

浓雾 nóng wù dense fog / 浓咖啡 nóng kāfēi strong coffee

nónghòu 浓厚 [comp: 浓 thick + 厚 thick] **ADJ** **1** (of smoke, cloud, etc.) thick **2** (of atmosphere, interest, etc.) strong, heavy

nòng 弄 **V** do, manage, get … done ■ 我弄饭，你去买点儿酒。 **Wǒ nòng fàn, nǐ qù mǎi diǎnr jiǔ.** *I'll do the cooking; you go and buy some wine.* ■ 这么多事儿，我今天弄不完。 **Zhème duō shìr, wǒ jīntiān nòng bu wán.** *There're so many things to do, I can't finish them all today.*

nú 奴 **N** slave

núlì 奴隶 **N** slave

nǔ 努 **V** work hard

nǔlì 努力 [comp: 努 physical effort + 力 strength] **ADJ** making great efforts ■ 我们大家努力工作，为了更好的明天。 **Wǒmen dàjiā nǔlì gōngzuò, wèile gèng hǎo de míngtiān.** *We all work hard for a better tomorrow.* ■ 他中文学习得很努力。 **Tā Zhōngwén xuéxí de hěn nǔlì.** *He studies Chinese very hard.*

nǚ 女 **ADJ** (of humans) female (ANTONYM 男 **nán**)

■ 请问，女洗手间在哪里？ **Qǐngwèn, nǚ xǐshǒujiān zài nǎli?** *Excuse me, where is the women's toilet?*

nǚ'ér 女儿 **N** daughter ■ 他们的三个孩子都是女儿，没有儿子。 **Tāmen de sān ge háizi dōu shì nǚ'ér, méiyǒu érzi.** *All their three children are daughters; they don't have a son.*

nǚ háizi 女孩子 **N** girl

nǚ qīngnián 女青年 **N** young woman

nǚrén 女人 [modif: 女 female human + 人 person] **N** woman, adult woman (ANTONYM 男人 **nánrén**)

nǚshēng 女生 **N** female student/pupil

nǚshì 女士 [modif: 女 female human + 士 gentleman, gentlewoman] **N** (respectful form of address or reference to a woman) Madam, Ms, lady, a woman ■ 王女士是我们城市的教育局局长。 **Wáng nǚshì shì wǒmen chéngshì de jiàoyùjú júzhǎng.** *Madam Wang is director of our city's education bureau.* ■ 女士们，先生们，请允许我代表市政府热烈欢迎大家。 **Nǚshìmen, xiānshengmen, qǐng yúnxǔ wǒ dàibiǎo shì zhèngfǔ rèliè huānyíng dàjiā.** *Ladies and gentlemen, allow me to extend you a warm welcome on behalf of the city government.*

nuǎn 暖 **ADJ** warm ■ 在中国很多地区，一到四月天就暖了。 **Zài Zhōngguó hěn duō dìqū, yídào Sìyuè tiān jiù nuǎn le.** *In many areas in China the weather becomes warm when April arrives.*

nuǎnhuo 暖和 [comp: 暖 warm + 和 (in this context) mild] **ADJ** pleasantly warm ■ 春天的太阳不太热，很暖和。 **Chūntiān de tàiyáng bú tài rè, hěn nuǎnhuo.** *The sunshine in spring is not hot; it's warm.* ■ 她的话说得我心里很暖和。 **Tā de huà shuō de wǒ xīnli hěn nuǎnhuo.** *What she said warmed my heart.*

nüè 虐 **ADJ** cruel, brutal

nüèdài 虐待 **V** abuse (a person), ill-treat

nuó 挪 **V** move, shift

nuóyòng 挪用 [comp: 挪 move + 用 use] **V** divert (funds)

挪用公款 nuóyòng gōngkuǎn misappropriate public funds

O

ō 噢 **INTERJ** (used to indicate understanding or a promise) ■ 噢，我明白了。 **Ō, wǒ míngbai le.** *Oh, I see.* ■ 噢，我忘不了。 **Ō, wǒ wàng bu liǎo.** *Yes, I won't forget it.*

ó 哦 **INTERJ** (used to indicate doubt) ■ 哦，他还会说日本话？ **Ó, tā hái huì shuō Rìběn huà?** *Well, he also speaks Japanese?*

ōu 欧 **TRAD** 歐 **N** Europe

Ōuméng 欧盟 **N** shortening for 欧洲联盟 **Ōuzhōu Liánméng**, the European Union

Ōuyuán 欧元 [modif: 欧 Europe + 元 dollar] **N** Euro ■ 一百欧元可以换多少美元？ **Yìbǎi Ōuyuán kěyǐ huàn duōshǎo Měiyuán?** *How many US dollars can a hundred Euros be exchanged for?*

Ōuzhōu 欧洲 [modif: 欧 Europe + 洲 continent] **N** Europe ■ 我有了钱，就去欧洲旅游。 **Wǒ yǒule qián, jiù qù Ōuzhōu lǚyóu.** *When I have the money, I'll go to Europe for a holiday.*

ōu 殴 TRAD 毆 **V** beat (people)

ōudǎ 殴打 [comp: 殴 beat + 打 beat] **V** beat up (people)

ǒu 呕 TRAD 嘔 **V** vomit

ǒutù 呕吐 [comp: 呕 vomit + 吐 vomit] **V** vomit ■ 我想呕吐。 **Wǒ xiǎng ǒutù.** *I feel sick.*

ǒu 偶¹ ADV **1** occasionally **2** accidentally

ǒu'ěr 偶尔 ADV occasionally

ǒurán 偶然 ADV accidentally

ǒu 偶² N even number

ǒushù 偶数 N even number (ANTONYM 奇数 **jīshù**)

ǒu 偶³ N human figure

ǒuxiàng 偶像 N idol

P

pā 趴 **V** prostrate, lie prone

pá 爬 **V** crawl, climb ■ 他们的儿子才一岁，还不会走路，只会在地上爬。 **Tāmen de érzi cái yí suì, hái bú huì zǒulù, zhǐ huì zài dì shang pá.** *Their son is only a year old; he still can't walk and can only crawl on the floor.*

páshān 爬山 **V & N** climb a hill or mountain; mountaineering

páxíng 爬行 **V** creep, crawl

páxíng dòngwù 爬行动物 N reptile

pà 怕 **1** **V** fear, be afraid ■ 一个人住这么大的房子，我有点儿怕。 **Yí ge rén zhù zhème dà de fángzi, wǒ yǒu diǎnr pà.** *I'm a bit afraid to live alone in such a big house.* ■ 我怕他没接到我的短信，又打了电话。 **Wǒ pà tā méi jiēdào wǒ de duǎnxìn, yòu dǎle diànhuà.** *I was afraid he might not get my text message, so I rang him.* **2** ADV same as 恐怕 **kǒngpà**, but with less force.

pāi 拍 **V** pat, clap ■ 孩子们拍手欢迎新老师。 **Háizimen pāishǒu huānyíng xīn lǎoshī.** *The children gave the new teacher a big hand.*

pāimài 拍卖 **V** auction, sell at a reduced price

pāishǒu 拍手 **V** clap, applaud

pāizhào 拍照 **V** take photos ■ 此处不准拍照。 **Cǐchù bùzhǔn pāizhào.** *No photographing here. Picture-taking not allowed here.*

pái 排 **I** **V 1** arrange in a definite order ■ 旅客排成一行，等待登机前检查。 **Lǚkè pái chéng yì háng, děngdài dēngjī qián jiǎnchá.** *The travelers stood in a line for the preflight inspection.* **2** remove **II** N row, rank ■ "你的票是几排几座？" "七排

四座。" "**Nǐ de piào shì jǐ pái jǐ zuò?**" "**Qī pái sì zuò.**" *"What is the seat and row in your ticket?" "Row 7, Seat 4."* ■ 我要坐在前排，后排听不清。 **Wǒ yào zuòzài qián pái, hòu pái tīng bu qīng.** *I want to sit in a front row. I can't hear clearly in the back seats.* **III** MEASURE WORD (for things arranged in a row) 一排椅子 yì pái yǐzi a row of chairs

páichì 排斥 [comp: 排 remove + 斥 denounce] **V** expel, reject

páichú 排除 [comp: 排 expel + 除 deduct] **V** rule out, eliminate 排除这种可能性 páichú zhè zhǒng kěnéngxìng rule out this possibility / 排除障碍 páichú zhàng'ài surmount an obstacle

páiduì 排队 **V** form a line, line up, queue up

páifàng 排放 **V** discharge (waste gas, sewage, etc.)

páijǐ 排挤 [comp: 排 expel + 挤 squeeze] **V** elbow out, push aside, squeeze out

páiliàn 排练 **V & N** rehearse; rehearsal

páiliè 排列 **V** arrange, put in order 按字母顺序排列 àn zìmǔ shùnxù páiliè arrange in alphabetical order

páiqiú 排球 [modif: 排 row + 球 ball] **N** volleyball (只 **zhī**) ■ 夏天我们常常在海边打排球。 **Xiàtiān wǒmen chángcháng zài hǎibiān dǎ páiqiú.** *In summer we often play volleyball at the seaside.*

páihuái 徘徊 **V** pace up and down, move hesitatingly

pái 牌¹ N playing cards (张 **zhāng**, 副 **fù**) ■ 他在火车上和别的旅客一起打牌。 **Tā zài huǒchē shang hé biéde lǚkè yìqǐ dǎpái.** *He played cards with fellow passengers on the train.* ■ 我不会打这种牌。 **Wǒ bú huì dǎ zhè zhǒng pái.** *I don't know how to play this card game.* 打牌 dǎpái play cards / 发牌 fāpái deal cards / 洗牌 xǐpái shuffle cards

NOTE: 扑克牌 **pūkèpái** is a more common word for *playing cards* (noun).

pái 牌² N brand name, brand ■ 你买的汽车是什么牌的？ **Nǐ mǎi de qìchē shì shénme pái de?** *What brand of car did you buy?* 名牌 míngpái famous brand, name brand

páizi 牌子 [suffix: 牌 signboard + 子 nominal suffix] **N 1** signboard (块 **kuài**) ■ 他在门口放了一块牌子，"减价出售"。 **Tā zài ménkǒu fàngle yí kuài páizi, "jiǎnjià chūshòu".** *He put up a signboard at the gate: "Discount sale."* **2** same as 牌² **pái** ■ 这种牌子的衣服特别贵。 **Zhè zhǒng páizi de yīfu tèbié guì.** *Clothes of this brand name are extremely expensive.*

pài 派¹ **V 1** dispatch ■ 公司派我到上海开发市场。 **Gōngsī pài wǒ dào Shànghǎi kāifā shìchǎng.** *The company sent me to Shanghai to develop the market.* **2** assign (a job) ■ 校长派我教三年

级。**Xiàozhǎng pài wǒ jiāo sān-nián jí.** *The principal assigned me to teach third grade.*

pài 派[2] N faction, school (of thought) ■ 在这个问题上有很多派。**Zài zhège wèntí shang yǒu hěn duō pài.** *There are many schools of thought on this issue.*

反对派 fǎnduì pài the opposing force, opponent

pàibié 派别 N faction, group, school (of thought)

pàichūsuǒ 派出所 N police station

pàiduì 派对 N (social) party ■ 我们搬进新房子以后要开一个派对。**Wǒmen bānjìn xīn fángzi yǐhòu yào kāi yí ge pàiduì.** *We'll give a party after moving into the new house.*

NOTE: 派对 **pàiduì** is a transliteration of (social) party, used among urban fashionable people. 聚会 **jùhuì** is a more formal word.

pàiqiǎn 派遣 V send, dispatch (troops, formal delegates, etc.)

pān 攀 V climb

pāndēng 攀登 [comp: 攀 climb + 登 ascend] V climb, scale

pán 盘 TRAD 盤 N dish, plate

pánxuán 盘旋 V (of a bird or aeroplane) spiral, circle

pánzi 盘子 [suffix: 盘 plate, dish + 子 nominal suffix] N plate, dish, tray (只 **zhī**) ■ 她在饭店里端盘子。**Tā zài fàndiàn li duān pánzi.** *She carries plates in a restaurant. (→ She is a waitress in a restaurant.)*

pàn 判 V judge

pànduàn 判断 [comp: 判 judge + 断 reach a verdict] V & N judge, decide; judgment, verdict ■ 他判断是非的能力很强。**Tā pànduàn shì-fēi de nénglì hěn qiáng.** *He is very good at telling right from wrong.* ■ 我的判断是这批货都是假的。**Wǒ de pànduàn shì zhè pī huò dōu shì jiǎ de.** *My judgment is that this batch of goods is counterfeit.*

pànjué 判决 V & N (of a court) pass judgment; court decision, judgment

pàn 叛 V betray, be disloyal to

pànbiàn 叛变 V turn traitor, become a turncoat

pànguó 叛国 V commit treason

pàn 盼 V expect

pànwàng 盼望 [comp: 盼 expect + 望 look forward to] V look forward to, long for ■ 母亲盼望孩子们都回家过春节。**Mǔqin pànwàng háizimen dōu huíjiā guò chūnjié.** *The mother longed for the homecoming of all her children for Chinese New Year.* ■ 我盼望不久就和你见面。**Wǒ pànwàng bùjiǔ jiù hé nǐ jiànmiàn.** *I look forward to meeting you soon.*

pàn 畔 N (river, lake, etc.) side, bank

páng 庞 TRAD 龐 ADJ big

pángdà 庞大 [comp: 庞 big + 大 big] ADJ huge, enormous

páng 旁 N side ■ 路旁都摆着各种各样的小摊

子。**Lùpáng dōu bǎizhe gè-zhǒng-gè-yàng de xiǎo tānzi.** *By the roadside are all kinds of stalls.*

pángbiān 旁边 [modif: 旁 aside + 边 side] N side ■ 王先生旁边那位先生是谁？**Wáng xiānsheng pángbiān nà wèi xiānsheng shì shéi?** *Who is the man beside Mr Wang?* ■ 小河旁边有一个农场。**Xiǎo hé pángbiān yǒu yí ge nóngchǎng.** *There's a farm by the small river.*

pángguān 旁观 V look on

pángguānzhě qīng 旁观者清 IDIOM The onlooker sees most of the game.

pàng 胖 ADJ fat, plump ■ 现在胖的人越来越多了。**Xiànzài pàng de rén yuèláiyuè duō le.** *There are more and more fat people now.*

pàngzi 胖子 N fat person, "fatty"

pāo 抛 V throw, hurl

pāoqì 抛弃 [comp: 抛 throw + 弃 discard] V abandon, forsake

páo 袍 N gown

长袍 cháng páo gown, robe (件 **jiàn**)

pǎo 跑 V run ■ 我们比一比，看谁跑得快。**Wǒmen bǐ yi bǐ, kàn shéi pǎo de kuài.** *Let's compete and see who runs faster.*

pǎobù 跑步 [modif: 跑 run + 步 steps] V jog ■ 每天早上很多人在公园里跑步。**Měi tiān zǎoshang hěn duō rén zài gōngyuán li pǎobù.** *Many people jog in the park early every morning.*

pǎodào 跑道 N runway, track (in a sports ground)

pào 炮 N cannon, gun (门 **mén**, 座 **zuò**) ■ 山顶上放着一门古炮。**Shāndǐng shang fàngzhe yì mén gǔ pào.** *On top of the hill stands an old cannon.*

pàobīng 炮兵 N artillery man

pào 泡 I N 1 bubble

肥皂泡 féizàopào soap bubble

2 blister II V soak, steep

pàomò 泡沫 [comp: 泡 bubble + 沫 foam] N bubble, foam

péi 陪 V accompany ■ 他妻子上街买衣服，他陪她去。**Tā qīzi shàngjiē mǎi yīfu, tā péi tā qù.** *His wife went out to buy clothes, and he went with her.* ■ 我今天没有空陪你去看电影。**Wǒ jīntiān méiyǒu kòng péi nǐ qù kàn diànyǐng.** *I don't have time to go to the movies with you.*

péi 培 V cultivate

péixùn 培训 [comp: 培 cultivate + 训 train] N training

培训班 péixùnbān training class, training course / 培训生 péixùnshēng trainee

péiyǎng 培养 [comp: 培 cultivate + 养 provide for] V 1 train, develop 2 cultivate, breed

péiyù 培育 [comp: 培 cultivate + 育 nurture] V bring up, nurture

培育下一代 péiyù xià yídài bring up the next generation, bring up one's children

péi 赔 TRAD 賠 V compensate, pay for (damage, loss, etc.) ■ 你借给我的书，我丢了。我赔你

吧。**Nǐ jiè gei wǒ de shū, wǒ diū le. Wǒ péi nǐ ba.** *I've lost the book you lent me. Let me pay for it.*

péicháng 赔偿 [comp: 赔 compensate + 偿 give back] **v & n** compensate for; compensation for

pèi 佩 **v** wear

pèifu 佩服 **v** admire ■ 我佩服自学成才的人。**Wǒ pèifu zì-xué-chéng-cái de rén.** *I admire those who become a success from being self-taught.*

NOTE: You can utter 佩服 **Pèifu** or 佩服！佩服！**Pèifu! Pèifu!** to express great admiration for a feat or a remarkable achievement, for example: ■ "你五门功课都是一百分？佩服！佩服！" **"Nǐ wǔ mén gōngkè dōu shì yìbǎi fēn? Pèifu! Pèifu!"** *"You got full marks for all the five subjects? Wow!"*

pèi 配 **v 1** match, blend **2** be worthy of, deserve 配得上 **pèi de shàng** be worth of, be good enough to be / 配不上 **pèi bu shàng** be not good enough to be, be unworthy of

pèibèi 配备 **v** allocate, provide with, be equipped with 每个教室配备一台电脑 **měige jiàoshì pèibèi yìtái diànnǎo** equip each classroom with a computer

pèihé 配合 [comp: 配 match + 合 cooperate] **v** cooperate, coordinate ■ 各个部门都要相互配合。**Gè ge bùmén dōu yào xiānghù pèihé.** *All the departments should cooperate with each other.* ■ 病人要和医生密切配合，才能早日恢复健康。**Bìngrén yào hé yīshēng mìqiè pèihé, cáinéng zǎorì huīfù jiànkāng.** *A patient should cooperate closely with his doctor so as to achieve a speedy recovery.*

pèi'ǒu 配偶 **n** spouse

pèitào 配套 **v** make up a complete set

pēn 喷 TRAD 噴 **v** sprinkle, spray ■ 这棵树上有虫子，要喷点儿药。**Zhè kē shù shang yǒu chóngzi, yào pēn diǎnr yào.** *This tree has insects on it and needs spraying.*

pén 盆 **n** basin, pot (个 **gè**) 花盆 **huāpén** flower pot / 洗脸盆 **xǐliǎnpén** wash-basin

péndì 盆地 **n** (in geography) basin

pēng 烹 **v** boil, cook

pēngrèn 烹饪 **n** cuisine

péng 朋 **n** companion

péngyou 朋友 [comp: 朋 companion + 友 friend] **n** friend ■ 朋友之间应该互相帮助。**Péngyou zhī jiān yīnggāi hùxiāng bāngzhù.** *Friends should help one another.* 跟/和…交朋友 **gēn/hé … jiāo péngyou** make friends with … ■ 他在中学的时候交了不少朋友。**Tā zài zhōngxué de shíhou jiāole bù shǎo péngyou.** *He made quite a few friends in high school.* 男朋友 **nánpéngyou** boyfriend / 女朋友 **nǚpéngyou** girlfriend

péng 膨 **v** swell

péngzhàng 膨胀 **v** extend, swell, expand

pěng 捧 **v 1** hold in both hands (with care, pride, etc.) ■ 他捧着一盆花回家。**Tā pěngzhe yì péng huā huíjiā.** *He came home with a pot of flowers in his hands.* **2** sing somebody's praise (especially insincerely), flatter ■ 你别捧我，我知道自己有几斤几两。**Nǐ bié pěng wǒ, wǒ zhīdào zìjǐ yǒu jǐ jīn jǐ liǎng.** *Don't flatter me. I know my worth.*

pèng 碰 **v** bump into, touch ■ 别碰我，我手里拿着水呢！**Bié pèng wǒ, wǒ shǒu li názhe shuǐ ne!** *Don't bump into me. I'm carrying water.*

pèngdao 碰到 **v** meet unexpectedly, run into ■ 我昨天在城里碰到一个老同学。**Wǒ zuótiān zài chénglǐ pèngdào yí ge lǎo tóngxué.** *I ran into an old classmate in town yesterday.*

pī 批 MEASURE WORD (for a batch of goods, and for things/people arriving at the same time) 一批新书 **yì pī xīn shū** a batch of new books (published at about the same time) / 两批旅游者 **liǎng pī lǚyóuzhě** two groups of tourists

pīfā 批发 **v** sell wholesale (ANTONYM 零售 **língshòu**)

pīpàn 批判 **v** criticize, repudiate

pīpíng 批评 [comp: 批 criticism + 评 comment] **v & n** criticize, scold; criticism (ANTONYM 表扬 **biǎoyáng**) ■ 老师批评他常常迟到。**Lǎoshī pīpíng tā chángcháng chídào.** *The teacher criticized him for being often late for class.* ■ 我接受你对我的批评。**Wǒ jiēshòu nǐ duì wǒ de pīpíng.** *I accept your criticism.*

pīzhǔn 批准 [comp: 批 express opinion + 准 approve, permit] **v** approve, ratify ■ 你的申请已经批准了。**Nǐ de shēnqǐng yǐjīng pīzhǔn le.** *Your application has been approved.*

pī 劈 **v** chop to split

pī 披 **v** drape over the shoulder ■ 他披着大衣，看孩子在雪地里玩。**Tā pīzhe dàyī, kàn háizi zài xuědì li wán.** *With an overcoat draped over his shoulders, he watched the children play in the snow.*

pí 皮 **n** skin, leather ■ 她从自行车上摔下来，擦破了点皮。**Tā cóng zìxíngchē shang shuāi xiàlai, cāpòle diǎn pí.** *She fell off the bike and scraped her skin.* 皮衣 **píyī** fur coat

pífū 皮肤 [comp: 皮 skin + 肤 skin] **n** skin (human) ■ 在海边住了一个夏天，他的皮肤晒黑了。**Zài hǎibiān zhùle yí ge xiàtiān, tā de pífū shài hēi le.** *After a summer by the sea, he was tanned.*

pígé 皮革 **n** leather, hide 皮革制品 **pígé zhìpǐn** leather product, leatherware

píxié 皮鞋 **n** leather shoes (双 **shuāng**)

pí 疲 ADJ fatigued

píbèi 疲惫 ADJ physically and mentally fatigued

pífá 疲乏 ADJ tired, weary

píjuàn 疲倦 [comp: 疲 fatigued + 倦 tired] ADJ weary, fed up

píláo 疲劳 ADJ fatigued, tired ■ 我连续工作了六小时，实在疲劳。**Wǒ liánxù gōngzuòle liù xiǎoshí,**

shízài píláo. *I have been working non-stop for six hours. I am indeed tired.*

pí 啤 N beer

píjiǔ 啤酒 N beer (瓶 **píng**, 杯 **bēi**) ■ 这种啤酒很好喝。 **Zhè zhǒng píjiǔ hěn hǎohē.** *This beer tastes good.* ■ 爸爸每星期五买很多啤酒。 **Bàba měi Xīngqīwǔ mǎi hěn duō píjiǔ.** *Daddy buys lots of beer every Friday.*

NOTE: 啤酒 **píjiǔ** is an example of semi-transliteration: 啤 **pí** represents the sound of English word "beer" and 酒 **jiǔ** means *alcoholic drink*.

pí 脾 N spleen

píqi 脾气 N temper ■ 王医生脾气好，很少生气。 **Wáng yīshēng píqi hǎo, hěn shǎo shēngqì.** *Dr Wang is good-tempered; he rarely gets angry.* 发脾气 fā píqi throw a tantrum, lose one's temper ■ 他为什么发脾气？ **Tā wèishénme fā píqi?** *Why did he lose his temper?*

pǐ 匹 MEASURE WORD (for horses) 一匹快马 yì pǐ kuài mǎ a fast horse

pì 辟 TRAD 闢 V open up (See **kāipì 开辟**.)

pì 僻 ADJ remote (See **piānpì 偏僻**.)

pì 屁 N flatulence, fart 放屁 fàng pì fart, break wind

pìgu 屁股 N bottom, buttocks

pìrú 譬如 CONJ same as 比如 **bǐrú**

piān 偏 ADV must (used to indicate that the action in question is contrary to one's expectation or wishes) ■ 明天有一个重要的考试，她偏今天病倒了。 **Míngtiān yǒu yí ge zhòngyào de kǎoshì, tā piān jīntiān bìngdǎo le.** *Just as there'll be an important exam tomorrow, what must she do but fall ill today?*

piānchā 偏差 N deviation, error

piānjiàn 偏见 [modif: 偏 impartial + 见 view] N prejudice, bias 对同性恋者有偏见 duì tóngxìngliànzhě yǒu piānjiàn hold prejudice against homosexuals

piānpì 偏僻 ADJ out-of-the-way, remote

piānpiān 偏偏 ADV as luck would have it ■ 我正在洗澡，手机偏偏响了。 **Wǒ zhèngzài xǐzǎo, shǒujī piānpiān xiǎng le.** *The cell phone must ring when I was taking a bath.*

piān 篇 MEASURE WORD (for a piece of writing) 一篇文章 yì piān wénzhāng an article/essay

pián 便 ADJ comfortable

piányi 便宜 ADJ inexpensive, cheap (ANTONYM 贵 guì) ■ 这家商店东西很便宜。 **Zhè jiā shāngdiàn dōngxi hěn piányi.** *Things are cheap in this store.* ■ 我想买便宜一点儿的衣服。 **Wǒ xiǎng mǎi piányi yìdiǎnr de yīfu.** *I want to buy less expensive clothes.*

piányihuò 便宜货 N cheap goods, bargain

piàn 片 I N thin and flat piece 肉片 ròupiàn meat slices

II MEASURE WORD (for thin, flat pieces) 一片面包 yí piàn miànbāo a slice of bread

piànduàn 片断 N fragment (of a writing, narrative, life experiences, etc.)

piànkè 片刻 N a brief moment, a short while

piànmiàn 片面 ADJ one-sided, unilateral (ANTONYM 全面 quánmiàn) ■ 我们应该全面考虑问题，不要有片面的观点。 **Wǒmen yīnggāi quánmiàn kǎolǜwèntí, bú yào yǒu piànmiàn de guāndiǎn.** *We should approach an issue from all sides and do not have a one-sided view.*

piàn 骗 TRAD 騙 V deceive, fool ■ 你受骗了！ **Nǐ shòu piàn le!** *You've been duped!* ■ 那个人骗我钱。 **Nàge rén piàn wǒ qián.** *That man cheated me out of my money.*

piànjú 骗局 N hoax, fraud

piànzi 骗子 N swindler, con man

piāo 飘 TRAD 飄 V flutter ■ 彩旗飘飘。 **Cǎiqí piāopiāo.** *Colorful banners fluttered in the breeze.*

piāoyáng 飘扬 V (of banners, flags, etc.) flutter, wave

piāo 漂 V float

piāofú 漂浮 V float

piào 票 N ticket (张 **zhāng**) ■ 这场电影票全卖完了。 **Zhè chǎng diànyǐng piào quán màiwán le.** *Tickets are all sold out for this movie show.* ■ 我买两张去香港的飞机票。 **Wǒ mǎi liǎng zhāng qù Xiānggǎng de fēijī piào.** *I want to buy two air tickets to Hong Kong.* 电影票 diànyǐng piào movie ticket / 飞机票 fēijī piào air ticket / 火车票 huǒchē piào train ticket / 门票 ménpiào admission ticket (to a show, sporting event, etc.) / 汽车票 qìchē piào bus/coach ticket

piào 漂 ADJ pretty

piàoliang 漂亮 ADJ pretty, good-looking ■ 这个小女孩真漂亮！ **Zhège xiǎo nǚhái zhēn piàoliang!** *This little girl is really pretty. (→ What a pretty little girl!)* ■ 你的汉字写得真漂亮。 **Nǐ de hànzì xiě de zhēn piàoliang.** *Your Chinese characters are beautifully written.*

piē 撇 V 1 discard, abandon 2 skim off from the surface of a liquid

pīn 拼 V fight bitterly

pīnbó 拼搏 [comp: 拼 fight bitterly + 搏 wrestle] V fight hard against formidable adversary (often figuratively) 拼搏精神 pīnbó jīngshen fierce fighting spirit

pīnmìng 拼命 [v+obj: 拼 fight bitterly + 命 one's life] V do all one can, risk one's life ■ 他拼命赚钱，都是为了什么呢？ **Tā pīnmìng zhuànqián, dōushì wèile shénme ne?** *He does everything possible to earn money, but for what purpose?*

pīnyīn 拼音 [v+obj: 拼 put together + 音 sound] I V spell, phonetize II N Romanized Chinese writing, *pinyin* ■ 老师，我不会写的汉字，可以写拼音吗？ **Lǎoshī, wǒ búhuì xiě de Hànzì, kěyǐ xiě pīnyīn**

ma? *Teacher, can I use pinyin for those Chinese characters I can't write?*

拼音文字 pīnyīn wénzì phonetic writing / 汉语拼音方案 Hànyǔ Pīnyīn Fāng'àn Phonetic System of the Chinese Language

pín 贫 TRAD 貧 ADJ poor, lacking

pínfá 贫乏 [comp: 贫 poor + 乏 lacking] ADJ poor in, short of

资源贫乏 zīyuán pínfá poor in natural resources

pínkùn 贫困 [comp: 贫 poor + 困 stranded] ADJ poor, destitute

pín 频 TRAD 頻 ADJ frequent

pínfán 频繁 ADJ frequent

pínlǜ 频率 [modif: 频 frequent + 率 rate] N frequency

pǐn 品 N article

pǐndé 品德 [comp: 品 quality + 德 virtue] N moral character

品德高尚 pǐndé gāoshàng of lofty (excellent) moral character

pǐnxíng 品行 [comp: 品 quality + 行 behavior] N moral quality and conduct, behavior

品行不良 pǐnxíng bùliáng of poor moral quality and behave badly

pǐnzhì 品质 N 1 (of people) moral character ■ 这个人很讨人喜欢，但是品质不好。 **Zhège rén hěn tǎorén xǐhuan, dànshì pǐnzhì bù hǎo.** *This guy is quite pleasant, but has bad moral character.* 2 (of products) quality

pǐnzhǒng 品种 [comp: 品 article + 种 kind] N variety, breed ■ 超级市场里的水果品种多得不得了，简直让人眼睛都看花了。 **Chāojíshìchǎng li de shuǐguǒ pǐnzhǒng duō de bùdeliǎo, jiǎnzhí ràng rén yǎnjing dōu kànhuā le.** *There is a huge variety of fruits in the supermarket. It is simply dazzling.*

pìn 聘 V appoint to a position, engage

pìnqǐng 聘请 V invite and appoint to a (professional or managerial) position

pīngpāngqiú 乒乓球 N table tennis, table tennis ball (只 zhī) ■ 很多中国人乒乓球打得很好。 **Hěn duō Zhōngguórén pīngpāngqiú dǎ de hěn hǎo.** *Many Chinese are good at table tennis.*

píng 平 ADJ flat, level, smooth ■ 这张桌子桌面不平。 **Zhè zhāng zhuōzi zhuōmiàn bù píng.** *The surface of the table is not level.*

píng'ān 平安 [comp: 平 peace + 安 peace] ADJ safe and sound ■ 祝你一路平安！ **Zhù nǐ yílù píng'ān!** *I wish you a safe journey! (→ Bon voyage!)* ■ 高高兴兴上班，平平安安回家。 **Gāo-gāo-xìng-xìng shàngbān, píng-píng-ān-ān huíjiā.** *Come to work in high spirits and return home safe and sound. (A Chinese slogan urging workers to observe occupational safety.)*

píngbǎn diànnǎo 平板电脑 N tablet (computer)

píngcháng 平常 [comp: 平 flat + 常 usual] I ADJ ordinary, common ■ 这位世界冠军的父母都是

平平常常的人。 **Zhè wèi shìjiè guànjūn de fùmǔ dōushì píng-píng-cháng-cháng de rén.** *The parents of this world champion are just ordinary people.* ■ 那是我一生中最不平常的一天。 **Nà shì wǒ yìshēng zhong zuì bù píngcháng de yì tiān.** *That was the most unusual day of my life.* II N ordinary time, usually, normally ■ 我平常不喝酒，只有节日的时候喝一点儿。 **Wǒ píngcháng bù hē jiǔ, zhǐyǒu jiérì de shíhou hē yìdiǎnr.** *I normally don't drink. I only drink a little on festive occasions.*

píngděng 平等 [modif: 平 flat + 等 grade] I ADJ equal (in status) ■ 法律面前人人平等。 **Fǎlù miànqián rénrén píngděng.** *Everyone is equal in the eyes of the law.* ■ 社会上还有很多不平等现象。 **Shèhuì shang háiyǒu hěn duō bù píngděng xiànxiàng.** *There are still many cases of inequality in society.* II N equality ■ 夫妻之间的平等是现代婚姻的基础。 **Fūqī zhījiān de píngděng shì xiàndài hūnyīn de jīchǔ.** *Equality between husband and wife is the foundation of modern marriage.*

píngfán 平凡 ADJ ordinary, common

píngfāng 平方 N square (mathematics) ■ 三平方公尺 **sān píngfāng gōngchǐ** 3 *square meters*

píngjìng 平静 [comp: 平 peace + 静 quiet] ADJ calm, quiet, uneventful ■ 没有一点风，大海十分平静。 **Méiyǒu yìdiǎn fēng, dàhǎi shífēn píngjìng.** *It is windless. The sea is perfectly calm.* ■ 老人平静的生活被这个消息打乱了。 **Lǎorén píngjìng de shēnghuó bèi zhège xiāoxi dàluàn le.** *The old man's peaceful life was shattered by this news.*

píngjūn 平均 ADJ average ■ 这个城市的人平均收入是一年一万元。 **Zhège chéngshì de rén píngjūn shōurù shì yì nián yíwàn yuán.** *The average per capita income of this city is 10,000 yuan a year.*

píngmiàn 平面 [modif: 平 flat + 面 face] N (in mathematics) plane

平面几何 píngmiànjǐhé plane geometry

píngshí 平时 [comp: 平 ordinary + 时 time] N ordinary time ■ 我平时六点半起床，周末八点多才起床。 **Wǒ píngshí liù diǎnbàn qǐchuáng, zhōumò bā diǎn duō cái qǐchuáng.** *I usually get up at half past six, but on weekends I get up after eight o'clock.*

píngtǎn 平坦 ADJ level and broad

píngxíng 平行 ADJ parallel

平行线 píngxíngxiàn parallel lines

píngyōng 平庸 ADJ mediocre, ordinary

píngyuán 平原 N flatland, plain ■ 中国东北地区是一个大平原。 **Zhōngguó dōngběi dìqū shì yí ge dà píngyuán.** *The northeast region of China is a huge plain.*

píng 评 TRAD 評 V comment

pínggū 评估 [comp: 评 appraise + 估 estimate] V & N assess, appraise; assessment

资产评估 zīchǎn pínggū assets assessment

píngjià 评价 [v+obj: 评 appraise + 价 value] V & N

appraise, evaluate; appraisal, evaluation
高度评价 gāodù píngjià place a high value on

pínglùn 评论 [comp: 评 comment + 论 discuss] **v & n** comment; commentary ∎ 我不想评论他们之间的矛盾。 **Wǒ bù xiǎng pínglùn tāmen zhījiān de máodùn.** *I have no comment on the conflict between them.*

píng 苹 TRAD 蘋 **n** apple

píngguǒ 苹果 [modif: 苹 apple + 果 fruit] **n** apple (个 gè) ∎ 这种苹果多少钱一公斤？ **Zhè zhǒng píngguǒ duōshǎo qián yì gōngjīn?** *How much is a kilo of these apples?*

píng 瓶 **I n** bottle **II** MEASURE WORD a bottle of 一瓶啤酒 yì píng píjiǔ a bottle of beer / 两瓶可口可乐 liǎng píng kěkǒukělè two bottles of Coca-Cola.

píngzi 瓶子 **n** bottle (个 gè)

píng 屏 **n** screen

píngmù 屏幕 **n** (film, TV) screen, (computer) monitor

píngzhàng 屏障 **n** barrier, protective screen

píng 凭 **I n** evidence, proof
真凭实据 zhēnpíng shíjù hard evidence
II v go by, base on
凭票入场 píngpiàorùchǎng admission by tickets

pō 坡 **n** slope ∎ 骑自行车上坡很累。 **Qí zìxíngchē shàng pō hěn lèi.** *Cycling up a slope is very tiring.*

pō 泼 TRAD 潑 **v** sprinkle (See huópo 活泼.)

pō 泊 **n** lake (See húpō 湖泊.)

pópo 婆婆 **n** husband's mother

pò 迫 **v** compel

pò bù jí dài 迫不及待 IDIOM brook no delay, too important to wait

pòhài 迫害 [comp: 迫 oppress + 害 harm] **v & n** persecute; prosecution

pòqiè 迫切 **ADJ** urgent, pressing ∎ 我们的迫切任务是了解市场情况。 **Wǒmen de pòqiè rènwù shì liǎojiě shìchǎng qíngkuàng.** *Our urgent task is to understand the market situation.*

pò 破 **I v** break, damage ∎ 你的衣服破了。 **Nǐ de yīfu pò le.** *Your clothes are torn.* **II ADJ** torn, damaged ∎ 这件破衣服不能穿了。 **Zhè jiàn pò yīfu bù néng chuān le.** *This torn coat is no longer wearable.* ∎ 花瓶打破了。 **Huāpíng dǎpò le.** *The vase is broken.*

pòchǎn 破产 **v & n** go bankrupt; bankruptcy ∎ 没有想到，这家大公司会宣布破产。 **Méiyǒu xiǎngdào, zhè jiā dà gōngsī huì xuānbù pòchǎn.** *It is quite unexpected that this big company should declare bankruptcy.*

pòhuài 破坏 [v+obj: 破 break + 坏 bad] **v** sabotage, damage ∎ 不准破坏公共财物。 **Bù zhǔn pòhuài gōnggòng cáiwù.** *Vandalism of public property is not allowed.*

pòlì 破例 **v** make an exception, break a rule

pò 魄 **n 1** soul, spirit **2** vigor

pòlì 魄力 [comp: 魄 vigor + 力 strength] **n** daring, resolution

pōu 剖 **v** cut open (See jiěpōu 解剖.)

pū 扑 TRAD 撲 **v 1** pounce on **2** flap

pū 铺 TRAD 鋪 **v** spread, unfold ∎ 桌子上铺着一块漂亮的桌布。 **Zhuōzi shang pūzhe yí kuài piàoliang de zhuōbù.** *A beautiful tablecloth was spread over the table.*

pútao 葡萄 **n** grape (颗 kē) ∎ 这里的葡萄又大又甜。 **Zhèlǐ de pútao yòu dà yòu tián.** *The grapes here are big and sweet.*

pútaojiǔ 葡萄酒 **n** grape wine, wine

pútaoyuán 葡萄园 **n** vineyard

pǔ 朴 TRAD 樸 **ADJ** plain

pǔshí 朴实 **ADJ 1** (of style) simple and plain, down-to-earth **2** (of people) sincere and honest

pǔsù 朴素 **ADJ** simple and plain ∎ 她喜欢穿朴素的衣服。 **Tá xǐhuan chuān pǔsù de yīfu.** *She likes to dress simply.*

pǔ 普 **ADJ** common

pǔbiàn 普遍 [comp: 普 common + 遍 everywhere] **ADJ** widespread, commonplace ∎ 在那个地方，少女母亲的现象很普遍。 **Zài nàge dìfang, shàonǚ mǔqin de xiànxiàng hěn pǔbiàn.** *In that area, teenage mothers are quite commonplace.* ∎ 人们普遍认为这种做法是不对的。 **Rénmen pǔbiàn rènwéi zhè zhǒng zuòfǎ shì bú duì de.** *People generally think this kind of behavior is wrong.*

pǔjí 普及 **v** popularize, make commonplace ∎ 智能手机现在很普及了。 **Zhìnéng shǒujī xiànzài hěn pǔjí le.** *Smartphones are very commonplace now.*

pǔtōng 普通 **ADJ** common, commonplace, ordinary ∎ 在这个城市里一座普通的房子要多少钱？ **Zài zhège chéngshì li yízuò pǔtōng de fángzi yào duóshǎo qián?** *How much is an ordinary house in this city?*

Pǔtōnghuà 普通话 [modif: 普通 common + 话 speech] **n** Standard Modern Chinese, Mandarin, Putonghua ∎ 大多数中国人都听得懂普通话。 **Dàduōshù Zhōngguórén dōu tīng de dǒng Pǔtōnghuà.** *Most Chinese people understand Putonghua.* ∎ 你说普通话不太标准，也不要紧。 **Nǐ shuō Pǔtōnghuà bú tài biāozhǔn, yě bú yàojǐn.** *It doesn't matter if you don't speak perfect Putonghua.*

NOTE: Modern Standard Chinese is known as 普通话 **Pǔtōnghuà** in China, 国语 **Guóyǔ** in Taiwan and 华语 **Huáyǔ** in Singapore and other Southeast Asian countries. They refer to the same language, though slight differences do exist among them.

pǔ 谱 TRAD 譜 **n** chart, guidebook
家谱 jiāpǔ family tree, genealogy

pù 瀑 **n** waterfall

pùbù 瀑布 **n** waterfall

Q

qī 七 NUMERAL seven
七百七十七 qībǎi qīshíqī seven hundred and seventy-seven (777)

qī 妻 N wife

qīzi 妻子 [suffix: 妻 wife + 子 nominal suffix] N wife ■ 丈夫和妻子应当互相爱护，互相尊重。 Zhàngfu hé qīzi yīngdāng hùxiāng àihù, hùxiāng zūnzhòng. *Husbands and wives should care for and respect each other.*

qī 期 I N fixed time
按期 àn qī according to the schedule, on time /
到期 dàoqī expire, due / 过期 guòqī overdue, expired
II v expect, anticipate

qīdài 期待 v expect, look forward to

qījiān 期间 N during the period of ■ 春节期间饭店的生意特别好。 Chūnjié qījiān fàndiàn de shēngyi tèbié hǎo. *During the Chinese New Year holidays, restaurants have particularly good business.*

qīwàng 期望 [comp: 期 expect + 望 look forward to] v & N expect, hope; expectations, hope
期望过高 qīwàng guògāo expect too much

qīxiàn 期限 N deadline, time limit
超过期限 chāoguò qīxiàn exceed the time limit, become overdue / 定一个期限 dìng yí ge qīxiàn set a deadline

qī 欺 v cheat, bully

qīfu 欺负 v bully, take advantage of (someone) ■ 他有了一点儿权，就要欺负别人。 Tā yǒu le yìdiǎnr quán, jiùyào qīfu biéren. *He tried to bully others once he'd got some power.*

qīpiàn 欺骗 [comp: 欺 cheat + 骗 deceive] v deceive ■ 这件事我完全了解，他无法欺骗我。 Zhè jiàn shì wǒ wánquán liǎojiě, tā wúfǎ qīpiàn wǒ. *I know this matter full well. There is no way he can deceive me.*

qī 凄 ADJ chilly, cold

qīliáng 凄凉 ADJ [comp: 凄 chilly + 凉 chilly] ADJ desolate, dreary, miserable

qī 戚 N relative (See qīnqi 亲戚.)

qí 齐 TRAD 齊 I ADJ neat, in a straight line ■ 书架上的书放得很齐。 Shūjià shang de shū fàng de hěn qí. *The books in the bookshelf are neatly arranged.* II v reach to the same height ■ 树长得齐屋顶了。 Shù zhǎng de qí wūdǐng le. *The trees have grown as tall as the roof.*

qíquán 齐全 ADJ complete, all in readiness
品种齐全 pǐnzhǒng qíquán have a complete range of products (goods)

qí xīn xié lì 齐心协力 IDIOM be of one mind and act in concerted effort

qí 岐 ADJ different, divergent

qíshì 歧视 v & N discriminate against; discrimination

种族歧视 zhǒngzú qíshì racial discrimination

qí 其 PRON this, that

qící 其次 ADV next, secondary, secondly ■ 他们离婚的原因首先是性格不合，其次是经济上有矛盾。 Tāmen líhūn de yuányīn shǒuxiān shì xìnggé bù hé, qící shì jīngjì shang yǒu máodùn. *The first reason they gave for divorcing was incompatibility of disposition and the second reason was financial conflict.*

qíshí 其实 ADV actually, as a matter of fact ■ 她说懂了，其实她还是不明白。 Tā shuō dǒng le, qíshí tā háishi bù míngbai. *She said she understood, but actually she still didn't comprehend it.*

qítā 其他 PRON other ■ 我只要买一台笔记本电脑，其它的什么都不要。 Wǒ zhǐyào mǎi yì tái bǐjìběn diànnǎo, qítā de shénme dōu bú yào. *I only want to buy a notebook computer. I don't want anything else.*

qíyú 其余 PRON the rest, the remainder ■ 我付了学费以后把其余的钱存进了银行。 Wǒ fùle xuéfèi yǐhòu bǎ qíyú de qián cúnjìnle yínháng. *After paying the tuition fee, I deposited the remainder of the money in the bank.*

qízhōng 其中 N among them, in it ■ 北京有很多名胜古迹，故宫是其中之一。 Běijīng yǒu hěn duō míngshèng gǔjì, gùgōng shì qízhōng zhī yī. *There are many scenic spots and historical sites in Beijing. The Palace Museum is one of them.*

qí 旗 N flag, banner (面 miàn)
旗杆 qígān flagstaff, flag pole / 国旗 guóqí national flag / 升旗 shēngqí hoist a flag

qízi 旗子 [suffix: 旗 flag, banner + 子 nominal suffix] N flag, banner (面 miàn) ■ 国旗是代表国家的旗子。 Guóqí shì dàibiǎo guójiā de qízi. *A national flag is one that symbolizes the country.*

qípáo 旗袍 N a woman's dress with a high neck and a slit up the side, *cheongsam*

qízhì 旗帜 N flag, banner, streamer

qí 奇 ADJ strange

qíguài 奇怪 [comp: 奇 strange + 怪 unusual] ADJ strange, unusual, odd ■ 他一年到头戴着一顶黄帽子，真奇怪。 Tā yì-nián-dào-tóu dàizhe yì dǐng huáng màozi, zhēn qíguài. *It is really odd that he wears a yellow cap all year long.* ■ 对这种奇怪的现象，我不能解释。 Duì zhè zhǒng qíguài de xiànxiàng, wǒ bù néng jiěshì. *I cannot explain this strange phenomenon.*

qíjì 奇迹 N miracle, wonder
创造奇迹 chuàngzào qíjì perform miracles, work wonders

qímiào 奇妙 ADJ marvelous, intriguing

qí 骑 TRAD 騎 v ride (a horse, bicycle, etc.)
骑自行车 qí zìxíngchē ride a bicycle ■ 我每天骑自行车去上学。 Wǒ měi tiān qí zìxíngchē qù shàngxué. *I go to school by bike every day.*

qí mǎ 骑马 ride a horse

qǐ 企 v hope

qǐtú 企图 v & N attempt, try; attempt ■ 恐怖分子企图破坏铁路和公路，制造大规模交通事故。**Kǒngbùfènzǐ qǐtú pòhuài tiělù hé gōnglù, zhìzào dà guīmó jiāotōng shìgù.** *Terrorists attempted to sabotage railways and highways to cause large-scale traffic accidents.* ■ 他们的企图失败了。**Tāmen de qǐtú shībài le.** *Their attempt failed.*

NOTE: 企图 **qǐtú** is usually used for negative situations. For example, we usually do not say 他企图帮助我。**Tā qǐtú bāngzhù wǒ.** *He tried to help me.* but 他企图欺骗我。**Tā qǐtú qīpiàn wǒ.** *He tried to deceive me.*

qǐyè 企业 N enterprise (家 **jiā**) ■ 管理一个大型企业是极其复杂的。**Guǎnlǐ yí ge dàxíng qǐyè shì jíqí fùzá de.** *To manage a large enterprise is an extremely complex undertaking.*

国有企业 guóyǒu qǐyè state-owned enterprise / 私有企业 sīyǒu qǐyè private enterprise

qǐyèjiā 企业家 N entrepreneur

qǐ 启 TRAD 啟 v open

qǐchéng 启程 v start a journey, set out

qǐfā 启发 [comp: 启 open + 发 release] v & N enlighten, arouse; enlightenment, inspiration ■ 我们应该启发孩子的学习兴趣。**Wǒmen yīnggāi qǐfā háizi de xuéxí xìngqù.** *We should arouse an interest to learn in children.* ■ 科学家常常从平常的自然现象得到启发。**Kēxuéjiā chángcháng cóng píngcháng de zìrán xiànxiàng dédào qǐfā.** *Scientists are often enlightened by commonplace natural phenomena.*

qǐméng 启蒙 v & N enlighten; enlightenment

qǐshì 启示 [comp: 启 enlighten + 示 indicate] N revelation, inspiration, enlightenment

qǐshì 启事 N public announcement

qǐ 起 v rise, get up

从 … 起 cóng … qǐ starting from … ■ 从晚上七点起，网吧就特别忙。**Cóng wǎnshang qī diǎn qǐ, wǎngbā jiù tèbié máng.** *Starting from seven o'clock in the evening, the Internet cafe is particularly busy.*

qǐcǎo 起草 v draft, make a draft of (a plan, a document, etc.)

qǐchū 起初 ADV at first, at the onset

qǐchuáng 起床 v get up (out of bed) ■ "你每天几点起床？" "平时七点，周末就晚一点。" "**Nǐ měi tiān jǐ diǎn qǐchuáng?**" "**Píngshí qī diǎn, zhōumò jiù wǎn yì diǎn.**" *"When do you get up every day?" "Seven o'clock usually, but a bit later on weekends."*

qǐfēi 起飞 v (of a plane) take off

qǐfú 起伏 v & N undulate, fluctuate; fluctuation, ups and downs

qǐhòng 起哄 v set up a commotion in a light-hearted or mocking manner

qǐlai 起来 v get up (out of bed), stand up ■ 校长走进教室，大家都站起来。**Xiàozhǎng zǒujìn jiàoshì, dàjiā dōu zhàn qǐlai.** *When the principal entered the classroom, everybody stood up.*

NOTE: 起来 **qǐlai** is often used after a verb as a complement to express various meanings. Among other meanings, 起来 **qǐlai** may be used after a verb to mean *begin to ...*, e.g. ■ 我们不等爸爸了，吃起来吧。**Wǒmen bù děng bàba le, chī qǐlai ba.** *We're not going to wait for daddy any longer. Let's start eating.*

qǐmǎ 起码 ADJ the very least, minimum

qǐsù 起诉 v sue, file a lawsuit against

qǐyì 起义 v & N rise in an uprising; uprising

qǐyuán 起源 [comp: 起 start + 源 source] N origin ■ 你知道人类的起源吗 **Nǐ zhīdào rénlèi de qǐyuán ma?** *Do you know the origin of humankind?*

qǐ 乞 v beg

qǐgài 乞丐 N beggar

qǐ 岂 TRAD 豈 ADV (forming rhetorical question)

qǐ yǒu cǐ lǐ 岂有此理 IDIOM preposterous, outrageous ■ 真是岂有此理！**Zhēn shi qǐ yǒu cǐ lǐ!** *How absurd! That's really outrageous!*

qì 气 TRAD 氣 v be angry, make angry ■ 知道他一直在骗我，我气极了。**Zhīdào tā yìzhí zài piàn wǒ, wǒ qì jíle.** *When I found that he had been deceiving me all the time, I was very angry.* ■ 你干吗说这种话气她？**Nǐ gànmá shuō zhè zhǒng huà qì tā?** *Why on earth did you say that and make her angry?*

qìfen 气氛 N atmosphere, ambiance ■ 我喜欢这家酒吧友好的气氛。**Wǒ xǐhuan zhè jiā jiǔbā yǒuhǎo de qìfen.** *I like the friendly ambiance of this bar.*

qìgài 气概 N lofty spirit, (heroic) mettle

qìgōng 气功 [modif: 气 breath + 功 skill] N a form of exercises involving deep breath, *qigong*

练气功 liàn qìgōng practice exercises of deep breath, practice *qigong*

qìhòu 气候 N climate ■ 地球上的气候在渐渐变暖。**Dìqiú shang de qìhòu zài jiànjiàn biàn nuǎn.** *The climate on earth is gradually becoming warmer.*

qìpò 气魄 N daring, boldness

qìqiú 气球 N balloon

热气球 rè qìqiú hot-air balloon

qìsè 气色 N complexion

qìshì 气势 N momentum

qìtǐ 气体 N gas

qìwèi 气味 N smell, odor ■ 这个剩菜气味不对，不能吃了。*The leftovers have a funny smell, and can't be eaten.*

qìwēn 气温 [modif: 气 atmosphere + 温 temperature] N atmospheric temperature ■ 今天最高气温十五度，最低气温八度。**Jīntiān zuì gāo qìwēn shíwǔ dù, zuì dī qìwēn bā dù.** *Today's maximum temperature is 15 degrees, and the minimum is 8 degrees.*

qìxiàng 气象 N meteorological phenomena, weather
气象预报 qìxiàng yùbào weather forecast ■ 你听今天的气象预报了吗？ **Nǐ tīng jīntiān de qìxiàng yùbào le ma?** *Have you heard today's weather forecast?*

qìxiàngtái 气象台 N meteorological observatory

qìxiàngxué 气象学 N meteorology

qìyā 气压 N atmospheric pressure

qìzhì 气质 N temperament, disposition

qì 汽 N vapor, steam

qìchē 汽车 [modif: 汽 vapor + 车 vehicle] N automobile, car (辆 **liàng**) ■ 我的汽车坏了。**Wǒde qìchē huài le.** *My car has broken down.*
开汽车 kāi qìchē drive a car ■ 你会开汽车吗？ **Nǐ huì kāi qìchē ma?** *Can you drive a car?*

NOTE: In everyday Chinese, 车 **chē** is often used instead of 汽车 **qìchē** to refer to a car, e.g. ■ 你会开车吗？ **Nǐ huì kāi chē ma?** *Can you drive a car?*

qìshuǐ 汽水 [modif: 汽 vapor + 水 water] N soda water, soft drink, soda, pop (瓶 **píng**, 杯 **bēi**) ■ 这瓶汽水是给你的。**Zhè píng qìshuǐ shì gěi nǐ de.** *This bottle of soda water is for you.* ■ 我不喝汽水，我喝水。**Wǒ bù hē qìshuǐ, wǒ hē shuǐ.** *I don't drink soft drinks. I drink water.*

qìyóu 汽油 N gasoline, gas, petrol ■ 我们的汽油快用完了，到前面的加油站要停下加油。**Wǒmen de qìyóu kuài yòngwán le, dào qiánmiàn de jiāyóuzhàn yào tíngxia jiāyóu.** *We've almost run out of gas. We'll have to stop for gas at the next gas station.*

qì 弃 TRAD 棄 V abandon (See fàngqì 放弃.)

qì 器 N utensil

qìcái 器材 [comp: 器 equipment + 材 material] N equipment, material

qìguān 器官 N (human and animal) organ

qì 迄 PREP up to

qì jīn wéi zhǐ 迄今为止 IDIOM up to this date, by now

qiā 掐 V pinch, nip

qià 洽 ADJ in harmony

qiàtán 洽谈 V consult, negotiate

qià 恰 ADV just, exactly

qiàdàng 恰当 ADJ appropriate, suitable, proper

qià dào hǎo chù 恰到好处 ADJ just right, hitting the spot ■ 你说的话，恰到好处。**Nǐ shuōde huà, qià dào hǎo chù.** *What you said hit the nail on the head.*

qiàqiǎo 恰巧 ADV as luck would have it, fortunately ■ 恰巧大家都在。**Qiàqiǎo dàjiā dōu zài.** *Fortunately everyone happened to be there.*

qiān 千 NUMERAL thousand ■ 一千零一夜 **yìqiān líng yí yè** *a thousand and one nights* ■ 四千五百八十 **sìqiān wǔbǎi bāshí** *four thousand, five hundred and eighty (4580)*

qiān fāng bǎi jì 千方百计 [comp: 千方 a thousand methods + 百计 a hundred plans] ADV trying a thousand and one ways, by every possible means

qiānwàn 千万 ADV be sure to, must never (used in an imperative sentence for emphasis) ■ 你开车千万要小心！**Nǐ kāichē qiānwàn yào xiǎoxīn!** *Be very, very careful while driving.* ■ 明天的会你千万别迟到。**Míngtiān de huì nǐ qiānwàn bié chídào.** *Be sure not to be late for tomorrow's meeting.*

qiān 迁 TRAD 遷 V move

qiānjiù 迁就 V accommodate oneself to, yield to

qiānxǐ 迁徙 V move, migrate

qiān 牵 V lead along by hand

qiānchě 牵扯 V involve, implicate

qiānzhì 牵制 V restrain, be bogged down

qiān 谦 TRAD 謙 ADJ modest

qiānxū 谦虚 [comp: 谦 modest + 虚 empty] ADJ modest, self-effacing ■ 他对自己的成绩非常谦虚。 *He is very modest about his achievements*

qiānxùn 谦逊 ADJ modest and unassuming

qiān 签 TRAD 簽 V sign, autograph

qiāndìng 签订 V sign (a treaty, an agreement, etc.) ■ 那家建筑公司和市政府签订了两份合同。**Nà jiā jiànzhù gōngsī hé shì zhèngfǔ qiāndìng le liǎng fèn hétong.** *The construction company has signed two contracts with the city government.*

qiānmíng 签名 [v+obj: 签 sign + 名 name] V & N autograph, sign one's name; autograph, signature
请歌星签名 qǐng gēxīng qiānmíng ask a singer for his/her autograph

qiānshǔ 签署 V sign (a treaty, a contract, etc.)

qiānzhèng 签证 N visa
入境签证 rùjìng qiānzhèng entry visa / 申请签证 shēnqǐng qiānzhèng apply for visa

qiān 铅 TRAD 鉛 N lead

qiānbǐ 铅笔 [modif: 铅 lead + 笔 pen] N pencil (支 **zhī**) ■ 我的红铅笔哪里去了？ **Wǒ de hóng qiānbǐ nǎlǐ qù le?** *Where's my red pencil?* ■ 我可以用一下你的铅笔吗？ **Wǒ kěyǐ yòng yíxià nǐ de qiānbǐ ma?** *May I use your pencil for a while?*

qiānbǐ dāo 铅笔刀 N pencil sharpener

qiānbǐ hé 铅笔盒 N pencil box

qián 前 N 1 front, in front of (ANTONYM 后 **hòu**) ■ 房子前有一块草地。**Fángzi qián yǒu yí kuài cǎodì.** *In front of the house there's a lawn.* ■ 中国人的姓名，姓在前，名在后。**Zhōngguórén de xìngmíng, xìng zài qián, míng zài hòu.** *In a Chinese person's name, the family name comes before the given name.* 2 same as 以前 **yǐqián**

NOTE: In everyday Chinese, 前 **qián** is seldom used alone to mean *front* or *in front of*. Often it is better to use 前边 **qiánbian**.

qiánbian 前边 [modif: 前 front + 边 side] N front (ANTONYM 后边 **hòubian**) ■ 房子前边有一块草

地。**Fángzi qiánbian yǒu yí kuài cǎodì.** *In front of the house, there's a lawn.* ■ 中国人的姓名姓在前边，名在后边。**Zhōngguórén de xìngmíng, xìng zài qiánbian, míng zài hòubian.** *In a Chinese person's name, the family name comes before the given name.*

qiánjìn 前进 [comp: 前 advance + 进 advance] v advance (ANTONYM 后退 **hòutuì**) ■ 我们的经济在过去一年又前进了一大步。**Wǒmen de jīngjì zài guòqù yì nián yòu qiánjìn le yí dà bù.** *Last year our economy took a big stride forward.*

qiánjǐng 前景 [modif: 前 front + 景 view] N prospect, vista ■ 前景不妙。**Qiánjǐng búmiào.** *The future doesn't look too promising.*

qiánmiàn 前面 N same as 前边 **qiánbian**

qiánnián 前年 N the year before last ■ 今年是2015年，前年是2013年。**Jīnnián shì èr-líng-yī-wǔ nián, qiánnián shì èr-líng-yī-sān nián.** *This year is 2015 and the year before last was 2013.* ■ 前年我刚开始学中文。**Qiánnián wǒ gāng kāishǐ xué Zhōngwén.** *I just began to learn Chinese the year before last.*

qiántí 前提 N **1** prerequisite, the prime consideration **2** (in logic) premise

qiántiān 前天 N the day before yesterday ■ 他前天去中国，今天我收到了他从中国发来的电子邮件。**Tá qiántiān qù Zhōngguó, jīntiān wǒ shōudàole tā cóng Zhōngguó fālai de diànzǐ yóujiàn.** *He left for China the day before yesterday, and today I got an e-mail he sent from China.*

qiántú 前途 [modif: 前 in front + 途 journey] N future, prospects, future prospects ■ 这次计划的成败将决定公司的前途。**Zhè cì jìhuà de chéngbài jiāng juédìng gōngsī de qiántú.** *The success or failure of this plan will determine the future prospects of the company.*

qián 潜 ADJ hidden, latent

qiánlì 潜力 [modif: 潜 hidden + 力 strength] N latent capacity, potential, potentiality

qiánshuǐ 潜水 v go underwater, dive

qiánshuǐyuán 潜水员 N diver, frogman

qián yí mò huà 潜移默化 IDIOM influence imperceptibly, act on subtly

qián 钱 TRAD 錢 N money (笔 **bǐ**) ■ 他在银行里有一大笔钱。**Tā zài yínháng li yǒu yí dà bǐ qián.** *He has a big sum of money in the bank.* ■ 他从来不向人借钱，也不借钱给别人。**Tā cónglái bú xiàng rén jiè qián, yě bú jiè qián gěi biéren.** *He never borrows money, nor does he lend money to others.*

qiánbāo 钱包 N wallet, purse

qiǎn 谴 TRAD 譴 v as in 谴责 **qiǎnzé**

qiǎnzé 谴责 v condemn, denounce

qiǎn 浅 TRAD 淺 ADJ **1** shallow (ANTONYM 深 **shēn**) ■ 这条河很浅，可以走过去。**Zhè tiáo hé hěn qiǎn, kěyǐ zǒu guòqù.** *This river is shallow. You can wade across it.* **2** easy, of low standard ■ 这

本书太浅，你不用看。**Zhè běn shū tài qiǎn, nǐ bú yòng kàn.** *This book is too easy for you; you don't have to read it.*

qiàn 欠 v owe, be in debt to ■ 他欠我一百元。**Tā qiàn wǒ yìbǎi yuán.** *He owes me a hundred yuan.*

qiàn rénqíng 欠人情 owe a debt of gratitude

qiàn 歉 N apology

qiànyì 歉意 N apology, regret 表达歉意 biǎodá qiànyì offer an apology

qiāng 枪 TRAD 槍 N small arms, gun, pistol (支 **zhī**, 把 **bǎ**) ■ 在我们国家，老百姓有枪是犯法的。**Zài wǒmen guójiā, lǎobǎixìng yǒu qiāng shì fànfǎ de.** *In our country, it's against the law for ordinary citizens to own guns.* 手枪 shǒuqiāng handgun (revolver, pistol)

qiāng 腔 N hollow part of a body, cavity 腹腔 fùqiāng abdominal cavity / 胸腔 xiōngqiāng thoracic cavity

qiáng 强 ADJ strong (ANTONYM 弱 **ruò**) ■ 她中文口语很强，但是写汉字的能力比较弱。**Tā Zhōngwén kǒuyǔ hěn qiáng, dànshì xiě Hànzì de nénglì bǐjiào ruò.** *She is strong in oral Chinese, but weak in writing characters.*

qiángdà 强大 [comp: 强 strong + 大 big] ADJ powerful (ANTONYM 弱小 **ruòxiǎo**) ■ 谁都希望自己的祖国强大。**Shéi dōu xīwàng zìjǐ de zǔguó qiángdà.** *Everybody wants their motherland to be a powerful country.*

qiángdào 强盗 N bandit, robber ■ 他十几岁的时候是个小偷，现在二十多岁成了一名强盗。**Tā shí jǐ suì de shíhou shì ge xiǎotōu, xiànzài èrshí duō suì chéngle yì míng qiángdào.** *When he was a teenager he was a thief. Now in his twenties, he has become a robber.*

qiángdiào 强调 [modif: 强 strong + 调 tone] v emphasize, lay stress on ■ 王老师强调语音准确的重要性。**Wáng lǎoshī qiángdiào yǔyīn zhǔnquè de zhòngyàoxìng.** *Teacher Wang emphasized the importance of correct pronunciation.*

qiángdù 强度 [modif: 强 strong + 度 degree] N intensity, strength ■ 这种材料的强度还不够。**Zhè zhǒng cáiliào de qiángdù hái bú gòu.** *This material does not have enough strength.*

qiángliè 强烈 [comp: 强 strong + 烈 raging] ADJ strong, intense, violent ■ 顾客们强烈要求退货。**Gùkèmen qiángliè yāoqiú tuìhuò.** *The customers firmly demanded a refund.*

qiángzhì 强制 v coerce, force, compel

qiáng 墙 TRAD 牆 N wall (道 **dào**) ■ 墙上有一张世界地图。**Qiáng shang yǒu yì zhāng shìjiè dìtú.** *There's a map of the world on the wall.*

qiǎng 抢 TRAD 搶 v seize, grab ■ 他的玩具手枪被一个大孩子抢走了。**Tā de wánjù shǒuqiāng bèi yí ge dà háizi qiǎngzǒu le.** *His toy pistol was snatched away by a big boy.*

qiǎngjié 抢劫 v rob, plunder

抢劫银行 qiǎngjié yínháng rob a bank

qiǎngjiù 抢救 **v** rescue, salvage

抢救病人 qiǎngjiù bìngrén rescue a patient, give emergency treatment to a patient

qiǎng 强 **v** make hard effort

qiǎngpò 强迫 **v** compel, coerce, force

qiāo 悄 **ADJ** quiet

qiāoqiāo 悄悄 **ADV** quietly, on the quiet ■ 他悄悄 对我说，"别在这里买，太贵了。" **Tā qiāoqiāo duì wǒ shuō, "Bié zài zhèli mǎi, tài guì le."** *He whispered to me, "Don't buy it here; it's too expensive."*

qiāo 敲 **v** knock ■ 有人敲门。**Yǒu rén qiāo mén.** *Someone is knocking at the door.*

qiáo 桥 **TRAD** 橋 **N** bridge (座 zuò) ■ 长江上有很 多大桥。**Chángjiāng shang yǒu hěn duō dà qiáo.** *There are many big bridges across the Yangtze River.*

过桥 guò qiáo cross a bridge

qiáoliáng 桥梁 **N** big bridge (座 zuò) ■ 他的专业 是桥梁建造。**Tā de zhuānyè shì qiáoliáng jiànzào.** *His special field is bridge construction.*

qiáo 侨 **TRAD** 僑 **v** live abroad (See Huáqiáo 华侨.)

qiáo 瞧 **v** same as 看¹ **kàn** verb. Used as a colloquialism.

qiǎo 巧 ¹ **ADV** coincidence ■ 真巧，我正要找他， 他来了。**Zhēn qiǎo, wǒ zhèngyào zhǎo tā, tā láile.** *What a happy coincidence, he came just when I wanted to see him.* ■ 你要买的书最后一本刚卖 走，很不巧。**Nǐ yào mǎi de shū zuì hòu yì běn gāng màizǒu, hěn bù qiǎo.** *Unfortunately, the last copy of the book you want has just been sold.*

qiǎo 巧 ² **ADJ** skilled, clever ■ 他们的儿子手巧， 女儿嘴巧。**Tāmen de érzi shǒu qiǎo, nǚ'ér zuǐ qiǎo.** *Their son is clever with his hands and their daughter has the gift of the gab.*

qiǎokèlì 巧克力 **N** chocolate (块 kuài)

qiǎomiào 巧妙 [comp: 巧 skilled + 妙 wonderful] **ADJ** ingenious, very clever ■ 这台机器设计得很巧 妙。**Zhè tái jīqì shèjì de hěn qiǎomiào.** *This machine is ingeniously designed.* ■ 她的回答很巧妙。**Tā de huídá hěn qiǎomiào.** *She gave a clever answer.*

qiào 窍 **TRAD** 竅 **N 1** orifice **2** key (to something)

qiàomén 窍门 **N** key (to a problem), knack, trick

qiào 翘 **v** stick up, bend upward

qiào 壳 **N** shell, crust

dìqiào 地壳 the Earth's crust

qiē 切 **v** cut, slice ■ 爸爸把西瓜切成四块。**Bàba bǎ xīguā qiē chéng sì kuài.** *Dad cut the watermelon into four pieces.*

qiě 且 **CONJ** moreover (See érqiě 而且.)

qiè 切 **v** correspond to, be close to

qièshí 切实 **ADJ** feasible, practical

切实可行的办法 qièshí kěxíng de bànfǎ practical measure

qiè 窃 **TRAD** 竊 **v** steal, pilfer

qiètīng 窃听 **v** wiretap, bug

qiè 锲 **TRAD** 鍥 **v** carve

qiè ér bù shě 锲而不舍 **IDIOM** work with perseverance, make steady and unflagging effort

qīn 亲 **TRAD** 親 **N** blood relation

qīn'ài 亲爱 [comp: 亲 intimate + 爱 love] **ADJ** dear, beloved, darling ■ 我亲爱的祖母去年去世了，我 难受了好久。**Wǒ qīn'ài de zǔmǔ qùnián qùshì le, wǒ nánshòu le hǎojiǔ.** *My dear grandmother died last year; I was sad for a long time.*

NOTE: Although 亲爱 **qīn'ài** is glossed as *dear*, the Chinese reserve 亲爱 (的) **qīn'ài (de)** for the very few people who are really dear and close to their hearts.

qīnmì 亲密 [comp: 亲 close + 密 intimate] **ADJ** intimate, close

qīnqi 亲戚 **N** relative, relation ■ 他爸爸妈妈兄 弟姐妹很多，所以他亲戚很多。**Tā bàba māma xiōngdì jiěmèi hěn duō, suǒyǐ tā qīnqi hěn duō.** *His parents have many siblings, so he has many relatives.*

走亲戚 zǒu qīnqi visit a relative

qīnqiè 亲切 **ADJ** cordial ■ 过圣诞节的时候，朋 友们给我发来电子贺卡，表示亲切的问候。**Guò shèngdànjié de shíhou, péngyǒumen gěi wǒ fālai diànzǐ hèkǎ, biǎoshì qīnqiè de wènhòu.** *At Christmas, my friends sent me e-cards, conveying cordial greetings.*

qīnrè 亲热 [comp: 亲 intimate + 热 warm] **ADJ** affectionate, warm-hearted

qīnshēn 亲身 **ADV** same as 亲自 **qīnzì**

qīnzì 亲自 **ADV** by oneself ■ 李校长亲自来征求 对教学的意见。**Lǐ xiàozhǎng qīnzì lái zhēngqiú duì jiàoxué de yìjiàn.** *Mr Li, the principal, came himself to ask for our comments on teaching.*

qīn 钦 **TRAD** 欽 **v** admire

qīnpèi 钦佩 [comp: 钦 admire + 佩 admire] **v** admire, esteem

令人钦佩 lìngrén qīnpèi admirable

qīn 侵 **v** encroach

qīnfàn 侵犯 **v** encroach on, infringe upon, violate

侵犯知识产权 qīnfàn zhīshi chǎnquán infringe intellectual property right

qīnlüè 侵略 **v** invade (by force) ■ 侵略别国在国 际上是不允许的。**Qīnlüè bié guó zài guójì shang shì bù yǔnxǔ de.** *Invading another country is not permitted internationally.*

qín 禽 **N** fowl, birds

jiāqín 家禽 domestic fowl, poultry

qín 勤 **ADJ** diligent, hard-working

qínfèn 勤奋 **ADJ** diligent, applying oneself to

qínjiǎn 勤俭 [comp: 勤 diligent + 俭 frugal] **ADJ** diligent and frugal, hard-working and thrify ■ 勤 俭致富。**Qínjiǎn zhìfù.** *Industry and frugality leads to wealth.*

qínkěn 勤恳 **ADJ** diligent and conscientious

qínláo 勤劳 **ADJ** hard-working, industrious, diligent

qín 琴 **N** musical instrument

钢琴 gāngqín piano / 小提琴 xiǎotíqín violin

qīng 青 **ADJ** green

qīngchūn 青春 [modif: 青 green + 春 spring] **N** the quality of being young, youth

qīngchūnqī 青春期 puberty

qīngnián 青年 [modif: 青 green + 年 year] **N** young person, young people, youth (especially male) (位 wèi, 个 gè) ■ 青年工人往往没有多少经验。 *Qīngnián gōngrén wǎngwǎng méiyǒu duōshǎo jīngyàn. Young workers often don't have much experience.*

qīngshàonián 青少年 **N** adolescents and young people

qīngwā 青蛙 [modif: 青 green + 蛙 frog] **N** frog (只 zhī)

qīng 清 **ADJ** **1** clear (water), clean ■ 过去这条河的水很清，能看到河底的小石头。 *Guòqù zhè tiáo hé de shuǐ hěn qīng, néng kàndào hédǐ de xiǎo shítou. In the past this river had very clear water and you could see the little stones on the river bed.* **2** (of matters) clear, easy to understand ■ 这件事没有人能说得清。 *Zhè jiàn shì méiyǒu rén néng shuō de qīng. Nobody can give a clear account of this matter.*

qīngchè 清澈 **ADJ** crystal clear, limpid

qīngchén 清晨 **N** early morning

qīngchú 清除 [comp: 清 clear + 除 remove] **V** remove, clear away, delete

清除垃圾邮件 qīngchú lājī yóujiàn delete junk mail

qīngchu 清楚 [comp: 清 clear + 楚 clear-cut] **ADJ** clear (of speech or image) ■ 你的意思很清楚，我明白。 *Nǐ de yìsi hěn qīngchu, wǒ míngbai. Your meaning is clear. I understand it.* ■ 老师，黑板上的字我看不清楚。 *Lǎoshī, hēibǎn shang de zì wǒ kàn bu qīngchu. Teacher, I can't see the words on the blackboard clearly.* ■ 我说得清清楚楚，你怎么会误会呢？ *Wǒ shuōde qīng-qīng-chǔ-chǔ, nǐ zěnme huì wùhuì ne? I said it very clearly. How could you misunderstand it?*

qīngdàn 清淡 **ADJ** (of color, smell or taste) light and delicate

qīngjié 清洁 [comp: 清 clear + 洁 clean] **ADJ** clean, spotless

清洁工 qīngjiégōng cleaner

qīnglǐ 清理 [comp: 清 clear + 理 tidy up] **V** sort out, clear out

清理办公桌 qīnglǐ bàngōngzhuō clear out a desk

qīngxī 清晰 [comp: 清 clear + 晰 clear] **ADJ** very clear, distinct

qīngxǐng 清醒 [comp: 清 clear + 醒 awake] **ADJ** clear-headed, sober

qīngzhēn 清真 **ADJ** Islamic, Muslim

qīngzhēnsì 清真寺 **N** mosque

qīng 轻 **TRAD** 輕 **ADJ** **1** light (of weight) (**ANTONYM** 重 zhòng) ■ 油比水轻。 *Yóu bǐ shuǐ qīng. Oil is lighter than water.* **2** low, soft (of voice) ■ 她说话很轻，要仔细听，才能听清楚。 *Tā shuōhuà hěn qīng, yào zǐxì tīng, cái néng tīng qīngchu. She speaks softly. Only if you listen attentively, can you hear her clearly.* **3** of a low degree ■ 对他的处分太轻了。 *Duì tā de chǔfèn tài qīng le. The disciplinary action against him was not severe enough.*

qīng ěr yì jǔ 轻而易举 **ADJ** extremely easy to do, a piece of cake

qīngsōng 轻松 [comp: 轻 light + 松 loose] **ADJ** (of a job) easy, not requiring much effort ■ 这个工作很轻松，当然工资不高。 *Zhège gōngzuò hěn qīngsōng, dāngrán gōngzī bù gāo. This job is easy and requires no real effort; of course it is poorly paid.* ■ 上个周末我过得非常轻松愉快。 *Shàng ge zhōumò wǒ guò de fēicháng qīngsōng yúkuài. Last weekend I had a very relaxed and pleasant time.*

qīng 氢 **N** hydrogen (H)

qīng 倾 **V** incline, lean

qīngtīng 倾听 [comp: 倾 lean + 听 listen] **V** listen attentively

qīngxiàng 倾向 **N** tendency, inclination

qīngxié 倾斜 **V** tilt, incline

qíng 情 **N** **1** circumstance, situation **2** emotion, affection

qíngbào 情报 [modif: 情 situation + 报 report] **N** intelligence, information

军事情报 jūnshì qíngbào military intelligence

qíngjié 情节 **N** plot (of a story, movie, etc.), scenario

qíngjǐng 情景 [comp: 情 situation + 景 scene] **N** scene, occasion ■ 旅馆大楼在半夜着火了，人们从楼上跳下，真是可怕的情景。 *Lǚguǎn dàlóu zài bànyè zháohuǒ le, rénmen cóng lóushang tiàoxia, zhēn shì kěpà de qíngjǐng. When the hotel caught fire at midnight, people jumped from the upper floors. It was indeed a frightening scene.*

qíngkuàng 情况 [comp: 情 circumstance + 况 situation] **N** situation, circumstance ■ 他生病住院了，情况很严重。 *Tā shēngbìng zhùyuàn le, qíngkuàng hěn yánzhòng. He's been hospitalized. His condition is very serious.* ■ 我不大了解这个国家的情况。 *Wǒ bú dà liǎojiě zhège guójiā de qíngkuàng. I don't quite know the situation this country is in.*

qínglǐ 情理 [comp: 情 emotion + 理 reason] **N** common sense, reason

qíngxíng 情形 [comp: 情 situation + 形 shape] **N** circumstances, situation ■ 你能不能说说当时的情形？ *Nǐ néngbunéng shuō-shuō dāngshí de qíngxíng? Can you describe how things were at the time?*

qíngxù 情绪 [comp: 情 emotion + 绪 mood] N mood, feelings ■ 他看来情绪不好，你知道为什么吗？ **Tā kànlai qíngxù bù hǎo, nǐ zhīdào wèishénme ma?** *He seems to be in a bad mood. Do you know why?*

qíng 晴 ADJ fine, clear (of weather) ■ 今天上午晴，中午以后开始下雨了。 **Jīntiān shàngwǔ qíng, zhōngwǔ yǐhòu kāishǐ xià yǔ le.** *It was fine this morning. It began raining in the afternoon.* ■ 晴天比雨天舒服。 **Qíngtiān bǐ yǔtiān shūfu.** *A fine day is more comfortable than a rainy day.*

qínglǎng 晴朗 ADJ fine (weather), sunny

qǐng 请 TRAD 請 V 1 invite ■ 今天晚上我请你吃饭。 **Jīntiān wǎnshang wǒ qǐng nǐ chīfàn.** *I'll invite you to dinner tonight.* 2 ask, request ■ 学生请老师再说一遍。 **Xuésheng qǐng lǎoshī zài shuō yí biàn.** *The students asked the teacher to repeat it.*

NOTE: 请 **qǐng** is used to start a polite request, equivalent to *Please ...*, e.g. ■ 请您别在这里吸烟。 **Qǐng nín bié zài zhèli xīyān.** *Please don't smoke here.* ■ 请坐! **Qǐng zuò!** *Sit down, please!* ■ 请喝茶! **Qǐng hē chá.** *Have some tea, please!*

qǐngjià 请假 V ask for leave
请病假 **qǐng bìngjià** ask for sick leave / 请事假 **qǐng shìjià** ask for leave of absence

qǐngjiǎn 请柬 N letter of invitation, invitation card (份 **fèn**)

qǐngjiào 请教 [v+obj: 请 ask for + 教 teaching] V ask for advice, consult

NOTE: 请教 **qǐngjiào** is a polite word, used when you want to ask for advice or information, e.g. ■ 我能不能请教您一个问题？ **Wǒ néngbunéng qǐng jiào nín yí ge wèntí?** *Could I ask you a question, please?* ■ 请教，这个汉字是什么意思？ **Qǐngjiào, zhège Hànzì shì shénme yìsi?** *Would you please tell me the meaning of this Chinese character?*

qǐngkè 请客 [v+obj: 请 invite + 客 guest] V 1 invite to dinner, host a dinner party ■ 张先生这个星期六在家里请客吃饭。 **Zhāng xiānsheng zhège Xīngqīliù zài jiāli qǐngkè chīfàn.** *This Saturday Mr Zhang will give a dinner party at home.* 2 stand treat ■ 这次出去玩，车票、门票都是我请客。 **Zhè cì chūqu wán, chēpiào, ménpiào dōu shì wǒ qǐngkè.** *On this date, I'll pay for bus fares and admission tickets.*

qǐngqiú 请求 [comp: 请 request + 求 beseech] V & N request, ask for; request ■ 我请求你原谅我的错误。 **Wǒ qǐngqiú nǐ yuánliàng wǒ de cuòwù.** *I ask for your forgiveness of my mistake.* ■ 你们的请求已交委员会考虑。 **Nǐmen de qǐngqiú yǐ jiāo wěiyuánhuì kǎolǜ.** *Your request has been submitted to the committee for consideration.*

qǐngshì 请示 [v+obj: 请 request + 示 instruction] V ask (a person of superior position) for instruction

qǐngtiě 请帖 N letter of invitation, invitation card (份 **fèn**)

qǐngwèn 请问 IDIOM Excuse me, ... ■ 请问，您是上海来的张先生吗？ **Qǐngwèn, nín shì Shànghǎi lái de Zhāng xiānsheng ma?** *Excuse me, are you Mr Zhang from Shanghai?*

qìng 庆 TRAD 慶 V celebrate

qìngzhù 庆祝 [comp: 庆 celebrate + 祝 good wishes] V & N celebrate; celebration ■ 下个月他们的女儿大学毕业。他们打算好好庆祝一下。 **Xià ge yuè tāmen de nǚ'ér dàxué bìyè, tāmen dǎsuàn hǎohǎo qìngzhù yíxià.** *Their daughter will graduate from university next month. They plan to have a big celebration.*

qióng 穷 TRAD 窮 ADJ poor, poverty-stricken ■ 她家里以前比较穷。 **Tā jiālǐ yǐqián bǐjiào qióng.** *Her family used to be rather poor.*

qióngrén 穷人 N poor person, poor people

qiū 秋 N fall, autumn ■ 北京香山的秋景很美。 **Běijīng Xiāngshān de qiū jǐng hěn měi.** *The autumn scenery on Fragrance Hill in Beijing is very beautiful.*

qiūtiān 秋天 [modif: 秋 autumn + 天 day] N fall, autumn ■ 秋天不冷不热，十分舒服。 **Qiūtiān bù lěng bú rè, shífēn shūfu.** *Autumn is neither hot nor cold; it's very comfortable.*

qiū 丘 N mound, low and small hill

qiūlíng 丘陵 N hills, hilly land

qiú 求 V beseech, beg, ask for humbly ■ 你只有求他帮忙。 **Nǐ zhǐyǒu qiú tā bāngmáng.** *You can only ask him for help.* ■ 我求你再考虑考虑。 **Wǒ qiú nǐ zài kǎolǜ kǎolǜ.** *I beg you to give it further consideration.*

qiú 球 N 1 ball (只 **zhī**) ■ 花园里有一只球，是谁的？ **Huāyuán li yǒu yì zhī qiú, shì shéi de?** *There's a ball in the garden. Whose is it?* 2 ball game (场 **chǎng**) ■ 我们每星期六下午打一场球。 **Wǒmen měi Xīngqīliù xiàwǔ dǎ yì chǎng qiú.** *We have a ball game every Saturday afternoon.*
棒球 **bàngqiú** baseball / 比球 **bǐ qiú** have a (ball game) match / 打球 **dǎ qiú** play basketball, volleyball, etc. / 看球 **kàn qiú** watch a ball game / 篮球 **lánqiú** basketball / 排球 **páiqiú** volleyball / 踢球 **tī qiú** play soccer / 足球 **zúqiú** soccer

qiúchǎng 球场 N sports ground (especially where ball games are played)

qiúduì 球队 N (ball game) team

qiúmí 球迷 N (ball game) fan
足球迷 **zúqiú mí** football fan, soccer fan

qū 区 TRAD 區 N district (urban) ■ 中国的城市一般分成几个区。 **Zhōngguó de chéngshì yìbān fēnchéng jǐ ge qū.** *A city in China is usually divided into several districts.*
工业区 **gōngyèqū** industrial zone, industrial district / 商业区 **shāngyèqū** commercial area, business district / 住宅区 **zhù zháiqu** residential quarters

qūbié 区别 v & N distinguish between, differentiate; difference ■ 你能区别美国英语和英国英语吗？**Nǐ néng qūbié Měiguó Yīngyǔ hé Yīngguó Yīngyǔ ma?** *Can you tell American English from British English?* ■ 这两个词的意义没有多大区别。**Zhè liǎng ge cí de yìyì méiyǒu duōdà qūbié.** *There is not much difference in the meaning of the two words.*

qūfēn 区分 v & N put in different categories, differentiate; differentiation

qūyù 区域 N region, area

qū 曲 ADJ curved, bent, zigzag

qūzhé 曲折 I ADJ tortuous, winding II N complications, twists
曲折变化 qūzhé biànhuà twists and turns

qū 驱 TRAD 驅 v drive
驱车前往 qūchē qiánwǎng drive (in a car) to

qūzhú 驱逐 v drive out, banish
驱逐出境 qūzhú chūjìng deport, deportation

qū 屈 v bend, bow

qūfú 屈服 [comp: 屈 bend + 服 obey] v yield (to), knuckle under

qú 渠 N ditch, canal
灌溉渠 guàngàiqú irrigation channel

qúdào 渠道 [comp: 渠 ditch + 道 way] N 1 irrigation ditch 2 medium of communication, channel

qǔ 取 v fetch, collect

qǔdé 取得 [comp: 取 obtain + 得 get] v obtain, achieve ■ 我们去年取得很大成绩。**Wǒmen qùnián qǔdé hěn dà chéngjì.** *We made great achievements last year.*

qǔdì 取缔 v clamp down, ban, prohibit

qǔkuǎn 取款 v withdraw money
自动取款机 zìdòng qǔkuǎnjī ATM

qǔxiāo 取消 v cancel ■ 明天的会议已经取消了。**Míngtiān de huìyì yǐjīng qǔxiāo le.** *The meeting tomorrow has been called off.*

qǔ 娶 v (of a man) marry

NOTE: See note on 嫁 **jià.**

qǔ 曲 N melody, tune

qǔzi 曲子 N song, melody
熟悉的曲子 shúxī de qǔzi familiar tune

qù 去 v leave for, go to (来 lái) ■ 你什么时候去中国？**Nǐ shénme shíhou qù Zhōngguó?** *When are you going to China?* ■ 他下星期到美国去。**Tā xià xīngqī dào Měiguó qù.** *He's going to America next week.*

NOTE: 到 **dào** and 到 … 去 **dào … qù** have the same meaning and are normally interchangeable.

qùnián 去年 [modif: 去 what has gone + 年 year] N last year ■ 她去年才开始学中文。**Tā qùnián cái kāishǐ xué Zhōngwén.** *She began learning Chinese only last year.*

qùshì 去世 [v+obj: 去 leave + 世 the world] v die, pass away ■ 他的祖父在上个月去世了。**Tā de zǔfù zài shàngge yuè qùshì le.** *His grandfather passed away last month.*

NOTE: 去世 **qùshì** must be used when you want to show respect and/or love to the deceased. For instance, the normal word for *die*, 死 **sǐ**, would be totally inappropriate in the example sentence.

qù 趣 N interest (See **xìngqù** 兴趣, **yǒuqù** 有趣.)

qùwèi 趣味 [comp: 趣 interest + 味 taste] N 1 interest, delight 2 taste
低级趣味 dījí qùwèi vulgar taste

quān 圈 N circle, ring ■ 运动会的旗子上有五个圈。**Yùndònghuì de qízi shang yǒu wǔ ge quān.** *There are five circles on the flag of the Games.*

quāntào 圈套 N snare, trap
设下圈套 shè xià quāntào set a trap, lay a snare / 落入圈套 luòrù quāntào be caught in a trap, be snared

quán 全 ADJ whole, complete ■ 你的病还没全好，怎么能上班呢？**Nǐ de bìng hái méi quán hǎo, zěnme néng shàngbān ne?** *You haven't fully recovered. How can you go to work?* ■ 他说的不全是真话。**Tā shuō de bù quán shì zhēnhuà.** *He did not tell the whole truth.*
全国 quánguó the whole country / 全家 quánjiā the whole family / 全世界 quánshìjiè the entire world

quánbù 全部 [modif: 全 whole + 部 part] N all, without exception ■ 我爸爸全部的时间都放在工作上。**Wǒ bàba quánbù de shíjiān dōu fàng zài gōngzuò shang.** *My father devotes all his time to work.*

quánjú 全局 N overall situation

quán lì yǐ fù 全力以赴 IDIOM spare no efforts, go all out

quánmiàn 全面 [modif: 全 all + 面 side] ADJ all-round, comprehensive ■ 对这个问题，我们要做全面的考虑。**Duì zhège wèntí, wǒmen yào zuò quánmiàn de kǎolǜ.** *We will give thorough consideration to this issue.*

quántǐ 全体 [modif: 全 whole + 体 body] N all, each and every one (of a group of people) ■ 她代表全体学生向老师表示感谢。**Tā dàibiǎo quántǐ xuésheng xiàng lǎoshī biǎoshì gǎnxiè.** *On behalf of all the students she expressed gratitude to the teacher.*

quán 权 TRAD 權 N 1 authority, power 2 right

quánhéng 权衡 v judge the comparative importance of, weigh (options)

quánlì 权利 [comp: 权 power + 利 benefit] N right ■ 你要享受权利，就要尽一定的义务。**Nǐ yào xiǎngshòu quánlì, jiùyào jìn yídìng de yìwù.** *If you want to enjoy rights, you will have to fulfill certain obligations.*

quánlì 权力 [comp: 权 power + 力 strength] **N** authority, power ■ 校长有权力解雇教师吗? **Xiàozhǎng yǒu quánlì jiěgù jiàoshī ma?** *Does a principal have the authority to dismiss a teacher?*

quánwēi 权威 [comp: 权 power + 威 awe] **N** authority, authoritativeness
国际法权威 guójìfǎ quánwēi an authority in international law

quányì 权益 [comp: 权 power + 益 benefit] **N** rights and interests

quán 拳 **N** fist

quántou 拳头 [suffix: 拳 fist + 头 nominal suffix] **N** fist

quán 泉 **N** spring (water)
温泉 wēnquán hot spring

quǎn 犬 **N** dog
警犬 jǐngquǎn police dog

quàn 劝 TRAD 勸 **V** try to talk … into (or out of) doing something, advise ■ 他劝我不要把钱都存在那家银行。 **Tā quàn wǒ bú yào bǎ qián dōu cún zài nà jiā yínháng.** *He advised me not to put all my money in that bank.* ■ 我劝你改善和她的关系。 **Wǒ quàn nǐ gǎishàn hé tā de guānxi.** *I encourage you to improve your relationship with her.*

quē 缺 **V** lack, be short of ■ 要买智能手机,我还缺三百块钱。 **Yào mǎi zhìnéng shǒujī, wǒ hái quē sānbǎi kuài qián.** *I'm short of 300 yuan for the purchase of a smartphone.*
缺人手 quē rénshǒu short of hands

quēdiǎn 缺点 [v+obj: 缺 lack + 点 point] **N** shortcoming, defect ■ 你要克服粗心的缺点。 **Nǐ yào kèfú cūxīn de quēdiǎn.** *You should overcome the shortcoming of carelessness.*

quēfá 缺乏 **V** be deficient in, lack ■ 他知识丰富,但是缺乏实际经验。 **Tā zhīshi fēngfù, dànshì quēfá shíjì jīngyàn.** *He has very rich knowledge but lacks practical experience.*

quēkǒu 缺口 **N** breach, indentation

quēshǎo 缺少 **V** be short of, lack ■ 我们缺少一名球员,你愿意参加比赛吗? **Wǒmen quēshǎo yì míng qiúyuán, nǐ yuànyì cānjiā bǐsài ma?** *We're still short of one player. Are you willing to participate in the game?*

NOTE: 缺乏 **quēfá** and 缺少 **quēshǎo** are synonyms, but 缺乏 **quēfá** has abstract nouns as objects, while 缺少 **quēshǎo** takes as objects nouns denoting concrete persons or things.

quēxí 缺席 **V** be absent from (a meeting, a class, etc.)

quēxiàn 缺陷 **ADJ** defect, shortcoming

qué 瘸 **V** be lame

quézi 瘸子 **N** lame person, cripple

què 却 **ADV** unexpectedly, contrary to what may be normally expected, but, yet ■ 今天是星期天,他却起得比平时还早。 **Jīntiān shì Xīngqītiān, tā què qǐ de bǐ píngshí hái zǎo.** *It's Sunday today, but he got up earlier than on weekdays.* ■ 他很有钱,却并不幸福。 **Tā hěn yǒuqián, què bìng bù xìngfú.** *He is rich, but he is not happy.*

què 确 TRAD 確 **ADJ** certain

quèbǎo 确保 [modif: 确 firmly + 保 guarantee] **V** ensure, guarantee

quèdìng 确定 [comp: 确 true + 定 definite] **V** confirm, fix, determine ■ 他出国的日期已经确定。 **Tā chūguó de rìqī yǐjīng quèdìng.** *His date of departure overseas has been fixed.*

quèlì 确立 **V** establish, set up, fix

quèqiè 确切 **ADJ** precise, specific, accurate

quèrèn 确认 [modif: 确 firmly + 认 acknowledge] **V** affirm, confirm

quèshí 确实 [comp: 确 certain + 实 substantial] **ADJ** verified to be true, indeed ■ 这个消息不确实。 **Zhège xiāoxi bú quèshí.** *This news is not true.*

quèxìn 确信 [modif: 确 firmly + 信 believe] **V** firmly believe, be convinced

qún 裙 **N** skirt

qúnzi 裙子 [suffix: 裙 skirt + 子 nominal suffix] **N** skirt (条 tiáo) ■ 你穿白裙子很好看。 **Nǐ chuān bái qúnzi hěn hǎokàn.** *You look good in a white skirt.*

qún 群 MEASURE WORD a crowd of, a group of (for people or animals)
一群狗 yìqún gǒu a pack of dogs / 一群鸟 yìqún niǎo a flock of birds / 一群牛 yìqún niú a herd of cattle / 一群小学生 yìqún xiǎoxuéshēng a group of schoolchildren / 一群羊 yìqún yáng a flock of sheep

qúnzhòng 群众 [comp: 群 crowd + 众 multitude] **N** the masses (people), the general public ■ 在群众的帮助下,警察很快抓到了强盗。 **Zài qúnzhòng de bāngzhù xià, jǐngchá hěn kuài zhuādào le qiángdào.** *With the help of the general public, the police soon caught the robber.*

R

rán 然 **ADV** however

rán'ér 然而 **CONJ** same as 但是 **dànshì**. Usually used in writing.

ránhòu 然后 **CONJ** afterwards, ... and then
先 … 然后 … xiān … ránhòu … first ... and then … ■ 他每天早上先跑步,然后吃早饭。 **Tā měi tiān zǎoshang xiān pǎobù, ránhòu chī zǎofàn.** *Every morning he first jogs and then has breakfast.*

rán 燃 **V** burn

ránliào 燃料 [modif: 燃 burn + 料 material, stuff] **N** fuel

ránshāo 燃烧 [comp: 燃 burn + 烧 burn] **V** burn ■ 森林大火燃烧了三天三夜。 **Sēnlín dàhuǒ ránshāole sān tiān sān yè.** *The forest fire raged three days and nights.*

rǎn 染 v dye ■ 有些年轻人喜欢染头发。**Yǒuxiē niánqīngrén xǐhuan rǎn tóufa.** *Some young people like to dye their hair.*

rǎng 壤 N soil (See **tǔrǎng** 土壤.)

rǎng 嚷 v yell, shout ■ 别嚷了，有话好好说。**Bié rǎng le, yǒu huà hǎohǎo shuō.** *Stop yelling. Speak nicely if you have something to say.*

ràng 让 TRAD 讓 v 1 let, allow ■ 你应该让那辆车先行。**Nǐ yīnggāi ràng nà liàng chē xiānxíng.** *You should let that vehicle go first. (→ You should give way to that vehicle.)* ■ 让我想一想。**Ràng wǒ xiǎng yi xiǎng.** *Let me think.* 2 make ■ 他的话让我明白了许多道理。**Tā de huà ràng wǒ míngbaile xǔduō dàolǐ.** *What he said made me understand many things. (→ What he said enlightened me.)*

ràngbù 让步 v concede, give in

ráo 饶 TRAD 饒 v have mercy on, forgive ■ 饶了我吧！**Ráo le wǒ ba!** *Please spare me! Please don't kill (harm) me!*

ráoshù 饶恕 v spare punishment, forgive, pardon

rǎo 扰 TRAD 擾 v harass (See **dǎrǎo** 打扰.)

rǎoluàn 扰乱 v cause chaos, disrupt, harrass

rào 绕 TRAD 繞 v make a detour, bypass ■ 前面施工，车辆绕道。**Qiánmiàn shīgōng, chēliàng rào dào.** *Road works ahead. Vehicles must detour.*

rě 惹 v cause (something undesirable), invite (trouble, etc.) ■ 别惹麻烦了。**Bié rě máfan le.** *Don't ask for trouble.* ■ 你和这种人交朋友会惹爸爸生气。**Nǐ hé zhè zhǒng rén jiāo péngyou huì rě bàba shēngqì.** *It will make daddy angry if you make friends with such people.*

rěhuò 惹祸 v make serious trouble, court trouble

rè 热 TRAD 熱 ADJ hot (ANTONYM 冷 lěng) ■ 香港的夏天很热。**Xiānggǎng de xiàtiān hěn rè.** *Summer in Hong Kong is very hot.* ■ 我想喝一杯热水，不要冷水。**Wǒ xiǎng hē yì bēi rè shuǐ, bú yào lěng shuǐ.** *I want to drink a glass of hot water, not cold water.*

rè'ài 热爱 [modif: 热 hot + 爱 love] v love ardently, be in deep love with ■ 我热爱我的祖国。**Wǒ rè'ài wǒ de zǔguó.** *I love my motherland.*

rè lèi yíng kuàng 热泪盈眶 IDIOM eyes brimming with tears, tears welling up in one's eyes

rèliè 热烈 [comp: 热 hot + 烈 intense] ADJ warm, ardent ■ 热烈欢迎新同学。**Rèliè huānyíng xīn tóngxué!** *A warm welcome to the new students!*

rèmén 热门 N things or matters of great popular interest

热门货 rèménhuò commodity in great demand, "hotcakes"

rènao 热闹 [comp: 热 hot + 闹 noisy] ADJ noisy and exciting in a pleasant way, boisterous, bustling, lively (of a scene or occasion) ■ 中国人过年非常热闹。**Zhōngguórén guònián fēicháng rènao.** *When the Chinese celebrate their New Year's Day, it is a noisy and exciting occasion.*

rèqíng 热情 [modif: 热 hot + 情 emotion] ADJ enthusiastic, warm-hearted ■ 她对人很热情。**Tā duì rén hěn rèqíng.** *She's warm-hearted towards people.* ■ 他常常热情地帮助朋友。**Tá chángcháng rèqíng de bāngzhù péngyou.** *He often helps his friends enthusiastically.*

rèshuǐpíng 热水瓶 [modfi: 热 hot + 水 water + 瓶 bottle, flask] N thermos, thermos flask (只 **zhī**)

rèxīn 热心 [modif: 热 hot + 心 heart] ADJ warm-hearted, enthusiastic

对 … 热心 duì … rèxīn be warm-hearted towards, be enthusiastic about ■ 他对朋友很热心。**Tā duì péngyou hěn rèxīn.** *He is warm-hearted towards friends.*

rén 人 N human being, man, person ■ 你认识这个人吗？**Nǐ rènshi zhège rén ma?** *Do you know this person?* ■ 人和动物有什么区别？**Rén hé dòngwù yǒu shénme qūbié?** *What are the differences between humans and animals?*

réncái 人才 [modif: 人 human + 才 talent] N talented person, person of ability ■ 他自以为是个人才。**Tā zì yǐwéi shì ge réncái.** *He thinks himself quite talented.* ■ 我们公司需要电脑人才。**Wǒmen gōngsī xūyào diànnǎo réncái.** *Our company needs people with computer skills.*

réndào 人道 N humanity, humanitarianism

réndàozhǔyì 人道主义 N humanitarianism

人道主义援助 réndàozhǔyì yuánzhù humanitarian aid

réngé 人格 [modif: 人 personal + 格 quality] N personality, moral quality

以我的人格担保 yǐ wǒde réngé dānbǎo give (you) my personal guarantee

réngōng 人工 I ADJ artificial, man-made

人工智能 réngōng zhìnéng artificial intelligence II N manpower, man-day

rénjia 人家 PRON 1 other people ■ 人家能做到的，我也能做到。**Rénjia néng zuòdào de, wǒ yě néng zuòdào.** *What others can achieve, I can too.* 2 he, she, they (used to refer to another person or other people) ■ 人家不愿意，你别勉强。**Rénjia bú yuànyì, nǐ bié miǎnqiáng.** *If they aren't willing, don't force them to do it.* 3 I, me (used to refer to oneself, only used among intimate friends or family members)

rénjiān 人间 N the earth, the human world

人间天堂 rénjiān tiāntáng paradise on earth

rénkǒu 人口 [comp: 人 human + 口 mouth] N population (human) ■ 你们国家有多少人口？**Nǐmen guójiā yǒu duōshǎo rénkǒu?** *What is the population of your country?*

NOTE: It is interesting that the Chinese word for *population* is made up of 人 **rén** (human) and 口 **kǒu** (the mouth). It suggests that feeding people (mouths) has been the primary concern in China.

rénlèi 人类 [modif: 人 human + 类 kind] N humankind, mankind ■ 人类应该保护自然环境。**Rénlèi yīnggāi bǎohù zìrán huánjìng.** *Mankind should protect the natural environment.*

rénlèi xué 人类学 anthropology

rénmen 人们 [suffix: 人 person, people + 们 suffix indicating plural number] N people, the public ■ 春节那几天，人们都比较客气，避免争吵。**Chūnjié nà jǐ tiān, rénmen dōu bǐjiào kèqi, bìmiǎn zhēngchǎo.** *During the Chinese New Year, people are polite to each other to avoid quarrels.* ■ 人们都认为发展经济很重要。**Rénmen dōu rénwéi fāzhǎn jīngjì hěn zhòngyào.** *People think it is important to develop the economy.*

rénmín 人民 [comp: 人 human beings + 民 the people] N the people (of a state) ■ 政府应该为人民服务。**Zhèngfǔ yīnggāi wèi rénmín fúwù.** *The government should serve the people.*

Rénmínbì 人民币 [modif: 人民 the people + 币 currency, banknote] N the Chinese currency, Renminbi (RMB) ■ 我想用美元换人民币。**Wǒ xiǎng yòng Měiyuán huàn Rénmínbì.** *I want to change some US dollars to Renminbi.*

rénshēng 人生 N (one's entire) life ■ 人生苦短。**Rénshēng kǔ duǎn.** *It's sad that life is so short.*

rénshì 人事 [modif: 人 people + 事 matters] N human resources affairs

人事部门 **rénshì bùmén** human resources department, personnel department

rénshì 人士 N person/people with social standing, personality

rénwéi 人为 ADJ caused by humans, man-made, artificial

rénwù 人物 N well-known and important person, figure, personage (位 **wèi**) ■ 这位大学校长是世界著名人物。**Zhè wèi dàxué xiàozhǎng shì shìjiè zhùmíng rénwù.** *This university president is a famous figure in the world.*

rénxìng 人性 N human nature ■ 人性善，还是人性恶？**Rénxìng shàn, háishi rénxìng è?** *Is human nature good or evil?*

rényuán 人员 [comp: 人 human + 员 staff] N personnel, staff ■ 我校有教学人员五十六名，其他人员十八名。**Wǒ xiào yǒu jiàoxué rényuán wǔshí liù míng, qítā rényuán shíbā míng.** *This school has a teaching staff of 56 people and 18 other staff members.*

rénzào 人造 [modif: 人 man + 造 make] ADJ man-made, artificial

rénzhì 人质 N hostage

扣留人质 **kòuliú rénzhì** hold hostage

rén 仁 N & ADJ benevolence, being human; benevolent, humane

réncí 仁慈 [comp: 仁 benevolent + 慈 kind] ADJ benevolent, merciful

rěn 忍 V endure, tolerate, put up with ■ 你刚来，有的地方不习惯，还得忍一点。**Nǐ gāng lái, yǒude dìfang bù xíguàn, hái děi rěn yìdiǎn.** *You're new here, so there may be things you're not used to and will have to put up with for a while.*

忍不住 **rěn bu zhù** be unable to bear, cannot help ■ 她在电话里听到妈妈的声音，忍不住哭起来。**Tā zài diànhuà li tīngdào māma de shēngyīn, rěnbuzhù kū qǐlai.** *Hearing mom's voice on the phone, she couldn't help crying.*

忍得住 **rěn de zhù** can endure, can bear

rěnnài 忍耐 [comp: 忍 endure + 耐 endure] V show restraint, bear, put up with ■ 没有办法，只能忍耐。**Méiyǒu bànfǎ, zhǐ néng rěnnài.** *There's nothing we can do; we can only put up with it.*

rěnshòu 忍受 V tolerate, bear

rèn 认 TRAD 認 V 1 recognize ■ 两年不见，我几乎认不出你了！**Liǎng nián bú jiàn, wǒ jīhū rèn bu chū nǐ le!** *I haven't seen you for two years, and I can hardly recognize you.* 2 identify ■ 你认一下，这里这么多自行车，哪辆是你的？**Nǐ rèn yíxià, zhèli zhème duō zìxíngchē, nǎ liàng shì nǐ de?** *Among so many bicycles here, can you identify which one is yours?*

rènde 认得 V same as 认识 **rènshi**

rèndìng 认定 V be firmly convinced, maintain

rènkě 认可 V approve

质量认可书 **zhìliàng rènkě shū** certificate of quality approval

rènshi 认识 [comp: 认 recognize + 识 know] V know, understand ■ 认识你，很高兴。**Rènshi nǐ, hěn gāoxìng.** *I'm glad to make your acquaintance.* ■ 你认识这个汉字吗？**Nǐ rènshi zhège Hànzì ma?** *Do you know this Chinese character?*

rènwéi 认为 V think, consider (normally followed by a clause) ■ 我认为你说得不对。**Wǒ rènwéi nǐ shuōde bú duì.** *I think what you said is incorrect.*

rènzhēn 认真 [v+compl: 认 consider + 真 real] ADJ earnest, conscientious, serious ■ 他是个认真的学生。**Tā shì ge rènzhēn de xuésheng.** *She's a conscientious student.* ■ 老老实实做人，认认真真做事。**Lǎo-lǎo-shí-shí zuòrén, rèn-rèn-zhēn-zhēn zuòshì.** *Be an honest person and a conscientious worker.*

rèn 任 CONJ no matter

rènhé 任何 [comp: 任 no matter + 何 what] PRON any, whatever ■ 你任何时候都可以来找我。**Nǐ rènhé shíhou dōu kěyǐ lái zhǎo wǒ.** *You can come to see me at any time.* ■ 在任何情况下，都要遵守法律。**Zài rènhé qíngkuàng xià, dōu yào zūnshǒu fǎlù.** *One should abide by the law under any circumstances.*

任何人 **rènhé rén** anyone ■ 任何人都不可以那样做。**Rènhé rén dōu bù kěyǐ nàyàng zuò.** *No one is allowed to do that.*

任何事 **rènhé shì** any matter, anything, everything ■ 他做任何事都挺认真。**Tā zuò rènhé shì dōu tǐng**

rènzhēn. *He does everything conscientiously.*

rènmìng 任命 **v** appoint (to a position of importance)

任命他为副总裁 rènmìng tā wéi fùzǒngcái appoint him Vice CEO

rènwù 任务 [comp: 任 mission + 务 work] **N** assignment, mission ■ 李经理要派你一个重要任务。**Lǐ jīnglǐ yào pài nǐ yí ge zhòngyào rènwù.** *Mr Li, the manager, will give you an important assignment.*

rènxìng 任性 **ADJ** willful, headstrong

rènyì 任意 **ADJ & ADV** random; randomly, at random

rèn zhòng dào yuǎn 任重道远 **IDIOM** the burden is heavy and the road is long (→ be entrusted with an important mission with heavy responsibilities)

rēng 扔 **v** throw, toss ■ 不要乱扔垃圾。**Bú yào luàn rēng lājī.** *Do not discard rubbish everywhere. (→ Don't litter.)*

réng 仍 **ADV** same as 仍然 **réngrán**

réngjiù 仍旧 **ADV** same as 仍然 **réngrán**

réngrán 仍然 **ADV** still, as before ■ 他有这么多钱，仍然不满足。**Tā yǒu zhème duō qián, réngrán bù mǎnzú.** *He has so much money but he is still not satisfied.* ■ 我睡了十几个小时，仍然觉得累。**Wǒ shuìle shí jǐ ge xiǎoshí, réngrán juéde lèi.** *I slept for over ten hours but still feel tired.*

rì 日 **N** date, day ■ 三月二十四日 **Sānyuè èrshísì rì** *the twenty-fourth of March* ■ 九月一日 **Jiǔyuè yī rì** *the first of September*

NOTE: In writing, 日 **rì** is used for *dates* as shown above. However, in speech it is more common to say 号 **hào**. For example, to say *the twenty-fourth of March* 三月二十四号 **Sānyuè èrshí sì hào** is more natural than 三月二十四日 **Sānyuè èrshi sì rì**.

Rìběn 日本 **N** Japan

rìcháng 日常 [comp: 日 daily + 常 usual] **ADJ** daily, routine ■ 他不希望有规律的日常生活被打乱。**Tā bù xīwàng yǒu guīlǜ de rìcháng shēnghuó bèi dǎluàn.** *He does not want his regular everyday life to be upset.* ■ 这是我的日常工作，一点都不麻烦。**Zhè shì wǒ de rìcháng gōngzuò, yìdiǎn dōu bù máfan.** *It is part of my routine work. There is no trouble at all.*

rìchéng 日程 [modif: 日 daily + 程 journey] **N** daily schedule, schedule ■ 我们开一个会，安排一下工作日程。**Wǒmen kāi yí ge huì, ānpái yíxià gōngzuò rìchéng.** *Let's have a meeting to plan our work schedule.* ■ 今天的日程排得很满。**Jīntiān de rìchéng pái de hěn mǎn.** *We have a full schedule today.*

议事日程 yìshì rìchéng agenda

rìchéngbiǎo 日程表 **N** timetable (for a schedule), program

rìjì 日记 [modif: 日 daily + 记 record] **N** diary (本 **běn**, 篇 **piān**)

记日记 jì rìjì keep a diary ■ 我从十五岁生日那天

开始记日记。**Wǒ cóng shíwǔ suì shēngrì nà tiān kāishǐ jì rìjì.** *I have been keeping a diary since my fifteenth birthday.*

rìjìběn 日记本 **N** diary book

rìlì 日历 **N** calendar (of pages showing dates)

rìqī 日期 [comp: 日 day + 期 fixed time] **N** date (especially of an event) ■ 你知道考试日期吗？**Nǐ zhīdào kǎoshì rìqī ma?** *Do you know the date of the exam?*

过期日期 guòqī rìqī sell-by date

Rìwén 日文 [modif: 日 Japanese + 文 writing] **N** the Japanese language (especially the writing)

rì xīn yuè yì 日新月异 **IDIOM** make progress with each passing day and passing month (→ make fast and impressive progress)

rìyè 日夜 **N** day and night, round the clock

rìyì 日益 **ADV** day by day, increasingly

rìyòngpǐn 日用品 [modif: 日 daily + 用 use + 品 article] **N** daily necessities

Rìyǔ 日语 [modif: 日 Japan + 语 speech] **N** the Japanese language ■ 日语和汉语很不一样。**Rìyǔ hé Hànyǔ hěn bù yíyàng.** *Japanese is very different from Chinese.*

Rìyuán 日元 [modif: 日 Japan + 元 dollar] **N** Japanese currency, yen

rìzi 日子 [suffix: 日 day + 子 nominal suffix] **N 1** day, date ■ 今天这个日子对我来说特别重要。**Jīntiān zhège rìzi duì wǒ lái shuō tèbié zhòngyào.** *Today is particularly important to me.* ■ 今天是什么日子？为什么街上那么多人？**Jīntiān shì shénme rìzi? Wèishénme jiē shang nàme duō rén?** *What day is today? Why are there so many people in the street?* **2** life ■ 我们家的日子比过去好多了。**Wǒmen jiā de rìzi bǐ guòqù hǎo duō le.** *The life of my family is much better than before. (→ My family is better off now.)* ■ 我只想安安静静地过日子。**Wǒ zhǐ xiǎng ān-ān-jìng-jìng de guò rìzi.** *I only want to live a quiet and peaceful life.*

róng 荣 **TRAD** 榮 **ADJ** glorious, honored

róngxìng 荣幸 [comp: 荣 honored + 幸 happy] **ADJ** feeling honored and privileged

róngyù 荣誉 [modif: 荣 glorious + 誉 reputation] **N** honor, great credit

荣誉称号 róngyù chēnghào title of honor

róng 容 **v** tolerate

róngliàng 容量 [modif: 容 accommodating + 量 amount] **N** the amount that something can hold, capacity, volume

电容量 diàn róngliàng electric capacity

róngmào 容貌 **N** facial features, looks

róngnà 容纳 **v** have a capacity of, hold, contain

róngqì 容器 **N** container, vessel

róngrěn 容忍 [comp: 容 tolerate + 忍 endure] **v** tolerate, endure, put up with

róngyì 容易 [comp: 容 tolerant + 易 easy] **ADJ 1** easy, not difficult (**ANTONYM** 难 **nán**) ■ 这件事很

容易。**Zhè jiàn shì hěn róngyì.** *This is easy to do.*
2 having a tendency to, likely ■ 年轻人容易受朋友的影响。**Niánqīngrén róngyì shòu péngyou de yǐngxiǎng.** *Young people are susceptible to their friends' influence.*

róng 溶 **v** dissolve, melt

róngjiě 溶解 **v** dissolve, melt

róng 融 **v** melt, thaw

rónghuà 融化 **v** thaw, melt

róngqià 融洽 **ADJ** harmonious, very friendly

róng 绒 **TRAD** 絨 **N** light hair, down (See **yǔróng** 羽绒.)

róu 柔 **ADJ** soft, gentle

róuhé 柔和 [comp: 柔 soft + 和 mild] **ADJ** soft and mild, gentle
柔和的口气 **róuhe de kǒuqì** gentle and soothing voice

róu 揉 **v** rub, knead

róumiàn 揉面 **v** knead dough

ròu 肉 **N** flesh, meat ■ 在我们这儿肉比鱼便宜。**Zài wǒmen zhèr ròu bǐ yú piányi.** *Pork is cheaper than fish.*
鸡肉 **jīròu** chicken meat / 牛肉 **niúròu** beef / 羊肉 **yángròu** mutton / 鱼肉 **yúròu** fish meat / 猪肉 **zhūròu** pork

NOTE: The most popular meat in China is pork. Unspecified, 肉 **ròu** often refers to *pork*.

rú 如 **CONJ** same as 如果 **rúguǒ**. Used only in writing.

rúguǒ 如果 **CONJ** if ■ 如果明天下雨，我们就不去海边游泳。**Rúguǒ míngtiān xià yǔ, wǒmen jiù bú qù hǎibiān yóuyǒng.** *If it rains tomorrow, we won't go to the seaside to swim.*

NOTE: 如果 **rúguǒ** is usually used with 就 **jiù**.

rúhé 如何 **PRON** how, what ■ 你以为如何？**Nǐ yǐwéi rúhé?** *What do you think?*

NOTE: 如何 **rúhé** is one of the few remnants of Classical Chinese still used in Modern Chinese, but it is usually used in writing only. The same is true with 如此 **rúcǐ**, 如今 **rújīn** and 如同 **rútóng**.

rújīn 如今 **N** today, now

NOTE: See note on 如何 **rúhé**.

rútóng 如同 **v** be like, as

NOTE: See note on 如何 **rúhé**.

rú 儒 **N** scholar

rújiā 儒家 **N** Confucianism, Confucianists

rǔ 乳 **N 1** the breast **2** milk

rǔfáng 乳房 **N** the breast

rǔzhìpǐn 乳制品 **N** dairy product

rǔ 辱 **v & N** insult (See **wǔrǔ** 侮辱.)

rù 入 **v** enter ■ 病从口入。**Bìng cóng kǒu rù.** *Dis-*
ease enters the body by the mouth. (→ *Bad food causes disease.*)

rùkǒu 入口 **N** entry, entrance

ruǎn 软 **TRAD** 軟 **ADJ** soft, supple (ANTONYM 硬 **yìng**) ■ 这张床太软。**Zhè zhāng chuáng tài ruǎn.** *This bed is too soft.*

ruǎnjiàn 软件 [modif: 软 soft + 件 article] **N** computer software, software ■ 他除了买这台新电脑以外，还买了一些软件。**Tā chúle mǎi zhè tái xīn diànnǎo yǐwài, hái mǎile yìxiē ruǎnjiàn.** *In addition to the new computer he also bought some software.* ■ 他们设计了一个软件非常成功。**Tāmen shèjìle yí ge ruǎnjiàn fēicháng chénggōng.** *They have designed a very successful piece of software.*

ruì 锐 **TRAD** 銳 **ADJ** sharp (See **jiānruì** 尖锐.)

ruò 若 **CONJ** if
NUMERAL a certain number

ruògàn 若干 NUMERAL a certain number

ruò 弱 **ADJ** weak, feeble (ANTONYM 强 **qiáng**) ■ 他年老体弱，不能在田里干活了。**Tā nián-lǎo-tǐ-ruò, bù néng zài tián li gànhuó le.** *He is old and feeble, and is unable to work in the fields.* ■ 我使用电脑的能力比较弱，可是我的语言能力很强。**Wǒ shǐyòng diànnǎo de nénglì bǐjiào ruò, kěshì wǒ de yǔyán nénglì hěn qiáng.** *I'm rather weak in computer skills, but strong in languages.*

ruòdiǎn 弱点 **N** weak point, shortcoming

S

sā 撒 **v** cast, spread out
撒渔网 **sā yúwǎng** spread out a fishing net

sāhuǎng 撒谎 **v** same as 说谎 **shuōhuǎng**

sǎ 洒 **TRAD** 灑 **v** sprinkle, spray ■ 这片稻田有害虫，要洒一点儿药。**Zhè piàn dàotián yǒu hàichóng, yào sǎ yìdiǎnr yào.** *This paddy field is infested. You need to spray some pesticide on it.*

sāi 腮 **N** cheek

sāi 塞 **v** fill in, stuff

sāichē 塞车 **N** same as 堵车 **dǔchē**

sāizi 塞子 **N** stopper, plug, cork

sài 赛 **TRAD** 賽 **v** compete (See 比赛 **bǐsài**, 竞赛 **jìngsài**.)

sān 三 NUMERAL three
十三 **shísān** thirteen (13) / 三十 **sānshí** thirty (30)

sānjiǎo 三角 **N 1** triangle **2** trigonometry

sǎn 伞 **TRAD** 傘 **N** umbrella (把 **bǎ**) ■ 今天可能会下雨，带着伞吧。**Jīntiān kěnéng huì xià yǔ, dàizhe sǎn ba.** *It may rain today. Take your umbrella with you.* ■ 我的伞又丢了。**Wǒ de sǎn yòu diū le.** *I've lost my umbrella again.*

sǎn 散 **ADJ** fragmentary, loose

sǎnwén 散文 **N** prose, essay (篇 **piān**)

sàn 散 **v** disperse, distribute

sànbù 散步 [modif: 散 random + 步 step] **v** take

a short leisurely walk, stroll ■ 他俩沿着小河散步，直到天快黑了。**Tā liǎ yánzhe xiǎo hé sànbù, zhídào tiān kuài hēi le.** *The two of them took a walk along the stream till it was almost dark.*

sànbù 散布 v disseminate, spread
散布谣言 sànbù yáoyán spread rumor

sànfā 散发 v distribute, give out
散发广告纸 sànfā guǎnggào zhǐ pass out fliers

sāng 丧 TRAD 喪 N funeral
奔丧 bēnsāng travel to attend a funeral

sāngshì 丧事 N funeral arrangement, funeral
办丧事 bànsāngshì make funeral arrangements, perform a funeral ceremony

sāng 桑 N mulberry (See **bǎo jīng cāngsāng** 饱经沧桑.)

sǎng 嗓 N throat

sǎngzi 嗓子 [suffix: 嗓 throat + 子 nominal suffix] N 1 voice ■ 她嗓子很尖。**Tā sǎngzi hěn jiān.** *She has a high-pitched voice. (*or *Her voice is very shrill.)* 2 throat ■ 我嗓子疼。**Wǒ sǎngzi téng.** *I have a sore throat.*

sàng 丧 TRAD 喪 v lose

sàngshī 丧失 [comp: 丧 lose + 失 lose] v lose, forfeit

sāo 骚 TRAD 騷 v harass

sāorǎo 骚扰 v & N harass; harassment
性骚扰 xìng sāorǎo sexual harassment

sǎo 扫 TRAD 掃 v sweep ■ 秋天我得常常扫院子里的落叶。**Qiūtiān wǒ děi chángcháng sǎo yuànzi li de luòyè.** *In autumn, I have to often sweep away the fallen leaves in my courtyard.*

sǎo 嫂 N elder brother's wife

sǎozi 嫂子 [suffix: 嫂 elder brother's wife + 子 nominal suffix] N elder brother's wife, sister-in-law

NOTE: One's younger brother's wife is 弟妹 **dìmèi.**

sè 色 N color ■ 那座白色的大楼就是医院。**Nà zuò báisè de dàlóu jiù shì yīyuàn.** *That white building is the hospital.*

sècǎi 色彩 N color, hue
色彩丰富 sècǎi fēngfù a riot of color

sèqíng 色情 N sex urge, eroticism
色情狂 sèqíngkuáng sex mania, erotomania

sēn 森 N forest

sēnlín 森林 [comp: 森 forest + 林 woods] N forest ■ 防止火灾，保护森林。**Fángzhǐ huǒzāi, bǎohù sēnlín.** *Prevent fires; protect the forest.*

shā 杀 TRAD 殺 v kill, slay, put to death

shā 沙 N sand

shāfā 沙发 N upholstered chair, sofa, couch ■ 他买了一对单人沙发和一个双人沙发。**Tā mǎile yí duì dānrén shāfā hé yí ge shuāngrén shāfā.** *He bought a pair of upholstered chairs and a two-seat sofa.*

shāmò 沙漠 [modif: 沙 sand + 漠 desert] N desert

■ 沙漠里最需要的是水。**Shāmò li zuì xūyào de shì shuǐ.** *In a desert, what is most needed is water.*

shātān 沙滩 N sandy beach

shāzi 沙子 [suffix: 沙 sand + 子 nominal suffix] N sand, grit (粒 lì) ■ 我右眼里恐怕有一粒沙子，难受极了。**Wǒ yòuyǎn li kǒngpà yǒu yí lì shāzi, nánshòu jíle.** *I'm afraid there is a grain of sand in my right eye. It's so irritating!*

shāchē 刹车 v & N apply the brakes; brake
急刹车 jíshāchē brake suddenly

shá 啥 PRON what
有啥吃啥 yǒu shá chī shá eat whatever you've got

NOTE: 啥 **shá** is a dialectal word, used on very casual occasions.

shǎ 傻 ADJ foolish, stupid (ANTONYM 聪明 cōngmíng) ■ 你别看他模样傻，其实一点儿也不傻。**Nǐ bié kàn tā móyàng shǎ, qíshí yìdiǎnr yě bù shǎ.** *He may look stupid, but he is actually not at all stupid.* ■ 你怎么会相信他？真太傻了！**Nǐ zěnme huì xiāngxìn tā? Zhēn tài shǎ le!** *How could you have believed him? It was really foolish!*

shāi 筛 v sieve, sift

shāixuǎn 筛选 v select through elimination

shài 晒 TRAD 曬 v dry in the sun, bask
晒太阳 shài tàiyang sunbathe

shān 山 N mountain, hill (座 zuò) ■ 这座山真高啊！**Zhè zuò shān zhēn gāo a!** *How high this mountain is!* ■ 这个美丽的小城，前面是大河，背后是青山。**Zhège měilì de xiǎochéng, qiánmiàn shì dà hé, bèihòu shì qīng shān.** *In front of this beautiful town is a big river and behind it are green hills.*
爬山 páshān mountain climbing, mountaineering ■ 星期六我们去爬山吧！**Xīngqīliù wǒmen qù páshān ba!** *Let's go mountain climbing this Saturday.*

shānmài 山脉 [modif: 山 mountain + 脉 veins and arteries] N mountain range (条 tiáo) ■ 世界上最大的山脉—喜马拉雅山脉—在中国。**Shìjiè shang zuì dà de shānmài – Xǐmǎlāyǎ shānmài – zài Zhōngguó.** *The biggest mountain range in the world—the Himalayas—is in China.*

shānshuǐ 山水 N landscape ■ 中国浙江的山水很美。**Zhōngguó Zhèjiāng de shānshuǐ hěn měi.** *The landscape in Zhejiang, China, is beautiful.*
游山玩水 yóu shān wán shuǐ IDIOM go sightseeing ■ 他有钱，又有时间，所以经常出国游山玩水。**Tā yǒu qián, yòu yǒu shíjiān, suǒyǐ jīngcháng chūguó yóu-shān-wán-shuǐ.** *He's rich and he's got the time, so he often goes sightseeing overseas.*

shān 衫 N shirt (See **chènshān** 衬衫.)

shān 删 v delete (words)

shānchú 删除 v delete, remove, cross out

shǎn 闪 N flash

shǎndiàn 闪电 N lightning ■ 昨天夜里又打雷，

又闪电，真吓人。**Zuótiān yèlǐ yòu dǎléi, yòu shǎndiàn, zhēn xiàrén.** *Last night thunder boomed and lightning flashed. It was really frightening.*

shǎnshuò 闪烁 v twinkle, glitter

shàn 扇 I N fan II v wave a fan

shànzi 扇子 N fan（把 **bǎ**）

shàn 善 ADJ good

shànliáng 善良 [comp: 善 good + 良 good] ADJ kind-hearted, good-hearted

shànyú 善于 v be good at ■ 他善于理解，不善于表达。**Tā shànyú lǐjiě, bú shànyú biǎodá.** *He is good at understanding, but not good at expressing himself.*

shàn 擅 I v be good at II ADV (doing things) without authorization

shàncháng 擅长 v be expert in, have a special skill

擅长谈判 shàncháng tánpàn be especially good at negotiation, be an expert negotiator

shànzì 擅自 ADV without permission, without authorization

shāng 伤 TRAD 傷 I v wound, injure, hurt ■ 他踢球的时候伤了脚。**Tā tīqiú de shíhou shāngle jiǎo.** *He injured his foot playing football.* ■ 你这么做会伤他的感情。**Nǐ zhènme zuò huì shāng tā de gǎnqíng.** *Doing that will hurt his feelings.* II N wound, injury ■ 你的伤不重，很快就会好的。**Nǐ de shāng bú zhòng, hěn kuài jiù huì hǎo de.** *Your injury is not serious and will heal soon.*

受伤 shòushāng be wounded, be injured

shāngbā 伤疤 N scar

shāngfēng 伤风 N catch cold, have a cold

shānghài 伤害 [comp: 伤 injure + 害 harm] v harm, hurt ■ 她无意说的那句话，大大伤害了他的感情。**Tā wúyì shuōde nà jù huà, dàdà shānghài le tāde gǎnqíng.** *That casual remark of hers hurt him badly.*

shāng nǎojīn 伤脑筋 [v+obj: 伤 wound + 脑筋 the brains] ADJ knotty, vexing, troublesome

伤脑筋的问题 shāng nǎojīn de wèntí very difficult problem, thorny problem

shāngxīn 伤心 [v+obj: 伤 wound + 心 the heart] ADJ heartbreaking, heartbroken ■ 听到这个伤心的消息，玛丽忍不住哭了。**Tīngdào zhège shāngxīn de xiāoxi, Mǎlì rěn bu zhù kū le.** *Hearing this heartbreaking news, Mary couldn't help weeping.*

shāng 商 N commerce

shāngbiāo 商标 [modif: 商 commerce + 标 mark] N trademark

shāngchǎng 商场 [modif: 商 commerce + 场 place] N shopping center, mall（家 **jiā**, 座 **zuò**）■ 这座商场有近一百家大大小小的商店。**Zhè zuò shāngchǎng yǒu jìn yìbǎi jiā dà-dà-xiǎo-xiǎo de shāngdiàn.** *This shopping center has nearly a hundred shops, big and small.*

shāngdiàn 商店 N shop, store（家 **jiā**）■ 这家商店是卖什么的？**Zhè jiā shāngdiàn shì mài shénme de?** *What does this store sell?* ■ 我常去那家商店买东西。**Wǒ cháng qù nàjiā shāngdiàn mǎi dōngxi.** *I often shop at that store.*

开商店 kāi shāngdiàn open a shop, keep a shop

shāngliang 商量 [comp: 商 discuss + 量 weigh] v discuss, consult ■ 有重要的事，先和好朋友商量再决定。**Yǒu zhòngyào de shì, xiān hé hǎo péngyou shāngliang zài juédìng.** *When an important matter arises, discuss it with good friends before making a decision.* ■ 我想和你商量一件事，听听你的意见。**Wǒ xiǎng hé nǐ shāngliang yí jiàn shì, tīngtīng nǐ de yìjiàn.** *There is something I'd like to consult you over and hear your advice.*

shāngpǐn 商品 [modif: 商 commerce + 品 article] N commodity（件 **jiàn**, 种 **zhǒng**）■ 我们卖出的商品都有质量保证。**Wǒmen màichū de shāngpǐn dōu yǒu zhìliàng bǎozhèng.** *All the goods we sell have a quality guarantee.*

shāngwù 商务 N business affairs

shāngyè 商业 [modif: 商 commerce + 业 industry] N commerce, business ■ 这个城市商业十分发达。**Zhège chéngshì shāngyè shífēn fādá.** *Commerce is very well developed in this city.*

shāngyè guǎnlǐ 商业管理 N business administration

商业管理硕士 shāngyè guǎnlǐ shuòshì Master of Business Administration (MBA)

shāngyè qū 商业区 N business district

shǎng 赏 v **1** appreciate (See **xīnshǎng** 欣赏.) **2** award

shàng 上¹ N **1** on top of, on, above (ANTONYM 下 **xià**) ■ 山上有一座白房子。**Shān shang yǒu yí zuò bái fángzi.** *There's a white house on the hill.* **2** previous, last

上星期 shàng xīngqī last week / 上一课 shàng yí kè the previous class (lesson)

NOTE: 上 **shàng** is often used after a noun to form words of location. While its basic meaning is *on top,* 上 **shàng** may have various, often semi-idiomatic senses, e.g. 报纸上 **bàozhǐ shang** *in the newspaper* / 地上 **dìshang** *on the ground* / 工作上 **gōngzuò shang** *in work* / 会上 **huì shang** *at the meeting* 世界上 / **shìjiè shang** *in the world* / 手上 **shǒu shang** *in hand, in the hands of*

shàng 上² v **1** go upwards, ascend

上来 shànglai come up ■ 楼上有空房间，快上来吧！**Lóu shang yǒu kòng fángjiān, kuài shànglai ba!** *There's a vacant room upstairs. Please come up!*

上楼 shàng lóu go upstairs ■ 我坐电梯上楼。**Wǒ zuò diàntī shàng lóu.** *I take the lift upstairs.*

上去 shàngqu go up ■ 他们在楼上等你，快上去吧！**Tāmen zài lóu shang děng nǐ, kuài shàngqu ba!** *They're waiting for you upstairs. Please go upstairs.*

2 get on (a vehicle), go aboard (a plane, ship) ■ 火车来了，准备上车吧！**Huǒchē lái le, zhǔnbèi shàng chē ba!** *The train is coming. Let's get ready to board.*

上车 shàng chē get into a vehicle / 上船 shàng chuán board a ship / 上飞机 shàng fēijī get on the plane

3 attend (school), go to (work)

上班 shàngbān go to work, start work ■ 我母亲每天九点上班，五点下班。 **Wǒ mǔqin měi tiān jiǔ diǎn shàngbǎn, wǔ diǎn xiàbǎn.** *Every day my mother goes to work at nine and finishes at five.*

上课 shàngkè go to class, teach a class or attend a class ■ 明天放假，不上课。 **Míngtiān fàngjià, bú shàngkè.** *Tomorrow's a holiday. There're no classes.*

上学 shàngxué go to school ■ 你弟弟上学了吗？ **Nǐ dìdi shàngxué le ma?** *Has your younger brother started school yet?* ■ 我骑自行车上学。 **Wǒ qí zìxíngchē shàngxué.** *I go to school by bike.*

shàngbian 上边 [modif: 上 top, upper + 边 side] **N** above, high up (ANTONYM 下边 **xiàbian**) ■ 从那座大楼的上边可以看见飞机场。 **Cóng nà zuò dàlóu de shàngbian kěyǐ kànjiàn fēijīchǎng.** *From the top of that high building, one can see the airport.*

shàngdàng 上当 **v** be fooled, be duped ■ 他太老实了，容易上当受骗。 **Tā tài lǎoshí le, róngyì shàngdàng shòupiàn.** *He is too straightforward and easily duped.* ■ 你怎么又上她的当了？ **Nǐ zěnme yòu shàng tā de dàng le?** *How is it that you got fooled by her again?*

shàngjí 上级 [modif: 上 up, above + 级 step, grade] **N** higher authorities, superior ■ 上级发来通知，六月三十日停课。 **Shàngjí fālai tōngzhī, Liùyuè sānshí rì tíng kè.** *The authorities have advised that school be closed on June thirtieth.* ■ 你是我的上级，我当然要完成你分配的任务。 **Nǐ shì wǒ de shàngjí, wǒ dāngrán yào wánchéng nǐ fēnpèi de rènwù.** *You're my superior, so of course I will complete the task you assigned.*

shàngjìn 上进 **v** make progress, go forward

shàngjìnxīn 上进心 **N** the desire to do better, the urge for improvement

shàngmiàn 上面 **N** same as 上边 **shàngbian**

shàngrèn 上任 **I v** take a post as an official **II N** predecessor

shàngwǎng 上网 [v+obj: 上 get on + 网 Internet] **v** get on the Internet, surf the Internet ■ 他一般吃了晚饭，就上网半小时看看新闻。 **Tā yìbān chīle wǎnfàn jiù shàngwǎng bàn xiǎoshí kànkan xīnwén.** *After supper he usually gets on the Internet for half an hour to read the news.* ■ 这几天我忙得没有时间上网。 **Zhè jǐ tiān wǒ máng de méiyǒu shíjiān shàngwǎng.** *These days I'm so busy that I haven't got the time to get on the Internet.*

shàngwǎng běn 上网本 **N** netbook

shàngwǔ 上午 [modif: 上 upper half + 午 noon] **N** morning (usually from 8 a.m. to noon) (ANTONYM 下午 **xiàwù**) ■ 我们上午上三课。 **Wǒmen shàngwǔ shàng sān jié kè.** *We have three classes in the morning.* ■ 他一直睡到第二天上午十点左右。 **Tā yìzhí shuìdào dì-èr tiān shàngwǔ shí diǎn zuǒyòu.** *He slept until about ten o'clock the next morning.*

NOTE: 上午 **shàngwǔ** does not mean the whole morning. It denotes the part of morning *from about eight or nine o'clock to noon*. The period before eight or nine o'clock is 早晨 **zǎochén** or 早上 **zǎoshang**.

shàngyī 上衣 [modif: 上 upper + 衣 clothing] **N** upper garment, jacket (件 **jiàn**) ■ 你这件上衣很好看，在哪儿买的？ **Nǐ zhè jiàn shàngyī hěn hǎokàn, zài nǎr mǎi de?** *Your jacket looks good. Where did you buy it?*

shàngyǐn 上瘾 **v** be addicted, get into the habit of doing something

shàngyóu 上游 **N** upper reaches (of a river)

shàngzài 上载 **v** upload

shàng 尚 as in 尚且 **shàngqiě**

shàngqiě 尚且 **CONJ** even

shāo 捎¹ **v** take (something) along for (someone) 捎个话儿 shāo gè huàr take an (oral) message, relay a message

shāo 梢² **N** the thin tip of a long-shaped object 树梢儿 shùshāor treetops

shāo 稍 **ADV** same as 稍微 **shāowēi**. Often used in written Chinese.

shāowēi 稍微 [comp: 稍 slight + 微 tiny] **ADV** slightly, just a little bit ■ 我稍微有点儿头疼，休息一会儿就会好的。 **Wǒ shāowēi yǒu diǎnr tóuténg, xiūxi yíhuìr jiù huì hǎo de.** *I've a slight headache. I'll be all right after a short rest.*

shāo 烧 TRAD 燒 **v 1** burn ■ 市政府禁止烧垃圾。 **Shìzhèngfǔ jìnzhǐ shāo lājī.** *The city government bans the burning of rubbish.* **2** cook ■ 今天我给你们烧个鱼。 **Jīntiān wǒ gěi nǐmen shāo ge yú.** *Today I'll cook you a fish.* **3** have fever ■ 这孩子烧得厉害，得马上送医院！ **Zhè háizi shāo de lìhai, děi mǎshàng sòng yīyuàn!** *The child is running a very high fever. He must be sent to the hospital right now!*

sháo 勺 **N** spoon

sháozi 勺子 [suffix: 勺 ladle + 子 nominal suffix] **N** ladle, spoon (把 **bǎ**) ■ 她用勺子把汤分给大家。 **Tā yòng sháozi bǎ tāng fēn gei dàjiā.** *She gave soup to everyone with a ladle.*

shǎo 少 **I ADJ 1** small amount, few, little (ANTONYM 多 **duō**) ■ 中国地少人多。 **Zhōngguó dì shǎo rén duō.** *China has little arable land but a large population.* **2** not often, seldom ■ 我们虽然在同一个学校，但是很少见面。 **Wǒmen suīrán zài tóng yí ge xuéxiào, dànshì hěn shǎo jiànmiàn.** *Al-*

though we're in the same school, we seldom see each other. **II v** be short, be missing ■ 原来我有一百元，现在怎么少了二十元？ **Yuánlái wǒ yǒu yìbǎi yuán, xiànzài zěnme shǎole èrshí yuán?** *I originally had one hundred dollars. How is it that I have twenty dollars less now?* ■ 要和他们比赛，我们还少一个人。 **Yào hé tāmen bǐsài, wǒmen hái shǎo yí ge rén.** *We're still short of one person if we want to compete with them.*

shǎoshù 少数 [modif: 少 few, little + 数 number] **N** minority (**ANTONYM** 多数 **duōshù**) ■ 少数服从多数，这是民主的一条基本原则。 **Shǎoshù fúcóng duōshù, zhè shì mínzhǔ de yì tiáo jīběn yuánzé.** *The minority should submit to the majority—this is a fundamental principle of democracy.*

shǎoshù mínzú 少数民族 **N** ethnic minority (non-Han ethnic people in China)

shào 少 **ADJ** young, early youth

shàonián 少年 [modif: 少 young + 年 age] **N** young man (from around 10 to 16 years old), adolescent ■ 自古少年出英雄。 **Zìgǔ shàonián chū yīngxióng.** *Ever since ancient times, heroes have emerged from the young.*

NOTES: (1) A young woman of around 10 to 16 years old is called 少女 **shàonǚ**. (2) The word 青少年 **qīngshàonián** is often used to mean young people collectively.

shào 哨 **N 1** sentry **2** whistle

shàobīng 哨兵 **N** sentry, armed guard (名 **míng**)

shàozi 哨子 **N** whistle
吹哨子 chuī shàozi blow a whistle

shào 绍 **TRAD** 紹 **v** connect (See **jièshào** 介绍.)

shē 奢 **ADJ** excessive

shēchǐ 奢侈 [comp: 奢 excessive + 侈 wasteful] **ADJ** luxurious

shēchǐ pǐn 奢侈品 **N** luxury goods, luxury item

shé 舌 **N** tongue

shétou 舌头 [suffix: 舌 the tongue + 头 nominal suffix] **N** the tongue ■ 医生：你舌头伸出来，我看看。 **Yīshēng: Nǐ shétou shēn chūlai, wǒ kànkan.** *Doctor: Stick out your tongue and I'll have a look. (→ Show me your tongue.)*

shé 蛇 **N** snake (条 **tiáo**) ■ 她最怕蛇。 **Tā zuì pà shé.** *She finds snakes the most frightening [of all animals].*

shě 舍 **v** give up

shěbudé 舍不得 **v** be unwilling to give up, hate to part with ■ 我在伯伯、伯母家渡过了愉快的暑假，真舍不得跟他们告别。 **Wǒ zài bóbo, bó mǔ jiā dùguòle yúkuài de shǔjià, zhēn shěbudé gēn tāmen gàobié.** *After spending a happy summer vacation with my uncle and aunt, I could hardly tear away from them.*

shědé 舍得 **v** be willing to part with, not grudge ■ 她为了孩子，舍得花钱花时间。 **Tā wèile háizi,**

shěde huāqián huā shíjiān. *She is willing to spend time and money on her children.*

shè 设 **TRAD** 設 **v** equip

shèbèi 设备 **N** equipment, installation ■ 这座医院设备良好。 **Zhè zuò yīyuàn shèbèi liánghǎo.** *This hospital is well equipped.*

shèjì 设计 [comp: 设 plan + 计 calculate] **v & N** design ■ 工程师正在设计一种新型汽车。 **Gōngchéngshī zhèngzài shèjì yì zhǒng xīnxíng qìchē.** *Engineers are designing a car that does not use petrol.*

shèlì 设立 **v** establish, set up

shèshī 设施 **N** facilities, equipment

shèxiǎng 设想 **v** conceive, envision
不堪设想的后果 bùkān shèxiǎng de hòuguǒ inconceivable consequences

shèzhì 设置 **v** set up, establish

shè 社 **N** association

shèhuì 社会 [comp: 社 god of the earth + 会 gathering] **N** society ■ 我们每个人都应该关心社会。 **Wǒmen měi ge rén dōu yīnggāi guānxīn shèhuì.** *Each of us should be concerned for society.* ■ 今天的中国是个什么样的社会？ **Jīntiān de Zhōngguó shì ge shénmeyàng de shèhuì?** *What kind of society is China today?*
社会上 shèhuì shang in society

shèhuìxué 社会学 **N** sociology

shèhuì zhǔyì 社会主义 **N** socialism

shèjiāo 社交 **N** social contact, social life ■ 他的社交很广泛。 **Tā de shèjiāo hěn guǎngfàn.** *He has extensive social contacts.*

shèjiāo méitǐ 社交媒体 **N** social media

shèjiāo wǎngluò 社交网络 **N** social network

shèqū 社区 **N** community

shè 舍 **N** hut, shed (See **sùshè** 宿舍.)

shè 摄 **TRAD** 攝 **v** absorb, take in

shèqǔ 摄取 **v** absorb, take in

shèshìdù 摄氏度 **N** Celsius, centigrade
摄氏温度计 shèshì wēndùjì centigrade thermometer

NOTE: China uses Celsius (摄氏 **shèshì**), not Fahrenheit (华氏 **huáshì**). In everyday speech, people usually do not mention 摄氏度 **shèshì dù**. So if a Chinese person says 今天最高气温二十八度 **Jīntiān zuìgāo qìwēn èrshíbā dù,** it automatically means *The highest tempretaure today will be 28 degrees Celsius.*

shèxiàng 摄像 **v** make a video recording

shèxiàngtóu 摄像头 **N** webcam

shèyǐng 摄影 [v+obj: 摄 take + 影 shadow] **v & N** take a picture, shoot a movie, photograph; photography, cinematography ■ 这个电影的摄影十分成功。 **Zhège diànyǐng de shèyǐng shífēn chénggōng.** *The cinematography of this film is a spectacular success.*

shèyǐngshī 摄影师 **N** photographer

shè 射 **v** shoot

shèjī 射击 **v** shoot, fire

shè 涉 **v** involve

shèjí 涉及 **v** involve, touch on, have something to do with

shéi 谁 **TRAD** 誰 **PRON** same as 谁 **shuí**. Used colloquially.

shēn 申 **v** explain, state

shēnbào 申报 [comp: 申 state + 报 report] **v** 1 declare (at customs) ■ （在海关）我没有什么东西要申报. **(Zài hǎiguān) Wǒ méiyǒu shénme dōngxī yào shēnbào.** (At customs) I've nothing to declare. 2 submit an official report

shēnqǐng 申请 [comp: 申 state + 请 request] **v** apply for (a visa, a job, a permit, etc.) 申请表 shēnqǐngbiǎo application form / 申请人 shēnqǐngrén applicant / 申请书 shēnqǐngshū letter of application

shēn 伸 **v** stretch out, extend ■ 火车开的时候，你千万不要把头伸出车窗. **Huǒchē kāi de shíhou, nǐ qiānwàn bú yào bǎ tóu shēnchū chēchuāng.** Never stick your head out of the window when the train is moving.

shēn 绅 **TRAD** 紳 as in 绅士 **shēnshì**

shēnshì 绅士 **N** gentleman, gentry

shēn 呻 as in 呻吟 **shēnyín**

shēnyín 呻吟 **v** groan, moan

shēn 身 **I N** the human body ■ 他身高175公分. **Tā shēn gāo yìbǎi qīshí wǔ gōngfēn.** He is 175 centimeters tall. **II MEASURE WORD** (for clothes) 一身新衣服 yì shēn xīn yīfu a suit of new clothes

shēnbiān 身边 **N** close by one's side, on one's person ■ 我身边没有她的地址，我发电子邮件告诉你. **Wǒ shēnbiān méiyǒu tā de dìzhǐ, wǒ fā diànzǐ yóujiàn gàosu nǐ.** I don't have her address with me. I'll send it to you by e-mail. ■ 他出去身边总带着手机. **Tā chūqu shēnbiān zǒng dàizhe shǒujī.** He never goes anywhere without his cell phone.

shēncái 身材 **N** stature, figure 身材苗条 shēncái miáotiáo with a slender figure

shēnfen 身分 same as **shēnfen** 身份

shēnfen 身份 **N** social status, identity 身份不明 shēnfen bùmíng unknown identity

shēntǐ 身体 [comp: 身 body + 体 physical] **N** 1 human body ■ 少年儿童正处在长身体的时期. **Shàonián értóng zhèng chǔ zài zhǎng shēntǐ de shíqī.** Children and adolescents are at a stage of physical development. 2 health ■ 我爸爸年纪大了，但是身体还很好. **Wǒ bàba niánjì dà le, dànshì shēntǐ hái hěn hǎo.** My father is getting old, but is still in good health. ■ 你要注意身体. **Nǐ yào zhùyì shēntǐ.** You should pay attention to your health.

NOTE: Although its original meaning is the *body*, 身体 **shēntǐ** is often used in colloquial Chinese to mean *health*. Friends often ask about each other's health in greeting: ■ 你身体好吗? **Nǐ shēntǐ hǎo ma?** *How's your health?* ■ 你最近身体怎么样? **Nǐ zuìjìn shēntǐ zěnmeyàng?** *How's your health been recently?*

shēn 深 **ADJ** 1 deep (**ANTONYM** 浅 **qiǎn**) ■ 这条河深吗? **Zhè tiáo hé shēn ma?** *Is this river deep?* 2 difficult to understand, profound ■ 这本书太深了，我看不懂. **Zhè běn shū tài shēn le, wǒ kàn bu dǒng.** *This book is too difficult. I can't understand it.*

shēn'ào 深奥 **ADJ** abstruse, profound

shēnchén 深沉 [comp: 深 deep + 沉 heavy] **ADJ** deep, heavy 深沉的爱 shēnchén de ài deep love

shēnhòu 深厚 [comp: 深 deep + 厚 thick] **ADJ** deep, profound ■ 他对故乡有深厚的感情. **Tā duì gùxiāng yǒu shēnhòu de gǎnqíng.** *He has deep feelings for his hometown.*

shēnkè 深刻 [modif: 深 deep + 刻 carve] **ADJ** incisive, insightful, profound ■ 这位老人经历十分丰富，对人性有深刻的认识. **Zhè wèi lǎorén jīnglì shífēn fēngfù, duì rénxìng yǒu shēnkè de rènshi.** *This old man has had very rich experiences and has an incisive understanding of human nature.*

shēn qíng hòu yì 深情厚谊 **IDIOM** profound sentiments of friendship

shēnrù 深入 [modif: 深 deep + 入 enter, penetrate] **v** enter deeply into ■ 这一政策深入人心. **Zhè yí zhèngcè shēnrù rénxīn.** *This policy enters deeply into people's hearts. (→ This policy is extremely popular.)*

shēn rù qiǎn chū 深入浅出 **IDIOM** explain complicated theories or phenomena in simple, easy-to-understand language

shén 什 **PRON** what

shénme 什么 **PRON** what ■ 你要什么? **Nǐ yào shénme?** *What do you want?* ■ 你要什么菜? **Nǐ yào shénme cài?** *Which dish do you want? (or What would you like to order?)*

shénmede 什么的 **PRON** and so on, and so forth ■ 他们要了很多菜，有鱼、肉、蔬菜什么的. **Tāmen yàole hěn duō cài, yǒu yú, ròu, shūcài shénmede.** *They ordered lots of dishes, fish, meat, vegetables and so on.*

shén 神 **I N** god, supernatural being ■ 你相信神吗? **Nǐ xiāngxìn shén ma?** *Do you believe in gods?* 财神爷 cáishényé the God of Wealth, the God of Fortune **II ADJ** magical, wondrous

shénhuà 神话 [modif: 神 god + 话 story] **N** mythology, fairy-tales

shénjīng 神经 **N** 1 nerve ■ 我牙神经疼. **Wǒ yá shénjīng téng.** *My tooth nerve hurts.* 2 the mind,

mental state ■ 他神经有毛病。**Tā shénjīng yǒu máobìng.** *There is something wrong with his mind.*

shénjīngbìng 神经病 N neuropathy, mental disorder

NOTE: The formal word for *mental disorder* is 精神病 **jīngshénbìng**, hence 精神病人 **jīngshénbìngrén** (patient suffering from mental illness) and 精神病院 **jīngshénbìngyuàn** (psychiatric hospital, mental hospital).

shénmì 神秘 [comp: 神 god, supernatural + 秘 secret] ADJ mysterious, mythical ■ 有些西方人觉得汉字很神秘。**Yǒuxiē xīfāngrén juéde Hànzì hěn shénmì.** *Some Westerners find Chinese characters quite mysterious.*

shénqí 神奇 [comp: 神 magical + 奇 strange] ADJ miraculous, mystical

shénqì 神气 ADJ 1 looking arrogant and cocky 2 looking spirited and vigorous

shénqíng 神情 N facial expression, look, air

shénsè 神色 N expression, look

shénshèng 神圣 [comp: 神 god + 圣 sacred] ADJ sacred, holy

shéntài 神态 N bearing, appearance

shénxiān 神仙 [comp: 神 god + 仙 immortal] N god, immortal, celestial being (位 **wèi**)

shěn 审 V 1 examine 2 interrogate

shěnchá 审查 [comp: 审 examine + 查 investigate] V examine, investigate

shěnjì 审计 V audit

审计员 **shěnjìyuán** auditor

shěnlǐ 审理 V hear (a legal case), handle (a legal case)

shěnměi 审美 N appreciation of what is beautiful, aesthetics

shěnpàn 审判 [comp: 审 interrogate + 判 sentence] V examine and decide (on a legal case), try a case

shèn 甚 ADV much, very much

shènzhì 甚至 ADV even, so much so ■ 她到过中国很多地方, 甚至西藏也去过。**Tā dàoguo Zhōngguó hěn duō dìfang, shènzhì Xīzàng yě qù guò.** *She has been to many places in China, even to Tibet.*

shèn 渗 V seep

shèntòu 渗透 [v+compl: 渗 seep + 透 thorough] V seep into, permeate, infiltrate

shèn 慎 ADJ cautious

shènzhòng 慎重 [comp: 慎 cautious + 重 attach importance to] ADJ very cautious, discreet

shēng 升 V rise, go up ■ 昨天股票升了百分之零点五。**Zuótiān gǔpiào shēngle bǎifēn zhī líng diǎn wǔ.** *Shares rose by half a percent yesterday.*

shēng 生¹ V give birth to, grow ■ 他妻子上星期生了一个女儿。**Tā qīzi shàng xīngqī shēng le yí ge nǚ'ér.** *His wife gave birth to a girl baby last week.*

shēng 生² ADJ 1 raw, not cooked ■ 我不敢吃生鱼。**Wǒ bù gǎn chī shēng yú.** *I don't dare to eat raw fish.* 2 unripe ■ 苹果还太生, 要等一段时间才能吃。**Píngguǒ hái tài shēng, yào děng yí duàn shíjiān cái néng chī.** *The apples are not ripe yet. It will be some time before they'll be edible.*

shēngbìng 生病 V fall ill, get sick ■ 王老师生病了, 不能来上班。**Wáng Lǎoshī shēngbìng le, bù néng lái shàngbān.** *Teacher Wang is sick, and not able to come to work.*

shēngchǎn 生产 [comp: 生 grow + 产 produce] V produce, manufacture ■ 这家工厂去年生产一万辆汽车。**Zhè jiā gōngchǎng qùnián shēngchǎn yíwàn liàng qìchē.** *This factory manufactured 10,000 automobiles last year.*

shēngcí 生词 [modif: 生 unfamiliar + 词 word] N new word (in a language lesson) ■ 这些生词你都记住了吗？**Zhèxiē shēngcí nǐ dōu jìzhù le ma?** *Have you committed these new words to memory?* ■ 这个句子里有一个生词, 我不认识, 也不会念。**Zhège jùzi li yǒu yí ge shēngcí, wǒ bú rènshi, yě bú huì niàn.** *There's a new word in the sentence. I don't know it, nor do I know how to say it.*

记生词 jì shēngcí memorize new words

shēngcún 生存 [comp: 生 live + 存 exist] V & N survive, be alive; survival ■ 由于过分开发, 野生动物在这里无法生存。*Owing to excessive development, wild lives cannot survive here.*

shēngdòng 生动 [comp: 生 lively + 动 move] ADJ vivid, lively ■ 她在信里生动有趣地描写了旅行经历。**Tā zài xìn li shēngdòng yǒuqù de miáoxiěle lǚxíng jīnglì.** *In her letter she gives vivid and interesting accounts of her travel experiences.*

shēnghuó 生活 [comp: 生 living + 活 alive] V & N live a life; life ■ 我小时候生活得很愉快。**Wǒ xiǎoshíhou shēnghuó de hěn yúkuài.** *I lived a happy life in childhood. (→ I had a happy childhood.)* ■ 请您介绍一下中国大学生的生活。**Qǐng nín jièshào yíxià Zhōngguó dàxuéshēng de shēnghuó.** *Please tell us something about the life of Chinese university students.*

日常生活 rìcháng shēnghuó daily life

shēnghuófèi 生活费 N cost of living, living expenses

shēnghuó shuǐpíng 生活水平 N living standards

shēngjī 生机 N 1 chance of survival, lease on life 一线生机 yīxiànshēngjī a slim chance of survival 2 vitality

生机勃勃 shēngjī bóbó full of vigor and vitality

shēnglǐ 生理 [modif: 生 life + 理 theory] N the physical aspect of human life

生理学 shēnglǐxué physiology

shēngmìng 生命 [comp: 生 living + 命 life] N life (条 **tiáo**) ■ 他的生命处在危险中。**Tā de shēngmìng chǔ zài wēixiǎn zhōng.** *His life is in danger.* ■ 这只小猫也是一条小生命, 不能眼

看它死去。**Zhè zhī xiǎo māo yě shì yì tiáo xiǎo shēngmìng, bù néng yǎnkàn tā sǐqu.** *This kitten is also a life. We can't let it die without doing anything.*

shēngmìng kēxué 生命科学 N life science

shēngmìnglì 生命力 N life force

shēngqì 生气 V get angry, be offended ■ 别对他生气，他不是故意的。**Bié duì tā shēngqì, tā bú shì gùyì de.** *Don't get angry with him. He did not mean it.* ■ 你为了什么事生气?**Nǐ wèile shénme shì shēngqì?** *What are you angry about?*

shēngrì 生日 [modif: 生 birth + 日 day] N birthday ■ 你的生日是哪一天? **Nǐ de shēngrì shì nǎ yì tiān?** *Which date is your birthday? (→ When is your birthday?)* ■ 祝你生日快乐! **Zhù nǐ shēngrì kuàilè!** *I wish you a happy birthday!*

过生日 guò shēngrì celebrate a birthday ■ 你今年打算怎么过生日? **Nǐ jīnnián dǎsuàn zěnme guò shēngrì?** *How are you going to celebrate your birthday this year?*

shēngrì hèkǎ 生日贺卡 N birthday card

shēngrì lǐwù 生日礼物 N birthday present

shēngshū 生疏 ADJ not familiar (ANTONYM 熟悉 **shúxī**)

shēngtài 生态 [modif: 生 life + 态 condition] N ecology

shēngtài lǚyóu 生态旅游 N eco-tourism

shēngtàixué 生态学 N ecology

shēngwù 生物 [modif: 生 living + 物 thing] N living things ■ 生物一般分为动物和植物两大类。**Shēngwù yìbān fēnwéi dòngwù hé zhíwù liǎng dà lèi.** *Living things are generally categorized into animals and plants.*

shēngwù xué 生物学 N biology

shēngwù huàxué 生物化学 N chemical biology, biochemistry

shēngxiào 生肖 N the 12 symbolic animals used to denote the year of a person's birth

NOTE: The 12 animals are rat, ox, tiger, hare, Chinese dragon, snake, horse, sheep, monkey, rooster, dog, and pig. **Shēngxiào** 生肖 is also referred to as 属相 **shǔxiàng**. If you want to know what is the symbolic animal of the year of someone's birth, you ask 你属什么? **Nǐ shǔ shénme?**, and the answer is 我属 **Wǒ shǔ** + the animal, e.g. 我属鼠 **Wǒ shǔ shǔ**, meaning "I was born in a year of the rat."

shēngxiào 生效 V come into effect, go into effect, become valid

shēngxiù 生锈 V get rusty

shēngyi 生意 N business, trade ■ 他每天上网做生意。**Tā měi tiān shàngwǎng zuò shēngyi.** *He does trading over the Internet every day.* ■ 最近生意很不好。**Zuìjìn shēngyi hěn bù hǎo.** *Business has been slack lately.*

shēngyù 生育 V give birth to, bear

shēngzhǎng 生长 [comp: 生 living + 长 growing] V grow, grow up ■ 我生长在一个大城市里。**Wǒ shēngzhǎng zài yí ge dà chéngshì li.** *I grew up in a big city.* ■ 这种植物在河边生长得很好。**Zhè zhǒng zhíwù zài hébiān shēngzhǎng de hěn hǎo.** *This kind of plant grows well by the river.*

shēng 牲 N domesticated animal (See **xīshēng** 牺牲.)

shēngchù 牲畜 N livestock, domestic animal (头 tóu)

shēng 声 TRAD 聲 N sound, noise, voice ■ 机器声太大，我听不清你说什么。**Jīqì shēng tài dà, wǒ tīng bu qīng nǐ shuō shénme.** *The noise from the machine is too loud; I can't hear what you're saying.*

shēngdiào 声调 [modif: 声 voice + 调 tone] N tone of a Chinese word ■ 汉语的声调确实比较难学。**Hànyǔ de shēngdiào quèshí bǐjiào nánxué.** *The tones of Chinese are really rather difficult to learn.* ■ "这个字是哪个声调?" "这个字读第二声。" **"Zhège zì shì nǎge shēngdiào?" "Zhège zì dú dì-èr shēng."** *"Which tone should this character be read with? (or Which tone does this character have?)" "This character is read with the second tone."*

shēngmíng 声明 V & N make a formal statement, publicly declare; formal statement ■ 我声明，他做的任何事情都与我无关。**Wǒ shēngmíng, tā zuò de rènhé shìqing dōu yǔ wǒ wú guān.** *I declare that whatever he does has nothing to do with me.* ■ 外交部就这一事件发表了声明。**Wàijiāobù jiù zhè yī shìjiàn fābiǎole shēngmíng.** *The Minstry of Foreign Affairs issued a statement on this incident.*

shēngshì 声势 [comp: 声 sounds + 势 power] N power and influence, momentum

shēngyīn 声音 [comp: 声 voice + 音 sound] N voice, sound ■ 她的声音很好听。**Tā de shēngyīn hěn hǎotīng.** *Her voice is pleasant.* ■ 请你们说话声音轻一点。**Qǐng nǐmen shuōhuà shēngyīn qīng yìdiǎn.** *Please talk softly. (or Please don't talk so loudly.)*

shēngyù 声誉 N reputation, prestige

shéng 绳 TRAD 繩 N string, rope

shéngzi 绳子 [suffix: 绳 rope + 子 nominal suffix] N rope, cord (根 gēn, 条 tiáo) ■ 你拉一下这根绳子，窗子就会开。**Nǐ lā yíxià zhè gēn shéngzi, chuāngzi jiù huì kāi.** *Pull this cord and the window will open.*

shěng 省¹ N province ■ 中国一共有多少个省? **Zhōngguó yígòng yǒu duōshǎo ge shěng?** *How many provinces are there in China?*

shěnghuì 省会 N provincial capital

shěng 省² V save, economize ■ 这辆车用油很省。**Zhè liàng chē yòng yóu hěn shěng.** *This car uses little gas.*

shěngde 省得 CONJ in case, so as not to

shěnglüè 省略 v omit, leave out

shèng 胜 TRAD 勝 v triumph (over), be victorious, defeat ■ 上海队胜了北京队。**Shànghǎi duì shèngle Běijīng duì.** *The Shanghai team defeated the Beijing team.*

shèngfù 胜负 [comp: 胜 win + 负 lose] N win or lose, success or failure

shènglì 胜利 [comp: 胜 triumph + 利 gain benefit] v & N win victory; victory (ANTONYM 失败 **shībài**) ■ 我们胜利了! **Wǒmen shènglì le!** *We've won!* ■ 我们的胜利来得不容易。**Wǒmen de shènglì lái de bù róngyì.** *Our victory was hard-won.*

shèng 盛 ADJ 1 flourishing, prosperous 2 magnificent, grand 3 popular, common

shèngchǎn 盛产 v produce an abundance of, abound in

shèngkāi 盛开 v bloom luxuriantly, blossom luxuriantly

shèngqíng 盛情 N great kindness, lavish hospitality

shèngxíng 盛行 v be in vogue, be very popular

shèng 圣 TRAD 聖 ADJ holy, sacred

Shèngdànjié 圣诞节 N Christmas

shèng 剩 v be left over, have as surplus ■ 我原来有五百块钱，用了四百块，还剩一百块。**Wǒ yuánlái yǒu wǔbǎi kuài qián, yòngle sìbǎi kuài, hái shèng yìbǎi kuài.** *I originally had five hundred dollars; I've used four hundred dollars and now have one hundred dollars left.*

shèngcài 剩菜 N leftovers

shī 失 v lose

shībài 失败 [comp: 失 lose + 败 be defeated] I v be defeated, lose, fail (ANTONYMS 胜利 **shènglì**, 成功 **chénggōng**) ■ 他们的计划失败了。**Tāmen de jìhuà shībài le.** *Their plan failed.* II N defeat, loss, failure ■ 失败是成功之母。**Shībài shì chénggōng zhī mǔ.** *Failure is the mother of success.*

shīmián 失眠 [v+obj: 失 lose + 眠 sleep] N & V insomnia; suffer from insomnia ■ 她昨天夜里又失眠了。**Tā zuótiān yèlǐ yòu shīmián le.** *She suffered from insomnia again last night.*

shīqù 失去 [comp: 失 lose + 去 go away] v lose (something valuable) ■ 她渐渐对孩子失去耐心。**Tā jiànjiàn duì háizi shīqù nàixīn.** *She is running out of patience with the kids.*

shīshì 失事 v have an accident, meet with a disaster ■ 飞机失事了。**Fēijī shīshì le.** *The airplane (The flight) had an accident.*

shīwàng 失望 [v+obj: 失 lose + 望 hope] ADJ disappointed ■ 你们没有完成上个月的生产计划，我非常失望。**Nǐmen méiyǒu wánchéng shàng ge yuè de shēngchǎn jìhuà, wǒ fēicháng shīwàng.** *I am bitterly disappointed that you failed to complete last month's production plan.*

对 ... 失望 duì ... shīwàng be disappointed with ... ■ 我知道，我哥哥和嫂子对他们的孩子很失

望。**Wǒ zhīdào, wǒ gēge hé sǎozi duì tāmende háizi hěn shīwàng.** *I know my brother and his wife are disappointed with their children.*

shīwù 失误 [comp: 失 lose + 误 make a mistake] v & N miscalculate, muff; miscalculation, muff

shīyè 失业 [v+obj: 失 lose + 业 occupation, employment] v lose one's job, become unemployed ■ 经济情况不好，失业的人越来越多。**Jīngjì qíngkuàng bù hǎo, shīyè de rén yuèlaiyuè duō.** *As the economy is weak, more and more people lose their jobs.* ■ 我万一失业了，就再进大学念书。**Wǒ wànyī shīyè le, jiù zài jìn dàxué niànshū.** *If I lose my job, I will go back to university to study.*

shīzōng 失踪 [v+obj: 失 lose + 踪 foot print] v be missing, disappear

失踪人员 shīzōng rényuán missing person

shī 师 TRAD 師 N master, teacher

shīfàn 师范 N teachers' education

shīfàn xuéyuàn 师范学院 N teachers' college, college of education

shīfu 师傅 [comp: 师 teacher + 傅 tutor] N master worker (位 **wèi**) ■ 这位师傅技术很高。**Zhè wèi shīfu jìshù hěn gāo.** *This master worker is highly skilled.* ■ 这个机器坏了，要请一位师傅来看看。**Zhège jīqì huàile, yào qǐng yí wèi shīfu lái kànkan.** *This machine is not working properly. We need to ask a master worker to come and have a look.*

NOTE: 师傅 **shīfu** is also a polite form of address to a *worker.* For example, an electrician or mechanic can be addressed as 师傅 **shīfu** or, if his family name is 李 **Lǐ**, 李师傅 **Lǐ shīfu.**

shī 诗 TRAD 詩 N poem, poetry (首 **shǒu**) ■ 现在写诗、读诗的人越来越少了。**Xiànzài xiě shī, dú shī de rén yuèlaiyuè shǎo le.** *Nowadays fewer and fewer people write or read poems.*

shīgē 诗歌 N poem, poetry

shīrén 诗人 N poet

shī 施 v carry out, execute

shīgōng 施工 [v+obj: 施 execute + 工 work] v (construction work) be underway, be in progress ■ 前面施工，绕道通行。**Qiánmiàn shīgōng, rào dào tōngxíng.** *Road works ahead. Detour.*

shījiā 施加 v exert, bring to bear on

对 ... 施加压力 duì ... shījiā yālì put pressure on ...

shīzhǎn 施展 v put to good use, give free play to

shī 狮 TRAD 獅 N lion

shīzi 狮子 [suffix: 狮 lion + 子 nominal suffix] N lion (头 **tóu**)

shī 湿 TRAD 濕 ADJ damp, wet, (ANTONYM 干 **gān**) ■ 昨夜下过雨，早上路面还湿着。**Zuóyè xiàguo yǔ, zǎoshang lùmiàn hái shīzhe.** *It rained last night, so the roads were wet this morning.*

shīdù 湿度 [modif: 湿 wet + 度 degree] N humidity

shīrùn 湿润 [comp: 湿 wet + 润 moist] **ADJ** moist, damp

shī 尸 **TRAD** 屍 **N** dead body, corpse

shītǐ 尸体 **N** dead body, corpse (具 **jù**)

shí 十 **NUMERAL** ten

十五 shíwǔ fifteen (15) / 五十 wǔshí fifty (50)

shífēn 十分 [modif: 十 ten + 分 point] **ADV** one hundred percent, totally, fully ■ 我十分满意。**Wǒ shífēn mǎnyì.** *I'm totally satisfied.* ■ 我十分理解你们的心情。**Wǒ shífēn lǐjiě nǐmen de xīnqíng.** *I understand your feelings completely.*

shízú 十足 **ADV** 100 percent, out-and-out

shí 石 **N** stone

shítou 石头 [suffix: 石 stone, rock + 头 nominal suffix] **N** stone, rock (块 **kuài**) ■ 这座山上石头太多，不适合种树。**Zhè zuò shān shang shítou tài duō, bú shìhé zhòng shù.** *This hill is too rocky. It is not suitable for tree planting.* ■ 摸着石头过河。**Mōzhe shítou guò hé.** *Cross a river by feeling for stones. (→ Make decisions as you go along, act without a pre-meditated plan.)*

shíyóu 石油 [modif: 石 stone + 油 oil] **N** petroleum, oil ■ 必须在石油用尽以前，开发出新的能源。**Bìxū zài shíyóu yòngjìn yǐqián, kāifāchū xīn de néngyuán.** *New sources of energy must be developed before petroleum is exhausted.*

shí 识 **TRAD** 識 **V** know (See **rènshi** 认识, **zhīshi** 知识.)

shíbié 识别 **V** distinguish, identify, recognize

识别敌友 shíbié dí yǒu tell enemies from friends

shí 时 **TRAD** 時 **N** time, times

shíchā 时差 **N** time difference between time zones

shícháng 时常 **ADV** from time to time, often

shídài 时代 [comp: 时 time + 代 generation] **N** a historical period, epoch, age, times ■ 人类从石器时代到电脑时代，花了几千年的时间。**Rénlèi cóng shíqì shídài dào diànnǎo shídài, huāle jǐqiān nián de shíjiān.** *It took mankind thousands of years to move from the Stone Age to the Computer Age.*

shí'ér 时而 **ADV** occasionally, sometimes

shíguāng 时光 **N** time, used poetically

shíhou 时候 [comp: 时 time + 候 a certain point in time] **N** a certain point in time, (the time) when ■ 飞机什么时候开？**Fēijī shénme shíhou kāi?** *When will the plane depart?* ■ 他来的时候，我正在打电话。**Tā lái de shíhou, wǒ zhèngzài dǎ diànhuà.** *I was on the phone when he came.*

shíjī 时机 **N** opportunity, opportune moment

shíjiān 时间 [comp: 时 time + 间 moment] **N** time, a period of time ■ 时间不够，我没做完那道练习。**Shíjiān bú gòu, wǒ méi zuòwán nà dào liànxí.** *As there wasn't enough time, I did not finish that exercise.* ■ 我没有时间写信。**Wǒ méiyǒu shíjiān xiě xìn.** *I don't have time to write letters.*

shíkè 时刻 [comp: 时 time + 刻 a point] **N** at a particular point in time ■ 在关键时刻，可以看出一个人的本性。**Zài guānjiàn shíkè, kěyǐ kànchū yí ge rén de běnxìng.** *At critical moments, a person shows his true colors.*

shíkèbiǎo 时刻表 **N** (railway, coach) timetable

shímáo 时髦 **ADJ** fashionable, in vogue

shíqī 时期 [comp: 时 time + 期 period] **N** period of time, stage ■ 他在少年时期受到良好的教育。**Tā zài shàonián shíqī shòudào liánghǎo de jiàoyù.** *He received a very good education during his adolescence.*

shíshàng 时尚 **N** fashion, fad, vogue

shíshì 时事 **N** current affairs, current events

shízhuāng 时装 **N** fashionable dress, latest fashion

shí 实 **TRAD** 實 **ADJ** real, true

shíhuà 实话 [modif: 实 true + 话 words] **N** true fact, truth

实话实说 shíhuà shíshuō tell the truth

shíhuì 实惠 **I N** real benefit, material gain **II ADJ** substantial, solid

shíjì 实际 **I N** reality, actual situation ■ 这项政策脱离实际。**Zhè xiàng zhèngcè tuōlí shíjì.** *This policy is out of touch with reality.* **II ADJ** practical, realistic ■ 我们订计划要实际一点。**Wǒmen dìng jìhuà yào shíjì yìdiǎn.** *We should be practical when drawing up a plan.*

shíjiàn 实践 [comp: 实 fruit, fruition + 践 implement] **V & N** put into practice, apply; practice ■ 懂了这个道理，就要实践。**Dǒngle zhège dàolǐ, jiù yào shíjiàn.** *After you've understood this principle, you should put it into practice.* ■ 实践出真知。**Shíjiàn chū zhēnzhī.** *Practice leads to genuine knowledge.*

shílì 实力 [modif: 实 true + 力 strength] **N** actual strength, strength, power

军事实力 jūnshì shílì military strength, military power

shíshī 实施 **V** put into effect, carry out, implement

shí shì qiú shì 实事求是 **IDIOM** seek truth from facts, be realistic

shíxiàn 实现 [comp: 实 fruit, fruition + 现 materialize] **V** materialize, realize ■ 我一定要实现这个计划。**Wǒ yídìng yào shíxiàn zhège jìhuà.** *I must realize this plan.* ■ 他终于实现了自己的理想。**Tā zhōngyú shíxiànle zìjǐ de lǐxiǎng.** *He finally realized his aspirations.*

shíxíng 实行 **V** put into practice, take effect, implement, carry out, institute ■ 有的大学实行一年三学期的制度。**Yǒude dàxué shíxíng yì nián sān xuéqī de zhìdù.** *Some universities implement the system of three terms a year.* ■ 他的新年决心实行了多久？**Tā de xīnnián juéxīn shíxíngle duōjiǔ?** *How long did he put his New Year's resolutions into practice?*

shíyàn 实验 [modif: 实 practical + 验 testing] **N** experiment, test (项 **xiàng**, 次 **cì**) ■ 学化学一定要做实验。**Xué huàxué yídìng yào zuò shíyàn.** *To*

study chemistry, one must do experiments. ■ 有人反对用动物做实验。 **Yǒurén fǎnduì yòng dòngwù zuò shíyàn.** *Some people oppose experiments on animals.*

shíyànshì 实验室 N laboratory

shíyànyuán 实验员 N laboratory technician

shíyòng 实用 [modif: 实 practical + 用 use] ADJ practical (for use), useful, handy ■ 这套工作服穿着不好看，但是十分实用。 **Zhè tào gōngzuòfú chuānzhe bù hǎokàn, dànshì shífēn shíyòng.** *This set of work clothes does not look beautiful, but it is very practical.* ■ 这本词典非常实用。 **Zhè běn cídiǎn fēicháng shíyòng.** *This dictionary is very useful.*

shízài 实在 ADJ 1 honest, truthful ■ 他说的话你听了可能不高兴，但却很实在。 **Tā shuō de huà nǐ tīngle kěnéng bù gāoxìng, dàn què hěn shízài.** *What he said may have made you unhappy, but it was truthful.* 2 indeed, really ■ 我记不起你的名字了，实在抱歉。 **Wǒ jì bu qǐ nǐ de míngzi le, shízài hěn bàoqiàn.** *I'm really sorry I can't remember your name.*

shízhì 实质 N substance, essence
实质上 shízhì shàng in essence, practically, virtually

shí 拾 V pick up (from the ground) (See shōushi 收拾.)

shí 食 N food

shípǐn 食品 [modif: 食 food + 品 article] N foodstuff (as commodities) (件 jiàn) ■ 新西兰生产的食品质量很高。 **Xīnxīlán shēngchǎn de shípǐn zhìliàng hěn gāo.** *The foodstuffs produced in New Zealand are of very high quality.*

shítáng 食堂 [modif: 食 food + 堂 hall] N dining hall ■ 吃饭的时候，食堂里人很多。 **Chīfàn de shíhou, shítáng li rén hěn duō.** *At mealtimes, there're many people in the dining hall.*

shíwù 食物 [modif: 食 food + 物 things] N food ■ 空气、水和食物都是绝对必要的。 **Kōngqì, shuǐ hé shíwù dōu shì juéduì bìyào de.** *Air, water and food are absolutely indispensable.*

shǐ 史 N history (See lìshǐ 历史.)

shǐ 使 V make, enable ■ 这次旅行使我学到很多知识。 **Zhè cì lǚxíng shǐ wǒ xuédào hěn duō zhīshi.** *This trip enabled me to gain a great deal of knowledge.* ■ 岁月使人老。 **Suìyuè shǐ rén lǎo.** *Time makes one old.*

shǐjìngr 使劲儿 [v+obj: 使 apply + 劲 strength] V exert all one's strength

shǐmìng 使命 N mission, important duty
不辱使命 bùrǔ shǐmìng mission accomplished

shǐyòng 使用 [comp: 使 use + 用 use] V use, apply ■ 你会使用这台电脑吗？ **Nǐ huì shǐyòng zhè tái diànnǎo ma?** *Do you know how to use this computer?* ■ 这辆车是公司的，只有办公事才能使用。 **Zhè liàng chē shì gōngsī de, zhǐyǒu bàn gōngshì cái néng shǐyòng.** *This car belongs to the company;*

you can use it on company business only.

shǐ 始 V begin, start, commence

shǐzhōng 始终 [comp: 始 beginning + 终 end] ADV from beginning to end, throughout, ever ■ 他始终爱着初恋的情人。 **Tā shǐzhōng àizhe chūliàn de qíngrén.** *He loved his first love all his life.*

shì 士 N 1 gentleman, scholar (See shēnshì 绅士.) 2 soldier, serviceman

shìbīng 士兵 N rank-and-file soldier

shì 示 V show, indicate

shìfàn 示范 [v+obj: 示 show + 范 example] V & N set an example, demonstrate; demonstration

shìwēi 示威 [v+obj: 示 show + 威 power] V put on a show of force, demonstrate
抗议示威 kàngyì shìwēi protest demonstration

shìyì 示意 V hint, signal, motion

shìyìtú 示意图 N sketch map

shì 世 N 1 the world 2 lifetime 3 generation

shìdài 世代 [comp: 世 generation + 代 generation] N from generation to generation, for generations
世代经商 shìdài jīngshāng have been businessmen for generations

shìjì 世纪 [modif: 世 generation + 纪 age] N century ■ 公元两千年，世界迎来了一个新世纪——二十一世纪。 **Gōngyuán liǎngqiān nián, shìjiè yíngláile yí ge xīn shìjì – èrshíyī shìjì.** *In the year AD 2000, the world greeted a new century—the twenty-first century.*

shìjiè 世界 [comp: 世 world + 界 boundary] N the world ■ 世界每天都在变。 **Shìjiè měi tiān dōu zài biàn.** *The world is changing every day.*
世界上 shìjiè shang in the world ■ 世界上的事情都很复杂。 **Shìjiè shang de shìqing dōu hěn fùzá.** *Everything in the world is complicated.*

shìjièguān 世界观 N world outlook, worldview

shì 势 TRAD 勢 N power, force

shìbì 势必 ADV be bound to, be sure to

shìlì 势力 N force, power, influence

shì 事 N affair, matter (件 jiàn) ■ 这件事很重要，一定要办好。 **Zhè jiàn shì hěn zhòngyào, yídìng yào bànhǎo.** *This is an important matter and must be done well.* ■ 大家都很关心这件事。 **Dàjiā dōu hěn guānxīn zhè jiàn shì.** *Everybody is concerned over this matter.*

NOTE: In many cases, as in the two examples above, 事 **shì** may be replaced by 事情 **shìqing**. 事 **shì** or 事情 **shìqing** is a noun that can be applied widely, denoting *any affair, matter or business to be done or considered.* Here are more examples: ■ 我今天晚上没有事情做。 **Wǒ jīntiān wǎnshang méiyǒu shìqing zuò.** *I've nothing to do this evening.* ■ 我跟你说一件事。 **Wǒ gēn nǐ shuō yí jiàn shì.** *I want to tell you something.* ■ 他们在路上出事了。 **Tāmen zài lùshang chūshì le.** *They had an accident on the way.*

shìgù 事故 N accident, mishap (件 **jiàn**) ∎ 昨天工厂发生了一件严重事故。**Zuótiān gōngchǎng fāshēngle yí jiàn yánzhòng shìgù.** *A serious accident took place in the factory yesterday.* ∎ 有关部门正在调查事故的原因。**Yǒuguān bùmén zhèngzài diàochá shìgù de yuányīn.** *The departments concerned are investigating the cause of the accident.*

事故现场 shìgù xiànchǎng scene of an accident / 工伤事故 gōngshāng shìgù industrial accident / 交通事故 jiāotōng shìgù traffic accident, road accident

shìjiàn 事件 N (historic) event, incident

shìqing 事情 N see note on 事 **shì**

shìshí 事实 [comp: 事 thing + 实 truth] N fact (件 **jiàn**) ∎ 我的报告是根据事实写的。**Wǒ de bàogào shì gēnjù shìshí xiě de.** *My report is based on facts.* ∎ 你应该先调查事实, 再作结论。**Nǐ yīnggāi xiān diàochá shìshí, zài zuò jiélùn.** *You should check the facts before drawing a conclusion.*

事实上 shìshí shang in fact, as a matter of fact

shìtài 事态 N state of affairs, situation

shìwù 事物 N thing, object, reality

shìwù 事务 N matters to attend to, work

事务工作 shìwù gōngzuò routine work

shìxiān 事先 N beforehand, in advance ∎ 他上星期去中国工作了, 事先没有告诉任何人。**Tā shàng xīngqī qù Zhōngguó gōngzuò le, shìxiān méiyǒu gàosu rènhé rén.** *He went to work in China last week. He had not told anybody beforehand.*

shìxiàng 事项 N item, matter

注意事项 zhùyì shìxiàng points for attention

shìyè 事业 [comp: 事 work + 业 cause] N 1 career ∎ 要事业, 还是要家庭? 她决定不了。**Yào shìyè, háishi yào jiātíng? Tā juédìng bù liǎo.** *She can't make up her mind whether to pursue a career or have a family.* 2 cause, undertaking ∎ 他为世界和平事业作出了巨大贡献。**Tā wèi shìjiè hépíng shìyè zuòchū le jùdà gòngxiàn.** *He made tremendous contributions to the cause of world peace.*

shì 试 TRAD 試 V test, try ∎ 你的办法不行, 试试我的办法。**Nǐ de bànfǎ bù xíng, shìshì wǒ de bànfǎ.** *Your method didn't work. Try my method.* ∎ 这种新药, 病人试过没有? **Zhè zhǒng xīnyào, bìngrén shìguo méiyǒu?** *Has the patient tried this new drug?*

试试/试一下 shìshì/shì yíxià have a try

shìjuàn 试卷 N examination paper, test paper (份 **fèn**)

shìtú 试图 V attempt, try

shìyàn 试验 [comp: 试 test + 验 test] V test, experiment (项 **xiàng**, 次 **cì**) ∎ 研究人员正在动物身上试验这种新药。**Yánjiū rényuán zhèngzài dòngwù shēnshang shìyàn zhè zhǒng xīn yào.** *Researchers are testing this new medicine on animals.*

shì 视 TRAD 視 V watch (See **diànshì 电视**, **zhòngshì 重视**.)

shìlì 视力 [modif: 视 vision + 力 power] N eyesight, sight

视力测验 shìlì cèyàn eyesight test

shìpín 视频 N video frequency

视频光盘 shìpín guāngpán video compact disc, VCD

shìxiàn 视线 [modif: 视 vision + 线 line] N line of sight, line of vision

挡住了视线 dǎngzhù le shìxiàn block one's view

shìyě 视野 N field of vision, field of view

shì 市 N municipality, city ∎ 下午我要到市里去。**Xiàwǔ wǒ yào dào shìli qù.** *I'm going to the city this afternoon.*

shìchǎng 市场 [modif: 市 market + 场 ground] N marketplace, market ∎ 她在市场上买了一只活鸡, 两条活鱼。**Tā zài shìchǎng shang mǎile yì zhī huó jī, liǎng tiáo huóyú.** *She bought a live chicken and two live fish from the market.* ∎ 市场上需要什么, 他们就生产什么。**Shìchǎng shang xūyào shénme, tāmen jiù shēngchǎn shénme.** *They produce whatever the market needs.*

菜市场 cài shìchǎng vegetable market, food market / 市场经济 shìchǎng jīngjì market economy

shì 式 N form, pattern (See **fāngshì 方式**, **xíngshì 形式**, etc.)

shì 似 as in 似的 **shìde**

shìde 似的 PARTICLE be like, as … as

shì 是 V 1 be, yes ∎ "你们的中文老师是不是北京人?" "是的." **"Nǐmen de Zhōngwén lǎoshī shì bu shì Běijīngrén?" "Shì de."** *"Is your Chinese teacher from Beijing?" "Yes."* ∎ "这本书是你的吗?" "不是, 不是我的。" **"Zhè běn shū shì nǐ de ma?" "Bú shì, bú shì wǒ de."** *"Is this book yours?" "No."* 2 (indicating existence of), (there) be ∎ 小学旁边是一座公园。**Xiǎoxué pángbian shì yí zuò gōngyuán.** *There is a park by the primary school.* ∎ 张教授的办公室里到处是书。**Zhāng jiàoshòu de bàngōngshì li dàochù shì shū.** *There are books everywhere in Professor Zhang's office.* 3 (used to emphasize the words following it) ∎ 他这么做是出于好心。**Tā zhème zuò shì chūyú hǎoxīn.** *He did it out of kindness.* ∎ 那个电话是谁打来的? **Nàge diànhuà shì shéi dǎ lai de?** *Who rang?*

shìfēi 是非 [comp: 是 yes + 非 no] N right and wrong, truth and falsehood

明辨是非 míngbiàn shìfēi distinguish clearly between right and wrong

shìfǒu 是否 ADV whether or not, yes or no

shì 室 N room (See **bàngōngshì 办公室**, **jiàoshì 教室**, etc.)

shì 柿 N persimmon

shìzi 柿子 N persimmon

shì 适 TRAD 適 V suit, fit

shìdàng 适当 [comp: 适 suitable + 当 ought to] **ADJ** appropriate, suitable ■ 我会在适当的时候批评他。**Wǒ huì zài shìdàng de shíhou pīpíng tā.** *I will criticize him at an appropriate moment.* ■ 在中国送钟给老年人当礼物，是不适当的，因为"送钟"和"送终"同音。**Zài Zhōngguó sòng zhōng gěi lǎoniánrén dāng lǐwù, shì bú shìdàng de, yīnwèi "sòng zhōng" hé "sòng zhōng" tóngyīn.** *In China it is not appropriate to give an old person a clock as a gift because "give a clock"* (sòng zhōng) *is pronounced the same as "pay last tribute"* (sòng zhōng).

shìhé 适合 [comp: 适 suit + 合 be harmonious] **V** suit, fit ■ 他善于交际，适合做生意。**Tā shànyú jiāojì, shìhé zuò shēngyi.** *He is good at social dealings, and is suited to be a businessman.*

shìyí 适宜 **ADJ** suitable, appropriate

shìyìng 适应 **V** be able to adapt to ■ 你已经适应新环境了吗？**Nǐ yǐjīng shìyìng xīn huánjìng le ma?** *Have you been able to adapt to your new situation?*

shìyòng 适用 [v+obj: 适 suit + 用 use, application] **ADJ** applicable, suitable ■ 你的方法很先进，但是在这里不适用。**Nǐ de fāngfǎ hěn xiānjìn, dànshì zài zhèlǐ bú shìyòng.** *Your method is very advanced, but it cannot be applied here.*

shì 逝 **V** pass, leave

shìshì 逝世 [v+obj: 逝 leave + 世 the world] **V** pass away, die

NOTE: See note on 去世 **qùshì.**

shì 释 **TRAD** 釋 **V 1** clarify (See **jiěshì** 解释.) **2** let go (See **ài bú shì shǒu** 爱不释手.)

shìfàng 释放 **V** release, set free

shi 匙 See **yàoshi** 钥匙

shōu 收 **V 1** receive, accept ■ 我昨天收到一封信。**Wǒ zuótiān shōudào yì fēng xìn.** *I received a letter yesterday.* ■ 请你收下这件小礼物。**Qǐng nǐ shōuxia zhè jiàn xiǎo lǐwù.** *Please accept this small gift.* **2** collect (fee), charge ■ 这种服务是要收费的。**Zhè zhǒng fúwù shì yào shōufèi de.** *This service will incur a fee.*

收到 shōudào receive / 收回 shōuhuí take back, recall / 收下 shōuxia accept

shōucáng 收藏 **V** collect (antiques, collectibles, etc.)

收藏中国明代花瓶 shōucáng Zhōngguó Míngdài huāpíng collect Chinese Ming vases

shōuhuò 收获 [comp: 收 collect + 获 gain] **V & N** gather in crops, harvest; gain (of work), achievement, reward ■ 今年这位农民收获了五千公斤小麦。**Jīnnián zhè wèi nóngmín shōuhuòle wǔqiān gōngjīn xiǎomài.** *This year the farmer harvested five thousand kilograms of wheat.* ■ 这次试验取得了大量数据，收获很大。**Zhè cì shìyàn qǔdéle dàliàng shùjù, shōuhuò hěn dà.** *A large amount of*

data has been obtained from the test, which is a big achievement.

shōujù 收据 **N** receipt

shōurù 收入 [comp: 收 collect + 入 entry] **V & N** earn, receive; income ■ 我不想告诉他我去年收入多少钱。**Wǒ bù xiǎng gàosu tā wǒ qùnián shōurù duōshǎo qián.** *I didn't want to tell him how much I earned last year.*

人均收入 rén jūn shōurù average income per capita

shōushi 收拾 [comp: 收 gather in + 拾 pick up] **V** put in order, tidy up ■ 桌子上的书和报纸太多，我要收拾一下。**Zhuōzi shang de shū hé bàozhǐ tài duō, wǒ yào shōushi yíxià.** *There are too many newspapers and books on the table. I'll tidy it up.*

shōusuō 收缩 **V** contract, shrink

shōuyì 收益 **N** profit, earnings

shōuyīnjī 收音机 [modif: 收音 receive sound + 机 machine] **N** radio (台 tái, 架 jià) ■ 这台收音机还是我爷爷买的。**Zhè tái shōuyīnjī háishì wǒ yéye mǎide.** *This radio was bought by my grandpa.*

shǒu 手 **N** hand (只 zhī, 双 shuāng) ■ 我的手不干净，要洗一下才能吃饭。**Wǒ de shǒu bù gānjing, yào xǐ yíxià cái néng chīfàn.** *My hands are not clean. I have to wash them before eating my meal.*

shǒu shang 手上 in the hand ■ 他手上拿着一本书。**Tā shǒu shang názhe yì běn shū.** *He's holding a book in his hand.*

右手 yòushǒu the right hand / 左手 zuǒshǒu the left hand

shǒubiǎo 手表 [modif: 手 hand + 表 watch] **N** wristwatch (块 kuài) ■ 我的手表慢了，你的手表几点？**Wǒ de shǒubiǎo màn le, nǐ de shǒubiǎo jǐ diǎn?** *My watch is slow. What time is it by your watch?*

NOTE: In everyday usage, 手表 **shǒubiǎo** is often shortened to 表 **biǎo**: 我的表慢了，你的表几点？**Wǒ de biǎo màn le, nǐ de biǎo jǐ diǎn?** *My watch is slow. What time is it by your watch?*

shǒuduàn 手段 **N** means, measure ■ 我不赞成使用不合理的手段来达到目的。**Wǒ bú zànchéng shǐyòng bù hélǐ de shǒuduàn lái dádào mùdì.** *I don't endorse the use of unjustifiable means to achieve your ends.*

shǒufǎ 手法 **N** trick, gimmick

shǒugōng 手工 [modif: 手 hand + 工 work] **N** done by hand, made by hand, manual ■ 这件丝绸衬衫是手工做的，所以比较贵。**Zhè jiàn sīchóu chènshān shì shǒugōng zuòde, suǒyǐ bǐjiào guì.** *This silk shirt was handmade, so it is rather expensive.*

shǒugōngyè 手工业 **N** handicraft industry

shǒugōngyì 手工艺 **N** arts and crafts, handicraft

shǒujī 手机 [modif: 手 hand + 机 machine] **N** cell phone, mobile telephone (只 zhī) ■ 上飞机以前，要关上手机。**Shàng fēijī yǐqián, yào guānshang shǒujī.** *Switch off your cell phone before boarding*

a plane. ■ 他又换了一只手机。**Tā yòu huànle yì zhī shǒujī.** *He changed his cell phone again.*

shǒujuàn 手绢 N handkerchief (块 **kuài**) ■ 手绢要每天换。**Shǒujuàn yào měi tiān huàn.** *Handkerchiefs should be changed daily. (→ You have to use a clean handkerchief every day.)*

shǒushì 手势 N hand signal, gesture
打手势 dǎ shǒushì make a hand signal, make a gesture

shǒushù 手术 N surgical operation, operation
做手术 zuò shǒushù perform an operation, operate ■ 外科主任亲自做这个手术。**Wàikē zhǔrèn qīnzì zuò zhè ge shǒushù.** *The chief surgeon will perform the operation himself.*

shǒushùjiān 手术间 N operating room, surgery room

shǒutào 手套 [modif: 手 hand + 套 covering] N glove (只 **zhī**, 副 **fù**) ■ 今天真冷，我戴了手套、帽子，还觉得冷！**Jīntiān zhēn lěng, wǒ dàile shǒutào, màozi, hái juéde lěng!** *It's really cold today. I'm wearing gloves and a hat, but still feel cold!*

shǒuxù 手续 N formalities, procedure
办手续 bàn shǒuxù go through the formalities ■ 买卖房子，要办法律手续。**Mǎimài fángzi, yào bàn fǎlǜ shǒuxù.** *You will have to complete the legal formalities when you buy or sell a house.*

shǒuyì 手艺 [modif: 手 hand + 艺 art] N craftsmanship, workmanship

shǒuzhǐ 手指 N finger, thumb ■ 她的手指又细又长。**Tā de shǒuzhǐ yòu xì yòu cháng.** *Her fingers are slender and long.*

NOTE: In Chinese the thumb 拇指 **mǔzhǐ**, or 大拇指 **dàmǔzhǐ** is considered just one of the fingers. So it is correct to say: 我有十个手指。**Wǒ yǒu shí ge shǒuzhǐ.** *I have ten fingers.*

shǒu 守 V 1 observe, abide by (See **zūnshǒu** 遵守.) 2 keep watch, guard

shǒuhù 守护 V guard and defend

shǒu 首 MEASURE WORD (for songs and poems)
一首歌 yì shǒu gē a song

shǒudū 首都 [modif: 首 the head, first + 都 metropolis] N capital city ■ 中国的首都是北京。**Zhōngguó de shǒudū shì Běijīng.** *China's capital city is Beijing.*

shǒushi 首饰 N jewelry (ring, earring, bracelet, etc.)

shǒuxiān 首先 [comp: 首 first + 先 before] ADV first, first of all ■ 首先，请允许我自我介绍一下。**Shǒuxiān, qǐng yǔnxǔ wǒ zìwǒ jièshào yíxià.** *First of all, allow me to introduce myself.*

shǒuyào 首要 [comp: 首 first + 要 important] ADJ of primary importance

shòu 受 V 1 receive, accept ■ 每个人都有受教育的权利。**Měi ge rén dōu yǒu shòu jiàoyù de quánlì.** *Everyone has the right to receive an edu-*

cation. ■ 他因为上班迟到而受批评了。**Tā yīnwèi shàngbān chídào ér shòu pīpíng le.** *He was criticized for being late for work.* 2 bear, endure
受不了 shòu bu liǎo cannot stand/endure ■ 有些人受不了东北严寒的冬天。**Yǒu xiē rén shòu bu liǎo Dōngběi yánhán de dōngtiān.** *Some people cannot stand the severe winter in China's Northeast.*

shòudào 受到 V have received, have suffered
受到很好的教育 shòudào hěn hǎo de jiàoyù have received an excellent education, very well-educated / 受到公司的警告 shòudào gōngsī de jǐnggào have received a warning from the company

shòufá 受罚 [v+obj: 受 suffer + 罚 penalty] V be punished, be penalized ■ 拖延付款要受罚。**Tuōyán fùkuǎn yào shòufá.** *Late payment will be penalized*

shòushāng 受伤 [v+obj: 受 suffer + 伤 wound] V be wounded, be injured

shòuzuì 受罪 V endure hardship, have a very hard time

shòu 授 V give, award

shòuyǔ 授予 V confer, award
授予学位 shòuyǔ xuéwèi confer an academic degree

shòu 瘦 ADJ thin, lean ■ 她比以前瘦多了。**Tā bǐ yǐqián shòu duō le.** *She is much thinner than before.* ■ 别以为越瘦越好看。**Bié yǐwéi yuè shòu yuè hǎokàn.** *Do not think that the thinner you are, the more beautiful you become.*

shòuròu 瘦肉 N lean meat ■ 她只吃瘦肉，不吃肥肉。**Tā zhǐ chī shòuròu, bù chī féiròu.** *She eats only lean meat, and does not eat fatty meat.*

shòu 售 V sell

shòuhuòyuán 售货员 [suffix: 售 sell + 货 goods + 员 nominal suffix] N shop assistant, salesperson ■ 售货员帮我挑选皮鞋。**Shòuhuòyuán bāng wǒ tiāoxuǎn píxié.** *The shop assistant helped me choose a pair of shoes.*

shòu 寿 TRAD 壽 N life, lifespan
长寿 chángshòu longevity ■ 祝您老人家健康长寿！**Zhù nín lǎorenjia jiànkāng chángshòu!** *(to an elderly person) Wish you good health and longevity!*

shòumìng 寿命 [comp: 寿 life + 命 life] N lifespan

shòu 兽 TRAD 獸 N beast, four-legged mammal (See **yěshòu** 野兽.)

shū 书 TRAD 書 N book (本 **běn**) ■ 这本书很有意思，你看过没有？**Zhè běn shū hěn yǒu yìsi, nǐ kànguo méiyǒu?** *This book is very interesting. Have you read it?* ■ 她常常去图书馆借书。**Tā chángcháng qù túshūguǎn jiè shū.** *She often goes to the library to borrow books.*
看书 kàn shū read, do reading ■ 我喜欢看书。**Wǒ xǐhuan kàn shū.** *I like reading.*

shūbāo 书包 [modif: 书 book + 包 bag] N schoolbag, satchel (只 **zhī**) ■ 小学生的书包为什么这么

重？**Xiǎoxuéshēng de shūbāo wèishénme zhème zhòng?** *Why are children's schoolbags so heavy?*

shūdiàn 书店 [modif: 书 book + 店 store, shop] **N** bookstore, bookshop (家 **jiā**) ■ 你们这里哪家书店最好？ **Nǐmen zhèlǐ nǎ jiā shūdiàn zuì hǎo?** *Which is the best bookstore here?*

shūfǎ 书法 **N** calligraphy

shūfǎjiā 书法家 **N** calligrapher

shūjí 书籍 **N** books (collectively)

shūjì 书记 **N** head of the Chinese Communist Party or Chinese Communist Youth League organizations at various levels, Party secretary, League secretary

shūjià 书架 [modif: 书 book + 架 shelf] **N** bookshelf ■ 王老师的办公室有一个大书架。 **Wáng lǎoshī de bàngōngshì yǒu yí ge dà shūjià.** *There is a big bookshelf in Teacher Wang's office.*

shūmiàn 书面 **ADJ** in written form, written (**ANTONYM** 口头 **kǒutóu**)

书面邀请 **shūmiàn yāoqǐng** written invitation

shū 叔 **N** father's younger brother

shūshu 叔叔 **N** father's younger brother, uncle ■ 我叔叔是设计电脑软件的。 **Wǒ shūshu shì shèjì diànnǎo ruǎnjiàn de.** *My father's younger brother designs computer software.*

NOTE: 叔叔 **shūshu** is a form of address used by a child for a man around his/her father's age. It is common to put a family name before 叔叔 **shūshuí**, e.g. 张叔叔 **Zhāng shūshu.** Also see note on 阿姨 **āyí.**

shū 殊 **ADJ** different (See 特殊 **tèshū.**)

shūzi 梳子 [suffix: 梳 comb + 子 nominal suffix] **N** comb (把 **bǎ**)

shū 舒 **V** stretch, unfold

shūchàng 舒畅 [comp: 舒 relaxing + 畅 uninhibited] **ADJ** entirely free from worry, happy

心情舒畅 **xīnqíng shūchàng** have ease of mind, feel carefree and happy

shūfu 舒服 [comp: 舒 relaxing + 服 conceding] **ADJ** comfortable ■ 这把椅子很舒服，你坐下去就不想起来了。 **Zhè bǎ yǐzi hěn shūfu, nǐ zuò xiàqu jiù bù xiǎng qǐlái le.** *This chair is very comfortable. Sit on it and you don't want to get up.* ■ 他们不是非常有钱，但是生活过得挺舒服。 **Tāmen bú shì fēicháng yǒu qián, dànshì shēnghuó guò de tǐng shūfu.** *They are not wealthy, but they live comfortably.*

不舒服 **bù shūfu** (of a person) not very well, be under the weather ■ 我今天不舒服，想早点回家。 **Wǒ jīntiān bù shūfu, xiǎng zǎo diǎn huíjiā.** *I'm unwell today. I want to go home early.*

shūshì 舒适 **ADJ** comfortable, cosy

shū 疏 **I ADJ 1** sparse, scattered **2** (of relationships) not intimate, distant **II v** neglect, overlook

shūhu 疏忽 [comp: 疏 neglect + 忽 overlook] **V & N** neglect, overlook; oversight, omission

shūyuǎn 疏远 [comp: 疏 distant + 远 distant] **ADJ** (of relationships) not close, estranged

shū 蔬 **N** vegetable

shūcài 蔬菜 **N** vegetable ■ 多吃蔬菜，少吃肉，对健康有利。 **Duō chī shūcài, shǎo chī ròu, duì jiànkāng yǒulì.** *Eating lots of vegetables and little meat is good for your health.*

shū 输¹ **TRAD** 輸 **v** lose (a game, a bet) (**ANTONYM** 赢 **yíng**) ■ 上回我们队输了，这回一定要赢！ **Shàng huí wǒmen duì shū le, zhè huí yídìng yào yíng!** *Our team lost the game the last time; this time we must win!* ■ 客队输了两个球。 **Kèduì shūle liǎng ge qiú.** *The visiting team lost two points.*

shū 输² **TRAD** 輸 **v** transport

shūchū 输出 **v 1** output **2** send out, export

shūrù 输入 **v 1** input **2** bring in, introduce

shūsòng 输送 **v** transport, convey

shūxuè 输血 **N** blood transfusion

shú 熟 **ADJ 1** ripe, cooked ■ 苹果还没有熟，很酸。 **Píngguǒ hái méiyǒu shú, hěn suān.** *The apples are not yet ripe. They're sour.* ■ 肉熟了就可以吃饭。 **Ròu shúle jiù kěyǐ chīfàn.** *We can have our meal when the meat is done.* **2** familiar with, know well ■ 这个城市我不熟。 **Zhège chéngshì wǒ bù shú.** *I don't know this city very well.*

shúliàn 熟练 [comp: 熟 familiar with + 练 practiced] **ADJ** skilful, skilled ■ 我们工厂缺乏熟练工人。 **Wǒmen gōngchǎng quēfá shúliàn gōngrén.** *Our factory is short of skilled workers.*

shúxī 熟悉 [comp: 熟 familiar with + 悉 knowing] **ADJ & V** familiar with; be familiar with, know well ■ 他和熟悉的人在一起的时候话很多。 **Tā hé shúxī de rén zài yìqǐ de shíhou huà hěn duō.** *He is talkative in the company of the people he knows well.* ■ 我对这个地方不熟悉。 **Wǒ duì zhège dìfang bù shúxī.** *I am not familiar with this place.*

shǔ 数 **TRAD** 數 **v** count ■ 我来数一下，这里有多少人，一、二、三、… **Wǒ lái shǔ yíxià, zhèlǐ yǒu duōshǎo rén, yī, èr, sān…** *Let me count to see how many people there are here. One, two, three…*

shǔ 暑 **N** heat

shǔjià 暑假 [modif: 暑 summer + 假 holiday, vacation] **N** summer holiday, summer vacation ■ 你暑假有什么打算？ **Nǐ shǔjià yǒu shénme dǎsuàn?** *What is your plan for the summer holiday?*

shǔ 属 **TRAD** 屬 **v** belong to

shǔxiàng 属相 (See note on 生肖 **shēngxiāo.**)

shǔyú 属于 **v** belong to ■ 这些书不是我个人的，而是属于学校图书馆。 **Zhèxiē shū bú shì wǒ gèrén de, érshì shǔyú xuéxiào túshūguǎn.** *These books are not mine, but belong to the school library.*

shǔ 鼠 **N** rat, mouse

shǔbiāo 鼠标 (computer) mouse

shù 术 **TRAD** 術 **N** skill, art, craft (See jìshù 技术, měishù 美术, etc.)

shù 束 **N** knot

shùfù 束缚 [comp: 束 knot + 缚 tie up] **v** bind up, fetter

shù 述 **v** narrate (See **fùshù** 复述.)

shù 树 TRAD 樹 **N** tree (棵 **kē**) ■ 这棵树又高又大，树下很凉快。**Zhè kē shù yòu gāo yòu dà, shù xia hěn liángkuai.** *This tree is big and tall; it's cool under it.* ■ 我爸爸在花园里种了两棵树。**Wǒ bàba zài huāyuán li zhòngle liǎng kē shù.** *My father planted two trees in the garden.*

shùlì 树立 **v** set up, establish

shùlín 树林 [comp: 树 tree + 林 wood] **N** wood, woods ■ 在树林里有很多种鸟。**Zài shùlín li yǒu hěn duō zhǒng niǎo.** *There are many kinds of birds in the woods.*

shù 竖 **ADJ** vertical (ANTONYM 横 **héng**)

shù 恕 **v** forgive (See **ráoshù** 饶恕.)

shù 数 TRAD 數 **N** number, figure ■ 说这种语言的人数在不断减少。**Shuō zhè zhǒng yǔyán de rénshù zài búduàn jiǎnshǎo.** *The number of speakers of this language is on the decline.*

shù'é 数额 **N** fixed amount, quota

shùjù 数据 [modif: 数 number + 据 evidence] **N** datum, data ■ "你能肯定这些数据是准确的吗？" "能肯定." **Nǐ néng kěndìng zhèxiē shùjù shì zhǔnquè de ma?" "Néng kěndìng."** *"Are you sure these data are accurate?" "Positive."*

shùjùkù 数据库 **N** database

shùliàng 数量 [comp: 数 number + 量 quantity] **N** quantity, amount ■ 电视节目的数量在增加，但质量怎么样呢？**Diànshì jiémù de shùliàng zài zēngjiā, dàn zhìliàng zěnmeyàng ne?** *The quantity of TV programs is increasing, but how about their quality?*

shùmǎ 数码 **ADJ** digital

数码化 **shùmǎhuà** digitalize, digitalization

shùmù 数目 **N** number, amount

shùxué 数学 [modif: 数 number + 学 knowledge, study of] **N** mathematics, math ■ 我看，数学和语文是学校里最重要的两门课。**Wǒ kàn, shùxué hé yǔwén shì xuéxiào li zuì zhòngyào de liǎng mén kè.** *In my view, mathematics and Chinese are the two most important subjects in schools.* ■ 我们明天考数学。**Wǒmen míngtiān kǎo shùxué.** *We're having a mathematics examination tomorrow.*

shùzì 数字 [modif: 数 number + 字 written word] **N** 1 numeral (in writing) ■ 我认为写中文的时候，一般应该写中文数字，如 "一," "二" "三。" **Wǒ rènwéi xiě Zhōngwén de shíhou, yìbān yīnggāi xiě Zhōngwén shùzì, rú "yī," "èr," "sān."** *I think when we're writing Chinese, we should generally use Chinese numerals, such as "一," "二" and "三." * 2 figure, number ■ 每个月都节省一点钱，几年以后就是一笔不小的数字。**Měi ge yuè dōu jiéshěng yìdiǎn qián, jǐ nián yǐhòu jiùshì yìbǐ bù xiǎo de shùzì.** *If you save some money every month, years later you will have a quite large sum.*

shuā 刷 **v** brush

shuāyá 刷牙 **v** brush teeth ■ 我每天睡觉前刷牙。**Wǒ měi tiān shuìjiào qián shuā yá.** *I brush my teeth before going to bed every night.*

shuāzi 刷子 **N** brush (把 **bǎ**)

shuǎ 耍 **v** play, play with, perform

shuāi 摔 **v** 1 fall, fumble ■ 她从自行车上摔下来，擦破了手。**Tā cóng zìxíngchē shang shuāi xiàlai, cāpòle shǒu.** *She fell off the bicycle and scraped her hand.* 2 fall and break, cause to fall and break ■ 我不小心把茶杯摔了。**Wǒ bù xiǎoxīn bǎ chábēi shuāi le.** *I accidentally broke the teacup.*

shuāidǎo 摔倒 **v** fall, trip and fall

shuāi 衰 **v** decline, decay

shuāilǎo 衰老 [comp: 衰 decline + 老 old] **ADJ** old and in declining health, old and frail

shuāituì 衰退 [comp: 衰 decline + 退 regress] **v** become weaker, decline

经济衰退 **jīngjì shuāituì** economic recession

shuǎi 甩 **v** swing, throw

shuài 率 **v** lead, command

shuàilǐng 率领 [comp: 率 lead + 领 lead] **v** lead, command (troops)

shuài 帅 TRAD 帥 **I N** commander in chief

元帅 **yuánshuài** marshal

II ADJ handsome, smart

shuàigē 帅哥 **N** handsome young man

shuàn 涮 **v** rinse meat slice in boiling water

shuàn huǒguǒ 涮火锅 **v** have a hot-pot dinner

shuāng 双 TRAD 雙 MEASURE WORD a pair of (shoes, chopsticks, etc.)

一双鞋 **yì shuāng xié** a pair of shoes / 两双筷子 **liǎng shuāng kuàizi** two pairs of chopsticks

shuāngbāotāi 双胞胎 **N** twins

shuāngfāng 双方 [modif: 双 both + 方 side, party] **N** both sides, both parties ■ 双方同意加强合作。**Shuāngfāng tóngyì jiāqiáng hézuò.** *Both parties agree to strengthen their cooperation.*

shuāng 霜 **N** frost

shuǎng 爽 **ADJ** 1 crisp, refreshing 2 straightforward, open-hearted

shuǎngkuài 爽快 **ADJ** 1 refreshed 2 straightforward, frank 3 readily, without hesitation ■ 你有什么话，就爽快地说吧。**Nǐ yǒu shénme huà, jiù shuǎngkuài de shuō ba.** *If you've got anything to say, just be frank and speak up.*

shuí 谁 TRAD 誰 PRON 1 who, whom ■ 谁是你们的中文老师？**Shuí shì nǐmen de Zhōngwén lǎoshī?** *Who's your Chinese teacher?* ■ 你找谁？**Nǐ zhǎo shuí?** *Who are you looking for?* 2 everyone, anybody, whoever, no matter who ■ 谁都希望生活过得幸福。**Shuí dōu xīwàng shēnghuó guò de xìngfú.** *Everybody hopes to live a happy life.* ■ 谁也不能保证永远不犯错误。**Shuí yě bù néng bǎozhèng yǒngyuǎn bú fàn cuòwù.** *Nobody can guarantee that he will never make a mistake.*

shuǐ 水 N water ■ 我口渴，要喝水。**Wǒ kǒu kě, yào hē shuǐ.** *I'm thirsty. I want to drink some water.*
自来水 zìláishuǐ running water, tap water ■ 这里的自来水能喝吗？**Zhèlǐ de zìláishuǐ néng hē ma?** *Is the tap water here drinkable?*
开水 kāishuǐ boiled water

shuǐdào 水稻 [modif: 水 water + 稻 paddy rice] N paddy rice, rice ■ 这些年水稻产量有了相当大的提高。**Zhèxiē nián shuǐdào chǎnliàng yǒule xiāngdāng dà de tígāo.** *The yield of paddy rice has increased considerably in recent years.*

shuǐguǒ 水果 [modif: 水 water + 果 fruit] N fruit ■ 水果人人都爱吃。**Shuǐguǒ rénrén dōu ài chī.** *Everybody loves to eat fruit.* ■ 我要去商店买一些水果。**Wǒ yào qù shāngdiàn mǎi yìxiē shuǐguǒ.** *I'll go to the store to buy some fruit.*

shuǐlì 水利 [modif: 水 water + 利 benefit] N water conservancy, irrigation works
水利工程 shuǐlì gōngchéng water conservancy project

shuǐlóngtóu 水龙头 N water tap, faucet

shuǐní 水泥 [comp: 水 water + 泥 mud] N cement ■ 我要买两袋优质水泥，多少钱？**Wǒ yào mǎi liǎng dài yōuzhì shuǐní, duōshǎo qián?** *I want two sacks of quality cement. How much is it?*

shuǐpíng 水平 N 1 level, standard ■ 政府努力提高人民的生活水平。**Zhèngfǔ nǔlì tígāo rénmín de shēnghuó shuǐpíng.** *The government is working hard to raise the people's living standard.* 2 proficiency (in language) ■ 我的中文水平不高，请您多多帮助。**Wǒ de Zhōngwén shuǐpíng bù gāo, qǐng nín duōduō bāngzhù.** *My proficiency in Chinese is not very high. Please help me.*
提高 … 水平 tígāo … shuǐpíng raise the standard of … / 生活水平 shēnghuó shuǐpíng living standard / 文化水平 wénhuà shuǐpíng cultural level, educational experience

shuì 税 N tax, duty ■ 每个公民都有交税的义务。**Měi ge gōngmín dōu yǒu jiāo shuì de yìwù.** *Every citizen has an obligation to pay taxes.*
关税 guānshuì tariff

shuìwùjú 税务局 N tax bureau, Inland Revenue Service

shuì 睡 V sleep ■ 爸爸睡了，你明天再跟他说吧。**Bàba shuì le, nǐ míngtiān zài gēn tā shuō ba.** *Daddy's sleeping. Talk to him tomorrow.* ■ 我一般夜里睡得挺好，可是昨天没睡好，因为心里有事。**Wǒ yìbān yèlǐ shuì de tǐng hǎo, kěshì zuótiān méi shuì hǎo, yīnwèi xīnli yǒushì.** *I usually sleep well at night, but I did not sleep well last night as I had something on my mind.*
睡着 shuìzháo fall asleep ■ 昨天我十点上床，到十二点左右才睡着。**Zuótiān wǒ shí diǎn shàngchuáng, dào shí'èr diǎn zuǒyòu cái shuì zháo.** *I went to bed at ten yesterday and didn't fall asleep until about twelve o'clock.*

shuìjiào 睡觉 [comp: 睡 sleep + 觉 sleep] V sleep, go to bed ■ "你每天什么时候睡觉？" "十点钟以后。" **"Nǐ měi tiān shénme shíhou shuìjiào?" "Shí diǎnzhōng yǐhòu."** *"When do you go to bed every day?" "After ten o'clock."* ■ 这么晚了，你还不睡觉？**Zhème wǎn le, nǐ hái bú shuìjiào?** *It's so late. You're not going to bed?*

NOTES: (1) 睡 **shuì** and 睡觉 **shuìjiào** are often interchangeable. (2) 觉 is pronounced **jiào** in 睡觉 **shuìjiào,** but **jué** in 觉得 **juéde.**

shuìyī 睡衣 N pajamas, dressing gown

shùn 顺 TRAD 順 ADJ smooth

shùnbiàn 顺便 [comp: 顺 smooth + 便 convenient] ADV in passing, incidentally ■ 你回家的路上，顺便给我买一份晚报，好吗？**Nǐ huíjiā de lùshang, shùnbiàn gěi wǒ mǎi yífèn wǎnbào, hǎo ma?** *Could you buy me an evening paper on your way home?* ■ 顺便说一句，下个月我要请两天假。**Shùnbiàn shuō yíjù, xià ge yuè wǒ yào qǐng liǎngtiān jià.** *Incidentally, I'm going to ask for a couple of days' leave next month.*

shùnlì 顺利 [comp: 顺 smooth + 利 favorable] ADJ smooth, without a hitch, successful ■ 我们的计划执行得很顺利。**Wǒmen de jìhuà zhíxíng de hěn shùnlì.** *Our plan has been carried out smoothly.* ■ 他一生都很顺利。**Tā yìshēng dōu hěn shùnlì.** *All his life has been plain sailing. (→ He has had an easy life.)*

shùnxù 顺序 N sequence, order

shùn 瞬 V wink

shùnjiān 瞬间 N in the twinkling of an eye

shuō 说 TRAD 說 V 1 say, speak ■ 他说今天晚上没有时间。**Tā shuō jīntiān wǎnshang méiyǒu shíjiān.** *He said he did not have time this evening.* ■ 他说什么？**Tā shuō shénme?** *What did he say?* 2 explain, tell ■ 你说说，这个菜怎么做？**Nǐ shuōshuo, zhège cài zěnme zuò?** *Will you tell me how to cook this dish?* ■ 她很聪明，老师一说她就懂。**Tā hěn cōngmíng, lǎoshī yì shuō tā jiù dǒng.** *She is very bright. As soon as the teacher has explained, she understands.*
说笑话 shuō xiàohua tell a joke, kid

shuō bu dìng 说不定 ADV 1 probably, likely 2 not for sure, indefinitely

shuōfú 说服 [v+compl: 说 speak + 服 obey] V 1 persuade ■ 妈妈说服了爸爸提前退休。**Māma shuōfú le bàba tí qián tuìxiū.** *Mom has persuaded Dad to have an early retirement.* 2 convince ■ 他说的话没有道理，我没有被说服。**Tā shuō de huà méiyǒu dàolǐ, wǒ méiyǒu bèi shuōfú.** *What he said was not reasonable; I was not convinced.*

shuōhuà 说话 V speak, talk ■ 上课了，不要说话了。**Shàngkè le, bú yào shuōhuà le.** *Class has started; don't talk any more.*

shuōhuǎng 说谎 说谎 V tell a lie, lie ■ 好孩子是不说

谎的。**Hǎo háizi shì b shuōhuǎng de.** *A good child does not tell lies.*

shuōmíng 说明 [v+compl: 说 say + 明 clear] **v & N** explain, show; explanation, manual ■ 我来说明一下，为什么我最近有时候迟到。**Wǒ lái shuōmíng yíxià, wèishénme wǒ zuìjìn yǒu shíhou chídào.** *Let me explain why I've been sometimes late recently.* ■ 这个电脑怎么用，我要看一下说明。**Zhège diànnǎo zěnme yòng, wǒ yào kàn yíxià shuōmíng.** *As to how to use this computer, I need to read the manual.*

shuò 硕 **TRAD** 碩 **ADJ** large, big

shuòshì 硕士 [modif: 硕 big + 士 scholar] **N** holder of a master's degree
硕士学位 **shuòshì xuéwèi** master's degree, masterate

sī 司 **v** take charge of

sīfǎ 司法 [v+obj: 司 take charge of + 法 law] **N** administration of justice, judicature
司法机关 **sīfǎ jīguān** judicial office, judicial system

sījī 司机 [v+obj: 司 take charge + 机 machine] **N** (professional) automobile driver, train driver ■ 出租汽车司机态度很好。**Chūzū qìchē sījī tàidu hěn yóuhǎo.** *The taxi driver is very friendly.*

sīlìng 司令 **N** commander, commanding officer

sīlìngbù 司令部 **N** (military) headquarters

sī 撕 **v** tear (a piece of paper)
撕得粉碎 **sī de fěnsuì** tear into tiny pieces, tear up

sī 私 **ADJ** private

sīrén 私人 [modif: 私 private + 人 person] **I ADJ** private, personal ■ 私人财产受到法律保护。**Sīrén cáichǎn shòudào fǎlǜ bǎohù.** *Private property is protected by the law.* **II N** personal relationship ■ 我和他只是同事，没有私人关系。**Wǒ hé tā zhǐshì tóngshì, méiyǒu sīrén guānxi.** *He and I are colleagues only; we do not have any personal relationship.*

sīzì 私自 **ADV** without permission, secretly
私自决定 **sīzì juédìng** make a decision all by oneself and without permission from the authorities

sī 思 **v** think

sīkǎo 思考 [comp: 思 think + 考 examine] **v** ponder over, reflect on, think seriously
独立思考 **dúlì sīkǎo** think things out for oneself, think independently

sīniàn 思念 [comp: 思 think + 念 miss] **v** miss, think of longingly
思念亲友 **sīniàn qīnyǒu** miss one's family and friends

sīsuǒ 思索 [comp: 思 think + 索 search] **v** think deeply, rack one's brains

sīwéi 思维 **N** thought, thinking, the process of thinking

sīxiǎng 思想 [comp: 思 think + 想 think] **N** thought, thinking ■ 人们的思想是什么决定的？**Rénmen de sīxiǎng shì shénme juédìng de?** *What determines people's thoughts?* ■ 这个孩子怎么会有这种思想呢？**Zhège háizi zěnme huì yǒu**

zhè zhǒng sīxiǎng ne? *How did the child have this kind of thinking?*

sīxù 思绪 **N** train of thought, thoughts

sī 丝 **TRAD** 絲 **N** silk

sīchóu 丝绸 [comp: 丝 silk + 绸 silk cloth] **N** silk, silk cloth ■ 我要买一些丝绸产品，带回去送朋友。**Wǒ yào mǎi yìxiē sīchóu chǎnpǐn, dài huíqu sòng péngyou.** *I want to buy some silk products to take home as gifts for friends.*

sīháo 丝毫 **N** the slightest, in the least
没有丝毫变化 **méiyǒu sīháo biànhuà** without the slightest change, haven't changed in the least

NOTE: 丝毫 **sīháo** is usually used alongside with a negative word, as is shown in the example.

sī 斯 **PRON** this

NOTE: This character was used in Classical Chinese to mean *this*. In Modern Chinese it is normally used just to transliterate foreign names, e.g. 查尔斯 **Chá'ěrsī** for the English name *Charles*.

sīwén 斯文 **ADJ** gentle and mild, refined

sǐ 死 **v** die (**ANTONYM** 活 **huó**) ■ 我家的狗昨天死了。**Wǒ jiā de gǒu zuótiān sǐ le.** *Our family dog died yesterday.* ■ 人总有一死，谁都不能避免。**Rén zǒng yǒu yì sǐ, shuí dōu bù néng bìmiǎn.** *People eventually die. No one can avoid this.*

NOTE: See note on 去世 **qùshì**.

sǐwáng 死亡 **v & N** die, perish; death, doom (**ANTONYM** 生存 **shēncún**)
死亡证 **sǐwáng zhèng** death certificate

sì 四 **NUMERAL** four
四十四 **sìshí sì** forty-four (44) / 四海为家 **sì hǎi wéi jiā** Make the four seas one's home (→ Make one's home wherever one is.)

sìzhī 四肢 **N** the four limbs, arms and legs
四肢发达 **sìzhī fādá** physically strong

sì 寺 **N** monastery, temple

sìmiào 寺庙 **N** temples and monasteries

sì 饲 **TRAD** 飼 **v** raise (animals)

sìyǎng 饲养 [comp: 饲 raise + 养 raise, keep] **v** raise (animals) ■ 这位农民饲养了一百多头猪。**Zhè wèi nóngmín sìyǎng le yībǎi duō tóu zhū.** *This farmer raises over 100 pigs.*

sì wú jì dàn 肆无忌惮 **IDIOM** unbridled, wanton

sì 似 **v** seem

sìhū 似乎 **ADV** it seems, as if ■ 他听了我的话，似乎不大高兴。**Tā tīngle wǒ de huà, sìhū bú dà gāoxìng.** *He seemed unhappy to hear what I had to say.* ■ 我似乎在哪儿见到过他。**Wǒ sìhū zài nǎr jiàndàoguo tā.** *I seem to have met him before somewhere.*

sōng 松 **TRAD** 鬆 **I ADJ** lax, weak (**ANTONYM** 紧 **jǐn**) ■ 这个学校对学生的要求太松。**Zhège xuéxiào duì xuésheng de yāoqiú tài sōng.** *This school demands*

too little of the students. (→ This school does not set a high standard for students.) **II v** loosen, slacken ■ 带子太紧了，要松一下。 **Dàizi tài jǐn le, yào sōng yíxià.** *The belt is too tight. It needs to be loosened.*

sǒng 耸 **TRAD** 聳 **v 1** alarm, alert **2** rise up
耸耸肩膀 sǒng sǒng jiānbǎng shrug one's shoulders

sòng 颂 **TRAD** 頌 **v** praise (See **gēsòng** 歌颂.)

sòng 送 **v 1** give as a gift ■ 去年圣诞节，爸爸送给他一辆自行车。 **Qùnián shèngdànjié, bàba sòng gei tā yí liàng zìxíngchē.** *Last Christmas his father gave him a bike.* **2** deliver ■ 我们可以把你买的电脑送到你家。 **Wǒmen kěyǐ bǎ nǐ mǎi de diànnǎo sòngdào nǐ jiā.** *We can deliver the computer you've bought to your home.* **3** accompany, take, escort ■ 天太晚了，我开车送你回家吧。 **Tiān tài wǎn le, wǒ kāi chē sòng nǐ huíjiā ba.** *It's too late. Let me drive you home.*

sòng 诵 **TRAD** 誦 **v** chant, recite (See **bèisòng** 背诵.)

sōu 搜 **v** search

sōuchá 搜查 [comp: 搜 search + 查 check] **v** search, ransack
搜查证 sōuchá zhèng search warrant

sōují 搜集 [comp: 搜 search + 集 gather] **v** collect, gather
搜集资料 sōují zīliào collect data, data-gathering

sōusuǒ 搜索 **v** search
搜索队 sōusuǒduì search party

sōusuǒ yǐnqíng 搜索引擎 **N** search engine

sōu 艘 **MEASURE WORD** (used with nouns denoting boats and ships)
一艘渔轮 yì sōu yúlún a fishing boat

sòu 嗽 **N** cough (See **késou** 咳嗽.)

sū 苏 **TRAD** 蘇 **v** revive

sūxǐng 苏醒 [comp: 苏 revive + 醒 awake] **v** regain consciousness, come to

sú 俗 **N** custom, convention

súhuà 俗话 **N** traditional saying, common saying

sù 诉 **TRAD** 訴 **v** tell (See **gàosu** 告诉.)

sùsòng 诉讼 **N** lawsuit, litigation
对 … 提出诉讼 duì … tíchū sùsòng file a lawsuit against

sù 肃 **TRAD** 肅 **ADJ** solemn (See **yánsù** 严肃.)

sù 速 **N** speed

sùdù 速度 [modif: 速 speed + 度 degree] **N** speed, velocity ■ 以这样的速度，我们可以在两小时之内到达目的地。 **Yǐ zhèyàng de sùdù, wǒmen kěyǐ zài liǎng xiǎoshí zhīnèi dàodá mùdìdì.** *At this speed, we can reach our destination in two hours.* ■ 你开车超过了限定的速度。 **Nǐ kāichē chāoguòle xiàndìng de sùdù.** *You have exceeded the speed limit.*

sù 素 **ADJ 1** plain, simple (See **pǔsù** 朴素.)
2 vegetarian, non-meat

sùshí 素食 **N** vegetarian food

sùshí zhǔyì 素食主义 **N** vegetarianism
素食主义者 sùshí zhǔyì zhě vegetarian (a person)

sùzhì 素质 **N** (of a person) true quality, very nature

sù 宿 **v** stay overnight

sùshè 宿舍 [modif: 宿 stay overnight + 舍 lodge] **N** hostel, dormitory ■ 我的书忘在宿舍里了！ **Wǒ de shū wàng zài sùshè li le!** *I've left my book in the dormitory.*
学生宿舍 xuésheng sùshè students' hostel (dormitory)

sù 塑 **v** mold

sùliào 塑料 **N** plastic ■ 这种桌椅是用塑料做的，又轻又便宜。 **Zhè zhǒng zhuōyǐ shì yòng sùliào zuò de, yòu qīng yòu piányi.** *These tables and chairs are made of plastic; they are light and inexpensive.*
塑料袋 sùliào dài plastic bag

sùzào 塑造 [comp: 塑 mold + 造 make] **v** sculpture, portray

suān 酸 **ADJ** sour ■ 我不喜欢吃酸的东西。 **Wǒ bù xǐhuan chī suān de dōngxi.** *I don't like to eat sour food.* ■ 这种酒太酸了一点儿。 **Zhè zhǒng jiǔ tài suānle yìdiǎnr.** *This wine is a bit too sour.*

suàn 算 **v 1** calculate ■ 我算一下这个星期花了多少钱。 **Wǒ suàn yíxià zhège xīngqī huāle duōshǎo qián.** *Let me calculate how much money I've spent this week.* ■ 完成这项工程需要多少人工，你算过没有？ **Wánchéng zhè xiàng gōngchéng xūyào duōshǎo réngōng, nǐ suànguo méiyǒu?** *Have you calculated how many man-days will be needed to finish this project?* **2** may be considered as ■ 今天不算冷，昨天才冷呢！ **Jīntiān bú suàn lěng, zuótiān cái lěng ne!** *Today can't be considered as cold. Yesterday was really cold.*

suànle 算了 **v** let it be, forget it

suànshù 算数 **v** count ■ 我说话是算数的。 **Wǒ shuōhuà shì suàn shù de.** *Whatever I say counts. (→ I mean what I say.)*

suī 虽 **TRAD** 雖 **CONJ** although

suīrán 虽然 **CONJ** although, though ■ 虽然已经是秋天了，这两天天气还是很热。 **Suīrán yǐjīng shì qiūtiān le, zhè liǎng tiān tiānqì háishì hěn rè.** *Although it's already autumn, it's still hot these days.* ■ 他虽然赚了很多钱，但是还不满足。 **Tā suīrán zhuànle hěn duō qián, dànshì hái bù mǎnzú.** *Although he's earned a lot of money, he is still dissatisfied.*

NOTE: 虽然 **suīrán** is often used together with 但是 **dànshì** or 但 **dàn** to form the pattern 虽然 … 但(是).

suí 随 **TRAD** 隨 **v** let (somebody do as he pleases), as you wish ■ 这件事和我没有关系，随你处理。 **Zhè jiàn shì hé wǒ méiyǒu guānxi, suí nǐ chǔlǐ.** *This matter is none of my businesses. You can deal with it the way you like.*

suíbiàn 随便 **ADJ** casual, informal ■ 中饭我们

随便吃一点，晚上我请你到饭店去好好吃一顿。**Zhōngfàn wǒmen suíbiàn chī yìdiǎn, wǎnshang wǒ qǐng nǐ dào fàndiàn qu hǎohǎo chī yí dùn.** *For lunch we'll have a casual meal. In the evening I'll take you to a restaurant for a square meal.*

NOTE: 随便 **suíbiàn** is often used in casual conversation to mean something like *as you wish, anything you like,* or *I have no objection whatsoever.* e.g. ■ "你喝红茶还是绿茶？""随便。" **"Nǐ hē hóngchá háishì lǜchá?" "Suíbiàn."** *"Do you want to drink black tea or green tea?" "Anything's fine with me."*

suíjí 随即 ADV immediately, soon after

suíshēn 随身 ADV (carry) on one's person, bring with one

suíshí 随时 ADV whenever, at any moment ■ 你有问题，可以随时给我打电话。**Nǐ yǒu wèntí, kěyǐ suíshí gěi wǒ dǎ diànhuà.** *If you have a problem, you can call me anytime.*

suíshǒu 随手 ADV 1 immediately ■ 请随手关门。**Qǐng suíshǒu guānmén.** *Please close the door after you.* 2 casually, without much thought

随手乱放 **suíshǒu luàn fàng** put … somewhere casually and without much thought

suíyì 随意 ADV 1 as one pleases, casually 2 random

随意抽样 **suíyì chōuyàng** random sampling

suízhe 随着 PREP along with, in the wake of

suì 岁 TRAD 歲 MEASURE WORD year (of age) ■ 我小弟弟今年八岁。**Wǒ xiǎo dìdi jīnnián bā suì.** *My younger brother is eight years old.*

NOTE: See 年纪 **niánjì**.

suìyuè 岁月 N years and months, time

suì 碎 ADJ broken, fragmentary ■ 车窗的玻璃被一块石头打碎了。**Chēchuāng de bōli bèi yí kuài shítou dǎ suì le.** *The car window was shattered by a stone.*

suì 隧 N tunnel

suìdào 隧道 N underground passage, tunnel

sūn 孙 TRAD 孫 N grandchild

sūnnǚ 孙女 N granddaughter

sūnzi 孙子 N grandson

sǔn 损 TRAD 損 V damage

sǔnhuài 损坏 [v+compl: 损 damage + 坏 out of order] V damage to render unusable, damage

损坏公物 **sǔnhuài gōngwù** damage public property

sǔnshī 损失 [comp: 损 damage + 失 loss] V & N lose, suffer from damage and/or loss; loss, damage ■ 由于他的错误决定，公司损失了五十万元。**Yóuyú tā de cuòwù juédìng, gōngsī sǔnshīle wǔshíwàn yuán.** *Owing to his wrong decision, the company lost half a million yuan.* ■ 这次水灾造成巨大损失。**Zhè cì shuǐzāi zàochéng jùdà sǔnshī.** *This flooding caused huge losses.*

suō 缩 TRAD 縮 V shrink (ANTONYM 胀 **zhàng**) ■ 棉布下水以后会缩。**Miánbù xiàshuǐ yǐhòu huì suō.** *Cotton cloth will shrink in the wash.*

suōduǎn 缩短 [v+compl: 缩 shrink + 短 short] V shorten ■ 由于使用了新型飞机，这段航程的时间缩短了一小时。**Yóuyú shǐyòng le xīnxíng fēijī, zhè duàn hángchéng de shíjiān suōduǎn le yī xiǎoshí.** *Thanks to the use of a new model airplane, the flight time is shortened by one hour.*

suǒ 所 MEASURE WORD (for houses or institutions housed in a building)

一所医院 **yì suǒ yīyuàn** a hospital / 两所大学 **liǎng suǒ dàxué** two universities

suǒwèi 所谓 ADJ what is called, so-called ■ 他所谓的"理由"完全站不住脚。**Tā suǒwèi de "lǐyóu" wánquán zhàn bu zhù jiǎo.** *His so-called "reason" does not have a leg to stand on.*

suǒyǐ 所以 CONJ therefore, so ■ 因为家里有事，所以她今天没来上班。**Yīnwèi jiā li yǒu shì, suǒyǐ tā jīntiān méi lái shàngbān.** *There was an emergency in her family; therefore, she did not come to work today.*

NOTE: See note on 因为 **yīnwèi**.

suǒyǒu 所有 ADJ all ■ 所有的朋友都反对他的计划。**Suǒyǒu de péngyou dōu fǎnduì tā de jìhuà.** *All his friends are opposed to his plan.*

NOTES: 所有 **suǒyǒu** is (1) used only as an attribute, (2) always followed by 的 **de,** and (3) often used together with 都 **dōu.**

suǒ 索 V search

suǒpéi 索赔 [v+obj: 索 search for + 赔 compensation] V claim damages, claim indemnity

suǒqǔ 索取 [comp: 索 search + 取 take] V ask for, exact

索取报名单 **suǒqǔ bàomíngdān** ask for an application form

suǒxìng 索性 ADV might as well, simply

suǒ 锁 TRAD 鎖 N & V lock ■ 门打不开，恐怕是锁坏了。**Mén dǎ bu kāi, kǒngpà shì suǒ huài le.** *The door can't be opened. I'm afraid something is wrong with the lock.* ■ 离开以前一定要把办公室的门锁上。**Líkāi yǐqián yídìng yào bǎ bàngōngshì de mén suǒ shàng.** *Before you leave, make sure you lock the office door.*

T

tā 他 PRON he, him ■ "他是谁？""他是我的同学。" **"Tā shì shéi?" "Tā shì wǒ de tóngxué."** *"Who's he?" "He's my classmate."* ■ 他的朋友都叫他小王。**Tā de péngyou dōu jiào tā Xiǎo Wáng.** *His friends all call him Xiao Wang.*

tāmen 他们 [suffix: 他 he, him + 们 suffix de-

noting a plural number] PRON they, them ■ 他们
有困难，我们要帮助他们。**Tāmen yǒu kùnnan,
wǒmen yào bāngzhù tāmen.** *As they're in difficulty, we should help them.* ■ 这是他们的问题，
我们没有办法。**Zhè shì tāmen de wèntí, wǒmen
méiyǒu bànfǎ.** *This is their problem. There's nothing we can do.*

tā 它 PRON it ■ 它是我的小狗。**Tā shì wǒ de xiǎo
gǒu.** *It's my puppy.*

tāmen 它们 [suffix: 它 it + 们 suffix denoting a
plural number] PRON (non-human) they, them (plural form of 它 **tā**)

tā 她 PRON she, her ■ 她是我班上的女同学。**Tā shì
wǒ bānshang de nǚ tóngxué.** *She's a girl student in
my class.*

tāmen 她们 [suffix: 她 she, her + 们 suffix denoting a plural number] PRON (female) they, them

tā 塌 V collapse, cave

tāshi 踏实 ADJ 1 down-to-earth, steadfast 2 peace
of mind, free from anxiety

tǎ 塔 N pagoda, tower (座 **zuò**) ■ 在中国几乎每一
个城市都有一座古塔。**Zài Zhōngguó jīhū měi yí
ge chéngshì dōu yǒu yí zuò gǔ tǎ.** *In China almost
every town has an ancient tower.*

tāi 胎 N 1 fetus, embryo 2 padding, stuffing (See
lúntāi 轮胎.)

tái 台 TRAD 檯 I N table, desk (张 **zhāng**) ■ 董事长
坐在一张大写字台后面。**Dǒngshìzhǎng zuò zai yì
zhāng dà xiězìtái hòumiàn.** *The chairman of the
board sat behind a large desk.* II MEASURE WORD (for
machines, big instruments, etc.)

一台机器 yì tái jīqì a machine

táifēng 台风 N typhoon, tropical cyclone
(场 **cháng**)

táijiē 台阶 N flight of steps, step

táishìjī 台式机 N desktop PC

Táiwān 台湾 N Taiwan

tái 抬 V lift, raise ■ 来，咱们俩把桌子抬到外边
去。**Lái, zánmen liǎ bǎ zhuōzi táidào wàibian qù.**
Come on; let's move the table outside.

抬高 táigāo raise (prices)

tài 太 ADV 1 excessively, too ■ 今天我太累了，不
去游泳了。**Jīntiān wǒ tài lèi le, bú qù yóuyǒng le.**
Today I'm too tired to go swimming. ■ 这个房间
太小，坐不下二十个人。**Zhège fángjiān tài xiǎo,
zuò bu xià èrshí ge rén.** *This room is too small. It
can't seat twenty people.* 2 extremely, really ■ 太
好了！**Tài hǎo le!** *That's wonderful!* ■ 你们现在
抬高物价，太不讲道理了。**Nǐmen xiànzài táigāo
wùjià, tài bù jiǎng dàolǐ le.** *It is extremely unreasonable of you to raise prices now.*

Tàijíquán 太极拳 N shadow boxing, Taichi

tàikōng 太空 N outer space, firmament

tàitai 太太 N 1 Mrs ■ 王先生和王太太常在家
里请客吃饭。**Wáng xiānsheng hé Wáng tàitai
chángcháng zài jiā li qǐngkè chīfàn.** *Mr and Mrs*

Wang often give dinner parties in their home.
2 wife ■ 您太太刚才打电话来。**Nín tàitai gāngcái
dǎ diànhuà lai.** *Your wife called just now.* ■ 今天
是我太太生日，我要早一点回家。**Jīntiān shì wǒ
tàitai shēngrì, wǒ yào zǎo yìdiǎn huíjiā.** *Today's my
wife's birthday. I need go home earlier.*

NOTE: (1) While *Mrs* is used in English-speaking
countries regardless of class or social status, its
Chinese counterpart 太太 **tàitai** is only used in
middle-class or upper-class circles. (2) Although
Chinese women often retain their family names
after marriage, 太太 **tàitai** as a form of address must
be prefixed by the husband's family name.

tàiyang 太阳 [modif: 太 big, super + 阳 open,
overt, masculine] N the sun, sunshine ■ 今天的
太阳真好。**Jīntiān de tàiyang zhēn hǎo.** *The sunshine's beautiful today.*

NOTE: (1) Put together, 太 **tài** (meaning *big, great* in
classical Chinese) and 阳 **yáng** (meaning *Yang of
ancient Chinese thought*) mean the ultimate *Yang,*
as the sun is the ultimate symbol of *Yang.* The ultimate symbol of *Yin* is the moon 月 **yuè.** (2) In 太阳
tàiyang, 阳 **yang** is pronounced in the neutral tone.

tài 态 TRAD 態 N stance

tàidu 态度 [comp: 态 stance + 度 appearance,
bearing] N attitude, approach ■ 这位服务员的服务
态度很好。**Zhè wèi fúwùyuán de fúwù tàidu hěn
hǎo.** *This attendant's work attitude is good.* ■ 这孩
子说话态度不好，常惹人生气。**Zhè háizi shuōhuà
tàidu bù hǎo, cháng rě rén shēngqì.** *This child's
manner of speaking is bad, and is often offensive.*

NOTE: Though 态度 **tàidu** is glossed as *attitude* or
approach, it is more commonly used in Chinese
than its equivalents in English.

tài 泰 ADJ peace, safe ■ 国泰民安 **Guó tài mín ān**
The country is safe and the people live in peace

tàidǒu 泰斗 N authority, guru, master

tān 贪 TRAD 貪 I V be greedy II ADJ corrupt

tānguān 贪官 N corrupt official

tānlán 贪婪 ADJ greedy, avaricious

tānwū 贪污 [comp: 贪 corrupt + 污 filthy] V & N
embezzle, be involved in corruption; embezzle-
ment, corruption

贪污犯 tānwūfàn embezzler, grafter / 贪污公款
tānwū gōngkuǎn embezzle public funds

tān 摊 TRAD 攤 N vendor's stand, stall

摊儿 tānr vendor's stand, stall ■ 路两边摆了很多
摊儿，有卖吃的，也有卖工艺品的。**Lù liǎngbiān
bǎile hěn duō tānr, yǒu mài chī de, yě yǒu mài
gōngyìpǐn de.** *There are many stands on the two
sides of the street; some sell food and others sell
small handicraft articles.*

tān 瘫 TRAD 癱 V be paralyzed

tānhuàn 瘫痪 **v & n** be paralyzed; paralysis
全身瘫痪 quánshēn tānhuàn complete paralysis

tán 谈 **trad** 談 **v** talk, discuss ■ 我想跟你谈一件
事。**Wǒ xiǎng gēn nǐ tán yí jiàn shì.** *I'd like to
discuss something with you.*
谈一下 tán yíxià talk briefly about, give a brief
talk about ■ 请你谈一下去中国旅行的情况。**Qǐng
nǐ tán yíxià qù Zhōngguó lǚxíng de qíngkuàng.**
Please give a brief talk about your trip to China.

tánhuà 谈话 [comp: 谈 talk + 话 talk] **v & n**
have a (serious, formal) talk; talk ■ 校长找我谈
话。**Xiàozhǎng zhǎo wǒ tánhuà.** *The principal
summoned me for a talk.*

tánpàn 谈判 **v & n** negotiate; negotiation ■ 双方正
在为签订一项合同谈判。**Shuāngfāng zhèngzài wèi
qiāndìng yí xiàng hétóng tánpàn.** *The two sides
are negotiating the signing of a contract.* ■ 这项
谈判在进行了三个星期以后终于取得双方满意的
结果。**Zhè xiàng tánpàn zài jìnxíngle sān ge xīngqī
yǐhòu zhōngyú qǔdé shuāngfāng mǎnyì de jiéguǒ.**
*After three weeks the negotiations finally reached
a conclusion that satisfied both parties.*

tántiān 谈天 **v** chat, chitchat ■ 上班的时候，不能
谈天。**Shàngbān de shíhou, bù néng tántiān.** *You
are not supposed to chat during working hours.*

tán 弹 **trad** 彈 **v** pluck, catapult

tán gāngqín 弹钢琴 **v** play the piano

tánxìng 弹性 **n** elasticity, flexibility
有弹性的 yǒu tánxìng de flexible

tán 坛 **trad** 壇 **n** altar
天坛 tiāntán the Temple of Heaven (in Beijing)

tǎn 毯 **n** blanket, rug, tapestry, carpet
羊毛毯 yángmáotǎn woolen blanket

tǎnzi 毯子 [suffix: 毯 blanket + 子 nominal suffix]
n blanket (条 tiáo) ■ 中国人一般不用毯子，而用
被子。**Zhōngguórén yìbān bú yòng tǎnzi, ér yòng
bèizi.** *The Chinese usually do not use blankets, but
use quilts.*

tǎn 坦 **adj** 1 candid, frank 2 level, smooth
平坦 píngtǎn (of land) level and expansive

tǎnbái 坦白 **v** 1 confess to (crimes or wrongdoing), owe up to ■ 坦白从宽，抗拒从严。**Tǎnbái
cóng kuān, kàngjù cóng yán.** *Leniency to those
who confess and severity to those who refuse to.*
2 be frank, be candid, guileless

tǎnshuài 坦率 **adj** frank, candid
坦率地说 tǎnshuài de shuō to be frank with you,
to tell the truth

tàn 探 **v** explore

tàncè 探测 [comp: 探 explore + 测 test] **v** survey,
probe

tànsuǒ 探索 [comp: 探 explore + 索 search] **v**
explore, seek, search for ■ 医生们正在探索医治这
种疾病的方法。**Yīshēngmen zhèngzài tànsuǒ yīzhì
zhè zhǒng jíbìng de fāngfǎ.** *Doctors are searching
for a way to cure this disease.*

tàntǎo 探讨 [comp: 探 explore + 讨 discuss] **v**
explore and discuss, inquire into
探讨… 的可行性 tàntǎo… de kěxíngxìng explore
the feasibility of …

tànwàng 探望 [comp: 探 visit + 望 see] **v** go to
see, visit
探望病人 tànwàng bìngrén visit someone who is
sick, visit a patient

tànxiǎn 探险 [v+obj: 探 explore + 险 danger] **v**
venture into, explore

tànxiǎn duì 探险队 **n** exploration team

tànxiǎn jiā 探险家 **n** explorer

tàn 叹 **trad** 嘆 **v** sigh

tànqì 叹气 [v+obj: 叹 sigh + 气 air] **v** heave a
sigh, sigh

tàn 碳 **n** carbon (See **èr yǎng huà tàn** 二氧化
碳.)

tāng 汤 **trad** 湯 **n** soup (碗 **wǎn**) ■ 妈妈做的汤真
好喝。**Māma zuò de tāng zhēn hǎohē.** *The soup
mom prepared is really delicious.*
喝汤 hē tāng eat soup

táng 堂 **n** hall, main room (See **lǐtáng** 礼堂, **shítáng** 食堂.)

táng 糖 **n** sugar, candy (块 **kuài**) ■ "你的咖啡里
要放糖吗？" "要，请放一块糖。" **"Nǐ de kāfēi
li yào fàng táng ma?" "Yào, qǐng fàng yí kuài
táng."** *"Do you want sugar in your coffee?" "Yes,
a lump of sugar, please."*

tángguǒ 糖果 **n** candy, sweets ■ 小孩儿一般
都喜欢吃糖果。**Xiǎo háir yìbān dòu xǐhuan chī
tángguǒ.** *Children usually love candy.*

táng húlu 糖葫芦 **n** sugar-coated haws, crab
apples, etc. stringed on a stick

tǎng 倘 **conj** if, in case

tǎngruò 倘若 **conj** if, in case

tǎng 躺 **v** lie ■ 她喜欢躺在床上看书。**Tā xǐhuan
tǎng zài chuángshang kànshū.** *She likes to lie on
bed and read.* ■ 你既然醒了，就起床吧，别躺在
床上了。**Nǐ jìrán xǐngle, jiù qǐchuáng ba, bié tǎng
zài chuángshang le.** *Now that you've been awake,
you should get up. Don't lie in bed.*

tàng 趟 **measure word** (for trips) ■ 我去了两
趟，都没找到他。**Wǒ qùle liǎng tàng, dōu méi
zhǎodào tā.** *I made two trips but did not find him.*

tàng 烫 **trad** 燙 **adj** boiling hot, scalding hot, burning hot ■ 这碗汤太烫了，没法喝。**Zhè wǎn tāng tài
tàng le, méifǎ hē.** *This bowl of soup is too hot to eat.*

tāo 掏 **v** pull out, draw out
掏耳朵 tāo ěrduo pick one's ears

tāo 滔 **v** inundate, flood

tāo tāo bù jué 滔滔不绝 **idiom** talking on and on
in a flow of eloquence

táo 逃 **v** flee, run away (from danger, punishment,
etc.) ■ 警察来的时候，强盗已经逃走了。**Jǐngchá
lái de shíhou, qiángdào yǐjīng táozǒu le.** *By the
time the policemen arrived, the robbers had fled.*

táobì 逃避 [comp: 逃 flee + 避 avoid] v evade, shirk 逃避责任 táobì zérèn evade responsibility

táo 陶[1] N pottery

táocí 陶瓷 [comp: 陶 pottery + 瓷 porcelain] N pottery and porcelain, ceramics

táoqì 陶器 N pottery, earthenware

táo 陶[2] ADJ contented and happy

táozuì 陶醉 [comp: 陶 contented and happy + 醉 drunk] v revel in, be intoxicated

táo 淘 v wash in a pan or basket

táoqì 淘气 ADJ naughty, mischievous

táotài 淘汰 v eliminate through competition

táotàisài 淘汰赛 N (in sports) elimination series, knock-out rounds

tǎo 讨 TRAD 討 v ask for

tǎohǎo 讨好 v 1 fawn on, toady to 2 be rewarded with good results 吃力不讨好 chīlì bù tǎohǎo work hard only to get negative results, do a thankless job

tǎo jià huán jià 讨价还价 v haggle over prices, bargain

tǎolùn 讨论 [comp: 讨 explore + 论 discuss] v & N discuss; discussion ■ 我们要讨论一下才能作出决定。**Wǒmen yào tǎolùn yíxià cái néng zuòchū juédìng.** We must have a discussion before we can make a decision. ■ 这次讨论对我们很有用。**Zhè cì tǎolùn duì wǒmen hěn yǒuyòng.** This discussion is useful to us.

tǎoyàn 讨厌 [v+obj: 讨 ask for + 厌 boredom, vexation] v & ADJ loathe, dislike; disgusting, annoying ■ 我讨厌连续下雨的天气。**Wǒ tǎoyàn liánxù xiàyǔ de tiānqì.** I hate incessant rain. ■ 这种电视广告讨厌得很。**Zhè zhǒng diànshì guǎnggào tǎoyàn de hěn.** This kind of TV commercial is disgusting.

tào 套 MEASURE WORD set, suit, suite (for a collection of things) 一套衣服 yí tào yīfu a suit of clothes / 两套家具 liǎng tào jiājù two sets of furniture

tè 特 ADV particularly, especially

tèbié 特别 [comp: 特 special + 别 other, unusual] ADJ special, especially ■ 他病得很重，住在特别病房。**Tā bìng de hěn zhòng, zhù zài tèbié bìngfáng.** He's seriously ill and stays in the special ward.

tècháng 特长 N one's special skill, strong points

tèdiǎn 特点 [modif: 特 special + 点 point] N special features, characteristic ■ 中国文化有什么特点？**Zhōngguó wénhuà yǒu shénme tèdiǎn?** What are the special features of Chinese culture?

tèdìng 特定 [comp: 特 special + 定 definite] ADJ specific, specified, special 特定的条件 tèdìngde tiáojiàn special condition

tèsè 特色 [modif: 特 special + 色 color] N salient feature, characteristic

tèshū 特殊 [comp: 特 special + 殊 different] ADJ special, unusual, exceptional ■ 你只有在特殊情

况下才能采取这一措施。**Nǐ zhǐyǒu zài tèshū qíngkuàng xia cái néng cǎiqǔ zhè yí cuòshī.** Only under special circumstances can you take this step. ■ 每个公民都必须遵守法律，没有人可以特殊。**Měi ge gōngmín dōu bìxū zūnshǒu fǎlù, méiyǒu rén kéyǐ tèshū.** Every citizen must obey the law and nobody can be an exception.

tèyì 特意 [modif: 特 special + 意 intention] ADV for a special purpose, specially

tèzhēng 特征 [modif: 特 special + 征 feature] N characteristic, feature

téng 疼 v 1 ache, hurt ■ 我头疼，得躺一会儿。**Wǒ tóu téng, děi tǎng yíhuìr.** I have a headache. I have to lie down for a while. 头疼 tóu téng headache, have a headache

NOTE: 疼 **téng** in the sense of *ache, hurt* is a colloquial word. You can use 痛 **tòng** instead of 疼 **téng** to mean *ache, hurt.*

2 love dearly ■ 我小时候，我奶奶可疼我了。**Wǒ xiǎoshíhou, wǒ nǎinai kě téng wǒ le.** When I was a child, my granny really loved me dearly.

téngài 疼爱 same as 疼 **téng 2**

tī 梯 N ladder, steps (See **diàntī** 电梯, **lóutī** 楼梯.)

tī 踢 v kick 踢球 tī qiú play soccer / tī zúqiú 踢足球 play soccer

tí 提 v 1 carry in the hand (with the arm down) ■ 我可以提这个小皮箱上飞机吗？**Wǒ kéyǐ tí zhège xiǎo píxiāng shàng fēijī ma?** Can I carry this small bag on board the plane? **2** mention ■ 你见到他的时候，别提这件事。**Nǐ jiàndào tā de shíhou, bié tí zhè jiàn shì.** Don't mention this matter when you see him. 提建议 tí jiànyì put forward a proposal, make a suggestion / 提问题 tí wèntí raise a question

tíbá 提拔 v promote (to a higher position) 提拔为部门经理 tíba wéi bùmén jīnglǐ promote to branch manager

tíchàng 提倡 [comp: 提 put forward + 倡 advocate] v advocate, recommend ■ 政府提倡一对夫妻只生一个孩子。**Zhèngfǔ tíchàng yí duì fūqī zhǐ shēng yí ge háizi.** The government recommends that every couple has only one child.

tígāng 提纲 N outline

tígāo 提高 [v+compl: 提 raise + 高 high] v raise, advance ■ 我要提高自己的中文水平。**Wǒ yào tígāo zìjǐ de Zhōngwén shuǐpíng.** I want to raise my proficiency in Chinese. ■ 我们不断提高产品的质量。**Wǒmen búduàn tígāo chǎnpǐn de zhìliàng.** We work constantly to improve the quality of our products.

tígōng 提供 [comp: 提 put forward + 供 supply] v provide, supply ■ 我们提供售后服务。**Wǒmen tígōng shòuhòu fúwù.** We provide after-sales service. ■ 这项研究为决定政策提供了有力的数

据。 **Zhè xiàng yánjiū wèi juédìng zhèngcè tígōngle yǒulì de shùjù.** *This research provided solid data for policy-making.*

tíliàn 提炼 v extract and purify, refine

tíqián 提前 [v+obj: 提 put forward + 前 forward] v put ahead of schedule, advance ■ 你知道吗？考试提前两天举行。 **Nǐ zhīdào ma? Kǎoshì tíqián liǎng tiān jǔxíng.** *Do you know that the examination will be held two days earlier?*

tíshì 提示 v hint, tip ■ 给我一个提示，好吗？ **Gěi wǒ yí ge tíshì, hǎoma?** *Can you give me a hint?*

tíwèn 提问 v put questions to, quiz

tíxǐng 提醒 v remind, call attention to

tíyì 提议 v & n propose; proposal ■ 我提议为主人的健康干杯！ **Wǒ tíyì wèi zhǔrén de jiànkāng gānbēi!** *May I propose a toast to the health of our host?*

tí 题 TRAD 題 n topic, question

tícái 题材 [comp: 题 topic + 材 material] n subject matter, theme

tímù 题目 n 1 question for an examination, school exercises, etc. (道 **dào**) ■ 这次测验一共有十道题目。 **Zhè cì cèyàn yígòng yǒu shí dào tímù.** *There will be ten questions in this test.* 2 title, subject ■ 他要给文章取一个好题目。 **Tā yào gěi wénzhāng qǔ yí ge hǎo tímù.** *He will give his essay a good title.*

tǐ 体 TRAD 體 I n human body, body II v experience personally, feel intimately

tǐcái 体裁 n literary genre

tǐhuì 体会 [comp: 体 experience personally + 会 understand] v & n gain intimate knowledge through personal experience, realize; personal understanding through experience ■ 他当了一年爸爸，体会到当父母是多么不容易。 **Tā dāngle yì nián bàba, tǐhuì dào dāng fùmǔ shì duōme bù róngyì.** *After being a father for a year, he realized how difficult parenting was.* ■ 请你谈谈你在中国工作的体会。 **Qǐng nǐ tántan nǐ zài Zhōngguó gōngzuò de tǐhuì.** *Please tell us what you have learned from working in China.*

tǐjī 体积 n volume (mathematics) ■ 这个箱子体积不大，为什么这么重？ **Zhège xiāngzi tǐjī bú dà, wèishénme zhème zhòng?** *This box is not big. Why is it so heavy?*

tǐliàng 体谅 [comp: 体 experience personally + 谅 forgive] v show understanding toward, be sympathetic to, make allowance for

体谅他人的难处 **tǐliàng tārén de nánchu** understand and sympathize with other people's difficulties

tǐmiàn 体面 I ADJ respectable, decent II n dignity, face

tǐtiē 体贴 v give every consideration to, give loving care to

tǐwēn 体温 n (body) temperature

NOTE: See the notes on 温度 **wēndù.**

tǐxì 体系 n system, setup

tǐxiàn 体现 v give expressions to, embody

tǐyàn 体验 n & v personal experience; learn through one's personal experience

tǐyù 体育 [modif: 体 physical + 育 education] n physical education, sports ■ 体育和学习，哪个更重要？ **Tǐyù hé xuéxí, nǎge gèng zhòngyào?** *Sports or study, which is more important?*

tǐyùchǎng 体育场 [modif: 体育 sports + 场 ground] n stadium ■ 体育场里正在举行一场精彩的足球比赛。 **Tǐyùchǎng li zhèngzài jǔxíng yì chǎng jīngcǎi de zúqiú bǐsài.** *A thrilling football match is going on in the stadium.*

tǐyùguǎn 体育馆 [modif: 体育 sports + 馆 building] n gymnasium ■ 这个体育馆有多少座位？ **Zhège tǐyùguǎn yǒu duōshǎo zuòwèi?** *How many seats are there in this gymnasium?*

tǐyù kè 体育课 n physical education (PE) lesson

tì 替 v 1 replace, substitute ■ 万一他生病了，谁来替他呢？ **Wànyī tā shēngbìng le, shuí lái tì tā ne?** *If he falls ill, who will replace him?* 2 same as 给 **gěi** PREP

tiān 天 n 1 sky, heaven ■ 秋天，天特别蓝。 **Qiūtiān, tiān tèbié lán.** *In autumn, the sky is especially blue.* 2 day ■ 我在朋友家住了三天。 **Wǒ zài péngyou jiā zhùle sān tiān.** *I stayed with my friend for three days.* ■ 这位老人下雨天一般不出去。 **Zhè wèi lǎorén xià yǔ tiān yìbān bù chūqu.** *This old man normally does not go out on rainy days.* 3 weather ■ 农民还是靠天吃饭。 **Nóngmín háishì kào tiān chīfàn.** *Peasants still depend on the weather to make a living.* 4 abode of gods, Heaven ■ 天知道! **Tiān zhīdào!** *Only God knows!*

老天爷 **Lǎotiānyé** Heavens (a colloquial term that denotes "God" or "Nature") ■ 老天爷再不下雨，就要闹灾了。 **Lǎotiānyé zài bú xià yǔ, jiù yào nào zāi le.** *If it does not rain, there'll be disaster.*

tiāncái 天才 [modif: 天 heavenly + 才 talent] n genius ■ 他们的儿子非常聪明，但是并不是天才。 **Tāmen de érzi fēicháng cōngming, dànshì bìng bù shì tiāncái.** *Their son is very smart, but he isn't a genius.*

tiānfù 天赋 n natural gift, great talent

tiānkōng 天空 [comp: 天 sky + 空 empty] n sky

tiānlún 天伦 n natural bonds and ethical relationships among members of a family

tiānlún zhī lè 天伦之乐 n happiness out of the natural bonds and ethical relationship among family members, family happiness

tiānqì 天气 [comp: 天 weather + 气 weather] n weather ■ 天气变化很大。 **Tiānqì biànhuà hěn dà.** *The weather changes dramatically.* ■ 明天的天气怎么样？ **Míngtiān de tiānqì zěnmeyàng?** *How will the weather be tomorrow?*

tiānrán 天然 ADJ natural

tiānránqì 天然气 n natural gas

tiānshang 天上 **ADV** in the sky

tiānshēng 天生 **ADJ** inherent, natural

tiāntáng 天堂 [modif: 天 heaven + 堂 hall] **N** paradise

tiāntiān 天天 **ADV** every day, from day to day

tiānwén 天文 **N** astronomy

tiānwéntái 天文台 **N** astronomical observatory

tiānwénxué 天文学 **N** astronomy

tiānxià 天下 **ADV** under heaven, in the world, on earth

tiānzhēn 天真 [comp: 天 natural + 真 genuine] **ADJ** 1 simple and unaffected, ingenuous ■ 和天真的孩子说话，是一种享受。**Hé tiānzhēn de háizi shuōhuà, shì yì zhǒng xiǎngshòu.** *Talking with innocent children is an enjoyment.* 2 naive, gullible ■ 你怎么会相信这种广告？太天真了！**Nǐ zěnme huì xiāngxìn zhè zhǒng guǎnggào? Tài tiānzhēn le!** *How could you believe such advertisements? You're too naive!*

tiān 添 **V** add ■ 你这么忙，我不想给你添麻烦。**Nǐ zhème máng, wǒ bù xiǎng gěi nǐ tiān máfan.** *You're so busy. I don't want to add to your trouble.*

tián 田 **N** farmland (especially paddy fields), fields ■ 他在田里干活。**Tā zài tián li gànhuó.** *He was working in the fields.*

种田 zhòngtián grow crops, farm ■ 在中国光靠种田，很难富。**Zài Zhōngguó guāng kào zhòngtián, hěn nán fù.** *In China, it's difficult to get rich simply by growing crops.*

tiánjìng 田径 **N** track and field events

tiányě 田野 [comp: 田 fields, farmland + 野 old country] **N** farmland and open country ■ 城里人有时候喜欢到田野走走。**Chénglǐrén yǒushíhou xǐhuan dào tiányě zǒuzǒu.** *City people like to take an occasional walk in the open country.*

tián 填 **V** fill in (a form, blanks as in an exercise) ■ 进入一个国家要填表，离开一个国家也要填表。**Jìnrù yí ge guójiā yào tián biǎo, líkāi yí ge guójiā yě yào tián biǎo.** *To enter a country you need to fill in a form, and to leave a country you need to fill in a form as well.*

tiánkòng 填空 **V** fill in blanks

tián 甜 **ADJ** sweet, honeyed

tiánshí 甜食 **N** sweet food, dessert

tiǎn 舔 **V** lick, lap

tiāo 挑 **V** take one's pick, choose, select ■ 商店里这么多鞋子，你还挑不到一双喜欢的？**Shàngdiàn li zhème duō xiézi, nǐ hái tiāo bu dào yì shuāng xǐhuan de?** *There are so many shoes in the store, and you still can't choose a pair you like?*

东挑西拣 dōng tiāo xī jiǎn choose this and pick that, spend a long time choosing, be very choosy

tiāotī 挑剔 **V** nitpick, be hypercritical, be fastidious

tiāoxuǎn 挑选 [comp: 挑 take one's pick + 选 select] **V** select ■ 董事会要从经理中挑选出一名总经理。**Dǒngshìhuì yào cóng jīnglǐ zhong tiāoxuǎnchu yì míng zǒngjīnglǐ.** *The board of directors will select a chief executive officer from the executives.* ■ 有时候可以挑选的东西太多，很难决定。**Yǒushíhou kěyǐ tiāoxuǎn de dōngxi tài duō, hěn nán juédìng.** *Sometimes when there are too many things to choose from, it's difficult to decide.*

tiáo 条 **TRAD** 條 **MEASURE WORD** (for things with a long, narrow shape)

一条河 yì tiáo hé a river / 两条鱼 liǎng tiáo yú two fish

tiáojiàn 条件 **N** 1 condition ■ 这个地区的自然条件不好。**Zhège dìqū de zìrán tiáojiàn bù hǎo.** *The natural conditions of this region are rather poor.*

生活条件 shēnghuó tiáojiàn living conditions ■ 他们那里的生活条件比较差。**Tāmen nàlǐ de shēnghuó tiáojiàn bǐjiào chà.** *Their living conditions are rather poor.*

工作条件 gōngzuò tiáojiàn working conditions ■ 工人们要求改善工作条件。**Gōngrénmen yāoqiú gǎishàn gōngzuò tiáojiàn.** *Workers demand that their working conditions be improved.*

2 requirement, prerequisite ■ 她找对象的条件非常高。**Tā zhǎo duìxiàng de tiáojiàn fēicháng gāo.** *She has very high requirements of a fiancé.* ■ 对方的条件太高，我们无法合作。**Duìfāng de tiáojiàn tài gāo, wǒmen wúfǎ hézuò.** *The other party's requirements are too high for us to work with them.*

tiáokuǎn 条款 **N** clause (in a contract, an agreement, etc.) (项 **xiàng**)

tiáolǐ 条理 **N** orderliness

有条理 yǒu tiáolǐ well-organized

tiáoyuē 条约 [comp: 条 article (of a treaty) + 约 agreement] **N** treaty, pact (份 **fèn**) ■ 两国将签订条约，以加强合作。**Liǎng guó jiāng qiāndìng tiáoyuē, yǐ jiāqiáng hézuò.** *The two countries will sign a treaty in order to strengthen cooperation.*

tiáo 调 **TRAD** 調 **V** adjust

tiáohé 调和 **V** 1 mediate, reconcile 2 comprise

tiáojì 调剂 **V** adjust, regulate

tiáojié 调节 **V** regulate, adjust

调节器 tiáojiéqì regulator, conditioner

tiáojiě 调解 [comp: 调 adjust + 解 solve] **V** mediate, make peace

调解纠纷 tiáojiě jiūfēn mediate a dipute

tiáoliào 调料 **N** condiment, seasoning

tiáopí 调皮 **ADJ** naughty, mischievous

tiáozhěng 调整 [comp: 调 adjust + 整 rectify] **V** adjust, rectify ■ 教育部打算调整中小学的师生比例。**Jiàoyùbù dǎsuàn tiáozhěng zhōng-xiǎoxué de shīshēng bǐlì.** *The Ministry of Education plans to adjust the teacher-student ratio in schools.*

tiǎo 挑 **V** poke, pick up

tiǎobō 挑拨 [comp: 挑 poke + 拨 stir] **V** sow discord, instigate

挑拨同事之间的关系 tiǎobō tóngshì zhījiān de guānxi sow discord among colleagues

tiǎoxìn 挑衅 [v+obj: 挑 pick up + 衅 quarrel] **v & N** provoke; provocation

故意挑衅 gùyì tiǎoxìn deliberate provocation

tiǎozhàn 挑战 v & N challenge to battle, challenge to a contest, throw down the gauntlet; challenge

tiào 跳 v jump ■ 他跳得很高，所以篮球打得好。**Tā tiào de hěn gāo, suǒyǐ lánqiú dǎ de hǎo.** *He can jump high, so he plays basketball well.*

tiàogāo 跳高 N high jump

tiàoshéng 跳绳 N rope-skipping, rope-jumping

tiàoshuǐ 跳水 v & N dive; diving

tiàowǔ 跳舞 [comp: 跳 jump + 舞 dance] **v** dance ■ 我可以请您跳舞吗？**Wǒ kěyǐ qǐng nín tiàowǔ ma?** *May I have a dance with you?* ■ 她跳舞跳得很美。**Tā tiàowǔ tiào de hěn měi.** *She dances beautifully.*

tiàoyuǎn 跳远 N long jump

tiàoyuè 跳跃 v jump, leap

tiē 贴 TRAD 貼 v paste, stick ■ 他回到办公室，发现门上贴了一张便条。**Tā huídào bàngōngshì, fāxiàn mén shang tiēle yì zhāng biàntiáo.** *When he came back to the office, he found a note stuck on the door.*

tiě 帖 N note, card

tiě 帖子 N brief note, message (张 **zhāng**, 份 **fèn**)

tiě 铁 TRAD 鐵 N iron ■ 花园里的那条长椅是铁做的。**Huāyuán li de nà tiáo chángyǐ shì tiě zuò de.** *The bench in the garden is made of iron.*

tiělù 铁路 [modif: 铁 iron + 路 road] **N** railway (条 **tiáo**) ■ 这条铁路伸进大山脉。**Zhè tiáo tiělù shēnjìn dà shānmài.** *This railway extends all the way to the great mountain range.*

tīng 厅 TRAD 廳 N hall (See **cāntīng** 餐厅.)

tīng 听 TRAD 聽 v 1 listen ■ 他每天早上都听广播。**Tā měi tiān zǎoshang dōu tīng guǎngbō.** *He listens to the radio early every morning.*

听见 tīngjiàn hear ■ 我听见有人在花园里叫我。**Wǒ tīngjiàn yǒu rén zài huāyuán li jiào wǒ.** *I heard somebody calling me in the garden.*

2 heed, obey ■ 你不听他的话，会后悔的。**Nǐ bù tīng tā de huà, huì hòuhuǐ de.** *You will be sorry if you don't heed his advice (or warning).*

tīnghuà 听话 v heed, be obedient ■ 中国家长喜欢听话的孩子。**Zhōngguó jiāzhǎng xǐhuan tīnghuà de háizi.** *Chinese parents like obedient children.*

tīngshuō 听说 v hear of, people say ■ 听说张先生一家搬走了。**Tīngshuō Zhāng xiānsheng yìjiā bānzǒu le.** *I've heard that Mr Zhang's family has moved.*

tīngxiě 听写 N & v dictation; do dictation

tíng 停 v stop, park (a vehicle) ■ 路上车辆太多了，我们停停开开，花了一个小时才回到家。**Lùshang chēliàng tài duō le, wǒmen tíng tíng kāi kāi, huāle yí ge xiǎoshí cái huídào jiā.** *Traffic was heavy. We were continually stopping and it took*

us one hour to arrive home. ■ 我可以把车停在这里吗？**Wǒ kěyǐ bǎ chē tíng zai zhèlǐ ma?** *May I park my car here?*

停下来 tíng xiàlai come to a stop ■ 前面是红灯，车子要停下来。**Qiánmiàn shì hóngdēng, chēzi yào tíng xiàlai.** *It's a red light in front. The car must stop.*

tíngbó 停泊 v (of ships) lie at anchor, anchor

tíngchē 停车 [v+obj: 停 park + 车 car] **v** stop a cars, park a car

tíngchēchǎng 停车场 N parking lot, car park

tíngdùn 停顿 v pause, halt

tíngzhǐ 停止 [comp: 停 stop + 止 stop] **v** stop, cease ■ 那家公司停止营业了，那他们欠我们的钱怎么办呢？**Nà jiā gōngsī tíngzhǐ yíngyè le, nà tāmen qiàn wǒmen de qián zěnme bàn ne?** *That company has gone out of business. Then what about the money they owe us?* ■ 请你们立即停止这种影响他人的行为。**Qǐng nǐmen lìjí tíngzhǐ zhè zhǒng yǐngxiǎng tārén de xíngwéi.** *Stop such disruptive behavior immediately, please.*

tíngzhì 停滞 v stagnate, come to a standstill

tíng 亭 N pavilion, kiosk

tíngzi 亭子 N pavilion, kiosk

tíng 庭 N front courtyard (See **jiātíng** 家庭.)

tǐng 挺¹ ADV very ■ 她学习挺认真。**Tā xuéxí tǐng rènzhēn.** *She studies conscientiously.*

NOTE: 挺 **tǐng** and 很 **hěn** share the same meaning, but 挺 **tǐng** is a colloquial word.

tǐng 挺² ADJ hard and straight

tǐngbá 挺拔 ADJ tall and straight

tǐng 艇 N light boat

救生艇 jiù shēngtǐng lifeboat

tōng 通 v 1 (of roads, railways) lead to, go to ■ 这条路通到哪里？**Zhè tiáo lù tōngdào nǎlǐ?** *Where does this road lead to?* ■ 条条大路通罗马。**Tiáotiáo dàlù tōng Luómǎ.** *All roads lead to Rome.* **II ADJ** logical, coherent, reasonable ■ 这句话不通，但是我说不出错在哪里。**Zhè jù huà bù tōng, dànshì wǒ shuō bu chū cuò zài nǎlǐ.** *This sentence is not quite right, but I can't identify where the mistake is.*

tōngcháng 通常 ADJ general, usual

tōngguò 通过 [comp: 通 go through + 过 pass] **I v** pass through ■ 从我家到机场，要通过城里。**Cóng wǒ jiā dào jīchǎng, yào tōngguò chénglǐ.** *Going from my home to the airport, one has to pass through the city center.* **II PREP** through, as a result of ■ 通过这次访问，我更了解中国了。**Tōngguò zhè cì fǎngwèn, wǒ gèng liǎojiě Zhōngguó le.** *As a result of this visit, I understand China better.*

tōnghuò 通货 N currency, money

tōnghuò péngzhàng 通货膨胀 N inflation

抑制通货膨胀 yìzhì tōnghuò péngzhàng check inflation

tōngjī 通缉 v list someone as wanted

tōngsú 通俗 ADJ easily understood and accepted by common folks, popular

通俗读物 tōngsú dúwù light reading

tōngxùn 通讯 [v+obj: 通 communicate + 讯 message] N communications

tōngyòng 通用 v be in common use, be current

tōngzhī 通知 v & N notify, inform; notice, circular ■ 科长通知我们，明天上午开会。**Kēzhǎng tōngzhī wǒmen, míngtiān shàngwǔ kāihuì.** *The section head has informed us that there will be a meeting tomorrow morning.* ■ 市政府在报上发了一个通知。**Shì zhèngfǔ zài bào shang fāle yí ge tōngzhī.** *The city government has published a notice in the paper.*

tóng 同 I PREP with, along with ■ 同你在一起，我感到很愉快。**Tóng nǐ zài yìqǐ, wǒ gǎndào hěn yúkuài.** *I find it a pleasure to be with you.* II CONJ and

tóngbāo 同胞 N fellow-countryman, compatriot

tóngqíng 同情 [modif: 同 same + 情 emotion] v & N sympathize with; sympathy ■ 我很同情这位在交通事故中失去儿子的母亲。**Wǒ hěn tóngqíng zhè wèi zài jiāotōng shìgù zhong shīqù érzi de mǔqin.** *I sympathize with the mother who lost her son in the traffic accident.* ■ 他的痛苦经历，引起了我的同情。**Tā de tòngkǔ jīnglì, yǐnqǐle wǒ de tóngqíng.** *His painful experience aroused my sympathy.*

tóngshí 同时 [modif: 同 same + 时 time] N at the same time, simultaneously ■ 我和她同时开始学中文。**Wǒ hé tā tóngshí kāishǐ xué Zhōngwén.** *She and I began to learn Chinese at the same time.*

tóngshì 同事 [modif: 同 same + 事 job] N colleague ■ 同事之间要建立合作关系。**Tóngshì zhījiān yào jiànlì hézuò guānxi.** *Colleagues should build a cooperative relationship among themselves.*

tóngwū 同屋 [modif: 同 same + 屋 room] N roommate, flatmate ■ 他是我的同学，也是我的同屋。**Tā shì wǒ de tóngxué, yě shì wǒ de tóngwū.** *He is my classmate, and my roommate as well.*

tóngxué 同学 [modif: 同 together + 学 study] N classmate, schoolmate

老同学 lǎotóngxué former schoolmate ■ 他利用老同学的关系，取得了那份合同。**Tā lìyòng lǎotóngxué de guānxi, qǔdéle nà fèn hétóng.** *He got the contract through the connection of an old schoolmate.*

NOTE: In Chinese schools, teachers address students as 同学们 **tóngxuémen**, e.g. ■ 同学们，我们现在上课了。**Tóngxuémen, wǒmen xiànzài shàngkè le.** *Class, we're starting class now.*

tóngyàng 同样 [modif: 同 same + 样 way] ADJ same ■ 他和妻子有同样的爱好，同样的理想。**Tā**

hé qīzi yǒu tóngyàng de àihào, tóngyàng de lǐxiǎng. *He and his wife share the same hobby and the same dream.*

tóngyì 同意 [modif: 同 same + 意 opinion] v agree, approve (ANTONYM 反对 **fǎnduì**) ■ 我不同意你说的话。**Wǒ bù tóngyì nǐ shuō de huà.** *I don't agree with what you said.* ■ 我不反对你的计划，但是不同意立即执行。**Wǒ bù fǎnduì nǐ de jìhuà, dànshì bù tóngyì lìjí zhíxíng.** *I don't oppose your plan, but I don't agree to its immediate implementation.*

tóngzhì 同志 [comp: 同 same + 志 aspiration] N comrade

NOTE: 同志 **tóngzhì** used to be the most common form of address in China before 1980. Now it is seldom used. 同志 **tóngzhì** is almost never used between a Chinese and a foreigner. The common forms of address in China today are 先生 **xiānsheng** (to men) and 小姐 **xiǎojiě** (to women, especially young women). In some places 同志 **tóngzhì** has acquired the meaning of *a fellow homosexual.*

tóng 铜 TRAD 銅 N copper (Cu) ■ 铜是一种重要金属。**Tóng shì yì zhǒng zhòngyào jīnshǔ.** *Copper is an important metal.*

tóngkuàng 铜矿 N copper mine

tóng 童 N child (See **értóng** 儿童.)

tónghuà 童话 N children's story, fairy tale

tóngnián 童年 N childhood

tǒng 桶 N bucket, pail (只 **zhī**) ■ 他提了一桶水去洗车。**Tā tíle yì tǒng shuǐ qù xǐ chē.** *He carried a bucket of water over to wash his car.*

tǒng 统 TRAD 統 ADJ together

tǒng chóu jiān gù 统筹兼顾 IDIOM overall planning and all-round consideration

tǒngjì 统计 [modif: 统 together + 计 calculate] v & N add up; statistics

tǒngtǒng 统统 ADV all, entirely

tǒngyī 统一 I v unify, integrate ■ 关于这个问题，我们需要统一认识。**Guānyú zhège wèntí, wǒmen xūyào tǒngyī rènshi.** *We need to reach a common understanding on this issue.* II ADJ unified ■ 这些国家已经形成一个统一的市场。**Zhèxiē guójiā yǐjīng xíngchéng yí ge tǒngyī de shìchǎng.** *These countries have already formed a common market.*

tǒngzhì 统治 [comp: 统 lead + 治 govern] v control and run a country, rule

tòng 痛 v same as 疼 **téng 1** v

tòngkǔ 痛苦 [comp: 痛 painful + 苦 bitter] ADJ painful, tortuous ■ 他不想回忆那段痛苦的生活。**Tā bù xiǎng huíyì nà duàn tòngkǔ de shēnghuó.** *He does not want to recall that painful period of his life.*

tòngkuai 痛快 [comp: 痛 to one's heart's content + 快 delight] ADJ overjoyed, very delighted ■ 我在会上说了一直想说的话，心里很痛快。**Wǒ zài**

huìshang shuōle yìzhí xiǎng shuō de huà, xīnli hěn tòngkuai. *At the meeting I said that I'd been wanting to say, and felt extremely pleased.* ■ 上星期日我们玩得真痛快。**Shàng Xīngqīrì wǒmen wán de zhēn tòngkuai.** *We had a terrific time last Sunday.*

tōu 偷 v steal, pilfer ■ 我的钱包让人偷了！**Wǒ de qiánbāo ràng rén tōu le!** *My wallet's been stolen!*

tōutōu 偷偷 ADV stealthily, on the quiet ■ 我看见一个人偷偷走进校长办公室。**Wǒ kànjiàn yí ge rén tōutōu zǒujìn xiàozhǎng bàngōngshì.** *I saw a figure walking stealthily into the principal's office. (→ I saw someone sneak into the principal's office.)*

tóu 头 TRAD 頭 I N 1 the head ■ 我头疼。**Wǒ tóu téng.** *My head aches. (→ I have a headache.)* 2 foreman, chief ■ 你们的头儿呢？我要找他说话。**Nǐmen de tóur ne? Wǒ yào zhǎo tā shuōhuà.** *Who's your foreman? (or Who's in charge here?) I want to talk to him.* II ADJ first, first few ■ 我刚来的头几个星期，几乎天天下雨。**Wǒ gāng lái de tóu jǐge xīngqī, jīhū tiāntiān xiàyǔ.** *The first few weeks after I arrived, it rained almost every day.* III MEASURE WORD (for cattle or sheep)
一头牛 yì tóu niú a head of cattle (or buffalo/cow) / 两头羊 liǎng tóu yáng two sheep

tóufa 头发 [modif: 头 head + 发 hair] N hair (of the human head) (根 **gēn**) ■ 爸爸的头发渐渐白了。**Bàba de tóufa jiànjiàn bái le.** *Daddy's hair is turning gray.*

tóu 投 v throw

tóujī 投机[1] I v & N speculate, engage in speculation; speculation
货币投机 huòbì tóujī currency speculation
II ADJ opportunistic
投机分子 tóujīfènzǐ opportunist

tóujī 投机[2] ADJ agreeable, congenial, of the same mind
谈得很投机 tán de hěn tóujī have a most agreeable conversation

tóupiào 投票 v cast a vote, vote

tóurù 投入 [comp: 投 throw + 入 enter] v put into, invest ■ 他们在孩子的教育上投入很多钱。**Tāmen zài háizi de jiàoyù shang tóurù hěn duō qián.** *They put lots of money into their children's education.*

tóuxiáng 投降 v surrender, capitulate

tóuzhì 投掷 [comp: 投 throw + 掷 throw] v throw, hurl

tóuzī 投资 [v+obj: 投 put + 资 capital] v & N invest; investment
投资在一家合资企业 tóuzī zài yìjiā hézī qǐ yè invest in a joint-venture / 投资的回报 tóuzī de huíbào return on an investment

tòu 透 I v penetrate, pass through ■ 月光透进房间。**Yuèguāng tòujìn fángjiān.** *Moonlight came into the room.* II ADJ thorough ■ 王老师把这个语法问题讲得很透。**Wáng lǎoshī bǎ zhège yǔfǎ**

wèntí jiǎng de hěn tòu. *Teacher Wang explained this grammar point thoroughly.*

tòulù 透露 v let on about, leak, disclose

tòumíng 透明 [comp: 透 thorough + 明 clear, bright] ADJ transparent

tòumíngdù 透明度 N transparency

tū 秃 ADJ having no hair, bald

tū 突 ADJ protruding

tūchū 突出 [comp: 突 protrude + 出 out] I v give prominence, highlight, emphasize ■ 他在这篇文章中突出市场调查的重要性。**Tā zài zhè piān wénzhāng zhōng tūchūle shìchǎng diàochá de zhòngyàoxìng.** *In this article he emphasizes the importance of market research.* II ADJ prominent, conspicuous ■ 火车上只有他一个外国人，显得很突出。**Huǒchē shang zhǐyǒu tā yí ge wàiguórén, xiǎnde hěn tūchū.** *He is the only foreigner on the train and is very conspicuous.*

tūpò 突破 [modif: 突 sudden + 破 break] v & N break through, make a breakthrough; breakthrough

tūrán 突然 [suffix: 突 sudden + 然 adjectival suffix] ADJ & ADV sudden, suddenly ■ 突然发生这件事，我真不知道怎么办。**Tūrán fāshēng zhè jiàn shì, wó zhēn bù zhīdào zěnme bàn.** *I really don't know what to do about this sudden incident.*

tú 图 TRAD 圖 N picture, drawing, chart, diagram (张 **zhāng**) ■ 他画了一张图，说明这种药不同成分的比例。**Tā huàle yì zhāng tú, shuōmíng zhè zhǒng yào bùtóng chéngfèn de bǐlì.** *He drew a chart to show the proportion of the various ingredients in this medicine.*

tú'àn 图案 N pattern, design

túshūguǎn 图书馆 [modif: 图书 books + 馆 building] N library (座 **zuò**) ■ 我们学校的图书馆没有多少中文书。**Wǒmen xuéxiào de túshūguǎn méiyǒu duōshǎo Zhōngwén shū.** *The library in our school doesn't have many Chinese books.*

tú 涂 TRAD 塗 v smear, spread on ■ 她在面包上涂了一层黄油。**Tā zài miànbāo shang túle yì céng huángyóu.** *She spread butter on the bread.*

tú 徒 N apprentice

túdì 徒弟 [comp: 徒 apprentice + 弟 younger brother] N apprentice, pupil

tú 途 N way, route

tújìng 途径 [comp: 途 way + 径 footpath] N way, road, path

tǔ 土 N soil, earth ■ 你鞋上怎么全是土？**Nǐ xié shang zěnme quán shì tǔ?** *How come your shoes are covered with dirt?*

tǔdì 土地 [comp: 土 soil + 地 land] N land ■ 对农民来说，最重要的资源是土地。**Duì nóngmín lái shōu, zuì zhòngyào de zīyuán shì tǔdì.** *To farmers, the most important resource is land.*

tǔdòu 土豆 [modif: 土 soil + 豆 bean] N potato (只 **zhī**, 块 **kuài**) ■ "土豆烧牛肉"是一道有名的西菜。**"Tǔdòu shāo niúròu" shì yí dào yǒumíng**

de xīcài. *"Beef and potato stew" (*or *Hungarian goulash) is a famous Western dish.*

tǔrǎng 土壤 N soil
肥沃的土壤 féiwò de tǔrǎng fertile soil

tǔ 吐 v spit, exhale ■ 她吓得半天才吐出一口气。**Tā xià de bàntiān cái tǔ chū yì kǒu qì.** *She was so terrified that she held her breath.*

tù 吐 v vomit ■ 他酒喝得太多，吐了。**Tā jiǔ hē de tài duō, tù le.** *He vomited because he drank too much.* ■ 我想吐。**Wǒ xiǎng tù.** *I want to vomit (→ I feel sick).*

tù 兔 N rabbit, hare

tùzi 兔子 [suffix: 兔 rabbit, hare + 子 nominal suffix] N rabbit, hare (只 **zhī**) ■ 我小时候养过两只兔子。**Wǒ xiǎoshíhou yǎngguo liǎng zhī tùzi.** *When I was a child I once kept two rabbits.*

tuán 团 TRAD 團 N (military) regiment; group, team ■ 你打算参加旅行团，还是自己一个人去中国？**Nǐ dǎsuàn cānjiā lǚxíngtuán, háishi zìjǐ yígerén qù Zhōngguó?** *Do you plan to tour China in a tourist group or all by yourself?*
代表团 dàibiǎotuán delegation / 旅行团 lǚxíngtuán tour group / 歌舞团 gēwǔtuán song and dance troupe

tuánjié 团结 [comp: 团 rally around + 结 tie up] v unite, be in solidarity with ■ 这一家的兄弟姐妹很团结。**Zhè yì jiā de xiōng-dì-jiě-mèi hěn tuánjié.** *The siblings in this family are united.* ■ 团结就是力量。**Tuánjié jiù shì lìliàng.** *Unity is strength.*

tuántǐ 团体 N organization, group

tuányuán 团圆 V & N reunite with family members; family reunion

tuī 推 v push ■ 你要推这个门，不要拉。**Nì yào tuī zhège mén, bú yào lā.** *You should push this door; not pull it.* ■ 他推着自行车上坡。**Tā tuīzhe zìxíngchē shàng pō.** *He pushed the bicycle up the slope.*

tuīcè 推测 v infer, suppose

tuīchí 推迟 [v+compl: 推 push + 迟 late] v postpone ■ 旅行团出发的日期要推迟三天。**Lǚxíngtuán chūfā de rìqī yào tuīchí sān tiān.** *The date of the tourist group departure will be postponed for three days.*

tuīcí 推辞 v decline, turn down

tuīdòng 推动 [v+compl: 推 push + 动 move] v push forward, promote ■ 中国迅速的经济发展推动了中文教学。**Zhōngguó xùnsù de jīngjì fāzhǎn tuīdòngle Zhōngwén jiàoxué.** *China's rapid economic development has promoted teaching and learning of the Chinese language.*

tuīfān 推翻 [v+compl: 推 push + 翻 turn over] v overturn, overthrow

tuīguǎng 推广 [v+compl: 推 push + 广 wide] v popularize, spread ■ 中国大力推广普通话，已经取得了成功。**Zhōngguó dàlì tuīguǎng Pǔtōnghuà, yǐjīng qǔdéle chénggōng.** *China's tremendous*

efforts to popularize Putonghua have been successful.

tuījiàn 推荐 [comp: 推 push + 荐 recommend] v recommend ■ 王老师给我推荐一本汉英词典。**Wáng lǎoshī gěi wǒ tuījiàn yì běn Hànyīng cídiǎn.** *Teacher Wang recommended me a Chinese-English dictionary.* ■ 你能不能给我推荐一位会说英语的牙医？**Nǐ néng bu néng gěi wǒ tuījiàn yí wèi huì shōu Yīngyǔ de yáyī?** *Could you recommend me a dentist who speaks English?*

tuīlǐ 推理 V & N infer, reason; reasoning by way of inference, inference, rationalization

tuīlùn 推论 V & N infer, deduce; conclusion based on inference

tuīxiāo 推销 [v+obj: 推 push + 销 sale] v promote (sale), market
推销新产品 tuīxiāo xīnchǎnpǐn promote a new product

tuǐ 腿 N leg (条 **tiáo**) ■ 他腿长，跑得快。**Tā tuǐ cháng, pǎo de kuài.** *He's got long legs and runs fast.*

tuì 退 v move back, retreat ■ 请你退到黄线后面。**Qǐng nǐ tuìdào huángxiàn hòumiàn.** *Please step back behind the yellow line.*

tuìbù 退步 v retrogress, lag behind

tuìkuǎn 退款 v refund, ask for refund ■ 你对商品不满意，可以退款。**Nǐ duì shāngpǐn bù mǎnyì, kěyǐ tuìkuǎn.** *If you are not satisfied with your purchase, you can ask for a refund.*

tuìxiū 退休 V & N retire (from employment); retirement

tuìxiūjīn 退休金 N pension, superannuation

tūn 吞 v swallow

tūn tūn tǔ tǔ 吞吞吐吐 IDIOM hesitant in speech, hum and haw

tūnyàn 吞咽 v swallow, gulp down

tuō 托 v entrust, ask ■ 你进城吗？我托你办一件事，行吗？**Nǐ jìnchéng ma? Wǒ tuō nǐ bàn yí jiàn shì, xíng ma?** *Are you going to town? May I ask you to do something?*

tuōyùn 托运 v consign for shipment

tuō 拖 v drag on, defer, procrastinate ■ 这件事不能再拖了，得马上决定。**Zhè jiàn shì bù néng zài tuō le, děi mǎshàng juédìng.** *We cannot defer any longer but have to make an immediate decision on this matter.*

tuōyán 拖延 [comp: 拖 drag + 延 postpone] v delay, put off

tuō 脱 v take off (clothes, shoes, etc.)
脱衣服 tuō yīfu take off clothes ■ 这个小孩儿会自己脱衣服吗？**Zhège xiǎoháir huì zìjǐ tuō yīfu ma?** *Can the child take off his clothes by himself? (→ Can this child undress himself?)*
脱帽子 tuō màozi take off one's hat / 脱鞋 tuō xié take off one's shoes

tuōlí 脱离 [comp: 脱 get out of + 离 leave] v

break away from, sever ■ 此人已与本公司脱离一切关系。 **Cǐ rén yǐ yú běn gōngsī tuōlí yíqiè guānxi.** *This person has severed all ties with this company.*

tuǒ 妥 ADJ appropriate, proper

tuǒdàng 妥当 ADJ appropriate, proper

tuǒshàn 妥善 [comp: 妥 appropriate + 善 good] ADJ appropriate and satisfactory

tuǒxié 妥协 V & N avoid conflict by concession; compromise
达成妥协 dáchéng tuǒxié reach a compromise

tuǒyuán 椭圆 N oval
椭圆形 tuǒyuánxíng oval shape

tuò 唾 N saliva

tuòmo 唾沫 N saliva, spittle

tuòqì 唾弃 V spurn with contempt, disdain and reject

W

wā 挖 V dig, scoop, excavate

wājué 挖掘 V dig, excavate

wā 哇 PARTICLE same as 啊 **ā**, II

wā 蛙 N frog
青蛙 qīngwā frog

wá 娃 N baby, child
娃娃 wáwa baby, small child (个 **gè**)

wǎ 瓦 N tile (片 **piàn**)

wǎjiě 瓦解 V disintegrate, collapse

wà 袜 TRAD 襪 N stocking

wàzi 袜子 [suffix: 袜 stocking + 子 nominal suffix] N stocking, sock (只 **zhī**, 双 **shuāng**) ■ 我的袜子破了。 **Wǒ de wàzi pò le.** *My socks have holes.*
穿袜子 chuān wàzi put on socks, wear socks / 脱袜子 tuō wàzi take off socks

wāi 歪 ADJ not straight, askew, crooked ■ 这幅画挂歪了。 **Zhè fú huà guà wāi le.** *The picture hangs askew.*

wāiqū 歪曲 [comp: 歪 askew + 曲 bend] V distort, misinterpret ■ 我不是那个意思，你歪曲了我的话。 **Wǒ bú shì nàge yìsi, nǐ wāiqū le wǒde huà.** *That's not what I meant; you've distorted my remarks.*

wài 外 N outside (ANTONYM 里 **lǐ**) ■ 墙外是一条安静的小街。 **Qiáng wài shì yì tiáo ānjìng de xiǎo jiē.** *Beyond the wall is a quiet by-street.*

wàibian 外边 [modif: 外 outside + 边 side] N outside (ANTONYM 里边 **lǐbian**) ■ 外边凉快，我们到外边去吧。 **Wàibian liángkuai, wǒmen dào wàibian qù ba.** *It's cool outside. Let's go outside.* ■ 外边下雨呢，带着伞吧! **Wàibian xià yǔ ne, dàizhe sǎn ba!** *It's raining outside. Bring an umbrella with you.*

wàibiǎo 外表 N outward appearance, exterior

wàidì 外地 [modif: 外 outside + 地 place] N parts of the country other than where one is (ANTONYM 本

地 **běndì**) ■ 他经常到外地去开会。 **Tā jīngcháng dào wàidì qù kāihuì.** *He often travels to other parts of the country to attend conferences.*

wàidìrén 外地人 N one who is from other parts of the country, not a native ■ 她的丈夫是外地人。 **Tāde zhàngfu shì wàidìrén.** *Her husband is from another part of the country.*

wàigōng 外公 N (maternal) granddad

wàiguó 外国 [modif: 外 outside + 国 country] N foreign country ■ 你去过外国吗? **Nǐ qùguo wàiguó ma?** *Have you ever been abroad?*

wàiguórén 外国人 N foreigner

wàiguóhuò 外国货 N foreign products, foreign goods

wàiháng 外行 ADJ & N lay, not trained, unprofessional; layman, nonprofessional

wàijiāo 外交 [modif: 外 external + 交 deal with] N foreign affairs, diplomacy

Wàijiāobù 外交部 N Ministry of Foreign Affairs

Wàijiāo bùzhǎng 外交部长 N Minister of Foreign Affairs

wàijiāoguān 外交官 N diplomat

wàijiè 外界 N outside community, external world

wàimiàn 外面 N same as 外边 **wàibian**

wàipó 外婆 N (maternal) grandma

wàiwén 外文 [modif: 外 foreign + 文 writing] N foreign language (especially its writing) (门 **mén**) ■ 这封信是用外文写的，我看不懂。 **Zhè fēn xìn shì yòng wàiwén xiě de, wǒ kàn bu dǒng.** *This letter is written in a foreign language. I can't read it.* ■ 这本书已经翻译成多种外文。 **Zhè běn shū yǐjīng fānyì chéng duō zhǒng wàiwén.** *This book has been translated into many foreign languages.*

wàixiàng 外向 ADJ extrovert (ANTONYM 内向 **nèixiang**)

wàixiàngxíng 外向型 ADJ export-oriented
外向型经济 wàixiàngxíng jīngjì export-oriented economy

wàiyǔ 外语 [modif: 外 foreign + 语 language] N foreign language (门 **mén**) ■ 懂一门外语很有用。 **Dǒng yì mén wàiyǔ hěn yǒuyòng.** *Knowing a foreign language is useful.*

wān 弯 TRAD 彎 ADJ curved, tortuous ■ 你这条线划得不直，划弯了。 **Nǐ zhè tiáo xiàn huà de bù zhí, huà wān le.** *You did not draw this line straight; it's curved.*

wān 湾 TRAD 灣 N bay, gulf (See **Táiwān** 台湾)

wán 丸 N bolus, pill (粒 **lì**, 颗 **kē**)

wán 完 V finish, end ■ 电影什么时候完? **Diànyǐng shénme shíhou wán?** *When will the movie end?*
吃完 chīwán finish eating, eat up ■ 我吃完饭就去开会。 **Wǒ chīwán fàn jiù qù kāihuì.** *I'm going to a meeting as soon as I finish my meal.*
看完 kànwán finish reading/watching ■ 我昨天看完电视已经十二点了。 **Wǒ zuótiān kànwán diànshì yǐjīng shí'èr diǎn le.** *It was already twelve*

o'clock when I finished watching TV last night.
做完 zuòwán finish doing ■ 你什么时候可以做
完作业？ **Nǐ shénme shíhou kěyǐ zuòwán zuòyè?**
When can you finish your homework?
用完 yòngwán use up ■ 我的钱用完了，我要到
银行去取钱。 **Wǒ de qián yòngwán le, wǒ yào dào
yínháng qu qǔ qián.** *I've used up my money. I'll
go to the bank to get some cash.*

wánbèi 完备 [comp: 完 finished + 备 provided]
ADJ having all the necessary parts, perfect, complete

wánbì 完毕 **v** complete, finish

wánchéng 完成 [comp: 完 finish + 成 accom-
plish] **v** accomplish, fulfill ■ 这个计划在明年六月
完成。 **Zhège jìhuà zài míngnián liùyuè wánchéng.**
This plan will be fulfilled in June next year. ■ 我
们完成这个任务后要好好庆祝一下。 **Wǒmen wán-
chéng zhège rènwù hòu yào hǎohǎo qìngzhù yíxià.**
*We will have a good celebration after we have
accomplished this task.*

wánměi 完美 **ADJ** perfect, flawless
不完美 bù wánměi imperfect

wánquán 完全 [comp: 完 finished + 全 all] **ADJ**
complete ■ 你提供的资料不完全。 **Nǐ tígōng de
zīliào bù wánquán.** *The data you have supplied
are not complete.* ■ 你完全不懂我的意思。 **Nǐ
wánquán bù dǒng wǒ de yìsi.** *You completely fail
to see my point.*

wánshàn 完善 **I ADJ** complete and perfect, consummate **II v** make perfect, improve

wánzhěng 完整 [comp: 完 complete + 整 whole]
ADJ complete, integrated ■ 请你用一个完整的句子
来回答。 **Qǐng nǐ yòng yí ge wánzhěng de jùzi lái
huídá.** *Please answer in a complete sentence.*

wánr 玩儿 [suffix: 玩 play + 儿 suffix] **v** play;
have fun ■ 我们一块儿到公园去玩儿吧。 **Wǒmen
yíkuàir dào gōngyuán qù wánr ba.** *Let's go to the
park to have fun!*

NOTE: Though 玩儿 **wánr** is often glossed as *to play*,
its basic meaning is *to have fun* or *to have a good time*.
It can refer to many kinds of activities and therefore
has a very wide application. More examples: ■ 我们常
常到小明家去玩儿。 **Wǒmen chángcháng dào Xiǎo
Míng jiā qu wánr.** *We often go to Xiao Ming's home
to have a good time. (e.g. singing, dancing, playing
cards, playing games or just chatting.)* ■ 上星期天我
们在海边玩儿得真高兴！ **Shàng Xīngqītiān wǒmen
zài hǎibiān wánr de zhēn gāoxìng!** *We had a wonderful time by the seaside last Sunday.* ■ 我想去香港
玩儿。 **Wǒ xiǎng qù Xiānggǎng wánr.** *I want to have
a holiday in Hong Kong.*

wánjù 玩具 **N** toy
wánnòng 玩弄 **v** play with, toy with
wányìr 玩意儿 **N 1** plaything **2** stuff, thing

NOTE: 玩意儿 **wányìr** is normally used with some
contempt to suggest "insignificance" or "unworthi-
ness", similar to 东西 **dōngxi**. The expletives 什么玩
意儿？ **Shénme wányìr?** and 他是个什么玩意儿？ **Tā
shìgè shénme wányìr?** may be roughly translated
respectively into *What trash!* and *Who does he think
he is?*

wángù 顽固 **ADJ** stubborn, obstinate, pig-headed
wánqiáng 顽强 **ADJ** tenacious, indomitable
wǎn 挽 **v** salvage
wǎnhuí 挽回 **v** reverse the unfavorable situation,
turn the table
wǎnjiù 挽救 **v** rescue, save
wǎn 晚 **ADJ** late, not on time ■ 对不起，我来晚
了。 **Duìbuqǐ, wǒ lái wǎn le.** *I'm sorry I'm late.*
■ 时间太晚了，我得走了。 **Shíjiān tài wǎn le, wǒ
děi zǒu le.** *It's very late; I've got to go.*
wǎnfàn 晚饭 [modif: 晚 supper + 饭 meal] **N** evening meal, supper, dinner (顿 **dùn**) ■ 你们家一般什
么时候吃晚饭？ **Nǐmen jiā yìbān shénme shíhou chī
wǎnfàn?** *When do you usually have supper at home?*
做晚饭 zuò wǎnfàn prepare supper
wǎnhuì 晚会 [modif: 晚 evening + 会 assembly] **N**
evening party, an evening of entertainment ■ 很多重
要的人要来参加今天的晚会。 **Hěn duō zhòngyào de
rén yào lái cānjiā jīntiān de wǎnhuì.** *Many important
people will attend this evening's party.*
wǎnnián 晚年 **N** old age
安度晚年 āndù wǎnnián enjoy one's old age in
peace
wǎnshang 晚上 **N** evening ■ 你今天晚上打算做
什么？ **Nǐ jīntiān wǎnshang dǎsuàn zuò shénme?**
What do you plan to do this evening? ■ 他往往晚
上还要工作两三个小时。 **Tā wǎngwǎng wǎnshang
háiyào gōngzuò liǎng-sān ge xiǎoshí.** *He usually
has to work two or three hours in the evening.*
今天晚上（今晚） jīntiān wǎnshang (jīnwǎn) this
evening / 昨天晚上（昨晚） zuótiān wǎnshang
(zuówǎn) yesterday evening
wǎn 惋 **v** sympathize with
wǎnxī 惋惜 [comp: 惋 sympathize with + 惜 pity]
v feel sorry for (about), commiserate
为浪费人才而惋惜 wéi làngfèi réncái ér wǎnxī
feel sorry about the waste of talents
wǎn 碗 **N** bowl (只 **zhī**) ■ 中国人吃饭一般用碗，大
碗放菜，小碗放米饭。 **Zhōngguórén chīfàn yìbān
yòng wǎn, dà wǎn fàng cài, xiǎo wǎn fàng mǐfàn.**
*Chinese people usually use bowls for meals: big
bowls for dishes and small ones for cooked rice.*
… 碗饭 … wǎnfàn ... bowl(s) of rice ■ "你一顿
吃几碗饭？" "两碗饭。" **"Nǐ yí dùn chī jǐ wǎn
fàn?" "Liǎng wǎn fàn."** *"How many bowls of rice
do you have for one meal?" "Two."*
菜碗 càiwǎn dish bowl, big bowl / 饭碗 fànwǎn
rice bowl; livelihood, job

wàn 万 TRAD 萬 NUMERAL ten thousand
一万两千三百 yíwàn liǎngqiān sānbǎi twelve thousand and three hundred (12,300) / 二十万 èrshí wàn two hundred thousand (200,000) / 一百万 yì bǎiwàn one million (1,000,000)/ 一千万 yì qiānwàn ten million (10,000,000)

NOTE: 万 wàn (ten thousand) is an important number in Chinese. While English has four basic digits (one, ten, hundred and thousand), Chinese has five (个 gè one, 十 shí ten, 百 bǎi hundred, 千 qiān thousand, 万 wàn ten thousand). The Chinese use 万 wàn to mean ten thousand. Therefore a hundred thousand is 十万 shí wàn. In Chinese-speaking communities in Southeast Asia, some people use 十千 shíqiān for ten thousand, e.g. 三十千 sānshíqiān 30,000. This is, however, not acceptable in standard Chinese.

wànfēn 万分 ADV extremely
wànyī 万一 I CONJ in the unlikely event of, in case ■ 万一飞机失事，不要惊慌。 Wànyī fēijī shīshì, búyào jīnghuāng. In case of a flying accident, do not panic. II ADJ unlikely but possible
万一的情况 wànyī de qíngkuàng contingency
wáng 王 N king
国王 guówáng king (of a kingdom)
wángguó 王国 N kingdom
丹麦王国 Dānmài wángguó the Kingdom of Denmark
wánghòu 王后 N queen (位 wèi)
wángzǐ 王子 N prince (位 wèi)
wáng 亡 V die, perish (See sǐwáng 死亡.)
wǎng 网 TRAD 網 N net
wǎngbā 网吧 [modif: 网 net, network + 吧 bar] N Internet café (座 zuò, 家 jiā) ■ 这家网吧吸引很多年轻人。 Zhè jiā wǎngbā xīyǐn hěn duō niánqīngrén. This Internet café attracts many young people. ■ 他不在家，就在网吧。 Tā bú zài jiā, jiù zài wǎngbā. If he is not home, then he must be at the Internet café.
wǎngguò 网购 V & N shop online; online shopping
wǎngluò 网络 [modif: 网 net + 络 net, network] N Internet, network
网络营销 wǎngluò yíngxiāo Internet marketing
wǎngmín 网民 N netizen
wǎngqiú 网球 [modif: 网 net + 球 ball] N tennis ■ 我们来打一场网球吧。 Wǒmen lái dǎ yì chǎng wǎngqiú ba. Let's have a game of tennis.
wǎngqiúchǎng 网球场 tennis court
wǎngzhàn 网站 [modif: 网 net, network + 站 station] N website ■ 欢迎您访问我的个人网站。 Huānyíng nín fǎngwèn wǒ de gèrén wǎngzhàn. You are welcome to visit my personal website.
wǎngzhàn yùnyíng 网站运营 website operation
wǎng 往 PREP towards, in the direction of ■ 你往前走，到红绿灯的地方，往左拐，就可以到火车站。 Nǐ wǎng qián zǒu, dào hónglǜdēng de dìfang,

wǎng zuǒ guǎi, jiù kěyǐ dào huǒchēzhàn. Walk straight on, and turn left at the traffic lights. Then you'll reach the railway station.
wǎngcháng 往常 ADV habitually in the past, used to
wǎngfǎn 往返 V journey to and from, make a round trip
wǎngshì 往事 N past events, the past
回忆往事 huíyì wǎngshì recollect past events, reflect upon the past
wàng 妄 ADJ preposterous
wàngxiǎng 妄想 V & N make a vain attempt; wild fantasy, vain hope
wàng 忘 V forget ■ 别忘了寄这封信。 Bié wàngle jì zhè fēng xìn. Don't forget to post this letter. ■ 他叫什么名字？ 我忘了。 Tā jiào shénme míngzi? Wǒ wàngle. What's his name? I've forgotten it.
wàngjì 忘记 V same as 忘 wàng
wàng 望 V look at, gaze into the distance ■ 举头望明月。 Jǔ tóu wàng míngyuè. I look up to gaze at the bright moon. (a line from a poem by the Tang Dynasty poet Li Bai)
wàng 旺 ADJ flourishing, thriving (See xīngwàng 兴旺.)
wēi 危 ADJ perilous
wēihài 危害 [comp: 危 endanger + 害 damage] V & N harm severely, jeopardize; serious harm, severe damage ■ 降低农产品价格会危害农民的利益。 Jiàngdī nóngchǎnpǐn jiàgé huì wēihài nóngmín de lìyì. Lowering produce prices will severely harm the farmers' interest. ■ 森林面积的减少给环境造成很大危害。 Sēnlín miànjī de jiǎnshǎo gěi huánjìng zàochéng hěn dà wēihài. The reduction of forest areas causes severe damage to the environment.
wēijī 危机 [motif: 危 perilous + 机 situation] N crisis ■ 要解决危机，先要了解危机是怎么发生的。 Yào jiějué wēijī, xiānyào liáojiě wēijī shì zěnme fāshēng de. In order to resolve a crisis, one should first of all learn how it came into being.
wēixiǎn 危险 [comp: 危 perilous + 险 risky] I ADJ dangerous, in danger ■ 下雪天开车比较危险。 Xià xuě tiān kāichē bǐjiào wēixiǎn. It's dangerous to drive in snow. II N danger, risk ■ 病人已经脱离危险。 Bìngrén yǐjīng tuōlí wēixiǎn. The patient is out of danger.
wēi 威 N awesome force
wēifēng 威风 N power and prestige, manner or style showing power and prestige
耍威风 shuǎ wēifēng throw one's weight around
wēilì 威力 N formidable force, power
wēiwàng 威望 N enormous prestige
wēixié 威胁 V & N pose a threat, threaten; threat ■ 森林面积越来越小，威胁到野生动物的生存。 Sēnlín miànjī yuèláiyuè xiǎo, wēixié dào yěshēng dòngwù de shēngcún. Forests are getting smaller

and smaller, which threatens the survival of wild animals.

wēixìn 威信 N popular trust, prestige
在同事中享有很高威信 zài tóngshì zhōng xiǎngyǒu hěn gāo wēixìn enjoy high prestige among colleagues

wēi 微 ADJ small

wēibó 微博 N microblog, microblogging

wēi bù zú dào 微不足道 ADJ negligibly small, extremely tiny

wēiguān 微观 ADJ microcosmic, micro- (**ANTONYM** 宏观 hóngguān)

wēixiào 微笑 [modif: 微 small + 笑 smile, laugh] **v** smile ■ 她微笑着说，"谢谢你了。" Ta wēixiàozhe shuō, "Xièxie nǐ le." *She said, smiling, "Thank you."*

wēixìn 微信 N micro-channel, WeChat

wéi 围 TRAD 圍 v enclose, surround ■ 他建了一道墙，把自己的房子围起来。Tā jiànle yí dào qiáng, bǎ zìjǐ de fángzi wéi qǐlai. *He built a wall to enclose his home.*

wéirào 围绕 [comp: 围 enclose + 绕 around] **v 1** move around, encircle ■ 地球围绕太阳转。Dìqiú wéirào tàiyang zhuàn. *The earth moves around the sun.* **2** center on, focus on ■ 请大家围绕这个问题谈，不要离题。Qǐng dàjiā wéirào zhè ge wèntí tán, bú yào lítí. *Please focus on this question. Do not digress.*

wéi 为 TRAD 為 v be, become

wéinán 为难 v 1 make things difficult for ■ 我不想为难你。Wǒ bùxiǎng wéinán nǐ. *I don't want to make things difficult for you.* **2** feel awkward 为难的事情 wéinán de shì qíng something one finds difficult to cope with

wéiqī 为期 v (to be completed) by a definite date 为期不远 wéiqī bù yuǎn will take place soon / 为期一周 wéiqī yì zhōu will last a week

wéishǒu 为首 ADJ headed by

wéi 违 TRAD 違 v disobey

wéibèi 违背 [comp: 违 disobey + 背 in opposition to] **v** go against, violate ■ 你们这样做，违背了总公司的意愿。Nǐmen zhèyàng zuò, wéibèi le zǒnggōngsī de yìyuàn. *What you've done goes against the will of the headquarters.*

wéifǎn 违反 [comp: 违 disobey + 反 counter] **v** run counter to, violate ■ 婚外恋违法道德标准。Hūnwàiliàn wéifǎ dàodé biāozhǔn. *Extramarital affairs violate the moral code.*

wéi 唯 ADV only

NOTE: In some cases, 唯 is also written as 惟.

wéidú 唯独 ADV only, alone
wéiwùlùn 唯物论 N materialism
wéixīnlùn 唯心论 N idealism
wéiyī 唯一 [comp: 唯 only + 一 one] **ADJ** the only one, sole ■ 他唯一的爱好是打麻将，一有空就

打。Tā wéiyī de àihào shì dǎ májiàng, yì yǒukòng jiù dǎ. *His only hobby is playing mahjong. He plays mahjong whenever he has time.*

wéi 维 TRAD 維 v preserve, safeguard

wéichí 维持 v maintain, keep

wéihù 维护 [comp: 维 preserve + 护 protect] **v** safeguard, defend ■ 为了维护国家安全，必须要有一支强大的军队。Wèile wéihù guójiā ānquán, bìxū yào yǒu yì zhī qiángdà de jūnduì. *To ensure national security, we must maintain strong armed forces.*

wéishēng sù 维生素 N vitamins

wéixiū 维修 [comp: 维 preserve + 修 repair] **v** keep in good repair, maintain (a machine, a house, etc.)

wěi 伟 TRAD 偉 ADJ big

wěidà 伟大 [comp: 伟 big + 大 big] **ADJ** great, grand, outstanding ■ 孙中山是中国历史上的一位伟大人物。Sūn Zhōngshān shì Zhōngguó lìshǐ shang de yí wèi wěidà rénwù. *Dr Sun Yat-sen is a great man in Chinese history.*

wěi 尾 N tail, end

wěiba 尾巴 N tail (条 tiáo) ■ 狗摇尾巴，是表示高兴。Gǒu yáo wěiba, shì biǎoshì gāoxìng. *When a dog wags its tail, it indicates happiness.*

wěi 伪 TRAD 偽 ADJ false

wěizào 伪造 v forge, counterfeit
一份伪造的文件 yí fèn wěizào de wénjiàn a forged document

wěi 委 v entrust

wěiqū 委屈 v feel wronged, nurse a grievance

wěituō 委托 [comp: 委 entrust + 托 entrust] **v** entrust, delegate ■ 公司委托律师正式回答用户的投诉。Gōngsī wěituō lǜshī zhèngshì huídá yònghù de tóusù. *The company has entrusted its lawyer with a formal reply to the consumers' complaint.*

wěiyuán 委员 N member of a committee

wěiyuánhuì 委员会 N committee (个 gè) ■ 这个委员会的任务是制定教育政策。Zhège wěiyuánhuì de rènwù shì zhìdìng jiàoyù zhèngcè. *This committee's mission is to set policies on education.*

wèi 卫 TRAD 衛 v defend, protect

wèishēng 卫生 [v+obj: 卫 defend + 生 life] **N** hygiene, sanitation ■ 保持个人卫生和公共卫生，有利于人民的身体健康。Bǎochí gèrén wèishēng hé gōnggòng wèishēng, yǒulì yú rénmín de shēntǐ jiànkāng. *Maintaining good personal hygiene and public sanitation is beneficial to people's health.*
个人卫生 gèrén wèishēng hygiene, personal hygiene / 公共卫生 gōnggòng wèishēng sanitation, public sanitation / 环境卫生 huánjìng wèishēng environmental sanitation

wèishēngjiān 卫生间 N bathroom, washroom, toilet

wèishēngjú 卫生局 N Bureau of Public Health, Health Department,

wèixīng 卫星 [modif: 卫 encircling + 星 star] **N** satellite ■ 月球是地球的卫星。**Yuèqiú shì dìqiú de wèixīng.** *The moon is a satellite of the earth.* 人造卫星 rénzào wèixīng man-made satellite

wèi 为 **TRAD** 為 **PREP** (do, work) for the benefit of ■ 我为人人，人人为我。**Wǒ wèi rénrén, rénrén wèi wǒ.** *I work for everybody else as everybody else works for me. (→ One for all and all for one.)*

wèile 为了 **V & PREP** for the purpose of ■ 他这样辛辛苦苦地工作，都是为了孩子。**Tā zhèyàng xīn-xīn-kǔ-kǔ de gōngzuò, dōu shì wèile háizi.** *He works so hard, all for his children.* ■ 为了健康，他不吸烟不喝酒，每天锻炼身体。**Wèile jiànkāng, tā bù xīyān bù hē jiǔ, měi tiān duànliàn shēntǐ.** *In order to keep fit he does not smoke or drink, and exercises every day.*

NOTE: Both 为 **wèi** and 为了 **wèile** can be used as prepositions and have similar meanings, but 为了 **wèile** is more commonly used in everyday Chinese.

wèishénme 为什么 [v+obj: 为 for + 什么 what] **ADV** why, what for ■ 你昨天为什么没有来上课？**Nǐ zuótiān wèishénme méiyǒu lái shàngkè?** *Why didn't you come to school yesterday?*

wèi 未 **ADJ** have not, did not ■ 该生未经批准不来上课，将受处分。**Gāishēng wèi jīng pīzhǔn bù lái shàngkè, jiāng shòu chǔfèn.** *This student was absent from class without permission and will be disciplined.*

NOTE: 未 **wèi** is only used in rather formal, written styles. In everyday Chinese, 没有 **méiyǒu** is used instead.

wèibì 未必 **ADV** not necessarily, may not

wèilái 未来 **N** future ■ 少年儿童是国家的未来。**Shàonián értóng shì guójiā de wèilái.** *Teenagers and children are the future of a nation.* ■ 我们对未来有信心。**Wǒmen duì wèilái yǒu xìnxīn.** *We have confidence in the future.*

wèimiǎn 未免 **ADV** rather, a bit too

wèi 位[1] **MEASURE WORD** (a polite measure word used with people) 一位老师 yí wèi lǎoshī a teacher ■ 那位先生是谁？**Nà wèi xiānsheng shì shuí?** *Who is that gentleman?*

wèi 位[2] **N** place, location

wèiyú 位于 **V** be located in, be situated

wèizhi 位置 [comp: 位 seat + 置 locate] **N** 1 place, location ■ 没有人能确定沉船的位置。**Méiyǒu rén néng quèdìng chénchuán de wèizhi.** *Nobody can determine the location of the sunken ship.* 2 (abstract) position, post ■ 人力资源经理是公司里一个极其重要的位置。**Rénlì zīyuán jīnglǐ shì gōngsī li yí ge jíqí zhòngyào de wèizhi.** *The human resources manager holds an extremely important position in a company.*

wèi 味 **N** taste, flavor

wèidao 味道 **N** taste ■ 这个菜味道好极了。**Zhège cài wèidao hǎo jíle.** *This dish is very delicious indeed.* ■ 我觉得这个菜味道太淡，我喜欢味道浓一点的菜。**Wǒ juéde zhège cài wèidao tài dàn, wǒ xǐhuan wèidao nóng yìdiǎn de cài.** *I find this dish too bland. I like strongly-flavored dishes.*

wèi 胃 **N** stomach ■ 我胃疼。**Wǒ wèi téng.** *I have a stomachache.* ■ 她的胃不太好，多吃一点儿就不舒服。**Tā de wèi bú tài hǎo, duō chī yìdiǎnr jiù bù shūfu.** *She has a weak stomach. If she eats a little too much, she feels uncomfortable.*

wèikǒu 胃口 **N** appetite, interest (in something)

wèi 谓 **TRAD** 謂 **V** be called (See suǒwèi 所谓.)

wèi 慰 **V** console (See ānwèi 安慰.)

wèiwèn 慰问 [comp: 慰 console + 问 ask] **V** express sympathy and solicitude for

wèi 畏 **V** fear

wèijù 畏惧 [comp: 畏 fear + 惧 dread] **V & N** fear, dread

wèi 喂[1] **INTERJ** 1 hey ■ 喂，你的票呢？**Wèi, nǐ de piào ne?** *Hey, where's your ticket?* 2 hello, hi ■ 喂，这里是大华公司，您找谁？**Wèi, zhèlǐ shì Dàhuá Gōngsī, nín zhǎo shuí?** *Hello, this is Dahua Company. Who would you like to speak to?*

NOTE: In telephone conversation 喂 **wèi** is equivalent to *hello*. In other contexts, 喂 **wèi** is a rude way of getting people's attention. It is more polite to say 对不起 **duìbuqǐ**, e.g. ■ 对不起，先生，您的票呢？**Duìbuqǐ, xiānsheng, nín de piào ne?** *Excuse me, sir, where's your ticket?*

wèi 喂[2] **V** feed ■ 她每天夜里起来给孩子喂奶。**Tā měitiān yèli qǐlai gěi háizi wèi nǎi.** *Every night she gets up to feed her baby.*

wèilán 蔚蓝 **ADJ** azure, sky blue

wēn 温 **ADJ** warm, temperate, gentle

wēndài 温带 [modif: 温 warm + 带 zone] **N** temperate zone 北温带 Běiwēndài the North Temperate Zone

wēndù 温度 [modif: 温 warmth + 度 degree] **N** (atmospheric) temperature ■ 今天温度比较低，但是没有风，所以不觉得怎么冷。**Jīntiān wēndù bǐjiào dī, dànshì méiyǒu fēng, suǒyǐ bù juéde zěnme lěng.** *The temperature is rather low today but it is not windy. So you don't feel very cold.*

NOTE: (1) 温度 **wēndù** generally refers to atmospheric temperature only. For body temperature the expression is 体温 **tǐwēn**, e.g. ■ 人的正常体温是多少？**Rénde zhèngcháng tǐwēn shì duōshǎo?** *What is the normal temperature of a human being?* When a person has a fever, however, 热度 **rèdù** is used to refer to his/her temperature, e.g. ■ 他今天热度还很高。**Tā jīntiān rèdù hái hěn gāo.** *He is still running a fever.* (2) The Chinese use the centigrade system, which is called 摄氏 **shèshì**, e.g. ■ 今天最高温度摄氏

二十八度。**Jīntiān zuì gāo wēndù shèshì érshíbā dù.** *Today's maximum temperature is 28 degrees centigrade.* In everyday usage, however, people usually omit 摄氏 **shèshì.**

wēnhé 温和 [comp: 温 warm + 和 mild] ADJ 1 (of climate) temperate, without extreme temperature 温和的气候 wēnhé de qìhòu mild, temperate climate

2 (of people) gentle, mild 语气温和 yǔqì wēnhé mild tone

wēnnuǎn 温暖 [comp: 温 warm + 暖 warm] ADJ warm

wēnróu 温柔 [comp: 温 gentle + 柔 soft] ADJ (of people) gentle and soft, soothing

wén 文 N culture

wénběn 文本 text file

wénhuà 文化 N culture ■ 语言中有很多文化知识。**Yǔyán zhong yǒu hěn duō wénhuà zhīshi.** *A language contains a great deal of cultural knowledge.* ■ 我对中国文化知道得不多。**Wǒ duì Zhōngguó wénhuà zhīdào de bù duō.** *I don't know much about Chinese culture.*

wénjiàn 文件 N document, file (份 **fèn**) ■ 这个文件你保留在电脑里了吗？**Zhège wénjiàn nǐ bǎoliú zài diànnǎo li le ma?** *Have you saved this file in the computer?*
文件管理 wénjiàn guǎnlǐn file management

wénjù 文具 N stationery, writing material

wénmíng 文明 [comp: 文 culture + 明 enlightenment] I N civilization, culture ■ 各种文明各有优点，各有缺点。**Gè zhǒng wénmíng gè yǒu yōudiǎn, gè yǒu quēdiǎn.** *Each of the civilizations has its merits and shortcomings.* II ADJ civilized ■ 在文明社会不应该存在这种现象。**Zài wénmíng shèhuì bù yīnggāi cúnzài zhè zhǒng xiànxiàng.** *Such a phenomenon should not exist in a civilized society.*

wénpíng 文凭 N diploma, certificate of academic achievements (张 **zhāng**)

wénwù 文物 [modif: 文 cultural + 物 object] N cultural relic, artifact
文物商店 wénwù shāngdiàn antique shop

wénxiàn 文献 N document, literature of historical value

wénxué 文学 N literature ■ 我姐姐在大学念英国文学。**Wǒ jiějie zài dàxué niàn Yīngguó wénxué.** *My elder sister studies English literature in university.*
文学家 wénxuéjiā (great) writer

wényǎ 文雅 ADJ cultured and refined, elegant and polished

wényì 文艺 [comp: 文 literature + 艺 art] N literature and art; performing arts ■ 我妈妈喜欢文艺，我爸爸喜欢体育。**Wǒ māma xǐhuan wényì, wǒ bàba xǐhuan tǐyù.** *My mother likes literature and art while my father likes sports.*

wényì wǎnhuì 文艺晚会 an evening of entertainment, soirée

wénzhāng 文章 [comp: 文 writing + 章 chapter] N essay, article (篇 **piān**) ■ 昨天晚报上有一篇很有意思的文章。**Zuótiān wǎnbào shang yǒu yì piān hěn yǒu yìsi de wénzhāng.** *There's an interesting article in yesterday's evening paper.* ■ 他文章写得又快又好。**Tā wénzhāng xiě de yòu kuài yòu hǎo.** *He writes good essays, and he writes them quickly.*

wénzi 文字 [comp: 文 writing + 字 script] N written language, script, character ■ 这本小说已经翻译成六种文字了。**Zhè běn xiǎoshuō yǐjīng fānyì chéng liù zhǒng wénzì le.** *This novel has been translated into six languages.*
文字处理 wénzì chǔlǐ word processing

wén 纹 TRAD 紋 N lines, veins (See **zhòuwén** 皱纹.)

wén 蚊 N mosquito

wénzi 蚊子 [suffix: 蚊 mosquito + 子 nominal suffix] N mosquito (只 **zhī**) ■ 这里夏天有蚊子吗？**Zhèli xiàtiān yǒu wénzi ma?** *Are there mosquitoes here in summer?*

wén 闻 TRAD 聞 N what is heard (See **xīnwén** 新闻.)

wěn 稳 TRAD 穩 ADJ steady, stable ■ 等车停稳了再下车。**Děng chē tíng wěnle zài xià chē.** *Do not get off the car (or bus) before it comes to a complete stop.*

wěndìng 稳定 [comp: 稳 stable + 定 fixed] ADJ stable ■ 现在的形势十分稳定。**Xiànzài de xíngshì shífēn wěndìng.** *The present situation is very stable.*

wěn 吻 V & N kiss ■ 每天晚上儿子睡觉前，她都要吻吻他。**Měitiān wǎnshang érzi shuìjiào qián, tā dōu yào wěn wěn tā.** *Before her son went to sleep every evening, she would kiss him.*

wèn 问 TRAD 問 V ask (a question), inquire ■ 我可以问你一个问题吗？**Wǒ kěyǐ wèn nǐ yí ge wèntí ma?** *May I ask you a question?*

wèn hǎo 问好 V ask after, give greetings to ■ 请代问您父母亲好。**Qǐng dài wèn nín fù-mǔqin hǎo.** *Please give my regards to your parents.*

wènhòu 问候 V give regards to, send regards to, ask after ■ 见到王老师，替我问候他。**Jiàndào Wáng lǎoshī, tì wǒ wènhòu tā.** *When you see Teacher Wang, please give him my regards.* ■ 我在信里问候她全家。**Wǒ zài xìnli wènhòu tā quán jiā.** *In the letter I sent my regards to his family.*

wènlù 问路 V ask the way

wènshì 问世 V be published, come into being

wèntí 问题 [comp: 问 inquiry + 题 question] N question ■ "有什么问题吗？" "有，我有一个问题。" **"Yǒu shénme wèntí ma?" "Yǒu, wǒ yǒu yí ge wèntí."** *"Do you have any questions?" "Yes, I do."*

wō 窝 N nest, lair

乌窝 niǎowō bird nest

wǒ 我 **PRON** I, me ■ 我叫张明，我是中国人。**Wǒ jiào Zhāng Míng, wǒ shì Zhōngguórén.** *My name is Zhang Ming. I'm Chinese.*

wǒmen 我们 [suffix: 我 I, me + 们 suffix denoting a plural number] **PRON** we, us ■ 我们是学中文的学生。**Wǒmen shì xué Zhōngwén de xuésheng.** *We're students of Chinese.*

wò 卧 **V** lie

卧床休息 wòchuáng xiūxi lie in bed and rest

wòshì 卧室 **N** bedroom (间 **jiān**)

wò 握 **V** hold, grasp

wòshǒu 握手 [v+obj: 握 hold + 手 hand] **V** shake hands ■ 他和新认识的朋友握手。**Tā hé xīn rènshi de péngyou wòshǒu.** *He shook hands with his new friends.*

wū 乌 **TRAD** 烏 **ADJ** black, dark

wūhēi 乌黑 **ADJ** pitch-black, jet-black

wū 污 **N** filth

wūmiè 污蔑 **V & N** slander, vilify; slander

wūrǎn 污染 [comp: 污 soil + 染 dye] **V & N** pollute; pollution ■ 这家化工厂严重污染环境，必须关闭。**Zhè jiā huàgōngchǎng yánzhòng wūrǎn huánjìng, bìxū guānbì.** *This chemical plant is seriously polluting the environment and must be closed down.* ■ 空气污染影响了生活质量。**Kōngqì wūrǎn yǐngxiǎngle shēnghuó zhìliàng.** *Air pollution affects the quality of life.*

wūrǔ 污辱 same as 侮辱 **wǔrǔ**

wū 诬 **TRAD** 誣 **V** accuse falsely

wūxiàn 诬陷 **V** frame (somebody)

诬陷好人 wūxiàn hǎorén frame an innocent person

wū 屋 **N** house, room

wūzi 屋子 [suffix: 屋 house, room + 子 nominal suffix] **N** room (间 **jiān**) ■ 这个房子有几间屋子？**Zhège fángzi yǒu jǐ jiān wūzi?** *How many rooms are there in the house?*

NOTE: 屋子 **wūzi** in the sense of *room* is only used in north China. To southern Chinese 屋子 **wūzi** may mean *house*. To avoid ambiguity, it is better to use the word 房间 **fángjiān** for *room*.

wú 无 **TRAD** 無 **V** have no (**ANTONYM** 有 **yǒu**) ■ 我们无法解决这个问题。**Wǒmen wú fǎ jiějué zhège wèntí.** *We have no way to solve this problem.*

wúbǐ 无比 **ADJ** matchless, unparalleled

wúcháng 无偿 [v+obj: 无 have no + 偿 compensation] **ADJ** free, gratis

无偿服务 wúcháng fúwù voluntary service

wúchǐ 无耻 [modif: 无 have no + 耻 shame] **ADJ** shameless, brazen

wúcóng 无从 **V** have no way (of doing something), be not in a position (to do something)

wú dòng yú zhōng 无动于衷 **IDIOM** unmoved, untouched, indifferent

wúfēi 无非 **ADV** nothing but, no more than ■ 他无非是为了钱。**Tā wúfēi shì wèile qián.** *He wants nothing but money.*

wúgū 无辜 **ADJ** innocent, not guilty

wú jīng dǎ cǎi 无精打采 **ADJ** in low spirits, listless

wú kě fèng gào 无可奉告 **IDIOM** no comment

wú kě nàihé 无可奈何 **IDIOM** there is no way out, have no alternative, helpless

wúlài 无赖 **I N** rascal **II ADV** rascally

wú lǐ qǔ nào 无理取闹 **V** willfully make trouble, be deliberately provocative

wúliáo 无聊 **ADJ 1** bored **2** silly, meaningless

wúlùn 无论 **CONJ** same as 不管 **bùguǎn**. Tends to be used in writing.

wúnài 无奈 **ADV** having no alternative, helplessly

wú néng wéi lì 无能为力 **V** be totally powerless

wú qióng wú jìn 无穷无尽 **ADJ** infinite, endless, boundless

wúshù 无数 [modif: 无 no + 数 number] **ADJ** innumerable, countless ■ 无数事实证明，那种社会制度是行不通的。**Wúshù shìshí zhèngmíng, nà zhǒng shèhuì zhìdù shì xíngbutōng de.** *Innumerable facts have proven that kind of social system does not work.*

wúsuǒwèi 无所谓 **I V** doesn't matter ■ 他同意不同意，无所谓；反正我已经决定了。**Tā tóngyì bù tóngyì, wúsuǒwèi; fǎnzheng wǒ yǐjing juédìngle.** *It doesn't matter whether he approves or not – I've made up my mind anyway.* **II** indifferent, apathetic ■ 哪个队赢，哪个队输，我都无所谓。**Nǎge duì yíng, nǎge duì shū, wǒ dōu wúsuǒwèi.** *Which team will win, which team will lose, I am indifferent.* (→ *I don't care about the outcome of the game.*)

wú wēi bú zhì 无微不至 **ADJ** meticulous, sparing no effort, paying attention to every detail

无微不至的照顾 wú wēi búzhì de zhàogù meticulous care

wú yōu wú lǜ 无忧无虑 **ADJ** totally carefree

wúzhī 无知 **ADJ** ignorant

wǔ 五 **NUMERAL** five ■ 五五二十五。**Wǔ wǔ èrshíwǔ.** *Five times five is twenty-five.* (5x5=25)

五星红旗 wǔ xīng hóng qí the five-star red flag (the Chinese national flag)

wǔ 午 **N** noon

wǔfàn 午饭 [modif: 午 noon + 饭 meal] **N** lunch (顿 **dùn**) ■ 我在学校吃午饭。**Wǒ zài xuéxiào chī wǔfàn.** *I have lunch in school.* ■ 工人有一小时的午饭时间。**Gōngrén yǒu yì xiǎoshí de wǔfàn shíjiān.** *The workers have a one-hour lunch break.*

wǔ 武 **N** military

wǔqì 武器 [modif: 武 military + 器 artifact] **N** weapon (件 **jiàn**) ■ 不准带任何武器上飞机。**Bù zhǔn dài rènhé wǔqì shàng fēijī.** *It is forbidden to bring a weapon of any kind on board the plane.*

大规模杀伤武器 dàguīmó shāshāng wǔqì weapon of mass destruction (WMD)

wǔshù 武术 [modif: 武 martial + 术 arts] **N** martial arts ■ 他在中国学了三年武术。**Tā zài Zhōngguó xuéle sān nián wǔshù.** *He studied martial arts in China for three years.*

wǔxiá 武侠 **N** swordsman, knight

wǔzhuāng 武装 **V & N** arm, get armed; arms 武装到牙齿 wǔzhuāng dào yáchǐ be armed to the teeth / 解除武装 jiěchú wǔzhuāng lay down arms, be disarmed

wǔ 侮 **V** insult

wǔrǔ 侮辱 [comp: 侮 insult + 辱 insult] **V & N** insult, humiliate; insult, humiliation ■ 我不能容忍别人侮辱我的父母。**Wǒ bùnéng róngrěn biéren wǔrǔ wǒde fùmǔ.** *I can't tolerate someone insulting my parents.* ■ 你这么说，是对我的侮辱。**Nǐ zhème shuō, shì duì wǒde wǔrǔ.** *What you said was an insult to me.*

wǔ 舞 **N** dance

wǔdǎo 舞蹈 **V & N** dance

wǔtái 舞台 **N** stage, arena

wù 务 **TRAD** 務 **V** work

wùbì 务必 **ADV** must, be sure to

wùshí 务实 **ADJ** pragmatic, practical

wù 勿 **V** do not, don't ■ 请勿吸烟。**Qǐngwù xīyān.** *Please do not smoke (→ No smoking. Smoke-free.)*

wù 物 **N** things, objects

wùjià 物价 [modif: 物 thing + 价 price] **N** price, commodity price ■ 最近的物价比较稳定。**Zuìjìn de wùjià bǐjiào wěndìng.** *Prices have been quite stable recently.*

wùlǐ 物理 [modif: 物 things, objects + 理 pattern, rule] **N** physics ■ 我弟弟物理、数学都挺好。**Wǒ dìdi wùlǐ, shùxué dōu tíng hǎo.** *My younger brother is good at physics and mathematics.*

wù měi jià lián 物美价廉 **IDIOM** the goods are satisfactory and the prices reasonable, good and inexpensive

wùtǐ 物体 **N** object, substance

wùyè 物业 **N** real estate, property 物业管理 wùyè guǎnlǐ property management

wùzhì 物质 **N** matter, substance

wùzī 物资 **N** goods and materials, supplies

wù 雾 **TRAD** 霧 **N** fog, mist ■ 今天早上有大雾，很多人迟到。**Jīntiān zǎoshang yǒu dà wù, hěn duō rén chídào.** *Many people were late for work this morning because of the heavy fog.* ■ 有雾天气，开车要特别小心。**Yǒu wù tiānqì, kāichē yào tèbié xiǎoxīn.** *You should be particularly careful when driving in foggy weather.*

wùmái 雾霾 **N** smog

wù 误 **TRAD** 誤 **ADJ** erroneous

wùchà 误差 **N** (in physics) error

wùhuì 误会 [modif: 误 mistaken + 会 understanding] **V & N** misunderstand, misconstrue; misunderstanding ■ 你误会了我的意思。**Nǐ wùhuìle wǒ de**

yìsi. *You've misconstrued my meaning.* ■ 我没有说清楚，造成了误会，很抱歉。**Wǒ méiyǒu shuō qīngchu, zàochéngle wùhuì, hěn bàoqiàn.** *I did not make it clear, which has caused a misunderstanding. I apologize.*

wùjiě 误解 **V & N** misunderstand; misunderstanding ■ 你误解了我的意思。**Nǐ wùjiě le wǒde yìsi.** *You misunderstood my meaning.*

xī 西 **N** west, western ■ 河东是一座小城，河西是一大片农场。**Hé dōng shì yí zuò xiǎo chéng, hé xī shì yí dà piàn nóngchǎng.** *East of the river is a small town, and on the west is a big farm.*

xīběi 西北 [comp: 西 west + 北 north] **N** northwest, the Northwest ■ 中国正在努力开发大西北。**Zhōngguó zhèngzài nǔlì kāifā dà xīběi.** *China is making efforts to develop her northwest region.*

xībian 西边 [modif: 西 west + 边 side] **N** west side, to the west, in the west ■ 太阳在西边下山。**Tàiyang zài xībian xiàshān.** *The sun sets in the west.*

xīcān 西餐 [modif: 西 West + 餐 meal] **N** Western-style meal ■ 走，我请你吃西餐。**Zǒu, wǒ qǐng nǐ chī xīcān.** *Let's go. I'll treat you to a Western-style meal.*

xīcānguǎn 西餐馆 **N** Western-style restaurant (家 **jiā**)

xīfāng 西方 [modif: 西 West + 方 direction, part] **N** the West, Occident ■ 西方文明有什么重要特点？**Xīfāng wénmíng yǒu shénme zhòngyào tèdiǎn?** *What are the major characteristics of Western civilization?*

xīfú 西服 [modif: 西 West + 服 clothes] **N 1** Western-style clothes **2** Western-style coat (件 **jiàn**)

xīguā 西瓜 **N** watermelon (只 **zhī**) ■ 中国人夏天最喜欢吃西瓜。**Zhōngguórén xiàtiān zuì xǐhuan chī xīguā.** *The Chinese people's favorite fruit in summer is the watermelon.*

xīhóngshì 西红柿 [modif: 西 Western + 红 red + 柿 persimmon] **N** tomato (只 **zhī**) ■ 我要买一公斤西红柿。**Wǒ yào mǎi yì gōngjīn xīhóngshì.** *I want to buy a kilogram of tomatoes.*

xīnán 西南 [comp: 西 west + 南 south] **N** southwest, the Southwest ■ 中国西南地方有很多少数民族。**Zhōngguó xīnán dìfang yǒu hěn duō shǎoshù mínzú.** *There are many national minorities in China's southwestern region.*

xī 牺 **TRAD** 犧 **N** sacrifice

xīshēng 牺牲 [v+obj: 牺 sacrifice + 牲 domestic animal] **V & N 1** give up, offer, at the expense of; giving up, sacrifice ■ 他们为子女牺牲了大量时间和金钱。**Tāmen wèi zǐnǔ xīshēngle dàliàng shíjiān hé jīnqián.** *They gave up a great deal of time and*

money for their children. ■ 她为家庭作出了巨大牺牲。**Tā wèi jiātíng zuòchule jùdà xīshēng.** *She made great sacrifices for the family.* **2** give one's life for, die a martyr's death

xī 吸 v inhale, suck

xīqǔ 吸取 [comp: 吸 absorb + 取 take] **v** absorb, draw
吸取教训 xīqǔ jiàoxun learn a lesson (from past experience)

xīshōu 吸收 [comp: 吸 suck + 收 receive] **v** suck up, absorb ■ 我们要吸收别人的好经验。**Wǒmen yào xīshōu biérén de hǎo jīngyàn.** *We should draw from other people's positive experiences.*

xīyān 吸烟 v smoke (a cigarette, a cigar, etc) ■ 这里不准吸烟。**Zhèli bù zhǔn xīyān.** *Smoking is not allowed here.*

xīyǐn 吸引 [comp: 吸 suck + 引 guide] **v** attract ■ 我们想吸引更多的旅游者来我国游览。**Wǒmen xiǎng xīyǐn gèng duō de lǚyóuzhě lái wǒguó yóulǎn.** *We want to attract more tourists to our country.*
吸引力 xīyǐnlì attraction, appeal / 有吸引力 yǒu xīyǐnlì attractive, appealing

xī 希 v wish

xīwàng 希望 [comp: 希 wish + 望 look forward to] **v & N** hope, wish ■ 希望你旅行愉快！**Xīwàng nǐ lǚxíng yúkuài!** *I wish you a happy journey. (→ Bon voyage!)* ■ 孩子是父母的希望。**Háizi shì fùmǔ de xīwàng.** *Children are their parents' hope.*

xī 稀 ADJ rare (See **zhēnxī 珍稀**.)

xī 夕 N dusk, twilight

xīyáng 夕阳 N the setting sun

xī 昔 N bygone days, old times

xīrì 昔日 N former days, yesteryears

xī 惜 v 1 cherish, treasure (See **zhēnxī 珍惜**.) **2** have pity on (See **kěxī 可惜**.)

xī 悉 v know (See **shúxi 熟悉**.)

xī 溪 N small stream
小溪 xiǎoxī small stream

xī 息 v cease (See **xiūxi 休息**.)

xī 熄 v extinguish (fire)

xīmiè 熄灭 v (of fire) die out, be extinguished

xī 膝 N knee

xīgài 膝盖 N knee

xí 习 TRAD 習 v practice

xíguàn 习惯 [comp: 习 be familiar with + 惯 be accustomed to] **v & N** be accustomed to, be used to; habit ■ 很多中国人不习惯吃西餐。**Hěn duō Zhōngguórén bù xíguàn chī xīcān.** *Many Chinese are not used to eating Western-style meals.* ■ 他有一个坏习惯，我希望他改掉。**Tā yǒu yí ge huài xíguàn, wǒ xīwàng tā gǎidiào.** *He has a bad habit. I hope he'll get rid of it.*
习惯上 xíguàn shang habitually

xísú 习俗 [comp: 习 practice + 俗 custom] **N** customs and habits, custom

xí 袭 TRAD 襲 v attack

xíjī 袭击 v (of troops) attack, raid
突然袭击 tūrán xíjī sudden attack, launch a sudden attack

xí 媳 N daughter–in-law

xífù 媳妇 N daughter-in-law
儿媳妇 érxífù daughter-in-law

NOTE: In some dialects, 媳妇 **xífù** may also refer to a *wife*, e.g. 娶媳妇 **qǔ xífù** to get a wife, (for men) *to get married.*

xí 席 N seat (See **chūxí 出席, zhǔxí 主席**.)

xǐ 洗 v wash ■ 吃饭前要洗手。**Chīfàn qián yào xǐ shǒu.** *You should wash your hands before having a meal.*

xǐshǒujiān 洗手间 N toilet, restroom, washroom ■ 请问，洗手间在哪里？**Qǐngwèn, xǐshǒujiān zài nǎli?** *Excuse me, where's the washroom?*

NOTE: 洗手间 **xǐshǒujiān** is a common euphemism for *toilet.*

xǐyījī 洗衣机 [modif: 洗衣 wash clothes + 机 machine] **N** washing machine (台 **tái**) ■ 洗衣机又坏了，得买一台新的了。**Xǐyījī yòu huàile, děi mǎi yì tái xīnde le.** *The washing machine broke down again. We've got to buy a new one.*

xǐzǎo 洗澡 [comp: 洗 wash + 澡 bath, take a bath] **v** take a bath, take a shower ■ 有人每天早上洗澡，有人每天晚上洗澡。**Yǒurén měi tiān zǎoshang xǐzǎo, yǒurén měi tiān wǎnshang xǐzǎo.** *Some people take a bath early every morning, and others in the evening.* ■ 他习惯临睡前洗一个热水澡。**Tā xíguàn línshuì qián xǐ yí ge rèshuǐ zǎo.** *He is used to taking a hot bath just before going to bed.*
洗澡间 xǐzǎojiān bathroom, shower room (same as 浴室 **yùshì**.)

xǐ 喜 v be fond of

xǐhuan 喜欢 [comp: 喜 be fond of + 欢 pleasure] **v** like, be fond of ■ 你喜欢不喜欢中国音乐？**Nǐ xǐhuan bu xǐhuan Zhōngguó yīnyuè?** *Do you like Chinese music?* ■ 他喜欢一边喝啤酒，一边看体育节目。**Tā xǐhuan yìbiān hē píjiǔ, yìbiān kàn tǐyù jiémù.** *He likes to drink beer while watching sports programs.*

xǐ wén lè jiàn 喜闻乐见 IDIOM love to see and hear, appealing

xǐyuè 喜悦 [comp: 喜 happy + 悦 joy] **ADJ** happy, joyful

xì 戏 TRAD 戲 N drama, play (出 **chū**) ■ 今天晚上我们去看戏。**Jīntiān wǎnshang wǒmen qù kàn xì.** *We're going to watch a play this evening.*

xìjù 戏剧 N drama, play, theater

xì 系 N department (of a university) ■ 这座大学有十二个系，最大的是电脑系。**Zhè zuò dàxué yǒu shí'èr ge xì, zuì dà de shì diànnǎo xì.** *This univer-*

sity has twelve departments; the biggest is the Computing Science Department.

系主任 xì zhǔrèn chair of a (university) department

xìliè 系列 **N** series

一系列 yíxìliè a series of

xìtǒng 系统 **N** a group of items serving a common purpose, system (套 **tào**) ■ 系统中只要有一个地方出毛病，整套系统就不能正常工作。**Xìtǒng zhōng zhǐyào yǒu yí ge dìfang chū máobìng, zhěngtào xìtǒng jiù bù néng zhèngcháng gōngzuò.** *If only one part of a system goes wrong, the entire system will not be able to function properly.*

xì 细 **TRAD** 細 **ADJ** thin, slender (of objects shaped like a strip) (**ANTONYM** 粗 **cū**) ■ 中国的面条又细又长，是我最喜欢吃的东西。**Zhōngguó de miàntiáo yòu xì yòu cháng, shì wǒ zuì xǐhuan chī de dōngxi.** *Chinese noodles are thin and long; they are my favorite food.* ■ 他把计划的各个方面都考虑得很细。**Tā bǎ jìhuà de gè ge fāngmiàn dōu kǎolǜ de hěn xì.** *He considered every single aspect of the plan very carefully.*

xìbāo 细胞 **N** (in biology) cell

xìjié 细节 **N** detail ■ 这件事的细节我不清楚。**Zhè jiàn shì de xìjié wǒ bùqīngchu.** *I'm not clear about the details of this matter.*

xìjūn 细菌 [modif: 细 tiny + 菌 bacterium] **N** bacterium, germ ■ 科学家还没有找到引起这种病的细菌。**Kēxuéjiā hái méiyǒu zhǎodào yǐnqǐ zhè zhǒng bìng de xìjūn.** *Scientists have not identified the bacterium that causes this disease.*

xìxīn 细心 [modif: 细 tiny + 心 the heart] **ADJ** very careful, meticulous ■ 她做完数学练习后总要细心地检查一遍。**Tā zuòwán shùxué liànxí hòu zǒngyào xìxīn de jiǎnchá yíbiàn.** *After doing mathematics exercises she checks every question very carefully.*

xìzhì 细致 **ADJ** careful, meticulous

xiā 瞎 **ADJ** blind

xiá 峡 **TRAD** 峽 **N** gorge

xiágǔ 峡谷 **N** gorge, canyon

xiá 狭 **TRAD** 狹 **ADJ** narrow

xiá'ài 狭隘 **ADJ** narrow, narrow-minded

心胸狭隘 xīnxiōng xiá'ài narrow-minded, intolerant

xiázhǎi 狭窄 **ADJ** cramped, narrow

xiá 侠 **TRAD** 俠 **N** knight errant

xiá 霞 **N** rosy clouds, morning or evening glow

xià 下¹ **N** below, under, underneath (**ANTONYM** 上 **shàng**) ■ 树下很凉快。**Shù xià hěn liángkuài.** *It's cool under the tree.*

山下 shānxia at the foot of a mountain or hills

xià 下² **V** go/come down (**ANTONYM** 上 **shàng**) ■ 他常常走下楼。**Tā chángcháng zǒu xià lóu.** *He often walks downstairs.*

下班 xiàbān get off work ■ 我下班以后要去买

菜。**Wǒ xiàbān yǐhòu yào qù mǎi cài.** *I'll go and do grocery shopping after work.*

下车 xiàchē get off a vehicle ■ 到了，下车吧！**Dàole, xiàchē ba!** *Here we are. Let's get off the car (or bus).*

下课 xiàkè finish class ■ 你们每天几点钟下课？**Nǐmen měi tiān jǐ diǎnzhōng xiàkè?** *When does school finish every day?*

下来 xiàlai come down ■ 晚饭做好了，快下来吃吧！**Wǎnfàn zuòhǎo le, kuài xiàlai chī ba!** *Supper is ready. Come down and eat!*

下去 xiàqu go down ■ 时间不早了，我们(从山上)下去吧。**Shíjiān bù zǎo le, wǒmen (cóng shānshang) xiàqu ba.** *It's quite late. Let's go down (the hill).*

xià 下³ **MEASURE WORD** (used with certain verbs to indicate the number of times the action is done) ■ 我试了几下，都不行。**Wǒ shìle jǐ xià, dōu bù xíng.** *I tried several times, but it didn't work.*

… 一下 … yíxià (used after a verb to indicate the action is done briefly or tentatively) ■ 我看一下电视就去洗澡。**Wǒ kàn yíxià diànshì, jiù qù xǐzǎo.** *I'll watch TV for a short while before taking a bath.*

xiàbian 下边 [modif: 下 below, underneath + 边 side] **N** below, under (**ANTONYM** 上边 **shàngbian**) ■ 椅子下边有几本书，是谁的？**Yǐzi xiàbian yǒu jǐ běn shū, shì shéi de?** *There are some books under the chair. Whose are they?*

xiàgǎng 下岗 [v+obj: 下 leave + 岗 post, job] **V** be laid off, be unemployed ■ 张师傅下岗好几年了，生活很困难。**Zhāng shīfu xiàgǎng hǎo jǐ nián le, shēnghuó hěn kùnnan.** *Master worker Zhang was laid off several years ago and has been living a hard life.*

下岗工人 xiàgǎng gōngrén worker who has been laid off, unemployed worker

xiàmiàn 下面 **N** same as 下边 **xiàbian**

xiàshǔ 下属 **N** subordinate (person), lower-level

xiàwǔ 下午 [modif: 下 lower half + 午 noon] **N** afternoon (**ANTONYM** 上午 **shàngwǔ**) ■ 上午多云，下午天晴了。**Shàngwǔ duō yún, xiàwǔ tiān qíng le.** *It was cloudy in the morning, but it cleared up in the afternoon.*

xiàzài 下载 [modif: 下 down, downward + 载 carry] **V** download

xià 吓 **TRAD** 嚇 **V** frighten, scare, be frightened, be scared ■ 我不是吓你，你父亲的病极其严重。**Wǒ bú shì xià nǐ, nǐ fùqin de bìng jíqí yánzhòng.** *I don't want to frighten you, but your father's illness is extremely severe.* ■ 她看到强盗手里拿着刀，吓得尖叫起来。**Tā kàndào qiángdào shǒuli názhe dāo, xià de jiānjiào qǐlai.** *When she saw the robber holding a knife in hand, she was so frightened that she screamed.*

xià 夏 **N** summer

xiàlìngyíng 夏令营 **N** summer camp

xiàtiān 夏天 [modif: 夏 summer + 天 days] **N** summer ■ 北京的夏天热吗？ *Běijīng de xiàtiān rè ma? Is summer in Beijing hot?* ■ 我们夏天常常到海边去游泳。 *Wǒmen xiàtiān chángcháng dào hǎibiān qù yóuyǒng. We often go swimming by the seaside in summer.*

xiān 先 **ADV** first (in time sequence) (ANTONYM 后 hòu) ■ 他早上先跑步，再吃早饭。 *Tā zǎoshang xiān pǎobù, zài chī zǎofàn. Early in the morning he first jogs and then has breakfast.* ■ 您先请。 *Nín xiān qǐng. After you.*

先 … 再 … xiān … zài … first ... and then...

xiānhòu 先后 [comp: 先 before + 后 later] **ADV** one after another, successively ■ 他们四个孩子大学毕业后先后离家。 *Tāmen sì ge háizi dàxué bìyè hòu xiānhòu lí jiā. After graduation from university their four sons and daughters left home one after another.* ■ 他的祖父和祖母在去年先后去世。 *Tā de zǔfù hé zǔmǔ zài qùnián xiānhòu qùshì. His grandfather and grandmother died one after another last year.*

xiānjìn 先进 [modif: 先 in advance + 进 go forward] **ADJ** advanced ■ 这种照相机使用最先进的技术。 *Zhè zhǒng zhàoxiàngjī shǐyòng zuì xiānjìn de jìshù. This camera uses the most advanced technology.*

xiānqián 先前 **ADV** previously

xiānsheng 先生 [modif: 先 first, before + 生 born] **N 1** Mr ■ 王先生，这位是张先生。 *Wáng xiānsheng, zhè wèi shì Zhāng xiānsheng. Mr Wang, this is Mr Zhang.* **2** sir, gentleman ■ 先生，有事吗？ *Xiānsheng, yǒu shì ma? Is there anything I can do for you, sir?* ■ 有一位先生要见你。 *Yǒu yí wèi xiānsheng yào jiàn nǐ. There's a gentleman wanting to see you.* **3** husband ■ 您先生在哪儿工作？ *Nín xiānsheng zài nǎr gōngzuò? Where does your husband work?*

xiān 仙 **N** immortal, fairy (See **shénxiān** 神仙.)

xiān 鲜 TRAD 鮮 **ADJ** fresh ■ 她买了几根鲜黄瓜回家做凉菜。 *Tā mǎile jǐ gēn xiān huánggua huíjiā zuò liángcài. She bought several fresh cucumbers and brought them home to prepare a cold dish.*

xiānhuā 鲜花 [modif: 鲜 fresh + 花 flower] **N** fresh flower, flower (朵 duǒ) ■ 他采了路边的一朵鲜花，送给女朋友。 *Tā cǎile lùbiān de yì duǒ xiānhuā, sòng gei nǚpéngyou. He picked a fresh flower by the roadside and gave it to his girlfriend.*

xiānmíng 鲜明 [comp: 鲜 bright + 明 bright] **ADJ** bright, clear, distinct

xiānyàn 鲜艳 [comp: 鲜 bright + 艳 fresh and attractive] **ADJ** bright-colored, gaily-colored

xiān 纤 TRAD 纖 **ADJ** minute, fine

xiānwéi 纤维 **N** fiber ■ 有了化学纤维，衣服便宜多了。 *Yǒule huàxué xiānwéi, yīfu piányi duōle.*

With (the invention of) chemical fiber, clothes have become much cheaper.

xiān 掀 **V** lift, lift up

xiānqǐ 掀起 **V** set off, start

xián 咸 TRAD 鹹 **ADJ** salty ■ 你盐放多了，这个菜太咸。 *Nǐ yán fàngduōle, zhège cài tài xián. You've put too much salt in the dish; it's too salty.*

xián 闲 TRAD 閑 **ADJ** idle, unoccupied ■ 有的人挺忙，有的人闲着：分工不合理。 *Yǒude rén tǐng máng, yǒude rén xiánzhe: fēngōng bù hélǐ. While some are very busy, others are idle. The division of labor is irrational.*

清闲 qīngxián **ADJ** leisurely, carefree

xiánhuà 闲话 [modif: 闲 idle + 话 talk] **N 1** digression ■ 闲话别说了，你有什么事直接说吧。 *Xiánhuà bié shuō le, nǐ yǒu shénme shì zhíjiē shuō ba. No more digression; if you've got something to say, say it straightaway (→ come right to the point.)* **2** gossip, complaint ■ 他喜欢说人家闲话。 *Tā xǐhuan shuō rénjia xiánhuà. He likes to gossip about others.*

xiánrén 闲人 **N** idler, uninvolved person

xiánshì 闲事 **N** matter that does not concern you ■ 别管闲事。 *Bié guǎn xiánshì. It's none of your business.*

xián 贤 TRAD 賢 **ADJ** virtuous

xiánhuì 贤惠 [comp: 贤 virtuous + 惠 kind] **ADJ** (of women) kind and wise, virtuous

xián 弦 **N** string (of a musical instrument), bowstring

xián 衔 TRAD 銜 **V** hold in the mouth

xiánjiē 衔接 **V** link up, join

xián 嫌 **I V** dislike, complain **II N** suspicion

避嫌 bìxián avoid suspicion

xiányí 嫌疑 [comp: 嫌 suspicion + 疑 doubt] **V & N** suspect; suspicion

xiǎn 显 TRAD 顯 **V** appear, look

xiǎnde 显得 **V** appear to be, seem to be ■ 他穿了黑衣服显得更瘦。 *Tā chuānle hēi yīfu xiǎnde gèng shòu. Dressed in a black suit, he appeared all the thinner.*

xiǎnrán 显然 **ADJ, ADV** obvious; obviously ■ 这道题目显然答错了。 *Zhè dào tímù xiǎnrán dá cuò le. The answer to this question is obviously wrong.* ■ 她的计划显然不可行。 *Tā de jìhuà xiǎnrán bù kě xíng. It's obvious that her plan is not feasible.*

xiǎnshì 显示 [comp: 显 display + 示 show] **V** show, manifest

xiǎnzhù 显著 **ADJ** remarkable, outstanding, notable ■ 今年我们公司在开发新产品方面取得了显著成就。 *Jīnnián wǒmen gōngsī zài kāifā xīn chǎnpǐn fāngmiàn qǔdéle xiǎnzhù chéngjiù. This year our company has made notable achievements in developing new products.*

xiǎn 险 TRAD 險 **ADJ** dangerous (See **wēixiǎn** 危险.)

xiàn 县 TRAD 縣 **N** (rural) county ■ 中国有两千左

右个县。**Zhōngguó yǒu liǎngqiān zuǒyòu ge xiàn.** *China has around 2,000 counties.*

xiànchéng 县城 **N** county town, county seat

xiànzhǎng 县长 **N** mayor of a county

xiàn 现 TRAD 現 ADJ present, ready

xiànchǎng 现场 **N 1** (crime, accident, disaster, etc.) scene

犯罪现场 fànzuì xiànchǎng crime scene / 事故现场 shìgù xiànchǎng accident scene

2 on the site, on the spot

xiànchéng 现成 ADJ ready-made

吃现成饭 chī xiànchéng fàn eat a ready-made meal, enjoy the fruit of others' labor

xiàndài 现代 [modif: 现 present + 代 generation] **N** modern times, the contemporary age ■ 我祖父不喜欢现代音乐。**Wǒ zǔfù bù xǐhuan xiàndài yīnyuè.** *My grandfather does not like modern music.* ■ 在这座古庙前，盖了这么一个现代建筑，很不合适。**Zài zhè zuò gǔ miào qián, gàile zhème yí ge xiàndài jiànzhù, hěn bù héshì.** *It is inappropriate to put up such a modern building in front of this ancient temple.*

xiàndàihuà 现代化 **V & N** modernize; modernization ■ 我们的教学手段应该现代化。**Wǒmen de jiàoxué shǒuduàn yīnggāi xiàndàihuà.** *Our means of teaching and learning should be modernized.* ■ 办公设备的现代化提高了工作效率。**Bàngōng shèbèi de xiàndàihuà tígāole gōngzuò xiàolǜ.** *The modernization of office equipment has increased work efficiency.*

xiànjīn 现金 [comp: 现 now, ready + 金 gold, money] **N** ready money, cash

xiànshí 现实 [comp: 现 present + 实 real] **N & ADJ** what is real, reality, actuality; realistic, practical ■ 现实往往不那么美好。**Xiànshí wǎngwǎng bú nàme měihǎo.** *The reality is often not so perfect.* ■ 这个计划不太现实。**Zhège jìhuà bú tài xiànshí.** *This plan is not very realistic.*

xiànxiàng 现象 **N** phenomenon ■ 有些自然现象还不能解释。**Yǒuxiē zìrán xiànxiàng hái bù néng jiěshì.** *Some natural phenomena still cannot be explained.*

xiànzài 现在 [comp: 现 present + 在 being] **N** the present time, now ■ 我现在没有时间，晚上再打电话给他。**Wǒ xiànzài méiyǒu shíjiān, wǎnshang zài dǎ diànhuà gěi tā.** *I don't have time now, I'll ring him this evening.* ■ 现在几点钟？**Xiànzài jǐ diǎn zhōng?** *What time is it?*

xiànzhuàng 现状 [modif: 现 now + 状 situation] **N** current situation

xiàn 线 TRAD 線 **N** string, thread, wire (根 **gēn**) ■ 这根线太短，有没有长一点的？**Zhè gen xiàn tài duǎn, yǒu méi yǒu cháng yìdiǎn de?** *This string is too short. Do you have a longer one?*

xiànsuǒ 线索 **N** clue, lead (e.g. in a police case) 发现线索 fāxiàn xiànsuǒ discover a clue, find a lead

xiàn 宪 TRAD 憲 **N** statute

xiànfǎ 宪法 **N** constitution ■ 根据宪法，公民享有言论自由。**Gēnjù xiànfǎ, gōngmín xiǎngyǒu yánlùn zìyóu.** *According to the Constitution, citizens enjoy freedom of speech.*

xiàn 陷 **V** get bogged down, get trapped

xiànhài 陷害 [comp: 陷 get bogged down + 害 harm] **V** make a trumped-up charge against, frame

xiànjǐng 陷阱 **N** pitfall, trap

xiàn 馅 TRAD 餡 **N** filling, stuffing

xiànr 馅儿 **N** filling, stuffing

xiàn 限 **V** limit

xiànzhì 限制 [comp: 限 limit + 制 control] **V** limit, restrict, confine ■ 为了减肥，她限制自己一天吃两顿饭。**Wèile jiǎnféi, tā xiànzhì zìjǐ yì tiān chī liǎng dùn fàn.** *To reduce weight she restricted herself to two meals a day.* ■ 政府限制进口汽车的数量。**Zhèngfǔ xiànzhì jìnkǒu qìchē de shùliàng.** *The government restricts the number of imported cars.*

xiàn 羡 TRAD 羨 **V** admire, envy

xiànmù 羡慕 [comp: 羡 envy + 慕 envy] **V** envy ■ 她的家庭这么美满，真让人羡慕。**Tā de jiātíng zhème měimǎn, zhēn ràng rén xiànmù!** *Her perfectly happy family really makes one envious.* ■ 我很羡慕记忆力好的人。**Wǒ hěn xiànmù jìyìlì hǎo de rén.** *I envy those who have a good memory.*

xiàn 献 TRAD 獻 **V** offer (See **gòngxiàn** 贡献.)

xiāng 乡 TRAD 鄉 **N** rural town ■ 乡比县小，比村大。**Xiāng bǐ xiàn xiǎo, bǐ cūn dà.** *A rural town is smaller than a county, but bigger than a village.*

xiāngxia 乡下 **N** countryside, rural area ■ 他的爷爷奶奶住在乡下。**Tā de yéye nǎinai zhù zài xiāngxia.** *His grandpa and grandma live in the country.*

xiāngzhèn 乡镇 [comp: 乡 rural town + 镇 township] **N** townships and villages 乡镇企业 xiāngzhèn qǐyè township and village enterprise, rural industry

xiāng 相 ADV each other, mutually

xiāngchà 相差 **V** differ, differ from

xiāngchǔ 相处 **V** get along (with each other)

xiāngdāng 相当 **I** ADJ suitable, appropriate ■ 我在翻译的时候，常常想不出一个相当的词。**Wǒ zài fānyì de shíhou, chángcháng xiǎng bu chū yí ge xiāngdāng de cí.** *When I do translation I often cannot find a suitable word.* **II** ADV fairly, rather, quite ■ 他中文说得相当不错。**Tā Zhōngwén shuō de xiāngdāng búcuò.** *He speaks Chinese rather well.*

xiāngděng 相等 **V** be equal

xiāngduì 相对 ADV relatively, comparatively (ANTONYM 绝对 **juéduì**) 相对来说 xiāngduì láishuō relatively speaking / 相对论 xiāngduìlùn the theory of relativity

xiāngfǎn 相反 ADJ opposite, contrary ■ 不同的

意见，甚至相反的意见都要听。**Bùtóng de yìjiàn, shènzhì xiāngfǎn de yìjiàn dōu yào tīng.** *We should hear out different, even opposing, opinions.*

xiāng fǔ xiāng chéng 相辅相成 **IDIOM** supplement and complement each other

xiāngguān 相关 **v** be related to, be interrelated

xiānghù 相互 **ADJ** mutual, each other ■ 一对年轻人必须相互了解才能考虑婚姻。**Yíduì niánqīngrén bìxū xiānghù liǎojiě cái néng kǎolǜ hūnyīn.** *A young man and a young woman must know each other well before contemplating marriage.*

xiāngsì 相似 **ADJ** similar to, be alike ■ 你提出的方案和我的想法很相似。**Nǐ tíchū de fāng'àn hé wǒ de xiǎngfǎ hěn xiāngsì.** *Your plan is similar to my ideas.* ■ 他们姐妹俩长得很相似，但是脾气性格不一样。**Tāmen jiě-mèi liǎ zhǎng de hěn xiāngsì, dànshì píqì xìnggé bù yíyàng.** *The two sisters resemble each other, but have different temperaments.*

xiāngtóng 相同 **ADJ** identical, same ■ 相同的年龄，相同的经历使他们有很多共同语言。**Xiāngtóng de niánlíng, xiāngtóng de jīnglì shǐ tāmen yǒu hěn duō gòngtóng yǔyán.** *The same age and the same experiences give them lots of common language.*

xiāngxìn 相信 **v** believe, believe in ■ 我不相信他会做这种事。**Wǒ bù xiāngxìn tā huì zuò zhè zhǒng shì.** *I don't believe that he would do such a thing.* ■ 你相信鬼故事吗？**Nǐ xiāngxìn guǐ gùshi ma?** *Do you believe ghost stories?*

xiāngyìng 相应 **ADJ** corresponding, relevant

相应措施 xiāngyìng cuòshī appropriate measures

xiāng 箱 **N** box, chest

xiāngzi 箱子 [suffix: 箱 trunk + 子 nominal suffix] **N** trunk, chest, box, suitcase ■ 这个箱子是她奶奶传给她的。**Zhège xiāngzi shì tā nǎinai chuán gei tā de.** *This trunk was passed down to her from her grandmother.*

xiāng 镶 **TRAD** 鑲 **v 1** set into, set **2** mount

xiāng 香 **ADJ** fragrant, sweet-smelling, aromatic ■ 这花真香！**Zhè huā zhēn xiāng!** *How sweet this flower smells!* ■ 我闻到烤肉的香味。**Wǒ wéndào kǎoròu de xiāngwèi.** *I smell the delicious aroma of roast beef.*

xiāngcháng 香肠 [modif: 香 savory + 肠 intestine] **N** sausage (根 **gēn**) ■ 中国的香肠和西方的香肠味道不一样。**Zhōngguó de xiāngcháng hé xīfāng de xiāngcháng wèidao bù yíyàng.** *Chinese sausages and Western sausages taste very different.*

Xiānggǎng 香港 [modif: 香 fragrant + 港 harbor] **N** Hong Kong

xiāngjiāo 香蕉 [modif: 香 fragrant + 蕉 banana] **N** banana (根 **gēn**) ■ 这些香蕉还没有熟，过两天再吃吧。**Zhèxiē xiāngjiāo hái méiyǒu shú, guò liǎngtiān zài chī ba.** *These bananas are not ripe yet. Let's wait a few days before eating them.*

xiāngzào 香皂 [modif: 香 fragrant + 皂 soap] **N** toilet soap, bath soap (块 **kuài**) ■ 这块香皂很好闻。**Zhè kuài xiāngzào hěn hǎowén.** *This soap smells nice.*

xiáng 详 **TRAD** 詳 **ADJ** detailed

xiángxì 详细 [comp: 详 in detail + 细 tiny] **ADJ** in detail, detailed ■ 我只知道大概的情况，详细情况不清楚。**Wǒ zhǐ zhīdào dàgài de qíngkuàng, xiángxì qíngkuàng bù qīngchu.** *I only know the general situation and am not clear about the details.* ■ 他详细说明了全部经过。**Tā xiángxì shuōmíngle quánbù jīngguò.** *He told the whole story in detail.*

xiáng 降 **v** surrender (See **tóuxiáng** 投降.)

xiǎng 享 **v** enjoy

xiǎngshòu 享受 [comp: 享 enjoy + 受 experience] **v** enjoy ■ 在有些方面现代人享受的比古代皇帝还多。**Zài yǒuxiē fāngmiàn xiàndàirén xiǎngshòu de bǐ gǔdài huángdì hái duō.** *In some respects a modern man enjoys more things than an emperor did in ancient times.* ■ 忙了半个月，今天可以享受一下清闲了。**Mángle bàn ge yuè, jīntiān kěyǐ xiǎngshòu yíxià qīngxián le.** *After half a month's busy work, I can enjoy carefree leisure today.*

xiǎng 响 **TRAD** 響 **ADJ** loud, noisy ■ 教室里在考试，你们说话声音别这么响。**Jiàoshì li zài kǎoshì, nǐmen shuōhuà shēngyīn bié zhènme xiǎng.** *There's an examination in progress in the classroom. Don't talk so loudly.*

xiǎngliàng 响亮 **ADJ** loud and clear, resounding

xiǎngyìng 响应 **v** respond, answer

xiǎng 想 **v** think ■ 这个问题我要想想。**Zhège wèntí wǒ yào xiǎngxiǎng.** *I need to think over this problem.* ■ 我想这个手续不会太麻烦。**Wǒ xiǎng zhè shǒuxù bú huì tài máfan.** *I don't think this procedure will be very complicated.*

想一下 xiǎng yíxià think for a while, give ... some thought ■ 明天晚上跟不跟他一块儿去看电影？让我想一下。**Míngtiān wǎnshang gēn bu gēn tā yíkuàir qù kàn diànyǐng? Ràng wǒ xiàng yì xiǎng.** *Shall I go to the movie with him tomorrow evening? Let me think it over.*

想办法 xiǎng bànfǎ think of a way (to do something) ■ 没关系，我来想办法。**Méiguānxi, wǒ lái xiǎng bànfǎ.** *It's OK. I'll think of a way.*

xiǎngfǎ 想法 [modif: 想 thinking + 法 way, method] **N** what one thinks, idea, opinion ■ 你有什么想法，尽管谈。**Nǐ yǒu shénme xiǎngfǎ, jìnguǎn tán.** *Feel free to say whatever you have in mind.* ■ 老师想了解一下学生对开口语课的想法。**Lǎoshī xiǎng liáojiě yíxià xuésheng duì kāi kǒuyǔ kè de xiǎngfǎ.** *The teacher wants to find out what the students think of introducing an oral Chinese class.*

xiǎng fāng shè fǎ 想方设法 **v** try every means, do all one can

xiǎngniàn 想念 [comp: 想 think + 念 miss (someone)] **v** miss, remember with longing ■ 祖母去世两年了，我还非常想念她。*Zǔmǔ qùshì liǎng nián le, wǒ hái fēicháng xiǎngniàn tā. It's over two years since Granny died, but I still miss her very much.*

xiǎngxiàng 想象 [v+obj: 想 think + 象 image] **v** imagine ■ 小女孩常常想象自己是一位美丽的舞蹈演员。*Xiǎonǚhái chángcháng xiǎngxiàng zìjǐ shì yí wèi měilì de wǔdǎo yǎnyuán. The little girl often imagines herself to be a beautiful dancer.* ■ 我不能想象，没有音乐，怎么生活。*Wǒ bù néng xiǎngxiàng, méiyǒu yīnyuè, zěnme shēnghuó. I cannot imagine how one can live without music.*

xiàng 项 TRAD 項 MEASURE WORD item of something (for things that are composed of items or things considered to be component) 一项任务 yí xiàng rènwù a mission / 两项文件 liǎng xiàng wénjiàn two documents

xiàngliàn 项链 **n** necklace (条 **tiáo**) 戴一条珍珠项链 dài yì tiáo zhēnzhū xiàngliàn wear a pearl necklace

xiàngmù 项目 [comp: 项 item + 目 item] **n** item ■ 他负责一个重要的研究项目。*Tā fùzé yíge zhòngyào de yánjiū xiàngmù. He is in charge of an important research project.*

xiàng 象¹ same as 大象 **dàxiàng**

xiàng 象² I **n** appearance, shape, image II **v** imitate

xiàngqí 象棋 **n** chess (副 **fù**, 盘 **pán**) 国际象棋 guójì xiàngqí Western chess / 中国象棋 Zhōngguó xiàngqí Chinese chess / 下一盘象棋 xià yìpán xiàngqí play a game of chess

xiàng shēng zì 象声字 **n** sound-imitating word, onomatopoeia

xiàng xíng zì 象形字 **n** pictographic character, pictograph

xiàngzhēng 象征 **v & n** symbolize; symbol

xiàng 像 I **v** resemble, bear resemblance to, be like ■ 她很像妈妈。*Tā hěn xiàng māma. She takes after her mother.* ■ 他的脾气一点也不像他爸爸。*Tā de píqì yìdiǎn yě bú xiàng tā bàba. His temperament is not at all like his father's.* II **n** likeness of (a human being), portrait ■ 墙上挂着祖父的像。*Qiáng shang guàzhe zǔfù de xiàng. On the wall hangs a portrait of their grandfather.*

xiàng 橡 **n** oak

xiàngjiāo 橡胶 **n** rubber 橡胶树 xiàngjiāoshù rubber tree

xiàngpí 橡皮 **n** eraser (a piece of rubber) (块 **kuài**)

xiàng 向 I PREP in the direction of, towards ■ 中国的长江、黄河都向东流。*Zhōngguó de Chángjiāng, Huánghé dōu xiàng dōng liú. China's Yangtze River and Yellow River flow to the east.* II **v** face ■ 这个房间有两个窗子，一个向南，一个向东。*Zhège fángjiān yǒu liǎng ge chuāngzi, yí ge xiàng nán, yí ge xiàng dōng. There are two windows in the room. One faces south and the other faces east.*

xiàngdǎo 向导 **n** guide 旅游向导 lǚyóu xiàngdǎo tourist guide

xiànglái 向来 ADV always, all along

xiàngwǎng 向往 **v** yearn for, look forward to

xiàng 巷 **n** narrow street, alley (条 **tiáo**) 一条深巷 yìtiáo shēn xiàng a long alley

xiàng 相 **v** assist

xiàngsheng 相声 **n** comic dialogue, comic cross-talk

xiāo 削 **v** peel 削苹果 xiāo píngguǒ peel an apple / 削铅笔 xiāo qiānbǐ sharpen a pencil

xiāo 消 **v** vanish

xiāochú 消除 [comp: 消 remove + 除 get rid of] **v** clear up, dispel ■ 我跟他好好谈了一次，消除了我们之间的误会。*Wǒ gēn tā hǎohǎo tánle yícì, xiāochúle wǒmen zhījiān de wùhuì. I had a good talk with him and cleared up the misunderstanding between us.*

xiāodú 消毒 [v+obj: 消 dispel + 毒 toxin] **v** disinfect, sterilize

xiāofáng 消防 **n** fire-prevention and fire-fighting 消防车 xiāofángchē fire engine / 消防队 xiāofángduì fire brigade, fire department

xiāofèi 消费 **v** consume ■ 生活水平提高了，人们消费的商品就越来越多。*Shēnghuó shuǐpíng tígāole, rénmen xiāofèi de shāngpǐn jiù yuèláiyuè duō. As people's living standard rises, they consume more and more goods.* 消费品 xiāofèipǐn consumer commodities, consumer goods / 消费者 xiāofèizhě consumer

xiāohào 消耗 **v** consume

xiāohuà 消化 [comp: 消 eliminate + 化 exterminate] **v** digest ■ 我中饭还没有消化呢，不想吃晚饭。*Wǒ zhōngfàn hái méiyǒu xiāohuà ne, bù xiǎng chī wǎnfàn. I still haven't digested my lunch. I don't want to eat supper.* ■ 今天老师讲了这么多，我还没有完全消化。*Jīntiān lǎoshī jiǎngle zhème duō, wǒ hái méiyǒu wánquán xiāohuà. The teacher gave us so much information today; I haven't entirely digested it.*

xiāojí 消极 ADJ lacking enthusiasm, passive (ANTONYM 积极 **jījí**)

xiāomiè 消灭 [comp: 消 eliminate + 灭 exterminate] **v** eliminate, wipe out ■ 这种害虫在本地区基本消灭。*Zhè zhǒng hàichóng zài běn dìqū jīběn xiāomiè. This pest has been mainly exterminated in this region.*

xiāoshī 消失 [comp: 消 vanish + 失 lose] **v** disappear, vanish ■ 太阳出来以后，雾渐渐消失了。*Tàiyang chūlai yǐhòu, wù jiànjiàn xiāoshī le. As the sun came out, the fog dissipated.*

xiāoxi 消息 [comp: 消 information + 息 news] **n** news (条 **tiáo**) ■ 我告诉你一个好消息。*Wǒ gàosu*

nǐ yí ge hǎo xiāoxi. *I'll tell you a piece of good news.* ■ 一有关于他的消息，请马上告诉我。**Yì yǒu guānyú tā de xiāoxi, qǐng mǎshàng gàosu wǒ.** *Please let me know as soon as you've got news about him.*

xiāo 销 **TRAD** 銷 **v** melt (metal)

xiāohuǐ 销毁 [comp: 销 annual + 毁 destroy] **v** destroy (especially by burning)

销毁罪证 xiāohuǐzuìzhèng destroy incriminating evidence

xiāoshòu 销售 [comp: 销 sell + 售 sell] **v & N** sell; market ■ 你们销售这家汽车制造厂的零件吗？**Nǐmen xiāoshòu zhè jiā qìchē zhìzàochǎng de língjiàn ma?** *Do you sell parts of this auto manifacturer?*

销售部 xiāoshòu bù sales department / 销售额 xiāoshòu'é money sales bring to a company, sales, takings / 销售量 xiāoshòuliàng sales volume

xiāo 潇 **TRAD** 瀟 **ADJ** deep and clear

xiāosǎ 潇洒 **ADJ** natural and unrestrained, with an easy and natural bearing

xiāo 宵 **N** night (See **yuánxiāo** 元宵.)

xiāo 小 **ADJ** 1 small, little (**ANTONYM** 大 **dà**) ■ 这双鞋太小了，有没有大一点儿的？**Zhè shuāng xié tài xiǎo le, yǒu méiyǒu dà yìdiǎnr de?** *This pair of shoes is too small. Do you have a bigger size?* 2 young ■ 我小时候，放暑假的时候，常常住在奶奶家。**Wǒ xiǎo shíhou, fàng shǔjià de shíhou, chángcháng zhù zai nǎinai jiā.** *When I was a child, I often stayed with granny during the summer holidays.* ■ 我姓李，您就叫我小李吧。**Wǒ xìng Lǐ, nín jiù jiào wǒ Xiǎo Lǐ ba.** *My family name is Li. You can call me Xiao Li.*

NOTE: "小 **xiǎo** + family name," like 小李 **Xiǎo Lǐ**, is a casual, friendly form of address to a person younger than oneself. See note on 老 **lǎo** for forms of address like 老李 **Lǎo Lǐ**.

xiǎochī 小吃 **N** small and inexpensive dishes, snacks

xiǎofèi 小费 **N** tip, gratuity

xiǎoháir 小孩儿 **N** same as 孩子 **háizi**

xiǎohuǒzi 小伙子 **N** young man, lad ■ 这些农村来的小伙子又老实又肯干。**Zhèxiē nóngcūn lái de xiǎohuǒzi yòu lǎoshí yòu kěngàn.** *These country lads are honest and hardworking.*

NOTE: See note on 姑娘 **gūniang**.

xiǎojiě 小姐 [comp: 小 young + 姐 elder sister] **N** young lady; Miss ■ 有一位小姐要见你。**Yǒu yí wèi xiǎojiě yào jiàn nǐ.** *There's a young lady wanting to see you.* ■ 王先生、王太太和他们的女儿王小姐都在美国旅行。**Wáng xiānsheng, Wáng tàitai hé tāmen de nǚ'ér Wáng xiǎojiě dōu zài Měiguó lǚxíng.** *Mr and Mrs Wang, with their daughter Miss Wang, are all traveling in the United States.*

NOTE: 小姐 **xiǎojiě** is a common form of address to a *young (or not so young)* woman. If her family name is not known, just use 小姐 **xiǎojiě**. 小姐 **xiǎojiě** is also the form of address for *a waitress* or *female attendant*, e.g. ■ 小姐，请给我一杯水。**Xiǎojiě, qǐng gěi wǒ yì bēi shuǐ.** *Please give me a glass of water.*

xiǎomài 小麦 **N** wheat ■ 在中国北方粮食以小麦为主。**Zài Zhōngguó běifang liángshi yǐ xiǎomài wéi zhǔ.** *In northern China, wheat is the main cereal crop.*

xiǎopéngyou 小朋友 **N** (a friendly form of address or reference to a child) ■ 小朋友，你们校长办公室在哪里？**Xiǎopéngyou, nǐmen xiàozhǎng bàngōngshì zài nǎlǐ?** *Where's your headmaster's office, children?*

xiǎoqì 小气 **ADJ** stingy, miserly

xiǎoshí 小时 [modif: 小 small + 时 time] **N** hour ■ 我等你等了一个半小时了。**Wǒ děng nǐ děngle yí ge bàn xiǎoshí le.** *I've been waiting for you for an hour and a half.*

半小时 bàn xiǎoshí half an hour

xiǎoshuō 小说 [modif: 小 small + 说 talk] **N** novel (本 **běn**, 篇 **piān**) ■ 这本小说的作者有丰富的生活经历。**Zhè běn xiǎoshuō de zuòzhě yǒu fēngfù de shēnghuó jīnglì.** *The author of this novel has had rich life experiences.* ■ 这篇小说语言优美，但是没有多大意思。**Zhè piān xiǎoshuō yǔyán yōuměi, dànshì méiyǒu duō dà yìsi.** *The language of this story is beautiful but it is not very meaningful.*

爱情小说 àiqíng xiǎoshuō romance novel / 长篇小说 chángpiān xiǎoshuō novel / 短篇小说 duǎnpiān xiǎoshuō short story, story / 历史小说 lìshǐ xiǎoshuō historical novel

xiǎoshuōjiā 小说家 **N** (accomplished) novelist

xiǎotōu 小偷 [modif: 小 small, petty + 偷 thief] **N** thief ■ 抓小偷！抓小偷！**Zhuā xiǎotōu! Zhuā xiǎotōu!** *Stop thief! Stop thief!*

xiǎoxīn 小心 [modif: 小 small + 心 the heart] **ADJ** careful, cautious ■ 他说话、做事都很小心。**Tā shuōhuà, zuòshì dōu hěn xiǎoxīn.** *He is cautious in speech and action.*

xiǎoxīn yìyì 小心翼翼 **ADJ** with the greatest of care, extremely cautious ■ 今天有雾，开车要特别小心。**Jīntiān yǒu wù, kāichē yào tèbié xiǎoxīn.** *It's foggy today. You need to be particularly careful while driving.*

xiǎoxué 小学 [modif: 小 small + 学 school] **N** primary school (座 **zuò**, 所 **suǒ**) ■ 这座小学操场太小，孩子没地方玩。**Zhè zuò xiǎoxué cāochǎng tài xiǎo, háizi méi dìfang wán.** *This primary school's sports ground is too small and the children have nowhere to play.*

xiǎozǔ 小组 **N** small group (for work or study)

xiǎo 晓 **TRAD** 曉 **v** know

xiǎode 晓得 **v** same as 知道 **zhīdào**. Only used in colloquial Chinese.

xiào 孝 N filial piety

xiàoshùn 孝顺 [comp: 孝 filial piety + 顺 obedience] V & N perform one's filial duties faithfully, be obedient and considerate of one's parents; filial piety ■ 他很孝顺父母。**Tā hěn xiàoshùn fùmǔ.** *He is obedient and considerate of his parents.*

xiào 效 N effect

xiàoguǒ 效果 [comp: 效 effect + 果 result] N effect, result ■ 对孩子太严格，往往效果不好。**Duì háizi tài yángé, wǎngwǎng xiàoguǒ bù hǎo.** *Being too strict with children often gives poor results.* ■ 这种新方法效果怎么样？**Zhè zhǒng xīn fāngfǎ xiàoguǒ zěnmeyàng?** *How effective is this new method?*

xiàolǜ 效率 [modif: 效 effect + 率 rate] N efficiency ■ 我们必须不断提高工作效率。**Wǒmen bìxū búduàn tígāo gōngzuò xiàolǜ.** *We must constantly increase work efficiency.*

xiàoyì 效益 N beneficial (economic) results, economic benefits

xiào 校 N school

xiàozhǎng 校长 [modif: 校 school + 长 chief] N headmaster, principal, university president, university vice chancellor ■ 这位校长得到大多数教师的拥护。**Zhèwèi xiàozhǎng dédào dàduōshù jiàoshī de yōnghù.** *This principal enjoys the support of most of the teachers.* ■ 在中文里，小学、中学、大学的负责人都叫 "校长"。**Zài Zhōngwén li, xiǎoxué, zhōngxué, dàxué de fùzérén dōu jiào "xiàozhǎng".** *In Chinese, people in charge of primary schools, high schools or universities are all called "xiaozhang."*

xiào 笑 V laugh, smile (ANTONYM 哭 **kū**) ■ 你笑什么？**Nǐ xiào shénme?** *What are you laughing at?* ■ 笑一笑，十年少。**Xiào yi xiào, shí nián shào.** *Laugh and you'll be ten years younger.* (→ *Laughter is the best medicine.*)

大笑 **dàxiào** laugh

xiàohua 笑话 [modif: 笑 laughing + 话 talk] I N joke ■ 我来讲个笑话。**Wǒ lái jiǎng ge xiàohua.** *I'll tell you a joke.* ■ 他很会讲笑话。**Tā hěn huì jiǎng xiàohua.** *He is good at telling jokes.* II V laugh at ■ 我中文讲得不好，你们别笑话我。**Wǒ Zhōngwén jiǎng de bù hǎo, nǐmen bié xiàohua wǒ.** *I don't speak Chinese very well. Please don't laugh at me.*

xiào 肖 V resemble, be like

xiàoxiàng 肖像 N portrait (幅 **fú**)

xiē 些 MEASURE WORD some, a few, a little ■ 午饭我吃了一些面包。**Wǔfàn wǒ chīle yìxiē miànbāo.** *I had some bread for lunch.*

好些 **hǎoxiē** lots of, quite a few ■ 昨天晚上他和老朋友谈了很久，喝了好些酒。**Zuótiān wǎnshang tā hé lǎo péngyou tánle hěn jiǔ, hēle hǎoxiē jiǔ.** *Yesterday evening he chatted with his old friends for a long time and drank lots of wine.*

xiē 歇 V take a rest ■ 我走不动了，歇会儿吧。**Wǒ zǒu bu dòng le, xiē huìr ba.** *I can't walk any further. Let's take a break.*

xié 斜 ADJ oblique, slanting ■ 他斜穿过马路。**Tā xié chuānguo mǎlù.** *He crossed the street diagonally.*

xié 鞋 N shoe (只 **zhī**, 双 **shuāng**) ■ 他总是穿一双黑鞋。**Tā zǒngshi chuān yì shuāng hēi xié.** *He always wears a pair of black shoes.*

凉鞋 **liáng xié** sandals / 皮鞋 **pí xié** leather shoes / 拖鞋 **tuō xié** slippers / 雨鞋 **yǔ xié** rubber boots / 运动鞋 **yùndòng xié** sports shoes

xié dài 鞋带 N shoelace, shoestring (条 **tiáo**, 根 **gēn**)

xié 协 TRAD 協 V join, assist

xiédìng 协定 [comp: 协 joint + 定 decision] N agreement, treaty ■ 两家公司签订了技术合作的协定。*The two companies signed an agreement on technological cooperation.*

xiéhuì 协会 N association (an organization), society

环境保护者协会 **huánjìng bǎohù zhě xiéhuì** Environmentalists' Association

xiéshāng 协商 V discuss and seek advice, consult

xiétiáo 协调 I V coordinate, bring into line II ADJ in a concerted way, balanced

xiéyì 协议 N agreement (a document) (份 **fèn**)

达成协议 **dáchéng xiéyì** reach an agreement

xiézhù 协助 [comp: 协 assist + 助 help] V & N assist; assistance ■ 由于当地居民的协助，警方很快逮捕了罪犯。**Yóuyú dāngdì jūmín de xiézhù, jǐngfāng hěn kuài dàibǔle zuìfàn.** *Thanks to the assistance by local residents, the police arrested the criminal in no time.*

xié 携 V 1 carry, take with 2 take by the hand

xiédài 携带 V carry, take along ■ 以下物品不准携带上机：... **Yǐxià wùpǐn bùzhǔn xiédài shàngjī: ...** *It is forbidden to carry the following objects on the plane: ....*

xiě 血 N same as **xuè** 血. Used only in colloquial Chinese.

xiě 写 TRAD 寫 V write, write with a pen ■ 这个汉字怎么写？**Zhège Hànzì zěnme xiě?** *How do you write this Chinese character?* ■ 我经常用电脑，不大写字。**Wǒ jīngcháng yòng diànnǎo, bú dà xiě zì.** *I often use computers and seldom write with a pen.*

xiězuò 写作 V & N write as a professional writer, compose essays; writing

xiè 泻 TRAD 瀉 V have loose bowels (See **fùxiè** 腹泻.)

xièdù 泻肚 same as 腹泻 **fùxiè**

xiè 械 N tool (See **jīxiè** 机械.)

xiè 泄 V allow air or liquid to escape, let out, leak

xièlòu 泄露 [comp: 泄 leak + 露 expose] V leak (information)

xièqì 泄气 [v+obj: 泄 let out + 气 air] V lose heart, feel discouraged

xiè 屑 N bits, crumbs

xiè 谢 TRAD 謝 V thank

xièjué 谢绝 V decline (an invitation, an offer, etc.), refuse politely

xièxie 谢谢 V thank ■ "谢谢你。" "不客气。" **"Xièxie nǐ." "Bú kèqi."** *"Thank you." "You're welcome."* ■ 你给我这么大帮助，我不知道怎样谢谢你才好。**Nǐ gěi wǒ zhème dà bāngzhù, wǒ bù zhīdào zěnyàng xièxie nǐ cái hǎo.** *You've given me so much help. I don't know how to thank you.*

NOTE: There are many ways of replying to 谢谢你 **xièxie nǐ**, e.g. ■ 不客气。**Bú kèqi.** *You don't have to be so polite.* ■ 不用谢。**Bú yòng xiè.** *You don't have to thank me.* ■ 没关系。**Méi guānxi.** *It doesn't matter.*

xiè 卸 V unload, discharge (See **zhuāngxiè** 装卸.)

xīn 心 N the heart ■ 这个人心真好！**Zhège rén xīn zhēn hǎo!** *This person is really kind-hearted.* 用心 **yòngxīn** apply oneself to ■ 你学习不太用心。**Nǐ xuéxí bú tài yòngxīn.** *You don't really apply yourself to studying.*

开心 **kāixīn** be joyous / 痛心 **tòngxīn** pained, agonized / 伤心 **shāngxīn** heartbroken

xīndé 心得 N what one has learned from work, study, etc., gain in understanding

xīn gān qíng yuàn 心甘情愿 ADJ most willing to, perfectly happy to

xīnlǐ 心理 [comp: 心 the heart + 理 theory] N mentality, psychology

心理分析 **xīnlǐfēnxī** psychoanalysis / 心理咨询 **xīnlǐ zīxún** psychological consultation

xīnlǐxué 心理学 N (the science of) psychology

xīnlíng 心灵 [comp: 心 the heart + 灵 spirit] N soul, spirit

心灵深处 **xīnlíng shēnchù** deep down in one's heart, inner soul

xīnqíng 心情 [comp: 心 the heart + 情 emotion] N state of mind, mood ■ 她孩子又生病了，她心情怎么会好？**Tā háizi yòu shēngbìng le, tā xīnqíng zěnme huì hǎo?** *Her child has fallen ill again. How can she be in a good mood?*

xīntài 心态 N mental state, mentality

xīnténg 心疼 V 1 love dearly 2 make one's heart ache, feel sorry

xīnxuè 心血 [comp: 心 the heart + 血 blood] N painstaking effort

付出很大心血 **fùchū hěn dà xīnxuè** put in a great deal of painstaking effort

xīnyǎnr 心眼儿 N heart, mind

没安什么好心眼儿 **méi ān shénme hǎoxīnyǎnr** do not mean well, have some bad intention

xīnzàng 心脏 [modif: 心 the heart + 脏 human organ] N the heart (as a medical term) ■ 经过检查，医生确定他有心脏病。**Jīngguò jiǎnchá,**

yīshēng quèdìng tā yǒu xīnzàng bìng. *After examination, the doctor confirmed that he had heart trouble.*

xīn 辛 ADJ spicy hot

xīnkǔ 辛苦 [comp: 辛 spicy hot + 苦 bitter] I ADJ 1 hard and toilsome (job) ■ 这个工作很辛苦。**Zhège gōngzuò hěn xīnkǔ.** *This is a tough job.* ■ 你们辛苦了。**Nǐmen xīnkǔ le.** *You've been working hard.* 2 harsh, difficult (life) ■ 很多农民的生活很辛苦。**Hěn duō nóngmín de shēnghuó hěn xīnkǔ.** *Many peasants live a hard life.* II V (used to request somebody's service) ■ 辛苦你把这几只箱子搬到楼上去。**Xīnkǔ nǐ bǎ zhè jǐ zhī xiāngzi bān dào lóu shang qù.** *Would you please carry these suitcases upstairs?*

NOTE: 你们辛苦了！**Nǐmen xīnkǔ le.** is used by a superior to express appreciation of hard work done by subordinate(s). When somebody has done you a service, you can say 辛苦你了！**Xīnkǔ nǐ le!**

xīnqín 辛勤 ADJ industrious, hard-working

xīn 欣 I ADJ joyful II V enjoy

xīnshǎng 欣赏 [comp: 欣 enjoy + 赏 appreciate] V 1 admire and enjoy

欣赏美丽的风光 **xīnshǎng měilì de fēngguāng** admire and enjoy beautiful sceneries 2 appreciate, like

xīnwèi 欣慰 [comp: 欣 joyful + 慰 sooth] ADJ pleased and satisfied, gratified

xīn xīn xiàng róng 欣欣向荣 ADJ flourishing, prosperous

xīn 新 ADJ new (ANTONYM 旧 **jiù**) ■ 你觉得我这件新衣服怎么样？**Nǐ juéde wǒ zhè jiàn xīn yīfu zěnmeyàng?** *What do you think of my new dress?* ■ 旧的不去，新的不来。**Jiù de bú qù, xīn de bù lái.** *If old stuff doesn't go away, new stuff won't come. (→ If you don't discard old things, you won't be able to use new things.)*

xīn chén dài xiè 新陈代谢 IDIOM supersede the old by new, metabolize, metabolism

Xīnjiāpō 新加坡 N Singapore

xīnláng 新郎 [modif: 新 new + 郎 person] N bridegroom

xīnnián 新年 [modif: 新 new + 年 year] N New Year ■ 新年好！**Xīnnián hǎo!** *Happy New Year!* ■ 祝您新年快乐！**Zhù nín Xīnnián kuàile!** *I wish you a happy New Year!*

新年贺卡 **Xīnnián hèkǎ** New Year card

xīnniáng 新娘 [modif: 新 new + 娘 young woman] N bride

xīnwén 新闻 [modif: 新 new + 闻 what is heard] N news (of current affairs) (条 **tiáo**) ■ 你是怎么样得到新闻的—读报纸，听广播，还是看电视？**Nǐ shì zěnmeyàng dédào xīnwén de—dú bàozhǐ, tīng guǎngbō, háishì kàn diànshì?** *How do you get news—by reading newspapers, listening to radio*

or watching television? ■ 他每天一边吃晚饭，一边看电视新闻。**Tā měi tiān yìbiān chī wǎnfàn, yìbiān kàn diànshì xīnwén.** *Every day he watches TV news while having supper.*

Xīnxīlán 新西兰 **N** New Zealand

xīnxiān 新鲜 [comp: 新 new + 鲜 fresh] **ADJ** fresh ■ 我们每天都要吃新鲜蔬菜。**Wǒmen měi tiān dōu yào chī xīnxiān shūcài.** *We should eat fresh vegetables every day.* ■ 这条鱼不新鲜了。**Zhè tiáo yú bù xīnxiān le.** *This fish is no longer fresh.*

xīnyǐng 新颖 **ADJ** new and original, novel

xīn 薪 **N 1** firewood **2** salary

高薪养廉 gāoxīn yǎnglián the policy of high salary for civil servants in order to cultivate clean government

xīnshuǐ 薪水 [comp: 薪 firewood + 水 water] **N** salary, pay

xìn 信[1] **V** believe ■ 我不信他一天能干这么多活。**Wǒ bú xìn tā yì tiān néng gàn zhème duō huó.** *I don't believe he could have done so much work in a day.*

xìnlài 信赖 **V & N** trust, count on; trust

可以信赖的 kěyǐ xìnlài de trustworthy, reliable

xìnniàn 信念 **N** faith, conviction

xìnrèn 信任 [comp: 信 trust + 任 entrust] **V & N** have confidence in (somebody), trust; confidence (in somebody), trust ■ 你既然请他做这么重要的工作，一定很信任他。**Nǐ jìrán qǐng tā zuò zhème zhòngyào de gōngzuò, yídìng hěn xìnrèn tā.** *Since you've asked him to do such an important job, you must really trust him.* ■ 他得到董事会的信任，到外地去开展业务。**Tā dédào dǒngshìhuì de xìnrèn, dào wàidì qù kāizhǎn yèwù.** *He earned the trust of the board and has gone to other parts of the country to develop the company business.*

xìnxīn 信心 [modif: 信 believe + 心 the heart] **N** confidence ■ 我对公司的前途充满信心。**Wǒ duì gōngsī de qiántú chōngmǎn xìnxīn.** *I have full confidence in the company's future.* ■ 他对自己缺乏信心。**Tá duì zìjǐ quēfá xìnxīn.** *He lacks self-confidence.*

xìnyòng 信用 **N** trustworthiness, credit

讲信用 jiǎng xìnyòng keep one's word, trustworthy

xìnyòngkǎ 信用卡 **N** credit card

xìnyǎng 信仰 **V & N** firmly believe in, have faith in; faith, belief, conviction

宗教信仰 zōngjiào xìnyǎng religious belief

xìnyù 信誉 **N** prestige, credit, reputation

xìn 信[2] **N 1** letter ■ 现在人们很少写信。**Xiànzài rénmen hěn shǎo xiě xìn.** *People don't often write letters now.*

寄信 jì xìn post a letter / 介绍信 jièshàoxìn letter of recommendation, reference / 收到信 shōudào xin receive a letter / 祝贺信 zhùhèxìn letter of congratulation / 信封 xìnfēng envelope

2 message

xìnhào 信号 **N** signal

xìnxī 信息 [comp: 信 message + 息 news, tiding] **N** information ■ 这台电脑处理信息十分迅速。**Zhè tái diànnǎo chǔlǐ xìnxī shífēn xùnsù.** *This computer processes information rapidly.* ■ 你有关于他的信息吗？**Nǐ yǒu guānyú tā de xìnxī ma?** *Do you have any information about him?*

xīng 兴 **TRAD** 興 **ADJ** flourishing

xīngfèn 兴奋 [comp: 兴 flourishing + 奋 excited] **ADJ** excited, overjoyed ■ 她们得了冠军，兴奋得跳了起来。**Tāmen déle guànjūn, xīngfèn de tiàole qǐlai.** *When they got the championship, they were so overjoyed that they jumped.* ■ 不要在兴奋的时候，做任何决定。**Bú yào zài xīngfèn de shíhou, zuò rènhé juédìng.** *Don't make decisions when you are excited.*

xīngfènjì 兴奋剂 **N** stimulant, dope

xīnglóng 兴隆 **ADJ** thriving, brisk, flourishing

xīngwàng 兴旺 **ADJ** prosperous, thriving

xīng 星 **N** celestial body, star (颗 kē) ■ 太阳系有九大行星。**Tàiyángxì yǒu jiǔ dà xíngxīng.** *There are nine planets in the solar system.*

恒星 héngxīng fixed star, star / 流星 liúxīng meteor / 行星 xíngxīng planet

NOTE: In everyday Chinese 星星 **xīngxīng** is normally used instead of 星 **xīng**, e.g. ■ 今天晚上的星星真亮。**Jīntiān wǎnshang de xīngxing zhēn liàng.** *Tonight the stars are really bright.*

xīngqī 星期 **N** week ■ 一年有五十二个星期。**Yì nián yǒu wǔshí èr ge xīngqī.** *There're fifty-two weeks in a year.*

星期一 Xīngqīyī Monday / 星期二 Xīngqī'èr Tuesday / 星期三 Xīngqīsān Wednesday / 星期四 Xīngqīsì Thursday / 星期五 Xīngqīwǔ Friday / 星期六 Xīngqīliù Saturday / 星期日 Xīngqīrì Sunday / 星期天 Xīngqītiān Sunday / 上星期 shàng xīngqī last week / 下星期 xià xīngqī next week

xīng 腥 **ADJ** bad fish-smelling

xíng 刑 **ADJ** penal, criminal

xíngshì 刑事 [modif: 刑 penal + 事 affair] **ADJ** criminal, penal

刑事犯 xíngshìfàn criminal offender, convict / 刑事案件 xíngshì ànjiàn criminal case

xíng 行[1] **I V 1** travel, go ■ 三人行，必有我师。（孔子）**Sān rén xíng, bì yǒu wǒ shī. (Kǒngzǐ)** *When three people are walking together, at least one of them must be my teacher (Confucius). (→ One can always find someone good enough to be one's teacher.)* **2** practice **II N** trip

xíng 行[2] **I V** all right, OK, (that) will do ■ "我可以用一下你的词典吗？" "行。" **"Wǒ kěyǐ yòng yíxià nǐ de cídiǎn ma?" "Xíng."** *"May I use your dictionary?" "OK."* ■ 学中文不学汉字不行。**Xué Zhōngwén bù xué hànzì bù xíng.** *It won't do to learn Chinese without learning Chinese charac-*

ters. **II** ADJ competent, capable ■ 你又赢了，真行！ *Nǐ yòu yíng le, zhēn xíng! You've won again. You're really great!* ■ 我踢足球不行，打篮球还可以。 *Wǒ tī zúqiú bù xíng, dǎ lánqiú hái kěyǐ. I'm not good at soccer but I'm not too bad at basketball.*

xíngdòng 行动 [comp: 行 work + 动 move] V & N move around; action, behavior, movement ■ 老人行动不便，不愿多外出。 *Lǎorén xíngdòng búbiàn, bú yuàn duō wàichū. The old man has difficulty moving about and is reluctant to go out very often.* ■ 不但要听他说什么，而且要看他的行动。 *Búdàn yào tīng tā shuō shénme, érqiě yào kàn tā de xíngdòng. We should not only listen to what he says but also look at what he does.*

xíngli 行李 N luggage, baggage (件 **jiàn**) ■ 你有几件行李？ *Nǐ yǒu jǐ jiàn xíngli? How many pieces of luggage do you have?* ■ 你的行李超重了，要付一百元。 *Nǐ de xíngli chāozhòng le, yào fù yìbǎi yuán. Your luggage is overweight. You need to pay 100 yuan.*

xíngrén 行人 [modif: 行 travel, go + 人 person] N pedestrian

行人道 xíngréndào sidewalk / 行人横道线 xíngrén héngdào xiàn pedestrian crossing

xíngwéi 行为 N behavior, conduct, act ■ 他的行为不符合他教师的身分。 *Tāde xíngwéi bù fúhé tā jiàoshī de shēnfēn His behavior does not befit his status as a teacher.*

xíngzhèng 行政 [v+obj: 行 exercise + 政 governance] N administration

行政部门 xíngzhèng bùmén administrative department / 行政命令 xíngzhèng mìnglìng executive order

xíng 形 N form, shape

xíngchéng 形成 [v+obj: 形 form + 成 become] V take shape, form ■ 习惯形成以后，就很难改变。 *Xíguàn xíngchéng yǐhòu, jiù hěn nán gǎibiàn. After a habit is formed, it is difficult to break.*

xíngróng 形容 V describe ■ 我形容不出来那个小偷长的样子。 *Wǒ xíngróng bu chūlāi nà ge xiǎotōu zhǎng de yàngzi. I can't describe what the thief looks like.*

xíngshì 形式 [comp: 形 shape + 式 manner] N form, shape (ANTONYM 内容 **nèiróng**) ■ 道歉是必要的，用什么形式还要考虑。 *Dàoqiàn shì bìyào de, yòng shénme xíngshì háiyào kǎolǜ. While an apology is necessary, we need to think over the form it should take.*

xíngshì 形势 [comp: 形 shape + 势 force] N situation ■ 目前的形势对我们有利。 *Mùqián de xíngshì duì wǒmen yǒulì. The present situation is in our favor.*

xíngtài 形态 N form, pattern

xíngxiàng 形象 [comp: 形 shape + 象 image] N image ■ 公司要注意公共关系，改善社会形象。 *Gōngsī yào zhùyì gōnggòng guānxi, gǎishàn

shèhuì xíngxiàng. The company should pay attention to public relations and improve its public image.*

xíngzhuàng 形状 [comp: 形 shape + 状 shape] N appearance, shape, form ■ 这座山的形状象一只猴子，因此人们就叫它猴山。 *Zhè zuò shān de xíngzhuàng xiàng yì zhī hóuzi, yīncǐ rénmen jiù jiào tā hóushān. The hill has the shape of a monkey and is therefore called Monkey Hill.*

xíng 型 N model, type (See **dàxíng** 大型.)

xíng 醒 V wake, wake up ■ 我今天很早就醒了。 *Wǒ jīntiān hěn zǎo jiù xǐng le. I woke up very early this morning.*

睡醒 shuìxǐng have enough sleep ■ 睡醒了没有？ *Shuì xǐngle méiyǒu? Have you had enough sleep?*

叫醒 jiàoxǐng wake somebody up ■ 你明天早上五点钟叫醒我，好吗？ *Nǐ míngtiān zǎoshang wǔ diǎnzhōng jiàoxǐng wǒ, hǎo ma? Could you wake me up tomorrow morning at five?*

xìng 兴 TRAD 興 ADJ joyful

xìng gāo cǎi liè 兴高采烈 ADJ jubilant, in high spirits

xìngqù 兴趣 [comp: 兴 joy + 趣 interest] N interest ■ 这孩子对动物很感兴趣。 *Zhè háizi duì dòngwù hěn gǎn xìngqù. This child is very interested in animals.* ■ 我对别人的私事没有兴趣。 *Wǒ duì biéren de sīshì méiyǒu xìngqù. I'm not interested in other people's private matters.*

对 … 感兴趣 duì … gǎn xìngqù be interested in … / 对 … 有兴趣 duì … yǒu xìngqù be interested in … / 对 … 不感兴趣 duì … bù gǎn xìngqù be uninterested in … / 对 … 没有兴趣 duì … méiyǒu xìngqù be uninterested in …

xìngzhì bóbó 兴致勃勃 ADJ keenly interested and all excited about, full of zest,

xìng 性 N 1 nature, character 2 sex, gender

xìngbié 性别 N gender, sex

xìnggǎn 性感 N sex appeal, sexiness

xìnggé 性格 N person's character, disposition, temperament ■ 她性格很坚强。 *Tā xìnggé hěn jiānqiáng. She has a strong character.*

xìngmìng 性命 N (human) life ■ 这是性命交关的事啊！ *Zhè shì xìngmìngjiāoguān de shì a! This is a matter of life and death.*

xìngnéng 性能 N function, performance

性能良好 xìngnéng liánghǎo (of a machine) perform well, with satisfactory performance

xìngqíng 性情 [comp: 性 nature + 情 emotion] N disposition, temperament

xìngyù 性欲 N sexual desire, sex urge

xìngzhì 性质 [comp: 性 nature + 质 substance] N nature (of a matter, an event, etc.), basic quality ■ 这一事件的性质是新旧力量之间的一场政治斗争。 *Zhè yí shìjiàn de xìngzhì shì xīn jiù lìliang zhījiān de yì chǎng zhèngzhì dòuzhēng. This inci-

dent is in nature a political struggle between the new and old forces.

xìng 幸 N good fortune

xìngfú 幸福 [comp: 幸 good fortune + 福 happiness] ADJ happy, fortunate ■ 多么幸福的家庭! **Duōme xìngfú de jiātíng!** *What a happy family!* ■ 她实现了自己的理想，感到很幸福。**Tā shíxiàn le zìjǐ de líxiǎng, gǎndào hěn xìngfú.** *She feels happy as she has realized her aspiration.*

NOTE: 幸福 **xìngfú** is used in a sublime sense, denoting *a profound and almost perfect happiness.* So it has a much more limited use than its English equivalents *happy* or *fortunate*. The usual Chinese word for *happy*, as in "I'm happy to hear the news," is 高兴 **gāoxìng**, e.g. ■ 听到这个消息，我很高兴。**Tīngdào zhège xiāoxi, wǒ hěn gāoxìng.** *I'm happy to hear the news.*

xìnghǎo 幸好 ADV fortunately, luckily

xìngkuī 幸亏 ADV fortunately, luckily

xìngyùn 幸运 N good fortune, good luck

xìng 姓 N family name ■ 中国人最常用的三个姓是李、王、张。**Zhōngguórén zuì chángyòng de sān ge xìng shì Lǐ, Wáng, Zhāng.** *The three most common family names of the Chinese are Li, Wang and Zhang.*

贵姓 guìxìng your family name (polite usage, normally in a question) ■ "您贵姓？" "我姓王。" **"Nín guìxìng?" "Wǒ xìng Wáng."** *"What's your family name?" "Wang."*

NOTE: The character 姓 **xìng** has the signific graph of 女 **nǚ**, meaning *female*, an indication that the Chinese once had a matriarchal society.

xìngmíng 姓名 [comp: 姓 family name + 名 given name] N full name ■ 请你在这里写上自己的姓名。**Qǐng nǐ zài zhèli xiěshang zìjǐ de xìngmíng.** *Please write down your full name here.*

xiōng 兄 N elder brother

xiōngdì 兄弟 [comp: 兄 elder brother + 弟 younger brother] N brother(s) ■ 他们兄弟之间关系很好，一人有事，大家帮忙。**Tāmen xiōngdì zhījiān guānxi hěn hǎo, yì rén yǒu shì, dàjiā bāngmáng.** *The brothers have a very good relationship—when one of them is in difficulty, the others will come to help him.*

xiōng 凶 TRAD 兇 ADJ ferocious, fierce: ■ 有话好好说，别这么凶。**Yǒu huà hǎohǎo shuō, bié zhème xiōng.** *If you've got something to say, say it nicely; don't be so ferocious.*

xiōng'è 凶恶 [comp: 凶 ferocious + 恶 bad, evil] ADJ ferocious, fierce ■ 癌是人类的凶恶敌人。**Ái shì rénlèi de xiōng'è dírén.** *Cancer is a ferocious enemy of the humankind.*

xiōngshǒu 凶手 [comp: 凶 ferocious + 手 hand] N murderer, assailant

xiōngyǒng 汹涌 ADJ turbulent, surging

xiōng 胸 N the chest, thorax

xiōnghuái 胸怀¹ V cherish

胸怀大志 xiōnghuái dàzhì have lofty aspirations, cherish high ideals

xiōnghuái 胸怀² N mind, breadth of mind, heart

胸怀宽广 xiōnghuái kuānguǎng broad-minded

xiōngtáng 胸膛 N the chest (of the human body)

xióng 雄 ADJ 1 male (of animals) (ANTONYM 雌 **cí**) ■ 雄狮子比雌狮子大得多。**Xióng shīzi bǐ cí shīzi dà de duō.** *Male lions are much bigger than female ones.* 2 grand

xiónghòu 雄厚 [comp: 雄 grand + 厚 thick] ADJ abundant, rich

资金雄厚 zījīnxiónghòu with abundant funds, very well-financed

xióngwěi 雄伟 [comp: 雄 male + 伟 great] ADJ grand, magnificent ■ 这个城市有很多雄伟的建筑。**Zhège chéngshì yǒu hěn duō xióngwěi de jiànzhù.** *This city boasts many grand buildings.*

xióng 熊 N bear (只 **zhī**)

xióngmāo 熊猫 [comp: 熊 bear + 猫 cat] N panda, giant panda (只 **zhī**) ■ 熊猫只吃竹子。**Xióngmāo zhǐ chī zhúzi.** *Pandas eat only bamboo.*

xiū 修 V 1 same as 修理 **xiūlǐ** 2 build, construct (a building, bridge, road, etc.) ■ 这条江上要修一座大桥。**Zhè tiáo jiāng shang yào xiū yí zuò dà qiáo.** *A big bridge will be built across this river.*

xiūfù 修复 V restore (a work of art)

xiūgǎi 修改 [comp: 修 repair + 改 alter] V amend, revise ■ 这份报告要修改一下，再送董事会。**Zhè fèn bàogào yào xiūgǎi yíxià, zài sòng dǒngshìhuì.** *This report needs some revision before being submitted to the board of directors.*

xiūjiàn 修建 [comp: 修 build + 建 build] V build, construct

修建高速铁路 xiūjiàn gāosù tiělù build high speed railroad

xiūlǐ 修理 V repair, fix ■ 自行车坏了，你会修理吗？**Zìxíngchē huài le, nǐ huì xiūlǐ ma?** *The bike is broken. Can you fix it?* ■ 这台机器很旧了，不值得再修理了。**Zhè tái jīqì hěn jiù le, bù zhídé zài xiūlǐ le.** *This machine is very old and is not worth repairing any more.*

xiūyǎng 修养 N 1 accomplishment in self-cultivation, self-possession ■ 他修养很好，一般不会发脾气。**Tā xiūyǎng hěn hǎo, yìbān bú huì fān píqi.** *He is self-possessed, and seldom loses his temper.* 2 accomplishment and mastery of knowledge

xiū 休 N leisure

xiūxi 休息 [comp: 休 leisure + 息 pause] V rest, take a rest, have a day off ■ 我们工作了两个小时了，休息一会儿吧。**Wǒmen gōngzuòle liǎng ge xiǎoshí le, xiūxi yíhuìr ba.** *We've been working for over two hours. Let's take a break.* ■ 我感到很疲

劳，需要休息几天。**Wǒ gǎndào hěn píláo, xūyào xiūxi jǐtiān.** *I feel worn out. I need a few days' rest.*

xiūxián 休闲 [comp: 休 leisure + 闲 idle] N leisure

休闲服 xiūxián fú casual clothes

xiū 羞 v be shy, be bashful

xiūchǐ 羞耻 N sense of shame

不知羞耻 bùzhī xiūchǐ have no sense of shame, shameless

xiù 秀 ADJ elegant (See **yōuxiù** 优秀.)

xiù 锈 TRAD 鏽 N rust

xiù 嗅 v smell, sniff

xiù 袖 N sleeve

xiùzi 袖子 N sleeve

xū 须 TRAD 須 MODAL V must (See **bìxū** 必须.)

xūzhī 须知 N (important) notice, essential information

考生须知 kǎoshēng xūzhī important notice to examinees

xū 虚 ADJ void

xūjiǎ 虚假 ADJ false, sham

xūróng 虚荣 N vanity

xūwěi 虚伪 ADJ & N hypocritical; hypocrisy

虚伪的人 xūwěi de rén hypocrite

xūxīn 虚心 [modif: 虚 empty + 心 the heart] ADJ open-minded and modest ■ 我们虚心地请您提意见。**Wǒmen xūxīn de qǐng nín tí yìjian.** *We sincerely request your comments.* ■ 他很不虚心，总是认为自己了不起。**Tā hěn bù xūxīn, zǒngshi rènwéi zìjǐ liǎobuqǐ.** *He is very arrogant, always thinking himself terrific.*

xū 需 v need

xūqiú 需求 N demand, requirement

xūyào 需要 [comp: 需 need + 要 want] v need, be in need of ■ 我需要一本中文词典。**Wǒ xūyào yì běn Zhōngwén cídiǎn.** *I need a Chinese dictionary.* ■ "你有什么需要，可以跟我说。""谢谢，没有什么需要。" **"Nǐ yǒu shénme xūyào, kěyǐ gēn wǒ shuō." "Xièxie, méiyǒu shénme xūyào."** *"If there's anything you need, let me know." "Thank you, but there's nothing I need."*

xǔ 许 TRAD 許 v same as 允许 **yúnxǔ**

xǔduō 许多 [comp: 许 approximate + 多 many, much] ADJ many, much ■ 妈妈买回来许多好吃的东西。**Māma mǎi huílai xǔduō hǎochī de dōngxi.** *Mom bought lots of delicious food.*

xǔkě 许可 v permit, allow

许可证 xǔkězhèng permit, license

xù 序 N sequence, order (See **zhìxù** 秩序.)

xùyán 序言 N preface

xù 畜 v keep domesticated animals

xùchǎnpǐn 畜产品 N animal products

xùmù 畜牧 N keeping livestock

xùmùyè 畜牧业 N animal husbandry

xùjiǔ 酗酒 v drink excessively, get drunk

xù 续 TRAD 續 v continue (See **jìxù** 继续, **liánxù** 连续, etc.)

xù 绪 TRAD 緒 N mood (See **qíngxù** 情绪.)

xù 叙 TRAD 敍 v 1 chat 2 narrate

xùshù 叙述 v narrate

xuān 宣 v declare, publicize

xuānbù 宣布 v declare, announce ■ 校长在大会上宣布了对他的处分。**Xiàozhǎng zài dàhuì shang xuānbùle duì tā de chǔfèn.** *At the assembly the principal announced the disciplinary action against him.*

xuānchuán 宣传 [comp: 宣 announce + 传 spread] v & N disseminate, publicize; dissemination of information, propaganda ■ 卫生部正在大力宣传吸烟的害处。**Wèishēngbù zhèngzài dàlì xuānchuán xīyān de hàichu.** *The Ministry of Health is making efforts to disseminate information regarding the harm that smoking does.* ■ 这完全是宣传，不能相信。**Zhè wánquán shì xuānchuán, bù néng xiāngxìn.** *This is propaganda, pure and simple. You mustn't believe it.*

xuānshì 宣誓 v swear an oath, make a vow, make a pledge

宣誓仪式 xuānshì yíshì swearing-in ceremony

xuānyáng 宣扬 v publicize, promote

xuān 喧 ADJ noisy

xuānhuá 喧哗 v & N make an uproar, make a racket; confused loud noise, uproar

xuán 悬 TRAD 懸 v hang, suspend

xuánguà 悬挂 v hang

xuánniàn 悬念 N suspense

xuányá 悬崖 N overhanging cliff, precipice

悬崖勒马 xuányá lèmǎ rein in at the brink of the precipice (→ avoid an imminent danger at the last moment)

xuányá qiàobì 悬崖峭壁 N sheer precipices and overhanging rocks

xuán 旋 v circle, spin

xuánlǜ 旋律 N melody

xuánzhuǎn 旋转 [comp: 旋 spin + 转 turn] v revolve, spin, gyrate

xuǎn 选 TRAD 選 v 1 vote for 2 select, choose ■ 不同牌子的电视机都差不多，很难选。**Bùtóng páizi de diànshìjī dōu chàbuduō, hěn nán xuǎn.** *TV sets of different brands are more or less the same; it is difficult to select one.*

xuǎnbá 选拔 v select, choose

xuǎnjǔ 选举 [comp: 选 select + 举 recommend] v & N elect, vote; election, voting ■ 我们下午选举班长。**Wǒmen xiàwǔ xuǎnjǔ bānzhǎng.** *We're going to elect a class monitor this afternoon.* ■ 参加大会的代表必须由选举产生。**Cānjiā dàhuì de dàibiǎo bìxū yóu xuǎnjǔ chǎnshēng.** *The delegates to the congress must be chosen by election.*

xuǎnshǒu 选手 N (of sports) selected contestant, player, athlete, competing athlete

xuǎnzé 选择 [comp: 选 select + 择 choose] v & N select, choose; choice, alternative ■ 人生的道路

要自己选择。 **Rénshēng de dàolù yào zìjǐ xuǎnzé.** *One should decide for oneself what kind of life to lead.* ■ 我们除此以外，别无选择。 **Wǒmen chú cǐ yǐwài, bié wú xuǎnzé.** *We have no choice but to do this.*

xuàn 炫 v dazzle

xuànyào 炫耀 v make a display of one's prowess
炫耀武力 xuànyào wǔlì flaunt one's military power

xuē 削 v cut

xuējiǎn 削减 [comp: 削 cut + 减 decrease] v cut down, reduce

xuēruò 削弱 v weaken, enfeeble

xué 学 TRAD 學 v learn, study ■ "你在大学学什么？" "学电脑。" **"Nǐ zài dàxué xué shénme?" "Xué diànnǎo."** *What do you study at university?" "Computing science."* ■ 活到老，学到老。 **Huó dào lǎo, xué dào lǎo.** *One should keep learning as long as one lives.*

xuéfèi 学费 [modif: 学 study + 费 fee] N tuition, tuition fee ■ 你们学校国际学生的学费是多少？ **Nǐmen xuéxiào guójì xuésheng de xué fèi shì duōshǎo?** *How much is the tuition fee for international students in your school?*

xuélì 学历 N record of formal schooling, record of education

xuéqī 学期 [modif: 学 study + 期 period] N semester, term ■ 中国的学校一般分上学期和下学期两个学期。 **Zhōngguó de xuéxiào yìbān fēn shàng xuéqī he xià xuéqī liǎng ge xuéqī.** *Chinese schools generally have two terms: the first term and the second term.*

xuésheng 学生 [modif: 学 study + 生 scholar] N student, pupil (个 gè, 名 míng) ■ "这个班有多少学生？" "三十二个。" **"Zhège bān yǒu duōshǎo xuésheng?" "Sānshí'èr ge."** *How many students are there in this class?" "Thirty-two."*

xuéshù 学术 N learning, scholarship
学术会议 xuéshù huìyì (scholarly or scientific) conference, symposium

xuéshuō 学说 N systematic theory, doctrine

xuéwèi 学位 [modif: 学 study + 位 position] N academic degree
学士学位 xuéshì xuéwèi bachelor degree / 硕士学位 shuòshì xuéwèi master's degree, masterate / 博士学位 bóshì xuéwèi Ph.D. degree, doctorate

xuéwèn 学问 [comp: 学 study + 问 ask] N learning, knowledge ■ 这位老教授很有学问。 **Zhè wèi lǎo jiàoshòu hěn yǒu xuéwèn.** *This old professor has a great deal of learning.*

xuéxí 学习 [comp: 学 learn + 习 practice] V & N study, learn; study, studies ■ 年轻的时候，应该多学习些知识。 **Niánqíng de shíhou, yīnggāi duō xuéxí xiē zhīshi.** *One should learn lots of knowledge when young.* ■ 学生应该把学习放在第一位。 **Xuésheng yīnggāi bǎ xuéxí fàng zai dì-yī wèi.** *Students should give priority to their studies.*

向 … 学习 xiàng … xuéxí learn from ..., emulate … ■ 你工作很认真，我要向你学习。 **Nǐ gōngzuò hěn rènzhēn, wǒ yào xiàng nǐ xuéxí.** *You work conscientiously. I must emulate you.*

xuéxiào 学校 [comp: 学 study + 校 school] N school (座 zuò) ■ 王老师每天八点前就到学校来了。 **Wáng lǎoshī měi tiān bā diǎn qián jiù dào xuéxiào lái le.** *Teacher Wang comes to school before eight o'clock every day.* ■ 市政府去年新建了两座学校。 **Shì zhèngfǔ qùnián xīn jiànle liǎng zuò xuéxiào.** *The city government built two schools last year.*

xuéyuàn 学院 [comp: 学 study + 院 place (for certain activities)] N college, institute ■ 在中国有些高等学校叫"学院"，例如"教育学院"。 **Zài Zhōngguó yǒuxiē gāoděng xuéxiào jiào "xuéyuàn", lìrú "jiàoyù xuéyuàn".** *In China some institutions of higher learning are called "college," for example "college of education."*

xuě 雪 N snow
下雪 xià xuě to snow

xuě bái 雪白 ADJ snow-white, pure white

xuě shàng jiā shuāng 雪上加霜 IDIOM add frost to snow, make a bad situation even worse

xuě 血 N blood ■ 流了一点血，不要紧。 **Liúle yìdiǎn xuě, bú yàojǐn.** *It's just a little bleeding, nothing serious.*

xuèyà 血压 [modif: 血 blood + 压 pressure] N blood pressure
高血压 gāoxuèyā high blood pressure, hypertension / 低血压 dīxuèyā low blood pressure, hypotension

xuěyè 血液 [modif: 血 blood + 液 liquid] N blood (as a technical term) ■ 你要化验血液。 **Nǐ yào huàyàn xuěyè.** *You should have your blood tested.*

xūn 熏 TRAD 燻 v treat with smoke, smoke
熏鱼 xūnyú smoked fish

xūntáo 熏陶 v exert a gradual and uplifting influence on, nurture, edify

xún 寻 TRAD 尋 v seek

xúnmì 寻觅 v seek, look for

xúnzhǎo 寻找 [comp: 寻 seek + 找 look for] v look for, seek ■ 他家的猫不见了，他们正在到处寻找。 **Tā jiā de māo bú jiàn le, tāmen zhèngzài dàochù xúnzhǎo.** *Their cat has disappeared, and they are looking for it everywhere.*

xún 巡 v patrol

xúnluó 巡逻 v patrol, go on patrol
巡逻艇 xúnluótǐng patrol boat

xún 循 v abide by, follow

xúnhuán 循环 v & N circulate; circulation
血液循环 xuèyè xúnhuán blood circulation

xún xù jiàn jìn 循序渐进 IDIOM proceed step by step in an orderly way

xún 询 TRAD 詢 v inquire

xúnwèn 询问 [comp: 询 inquire + 问 ask] v in-

quire, ask ■ 你可以打电话询问报名细节。 **Nǐ kěyǐ dǎ diànhuà xúnwèn bàomíng xìjié.** *You may call to inquire the details about the application (for a seat in a school).*

xùn 讯 TRAD 訊 N message (See **tōngxùn** 通讯.)

xùn 迅 ADJ rapid

xùnsù 迅速 [comp: 迅 rapid, speedy + 速 swift] ADJ rapid, speedy, swift ■ 这件事很急， 要迅速处理。 **Zhè jiàn shì hěn jí, yào xùnsù chǔlǐ.** *This is an urgent matter, and should be dealt with without delay.*

xùn 训 TRAD 訓 V train

xùnliàn 训练 [comp: 训 train + 练 practice] V train ■ 全国运动会快开了， 运动员正在紧张训练。 **Quánguó yùndònghuì kuài kāi le, yùndàngyuán zhèngzài jǐnzhāng xùnliàn.** *The national games will be held soon. Athletes are engaged in intense training.*

Y

yā 压 TRAD 壓 V press, push down ■ 这纸盒不能压。 **Zhè zhǐhé bù néng yā.** *This paper box mustn't be crushed.*

yājià 压价 V undersell

yālì 压力 N pressure

yāpò 压迫 [comp: 压 press + 迫 force, compel] V & N oppress; oppression ■ 在有些国家， 妇女仍然受到压迫。 **Zài yǒuxiē guójiā, fùnǚ réngrán shòudào yāpò.** *In some countries, women still suffer from oppression.*

yāsuìqián 压岁钱 N money given to children as a lunar New Year gift

yāsuō 压缩 [v+compl: 压 press + 缩 shrink] V compress, condense
空气压缩机 **kōngqì yāsuōjī** compressor

yāyì 压抑 [comp: 压 press + 抑 suppress] V suppress, constrain, inhibit
压抑自己的愤怒 **yāyì zìjǐ de fènnù** suppress one's anger

yāzhà 压榨 [comp: 压 press + 榨 squeeze] V extract (juice) by pressure, press

yāzhì 压制 V repress, stifle

yā 呀 INTERJ oh, ah (expressing surprise) ■ 呀， 这不是约翰吗， 没想到在这里见到你！ **Yā, zhè bú shì Yuēhàn ma, méi xiǎngdào zài zhèlǐ jiàndào nǐ!** *Oh, isn't it John? Fancy seeing you here!* ■ 呀， 你还会说上海话！ **Yā, nǐ hái huì shuō Shànghǎi huà!** *Oh, you also speak the Shanghai dialect!*

yā 押 V detain, take into custody

yājīn 押金 N cash pledge, deposit

yā 鸭 TRAD 鴨 N duck

yāzi 鸭子 N duck (只 **zhī**)

yā 鸦 TRAD 鴉 N crow
乌鸦 **wūyā** crow (只 **zhī**)

yā què wú shēng 鸦雀无声 IDIOM not even a crow or sparrow can be heard, all is quiet

yá 牙 N tooth, teeth ■ 我牙疼。 **Wǒ yá téng.** *I have a toothache.*

yáchǐ 牙齿 [comp: 牙 tooth + 齿 tooth] N tooth, teeth (颗 **kē**)

yágāo 牙膏 [modif: 牙 tooth + 膏 paste, cream] N toothpaste (管 **guǎn**)

yáshuā 牙刷 [modif: 牙 tooth + 刷 brush] N toothbrush (把 **bǎ**) ■ 我忘了带牙刷， 要买一把。 **Wǒ wàngle dài yáshuā, yào mǎi yì bǎ.** *I forgot to bring my toothbrush. I need to buy one.*

yáyī 牙医 N dentist, dentistry

yá 芽 N sprout (See **méngyá** 萌芽.)

yǎ 哑 TRAD 啞 ADJ mute

yǎba 哑巴 N speech-impaired person, dumb person

yǎ 雅 ADJ refined (See **wényǎ** 文雅.)

yà 亚 TRAD 亞 ADJ inferior; Asia

yàjūn 亚军 N (in sports) second place, runner-up

Yàzhōu 亚洲 [modif: 亚 Asia + 洲 continent] N Asia ■ 亚洲是世界上最大的一个洲。 **Yàzhōu shì shìjiè shang zuì dà de yí ge zhōu.** *Asia is the largest continent in the world.*

ya 呀 PARTICLE same as 啊² **ā** PARTICLE. Used after a, e, i, o, u. ■ 这个苹果真大呀！ **Zhège píngguǒ zhēn dà ya!** *How big this apple is!*

yān 烟 TRAD 煙 N 1 smoke 2 same as 香烟 **xiāngyān** ■ 请勿吸烟 **qǐngwù xīyān** No smoking.
禁烟区 **jìnyān qū** smoke-free area

yānhuā bàozhú 烟花爆竹 N fireworks and firecrackers

yān 淹 V submerge, inundate

yānmò 淹没 V submerge, flood

yán 延 V extend

yáncháng 延长 [v+compl: 延 extend + 长 long] V prolong, extend ■ 会议延长两天。 **Huìyì yáncháng liǎng tiān.** *The conference was extended two more days.*

yánqī 延期 [v+obj: 延 extend + 期 date] V postpone, defer ■ 会议延期一周举行。 **Huìyì yánqī yīzhōu jǔxíng.** *The meeting (conference) will be postponed for a week.*

yánshēn 延伸 [comp: 延 extend + 伸 reach] V stretch, extend

yánxù 延续 [comp: 延 extend + 续 continue] V continue, go on

yán 严 TRAD 嚴 ADJ strict, severe

yángé 严格 ADJ strict, stringent, rigorous ■ 在中国的传统中， 一位严格的老师才是好老师。 **Zài Zhōngguó de chuántǒng zhong, yí wèi yángé de lǎoshī cái shì hǎo lǎoshī.** *In the Chinese tradition, only a strict teacher was a good one.*

yánhán 严寒 ADJ severe cold

yánjìn 严禁 V strictly forbid ■ 此处严禁停车。 **Cǐchù yánjìn tíngchē.** *Parking is strictly forbidden here.*

yánjùn 严峻 ADJ severe, rigorous, grim
严峻的考验 yánjùn de kǎoyàn severe test

yánlì 严厉 [comp: 严 severe + 厉 harsh] ADJ stern, severe
严厉的警告 yánlì de jǐnggào stern warning

yánmì 严密 ADJ tight, watertight

yánsù 严肃 [comp: 严 severe + 肃 solemn] ADJ serious, solemn ■ 李校长为什么总是这么严肃？ Lǐ xiàozhǎng wèishénme zǒngshì zhème yánsù? *Why does Mr Li, the principal, always look so serious?*

yánzhòng 严重 [comp: 严 severe + 重 weighty] ADJ serious, critical ■ 这是一个严重的问题，必须认真对付。 Zhè shì yí ge yánzhòng de wèntí, bìxū rènzhēn duìfu. *This is a serious problem and must be dealt with earnestly.* ■ 她的病情很严重。 Tā de bìngqíng hěn yánzhòng. *She is critically ill.*

yán 言 N speech

yánlùn 言论 N opinion on public affairs, expression of one's political views
言论自由 yánlùn zìyóu freedom of speech

yán 岩 N rock

yánshí 岩石 N rock (块 kuài)

yán 炎 ADJ scorching

yánrè 炎热 ADJ scorching hot

yán 沿 PREP along ■ 沿街有很多小商店。 Yán jiē yǒu hěn duō xiǎo shāngdiàn. *There are numerous small shops along the street.* ■ 你沿着公园一直走，就到市中心了。 Nǐ yánzhe gōngyuán yì zhí zǒu, jiù dào shìzhōngxīn le. *Walk along the park and you will get to the city center.*

yánhǎi 沿海 N (places) along the coast
沿海城市 yánhǎi chéngshì coastal city

yán 研 V study, research

yánjiū 研究 [comp: 研 research + 究 investigate] V & N consider carefully, research, study; research, study ■ 科学家们正在研究一种新药。 Kēxuéjiāmen zhèngzài yánjiū yì zhǒng xīn yào. *Scientists are researching a new medicine.* ■ 公司已经研究了你的计划，认为是可行的。 Gōngsī yǐjīng yánjiūle nǐ de jìhuà, rènwéi shì kěxíng de. *The company has considered your plan carefully and believes it is feasible.*

yánjiūshēng 研究生 N graduate student, post-graduate student
研究生院 yánjiūshēng yuàn graduate school (of a university)

yánjiūsuǒ 研究所 N research institute, research unit

yánjiūyuàn 研究院 N research institute

yán 盐 TRAD 鹽 N salt ■ 我吃得比较淡，你菜里少放点盐。 Wǒ chī de bǐjiào dàn, nǐ cài li shǎo fàng diǎn yán. *I prefer my food to be bland. Please don't put too much salt in the dish.*

yán 颜 TRAD 顏 N complexion

yánsè 颜色 [comp: 颜 complexion + 色 color] N color ■ "你最喜欢什么颜色？" "蓝颜色。" "Nǐ zuì xǐhuan shénme yánsè?" "Lán yánsè." *"What's your favorite color?" "Blue."* ■ 我们有各种颜色的墙纸。 Wǒmen yǒu gè zhǒng yánsè de qiángzhǐ. *We have wallpaper in various colors.*

yǎn 掩 V cover, cover up

yǎngài 掩盖 [comp: 掩 cover up + 盖 lid, cover] V cover, cover up
掩盖真相 yǎngài zhēnxiàng cover up the truth of the matter

yǎnhù 掩护 [comp: 掩 cover + 护 protect] V cover, shield

yǎnshì 掩饰 V cover up, gloss over, conceal
掩饰错误 yǎnshìcuòwù gloss over a mistake

yǎn 眼 N the eye, eye
左眼 zuǒyǎn the left eye / 右眼 yòuyǎn the right eye

yǎnguāng 眼光 N way of looking at things, eye
有审美眼光 yǒu shěnměi yǎnguāng have an eye for what is beautiful / 用老眼光看新问题 yòng lǎoyǎnguāng kàn xīn wèntí look at a new problem from an old point of view

yǎnkē yīshēng 眼科医生 N ophthalmologist

yǎnjìng 眼镜 [modif: 眼 eye + 镜 mirror] N glasses, spectacles (副 fù) ■ 那位戴眼镜的先生是谁？ Nà wèi dài yǎnjìng de xiānsheng shì shuí? *Who is the gentleman wearing glasses over there?*
太阳眼镜 tàiyang yǎnjìng sunglasses

yǎnjing 眼睛 [comp: 眼 eye + 睛 eyeball] N eye ■ 打电脑的时间太长，我的眼睛累了。 Dǎ diànnǎo de shíjiān tài cháng, wǒ de yǎnjing lèi le. *I've been working on the computer for too long; my eyes are tired.*

yǎnlèi 眼泪 [modif: 眼 eye + 泪 tear] N tear (滴 dī)
流眼泪 liú yǎnlèi shed tears

yǎnqián 眼前 N 1 before one's eyes ■ 那件交通事故就发生在他眼前。 Nà jiàn jiāotóng shìgù jiù fāshēng zài tā yǎnqián. *The road accident happened right in front of him.* 2 at present, at this moment ■ 眼前我们有些困难，但很快能克服的。 Yǎnqián wǒmen yǒuxiē kùnnan, dàn hěn kuài néng kèfú de. *At present we have some difficulties, but they can be overcome very soon.*

yǎnsè 眼色 [modif: 眼 eye + 色 color] N meaningful glance
交换眼色 jiāohuàn yǎnsè exchange meaningful glances

yǎnshén 眼神 [modif: 眼 eye + 神 spirit] N looks or expressions in one's eyes

yǎnxià 眼下 N at present, at this moment, now

yǎn 演 V 1 act, perform, show ■ 他很会演戏。 Tā hěn huì yǎn xì. *He is good at acting.* 2 show (a film) ■ 今天电影院演什么电影？ Jīntiān diànyǐngyuàn yǎn shénme diànyǐng? *What movies are being shown at the cinema today?* 3 develop, evolve

yǎnbiàn 演变 [comp: 演 evolve + 变 change]

V & N evolve, unfold; evolution

yǎnchū 演出 **V** put on a theatrical performance, perform; theatrical performance ■ 这次音乐会有两位有名的歌唱家演出。**Zhè cì yīnyuèhuì yǒu liǎng wèi yǒumíng de gēchàngjiā yǎnchū.** *Two well-known singers will perform at the concert.* ■ 他们的演出精彩极了！**Tāmen de yǎnchū jīngcǎi jíle.** *How wonderful their performance was!*

yǎnjiǎng 演讲 [comp: 演 perform + 讲 speak] **V** deliver a formal speech, give a formal lecture

yǎnxí 演习 **N** military exercise, drill, practice 军事演习 jūnshì yǎnxí military exercise

yǎnyì 演绎 **V & N** deduce; deduction

yǎnyuán 演员 [modif: 演 act + 员 person] **N** actor, actress ■ 在中国要当演员一定要会说标准的普通话。**Zài Zhōngguó yào dāng yǎnyuán yídìng yào huì shuō biāozhǔn de Pǔtōnghuà.** *In China if one wants to be an actor one must be able to speak standard Putonghua.*

yǎnzòu 演奏 **V** give an instrument performance

yàn 厌 **TRAD** 厭 **V** detest (See **tǎoyàn** 讨厌.)

yànwù 厌恶 [comp: 厌 detest + 恶 loathe] **V** detest, be digusted with

yàn 咽 **V** swallow ■ 我要喝一点水，才能把药片咽下去。**Wǒ yào hē yìdiǎn shuǐ, cái néng bǎ yàopiàn yàn xiàqu.** *I must drink a bit of water to be able to swallow the pill.*

yàn 宴 **N** feast

yànhuì 宴会 [modif: 宴 feast + 会 meet] **N** banquet, feast ■ 他们回国以前，举行了告别宴会。**Tāmen huíguó yǐqián, jǔxíng le gàobié yànhuì.** *Before returning to their country, they gave a farewell banquet.* ■ 明天晚上我要去参加朋友的结婚宴会。**Míngtiān wǎnshang wǒ yào qù cānjiā péngyou de jiéhūn yànhuì.** *Tomorrow night I'll be attending a friend's wedding banquet.*

参加宴会 cānjiā yànhuì attend a banquet / 告别宴会 gàobié yànhuì farewell banquet / 欢迎宴会 huānyíng yànhuì welcome banquet / 结婚宴会 jiéhūn yànhuì wedding banquet

yàn 验 **TRAD** 驗 **V** examine (See **cèyàn** 测验, **jīngyàn** 经验, etc.)

yànshōu 验收 [comp: 验 examine + 收 accept] **V** check and accept, check upon delivery

yànzhèng 验证 [comp: 验 examine + 证 verify] **V** test to verify

yáng 羊 **N** sheep, goat, lamb (头 **tóu**) ■ 春天是生小羊的时候。**Chūntiān shì shēng xiǎoyáng de shíhou.** *Spring is the lambing season.*

山羊 shānyáng goat / 小羊 xiǎoyáng lamb

yáng 阳 **TRAD** 陽 **N** what is open, overt, masculine, the sun

yángguāng 阳光 [modif: 阳 the sun + 光 light] **N** sunshine, sunlight ■ 这里的阳光太强了。**Zhèlǐ de yángguāng tài qiáng le.** *The sunshine here is too intense.*

yángtái 阳台 **N** balcony

yángxìng 阳性 **ADJ** (of medical test result) positive (**ANTONYM** 阴性 **yīnxìng**)

yáng 扬 **TRAD** 揚 **V** raise, make known (See **biǎoyáng** 表扬.)

yáng 洋 **N** ocean (See **hǎiyáng** 海洋.)

yǎng 养 **TRAD** 養 **V 1** provide for, support ■ 爸爸妈妈辛辛苦苦地工作，把我养大。**Bàba māma xīn-xīn-kǔ-kǔ de gōngzuò, bǎ wǒ yǎng dà.** *Dad and mom worked hard to provide for me.* **2** raise, keep as pet ■ 我一直想养一只狗。**Wǒ yìzhí xiǎng yǎng yì zhī gǒu.** *I have always wanted to have a dog.*

yǎng 氧 **N** oxygen (O)

yǎngqì 氧气 **N** oxygen (O)

yǎng 痒 **V** itch, tickle 发痒 fāyǎng itch ■ 我背上发痒。**Wǒ bēishàng fāyǎng.** *My back itches.*

yàng 样 **TRAD** 樣 **MEASURE WORD** kind, category, type ■ 他做了几样菜，招待朋友。**Tā zuòle jǐ yàng cài, zhāodài péngyou.** *He prepared several dishes to entertain his friends.*

yàngpǐn 样品 **N** sample, sample product, specimen

yàngzi 样子 **N** appearance, manner ■ 几年不见，你还是以前的样子。**Jǐ nián bú jiàn, nǐ hái shì yǐqián de yàngzi.** *It's been years since I last saw you and you still look the same as before.*

yāoqiú 要求 [comp: 要 ask + 求 request] **V & N** ask, demand, require; demand, requirement ■ 市场要求我们不断开发新产品。**Shìchǎng yāoqiú wǒmen búduàn kāifā xīn chǎnpǐn.** *The market demands that we constantly develop new products.* ■ 我想提两个要求，可以吗？**Wǒ xiǎng tí liǎng ge yāoqiú, kěyǐ ma?** *May I make two demands?* 满足顾客的要求 mǎnzú gùkè de yāoqiú meet our clients' demands

yāo 腰 **N** waist, small of the back

yāo 邀 **V** invite

yāoqǐng 邀请 [comp: 邀 invite + 请 ask] **V & N** invite; invitation ■ 他邀请很多朋友来参加他的二十一岁生日宴会。**Tā yāoqǐng hěn duō péngyou lái cānjiā tā de èrshíyī suì shēngrì yànhuì.** *He invited many friends to his twenty-first birthday dinner party.* ■ 我昨天发出了邀请，他们大约明天会收到。**Wǒ zuótiān fāchūle yāoqǐng, tāmen dàyuē míngtiān huì shōudào.** *I sent the invitation yesterday, and they'll probably receive it tomorrow.* 邀请信 yāoqǐngxìn letter of invitation

yáo 谣 **TRAD** 謠 **N 1** rumor **2** ballad, rhyme 民谣 mínyáo folk ballad, ballad

yáoyán 谣言 [modif: 谣 rumor + 言 word] **N** malicious rumor, rumor ■ 我不信谣言，也不传谣言。**Wǒ bù xìn yáoyán, yě bù chuán yáoyán.** *I don't believe rumors, nor do I spread them.*

yáo 摇 **V** shake, wave ■ 点头表示同意，摇头表示反对。**Diǎntóu biǎoshì tóngyì, yáo tóu biǎoshì**

fǎnduì . *Nodding the head indicates agreement and shaking the head signals disagreement.*

yáobǎi 摇摆 v move back and forth, swing, sway

yáogǔnyuè 摇滚乐 N rock and roll, rock (music)

yáohuàng 摇晃 v sway, swing, rock

yáo 遥 ADJ faraway

yáokòng 遥控 v remote control

遥控器 yáokòngqì (a device of) remote control

yáoyuǎn 遥远 [comp: 遥 faraway + 远 distant] ADJ faraway, remote, distant

yǎo 咬 v bite ■ 我给蚊子咬了一口。**Wǒ gěi wénzi yǎole yì kǒu.** *I was bitten by a mosquito.*

yǎo yá qiè chǐ 咬牙切齿 v gnash one's teeth in rage or hatred

yào 药 TRAD 藥 N medicine, drug ■ 这种药你一天吃两次，每次吃一片。**Zhè zhǒng yào nǐ yì tiān chī liǎng cì, měi cì chī yí piàn.** *You should take this medicine twice a day, one pill each time.* ■ 现在还没有药治这种病。**Xiànzài hái méiyǒu yào zhì zhè zhǒng bìng.** *At present there is no medicine that cures this disease.*

草药 cǎoyào herbal medicine / 吃药 chī yào take medicine / 配药 pèi yào fill a prescription / 西药 xīyào Western medicine / 中药 zhōngyào traditional Chinese medicine

yàofāng 药方 N prescription

开药方 kāi yàofāng write a prescription

yàofáng 药房 N pharmacist's, pharmacy

yàopiàn 药片 N pill

yàoshuǐ 药水 N liquid medicine

yào 要 ¹ I want, ask for, would like ■ 我要一间安静的房间。**Wǒ yào yì jiān ānjìng de fángjiān.** *I want a quiet room.* ■ 我哥哥要我问你好。**Wǒ gēge yào wǒ wèn nǐ hǎo.** *My brother asked me to give you his regards.* II MODAL V should, must ■ 你想学好中文，就要多听，多讲。**Nǐ xiǎng xuéhǎo Zhōngwén, jiù yào duō tīng, duō jiǎng.** *If you want to learn Chinese well, you should listen more and speak more.*

yào 要 ² ADJ important, essential

yàobu 要不 CONJ otherwise, or else

yàoburán 要不然 same as 要不 **yàobu**

yàodiǎn 要点 [modif: 要 important + 点 point] N key point, major point

yàojǐn 要紧 ADJ important, urgent, serious ■ 考试的时候，最要紧的是看清考题。**Kǎoshì de shíhou, zuì yàojǐn de shì kànqīng kǎotí.** *The most important thing at examinations is to understand the question clearly.*

不要紧 búyàojǐn it doesn't matter ■ "对不起。" "不要紧。" **"Duìbuqǐ." "Búyàojǐn."** *"I'm sorry." "It doesn't matter."*

yàomìng 要命 ADJ extreme ■ 我这两天忙得要命。**Wǒ zhè liǎng tiān máng de yàomìng.** *I'm extremely busy these days.*

yàoshì 要是 CONJ if ■ 要是你明天不能来，请给我打个电话。**Yàoshì nǐ míngtiān bù néng lái, qǐng gěi wǒ dǎ ge diànhuà.** *If you're not able to come tomorrow, please give me a call.*

NOTE: Both 如果 **rúguǒ** and 要是 **yàoshì** mean *if*. While 如果 **rúguǒ** is for general use, 要是 **yàoshì** is a colloquialism.

yàosù 要素 N essential element

yào 耀 v shine, dazzle

yàoyǎn 耀眼 [v+obj: 耀 dazzle + 眼 the eyes] v dazzling

yào 钥 TRAD 鑰 See **yàoshi** 钥匙

yàoshi 钥匙 N key (把 **bǎ**) ■ 钥匙一定要放好。**Yàoshi yídìng yào fànghǎo.** *You must keep the keys in a safe place.*

yé 爷 TRAD 爺 N paternal grandfather

yéye 爷爷 N same as 祖父 **zǔfù**. Used in colloquial Chinese.

yě 也 I ADV also, too ■ 我喜欢打球，也喜欢游泳。**Wǒ xǐhuan dǎ qiú, yě xǐhuan yóuyǒng.** *I like ball games, and I also like swimming.* ■ 你想去北京学习，我也想去北京学习。**Nǐ xiǎng qù Běijīng xuéxí, wǒ yě xiǎng qù Běijīng xuéxí.** *You want to study in Beijing, so do I.* II CONJ neither, nor ■ 你没有看过这个电影，我也没看过这个电影。**Nǐ méiyǒu kànguo zhège diànyǐng, wǒ yě méi kànguo zhège diànyǐng.** *You haven't seen this movie, nor have I.*

yěxǔ 也许 ADV perhaps, maybe ■ 天上有大块的云，也许会下雨。**Tiān shang yǒu dà kuài de yún, yěxǔ huì xiàyǔ.** *It's very cloudy. Perhaps it'll rain.* ■ "他今天会给我们发电子邮件吗？" "也许。" **"Tā jīntiān huì gěi wǒmen fā diànzǐ yóujiàn ma?" "Yěxǔ."** *"Will he send us an e-mail today?" "Perhaps."*

NOTE: See note on 恐怕 **kǒngpà**.

yě 野 ADJ open country, wild

yěmán 野蛮 [comp: 野 wild + 蛮 rough] ADJ savage, barbaric

yěshēng 野生 [modif: 野 wild + 生 living] ADJ wild (animal or plant)

野生动物 yěshēng dòngwù wildlife / 野生植物 yěshēng zhíwù wild plant

yěshòu 野兽 [modif: 野 wild + 兽 beast] N wild beast, wild animal

yěwài 野外 N open country, field

野外作业 yěwàizuòyè field work

yěxīn 野心 [modif: 野 wild + 心 heart] N wild ambition

yè 业 TRAD 業 N industry

yèwù 业务 [comp: 业 occupation + 务 business] N 1 professional work, vocational work ■ 她业务水平很强。**Tā yèwù shuǐpíng hěn qiáng.** *She is very efficient professionally.* 2 business ■ 公司的业务开展很顺利。**Gōngsī de yèwù kāizhǎn hěn shùnlì.** *The business of the company has developed smoothly.*

yèyú 业余 ADJ spare time, amateur ■ 你业余时间做什么? **Nǐ yèyú shíjiān zuò shénme?** *What do you do in your spare time?* ■ 他是一位中学老师，也是业余音乐家。**Tā shì yí wèi zhōngxué lǎoshī, yě shì yèyú yīnyuèjiā.** *He is a high school teacher and also an amateur musician.*

yè 叶 TRAD 葉 N leaf

yèzi 叶子 [suffix: 叶 leaf + 子 nominal suffix] N leaf (片 **piàn**) ■ 秋天，叶子都黄了。**Qiūtiān, yèzi dōu huáng le.** *In autumn, leaves turn yellow.*

yè 页 TRAD 頁 N page ■ 这本词典有三百多页。**Zhè běn cídiǎn yǒu sānbǎi duō yè.** *This dictionary has over three hundred pages.* ■ 请把书翻到二十页。**Qǐng bǎ shū fān dào èrshí yè.** *Please turn to page twenty of your book.*

yè 夜 N night, evening ■ 他昨夜十一点钟才回家。**Tā zuó yè shíyī diǎnzhōng cái huíjiā.** *Last night she returned home as late as eleven o'clock.*

夜班 yèbān night shift / 夜车 yèchē night train / 半夜 bànyè midnight

yèli 夜里 N at night ■ 这条大街夜里也车辆不断。**Zhè tiáo dàjiā yèli yě chēliàng bú duàn.** *There is constant traffic on this main street even at night.* ■ 这个人喜欢白天睡觉，夜里工作，是个"夜猫子"。**Zhège rén xǐhuan báitiān shuìjiào, yèli gōngzuò, shì ge "yè māozi."** *This guy likes sleeping in the day and working at night, just like an owl.*

yèwǎn 夜晚 N same as 夜里 **yèli**

yè 液 N liquid, fluid

yètǐ 液体 N liquid

yī 一 NUMERAL one ■ 一万一千一百十一 **yíwàn yìqiān yìbǎi shíyī** *eleven thousand, one hundred and eleven (11,111)*

NOTES: (1) 一 undergoes tone changes (tone sandhi). When standing alone, 一 is pronounced with the first tone, i.e. **yī**. When followed by a sound in the fourth tone, 一 changes to the second tone, e.g. 一定 **yídìng**. 一 is pronounced in the fourth tone in all other circumstances, e.g. 一般 **yìbān**, 一同 **yìtóng**, 一起 **yìqǐ**. Pay attention to the various tones of 一 here and in following words. (2) When saying a number (e.g. a telephone number) people may pronounce 一 as **yāo** for clarity, e.g. ■ 我的电话号码是五八一三九。**Wǒ de diànhuà hàomǎ shì wǔ-bā-yāo-sān-jiǔ.** *My telephone number is 58139.*

yíbàn 一半 N half, one half ■ 他一半时间念书，一半时间做工。**Tā yíbàn shíjiān niànshū, yíbàn shíjiān zuògōng.** *He spends half his time studying and the other half working.*

yìbān 一般 ADJ 1 generally speaking, ordinarily ■ 每星期一上午我们一般都开会。**Měi Xīngqīyī shàngwǔ wǒmen yìbān dōu kāihuì.** *We usually have a meeting every Monday morning.* 2 average, commonplace ■ 他的学习成绩一般。**Tā de**

xuéxí chéngjì yìbān. *His school record is average.* 3 same as, as … as ■ 哥哥长得和爸爸一般高了。**Gēge zhǎng de hé bàba yìbān gāo le.** *My elder brother is now as tall as Daddy.*

yíbèizi 一辈子 N one's entire life

yìbiān 一边 N one side ■ 在这场争论中，我站在你们一边。**Zài zhè chǎng zhēnglùn zhōng, wǒ zhàn zài nǐmen yìbiān.** *In this debate I am on your side.*

yìbiān … yìbiān … 一边 … 一边 … CONJ while … at the same time ■ 不少大学生一边学习一边工作。**Bùshǎo dàxuéshēng yìbiān xuéxí yìbiān gōngzuò.** *Quite a few university students study and work at the same time.*

NOTE: 一边 … 一边 … **yìbiān … yìbiān …** links two verbs to indicate that the two actions denoted by the verbs take place simultaneously. Another example: ■ 他常常一边做作业一边听音乐。**Tā chángcháng yìbiān zuò zuòyè yìbiān tīng yīnyuè.** *He often does his homework while listening to music.* When the verbs are monosyllabic, 边 … 边 … **biān … biān …** may be used instead of 一边 … 一边 … **yìbiān … yìbiān … ,** e.g. ■ 孩子们边走边唱。**Háizimen biān zǒu biān chàng.** *The children sang while walking.* ■ 我们边吃边谈吧。**Wǒmen biān chī biān tán ba.** *Let's carry on the conversation while eating.*

yídàn 一旦 CONJ once, some day ■ 一旦有她的消息，马上告诉我。**yídàn yǒu tāde xiāoxi, mǎshàng gàosu wǒ.** *Once you've got news about her, let me know immediately.*

yídào 一道 ADV same as 一起 **yìqǐ**

yìdiǎnr 一点儿 N a tiny amount, a bit ■ 那个菜不好吃，我只吃了一点儿。**Nàge cài bù hǎo chī, wǒ zhǐ chīle yìdiǎnr.** *That dish is not tasty. I ate only a tiny bit of it.*

yídìng 一定 ADJ 1 fixed, specified ■ 他吃饭没有一定的时间。**Tā chīfàn méiyǒu yídìng de shíjiān.** *He has no fixed mealtimes.* 2 to a certain degree, fair, limited ■ 你的中文已经达到了一定水平。**Nǐ de Zhōngwén yǐjīng dádàole yídìng shuǐpíng.** *You've already reached a certain level of proficiency in Chinese.* 3 certainly, definitely ■ 我们的目标一定能达到。**Wǒmen de mùbiāo yídìng néng dádào.** *We can certainly reach our goal.*

yídù 一度 ADV once, for a time ■ 他一度得过忧郁症。**Tā yīdù dé guò yōuyùzhèng.** *He once suffered from depression.*

yì fān fēng shùn 一帆风顺 IDIOM all plain sailing

yìfāngmiàn … yìfāngmiàn … 一方面 … 一方面 … CONJ on the one hand … on the other hand … ■ 我们一方面要发展经济，一方面要保护环境。**Wǒmen yìfāngmiàn yào fāzhǎn jīngjì, yìfāngmiàn yào bǎohù huánjìng.** *We should on the one hand develop the economy and on the other hand protect the environment.*

yígòng 一共 **ADJ** in all, total, altogether ■ 你们学校一共有多少学生？ *Nǐmen xuéxiào yígòng yǒu duōshǎo xuésheng? How many students are there altogether in your school? (→ What is the total number of students in your school?)* ■ 我们去年一共学了五百二十个汉字。 *Wǒmen qùnián yígòng xuéle wǔbǎi érshí ge Hànzì. Last year we learned 520 Chinese characters in total.*

yíguàn 一贯 **ADV** all along, always

yíhuìr 一会儿 **ADV** in a very short time, in a moment ■ 不用麻烦倒茶，我一会儿就走。 *Bú yòng máfan dào chá, wǒ yíhuìr jiù zǒu. Please don't bother making tea. I'll be leaving in a moment.* ■ 他只休息了一会儿，就又干起来了。 *Tā zhǐ xiūxile yíhuìr, jiù yòu gàn qǐlai le. He took only a brief break and started working again.*

yī … jiù … 一 … 就 … **CONJ** as soon as, no sooner … than … ■ 妈妈一回家，就做晚饭。 *Māma yì huíjiā, jiù zuò wǎnfàn. Mom cooks supper as soon as she gets back home.* ■ 我一上火车，车就开了。 *Wǒ yí shàng huǒchē, chē jiù kāi le. No sooner did I board the train than it started.*

yì jǔ liǎng dé 一举两得 **IDIOM** gain two ends at once, kill two birds with one stone

yíkuàir 一块儿 **ADV** same as 一起 **yìqǐ**. Tends to be used in colloquial Chinese.

yìliú 一流 **ADJ** first-rate, first-class, top-notch

yílǜ 一律 **ADV** all, without exception

yí mù liǎorán 一目了然 **IDIOM** clear at one glance

yìqí 一齐 **ADV** same as 一起 **yìqǐ**

yìqǐ 一起 **ADV** together ■ 我们一起去吃饭吧。 *Wǒmen yìqǐ qù chīfàn ba. Let's have a meal together.* ■ 他们夫妻俩在同一公司工作，常常一起上班，一起回家。 *Tāmen fūqī liǎ zài tóng yì gōngsī gōngzuò, chángcháng yìqǐ shàngbān, yìqǐ huíjiā. That couple work in the same company, so they often go to work together and come home together.*

yíqiè 一切 **I ADJ** all, every and each without exception ■ 一切工作都做完了，才能放假。 *Yíqiè gōngzuò dōu zuòwánle, cái néng fàngjià. You can have your holiday only after all the work is done.* ■ 出国的一切手续都办完，要多长时间？ *Chūguó de yíqiè shǒuxù dōu bànwán yào duō cháng shíjiān? How long will it take to go through all the formalities for going abroad?* **II PRON** all, everything ■ 我了解她的一切。 *Wǒ liǎojiě tā de yíqiè. I know everything about her.* ■ 他做的一切都是为了赚更多的钱。 *Tā zuò de yíqiè dōushì wèile zhuàn gèng duō de qián. Everything he does, he does to make more money.*

yì rú jì wǎng 一如既往 **ADV** just as in the past, as before

yìshēng 一生 **N** all one's life, lifetime ■ 这位老人一生都住在这个山区。 *Zhè wèi lǎorén yìshēng dōu zhù zài zhège shānqū. This old man has lived in this mountainous area all his life.*

yìshí 一时 **N** for the time being, momentarily ■ 这个字我认识，但是一时记不起来了。 *Zhège zì wǒ rènshi, dànshì yìshí jì bu qǐlái le. I do know the word, but I just don't remember at this moment.*

yì sī bù gǒu 一丝不苟 **IDIOM** not the least bit negligent, attention to every detail, meticulous

yìtóng 一同 **ADV** same as 一起 **yìqǐ**

yíxià 一下 **ADV** (used after a verb to indicate the action is done briefly or casually) ■ 请您等一下，王先生马上就来。 *Qǐng nín děng yíxià, Wáng xiānsheng mǎshàng jiù lái. Please wait for a while. Mr Wang will be here in a moment.*

NOTE: It is very common in spoken Chinese to use 一下 **yíxià** after a verb, especially as an informal request. Some Northern Chinese speakers use 一下儿 **yíxiàr** instead of 一下 **yíxià**. More examples: ■ 请您来一下儿。 *Qǐng nín lái yíxiàr. Please come over for a while.* ■ 我们在这里停一下儿吧。 *Wǒmen zài zhèlǐ tíng yíxiàr ba. Let's stop here for a while.* ■ 让我想一下儿再回答。 *Ràng wǒ xiǎng yíxiàr zài huídá. Let me think a while before I answer.*

yíxiàzi 一下子 **ADV** all at once, all at a sudden ■ 这么多事一下子做不完，明天再做吧。 *Zhème duō shì yíxiàzi zuò bu wán, míngtiān zài zuò ba. We can't finish so many things at once. Let's continue tomorrow.*

yíxiàng 一向 **ADV** all along, always

yìxiē 一些 **MEASURE WORD** a small amount of, a bit of ■ 请你在我的茶里放一些糖。 *Qǐng nǐ zài wǒ de chá li fàng yìxiē táng. Please put a little sugar in my tea.* ■ 我这里有一些书，你看看还有没有用。 *Wǒ zhèlǐ yǒu yìxiē shū, nǐ kànkan hái yǒu méiyǒu yòng. I have a few books here. Have a look to see if they are still useful.*

yíyàng 一样 **ADJ** same, identical ■ "一下"和"一下儿"是一样的。 *"Yíxià" hé "yíxiàr" shì yíyàng de. "Yixia" and "Yixiar" are the same.* ■ 你今天去，明天去，都一样。 *Nǐ jīntiān qù, míngtiān qù, dōu yíyàng. It's all the same whether you go today or tomorrow.*

yízài 一再 **ADV** time and again, repeatedly

yìzhí 一直 **ADV** always, all the time ■ 我一直住在这个城市。 *Wǒ yìzhí zhù zài zhège chéngshì. I've always been living in this city.* ■ 他一直很关心你，常打听你的消息。 *Tā yìzhí hěn guānxīn nǐ, cháng dǎtīng nǐ de xiāoxi. He is always concerned for you and asks after you.*

yízhì 一致 **ADJ** unanimous, identical ■ 会上没有取得一致的意见。 *Huìshang méiyǒu qǔdé yízhì de yìjiàn. No consensus of opinion was reached at the meeting.*

yī 衣 **N** clothing

yīfu 衣服 [comp: 衣 clothing + 服 clothing] **N** clothes, a piece of clothing (件 **jiàn**) ■ 她每年花很多钱买衣服。 *Tā měi nián huā hěn duō qián mǎi*

yīfu. *She spends lots of money every year buying clothes.* ■ 她很会穿衣服。**Tā hěn huì chuān yīfu.** *She has good dress sense.*

NOTE: 衣服 **yīfu** may denote *clothes* or *a piece of clothing.* 一件衣服 **yí jiàn yīfu** may be *a jacket, a coat, a dress* or *a sweater,* but not *a pair of trousers,* which is 一条裤子 **yì tiáo kùzi.**

yīshang 衣裳 N same as 衣服 **yīfu**

yī 依 V rely on

yīcì 依次 V in proper order, one by one

yījiù 依旧 ADJ as before, still

yījù 依据 V & N be based on; basis, foundation
依据最新资料 yījù zuìxīn zīliào based on the latest data / 没有依据的指控 méiyǒu yījù de zhǐkòng unfounded allegation

yīkào 依靠 [comp: 依 rely on + 靠 lean on] V rely on, depend on ■ 公司的成功要依靠全体职工的努力。**Gōngsī de chénggōng yào kào quántǐ zhígōng de nǔlì.** *The success of the company depends on the efforts of all staff.*

yīlài 依赖 [comp: 依 rely on + 赖 rely on] V rely on, be dependent on

yītuō 依托 V rely on, depend on

yī 医 TRAD 醫 V heal, cure

yīshēng 医生 [modif: 医 medicine + 生 scholar] N medical doctor (位 **wèi**) ■ 你要听医生的话。**Nǐ yào tīng yīshēng de huà.** *You should follow the doctor's advice.* ■ 我们的家庭医生是张医生。**Wǒmen de jiātíng yīshēng shì Zhāng yīshēng.** *Our family physician is Dr Zhang.*

yīwùshì 医务室 [modif: 医 medical + 务 affair + 室 room] N clinic (in a school, factory, etc.) ■ 我们学校的医务室只有一位护士。**Wǒmen xuéxiào de yīwùshì zhǐyǒu yí wèi hùshi.** *There is only a nurse in our school clinic.*

yīxué 医学 [modif: 医 medical + 学 study] N medical science, medicine ■ 医学正在经历一场革命。**Yīxué zhèngzài jīnglì yì chǎng gémìng.** *Medical science is experiencing a revolution.*
医学院 yīxuéyuàn medical school

yīyuàn 医院 [modif: 医 medicine + 院 place (for certain activities)] N hospital (座 **zuò**) ■ 马上送医院！**Mǎshàng sòng yīyuàn!** *Take him to the hospital right now!* ■ 请问，最近的医院在哪儿？**Qǐng wèn, zuì jìn de yīyuàn zài nǎr?** *Excuse me, where is the nearest hospital?*
送 … 去医院 sòng … qù yīyuàn take … to the hospital / 住(医)院 zhù (yī) yuàn be hospitalized ■ 他病得很重，得住医院。**Tā bìng de hěn zhòng, děi zhù yīyuàn.** *He's seriously ill and has to be hospitalized.*

yí 仪 TRAD 儀 N instrument

yíqì 仪器 [comp: 仪 instrument + 器 utensil] N instrument (件 **jiàn**) ■ 做这个试验需要很多仪器。**Zuò zhège shìyàn xūyào hěn duō yíqì.** *This

test requires many instruments.*

yíshì 仪式 N ceremony, function, rite
举行仪式 jǔxíng yíshì hold a ceremony

yí 移 V move, shift ■ 窗前的阳光太强，我要把桌子往边上移。**Chuāngqián de yángguāng tài qiáng, wǒ yào bǎ zhuōzi wǎng biānshang yí.** *The sunshine is too strong by the window. I want to move my desk to the side.*

yídòng 移动 [comp: 移 move + 动 move] V move, shift ■ 强冷空气正在向东移动。**Qiáng lěng kōngqì zhèngzài xiàng dōng yídòng.** *Strong cold air is moving eastward.*

yídòng diànhuà 移动电话 N cordless telephone

yímín 移民 V & N immigrate, emigrate; immigrant, emigrant; immigration
移民局 Yímínjú Immigration Services

yí 疑 V doubt

yíhuò 疑惑 [comp: 疑 doubt + 惑 be puzzled] V feel uncertain, doubt
疑惑不解 yíhuò bù jiě feel puzzled, bewildered

yíwèn 疑问 [comp: 疑 doubt + 问 inquire] N doubt ■ 这个计划一定要实现，这是毫无疑问的。**Zhège jìhuà yídìng yào shíxiàn, zhè shì háowú yíwèn de.** *It is beyond any doubt that this plan will materialize.*

yí 遗 TRAD 遺 V leave behind

yíchǎn 遗产 [modif: 遗 leave behind + 产 property] N inheritance, legacy, heritage

yíchuán 遗传 [comp: 遗 leave behind + 传 transmit] V pass to the next generation, be hereditary

yíchuánbìng 遗传病 N hereditary disease

yíchuán gōngchéng 遗传工程 N genetic engineering

yíchuánxué 遗传学 N genetics

yíhàn 遗憾 V & ADJ regret; regretful ■ 部长非常遗憾，不能接受你们的邀请。**Bùzhǎng fēicháng yíhàn, bù néng jiēshòu nǐmen de yāoqǐng.** *The Minister regrets he is unable to accept your invitation.* ■ 我错过了那场音乐会，真是很遗憾。**Wǒ cuòguole nà chǎng yīnyuèhuì, zhēn shì hěn yíhàn.** *It is a pity that I missed the concert.*

yíliú 遗留 V leave behind, hand down

yíshī 遗失 V lose, be lost ■ 那份遗失的文件找到了。**Nà fèn yíshī de wénjiàn zhǎodào le.** *The lost document was recovered.*

yǐ 已 ADJ same as 已经 **yǐjīng**. Used in written Chinese.

yǐjīng 已经 ADJ already ■ 我已经学了三年中文了。**Wǒ yǐjīng xuéle sān nián Zhōngwén le.** *I've already been studying Chinese for three years.* ■ 她已经三十五岁了，还没有结婚。**Tā yǐjīng sānshíwǔ suì le, hái méiyǒu jiéhūn.** *She is already thirty-five years old and is not married yet.*

yǐ 乙 N the second of the ten Heavenly Stems, second

yǐ 以¹ PREP 1 with, in the manner of ■ 我们要以高

标准严格要求自己。**Wǒmen yào yǐ gāo biāozhǔn yángé yāoqiú zìjǐ.** *We should set high standards for ourselves.* **2** for, because of ■ 这个地方以风景优美著名。**Zhège dìfang yǐ fēngjǐng yōuměi zhùmíng.** *This place is famous for its beautiful scenery.*

yǐ 以² CONJ in order to, so as to ■ 应该推广新技术以提高工作效率。**Yīnggāi tuīguǎng xīn jìshù yǐ tígāo gōngzuò xiàolǜ.** *We should promote new technology so as to increase efficiency.*

yǐbiàn 以便 CONJ so that, in order that ■ 请你尽早通知我们，以便及时做好准备。**Qǐng nǐ jìnzǎo tōngzhī wǒmeà yǐbiàn jíshí zuòhǎo zhǔnbèi.** *Please let us know as soon as possible so that we can get ready in time.*

yǐhòu 以后 N after, later (ANTONYM 以前 **yǐqián**) ■ 做完作业以后，要检查一下。**Zuòwán zuòyè yǐhòu, yào jiǎnchá yíxià.** *After you've done an assignment, you should check it [for mistakes].* ■ 这个问题我们以后再谈。**Zhège wèntí wǒmen yǐhòu zài tán.** *We'll discuss this problem later.*

yǐjí 以及 CONJ same as 和¹ **hé** CONJ. Used in formal Chinese.

yǐlái 以来 PARTICLE since, in the past … ■ 今年以来，天气一直不正常。**Jīnnián yǐlái, tiānqì yìzhí bú zhèngcháng.** *Since the beginning of this year the weather has been quite abnormal.* ■ 三个月以来，你的中文口语有了很大进步。**Sān ge yuè yǐlái, nǐ de Zhōngwén kǒuyǔ yǒule hěn dà jìnbù.** *In the past three months you have made good progress in spoken Chinese.*

yǐmiǎn 以免 CONJ in order to avoid, so as not to

yǐnèi 以内 N within, during ■ 三天以内我一定把报告交给你。**Sān tiān yǐnèi wǒ yídìng bǎ bàogào jiāo gei nǐ.** *I will definitely submit my report to you in three days.*

yǐqián 以前 N before, some time ago (ANTONYM 以后 **yǐhòu**) ■ 回答问题以前，先要想一下。**Huídá wèntí yǐqián, xiān yào xiǎng yíxià.** *Before you answer a question, you should think first.* ■ 他不久以前身体不大好。**Tā bùjiǔ yǐqián shēntǐ bú dà hǎo.** *He was in poor health not long ago.*

不久以前 **bùjiǔ yǐqián** not long ago

yǐshàng 以上 N over, more than (ANTONYM 以下 **yíxià**)

yǐwài 以外 N beyond, outside, other than ■ 八小时以外你可以做自己喜欢做的事。**Bā xiǎoshí yǐwài nǐ kěyǐ zuò zìjǐ xǐhuan zuò de shì.** *You can do what you enjoy doing outside the eight working hours.*

yǐwǎng 以往 N formerly, in the past

yǐwéi 以为 V think (usually incorrectly) ■ 呀，你还在工作？我以为你已经回家了。**Yǎ, nǐ háizài gōngzuò? Wǒ yǐwéi nǐ yǐjīng huíjiā le.** *Oh, you're still working. I thought you'd gone home.* ■ 我一直以为他是日本人，现在才知道他是中国人。**Wǒ yìzhí yǐwéi tā shì Rìběnrén, xiànzài cái zhīdào tā shì Zhōngguórén.** *I always thought he was*

Japanese; only now I know he is Chinese.

yíxià 以下 N below, less than (ANTONYM 以上 **yǐshàng**) ■ 他们的年收入在一万元以下。**Tāmen de nián shōurù zài yíwàn yuán yíxià.** *Their annual income is less than 10,000 yuan.*

yǐzhì 以至 CONJ **1** up to

以至无穷 **yǐzhì wúqióng** into infinity

2 so as to, so…that

yǐzhì 以致 CONJ consequently, as a result

yǐ 椅 N chair

yǐzi 椅子 [suffix: 椅 chair + 子 nominal suffix] N chair (把 **bǎ**) ■ 房间里有一张桌子和四把椅子。**Fángjiān li yǒu yì zhāng zhuōzi hé sì bǎ yǐzi.** *There are a table and four chairs in the room.*

yì 亦 ADV also

yì 谊 TRAD 誼 N friendship (See **yǒuyì 友谊**.)

yì 义 TRAD 義 ADJ righteous

yìwù 义务 N duty, obligation ■ 交税是每一个公民的义务。**Jiāo shuì shì měi yí ge gōngmín de yìwù.** *Paying taxes is the duty of every citizen.*

yìwù gōngzuò (yìgōng) 义务工作（义工） N voluntary work

yìwù jiàoyù 义务教育 N compulsory education

yì 亿 TRAD 億 NUMERAL one hundred million ■ 中国有十三亿人口。**Zhōngguó yǒu shísān yì rénkǒu.** *China has a population of 1.3 billion.*

十亿 **shíyì** billion / 万亿 **wànyì** trillion

yì 忆 TRAD 憶 V recall (See **huíyì 回忆**, **jìyì 记忆**.)

yì 艺 TRAD 藝 N art

yìshù 艺术 [modif: 艺 art + 术 craft, skill] N art ■ 我不大懂现代艺术。**Wǒ bú dà dǒng xiàndài yìshù.** *I don't quite understand modern art.* ■ 他是搞艺术的。**Tā shì gǎo yìshù de.** *He is engaged in art. (→ He is an artist.)*

艺术作品 **yìshù zuòpǐn** a work of art

yìshùjiā 艺术家 N (accomplished, recognized) artist

yì 译 TRAD 譯 V translate (See **fānyì 翻译**.)

yì 异 TRAD 異 ADJ different

yìcháng 异常 [v+obj: 异 differ from + 常 the usual] ADJ abnormal, unusual ■ 环境遭到破坏，造成天气异常。**Huánjìng zāodào pòhuài, zàochéng tiānqì yìcháng.** *As the environment is damaged, abnormal weather results.*

yì 易¹ ADJ easy, not difficult (See **róngyì 容易**.)

yì 易² V exchange (See **màoyì 贸易**.)

yì 意 N idea, meaning

yìjiàn 意见 [comp: 意 idea + 见 viewpoint] N **1** opinion, view (条 **tiáo**) ■ 对这个问题你有什么意见？**Duì zhège wèntí nǐ yǒu shénme yìjiàn?** *What is your opinion on this issue?* ■ 在这个问题上我们已经取得了一致的意见。**Zài zhège wèntí shang wǒmen yǐjīng qǔdéle yízhì de yìjiàn.** *We have reached consensus on this issue.* **2** complaint, objection ■ 我对他处理这件事的方法很有意见。**Wǒ duì tā chǔlǐ zhè jiàn shì de fāngfǎ hěn yǒu yìjiàn.**

I have objections to the way he dealt with this matter. ■ 他只想到自己，我对他有意见。**Tā zhǐ xiǎngdào zìjǐ, wǒ duì tā yǒu yìjiàn.** *My complaint against him is that he thinks only about himself.* 提意见 tí yìjiàn make a comment (on an issue, a proposal etc.), make a complaint

yìliào 意料 **v & n** expect, anticipate; expectation, anticipation
意料之中 yìliào zhīzhōng in line with expectations / 出乎意料 chūhū yìliào out of expectations, not anticipated

yìshi 意识 **v & n** be conscious of, be aware of; consciousness

yìsi 意思 [comp: 意 meaning + 思 thought] **n** meaning ■ 这个字是什么意思？**Zhège zì shì shénme yìsi?** *What's the meaning of this character?* ■ 这句话的意思不清楚。**Zhè jù huà de yìsi bù qīngchu.** *The meaning of this sentence is not clear.* ■ 他的意思是你最好别去。**Tā de yìsi shì nǐ zuìhǎo bié qù.** *What he meant is that you'd better not go.*

yìtú 意图 **n** intention, intent
了解他们的意图 liǎojiě tāmende yìtú find out their intentions

yìwài 意外 **I** **adj** unexpected, unforeseen ■ 这个消息很意外。**Zhège xiāoxi hěn yìwài.** *This is unexpected news.* ■ 她平时常常迟到，今天这么早就来了，让人感到意外。**Tā píngshí chángcháng chídào, jīntiān zhème zǎo jiù lái le, ràng rén gǎndào yìwài.** *She is usually late for work, but she came so early today. It's quite unexpected.*
II **n** mishap, accident ■ 我们要采取安全措施，以防止意外。**Wǒmen yào cǎiqǔ ānquán cuòshī, yǐ fángzhǐ yìwài.** *We should take safety measures to prevent accidents.*

yìwèizhe 意味着 **v** mean, signify, imply

yìxiàng 意向 **n** intent, purpose
意向书 yìxiàngshū letter of intent; agreement of intent

yìyì 意义 [comp: 意 meaning + 义 meaning] **n** significance ■ 这件事有很大的历史意义。**Zhè jiàn shì yǒu hěn dà de lìshǐ yìyì.** *This event has great historical significance.* ■ 生活的意义是什么？**Shēnghuó de yìyì shì shénme?** *What is the meaning of life?*

yìzhì 意志 [comp: 意 will + 志 aspiration] **n** will ■ 这位运动员意志坚强，受了伤还每天锻炼。**Zhè wèi yùndòngyuán yìzhì jiānqiáng, shòule shāng hái měi tiān duànliàn.** *This athlete is strong-willed. He trains everyday despite his injury.*

yì 益 **n** benefit (See lìyì 利益.)

yì 毅 **adj** firm, resolute

yìlì 毅力 [modif: 毅 resolute + 力 strength] **n** indomitable will, strong willpower

yìrán 毅然 **adv** resolutely

yì 议 **trad** 議 **v** discuss

yìlùn 议论 [comp: 议 discuss + 论 comment] **v** comment, discuss, talk ■ 我从来不在背后议论别人。**Wǒ cónglái bú zài bèihòu yìlùn biérén.** *I never talk about people behind their backs.* ■ 我看你别议论政治了，挺危险的。**Wǒ kàn nǐ bié yìlùn zhèngzhì le, tǐng wēixiǎn de.** *I suggest you stop commenting on politics. It is rather dangerous.*

yì 抑 **v** press down

yìzhì 抑制 **v & n** inhibit, restrain; inhibition, restraint

yīn 因 **conj** because

yīncǐ 因此 **conj** therefore, so ■ 这种产品质量极好，因此价格比较高。**Zhè zhǒng chǎnpǐn zhìliàng jí hǎo, yīncǐ jiàgé bǐjiào gāo.** *This product is of excellent quality and is therefore rather expensive.*

yīn'ér 因而 same as 因此 **yīncǐ**

yīnsù 因素 **n** factor, element ■ 坚强的意志是事业成功的因素。**Jiānqiáng de yìzhì shì shìyè chénggōng de yīnsù.** *A strong will is an important factor for a successful career.* ■ 目前的这种情况，是由很多因素造成的。**Mùqián de zhè zhǒng qíngkuàng, shì yóu hěn duō yīnsù zàochéng de.** *The present situation was brought about by many factors.*

yīnwèi 因为 **conj** because ■ 因为没有时间，所以我很少去看朋友。**Yīnwèi méiyǒu shíjiān, suǒyǐ wǒ hěnshǎo qù kàn péngyou.** *I seldom go visiting friends because I don't have the time.* ■ 因为大多数人都反对，所以这个计划放弃了。**Yīnwèi dàduōshù rén dōu fǎnduì, suǒyǐ zhège jìhuà fàngqì le.** *Because the majority opposed the plan, it was abandoned.*

NOTE: 因为 **yīnwèi** is usually followed by 所以 **suǒyǐ**: 因为 … 所以 … **yīnwèi** … **suǒyǐ**… *because ... so/therefore*

yīn 阴 **trad** 陰 **adj** cloudy, overcast ■ 昨天上午天晴，下午阴天，晚上下雨。**Zuótián shàngwǔ tiānqíng, xiàwǔ yīntiān, wánshang xiàyǔ.** *Yesterday it was fine in the morning, cloudy in the afternoon and it rained in the evening.*

yīnmóu 阴谋 [modif: 阴 hidden + 谋 plot] **n** conspiracy
揭露一项国际阴谋 jiēlù yí xiàng guójì yīnmóu uncover an international conspiracy

yīntiān 阴天 cloudy day

yīnxìng 阴性 **adj** (of test result) negative (**antonym** 阳性 **yángxìng**)

yīn 姻 **n** marriage (See hūnyīn 婚姻.)

yīn 音 **n** sound

yīnxiǎng 音响 **n** 1 sounds, acoustics 2 stereo set

yīnyuè 音乐 [comp: 音 sound + 乐 music] **n** music ■ 星期天我常常跟朋友一块儿听音乐。**Xīngqītiān wǒ chángcháng gēn péngyou yíkuàir tīng yīnyuè.** *I often listen to music with my friends on Sundays.* ■ 你喜欢什么样的音乐？**Nǐ**

xǐhuan shénmeyàng de yīnyuè? *What kind of music do you like?*

轻音乐 qīng yīnyuè light music

yīnyuè huì 音乐会 N musical performance, concert

yīnyuè jiā 音乐家 N (accomplished) musician

yīnyuè xuéyuàn 音乐学院 N music school, conservatory

yín 银 TRAD 銀 N silver ■ 银是一种贵金属。 **Yín shì yì zhǒng guì jīnshǔ.** *Silver is a precious metal.*

yínháng 银行 [modif: 银 silver, money + 行 firm] N bank (家 **jiā**) ■ 他打算到银行去借钱。 **Tā dǎsuàn dào yínháng qù jiè qián.** *He plans to ask for a loan from the bank.* ■ 这里的银行几点钟 开始营业？ **Zhèli de yínháng jǐ diǎnzhōng kāishǐ yíngyè?** *What time do the banks here open for business?*

yǐn 引 V lead, provoke

yǐndǎo 引导 V guide, lead

yǐnqǐ 引起 V give rise to, lead to, cause, arouse ■ 连续三天大雨，引起了水灾。 **Liánxù sān tiān dà yǔ, yǐnqǐle shuǐzāi.** *Three days of incessant heavy rain caused flooding.*

yǐnqíng 引擎 N engine, especially heat engine

yǐnyòng 引用 V quote, cite

yǐn 饮 TRAD 飲 V drink

yǐnliào 饮料 [modif: 饮 drink + 料 stuff] N drink, beverage ■ "你要什么饮料？""我要一杯橘子水，谢谢。" **"Nǐ yào shénme yǐnliào?" "Wǒ yào yì bēi júzi shuǐ, xièxie."** *"What drink would you like to have?" "A glass of orange juice, thank you."*

yǐnshí 饮食 N food and drink

yǐnshíyè 饮食业 N catering industry, catering

yǐnyòngshuǐ 饮用水 N drinking water

非饮用水 fēi yǐnyòngshuǐ non-drinking water

yǐn 隐 TRAD 隱 V hide, conceal

yǐnbì 隐蔽 [comp: 隐 hide + 蔽 hide] V take cover, conceal

yǐnhuàn 隐患 N hidden trouble, hidden danger

yǐnmán 隐瞒 V conceal (facts)

隐瞒真相 yǐnmán zhēnxiàng cover up truth

yǐnsī 隐私 TRAD 隱私 N one's secrets, private matters, privacy

yǐnyuē 隐约 ADJ indistinct, faint, vague

yǐn 瘾 TRAD 癮 N addiction (See **shàngyǐn** 上瘾.)

yìn 印 V print ■ 这张照片，我想印三份。 **Zhè zhāng zhàopiàn, wǒ xiǎng yìn sān fèn.** *I want three prints of this photo.*

影印 yǐngyìn photocopy / 影印机 yǐngyìnjī photocopier

yìnshuā 印刷 [comp: 印 print + 刷 brush] V print (books, pamphlets, etc.) ■ 本店印刷各类文件。 **Běn diàn yìnshuā gè lèi wénjiàn.** *This shop prints all kinds of documents.*

印刷厂 yìnshuāchǎng print shop / 印刷机 yìnshuājī printing machine, press / 印刷品 yìnshuāpǐn printed matter

yìnxiàng 印象 [comp: 印 print + 象 image] N impression ■ 这个展览会给我留下深刻印象。 **Zhège zhǎnlǎnhuì gěi wǒ liúxià shēnkè yìnxiàng.** *This exhibition has left a deep impression on me.*

给 … 留下印象 gěi … liúxià yìnxiàng leave an impression on …

yīng 应 TRAD 應 MODAL V same as 应该 **yīnggāi**

yīngdāng 应当 MODAL V same as 应该 **yīnggāi**

yīnggāi 应该 MODAL V should, ought to ■ 你应该 早一点告诉我。 **Nǐ yīnggāi zǎo yìdiǎn gàosu wǒ.** *You should have told me earlier.* ■ 不用谢，这是 我应该做的。 **Búyòng xiè, zhè shì wǒ yīnggāi zuò de.** *Don't mention it. This is what I should do.*

yīng 英 ADJ heroic

Yīngguó 英国 N Britain, the UK

yīngjùn 英俊 ADJ (of men) handsome, attractive

英俊青年 yīngjùn qīngnián handsome young man

yīngmíng 英明 ADJ wise, brilliant

yīngtèwǎng 英特网 [modif: 英特 Internet + 网 net] N same as 互联网 **hùliánwǎng**

Yīngwén 英文 [modif: 英 English + 文 writing] N the English language (especially the writing)

yīngxióng 英雄 N talented and brave person, hero ■ 是英雄创造历史，还是历史产生英雄？ **Shì yīngxióng chuàngzào lìshǐ, háishì lìshǐ chǎnshēng yīngxióng?** *Do heroes create history or does history produce heroes?*

yīngyǒng 英勇 ADJ exceptionally brave, valiant, heroic

Yīngyǔ 英语 [modif: 英 English + 语 language] N the English language ■ 英语是世界上最通用的 国际语言。 **Yīngyǔ shì shìjiè shang zuì tōngyòng de guójì yǔyán.** *English is the world's most widely used international language.*

yīng 婴 TRAD 嬰 N baby

yīng'ér 婴儿 N baby (个 **gè**)

yíng 迎 V meet

yíngjiē 迎接 [comp: 迎 meet + 接 receive] V meet, greet ■ 今天下午我们要去机场迎接外国客 人。 **Jīntiān xiàwǔ wǒmen yào qù jīchǎng yíngjiē wàiguó kèren.** *This afternoon we are going to the airport to meet visitors from overseas.*

yíngmiàn 迎面 ADV head-on, in one's face

yíng 荧 TRAD 熒 ADJ glimmering, shimmering

yíngpíng 荧屏 N fluorescent screen, TV screen

yíng 营 TRAD 營 V operate

yíngyǎng 营养 N nutrition, nourishment ■ 这种 水果营养特别丰富。 **Zhè zhǒng shuǐguǒ yíngyǎng tèbié fēngfù.** *This fruit is particularly rich in nutrition.*

yíngyè 营业 V (of a commercial or service establishment) do business ■ 本店营业范围广 泛。 **Běn diàn yíngyè fànwéi guǎngfàn.** *This shop has an extensive range of business interests.*

营业时间 yíngyè shíjiān business hours

yíngyèyuán 营业员 **N** shop assistant, salesperson

yíng 盈 **N** surplus

yínglì 盈利 **V & N** make profit, reap profit; profit, profit margin

yíng 蝇 **TRAD** 蠅 **N** fly (See 苍蝇 **cāngying**.)

yíng 赢 **V** win (a game), beat (a rival) ■ 昨天的球赛谁赢了？ **Zuótiān de qiúsài shéi yíng le?** *Who won the ball game yesterday?* ■ 他买彩票赢了一千块钱。 **Tā mǎi cǎipiào yíngle yìqiān kuài qián.** *He won 1,000 yuan in the lottery.*

yíng 影 **N** shadow

yǐngxiǎng 影响 [comp: 影 shadow + 响 sound] **V & N** influence, affect; influence ■ 经济发展慢，影响了生活水平的提高。 **Jīngjì fāzhǎn màn, yǐngxiǎngle shēnghuó shuǐpíng de tígāo.** *Slow economic development affects the improvement of living standards.* ■ 中学生受谁的影响大—父母，还是朋友？ **Zhōngxuéshēng shòu shuí de yǐngxiǎng dà – fù-mǔ, háishì péngyou?** *Who has more influence on high school students—parents or friends?*

yǐngzi 影子 **N** shadow, reflection

yìng 应 **TRAD** 應 **V** respond

yìngchou 应酬 **V** engage in social activities, entertain

yìngfu 应付 **V 1** cope with ■ 顾客多的时候，一个售货员应付不了。 **Gùkè duō de shíhou, yí ge shòuhuòyuán yìngfu bùliǎo.** *When there's many cusomers, one sales clerk can't cope.* **2** act perfunctorily

yìngpìn 应聘 **V** accept an offer of an employment

yìngyāo 应邀 **ADJ** at the invitation of, on invitation

yìngyòng 应用 **V** apply ■ 这项新技术还不能应用在工业上。 **Zhè xiàng xīn jìshù hái bù néng yìngyòng zài gōngyè shang.** *This new technology cannot be applied in industry yet.*
应用程序 **yìngyòng chéngxù** app, application (program) / 应用科学 **yìngyòng kēxué** applied science

yìng 映 **V** reflect (See **fǎnyìng** 反映.)

yìng 硬 **ADJ** (of substance) hard, tough (**ANTONYM** 软 **ruǎn**) ■ 这种材料非常硬。 **Zhè zhǒng cáiliào fēicháng yìng.** *This material is very hard.*

yìngjiàn 硬件 **N** (in computing) hardware

yōng 拥 **TRAD** 擁 **V** embrace

yōngbào 拥抱 [comp: 拥 embrace + 抱 hold in arms] **V** embrace, hug ■ 中国人一般不习惯和人拥抱。 **Zhōngguórén yìbān bù xíguàn hé rén yōngbào.** *The Chinese are generally unaccustomed to hugging.*

yōnghù 拥护 **V** agree to and fully support, uphold

yōngjǐ 拥挤 **I V** push, push and shove ■ 不要拥挤，前面有小孩子！ *Don't push; there're kids before me!* **II ADJ** crowded ■ 现在这个时候公共汽车很拥挤，我们还是叫出租汽车吧。 **Xiànzài zhège shíhou gōnggòng qìchē hěn yōngjǐ, wǒmen háishi jiào chūzū qìchē ba.** *The buses are crowded at this moment; let's call a taxi.*

yōngyǒu 拥有 **V** possess, own

yōng 佣 **TRAD** 傭 **V** employ, hire
女佣 **nǚyōng** woman servant, maid

yōngrén 佣人 **N** servant

yōng 庸 **ADJ 1** mediocre
平庸 **píngyōng** mediocre, commonplace
2 vulgar

yōngsú 庸俗 **ADJ** vulgar, of low taste

yǒng 永 **ADV** forever

yǒnghéng 永恒 **ADJ** forever, permanent

yǒngyuǎn 永远 [comp: 永 forever + 远 remote] **ADV** forever ■ 我们永远是朋友。 **Wǒmen yǒngyuǎn shì péngyou.** *We'll be friends forever.* ■ 他永远不会做对家庭有害的事。 **Tā yǒngyuǎn bú huì zuò duì jiātíng yǒuhài de shì.** *He would never do anything that may harm his family.*

yǒng 勇 **N** courage

yǒnggǎn 勇敢 [comp: 勇 bold + 敢 daring] **ADJ** brave, bold, fearless ■ 他勇敢地从大火中救出两个孩子。 **Tā yǒnggǎn de cóng dà huǒ zhōng jiùchū liǎng ge háizi.** *He bravely saved two children from the fire.*

yǒngqì 勇气 [modif: 勇 courage + 气 quality] **N** courage ■ 你要有勇气承认错误。 **Nǐ yào yǒu yǒngqì chéngrèn cuòwù.** *You should have the courage to admit your mistake.*

yǒngyú 勇于 **V** have the courage to
勇于认错 **yǒngyú rèncuò** have the courage to admit one's own mistake

yǒng 涌 **V** gush, surge

yǒngxiàn 涌现 **V** emerge in large numbers

yǒng 踊 **V** leap up

yǒngyuè 踊跃 **I V** leap, jump **II ADV** eagerly, enthusiastically

yǒng 泳 **V** swim (See **yóuyǒng** 游泳.)

yòng 用 **V** use, (do something) with ■ 我可以用一下你的自行车吗？ **Wǒ kěyǐ yòng yíxià nǐ de zìxíngchē ma?** *May I use your bicycle?* ■ 我会用电脑写汉字。 **Wǒ huì yòng diànnǎo xiě Hànzì.** *I can use a computer to write Chinese characters.*

yòngbuzháo 用不着 **IDIOM 1** there is no need to ■ 这点小事，用不着请别人帮忙。 **Zhè diǎn xiǎo shì, yòngbuzháo qǐng biéren bāngmáng.** *This is a trivial matter and there is no need to ask for help.* **2** useless ■ 用不着的书别放在书架上。 **Yòngbuzháo de shū bié fàng zài shūjià shang.** *Don't put useless books on the bookshelf.*

yòngchu 用处 [modif: 用 use + 处 place] **V** use ■ 这个应用程序用处不大，就别买了。 **Zhè ge yìngyòng chéngxù yòngchu bú dà, jiù bié mǎi le.** *This app isn't of much use. Let's not buy it.*

yònggōng 用功 [v+obj: 用 use + 功 efforts] **ADJ** hardworking, diligent (student) ■ 她学习非常用功。 **Tā xuéxí fēicháng yònggōng.** *She studies diligently.* ■ 这学期我没有好好学习，下学期要

用功点。**Zhè xuéqī wǒ méiyǒu hǎohǎo xuéxí, xià xuéqī yào yònggōng diǎn.** *I did not study well this semester. I will work harder in the next semester.*

yònghù 用户 [modif: 用 use + 户 household] N user (of a product), consumer

yònglì 用力 [v+obj: 用 use + 力 strength] V exert oneself (physically) ■ 他用力把桌子推到一边。**Tā yònglì bǎ zhuōzi tuīdào yìbiān.** *He made an effort to push the desk to the side.*

yòngtú 用途 N use, function ■ 这种新型汽车用途很广。**Zhè zhǒng xīnxíng qìchē yòngtú hěn guǎng.** *This new model automobile has a wide range of uses.*

yōu 优 TRAD 優 ADJ excellent

yōudiǎn 优点 [modif: 优 excellent + 点 point] N strong point, merit (ANTONYM 缺点 **quēdiǎn**) ■ 每个人都有优点和缺点。**Měi ge rén dōu yǒu yōudiǎn hé quēdiǎn.** *Everybody has their strong points and weak points.* ■ 这个产品有什么优点? **Zhège chǎnpǐn yǒu shénme yōudiǎn?** *What are the merits of this new product?*

yōuhuì 优惠 ADJ preferential, favorable
优惠价 **yōuhuìjià** preferential price

yōuliáng 优良 [comp: 优 excellent + 良 good] ADJ fine, good ■ 政府正在推广小麦优良品种。**Zhèngfǔ zhèngzài tuīguǎng xiǎomài yōuliáng pǐnzhǒng.** *The government is promoting a fine variety of wheat.* ■ 她的儿子年年考试成绩优良。**Tā de érzi niánnián kǎoshì chéngjì yōuliáng.** *Her son gets good examination results every year.*

yōuměi 优美 [comp: 优 excellent + 美 beautiful] ADJ beautiful, graceful ■ 这里优美的风景吸引大批游览者。**Zhèli yōuměi de fēngjǐng xīyǐn dàpī yóulǎnzhě.** *The beautiful landscape here attracts large numbers of tourists.*

yōushèng 优胜 ADJ winning, superior
优胜者 **yōushèngzhě** winner

yōu shèng liè tài 优胜劣汰 IDIOM the superior wins and the inferior loses, survival of the fittest

yōushì 优势 [modif: 优 superior + 势 power] N superiority, advantage, dominant position ■ 这个国家人力资源丰富, 是发展经济的优势。**Zhège guójiā rén lì zīyuán fēngfù, shì fāzhǎn jīngjì de yōushì.** *Rich human resources are an advantage the country has in economic development.*

yōuxiān 优先 [comp: 优 superior + 先 first] ADJ taking precedence, having priority

yōuxiù 优秀 [comp: 优 excellent + 秀 elegant] ADJ outstanding, excellent ■ 这位青年是我们公司的优秀人才。**Zhè wèi qīngnián shì wǒmen gōngsī de yōuxiù réncái.** *This young man is an outstanding talent of our company.*

yōuyì 优异 [comp: 优 excellent + 异 unique] ADJ outstanding, exceptional

yōuyuè 优越 ADJ superior ■ 别以为自己比别人优越。**Bié yǐwéi zìjǐ bǐ biéren yōuyuè.** *Don't think*

you're superior to others (→ *None of your "holier-than-thou" attitude.*)
优越感 **yōuyuègǎn** superiority complex

yōu 悠 ADJ remote

yōujiǔ 悠久 [comp: 悠 remote + 久 long] ADJ very long, long-standing, time-honored ■ 中国历史悠久, 人口众多。**Zhōngguó lìshǐ yōujiǔ, rénkǒu zhòngduō.** *China has a long history and a large population.*

yōu 幽 ADJ quiet, serene

yōumò 幽默 N humor
有幽默感 **yǒu yōumògǎn** have a sense of humor

yōu 忧 TRAD 憂 V worry

yōuyù 忧郁 [comp: 忧 worried + 郁 gloomy] ADJ depressed, depressive

yōuyùzhèng 忧郁症 N (in medicine) depression
忧郁症患者 **yōuyùzhèng huànzhě** one who suffers from depression

yóu 尤 ADV especially

yóuqí 尤其 ADV especially ■ 我喜欢吃中国菜, 尤其喜欢吃广东菜。**Wǒ xǐhuan chī Zhōngguó cài, yóuqí xǐhuan chī Guǎngdōng cài.** *I love Chinese food, especially Cantonese food.*

yóu 由 PREP 1 (introducing the agent of an action), by ■ 技术问题由你们解决。**Jìshù wèntí yóu nǐmen jiějué.** *Technical problems will be solved by you.* (→ *You are responsible for solving technical problems.*) 2 (introducing manner or cause of an action), with ■ 很多交通事故都是由车速太快造成的。**Hěn duō jiāotōng shìgù dōu shì yóu chēsù tài kuài zàochéng de.** *Many road accidents are caused by speeding.*

yóuyú 由于 PREP & CONJ because of, owing to, due to; because, as ■ 由于家庭她不得不放弃事业。**Yóuyú jiātíng tā bùdébù fàngqì shìyè.** *She had no choice but give up her career because of her family.* ■ 由于丈夫身体不好, 她不能出国工作。**Yóuyú zhàngfu shēntǐ bù hǎo, tā bù néng chūguó gōngzuò.** *She was not able to go abroad to work because her husband was in poor health.*

yóu 邮 TRAD 郵 N post

yóujú 邮局 [modif: 邮 post + 局 office] N post office ■ 请问, 附近有没有邮局? **Qǐngwèn, fùjìn yǒu méiyǒu yóujú?** *Excuse me, is there a post office nearby?* ■ 由于电脑的广泛使用, 邮局已经没有以前那么重要了。**Yóuyú diànnǎo de guǎngfàn shǐyòng, yóujú yǐjīng méiyǒu yǐqián nàme zhòngyào le.** *Thanks to extensive use of the computer, the post office is no longer as important as before.*

yóupiào 邮票 [modif: 邮 post + 票 ticket] N postal stamp (张 **zhāng**) ■ 这封信寄到台湾, 要多少邮票? **Zhè fēng xìn jìdào Táiwān, yào duōshǎo yóupiào?** *How much is the postage for this letter to Taiwan?* ■ 我买十块钱邮票。**Wǒ mǎi shí kuài qián yóupiào.** *I want to buy ten yuan worth of stamps.*

yóu 犹 TRAD 猶 PREP like, as

yóurú 犹如 PREP just like, just as

yóuyù 犹豫 ADJ hesitant, wavering, procrastinating ■ 去不去国外找工作，我还有点犹豫。**Qù bu qù guówài zhǎo gōngzuò, wǒ hái yǒudiǎn yóuyù.** *I'm still wavering over going job hunting abroad.* ■ 不能犹豫了，得马上决定。**Bú néng yóuyù le, děi mǎshàng juédìng.** *You can't hesitate any more. You've got to decide right now.*

yóu 油 I N oil ■ 油比水轻。**Yóu bǐ shuǐ qīng.** *Oil is lighter than water.* II ADJ greasy (food) ■ 这个菜太油了，我不能吃。**Zhège cài tài yóu le, wǒ bù néng chī.** *This dish is too greasy. I can't eat it.*

食油 shíyóu edible oil, cooking oil / 石油 shíyóu petroleum, oil

yóuhuà 油画 [modif: 油 oil + 画 painting] N oil painting (幅 **fú**)

yóunì 油腻 ADJ greasy, oily, fatty

yóuqī 油漆 V & N coat with paint, paint; paint

yóutián 油田 [modif: 油 oil + 田 field] N oil field

yóuzhà 油炸 V & ADJ deep fry; deep fried

yóu 游 V play

yóulǎn 游览 [comp: 游 play + 览 see] V go sightseeing, tour for pleasure ■ 每年很多人去香港游览。**Měi nián hěn duō rén qù Xiānggǎng yóulǎn.** *Every year many people go to Hong Kong on holiday.*

游览者 yóulǎnzhě tourist

yóuyǒng 游泳 V swim ■ 他游泳游得很好。**Tā yóuyǒng yóu de hěn hǎo.** *He swims very well.* ■ 我一星期游两次泳。**Wǒ yì xīngqī yóu liǎng cì yǒng.** *I swim twice a week.*

游泳池 yóuyǒngchí swimming pool / 游泳裤 yóuyǒng kù swimming trunks / 游泳衣 yóuyǒng yī swimsuit / 温水游泳池 wēnshuǐ yóuyǒngchí heated swimming pool

yóuxì 游戏 [modif: 游 play + 戏 have fun] N game ■ 我们来做游戏！**Wǒmen lái zuò yóuxì!** *Let's play a game!*

电脑游戏 diànnǎo yóuxì computer game

yóuxìjī 游戏机 N play station, console

yǒu 友 N friend

yǒuhǎo 友好 [comp: 友 friendly + 好 amiable] ADJ friendly ■ 她对所有的人都很友好。**Tā duì suǒyǒu de rén dōu hěn yǒuhǎo.** *She is friendly to everyone.* ■ 你这么做不大友好。**Nǐ zhème zuò bú dà yǒuhǎo.** *It's not friendly of you to do so.*

yǒuyì 友谊 [comp: 友 friendly + 谊 friendship] N friendship ■ 我希望我们能发展我们之间的友谊。**Wǒ xīwàng wǒmen néng fāzhǎn wǒmen zhī jiān de yǒuyì.** *I hope we will be able to develop the friendship between us.* ■ 友谊天长地久。**Yǒuyì tiān-cháng-dì-jiǔ.** *Our friendship will last forever.*

yǒu 有 V 1 possess, have ■ 他们有一座房子、一辆汽车；在银行里还有一些钱。**Tāmen yǒu yí zuò fángzi, yí liàng qìchē, zài yínháng li háiyǒu yìxiē qián.** *They have a house, a car and some money in the bank.* **2** exist, there is (are) ■ 世界上有多少国家？**Shìjiè shang yǒu duōshǎo guójiā?** *How many countries are there in the world?*

没有 méiyǒu do not possess, have no; do not exist, there is no ■ 我没有汽车。**Wǒ méiyǒu qìchē.** *I don't have a car.* ■ 教室里没有人。**Jiàoshì li méiyǒu rén.** *There is nobody in the classroom.*

yǒude 有的 PRON some ■ 有的人喜欢体育，有的人喜欢艺术，也有的人什么也不喜欢。**Yǒude rén xǐhuan tǐyù, yǒude rén xǐhuan yìshù, yě yǒude rén shénme yě bù xǐhuan.** *Some people are fond of sports, others are fond of the arts and still others are not fond of anything.*

yǒudeshì 有的是 V be plenty of, be abundant, not in short supply ■ 大学毕业生有的是。**Dàxué bìyèshēng yǒudeshì.** *There are plenty of university graduates.*

yǒu(yì)diǎnr 有(一)点儿 ADV slightly, a little, somewhat ■ 我今天有点儿累了，明天再谈吧。**Wǒ jīntiān yǒudiǎnr lèi le, míngtiān zài tán ba.** *I'm a bit tired today. Let's talk tomorrow.* ■ 他这么回答，她有一点失望。**Tā zhème huídá, tā yǒuyìdiǎn shīwàng.** *She is somewhat disappointed at his reply.*

NOTE: 有点 **yǒudiǎn,** 有点儿 **yǒudiǎnr,** 有一点 **yǒuyìdiǎn,** 有一点儿 **yǒuyìdiǎnr** mean the same thing. 有点儿 **yǒudiǎnr** and 有一点儿 **yǒuyìdiǎnr** are only used in colloquial Chinese.

yǒuguān 有关 V have a bearing on, have something to do with, be related to (ANTONYM 无关 wúguān) ■ 这件事与你有关。**Zhè jiàn shì yú nǐ yǒuguān.** *This matter has something to do with you. (→ This matter concerns you.)* ■ 一个人的性格和事业成功与否有关。**Yí ge rén de xìnggé hé shìyè chénggōng yúfǒu yǒuguān.** *A person's disposition has a bearing on whether his career is successful or not.*

yǒulì 有力 [v+obj: 有 have + 力 force] ADJ forceful, powerful, strong ■ 我们要采取有力措施节水节电。**Wǒmen yào cǎiqǔ yǒulì cuòshī jié shuǐ jié diàn.** *We should take strong measures to save water and electricity.*

yǒulì 有利 [v+obj: 有 have + 利 benefit] ADJ favorable, advantageous (ANTONYM 不利 búlì) ■ 我们要在那里发展业务有有利条件，也有不利条件。**Wǒmen yào zài nàli fāzhǎn yèwù yǒu yǒulì tiáojiàn, yě yǒu búlì tiáojiàn.** *There are both favorable and unfavorable conditions for our developing our business there.*

yǒumíng 有名 [v+obj: 有 have + 名 name, fame] ADJ famous, well-known ■ 这座大学很有名。**Zhè zuò dàxué hěn yǒumíng.** *This is a famous university.* ■ 这是一本很有名的小说。**Zhè shì yì běn hěn**

yǒumíng de xiǎoshuō. *This is a well-known novel.*

yǒuqián 有钱 [v+obj: 有 have + 钱 money] ADJ rich, wealthy ■ 他爸爸很有钱，但是他从来不乱花钱。 **Tā bàba hěn yǒuqián, dànshì tā cónglái bù luàn huā qián.** *His father is very wealthy, but he is quite frugal* ■ 她想找一个有钱人结婚。 **Tā xiǎng zhǎo yí ge yǒu qián rén jiéhūn.** *She wants to find a rich man to marry.*

NOTE: See note on 富 **fù.**

yǒuqù 有趣 [v+obj: 有 have + 趣 fun] ADJ interesting, amusing ■ 我给你讲一个有趣的故事。 **Wǒ gěi nǐ jiǎng yí ge yǒuqù de gùshi.** *I'll tell you an interesting story.* ■ 他在旅行的时候，遇到很多有趣的事。 **Tā zài lǚxíng de shíhou, yùdào hěn duō yǒuqù de shì.** *He had many interesting experiences on his journey.*

yǒushí 有时 ADV same as 有时候 **yǒushíhou**

yǒushíhou 有时候 ADV sometimes ■ 爸爸有时候忙，有时候不那么忙。 **Bàba yǒushíhou máng, yǒushíhou bú nàme máng.** *Sometimes my father is busy; sometimes he isn't so busy.* ■ 他工作一般都很认真，但有时候也会马虎。 **Tā gōngzuò yìbān dōu hěn rènzhēn, dàn yǒushíhou yě huì mǎhu.** *He is generally a conscientious worker, but he can be careless sometimes.*

yǒu tiáo bù wěn 有条不紊 ADJ in an orderly way, methodically

yǒuxiào 有效 [v+obj: 有 have + 效 effect] ADJ 1 effective, efficacious ■ 王老师教我们记生词的办法很有效。 **Wáng lǎoshī jiāo wǒmen jì shēngcí de bànfǎ hěn yǒuxiào.** *Teacher Wang taught us an effective method of memorizing new words.* 2 valid ■ 我的护照还有效。 **Wǒ de hùzhào hái yǒuxiào.** *My passport is still valid.*

有效期 yǒuxiàoqī term of validity, expiry date

yǒuxiē 有些 PRON same as 有的 **yǒude**

yǒu yìsi 有意思 [v+obj: 有 have + 意思 meaning] ADJ meaningful, interesting ■ 这本书很有意思，每个人都应该看。 **Zhè běn shū hěn yǒu yìsi, měi ge rén dōu yīnggāi kàn.** *This book is very meaningful. Everybody should read it.* ■ 董事长讲话的最后几句很有意思。 **Dǒngshìzhǎng jiǎnghuà de zuì hòu jǐ jù hěn yǒu yìsi.** *The last few sentences in the Chairman's speech are rather meaningful.*

没有意思 méiyǒu yìsi uninteresting, meaningless ■ 那个电影没有意思。 **Nàge diànyǐng méiyǒu yìsi.** *That movie isn't interesting.*

yǒuyòng 有用 [v+obj: 有 have + 用 use] ADJ useful ■ 我相信中文会越来越有用。 **Wǒ xiāngxìn Zhōngwén huì yuèláiyuè yǒuyòng.** *I believe the Chinese language will be more and more useful.* ■ 这本词典很有用。 **Zhè běn cídiǎn hěn yǒuyòng.** *This dictionary is very useful.*

没有用 méiyǒu yòng useless ■ 这本书太旧了，没

有什么用了。 **Zhè běn shū tài jiù le, méiyǒu shénme yòng le.** *This book is too outdated, and is not of much use.*

yòu 右 N the right side (ANTONYM 左 **zuǒ**) ■ 你右边的那座房子就是图书馆。 **Nǐ yòubian de nà zuò fángzi jiù shì túshūguǎn.** *The building on your right is the library.*

yòubian 右边 [modif: 右 right + 边 side] N the right side, the right-hand side ■ 超级市场的右边是个停车场。 **Chāojí shìchǎng de yòubian shì yí ge tíngchēchǎng.** *On the right side of the supermarket is a car park.*

yòu 幼 ADJ very young

yòu'ér 幼儿 [modif: 幼 very young + 儿 child] N young child between 2 and 6 years old

yòu'éryuán 幼儿园 [modif: 幼儿 young child + 园 garden] N kindergarten

yòuzhì 幼稚 ADJ naive, childish

yòu 诱 TRAD 誘 V induce

yòuhuò 诱惑 [comp: 诱 induce + 惑 confuse] V entice, seduce

yòu 又 ADV 1 again ■ 电脑昨天刚修好，今天又坏了。 **Diànnǎo zuótiān gāng xiūhǎo, jīntiān yòu huài le.** *The computer was fixed yesterday, but it broke down again today.* ■ 晴了半天，又下雨了。 **Qíngle bàntiān, yòu xià yǔ le.** *After just half a day's fine weather, it rained again.* 2 moreover, additionally ■ 这个菜味道好，营养又丰富。 **Zhège cài wèidao hǎo, yíngyǎng yòu fēngfù.** *This dish is tasty and also very nutritious.* ■ 吸烟很花钱，又对身体有害。 **Xīyān hěn huāqián, yòu duì shēntǐ yǒuhài.** *Smoking is costly and, moreover, harmful to your health.*

又 … 又 … yòu … yòu … and also …, both … and … ■ 他们的小女儿又聪明又可爱。 **Tāmen de xiǎo nǚ'ér yòu cōngmíng yòu kě'ài.** *Their young daughter is bright and lovely.*

NOTE: See note on 再 **zài.**

yú 于 TRAD 於 PREP in, at (only used in written Chinese) ■ 他生于一九八零年。 **Tā shēng yú yī-jiǔ-bā-líng nián.** *He was born in 1980.*

yúshì 于是 CONJ as a result, consequently ■ 他爸爸在上海找到了工作，于是全家搬到上海去了。 **Tā bàba zài Shànghǎi zhǎodào le gōngzuò, yúshì quán jiā bāndào Shànghǎi qù le.** *His father found a job in Shanghai; as a result the family moved to Shanghai.*

yú 余 TRAD 餘 V spare (See 其余 **qíyú**, 业余 **yèyú**.)

yú 鱼 TRAD 魚 N fish (条 **tiáo**) ■ 河里有鱼吗？ **Hé li yǒu yú ma?** *Is there any fish in the river?*

yú 渔 TRAD 漁 N fishing, fishery ■ 授人以鱼，不如授之以渔。（老子） **Shòu rén yǐ yú, bùrú shuò zhī yǐ yú. (Lǎozǐ)** *Giving someone a fish is not so good as teaching him how to fish. (Laozi)*

yúchuán 渔船 N fishing boat (艘 **sōu**)

yúmín 渔民 N fisherman

yúwǎng 渔网 N fishing net (张 **zhāng**)

yú 愚 ADJ foolish

yúchǔn 愚蠢 [comp: 愚 foolish + 蠢 stupid] ADJ foolish, stupid

yúmèi 愚昧 [comp: 愚 foolish + 昧 ignorant] ADJ ignorant and foolish

yú 與 TRAD 舆 N chariot

yúlùn 舆论 N public opinion

yú 娱 TRAD 娱 V amuse, give pleasure to

yúlè 娱乐 [comp: 娱 amuse + 乐 amuse] V & N entertain, amuse; entertainment, amusement
娱乐活动 **yúlè huódòng** recreation, recreational activities

yú 愉 N pleasure

yúkuài 愉快 [comp: 愉 pleasant + 快 delightful] ADJ 1 pleasant, joyful ■ 祝你假期愉快！**Zhù nǐ jiàqī yúkuài!** *I wish you a joyful holiday.* ■ 和你一起工作是很愉快的。**Hé nǐ yìqǐ gōngzuò shì hěn yúkuài de.** *Working with you is very pleasant.* ■ 我永远不会忘记那段愉快的经历。**Wǒ yóngyuǎn bú huì wàngji zhè duàn yúkuài de jīnglì.** *I will never forget that pleasant experience.* **2** pleased, happy ■ 我听到这句话，很不愉快。**Wǒ tīngdào zhè jù huà, hěn bù yúkuài.** *I feel displeased to hear this.*

yǔ 与 TRAD 與 same as 和 **hé** and 跟 **gēn**. Only used in written Chinese.

yǔ cǐ tóng shí 与此同时 IDIOM at the same time

yǔhuì 与会 V be present at a meeting (conference)

yǔqí ... bùrú 与其 ... 不如 CONJ would rather ... than ■ 与其坐着谈，不如起而行。**Yǔqí zuòzhe tán, bùrú qǐ ér xíng.** *We would rather get up and do something than sit here talking.*

NOTE: Pay attention to the different word orders of 与其 ... 不如 **yǔqí ... bùrú** *would rather... than*: while it is 与其 A 不如 B in Chinese, in English it is *would rather B than A.*

yǔ rì jù zēng 与日俱增 V grow with each passing day, be steadily on the increase

yǔ 屿 TRAD 嶼 N small island, isle (See **dǎoyǔ** 岛屿.)

yǔ 宇 N space

yǔzhòu 宇宙 [comp: 宇 space + 宙 time] N the universe

yǔ 雨 N rain ■ 这里夏天多雨。**Zhèli xiàtiān duō yǔ.** *It often rains here in summer.* ■ 我看马上要下雨了。**Wǒ kàn mǎshàng yào xià yǔ le.** *It seems to me that it's going to rain soon.*
雨天 **yǔtiān** rainy day / 雨衣 **yǔyī** raincoat / 下雨 **xià yǔ** to rain

yǔ 羽 N feather

yǔmáoqiú 羽毛球 [modif: 羽毛 feather + 球 ball] V badminton, shuttlecock (只 **zhī**) ■ 我常常跟朋友在体育馆打羽毛球。**Wǒ chángcháng gēn péngyou zài tǐyùguǎn dǎ yǔmáoqiú.** *I often play badminton with my friends in the gym.*

yǔróng 羽绒 [comp: 羽 feather + 绒 down] N eiderdown

yǔróngfú 羽绒服 N eiderdown clothes, eiderdown coat (件 **jiàn**)

yǔ 语 TRAD 語 N language

yǔdiào 语调 [modif: 语 speech + 调 tune] N intonation ■ 中文的声调不容易掌握，语调也很难。**Zhōngwén de shēngdiào bù róngyì zhǎngwò, yǔdiào yě hěn nán.** *While it is not easy to have a good command of Chinese tones, Chinese intonation is also difficult.*

yǔfǎ 语法 [modif: 语 language + 法 law, rule] N grammar ■ 我不大懂汉语语法，我想学一点儿。**Wǒ bú dà dǒng Hànyǔ yǔfǎ, wǒ xiǎng xué yìdiǎnr.** *I don't quite understand Chinese grammar; I want to learn a bit.*

yǔqì 语气 [modif: 语 speech + 气 quality] N tone, manner of speaking ■ 同样一句话，语气不同，听了感觉就不同。**Tóngyàng yí jù huà, yǔqì bùtóng, tīngle gǎnjué jiù bùtóng.** *Saying the same sentence in different tones of the voice produces different feelings in the hearers.*

yǔyán 语言 [comp: 语 language + 言 speech] N language (门 **mén**, 种 **zhǒng**) ■ 要了解一个民族，就要学它的语言。**Yào liǎojiě yí ge mínzú, jiù yào xué tā de yǔyán.** *If you want to understand an ethnic group, you should study its language.* ■ 学一门语言，就是多一个观察世界的窗户。**Xué yì mén yǔyán, jiù shì duō yí ge guānchá shìjiè de chuānghu.** *To learn a language is to have one more window from which to look at the world.*

yǔyǐ 予以 V grant, give

yù 玉 TRAD 玉 N jade

yùmǐ 玉米 [modif: 玉 jade + 米 rice] N corn, maize (根 **gēn**) ■ 肚子饿了，先吃一根玉米吧。**Dùzi è le, xiān chī yì gēn yùmǐ ba.** *If you're hungry, eat some corn first.*

yùqì 玉器 N jade article, jadeware

yù 育 V educate, nurture (See **jiàoyù** 教育, **tǐyù** 体育, etc.)

yù 浴 V bathe

yùshì 浴室 [modif: 浴 bathe + 室 room] N bathroom (间 **jiān**) ■ 这套房子很大，有两间浴室。**Zhè tào fángzi hěn dà, yǒu liǎng jiān yùshì.** *This is a big flat with two bathrooms.*

yù 狱 TRAD 獄 N prison
地狱 **dìyù** hell

yù 遇 V encounter

yùdào 遇到 V encounter, come across ■ 我在国外旅行的时候，遇到不少好心人。**Wǒ zài guówài lǚxíng de shíhou, yùdào bùshǎo hǎoxīnrén.** *When I traveled overseas, I came across many kindhearted people.* ■ 在工作中总会遇到困难。**Zài gōngzuò zhōng zǒng huì yùdào kùnnan.** *One is bound to encounter difficulties in work.*

yùjiàn 遇见 v meet (someone) unexpectedly, come across, run into ■ 我昨天在超级市场遇见一个老同学。**Wǒ zuótiān zài chāojí shìchǎng yùjiàn yí ge lǎo tóngxué.** *I ran into an old classmate of mine in the supermarket yesterday.*

yù 预 TRAD 預 ADV in advance

yùbào 预报 [modif: 预 in advance + 报 report] N forecast, prediction ■ 你听过今天的天气预报吗？**Nǐ tīngguo jīntiān de tiānqì yùbào ma?** *Have you listened to the weather forecast for today?*

yùbèi 预备 [modif: 预 in advance + 备 prepare] v prepare, get ready ■ 他们在春节前一个星期，就开始预备春节时的饭菜了。**Tāmen zài chūnjié qián yí ge xīngqī, jiù kāishǐ yùbèi chūnjié shí de fàncài le.** *They began preparing the food for the Spring Festival a week before.*

预备会议 yùbèi huìyì preparatory meeting / 预备学校 yùbèi xuéxiào preparatory school

yùdìng 预订 v book, place an order ■ 我已经在餐馆预订了席位。**Wǒ yǐjīng zài cānguǎn yùdìng le xíwèi.** *I've booked seats in the restaurant.*

yùfáng 预防 [modif: 预 in advance + 防 defend] V & N take precautionary measures to prevent, prevent; prevention ■ 预防重于治疗。**Yùfáng zhòngyú zhìliáo.** *Prevention (of disease) is more important than treatment.*

yùliào 预料 v predict, expect

yùqī 预期 [comp: 预 in advance + 期 expect] v expect, anticipate

yùsuàn 预算 [comp: 预 in advance + 算 calculate] N budget

yùxí 预习 [modif: 预 preparatory + 习 study] v prepare lessons before class, preview ■ 明天上语法课，我要想预习一下。**Míngtiān shàng yǔfǎ kè, wǒ yào xiān yùxí yíxià.** *Tomorrow there'll be a grammar lesson, and I'll prepare for it.*

yùxiān 预先 ADV in advance, beforehand

yùyán 预言 V & N predict; prediction, prophecy 古代圣人的预言 gǔdài shèngrén de yùyán prophecy made by ancient sages

yùzhào 预兆 N omen, presage, harbinger

yù 欲 N desire 食欲 shíyù desire for food, appetite / 性欲 xìngyù sexual desire, sex drive

yùwàng 欲望 [comp: 欲 desire + 望 hope] N desire 求知的欲望 qiúzhī de yùwàng desire to have more knowledge, hunger for knowledge

yù 寓 v imply

yùyán 寓言 N fable, parable

yù 愈 I v recover from illness 大病初愈 dàbìng chū yù have just recovered from a serious illness

II ADV more

yù 豫 N comfort (See yóuyù 犹豫.)

yuān 冤 N injustice, wrong

yuānwang 冤枉 v be wronged with false charges

■ 别冤枉好人。**Bié yuānwang hǎorén.** *Don't wrong innocent people.*

yuán 元 [1] ADJ first, primary

yuándàn 元旦 [modif: 元 first + 旦 dawn] N the New Year's Day

yuánjiàn 元件 N component part, component

yuánshǒu 元首 [modif: 元 first + 首 head] N head of state ■ 中华人民共和国主席是中国元首。**Zhōnghuá Rénmín Gònghéguó zhǔxí shì Zhōngguó yuánshǒu.** *The President of the People's Republic of China is China's head of state.*

yuánsù 元素 N (chemical) element

yuánxiāo 元宵 [modif: 元 first + 宵 night] N 1 also known as 元宵节 **Yuánxiāojié**, the Lantern Festival (the 15th of the first month in the Chinese Lunar Calendar, when the full moon appears for the first time in a year.) 2 the traditional sweet dumpling for the Lantern Festival

yuán 元 [2] MEASURE WORD (the basic unit of Chinese currency: 1 元 yuán = 10 角 jiǎo/毛 máo = 100 分 fēn), yuan, dollar

美元 Měiyuán US dollar / 日元 Rìyuán Japanese yen

NOTE: 元 **yuán** is the formal word for the basic unit of Chinese currency. In spoken Chinese 块 **kuài** is more common. For instance, the sum of 50 yuan is usually written as 五十元 **wǔshí yuán**, but spoken of as 五十块 **wǔshí kuài** or 五十块钱 **wǔshí kuài qián**.

yuán 员 TRAD 員 N member

yuángōng 员工 N staff, personnel

yuán 园 TRAD 園 N garden

yuánlín 园林 N garden, park, gardens and parks

yuán 原 ADJ original, former

yuángào 原告 N plaintiff, prosecutor

yuánlái 原来 ADJ original, former ■ 她原来的计划是去英国工作一段时间。**Tā yuánlái de jìhuà shì qù Yīngguó gōngzuò yí duàn shíjiān.** *Her original plan was to go to England and work there for a period of time.* ■ 古建筑遭到破坏，不能恢复原来的样子。**Gǔ jiànzhù zāodào pòhuài, bù néng huīfù yuánlái de yàngzi.** *The ancient building is damaged and cannot be restored to its former appearance.*

yuánlǐ 原理 N principle, tenet 生物学原理 shēngwùxué yuánlǐ principles of biology

yuánliàng 原谅 v pardon, excuse, forgive ■ 我今天上午没有能到飞机场去接你，请多原谅。**Wǒ jīntiān shàngwǔ méiyǒu néng dào fēijīchǎng qù jiē nǐ, qǐng duō yuánliàng.** *Please forgive me for not having been able to meet you at the airport this morning.* ■ 你这么做，我不能原谅。**Nǐ zhème zuò, wǒ bù néng yuánliàng.** *I can't forgive you for such behavior.*

yuánliào 原料 [modif: 原 original + 料 material] N raw material ■ 原料价格又涨了。**Yuánliào jiàgé yòu zhǎng le.** *The price of raw materials has risen again.*

yuánshǐ 原始 [comp: 原 original + 始 beginning]
ADJ 1 primitive, primal
原始森林 yuánshǐ sēnlín primitive forests
2 primal, first-hand, original
原始资料 yuánshǐ zīliào first-hand data

yuánxiān 原先 **ADV** original, former

yuányīn 原因 [modif: 原 origin + 因 cause] **N**
cause, reason ■ 出了问题，一定要找出原因。
Chūle wèntí, yídìng yào zhǎochū yuányīn. When
something has gone wrong we must identify the
cause.

yuánzé 原则 **N** principle ■ 不管发生什么，我都
不会放弃原则。 **Bùguǎn fāshēng shénme, wǒ dōu
bú huì fàngqì yuánzé.** I will not abandon my principles, no matter what. ■ 有时候坚持原则是不容
易的。 **Yǒushíhou jiānchí yuánzé shì bù róngyì de.**
Sometimes it is not easy to adhere to one's principles.

yuán 圆 **TRAD** 圓 **ADJ** round, circular ■ 在古代，
人们不知道地球是圆的。 **Zài gǔdài rénmen bù
zhīdào dìqiú shì yuán de.** In ancient times people
did not know that the earth was round.

yuánmǎn 圆满 [comp: 圆 round + 满 full] **ADJ**
totally satisfactory, perfect

yuán 缘 **N** reason

yuángù 缘故 **N** reason, cause

yuán 援 **v** help (See **zhīyuán** 支援.)

yuán 源 **N** source

yuánquán 源泉 **N** source, fountainhead

yuǎn 远 **TRAD** 遠 **ADJ** far, distant, remote (**ANTONYM**
近 **jìn**) ■ "这里离火车站有多远？" "大概两
公里。" **"Zhèli lí huǒchēzhàn yǒu duō yuǎn?"
"Dàgài liǎng gōnglǐ."** "How far is it from here to
the railway station?" "About two kilometers."
… lí … yuǎn … 离 … 远 … is far from … ■ 我家离
学校不远。 **Wǒ jiā lí xuéxiào bù yuǎn.** My home is
not far from school.

yuàn 院 **N** courtyard

yuànzi 院子 [suffix: 院 courtyard + 子 nominal
suffix] **N** courtyard, compound ■ 下午四点钟以后
很多孩子在院子里玩。 **Xiàwǔ sì diǎnzhōng yǐhòu
hěn duō háizi zài yuànzi li wán.** After four o'clock
many children will play in the courtyard.

yuàn 愿 **TRAD** 願 **v** wish, hope

yuànwàng 愿望 [comp: 愿 wish + 望 hope]
N wish, aspiration, desire ■ 我的愿望终于实现
了。 **Wǒ de yuànwàng zōngyú shíxiàn le.** My wish
has come true at last! ■ 谁也不能满足他的愿
望。 **Shuí yě bù néng mǎngzú tā de yuànwàng.**
Nobody can satisfy his desire.

yuànyì 愿意 [comp: 愿 wish + 意 desire] **I MODAL**
v be willing, will ■ 我愿意帮助你。 **Wǒ yuànyì
bāngzhù nǐ.** I'm willing to help you. ■ 你愿意去
就去，不愿意去别别去。 **Nǐ yuànyì qù jiù qù, bú
yuànyì qù jiù bié qù.** If you're willing to go, you
can go; if you're not willing to go, you don't have

to go. **II v** wish, want ■ 父母都愿意自己的孩子幸
福。 **Fùmǔ dōu yuànyì zìjǐ de háizi xìngfú.** All parents want their children to be happy.

yuàn 怨 **v** resent, complain (See **mányuàn**
埋怨.)

yuē 约 **TRAD** 約 **ADV** same as 大约 **dàyuē**. Used in
written Chinese.

yuēhuì 约会 [v+obj: 约 arrange + 会 meeting]
N (social) appointment, engagement, date ■ 她
今天打扮得这么漂亮，看来有约会。 **Tā jīntiān
dǎbàn de zhème piàoliang, kànlai yǒu yuēhuì.** She
dressed up beautifully today, she probably has a
date.

yuēshù 约束 **v** restrain, bind

yuè 月 **N 1** month ■ 我在那里住了八个月。 **Wǒ
zài nàli zhùle bā ge yuè.** I stayed there for eight
months. **2** the moon ■ 明月当空。 **Míng yuè dāng
kōng.** The bright moon shines in the sky.

yuèliang 月亮 **N** the moon ■ 今天晚上的月亮
真好！ **Jīntiān wǎnshang de yuèliang zhēn hǎo!**
What a fine moon it is, tonight!

yuèqiú 月球 **N** the Moon (as a scientific term)

yuè 乐 **TRAD** 樂 **N** music

yuèduì 乐队 [modif: 乐 music + 队 team] **N** band,
orchestra

yuèqì 乐器 [modif: 乐 music + 器 implement] **N**
musical instrument

yuèpǔ 乐谱 **N** music score, sheet music

yuèqǔ 乐曲 **N** melody

yuè 越 **ADV** even more

yuè … yuè … 越 … 越 … **ADV** the more … the
more … ■ 你真是越活越年轻了。 **Nǐ zhēn shì yuè
huó yuè niánqīng le.** You seem to get younger and
younger. ■ 学生越用功，老师越高兴。 **Xuésheng
yuè yònggōng, lǎoshī yuè gāoxìng.** The harder students study, the more delighted their teachers.

yuèláiyuè 越来越 **ADV** more and more ■ 学中文
的人越来越多。 **Xué Zhōngwén de rén yuèláiyuè
duō.** More and more people are learning Chinese.
■ 这孩子长得越来越像他爸爸了。 **Zhè háizi
zhǎngde yuèláiyuè xiàng tā bàba le.** This child is
becoming more and more like his father.

yuè 阅 **TRAD** 閱 **v** read

yuèdú 阅读 [comp: 阅 read + 读 read] **v** read
seriously ■ 总经理每天花很多时间阅读各部门的
报告。 **Zǒngjīnglǐ měi tiān huā hěn duō shíjiān
yuèdú gè bùmén de bàogào.** The general manager
spends a lot of time every day reading reports
submitted by various departments.

yuèlǎnshì 阅览室 [modif: 阅览 read, browse +
室 room] **N** reading room (间 **jiān**) ■ 阅览室里的图
书杂志不能带出室外。 **Yuèlǎnshì li de túshū zázhì
bù néng dàichū shìwài.** You are not allowed to take
books and periodicals out of the reading room.

yuè 跃 **TRAD** 躍 **v** leap (See **huóyuè** 活跃.)

yuè 岳 **N** high mountain

yuèfù 岳父 N wife's father
yuèmǔ 岳母 N wife's mother
yūn 晕 TRAD 暈 V dizzy, giddy
头晕 tóu yūn feel dizzy
yún 云 TRAD 雲 N cloud ■ 蓝天白云，好看极
了！**Lán tiān bái yún, hǎokàn jíle!** *White clouds
in the blue sky, how beautiful!*
多云 duōyún cloudy ■ 今天多云。**Jīntiān duōyún.**
It's cloudy today.
yǔn 允 V allow
yǔnxǔ 允许 [comp: 允 allow + 许 permit] V allow,
permit ■ 这里不允许停车。**Zhèlǐ bù yǔnxǔ tíng
chē.** *Parking is not allowed here.* ■ 我们不允许
任何反社会行为。**Wǒmen bù yǔnxǔ rènhé fǎn
shèhuì xíngwéi.** *We do not allow any anti-social
behavior.*
yùn 孕 ADJ pregnant
yùnyù 孕育 V be pregnant, breed, give rise to
yùn 运 TRAD 運 V transport, carry ■ 中国主要靠火
车运货。**Zhōngguó zhǔyào kào huǒchē yùn huò.**
China mainly uses trains to transport cargo.
yùndòng 运动 [comp: 运 move + 动 move] V &
N do physical exercises; physical exercises ■ "
你每天做什么运动？" "我有时候打球，有时
候跑步。" **"Nǐ měi tiān zuò shénme yùndòng?"
"Wǒ yǒushíhou dǎ qiú, yǒushíhou pǎobù."** *"What
physical exercises do you do every day?" "Sometimes I play ball games and sometimes I jog."*
■ 生命在于运动。**Shēngmìng zài yú yùndòng.** *Life
lies in physical exercise.*
yùndònghuì 运动会 [modif: 运动 sports + 会
meeting] N sports meet, games ■ 这个中学每年十
月举行运动会。**Zhège zhōngxué měi nián Shíyuè
jǔxíng yùndònghuì.** *This high school holds a
sports meet every October.*
yùndòngxié 运动鞋 N sport shoes
yùndòngyuán 运动员 [modif: 运动 sports +
员 person] N athlete, sportsman, sportswoman
■ 我叔叔年轻的时候是一名长跑运动员。**Wǒ
shūshu niánqīng de shíhou shì yì míng chángpǎo
yùndòngyuán.** *When young, my uncle was a long-
distance runner*
yùnqi 运气 N good luck ■ 他运气真好，又中彩票
了！*He is really lucky – he has won lottery again!*
yùnshū 运输 [comp: 运 transport + 输 transport]
V & N transport, carry; transportation ■ 你们用什
么把煤运输到港口？**Nǐmen yòng shénme bǎ méi
yùnshū dào gǎngkǒu?** *How do you transport coal
to the port?* ■ 修建了这条铁路，运输问题就基本
解决了。**Xiūjiànle zhè tiáo tiělù, yùnshū wèntí jiù
jīběn jiějué le.** *When this railway is built, transportation problems will be basically solved.*
yùnsuàn 运算 V & N operate (a mathematical
problem), calculate; calculation
yùnxíng 运行 V **1** revolve in cycles **2** be in
operation, be in motion

yùnyòng 运用 V use, apply, put into use ■ 我们
现在运用电脑来控制生产过程。**Wǒmen xiànzài
yùnyòng diànnǎo lái kòngzhì shēngchǎn guòchéng.**
*Now we use computers to control the production
process.*
yùn 酝 TRAD 醞 V brew, make wine
yùnniàng 酝酿 V **1** brew, ferment **2** deliberate,
prepare mentally
yùn 蕴 TRAD 蘊 V hold in store
yùncáng 蕴藏 V hold in store, contain
石油蕴藏量 shíyóu yùncángliàng oil reserves
yùn 熨 V iron (clothes), press
yùndǒu 熨斗 N iron (for pressing clothes)

Z

zá 杂 TRAD 雜 ADJ miscellaneous, sundry, all sorts
of ■ 我还有些杂事要办完才能回家。**Wǒ hái yǒu
xiē zá shì yào bànwán cái néng huí jiā.** *I still have
some miscellaneous things to deal with before I
can go home.*
záfèi 杂费 N sundry charges
zájì 杂技 [modif: 杂 miscellaneous + 技 skills] N
acrobatics ■ 听说中国的杂技很有名。**Tīngshuō
Zhōngguó de zájì hěn yǒumíng.** *I've heard people
say that Chinese acrobatics are very famous*
杂技团 zájìtuán acrobatics troupe / 杂技演员 zájì
yǎnyuán acrobat
zájiāo 杂交 V hybridize, crossbreed
zázhì 杂志 [modif: 杂 miscellaneous + 志 record]
N magazine (本 **běn**, 种 **zhǒng**) ■ 他订了两种杂
志。**Tā dìngle liǎng zhǒng zázhì.** *He subscribes to
two magazines.*
zá 砸 V **1** pound, tamp **2** break, smash
zǎ 咋 ADV how, why (Only used as a dialectal word.)
zāi 灾 TRAD 災 N disaster, calamity ■ 中国每年都
有地方受灾。**Zhōngguó měi nián dōu yǒu dìfang
shòu zāi.** *Every year there are places in China
that are hit by calamities.*
火灾 huǒzāi fire disaster, fire / 水灾 shuǐzāi flooding, floods
zāihài 灾害 [comp: 灾 disaster + 害 damage] N
disaster, calamity ■ 由于各种灾害，全国每年损
失几千亿元。**Yóuyú gè zhǒng zāihài, quánguó měi
nián sǔnshī jǐ qiān yì yuán.** *Owing to disasters of
all kinds the country loses hundreds of billions of
dollars every year.*
自然灾害 zìrán zāihài natural disaster
zāinàn 灾难 N great suffering caused by a natural
disaster, calamity (场 **cháng**)
灾难性后果 zāinànxìng hòuguǒ disastrous consequences
zāi 栽 V plant
zāipéi 栽培 [comp: 栽 plant + 培 cultivate] V cultivate and grow

zǎi 宰 v 1 slaughter 2 overcharge, fleece ■ 你挨宰了！**Nǐ āi zǎi le!** *You were fleeced!*

zài 再 ADV again ■ 我没听清楚，请您再说一遍。**Wǒ méi tīng qīngchu, qǐng nín zài shuō yí biàn.** *I did not hear it clearly. Please say it again.* ■ 你的电脑修好了，要是再坏，我就没有办法了。**Nǐ de diànnǎo xiūhǎo le, yàoshì zài huài, wǒ jiù méiyǒu bànfǎ le.** *Your computer has been repaired. If it breaks down again, there'll be nothing I can do.*

NOTE: 再 **zài** and 又 **yòu** are both glossed as *again*, but they have different usage: 又 **yòu** is used in the context of a past situation while 再 **zài** is used for a future situation. Here is another pair of examples: ■ 她昨天又迟到了。**Tā zuótiān yòu chídào le.** *She was late (for work, school, etc.) again yesterday.* ■ 明天你不要再迟到了。**Míngtiān nǐ bú yào zài chídào le.** *Please do not be late again tomorrow.*

zàijiàn 再见 [modif: 再 again + 见 see] v see you again, goodbye ■ "我回家了，再见！""再见，明天见。" "**Wǒ huíjiā le, zàijiàn!**" "**Zàijiàn, míngtiān jiàn.**" *"I'm going home, goodbye!" "Bye! See you tomorrow."*

zài jiē zài lì 再接再厉 v make persistent efforts, continue to exert oneself, persevere

zàisān 再三 [comp: 再 again + 三 three (times)] ADV over and over again ■ 她再三要求，才让她参加了考试。**Tā zàisān yāoqiú, cái ràng tā cānjiā le kǎoshì.** *It was only after her repeated requests that she was allowed to sit for the examination.*

zài 在¹ I PREP in, on, at ■ 在新加坡很多人会说中文。**Zài Xīnjiāpō hěn duō rén huì shuō Zhōngwén.** *In Singapore many people speak Chinese.* ■ 我在两年以前开始学中文。**Wǒ zài liǎngnián yǐqián kāishǐ xué Zhōngwén.** *I began to learn Chinese two years ago.* II v be in ■ 你爸爸在家吗？他不在家。"**Nǐ bàba zài jiā ma?**" "**Tā bú zài jiā.**" *"Is your father home?" "No, he isn't."* ■ "小明在哪里？" "他在操场上。" "**Xiǎo Míng zài nǎlǐ?**" "**Tā zài cāochàng shang.**" *"Where's Xiao Ming?" "He's on the sports ground."*

在 … 里 zài … li in ■ 他在房间里休息。**Tā zài fángjiān li xiūxi.** *He's taking a rest in the room.*

在 … 上 zài … shang on ■ 在桌子上有两本书。**Zài zhuōzi shang yǒu liǎng běn shū.** *There are two books on the desk.*

在 … 下 zài … xia under … ■ 在床下有一双鞋。**Zài chuáng xia yǒu yì shuāng xié.** *There's a pair of shoes under the bed.*

在 … 之间 zài … zhī jiān between ■ 我要在这两棵树之间种一些花。**Wǒ yào zài zhè liǎng kē shù zhī jiān zhòng yìxiē huā.** *I'm going to plant some flowers between the two trees.*

zài 在² ADV (used to indicate an action in progress) ■ "你在做什么？" "我在找东西。" "**Nǐ zài zuò shénme?**" "**Wǒ zài zhǎo dōngxi.**" *"What are you*

doing?" "I'm looking for something."

zàihu 在乎 v care, care about ■ 她不在乎别人的闲话。**Tā búzàihu biéren de xiánhuà.** *She doesn't care about people's gossip.*

NOTE: 在乎 **zàihu** is normally used in a negative sentence, or a question. The same is true with 在意 **zàiyì**.

zàiyì 在意 v take notice of, mind, care ■ 我抽烟，你在意吗？**Wǒ chōuyān, nǐ zàiyì ma?** *Do you mind if I smoke?*

NOTE: See note on 在乎 **zàihu**.

zàiyú 在于 v lie in, rest with

zán 咱 PRON same as 咱们 **zánmen**

zánmen 咱们 [suffix: 咱 we, us + 们 suffix denoting a plural number] PRON we, us (including the person or persons spoken to) ■ 你在学中文，我也在学中文，咱们都在学中文。**Nǐ zài xué Zhōngwén, wǒ yě zài xué Zhōngwén, zánmen dōu zài xué Zhōngwén.** *You're learning Chinese; I'm learning Chinese. We're both learning Chinese.* ■ 咱们去吃饭吧！**Zánmen qù chīfàn ba!** *Let's go and have our meal.*

NOTE: 咱们 **zánmen** is only used in colloquial Chinese, and has a northern dialect flavor. You can always just use 我们 **wǒmen**, even to include the person(s) spoken to. The following examples are perfectly acceptable: ■ 你在学中文，我也在学中文，我们都在学中文。**Nǐ zài xué Zhōngwén, wǒ yě zài xué Zhōngwén, wǒmen dōu zài xué Zhōngwén.** *You're learning Chinese. I'm learning Chinese. We're both learning Chinese.* ■ 我们去吃饭吧！**Wǒmen qù chīfàn ba!** *Let's go and have a meal.*

zǎn 攒 TRAD 攢 v save (money)

zàn 暂 TRAD 暫 ADJ temporary

zànqiě 暂且 ADV for the time being, for the moment

zànshí 暂时 [comp: 暂 temporary + 时 time] ADJ temporary, for the time being ■ 你暂时在这里住一下，大房间一空出来就可以搬进去。**Nǐ zànshí zài zhèli zhù yíxià, dà fángjiān yí kòng chūlai jiù kěyǐ bān jìnqu.** *Please stay here for the time being. You can move to the bigger room as soon as it is vacated.*

zàn 赞 TRAD 贊 v support

zànchéng 赞成 v approve of, support, be in favor of ■ 我不赞成他代表我们公司去参加会议。**Wǒ bú zànchéng tā dàibiǎo wǒmen gōngsī qù cānjiā huìyì.** *I don't approve his being our company representative at the conference.* ■ 赞成的，请举手！**Zànchéng de, qǐng jǔshǒu!** *Those in favor, please raise your hands.*

zànměi 赞美 [comp: 赞 praise + 美 beautify] v eulogize, praise highly

zàntàn 赞叹 [comp: 赞 praise + 叹 sigh] v gasp in admiration

zàntóng 赞同 v heartily approve of, agree with

zànyáng 赞扬 v speak highly of, praise, applaud

zànzhù 赞助 [comp: 赞 praise + 助 help] v support, sponsor
赞助人 zànzhù rén sponsor

zāng 脏 TRAD 髒 ADJ dirty (ANTONYM 干净 gānjìng) ■ 这些衣服脏了，要洗一下。**Zhèxiē yīfu zāng le, yào xǐ yíxià.** *These clothes are dirty and need washing.*

zàng 脏 TRAD 臟 N internal organs of the body (See **xīnzàng** 心脏.)

zāo 遭 v meet with (misfortune)

zāodào 遭到 v suffer, encounter, meet with ■ 公用电话常常遭到破坏。**Gōngyòng diànhuà chángcháng zāodào pòhuài.** *Public telephones are often vandalized.*

zāoshòu 遭受 v suffer, be subjected to ■ 去年这个地区连续遭受自然灾害。**Qùnián zhège dìqū liánxù zāoshòu zìrán zāihài.** *Last year this area suffered repeated natural disasters.*

zāoyāng 遭殃 [v+obj: 遭 suffer + 殃 disaster] v suffer disaster, suffer terribly

zāoyù 遭遇 [comp: 遭 encounter + 遇 meet] v encounter, meet with

zāo 糟 ADJ messy

zāogāo 糟糕 [modif: 糟 messy + 糕 cake] I ADJ in a mess, terrible, very bad ■ 我这次考试很糟糕。**Wǒ zhè cì kǎoshì hěn zāogāo.** *I did very poorly in the exam.* ■ 情况很糟糕。**Qíngkuàng hěn zāogāo.** *The situation is in a shambles.* II INTERJ How terrible! What bad luck! ■ 真糟糕，我的钥匙丢了。**Zhēn zāogāo, wǒ de yàoshi diū le.** *How terrible! I've lost my keys!*

zāota 糟蹋 v waste, ruin

zǎo 早 ADJ early ■ 现在才三点钟，还早呢！**Xiànzài cái sān diǎnzhōng, hái zǎo ne!** *It's only three o'clock. It's still early!* ■ 李先生每天很早上班，很晚下班。**Lǐ xiānsheng měi tiān hěn zǎo shàngbān, hěn wǎn xiàbān.** *Every day Mr Li goes to work early and comes off work late.*

NOTE: A common greeting among the Chinese when they meet in the morning is 早 **zǎo** or 你早 **Nǐ zǎo.**

zǎochén 早晨 [modif: 早 early + 晨 early morning] N early morning (approximately 6–9 a.m.) ■ 他早晨六点半起床。**Tā zǎochén liù diǎn bàn qǐchuáng.** *He gets up at half past six in the morning.* ■ 很多人喜欢在早晨锻炼身体。**Hěn duō rén xǐhuan zài zǎochén duànliàn shēntǐ.** *Many people like to exercise in the early morning.*

zǎofàn 早饭 [modif: 早 early + 饭 meal] N breakfast (顿 **dùn**) ■ 我今天起得太晚了，没有时间吃早饭。**Wǒ jīntiān qǐ de tài wǎn le, méiyǒu shíjiān chī zǎofàn.** *I got up too late today and didn't have time for breakfast.*

zǎoshang 早上 N same as 早晨 **zǎochén**

zǎo 澡 N bath (See **xǐzǎo** 洗澡.)

zào 皂 N soap (See **xiāngzào** 香皂.)

zào 造 v make, build ■ 中国人在公元一世纪就会造纸。**Zhōngguórén zài gōngyuán yī shìjì jiù huì zào zhǐ.** *The Chinese knew how to make paper as early as in the first century.*

zàochéng 造成 result in, give rise to ■ 不幸的童年造成他性格上的很多缺点。**Búxìng de tóngnián zàochéng tā xìnggé shang de hěn duō quēdiǎn.** *An unhappy childhood gave rise to many faults in his character.*

zàofǎn 造反 V & N rebel; rebellion

zàojù 造句 V & N make sentences; sentence-making
用所给的词语造句 yòng suǒ gěi de cíyǔ zàojù Make sentences with the given words

zàoxíng 造型 N modelling

zào 噪 ADJ noisy

zàoyīn 噪音 N noise
噪音污染 zàoyīnwūrǎn noise pollution, white pollution

zào 燥 ADJ dry (See **gānzào** 干燥.)

zé 则 TRAD 則 CONJ in that case, then ■ 不进则退。**Bú jìn zé tuì.** *If you don't make progress, then you'll fall behind.*

NOTE: 则 **zé** is only used in formal Chinese. In everyday Chinese, use 那 **nà** or 那么 **nàme** instead. See note on 那么 **nàme.**

zé 责 TRAD 責 N duty

zébèi 责备 v reproach, blame
责备的口气 zébèi de kǒuqì reproachful tone

zéguài 责怪 [comp: 责 scold + 怪 blame] v blame, reproach ■ 出了差错，他总是责怪别人。**Chūle chācuò, tā zǒngshì zéguài biéren.** *When something goes wrong, he would blame others.*

zérèn 责任 N 1 responsibility, duty ■ 教育孩子是父母的责任。**Jiàoyù háizi shì fù-mǔ de zérèn.** *It is the parents' responsibility to educate their children.* 2 responsibility for an accident, fault ■ 这次交通事故责任主要在开快车的那一方。**Zhè cì jiāotōng shìgù zérèn zhǔyào zài kāi kuàichē de nà yì fāng.** *The person who was speeding is mainly to blame for this traffic accident.*

zérèngǎn 责任感 N sense of responsibility ■ 这个男人缺点很多，但是责任感很强，很顾家。**Zhège nánrén quēdiǎn hěn duō, dànshì zérèngǎn hěn qiáng, hěn gù jiā.** *This man may have many shortcomings, but he has a strong sense of responsibility and cares for his family.*

zé 择 TRAD 擇 v choose, select (See **xuǎnzé** 选择.)

zéi 贼 TRAD 賊 N thief

zěnme 怎么 PRON 1 how, in what manner ■ 这

个汉字怎么写? *Zhège Hànzi zěnme xiě? How do you write this Chinese character?* ■ 对不起, 请问去北京大学怎么走? **Duìbuqǐ, qǐng wèn qù Běijīng Dàxué zěnme zǒu?** *Excuse me, could you please tell me how to get to Beijing University?* **2** no matter how (used with 都 **dōu** or 也 **yě**) ■ 是这把钥匙吗? 我怎么都开不开这个门。**Shì zhè bǎ yàoshi ma? Wǒ zěnme dōu kāi bu kāi zhège mén.** *Is this the right key? No matter how I tried, I couldn't open the door.* ■ 他怎么也找不到那本书。**Tā zěnme yě zhǎo bu dào nà běn shū.** *No matter how hard he tried, he couldn't find the book.* **3** why, how come ■ 你怎么又迟到了? **Nǐ zěnme yòu chídào le?** *Why are you late again?* ■ 她今天怎么这么高兴? **Tā jīntiān zěnme zhème gāoxìng?** *Why is she so happy today?* **4** how can ... ■ 这么多作业, 我今天怎么做得完? **Zhème duō zuòyè, wǒ jīntiān zěnme zuò de wán?** *How can I finish so many assignments today?* ■ 你说这种话, 妈妈怎么会不生气? **Nǐ shuō zhè zhǒng huà, māma zěnme huì bù shēngqì?** *How would mom not feel angry, when you had said such things?*

zěnmebàn 怎么办 **PRON** what's to be done? ■ 要是飞机票卖完了, 怎么办? **Yàoshì fēijīpiào mài-wán le, zěnmebàn?** *What should we do if the air tickets are sold out?*

zěnmele 怎么了 **PRON** what happened? ■ 怎么了, 她怎么哭了? **Zěnmele, tā zěnme kū le?** *What happened? Why is she crying?*

zěnmeyàng 怎么样 **PRON 1** (same as 怎么 **zěnme**) **2** how ■ 你今天觉得怎么样? **Nǐ jīntiān juéde zěnmeyàng?** *How are you feeling today?* ■ 他使用电脑的能力怎么样? **Tā shǐyòng diànnǎo de nénglì zěnmeyàng?** *How competent is he in using the computer?* **3** how's that? is it OK? ■ 我们每个人讲一个故事, 怎么样? **Wǒmen měi ge rén jiǎng yí ge gùshi, zěnmeyàng?** *We each tell a story, how about that?* ■ 我晚上开车来接你, 怎么样? **Wǒ wǎnshang kāichē lái jiē nǐ, zénmeyàng?** *I'll pick you up this evening. Is it OK?*

zěnyàng 怎样 **PRON** Same as 怎么样 **zěnmeyàng**. (used in writing.)

zēng 增 **v** increase

zēngjiā 增加 [comp: 增 increase + 加 add] **v** increase ■ 去年他家的收入增加了两千元。**Qùnián tā jiā de shōurù zēngjiāle liǎngqiān yuán.** *Last year his family income increased by 2,000 yuan.*

zēngtiān 增添 **v** provide (additional equipment, evidence, etc.) 增添人员和设备 zēngtiān rényuán hé shèbèi provide more personnel and equipment

zēngzhǎng 增长 [comp: 增 increase + 长 grow] **v** increase, grow ■ 旅行增长知识。**Lǚxíng zēngzhǎng zhīshi.** *Traveling increases one's knowledge.* ■ 大学生人数在五年中增长百分之三十以上。**Dàxuéshēng rénshù zài wǔ nián zhōng**

zēngzhǎng bǎifēn zhī sānshí yǐ shàng. *In the past five years the number of university students has grown by more than thirty percent.*

zèng 赠 **TRAD** 贈 **v** present a gift

zèngsòng 赠送 **v** present as a gift 向主人赠送礼物 xiàng zhǔrén zèngsòng lǐwù present a gift to the host

zhā 扎 **v** prick, stab

zhāshi 扎实 **ADJ** solid, sturdy

zhā 渣 **N** dregs, residue 煤渣 méizhā coal cinders

zhǎ 眨 **v** blink, wink 向我眨了眨眼 xiàng wǒ zhǎ le zhǎ yǎn winked at me

zhà 诈 **v** cheat, swindle

zhàpiàn 诈骗 [comp: 诈 cheat + 骗 deceive] **v** defraud, swindle 诈骗犯 zhàpiànfàn swindler

zhà 炸 **v 1** blow up, blast, bomb (See **bàozhà** 爆炸.) **2** deep fry (See **yóuzhà** 油炸.)

zhà 榨 **v** squeeze (See **yāzhà** 压榨.)

zhāi 摘 **v** pick, pluck ■ 星期天跟我们一起去果园摘苹果吧。**Xīngqītiān gēn wǒmen yìqǐ qù guǒyuán zhāi píngguǒ ba.** *Do go to the orchard with us on Sunday to pick apples.*

zhāiyào 摘要 [v+obj: 摘 pick + 要 what is impor-tant] **V & N** make a summary; abstract, summary 论文摘要 lùnwén zhāiyào abstract of an academic or scholarly paper

zhái 宅 **N** residence (See **zhùzhái** 住宅.)

zhǎi 窄 **ADJ** narrow (**ANTONYM** 宽 **kuān**) ■ 这条街太窄, 汽车开不进去。**Zhè tiáo jiē tài zhǎi, qìchē kāi bu jìnqu.** *This street is too narrow for a car to enter.*

zhài 债 **TRAD** 債 **N** debt ■ 借了债, 就要还。**Jièle zhài, jiùyào huán.** *If you owe a debt, you'll have to repay it.* 还债 huánzhài to pay off a debt, to settle a debt / 借债 jièzhài to borrow money, to ask for a loan / 欠债 qiànzhài to owe a debt

zhàiquàn 债券 **N** public or government bond

zhàiwù 债务 **N** debt, liabilities 债务人 zhàiwùrén debtor

zhàizhǔ 债主 **N** creditor

zhān 粘 **v** paste

zhānguāng 沾光 **v** benefit from association, sponge off

zhāntiē 粘贴 **v** paste, glue, stick

zhān 瞻 **v** look up

zhānyǎng 瞻仰 **v** look up with reverence, pay homage to

zhǎn 斩 **TRAD** 斬 **v** chop, cut

zhǎn dīng jié tiě 斩钉截铁 **IDIOM** resolute and decisive, without the slightest hesitation

zhǎnxīn 崭新 **ADJ** brand-new, nascent

zhǎn 展 **v** display

zhǎnchū 展出 [v+compl: 展 show + 出 out] v be on show, put on display ■ 这两天商场展出最新夏装。**Zhè liǎngtiān shāngchǎng zhǎnchū zuì xīn xiàzhuāng.** *These days the latest summer wear is on display in the shopping center.*

zhǎnkāi 展开 v carry out, launch ■ 政府将要展开交通安全的活动。**Zhèngfǔ jiāngyào zhǎnkāi jiāotōng ānquán de huódòng.** *The government will carry out activities to promote traffic safety.*

zhǎnlǎn 展览 [modif: 展 display + 览 view] v & N put on display, exhibit; exhibition, show ■ 这个画儿画得真好，可以去展览。**Zhège huàr huà de zhēn hǎo, kěyǐ qù zhǎnlǎn.** *This picture is done so well that it can be put on display.* ■ 我上个星期参观了一个很有意思的展览。**Wǒ shàngge xīngqī cānguānle yí ge hěn yǒu yìsi de zhǎnlǎn.** *Last week I visited a very interesting exhibition.*

zhǎnlǎnhuì 展览会 N exhibition, show

zhǎnshì 展示 v display, show

zhǎnwàng 展望 v & N look into the distance, look into the future; general view regarding future development

展望未来 zhǎnwàngwèilái foresee the future, predict the future

zhǎnxiàn 展现 v present before one's eyes

zhǎnxiāo 展销 v show and advertise (products)

zhǎnxiāohuì 展销会 commodities fair

汽车展销会 qìchē zhǎnxiāohuì auto fair, car show

zhàn 占 v occupy ■ 你一个人不能占两个座位。**Nǐ yí ge rén bù néng zhàn liǎng ge zuòwèi.** *You're only one person and can't take two seats.*

zhànjù 占据 v seize and occupy, hold by force

zhànlǐng 占领 v capture, occupy, seize

占领军 zhànlǐngjūn occupation troops

zhàn piányi 占便宜 v gain unfair advantage

zhànxiàn 占线 v (of a telephone line) engaged, busy

zhànyǒu 占有 v own, possess

zhàn 站¹ v stand ■ 房间里有些人站着，有些人坐着。**Fángjiān li yǒuxiē rén zhànzhe, yǒuxiē rén zuòzhe.** *In the room some people are standing, and others are seated.* ■ 站在高山上，可以看得很远。**Zhàn zài gāoshān shang, kěyǐ kàn de hěn yuǎn.** *Standing on a high mountain, one can see very far.*

zhàn qǐlai 站起来 stand up ■ 老师走进教室，学生们都站起来。**Lǎoshī zǒujìn jiàoshì, xuéshengmen dōu zhàn qǐlai.** *When the teacher came into the classroom, all the students stood up.*

zhàn 站² N station, stop ■ 我要一辆出租车去火车站。**Wǒ yào yí liàng chūzū qchē qù huǒchē zhàn.** *I want a taxi to go to the railway station.*

站长 zhànzhǎng railway/coach stationmaster / 出租汽车站 chūzū qìchē zhàn taxi stand / 火车站 huǒchē zhàn railway station / 汽车站 qìchē zhàn coach/bus station; bus stop

zhàn 战 TRAD 戰 v battle

zhàndòu 战斗 v combat, fight

zhànlüè 战略 N military strategy, strategy

zhànshèng 战胜 [v+compl: 战 fight + 胜 victorious] N triumph over, defeat ■ 人不可能战胜自然。**Rén bù kěnéng zhànshèng zìrán.** *It is impossible for man to triumph over nature.*

zhànshi 战士 [modif: 战 fighting + 士 person] N soldier, fighter ■ 不管天冷天热，战士们坚持军事训练。**Bùguǎn tiān-lěng-tiān-rè, zhànshimen jiānchí jūnshì xùnliàn.** *The soldiers persist in military training regardless of the weather conditions.*

zhànshù 战术 N military tactics

zhànyì 战役 N military campaign

zhànzhēng 战争 [comp: 战 fight + 争 strife] N war ■ 在二十一世纪，人类能避免大规模战争吗？**Zài èrshíyī shìjì, rénlèi néng bìmiǎn dà guīmó zhànzhēng ma?** *Can mankind avoid large-scale wars in the twenty-first century?*

zhāng 张¹ TRAD 張 MEASURE WORD (for paper, bed, table etc.)

一张纸 yì zhāng zhǐ a piece of paper / 两张床 liǎng zhāng chuáng two beds / 三张桌子 sān zhāng zhuōzi three tables/desks

Zhāng 张² TRAD 張 N a common family name ■ 张先生/太太/小姐 **Zhāng xiānsheng/tàitai/xiǎojiě** Mr/Mrs/Miss Zhang

zhāng 章 N chapter

zhāngchéng 章程 N regulations (for an organization), rules

zhǎng 长¹ TRAD 長 v 1 grow ■ 孩子长高了。**Háizi zhǎnggāo le.** *The child has grown taller.* ■ 孩子长大成人，父母也老了。**Háizi zhǎngdà chéngrén, fù-mǔ yě lǎo le.** *The parents will be old when their children are grown up.* 2 grow to be, look ■ 他们的女儿长得很漂亮。**Tāmen de nǚ'ér zhǎng de hěn piàoliang.** *Their daughter is very pretty.* ■ 今年的庄稼长得真好。**Jīnnián de zhuāngjia zhǎng de zhēn hǎo.** *The crops this year are really good.*

zhǎng 长² TRAD 長 N chief

zhǎngbèi 长辈 N people of the older generation, elder member of a family, elder

zhǎng 涨 TRAD 漲 v rise, go up ■ 水涨船高。**Shuǐ zhǎng chuán gāo.** *When the river rises the boat goes up. (→ When the general situation improves, particular things improve.)* ■ 上周股票涨了很多。**Shàng zhōu gǔpiào zhǎngle hěn duō.** *Last week shares rose greatly.*

zhǎng 掌 N hand, palm

zhǎngwò 掌握 [comp: 掌 be in charge + 握 take ... in one's hands] v have a good command of, know well ■ 要掌握一门外语是不容易的。**Yào zhǎngwò yì mén wàiyǔ shì bù róngyi de.** *It is not easy to gain a good command of a foreign language.*

zhàng 丈 N senior

zhàngfu 丈夫 N husband (ANTONYM 妻子 qīzi) ■ 你

认识她的丈夫吗？**Nǐ rènshi tā de zhàngfu ma?** *Do you know her husband?*

zhàng 账 **TRAD** 賬 **N** account
查账 cházhàng examine an account, audit / 算账 suàn zhàng compute income and expense, settle accounts

zhàngdān 账单 **N** bill
付电话账单 fù diànhuà zhàngdān pay phone bills

zhànghù 账户 **N** account
账户号 zhànghù hào account number

zhàngmù 账目 **N** items of an account
账目不清 zhàngmù bùqīng accounts in disorder

zhàng 帐 **TRAD** 帳 **N** curtain, canopy

zhàngpeng 帐篷 **N** tent
搭帐篷 dāzhàngpéng pitch a tent

zhàng 胀 **TRAD** 脹 **V** expand (**ANTONYM** 缩 **suō**)
热胀冷缩 rè zhàng lěng suō expand when heated, and contract when cooled

zhàng 障 **V** hinder, obstruct

zhàng'ài 障碍 [comp: 障 hinder + 碍 hinder] **N** obstacle, barrier
排除障碍 páichúzhàng'ài clear an obstacle

zhàng 仗 **N** battle, war (See **dǎ zhàng** 打仗.)

zhāo 招 **V** beckon, attract

zhāobiāo 招标 **V** invite bids, invite tenders

zhāodài 招待 **V** receive or entertain (a guest)
■ 他们用好酒好菜招待客人。**Tāmen yòng hǎo jiǔ hǎo cài zhāodài kèren.** *They entertained their guests with good wine and good food.*

zhāodàihuì 招待会 **N** reception
记者招待会 jìzhě zhāodàihuì press conference, news conference

zhāohu 招呼 [comp: 招 beckon + 呼 call] **V** call, shout at ■ 马路对面有人在招呼我。**Mǎlù duìmiàn yǒurén zài zhāohu wǒ.** *There's someone calling me on the other side of the road.*
打招呼 dǎ zhāohu **1** greet ■ 他进屋就跟大家打招呼。**Tā jìn wū jiù gēn dàjiā dǎ zhāohu.** *He greeted everybody when he came into the room.* **2** inform casually, tell ■ 他没跟我打招呼就把我的自行车骑走了。**Tā méi gēn wǒ dǎ zhāohu jiù bǎ wǒ de zìxíngchē qízǒu le.** *He rode off on my bicycle without telling me.*

zhāopìn 招聘 [comp: 招 attract + 聘 invite for service] **V** advertise for a position, recruit (employees) ■ 我们学校正在招聘一名中文老师。**Wǒmen xuéxiào zhèngzài zhāopìn yì míng Zhōngwén lǎoshī.** *Our school is advertising for a Chinese teacher.*
招聘广告 zhāopìn guǎnggào advertisement for staff (e.g. a teacher, a chef)

zhāoshōu 招收 **V** recruit
招收工人 zhāoshōu gōngrén recuit workers / 招收学生 zhāoshōu xuésheng enroll new students

zhāo 朝 **N** early morning

zhāoqì 朝气 [modif: 朝 early morning + 气 atmosphere] **N** youthful spirit

zhāoqì péngbó 朝气蓬勃 **IDIOM** full of youthful spirit, full of vigor and vitality

zháo 着 **V** touch, catch

zháohuǒ 着火 **V** catch fire, be caught fire
■ 着火了！着火了！**Zháohuǒ le! Zháohuǒ le!** *Fire! Fire!*

zháojí 着急 **V** be anxious, be worried ■ 已经十二点了，女儿还没回家，妈妈很着急。**Yǐjīng shí'èr diǎn le, nǚ'ér hái méi huíjiā, māma hěn zháojí.** *It was almost twelve o'clock and her daughter was still not home. The mother felt very worried.* ■ 你着急有什么用呢？慢慢想办法吧。**Nǐ zháojí yǒu shénme yòng ne? Mànman xiǎng bànfǎ ba.** *What's the use of being worried? Let's think of a plan.*
别着急 bié zháojí don't worry

zháoliáng 着凉 **V** catch a cold

zháomí 着迷 **V** be fascinated, be captivated

zhǎo 找 **V** look for, search for ■ "你在找什么？" "我在找我的手机。" **"Nǐ zài zhǎo shénme?" "Wǒ zài zhǎo wǒ de shǒujī."** *"What are you looking for?" "I'm looking for my cell phone."* ■ 你真的关心她，就帮她找个对象吧。**Nǐ zhēn de guānxīn tā, jiù bāng tā zhǎo ge duìxiàng ba.** *If you are really concerned for her, help her to find a fiancé.*
找到 zhǎodào find

zhǎo 沼 **N** pond

zhǎozé 沼泽 **N** swamp, marsh
沼泽地 zhǎozédì swamp, marshland

zhào 召 **V** summon

zhàokāi 召开 [comp: 召 summon + 开 open] **V** convene (a conference) ■ 下星期校长要召开全体教师会议，讨论明年工作安排。**Xià xīngqī xiàozhǎng yào zhàokāi quántǐ jiàoshī huìyì, tǎolùn míngnián gōngzuò ānpái.** *Next week the [high school] principal will convene a meeting of all teaching staff to discuss next year's work.*

zhào 照[1] **V 1** take a photo ■ 麻烦您给我们照一张相。**Máfan nín gěi wǒmen zhào yì zhāng xiàng.** *Would you please take a photo of us?* ■ 这儿风景不错，我想照一张相。**Zhèr fēngjǐng bú cuò, wǒ xiǎng zhào yì zhāng xiàng.** *The scenery is good here. I'd like to have a picture taken.* **2** look in a mirror ■ 他们的小男孩从来不照镜子，小女孩是照镜子。**Tāmen de xiǎo nánhái cónglái bú zhào jìngzi, xiǎo nǚhái lǎoshì zhào jìngzi.** *Their little boy never looks in the mirror but their little girl always looks in the mirror.* **3** shine, light up ■ 冬天的太阳照在脸上，暖暖的，很舒服。**Dōngtiān de tàiyang zhào zài liǎnshang, nuǎnnuǎn de, hěn shūfu.** *In winter when the sun shines on your face you feel warm and comfortable.*

zhào 照[2] **PREP** according to, in the manner of
■ 我们还是照以前的方法付款。**Wǒmen háishì zhào yǐqián de fāngfǎ fùkuǎn.** *We will pay in the same way as before.* ■ 照我说的去办，肯定不会

错。**Zhào wǒ shuōde qù bàn, kěndìng bú huì cuò.** *Do as I say and you will definitely not go wrong.*

zhàocháng 照常 [v+obj: 照 according to + 常 usual] ADJ as usual ■ 本店春节照常营业。**Běn diàn chūnjié zhàocháng yíngyè.** *Business as usual during the Spring Festival.*

zhàogù 照顾 [comp: 照 look after + 顾 attend to] V look after, care for ■ 他每个星期六到老人院去照顾老人。**Tā měi ge Xīngqīliù dào lǎorényuàn qù zhàogù lǎorén.** *Every Saturday afternoon she goes to a senior citizens' home to look after the senior citizens there.* ■ 我在阿姨家过暑假的时候，她一家对我照顾得很好。**Wǒ zài āyí jiā guò shǔjià de shíhou, tā yìjiā duì wǒ zhàogù de hěn hǎo.** *When I stayed with my aunt's family for the summer holidays, they took good care of me.*

zhàoliào 照料 V take care of, look after

zhàopiàn 照片 N photograph, picture, snapshot (张 zhāng) ■ 申请签证，要交三张照片。**Shēnqǐng qiānzhèng, yào jiāo sān zhāng zhàopiàn.** *To apply for visa, you need to submit three photos.* ■ 老人常常看看老照片，回忆过去的生活。**Lǎorén chángcháng kànzhe lǎo zhàopiàn, huíyì guòqù de shēnghuó.** *The old man (or woman) often looks at old photos, recalling life in the past.*

zhàoxiàng 照相 [v+obj: 照 illuminate + 相 photograph] V take a picture ■ 请你给我们照个相。**Qǐng nǐ gěi wǒmen zhào ge xiàng.** *Please take a picture of us.* ■ 人们喜欢站在那幅画前照相。**Rénmen xǐhuan zhàn zài nà fù huà qián zhàoxiàng.** *People like to take photos standing in front of that painting.*

zhàoxiàngguǎn 照相馆 N photographic studio

zhàoxiàngjī 照相机 N camera ■ 明天出去玩，别忘了带照相机！**Míngtiān chūqu wán, bié wàngle dài zhàoxiàngjī!** *Don't forget to bring a camera with you on your outing tomorrow!*

zhàoyàng 照样 ADV in the same old way

zhàoyào 照耀 V shine, illuminate

zhàoyìng 照应 V look after, take care of

zhào 罩 V cover, overspread (See **lǒngzhào** 笼罩.)

zhē 折 V roll over

zhēteng 折腾 V turn from side to side, toss about

zhē 遮 V hide from view

zhēdǎng 遮挡 V shelter from, keep out

zhé 折¹ I V convert to, amount to ■ 一美元折多少日元？**Yì Měiyuán zhé duōshǎo Rìyuán?** *How many Japanese yen does an American dollar amount to?* II N discount, reduction (in price) ■ 这些书现在打八折。**Zhèxiē shū xiànzài dǎ bā zhé.** *These books are under a twenty percent discount now.*

zhé 折² V break

zhémó 折磨 V & N cause much mental or physical suffering; suffering

受病痛的折磨 shòu bìngtòng de zhémó suffer terribly from the disease

zhé 哲 ADJ wise

zhéxué 哲学 N philosophy ■ 我对东方哲学感兴趣。**Wǒ duì dōngfāng zhéxué gǎn xìngqù.** *I am interested in Eastern philosophy.*

zhéxuéjiā 哲学家 N philosopher

zhě 者 SUFFIX (a nominal suffix denoting a person or people) (See **dúzhě** 读者, **jìzhě** 记者, etc.)

zhè 这 TRAD 這 PRON this ■ 这是什么？**Zhè shì shénme?** *What's this?* ■ 这也不行，那也不行，你到底要我怎么办？**Zhè yě bù xíng, nà yě bù xíng, nǐ dàodǐ yào wǒ zěnmebàn?** *This won't do and that won't do either. What do you expect me to do?*

zhège 这个 [modif: 这 this + 个 one] PRON this one, this ■ 这个太大，给我小一点儿的。**Zhège tài dà, gěi wǒ xiǎo yìdiǎnr de.** *This one is too big. Give me a smaller one.* ■ 你为了这个生气，值得吗？**Nǐ wèile zhège shēngqì, zhídé ma?** *Is it worth getting angry over this?*

zhèli 这里 PRON this place, here ■ 你在这里住了几年了？**Nǐ zài zhèli zhùle jǐ nián le?** *How long have you been living here?* ■ 我刚来的时候，不习惯这里的天气。**Wǒ gāng lái de shíhou, bù xíguàn zhèli de tiānqì.** *When I first came, I wasn't used to the weather here.*

NOTE: In spoken Chinese 这里 **zhèli** can be replaced by 这儿 **zhèr**.

zhème 这么 PRON like this, in this manner, so ■ 这件衣服这么贵，我没想到。**Zhè jiàn yīfu zhème guì, wǒ méi xiǎngdào.** *I did not expect this dress to be so expensive.* ■ 你这么快就把文章写好了，佩服佩服！**Nǐ zhème kuài jiù bǎ wénzhāng xiě hǎo le, pèifu pèifu!** *It is simply admirable that you wrote the article so fast!*

zhèxiē 这些 PRON these ■ 这些书你都看过吗？**Zhèxiē shū nǐ dōu kànguo ma?** *Have you read all these books?*

zhèyàng 这样 PRON 1 same as 这么 **zhème**. Used only in writing. 2 such ■ 他就是这样的一个人，根本靠不住。**Tā jiùshì zhèyàng de yí ge rén, gēnběn kào bu zhù.** *He is just such a person (→ That's just typical of him). He is not reliable at all.*

zhe 着 PARTICLE (used after a verb to indicate the action or state is going on) ■ 门开着，灯亮着，可是房间里没有人。**Mén kāizhe, dēng liàngzhe, kěshì fángjiān li méiyǒu rén.** *The door was open and the light was on but there was no one in the room.*

zhèi 这 TRAD 這 PRON same as 这 **zhè**. Used colloquially.

zhēn 真¹ ADV really, truly, indeed ■ 中国真大呀！**Zhōngguó zhēn dà ya!** *China is really big!* ■ 我真不愿意去参加那个晚会。**Wǒ zhēn bú yuànyì qù cānjiā nàge wǎnhuì.** *I really don't want to attend that evening party.*

zhēn 真² ADJ true, real (ANTONYM 假 **jiǎ**) ■ 这个电影是根据真人真事编写的。**Zhège diànyǐng shì gēnjù**

zhēn rén zhēn shì biānxiě de. *This movie is based on a real-life story.*

zhēnhuà 真话 N truth ■ 这家报纸很少说真话。 **Zhè jiā bàozhǐ hěn shǎo shuō zhēnhuà.** *This newspaper rarely tells the truth.*

zhēnkōng 真空 N vacuum

真空包装 zhēnkōng bāozhuāng vacuum-packed

zhēnlǐ 真理 [modif: 真 true + 理 reasoning, principle] N truth ■ 真理往往掌握在少数人手里。 **Zhēnlǐ wǎngwǎng zhǎngwò zài shǎoshù rén shǒuli.** *Truth is very often in the hands of the minority.*

zhēnshí 真实 [comp: 真 real + 实 substance] ADJ true, real, authentic ■ 到底发生了什么？没有人知道真实的情况。 **Dàodǐ fāshēngle shénme? Méiyǒu rén zhīdào zhēnshí de qíngkuàng.** *What on earth happened? Nobody knows the true situation.*

zhēnxiàng 真相 N the real situation, actual facts

zhēnxīn 真心 N sincerity

zhēnzhèng 真正 ADJ true, real, genuine ■ 真正的友谊是天长地久的。 **Zhēnzhèng de yǒuyì shì tiāncháng-dì-jiǔ de.** *Genuine friendship is everlasting.* ■ 他在农村各地旅行了一年多，才真正了解中国。 **Tā zài nóngcūn gèdì lǚxíngle yì nián duō, cái zhēnzhèng liǎojiě Zhōngguó.** *It was only after he traveled in various parts of rural China for over a year that he really came to understand China.*

zhēnzhì 真挚 ADJ sincere, truthful

zhēn 侦 TRAD 偵 V detect, investigate

zhēnchá 侦察 V reconnoiter, scout

侦察卫星 zhēnchá wèixīng reconnaissance (spy) satellite

zhēntàn 侦探 V & N do detective work, spy; detective, private investigator, spy

私人侦探 sīrén zhēntàn private detective, private eye

zhēn 珍 ADJ valuable

zhēnguì 珍贵 [comp: 珍 valuable + 贵 precious] ADJ precious, valuable ■ 这些文物有两千年的历史，多么珍贵啊！ **Zhè xiē wénwù yǒu liǎngqiān nián de lìshǐ, duōme zhēnguì a!** *These cultural relics are 2,000 years old; how precious they are!*

zhēnxī 珍惜 [modif: 珍 valuable + 惜 cherish] V cherish dearly, value highly

zhēnxī 珍稀 [comp: 珍 valuable + 稀 rare] ADJ rare and precious

zhēnzhū 珍珠 [modif: 珍 valuable + 珠 bead] N pearl (颗 kē)

珍珠项链 zhēnzhū xiàngliàn pearl necklace

zhēn 斟 V pour tea or wine

zhēnzhuó 斟酌 V consider, deliberate, weigh pros and cons

zhēn 针 TRAD 針 N 1 needle (根 gēn) ■ 我要一根缝衣针。 **Wǒ yào yì gēn féngyī zhēn.** *I want a sewing needle.* 2 injection

打针 dǎzhēn give an injection, get an injection ■ 护士给他打了一针。 **Hùshi gěi tā dǎ le yì zhēn.**

The nurse gave him an injection.

zhēnduì 针对 V aim at, be aimed at ■ 这次反吸烟运动主要针对青少年。 **Zhè cì fǎn xīyān yùndòng zhǔyào zhēnduì qīngshàonián.** *This anti-smoking campaign is mainly aimed at teenagers.* ■ 厂长的话是针对经常迟到的工人说的。 **Chǎngzhǎng de huà shì zhēnduì jīngcháng chídào de gōngrén shuō de.** *The factory manager's words are directed at workers who often come late for work.*

zhēnjiǔ 针灸 [comp: 针 needle + 灸 moxibustion] V & N give or receive acupuncture and moxibustion treatment; acupuncture and moxibustion ■ 他针灸了几次，肩就不痛了。 **Tā zhēnjiǔle jǐ cì, jiān jiù bú tòng le.** *After a few sessions of acupuncture and moxibustion, his shoulder no longer hurts.* ■ 他学中文的目的是为了研究针灸。 **Tā xué Zhōngwén de mùdì shì wèile yánjiū zhēnjiǔ.** *His purpose of learning Chinese is to study acupuncture and moxibustion.*

zhěn 诊 TRAD 診 V examine (a patient)

zhěnduàn 诊断 V & N diagnose; diagnosis

诊断为良性肿瘤 zhěnduàn wéi liángxìngzhǒngliú diagnosed as benign tumor / 做出诊断 zuòchū zhěnduàn make a diagnosis

zhěn 枕 N pillow

zhěntou 枕头 N pillow (只 zhī)

zhèn 阵 TRAD 陣 MEASURE WORD (for an action or event that lasts for some time) ■ 雨下了一阵停了。 **Yǔ xiàle yí zhèn tíng le.** *The rain stopped after a while.* ■ 刮了一阵大风，院子里满是落叶。 **Guāle yí zhèn dà fēng, yuànzi li mǎnshì luòyè.** *A strong wind blew for a while and the courtyard was full of fallen leaves.*

zhèndì 阵地 N (military) position

zhènróng 阵容 N layout of troops

zhènyǔ 阵雨 N brief period of rain, shower

zhèn 振 V arouse to action

zhèndòng 振动 V & N vibrate, oscillate; vibration, oscillation

zhènfèn 振奋 V stimulate, excite, arouse

令人振奋的消息 lìngrén zhènfèn de xiāoxi exciting news

zhènxīng 振兴 V rejuvenate, revitalize, revigorate

振兴中华 zhènxīng Zhōnghuá rejuvenate China, make China strong again

zhèn 震 V shake, shock

地震 dìzhèn earthquake

zhènhàn 震撼 [v+compl: 震 shake + 撼 move] V shake, vibrate

zhènjīng 震惊 [v+compl: 震 shake + 惊 be surprised] V shock, amaze, astonish

zhèn 镇[1] TRAD 鎮 N rural town

zhèn 镇[2] TRAD 鎮 V suppress

zhèndìng 镇定 ADJ unperturbed, calm,

zhènjìng 镇静 ADJ composed, calm ■ 遇到危险，

千万要保持镇静。**Yùdào wēixiǎn, qiānwàn yào bǎochí zhènjìng.** *Be sure to keep calm when in danger.*

zhènjìngjì 镇静剂 **N** sedative, tranquillizer

zhènyā 镇压 **V** (politically) suppress, repress, put down

zhēngyuè 正月 **N** the first month of the lunar year

zhēng 争 **TRAD** 爭 **V** argue ■ 别争了，争到明天也争不出结果来。**Bié zhēng le, zhēng dào míngtiān yě zhēng bu chū jiéguǒ lai.** *Stop arguing. Even if you argue till tomorrow there will be no conclusion.*

zhēngduān 争端 **N** controversial issue, a bone of contention

zhēngduó 争夺 **V** scramble for, fight for
争夺资源和市场 zhēngduó zīyuán hé shìchǎng scramble for resources and markets

zhēnglùn 争论 [comp: 争 argue + 论 comment] **V** dispute, debate ■ 他喜欢和朋友争论哲学问题。**Tā xǐhuan hé péngyou zhēnglùn zhéxué wèntí.** *He likes to debate philosophical issues with his friends.*

zhēngqì 争气 **V** work hard to win honor
为父母争气 wéi fùmǔ zhēngqì work hard to win honor for one's parents

zhēngqǔ 争取 [comp: 争 strive + 取 obtain] **V** strive for, fight for ■ 我们争取提前完成计划 **Wǒmen zhēngqǔ tíqián wánchéng jìhuà.** *We strive to fulfill the plan ahead of schedule.*

zhēng xiān kǒng hòu 争先恐后 **V** strive to be the first and fear to lag behind

zhēngyì 争议 **N** dispute
有争议的问题 yǒu zhēngyì de wèntí an issue in dispute, a controversial matter

zhēng 征 **TRAD** 徵 **V** solicit

zhēngfú 征服 **V** conquer, subjugate

zhēngqiú 征求 [comp: 征 solicit + 求 request] **V** solicit, ask for ■ 老师征求学生对教学的意见。**Lǎoshī zhēngqiú xuésheng duì jiàoxué de yìjiàn.** *The teachers solicit students' comments on their teaching.*

zhēngshōu 征收 **V** impose (taxes, etc.), levy, collect

zhēng 挣 **TRAD** 掙 **V** struggle to free oneself

zhēngzhá 挣扎 **V** struggle desperately

zhēng 睁 **TRAD** 睜 **V** open (the eyes) ■ 对这种行为，不能睁一只眼，闭一只眼。**Duì zhè zhǒng xíngwéi, bù néng zhēng yì zhī yǎn, bì yì zhī yǎn.** *We must not turn a blind eye to such behavior.*

zhēng 蒸 **V** steam ■ 馒头刚蒸好，快来吃吧！*The steamed buns are just ready, come and eat them!*

zhēngfā 蒸发 [comp: 蒸 steam + 发 give off] **V** evaporate

zhěng 整¹ **ADJ** whole, full, entire ■ 她昨天整夜没睡。**Tā zuótiān zhěngyè méi shuì.** *She didn't sleep the entire night.*

zhěngge 整个 **ADJ** whole, entire ■ 整个工程都是

他负责。**Zhěngge gōngchéng dōu shì tā fùzé.** *He is in charge of the entire project.*

zhěng 整² **V** put in order

zhěngdùn 整顿 **V** put in order, improve, reorganize
整顿纪律 zhěngdùnjìlǜ enforce discipline

zhěnglǐ 整理 [comp: 整 put in order + 理 tidy up] **V** put in order, tidy up ■ 客人来前，整理一下房间。**Kèren lái qián, zhěnglǐ yíxià fángjiān.** *Tidy up the rooms before guests arrive.*

zhěngqí 整齐 [comp: 整 neat + 齐 orderly] **ADJ** in good order, neat and tidy (**ANTONYM** 乱 **luàn**)

zhěngtǐ 整体 **N** whole, entirety, (something) as a whole
从整体上说 cóng zhěngtǐ shàng shuō on the whole

zhěngtiān 整天 **N** the whole day, all the time
整天抱怨 zhěngtiān bàoyuàn grumble all the time

zhèng 正 **ADJ** straight, upright (**ANTONYMS** 歪 **wāi**, 斜 **xié**) ■ 帮我看看，这幅画挂得正不正？**Bāng wǒ kànkan, zhè fú huà guà de zhèng bu zhèng?** *Have a look to see if this picture is hung straight.*

zhèngcháng 正常 [comp: 正 normal + 常 usual] **ADJ** normal, regular (**ANTONYM** 反常 **fǎncháng**) ■ 这几天，车间里一切正常。**Zhè jǐ tiān, chējiān li yíqiè zhèngcháng.** *Everything is normal in the workshop these days.* ■ 在正常的情况下，他一周给父母发一份电子邮件。**Zài zhèngcháng de qíngkuàng xià, tā yì zhōu gěi fùmǔ fā yí fèn diànzǐ yóujiàn.** *Under normal circumstances he sends his parents an e-mail once a week.*

zhèngdàng 正当 **ADJ** proper, legitimate
正当权益 zhèngdàng quányì legitimate rights and interests

zhèngfù 正负 **N** positive and negative

zhèngguī 正规 **ADJ** regular, standard

zhènghǎo 正好 [modif: 正 just + 好 good] **ADJ** 1 just right ■ 我穿这双鞋正好。**Wǒ chuān zhè shuāng xié zhènghǎo.** *These shoes are just the right size for me.* ■ 你来得正好，我正要找你呢。**Nǐ lái de zhènghǎo, wǒ zhèngyào zhǎo nǐ ne.** *You've come at the right moment; I was just looking for you.* 2 chance to, by coincidence ■ 我正好那天下午没课，可以陪她进城。**Wǒ zhènghǎo nà tiān xiàwǔ méi kè, kěyǐ péi tā jìnchéng.** *It happened that I did not have class that afternoon, so I could go to town with her.*

zhèngjing 正经 **ADJ** 1 decent, proper 2 serious, not frivolous
一本正经 yì běn zhèngjīng in all seriousness, sanctimonious

zhèngqì 正气 **N** healthy atmosphere, moral integrity

zhèngquè 正确 [comp: 正 proper + 确 true] **ADJ** correct, accurate (**ANTONYM** 错误 **cuòwù**) ■ 你的回答不正确。**Nǐ de huídá bú zhèngquè.** *Your answer is not correct.* ■ 你要听各方面的意见，才能形成

正确的观点。**Nǐ yào tīng gè fāngmiàn de yìjiàn, cáinéng xíngchéng zhèngquè de guāndiǎn.** *You can form the correct viewpoint only after hearing out opinions from all sides.*

zhèngshì 正式 [modif: 正 formal + 式 manner] ADJ formal, official ■ 公司正式通知职工，明年一月起工资提高百分之十。**Gōngsī zhèngshì tōngzhī zhígōng, míngnián Yīyuè qǐ gōngzī tígāo bǎifēn zhī shí.** *The company has formally informed the staff that they will get a ten-percent raise starting next January.*

zhèngyì 正义 ADJ & N just, righteous; justice, righteousness

zhèngzài 正在 ADV (used before a verb to indicate the action is in progress) ■ 他正在看电视。**Tā zhèngzài kàn diànshì.** *He's watching TV.*

NOTE: 正在 … 呢 **zhèngzài ... ne** is the same as 正在 **zhèngzài**, but with a casual, friendly tone.

zhèngzōng 正宗 ADJ authentic, genuine
zhèng 证 TRAD 證 N proof, certificate
zhèngjiàn 证件 [modif: 证 proof + 件 article] N paper or document proving one's identity, e.g an a passport, an ID card ■ 在国外旅行，一定要保管好自己的证件。**Zài guówài lǚxíng, yí dìng yào bǎo guǎnhǎo zìjǐ de zhèngjiàn.** *When you're traveling in a foreign country, you must take very good care of your personal papers.*

zhèngjù 证据 N evidence, proof ■ 说话要有证据。**Shuōhuà yào yǒu zhèngjù.** *When you make a claim, you must have evidence.*

zhèngmíng 证明 [v+compl: 证 prove + 明 clear] V & N prove, testify; proof, certificate ■ 事实证明，他的想法行不通。**Shìshí zhèngmíng, tā de xiǎngfǎ xíng bu tōng.** *Facts have proven that his ideas do not work.* ■ 你要请医生开一张病假证明。**Nǐ yào qǐng yīshēng kāi yì zhāng bìngjià zhèngmíng.** *You should ask your doctor to issue a certificate for medical leave.*

出证明 chū zhèngmíng issue a certificate
zhèngshí 证实 V verify, prove
zhèngshū 证书 N certificate (份 fèn, 张 zhāng)
毕业证书 bìyè zhèngshū diploma / 结婚证书 jiéhūn zhèngshū marriage license, marriage certificate
zhèngzhòng 郑重 ADJ solemn, serious
zhèng 政 N governance
zhèngcè 政策 [modif: 政 government + 策 policy] N government policy ■ 政府的移民政策可能会变化。**Zhèngfǔ de yímín zhèngcè kěnéng huì biànhuà.** *The government immigration policy may change.*

zhèngfǔ 政府 [modif: 政 governance + 府 building] N government ■ 政府有关部门正在研究这个问题。**Zhèngfǔ yǒuguān bùmén zhèngzài yánjiū zhège wèntí.** *The government departments concerned are studying this issue.*

zhèngquán 政权 [modif: 政 political + 权 power] N political power, government, regime ■ 军人发动政变，建立了新政权。**Jūnrén fādòng zhèngbiàn, jiànlì le xīn zhèngquán.** *Soldiers launched a coup d'etat, and established a new government.*

zhèngzhì 政治 [comp: 政 governance + 治 administering] N politics, governance ■ 我对这个国家的政治情况了解不多。**Wǒ duì zhège guójiā de zhèngzhì qíngkuàng liǎojiě bù duō.** *I don't know much about the political situation in this country.*

zhèng 症 N disease
急症 jízhèng acute disease, (medical) emergency / 急症室 jízhèng shì emergency room (ER)
zhèngzhuàng 症状 N symptom
zhèng 挣 V work to earn (money)
挣钱养活全家 zhèngqián yǎnghuo quánjiā work to earn money so as to provide for the family
zhī 之 PARTICLE same as 的 de. Used in written Chinese or certain set expressions.
zhī hòu 之后 after, behind ■ 他退休之后，要搬到故乡去住。**Tā tuìxiū zhī hòu, yào bāndào gùxiāng qù zhù.** *After retirement he will move to his hometown.*
之际 zhījì 1 between 2 at the moment when
之间 zhī jiān between ■ 两座大楼之间有一座小公园。**Liǎng zuò dàlóu zhī jiān yǒu yí zuò xiǎo gōngyuán.** *There is a small park between the two buildings.* ■ 我们之间存在着一些误会。**Wǒmen zhījiān cúnzàizhe yìxiē wùhuì.** *There is some misunderstanding between us.*
之前 zhī qián before ■ 你要在六月之前给我回信。**Nǐ yào zài Liùyuè zhī qián gěi wǒ huíxìn.** *You should give me a reply before June.*
之外 zhī wài outside, apart from ■ 地球之外，还有其他地方有生命吗？**Dìqiú zhī wài, háiyǒu qítā dìfang yǒu shēngmìng ma?** *Apart from the Earth, is there life anywhere else?*
之下 zhī xià below, under ■ 三层楼之下是一个大餐厅。**Sāncéng lóu zhī xià shì yí ge dà cāntīng.** *Below the third floor is a large restaurant.*
之一 zhī yī one of ■ 杭州是中国名胜之一。**Hángzhōu shì Zhōngguó míngshèng zhī yī.** *Hangzhou is one of China's tourist attractions.*
之中 zhī zhōng between, among ■ 她的朋友之中，没有人会说中文。**Tā de péngyou zhī zhōng, méiyǒu rén huì shuō Zhōngwén.** *There is none among her friends who speaks Chinese.*
zhī 支[1] MEASURE WORD (for stick-like things)
一支笔 yì zhī bǐ a pen
zhī 支[2] V support, prop
zhīchēng 支撑 [comp: 支 prop up + 撑 prop up] V prop up, shore up
zhīchí 支持 [comp: 支 prop up, support + 持 hold] V support ■ 同事之间要相互合作，相互支持。**Tóngshì zhī jiān yào xiānghù hézuò, xiānghù**

zhīchí. *Colleagues should cooperate and support each other.*

zhīchū 支出 **V & N** pay, expend; expenditure, expenses

zhīliú 支流 [modif: 支 branch + 流 flow] **N** tributary

zhīpèi 支配 **V 1** allocate, arrange
合理支配有限的资金 hélǐ zhīpèi yǒuxiàn de zījīn rationally allocate the limited funds **2** control, determine

zhīpiào 支票 **N** (in banking) check, cheque (张 **zhāng**)
兑现支票 duìxiàn zhīpiào cash a check

zhīyuán 支援 [comp: 支 prop up, support + 援 aid] **V & N** support, aid ■ 全国支援受灾地区。**Quánguó zhīyuán shòuzāi dìqū.** *The whole country aided the disaster-stricken region.* ■ 感谢你们给我们的宝贵支援。**Gǎnxiè nǐmen gěi wǒmen de bǎoguì zhīyuán.** *Our thanks for your precious aid.*

zhīzhù 支柱 [comp: 支 prop + 柱 column] **N** mainstay, pillar

zhī 枝 **N** twig, branch (根 **gēn**)

zhī 只 **TRAD** 隻 **MEASURE WORD** (used with certain nouns denoting animals or utensils, or objects normally occurring in pairs)
一只手 yì zhī shǒu a hand / 两只狗 liǎng zhī gǒu two dogs

zhī 汁 **N** juice (See **guǒzhī** 果汁.)

zhī 知 **V** know

zhīdào 知道 **V** know ■ 我不知道这件事。**Wǒ bù zhīdào zhè jiàn shì.** *I don't know about this matter.* ■ 你知道这家公司的传真号码吗？**Nǐ zhīdào zhè jiā gōngsī de chuánzhēn hàomǎ ma?** *Do you know the fax number of this company?*

zhījué 知觉 [comp: 知 know + 觉 be aware] **N** consciousness, senses
失去知觉 shīqù zhījué lose consciousness / 恢复知觉 huīfù zhījué regain consciousness, come to

zhīshi 知识 **N** knowledge ■ 旅行使人学到知识。**Lǚxíng shǐ rén xuédào zhīshi.** *Traveling enables one to learn knowledge.* ■ 他这一方面的知识很丰富。**Tā zhè yì fāngmiàn de zhīshi hěn fēngfù.** *He has rich knowledge in this aspect.*

zhī zú cháng lè 知足长乐 **IDIOM** Contentment brings happiness.

zhī 脂 **N** fat, grease

zhīfáng 脂肪 **N** fat

zhī 织 **TRAD** 織 **V** weave (See **fǎngzhī** 纺织, **zǔzhī** 组织.)

zhī 执 **TRAD** 執 **V** grasp, persist

zhíxíng 执行 **V** carry out, implement, execute ■ 坚决执行上级交给我们的任务。**Jiānjué zhíxíng shàngjí jiāo gěi wǒmen de rènwù.** *We will resolutely carry out the mission entrusted to us by the higher authorities.* ■ 这个计划很难执行。**Zhège jìhuà hěn nán zhíxíng.** *This plan is difficult to implement.*

zhízhào 执照 **N** license, permit
驾驶执照 jiàshǐ zhízhào driver's license

zhízhuó 执著 **ADJ** persevering, persistent, determined

zhí 直 **I ADJ** straight (**ANTONYM** 弯 **wān**) ■ 用尺划一条直线。**Yòng chǐ huà yì tiáo zhí xiàn.** *Draw a straight line using a ruler.* **II ADV** straight, directly ■ 这个航班直飞香港，中间不停。**Zhè ge hángbān zhí fēi Xiānggǎng, zhōngjiān bù tíng.** *This airliner flies direct to Hong Kong without any stopover.*

zhíbō 直播 **N 1** live broadcast, transmission **2** (farming) direct seeding

zhídào 直到 [modif: 直 straight + 到 arrive] **PREP** until, till ■ 孩子们在花园里玩，直到天黑。**Háizimen zài huāyuán lǐ wán, zhídào tiānhēi.** *The children played in the garden till it was dark.* ■ 他一直住在家乡，直到念完中学。**Tā yìzhí zhù zai jiāxiāng, zhídào niànwán zhōngxué.** *He lived in his hometown until he had finished high school.*

zhíjiē 直接 [modif: 直 direct + 接 join] **ADJ** direct ■ 你可以直接找房东，不用通过中间人。**Nǐ kěyǐ zhíjiē zhǎo fángdōng, bú yòng tōngguò zhōngjiānrén.** *You can make direct contact with the landlord without going through the middleman.*

zhíjìng 直径 **N** diameter

zhí 值 **N** value

zhíbān 值班 **V** be on duty

zhíde 值得 **V** be worth ■ 为了这件小事生气，不值得。**Wèile zhè jiàn xiǎoshì shēngqì, bù zhíde.** *Such a small matter is not worth getting angry over.* ■ 这本词典虽然不便宜，还是值得买。**Zhè běn cídiǎn suīrán bù piányi, háishì zhíde mǎi.** *Although this dictionary is not cheap, it is worth buying.*

zhí 职 **TRAD** 職 **N** job

zhígōng 职工 [comp: 职 clerk + 工 worker] **N** staff (of a factory, a company, an enterprise, etc.), employee(s) ■ 我们公司总共有一千八百五十名职工。**Wǒmen gōngsī zǒnggòng yǒu yìqiān bābǎi wǔshí míng zhígōng.** *Our company has 1,850 employees in total.*

zhínéng 职能 **N** function

zhíwèi 职位 **N** position, post

zhíwù 职务 **N** official duties and obligations, post

zhíyè 职业 [comp: 职 job + 业 occupation] **N** occupation, profession, vocation ■ 他的职业是医生，也是一位业余作家。**Tā de zhíyè shì yīshēng, yě shì yí wèi yèyú zuòjiā.** *He is a doctor by profession but he is also a writer in his spare time.*
职业介绍所 zhíyè jièshàosuǒ employment agency

zhíyèbìng 职业病 **N** occupational disease

zhí 殖 **V** breed

zhímín 殖民 **V** colonize
殖民地 zhímíndì colony / 殖民主义 zhímín zhǔyì colonialism

zhí 植 **V** plant, grow

zhíwù 植物 [modif: 植 plant + 物 thing] N plant, flora ∎ 这种植物很少见，应该受到保护。**Zhè zhǒng zhíwù hěn shǎojiàn, yīnggāi shòudào bǎohù.** *This plant is rare and should be protected.*

zhíwùxué 植物学 N botany
植物学家 zhíwùxuéjiā botanist

zhíwùyuán 植物园 N botanical garden

zhí 侄 N one's brother's child

zhínǚ 侄女 N one's brother's daughter, niece

zhízi 侄子 N one's brother's son, nephew

zhǐ 只 TRAD 祇 ADV only ∎ 我只有一个弟弟，没有哥哥，也没有姐妹。**Wǒ zhǐ yǒu yí ge dìdi, méiyǒu gēge, yě méiyǒu jiě-mèi.** *I've only got a younger brother. I don't have an elder brother or sister.* ∎ 她只喝水，不喝酒。**Tā zhǐ hē shuǐ, bù hē jiǔ.** *She only drinks water and does not drink wine.*

zhǐhǎo 只好 ADV have no choice but ∎ 他自行车坏了，只好走路去上学。**Tā zìxíngchē huài le, zhǐhǎo zǒu lù qù shàngxué.** *His bicycle has broken down, so he has to walk to school.* ∎ 飞机票全卖完了，我们只好坐火车去。**Fēijī piào quán màiwánle, wǒmen zhǐhǎo zuò huǒchē qù.** *As air tickets were sold out we had no choice but go by train.*

zhǐshì 只是 ADV only, just ∎ 我很想认真了解中国的历史，只是没有时间。**Wǒ hěn xiǎng rènzhēn liǎojiě Zhōngguó de lìshǐ, zhǐshì méiyǒu shíjiān.** *I'd like to learn Chinese history earnestly; it's just that I don't have the time.* ∎ 她很想去听音乐会，只是买不起门票。**Tā hěn xiǎng qù tīng yīnyuèhuì, zhǐshì mǎi buqǐ ménpiào.** *She wants to go to the concert badly, but unfortunately she can't afford the ticket.*

zhǐyào 只要 CONJ so long as, provided that, if only ∎ 只要身体好，就能享受生活。**Zhǐyào shēntǐ hǎo, jiù néng xiǎngshòu shēnghuó.** *As long as you are in good health, you can enjoy life.* ∎ 只要打一个电话，饭店就会马上把菜送来。**Zhǐyào dǎ yí ge diànhuà, fàndiàn jiù huì mǎshàng bǎ cài sònglai.** *You only need give the restaurant a call and they will deliver your order immediately.*

zhǐyǒu 只有 I ADV can only, have no choice but ∎ 既然答应帮助他，只有尽力而为了。**Jìrán dāyìng bāngzhù tā, zhǐyǒu jìn lì ér wéi le.** *Now that I've promised to help him, I can only do my best.* II CONJ only, only if ∎ 只有认真地学，才能学好中文。**Zhǐyǒu rènzhēn de xué, cáinéng xuéhǎo Zhōngwén.** *Only if you study in earnest, can you gain a good command of Chinese.* ∎ 只有经理亲自道歉，顾客才会满意。**Zhǐyǒu jīnglǐ qīnzì dàoqiàn, gùkè cáihuì mǎnyì.** *Only if the manager himself apologizes, will the customer be satisfied.*

zhǐ 纸 TRAD 紙 N paper (张 zhāng) ∎ 请给我几张纸。**Qǐng gěi wǒ jǐ zhāng zhǐ.** *Please give me some paper.*

zhǐ 止 V stop, suspend (See **tíngzhǐ** 停止.)
止痛片 zhǐ tòng piàn painkiller

zhǐ 址 N location (See **dìzhǐ** 地址.)

zhǐ 指 V 1 point at, point to ∎ 你不知道那东西叫什么，就用手指。**Nǐ bù zhīdào nà dōngxi jiào shénme, jiù yòng shǒu zhǐ.** *If you don't know what it's called, just point to it with your finger.* ∎ 他指着自己的鼻子说，"就是我。" **Tā zhǐzhe zìjǐ de bízi shuō, "Jiù shì wǒ."** *Pointing at his own nose, he said, "It's me."* 2 refer to, allude to, mean ∎ 他说有些人工作不负责，不知道是指谁。**Tā shuō yǒuxiē rén gōngzuò bú fùzé, bù zhīdào shì zhǐ shuí.** *I don't know to whom he was referring when he said some people were not responsible in their work.*

zhǐbiāo 指标 N target, quota

zhǐchū 指出 [v+obj: 指 point + 出 out] V point out ∎ 老师指出了我发音中的问题。**Lǎoshī zhǐchūle wǒ fāyīn zhōng de wèntí.** *The teacher pointed out the problems in my pronunciation.* ∎ 这篇文章指出，社会必须照顾弱者。**Zhè piān wénzhāng zhǐchū, shèhuì bìxū zhàogù ruòzhě.** *This article points out that the society must take care of the weak.*

zhǐdǎo 指导 [comp: 指 point + 导 guide] V guide, direct, supervise ∎ 工程师指导技术员修理机器。**Gōngchéngshī zhǐdǎo jìshùyuán xiūlǐ jīqì.** *The engineer supervised technicians in repairing the machine.*

zhǐdǎoyuán 指导员 N political instructor (in the Chinese People's Liberation Army)

zhǐdìng 指定 V appoint, designate
指定法律代表 zhǐdìng fǎlǜ dàibiǎo appoint a legal representative

zhǐhuī 指挥 V command, direct, conduct
指挥部 zhǐhuībù headquarters

zhǐjia 指甲 N fingernail
修指甲 xiū zhǐjia do fingernails, manicure fingernails

zhǐlìng 指令 N instruction, order

zhǐnánzhēn 指南针 N compass

zhǐshì 指示 V & N 1 instruct; instruction 2 indicate; indication

zhǐwàng 指望 V count on, expect ∎ 别指望他会来帮助你。**Bié zhǐwàng tā huì lái bāngzhù nǐ.** *Don't count on his help.*

zhǐzé 指责 V censure, blame, find fault with

zhǐzhēn 指针 N (needle) indicator, pointer

zhì 至 V to, until (only used in written Chinese) ∎ 银行营业时间是上午九时至下午五时。**Yínháng yíngyè shíjiān shì shàngwǔ jiǔ shí zhì xiàwǔ wǔ shí.** *The business hours of the bank are from nine o'clock in the morning till five o'clock in the afternoon.*

zhìjīn 至今 [v+obj: 至 to, until + 今 today] ADV till now, to this day, so far ∎ 至今已有七十多人报名学习中文。**Zhìjīn yǐ yǒu qīshí duō rén bàomíng xuéxí Zhōngwén.** *So far over seventy people have applied to study Chinese.* ∎ 我至今还不明白她为什么突然离家。**Wǒ zhìjīn hái bù míngbai tā**

wèishénme tūrán líjiā. *To this day I still do not understand why she left home all of a sudden.*

zhìshǎo 至少 **ADV** at least ■ 我今年学了至少三百个汉字。 **Wǒ jīnnián xuéle zhìshǎo sānbǎi ge hànzì.** *I have learnt at least 300 Chinese characters this year.* ■ 孩子至少懂得了为什么不应该说假话。 **Háizi zhìshǎo dǒngdele wèishénme bù yīnggāi shuō jiǎhuà.** *At least the child has understood why one should not tell lies.*

zhì 志 **N** will, willpower

zhìqì 志气 **N** aspiration, ambition
有志气 yǒu zhìqì have lofty aspirations

zhìyuàn 志愿 **I V** volunteer **II N** wish, ideal

zhìyuànzhě 志愿者 **N** volunteer (a person)

zhì 制¹ **TRAD** 製 **V** make, work out

zhìzào 制造 [comp: 制 make + 造 make] **V** make, manufacture ■ "中国制造" 的商品越来越多。 **"Zhōngguó zhìzào" de shāngpǐn yuèláiyuè duō.** *There are more and more goods labeled "Made in China."*
制造业 zhìzàoyè manufacturing industry

zhìzuò 制作 **V** same as 制造 **zhìzào**

zhì 制² **I V** control, rule **II N** system
公制 gōng zhì the metric system (of measurements)

zhìcái 制裁 **N** sanction
制裁那个国家 zhìcái nàge guójiā establish sanction against that country

zhìdìng 制定 [comp: 制 work out + 定 decide] **V** lay down, draw up ■ 他们在每年年底制定第二年的计划。 **Tāmen zài měi nián niándǐ zhìdìng dì-èr nián de jìhuà.** *They draw up the plan for the next year at the end of a year.*

zhìdù 制度 **N** system ■ 目前的教育制度存在很多问题。 **Mùqián de jiàoyù zhìdù cúnzài hěn duō wèntí.** *There are many problems in the current educational system.*

zhìfú 制服 **N** uniform (件 **jiàn**, 套 **tào**)

zhìyuē 制约 **V** constrain, restrain
受条件的制约 shòu tiáojiàn de zhìyuē constrained by one's circumstances

zhìzhǐ 制止 **V** stop, curb

zhì 治 **V** treat (disease) ■ 医生的责任是治病救人。 **Yīshēng de zérèn shì zhì bìng jiù rén.** *It is the responsibility of a doctor to treat diseases and save lives.* ■ 他的病恐怕治不好了。 **Tā de bìng kǒngpà zhì bu hǎo le.** *I'm afraid his disease cannot be cured.*

zhì'ān 治安 **N** public order, public security ■ 新加坡的治安情况很不错。 **Xīnjiāpō de zhì'ān qíngkuàng hěn búcuò.** *The public security situation in Singapore is not bad. (→ Singapore is orderly and has low crime rates.)*

zhìlǐ 治理 **V** govern, administrate

zhìliáo 治疗 **V** treat (a patient, a disease); treatment
治疗无效 zhìliáo wúxiào Medical treatment failed.

zhì 致¹ **V** reach (See yízhì 一致.)

zhì 致² **V** send, extend

zhìcí 致辞 **V** make a (short formal) speech

zhìlìyú 致力于 **V** devote one's efforts to, commit oneself to

zhìshǐ 致使 **V** lead to, result in, cause

zhì 质 **TRAD** 質 **N** nature, character

zhìliàng 质量 **N** quality (**ANTONYM** 数量 **shùliàng**) ■ 这个牌子的汽车质量好，价格又便宜。 **Zhège páizi de qìchē zhìliàng hǎo, jiàgé yòu piányi.** *Cars of this make are of good quality and inexpensive.* ■ 你觉得这种产品的质量如何？ **Nǐ juéde zhè zhǒng chǎnpǐn de zhìliàng rúhé?** *How do you find the quality of this product?*

zhì 秩 **N** order, rank

zhìxù 秩序 [comp: 秩 order + 序 sequence] **N** order, proper sequence ■ 运动场内秩序良好。 **Yùndòngchǎng nèi zhìxù liánghǎo.** *In the stadium the audience maintains good order.*

zhì 智 **ADJ** wise, intelligent
智者 zhìzhě wise man

zhìhuì 智慧 **N** wisdom

zhìlì 智力 [modif: 智 intelligent + 力 power] **N** intelligence, intellect
智力发达 zhìlì fādá highly intelligent

zhìnéng 智能 [modif: 智 intelligent + 能 ability] **N** intelligence and capability
人工智能 réngōng zhìnéng artificial intelligence (AI)

zhìnéng shǒujī 智能手机 **N** smartphone

zhìshāng 智商 **N** intelligence quotient (IQ)

zhì 置 **V** place (See wèizhì 位置.)

zhì 滞 **TRAD** 滯 **V** stagnate

zhìliú 滞留 **V** be held up, be detained

zhōng 中 **I N** center, middle
东南西北中 dōng, nán, xī, běi, zhōng the east, the south, the west, the north and the center **II ADJ** middle, medium

zhōngcān 中餐 [modif: 中 Chinese + 餐 meal] **N** Chinese cuisine, Chinese food ■ 我们用中餐招待客人。 **Wǒmen yòng zhōngcān zhāodài kèren.** *We entertain guests with Chinese food.*
中餐馆 zhōngcānguǎn Chinese restaurant / 中餐厅 zhōngcāntīng Chinese restaurant (in a hotel, etc.)

zhōngduàn 中断 **V** discontinue, interrupt

Zhōngguó 中国 [modif: 中 middle, central + 国 kingdom, country] **N** China ■ 中国历史长，人口多。 **Zhōngguó lìshǐ cháng, rénkǒu duō.** *China has a long history and a large population.*

Zhōnghuá 中华 **N** China, Chinese ■ 中华文明对东亚各国有很大影响。 **Zhōnghuá wénmíng duì Dōng-Yà gè guó yǒu hěn dà yǐngxiǎng.** *Chinese civilization has had great influence on countries in East Asia.*

NOTE: Both 中国 **Zhōngguó** and 中华 **Zhōnghuá** may refer to *China*, but 中华 **Zhōngghuá** has historical and cultural connotations.

zhōngjiān 中间 N center, middle, among ■ 花园的中间有一棵大树。**Huāyuán de zhōngjiān yǒu yì kē dà shù.** *In the center of the garden there is a very big tree.* ■ 我的朋友中间，他体育最好。**Wǒ de péngyou zhōngjiān, tā tǐyù zuì hǎo.** *Among my friends he is the best athlete.*

zhōngjiè 中介 N **1** medium, intermedium **2** same as 中介人 **zhōngjièrén**

zhōngjièrén 中介人 N agent, intermediary

zhōnglì 中立 ADJ neutral
中立国 zhōnglìguó neutral state

zhōngnián 中年 N middle age
中年人 zhōngniánrén middle-aged person

Zhōngqiūjié 中秋节 N the Mid-Autumn Festival (the 15th day of the 8th month in the Chinese lunar calendar)

Zhōngwén 中文 [modif: 中 China + 文 writing] N the Chinese language (especially the writing) ■ 世界上有十几亿人用中文。**Shìjiè shang yǒu shí jǐ yì rén yòng Zhōngwén.** *Over a billion people in the world use Chinese.*

NOTE: See note on 汉语 **Hànyǔ.**

zhōngwǔ 中午 [modif: 中 middle + 午 noon] N noon ■ 我们中午休息一个小时。**Wǒmen zhōngwǔ xiūxi yí ge xiǎoshí.** *We have a one-hour break at noon.*

zhōngxīn 中心 [modif: 中 central + 心 the heart] N central part, center ■ 城市的中心是一座大公园。**Chéngshì de zhōngxīn shì yí zuò dà gōngyuán.** *There is a big park in the center of the city.* ■ 他讲话的中心思想是必须保证产品的质量。**Tā jiǎnghuà de zhōngxīn sīxiǎng shì bìxū bǎozhèng chǎnpǐn de zhìliàng.** *The central idea of his speech is that product quality must be guaranteed.*
市中心 shìzhōngxīn city center, CBD / 研究中心 yánjiū zhōngxīn research center

zhōngxué 中学 [modif: 中 middle + 学 school] N secondary school, high school, middle school (座 **zuò,** 所 **suǒ**) ■ 在中国，中学分初中、高中两部分。**Zài Zhōngguó, zhōngxué fēn chūzhōng, gāozhōng liǎng bùfen.** *In China, high schools are divided into junior high and senior high.*

zhōngxún 中旬 N middle ten days of a month (11th to 20th)

zhōngyāng 中央 N **1** center, middle **2** the highest leading body of a state or party
党中央 dǎng zhōngyāng the Central Committee of the Chinese Commmunist Party, the top leadership of the Chinese Commmunist Party

zhōngyào 中药 [modif: 中 Chinese + 药 medicine, drug] N traditional Chinese medicine (e.g. herbs) ■ 很多常见的植物都是重要的中药。**Hěn duō chángjiàn de zhíwù dōu shì zhòngyào de zhōngyào.** *Many common plants are an important part of traditional Chinese medicine.*

zhōngyī 中医 [modif: 中 Chinese + 医 medicine, medical science] N **1** traditional Chinese medicine ■ 中医和古代哲学思想有关。**Zhōngyī hé gǔdài zhéxué sīxiǎng yǒuguān.** *Traditional Chinese medicine is related to ancient Chinese philosophical thought.* **2** one who practices Traditional Chinese medicine ■ 你这个病可以请一位中医看看。**Nǐ zhège bìng kěyǐ qǐng yí wèi zhōngyī kànkan.** *You can consult a traditional Chinese doctor on your illness.*

zhōng 忠 ADJ loyal

zhōngchéng 忠诚 [comp: 忠 loyal + 诚 sincere] ADJ loyal and faithful, staunch

zhōngshí 忠实 ADJ faithful and trustworthy, true-hearted

zhōng 钟 TRAD 鐘 N clock (座 **zuò**) ■ 这座钟慢了三分钟。**Zhè zuò zhōng mànle sān fēnzhōng.** *This clock is three minutes slow.*

zhōnglóu 钟楼 N clock tower

zhōngtóu 钟头 N same as 小时 **xiǎoshí** (used in spoken Chinese)

zhōng 终 TRAD 終 N end, finish

zhōngdiǎn 终点 N end point, destination

zhōngduān 终端 [modif: 终 end + 端 extreme] N terminal

zhōngjiū 终究 ADV after all, in the end

zhōngnián 终年 ADV all year round, throughout the year

zhōngshēn 终身 N all one's life, lifelong ■ 王医生把终身献给了医疗事业。**Wáng yīshēng bǎ zhōngshēn xiàngěile yīliáo shìyè.** *Dr Wang gave all his life to medicine.*

zhōngyú 终于 ADV finally, in the end ■ 他终于实现了自己的愿望。**Tā zhōngyú shíxiànle zìjǐ de yuànwàng.** *He finally realized his aspirations.* ■ 我终于找到了他的家。**Wǒ zhōngyú zhǎodàole tā de jiā.** *I finally found his home.*

zhōngzhǐ 终止 V terminate, end

zhōng 衷 N innermost feelings
言不由衷 yán bù yóu zhōng speak insincerely

zhōngxīn 衷心 ADJ sincere, whole-hearted

zhǒng 肿 TRAD 腫 V swell

zhǒngliú 肿瘤 N tumor
恶性肿瘤 èxìng zhǒngliú malignant tumor, cancer / 良性肿瘤 liángxìng zhǒngliú benign tumor

zhǒng 种 TRAD 種 I MEASURE WORD kind, sort, type ■ 这里有三种酒，你想喝哪一种？**Zhèli yǒu sān zhǒng jiǔ, nǐ xiǎng hē nǎ yì zhǒng?** *Here are three kinds of wine. Which one would you like to drink?* 各种各样 gè zhǒng gè yàng all sorts of, all kinds of II N seed

zhǒnglèi 种类 N kind, category

zhǒngzi 种子 [suffix: 种 seed + 子 nominal suffix] N seed ■ 这家公司向农民提供各类优质种子。**Zhè jiā gōngsī xiàng nóngmín tígōng gè lèi yōuzhì zhǒngzí.** *This company provides farmers with all kinds of high quality seeds.*

zhǒngzú 种族 N race

种族主义 zhǒngzúzhǔyì racism

zhòng 众 TRAD 眾 N crowd (See **guānzhòng** 观众, **qúnzhòng** 群众.)

zhòng suǒ zhōu zhī 众所周知 IDIOM as is known to all

zhòng 种 TRAD 種 V plant ■ 爸爸在我们家小花园里种了一些花。**Bàba zài wǒmen jiā xiǎo huāyuán li zhòngle yìxiē huā.** *Dad planted some flowers in our little garden.*

zhòngzhí 种植 V plant, grow

zhòng 重 ADJ 1 heavy (ANTONYM 轻 **qīng**) ■ 这个机器太重了，我们两个人搬不动。**Zhège jīqì tài zhòng le, wǒmen liǎng ge rén bān bu dòng.** *This machine is too heavy for the two of us to move.* 2 important ■ 他把钱看得太重。**Tā bǎ qián kànde tài zhòng.** *He attaches too much importance to money.*

zhòngdà 重大 [comp: 重 weighty + 大 big] ADJ major, great ■ 去年国际上有哪些重大事件？**Qùnián guójì shang yǒu nǎxiē zhòngdà shìjiàn?** *What were the major international events last year?* ■ 他在决定政策方面起重大作用。**Tā zài juédìng zhèngcè fāngmiàn qǐ zhòngdà zuòyòng.** *He played a major role in policy making.*

zhòngdiǎn 重点 [comp: 重 weighty + 点 point] N main point, focal point, emphasis ■ 中文一年级的学习重点应该是发音和口语。**Zhōngwén yī niánjí de xuéxí zhòngdiǎn yīnggāi shì fāyīn hé kǒuyǔ.** *The emphasis in first-year Chinese studies should be on pronunciation and spoken Chinese.* ■ 我今年要把重点放在学习语法上。**Wǒ jīnnián yào bǎ zhòngdiǎn fàng zai xuéxí yǔfǎ shang.** *This year I will put stress on the study of Chinese grammar.*

zhòngliàng 重量 [modif: 重 heavy + 量 amount] N weight ■ 称一下这件行李的重量。**Chēng yíxià zhè jiàn xíngli de zhòngliàng.** *Weigh this piece of luggage to see how heavy it is.*

zhòngshì 重视 [modif: 重 weighty + 视 view] V attach importance to, value ■ 老年人一般比较重视身体健康。**Lǎoniánrén yìbān bǐjiào zhòngshì shēntǐ jiànkāng.** *Old people generally value good health.* ■ 中国人一般重视子女的教育—主要是知识教育。**Zhōngguórén yìbān zhòngshì zǐnǚ de jiàoyù – zhǔyào shì zhīshi jiàoyù.** *Generally speaking, Chinese people attach much importance to their children's education—mainly knowledge education.*

zhòngxīn 重心 N 1 barycenter, center of gravity, center of mass

重心不稳 zhòngxīn bù wěn not stable, wobbling 2 focus, point of emphasis

问题的重心 wèntí de zhòngxīn the heart of a matter, the crux of a problem

zhòngyào 重要 [comp: 重 heavy + 要 (in this context) important] ADJ important ■ 这件事非常重要，你别忘了！**Zhè jiàn shì fēicháng zhòngyào, nǐ bié wàng le!** *This matter is very important. Don't you forget it!* ■ 我有一个重要的消息告诉你。**Wǒ yǒu yí ge zhòngyào de xiāoxi gàosu nǐ.** *I have important news to tell you.*

zhōu 舟 N boat

zhōu 州 N 1 administrative district in ancient China, prefecture 2 state (in the US)

纽约州 Niǔyuēzhōu the State of New York

zhōu 洲 N continent (See **Yàzhōu** 亚洲, **Ōuzhōu** 欧洲 etc.)

zhōu 周 TRAD 週 N week ■ "你们学校寒假放几周？" "三周。" **"Nǐmen xuéxiào hánjià fàng jǐ zhōu?" "Sān zhōu."** *"How many weeks of winter holiday does your school have?" "Three weeks."*

NOTES: (1) 周 **zhōu** and 星期 **xīngqī** both mean *week*, but 周 **zhōu** is usually used in writing only. Normally 星期 **xīngqī** is the word to use. (2) 周 **zhōu** is not used with any measure word .

zhōubiān 周边 same as **zhōuwéi** 周围

zhōudào 周到 [modif: 周 circumference, all sides + 到 reach] ADJ thorough, thoughtful ■ 这个旅馆的服务很周到。**Zhège lǚguǎn de fúwù hěn zhōudào.** *This hotel provides thoughtful service.* ■ 你们都准备好了，想得真周到。**Nǐmen dōu zhǔnbèi hǎole, xiǎngde zhēn zhōudào.** *It is really thoughtful of you to get everything ready.*

zhōumì 周密 ADJ careful and thorough, attentive to every detail

zhōumò 周末 [modif: 周 week + 末 end] N weekend ■ "上个周末你过得好吗？" "过得很愉快。" **"Shàng ge zhōumò nǐ guòde hǎo ma?" "Guò de hěn yúkuài."** *"Did you have a good time last weekend?" "Yes, I had a very pleasant time."*

zhōunián 周年 N anniversary

结婚十周年 jiéhūn shí zhōunián the tenth anniversary of one's wedding

zhōuqī 周期 N cycle, period

zhōuwéi 周围 [comp: 周 circuit + 围 encircle] N surrounding area, all around ■ 新西兰周围都是大海。**Xīnxīlán zhōuwéi dōu shì dàhǎi.** *All around New Zealand is the sea.*

zhōuzhé 周折 N twists and turns, setbacks

zhōuzhuǎn 周转 N (of funds) flow, cash flow

周转不灵 zhōuzhuǎnbùlíng not have enough cash for business operation

zhōu 粥 N porridge, gruel

喝粥 hē zhōu eat porridge / 小米粥 xiǎomǐzhōu millet gruel

zhòu 昼 TRAD 晝 N daytime

zhòuyè 昼夜 [comp: 昼 day + 夜 night] N day and night, round the clock, 24/7

昼夜服务 zhòuyè fúwù round-the-clock service

zhòu 皱 TRAD 皺 V wrinkle, crease

zhòuwén 皱纹 [comp: 皱 wrinkle + 纹 lines] **N** wrinkle (on skin), lines

zhū 猪 **TRAD** 豬 **N** pig (头 **tóu**) ■ 这家农民养了十头猪。**Zhè jiā nóngmín yǎngle shí tóu zhū.** *This peasant household keeps ten pigs.* ■ 中国人一般吃猪肉, 不大吃牛肉、羊肉。**Zhōngguórén yìbān chī zhūròu, bú dà chī niúròu, yángròu.** *The Chinese normally eat pork and don't eat much beef or mutton.*

zhū 株 **MEASURE WORD** (for plants and small trees)

zhū 诸 **TRAD** 諸 **ADJ** all, various

zhūwèi 诸位 **PRON** everybody, ladies and gentlemen

zhú 竹 **N** bamboo

zhúzi 竹子 [suffix: 竹 bamboo + 子 nominal suffix] **N** bamboo (棵 **kē**) ■ 古代中国人特别喜爱竹子。**Gǔdài Zhōngguórén tèbié xǐ'ài zhúzi.** *The ancient Chinese were particularly fond of bamboo.*

zhú 逐 **ADV** successive

zhúbù 逐步 [modif: 逐 successive + 步 step] **ADV** step by step, progressively, gradually ■ 我们的中文水平在逐步提高。**Wǒmen de Zhōngwén shuǐpíng zài zhúbù tígāo.** *Our Chinese proficiency is progressively improving.*

zhújiàn 逐渐 [comp: 逐 successive, one by one + 渐 gradual] **ADV** gradually, step by step ■ 地球正在逐渐变暖。**Dìqiú zhèngzài zhújiàn biàn nuǎn.** *The Earth is gradually warming up.* ■ 他逐渐能听懂中文广播了。**Tā zhújiàn néng tīngdǒng Zhōngwén guǎngbō le.** *Gradually he could understand Chinese broadcasts.*

zhúnián 逐年 **ADV** one year after another, year by year

zhǔ 主 **N** master, owner

zhǔbàn 主办 **V** host (a conference, an event, etc.) ■ 这个展览会由城市博物馆主办。**Zhège zhǎnlǎnhuì yóu chéngshì bówùguǎn zhǔbàn.** *This exhibition is hosted by the city museum.*

zhǔcài 主菜 **N** main course (of a dinner)

zhǔchí 主持 **V** be in charge of, host (a TV program), chair (a meeting) 节目主持人 jiémù zhǔchírén host/hostess of a TV/radio show

zhǔdǎo 主导 **ADJ** guiding, dominant

zhǔdòng 主动 [modif: 主 self + 动 act] **ADJ** of one's own accord, taking the initiative ■ 他主动提出帮助我们。**Tā zhǔdòng tíchū bāngzhù wǒmen.** *He offered to help us without being asked.* ■ 在谈恋爱的时候, 一般是小伙子主动一点。**Zài tán liàn'ài de shíhou, yìbān shì xiǎohuǒzi zhǔdòng yìdiǎn.** *Normally young men take the initiative in courtship.*

zhǔguān 主观 [modif: 主 subjective + 观 view] **ADJ** subjective ■ 你这种说法只是建立在你个人的经历上, 所以比较主观。**Nǐ zhè zhǒng shuōfǎ zhǐshì jiànlì zài nǐ gèrén de jīnglì shang, suǒyǐ bǐjiào zhǔguān.** *Your arguments are rather subjec-tive because they are only based on your personal experiences.*

zhǔguǎn 主管 **I V** be in charge, be responsible for ■ 这位副校长主管财务工作。**Zhè wèi fùxiàozhǎng zhǔguǎn cáiwù gōngzuò.** *This deputy principal is responsible for the finance of the school.* **II N** person in charge ■ 谁是这里的主管? **Shuí shì zhèli de zhǔguǎn?** *Who is in charge here?*

zhǔliú 主流 **N** mainstream

zhǔquán 主权 **N** sovereign rights, sovereignty

zhǔrén 主人 [modif: 主 master + 人 person] **N** **1** host (**ANTONYM** 客人 **kèrén**) ■ 客人都来了, 主人呢? **Kèrén dōu lái le, zhǔrén ne?** *The guests have all arrived, but where is the host?* **2** owner, proprietor ■ 我是这辆车的主人, 你们为什么把车拖走? **Wǒ shì zhè liàng chē de zhǔrén, nìmen wèishénme bǎ chē tuōzǒu?** *I'm the owner of this car. Why did you tow it away?*

zhǔrèn 主任 [modif: 主 principal + 任 appointed] **N** chairman (of a committee), director (of a department) ■ 这个委员会的主任由一位教授担任。**Zhège wěiyuánhuì de zhǔrèn yóu yí wèi jiàoshòu dānrèn.** *The chair of this committee was held by a professor.* 主任医生 zhǔrèn yīshēng chief physician, chief surgeon / 办公室主任 bàngōngshì zhǔrèn office manager / 车间主任 chējiān zhǔrèn head of a workshop (in a factory)

zhǔshí 主食 **N** staple food (usually cereal)

zhǔtí 主题 **N** theme (电影的)主题歌 (diànyǐng de) zhǔtígē theme song (of a movie)

zhǔxí 主席 [modif: 主 principal + 席 seat] **N** chairman, chairperson ■ 中华人民共和国的主席是中国的国家元首。**Zhōnghuá Rénmín Gònghéguó de zhǔxí shì Zhōngguó de guójiā yuánshǒu.** *The Chairman of the People's Republic of China is the head of state of China.*

zhǔyào 主要 [comp: 主 major + 要 (in this context) important] **ADJ** major, chief, main ■ 这不是主要的问题, 可以以后再讨论。**Zhè bú shì zhǔyào de wèntí, kěyǐ yǐhòu zài tǎolùn.** *This is not a major issue. We can discuss it later.* ■ 纠正错误是主要的, 谁该负责以后再说。**Jiūzhèng cuòwù shì zhǔyào de, shuí gāi fùzé yǐhòu zài shuō.** *Rectifying the mistake is the main thing. The question of who is to blame can wait till later.*

zhǔyì 主义 **N** doctrine, -ism

zhǔyi 主意 [comp: 主 major + 意 idea] **N** definite view, idea ■ 这件事我没有什么主意, 你看呢? **Zhè jiàn shì wǒ méiyǒu shénme zhǔyi, nǐ kàn ne?** *I don't have any definite views on this matter. What do you think?* ■ 他打定主意要去北京学中文。**Tā dǎdìng zhcyi yào qù Běijīng xué Zhōngwén.** *He has made up his mind to go to Beijing to learn Chinese.*

zhǔzhāng 主张 **v & n** advocate, stand for; proposition, idea, what one stands for ■ 她不主张借钱买车。 **Tā bù zhǔzhāng jiè qián mǎi chē.** *She does not favor borrowing to buy a car.* ■ 你的主张很有道理，但是恐怕很难实行。 **Nǐ de zhǔzhāng hěn yǒu dàolǐ, dànshì kǒngpà hěn nán shíxíng.** *Your idea is very reasonable but I'm afraid it's difficult to implement.*

zhǔ 煮 **v** boil, cook ■ 这块牛肉至少要煮一小时才能吃。 **Zhè kuài niúròu zhìshǎo yào zhǔ yì xiǎoshí cáinéng chī.** *This piece of beef should be boiled for at least one hour before it is edible.*

zhǔ 嘱 **TRAD** 囑 **v** advise

zhǔfù 嘱咐 [comp: 嘱 advice + 咐 tell] **v** exhort, tell (somebody to do something) earnestly, advise ■ 老人去世前，嘱咐子女要互相爱护、互相照顾。 **Lǎorén qùshì qián, zhǔfù zǐnǚ yào hùxiāng àihù, hùxiāng zhàogù.** *Before his death the old man exhorted his children to love and care for each other.*

zhù 柱 **n** pillar, column

柱子 **zhùzi** **n** pillar, column (根 **gēn**)

zhù 助 **v** assist (See **bāngzhù** 帮助.)

zhùlǐ 助理 **n** assistant

助理局长 **zhùlǐ júzhǎng** assistant director of the bureau / 局长助理 **júzhǎng zhùlǐ** assistant to director of the bureau

zhùshǒu 助手 [modif: 助 assist + 手 hand] **n** assistant

zhù 住 **v** live, stay ■ "你住在哪里？" "我住在学校附近。" **"Nǐ zhù zài nǎli?" "Wǒ zhù zài xuéxiào fùjìn."** *"Where do you live?" "I live near the school."*

zhùyuàn 住院 **n** be hospitalized

zhùzhái 住宅 **n** residence, home

住宅区 **zhùzháiqū** residential quarters

zhù 注 **v** add, pour

zhùcè 注册 **v** register

注册商标 **zhùcè shāngbiāo** registered trademark

zhùjiě 注解 **v & n** annotate, explain with notes; explanatory note, note

zhùshè 注射 [comp: 注 pour + 射 shoot] **v & n** inject; injection

zhùshì 注释 **n** same as 注解 **zhùjiě**

zhùshì 注视 **v** look attentively, gaze at

zhùyì 注意 **v** pay attention to, take notice of ■ 说话的时候，要注意语法。 **Shuōhuà de shíhou, yào zhùyì yǔfǎ.** *One should pay attention to grammar when speaking.* ■ 请大家注意！明天张老师要开一个重要的会，所以不上课。 **Qǐng dàjiā zhùyì! Míngtiān Zhāng lǎoshī yào kāi yí ge zhòngyào de huì, suǒyǐ bú shàngkè.** *Attention, please! Tomorrow Teacher Zhang will be attending an important meeting, so there will be no class.*

zhùzhòng 注重 **v** pay great attention to, attach importance to, emphasize

注重售后服务 **zhùzhòng shòuhòufúwù** pay much attention to after-sale service

zhù 驻 **TRAD** 駐 **v** stay

zhùzhā 驻扎 **v** (of troops) be stationed

zhù 祝 **v** express good wishes, wish ■ 祝你生日快乐！ **Zhù nǐ shēngrì kuàilè!** *I wish you a happy birthday!*

zhùfú 祝福 **v** give one's blessing to, wish somebody happiness

zhùhè 祝贺 [comp: 祝 wish well + 贺 congratulate] **v** congratulate ■ 祝贺你大学毕业！ **Zhùhè nǐ dàxué bìyè!** *Congratulations on your graduation!*

zhù 著 **v** write

zhùmíng 著名 **ADJ** famous, well-known ■ 我们的中文老师是一位著名的小说家。 **Wǒmen de Zhōngwén lǎoshī shì yí wèi zhùmíng de xiǎoshuōjiā.** *Our Chinese teacher is a famous novelist.*

zhùzuò 著作 [v+obj: 著 write + 作 (literary) work] **n** writings, (literary) work ■ 他的著作被翻译为十多种语言。 **Tā de zhùzuò bèi fānyìwéi shí duō zhǒng yǔyán.** *His works have been translated into a dozen foreign languages.*

zhù 铸 **TRAD** 鑄 **v** cast

zhùzào 铸造 **n** cast, foundry

zhù 筑 **TRAD** 築 **v** build, construct (See **jiànzhù** 建筑.)

zhuā 抓 **v** grab, seize ■ 他抓住小偷的胳膊。 **Tā zhuāzhù xiǎotōu de gēbo.** *He grabbed the thief by the arm.*

zhuājǐn 抓紧 [v+obj: 抓 grab + 紧 tight] **v** grasp firmly ■ 你要抓紧时间，在下星期一前写完报告。 **Ni yào zhuājǐn shíjiān, zài xià Xīngqīyī qián xiě wán bàogào.** *You should make the best use of your time and write up the report before next Monday.*

zhuāi 拽 **v** fling, throw

zhuān 专 **TRAD** 專 **ADJ** concentrated, focused

zhuāncháng 专长 **n** special skill, specialist field, expertise

zhuānchéng 专程 **ADV** (make a trip) specially for

zhuānjiā 专家 [modif: 专 specialist + 家 expert] **n** expert, specialist ■ 他是计算机专家，关于计算机的事没有不知道的。 **Tā shì jìsuànjī zhuānjiā, guānyú jìsuànjī de shì tā méiyǒu bù zhīdào de.** *He is a computer expert and knows everything there is to know about computers.*

zhuānkē 专科 **n** special field of study, speciality

专科医生 **zhuānkē yīshēng** medical specialist

zhuānlì 专利 **n** patent

申请专利 **shēnqǐng zhuānlì** apply for patent

zhuānmén 专门 **ADJ** specialized, specialist ■ 他发表过很多语言学专门著作。 **Tā fābiǎoguo hěn duō yǔyánxué zhuānmén zhùzuò.** *He has published many specialist works on linguistics.*

zhuāntí 专题 [modif: 专 special + 题 topic, theme] **N** special topic, special subject

zhuānxīn 专心 [modif: 专 concentrate + 心 the heart] **ADJ** concentrate on, be absorbed in ■ 妹妹正在专心地做数学练习。 **Mèimei zhèngzài zhuānxīn de zuò shùxué liànxí.** *My younger sister is absorbed in doing her mathematics exercises.* ■ 他做事不专心，所以一事无成。 **Tā zuòshì bù zhuānxīn, suǒyǐ yí shì wú chéng.** *He does everything half-heartedly and, as a result, has accomplished nothing.*

zhuānyè 专业 [modif: 专 specialist + 业 profession] **N** specialist field of study, specialty ■ 他的专业是中国农村经济。 **Tā de zhuānyè shì Zhōngguó nóngcūn jīngjì.** *His specialist field is Chinese rural economics.*

zhuān 砖 **TRAD** 磚 **N** brick
砖头 zhuāntóu brick (块 **kuài**)

zhuānwǎ 砖瓦 **N** bricks and tiles, building material

zhuǎn 转 **TRAD** 轉 **V** **1** turn, change ■ 今天下午雨转晴。 **Jīntiān xiàwǔ yǔ zhuǎn qíng.** *This afternoon it'll change from a rainy day to a fine day.* **2** pass on, forward ■ 我已经把他的电子邮件转给他姐姐了。 **Wǒ yǐjīng bǎ tā de diànzǐ yóujiàn zhuǎn gěi tā jiějie le.** *I have forwarded his e-mail message to his sister.*
转车 zhuǎnchē transfer to another train (or bus) / 转学 zhuǎnxué transfer to another school

zhuǎnbiàn 转变 [comp: 转 turn + 变 change] **V** change, transform (usually for the better) ■ 他从一个小偷转变成一个对社会有用的公民。 **Tā cóng yí ge xiǎotōu zhuǎnbiàn chéng yí ge duì shèhuì yǒuyòng de gōngmín.** *He has transformed from a thief to a useful member of society.* ■ 她的态度转变了 — 从怀疑到信任。 **Tā de tàidù zhuǎnbiàn le – cóng huáiyí dào xìnrèn.** *Her attitude changed—from doubt to trust.*

zhuǎndá 转达 **V** pass on (a piece of information)

zhuǎngào 转告 [modif: 转 transfer + 告 tell] **V** pass along (word) ■ 请你把这个消息转告全班同学。 **Qǐng nǐ bǎ zhège xiāoxi zhuǎngào quán bān tóngxué.** *Please pass on the news to all your classmates.*

zhuǎn jīyīn 转基因 **ADJ** genetic modified
转基因食品 zhuǎn jīyīn shípǐn genetic modified food

zhuǎnràng 转让 **V** transfer (a property, rights, etc.)

zhuǎnyí 转移 [comp: 转 transfer + 移 move] **V** shift, transfer, divert

zhuǎnzhé 转折 **N** turn in the course of events

zhuàn 传 **TRAD** 傳 **N** biography
自传 zizhuàn autobiography

zhuànjì 传记 **N** biography

zhuàn 赚 **TRAD** 賺 **V** make money, make a profit

■ 现在赚钱不容易。 **Xiànzài zhuàn qián bù róngyì.** *It is not easy to make any money now.* ■ 这家小小的西餐馆去年赚了十万多。 **Zhè jiā xiǎoxiǎo de xīcānguǎn qùnián zhuànle shí wàn duō.** *This small Western-style restaurant made a profit of over 100,000 yuan last year.*

zhuāng 庄 **TRAD** 莊 **N** village

zhuāngjia 庄稼 **N** crop ■ 光种庄稼，很难富起来。 **Guāng zhòng zhuāngjia, hěn nán fù qǐlai.** *It is difficult to get rich raising crops only.*
庄稼人 zhuāngjiarén farmer (especially one that grows crops) / 庄稼地 zhuāngjiadì farmland

zhuāngyán 庄严 [comp: 庄 grave + 严 grave] **ADJ** solemn, dignified, stately

zhuāngzhòng 庄重 [comp: 庄 grave + 重 heavy] **ADJ** serious, grave, solemn

zhuāng 装 **TRAD** 裝 **V** pretend ■ 她不想跟他说话，所以装着没看见。 **Tā bù xiǎng gēn tā shuōhuà, suǒyǐ zhuāngzhe méi kànjiàn.** *She did not want to talk to him, so she pretended not to see him.* ■ 不懂就是不懂，你干吗装懂？ **Bù dǒng jiù shì bù dǒng, nǐ gànmá zhuāng dǒng?** *It's all right if you don't understand. Why do you pretend to understand?*

zhuāngbèi 装备 **V & N** equip; equipment, outfit
军事装备 jūnshì zhuāngbèi armament

zhuāngshì 装饰 **V & N** decorate; decoration ■ 他们用中国工艺品装饰客厅。 **Tā men yòng Zhōngguó gōngyìpǐn zhuāngshì kètīng.** *They decorated their living room with Chinese handicrafts.*
装饰品 zhuāngshì pǐn article for decoration, ornament

zhuāngxiè 装卸 **V** load and unload

zhuāngxiū 装修 **V** fit up (e.g. a house)

zhuàng 状 **TRAD** 狀 **N** form, shape

zhuàngkuàng 状况 [comp: 状 shape (of things) + 况 situation] **N** shape (of things), situation, condition ■ 目前全国的经济状况很好。 **Mùqián quánguó de jīngjì zhuàngkuàng hěn hǎo.** *At present the national economy is in good shape.* ■ 你爷爷的身体状况怎么样？ **Nǐ yéye de shēntǐ zhuàngkuàng zěnmeyàng?** *How is your grandpa's health?*

zhuàngtài 状态 [comp: 状 shape (of things) + 态 condition] **N** state (of affairs), appearance ■ 运动员的精神状态非常重要。 **Yùndòngyuán de jīngshén zhuàngtài fēicháng zhòngyào.** *It is important for an athlete to be in a good mental state.*

zhuàng 壮 **TRAD** 壯 **ADJ** **1** robust, sturdy **2** magnificent

zhuàngguān 壮观 [modif: 壮 magnificent + 观 view] **N** magnificent sight

zhuànglì 壮丽 [comp: 壮 magnificent + 丽 beautiful] **ADJ** beautiful and magnificent, grand and glorious

zhuàngliè 壮烈 **ADJ** heroic, brave

zhuàng 撞 **V** bump against, collide ■ 两辆汽车相撞，造成重大交通事故。 **Liǎng liàng qìchē xiāng**

zhuàng, zàochéng zhòngdà jiāotōng shìgù. *The two cars collided and caused a major road accident.*

zhuàng 幢 MEASURE WORD (for houses)
一幢大楼 yí zhuàng dàlóu a big (multi-storied) building

zhuī 追 v chase, run after ■ 孩子们在操场上你追我、我追你。**Háizimen zài cāochǎng shang nǐ zhuī wǒ, wǒ zhuī nǐ.** *Children chased one another on the playground.*
追上 zhuīshang catch up with, catch ■ 我追不上他。**Wǒ zhuī bu shang tā.** *I can't catch up with him.*

zhuīdào 追悼 v mourn over (the death of somebody)

zhuīdàohuì 追悼会 N memorial service, memorial meeting

zhuījiū 追究 v get to the roots, investigate the origin
追究责任 zhuījiū zérèn investigate to find out who is responsible for something (e.g. rumor, accident)

zhuīqiú 追求 [comp: 追 chase + 求 seek] v pursue, seek ■ 人人追求幸福。*Everyone pursues happiness.*

zhuì 坠 TRAD 墜 v fall, drop

zhǔn 准 TRAD 準 ADJ accurate, exact ■ 电子手表一般都很准。**Diànzǐ shǒubiǎo yìbān dōu hěn zhǔn.** *Electronic watches are usually quite accurate.*

zhǔnbèi 准备 V & N prepare; preparation ■ 他正在准备在下午会议上的发言。**Tā zhèngzài zhǔnbèi zài xiàwǔ huìyì shang de fāyán.** *He is preparing the speech to be delivered at this afternoon's meeting.* ■ 老师上课前要做很多准备。**Lǎoshī shàngkè qián yào zuò hěn duō zhǔnbèi.** *The teacher needs to do a lot of preparation before class.*
准备好 zhǔnbèi hǎo be well prepared

zhǔnquè 准确 [comp: 准 accurate + 确 verified] ADJ accurate, exact ■ 发音不准确，有时候会闹笑话。**Fāyīn bù zhǔnquè, yǒushíhou huì nào xiàohua.** *Inaccurate pronunciation can sometimes have comical effects.* ■ 你的计算不够准确。**Nǐ de jìsuàn bú gòu zhǔnquè.** *Your calculation is not accurate enough.*

zhǔnshí 准时 ADJ punctual, on time ■ 这里的火车非常准时。**Zhèlǐ de huǒchē fēicháng zhǔnshí.** *The trains here are very punctual.* ■ 我从小养成了准时的习惯。**Wǒ cóngxiǎo yǎngchéngle zhǔnshí de xíguàn.** *In my childhood I formed the habit of being punctual.*

zhǔnzé 准则 N norm, standard
行为准则 xíngwéi zhǔnzé code of conduct

zhuō 捉 v catch, capture ■ 你怎么捉得住猫？你怎么捉得住猫？**Nǐ zěnme zhuō de zhù māo?** *How can you catch a cat?*

zhuōzi 桌子 [suffix: 桌 table + 子 nominal suffix] N table, desk (张 **zhāng**) ■ 桌子上有几本书和一个杯子。**Zhuōzi shang yǒu jǐ běn shū hé yí ge bēizi.** *There are some books and a cup on the table.*

zhuó 卓 ADJ outstanding

zhuóyuè 卓越 ADJ outstanding, exceptional, brilliant

zhuó 着 v apply, use

zhuóshǒu 着手 [v+obj: 着 apply + 手 hand] v begin, set out

zhuóxiǎng 着想 v consider (somebody's interest) ■ 我是为你着想。**Wǒ shì wèi nǐ zhuóxiǎng.** *I'm considering your interest. (→ I'm doing this for your good.)*

zhuózhòng 着重 v emphasize, underline, stress

zhuó 琢 v chisel, carve

zhuómó 琢磨 v carve and polish

NOTE: See note on 琢磨 **zuómo.**

zī 咨 v consult

zīxún 咨询 [comp: 咨 consult + 询 inquire] V & N seek advice from, consult

zī 姿 N looks, appearance

zīshì 姿势 N posture, carriage

zītài 姿态 N 1 posture 2 attitude, pose
保持低姿态 bǎochí dīzītài keep a low profile

zī 资 TRAD 資 N money, property

zīběn 资本 [comp: 资 capital + 本 principal] N capital ■ 他开工厂的资本是从银行借来的。**Tā kāi gōngchǎng de zīběn shì cóng yínháng jièlai de.** *The capital with which he opened his factory was borrowed from the bank.*
资本主义 zīběn zhǔyì capitalism

zīchǎn 资产 N asset, property, estate

zīgé 资格 N qualification ■ 她通过考试，终于取得了教师资格。**Tā tōngguò kǎoshì, zhōngyú qǔdé le jiàoshī zīgé.** *She passed the exams and got teaching qualification.*

zījīn 资金 [comp: 资 capital + 金 gold, fund] v fund ■ 学校向教育局申请建造教室的资金。**Xuéxiào xiàng jiàoyùjú shēnqǐng jiànzào jiàoshì de zījīn.** *The school applied to the education bureau for funds to build new classrooms.*

zīliào 资料 [comp: 资 capital + 料 material] N material, data ■ 王老师从北京带回来很多中文教学的参考资料。**Wáng lǎoshī cóng Běijīng dài huílai hěn duō Zhōngwén jiàoxué de cānkǎo zīliào.** *Teacher Wang brought back from Beijing a great deal of reference materials for teaching and learning Chinese.*

zīshēn 资深 ADJ having high credentials or seniority, senior

zīyuán 资源 [modif: 资 capital + 源 source] N natural resources ■ 我们要开发海洋资源。**Wǒmen yào kāifā hǎiyáng zīyuán.** *We will develop the natural resources of seas and oceans.*

zīzhù 资助 v provide financial support, fund

zī 滋 v grow

zīrùn 滋润 ADJ & v moist; moisten

zīwèi 滋味 N taste, flavor, relish

zīzhǎng 滋长 v grow, develop, engender

zǐ 子 N son

长子 **zhǎngzi** the first son

zǐdàn 子弹 N bullet, cartridge

zǐdì 子弟 N children and younger family members

zǐsūn 子孙 N children and grandchildren, descendants

子孙后代 **zǐsūn hòudài** descendants, posterity

zǐ-nǚ 子女 N sons and daughters, one's children

zǐ 仔 ADJ careful

zǐxì 仔细 ADJ very careful, paying attention to details ■ 考试的时候一定要仔细看清题目。 *Kǎoshì de shíhou yídìng yào zǐxì kànqīng tímù. At an examination be sure to read the questions very, very carefully.*

zǐ 紫 ADJ purple ■ 他冻得脸都发紫了。 *Tā dòng de liǎn dōu fā zǐ le. He was so cold that his face turned purple.*

zì 自 PREP same as 从 **cóng**. Only used in written Chinese.

zìbēi 自卑 [modif: 自 self + 卑 abase] v feel oneself inferior

自卑感 **zìbēigǎn** inferiority complex, sense of inferiority

zìcóng 自从 [comp: 自 from + 从 from] PREP from, since ■ 自从2001年9月11日，世界各地的飞机场都加强了行李检查。 *Zìcóng èr-líng-líng-yī nián Jiǔyuè shíyī rì, shìjiè gèdì de fēijīchǎng dōu jiāqiángle xíngli jiǎnchá. Since September 11, 2001, airports all over the world have strengthened their luggage check system.* ■ 自从认识他以来，我渐渐对他产生了好感。 *Zìcóng rènshi tā yǐlái, wǒ jiànjiàn duì tā chǎnshēngle hǎogǎn. Since I came to know him, I have gradually grown fond of him.*

zìdòng 自动 [modif: 自 self + 动 act] ADJ automatic ■ 这台机器会自动关闭。 *Zhè tái jīqì huì zìdòng guānbì. This machine will turn off automatically.*

自动化 **zìdònghuà** automatic, automation

zìfā 自发 ADJ spontaneous

zìfèi 自费 [modif: 自 self + 费 cost] ADJ self-supporting, paid by oneself ■ 我不明白，他们怎么有钱送孩子去国外自费留学？ *Wǒ bù míngbái, tāmen zěnme yǒu qián sòng háizi qù guówài zìfèi liúxué? I don't understand how they could afford to send their child overseas as a self-supporting student.*

自费留学生 **zìfèi liúxuéshēng** self-supporting foreign student, fee-paying foreign student

zìháo 自豪 [modif: 自 self + 豪 pride] v be very proud of oneself

zìjǐ 自己 PRON self, one's own ■ 自己的工作自己做。 *Zìjǐ de gōngzuò zìjǐ zuò. Each must do their own work.* ■ 你不能只想到自己。 *Nǐ bù néng zhǐ xiǎngdào zìjǐ. You mustn't think of yourself only.*

你自己 **nǐ zìjǐ** yourself / 你们自己 **nǐmen zìjǐ**

yourselves / 他/她自己 **tā zìjǐ** himself/herself / 他们自己 **tāmen zìjǐ** themselves / 我自己 **wǒ zìjǐ** myself / 我们自己 **wǒmen zìjǐ** ourselves

zìjué 自觉 [modif: 自 self + 觉 conscious, aware] ADJ being aware of, being conscious of, voluntary, conscientious ■ 孩子自觉帮助做家务。 *Háizi zìjué bāngzhù zuò jiāwù. The child helps with the household chores voluntarily.* ■ 他犯这个错误不是自觉的。 *Tā fàn zhège cuòwù bú shì zìjué de. He made the mistake without being aware of it.*

zì lì gēng shēng 自力更生 v rely on one's own efforts, self-reliant

zìmǎn 自满 [modif: 自 self + 满 full] ADJ complacent, self-satisfied ■ 我们取得了很好的成绩，但是不能自满。 *Wǒmen qǔdé le hěn hǎode chéngjì, dànshì bùnéng zìmǎn. We've made good achievements, but we mustn't be complacent.*

zìrán 自然 I N nature ■ 哲学问题之一就是人和自然的关系。 *Zhéxué wèntí zhī yī jiù shì rén hé zìrán de guānxi. One philosophical issue is the relationship between humankind and nature.* II ADJ natural ■ 父母爱子女是自然的。 *Fù-mǔ ài zǐnǚ shì zìrán de. It is only natural that parents love their children.* ■ 她说话的样子很不自然。 *Tā shuōhuà de yàngzi hěn bú zìrán. The way she speaks is quite affected.*

zìshā 自杀 v & N attempt or commit suicide; suicide

zìsī 自私 [comp: 自 self + 私 private] ADJ selfish, egoistic ■ 独生子女往往比较自私，对不对？ *Dúshēngzǐ nǚ wǎngwǎng bǐjiào zìsī, duì búduì? Is it true that an only child tends to be selfish?*

zìxìn 自信 ADJ self-confident

缺乏自信 **quēfá zìxìn** lacking in self-confidence

zìxíngchē 自行车 [modif: 自 self + 行 walking + 车 vehicle] N bicycle (辆 **liàng**) ■ 我会骑自行车，但是不会修自行车。 *Wǒ huì qí zìxíngchē, dànshì bú huì xiū zìxíngchē. I can ride a bicycle, but I can't fix it.*

zìxué 自学 [modif: 自 self + 学 study] v study independently, teach oneself ■ 他自学日语三年，已经能看懂日文书了。 *Tā zìxué Rìyǔ sān nián, yǐjīng néng kàndǒng Rìwén shū le. He taught himself Japanese for three years and is now able to read Japanese books.* ■ 我佩服自学成才的人。 *Wǒ pèifu zìxué chéngcái de rén. I admire those who have made themselves useful through self-study.*

zìyóu 自由 ADJ & N free, unrestrained; freedom, liberty ■ 他不愿意结婚，因为他喜欢自由。 *Tā bú yuànyì jiéhūn, yīnwèi tā xǐhuan zìyóu. He is unwilling to marry because he enjoys his freedom.* ■ 他觉得和父母住在一起不自由。 *Tā juéde hé fù-mǔ zhù zài yìqǐ bú zìyóu. Living with his parents, he does not feel free.*

zìyuàn 自愿 [modif: 自 self + 愿 willing] ADJ voluntary, of one's own accord

zìzhǔ 自主 **v** act on one's own, keep the initiative in one's own hands

zìzhùcān 自助餐 [modif: 自助 self-help + 餐 meal] **n** buffet dinner, buffet

zì 字 **n** Chinese character ■ 中国字很有意思。**Zhōngguó zì hěn yǒu yìsi.** *Chinese characters are very interesting.* ■ 这个字是什么意思？怎么念？ **Zhège zì shì shénme yìsi? zěnme niàn?** *What is the meaning of this Chinese character? How is it pronounced?*

zìmǔ 字母 **n** letter (of an alphabet)
字母表 **zìmǔbiǎo** alphabet

zìmù 字幕 **n** caption, subtitle

zi 子 **suffix** (forming a noun, e.g. **bēizi** 杯子, **xiāngzi** 箱子, etc.)

zōng 宗 **n** ancestor

zōngjiào 宗教 **n** religion
宗教信仰 **zōngjiào xìnyǎng** religious belief

zōngzhǐ 宗旨 **n** primary purpose, aim

zōng 棕 **n** palm, palm fiber

zōngsè 棕色 **n** brown

zōng 综 **trad** 綜 **adj** comprehensive

zōnghé 综合 **adj** comprehensive, synthetical

zōng 踪 **n** footprint
跟踪 **gēnzōng** follow the tracks of, shadow (somebody)

zōngjì 踪迹 [comp: 踪 footprint + 迹 trace] **n** trace, track

zǒng 总 **trad** 總 **adv** always, invariably ■ 他总觉得自己正确。**Tā zǒng juéde zìjǐ zhèngquè.** *He always thinks himself correct.* ■ 你为什么总这么晚起床？ **Nǐ wèishénme zǒng zhème wǎn qǐchuáng?** *Why do you always get up so late?*

zǒngcái 总裁 **n** CEO, director general

zǒng ér yán zhī 总而言之 **idiom** same as 总之 **zǒngzhī**

zǒnggòng 总共 [comp: 总 total + 共 altogether] **adv** in all, altogether

zǒnghé 总和 [modif: 总 total + 和 sum] **n** sum total

zǒngjié 总结 [modif: 总 general + 结 conclude, conclusion] **v & n** sum up, do a review of one's past work or life experiences; summary, a general view of one's past work or life experiences ■ 每年年底，公司都要总结一年的工作。**Měi nián niándǐ, gōngsī dōuyào zǒngjié yì nián de gōngzuò.** *At the end of every year the company does a general review of the work done.* ■ 这个计划已经完成，我们应该做一个总结了。**Zhège jìhuà yǐjīng wánchéng, wǒmen yīnggāi zuò yí ge zǒngjié le.** *Now that this plan is fulfilled, we should do a general review.*

zǒnglǐ 总理 [modif: 总 general + 理 administer] **n** premier, prime minister ■ 中国的国务院总理是政府首脑。**Zhōngguó de guówùyuàn zǒnglǐ shì zhèngfǔ shǒunǎo.** *The premier of the Chinese State Council is China's head of government.*

zǒngshì 总是 **adv** same as 总 **zǒng**

zǒngsuàn 总算 **adv** at long last, finally ■ 今天总算是星期五了。**Jīntiān zǒngsuàn shì xīngqīwǔ le.** *At long last, it's Friday today.*

zǒngtǒng 总统 [modif: 总 general + 统 rule, command] **n** president (of a country) ■ 美国每四年举行总统选举。**Měiguó měi sì nián jǔxíng zǒngtǒng xuǎnjǔ.** *The USA holds its presidential election every four years.*

zǒngzhī 总之 **adv** in a word, in short ■ 总之，你的计划是不可行的。**Zǒngzhī, nǐde jìhuà shì bùkě xíng de.** *Your plan, in short, is not feasible.*

zòng 纵 **trad** 縱 **adv** from north to south, lengthwise, vertical

zònghéng 纵横 **adv** in length and breadth, vertically and horizontally

zǒu 走 **v** walk; leave ■ 我家离学校很近，我每天走到学校。**Wǒ jiā lí xuéxiào hěn jìn, wǒ měi tiān zǒudào xuéxiào.** *My home is close to the school. I walk to school every day.* ■ 时间不早了，我们得走了。**Shíjiān bù zǎo le, wǒmen děi zǒu le.** *It's quite late. We've got to go.*

zǒuláng 走廊 [modif: 走 walk + 廊 corridor, porch] **n** corridor, hallway

zǒulòu 走漏 **v** leak (information)

zǒusī 走私 **v** smuggle
走私犯 **zǒusīfàn** smuggler

zòu 奏 **v** play a musical instrument (See **yǎnzòu** 演奏.)

zòu 揍 **v** beat, hit
挨揍 **áizòu** get a thrashing, be beaten up

zū 租 **v & n** rent, hire, charter; rent (money) ■ 在这座大楼租一个办公室，要多少钱？**Zài zhè zuò dàlóu zū yí ge bàngōngshì, yào duōshaoqián?** *How much is it to rent an office in this building?*
房租 **fángzū** (housing) rent

zūjīn 租金 [modif: 租 rent + 金 gold] **n** money paid for lease or hiring, rent

zūlìn 租赁 **v 1** hire, rent **2** lease, lease out

zú 足 **n** foot

zúqiú 足球 [modif: 足 foot + 球 ball] **n** soccer ■ 我爸爸年轻的时候，常常踢足球，现在还爱看足球比赛。**Wǒ bàba niánqīng de shíhou, chángcháng tī zúqiú, xiànzài hái ài kàn zúqiú bǐsài.** *My father often played soccer when he was young, and now he still enjoys watching soccer games.*

zúyǐ 足以 **adv** enough, sufficient

zú 族 **n** clan, nationality (See **mínzú** 民族.)

zǔ 阻 **v 1** resist, prevent **2** hinder, block

zǔ'ài 阻碍 [comp: 阻 hinder + 碍 hinder] **v** hinder, obstruct, impel

zǔlán 阻拦 [comp: 阻 stop + 拦 obstruct] **v** bar the way, stop

zǔlì 阻力 [modif: 阻 resist + 力 strength, force] **n** resistance, obstacle

zǔnáo 阻挠 [comp: 阻 hinder + 挠 obstruct] **v** obstruct, thwart, stand in the way

zǔzhǐ 阻止 [comp: 阻 stop + 止 stop] **v** prevent, stop, hold back

zǔ 祖 **N** ancestor

zǔfù 祖父 [modif: 祖 ancestor + 父 father] **N** grandfather ■ 我祖父七十多岁了，还每天锻炼身体。 **Wǒ zǔfù qīshí duō suì le, hái měi tiān duànliàn shēntǐ.** *My grandfather is over seventy and still does physical exercise every day.*

zǔguó 祖国 [modif: 祖 ancestor + 国 country] **N** motherland, fatherland ■ 我爱祖国。 **Wǒ ài zǔguó.** *I love my motherland.* ■ 他虽然住在国外，但深深地关心祖国。 **Tā suīrán zhù zai guówài, dàn shēnshēn de guānxīn zǔguó.** *Although living in a foreign country, he is still deeply concerned for his motherland.*

zǔmǔ 祖母 [modif: 祖 ancestor + 母 mother] **N** grandmother ■ 我祖母一个人住，我们常去看她。 **Wǒ zǔmǔ yígerén zhù, wǒmen cháng qù kàn tā.** *My grandmother lives by herself. We often go to see her.*

zǔxiān 祖先 [comp: 祖 ancestor + 先 first] **N** ancestor, ancestry

zǔ 组 **TRAD** 組 **N** group ■ 老师把全班分为三个组，练习口语。 **Lǎoshī bǎ quán bān fēn wéi sān ge zǔ, liànxí kǒuyǔ.** *The teacher divided the class into three groups for oral Chinese practice.*

zǔchéng 组成 **v** make up, compose, consist of ■ 这个专家组由五名世界级科学家组成。 **Zhège zhuānjiāzǔ yóu wǔ míng shìjiè jí kēxuéjiā zǔchéng.** *This expert panel is made up of five world-class scientists.*

zǔhé 组合 **I v** make up, compose, constitue **II N** association, combination

zǔzhī 组织 [comp: 组 to group + 织 to weave] **v & N** organize, arrange for; organization, organized system ■ 学校正在组织去北京旅游。 **Xuéxiào zhèngzài zǔzhī qù Běijīng lǚyóu.** *The school is organizing a trip to Beijing.* ■ 我父亲不参加任何组织。 **Wǒ fùqin bù cānjiā rènhé zǔzhī.** *My father did not join any organization.*

zuān 钻¹ **TRAD** 鑽 **N** drill

zuānyán 钻研 [comp: 钻 drill, bore into + 研 study, research] **v** study in great depth, study intensively ■ 这位科学家有时候钻研一个问题而忘了吃饭。 **Zhè wèi kēxuéjiā yǒushíhou zuānyán yí ge wèntí ér wàngle chīfàn.** *Sometimes this scientist studies a problem so intensively that he forgets his meals.*

zuàn 钻² **TRAD** 鑽 **N** diamond

zuànshí 钻石 **N** diamond (粒 **lì**, 颗 **kē**) 一枚三克拉的钻石戒指 yīméi sān kèlā de zuànshí jièzhi a 3-carat diamond ring

zuǐ 嘴 **N** mouth ■ 不要用嘴呼吸，要用鼻子呼吸。 **Bú yào yòng zuǐ hūxī, yào yòng bízi hūxī.** *Breathe through the nose, not the mouth.*

zuǐchún 嘴唇 **N** lip

zuì 最 **ADV** most (used before an adjective to indicate the superlative degree) ■ 中国是世界上人口最多的国家。 **Zhōngguó shì shìjiè shang rénkǒu zuì duō de guójiā.** *China is the most populous country in the world.* ■ 我最讨厌电视广告。 **Wǒ zuì tǎoyàn diànshì guǎnggào.** *I detest TV commercials most.*

zuìchū 最初 **N** the initial stage, initially ■ 最初我不习惯那里的生活。 **Zuìchū wǒ bù xíguàn nàli de shēnghuó.** *Initially I was not used to the life there.*

zuìhǎo 最好 [modif: 最 most + 好 good] **ADV** had better ■ 你最好常去看望奶奶。 **Nǐ zuìhǎo cháng qù kànwàng nǎinai.** *You'd better visit your grandma often.*

zuìhòu 最后 **N** the final stage, finally ■ 笑得最后，才笑得最好。 **Xiào de zuìhòu, cái xiào de zuìhǎo.** *He who laughs last laughs best.* ■ 最后他同意了我们的观点。 **Zuìhòu tā tóngyìle wǒmen de guāndiǎn.** *Finally, he accepted our views.*

zuìjìn 最近 **N** recently, recent time ■ 我最近特别忙。 **Wǒ zuìjìn tèbié máng.** *I'm particularly busy these days.* ■ 你最近看过什么好电影吗？ **Nǐ zuìjìn kànguo shénme hǎo diànyǐng ma?** *Have you seen any good movies lately?*

zuì 醉 **v** get drunk, be intoxicated ■ 我没醉，我还能喝。 **Wǒ méi zuì, wǒ hái néng hē.** *I'm not drunk. I can drink more.* ■ 他昨天晚上喝醉了，今天头疼。 **Tā zuótiān wǎnshang hē zuì le, jīntiān tóuténg.** *He was drunk last night and this morning he has a headache.*

zuì 罪 **N** crime, offense ■ 被告不承认自己有罪。 **Bèigào bùchéngrèn zìjǐ yǒuzuì.** *The defendant did not admit to any offense. (→ The defendant pleaded not guilty.)*

zuìfàn 罪犯 **N** criminal, offender, culprit ■ 警察在案发第二天就抓到了罪犯。 **Jǐngchá zài'àn fā dì èr tiān jiù zhuā dào le zuìfàn.** *The police caught the criminal the day after the crime.*

zūn 尊 **v** respect

zūnjìng 尊敬 [comp: 尊 respect + 敬 respect] **v** respect, honor ■ 中国的传统是尊敬老人。 **Zhōngguó de chuántǒng shì zūnjìng lǎorén.** *A tradition of the Chinese is to respect the aged.*

zūnyán 尊严 **N** dignity, honor

zūnzhòng 尊重 **v** respect, esteem, value

zūn 遵 **v** obey

zūnshǒu 遵守 [comp: 遵 obey + 守 abide by] **v** observe, abide by ■ 你既然在这个学校学习，就要遵守学校的各项规定。 **Nǐ jìrán zài zhège xuéxiào xuéxí, jiù yào zūnshǒu xuéxiào de gè xiàng guīdìng.** *Since you are studying in this school, you should observe its regulations.*

zūnxún 遵循 **v** follow faithfully, adhere to

zuó 昨 **N** yesterday

zuótiān 昨天 [modif: 昨 past + 天 day] N yesterday ■ 你昨天晚上去哪里了？ **Nǐ zuótiān wǎnshang qù nǎli le?** *Where were you yesterday evening?*

zuó 琢 as in 琢磨 **zuómo**

zuómo 琢磨 V turn over in one's mind, think over, ponder

NOTE: **zuómo** 琢磨 is different from 琢磨 **zhuómó** in pronunciation and meaning.

zuǒ 左 N the left side ■ 我弟弟用左手吃饭、写字。 **Wǒ dìdi yòng zuǒshǒu chīfàn, xiězì.** *My younger brother eats and writes with the left hand.*

zuǒbian 左边 [modif: 左 left + 边 side] N the left side, the left-hand side ■ 坐在李先生左边的那位小姐是谁？ **Zuò zai Lǐ xiānsheng zuǒbian de nà wèi xiǎojiě shì shuí?** *Who is the young lady sitting on the left of Mr Li?*

zuǒyòu 左右 [comp: 左 left + 右 right] ADV approximately, nearly, about ■ 今天最高温度二十度左右。 **Jīntiān zuìgāo wēndù èrshí dù zuǒyòu.** *Today's maximum temperature is about twenty degrees.*

zuò 坐 V sit ■ 请坐！ **Qǐng zuò!** *Sit down, please!* ■ 她正坐在窗边看书。 **Tā zhèng zuò zài chuāngbiān kànshū.** *She's sitting by the window, reading.*

zuò 作 V same as 做 **zuò**

NOTE: 做 **zuò** and 作 **zuò** have the same pronunciation and often the same meaning, but 做 **zuò** is much more commonly used while 作 **zuò** occurs only in certain set expressions.

zuòbì 作弊 V practice fraud, cheat
考试作弊 **kǎoshì zuòbì** cheat in an examination

zuòfèi 作废 V become invalid

zuòfēng 作风 N way of behavior, way of working, style
独断独行的领导作风 **dúduàndúxíng de lǐngdǎo zuòfēng** autocratic style of leadership

zuòjiā 作家 [modif: 作 create + 家 expert] N writer (especially of literary works, e.g. novels, stories) ■ 在过去，作家是很受人尊敬的。 **Zài guòqù, zuòjiā shì hěn shòu rén zūnjìng de.** *In the past writers were very much respected.*

zuòpǐn 作品 [modif: 作 create + 品 article] N literary or artistic work ■ 这位作家又有新作品了。 **Zhè wèi zuòjiā yòu yǒu xīn zuòpǐn le.** *This writer has written another work.*

zuòwéi 作为 PREP as, in the capacity of

zuòwén 作文 [modif: 作 create + 文 writing] N (student's) composition ■ 她的作文经常得到老师的表扬。 **Tā de zuòwén jīngcháng dédào lǎoshī de biǎoyáng.** *Her compositions are often commended by the teacher.*

zuòxī 作息 N work and rest
作息制度 **zuòxī zhìdù** daily schedule, timetable

zuòyè 作业 N school assignment, homework

■ 中国的中小学生每天要做很多作业。 **Zhōngguó de zhōng-xiǎo xuéshēng měi tiān yào zuò hěn duō zuòyè.** *School children in China have lots of homework to do every day.*

zuòyòng 作用 [comp: 作 work + 用 use] N function, role ■ 他在这次谈判中起了很大作用。 **Tā zài zhè cì tánpàn zhong qǐle hěn dà zuòyòng.** *He played a major role in the negotiations.*
zài … zhōng qǐ zuòyòng 在 … 中起作用 play a role in …, perform a function in …

zuòzhě 作者 [suffix: 作 create + 者 nominal suffix] N author ■ 这本书的作者是一位女作家。 **Zhè běn shū de zuòzhě shì yí wèi nǚ zuòjiā.** *The author of this book is a woman writer.*

zuò 座 MEASURE WORD (for large and solid objects, such as a large building)
一座城市 yí zuò chéngshì a city / 一座大楼 yí zuò dàlóu a big building / 一座大学 yí zuò dàxué a university / 一座工厂 yí zuò gōngchǎng a factory / 一座桥 yí zuò qiáo a bridge / 一座山 yí zuò shān a mountain, a hill

zuòtán 座谈 [comp: 座 seat + 谈 talk] V have an informal discussion, have an informal meeting ■ 校长今天下午和一年级学生座谈。 **Xiàozhǎng jīntiān xiàwǔ hé yī niánjí xuésheng zuòtán.** *The principal will have an informal discussion with first-year students this afternoon.*

zuòtánhuì 座谈会 N an informal discussion, forum

zuòwèi 座位 [comp: 座 seat + 位 seat] N seat ■ 请你给我留一个座位，我马上就到。 **Qǐng nǐ gěi wǒ liú yí ge zuòwèi, wǒ mǎshàng jiù dào.** *Please save a seat for me. I'll be there soon.* ■ 这个座位有人吗？ **Zhège zuòwèi yǒu rén ma?** *Is this seat taken?*

zuòyòumíng 座右铭 N motto ■ "为社会做贡献" 是我的座右铭。 **"Wèi shèhuì zuò gòngxiàn" shì wǒde zuòyòumíng.** *"Contribute to the society" is my motto.*

zuò 做 V 1 do ■ 这件事我不会做。 **Zhè jiàn shì wǒ bú huì zuò.** *I don't know how to do this.* ■ "你会做这个作业吗？" "会，我已经做好了。" **"Nǐ huì zuò zhège zuòyè ma?" "Huì, wǒ yǐjīng zuòhǎo le."** *"Can you do this assignment?" "Yes, I can. I've already done it."* 2 make ■ 这张桌子是我爸爸做的。 **Zhè zhāng zhuōzi shì wǒ bàba zuò de.** *This table was made by my father.* ■ 中国酒是用米做的。 **Zhōngguó jiǔ shì yòng mǐ zuò de.** *Chinese wine is made from rice.*

NOTE: See note on 作 **zuò**.

zuòdōng 做东 V play host, stand the treat

zuòfǎ 做法 [modif: 做 do + 法 method] N way of doing things, method, practice ■ 他这种做法不讲原则，我不赞成。 **Tā zhè zhǒng zuòfǎ bù jiǎng yuánzé, wǒ bú zànchéng.** *This kind of practice of his is unprincipled and I don't approve of it.*

Z

zuòfàn 做饭 N cook, prepare a meal ■ "你们家里谁做饭？" "我，经常是我做饭。" **"Nǐmen jiāli shuí zuòfàn?" "Wǒ, jīngcháng shì wǒ zuòfàn."** *"Who does the cooking in your family?" "I do. I usually do the cooking."*

zuògōng 做工 V do manual work, work ■ 今年夏天你要去哪里做工？ **Jīnnián xiàtiān nǐ yào qù nǎlǐ zuògōng?** *Where are you going to work this summer?*

zuòkè 做客 V be a guest, visit

zuòmèng 做梦 N & V 1 dream; have a dream 2 daydream; have a pipe dream 别做梦了。 Bié zuòmèng le. Don't be daydreaming.

zuòzhǔ 做主 V be one's own master, decide for oneself ■ 我自己的事自己作主。 **Wǒ zìjǐ de shì zìjǐ zuòzhǔ.** *I'll decide my matters by myself. (→ I'll be my own master.)*

English-Chinese Word Finder

A

abandon **fàngqì** 放弃 55, **pāoqì** 抛弃 138

abdomen **dùzi** 肚子 47

abide by **zūnshǒu** 遵守 244

ability **běnlǐng** 本领 9, **běnshì** 本事 9, **nénglì** 能力 134

able (person) **nénggàn** 能干 134

able to **huì** 会 84, **néng** 能 134, **nénggòu** 能够 134

abnormal **yìcháng** 异常 213, **fǎncháng** 反常 52

about **dàyuē** 大约 36, **guānyú** 关于 71

above **shàng** 上 157, **shàngbian** 上边 158, **shàngmiàn** 上面 158

absent (from a meeting, a class, etc.) **quēxí** 缺席 151

absent (from school without leave) **kuàngkè** 旷课 112

absent (from work without leave) **kuànggōng** 旷工 112

absolute **juéduì** 绝对 105

absorb **xīshōu** 吸收 191

abstract **chōuxiàng** 抽象 27

absurd **huāngmiù** 荒谬 82

abundant **fēngfù** 丰富 57, **chōngpèi** 充沛 27

academic degree **xuéwèi** 学位 205

academy of science **kēxuéyuàn** 科学院 108

accept **jiēshòu** 接受 98, **shōuxia** 收下 167

accident **shìgù** 事故 166

accompany **péi** 陪 138

accomplish **wánchéng** 完成 185

accord with **fúhé** 符合 59

according to **ànzhào** 按照 2, **gēnjù** 根据 65

according to a fixed time **ànshí** 按时 2

account for **jiěshì** 解释 99

accountant/accounting **kuàijì** 会计 112

accumulate **jīlěi** 积累 87

accurate **jīngquè** 精确 102, **zhǔnquè** 准确 241

(be) accustomed **xíguàn** 习惯 192

ache (v.) **tòng** 痛 181

achieve **dádào** 达到 33, **qǔdé** 取得 150

achievement **chéngguǒ** 成果 25, **chéngjì** 成绩 25, **shōuhuò** 收获 167

achievement (great) **chéngjiù** 成就 25

acknowledge **chéngrèn** 承认 26, **kěndìng** 肯定 110

acquire experience **qǔdé jīngyàn** 取得经验 102

acrobat **zájì yǎnyuán** 杂技演员 223

acrobatics **zájì** 杂技 223

act (v.) **yǎn** 演 207

action **xíngdòng** 行动 202

active **huóyuè** 活跃 85, **jījí** 积极 87

activity **huódòng** 活动 85

actor/actress **yǎnyuán** 演员 208

actual facts **zhēnxiàng** 真相 230

actuality **xiànshí** 现实 195

actually **qíshí** 其实 143

acupuncture and moxibustion **zhēnjiǔ** 针灸 230

acute **jùliè** 剧烈 105

acute (disease) **jíxìng** 急性 88

AD (Anno Domini) **gōngyuán** 公元 67

add **jiā** 加 90, **tiān** 添 179

add up to **gòngjì** 共计 67

additionally **yòu** 又 219

address (n.) **dìzhǐ** 地址 42

adequate **chōngfèn** 充分 27, **chōngzú** 充足 27

adjust **tiáozhěng** 调整 179, **tiáojié** 调节 179

administer **guǎnlǐ** 管理 71

administration **xíngzhèng** 行政 202

administration charge **guǎnlǐ fèi** 管理费 56

administrative department **xíngzhèng bùmén** 行政部门 202

admiration ticket **ménpiào** 门票 140

admission by tickets **píngpiàorùchǎng** 凭票入场 142

admit (mistakes, errors, etc.) **chéngrèn** 承认 26

adolescent **shàonián** 少年 159

adopt **cǎiqǔ** 采取 18

adult **chéngrén** 成人 25

advance **cùjìn** 促进 32, **tígāo** 提高 177, **tíqián** 提前 178

advanced **gāojí** 高级 63, **xiānjìn** 先进 194

advantageous **yǒulì** 有利 218

advertisement **guǎnggào** 广告 72

advise **quàn** 劝 151, **zhǔfù** 嘱咐 239

advisor **gùwèn** 顾问 69

advocate (v.) **tíchàng** 提倡 177, **zhǔzhāng** 主张 239

affair **shì** 事 165, **shìqing** 事情 166

affect **guānxi** 关系 70, **yǐngxiǎng** 影响 216

affection **gǎnqíng** 感情 62

affectionate **qīnrè** 亲热 147

affirmative **kěndìng** 肯定 110

after **yǐhòu** 以后 213, **zhī hòu** 之后 232

after all **bìjìng** 毕竟 10

afternoon **xiàwǔ** 下午 193

afterwards **hòulái** 后来 79, **ránhòu** 然后 151

(be) afraid **pà** 怕 137

again **yòu** 又 219, **zài** 再 224

age (n.) **niánjì** 年纪 135, **niánlíng** 年龄 135

agenda **yìshì rìchéng** 议事日程 154

agent **dàilǐrén** 代理人 36

aggravate **jiājù** 加剧 90, **èhuà** 恶化 50

agile **líng** 灵 120, **mǐnjié** 敏捷 129

agitate **gǔdòng** 鼓动 69

agonized **bēitòng** 悲痛 8, **tòngxīn** 痛心 200

agree **tóngyì** 同意 181

agreement **hétóng** 合同 77

agreement of intent **yìxiàngshū** 意向书 214

agriculture **nóngyè** 农业 136

ah **ā** 啊 1, **yā** 呀 206

aid **zhīyuán** 支援 233

aim (n.) **mùdì** 目的 131

aim at **zhēnduì** 针对 230

air (n.) **kōngqì** 空气 110

air conditioner **kōngtiáojī** 空调机 110

air conditioning **kōngtiáo** 空调 110

air force **kōngjūn** 空军 106

air ticket **fēijī piào** 飞机票 55, 140

airline **hángkōng gōngsī** 航空公司 76

airplane **fēijī** 飞机 55

airport **fēijī chǎng** 飞机场 55, **jīchǎng** 机场 86

airport tax **jīchǎng fèi** 机场费 56

alarm **jīngdòng** 惊动 102

alarmed **chījīng** 吃惊 26

alas **āi** 唉 1

alcohol **jiǔjīng** 酒精 103

alcoholic beverage **jiǔ** 酒 103

(be) alike **xiāngsì** 相似 196

all **suǒyǒu** 所有 175, **yíqiè** 一切 211

all around **zhōuwéi** 周围 237

all kinds of **gè zhǒng** 各种 64, **gè zhǒng gè yàng** 各种各样 236

all one's life/lifelong **zhōngshēn** 终身 236

all over the body **húnshēn** 浑身 85

all right **hǎo** 好 76

all the time **yìzhí** 一直 211

all-round **quánmiàn** 全面 150

allergic **guòmǐn** 过敏 74

Word Finder

alleviate **jiǎnqīng** 减轻 93, **huǎnjiě** 缓解 93

allocate **fēnpèi** 分配 56

allow **ràng** 让 152, **yǔnxǔ** 允许 223

allude to **zhǐ** 指 234

almost **chàbuduō** 差不多 21, **jīhū** 几乎 86

alone **dāndú** 单独 37

along **yán** 沿 207

along with **tóng** 同 181

alphabet **zìmǔbiǎo** 字母表 243

already **yǐjīng** 已经 212

also **yě** 也 209

alter **gǎi** 改 60

although **suīrán** 虽然 173

altitude **gāodù** 高度 63

altogether **gòng** 共 67, **yígòng** 一共 211

always **cónglái** 从来 32, **yìzhí** 一直 211, **zǒngshì** 总是 243

amateur (adj.) **yèyú** 业余 210

amazed **jīngqí** 惊奇 102

ambassador **dàshǐ** 大使 35

ambiguous **hánhu** 含糊 75, **àimèi** 暧昧 2

ambulance **jiùhùchē** 救护车 104

ameliorate/amelioration **gǎishàn** 改善 61

amend **xiūgǎi** 修改 203

America **Měiguó** 美国 126

among **zhī zhōng** 之中 232, **zhōngjiān** 中间 236

amount **shùliàng** 数量 170

ample **chōngfèn** 充分 27

amusing **yǒuqù** 有趣 219

anaesthesia/anaesthetize **mázuì** 麻醉 123

anaesthetist **mázuì shī** 麻醉师 123

analysis/analyze **fēnxī** 分析 56

ancient **gǔlǎo** 古老 68

ancient times **gǔdài** 古代 68

and **hé** 和 78, **jí** 及 87, **tóng** 同 181, **yǐjí** 以及 213

angle (= to fish) **diào** 钓 44

angle (n.) **jiǎodù** 角度 96

anger/angry **fènnù** 愤怒 57, **shēngqì** 生气 162

animal **dòngwù** 动物 46

animal husbandry **xùmùyè** 畜牧业 204

animal products **xùchǎnpǐn** 畜产品 204

anniversary **zhōunián** 周年 237

annual report **niándù bàogào** 年度报告 135

announce **xuānbù** 宣布 204

annoyed **nǎohuǒ** 恼火 133

another **lìngwài** 另外 121

answer (n.) **dá'àn** 答案 33

answer (v.) **huídá** 回答 83, **jiědá** 解答 99

answer a telephone call **tīng diànhuà** 听电话 43

ant **mǎyǐ** 蚂蚁 124

antagonize **duìkàng** 对抗 48

anthropology **rénlèi xué** 人类学 153

antique **gǔdǒng** 古董 69

anxious **zuò-lì-bù-ān** 坐立不安 117, **zháojí** 着急 228, **jiāojí** 焦急 96

any **rènhé** 任何 153

anyone **rènhé rén** 任何人 153

anything **rènhé shì** 任何事 153

anyway **fǎnzheng** 反正 53

aorta **zhǔdòngmài** 主动脉 46

apart from **zhī wài** 之外 232

apartment house **gōngyù** 公寓 67

apathetic **lěngdàn** 冷淡 115

ape (v.) **mófǎng** 模仿 130

aperture **kǒng** 孔 110

apologetic **bàoqiàn** 抱歉 7

apologize **dàoqiàn** 道歉 40

apology **qiànyì** 歉意 147

app/application program **yìngyòng chéngxù** 应用程序 216

apparel **fúzhuāng** 服装 59

apparent **míngxiǎn** 明显 130

appeal (v.) **hàozhào** 号召 77, **hūyù** 呼吁 79

appear **chūxiàn** 出现 28

appear to be **xiǎnde** 显得 194

appearance **miànmào** 面貌 128, **xíngzhuàng** 形状 202

appendix **fùjiàn** 附件 60

appetite **wèikǒu** 胃口 188, **shíyù** 食欲 221

applaud **gǔzhǎng** 鼓掌 69, **pāishǒu** 拍手 137

apple **píngguǒ** 苹果 142

applicable **shìyòng** 适用 167

applicant **shēnqǐngrén** 申请人 160

application form **shēnqǐngbiǎo** 申请表 160

applied science **yìngyòng kēxué** 应用科学 216

apply **yìngyòng** 应用 216, **yùnyòng** 运用 223

apply for (a visa, a job, etc.) **shēnqǐng** 申请 160

appoint (to a position of importance) **rènmìng** 任命 154

appointment (social) **yuēhuì** 约会 222

appraisal **gūjì** 估计 68

apprentice **túdì** 徒弟 182

approach (n.) **tàidu** 态度 175

appropriate (adj.) **héshì** 合适 77, **shìdàng** 适当 167

appropriate (v.) **bōkuǎn** 拨款 14

approve **pīzhǔn** 批准 139, **tóngyì** 同意 181

approve of **zànchéng** 赞成 224

approximately **dàyuē** 大约 36

Arabic (language) **Ālābóyǔ** 阿拉伯语 1

arable land **kěgēngdì** 可耕地 65

archaeologist **kǎogǔxué jiā** 考古学家 108

archaeology **kǎogǔxué** 考古学 108

archive **dàng'àn** 档案 39

architect **jiànzhùshī** 建筑师 94

architecture **jiànzhùxué** 建筑学 94

ardent **rèliè** 热烈 152

arduous **jiānnán** 艰难 92

area **dìfang** 地方 41, **dìqū** 地区 42

area (mathematics) **miànjī** 面积 128

argue **zhēng** 争 231

arid **gānhàn** 干旱 61

aristocrat/aristocracy **guìzú** 贵族 73

(the) arm (n.) **shǒubì** 手臂 10

armed forces **jūnduì** 军队 106

arms and ammunition **jūnhuǒ** 军火 106

army **bùduì** 部队 17, **lùjūn** 陆军 106

army uniform **jūnzhuāng** 军装 106

aromatic **xiāng** 香 196

arouse **yǐnqǐ** 引起 215, **jīfā** 激发 87

arrange **ānpái** 安排 2

arrest **dàibǔ** 逮捕 37

arrive **dàodá** 到达 39, **dǐdá** 抵达 41

arrogant **jiāo'ào** 骄傲 96

arrow **jiàn** 箭 94

art **yìshù** 艺术 213

art museum **měishùguǎn** 美术馆 126

artery **dòngmài** 动脉 46

article (writing) **wénzhāng** 文章 189

artificial **rénzào** 人造 153

artificial intelligence **réngōng zhìnéng** 人工智能 235

artificial leg **jiǎtuǐ** 假腿 91

artillery man **pàobīng** 炮兵 138

artist **huàjiā** 画家 81, **měishùjiā** 美术家 126, **yìshùjiā** 艺术家 213

artistic model **réntǐ mótè** 人体模特 130

artistic work **zuòpǐn** 作品 245

as **jì** 既 90, **jìrán** 既然 90

as a matter of fact **qíshí** 其实 143, **shìshí shang** 事实上 166

as a result **yúshì** 于是 219

as if **sìhū** 似乎 172

as soon as **yī ... jiù ...** 一 ... 就 ... 211

as soon as possible **jìn kuài** 尽快 100, **jízǎo** 及早 87

as usual **zhàocháng** 照常 229

ascend **shàng** 上 157

ashamed **cánkuì** 惭愧 19

Asia **Yàzhōu** 亚洲 206

ask **qǐng** 请 148, **wèn** 问 189, **yāoqiú** 要求 208, **yào** 要 209

ask after **wènhòu** 问候 189

ask for **qǐngqiú** 请求 149

askew **wāi** 歪 184

aspect **fāngmiàn** 方面 54

aspiration **lǐxiǎng** 理想 117, **yuànwàng** 愿望 222

assemble **jíhé** 集合 88

assembly **dàhuì** 大会 84

assembly hall **lǐtáng** 礼堂 116

assess /assessment **pínggū** 评估 141

assiduous **kèkǔ** 刻苦 109

assign (a job) **pài** 派 137

assignment **rènwù** 任务 154

assignment (in school) **zuòyè** 作业 245

assist **bāngzhù** 帮助 5, **fǔzhù** 辅助 59

assistant (n.) **zhùlǐ** 助理 239, **zhùshǒu** 助手 239

Word Finder

birthday present **shēngrì lǐwù** 生日礼物 116, 162

birthplace **chūshēng dì** 出生地 28

biscuit **bǐnggān** 饼干 13

bit **diǎn** 一点儿 210

bitch **mǔ gǒu** 母狗 68

bite **yǎo** 咬 209

bitter **kǔ** 苦 111

black **hēi** 黑 78

black tea **hóngchá** 红茶 79

blackboard **hēibǎn** 黑板 78

blame **guài** 怪 70, **zéguài** 责怪 225

bland **dàn** 淡 38

blank (space) **kòngbái** 空白 111

blanket (n.) **bèizi** 被 8, **tǎnzi** 毯子 176

bleak **huāngliáng** 荒凉 83

blind **mángmù** 盲目 125

blind person **mángrén** 盲人 125

block (v.) **dǎng** 挡 39, **dǔ** 堵 47

blog (web log)/blogger **bókè** 博客 14

blood **xuè** 血 206, **xuèyè** 血液 205

blood transfusion **shūxuè** 输血 169

blow (v.) **chuī** 吹 30, **guā** 刮 70

blue **lán** 蓝 113

blurred **móhú** 模糊 130

boarding card **dēng jī pái** 登机牌 41

boast (v.) **chuīniú** 吹牛 30

boat **chuán** 船 30

(dead) body **shītǐ** 尸体 164

boil **zhǔ** 煮 239

boiled water **kāishuǐ** 开水 107

boisterous **rènao** 热闹 152

bold **dàdǎn** 大胆 34, **yǒnggǎn** 勇敢 216

bond (n.) **zhàiquàn** 债券 226

bone **gǔtou** 骨头 69

bonus **jiǎngjīn** 奖金 95

book (n.) **shū** 书 168

book (v.) **yùdìng** 预订 221

book a table/seat **dìng zuò** 订座 45

book a ticket **dìng piào** 订票 44

bookcase **shūguì** 书柜 73

bookshelf **shūjià** 书架 168

bookshop/bookstore **shūdiàn** 书店 169

border **biānjiè** 边界 11, **biānjìng** 边境 11

borderline case **biānyuán zhuàngtài** 边缘状态 11

boring (adj.) **chénmèn** 沉闷 24

(be) born **chūshēng** 出生 28

borrow **jiè** 借 99

boss (n.) **lǎobǎn** 老板 114

botanical garden **zhíwùyuán** 植物园 234

botanist **zhíwùxuéjiā** 植物学家 234

botany **zhíwùxué** 植物学 234

both **dōu** 都 46

both sides **shuāngfāng** 双方 170

both … and … **yòu … yòu …** 又 … 又 … 219

bother (v.) **máfan** 麻烦 123

bottle **píng** 瓶 142

boundary **biānjiè xiàn** 边界线 11

bow (v.) **jūgōng** 鞠躬 104

bowl **wǎn** 碗 185

box **hézi** 盒子 78, **xiāngzi** 箱子 196

boxing **quánjī** 拳击 88

boy **nán háizi** 男孩子 133

boycott **dǐzhì** 抵制 41

boyfriend **nánpéngyou** 男朋友 139

brag (v.) **chuīniú** 吹牛 30

braid **biànzi** 辫子 12

brain **nǎozi** 脑子 133

brake/apply the brakes **shāchē** 刹车 156

branch (of company) **fēn gōngsī** 分公司 67

brand (n.) **pái** 牌 137, **páizi** 牌子 137

brave **yǒnggǎn** 勇敢 216, **dǎndà** 胆大 37

blaze a trail **chuàngxīn** 创新 30

bread **miànbāo** 面包 128

break (v.) **duàn** 断 48, **pò** 破 142

break a rule **fàn guī** 犯规 53

break away from **bǎituō** 摆脱 4

break down **huài** 坏 55

break off **duàn** 断 48

break the law **fànzuì** 犯罪 53

(mechanical) breakdown **gùzhàng** 故障 69

breakdown **máobìng** 毛病 125

breakfast **zǎofàn** 早饭 225

(the) breast **rǔfáng** 乳房 155

breathe **hūxī** 呼吸 80

breed (n.) **pǐnzhǒng** 品种 141

brew coffee **zhǔ kāfēi** 煮咖啡 106

bribe **huìlù** 贿赂 84

bribery **huìlù** 贿赂 84, **hóngbāo** 红包 79

brick **zhuāntóu** 砖头 240

bride **xīnniáng** 新娘 200

bridegroom **xīnláng** 新郎 200

bridge (n.) **qiáo** 桥 147

brief and to the point **jiǎnyào** 简要 94

brief interval **kòngxì** 空隙 111

bright (clever) **cōngmíng** 聪明 32

bright (radiant) **liàng** 亮 119, **míngliàng** 明亮 129

brilliance/brilliant **guānghuī** 光辉 72

bring **dài** 带 36

brisk **huóyuè** 活跃 85

Britain **Yīngguó** 英国 215

broadband **kuāndài** 宽带 112

broadcast/broadcasting **guǎngbō** 广播 72

broadcasting company **guǎngbō gōngsī** 广播公司 72

broad-minded and outspoken **kāilǎng** 开朗 107

broken **suì** 碎 174

(elder) brother **gēge** 哥哥 64

(younger) brother **dìdi** 弟弟 42

brother(s) **xiōngdì** 兄弟 203

brown **zōngsè** 棕色 243

(computer) browser **liúlǎnqì** 浏览器 121

brush (v.) **shuā** 刷 170

brush (n.) **shuāzi** 刷子 170

bubble **pàomò** 泡沫 138

bucket **tǒng** 桶 181

bud **huālěi** 花蕾 81

Buddha **fó** 佛 58

Buddhism **fójiào** 佛教 58

budget **yùsuàn** 预算 221

buffalo **niú** 牛 135

buffet dinner/buffet **zìzhùcān** 自助餐 243

bug/wiretap (v.) **qiètīng** 窃听 147

build **zào** 造 225

build (n.) **gèzi** 个子 64

build (v.) **jiàn** 建, **jiànzhù** 建筑 94

build up **jīlěi** 积累 87

building (n.) **jiànzhù** 建筑 94, **lóu** 楼 121

bull **gōng niú** 公牛 135

bulletin **zǐdàn** 子弹 242

bully **qīfu** 欺负 143

bump against **zhuàng** 撞 240

bump into **pèng** 碰 139

(steamed) bun **mántou** 馒头 124

bun (steamed, stuffed) **bāozi** 包子 6

bungalow **píngfáng** 平房 54

bungler **hútu chóng** 糊涂虫 80

bureau chief/director **júzhǎng** 局长 104

burn **ránshāo** 燃烧 151, **shāo** 烧 158

burn a CD **kèlù guāngpán** 刻录光盘 72

burn the midnight oil **kāi yèchē** 开夜车 107

bury **mái** 埋 124

bury (a dead person) **máizàng** 埋葬 124

bus **gōnggòng qìchē** 公共汽车 66

(long-distance) bus/coach **chángtú qìchē** 长途汽车 22

bus/coach station **qìchē zhàn** 汽车站 227

bus/coach ticket **qìchē piào** 汽车票 140

business **shāngyè** 商业 158, **shēngyi** 生意 163

business administration **shāngyè guǎnlǐ** 商业管理 71, 157

business class (cabin) **shāngwù cāng** 商务舱 19

business deal/transaction **jiāoyì** 交易 96

business district **shāngyè qū** 商业区 149, 157

business hours **yíngyè shíjiān** 营业时间 215

bustling **rènao** 热闹 152

busy **máng** 忙 125, **mánglù** 忙碌 125

but **dànshì** 但是 37, **rán'ér** 然而 151

butter **huángyóu** 黄油 83

butterfly **húdié** 蝴蝶 80

button **niǔkòur** 纽扣儿 135

buy **mǎi** 买 124

(company) buyer **cǎigòu yuán** 采购员 18

by (introducing agent) **bèi** 被 8

by and by **jiànjiàn** 渐渐 *94*

bypass (v.) **rào** 绕 *152*

C

cabbage **báicài** 白菜 *3*

cabinet **guìzi** 柜子 *73*

cadre (communist) **gànbù** 干部 *62*

cage **lóngzi** 笼子 *121*

cake (n.) **dàngāo** 蛋糕 *38*

calamity **zāihài** 灾害 *223*, **zāinàn** 灾难 *223*

calculate **suàn** 算 *173*, **jìsuàn** 计算 *89*

calf **xiǎo niú** 小牛 *135*

call **jiào** 叫 *97*, **zhāohu** 招呼 *228*

call attention to **tíxǐng** 提醒 *178*

call on **kànwàng** 看望 *108*

call upon **hàozhào** 号召 *77*

calligraphy **shūfǎ** 书法 *168*

calm (adj.) **píngjìng** 平静 *141*, **zhènjìng** 镇静 *230*

camera **zhàoxiàngjī** 照相机 *229*

can (modal v.) **huì** 会 *84*, **néng** 能 *134*, **nénggòu** 能够 *134*

can (n.) **guàntou** 罐头 *71*

Canada **Jiānádà** 加拿大 *91*

cancel **qǔxiāo** 取消 *150*

cancer **ái(zhèng)** 癌(症) *1*

candidate (for an election or selection) **hòuxuǎnrén** 候选人 *80*

candle **làzhú** 蜡烛 *113*

candy **táng, tángguǒ** 糖, 糖果 *176*

canned food **guàntou shípǐn** 罐头食品 *71*

cannon **pào** 炮 *138*

cannot help **rěn bu zhù** 忍不住 *153*

cap (n.) **màozi** 帽子 *125*

capability **běnlǐng** 本领, **běnshì** 本事 *9*

capable **nénggàn** 能干 *134*

capital **zīběn** 资本 *241*

capital city **shǒudū** 首都 *168*, **jīng** 京 *102*

capitalism **zīběn zhǔyì** 资本主义 *241*

capitulate **tóuxiáng** 投降 *182*

capture (v.) **zhuō** 捉 *241*

car **qìchē** 汽车 *145*

car accident **chēhuò** 车祸 *86*

car mechanic **qìchē jiǎnxiū gōng** 汽车检修工 *93*

car park **tíngchēchǎng** 停车场 *23*, *180*

card (v.) **kǎ** 卡 *106*

care for **guānxīn** 关心 *70*, **zhàogù** 照顾 *229*

career **shìyè** 事业 *166*

carefree **qīngxián** 清闲 *194*

careful **xiǎoxīn** 小心 *198*

careless **mǎhu** 马虎 *123*, **cǎoshuài** 草率 *20*

caress **fǔmó** 抚摩 *59*

caricature **mànhuà** 漫画 *106, 125*

carpet **dìtǎn** 地毯 *42*

carrot **hú luóbo** 胡萝卜 *123*

carry **duān** 端 *47*, **yùn** 运 *223*

carry (on back) **bēi** 背 *8*

carry (in hand) **ná** 拿 *131*

carry out **guànchè** 贯彻 *71*, **zhíxíng** 执行 *234*

cartoon **mànhuà** 漫画 *125*, **kǎtōng** 卡通 *106*

carve **kè** 刻 *109*, **diāokè** 雕刻 *44*

(legal) case **ànjiàn** 案件 *2*

cash (n.) **xiànjīn** 现金 *195*

cash (v.) **duìxiàn** 兑现 *49*

cash flow **zhōuzhuǎn** 周转 *237*

cash pledge **yājīn** 押金 *206*

casual **suíbiàn** 随便 *173*

cat **māo** 猫 *125*

catch **zhuō** 捉 *241*

catch a cold **gǎnmào** 感冒 *62*, **shāngfēng** 伤风 *157*

catch fire **zháo huǒ** 着火 *228*

catch up with **gǎn** 赶 *61*, **gēnshàng** 跟上 *65*, **zhuīshang** 追上 *241*

category **lèi** 类 *115*, **yàng** 样 *208*

catering industry **yǐnshíyè** 饮食业 *215*

cattle **niú** 牛 *135*

Caucasian **báirén** 白人 *3*

cause (n.) **yuányīn** 原因 *222*

cause (v.) **yǐnqǐ** 引起 *215*, **zhìshǐ** 致使 *235*

caution **jǐnggào** 警告 *102*

cautious **xiǎoxīn** 小心 *198*, **jǐnshèn** 谨慎 *100*

cave **dòng** 洞 *46*

cavity **dòng** 洞 *46*

CD (compact disc) **guāngdié** 光碟 *72*

cease **tíngzhǐ** 停止 *180*

celebrate/celebration **qìngzhù** 庆祝 *149*

(in biology) cell **xìbāo** 细胞 *193*

cell phone **shǒujī** 手机 *167*

cement **shuǐní** 水泥 *171*

cent **fēn** 分 *56*

center **zhōngjiān** 中间 *236*, **zhōngxīn** 中心 *236*

centimeter **límǐ** 厘米 *115*, **gōngfēn** 公分 *66*

central part **zhōngxīn** 中心 *236*

century **shìjì** 世纪 *165*

CEO (chief executive officer) **zǒngjīnglǐ** 总经理 *102*, **zǒngcái** 总裁 *243*

ceramics **táocí** 陶瓷 *177*

ceremony **yíshì** 仪式 *212*, **diǎnlǐ** 典礼 *43*

certain (pron.) **mǒu** 某 *131*

certainly **yídìng** 一定 *210*

certificate **zhèngmíng** 证明 *232*

chain stores **liánsuǒ diàn** 连锁店 *118*

chair **yǐzi** 椅子 *213*

chair (of a university department) **xì zhǔrèn** 系主任 *193*

chairman (of committee) **zhǔrèn** 主任 *238*

chairman (of the board) **dǒngshìzhǎng** 董事长 *45*

chairperson **zhǔxí** 主席 *238*

chalk **fěnbǐ** 粉笔 *57*

challenge **tiǎozhàn** 挑战 *180*

champion, championship **guànjūn** 冠军 *71*

chance to **zhènghǎo** 正好 *231*

change (money) **língqián** 零钱 *120*

change (n.) **biànhuà** 变化 *11*, **gǎibiàn** 改变 *60*

change (v.) **biàn** 变 *11*, **biànhuà** 变化 *11*

change into **biànchéng** 变成 *11*

chaotic **luàn** 乱 *123*, **hùnluàn** 混乱 *85*

character **běnzhì** 本质 *9*, **xìnggé** 性格 *202*

characteristic **tèdiǎn** 特点 *177*

charge (n.) **fèi** 费 *56*

charge (v.) **shōu** 收 *167*

charities (institutions of charity) **císhàn jīgòu** 慈善机构 *31*

charm **mèilì** 魅力 *127*

chase **zhuī** 追 *241*

chat **liáotiān** 聊天 *119*, **tántiān** 谈天 *176*

cheap **piányi** 便宜 *140*

cheat/practice fraud **zuòbì** 作弊 *245*

cheat in an examination **kǎoshì zuòbì** 考试作弊 *245*

check (v.) **chá** 查 *21*, **jiǎnchá** 检查 *93*

check/cheque (in banking) **zhīpiào** 支票 *233*

check and accept **yànshōu** 验收 *208*

check in **dēngjì** 登记 *41*

checking account **huóqī chǔxù** 活期储蓄 *29*

chemical biology **shēngwù huàxué** 生物化学 *162*

chemical fertilizer **huàféi** 化肥 *81*

chemical industry **huàxué gōngyè** 化学工业 *81*

chemical plant **huàgōngchǎng** 化工厂 *81*

chemical test **huàyàn** 化验 *81*

chemistry **huàxué** 化学 *81*

cherish **àihù** 爱护 *1*, **àixī** 爱惜 *2*

chess **xiàngqí** 象棋 *197*

chest (box) **xiōng** 胸 *203*

chest (box) **xiāngzi** 箱子 *196*

chew **jiáo** 嚼 *96*, **jǔjué** 咀嚼 *104*

chick **xiǎojī** 小鸡 *87*

chicken (n.) **jī** 鸡 *87*

chicken egg **jīdàn** 鸡蛋 *87*

chicken meat **jīròu** 鸡肉 *155*

chief (adj.) **zhǔyào** 主要 *238*

chief (n.) **tóu** 头 *182*

chief executive officer (CEO) **zǒngjīnglǐ** 总经理 *102*

chief of a bureau **júzhǎng** 局长 *104*

chief physician/surgeon **zhǔrèn yīshēng** 主任医生 *238*

child **értóng** 儿童 *50*, **háizi** 孩子 *75*

childhood **értóng shídài** 儿童时代 *50*

chilly (adj.) **liáng** 凉 *119*

China **Zhōngguó** 中国, **Zhōnghuá** 中华 *235*

Word Finder

complicated (adj.) **fùzá** 复杂 *60*, **máfan** 麻烦 *123*

compliment **chēngzàn** 称赞 *24*

component **chéngfèn** 成分 *24*

compose **biān** 编 *11*

composed **ānníng** 安宁 *2*, **zhènjìng** 镇静 *230*

(student's) composition **zuòwén** 作文 *245*

compound **yuànzi** 院子 *222*

comprehend **dǒng** 懂 *45*, **lǐjiě** 理解 *116*

comprehensive **quánmiàn** 全面 *150*

compromise **tuǒxié** 妥协 *184*

compulsory education **yìwù jiàoyù** 义务教育 *213*

computer **diànnǎo** 电脑 *43*, **jìsuànjī** 计算机 *89*

computer game **diànnǎo yóuxì** 电脑游戏 *218*

computer program **jìsuànjī chéngxù** 计算机程序 *26*

computer virus **diànnǎo bìngdù** 电脑病毒 *14*

comrade **tóngzhì** 同志 *181*

con man **piànzi** 骗子 *140*

conceal **cáng** 藏 *20*

conceal the truth **mán** 瞒 *124*

concede **ràngbù** 让步 *152*

conceited **jiāo'ào** 骄傲 *96*

concentrate/concentration **jízhōng** 集中 *88*

concentrate on **zhuānxīn** 专心 *240*

concept **gàiniàn** 概念 *61*, **guānniàn** 观念 *73*

concert **yīnyuè huì** 音乐会 *215*

conclusion **jiélùn** 结论 *98*

(hold) concurrent post **jiānzhí** 兼职 *92*

condemn **qiǎnzé** 谴责 *146*

condition **tiáojiàn** 条件 *179*, **zhuàngkuàng** 状况 *241*

conduct **xíngwéi** 行为 *202*

conference **huì** 会 *84*, **huìyì** 会议 *84*

confess (a wrongdoing) **jiāodài** 交代 *95*

confidence **xìnxīn** 信心 *201*, **xìnrèn** 信任 *201*

confidential **mìmì** 秘密 *127*

confine **xiànzhì** 限制 *195*

confirm **kěndìng** 肯定 *110*, **quèdìng** 确定 *151*, **quèrèn** 确认 *151*

conform to **fúhé** 符合 *59*

confuse right and wrong **hùnxiáo shìfēi** 混淆是非 *85*

confused (adj.) **hútu** 糊涂 *80*, **hùnluàn** 混乱 *85*

congratulate **zhùhè** 祝贺 *239*, **gōngxǐ** 恭喜 *67*

congress **dàhuì** 大会 *35*

connect **lián** 连 *118*

connection **guānxi** 关系 *70*, **liánxì** 联系 *118*

conquer **kèfú** 克服 *109*

conscience **liángxīn** 良心 *119*

conscientious **rènzhēn** 认真 *153*, **zìjué** 自觉 *242*

consciousness **zhījué** 知觉 *233*

consensus **gòngshí** 共识 *68*

consequence **jiéguǒ** 结果 *98*

consequences **hòuguǒ** 后果 *79*

consequently **jiéguǒ** 结果 *98*, **yúshì** 于是 *219*

conservative **bǎoshǒu** 保守 *6*

conservatory **yīnyuè xuéyuàn** 音乐学院 *215*

conserve **bǎo** 保, **bǎohù** 保护 *6*

consider **kǎolù** 考虑 *108*, **rènwéi** 认为 *153*

consider carefully **yánjiū** 研究 *207*

consign for shipment **tuōyùn** 托运 *183*

consist of **zǔchéng** 组成 *245*

console **ānwèi** 安慰 *2*

consolidate **gǒnggù** 巩固 *67*

conspicuous **tūchū** 突出 *183*

conspiracy **yīnmóu** 阴谋 *214*

constantly **lǎoshi** 老是 *114*

construct (v.) **jiàn** 建 *94*, **jiànshè** 建设 *94*

construction **jiégòu** 结构 *98*

construction work **gōngchéng** 工程 *65*

(diplomatic) consul **lǐngshì** 领事 *121*

consulate **lǐngshì guǎn** 领事馆 *121*

consult **shāngliang** 商量 *157*, **cuōshāng** 磋商 *33*

consultant **gùwèn** 顾问 *70*

(doctor's) consultation fee **guàhào fèi** 挂号费 *70*

consume **xiāofèi** 消费 *197*

consume (especially in a wasteful way) **hàofèi** 耗费 *77*

consumer **xiāofèizhě** 消费者 *197*

consumer goods **xiāofèipǐn** 消费品 *197*

contact **liánxì** 联系 *118*, **liánxì rén** 联系人 *118*

contact person **liánluò yuán** 联络员 *118*

contain **hán** 含 *75*, **bāohán** 包含 *6*

contemplate **dǎsuàn** 打算 *34*, **kǎolù** 考虑 *108*

contemporary **dāngdài** 当代 *38*

content (adj.) **ānxīn** 安心 *2*

content (n.) **nèiróng** 内容 *134*

contest **jìngsài** 竞赛 *103*

continent **dàlù** 大陆 *35*

contingency **jǐnjí zhuàngkuàng** 紧急状况 *10*, **wànyī de qíngkuàng** 万一的情况 *186*

continue **jìxù** 继续 *190*

continuously **búduàn** 不断 *15*

contract (n.) **hétóng** 合同 *78*

contract (v.) **shōusuō** 收缩 *167*

contradiction, contradictory **máodùn** 矛盾 *125*

contrary **xiāngfǎn** 相反 *195*

contrary to expectation **jìngrán** 竟然 *103*

contrast **bǐ** 比 *9*

contribute **gòngxiàn** 贡献 *68*

control **kòngzhì** 控制 *111*, **cāozòng** 操纵 *20*

convene (a conference) **zhàokāi** 召开 *228*

convenient **fāngbiàn** 方便 *54*

conversation **huìhuà** 会话 *84*

convince **shuōfú** 说服 *171*

convinced **fúqì** 服气 *58*

cook (v.) **shāo** 烧 *158*, **zuòfàn** 做饭 *246*, **zhǔ** 煮 *239*

cooked (adj.) **shú** 熟 *169*

cooked rice **fàn** 饭 *53*

cookie **bǐnggān** 饼干 *13*

cooking oil **shíyóu** 食油 *218*

cool (weather) **liáng** 凉, **liángkuai** 凉快 *118*

cool/relaxed and fashionable **kù** 酷 *112*

cool-headed **chénzhuó** 沉着 *24*, **lěngjìng** 冷静 *115*

cooperate **hézuò** 合作 *78*, **pèihé** 配合 *139*

cooperation **hézuò** 合作 *78*

coordinate **pèihé** 配合 *139*

cope with **duìfu** 对付 *48*

copper **tóng** 铜 *181*

copy (v.) **fùzhì** 复制 *60*

copy by hand **chāo** 抄 *23*, **chāoxiě** 抄写 *23*

cord **shéngzi** 绳子 *162*

cordial (adj.) **chéngzhì** 诚挚 *25*

cordless telephone **yídòng diànhuà** 移动电话 *212*

core **héxīn** 核心 *78*

corn **yùmǐ** 玉米 *220*

corner (n.) **jiǎo** 角 *96*, **jiǎoluò** 角落 *96*

corporation **gōngsī** 公司 *66*

corpse **shītǐ** 尸体 *164*

correct (adj.) **búcuò** 不错 *15*, **duì** 对 *48*, **zhèngquè** 正确 *231*

correct (v.) **gǎi** 改 *60*, **jiūzhèng** 纠正 *103*

correspondent **jìzhě** 记者 *89*

corridor **zǒuláng** 走廊 *243*

corrupt/corruption **fǔbài** 腐败 *59*, **tānwū** 贪污 *176*

corrupt official **tānguān** 贪官 *175*

cosmetics **huàzhuāngpǐn** 化妆品 *81*

cost (n.) **fèiyòng** 费用 *56*

cost (v.) **fèi** 费 *56*, **huā** 花 *80*

cost of living **shēnghuó fèiyòng** 生活费用 *56*, **shēnghuó fèi** 生活费 *161*

cost (a large amount) **hàofèi** 耗费 *77*

(business) cost **chéngběn** 成本 *24*

cosy up **bājie** 巴结 *2*

cotton **miánhuā** 棉花 *128*

couch **shāfā** 沙发 *156*

cough **késou** 咳嗽 *108*

cough lozenge **késou táng** 咳嗽糖 *108*

cough syrup **késou yàoshuǐ** 咳嗽药水 *108*

count (v.) **shǔ** 数 *169*

count on **zhǐwàng** 指望 *234*

Word Finder

describe **xíngróng** 形容 202, **miáoxiě** 描写 128

desert (n.) **shāmò** 沙漠 156

dessert **tiánshí** 甜食 179

design **shèjì** 设计 159

desire (n.) **yuànwàng** 愿望 222

desk **tái** 台 175, **zhuōzi** 桌子 241

desk lamp **táidēng** 台灯 41

desktop PC **táishì jī** 台式机 175

desolate **huāngliáng** 荒凉 83

despise **bǐshì** 鄙视 10

destination **zhōngdiǎn** 终点 236

destiny **mìngyùn** 命运 130

destroy **huǐmiè** 毁灭 84

detail **xìjié** 细节 193

detailed **xiángxì** 详细 196

detain **kòuyā** 扣押 111

detective **zhēntàn** 侦探 230

detergent powder **féizào fěn** 肥皂粉 56

determination **juéxīn** 决心 105

determine **juédìng** 决定 105, **quèdìng** 确定 151

determined (adj.) **jiānjué** 坚决 92

detestable **kěwù** 可恶 109

detour (v.) **rào** 绕 152

develop **fāzhǎn** 发展 51, **kāifā** 开发 106

developed (adj.) **fādá** 发达 51

developing country **fāzhǎnzhōng guójiā** 发展中国家 51

diagnose/diagnosis **zhěnduàn** 诊断 230

diagram **tú** 图 182

dialogue **duìhuà** 对话 48

diameter **zhíjìng** 直径 233

diarrhoea **fùxiè** 腹泻 60, **xièdù** 泻肚 199

diary **rìjì** 日记 154

dictation **tīngxiě** 听写 180

dictionary **cídiǎn** 词典 31

dictator **dúcáizhě** 独裁者 46

dictatorship **dúcái** 独裁 46

die **qùshì** 去世 150, **sǐ** 死 172

difference **qūbié** 区别 150

different **bùtóng** 不同 16

differentiate **qūbié** 区别 150, **fēnbiàn** 分辨 56

difficult/difficulty **kùnnan** 困难 112, **nán** 难 133

difficult (life) **xīnkǔ** 辛苦 200

dig **wājué** 挖掘 184

digest **xiāohuà** 消化 197

digital **shùmǎ** 数码 170

digitalize/digitalization **shùmǎhuà** 数码化 170

dignity **zūnyán** 尊严 244

digression **xiánhuà** 闲话 194

diligent **qínfèn** 勤奋 147

dim **àn** 暗 2

dining hall **shítáng** 食堂 165

diploma **wénpíng** 文凭 189

diplomacy **wàijiāo** 外交 184

diplomat **wàijiāo guān** 外交官 184

direct (adj.) **zhíjiē** 直接 233

direct (v.) **zhǐdǎo** 指导 234

direction **fāngxiàng** 方向 54

director (of department) **zhǔrèn** 主任 238

director of a bureau **júzhǎng** 局长 104

direct/director (a film or play) **dǎoyǎn** 导演 39

dirty **zāng** 脏 225

disabled **cánjí** 残疾 19

disabled person **cánjírén** 残疾人 19

disadvantage **huàichu** 坏处 76

disappear **xiāoshī** 消失 197, **shīzōng** 失踪 163

disappointed **shīwàng** 失望 163

(be) disappointed with… **duì … shīwàng** 对 … 失望 163

disaster **zāi** 灾, **zāihài** 灾害 223

disband **jiěsàn** 解散 99

disbelieve **huáiyí** 怀疑 82

discard **rēngdiao** 扔掉 44

discern **jiànbié** 鉴别 95

(be) discharged from hospital **chūyuàn** 出院 28

disciplinary action **chǔfèn** 处分 29

discipline **jìlǜ** 纪律 90

discontinue **zhōngduàn** 中断 235

discount (n.) **zhé** 折 229

(be) discouraged **huīxīn** 灰心 83

discover **fāxiàn** 发现 51

discriminate against/discrimination **qíshì** 歧视 143

discuss/discussion **tǎolùn** 讨论 177, **shāngliang** 商量 157

disease **bìng** 病 13, **jíbìng** 疾病 88

disease prevention **fángbìng** 防病 54

(be) disgraced **diūliǎn** 丢脸 119

disgusting **tǎoyàn** 讨厌 177

dish (n.) **pánzi** 盘子 138

(cooked) dish **càì cai** 菜 19

(be) disheartened **huīxīn** 灰心 83

disinfect **xiāodú** 消毒 197

disintegrate **wǎjiě** 瓦解 184, **jiětǐ** 解体 100

dismiss (an employee) **jiěgù** 解雇 99

disorderly **luàn** 乱 123

dispatch **pài** 派 137

display **chénliè** 陈列 24, **zhǎnlǎn** 展览 227

dispose of **chǔzhì** 处置 29

disposition **xìnggé** 性格 202

dispute **zhēngyì** 争议 231

disregard **bùgù** 不顾 16

dissect **jiěpōu** 解剖 99

disseminate **chuánbō** 传播 30, **xuānchuán** 宣传 204

dissertation **lùnwén** 论文 123

distance **jùlí** 距离 105

distant **yuǎn** 远 222

distinguish **fēnbié** 分别 56, **jiànbié** 鉴别 95

distinguished **jiéchū** 杰出 99

distribute/distribution **fēnbù** 分布 56

district (urban) **qū** 区 150

disturb **dǎrǎo** 打扰 34, **fáng'ài** 妨碍 54

disunity **máodùn** 矛盾 125

ditch **gōu** 沟 68

dive **qiánshuǐ** 潜水 146

diver **qiánshuǐyuán** 潜水员 146

divide **huàfēn** 划分 81, **fēn** 分 56

dividing line **jièxiàn** 界限 99

divorce **líhūn** 离婚 116

dizzy/feel dizzy **tóu yūn** 头晕 223

do **gàn** 干 62, **zuò zuò** 做 245, **zuò** 作 245

do business **zuò mǎimài** 做买卖 124

do manual labor **láodòng** 劳动 114

do not **búyào** 不要 15

do not have **méiyǒu** 没有 126

dock **mǎtóu** 码头 124

(medical) doctor **yīshēng** 医生 212, **dàifu** 大夫 36

Doctor (Ph.D.) **bóshì** 博士 14

doctor's consultation fee **guàhào fèi** 挂号费 70

doctrine/-ism **zhǔyì** 主义 238

document **wénjiàn** 文件 189

dodge **huíbì** 回避 83

dog (n.) **gǒu** 狗 68

dollar **yuán** 元 222

domain **lǐngyù** 领域 121

donate **juān** 捐 105

don't **bié** 别 13

door **mén** 门 127

doorway **ménkǒu** 门口 127

dope **xīngfènjì** 兴奋剂 201

dormitory **sùshè** 宿舍 173

dosage **jìliàng** 剂量 90

dot **diǎn** 点 42

double bed **shuāngrén chuáng** 双人床 30

doubt **yíwèn** 疑问 212, **huáiyí** 怀疑 82

dove **gēzi** 鸽子 64

download **xià zài** 下载 193

downstairs **lóu xia** 楼下 122

downtown **chénglǐ** 城里 25

doze/doze off **dǎ kēshui** 打瞌睡 34

draft (of a plan, proposal, a document, etc.) **cǎo'àn** 草案 20

draft (v.) **qǐcǎo** 起草 144

drag on **tuō** 拖 183

dragon **lóng** 龙 121

drama **xìjù** 戏剧 192, **xì** 戏 192

draw **huà** 画 81

draw up **zhìdìng** 制定 235

drawer **chōuti** 抽屉 27

drawing (n.) **huàr** 画儿 81, **tú** 图 182

(pencil) drawing **qiānbǐ huà** 铅笔画 81

dread **kǒngjù** 恐惧 110

dream **mèng** 梦, **zuòmèng** 做梦 127, 246

dress up **dǎban** 打扮 33

dressing gown **shuìyī** 睡衣 171

dressmaker **cáifeng** 裁缝 18

drill (n.) **liànxí** 练习 119

drink (v.) **hē** 喝 77

drink (n.) **yǐnliào** 饮料 215

drink excessively **xùjiǔ** 酗酒 204

drip (v.) **diǎn** 点 42

Word Finder

equipment **shèbèi** 设备 159, **qìcái** 器材 145

erroneous **cuòwù** 错误 33

error **cuòwù** 错误 33

erupt **bàofā** 爆发 7

especially **tèbié** 特别 177, **yóuqí** 尤其 217

espionage **jiàndié huódòng** 间谍 活动 95

essay **lùnwén** 论文 123, **sǎnwén** 散 文 155, **wénzhāng** 文章 189

essential **gēnběn** 根本 65

essential element **yàosù** 要素 209

establish **chénglì** 成立 25, **jiànlì** 建立 94

estimate **gūjì** 估计 68

et cetera, etc. **děng** 等 41

ethnic Chinese **Huárén** 华人 81

ethnic group **mínzú** 民族 129

ethics **dàodé** 道德 39

etiquette **lǐjié** 礼节 116

Euro **Ōuyuán** 欧元 137

Europe **Ōuzhōu** 欧洲 137

evade **bì** 避 83, **huíbì** 回避 83

evaporate **zhēngfā** 蒸发 231

even (adv.) **lián … dōu …** 连… 都… 118

even if **jiùshì** 就是 104, **nǎpà** 哪怕 132, **jíshǐ** 即使 88

even if/even though **jíshǐ** 即使 88, **jíbiàn** 即便 88

even more **gèng** 更, **gèngjiā** 更加 65

even though **jǐnguǎn** 尽管 100

evening **wǎnshang** 晚上 185, **yè** 夜 210

evening party **wǎnhuì** 晚会 185

(historic) event **shìjiàn** 事件 166

(sports) event **bǐsài xiàngmù** 比赛 项目 10

ever **cónglái** 从来 32, **shǐzhōng** 始终 165

every **gè** 各 64, **měi** 每 126

everybody **dàjiā** 大家 35

everybody (colloquial) **dàhuǒr** 大伙儿 35

every day **tiāntiān** 天天 179

everything **rènhé shì** 任何事 153, **yíqiè** 一切 211

everywhere **dàochù** 到处 39

evidence **zhèngjù** 证据 232

evolve **jìnhuà** 进化 101

exacerbate **jiājù** 加剧 90

exact **zhǔn** 准 241, **zhǔnquè** 准确 241

exaggerate **kuāzhāng** 夸张 111

examination **cèyàn** 测验 20, **kǎoshì** 考试 108

examination result **chéngjì** 成绩 25

examine **jiǎnchá** 检查 93, **kǎoshì** 考试 108

example **lìzi** 例子 118

(positive) example **bǎngyàng** 榜样 5

excavate **wājué** 挖掘 184

exceed **chāoguò** 超过 23

excellent **yōuxiù** 优秀 217

except **chúle … (yǐwài)** 除了 … (以外) 29

exception **lìwài** 例外 118

exceptional **tèshū** 特殊 177, **géwài** 格外 64

excessive **guòfèn** 过分 74

exchange **diào** 调 44, **jiāohuàn** 交换, **jiāoliú** 交流 96

(currency) exchange **duìhuàn** 兑换 49

(currency) exchange rate **huìlǜ** 汇率 85

excited **jīdòng** 激动 87, **xīngfèn** 兴奋 201

exciting **jīdòng** 激动 87

excuse (v.) **yuánliàng** 原谅 221

excuse (n.) **jièkǒu** 借口 99

Excuse me, … **qǐngwèn …** 请问… 149

execute **zhíxíng** 执行 233

executive order **xíngzhèng mìnglìng** 行政命令 202

exercise **liànxí** 练习 119

(physical) exercise **yùndòng** 运动 223

exert **yònglì** 用力 217

exhaust (v.) **jìn** 尽 100

exhausted **lèi** 累 115

exhibit (v.) **zhǎnlǎn** 展览 227

exhibition **zhǎnlǎn** 展览, **zhǎnlǎnhuì** 展览会 227

exhort **zhǔfu** 嘱咐 239

exist **cúnzài** 存在 33

exist (there is/are) **yǒu** 有 218

exit (n.) **chūkǒu** 出口 28

expand **kāizhǎn** 开展 107, **kuòdà** 扩大 112

expect/expectation **qīdài** 期待 143, **qīwàng** 期望 143

expenditure/expenses **kāizhī** 开支 108, **zhīchū** 支出 233

expense **fèiyòng** 费用 56

expensive **guì** 贵 73

experience (n.) **jīngyàn** 经验 102

experience (v.) **jīnglì** 经历 102

experienced **yǒu jīngyàn** 有经验 102

experiment **shíyàn** 实验 164, **shìyàn** 试验 166

expert **zhuānjiā** 专家 239

expertise **zhuāncháng** 专长 239

expire **dàoqī** 到期 143

expired **guòqī** 过期 143

expiry date **yǒuxiàoqī** 有效期 219

explain/explanation **jiěshì** 解释 99, **shuōmíng** 说明 172

exploration team **tànxiǎn duì** 探险 队 176

explore **tànsuǒ** 探索 176, **tànxiǎn** 探险 176

explore and discuss **tàntǎo** 探讨 176

explorer **tànxiǎnjiā** 探险家 176

export (v.) **chūkǒu** 出口 28

export-oriented **wàixiàngxíng** 外向 型 184

expose **jiēlù** 揭露 98

explosive **huǒyào** 火药 86

express (thoughts, emotions, etc.) **biǎodá** 表达 12

expressway **gāosù gōnglù** 高速公路 63

exquisite **jīngzhì** 精致 102

extend **shēn** 伸 160, **yáncháng** 延长 206

extensive **guǎngdà** 广大, **guǎngfàn** 广泛 72

extent **dù** 度 47

exterminate **huǐmiè** 毁灭 84, **mièwáng** 灭亡 129

extinguish **miè** 灭 129

extremely **jíqí** 极其 88, **jíle** 极了 88

(the) eye **yǎn** 眼, **yǎnjīng** 眼睛 207

eyebrow **méimao** 眉毛 127

F

fable **yùyán** 寓言 221

face (n.) **liǎn** 脸 119, **miànzi** 面子 128

face (v.) **cháo** 朝 23, **xiàng** 向 197

facial expression **biǎoqíng** 表情 12, **shénqíng** 神情 161

facilities **shèshī** 设施 159

fact **shìshí** 事实 166

factor **yīnsù** 因素 214

factory **gōngchǎng** 工厂 65

fail **shībài** 失败 163

failure **shībài** 失败 163

fair **gōngpíng** 公平 66

fairly **xiāngdāng** 相当 195

fairy tale **tónghuà** 童话 181

fake (goods) **jiǎhuò** 假货 91, **màopáihuò** 冒牌货 125

fall (season) **qiū** 秋, **qiūtiān** 秋天 149

fall (v.) **dǎo** 倒 39, **diē** 跌 44

fall apart **jiětǐ** 解体 99

fall asleep **shuìzháo** 睡着 171

fall ill **shēngbìng** 生病 162

fall unconscious **hūnmí** 昏迷 85

false **jiǎ** 假 91

familiar with **shú** 熟, **shúxi** 熟悉 169

family **jiā** 家 91, **jiātíng** 家庭 91

family member **jiāshǔ** 家属 91

family name **xìng** 姓 203

(your) family name **guìxìng** 贵姓 203

family reunion **tuányuán** 团圆 183

family tree **jiāpǔ** 家谱 142

famous **yǒumíng** 有名 218, **zhùmíng** 著名 239

(become) famous **chéng míng** 成名 25

famous brand **míngpái** 名牌 129

fantasize **huànxiǎng** 幻想 83

far **yuǎn** 远 222

far away from **lí … yuǎn** 离 … 远 116

farewell banquet **gàobié yànhuì** 告 别宴会 208

farewell party **huānsònghuì** 欢送 会 82

Word Finder

forest **sēnlín** 森林 *156*

forever **yǒngyuǎn** 永远 *216*

forgery **màopáihuò** 冒牌货 *125*

forget **wàng** 忘 *186*, **wàngdiao** 忘掉 *44*

(be) forgetful **diū sān là sì** 丢三落四 *45*

forgive **ráoshù** 饶恕 *152*

forgive **yuánliàng** 原谅 *221*

fork (n.) **chāzi** 叉子 *20*

form (n.) **biǎo** 表 *12*

form (n.) **xíngshì** 形式 *202*, **xíngzhuàng** 形状 *202*

form (v.) **gòuchéng** 构成 *68*, **xíngchéng** 形成 *202*

form a partnership **héhuǒ** 合伙 *77*

formal **zhèngshì** 正式 *232*

(make a) formal statement **shēngmíng** 声明 *162*

formalities **shǒuxù** 手续 *168*

format **géshì** 格式 *64*

former **yuánlái** 原来 *221*

formerly **céngjīng** 曾经 *20*

formidable **lìhai** 厉害 *117*

formula **gōngshì** 公式 *66*

fortunately **xìngkuī** 幸亏 *203*

fortune **cáifù** 财富 *18*

forum **zuòtánhuì** 座谈会 *245*

forward (v.) **zhuǎn** 转 *24*

fossil **huàshí** 化石 *81*

foul (in sports) **fàn guī** 犯规 *53*

found **jiàn chuànglì** 创立 *50*

foundation **jīchǔ** 基础 *87*

fountain pen **gāngbǐ** 钢笔 *63*

four **sì** 四 *172*

fragmentary **suì** 碎 *174*

fragrant **xiāng** 香 *196*

framework **kuàngjià** 框架 *112*

France **Fǎguó** 法国 *52*

fraud **piànjú** 骗局 *140*

free (adj.) **zìyóu** 自由 *242*

free of charge **miǎnfèi** 免费 *128*

free time **kòng** 空 *111*

freedom **zìyó1u** 自由 *242*

freeze **dòng** 冻 *46*

freezing cold **hánlěng** 寒冷 *75*

French (language) **Fǎwén** 法文 *52*, **Fǎyǔ** 法语 *52*

frequent **pínfán** 频繁 *141*

fresh **xiān** 鲜 *194*, **xīnxiān** 新鲜 *201*

fresh water/sweet water **dànshuǐ** 淡水 *39*

fret **fāchóu** 发愁 *51*

Friday **Xīngqīwǔ** 星期五 *201*

friend **péngyou** 朋友 *139*

friendly **yǒuhǎo** 友好 *218*

friendship **yǒuyì** 友谊 *218*

frighten, be frightened **xià** 吓 *193*

frightening **kěpà** 可怕 *109*

frog **qīngwā** 青蛙 *148*

from **cóng** 从 *32*, **zìcóng** 自从 *242*

from now on **jīnhòu** 今后 *100*

from… till… **cóng … dào…** 从 … 到 … *32*

front **qiánbiān** 前边 *145*, **qiánmiàn** 前面 *146*

frontier **biānjìng** 边境 *11*

frozen meat **dòngròu** 冻肉 *46*

(be) frugal **jiéshěng** 节省 *98*

fruit **shuǐguǒ** 水果 *171*

fruit jelly **shuǐguó dòng** 水果冻 *46*

fruit juice **guǒzhī** 果汁 *74*

frustration/setback **cuòzhé** 挫折 *33*

(shallow) fry **jiān** 煎 *92*

fuel **ránliào** 燃料 *151*

fulfill **wánchéng** 完成 *185*

full **mǎn** 满 *125*, **bǎo** 饱 *7*

full name **xìngmíng** 姓名 *204*

full of **chōngmǎn** 充满 *27*

fully **shífēn** 十分 *164*

fun **hǎowánr** 好玩儿 *77*

function (n.) **zuòyòng** 作用 *245*, **gōngnéng** 功能 *67*

function key(s) **gōngnéng jiàn** 功能键 *67*

fund **zījīn** 资金 *241*

fundamental **gēnběn** 根本 *65*, **jīběn** 基本 *87*

funeral /funeral arrangement **sāngshì** 丧事 *156*

fur coat **píyī** 皮衣 *140*

furious **měngliè** 猛烈 *127*

furniture **jiājù** 家具 *91*

further **jìnyíbù** 进一步 *101*

future **wèilái** 未来 *189*, **qiántú** 前途 *146*

future prospects **qiántú** 前途 *146*

fuzzy **móhú** 模糊 *130*

G

gallery **měishùguǎn** 美术馆 *126*

gamble **dǔbó** 赌博 *47*

game **yóuxì** 游戏 *215*

gang up with **gōujié** 勾结 *68*

garage **chēkù** 车库 *23*

garbage **lājī** 垃圾 *112*

garbage bin **lājī xiāng** 垃圾箱 *112*

garbage disposal **lājī chùlǐ** 垃圾处理 *112*

garden **huāyuán** 花园 *81*

garments **fúzhāng** 服装 *59*

garrulous **láodao** 唠叨 *114*

gas **qìtǐ** 气体 *144*

gasoline **qìyóu** 汽油 *145*

gasp **chuǎnqì** 喘气 *30*

gate **mén** 门 *127*, **dàmén** 大门 *127*

gather together **jíhé** 集合 *89*

gaze (v.) **dīng** 盯 *44*

gender **xìngbié** 性别 *202*

gene **jīyīn** 基因 *87*

genetic engineering **jīyīn gōngchéng** 基因工程 *87*, **yíchuán gōngchéng** 遗传工程 *212*

genetic modified **zhuǎn jīyīn** 转基因 *240*

genetic modified food **zhuǎn jīyīn shípǐn** 转基因食品 *240*

genetics **yíchuánxué** 遗传学 *212*

general (adj.) **dàgài** 大概 *35*

(armed forces) general **jiāngjūn** 将军 *95*

general manager **zǒngjīnglǐ** 总经理 *102*

(the) general public **qúnzhòng** 群众 *151*

generally speaking **yìbān** 一般 *210*

generation **dài** 代 *36*

generous **kāngkài** 慷慨 *108*, **dàfang** 大方 *35*

gentle and friendly **héqì** 和气 *78*

gentleman **shēnshì** 绅士 *160*, **jūnzǐ** 君子 *106*

genuine **zhēnzhèng** 真正 *230*, **zhèngzōng** 正宗 *232*

geography **dìlǐ** 地理 *42*

geographer **dìlǐxué jiā** 地理学家 *42*

germ **xìjūn** 细菌 *193*

German (language) **Déwén** 德文 *40*, **Déyǔ** 德语 *40*

Germany **Déguó** 德国 *40*

get **dé** 得 *40*, **huòdé** 获得 *86*

get in touch **liánxì** 联系 *118*

get on (a vehicle) **shàng** 上 *157*

get on the Internet **shàngwǎng** 上网 *158*

get ready **yùbèi** 预备 *221*

get rid of **chú** 除 *29*

get up **qǐ** 起 *144*

get up (out of bed) **qǐchuáng** 起床, **qǐlái** 起来 *144*

get … done **nòng** 弄 *136*

get worse **èhuà** 恶化 *50*

ghost **guǐ** 鬼 *73*

gift **lǐwù** 礼物 *116*

gigantic **jùdà** 巨大 *104*

girl **gūniang** 姑娘 *68*, **nǚ háizi** 女孩子 *74*

girlfriend **nǚpéngyou** 女朋友 *139*

give **gěi** 给 *89*

give an example **jǔ lìzi** 举例子 *118*

give the cold shoulder to **dàimàn** 怠慢 *37*

give as a gift **sòng** 送 *173*

give birth to **shēng** 生 *162*

give first aid **jiùhù** 救护 *103*

give incentive to **cìjī** 刺激 *31*

give off **fāchū** 发出 *51*, **mào** 冒 *125*

give rise to **yǐnqǐ** 引起 *215*, **zàochéng** 造成 *225*

glass **bōli** 玻璃 *14*

glasses **yǎnjìng** 眼镜 *207*

glitter **shǎnshuò** 闪烁 *157*

glorious **guāngróng** 光荣 *72*

glossy **guānghuá** 光滑 *72*

glove **shǒutào** 手套 *168*

glue **jiāoshuǐ** 胶水 *96*

gluttonous **zuǐchán** 嘴馋 *21*

gnaw **kěn** 啃 *110*

go aboard (a plane, ship) **shàng** 上 *158*

go abroad/overseas **chūguó** 出国 *28*

go ashore **shàng àn** 上岸 *2*

go back **huí** 回 *83*

go bankrupt **pòchǎn** 破产 *142*

go bust **dǎobì** 倒闭 *39*

go in **jìnqu** 进去 *101*

go into hiding **duǒcáng** 躲藏 *49*

Word Finder

go out **chūqu** 出去 28

go over **guòqu** 过去 74

go sightseeing **guānguāng** 观光 71

go to **qù** 去 150, **tōng** 通 180

go to class **shàngkè** 上课 158

go to extremes **zǒu jíduān** 走极端 88

go to work **shàngbān** 上班 158

go up **shēng** 升 161, **zhàng** 涨 227

go upwards **shàng** 上 157

go/come down **xià** 下 193

goal **mùbiāo** 目标 131

goat **shānyáng** 山羊 208

god(s) **shén** 神 161

gold **jīn, jīnzi** 金, 金子 100

gold mine **jīnkuàng** 金矿 112

good **hǎo** 好 76, **liánghǎo** 良好 119

(be) good at **shànyú** 善于 157

good fortune/good luck **xìngyùn** 幸运 203

good-looking **hǎokàn** 好看 76, **piàoliang** 漂亮 140

goods and materials **wùzī** 物资 191

goodbye **zàijiàn** 再见 224

goods **huò** 货 86

goose (n.) **é** 鹅 50

gorgeous **huálì** 华丽 81

gourd **guā** 瓜 70

governance **zhèngzhì** 政治 232

government **zhèngfǔ** 政府 232

government agency **jīgòu** 机构 86

government office **jīguān** 机关 86

government official **guān** 官 71

government policy **zhèngcè** 政策 232

grab **qiǎng** 抢 147, **zhuā** 抓 239

graceful **yōuměi** 优美 217

grade (in school) **niánjí** 年级 135

grade (n.) **děng** 等 41, **jí** 级 88

gradually **jiànjiàn** 渐渐 95, **zhúbù** 逐步 238, **zhújiàn** 逐渐 238

graduate (from school) **bìyè** 毕业 10

graduate school (of university) **yánjiūshēng yuàn** 研究生院 207

graduate student **yánjiūshēng** 研究生 207

grain **liángshí** 粮食 119

gram **kè** 克 109

grammar **yǔfǎ** 语法 221

grammatical **tōng** 通 180

grand **xióngwěi** 雄伟 203

granddaughter **sūnnǚ** 孙女 174

grandfather (paternal) **yéye** 爷爷 209, **zǔfù** 祖父 244

grandmother (paternal) **nǎinai** 奶奶 132, **zǔmǔ** 祖母 244

grandson **sūnzi** 孙子 174

granny (maternal) **āpó** 阿婆 1, **lǎolao** 姥姥 114, **wàipó** 外婆 184

grape **pútao** 葡萄 142

grasp firmly **zhuājǐn** 抓紧 239

grass **cǎo** 草 20

grassland **cǎoyuán** 草原 20

(be) grateful **gǎnxiè** 感谢 62

(be very) grateful **gǎnjī** 感激 62

gratuity **xiǎofèi** 小费 198

grave (n.) **fénmù** 坟墓 57

gray **huī** 灰 83

greasy (food) **yóu** 油 218

great **wěidà** 伟大 187, **zhòngdà** 重大 237

great achievement **chéngjiù** 成就 25

(the) Great Wall **chángchéng** 长城 22

green (adj.) **lǜ** 绿 122, **qīng** 青 148

greenback **Měiyuán** 美元 221

greet **dǎ zhāohu** 打招呼 228

greeting card **hèkǎ** 贺卡 78, 106

grieved (adj.) **bēitòng** 悲痛 8, **nánguò** 难过 133, **chéntòng** 沉痛 24

groan **shēnyín** 呻吟 160

ground (n.) **chǎng** 场 22

group (n.) **xiǎozǔ** 小组 198, **zǔ** 组 244

grouping **jítuán** 集团 89

grow **shēng** 生 162, **shēngzhǎng** 生长 162

grow up **chéngzhǎng** 成长 25, **shēngzhǎng** 生长 162

grown-up (n.) **dàren** 大人 35

grudging **miǎnqiǎng** 勉强 128

grumble **bàoyuàn** 抱怨 7

guarantee **bǎozhèng** 保证 6, **dānbǎo** 担保 37

guarantor **dānbǎorén** 担保人 37

guard against **fáng** 防 **fángzhǐ** 防止 54

guess **cāi** 猜 18

guest **kèren** 客人 110

guest room **kèfáng** 客房 54

guesthouse **bīnguǎn** 宾馆 13

guide (v.) **zhǐdǎo** 指导 234

guideline **gānglǐng** 纲领 63

gullible **tiānzhēn** 天真 179

gun **pào** 炮 138, **qiāng** 枪 172

gunpowder **huǒyào** 火药 86

gymnasium **tǐyùguǎn** 体育馆 71, 178, **jiànshēnfáng** 健身房 94

H

habit **xíguàn** 习惯 192

habitually **xíguàn shang** 习惯上 192

hack **kǎn** 砍 107

hacker **hēikè** 黑客 78

had better **zuìhǎo** 最好 244

haggle **jìjiào** 计较 89

hailstone/hailstorm **bīngbáo** 冰雹 13

hair **máo** 毛 125

hair (of the human head) **tóufa** 头发 182

hair salon **lǐfàdiàn** 理发店 116

hairdresser, hairstylist **lǐfàshī** 理发师 116

half **bàn** 半 5, **yíbàn** 一半 210

hall **táng** 堂 176

hammer **chuízi** 锤子 31

hamper (v.) **fáng'ài** 妨碍 54

hand **shǒu** 手 167

hand over **dì** 递 42, **jiāo** 交 95

handful of **bǎ** 把 5

handgun **shǒuqiāng** 手枪 146

handicraft **gōngyìpǐn** 工艺品 66

handicraft industry **shǒugōngyè** 手工业 167

handkerchief **shǒujuàn** 手绢 168

handle (n.) **bǎshǒu** 把手 29

handle (v.) **chǔlǐ** 处理 29, **cuò** 措 33

handmade **shǒugōng** 手工 167

(of men) handsome **yīngjùn** 英俊 215

handy **fāngbiàn** 方便 54

hang up (v.) **guà** 挂 70

happen **fāshēng** 发生 51

happy **gāoxìng** 高兴 63, **kuàilè** 快乐 112, **xìngfú** 幸福 203

(of marriage, family) happy **měimǎn** 美满 126

happy (to do) **lèyì** 乐意 115

harbor (n.) **gǎng** 港, **gǎngkǒu** 港口 63

hard **jiānkǔ** 艰苦 92, **yìng** 硬 216

hard (life) **kǔ** 苦 111

(in computing) hardware **yìngjiàn** 硬件 21

hardworking **kèkǔ** 刻苦 109, **qínláo** 勤劳 148

hare **tùzi** 兔子 183

harm (n.) **hàichu** 害处 75

harm (v.) **hài** 害 75

harmful **yǒuhài** 有害 75

harmonious **róngqià** 融洽 155

harmony, harmonious **héxié** 和谐 78

harsh (life) **xīnkǔ** 辛苦 200

harvest (v.) **shōuhuò** 收获 167

hasten **gǎnjǐn** 赶紧 62, **liánmáng** 连忙 118

hasty **jímáng** 急忙 88, **cāngcù** 仓促 19

hat **màozi** 帽子 125

hate **hèn** 恨 79

hateful **kěwù** 可恶 109

haunted house **guǐ wū** 鬼屋 73

have **yǒu** 有 218, **jùyǒu** 具有 105

have a dream **zuòmèng** 做梦 246

have a tendency to **róngyì** 容易 154

have as surplus **shèng** 剩 163

have fun **wánr** 玩儿 185

have no choice but **zhǐhǎo** 只好, **zhǐyǒu** 只有 234

have to **bùdebù** 不得不 15, **děi** 得 41

he **tā** 他 174

head (n.) **tóu** 头 182

head (v.) **dǐng** 顶 44

head of state **yuánshǒu** 元首 221

head of a workshop (in factory) **chējiān zhǔrèn** 车间主任 238

headache **tóu téng** 头疼 178

headline **biāotí** 标题 12

(military) headquarters **sīlìngbù** 司令部 172

health **jiànkāng** 健康 94, **shēntǐ** 身体 160

health club **jiànshēn fáng** 健身房 94

Health Department **wèishēngjú** 卫生局 187

260

healthy **jiànkāng** 健康 *94*

heap up **duī** 堆 *48*

hear **tīngjiàn** 听见 *180*

hear (a legal case) **shěnlǐ** 审理 *161*

hear of **tīngshuō** 听说 *180*

heart **xīn** 心 *200*

heart (medical term) **xīnzàng** 心脏 *200*

heartbreaking **shāngxīn** 伤心 *157*

heartbroken **shāngxīn** 伤心 *157, 200*

hearten **gǔwǔ** 鼓舞 *69*

heated swimming pool **wēnshuǐ yóuyǒngchí** 温水游泳池 *218*

heaven **tiān** 天 *178*

heavy **zhòng** 重 *237*, **chénzhòng** 沉重 *24*

heed **tīng** 听, **tīnghuà** 听话 *180*

height **gāodù** 高度 *63*

heir/heiress **jìchéngrén** 继承人 *90*

hello **wèi** 喂 *188*

help (n.) **bāngzhù** 帮助 *5*

help (v.) **bāng** 帮, **bāngzhù** 帮助, **bāngmáng** 帮忙 *5*

hen **jī** 鸡, **mǔjī** 母鸡 *87*

herbal medicine **cǎoyào** 草药 *209*

here **zhèlǐ** 这里 *229*, **cǐ** 此 *31*

here and now **cǐshícǐdì** 此时此地 *31*

hereditary disease **yíchuánbìng** 遗传病 *212*

hero **nánzǐhàn** 男子汉 *133*, **yīngxióng** 英雄 *215*

hesitant **yóuyù** 犹豫 *218*

hesitate **chíyí** 迟疑 *26*

hey, hi **wèi** 喂 *188*

hide **cáng** 藏 *20*

hide (oneself) **duǒ** 躲 *49*

hideous **chǒu'è** 丑恶 *28*

high **gāo** 高 *63*

high blood pressure/hypertension **gāoxuèyā** 高血压 *205*

(a) high degree **gāodù** 高度 *63*

high jump **tiào gāo** 跳高 *180*

high school **zhōngxué** 中学 *236*

high speed rail **gāosù tiělù** 高速铁路 *63*

high up **shàngmiàn** 上面 *158*, **shàngbian** 上边 *158*

high-level **gāojí** 高级 *63*

highland **gāoyuán** 高原 *63*

highlight **tūchū** 突出 *182*

highly **jí** 极, **jíqí** 极其 *88*

highway **gōnglù** 公路 *66*

hill **shān** 山 *156*

him **tā** 他 *174*

hinder **fáng'ài** 妨碍 *54*

hint **tíshì** 提示 *178*

historian **lìshǐxuéjiā** 历史学家 *117*

historic site **gǔjì** 古迹 *69*

historical novel **lìshǐ xiǎoshuō** 历史小说 *198*

historical period **shídài** 时代 *164*

history **lìshǐ** 历史 *117*

hit **dǎ** 打 *33*

hoax **piànjú** 骗局 *140*

hobby **àihào** 爱好 *1*

hold (v.) **ná** 拿 *131*

hold (in both hands) **pěng** 捧 *139*

hold (meeting/ceremony) **jǔxíng** 举行 *104*

hold a meeting **kāihuì** 开会 *106*

hold back **lán** 拦 *113*

hold in custody (for a given period of time) **jūliú** 拘留 *104*

hole **dòng** 洞 *46*, **kǒng** 孔 *111*

holiday period **jiàqī** 假期 *92*

holy **shénshèng** 神圣 *161*

home **jiā** 家 *91*

home village **gùxiāng** 故乡 *69*

hometown **gùxiāng** 故乡 *69*, **jiāxiāng** 家乡 *91*

homework **gōngkè** 功课 *67*, **zuòyè** 作业 *245*

honest **chéngshí** 诚实 *25*, **lǎoshi** 老实 *114*

honey **mì** 蜜 *127*

Hong Kong **Xiānggǎng** 香港 *196*

honor (n.) **miànzi** 面子 *128*

honor (v.) **zūnjìng** 尊敬 *244*

honorable **guāngróng** 光荣 *72*

honorary doctorate **míngyù bóshì** 名誉博士 *130*

hooligan **liúmáng** 流氓 *121*

hope **xīwàng** 希望 *192*

horizontal **héng** 横 *79*

horrible **bùdéliǎo** 不得了 *15*, **kǒngbù** 恐怖 *110*

horror movie **kǒngbù diànyǐng** 恐怖电影 *110*

horse **mǎ** 马 *123*

hospitable **hàokè** 好客 *77*

hospital **yīyuàn** 医院 *212*

(be) hospitalized **zhù (yī) yuàn** 住(医)院 *212, 239*

host (n.) **zhǔrén** 主人 *238*, **dōngdàozhǔ** 东道主 *45*

host (an event, a conference, etc.) **zhǔbàn** 主办 *238*, **jǔbàn** 举办 *104*

hostage **rénzhì** 人质 *153*

hostel **sùshè** 宿舍 *173*

hostile (to) **díshì** 敌视 *41*

hot **rè** 热 *152*

hot spring **wēnquán** 温泉 *151*

hot and stifling **mēnrè** 闷热 *127*

hot-air balloon **rèqì qiú** 热气球 *144*

(spicy) hot **là** 辣 *113*

hot (scalding) **tàng** 烫 *176*

hotel **lǚguǎn** 旅馆 *122*, **jiǔdiàn** 酒店 *103*

hour **xiǎoshí** 小时 *198*, **zhōngtóu** 钟头 *236*

house (n.) **fáng** 房 *54*, **fángzi** 房子 *54*

housefly **cāngyíng** 苍蝇 *19*

household **jiā** 家 *91*

household chores **jiāwù** 家务 *91*

housework **jiāwù** 家务 *91*

housing (n.) **fángzi** 房子 *54*

how **zěnme** 怎么 *225*, **zěnmeyàng** 怎么样 *226*

how can ... **zěnme** 怎么 *225*

how many/how much **duōshǎo** 多少 *49*

how much **duōshǎo qián** 多少钱 *49*

hug **bào** 抱 *7*, **yōngbào** 拥抱 *216*

huge **jùdà** 巨大 *104*, **pángdà** 庞大 *138*

hum (v.) **hēng** 哼 *79*

hum and hew **tūn tūn tǔ tǔ** 吞吞吐吐 *183*

human being **rén** 人 *152*

human body **shēn** 身 *160*, **shēntǐ** 身体 *160*

human population **rénkǒu** 人口 *152*

human resources affairs **rénshì** 人事 *153*

human nature **rénxìng** 人性 *153*

(the) human world **rénjiān** 人间 *152*

humankind **rénlèi** 人类 *153*

humor **yōumò** 幽默 *217*

hundred **bǎi** 百 *3*

hundred million **yì** 亿 *213*

hungry **è** 饿 *50*, **jī'è** 饥饿 *87*

hunt/hunting **dǎliè** 打猎 *34*

hurried (adj.) **jímáng** 急忙 *88*

hurry **cuī** 催 *32*

hurry up **gǎn** 赶 *61*

hurt **shāng** 伤 *157*, **tòng** 痛 *181*

husband **zhàngfu** 丈夫 *227*, **xiānsheng** 先生 *194*

husband's mother **pópo** 婆婆 *142*

husband and wife **fūqī** 夫妻 *58*

hygiene **wèishēng** 卫生 *187*

hypocritical/hypocrisy **xūwěi** 虚伪 *204*

I

I **wǒ** 我 *190*

I'm sorry **duìbuqǐ** 对不起 *48*

ice **bīng** 冰 *13*

ice cream **bīngjīlíng** 冰激凌 *13*

ice-skating **huábīng** 滑冰 *81*

idea **xiǎngfǎ** 想法 *196*, **zhǔyì** 主意 *238*

ideal **lǐxiǎng** 理想 *117*

identical **xiāngtóng** 相同 *196*, **yíyàng** 一样 *211*

identify **rèn** 认 *153*

idiom **chéngyǔ** 成语 *75*

idle **xián** 闲 *194*

idler **xiánrén** 闲人 *194*

if **rúguǒ** 如果 *155*, **yàoshì** 要是 *209*

if only **zhǐyào** 只要 *234*

(be) ill **bìng** 病 *13*

ill at ease **jūshù** 拘束 *104*

illegal **fēifǎ** 非法 *55*

illness **bìng** 病 *13*, **jíbìng** 疾病 *88*

image **xíngxiàng** 形象 *202*

imagine **xiǎngxiàng** 想象 *197*

imitate **mófǎng** 模仿 *130*

immediately **lìjí** 立即 *117*, **mǎshàng** 马上 *124*

immigrate, immigrant **yímín** 移民 *212*

immoral **bú dàodé** 不道德 *40*

immortal **shénxiān** 神仙 *161*

immunity **miǎnyì** 免疫 *128*

impatient/impetuous **jízào** 急躁 *88*

impatient/impetuous person **jíxìngzi**

Word Finder

262

invitation **yāoqǐng** 邀请 208

invitation card, letter of invitation **qǐngtiě** 请帖 149, **qǐngjiǎn** 请柬 149

invite **yāoqǐng** 邀请 208, **qǐng** 请 149

invite bids/tenders **zhāobiāo** 招标 228

involve **shèjí** 涉及 160

iron **tiě** 铁 180

iron (v.) **yùn** 熨 223

iron (n.) **yùndǒu** 熨斗 223

iron bar **tiěbàng** 铁棒 5

iron and steel **gāngtiě** 钢铁 63

irrigate/irrigation **guàngài** 灌溉 71, **jiāoguàn** 浇灌 96

irrigation ditch **qúdào** 渠道 150

irritate **cìjī** 刺激 31

island **dǎo** 岛 39

isolate **gélí** 隔离 64

isolation ward **gélí bìngfáng** 隔离病房 64

issue a certificate **chū zhèngmíng** 出证明 233

it **tā** 它 175

itch **yǎng** 痒, **fāyǎng** 发痒 208

item **xiàngmù** 项目 197

itinerary **lùxiàn** 路线 122

J

jacket **jiākèshān** 夹克衫 91, **shàngyī** 上衣 158

jade **yù** 玉 220

jadeware **yùqì** 玉器 220

jail **jiānyù** 监狱 92

Japan **Rìběn** 日本 154

Japanese (language) **Rìwén** 日文 154, **Rìyǔ** 日语 154

jealous **jídù** 嫉妒 88

jeans **niúzǎi kù** 牛仔裤 136

jellied meat **ròudòng** 肉冻 46

jelly (with fruit) **shuǐguó dòng** 水果冻 46

jeopardize **wēihài** 危害 186

jewelry **shǒushì** 首饰 168

job **gōngzuò** 工作 66, **fànwǎn** 饭碗 53

job (colloquial) **huór** 活儿 85

jog **pǎobù** 跑步 138

join **cānjiā** 参加 19, **lián** 联 118

jointly **gòng** 共 67

joke (n.) **xiàohua** 笑话 199

joke (v.) **kāi wánxiào** 开玩笑 107

journalist **xīnwén jìzhě** 新闻记者 89

journey (n.) **lǚtú** 旅途 122

joy **lèqù** 乐趣 115

joyful **huānlè** 欢乐 82

judge/judgment **pànduàn** 判断 138

jump **tiào** 跳 180

junior high school **chūzhōng** 初中 29

just/justice **gōngzhèng** 公正 67, **zhèngyì** 正义 232

just **gāngcái** 刚才 62, **zhǐshì** 只是 234

just a little bit **shāowēi** 稍微 158

just right **zhènghǎo** 正好 231

justification **lǐyóu** 理由 117

K

keep **bǎochí** 保持, **bǎocún** 保存 6

keep a shop **kāi shāngdiàn** 开商店 157

keep as pet **yǎng** 养 208

kettle **hú** 壶, **shuǐhú** 水壶 80

key **yàoshi** 钥匙 209

key point **yàodiǎn** 要点 209

keyboard **jiànpán** 键盘 95

kick (v.) **tī** 踢 177

kidnap **bǎngjià** 绑架 5

kill **shā** 杀 156

kilogram **gōngjīn** 公斤 66

kilometer **gōnglǐ** 公里 66

kind (n.) **yàng** 样 208, **zhǒng** 种 236

kindergarten **yòu'éryuán** 幼儿园 219

kind-hearted **shànliáng** 善良 157, **hǎoxīn** 好心 77

king **guówáng** 国王 186

kingdom **wángguó** 王国 186

kiosk **tíngzi** 亭子 180

kitchen **chúfáng** 厨房 29

kneel **guì** 跪 73

knife (n.) **dāo** 刀 39, **dāozi** 刀子 39

knit **biānzhī** 编织 11

knitting wool **máoxiàn** 毛线 125

knock (v.) **qiāo** 敲 147

know **zhīdào** 知道 233, **liǎojiě** 了解 120

know how to **huì** 会 84

know well **shúxi** 熟悉 169

knowledge **zhīshì** 知识 233

(be) known as **chēng** 称 24, **jiàozuo** 叫做 24

kung fu **gōngfu** 功夫 67

(the) Kuomintang **guómíndǎng** 国民党 74

L

labor **láodòng** 劳动 114

Labor Day (May 1st) **láodòng jié** 劳动节 114

laboratory **shíyànshì** 实验室 165, **huàyàn shì** 化验室 81

laboratory technician **shíyànyuán** 实验员 165, **huàyàn yuán** 化验员 81

laboratory test **huàyàn** 化验 81

lack **quēfá** 缺乏 151, **quēshǎo** 缺少 151

lad **xiǎohuǒzi** 小伙子 198

ladle (n.) **sháozi** 勺子 158

lag behind **tuìbù** 退步 183

(be) laid off **xiàgǎng** 下岗 193

lake **hú** 湖 80, **húpō** 湖泊 80

lakeside **húbiān** 湖边 80

lamb **xiǎoyáng** 小羊 208

lamp **dēng** 灯 41

lamplight **dēngguāng** 灯光 71

land (n.) **tǔdì** 土地 182

landlord/landlady **fángdōng** 房东 54

landscape **fēngjǐng** 风景 57, **shānshuǐ** 山水 156

language **yǔyán** 语言 220

large **dà** 大 34

large-scale **dàxíng** 大型 36

larynx **hóulóng** 喉咙 79

last year **qùnián** 去年 150

late **wǎn** 晚 185

(be) late **chídào** 迟到 26

later **yǐhòu** 以后 213

later on **hòulái** 后来 79

launch **kāizhǎn** 开展 107, **zhǎnkāi** 展开 227

launch (a rocket) **fāshè** 发射 51

law **fǎlǜ** 法律 52, **guīlǜ** 规律 72

law firm **lǜshī shìwùsuǒ** 律师事务所 123

lawsuit **sùsòng** 诉讼 173

lawn **cǎodì** 草地 20

lawyer **lǜshī** 律师 123

lax **sōng** 松 172

lay down **zhìdìng** 制定 235

lay off (staff) **cáiyuán** 裁员 18

layman **wàiháng** 外行 184

layout **géjú** 格局 64

lazy **lǎn** 懒 113, **lǎnduò** 懒惰 113

lead **lǐng** 领, **lǐngdǎo** 领导 120

lead (a life) **shēnghuó** 生活 161

lead (in a police case) **xiànsuǒ** 线索 195

lead to **yǐnqǐ** 引起 215, **chǎnshēng** 产生 22

leader **lǐngdǎo** 领导 120, **lǐngxiù** 领袖 121

leaf (n.) **yèzi** 叶子 210

leaflet **chuándān** 传单 30

leak **lòu** 漏 122

lean (adj.) **shòu** 瘦 168

lean meat **shòuròu** 瘦肉 168

learn **xué** 学 205, **tǐhuì** 体会 178

learn from … **xiàng … xuéxí** 向…学习 205

learning **xuéwèn** 学问 205

lease/lease out **zūlìn** 租赁 243

leather **pí** 皮 139

leave **lí** 离 116, **líkāi** 离开 116

leave application **jiàtiáo** 假条 92

leave work **xiàbān** 下班 4

lecture (n.) **jiǎngzuò** 讲座 95, **kè** 课 110

lecture (v.) **jiàoxùn** 教训 97

left hand **zuǒshǒu** 左手 167

(be) left over **shèng** 剩 163

left side **zuǒ** 左, **zuǒbian** 左边 245

leftovers **shèng cài** 剩菜 163

leg (n.) **tuǐ** 腿 183

legal person **fǎrén** 法人 52

legend **chuánshō** 传说 30

legitimate **héfǎ** 合法 77, **zhèngdàng** 正当 231

leisure **xiūxián** 休闲 204

leisurely **qīngxián** 清闲 194

lend **jiè** 借 99

less than **yíxià** 以下 213

lesson **kè** 课 110

lesson (from experience) **jiàoxùn** 教训 97, **jīngyàn** 经验 102

lest/so as not to **miǎnde** 免得 128

let **ràng** 让 152, **suí** 随 173

Word Finder

let down **gūfù** 辜负 *69*

letter (of an alphabet) **zìmǔ** 字母 *243*

letter **xìn** 信 *201*

letter of invitation **yāoqǐngxìn** 邀请信 *208*

letter received **láixìn** 来信 *113*

level (adj.) **píng** 平 *141*

level (n.) **chéngdù** 程度 *26*, **shuǐpíng** 水平 *171*

level (floor) **céng** 层 *20*

lever **gànggǎn** 杠杆 *63*

lewd **hào sè** 好色 *77*

liaison person **liánluò yuán** 联络员 *118*

libel **fěibàng** 诽谤 *56*

liberate/liberation **jiěfàng** 解放 *99*

liberty **zìyóu** 自由 *242*

library **túshūguǎn** 图书馆 *71, 182*

license **zhízhào** 执照 *233*

license plate (on vehicle) **chē pái** 车牌 *23*

lie (v.) **shuōhuǎng** 说谎 *171*

lie (n.) **jiǎhuà** 假话 *91*

lie (v.) **tǎng** 躺 *176*

life **rìzi** 日子 *154*, **shēnghuó** 生活 *161*, **shēngmìng** 生命 *161*

lifeboat **jiù shēng tǐng** 救生艇 *180*

lifestyle **shēnghuó fāngshì** 生活方式 *54*

lifetime **yìshēng** 一生 *211*

lift **jǔ** 举 *104*, **tái** 抬 *175*

light **guāng** 光 *71*, **diàndēng** 电灯 *41*

light (of weight) **qīng** 轻 *148*

light music **qīng yīnyuè** 轻音乐 *215*

light refreshments **diǎnxīn** 点心 *42*

light up **zhào** 照 *228*

lighten **jiǎnqīng** 减轻 *93*

lighting **dēng** 灯 *41*

lightning **shǎndiàn** 闪电 *156*

like **xǐhuan** 喜欢 *192*

(be) like **xiàng** 像 *197*

likely **róngyì** 容易 *154*

likeness of (a human being) **xiàng** 像 *197*

limit (n.) **júxiàn** 局限 *104*

limit (v.) **xiànzhì** 限制 *195*

limited (adj.) **yídìng** 一定 *210*

limits (n.) **fànwéi** 范围 *53*, **jièxiàn** 界限 *100*

line (measurement) **háng** 行 *76*

line up **páiduì** 排队 *138*

link **huánjié** 环节 *82*

lion **shīzi** 狮子 *163*

liquid **yètǐ** 液体 *210*

liquid medicine **yàoshuǐ** 药水 *209*

listen **tīng** 听 *180*

literary work **zhùzuò** 著作 *239*, **zuòpǐn** 作品 *245*

literature **wénxué** 文学 *189*

little **xiǎo** 小 *198*, **shǎo** 少 *158*

little girl **xiǎo gūniang** 小姑娘 *68*

live (a life) **guò rìzi** 过日子 *74*, **shēnghuó** 生活 *161*

live (in somewhere) **zhù** 住 *239*

---

lively **huópo** 活泼 *85*, **shēngdòng** 生动 *161*

livestock **shēngchù** 牲畜 *162*

liver **gān** 肝 *61*

living allowance **shēnghuó fèi** 生活费 *161*

living conditions **shēnghuó tiáojiàn** 生活条件 *179*

living expenses **shēnghuó fèiyòng** 生活费用 *56*

living room **kètīng** 客厅 *110*

living standard **shēnghuó shuǐpíng** 生活水平 *161, 171*

living things **shēngwù** 生物 *162*

loan (of money) **dàikuǎn** 贷款 *36*

local (n.) **dāngdì rén** 当地人 *38*

local time **dāngdì shíjiān** 当地时间 *38*

location **chù** 处 *29*, **dìfang** 地方 *41*, **wèizhì** 位置 *188*

lock **suǒ** 锁 *174*

lofty **chónggāo** 崇高 *27*

logic **luójì** 逻辑 *123*

logical **hélǐ** 合理 *77*

logistics **hòuqín** 后勤 *79*

lonely **jìmò** 寂寞 *90*, **gūdú** 孤独 *68*

long (adj.) **cháng** 长 *22*

long distance **chángtú** 长途 *22*

long-distance bus/coach **chángtú qìchē** 长途汽车 *22*

long-distance running **chángpǎo** 长跑 *22*

long for **pànwàng** 盼望 *138*

long jump **tiào yuǎn** 跳远 *179*

long-standing **lǎo** 老 *114*, **yōujiǔ** 悠久 *217*

long-winded **luōsuō** 啰唆 *123*

look **kàn** 看 *107*

look after **guānzhào** 关照 *71*, **zhàogù** 照顾 *229*

look at **wàng** 望 *186*

look down at **fǔshì** 俯视 *59*

look for **xúnzhǎo** 寻找 *205*, **zhǎo** 找 *228*

look forward to **pànwàng** 盼望 *138*, **qīdài** 期待 *143*

look on **pángguān** 旁观 *138*

look out for **liúshén** 留神 *121*

loosen **sōng** 松 *172*

lorry **kǎchē** 卡车 *106*

lose (a game/bet) **shū** 输 *169*

lose (something valuable) **shīqù** 失去 *163*

lose face **diūliǎn** 丢脸 *119*, **diū miànzi** 丢面子 *124*

lose one's job **shīyè** 失业 *163*

lose one's temper **fāhuǒ** 发火 *51*, **fā píqi** 发脾气 *140*

lose one's way **mílù** 迷路 *127*

loss **shībài** 失败 *163*, **sǔnshī** 损失 *174*

loss (in business) **kuīsǔn** 亏损 *112*

lots of **dàpī** 大批 *35*

loud **xiǎng** 响 *196*

loudly **dàshēng** 大声 *35*

lovable **kě'ài** 可爱 *109*

(romantic) love **àiqíng** 爱情 *1*, **liàn'ài** 恋爱 *119*

love (v.) **ài** 爱 *1*

love ardently **rè'ài** 热爱 *152*

love dearly **téng** 疼 *177*

low **dī** 低 *41*

low blood pressure/hypotension **dīxuèyā** 低血压 *205*

lower (v.) **dī** 低 *41*, **jiàng** 降 *96*, **jiàngdī** 降低 *96*

lozenge (for cough) **késou táng** 咳嗽糖 *109*

luckily **xìngkuī** 幸亏 *203*

luggage **xínglǐ** 行李 *202*

lunch **wǔfàn** 午饭 *190*

lungs **fèi** 肺 *56*

luxurious **háohuá** 豪华 *76*, **shēchǐ** 奢侈 *159*

luxury goods **shēchǐ pǐn** 奢侈品 *159*

M

machine **jīqì** 机器 *87*, **jīxiè** 机械 *87*

machine tool **jīchuáng** 机床 *86*

machinery **jīxiè** 机械 *87*

macroscopic **hóngguān** 宏观 *79*

magazine **zázhì** 杂志 *223*

magnetic tape **cídài** 磁带 *31*

magnificent **xióngwěi** 雄伟 *203*, **hóngwěi** 宏伟 *79*

magnifying glass **fàngdàjìng** 放大镜 *55*

magic **móshù** 魔术 *130*

magician **móshùshī** 魔术师 *130*

mahjong **májiàng** 麻将 *123*

mail (v.) **jì** 寄 *90*

mailbag **yóubāo** 邮包 *5*

main **zhǔyào** 主要 *238*

main course (of a dinner) **zhǔcài** 主菜 *238*

main point **zhòngdiǎn** 重点 *237*

main street **dàjiē** 大街 *35*

mainland **dàlù** 大陆 *35*

mainstream **zhǔliú** 主流 *238*

maintain (e.g. automobiles) **bǎoyǎng** 保养 *6*

maize **yùmǐ** 玉米 *220*

major (adj.) **zhòngdà** 重大 *237*, **zhǔyào** 主要 *238*

majority **dàduōshù** 大多数 *35*, **duōshù** 多数 *49*

make (v.) **shǐ** 使 *165*, **ràng** 让 *152*

make (v.) **zhìzào** 制造 *235*

make a decision **zuò juédìng** 做决定 *105*, **ná zhǔyi** 拿主意 *131*

make a fortune **fācái** 发财 *51*

make a mistake **fàn cuòwù** 犯错误 *33*

make a speech **fāyán** 发言 *51*

make a telephone call **dǎ diànhuà** 打电话 *40*

make a tough decision **xià hěnxīn** 下狠心 *78*

make a turn **guǎi** 拐 *70*

make a video recording **shèxiàng** 摄像 *159*

---

make a vow **xuānshì** 宣誓 *204*

make arrangement **ānpái** 安排 *2*

make clear **biǎomíng** 表明 *12*

make friends with ... **gēn/hé ... jiāo péngyou** 跟/和...交朋友 *139*

make known **fǎnyìng** 反映 *53*, **bàogào** 报告 *7*

make money/profit **zhuàn** 赚 *240*

make notes (while reading) **zuò bǐjì** 做笔记 *10*

make profit **yínglì** 盈利 *216*

make public **gōngkāi** 公开 *66*

make reservations **dìng zuò** 订座 *45*

make sentences **zàojù** 造句 *225*

make trouble **dǎoluàn** 捣乱 *39*

make up **dǎbàn** 打扮 *33*, **gòuchéng** 构成 *68*

make up one's mind **juédìng** 决定 *105*

make use of **lìyòng** 利用 *118*

make wine **niàng jiǔ** 酿酒 *135*

male (animal) **gōng** 公 *66*, **xióng** 雄 *203*

male (human) **nán** 男 *133*

mall **shāngchǎng** 商场 *157*

Mammon **cáishényé** 财神爷 *161*

man **rén** 人 *152*

man/men **nánrén** 男人 *133*, **nánzihàn** 男子汉 *133*

man-made **rénzào** 人造 *153*

manage **bàn** 办 *4*, **guǎnlǐ** 管理 *71*

manager **jīnglǐ** 经理 *102*

Mandarin (language) **Pǔtōnghuà** 普通话 *142*

manipulate **cāozòng** 操纵 *20*

mankind **rénlèi** 人类 *153*

manner **fāngshì** 方式 *54*, **yàngzi** 样子 *208*

manner of speaking **yǔqì** 语气 *221*

manpower **réngōng** 人工 *152*

manual **shuōmíng** 说明 *172*

manual (adj.) **shǒugōng** 手工 *167*

manufacture **shēngchǎn** 生产 *161*, **zhìzào** 制造 *235*

manufacturing industry **gōngyè** 工业 *66*, **zhìzàoyè** 制造业 *235*

manuscript **gǎojiàn** 稿件 *63*

many **xǔduō** 许多 *204*, **hǎo duō** 好多 *76*, **duō** 多 *49*

map **dìtú** 地图 *42*

maritime rights **hǎiyáng quán** 海洋权 *75*

market (n.) **shìchǎng** 市场 *166*

market (v.) **tuīxiāo** 推销 *183*

market economy **shìchǎng jīngjì** 市场经济 *102*, *166*

marketing manager **shìchǎng jīnglǐ** 市场经理 *102*

marketplace **shìchǎng** 市场 *166*

marriage **hūnyīn** 婚姻 *85*

marriage partner **duìxiàng** 对象 *48*

marry **jiéhūn** 结婚 *99*

martial arts **gōngfu** 功夫 *67*, **wǔshù** 武术 *191*

mascot **jíxiángwù** 吉祥物 *88*

mass media **dàzhòng méitǐ** 大众媒体 *126*

massage **ànmó** 按摩 *2*

massage parlor **ànmóyuàn** 按摩院 *2*

(be) master of **jīngtōng** 精通 *102*

master's degree/masterate **shuòshì xuéwèi** 硕士学位 *172*

Master of Business Administartion (MBA) **shāngyè guǎnlǐ shuòshì** 商业管理硕士 *157*

master worker **shīfu** 师傅 *163*

matchbox **huǒchái hé** 火柴盒 *86*

matchmaker **méirén** 媒人 *126*

(be a) matchmaker **zuòméi** 做媒 *126*

matchstick **huǒchái** 火柴 *86*

mate **huǒbàn** 伙伴 *86*

material **cáiliào** 材料 *18*, **zīliào** 资料 *241*

material incentive **wùzhì gǔlì** 物质鼓励 *69*

materialize **shíxiàn** 实现 *164*

maternal **mǔ** 母 *131*

maternal granny **ā pó** 阿婆 *1*

maternal instinct **mǔxìng** 母性 *131*

mathematics **shùxué** 数学 *170*

matter (n.) **shì** 事 *165*, **shìqing** 事情 *166*

mature **chéngshú** 成熟 *25*

may **kěnéng** 可能 *109*, **kěyǐ** 可以 *109*

maybe **yěxǔ** 也许 *209*

mayor of a county **xiànzhǎng** 县长 *195*

me **wǒ** 我 *190*

meager **bó** 薄 *14*

(a) meal **cān** 餐 *19*, **fàn** 饭 *53*

meals **huǒshí** 伙食 *86*

mean (v.) **zhǐ** 指 *234*

meaning **yìsi** 意思 *214*

(implied) meaning **hányì** 含义 *75*

meaningful **yǒu yìsi** 有意思 *219*

meaningless **méiyǒu yìsi** 没有意思 *219*

means (n.) **shǒuduàn** 手段 *167*

measure (n.) **cuòshī** 措施 *33*, **shǒuduàn** 手段 *167*

measure (v.) **liáng** 量 *119*, **cèliáng** 测量 *20*

measurements **chǐcùn** 尺寸 *27*

meat **ròu** 肉 *155*

mediate a dipute **tiáojiě jiūfēn** 调解纠纷 *179*

medical certificate **bìngjiàtiáo** 病假条 *92*

medical doctor **yīshēng** 医生 *212*

medical school **yīxuéyuàn** 医学院 *212*

medical science **yīxué** 医学 *212*

medical specialist **zhuānkē yīshēng** 专科医生 *239*

medicine **yào** 药 *209*, **yīxué** 医学 *212*

medium (n.) **méijiè** 媒介 *126*, **méitǐ** 媒体 *126*

meet **jiànmiàn** 见面 *94*, **huìjiàn** 会见 *84*

meet the needs of **mǎnzú** 满足 *124*

meet unexpectedly **pèngdao** 碰到 *139*, **yùjiàn** 遇见 *221*

meeting **huì** 会 *84*, **huìyì** 会议 *84*

melodious **hǎotīng** 好听 *77*

melody **xuánlǜ** 旋律 *204*

melon **guā** 瓜 *70*

melt **huà** 化 *81*, **rónghuà** 融化 *155*

member (of a family or group) **chéngyuán** 成员 *25*

membership (of an association) **huìjí** 会籍 *88*

memorandum/memo **bèiwànglù** 备忘录 *8*

memorial service **zhuīdàohuì** 追悼会 *241*

memorize **jìyì** 记忆 *89*

memorize new words **jì shēngcí** 记生词 *161*

memory **huíyì** 回忆 *84*, **jìyì** 记忆 *89*

mend **bǔ** 补 *14*

mental hospital **jīngshén bìng yīyuàn** 精神病医院 *102*

mental illness/disorder **jīngshénbìng** 精神病 *102*, *161*

mental state **shénjīng** 神经 *161*

mental work **nǎolì láodòng** 脑力劳动 *114*

mention (v.) **tí** 提 *177*

merciful **réncí** 仁慈 *153*

merely **jǐn** 仅 *100*, **jǐnjǐn** 仅仅 *100*

merge **hébìng** 合并 *77*

merit **yōudiǎn** 优点 *217*

(informal, written) message **biàntiáo** 便条 *11*

(text) message **duǎnxìn** 短信 *47*

metal **jīnshǔ** 金属 *100*

metaphor **bǐyù** 比喻 *10*

meteorological observatory **qìxiàngtái** 气象台 *145*

meteorological phenomena **qìxiàng** 气象 *145*

meteorology **qìxiàngxué** 气象学 *145*

meter (measurement) **gōngchǐ** 公尺 *27*, **mǐ** 米 *127*

method **bànfǎ** 办法 *4*, **fāngfǎ** 方法 *54*

meticulous **xìxīn** 细心 *193*, **jīngxīn** 精心 *102*

metric system (of measurements) **gōng zhì** 公制 *235*

micro-channel/WeChat **wēixìn** 微信 *187*

microphone **huàtǒng** 话筒 *82*, **màikèfēng** 麦克风 *124*

Mid-Autumn Festival (Moon Festival) **Zhōngqiūjié** 中秋节 *236*

middle **zhōng** 中 *235*, **zhōngjiān** 中间 *236*

middle age **zhōngnián** 中年 *236*

middle-aged person **zhōngniánrén** 中年人 *236*

middle school **zhōngxué** 中学 *236*

midnight **bànyè** 半夜 *5*, *210*

milestone **lǐchéng bēi** 里程碑 *116*

military affairs **jūnshì** 军事 *106*

Word Finder

(of medical test result) negative **yīnxìng** 阴性 *214*

negative effect **huàichu** 坏处 *82*

negative opinion **kànfǎ** 看法 *107*

neglect **hūlüè** 忽略, **hūshì** 忽视 *80*

negotiate/negotiation **tánpàn** 谈判 *176*

neighbor **línjū** 邻居 *120*

neither **yě** 也 *209*

nephew **zhízi** 侄子 *234*

nerve **shénjīng** 神经 *160*

nervous **jǐnzhāng** 紧张 *100*

netizen **wǎngmín** 网民 *186*

network **wǎngluò** 网络 *186*

neuropathy **shénjīngbìng** 神经病 *161*

neutral **zhōnglì** 中立 *236*

neutral state **zhōnglìguó** 中立国 *236*

never **cóngbù** 从不, **cónglái bù** 从来不 *32*

new **xīn** 新 *200*

New Year **xīnnián** 新年 *200*

(the) New Year's Day **yuándàn** 元旦 *221*

New Year's Day card **xīnnián hèkǎ** 新年贺卡 *200*

New Zealand **Xīnxīlán** 新西兰 *201*

news **xiāoxi** 消息 *197*, **xīnwén** 新闻 *200*

news conference **jìzhě zhāodàihuì** 记者招待会 *228*

news program **xīnwén jiémù** 新闻节目 *88*

news reporter **xīnwén jìzhě** 新闻记者 *89*

news story **bàodào** 报道 *7*

newspaper **bàozhǐ** 报纸 *7*

next **qícì** 其次 *143*

next door **gébì** 隔壁 *73*

next year **míngnián** 明年 *129*

nibble **kěn** 啃 *110*

niece **zhínǚ** 侄女 *234*

night **yè** 夜 *210*

(at) night **yèli** 夜里, **yèwǎn** 夜晚 *210*

nine **jiǔ** 九 *103*

no **bù** 不 *15*

no matter **bùguǎn** 不管 *16*, **wúlùn** 无论 *190*

no need **búyòng** 不用 *17*

nonsense **húshuō** 胡说 *80*

notebook (computer) **bǐjì běn (diànnǎo)** 笔记本（电脑）*10*

noble **gāoshàng** 高尚 *63*

noise **zàoyīn** 噪音 *225*

noise pollution **zàoyīn wūrǎn** 噪音污染 *225*

noisy **chǎo** 吵 *23*, **cáozá** 嘈杂 *20*

nonsense **fèihuà** 废话 *56*

noodles **miàntiáor** 面条儿 *128*

(instant) noodles **fāngbiàn miàn** 方便面 *54*

noon **zhōngwǔ** 中午 *236*

normal **zhèngcháng** 正常 *231*

normally **píngcháng** 平常 *141*

north **běi** 北 *8*

North Pole **běijí** 北极 *8*

north side **běibian** 北边, **běimiàn** 北面 *8*

North Star **běijíxīng** 北极星 *8*

northeast **dōngběi** 东北 *45*

northern **běi** 北 *8*

northern region **běibian** 北方 *8*

northwest **xīběi** 西北 *191*

nose **bízi** 鼻子 *9*

not **bù** 不 *15*

not allowed **bùxíng** 不行 *17*, **bùxǔ** 不许 *17*

not as...as **bùrú** 不如 *16*

not at all **háo bù** 毫不 *76*

not bad **búcuò** 不错 *15*

not enough time (to do something) **láibují** 来不及 *113*

not many **méiyǒu duōshǎo** 没有多少 *49*

not much **búdà** 不大 *15*, **méiyǒu duōshǎo** 没有多少 *49*

not only **búdàn** 不但 *15*, **bùjǐn** 不仅 *16*

not permitted **bùxǔ** 不许 *17*

not yet **hái méiyǒu** 还没有 *126*

notable **xiǎnzhù** 显著 *194*

notebook **běnzi** 本子 *9*, **bǐjì běn** 笔记本 *10*

(class, reading) notes **bǐjì** 笔记 *10*

notice **tōngzhī** 通知 *180*

(important) notice **xūzhī** 须知 *204*

notify **guānzhào** 关照 *71*, **tōngzhī** 通知 *181*

notion **gàiniàn** 概念 *61*

notarize **gōngzhèng** 公证 *67*

notary public **gōngzhèng rén** 公证人 *67*, **gōngzhèng chù** 公证处 *67*

nourishment **yíngyǎng** 营养 *215*

novel **xiǎoshuō** 小说 *198*, **chángpiān xiǎoshuō** 长篇小说 *198*

novelist **xiǎoshuōjiā** 小说家 *198*

now **xiànzài** 现在 *195*

nowadays **jìnlái** 近来 *101*

nuclear power plant **hédiànzhàn** 核电站 *78*

nuclear weapon **héwǔqì** 核武器 *78*

numb **mámù** 麻木 *123*

number **shù** 数 *169*, **shùzì** 数字 *170*

nurse **hùshi** 护士 *80*

nutrition **yíngyǎng** 营养 *215*

O

oar **jiǎng** 桨 *96*

oats **yànmài** 燕麦 *124*

(be) obedient **tīnghuà** 听话 *180*

obey **fúcóng** 服从 *58*

object (v.) **fǎnduì** 反对 *52*

objection **yìjiàn** 意见 *213*

objective (n.) **mùbiāo** 目标 *131*

obligation **yìwù** 义务 *213*

oblique **xié** 斜 *199*

observe **guānchá** 观察 *71*

observe a festival **guò jié** 过节 *74*

observer **guāncháyuán** 观察员 *71*

obstacle **zhàng'ài** 障碍 *228*

obstinate **gùzhi** 固执 *69*

obtain **huòdé** 获得 *86*, **qǔdé** 取得 *150*

obvious **míngxiǎn** 明显 *130*, **xiǎnrán** 显然 *194*

o'clock **diǎn** 点 *42*, **diǎnzhōng** 点钟 *43*

occasion **qíngjǐng** 情景 *148*, **chǎnghé** 场合 *22*

(the) Occident **xīfāng** 西方 *191*

occupation **zhíyè** 职业 *233*

occupy **zhàn** 占 *227*

ocean **hǎiyáng** 海洋 *75*

Oceania **Dàyángzhōu** 大洋洲 *36*

odd **guài** 怪 *70*, **qíguài** 奇怪 *143*

odd number **dānshù** 单数 *37*

odor **qìwèi** 气味 *144*

of course **dāngrán** 当然 *38*

offend **fàn** 犯 *53*

(be) offended **shēngqì** 生气 *162*

offer an apology **biǎodá qiànyì** 表达歉意 *146*

office **bàngōngshì** 办公室 *5*

office building **bàngōng dàlóu** 办公大楼 *5*

office hours **bàngōng shíjiān** 办公时间 *5*

office manager **bàngōngshì zhǔrèn** 办公室主任 *238*

official (adj.) **guān** 官 *71*, **zhèngshì** 正式 *232*

official (n.) **guānyuán** 官员 *71*

often **chángcháng** 常常 *22*, **jīngcháng** 经常 *101*

oil (n.) **shíyóu** 石油 *164*, **yóu** 油 *218*

oil painting **yóuhuà** 油画 *218*

oil well **yóujǐng** 油井 *103*

oilfield **yóukuàng** 油矿 *112*, **yóutián** 油田 *218*

OK **xíng** 行 *201*

old **lǎo** 老 *114*

old (things) **jiù** 旧 *103*

old and frail **shuāilǎo** 衰老 *170*

old age **wǎnnián** 晚年 *185*

old-fashioned **chénjiù** 陈旧 *24*

old person **lǎorén** 老人 *114*

omen **yùzhào** 预兆 *221*

omit **shěnglüè** 省略 *163*

on **guānyú** 关于 *71*, **shàng** 上 *157*, **zài** 在 *224*

on duty **zhíbān** 值班 *233*, *123*

(be) on holiday **fàngjià** 放假 *55*

on purpose **gùyì** 故意 *69*

on the one hand ... on the other hand ... **yìfāngmiàn ... yìfāngmiàn ...** 一方面 ... 一方面 ... *210*

on the spot **dāngcháng** 当场 *38*

on the whole **jīběn shang** 基本上 *87*

on time **ànshí** 按时 *2*, **àn qī** 按期 *143*, **zhǔnshí** 准时 *241*

on top of **shàng** 上 *157*

once again **chóng** 重, **chóngxīn** 重新 *27*

once upon a time **cóngqián** 从前 *32*

one **yī** 一 *210*

one after another **lùxù** 陆续 *122*, **xiānhòu** 先后 *194*, **jiēlián** 接连 *98*

Word Finder

paste (v.) **tiē** 贴 180

pasture **cǎoyuán** 草原 20

pat **pāi** 拍 137

patch (v.) **bǔ** 补 14

patent (n.) **zhuānlì** 专利 239

paternal grandfather **yéye** 爷爷 209

paternal grandmother **nǎinai** 奶奶 132

path **dàolù** 道路 40

patience **nàixīn** 耐心 132

patient (adj.) **nàifán** 耐烦 132, **nàixīn** 耐心 132

patient (n.) **bìngrén** 病人 14, **huànzhě** 患者 82

patrol **xúnluó** 巡逻 205

pavilion **tíngzi** 亭子 180

pay **fù** 付 59, **jiǎonà** 缴纳 97

pay attention to **zhùyì** 注意 239

pay fees **jiāo fèi** 交费 56

pay for (damage, loss, etc.) **péi** 赔 138

pay taxes **nàshuì** 纳税 132

payphone **gōngyòng diànhuà** 公用电话 67

peace **hépíng** 和平 78

peaceful **ān** 安 2, **ānjìng** 安静 2, **jìng** 静 102

peak (mountain) **shāndǐng** 山顶 44

peak (n.) **gāofēng** 高峰 63

peanut **huāshēng** 花生 81

peanut butter **huāshēng jiàng** 花生酱 81

pear **lí** 梨 116

pearl **zhēnzhū** 珍珠 230

peasant **nóngmín** 农民 136

pedestrian **xíngrén** 行人 202

pedestrian crossing **xíngrénhéngdào xiàn** 行人横道线 202

pedestrian street **bùxíng jiē** 步行街 98

Peking opera **jīngjù** 京剧 102

pen **bǐ** 笔 10

penalize/penalty **chéngfá** 惩罚 26

penalized **shòufá** 受罚 168

pencil **bǐ** 笔 10, **qiānbǐ** 铅笔 145

pencil drawing **qiānbǐ huà** 铅笔画 81

pencil sharpener **qiānbǐ dāo** 铅笔刀 39, 145

penetrate **tòu** 透 182

penknife **shuǐguǒ dāo** 水果刀 39

pension **tuìxiū jīn** 退休金 183

people **rénmen** 人们 153

(the) people (of a state) **rénmín** 人民 153

(hot) pepper **làjiāo** 辣椒 113

Pepsi[-Cola] **bǎishìkělè** 百事可乐 109

perceive **jiàn** 见 94

… percent **bǎi fēnzhī** … 百分之 … 57

percentage **bǎifēnbǐ** 百分比 4

perfect **wánměi** 完美 185

perform **biǎoxiàn** 表现 12, **biǎoyǎn** 表演 13

perform an operation **zuò shǒushù** 做手术 168

performance **biǎoyǎn** 表演 13, **yǎnchū** 演出 208

performing arts **wényì** 文艺 189

perhaps **kǒngpà** 恐怕 110, **yěxǔ** 也许 209, **huòxǔ** 或许 86

period of time **shíqī** 时期 164

periodical/magazine **kānwù** 刊物 107

periphery **biānyuán** 边缘 11

permeate **shèntòu** 渗透 161

permit (v.) **yǔnxǔ** 允许 223, **xǔkě** 许可 204

permit (n.)/license **xǔkě zhèng** 许可证 204

persecute/prosecution **pòhài** 迫害 142

persist **jiānchí** 坚持 92

person **rén** 人 152

person in charge **fùzérén** 负责人 59, **zhǔguǎn** 主管 238

personage **rénwù** 人物 153

personal **sīrén** 私人 172

personal experience **jīnglì** 经历 102

personal hygiene **gèrén wèishēng** 个人卫生 187

personal understanding **tǐhuì** 体会 178

personality **réngé** 人格 152, **gèxìng** 个性 64

personnel **rényuán** 人员 153

perspiration **hàn** 汗 75

perspire **chūhàn** 出汗 75

persuade **shuōfú** 说服 171

pessimistic **bēiguān** 悲观 8

pest (insect) **hàichóng** 害虫 75

(flower) petal **huābàn** 花瓣 81

petroleum **qìyóu** 汽油 145, **shíyóu** 石油 164

Ph.D. **bóshì** 博士 14

Ph.D. candidate **bóshì shēng** 博士生 14

Ph.D. degree/doctorate **bóshì xuéwèi** 博士学位 14, 205

Ph.D. supervisor **bóshì shēng dǎoshī** 博士生导师 14

pharmacy **yàofáng** 药房 209

phenomenon **xiànxiàng** 现象 195

philosopher **zhéxuéjiā** 哲学家 229

philosophy **zhéxué** 哲学 229

photocopier **yǐngyìnjī** 影印机 216, **fùyìn jī** 复印机 60

photocopy **yǐngyìn** 影印 216, **fùyìn** 复印 60

photograph (n.) **zhàopiàn** 照片 229

photograph (v.) **pāizhào** 拍照 137

photographer **shèyǐngshī** 摄影师 160

photographic studio **zhàoxiàngguǎn** 照相馆 229

photography/cinematography **shèyǐng** 摄影 159

physical education **tǐyù** 体育 178

physical strength **lìqi** 力气 117

physics **wùlǐ** 物理 191

physiology **shēnglǐxué** 生理学 161

piano **gāngqín** 钢琴 148

pick (v.) **cǎi** 采 18, **zhāi** 摘 226

pick up **jiǎn** 捡 93

pictorial **huàbào** 画报 81

picture (n.) **huàr** 画儿 81, **tú** 图 182, **zhàopiàn** 照片 229

pig **zhū** 猪 238

pile up **duī** 堆 48

pilfer **tōu** 偷 182

pill **yàopiàn** 药片 209

pillow **zhěntou** 枕头 230

pilot (v.) **kāi** 开 106, **kāi fēijī** 开飞机 55

pilot (n.) **jiàshǐyuán** 驾驶员 92

pinch (v.) **jiā** 夹 91

pioneering spirit **chuàngyè jīngshen** 创业精神 30

pipe-dream **kōngxiǎng** 空想 110

pipeline **guǎndào** 管道 71

pistol **qiāng** 枪 146

pitiful **kělián** 可怜 109

(be a) pity **kěxī** 可惜 109

place (n.) **dìfang** 地方 41, **wèizhi** 位置 188

place (v.) **bǎi** 摆 4, **gē** 搁 64

place an order **yùdìng** 预订 221

place of one's birth or origin **jíguàn** 籍贯 88

plain (n.) **píngyuán** 平原 141

plain boiled water **báikāishuǐ** 白开水 3

plaintiff **yuángào** 原告 221

plan (n.) **jìhuà** 计划 89

plan (v.) **dǎsuàn** 打算 34, **jìhuà** 计划 89

planet **xíngxīng** 行星 202

plant (n.) **zhíwù** 植物 234

plant (v.) **zhòng** 种 237

plastic **sùliào** 塑料 173

plate **pánzi** 盘子 138

plateau **gāoyuán** 高原 63

play (n.) **xì** 戏 192

play (v.) **wánr** 玩儿 185

play basketball **dǎ lánqiú** 打篮球 33

play cards **dǎpái** 打牌 137

play tricks **gǎo guǐ** 搞鬼 63

playground **cāochǎng** 操场 20, 22

playing cards (n.) **pūkèpái** 扑克牌 137

pleasant **yúkuài** 愉快 220

pleasantly warm **nuǎnhuo** 暖和 136

pleased **yúkuài** 愉快 220

pleasure **lèqù** 乐趣 115

pledge **bǎozhèng** 保证 6

plentiful **chōngpèi** 充沛 27

plot (of a story, movie, etc.), scenario **qíngjié** 情节 148

pluck (v.) **cǎi** 采 18, **zhāi** 摘 226

plump **pàng** 胖 138

plunder **lüèduó** 掠夺 123, **qiǎngjié** 抢劫 146

pluralism **duōyuánhuà** 多元化 49

plus **jiā** 加 90

pocket **kǒudài** 口袋 41, 111

pocket money **língqián** 零钱 120

poem **shī** 诗 163, **shīgē** 诗歌 163

poet **shīrén** 诗人 163

Word Finder

protect **bǎohù** 保护 6, **hànwèi** 捍卫 76

protein **dànbáizhì** 蛋白质 38

protest **kàngyì** 抗议 108

proud **jiāo'ào** 骄傲 96

prove **zhèngmíng** 证明 232

provide **gěi** 给 64, **tígōng** 提供 177

provide for **yǎng** 养 208

provided that **zhǐyào** 只要 234

province **shěng** 省 162

provincial capital **shěnghuì** 省会 162

provisional **línshí** 临时 120

provoke/provocation **tiǎoxìn** 挑衅 180

psychiatric patient **jīngshénbìng huànzhě** 精神病患者 82

psychiatrist **jīngshén bìng yīshēng** 精神病医生 102

psychoanalysis **xīnlǐfēnxī** 心理分析 200

psychological consultation **xīnlǐ zīxún** 心理咨询 200

(the science of) psychology **xīnlǐxué** 心理学 200

pub **jiǔbā** 酒吧 103

puberty **qīngchūnqī** 青春期 148

public **gōnggòng** 公共 66, **gōngkāi** 公开 66

(the) public **rénmen** 人们 153

public affair **gōngwù** 公务 67

public announcement **gōnggào** 公告 66, **qǐshì** 启事 144

public order **zhì'ān** 治安 235

public relations **gōnggòng guānxi** 公共关系 66

public road **gōnglù** 公路 66

public sanitation **gōnggòng wèishēng** 公共卫生 187

public security **gōng'ān** 公安 66

public telephone **gōngyòng diànhuà** 公用电话 67

public toilet **gōnggòng cèsuǒ** 公共厕所 66

publicize **fābiǎo** 发表 51, **xuānchuán** 宣传 204

(of a book) publish **chūbǎn** 出版 28

publish (in a newspaper, magazine, etc.) **kāndēng** 刊登 107

pull **lā** 拉 112

pullover (woolen) **máoyī** 毛衣 125

pulse **màibó** 脉搏 115

punctual **zhǔnshí** 准时 241

punctuation mark **biāodiǎn** 标点 12

punish/punishment **chéngfá** 惩罚 26

pupil **xuésheng** 学生 205

puppy **xiǎo gǒu** 小狗 78

(corporate) purchase **cǎigòu** 采购 18

purchasing agent **cǎigòu yuán** 采购员 18

pure **chúnjié** 纯洁 31

purple **zǐ** 紫 242

purpose **mùdì** 目的 131

purse **qiánbāo** 钱包 146

push (v.) **tuī** 推 183

push and shove **yōngjǐ** 拥挤 216

push down **yā** 压 206

put **bǎi** 摆 4, **fàng** 放 55

put in order **zhěnglǐ** 整理 231

put into **tóurù** 投入 182

put into practice **shíjiàn** 实践 164, **shíxíng** 实行 164

put on **chuān** 穿 29, **dài** 戴 37

put on a hat/cap **dài màozi** 戴帽子 125

put on make-up **huàzhuāng** 化妆 81

put up with **rěnnài** 忍耐, **rěn** 忍 153

put upside down **dào** 倒 39

puzzle/be puzzled **míhuò** 迷惑 127

Q

qualification **zīgé** 资格 241

qualified **hégé** 合格 77

quality **zhìliàng** 质量 235

quality control **zhìliàng jiěyàn** 质量检验 93

quantity **shùliàng** 数量 170

quarantine **gélí** 隔离 64

quarrel (v.) **chǎo** 吵 23, **chǎojià** 吵架 23

quarter of an hour **kè** 刻 109

quarter (of a year) **jìdù** 季度 90

queen **wánghòu** 王后 186

question **wèntí** 问题 189

queue up **páiduì** 排队 138

quick **kuài** 快 111

quick-witted **jīlíng** 机灵 87

quiet **ānjìng** 安静 2, **píngjìng** 平静 141

quietly **qiāoqiāo** 悄悄 147

quilt **bèizi** 被子 8

quite **bǐjiào** 比较 9, **xiāngdāng** 相当 195

quota **zhǐbiāo** 指标 234

R

rabbit **tùzi** 兔子 183

race **zhǒngzú** 种族 237

racial discrimination **zhǒngzú qíshì** 种族歧视 143

racism **zhǒngzú zhǔyì** 种族主义 237

radar **léidá** 雷达 115

radiance **guānghuī** 光辉 72

radio **shōuyīnjī** 收音机 168

(department of) radiology **fàngshèkē** 放射科 55

radiotherapy **fàngshè zhìliáo** 放射治疗 55

radio station **diàntái** 电台 43, **guǎngbō diàntái** 广播电台 72

radish **luóbo** 萝卜, **hóng luóbo** 红萝卜 123

railroad/railway **tiělù** 铁路 180

railroad/railway station **huǒchē zhàn** 火车站 227

rain (n.) **yǔ** 雨 220

rain (v.) **xià yǔ** 下雨 220

rainbow **cǎihóng** 彩虹 19

raincoat **yǔyī** 雨衣 220

raise **tígāo** 提高 177

raise (a child, an animal) **yǎng** 养 208

raise (prices) **táigāo** 抬高 175

rally (n.) **dàhuì** 大会 35, 84

random **rènyì** 任意 234

random sampling **suíyì chōuyàng** 随意抽样 174

range **fànwéi** 范围 53

rank and file **hángliè** 行列 76

rapid **xùnsù** 迅速 206

rare **hǎnjiàn** 罕见 76

rare and precious **zhēnxī** 珍稀 230

rat **lǎoshǔ** 老鼠 115

rather **xiāngdāng** 相当 195

ratify **pīzhǔn** 批准 139

raw **shēng** 生 161

raw material **yuánliào** 原料 221

ray (of light) **guāngróng** 光荣 72

reach **dádào** 达到 33, **dàodá** 到达 39

reaction **fǎnyìng** 反应 53

reactionary **fǎndòng** 反动 52

read **dú** 读 46, **dúshū** 读书 47, **kànshū** 看书 168

read aloud **niàn** 念 135

read aloud clearly **lǎngdú** 朗读 113

read seriously **yuèdú** 阅读 222

reader **dúzhě** 读者 47

reading room **yuèlǎnshì** 阅览室 222

real **zhēn** 真 229, **zhēnshí** 真正 230

real estate **wùyè** 物业 191

realistic/reality **shíjì** 实际 164, **xiànshí** 现实 195

realize **shíxiàn** 实现 164, **tǐhuì** 体会 178

really **díquè** 的确 41, **zhēn** 真 229

rear (n.) **hòu** 后 79, **hòubian** 后边 79

reason (n.) **dàolǐ** 道理 40, **lǐyóu** 理由 117

reasonable **yǒu dàolǐ** 有道理 40, **hélǐ** 合理 77

(of a person) reasonable **jiǎng dàolǐ** 讲道理 40

rebuild/rebuilding **gǎizào** 改造 61

recall (v.) **huíyì** 回忆 84, **shōuhuí** 收回 167

receipt **shōujù** 收据 167

receive **jiē** 接 98, **shōudào** 收到 167

receive (guest/visitor) **huìjiàn** 会见, **huìkè** 会客 84

recently **jìnlái** 近来 101, **zuìjìn** 最近 244

reception **zhāodàihuì** 招待会 228

(economic) recession **jīngjì shuāituì** 经济衰退 170

reckon **gūjì** 估计 68

reclaim **huíshōu** 回收 84

recognize **chéngrèn** 承认 26, **rèn** 认 153

recollect/recollection **huíyì** 回忆 84

recommend **tíchàng** 提倡 177, **tuījiàn** 推荐 183

(become) reconciled **héjiě** 和解 78

reconnoiter/scout **zhēnchá** 侦察 230

record **jìlù** 记录 89, **jì** 记 89

record of formal schooling **xuélì** 学历 205

Word Finder

Word Finder

Word Finder

Word Finder

terrorism **kǒngbù zhǔyì** 恐怖主义 110

terrorist **kǒngbù fènzǐ** 恐怖分子 110

test **cèyàn** 测验 20, **kǎoshì** 考试 108, **shìyàn** 试验 167

testify **zhèngmíng** 证明 232

text **kèwén** 课文 110

text message **duǎnxìn** 短信 47

textbook **jiàocái** 教材 97, **kèběn** 课本 110

textile goods **fǎngzhīpǐn** 纺织品 55

textile industry **fǎngzhī gōngyè** 纺织工业 55

thank **gǎnxiè** 感谢 62, **xièxie** 谢谢 200

that **nà** 那 132

that one **nàge** 那个 132

thatched cottage **cǎofáng** 草房 54

the only one **wéiyī** 唯一 187

theater **jùchǎng** 剧场 105

theatrical performance **yǎnchū** 演出 208

themselves **tāmen zìjǐ** 他们自己 242

then **dāngshí** 当时 38, **jiēzhe** 接着 98

theory **lǐlùn** 理论 117

there **nàlǐ** 那里 132

there (colloquial) **nàr** 那儿 132

there is/are no **méiyǒu** 没有 126

thereby **cóng'ér** 从而 32

therefore **suǒyǐ** 所以 174, **yīncǐ** 因此 214

thermos flask **rèshuǐpíng** 热水瓶 152

these **zhèxiē** 这些 229

thesis **lùnwén** 论文 123

they (human) **tāmen** 他们 174

they (human female) **tāmen** 她们 175

they (not human) **tāmen** 它们 175

thick **cū** 粗 32, **hòu** 厚 80

thick (gas/liquid) **nóng** 浓 136

thief **xiǎotōu** 小偷 198, **zéi** 贼 225

thin **báo** 薄 6, **shòu** 瘦 168, **xì** 细 193

thing **dōngxi** 东西 45

think **xiǎng** 想 196, **rènwéi** 认为 153

think (incorrectly) **yǐwéi** 以为 213

think up a plan **xiǎng bànfǎ** 想办法 196

thinking (n.) **sīxiǎng** 思想 172

thirsty **kě** 渴, **kǒukě** 口渴 111

this **zhè** 这, **zhège** 这个 229

thorax **xiōng** 胸 203

thorough **chèdǐ** 彻底 23, **tòu** 透 182

those **nàxiē** 那些 132

though **suīrán** 虽然 173

thought (n.) **sīxiǎng** 思想 172

thoughtful **zhōudào** 周到 237

thousand **qiān** 千 145

thread **xiàn** 线 195

threat/threaten **wēixié** 威胁 186

three **sān** 三 155

3-dimensional **lìtǐ** 立体 117

throat **sǎngzi** 嗓子 156

through **jīngguò** 经过 101, **tōngguò** 通过 180

throughout **shǐzhōng** 始终 165

throw **rēng** 扔 154

throw a tantrum **nào píqi** 闹脾气 133, **fā píqi** 发脾气 140

throw away **rēngdiào** 扔掉 44, **diū** 丢 67

thumb **shǒuzhǐ** 手指 168

thunder **léi** 雷, **dǎ léi** 打雷 115

thunderstorm **léi yǔ** 雷雨 115

Thursday **Xīngqīsì** 星期四 201

ticket **piào** 票 140

tidy **zhěngqí** 整齐 231

tidy up **shōushi** 收拾 167, **zhěnglǐ** 整理 231

tie/necktie **lǐngdài** 领带 120

tiger **lǎohǔ** 老虎 114

tight **jǐn** 紧 100

till (prep.) **zhídào** 直到 233

till now **zhìjīn** 至今 234

timber **mù** 木, **mùtou** 木头 131

time **shíjiān** 时间, **shíguāng** 时光 164

time and again **yízài** 一再 211, **lǚcì** 屡次 122

time difference between time zones **shíchā** 时差 164

time-honored **gǔlǎo** 古老 69, **yōujiǔ** 悠久 217

timely **jíshí** 及时 88

times **shídài** 时代 164

timetable **rìchéngbiǎo** 日程表 154

(railway, coach) timetable **shíkèbiǎo** 时刻表 164

timid **dǎnqiè** 胆怯 37

tin **guàntou** 罐头 71

tinned food **guàntou shípǐn** 罐头食品 71

tip (n.) **xiǎofèi** 小费 198

tired **lèi** 累 115, **píláo** 疲劳 139

title **tímù** 题目 178, **biāotí** 标题 12

title of honor **róngyù chēnghào** 荣誉称号 154

to some degree **bǐjiào** 比较 9

toast (with drink) **gānbēi** 干杯 61

today **jīntiān** 今天 100

tofu **dòufu** 豆腐 46

together **yídào** 一道, **yìqǐ** 一起 211, **yíkuàir** 一块儿 211

together with ... **gēn ... yìqǐ** 跟 ... 一起 65, **hé ... yìqǐ** 和 ... 一起 78

toilet **cèsuǒ** 厕所 20, **xǐshǒujiān** 洗手间 192

toilet soap **xiāngzào** 香皂 196

tolerant **kuānróng** 宽容 112

tolerate **rěn** 忍 153, **rěnshòu** 忍受 153

tomato **xīhóngshì** 西红柿 191

tomb **fénmù** 坟墓 57

tomorrow **míngtiān** 明天 130

ton **dūn** 吨 49

tone **yǔqì** 语气 220

tone (of Chinese word) **shēngdiào** 声调 162

tong **jiāzi** 夹子 91

tongue **shétou** 舌头 159

too **tài** 太 175, **yě** 也 209

tool **gōngjù** 工具 65

tooth/teeth **yá** 牙 206, **yáchǐ** 牙齿 206

toothbrush **yáshuā** 牙刷 206

toothpaste **yágāo** 牙膏 206

top grade **gāodàng** 高档 63

topic of conversation **huàtí** 话题 82

topple **dǎo** 倒 39

torn **pò** 破 142

tortuous **tòngkǔ** 痛苦 181

toss **rēng** 扔 154

(in) total **yígòng** 一共 211, **gòngjì** 共计 68

totally **shífēn** 十分 164

touch **diǎn** 点 42, **mō** 摸 130

touch emotionally **gǎndòng** 感动 62

touching (adj.) **dòngrén** 动人 46

tough **jiānkǔ** 艰苦 92, **yìng** 硬 216

tour bus **lǚyóuchē** 旅游车 122

tour for pleasure **lǚyóu** 旅游 122

tour group **lǚyóutuán** 旅游团 122, **lǚxíngtuán** 旅行团 183

tour itinerary **lǚyóu lùxiàn** 旅游路线 122

tourist **lǚyóuzhě** 旅游者 122, **yóulǎnzhě** 游览者 218

tourist company **lǚyóu gōngsī** 旅游公司 122

tourist guide **dǎoyóu** 导游 39

towards **cháo** 朝 23, **xiàng** 向 197

towel **máojīn** 毛巾 125

tower **tǎ** 塔 175

town **chéng** 城 25

(rural) town **xiāng** 乡 195

trace **hénjì** 痕迹 78

track (for sports) **pǎodào** 跑道 138, **guǐdào** 轨道 73

track and field events **tiánjìng** 田径 178

trade **màoyì** 贸易 125, **shēngyi** 生意 162

trade union **gōnghuì** 工会 65

trading company **màoyì gōngsī** 贸易公司 125

tradition **chuántǒng** 传统 30

traditional Chinese medical doctor **zhōngyī** 中医 236

traditional Chinese medicine **zhōngyào** 中药, **zhōngyī** 中医 236

traffic **jiāotōng** 交通 96

traffic accident **jiāotōng shìgù** 交通事故 96, 166, **chēhuò** 车祸 86

traffic jam **dǔchē** 堵车 47

traffic lights **hónglǜ dēng** 红绿灯 79

traffic police **jiāotōng jǐngchá** 交通警察 96

train (n.) **huǒchē** 火车 86

train (v.) **liànxí** 练习 119, **xùnliàn** 训练 206

train attendant **lièchē yuán** 列车员 120

train ticket **huǒchē piào** 火车票 140

trainee **péixùn shēng** 培训生 138

training class/training course **péixùnbān** 培训班 138

trample **jiàntà** 践踏 95

trampoline **bèngchuáng** 蹦床 9

tranquillizer **zhènjìng jì** 镇静剂 231

transfer (a property, rights, etc.) **zhuǎnràng** 转让 240

transfer to another school **zhuǎnxué** 转学 240

transfer to another train/bus **zhuǎnchē** 转车 240

transform **biàn** 变, **biànhuà** 变化 11, **gǎibiàn** 改变 60, **zhuǎnbiàn** 转变 240

transformation **biànhuà** 变化 11, **gǎibiàn** 改变 60

translate/translator **fānyì** 翻译 52

transparency **tòumíngdù** 透明度 182

transparent **tòumíng** 透明 182

transport (n.) **jiāotōng** 交通 96

transport (v.) **yùn** 运, **yùnshū** 运输 223

transportation **jiāotōng** 交通 96, **yùnshū** 运输 223

trap **quāntào** 圈套 150

travel (by car, train, plane, etc.) **chéng** 乘 26

travel (n.) **lǚtú** 旅途 122

travel (v.) **lǚxíng** 旅行 122

travel agency **lǚxíngshè** 旅行社 122

travel by boat/ship **zuòchuán** 坐船 30

travel for pleasure **lǚyóu** 旅游 122

tray **pánzi** 盘子 138

tread on **cǎi** 踩 19

treasured object/treasure **bǎobèi** 宝贝 6

treat (disease)/treatment **zhì** 治 235, **zhìliáo** 治疗 235

treat (v.) **dài** 待 36, **duì** 对 48

treat as **dàng** 当, **dàngzuò** 当做 39

treat (somebody) coldly **lěngluò** 冷落 115

treaty **tiáoyuē** 条约 179

tree **shù** 树 170

tremble **fādǒu** 发抖 51

tremendous **jùdà** 巨大 105

trend **cháoliú** 潮流 23

triangle **sānjiǎo** 三角 155

trillion **wànyì** 万亿 213

triumph **shèng** 胜 163

triumph over **zhànshèng** 战胜 227

throat **hóulóng** 喉咙 79

trolley bus **diànchē** 电车 43

troops **bùduì** 部队 17, **jūnduì** 军队 106

trophy **jiǎngbēi** 奖杯 95

trouble (n.) **máobìng** 毛病 125

trouble (v.) **nào** 闹 133

troublesome **máfan** 麻烦 123

trousers **kùzi** 裤子 111

truck **kǎchē** 卡车 106

true nature **běnzhì** 本质 9

true **zhēn** 真 229, **zhēnshí** 真实 230

truly **díquè** 的确 41, **zhēn** 真 229

trumpet **lǎba** 喇叭 112

trunk **xiāngzi** 箱子 196

trust **xìnrèn** 信任 201

trustworthy **kàodezhù** 靠得住 108, **kěkào** 可靠 109

truth **zhēnhuà** 真话, **zhēnlǐ** 真理 230

truthful **shízài** 实在 165

try **qǐtú** 企图 144, **shì** 试 166

Tuesday **Xīngqī'èr** 星期二 201

tuition fee **xué fèi** 学费 205

tumble **diē** 跌 44

tumor **zhǒngliú** 肿瘤 236

(benign) tumor **liángxìng zhǒngliú** 良性肿瘤 236

(malignant) tumor/cancer **èxìng zhǒngliú** 恶性肿瘤 236

tunnel **dìdào** 地道 41

turbulence **dòngdàng** 动荡 45

turn (v.) **fān** 翻 52, **guǎi** 拐 70, **zhuǎn** 转 240

turn a corner **guǎiwān** 拐弯 70

turn/do a somersault **fān jīndǒu** 翻筋斗 100

turn into **chéng** 成 24

turn off (v.) **guān** 关 70

turn on **kāi** 开 106

turn over **fān** 翻 52

turn the table **wǎnhuí** 挽回 185

turnip **luóbo** 萝卜, **bái luóbo** 白萝卜 123

tutor (n.) **fǔdǎo lǎoshī** 辅导老师 59

tutor (v.) **fǔdǎo** 辅导 59

tutorial **fǔdǎo kè** 辅导课 59

TV set **diànshì jī** 电视机 43

TV station **diànshì tái** 电视台 43

twins **shuāngbāotāi** 双胞胎 170

twinkle **shǎnshuò** 闪烁 157

twists and turns/setbacks **zhōuzhé** 周折 237

two **èr** 二 50, **liǎng** 两 119

type (category) **yàng** 样 208, **zhǒng** 种 236

type (v.) **dǎzì** 打字 34

typical **diǎnxíng** 典型 43

typical case **diǎnxíng shìlì** 典型事例 43

tyre/tire **lúntāi** 轮胎 123

U

ugly **nánkàn** 难看 133, **chǒu** 丑 28

ultimate **jíxiàn** 极限 88

umbrella **sǎn** 伞 155

unable to bear **rěn bu zhù** 忍不住 153

unanimous **yízhì** 一致 211

uncle (father's brother) **bófù** 伯父 14, **shūshu** 叔叔 169

uncomfortable **bièniu** 别扭 13

uncooked **shēng** 生 161

uncover **jiēlù** 揭露 97

under **dǐxia** 底下 41, **xiàmiàn** 下面 193

undergraduate **běnkē shēng** 本科生 8

undergraduate course **běnkē** 本科 8

underground **dìxià** 地下 42

underground passage **suìdào** 隧道 174

underneath **dǐxia** 底下 41, **xià** 下 193

underpass **dìdào** 地道 42

undersell **yājià** 压价 206

understand **dǒng** 懂 45, **lǐjiě** 理解 116

undertaking **shìyè** 事业 166

(be) underway **shīgōng** 施工 163

undulate **qǐfú** 起伏 144

(be) unemployed **xiàgǎng** 下岗 193

(become) unemployed **shīyè** 失业 163

uneventful **píngjìng** 平静 141

unexpected **yìwài** 意外 214

unexpectedly **què** 却 151, **búliào** 不料 16

unfamiliar **mòshēng** 陌生 131

unfold **pū** 铺 142

unforeseen **yìwài** 意外 214

unfortunate **búxìng** 不幸 17

unified (adj.) **tǒngyī** 统一 181

uniform **zhìfú** 制服 235

unify **tǒngyī** 统一 181

unilateral **piànmiàn** 片面 140

unique **dútè** 独特 46

unite **liánhé** 联合 118, **tuánjié** 团结 183

(the) United Nations Organization (UNO) **Liánhé Guó** 联合国 118

(the) United States of America **Měiguó** 美国 126

(the) universe **yǔzhòu** 宇宙 220

university **dàxué** 大学 36

university department **xì** 系 192

university professor **jiàoshòu** 教授 97

unlawful **fēifǎ** 非法 55

unless **chúfēi** 除非 29

unnecessarily **búbì** 不必 15

unoccupied **xián** 闲 194

unperturbed **zhèndìng** 镇定 230

unprecedented **kōngqián** 空前 110

unprofessional **wàiháng** 外行 184

unpromising **bùmiào** 不妙 129

unreliable **kàobuzhù** 靠不住 108

unrestrained **zìyóu** 自由 242

unripe **shēng** 生 161

unthinkable **bù kě sīyì** 不可思议 16

untie **jiě** 解 91

until **zhídào** 直到 233, **zhì** 至 234

until now **zhìjīn** 至今 234

untrue **jiǎ** 假 91

untrustworthy **kàobuzhù** 靠不住 108

unusual **qíguài** 奇怪 143, **tèshū** 特殊 177, **yìcháng** 异常 213

(be) unwell **bùshūfu** 不舒服 169

up to **dào** 到 39

upheaval **dòngdàng** 动荡 45

uphold **jiānchí** 坚持 92

upload **shàng zài** 上载 158

upper reaches (of a river) **shàngyóu** 上游 158

upright **gōngzhèng** 公正 67

ups and downs **qǐfú** 起伏 144

upstairs **lóu shang** 楼上 122

Word Finder